ANTITRUST

PRINCIPLES, CASES, AND MATERIALS

DANIEL FRANCIS

CHRISTOPHER JON SPRIGMAN

2023

INTRODUCTION

Welcome to *Antitrust: Principles, Cases, and Materials*! This is the first edition of a new antitrust casebook designed to offer an accessible, thorough, concise, and up-to-date introduction to the world of antitrust. Since May 2023 it has been available to all for free download pursuant to a Creative Commons license, and in a hard copy print-on-demand format priced at cost. The book is accompanied by a resource pack, including teaching slides and draft syllabuses, available to all on the same terms. You will find everything online at www.antitrustcasebook.org. We will update the materials each year.

In writing this book, we've been motivated by our hope that this casebook can play a role in making the antitrust classroom, and ultimately the antitrust profession, a more diverse, inclusive, and welcoming space. **Everyone belongs in the antitrust conversation!** Antitrust implicates countless fundamental questions about the rules that govern the economy, and about the place of the market in our shared life. It concerns each of us directly as consumers, workers, and citizens. And it is an endlessly rewarding field of study, work, and debate. We have aimed for an accessible and straightforward text, while acknowledging antitrust's many complexities and tensions. We have made a particular effort to capture recent materials: as a result, some older cases that are now primarily a matter of historical interest have received a briefer treatment or been omitted entirely. This has enabled us to maintain full coverage without undue length.

We are deeply grateful to those who have helped us improve this book before launch. In Fall 2022, a working draft of this book was used as the foundation for the antitrust courses at New York University and the University of Washington, and provided for comment to students in the antitrust class at George Mason University. And in Spring 2023, a revised draft of the book was used as the foundation for the antitrust courses at the University of Florida and New York University. We are profoundly grateful to the teachers who were willing to try out our book in beta-draft form, and to everyone—teachers, students, and colleagues—who took time to share feedback.

The book has also benefited enormously from the work of a board of distinguished and generous editorial consultants and commenters from all corners of the antitrust world. They are listed below, and we have been honored and grateful to have their help and support.

We want to express particular gratitude to Professor Douglas Ross of the University of Washington. His contribution to this project has been immense, including the structure and substance of the book as well as the teaching materials, which he helped to create. We also want to thank Jonathan Gleklen, 2021–22 Chair of the ABA Antitrust Section, for coming up with the idea for this project in the first place, and trusting us to take it forward.

Finally: the work of improvement is never done! We would love for you to help us improve this casebook. If you spot an error or a typo; if you want to suggest additional or alternative materials reflecting a broader array of perspectives; if there's something you really like; or if you want to suggest a cover image for the next edition: let us know! Shoot us an email at the addresses below with "Casebook Feedback" in the subject line. We will be very grateful for your input. You will be contributing to the quality of the product, and helping those who will use future versions.

Welcome to the world of antitrust. We hope you'll love it as much as we do.

Daniel Francis and Christopher Jon Sprigman
daniel.francis@law.nyu.edu; christopher.sprigman@nyu.edu
New York City, NY, May 2023

NOTES ON EXCERPTING

We have taken a free hand with edits to the excerpts, always in the interests of readability. In particular:

- We have freely eliminated footnotes, internal quotation marks, citations (including string cites), ellipses, and brackets, as well as subtitles, and we have amended or completed citations, without specifically indicating that we have done so.
- The ellipsis ". . ." signals the omission of less than one paragraph of material.
- The bracketed ellipsis "[. . .]" signals the omission of one paragraph or more.
- Editorial commentary is sometimes interpolated in the format: {*Eds.: Our comment here.*}
- Footnote numbers in excerpts generally follow the numbering in the original.

We have also applied the same rules, for the same reasons, to footnote citations throughout the book as appropriate, in the interests of clarity and readability.

ACKNOWLEDGEMENTS

Editorial Consultants and Commenters

For comments, ideas, suggestions, feedback, and criticism, we are deeply indebted to: Cem Akleman; Laura Alexander; Alexander Billy; Stephen Calkins; Michael A. Carrier; Ian R. Conner; Trish Conners; Eleanor Fox; Douglas Geho; Jonathan Gleklen; Nikolas Guggenberger; Scott Hemphill; Bruce Hoffman; Erik Hovenkamp; James Keyte; Keith Klovers; Sanjukta Paul; Alvaro Ramos; Douglas Ross; Steven C. Salop; Bilal Sayyed; Joseph Simons; Danny Sokol; Phillipp Tillmann; and Joanna Tsai.

Special Thanks

Professor Douglas Ross has been a friend to this project from the very beginning, and he has made huge contributions to the casebook and to the accompanying materials. We, and this book, owe him a special debt.

Professors Cem Akleman, Trish Conners, Jay Ezrielev, Bruce Hoffman, Mark Rosman, Nicole Sarrine, and Bilal Sayyed also volunteered to use our book in their respective antitrust classes (as the primary text at the University of Florida and a supplementary text at George Mason University) as part of our pilot program in 2022–23. We are very grateful for their trust and their helpful feedback.

Our colleagues and friends at the ABA Section of Antitrust Law have been immensely supportive. Jon Gleklen (Section Chair 2021–22) conceived the idea for this book and recruited us to write it back in the summer of 2021. We're grateful for his vision and trust! We are also grateful for the support of Tom Zych (Section Chair 2022–23) and Fiona Schaeffer (Section Chair 2022–23) in supporting this project through to launch, as well as to the Section's hard-working staff, who have generously contributed their time and skill.

Special thanks to Madhav Tankha for superb graphic design work, and to Taylor Owings for taking the cover photographs of Michael Lantz's sculpture *Man Controlling Trade* at FTC headquarters in Washington, DC.

Above all, thanks to the many students at NYU, the University of Washington, the University of Florida, and George Mason University who took time to share feedback on earlier drafts with us. We're very grateful.

*

Needless to say, while we have benefited enormously from the help and support of a village of wise and generous friends, everything herein is exclusively the authors' responsibility, including all errors, omissions, and views.

TABLE OF CONTENTS

I. THE ANTITRUST PROJECT

A. Overview

Welcome to antitrust! This chapter gives a very short introduction to the U.S. federal antitrust system: its basic purpose; its legal foundations; its main institutions; its historical origin and development; and some of its frontiers and controversies. Much of this material will be explored in detail in the rest of the book: for now, the point is simply to sketch out the shape of what we mean by "antitrust," introduce some of its most important features, and provide some basic context for the journey ahead.

We will start in Section B with some of the basic ideas underpinning antitrust, including its distinctive concern with competition and market power. Section C introduces antitrust's main legal rules, including the three central pillars of the antitrust system—the statutory prohibitions on restraints of trade, monopolization, and anticompetitive acquisitions—as well its basic enforcement architecture. Section D identifies the key federal antitrust statutes in order of enactment. Section E gives a very brief history of the antitrust project, including changing views of its economic and social mission. Finally, Section F highlights some questions and ambiguities within the idea of "competition" that will underpin many of the topics we will explore in the rest of the course.

B. The Idea of Antitrust

The most basic definition of U.S. federal antitrust is probably something like this: it is the project of interpreting, applying, and enforcing a specific set of federal statutes, of which the most important are the Sherman Act of 1890 and the Clayton Act of 1914.

The antitrust statutes confer on courts and enforcement agencies a specific set of functions, of which the most important are: (1) prohibiting and remedying anticompetitive agreements; (2) prohibiting and remedying certain kinds of anticompetitive conduct by businesses with significant market power; and (3) prohibiting and remedying anticompetitive mergers and acquisitions.

What unifies antitrust is its fundamental concern with two organizing ideas: "*competition*," on the one hand, by which we mean something like "the process of rivalry between suppliers, or between purchasers, to be chosen as trading partners" and "*market (or monopoly) power*," on the other, by which we mean something like "the ability of a supplier or purchaser to impose less desirable terms (price, quality, etc.) on trading partners by virtue of a lack of competitive pressure."[1]

Antitrust touches very deep normative questions: that is, questions about what we should do or what it would be best to do. Our instincts about antitrust rules and practices will depend, in part, on what else we think about trading, markets, freedom, power, welfare, and the relationship between law and economics. For example: what roles should agencies and courts play in regulating the exchange of goods, services, and money among persons or businesses? What is a "free" market and in what ways is it "free"? Is it good: and, if so, why and under what circumstances? Whose interests should we protect or promote in shaping rules about markets, and how can we best do so in light of our understanding of how the world really works? When exactly can we say that competition is "fair," "legitimate," or "on the merits," and when and how—if at all—can or should we try to make economic interactions conform to those categories? How good are businesses, agencies, and courts at accurately figuring out the likely effects of particular practices and transactions? How often, and how harmfully, are courts and agencies likely to err, and how should we react to the threat of error? The very broad range of views about answers to these

---

[1] Despite the name, antitrust has nothing to do with "trust" in the everyday sense. When the first federal antitrust law, the Sherman Act, was enacted in 1890, one means of extending a business organization across state lines, and/or of combining separate corporate actors, involved the use of the legal "trust" device: a vehicle through which legal ownership and beneficial interest are separated. Among other things, this device enabled a business organization to carry on activities in multiple states, despite limitations imposed at the time by state corporations laws. *See, e.g.*, Herbert Hovenkamp, ENTERPRISE AND AMERICAN LAW, 1836–1937 (1991), 259–67.

questions—and the changes in the relative ascendancy of particular views over time—creates plenty of room for reasonable disagreement, and makes antitrust a rich and rewarding field.

But almost everyone who is professionally concerned with the federal antitrust laws agrees that, at the most basic level, our antitrust system can be understood as an effort to protect the process of competition, and to set some guard rails around the ways in which market power can be created or maintained, as part of an effort to promote the public interest. Once we move beyond this very fundamental level, we will encounter plenty of disagreement: including disagreement about what "competition" is and when it is good; what "market power" is and when we should tolerate or prohibit practices that create or maintain it; and what "the public interest," correctly understood, really requires.

The United States was among the earliest adopters of antitrust,[2] but today almost every jurisdiction of significant size around the world pursues some version of the antitrust (or "competition law") project. The European Union, for example, enforces a set of competition-law provisions in the Treaty on the Functioning of the European Union ("TFEU"); China has an Anti-Monopoly Law; India has a Competition Act; and so on. And although there are major differences between these different systems—including the substantive rules they express and the institutional arrangements for enforcing them—they are united by their central concern with the promotion of competition, and with the control of market power and/or the means of obtaining such power.

The core of the U.S. antitrust system—as we will see later in this chapter and throughout the rest of the book—consists of three main prohibitions: a rule against anticompetitive agreements (agreements in "restraint of trade") in Section 1 of the Sherman Act; a rule against the improper creation or maintenance of monopoly power ("monopolization") in Section 2 of the Sherman Act; and a rule against anticompetitive mergers and acquisitions in Section 7 of the Clayton Act. We will call these the three pillars of U.S. antitrust. Most competition-law systems have something like these three functions at their core: in the European Union, for example, they are performed respectively by Article 101 TFEU, Article 102 TFEU, and the EU Merger Regulation; in China, they fall under Articles 3(1), 3(2), and 3(3) of the Anti-Monopoly Law; in India, Sections 3, 4, and 5 of the Competition Act 2002; and so on.

Of course, different jurisdictions define and interpret these core functions in different ways. One prominent difference between the United States and most of the rest of the world is that most other competition-law systems (including those of the European Union, China, and India) prohibit not only unilateral conduct by a monopolist or dominant business that tends to create or maintain monopoly power through exclusion of rivals, but also certain forms of unilateral "exploitation" or abuse of that power, even if the conduct does not contribute to the magnitude or duration of the power.

U.S. antitrust law is also distinctive in that it empowers persons who are injured by an antitrust violation to sue, not just for a compensatory measure of damages, but for *treble* the damages suffered. When combined with the provision under Federal Rule of Civil Procedure 23 for class-action litigation, this rule has contributed to a private antitrust litigation landscape in the United States that is vastly more active than in most other jurisdictions. And this reality, in turn, shapes how courts think about antitrust rules and their consequences.

The core U.S. antitrust project—protecting the competitive process and guarding against the improper acquisition or maintenance of market power—may sound pretty straightforward. But on closer inspection we will soon see that things are more complicated than they may at first appear.

For one thing: we will soon realize that not all "competition" among businesses is the kind of thing we really want to encourage. To pick some extreme examples, we surely do not want to encourage businesses to blow up their rivals' factories, or threaten violence against their rivals' customers, in an effort to maximize their profits. We might also not want to allow an incumbent to extract commitments from critical suppliers or distributors that they will

---

[2] But not the first! Canada enacted a national antitrust law in May 1889. And at the state level, Kansas moved even earlier, passing an antitrust statute in March 1889. *See, e.g.,* Yang Chen, *Sherman's Predecessors: Pioneers in State Antitrust Legislation,* 18 J. Reprints Antitrust L. & Econ. 93 (1988); David Millon, *The First Antitrust Statute,* 29 Washburn L.J. 141 (1990).

never work with any competitor of the incumbent; or to buy up all its competitors; or to coordinate with rivals on prices, terms, or markets.

Defining the *desirable* kind of "competition" (*i.e.*, the kind that we want to encourage, sometimes expressed as "competition on the merits," "legitimate competition," or "fair competition") turns out to be a very complicated matter. In particular, it can be difficult in some cases to tell the difference between behaviors that are—either in some individual case or in general—socially beneficial and those that are socially harmful. We will soon start to disagree with one another about the likely effects of particular practices or particular legal rules, and about the relative importance of various benefits, harms, risks, and possibilities. We may also have different intuitions about the wisdom and consequences of various kinds of state "interference" in the market, or about the values and risks of "unconstrained" competition.[3] For example, we might think that it is best to be very conservative and think of anything that sounds unusual to us—such as, for example, agreements between a buyer and seller that limit their respective freedom in any way—as something presumptively suspect. But we may soon conclude that such a narrow view will lead us to prevent businesses from doing things that make everyone better off in the long run, and that building policy in this very restrictive way will harm people and the economy.

Ultimately, if we want to protect a version of the competitive process that can plausibly be thought appealing, we will soon find that we will need *other* standards to identify the boundaries of desirable competition in the real world, and we may disagree about how to spot those boundaries in concrete cases. "Legitimate competition" or "competition on the merits" turns out to be hard to define! We may also find that we value different outcomes of "competitive" processes: better terms for trading partners and consumers (like lower prices or higher quality); the promotion of innovation and investment; decentralization and rivalry; a resilient, polycentic economy; and so on.

And just as it can be hard to tell what kinds of competition are desirable, it can be hard to tell when market power really reflects a problem we should try to solve. The existence of market power is not always a sign that something bad has happened or is likely to happen. To illustrate, suppose that there are five mousetrap-makers with roughly equal shares of the market, until one day one mousetrap-maker has a brilliant idea and makes a mousetrap that is twice as good but half as expensive to make. The competitors simply can't match it (perhaps because the innovator secures a patent on its new design, or because rivals can't figure out how the innovation was achieved), and the innovating manufacturer becomes effectively the only game in town, with the rivals making only minimal sales.

In this example, the mousetrap manufacturer has acquired a ton of market power on most plausible definitions: it has an overwhelming market share, faces little real constraint from rivals, and can probably charge a price comfortably in excess of its costs. But the changes in the world from our initial five-player situation all seem to be beneficial: a new desirable product has been created; consumers have gained access to a new option at a great price; and they are in a situation that they prefer overall. After all, if they didn't prefer the new mousetrap at the new price, they would just continue to buy old mousetrap designs from the other competitors!

It is true, of course, the other competitors are worse off than they were, but competition is *always* bad for less successful competitors. It is inherent in competitive rivalry that the successful competitor succeeds at the expense of a rival, and that businesses that are less efficient and effective will lose share and may eventually be forced to exit the market. If "competition" is what we want to support and protect, we must be comfortable with that reality.

As the mousetrap example suggests, an increase in market power can be understood as an increase in the strength of trading partners' preference for the products or services of one business, compared to the next best available options. Thus: market power may result from the worsening or elimination of alternative options, or from the improvement of an existing one, compared to the status quo ante. And, in practice, those two phenomena are often interlinked: the very same practices that make the products or services of one business more appealing may simultaneously make rivals' products and services less appealing. Real-world behaviors frequently have both of these effects. This makes designing and applying antitrust rules a complex task.

---

[3] The scare quotes allude to the fact that, on the one hand, given the foundational role of the state in defining and enforcing the rules underpinning a market, it is not at all obvious when state action affecting markets should be described as "interference," or when competition should be considered "unrestrained." *See generally, e.g.*, Bernard Harcourt, THE ILLUSION OF FREE MARKETS: PUNISHMENT AND THE MYTH OF NATURAL ORDER (2012).

So: both "competition" and "market power" turn out to be a bit more complicated than they may initially sound. For now, it is enough to think of antitrust law as an effort to define and protect a desirable version of the process of competition, and to limit the ways in which market power can be created or maintained. But you should keep in mind that both halves of this project raise deep complexities: not everything that can be labeled "competition" is beneficial, and not everything that results in "market power" is clearly bad, nor the product of conduct that is clearly bad. So: in defining the forms of competition that antitrust should protect, and in defining the circumstances under which expanding market power is unlawful, we will need to turn to other values and guideposts.

The Idea of "Consumer Welfare"

In modern law, the most common view about what should guide antitrust law and policy—albeit one that is more controversial than it used to be—is that it should operate to make people better off overall than they otherwise would be, by prohibiting certain kinds of marketplace practices and transactions that tend to cause social harm. As you might expect, reasonable minds disagree about how antitrust should accomplish this goal! At present, the most common (but not universal) view among courts, enforcers, and scholars is that antitrust should be shaped in ways that will ultimately make market participants better off overall with respect to their buying and selling activities, by improving the efficiency of markets.[4] This is sometimes described as the promotion of "consumer welfare." We will talk about some of the analytical foundations of this view in Chapter II.

There is plenty of disagreement even within the consumer-welfare tradition about *whose* welfare really counts in such an assessment, how it counts, how it can be evaluated or measured, and what rules or heuristics we should use to try to reflect the welfare stakes of real cases.[5] Among other things, some commentators suggest that only the welfare of consumers or other buyers should matter in the design and application of antitrust rules, while others argue that the welfare of workers, input producers, and other trading partners should also matter in various ways.[6] Moreover, there is considerable controversy today over whether the pursuit of consumer welfare and/or efficiency

---

[4] *See, e.g.*, Brooke Grp. Ltd. v. Brown & Williamson Tobacco Corp., 509 U.S. 209, 221 (1993) (noting "the antitrust laws' traditional concern for consumer welfare and price competition"); Jefferson Parish Hosp. Dist. No. 2 v. Hyde, 466 U.S. 2, 15 (1984) (referring to "the consumer—whose interests the [antitrust] statute was especially intended to serve"); Reiter v. Sonotone Corp., 442 U.S. 330, 343 (1979) (indicating that "Congress designed the Sherman Act as a consumer welfare prescription") (internal quotation marks and citation omitted); Broad. Music, Inc. v. Columbia Broad. Sys., Inc., 441 U.S. 1, 19–20 (1979) ("[When evaluating the possible application of a *per se* rule of illegality, a court should consider whether] the effect and . . . purpose of the practice are to threaten the proper operation of our predominantly free-market economy—that is, whether the practice facially appears to be one that would always or almost always tend to restrict competition and decrease output, and in what portion of the market, or instead one designed to increase economic efficiency and render markets more, rather than less, competitive.") (internal quotation marks and citation omitted); City of Lafayette, La. v. Louisiana Power & Light Co., 435 U.S. 389, 408 (1978) (noting "the efficiency of free markets which the regime of competition embodied in the antitrust laws is thought to engender"); Northern Pac. Ry. v. United States, 356 U.S. 1, 4 (1958) ("[The Sherman Act] rests on the premise that the unrestrained interaction of competitive forces will yield the best allocation of our economic resources, the lowest prices, the highest quality and the greatest material progress, while at the same time providing an environment conductive to the preservation of our democratic political and social institutions."; Siva v. Am. Bd. of Radiology, 38 F.4th 569 (7th Cir. 2022) (noting "antitrust's goal of promoting consumer welfare"); City of Oakland v. Oakland Raiders, 20 F.4th 441, 457 (9th Cir. 2021) ("The principal objective of antitrust policy is to maximize consumer welfare by encouraging firms to behave competitively[.]") (internal quotation marks, citation, and brackets omitted); United States v. Anthem, Inc., 855 F.3d 345, 366 (D.C. Cir. 2017) ("The principal objective of antitrust policy is to maximize consumer welfare by encouraging firms to behave competitively.") (internal quotation marks and citation omitted); Olympia Equipment Leasing Co. v. Western Union Telegraph Co., 797 F.2d 370, 375 (7th Cir. 1986) (noting shift "from the protection of competition as a process of rivalry to the protection of competition as a means of promoting economic efficiency").

[5] The current head of the Antitrust Division seems to have had this kind of thing in mind when he suggested that "consumer welfare is a catchphrase, not a standard." Jonathan Kanter, *Milton Handler Lecture* (remarks of May 18, 2022), https://www.justice.gov/opa/speech/assistant-attorney-general-jonathan-kanter-delivers-remarks-new-york-city-bar-association.

[6] *See, e.g.*, Laura Alexander & Steven C. Salop, *Antitrust Worker Protections: Rejecting Multi-Market Balancing as a Justification for Anticompetitive Harms to Workers*, 90 U. Chi. L. Rev. 273 (2023) (arguing that harms to workers should not be justifiable in antitrust analysis by benefits to consumers); Elyse Dorsey et al., *Consumer Welfare & the Rule of Law: The Case Against the New Populist Antitrust Movement*, 47 Pepperdine L. Rev. 861 (2020); Christine S. Wilson, *Welfare Standards Underlying Antitrust Enforcement: What You Measure is What You Get* (remarks of Feb. 15, 2019), 12–18 (outlining a case for a total-welfare standard); Steven C. Salop, *Question: What Is the Real and Proper Antitrust Welfare Standard? Answer: The True Consumer Welfare Standard*, 22 Loy. Consumer L. Rev. 336 (2010); *see also* Robert H. Bork, THE ANTITRUST PARADOX: A POLICY AT WAR WITH ITSELF (1978) (proposing a total-welfare standard under the label "consumer welfare"); A. Douglas Melamed, *Antitrust Law and its Critics*, 83 Antitrust L.J. 269, 271 (2020) ("[I]ncreased market power means the ability profitably to increase price or otherwise disadvantage trading partners through a reduction in the competitive efficacy of actual and potential rivals.").

is really a fair and accurate characterization of the best version of our antitrust project.[7] Certainly, in earlier decades, as we will see, courts and others had often characterized the goals of the antitrust laws in very different terms, including by reference to concerns with power, freedom, and the protection of small businesses.[8]

It is important to appreciate right from the start that promoting the welfare of society (or, at least, preventing certain things that harm it) might involve tolerating some practices that cause some harm in the short term.

To see this clearly, consider a price increase by a monopolist. Should we ban price increases—or maybe just "unreasonable" price increases—by monopolists? We might approach this question by pointing out that a price increase is obviously harmful to consumers in the short term: after all, they must pay more to get the product or service! But not so fast. That same price increase creates an opportunity and incentive for other competitors to enter the market and provide competition while making a profit. Moreover, imagine what would be necessary for antitrust law to *prohibit* such price increases: on the most natural versions of this exercise, an agency or a court would have to set a "correct" or "best" price for a product or service. And that decision, in turn, would have some consequences. For one thing, such a price cap would tend, by limiting the profits available from the provision of that product or service, to discourage businesses from investing in the first place (and to encourage them to put their capital, instead, into markets where no such price cap existed): so it would have the effect of reducing society's access to the relevant product or service, and stifling innovation that might otherwise take place. For another, it would also be a truly heroic task for government to figure out the "best" price (even if we could reach agreement on what we meant by "best" here) for even a single product or service, and to keep adjusting that price in light of changes in market conditions.

For these reasons among others, most economists agree that government price controls would do much more harm than good under most circumstances—at least when competitive markets are possible[9]—and that allowing businesses to charge whatever price they please for the products and services they supply is probably the general rule that best serves social welfare in the long run. Even John Sherman, the Senator who introduced the first federal antitrust law (which still bears his name), emphasized on the Senate floor during the debates that he did not intend antitrust law to disturb this principle, even for the least popular companies: "I am inclined to think that the Standard Oil Company can sell its product at just such prices as it pleases[.]"[10]

This point—that rushing to condemn or prohibit something that seems harmful or suspicious is not always in the long-run interests of society or consumers—can be generalized, with some caution. Many practices and

---

[7] *See, e.g.*, Sandeep Vaheesan, *The Profound Nonsense of Consumer Welfare Antitrust*, 64 Antitrust Bull. 479 (2019); Gregory T. Gundlach & Diana Moss, *The Role of Efficiencies in Antitrust Law: Introduction and Overview*, 60 Antitrust Bull. 91 (2015); Jonathan B. Baker & D. Daniel Sokol, *Economics and Politics: Perspectives on the Goals and Future of Antitrust*, 81 Fordham L. Rev. 2175 (2013); Joseph Farrell & Michael L. Katz, *The Economics of Welfare Standards in Antitrust*, 2 Comp. Pol'y Int'l 3 (2006); Richard A. Posner, ANTITRUST LAW (2001); Robert H. Lande, *Chicago's False Foundation: Wealth Transfers (Not Just Efficiency) Should Guide Antitrust*, 58 Antitrust L.J. 631 (1989); Eleanor Fox, *The Battle for the Soul of Antitrust*, 75 Calif. L. Rev. 917 (1987); John J. Flynn & James F. Ponsoldt, *Legal Reasoning and the Jurisprudence of Vertical Restraints: The Limitations of Neoclassical Economic Analysis in the Resolution of Antitrust Disputes*, 62 N.Y.U. L. Rev. 1125 (1987); Robert Pitofksy, *The Political Content of Antitrust*, 127 U. Pa. L. Rev. 1051 (1979); Kenneth G. Elzinga, *The Goals of Antitrust: Other Than Competition and Efficiency, What Else Counts?* 125 U. Pa. L. Rev. 1191 (1977).

[8] United States v. Topco Assocs., Inc., 405 U.S. 596, 610 (1972) ("Antitrust laws in general, and the Sherman Act in particular, are the Magna Carta of free enterprise. They are as important to the preservation of economic freedom and our free-enterprise system as the Bill of Rights is to the protection of our fundamental personal freedoms. And the freedom guaranteed each and every business, no matter how small, is the freedom to compete—to assert with vigor, imagination, devotion, and ingenuity whatever economic muscle it can muster."); Brown Shoe Co. v. United States, 370 U.S. 294 (1962) ("It is competition, not competitors, which the Act protects. But we cannot fail to recognize Congress' desire to promote competition through the protection of viable, small, locally owned business. Congress appreciated that occasional higher costs and prices might result from the maintenance of fragmented industries and markets. It resolved these competing considerations in favor of decentralization. We must give effect to that decision."); United States v. Alcoa, 148 F.2d 416, 428 (2d Cir. 1945) ("[A]mong the purposes of Congress in 1890 was a desire to put an end to great aggregations of capital because of the helplessness of the individual before them."); Appalachian Coals v. United States, 288 U.S. 344, 359 (1933) ("charter of freedom").

[9] This is not always the case! In some areas of economic activity, competition may not be sustainable, and in such areas policymakers might consider replacing the competitive market with a regulated monopoly supervised in various ways by the government. This is sometimes called "utility regulation." We will have little to say about regulated monopolies in the rest of this book: for when competition is impossible, antitrust usually has no role to play (at least so long as the regulated monopoly stays in the regulated market!). But the topic is a rich and important one. *See, e.g.*, Morgan Ricks, Ganesh Sitaraman, Shelley Welton, & Lev Menand, NETWORKS, PLATFORMS, AND UTILITIES: LAW & POLICY (2023).

[10] 21 Cong. Rec. 4090 (May 1, 1890).

transactions may seem at first to have some adverse impact on other market participants, including competitors. For example, when a large company enters into an exclusivity agreement with a valuable supplier, or when two rivals pool their resources to create a joint product, the downside for competition may be clear. After all, it is easy to just ask "why would they need to do that?" without really listening to the answer. But thorough antitrust analysis generally does <u>not</u> stop there. It asks, for example, whether those practices might be playing an important role in making possible some new or more efficient output that will be beneficial overall, and whether a prohibition on that practice might do more harm than good—including through its deterrent effects.

But caution and skepticism should go both ways. Just as there are dangers in being too quick to condemn a practice, there are dangers in being too willing to accept a flimsy justification from a business. In the real world, the subjects of antitrust scrutiny, and their executives and employees, very seldom throw up their hands and tearfully confess that their behavior is anticompetitive and harmful. Instead, businesses will often be able to point to some plausible "legitimate reason" for conduct, and that reason may even have been a genuine motivation for the practice. But this is usually the beginning, not the end, of antitrust analysis: conduct can nevertheless turn out to be both harmful and illegal even if an appealing label can be applied, or if it was undertaken with perfectly good intentions. Antitrust prohibits more than just the most flagrant and nakedly anticompetitive forms of wrongdoing.

The same caution and skepticism should also be applied to complaints and testimony from other market participants. Competitors and trading partners may be valuable witnesses in an investigation or litigation, but they too have their own interests. They may find it strategically helpful to cry foul to an agency or court in order to get one over on a market rival, or to extract some beneficial concession in exchange for support, or to increase pressure on a trading partner with whom they are locked in negotiations. And they may have an interest in opposing a practice or transaction simply because it makes a rival a more effective competitor. Similarly, a market participant might provide supportive testimony regarding the actual or probable effects of a practice because they stand to share in the profits of it, or because they do not fully understand its implications.[11]

All this means that good antitrust analysis requires penetrating through forms and labels, and grappling with the economic reality underneath. This usually requires more than a cursory glance at a practice or transaction (though sometimes this is enough!), and it *always* requires some even-handed skepticism of the viewpoints and labels offered by interested participants on both sides of an issue.

As you read through the cases and other materials in this book, ask yourself how each of the parties would characterize the practice or transaction at issue. It is good to get into the habit of seeing both sides whenever you can, realizing that each side may be in perfectly good faith about their understanding of what is "really" going on, and reflecting on which version you find more persuasive and why. It is also worth remembering that our record of evidence on many important (and even basic) issues of antitrust policy, including the effects of particular practices, or categories of practices, is often very far from complete. We all rely on our own intuitions and personal experiences in forming our views about what antitrust rules would be best—and those intuitions and experiences will differ!

As we have already noted, the dominant view today is that antitrust rules should be shaped to protect the participants in society, including consumers—and probably workers and other intermediate trading partners too—in their capacities as buyers and sellers of products and services. But some commenters and writers have different views. Some people think that the phrase "consumer welfare" has outlived its practical usefulness, and we should instead talk more specifically about whose welfare matters and how we will choose among different interests when they conflict. Other commenters reject the idea that antitrust should be motivated by welfare considerations at all. Some, for example, believe that antitrust law should be shaped and applied in ways that help to protect against political or social risks, like undue business size or power as such, rather than just harm from increased market power. Others believe that antitrust should independently pursue goals like commercial fairness or distributional equity, even when those goals conflict with the promotion of welfare. These debates are important, and it is worth spending some time familiarizing yourself with some of the writings from outside the

---

[11] One on occasion, Ronald Reagan's chief antitrust enforcer Bill Baxter said that "the most useful thing we can know about a merger is what the competitors think about it," and that when competitors oppose it, "my instinctive reaction is to approve the merger." Federal Antitrust Policy, Hearing Before the Committee on Small Business, U.S. Senate, 97th Cong. 111 (1981).

welfarist tradition. Those perspectives have not played an important role in influencing courts in recent decades, but some critics of the status quo have recently become prominent and influential in areas outside antitrust litigation. Antitrust is undergoing a process of deep examination and criticism, and some change may be in the wind. Only time will tell. In short: you have picked a very exciting time to study and think about antitrust!

C. Antitrust Law in a Nutshell

The phrase "antitrust laws" generally refers to a set of federal statutes and the enormous body of court and agency precedent interpreting and applying them. The most important antitrust statutes are the Sherman Act of 1890 and the Clayton Act of 1914 (as amended by the Celler-Kefauver Act of 1950); other important antitrust statutes, in chronological order, include the Federal Trade Commission Act of 1914; the Robinson-Patman Act of 1936; and the Hart-Scott-Rodino Act of 1976. Still other statutes—such as the Foreign Trade and Antitrust Improvements Act of 1998 and the Antitrust Criminal Penalty Enhancement and Reform Act of 2004—have amended or modified the basic antitrust framework in certain respects without disturbing the rules at the heart of the system.

As you might expect, these statutes contain many different provisions: too many to enumerate or discuss in this short introductory chapter, and more than we will meet in this entire book. Some of these provisions impose substantive obligations; some create institutional rules for government enforcement of the antitrust laws; others structure antitrust litigation among private actors. But three provisions in particular are of utterly central importance to modern antitrust: they effectively constitute the three foundational pillars of the U.S. antitrust system. Each of these three core rules is expressed in broad and general language: their meaning has been elaborated gradually over decades of adjudication, enforcement, and scholarship. Let's meet them in turn.

1. The Three Pillars

a) Sherman Act Section 1: Restraint of Trade

The first pillar of U.S. antitrust law is Section 1 of the Sherman Act (15 U.S.C. § 1), which prohibits agreements (specifically, "contracts," "combinations," and "conspiracies," although nothing turns on any distinction between them) that are "in restraint of trade." In modern law, Section 1 is understood to prohibit agreements that are unreasonably and unjustifiably anticompetitive. Section 1 provides in full:

> Every contract, combination in the form of trust or otherwise, or conspiracy, in restraint of trade or commerce among the several States, or with foreign nations, is declared to be illegal. Every person who shall make any contract or engage in any combination or conspiracy hereby declared to be illegal shall be deemed guilty of a felony, and, on conviction thereof, shall be punished by fine not exceeding $100,000,000 if a corporation, or, if any other person, $1,000,000, or by imprisonment not exceeding 10 years, or by both said punishments, in the discretion of the court.

Agreements are generally divided, for analytical purposes, into those between actual or potential competitors ("horizontal") and those between parties at different levels of a supply chain ("vertical"), with the former category generally attracting closer scrutiny from agencies and courts.

Analysis of an agreement under Section 1 involves the application of one of three main standards of legality. Horizontal agreements that are blatantly (or "nakedly") anticompetitive, with little or no redeeming procompetitive virtue, are usually considered automatically or "*per se*" illegal, regardless of their context, purpose, or effects. Bare agreements among competitors to fix prices or divide markets fall into this category. Agreements that are obviously harmful to competition but don't quite qualify for *per se* treatment are sometimes analyzed under a kind of intermediate standard often called "quick look" review, involving a presumption of illegality which the defendant has an opportunity to displace. Agreements that fall outside this category—representing the vast majority of agreements encountered by antitrust agencies and courts in the real world—are analyzed under a standard called the "rule of reason." Formulations of the rule of reason differ, but the core concept is that a court must determine whether the competitive harms of the agreement are outweighed or justified by its positive effects on competition.

We will talk at length about Section 1 in Chapters IV, V, and VI.

b) Sherman Act Section 2: Monopolization

The second pillar is Section 2 of the Sherman Act (15 U.S.C. § 2), which prohibits monopolization, attempted monopolization, and conspiracies to monopolize. In modern law, Section 2 is understood to prohibit conduct by a company with monopoly power, or something approaching such power, that impermissibly tends to create, maintain, or extend monopoly power. It provides in full:

> Every person who shall monopolize, or attempt to monopolize, or combine or conspire with any other person or persons, to monopolize any part of the trade or commerce among the several States, or with foreign nations, shall be deemed guilty of a felony, and, on conviction thereof, shall be punished by fine not exceeding $100,000,000 if a corporation, or, if any other person, $1,000,000, or by imprisonment not exceeding 10 years, or by both said punishments, in the discretion of the court.

Monopolization law is notoriously puzzling. Courts and agencies have not generally done a good job of explaining when exactly the acquisition, maintenance, or increase of monopoly power will constitute "monopolization" rather than lawful "competition on the merits." Cases are brought less often under this pillar by federal enforcers than under either of the other two pillars: in part, this may reflect the complexity and unpredictability of the underlying law; in part, it may reflect the fact that monopoly power is a high bar and monopolists are not common in our economy; and in part, it may also reflect a background reality that courts and agencies are particularly cautious about imposing liability under Section 2, perhaps for fear of punishing big companies for competing too aggressively.

However, despite the general confusion about the unifying principles, if any, animating Section 2, courts have provided somewhat greater clarity regarding the standards of legality that apply to specific kinds of practices, such as the use of exclusivity commitments to lock up suppliers or distributors, or the practice of "predatory pricing" (*i.e.*, charging an unsustainable low price to drive rivals out of the market, with the prospect of enjoying monopoly power thereafter).

We will focus on Section 2 in Chapter VII.

c) Clayton Act Section 7: Mergers and Acquisitions

The third pillar of our antitrust system is Section 7 of the Clayton Act (15 U.S.C. § 18), which prohibits the acquisition of stocks, shares, or assets, where "the effects of such acquisition may be substantially to lessen competition, or to tend to create a monopoly." The most important language provides in relevant part:

> No person engaged in commerce or in any activity affecting commerce shall acquire, directly or indirectly, the whole or any part of the stock or other share capital and no person subject to the jurisdiction of the Federal Trade Commission shall acquire the whole or any part of the assets of another person engaged also in commerce or in any activity affecting commerce, where in any line of commerce or in any activity affecting commerce in any section of the country, the effect of such acquisition may be substantially to lessen competition, or to tend to create a monopoly.

Mergers, like agreements, are generally divided for analytical purposes into "horizontal" transactions, which unite actual or potential competitors, and "vertical" transactions, which unite companies at different levels of the supply chain (or suppliers of complements[12]), with the former category generally attracting closer scrutiny from agencies and courts. Mergers that are neither horizontal nor vertical virtually never raise concerns today. Mergers may harm competition by creating or maintaining market power, either through the elimination of actual or potential

---

[12] In very general terms, complements are products or services that are more valuable together. More technically, they are products that exhibit negative cross-elasticity of demand: when the price of one goes up, demand for the other goes down. We will talk about complements below. *See infra* § II.C.2.

head-to-head competition between the parties (so-called "unilateral" competitive effects), or by facilitating tacit coordination, or interdependent parallel conduct, among the participants in the market (so-called "coordinated effects").

Merger law underpins the practice of "merger review," which is a major part of the work of the federal antitrust enforcers. Pursuant to the Hart-Scott-Rodino Act of 1976, proposed mergers and acquisitions that meet or exceed certain size thresholds must be notified to the antitrust agencies before they take effect, to give the agencies a chance to review them for competitive concerns and, if necessary, challenge them in court by seeking an injunction to block the deal. The agencies may also review proposed transactions that are not subject to HSR notification ("unreportable" deals) as well as transactions that have already closed ("consummated" deals), though it is widely recognized that it can be hard to unwind a deal that has already closed. The agencies have issued successive "Merger Guidelines" to explain the analytical framework that they use in analyzing mergers and acquisitions; these are periodically revised to reflect changes in economic learning and in enforcement practice.

We will turn to merger law in Chapter VIII.

2. Enforcement Architecture

The federal antitrust laws are enforced, in various ways, by the federal government, the states, and by private persons (including consumers, trading partners, and competitors).

Federal government enforcement includes both civil and criminal enforcement. Although both Sections 1 and 2 of the Sherman Act create felonies, federal criminal enforcement of the antitrust statutes, handled by the Department of Justice, is sharply limited today. For many decades, only a small subset of violations of Section 1 of the Sherman Act has been prosecuted criminally: namely, conduct that is "*per se* illegal," involving very flagrant violations of the antitrust laws, like outright price-fixing agreements. Penalties in criminal prosecutions can include imprisonment and criminal fines. DOJ extradites and prosecutes people who participate in cartels overseas that harm U.S. markets. In recent decades, the Department of Justice has not attempted to criminally prosecute conduct that is plausibly related to a procompetitive purpose, even if that conduct might constitute a civil violation of the law. In 2022, DOJ obtained a guilty plea to a criminal violation of Section 2 (*i.e.*, monopolization) for the first time in decades, launching an effort to revive criminal enforcement of monopolization law.[13]

Federal civil enforcement of the antitrust laws is handled by two agencies with overlapping jurisdiction: the Antitrust Division of the Department of Justice, on the one hand, and the Bureau of Competition of the Federal Trade Commission, on the other. DOJ enforces the antitrust laws directly; the FTC does so through the prohibition on "unfair methods of competition" in Section 5 of the FTC Act, on the basis that that phrase includes at least everything that is prohibited by the antitrust laws.[14] The two agencies have developed complementary bodies of experience and expertise over many years, and they allocate antitrust investigations between themselves through an informal (and largely nonpublic) process known as "clearance." There are some important differences between the agencies, including their structure, legal powers, and procedural options for investigating and challenging practices and transactions.[15] Federal civil enforcement generally results in injunctive relief to terminate and remedy unlawful conduct. Violations of an FTC cease-and-desist order may also result in the imposition of civil penalties.

States are empowered under the Sherman Act to bring claims under the antitrust laws for damages (whether suffered by the state directly or, in what is sometimes called a *parens patriae* claim, suffered by the state's residents) or injunctive relief. State enforcement is handled by the Offices of the Attorney General in each state or territory of the United States. Not every state AG office employs lawyers with antitrust expertise, but some (such as California, Texas, and New York) have large and experienced teams of antitrust enforcers. State Attorneys-General have played a leading role in some prominent recent antitrust matters, including the (unsuccessful) challenges to the Sprint / T-Mobile merger and certain "anti-steering" practices of American Express, and a range

---

[13] *See infra* § XI.C.2. (describing DOJ's criminal antitrust enforcement program).

[14] *See infra* § XI.B.2. (describing the FTC's powers).

[15] *See infra* § XI.D. (describing the two-agency model, its implications, and its complications).

of hospital merger challenges, as well as a number of lawsuits against large tech platforms. State civil enforcement may result in injunctive relief to terminate and remedy unlawful conduct, as well as an award of treble damages. Separately, most states also have their own state antitrust statutes, which are generally close to federal law but may differ in material respects. We will not discuss state antitrust statutes much in the rest of this book, but you should know that they exist and can be important.[16]

Most antitrust enforcement in the United States is private. Persons injured by antitrust violations—including customers, suppliers, competitors, and consumers—often have a right to sue the wrongdoer in federal court. Such suits may be brought individually or, in appropriate cases, pursuant to the class action mechanism in Federal Rule of Civil Procedure 23. Remedies may include injunctive relief to terminate and remedy unlawful conduct, and treble damages.

We will discuss government antitrust enforcement (including the FTC and DOJ, as well as the states) in some detail in Chapter XI, and private enforcement in Chapter XII.

3. Some Illustrative Easy and Hard Cases

To complete our nutshell tour, and to make concrete some of the general discussion above, it may be helpful to consider some concrete hypotheticals that would constitute "easy cases" under the antitrust laws, with a reasonably clear answer, and some that would constitute "hard cases," turning on a close assessment of the evidence.

Some easy cases include the following:

- **A price-fixing cartel.** Suppose that a group of competing hotel chains meet on video-conferencing software and agree that, rather than competing to offer the best room at the lowest price, they should simply set (or "fix") a uniform, higher price for hotel rooms.
  - o This is almost certainly an automatic (or "per se") violation of Section 1 of the Sherman Act, and could be prosecuted criminally by the Department of Justice. In addition, if the agreement took effect and consumers ended up paying higher prices as a result, those consumers could sue (probably as a class under Rule 23) to recover treble damages for their injury and to obtain injunctive relief to bring the cartel agreement to an end.

- **Unjustified use of highly exclusionary exclusivity.** Suppose that, for almost all uses, there is only one commercially viable supplier of touchscreens in the entire world. Upon learning that another firm is thinking about getting into the touchscreen-making business, the lone incumbent convinces all the world's major device manufacturers—who buy the touchscreens—to each commit that, for a period of twenty years, they will not purchase touchscreens from any other supplier. The commitment does not help to improve the efficiency of anyone's business operation: its only purpose, and only effect, is to lock up the key customers and kill the threat of competition from the potential entrant. Upon learning about these deals, the would-be rival abandons its plans and leaves the incumbent undisturbed in possession of the touchscreen market.
  - o This is almost certainly a violation of Section 1 of the Sherman Act, as an agreement in restraint of trade, and also a violation of Section 2 of the Sherman Act, as an act of monopolization (specifically "monopoly maintenance," as it involves protecting an already-acquired monopoly). DOJ or the FTC could sue for injunctive relief to eliminate the restriction on manufacturer freedom to buy from rivals. Injured parties (including trading partners and excluded rivals) could sue for treble damages and injunctive relief.

- **A plainly anticompetitive merger.** Suppose that there are only three book publishers in the United States, and that they have been locked in bitter competition for years, as each struggles to offer lower prices and better books to consumers, and to offer higher advance fees to authors. One day, two of the

---

[16] *See, e.g.*, ABA Section of Antitrust Law, STATE ANTITRUST PRACTICE AND STATUTES (2014).

publishers announce that they have reached an agreement to merge with one another, having calculated that this would significantly reduce the intensity of competition and significantly increase their profits.

- This is almost certainly a violation of Section 7 of the Clayton Act, as a transaction that may have the effect of substantially lessening competition, or the tendency to create a monopoly. DOJ or the FTC, and/or consumers or trading partners, could sue for injunctive relief to block the transaction before the deal closes.

On the other hand, some hard cases might include the following:

- **A joint venture in a somewhat concentrated market with serious procompetitive benefits.** Suppose that there are four or five reasonably competitive suppliers able to meet the federal government's need for an important defense product: say, a particular kind of radar system. Two of the leading suppliers propose to enter a joint bid rather than separate competing bids. They predict that the resulting team would be able to offer a product of higher quality than either competitor would manage alone; however, the elimination of one competitor seems likely to result in some lost competitive pressure.
  - This would raise concerns under Section 1 of the Sherman Act, as an agreement among competitors that could result in overall harm to competition. But the promise of serious competitive benefits from the collaboration—and perhaps other factors, such as the presence of a sophisticated and powerful buyer, the existence of multiple credible alternatives, and perhaps the nature and structure of the procurement process—could ultimately allay the concerns presented by the deal. Careful analysis would be needed to determine the harmful and beneficial tendencies of the transaction, and the extent to which cooperation was genuinely necessary to obtain any relevant benefits.

- **An exclusive deal with a monopolist device manufacturer regarding a valuable input.** Suppose that an incumbent device monopolist enters into an exclusive partnership with an important component supplier, which will support the development of new and valuable components, but which will deny rivals the opportunity to buy those components from the supplier for a period of five years. There is evidence that that supplier could achieve some of the research benefits independently; but the evidence also shows that the partnership will significantly increase the scope of what is technically possible, including by allowing the parties to share information and know-how more extensively than they would otherwise be able and willing to do.
  - This could raise concerns under Sections 1 of the Sherman Act, as an agreement that may have eliminated or restricted competition, and under Section 2 of the Sherman Act as conduct that may improperly increase or maintain the incumbent's monopoly power. But the significant benefits for competition, including the prospect of additional innovation that could not otherwise be achieved, and the fact that rivals have access to some plausible alternatives, will complicate matters. Ultimately, a court would have to determine whether the agreement will "substantially foreclose" rivals' access to inputs in ways that would threaten competition, and if so whether its benefits are sufficiently significant and likely to outweigh the harms.

- **A merger with ambiguous competitive effects.** Suppose that a major metropolitan center, with a river running through the center, was served by five hospitals, of which three were located on the west side of the river and two on the east side. Evidence suggests that travel around the city is generally fairly easy for most residents, although some residents prefer not to cross the river. Two of the three hospitals on the west side—the two smallest hospitals in the city—propose to merge, in order to access some significant complementarities and efficiencies that would not otherwise be available.
  - This would raise concerns under Section 7 of the Clayton Act, as a merger that may lead to a substantial lessening of competition by eliminating an important competitive constraint on the merged firm (particularly for the business of west-side residents that are unable or unwilling to cross the river), or by contributing to an environment of less vigorous price competition by facilitating strategic coordination ("tacit collusion") among the remaining hospitals. But the existence of other competitive alternatives, and the fact that the merged firm might be a more

aggressive competitor overall, could ultimately dispel competitive concerns. Careful analysis would be needed to determine the overall competitive consequences of the transaction.

NOTES

1) The United States has, by global standards, an unusually active antitrust private-litigation scene. How, if at all, do you think the availability of private treble-damages antitrust litigation should affect the content or interpretation of antitrust rules? How, if at all, do you think it should affect the antitrust agencies' choice of cases to investigate and prosecute?

2) What do you see as the principal advantages and disadvantages of a welfare-focused antitrust law? What do you think is the most attractive alternative and why?

3) Should antitrust law and enforcement be designed wholly with respect to the desirability of particular outcomes (what a philosopher might call "consequentialist" logic)? Are there particular rights, liberties, duties, or interests at stake here that antitrust should take seriously as well or instead?

4) What are your intuitions about the wisdom and utility of a rule against the mere exploitation of monopoly power, like the charging of high "monopoly" prices? If Congress wanted to introduce such a rule, how would you design its content and enforcement architecture?

5) Looking at the groups of "easy" and "hard" hypotheticals, are there any that you think antitrust law should or might better classify in the other group (in other words, should any of the easy cases be hard, or vice versa)?

6) What are the advantages and disadvantages of subjective intention as a measure of legality in antitrust cases?

7) Private plaintiffs lose the majority of antitrust cases that they file. How could we tell if they are losing "too many" in an overall sense: that is, if courts are systematically too pro-defendant? (And what values or objectives are you drawing on?) Outline an empirical study that would help us investigate this question.

D. The Federal Antitrust Statutes

1. The Sherman Act of 1890

The first federal antitrust statute was the Sherman Act of 1890. Enacted following popular discontent with large business consolidations in the United States—and particularly the conduct of certain large business consolidations toward agricultural and consumer interests—the Sherman Act introduced, in its first two sections, two of the three pillars of the U.S. antitrust system, in language that has remained essentially unchanged since then. As we have already seen, Section 1 established the prohibition on contracts, combinations, and conspiracies in restraint of trade, and Section 2 established the prohibition on monopolization, attempted monopolization, and conspiracy to monopolize, as described above.[17] As we will see later in this chapter, some of the Sherman Act legislators appear to have thought (or, at least, stated) that, at least to some extent, they were incorporating and codifying ideas that already existed at common law. But the Sherman Act turned out to mark a significant break with the common law, and a fresh start for what would become known as antitrust.

The Sherman Act gave federal courts jurisdiction over antitrust claims, gave injured persons the right to sue for treble damages, and empowered the United States to bring actions for injunctive relief "to prevent and restrain" violations of the new law.

2. The Federal Trade Commission Act of 1914

The Federal Trade Commission Act of 1914 was driven by dissatisfaction with the first generation of antitrust enforcement, which had generally been weak, inconsistent, and not always aimed at its original targets. This dissatisfaction led to calls for a new agency with a special focus on economic policy and competition enforcement. With support from President Woodrow Wilson and his economic adviser Louis Brandeis, the FTC was intended to offer unique expertise on the operation of markets and to help guard against anticompetitive practices.

---

[17] 15 U.S.C. §§ 1, 2.

The new agency was led by a bipartisan Commission of five members, nominated by the President and confirmed by the Senate, led by a Chair chosen by the President from among the five Commissioners. Section 5 of the Act empowered the FTC to prohibit "unfair methods of competition": a phrase designed to include, but reach more broadly than, the existing prohibitions of the Sherman Act.[18] More than two decades later—after the Supreme Court had made clear that Section 5 did not prohibit misconduct that did not distort competition[19]—Section 5 would be amended by the Wheeler-Lea Act of 1938 to introduce a second prohibition on "unfair or deceptive acts or practices." This would create the FTC's parallel consumer protection jurisdiction.

The FTC is not only an additional antitrust enforcer: it was also intended to be a complementary one. Accordingly, it had unique powers that differed from those of DOJ. Unlike DOJ, which enforced the antitrust laws by suing as a plaintiff in federal court, the FTC's original enforcement method was administrative. The FTC would issue a cease and desist order to a wrongdoer; if the wrongdoer subsequently violated that order, civil penalties would be imposed in an order enforcement proceeding.

It was not until 1973—in a provision introduced by the peculiar vehicle of the Trans-Alaska Pipeline Act—that the FTC gained a limited power to litigate in federal court. The new Section 13(b) of the FTC Act entitled the FTC to sue in federal court to obtain injunctive relief against a person who "is violating, or is about to violate" the laws that the FTC enforces.[20] This was a critical means of getting a preliminary injunction to stop proposed mergers: something that had previously been a serious problem for the FTC.[21] But 13(b) did not create a plenary power to litigate in federal court. In 2019, an appellate court held that this language meant that the FTC could not sue in federal court those who *had previously* violated the law but were no longer doing so.[22] And in 2021, the Supreme Court held that Section 13(b) did not authorize the Commission to obtain an injunction requiring the payment of money, such as disgorgement.[23]

3. The Clayton Act of 1914

Passed right on the heels of the FTC Act, the Clayton Act was a broader antitrust reform statute, containing a package of new measures. Perhaps most importantly, Section 7 of the Act introduced a prohibition on anticompetitive mergers and acquisitions: establishing the third pillar of the antitrust framework. Mergers had previously been successfully challenged as Sherman Act violations, but a question mark had hung over the limits of the Sherman Act as a merger-control tool: Section 7 was intended to remove all doubt. In its original form, Section 7 covered only acquisitions of stock (creating a peculiarly obvious loophole for transactions that involved the purchase of assets rather than shares) and was focused by its terms on loss of competition "between" the parties (raising a question of whether it was limited to transactions among actual or potential competitors: that is, what we would today call "horizontal" transactions).

The Clayton Act also contained a package of reforms to existing non-merger antitrust enforcement. Among other things, it introduced a reframed private right of action for victims of antitrust violations, allowing injured persons to sue wrongdoers for treble damages and injunctive relief. It also expressly exempted labor unions from the reach of antitrust condemnation, in an effort to stop the use of antitrust as an anti-union device. (The federal courts did not fully absorb this point until Congress came back to it again in the Norris-LaGuardia Act of 1932 and put the matter beyond reasonable doubt.) The Clayton Act also introduced specific rules prohibiting certain practices, such as: certain kinds of price discrimination; the use of exclusionary conditions in relation to the sale of commodities; and service as director or officer in multiple competing businesses (sometimes generally referred to as the creation of "interlocking directorates"). These rules were intended to complement and reinforce the existing Sherman Act prohibitions.

---

[18] 15 U.S.C. § 45.
[19] *See* FTC v. Raladam Co., 283 U.S. 643, 649 (1931).
[20] 15 U.S.C. § 53(b).
[21] *See* FTC v. Dean Foods Co., 384 U.S. 597, 607 (1966) ("[E]xperience shows that the Commission's inability to unscramble merged assets frequently prevents entry of an effective order of divestiture.").
[22] FTC v. Shire ViroPharma, Inc., 917 F.3d 147 (3d Cir. 2019).
[23] AMG Cap. Mgmt., LLC v. FTC, 141 S. Ct. 1341 (2021).

4. The Robinson-Patman Act of 1936

The Robinson-Patman Act was enacted in 1936, largely as a result of pressure from small businesses—especially independent grocery stores—unhappy with the better prices and terms being granted to large national chains.[24] The Robinson-Patman Act prohibits sellers from setting discriminatory prices for commodities where such discrimination may harm competition: (a) among the discriminating seller and its own competitors (so-called "primary line" discrimination); (b) among the buyers and their competitors (so-called "secondary line" discrimination); or (c) among the customers of the buyers (so-called "tertiary line" discrimination).[25] The Act creates defenses to what would otherwise be illegal discrimination, including on grounds that the discrimination was related to differences in the seller's costs, or that the discriminatory treatment was an effort to meet competition.[26] Either private plaintiffs or the federal government can bring suit for violations.[27]

The Robinson-Patman Act has been the subject of intensive criticism for many decades, because it is aimed at a practice—charging different prices to different sellers—that is generally good, not bad, for consumers.[28] (In brief, the point is that it may be profitable to offer a lower price to a more efficient, appealing, or successful buyer, or as part of an effort to induce entry or expansion, and that consumers will lose out, and overall prices will be higher, if that lower price is prohibited on the ground that it hurts other competitors.[29]) The Act's operation is exemplified by cases like *Morton Salt* (penalizing a salt manufacturer for offering volume discounts on salt to sellers who bought in larger quantities, despite the cost savings from doing so, with the result that consumer prices had to be raised in order to benefit smaller retailers)[30] and *Utah Pie* (imposing liability on market entrants for discounting to win share from a local incumbent in a highly competitive market).[31] The Act continues to play a role in private litigation, but the federal government has not brought an enforcement action in many years.[32] In 2022, the FTC signaled renewed interest in Robinson-Patman enforcement.[33]

5. The Celler-Kefauver Act of 1950

The Celler-Kefauver Amendments were a package of statutory amendments enacted in 1950 to amend Section 7 of the Clayton Act—that is, the merger control provision—to correct deficiencies and loopholes that, by that time, had become painfully clear. These amendments had three central purposes: *first*, to extend Section 7 to acquisitions of assets, as well as acquisitions of stock;[34] *second*, to clarify that Section 7 was not limited to what we would today call horizontal deals between competitors (the original version of Section 7 was focused on competition "between" the parties to the transaction[35]); and, *third*, to introduce the concept of a "line of commerce"—*i.e.*, what we would

---

[24] 15 U.S.C. § 13.

[25] Volvo Trucks North America, Inc. v. Reeder-Simco GMC, Inc., 546 U.S. 164, 176 (2006).

[26] *See generally* Hugh C. Hansen, *Robinson-Patman Law: A Review and Analysis*, 51 Fordham L. Rev. 1113, 1145–54 (1983); Gordon F. Hampton, *Defenses Under The Robinson-Patman Act*, 37 Antitrust L.J. 65 (1967).

[27] 15 U.S.C. §§ 15 (damages), 26 (injunction).

[28] *See, e.g.*, U.S. Department of Justice, *Department of Justice Report on the Robinson-Patman Act* (1977); Antitrust Modernization Committee, REPORT AND RECOMMENDATIONS (April 2007), 317-18.

[29] *See* Herbert Hovenkamp, *The Robinson-Patman Act and Competition: Unfinished Business*, 68 Antitrust L.J. 125 (2000); D. Daniel Sokol, *Analyzing Robinson-Patman*, 83 Geo. Wash. L. Rev. 2064 (2005).

[30] FTC v. Morton Salt Co., 334 U.S. 37 (1948).

[31] Utah Pie Co. v. Continental Baking Co., 386 U.S. 685 (1967).

[32] See, e.g., *Brief of* Amicus Curiae *The Federal Trade Commission in Support of Defendants-Appellants and Reversal*, Woodman's Food Market, Inc. v. The Clorox Co., Case No. 15-3001 (7th Cir. filed Nov. 2, 2015) 4 ("The FTC historically played a central role in enforcing the Robinson-Patman Act. . . . But the FTC has not brought an action to enforce Sections 2(d) or 2(e) since 1988."); Decision & Order, *In the matter of McCormick & Co.*, FTC Dkt. No. C-3939 (F.T.C. Apr. 27, 2020) (accepting consent decree). *See generally* Timothy J. Muris, *How History Informs Practice – Understanding the Development of Modern U.S. Competition Policy*, https://www.ftc.gov/sites/default/files/documents/public_statements/how-history-informs-practice-understanding-development-modern-u.s.competition-policy/murisfallaba.pdf (Nov. 19, 2003), 13 ("At the FTC, the decline in RP enforcement began in the 1970s and continued through the subsequent decades.").

[33] *See, e.g.*, Alvaro M. Bedoya, *Returning to Fairness* (remarks of Sept. 22, 2022), https://www.ftc.gov/system/files/ftc_gov/pdf/returning_to_fairness_prepared_remarks_commissioner_alvaro_bedoya.pdf.

[34] This limitation was a serious loophole in practice. *See, e.g.*, FTC Annual Report 1928, 18–19 (noting that "the effectiveness of the act has been materially lessened" as a result of decisions confirming that the Clayton Act, as it then stood, did not cover asset transactions).

[35] *See, e.g.*, Jason C. Blackford, *Vertical Acquisition and Section 7 of the Clayton Act*, 17 W. Res. L. Rev. 102, 106–10 (1965).

now call a "market"—as a replacement for a "section or community" as a zone in which competition might be harmed.[36] The Celler-Kefauver amendments created Section 7 as it exists today,[37] and they mark the last time Congress amended the core antitrust laws.

6. The Hart-Scott-Rodino Act of 1976

Congress returned to merger law in 1976 with the Hart-Scott-Rodino Act, which established a prior notification system for certain mergers and acquisitions.[38] Pursuant to the Act, proposed transactions must be notified to the federal antitrust agencies before the deal is "closed" or "consummated" if those transactions meet or exceed certain thresholds. The point of the HSR Act was to give the federal government an opportunity to spot and challenge competitively troubling mergers and acquisitions *before* the deal was consummated, to avoid the difficulties of breaking up a company back into separate viable competitors after the fact.

We will discuss the HSR Act in more detail in Chapter XI. In brief, an initial HSR merger notification is a fairly modest package of information and documents; the agencies then have a period of 30 days to conduct an initial review, within which the parties may not close their transaction. If the agencies issue a "Second Request" for further documents and information, the suspension obligation is extended, and another time period of 30 days commences once the parties have substantially complied with the request.[39] (The reviewing agency and the parties can agree to extend this deadline: why do you think parties might agree to do this?) If the agencies do not file a complaint before the expiration of the period, the parties may close their deal.

The HSR notification thresholds are updated every year. In very broad terms, effective February 2023: transactions valued up to $111.4 million are not reportable; transactions valued at more than $445.5 million are reportable; transactions valued at between $111.4 million and $445.5 million are reportable *if* one party has assets or annual sales of at least $22.3 million *and* the other has assets or annual sales of at least $222.7 million.[40]

7. Later Statutory Reforms

Statutory reforms since the 1970s have been relatively few and modest. For example, the Foreign Trade Antitrust Improvements Act ("FTAIA") clarified the application of the Sherman Act to international commerce[41]; the Antitrust Procedures and Penalties Act ("APPA" or "Tunney Act") introduced processes for the review of DOJ consent decrees[42]; the Antitrust Criminal Penalty Enhancement and Reform Act ("ACPERA") shored up DOJ's leniency program[43]; and the Merger Filing Fee Modernization Act of 2022 recalibrated merger filing fees.[44]

E. A Very Brief History of Antitrust

The history of the U.S. antitrust system is a long and rich story, and it is told at length in many excellent books and articles.[45] This section gives just a short sketch of the main arcs of the saga. It may be helpful to have this

---

[36] *See* Stephen Mann & Thomas M. Lewyn, *The Relevant Market under Section 7 of the Clayton Act: Two New Cases. Two Different Views*, 47 Va. L. Rev. 1014 (1961).

[37] For some early assessments of the impact of the Amendments, *see* M.A. Adelman, *The Antimerger Act, 1950 60*, 51 Am. Econ. Rev. 236, 236 (1961); Milton Handler & Stanley D. Robinson, *A Decade of Administration of the Celler-Kefauver Antimerger Act*, 61 COLUM. L. REV. 629 (1961).

[38] 15 U.S.C. § 18a.

[39] 15 U.S.C. § 18a(e)(2).

[40] *See infra* § XI.E. (describing the HSR system).

[41] 15 U.S.C. § 6a.

[42] 15 U.S.C. § 16(b)–16(e).

[43] 15 U.S.C. § 7a-1–7a-3.

[44] 16 C.F.R. § 803.9.

[45] For a variety of perspectives, *see, e.g.*, Amy Klobuchar, ANTITRUST: TAKING ON MONOPOLY POWER FROM GILDED AGE TO THE DIGITAL AGE (2021); Gregory J. Werden, THE FOUNDATIONS OF ANTITRUST (2020); Herbert Hovenkamp, ENTERPRISE AND AMERICAN LAW, 1836–1937 (1991); Hans B. Thorelli, THE FEDERAL ANTITRUST POLICY: ORIGINATION OF AN AMERICAN TRADITION (1955). Some of this section borrows from Daniel Francis, *Making Sense of Monopolization*, 84 Antitrust L.J. 779 (2022).

sketch in mind as context for the cases, principles, and enforcement practices that we will encounter in the rest of the book.

As you will see below and throughout the course, both doctrine and enforcement policy have undergone dramatic changes over antitrust's 130-year history, reflecting developments in changes in economic beliefs and understandings as well as changes in political and social circumstances. These changes have affected not only the content of doctrinal rules, but also the authoritative force of law from earlier periods. In the middle of the twentieth century, for example, the federal government and the Supreme Court routinely condemned mergers that combined very small players in highly competitive markets, and courts often expressed the view that superior efficiency could be a cause of antitrust concern. Today, many of these cases would not even be investigated, let alone litigated. But many earlier decisions have ceased to be followed in practice without ever having been formally overruled or repudiated. Indeed, some decisions even remain influential in some respects and totally without influence in others.[46] Likewise, the Robinson-Patman Act was enacted in the 1930s to empower the federal government, as well as private parties, to sue companies engaging in certain kinds of price discrimination. But, in light of mounting criticism of the Act's practical impact on consumers and competition, DOJ repudiated enforcement in the 1970s, and the FTC later followed suit.

All this means that it is helpful to have some sense of antitrust history before diving in and reading cases and statutes in detail. It also underscores the value of learning about the practice of courts and enforcement agencies, as well as formal doctrinal architecture. Anyone who tried to get a picture of antitrust law by just reading the text of binding court decisions would be terribly confused.[47]

1. Before 1890: Common Law

The federal antitrust statutes owe some conceptual debts to the Anglo-American common law that existed before 1890, but the magnitude of these debts have often been overstated, including by some of the Sherman Act legislators themselves.[48] Senator Sherman himself, among others, repeatedly described the Act as simply codifying common law into federal statute.[49] In particular, three strands of the common law are generally understood to have been particularly influential: the law of restraint of trade; the law of patent monopolies; and the law of anticompetitive combinations.

But, as we shall see, these strands of common-law doctrine did not really constitute or contain anything like a modern, competition-centric antitrust system. Anticompetitive agreements—even some naked price-fixing cartels—were often lawful. It was not generally illegal to use market practices like exclusivity or tying agreements to create or maintain monopoly power. And there was nothing at all that we would recognize as competition-focused merger control. However, each of these branches of common-law doctrine contained some conceptual material that proved influential and helpful to the framers of U.S. antitrust.

The first conceptual ancestor was the law of restraint of trade. From at least the 15th century, courts sometimes declined to enforce contractual obligations that unreasonably restrained the rights of persons to practice their trade

---

[46] Prominent examples of cases that remain important in some respects while uninfluential in others include *Alcoa* (influential regarding inference of monopoly power, uninfluential on definition of conduct that constitutes monopolization) and *Brown Shoe* (influential regarding market definition, uninfluential regarding thresholds for inferring harm from a change in market structure).

[47] *See, e.g.*, Herbert J. Hovenkamp, THE ANTITRUST ENTERPRISE: PRINCIPLE AND EXECUTION (2005) 208 ("While antitrust casebooks continue to print 1960s-vintage merger decisions that have never been overruled, no one, not even federal judges and certainly not government enforcement agencies, pay much attention to them."). As we will see later in this chapter and at points in the rest of the book, this is fractionally less cut-and-dried than it was in 2005, but it still captures a centrally important truth.

[48] *See, e.g.*, William L. Letwin, *The English Common Law Concerning Monopolies*, 21 U. Chi. L. Rev. 355, 355 (1954) ("The congressmen who drafted and passed the Sherman Antitrust Law thought they were merely declaring illegal offenses that the common law had always prohibited."); Donald Dewey, *The Common-Law Background of Antitrust Policy*, 1 Va. L. Rev. 759 (1955) ("During the debates on the Sherman bill, its backers on several occasions assured the floor that their object was to provide for federal enforcement of the common-law prohibitions of combinations contracts, and conspiracies in restraint of trade.")

[49] *See, e.g.*, 21 Cong. Rec. 2,456 (Mar. 21, 1890) ("[The bill] does not announce a new principle of law, but applies old and well-recognized principles of the common law to the complicated jurisdiction of our State and Federal Government."); 21 Cong. Rec. 2,461 (Mar. 21, 1890) ("Now, Mr. President, what is this bill? A remedial statute to enforce by civil process in the courts of the United States the common law against monopolies."); 21 Cong. Rec. 3,152 (Apr. 8, 1890) ("The great thing that this bill does, except affording a remedy, is to extend the common-law principles, which protected fair competition in trade in old times in England, to international and interstate commerce in the United States.").

or profession, similar to what we would call today a non-compete obligation.[50] The most famous early decision is *Dyer's Case* (1415), in which an English court refused to enforce a defendant's contractual obligation to refrain from work as a dyer.[51] The underlying concern in this and similar cases was something like unconscionable exclusion from a trade: courts were (inconsistently) concerned about the substantively unreasonable and oppressive impact of the agreement upon a worker with a valuable trade and a need to support his or her own existence. Subsequent prominent English cases included *Mitchel v. Reynolds* (1711), which articulated what amounts to a reasonableness test for contracts that restrained trade,[52] and later *Nordenfelt v. Maxim Nordenfelt* (1894), in which the highest English court was willing to approve even a worldwide restraint of 25 years' duration.[53] Informed and influenced by the English approach, American cases on restraint of trade in the decades before 1890 followed a similar pattern: intermittent concern about the unconscionability of contractual restraints that unreasonably precluded persons from practicing a trade.[54]

The second conceptual ancestor was the law constraining patent monopolies. For many centuries before 1890, governments had granted exclusive rights to engage in particular kinds of economic activity: to incentivize certain kinds of behavior, investment, or innovation; to reward loyal or influential supporters; or as part of a decision to substitute a regulated monopoly in place of a competitive regime (as in what we might call today utility-style regulation).[55] By the early seventeenth century, the longstanding practice of the British Crown of issuing "patent monopolies"—either for innovation or to reward political supporters—had become a major source of public complaint, as the holders of exclusive rights would often impose higher prices, and offer lower quality, than a competitive market would provide. Partial reform came in 1623 with the Statute of Monopolies, which invalidated some such monopolies and subjected others to a public-interest test; but, beginning with Edward Coke, some commenters began to assert that the common law itself imposed substantive limitations on the validity of patent monopolies, invalidating those that were unduly oppressive.[56] To a limited extent, saying it made it so: the assertions of Coke and others did in fact have some influence on courts and writers. (It helped that Coke became a very senior judge.) The nature and scope of the limits were not clearly articulated, and were inconsistently applied, but in at least some cases courts were willing to invalidate patent monopolies on the basis that they were contrary to the public interest.[57] However, well into the twentieth century one scholar was able to write that the common law of England "contains no special rule on the subject [of monopoly]. There is a principle of common law that 'restraints of trade are bad,' and that is all."[58]

More generally, antipathy to the "spirit of monopoly"—including monopolies created by the government, the already-declined trade guilds, and other tools of exclusion—permeated the political culture of the early United States.[59] Some state constitutions contained antimonopoly clauses limiting the grant of exclusive economic rights, and opposition to monopolies, especially state-created ones, was widespread.[60] By the mid-19th century, "Jacksonian" concerns about the capture of the state by private interests fueled public opposition to state

---

[50] *See, e.g.*, William L. Letwin, *The English Common Law Concerning Monopolies*, 21 U. Chi. L. Rev. 355, 373–79 (1954).

[51] Y.B. 2 Hen. V, 5B (1414).

[52] 24 Eng. Rep. 347 (Q.B. 1711).

[53] [1894] A.C. 535.

[54] Hans B. Thorelli, THE FEDERAL ANTITRUST POLICY: ORIGINATION OF AN AMERICAN TRADITION (1955) 36–53.

[55] *See generally, e.g.*, Christine MacLeod, INVENTING THE INDUSTRIAL REVOLUTION: THE ENGLISH PATENT SYSTEM 1660–1800 (2002); W.H. Price, THE ENGLISH PATENTS OF MONOPOLY (1906).

[56] *See, e.g.*, Edward Coke, 3 INSTITUTES Ch. 85 ("[A]ll grants of monopolies are against the ancient and fundamentall laws of this kingdome . . . it appeareth that a mans trade is accounted his life, because it maintaineth his life; and therefore the monopolist that taketh away a mans trade, taketh away his life, and therefore is so much the more odious, because he is vir sanguinis").

[57] *See generally, e.g.*, William L. Letwin, *The English Common Law Concerning Monopolies*, 21 U. Chi. L. Rev. 355, 356–67 (1954); E. F. Churchill, *Monopolies*, 41 L. Q. Rev. 275 (1925).

[58] F. D. Simpson, *How Far Does the Law of England Forbid Monopoly?*, 41 L. Q. Rev. 393, 393 (1925).

[59] *See, e.g.* , GORDON S. WOOD, THE RADICALISM OF THE AMERICAN REVOLUTION, 319 (1991). *See also* J.A.C. Grant, *The Gild Returns to America, I*, 4 J. POL. 303, 309 (1942). *See also* Letter from John Adams, Ben Franklin, and Thomas Jefferson, to Baron von Thulemeier (March 14, 1785) (criticizing reservation of exclusive rights "to particular persons or descriptions of persons" as fruit of "a very remote & unenlightened period").

[60] *See, e.g.*, Steven G. Calabresi & Larissa C. Leibowitz, *Monopolies and the Constitution: A History of Crony Capitalism*, 36 HARV. J.L. & PUB. POL'Y 983, 1109 et seq. (2013); J.D. Forrest, *Anti-Monopoly Legislation in the United States*, 1 Am. J. Soc. 411 (1896); *see also* Alexandra K. Howell, *Enforcing a Wall of Separation Between Big Business and State: Protection from Monopolies in State Constitutions*, 96 Notre Dame L. Rev. 859, 866 *et seq.* (2020).

involvement in economic activity, including grants of monopoly as well as other forms of regulation that suppressed competition and commercial freedom.

The third and final line of antitrust's common-law ancestry is the law of what we might call anticompetitive combinations. Today, we are accustomed to thinking of a naked price-fixing cartel as the clearest example of antitrust illegality. And certainly the older common law, particularly in the United States, contained some basis for condemning price-fixing.[61] But this record was very mixed, particularly with respect to combinations of producers.[62] In practice, skepticism was much more likely to be directed at the actions of organized labor than at price-fixing cartels by producers.[63]

The nineteenth century, with the ascendancy of freedom of contract and the rise of modern industrial and labor organization, saw England repeal many previous statutory anti-combination measures, and English and American courts adopt a more ambivalent and ambiguous approach to conspiracies, sustaining many that we would regard today as nakedly anticompetitive.[64] In the famous case of *Mogul Steamship* (1892), the English House of Lords held that, while a cartel agreement would not be enforced, it was not tortious.[65] Overall, the record of American and English courts regarding anticompetitive combinations was an inconsistent mess.[66] The "anticompetitive" character of an agreement or practice was not usually a reason to infer that it was tortious, criminal, or even suspect.

All in all, we can probably say two things about the pre-1890 common law background against which U.S. antitrust law was created. First, it contained some conceptual threads—including scrutiny of agreements that excluded willing traders from the market, and some concern about the control of at least some kinds of monopoly power—that were to be woven into the fabric of the Sherman Act. Second, competition as such was not a specially

---

[61] *See, e.g.*, John C. Peppin, *Price-Fixing Agreements under the Sherman Anti-Trust Law*, 28 Calif. L. Rev. 297, 310–24 (1940) (noting statutory and common-law basis for skepticism and condemnation of price fixing, and stating "down to the start of the nineteenth century agreements which directly fixed prices or wages were regarded as unlawful per se and also criminal at common law, whether or not the parties thereto controlled the market or any part thereof, and that the rule was applied indiscriminately both to price-fixing and wage-fixing agreements").

[62] Donald Dewey, *The Common-Law Background of Antitrust Policy*, 1 Va. L. Rev. 759, 768 (1955) ("So far as merchants were concerned, prosecutions [in England] for conspiracy to monopolize or restrain trade were virtually unknown."); Herbert Hovenkamp, *Labor Conspiracies in American Law, 1880–1930*, 66 Tex. L. Rev. 919, 922 (1988) ("During the first decades of the nineteenth century, American courts toyed with a conspiracy theory of labor organizing that condemned as unlawful two or more employees' coordinated work stoppage for the purpose of securing higher wages. . . . Indeed, a small number of early American courts concluded that combinations were illegal under received common law. Whether American courts ever actually adopted the conspiracy theory of labor activity is doubtful, although some scholars have concluded they did. Few if any American antebellum decisions examined the legality of a mere combination and strike for the purpose of raising wages, with no coercive activity directed at others."); John C. Peppin, *Price-Fixing Agreements under the Sherman Anti-Trust Law*, 28 Calif. L. Rev. 297, 336–49 (1940) (chronicling cases and noting "it certainly cannot be said that [before 1890] American courts held that agreements directly fixing prices or wages were unlawful *per se* at common law" and that "[o]n the contrary, it does not even appear that a presumption of illegality was raised against them"); Arthur M. Allen, *Criminal Conspiracies in Restraint of Trade at Common Law*, 23 Harv. L. Rev. 531 (1910).

[63] *See, e.g.*, Gary Minda, *The Common Law, Labor, and Antitrust*, 11 Indus. Relations L. J. 461, 484–85 (1989) (describing early case law and noting that "even though both sides could claim that the same rules protected their liberty, independence, and free will, the courts were much more inclined to find protection for only one side in the struggle").

[64] John C. Peppin, *Price-Fixing Agreements under the Sherman Anti-Trust Law*, 28 Calif. L. Rev. 297, 325–33 (1940). William L. Letwin, *The English Common Law Concerning Monopolies*, 21 U. Chi. L. Rev. 355, 379–84 (1954) ("The statute law governing combinations became increasingly lenient during the nineteenth century, in response to greater sympathy, abstract as well as sentimental, for the labor unions. The common law, influenced by a feeling that employers should not be denied rights granted to workers, matched the new legal power of the latter with a solicitous concern for employers' combinations; in the end it came to put a higher value on the freedom of entrepreneurs to use any means short of violence to outstrip competitors than on the right of the public to enjoy the advantages of competition.")

[65] Mogul Steamship Co. v. McGregor [1892] A.C. 25.

[66] *See, e.g.*, Donald Dewey, *The Common-Law Background of Antitrust Policy*, 1 Va. L. Rev. 759, 773–86 (1955) (noting inconsistent judicial practice); John C. Peppin, *Price-Fixing Agreements under the Sherman Anti-Trust Law*, 28 Calif. L. Rev. 297, 309 (1940) (noting the "frequent assertion" that price fixing was illegal at common law but that this view "cannot be supported" for either English or American law as of 1890); F. D. Simpson, *How Far Does the Law of England Forbid Monopoly?*, 41 L. Q. Rev. 393, 395 (1925) (noting that an anticompetitive combine may successfully defend against suits for harm inflicted on others and sue to enforce its contracts, but that may fail to sue to enforce the terms of the combination itself: "The cases show only one weakness in the legal position of combines. They cannot prevent one of their members leaving them, and they cannot always, even while he remains a member, enforce the contract against him."); *see also* United States v. Socony-Vacuum Oil Co., 310 U.S. 150, 224 n.59 (1940) ("Whatever may have been the status of price-fixing agreements at common law . . . the Sherman Act has a broader application to them than the common law prohibitions or sanctions.")

protected value at common law, nor was market or monopoly power in the economic sense, as such, a matter for legal concern or condemnation in virtually any circumstance.

Thus, the Sherman Act was a fresh start for the U.S. antitrust tradition, however much its authors and supporters might have thought or suggested otherwise.

2. 1890–1930s: Early Stirrings

President Benjamin Harrison signed the Sherman Act into life in July 1890, but neither he nor his immediate successors seemed particularly enthusiastic about the new law. Neither Harrison's Attorney General, William Miller, nor Grover Cleveland's first Attorney General, Richard Olney, were much interested in antitrust enforcement.[67] Cleveland's second Attorney General, Judson Harmon, appears to have taken the Act, and his own role in enforcing it, at least somewhat more seriously.[68] But the McKinley Administration presented "a lower water-mark equaled during no other period."[69] They were not alone: indeed, most professional economists of the time were skeptical, rather than supportive, of the new Sherman Act, with many believing "industrial monopoly was both inevitable and socially beneficial" given scale economies and natural-monopoly dynamics.[70] Organized labor, too, was only lukewarm.[71]

But Roosevelt, Taft, and Wilson were somewhat more interested in the antitrust project. Theodore Roosevelt probably does not quite deserve his modern reputation as a trustbuster: as one author writes, "Theodore Roosevelt did not favor busting trusts at any time in his public life, and over the course of his presidency, he became ever less fond of Sherman Act litigation."[72] He favored developing antitrust law in a manner that allowed the benefits of big business, but he supported government administrative regulation of the economy in a manner that would later be associated with the role of the Federal Trade Commission.[73] His administration did, however, bring the landmark *Northern Securities* case challenging the use of a holding company to combine competing railroads, which resulted in a Supreme Court-ordered breakup,[74] as well as the *Swift & Co.* case against the beef trust.[75] Roosevelt appears to have personally instigated the first and at least approved the second.[76]

William Taft, who had made a landmark contribution to antitrust law as a judge on the Sixth Circuit,[77] was a much more energetic antitrust prosecutor as President, and brought a blockbuster challenge to the U.S. Steel colossus (although it would ultimately fail in the Supreme Court).[78] He would go on to write an influential antitrust treatise after leaving the Presidency.[79] In the three-way election of 1912, antitrust played a prominent role.[80] And the victor, Woodrow Wilson, assisted by his advisor Louis Brandeis, would lead an effort for antitrust reform,

---

[67] Hans B. Thorelli, THE FEDERAL ANTITRUST POLICY: ORIGINATION OF AN AMERICAN TRADITION (1955) 373 *et seq.*

[68] *Id.* at 394 et seq.

[69] *Id.* at 405.

[70] Herbert Hovenkamp, ENTERPRISE AND AMERICAN LAW, 1836–1937 (1991) 219–20; Morton J. Horwitz, THE TRANSFORMATION OF AMERICAN LAW, 1870–1960: THE CRISIS OF LEGAL ORTHODOXY (1992), 80–85 (describing a "stunning reversal"); Hans B. Thorelli, THE FEDERAL ANTITRUST POLICY: ORIGINATION OF AN AMERICAN TRADITION (1955) 311–29.

[71] Richard Franklin Bensel, THE POLITICAL ECONOMY OF AMERICAN INDUSTRIALIZATION, 1877–1900 (2000) 343.

[72] Gregory J. Werden, THE FOUNDATIONS OF ANTITRUST (2020) 87. *See also, e.g.,* Leroy G. Dorsey, *Theodore Roosevelt and Corporate America, 1901-1909: A Reexamination,* 25 Pres. Stud. Q. 725 (1995).

[73] Gregory J. Werden, THE FOUNDATIONS OF ANTITRUST (2020) Ch. 9; William Letwin, LAW AND ECONOMIC POLICY IN AMERICA: THE EVOLUTION OF THE SHERMAN ANTITRUST ACT (1965) 195–238.

[74] Northern Securities Co. v. United States, 193 U.S. 197 (1904).

[75] Swift & Co. v. United States, 196 U.S. 375 (1905).

[76] Hans B. Thorelli, THE FEDERAL ANTITRUST POLICY: ORIGINATION OF AN AMERICAN TRADITION (1955) 424 (noting that "Roosevelt directed [AG] Knox to take action" in the *Northern Securities* matter), 427 (noting that the beef cases did not originate with field DOJ employees and concluding that the matter was at least the subject of "preliminary consultation" between the AG and the President).

[77] United States v. Addyston Pipe & Steel Co., 85 F. 271 (6th Cir. 1898).

[78] United States v. U.S. Steel Corp., 251 U.S. 417 (1920). For some context, *see* Guy B. Maseritz, *"No Inventions, No Innovations": Reassessing the Government's Antitrust Case Against United States Steel Corporation,* 7 J. Bus. & Tech. L. 247 (2012).

[79] W.H. Taft, THE ANTI-TRUST ACT AND THE SUPREME COURT (1914).

[80] Daniel A. Crane, *All I Really Need to Know About Antitrust I Learned in 1912,* 100 Iowa L. Rev. 2025 (2015); William Kolasky, *The Election of 1912: A Pivotal Moment in Antitrust History,* 25 Antitrust 82 (2011).

including the passage of the Clayton Act to augment antitrust enforcement and the creation of the Federal Trade Commission.[81]

The U.S. Supreme Court decisions of these early years show antitrust finding its feet in some fundamental respects. For example, after holding on constitutional grounds that the Sherman Act did not apply to conduct among manufacturers in *E.C. Knight* in 1895—a holding that would have marginalized antitrust right from the get-go—the Court walked this conclusion back in *Addyston Pipe & Steel* (1899) and *Swift & Co.* (1905).[82] After holding in *Trans-Missouri Freight* in 1897 (and the *Joint-Traffic* case the following year) that Section 1 invalidated all contracts that restrain trade, regardless of their reasonableness or effects[83]—a holding that would have made antitrust completely unworkable by prohibiting virtually every commercial agreement—the Court would course-correct in *Standard Oil* (1911) by adopting a more discriminating "rule of reason" approach to the legality of restraints.[84]

Despite President Wilson's enthusiasm for antitrust enforcement, it fell somewhat by the wayside with the advent of the First World War, the skepticism of the Supreme Court (which in 1920 rejected the government's blockbuster lawsuit against U.S. Steel[85]), and increasing public toleration for industrial concentration and cooperation.[86]

3. 1940s–1960s: The Rise of Structuralism

The beginning of the mid-century revival of antitrust enforcement is symbolized by FDR's appointment of Robert Jackson and then (and in particular) Thurman Arnold as successive heads of DOJ's Antitrust Division, which signaled the invigoration of antitrust enforcement as a serious and sustained federal project.[87] In a lengthy message to Congress in April 1938, President Roosevelt called for significant investment in antitrust enforcement and the augmentation of the antitrust statutes.[88] A string of antitrust enforcement actions were filed.[89] After years of effort,[90] the Celler-Kefauver Amendments of 1950 reinforced the merger-control standard in Section 7 of the Clayton Act.[91]

The rise of active antitrust enforcement was accompanied by an emerging view that would become known as structuralism: the idea that market structure (*i.e.*, the number, market share, and characteristics of market participants), and concentration in particular (*i.e.*, the domination of a market by a few large firms), should be the focus of antitrust intervention. The core structuralist idea was that concentrated markets tended to be less

---

[81] *See generally, e.g.*, Marc Winerman, *The Origins of the Federal Trade Commission: Concentration, Cooperation, Control, and Competition*, 71 Antitrust L.J. 1 (2003); G.erald Berk, LOUIS D. BRANDEIS AND THE MAKING OF REGULATED COMPETITION, 1900–1932 (2009); William Letwin, LAW AND ECONOMIC POLICY IN AMERICA: THE EVOLUTION OF THE SHERMAN ANTITRUST ACT (1965) 271–78.

[82] United States v. E. C. Knight Co., 156 U.S. 1 (1895); Addyston Pipe & Steel Co. v. U. S., 175 U.S. 211 (1899); Swift & Co. v. United States, 196 U.S. 375 (1905).

[83] United States v. Trans-Missouri Freight Ass'n, 166 U.S. 290 (1897); United States v. Joint-Traffic Ass'n, 171 U.S. 505 (1898).

[84] Standard Oil Co. of New Jersey v. United States, 221 U.S. 1 (1911).

[85] United States v. U.S. Steel Corp., 251 U.S. 417 (1920).

[86] *See, e.g.*, Harold J. Adam, *Anti-Trust (Anti-Monopoly) Policy and Application 1920-1929*, 4 Am. Econ. 9 (1960); Spencer Weber Waller, *The Antitrust Legacy of Thurman Arnold*, 78 St. John's L. Rev. 569, 577 (2004) ("Throughout the 1920s, the antitrust laws were barely enforced, if at all").

[87] *See generally* Spencer Weber Waller, *The Antitrust Legacy of Thurman Arnold*, 78 St. John's L. Rev. 569 (2004). See also Thurman W. Arnold, *Prosecution Policy under the Sherman Act*, 24 A.B.A. J. 417 (1938); Thurman W. Arnold, *Antitrust Activities of the Department of Justice*, 19 Or. L. Rev. 22, 22 (1939) ("The Antitrust Division of the Department of Justice interprets the war as a new challenge which intensifies the need for its activity. War has added to the task before us rather than subtracted from it because it has increased the opportunities for aggressive combinations to use war conditions as an excuse for the destruction of that industrial democracy on which political democracy depends."); *see also* John C. Peppin, *Price-Fixing Agreements under the Sherman Anti-Trust Law*, 28 Calif. L. Rev. 297 (1940) (noting "the current drive for vigorous enforcement of the antitrust laws"); Ellis W. Hawley, THE NEW DEAL AND THE PROBLEM OF MONOPOLY (1966) Chs. 22 & 23.

[88] Franklin D. Roosevelt, *Message to Congress on Curbing Monopolies* (Apr. 29, 1938), https://www.presidency.ucsb.edu/documents/message-congress-curbing-monopolies.

[89] For some highlight decisions of the 1940s, *see, e.g.*, United States v. Aluminum Co. of Am., 148 F.2d 416 (2d Cir. 1945); American Tobacco Co. v. United States, 328 U.S. 781 (1946); United States v Columbia Steel Co, 334 US 495 (1948); United States v. Paramount Pictures, 334 U.S. 131 (1948); Standard Oil Co. of California v. United States, 337 U.S. 293 (1949).

[90] See, e.g., Comment, *Corporate Consolidations and the Concentration of Economic Power: Proposals for Revitalization of Section 7 of the Clayton Act*, 57 Yale L.J. 613, 621–27 (1948) (chronicling a variety of proposals).

[91] Milton Handler & Stanley D. Robinson, *A Decade of Administration of the Celler-Kefauver Antimerger Act*, 61 Colum. L. Rev. 629 (1961).

competitive, with higher prices, markups, and profits.[92] Scholars proposed reforms that would tilt antitrust law and enforcement away from the existing conduct-focused paradigm that posed lengthy and difficult problems of proof, and toward a structure-focused approach that would allow intervention based on market structure alone and would favor structural remedies like corporate breakup.[93] A Presidential Task Force on Antitrust Policy proposed, among other things, a "Concentrated Industries Act" to break up oligopolistic markets.[94] However, despite later caricatures, structuralist writers were not necessarily or always hostile to size as such or to efficiency claims.[95]

Throughout the 1960s, the Supreme Court issued a series of decisions generally favoring government enforcement—including in cases that would not have been brought in earlier or later eras—in parallel with a surge in enforcement activity.[96] In the famous *Brown Shoe* decision (1962), for example, the Supreme Court indicated that mergers could be illegal even if they led only to very modest incremental increases in market concentration.[97] In *Continental Can* (1964) the Court prohibited a merger between a metal can manufacturer and a glass bottle manufacturer, relying on some very limited and generalized discussion about substitution between metal and glass containers, rather than a thorough analysis of the scope of competition for particular end-uses.[98] In *Von's Grocery* (1966) the Court prohibited a merger in a highly competitive market without any evidence that economic harm was plausible.[99] In *Pabst Brewing* (1966) the Court condemned a national merger between two brewing companies to a combined 4.5% share of the national market, relying primarily on the existence of somewhat higher—but still unimpressive—combined shares of sales in Wisconsin (24% combined share) and the Wisconsin-Illinois-Michigan "three state area" (11.32% combined share), without ever establishing whether the market in which competition took place was national, state-specific, or something in between.[100] And in *Procter & Gamble* (1968) the Court invalidated the acquisition of a liquid bleach brand by a consumer-products firm that did not sell bleach at all,

---

[92] The core of structuralism has recently been summarized in more technical terms as follows: "This empirical implementation of the paradigm typically involved regression analysis. The dependent variable was a market outcome such as profits, markups, or prices. The key explanatory variable sought to capture the structure of the market with a measure of concentration—usually the Herfindahl–Hirschman index, which is the sum of squared market shares. The regression also included a range of control variables intended to capture other exogenous reasons for variation. Structure is thus related to performance, with (unobservable) conduct captured as the estimated relationship between structure and performance. In this regression, the coefficient on the concentration measure is intended to capture how the toughness of competition changes as market concentration changes." Steven Berry, Martin Gaynor & Fiona Scott Morton, *Do Increasing Markups Matter? Lessons from Empirical Industrial Organization*, 33 J. Econ. Persp. 44, 46 (2019).

[93] *See, e.g.*, Joe S. Bain, INDUSTRIAL ORGANIZATION (1968) 651 ("[T]he law might be changed to state that structural situations (involving high concentration and impeded entry) which might be expected to have and demonstrably do have monopolistic performance tendencies are generally illegal, without particular reference to the lines of market conduct through which the undesirable structure has ben created, maintained, and exploited. . . . Furthermore, the law might instruct the courts that the usual remedy for illegal monopoly as defined should be dissolution or dismemberment of the principal firm or firms possessing the monopoly . . . provided that there would be no serious untoward side effects of such a remedy and that lesser remedies would not clearly suffice[.]"); Carl Kaysen & Donald F. Turner, ANTITRUST POLICY: AN ECONOMIC AND LEGAL ANALYSIS (1965) 46 ("We propose statutory authorization for the reduction of undue market power, whether individually or jointly possessed; this to be done normally by dissolution, divorcement, or divestiture. We would except market power derived from economies of scale, valid patents, or the introduction of new processes, products, or marketing techniques."); Joe S. Bain, BARRIERS TO NEW COMPETITION (1956) 212 ("[I]f it is found that the integration is not required for real economy and does not reduce costs, enforced disintegration of established firms, resulting in the establishment of non-integrated industries at both stages of production, may reduce the importance of scale economies . . . without offsetting disadvantages."); Derek C. Bok, *Section 7 of the Clayton Act and the Merging of Law and Economics*, 74 Harv. L. Rev. 226, 238–49 (1960).

[94] Phil C. Neal et al., *Report of the White House Task Force on Antitrust Policy*, 2 Antitrust L. & Econ. Rev. 11 (1968).

[95] *See, e.g.*, Joe S. Bain, BARRIERS TO NEW COMPETITION (1956) 207 ("[Entry barriers] resting on real economies of large-scale plant and firm (whatever their importance) should not and probably could not be removed, because of the adverse effects on efficiency of such removal."), 208 ("[T]he results of fairly high seller concentration might vary widely according to the condition of entry to the industry, and alteration of the condition of entry might constitute a generally more feasible regulatory technique than dissolution and dismemberment policies aimed just at reducing seller concentration.").

[96] *See, e.g.*, Donald Dewey, *Mergers and Cartels: Some Reservations about Policy*, 51 Am. Econ. Rev. 255, 255 (1961) ("In the last two decades, antitrust has finally been tried with a vengeance").

[97] Brown Shoe Co. v. United States, 370 U.S. 294, 343–44 (1962) ("If a merger achieving 5% control were now approved, we might be required to approve future merger efforts by Brown's competitors seeking similar market shares. The oligopoly Congress sought to avoid would then be furthered and it would be difficult to dissolve the combinations previously approved."); *but see id.* at 343 (noting higher concentration figures in some markets).

[98] United States v. Continental Can Co., 378 U.S. 441 (1964).

[99] United States v. Von's Grocery Co., 384 U.S. 270 (1966).

[100] United States v. Pabst Brewing Co., 384 U.S. 546 (1966).

apparently motivated primarily by a fear that the merged firm would enjoy economies of scope as a result of its presence in the consumer-products space.[101] Dissenting in *Von's Grocery*, Justice Potter Stewart famously griped: "The sole consistency that I can find is that in litigation under [Section] 7, the Government always wins."[102]

4. 1970s–2020s: Chicago and Post-Chicago

Structuralism eventually came under fire from both evolving perspectives in economics and changing political fortunes. In economic scholarship, structuralism was subject to increasing skepticism, including for difficulties in measuring key inputs to structuralist analysis (such as competitive performance) and in interpreting them (for example: do high profits imply desirable efficiencies, or undesirable anticompetitive harms?).[103] Ultimately the structure-conduct-performance paradigm became "discredited" in mainstream industrial organization economics.[104] Politically, too, the conditions favored realignment, with a broad move toward deregulatory economic policy in the United States and the ascendancy of the law and economics movement.[105]

Thus the 1970s proved to be a major turning point for antitrust law and policy, in what is known colloquially today as the "Chicago School Revolution." This multi-dimensional change in climate involved, among other things: (1) the normative orientation of antitrust policy toward maximizing the welfare of persons (with some debate and confusion about which persons counted and in what ways); (2) increased skepticism of the idea that business size and concentration were meaningfully correlated with consumer harm; (3) an increased emphasis on the efficiency-generating characteristics of many business practices that might lead to increased market power; and (4) a general turn—at the antitrust agencies, in the judiciary, and in academia—toward caution in matters of economic regulation, lest antitrust intervention end up suppressing the very competitive process that it was intended to encourage.

These views were most famously expressed by Robert Bork in a highly influential 1978 book called *The Antitrust Paradox*,[106] and by other leading "Chicago School" figures like Richard Posner and Frank Easterbrook.[107] The revolution in antitrust was also fueled by other currents and developments, including Joseph Schumpeter's account of "creative destruction" (which implied that the existence of monopoly was compatible with—and could be an

---

[101] FTC v. Procter & Gamble Co., 386 U.S. 568 (1967).

[102] United States v. Von's Grocery Co., 384 U.S. 270, 301 (1966) (Stewart, J., dissenting).

[103] *See, e.g.*, Sherril Shaffer, *Structure, conduct, performance, and welfare*, 9 Rev. Indus. Org. 435, 447 (1994) ("[W]elfare is not monotonically related to any of the dimensions of structure, conduct, or performance. . . . The findings emphasize that, apart from special conditions, there is no shortcut around the need to base public policy directly on total welfare. This conclusion has pessimistic implications for the potential usefulness of exercises designed to reduce welfare calculations to simple structural rules of thumb[.]"); Steven Berry, Martin Gaynor & Fiona Scott Morton, *Do Increasing Markups Matter? Lessons from Empirical Industrial Organization*, 33 J. Econ. Persp. 44, 46 (2019) ("Measuring concentration is inherently difficult because economic markets are not observed directly in the data. . . . Measuring economic outcomes was another problem for research in the structure-conduct-performance tradition. Most measures of profits use accounting measures, which are not economic profits. Markups are rarely directly observed in firm-level data at all[.] . . . But even if the structure and output variables were measured with precision and the analysis was within a single industry, structure-conduct-performance researchers . . . often grappled with the problem of interpreting their regressions [and particularly distinguishing between anticompetitive and procompetitive explanations.] . . . [T]here is no well-defined 'causal effect of concentration on price,' but rather a set of hypotheses that can explain observed correlations of the joint outcomes of price, measured markups, market share, and concentration."); T.F. Bresnahan, *Industries with Market Power* in 2 Richard Schmalensee & Robert Willig (eds.) HANDBOOK OF INDUSTRIAL ORGANIZATION (1989) 1012–13 (noting "dissatisfactions" regarding hypotheses in the structure-conduct-performance paradigm); Richard Schmalensee, *Inter-Industry Studies of Structure and Performance*, in Richard Schmalensee & Robert Willig (eds.), HANDBOOK OF INDUSTRIAL ORGANIZATION (1989) 974 (noting that many studies find "no statistically significant linear relation between domestic concentration and profitability").

[104] Steven Berry, Martin Gaynor & Fiona Scott Morton, *Do Increasing Markups Matter? Lessons from Empirical Industrial Organization*, 33 J. Econ. Persp. 44, 46 (2019).

[105] *See generally, e.g.*, George L. Priest, THE RISE OF LAW AND ECONOMICS: AN INTELLECTUAL HISTORY (2020); Martha Derthick & Paul J. Quirk, THE POLITICS OF DEREGULATION (1985); Stephen Breyer, REGULATION AND ITS REFORM (1985); Robert W. Crandall, *Deregulation: The U.S. Experience*, 139 J. Instit. & Theoret. Econ. 419 (1983); Guido Calabresi & A. Douglas Melamed, *Property Rules, Liability Rules and Inalienability: One View of the Cathedral*, 85 Harv. L. Rev. 1089 (1972); Guido Calabresi, THE COSTS OF ACCIDENTS: A LEGAL AND ECONOMIC ANALYSIS (1970). The roots of law and economics extend much further back in time. *See, e.g.*, Walton L. Hamilton, *Law and Economics*, 19 Am. Econ. Rev. 56 (1929).

[106] Robert H. Bork, THE ANTITRUST PARADOX: A POLICY AT WAR WITH ITSELF (1978); Robert H. Bork, *Legislative Intent and the Policy of the Sherman Act*, 9 J. L. & Econ. 7 (1966).

[107] *See, e.g.*, Richard Posner, ANTITRUST LAW: AN ECONOMIC PERSPECTIVE (1978); Frank H. Easterbrook, *The Limits of Antitrust*, 63 Tex. L. Rev. 1 (1984); Richard A. Posner, *The Rule of Reason and the Economic Approach: Reflections on the Sylvania Decision*, 45 U. Chi. L. Rev . 1 (1977); Aaron Director & Edward H. Levi, *Law and the Future: Trade Regulation*, 51 Nw. U. L. Rev. 281 (1956).

inducement to—intense dynamic competition)[108]; William Baumol's theory of "contestable markets" (which indicated that the threat of new entry from outside markets could discipline competition within them)[109]; and growing calls for efficiencies to be treated as a factor in favor of the legality of a merger or acquisition, rather than a reason for condemning it.[110] The antitrust agencies cut back their enforcement activities during the 1980s as the new view, and its adherents, became increasingly influential in the federal government.[111]

But, right from the start, the accommodation of "Chicago School" antitrust triggered a robust literature of "Post-Chicago" qualification and criticism. Scholars like Eleanor Fox, Steve Salop, Jon Baker, and Robert Pitofsky argued for more active antitrust doctrine and enforcement practices.[112] And the Supreme Court did not rush to embrace "hard Chicago" positions, instead generally favoring a middle position that was influenced by Chicagoan thinking, but less opposed to intervention and more focused on administrability (the "Harvard School").[113] Across a series of areas of antitrust doctrine, the Court cut back from bright-line prohibitions in favor of a case-specific effects-based analysis. Emblematic decisions in this vein included *General Dynamics* (1974) (holding that a structural case of illegality could be rebutted by evidence showing that the market shares presented a misleading picture of competition), *GTE Sylvania* (1977) (holding that it was not *per se* illegal for a seller to distribute its products through exclusive distribution territories), *BMI* (1979) (establishing that a combination among competitors to create a new product was not *per se* illegal even though it involved joint price-setting), *Jefferson Parish* (1984) (holding that tying one product to another could not be unlawful unless the business held market power in the product that provided the leverage to impose the condition), and *Northwest Wholesale Stationers* (1985) (holding that expulsion from a common buying cooperative was not *per se* illegal but required rule-of-reason analysis).[114]

In the age that was dawning, much "mainstream" scholarly debate about antitrust settled into a somewhat technocratic conversation about the economic tendencies of particular phenomena and practices. With antitrust's foundations established as the protection of consumers from economic harms, scholarship and argument often focused on whether and when the economic harms of particular practices (resale price maintenance, exclusive dealing, tying, and so on) might outweigh the benefits of tolerating them. In 2005, a leading antitrust scholar could open his survey of issues in antitrust law and policy by pointing out that, "[a]fter decades of debate, today we enjoy more consensus about the goals of the antitrust laws than at any time in the last half century."[115]

About ten years later, the consensus was sharply challenged. In the second decade of the 21st century, a school of "Neo-Brandeisian" critics—including Tim Wu, Lina Khan, and others—emerged to criticize modern antitrust as outdated, "defanged," and unfit for purpose, arguing in a series of writings that antitrust agencies and federal

---

[108] Joseph Schumpeter, CAPITALISM, SOCIALISM, AND DEMOCRACY (1942).

[109] William J. Baumol, CONTESTABLE MARKETS AND THE THEORY OF INDUSTRIAL STRUCTURE (1982).

[110] *See, e.g.,* Oliver E. Williamson, *Economies as an Antitrust Defense: The Welfare Tradeoffs*, 58 Am. Econ. Rev. 18 (1968); FTC v. Procter & Gamble Co., 386 U.S. 568 (1967) (Harlan, J., concurring).

[111] *See, e.g.,* F.M. Scherer, *Merger Policy in the 1970s and 1980s* in Robert J. Larner & James W. Meehan, Jr. (eds.), ECONOMICS AND ANTITRUST POLICY (1989) 90–94 ("Many mergers that almost surely would have drawn a challenge from past administrations were let through; and the number of challenges issued per year by the two enforcement agencies declined by half relative to 1960–1980 averages despite all-time peak levels of merger activity."); William E. Kovacic, *Failed Expectations: The Troubled Past and Uncertain Future of the Sherman Act as a Tool for Deconcentration*, 74 Iowa L. Rev. 1105 (1989) (1981–88 saw "the smallest number of [Section 2] prosecutions the . . . agencies have initiated in any eight-year period since 1900").

[112] *See, e.g.,* Robert Pitofsky (ed.), HOW THE CHICAGO SCHOOL OVERSHOT THE MARK: THE EFFECT OF CONSERVATIVE ECONOMIC ANALYSIS ON U.S. ANTITRUST (2008); Herbert Hovenkamp, *Post-Chicago Antitrust: A Review and Critique*, 2001 Colum. Bus. L. Rev. 257, 273 (2001); Jonathan B. Baker, *Recent Developments in Economics that Challenge Chicago School Views*, 58 Antitrust L.J. 645, 646 (1989); Eleanor M. Fox, *The Battle for the Soul of Antitrust*, 75 Calif. L. Rev. 917 (1987); Eleanor M. Fox, *Consumer Beware Chicago*, 84 Mich. L. Rev. 1714, 1715 (1986); Thomas G. Krattenmaker & Steven C. Salop, *Anticompetitive Exclusion: Raising Rivals' Costs to Achieve Power over Price*, 96 Yale L.J. 209 (1986); Herbert Hovenkamp, *Antitrust After Chicago*, 84 Mich. L. Rev. 213, 225 (1985).

[113] See, e.g., Einer Elhauge, H*arvard, Not Chicago: Which Antitrust School Drives Recent U.S. Supreme Court Decisions?* 3 Comp. Pol'y Int'l 59 (2007); William E. Kovacic, *The Intellectual DNA of Modern U.S. Competition Law for Dominant Firm Conduct: The Chicago/Harvard Double Helix*, 2007 Colum. Bus. L. Rev. 1, 36-38 (2007).

[114] *See* Continental Television v. GTE Sylvania, 433 U.S. 36 (1977); Broadcast Music, Inc. v. CBS, Inc. :: 441 US 1 (1979); Jefferson Parish Hospital District No. 2 v. Hyde, 466 US 2 (1984); Northwest Wholesale Stationers, Inc. v. Pacific Stationery & Printing Co., 472 U.S. 284 (1985).

[115] Herbert J. Hovenkamp, THE ANTITRUST ENTERPRISE: PRINCIPLE AND EXECUTION (2005), 1.

courts had been weak and ineffective stewards of the antitrust function, and that a radical shakeup was needed.[116] At the core of the emerging Neo-Brandeisian movement was an *antimonopoly* project: it centrally conceived of antitrust as a tool of opposition to monopoly power as such and as a means to pursue broader aims, including economic deconcentration, greater equality of economic opportunity, and equity. Following the Presidential election of 2020, Neo-Brandeisians were appointed to prominent leadership positions in the federal government.[117] This development, too, has elicited criticism, including for this school's emphasis on criticizing established practices rather than providing a workable and appealing alternative, and for its rejection of economic welfare as a guide to policy.[118] At the time of writing, there is no significant evidence that courts have been influenced by distinctively "Neo-Brandeisian" ideas. Changes at the agencies have been relatively limited: notable developments have included the pursuit of competition rulemaking at the FTC and efforts to revive criminal monopolization enforcement at DOJ. But these are early days!

It is far too soon to assess whether the Neo-Brandeisian intervention in U.S. antitrust discourse will lead to a meaningful and durable change in direction. Neo-Brandeisianism may turn out to be a brief phenomenon, or it may signal an impending generational shift in antitrust. But it has already made one valuable contribution to discussions about antitrust: it has helped to dispel the idea that antitrust is or could possibly be "neutral" or "above politics" in any relevant sense. By underscoring the importance of explicit normative debate about the functions, benefits, and limits of antitrust law, Neo-Brandeisian criticism has encouraged a more honest, searching, and inclusive conversation about what antitrust law is, and what it should be.[119]

Carl Shapiro, Antitrust in a Time of Populism
61 Intl. J. Indus. Org. (2018)

Antitrust is sexy again. Where does this take us?

American politicians are calling on antitrust to solve an array of problems associated with the excessive power of large corporations in the United States. [A recent] plan calls for much tougher merger enforcement and greater government oversight "to stop abusive conduct and the exploitation of market power where it already exists."

Not since 1912, when Teddy Roosevelt ran for President emphasizing the need to control corporate power, have antitrust issues had such political salience. While Roosevelt did not win, Congress passed the Federal Trade Commission Act and the Clayton Act in 1914, significantly strengthening the Sherman Act. Indeed, the Sherman Act itself was passed in 1890 in response to broad concerns about the political and economic power of large corporations in America [.] [. . .]

[T]he role of antitrust in promoting competition could well be undermined if antitrust is called upon or expected to address problems not directly relating to competition. Most notably, antitrust institutions are poorly suited to address problems associated with the excessive political power of large corporations. The courts and the antitrust enforcement agencies know how to assess economic power and the economic effects of mergers or challenged business practices, but there are no reliable methods by which they could assess the political power of large firms. Asking the DOJ, the FTC to evaluate mergers and business conduct based on the political power of the firms

---

[116] *See, e.g.*, Sanjukta Paul, *Recovering the Moral Economy Foundations of the Sherman Act*, 131 Yale L.J. 175 (2021); Matt Stoller, GOLIATH: THE 100-YEAR WAR BETWEEN MONOPOLY POWER AND DEMOCRACY (2019); Lina Khan, *The New Brandeis Movement: America's Antimonopoly Debate*, 9 J. Eur. Comp. L. & Prac. 131 (2018); Sandeep Vaheesan, *The Profound Nonsense of Consumer Welfare Antitrust*, 64 Antitrust Bull. 479 (2019); Zephyr Teachout, *Antitrust Law, Freedom, and Human Development*, 41 Cardozo L. Rev. 1081, 1104 (2019); Tim Wu, THE CURSE OF BIGNESS: ANTITRUST IN THE NEW GILDED AGE (2018); Lina M. Khan, *Amazon's Antitrust Paradox*, 126 Yale L.J. 710 (2017); Lina M. Khan & Sandeep Vaheesan, *Market Power and Inequality: The Antitrust Counterrevolution and its Discontents*, 11 Harv. L. & Pol'7 Rev. 235 (2017).

[117] *See* David McCabe & Cecilia Kang, *Biden Names Lina Khan, A Big-Tech Critic, as F.T.C. Chair*, N.Y. TIMES (June 17, 2021), https://www.nytimes.com/2021/06/15/technology/lina-khan-ftc.html; Cecilia Kang, *A Leading Critic of Big Tech Will Join the White House*, N.Y. TIMES (Mar. 5, 2021), https://www.nytimes.com/2021/03/05/technology/tim-wu-white-house.html.

[118] *See, e.g.*, Joshua D. Wright, Elyse Dorsey, Jonathan Klick & Jan M. Rybnicek, *Requiem For A Paradox: The Dubious Rise and Inevitable Fall of Hipster Antitrust*, 51 Ariz. St. L.J. 293 (2019); Daniel A. Crane, *How Much Brandeis Do The Neo-Brandeisians Want?* 64 Antitrust Bull. 531 (2019).

[119] That conversation is not just a domestic one: international cooperation is implicated also. *See, e.g.*, James Keyte, Frédéric Jenny & Eleanor Fox, *Buckle Up: The Global Future of Antitrust Enforcement and Regulation*, 35 ANTITRUST 32 (2021).

involved would invite corruption by allowing the executive branch to punish its enemies and reward its allies through the antitrust cases brought, or not brought, by antitrust enforcers. On top of that, asking the courts to approve or block mergers based on the political power of the merging firms would undermine the rule of law while inevitably drawing the judicial branch into deeply political considerations. Let me be clear: the corrupting power of money in politics in the United States is perhaps the gravest threat facing democracy in America. But this profound threat to democracy and to equality of opportunity is far better addressed through campaign finance reform, increased transparency, and anti-corruption rules than by antitrust. [. . .]

Until quite recently, few were claiming that there has been a substantial and widespread decline in competition in the United States since 1980. And even fewer were suggesting that such a decline in competition was a major cause of the increased inequality in the United States in recent decades, or the decline in productivity growth observed over the past 20 years. Yet, somehow, over the past two years, the notion that there has been a substantial and widespread decline in competition throughout the American economy has taken root in the popular press. In some circles, this is now the conventional wisdom, the starting point for policy analysis rather than a bold hypothesis that needs to be tested. [. . .]

Antitrust was born and then fortified during a period of populism in the United States in the late 19th and early 20th centuries. Likewise, today's populist sentiments—by which I mean the widespread and bipartisan concern that the deck is stacked in favor of large powerful firms—represent an opportunity, indeed a plea, to strengthen antitrust enforcement. [. . .]

Today's populist sentiments pose a threat as well as an opportunity for antitrust. The danger to effective antitrust enforcement is that today's populist sentiments are fueling a "big is bad" mentality, leading to policies that will slow economic growth and harm consumers. The rest of this article is devoted to identifying this threat and discussing how such an error can be avoided.

I take as my starting point the core principle guiding antitrust enforcement in the United States that has served us well for so many years: *antitrust is about protecting the competitive process so consumers receive the full benefits of vigorous competition.* None of the empirical evidence relating to growing concentration and growing corporate profits, which I have discussed at length in this article, provides a basis for abandoning this core principle. Applying this core principle, we understand quite well how to use antitrust to protect competition and consumers, at least conceptually. This enterprise centers on the economic notion of market power, and relies heavily on industrial organization economics. Of course, there is always room for improvement in practice, and right now that means stricter merger enforcement and vigilance regarding acts of monopolization, as already discussed. The fundamental danger that 21st century populism poses to antitrust is that populism will cause us to abandon this core principle and thereby undermine economic growth and deprive consumers of many of the benefits of vigorous but fair competition. Economic growth will be undermined if firms are discouraged from competing vigorously for fear that they will be found to have violated the antitrust laws, or for fear they will be broken up if they are too successful. [. . .]

My hope is that the intense energy of populism will empower stronger antitrust enforcement policy in the United States with the goal of protecting the competitive process and channeling more of the benefits of economic growth to consumers. To protect and preserve this mission, it is important to recognize that antitrust cannot be expected to solve the larger political and social problems facing the United States today. In particular, while antitrust enforcement does tend to reduce income inequality, antitrust cannot and should not be the primary means of addressing income inequality; tax policies and employment policies need to play that role. Nor can antitrust be the primary policy for dealing with the corruption of our political system and the excessive political power of large corporations; that huge problem is better addressed by campaign finance reform, a better-informed citizenry, stronger protections for voting rights, and far tougher laws to combat corruption. Trying to use antitrust to solve problems outside the sphere of competition will not work and could well backfire.

* * *

Lina M. Khan & Sandeep Vaheesan, Market Power and Inequality: The Antitrust Counterrevolution and Its Discontents

11 Harv. L. & Pol'y Rev. 235 (2017)

Antitrust laws historically sought to protect consumers and small suppliers from noncompetitive pricing, preserve open markets to all comers, and disperse economic and political power. The Reagan administration—with no input from Congress—rewrote antitrust to focus on the concept of neoclassical economic efficiency. In dramatically narrowing the goals of antitrust, executive branch officials and judges held that open-ended standards favorable to businesses with market power, rather than clear rules, should govern most forms of business conduct. This elastic standard has crippled plaintiffs' attempts to challenge illegal behavior and has permitted large corporations to engage in anticompetitive conduct.

The Reagan administration's overturning of antitrust has had sweeping effects. But antitrust laws can be restored to promote competitive markets once again. Doing so would also produce a more equitable distribution of wealth and power in American society. This requires two things: first, an intellectual shift that embraces the original goals of antitrust and second, the appointment of antitrust officials and federal judges committed to this approach. A determined administration should do a number of things to revive Congress's vision as expressed in 1890 and 1914. First, antitrust laws must be reoriented away from the current efficiency focus toward a broader understanding that aims to protect consumers and small suppliers from the market power of large sellers and buyers, maintain the openness of markets, and disperse economic and political power. Second, clear rules and presumptions must govern mergers, dominant firm conduct, and vertical restraints and replace the current rule of reason review and other amorphous standards, which heavily tilt the scales in favor of defendants. Third, by using existing legal powers or seeking additional authority from Congress, the agencies should challenge monopoly and oligopoly power that injures the public on account of duration or magnitude of harm. Fourth, strong structural remedies and blocking of anticompetitive mergers are necessary to ensure that competitive markets are restored and maintained. Fifth and finally, antitrust agencies must be subject to strong transparency duties to allow the public to understand the internal decision-making processes and choices over whether to pursue-or not to pursue-a particular case.

A revived antitrust movement could play an important role in reversing the dramatic rise in economic inequality. With public engagement and political will, the antitrust counterrevolution—which has produced monopolistic and oligopolistic markets and contributed to a captured political system—can be undone. To be clear, our argument is not that antitrust should embrace redistribution as an explicit goal, or that enforcers should harness antitrust in order to promote progressive redistribution. Instead we hold that the failure of antitrust to preserve competitive markets contributes to regressive wealth and income distribution and-similarly-restoring antitrust is likely to have progressive distributive effects.

NOTES

1) In choosing a direction for antitrust law and policy, how much do you think the intention of the Sherman Act legislators should matter? What about the concerns of those who supported the original antitrust legislation?

2) How could we tell whether antitrust enforcement has been too lax since the 1970s, or whether it was too strict before? What evidence or metrics could we look at?

3) What are the advantages and disadvantages of antitrust as a tool to respond to inequality in the United States?

4) In what way, or under what circumstances, do you think the increased use of economic analysis, and a focus on analyzing the effects of particular practices and transactions, might favor one side or other in antitrust cases?

5) How responsive should antitrust be to:
   a. Democratic change?
   b. Change in consensus among professional economists?
   c. Changes in social and economic conditions? (Which ones?)

F. What Is Competition?

As you navigate the rest of this book, it may be helpful to keep asking yourself: "What do we mean by 'competition on the merits'? How should we distinguish between "procompetitive" and "anticompetitive" practices?"

Earlier in this chapter we accepted a very general definition of competition: "the process of rivalry between suppliers, or between purchasers, to be chosen as trading partners." But that definition includes forms of "competitive" rivalry that antitrust law clearly has no truck with: it could include everything from blowing up rivals' factories to buying up all the competition. If we want the idea of "competition" to do some useful work *within* antitrust analysis—*i.e.*, if we want to use it to inform our view of how antitrust should treat particular phenomena or practices—we will need something narrower than "all forms of rivalry between market competitors."[120]

All too often, courts and commentators use the labels "procompetitive" and "anticompetitive" as if they have some obvious, but unstated, meaning. Be alert for this! Consider, for example, this famous formulation of the antitrust "rule of reason" under Section 1 of the Sherman Act in a challenge to a rule adopted by the Chicago Board of Trade:

> [The government, prosecuting this case] made no attempt to show that the rule was designed to or that it had the effect of limiting the amount of grain shipped to Chicago; or of retarding or accelerating shipment; or if raising or depressing prices; or of discriminating against any part of the public; or that it resulted in hardship to anyone. . . . [T]he legality of an agreement or regulation cannot be determined by so simple a test, as whether it restrains competition. Every agreement concerning trade, every regulation of trade, restrains. To bind, to restrain, is of their very essence. The true test of legality is whether the restraint imposed is such as merely regulates and perhaps thereby promotes competition or whether it is such as may suppress or even destroy competition. To determine that question the court must ordinarily consider the facts peculiar to the business to which the restraint is applied; its condition before and after the restraint was imposed; the nature of the restraint and its effect, actual or probable. The history of the restraint, the evil believed to exist, the reason for adopting the particular remedy, the purpose or end sought to be attained, are all relevant facts. This is not because a good intention will save an otherwise objectionable regulation or the reverse; but because knowledge of intent may help the court to interpret facts and to predict consequences.[121]

This language gets quoted a lot in ways that suggest it is very helpful and insightful, but the truth is that it is strikingly unhelpful for a reader trying to discern what it really means to "promote" rather than "suppress or even destroy" competition. The language at the beginning of the quotation suggests that output, speed of shipping, prices, discrimination, and hardship to "any one" might all be relevant, in some way. But it is not clear how, or why, or what to do if those metrics conflict. (What if output goes up but so do prices? What if there is hardship and discrimination but lower prices?) The Court is telling us what to look *at* (everything?), but not what to look *for*.

Similarly, regarding the monopolization offense in Section 2, the Supreme Court has given the following—equally famous (and perhaps almost equally vague)—guidance in *Trinko:*

> It is settled law that [the monopolization] offense requires, in addition to the possession of monopoly power in the relevant market, "the willful acquisition or maintenance of that power as distinguished from growth or development as a consequence of a superior product, business acumen, or historic accident." *United States v. Grinnell Corp.*, 384 U.S. 563, 570–71 (1966). The mere possession of monopoly power, and the concomitant charging of monopoly prices, is not only not unlawful; it is an important element of the free-market system. The opportunity to charge monopoly prices—at least for a short period—is what attracts "business acumen" in the first place; it induces risk taking that produces innovation and economic growth. To safeguard

---

[120] *See, e.g.,* Herbert Hovenkamp & Carl Shapiro, *Horizontal Mergers, Market Structure, and Burdens of Proof*, 127 Yale LJ. 1996, 2020 (2018) ("Does 'lessened competition' refer to lower output and higher price-cost margins, or rather to a market structure with fewer firms? If the former, then a merger creating a larger, more efficient firm that charges lower prices is welcome. If the latter, such a merger is unwelcome, especially if that firm will drive smaller, less-efficient firms out of business. Both of these are more or less consistent with the lay understanding of 'competition.'").

[121] Board of Trade of City of Chicago v. U.S., 246 U.S. 231, 238 (1918).

the incentive to innovate, the possession of monopoly power will not be found unlawful unless it is accompanied by an element of anticompetitive *conduct*.[122]

What does this tell us about when conduct is "anticompetitive"? At least the Court is clear here on the point that charging a monopoly price is not anticompetitive in the relevant sense. But the language quoted from *Grinnell* is little help. As one of us has argued elsewhere: "[T]his definition makes no sense: virtually every business seeks to win share from competitors—it willfully seeks monopoly—including through superior products and business acumen. No one thinks that 'willfulness' in chasing monopoly is bad or rare. Every monopolization defendant claims that its conduct facilitates 'superior' operation. And if the use of 'acumen' is exculpatory, then what remains? The first half of the Court's binary is not necessarily bad, the second part is not necessarily good, and they are in no real tension."[123]

The point is that the word "competition" is susceptible of many different definitions and understandings, and labels like "competition on the merits" and "anticompetitive conduct" are not self-applying. The beliefs, values, and assumptions that each of us brings to our work with antitrust will affect our intuitions about how we should understand the kind of "competition" that antitrust does and should protect. As you read the following extracts, and in the rest of the book, keep your eyes on the following questions (and the answers to them that judges and scholars seem to have in mind when they answer antitrust questions!).

When we interpret, apply, develop, and amend antitrust rules:

- **Goals and interests.** What are we trying to achieve or maximize? Whose interests matter and in what ways? Who should make this decision and how?
- **Competition and other values.** Do we want "maximum" competition (however defined), or do we want to balance competition against other desirable things? Who should make this decision and how?
- **Limits of regulators' knowledge.** How good do we think courts are, generally, at telling when a practice or transaction should be prohibited? What about agencies? How do we know?
- **Error costs.** Do we think that the costs of wrongly prohibiting business practices are generally higher or lower than the costs of wrongly permitting them? Are there circumstances under which the balance of costs might tip the other way?
- **Static v. dynamic effects.** How do we weigh static effects (like increased prices) against dynamic ones (like increased innovation)?
- **Probabilities.** How do we weigh high-probability outcomes against low-probability outcomes? And how do we assess these probabilities?
- **Tendencies and effects.** How do we know what effects practices like exclusivity arrangements, bundling pricing, and mergers have? How generalizable is that knowledge from one context to another?
- **Whose perspective?** Who is the "we" in these questions anyway? Do we have in mind judges, enforcement officials, economists, scholars, business executives, consumers, workers, union officials, employees, shareholders, citizens? Would the answers differ if we had different people in mind?

What kind of "competition" do the authors of the following extracts understand antitrust to protect? How do they seem to determine whether or not something is procompetitive or anticompetitive? Don't worry at this stage about the substantive antitrust law: just ask what version of "competition" is being valued and defended. For example: in what sense did the merger in *Von's Grocery* threaten to harm competition, and what facts suggested such harm? Is *Utah Pie* a tale of competitive harm, as the Court suggests—and if so what would "more competition" have looked like? Why didn't the plaintiff get what it wanted in *Cargill*? And what point is Judge Posner making about the intent to inflict harm through competition in *Olympia Equipment*? One very important note: neither *Von's Grocery* nor *Utah Pie* is representative of the current state of the law or the current practice of the courts. They are included here to demonstrate that the idea of "competition" can be (and has been) understood in very different ways, not to teach you anything about substantive antitrust law.

---

[122] Verizon Communications Inc. v. Law Offices of Curtis V. Trinko, LLP, 540 U.S. 398, 407 (2004).

[123] Daniel Francis, *Making Sense of Monopolization*, 84 Antitrust L.J. 779, 780 (2022).

United States v. Von's Grocery Co.

384 U.S. 270 (1966)

Justice Black.

[1] On March 25, 1960, the United States brought this action charging that the acquisition by Von's Grocery Company of its direct competitor Shopping Bag Food Stores, both large retail grocery companies in Los Angeles, California, violated s 7 of the Clayton Act[.] [. . .]

[2] The market involved here is the retail grocery market in the Los Angeles area. In 1958 Von's retail sales ranked third in the area and Shopping Bag's ranked sixth. In 1960 their sales together were 7.5% of the total two and one-half billion dollars of retail groceries sold in the Los Angeles market each year. . . . From 1948 to 1958 the number of Von's stores in the Los Angeles area practically doubled from 14 to 27, while at the same time the number of Shopping Bag's stores jumped from 15 to 34. . . . [T]he findings of the District Court show that the number of owners operating single stores in the Los Angeles retail grocery market decreased from 5,365 in 1950 to 3,818 in 1961. By 1963, three years after the merger, the number of single-store owners had dropped still further to 3,590. During roughly the same period, from 1953 to 1962, the number of chains with two or more grocery stores increased from 96 to 150. [. . .]

[3] Like the Sherman Act in 1890 and the Clayton Act in 1914, the basic purpose of the 1950 Celler-Kefauver Act was to prevent economic concentration in the American economy by keeping a large number of small competitors in business. In stating the purposes of their bill, both of its sponsors, Representative Celler and Senator Kefauver, emphasized their fear, widely shared by other members of Congress, that this concentration was rapidly driving the small businessman out of the market. . . . [In Section 7 of the Clayton Act] Congress sought to preserve competition among many small businesses by arresting a trend toward concentration in its incipiency before that trend developed to the point that a market was left in the grip of a few big companies. Thus, where concentration is gaining momentum in a market, we must be alert to carry out Congress' intent to protect competition against ever-increasing concentration through mergers.

[4] The facts of this case present exactly the threatening trend toward concentration which Congress wanted to halt. The number of small grocery companies in the Los Angeles retail grocery market had been declining rapidly before the merger and continued to decline rapidly afterwards. This rapid decline in the number of grocery store owners moved hand in hand with a large number of significant absorptions of the small companies by the larger ones. In the midst of this steadfast trend toward concentration, Von's and Shopping Bag, two of the most successful and largest companies in the area, jointly owning 66 grocery stores merged to become the second largest chain in Los Angeles. This merger cannot be defended on the ground that one of the companies was about to fail or that the two had to merge to save themselves from destruction by some larger and more powerful competitor. What we have on the contrary is simply the case of two already powerful companies merging in a way which makes them even more powerful than they were before. If ever such a merger would not violate s 7, certainly it does when it takes place in a market characterized by a long and continuous trend toward fewer and fewer owner-competitors which is exactly the sort of trend which Congress, with power to do so, declared must be arrested.

[5] Appellees' primary argument is that the merger between Von's and Shopping Bag is not prohibited by s 7 because the Los Angeles grocery market was competitive before the merger, has been since, and may continue to be in the future. Even so, s 7 requires not merely an appraisal of the immediate impact of the merger upon competition, but a prediction of its impact upon competitive conditions in the future; this is what is meant when it is said that the amended s 7 was intended to arrest anti-competitive tendencies in their incipiency. It is enough for us that Congress feared that a market marked at the same time by both a continuous decline in the number of small businesses and a large number of mergers would slowly but inevitably gravitate from a market of many small competitors to one dominated by one or a few giants, and competition would thereby be destroyed. Congress passed the Celler-Kefauver Act to prevent such a destruction of competition. Our cases since the passage of that Act have faithfully endeavored to enforce this congressional command. We adhere to them now.

* * *

Utah Pie Co. v. Continental Baking Co.
386 U.S. 685 (1967)

{Eds.: In the following extract some paragraphs have been broken up to make them easier to read.}

Justice White.

[1] This suit for treble damages and injunction ... was brought by petitioner, Utah Pie Company, against respondents, Continental Baking Company, Carnation Company and Pet Milk Company. The complaint charged a conspiracy under ss 1 and 2 of the Sherman Act, and violations by each respondent of ... the Robinson-Patman Act.... The Court of Appeals [considered] the single issue of whether the evidence against each of the respondents was sufficient to support a finding of probable injury to competition within the meaning of s 2(a) and holding that it was not. We granted certiorari. We reverse.

[2] The product involved is frozen dessert pies—apple, cherry, boysenberry, peach, pumpkin, and mince. The period covered by the suit comprised the years 1958, 1959, and 1960 and the first eight months of 1961. Petitioner is a Utah corporation which for 30 years had been baking pies in its plant in Salt Lake City and selling them in Utah and surrounding States. ... The frozen pie market was a rapidly expanding one: 57,060 dozen frozen pies were sold in the Salt Lake City market in 1958, 111,729 dozen in 1959, 184,569 dozen in 1960, and 266,908 dozen in 1961. Utah Pie's share of this market in those years was 66.5%[,] 34.3%[,] 45.5%, and 45.3% respectively, its sales volume steadily increasing over the four years. ...

[3] Each of the respondents is a large company and each of them is a major factor in the frozen pie market in one or more regions of the country. Each entered the Salt Lake City frozen pie market before petitioner began freezing dessert pies. None of them had a plant in Utah. By the end of the period involved in this suit Pet had plants in Michigan, Pennsylvania, and California; Continental in Virginia, Iowa, and California; and Carnation in California. The Salt Lake City market was supplied by respondents chiefly from their California operations. [. . .]

[4] The major competitive weapon in the Utah market was price. The location of petitioner's plant gave it natural advantages in the Salt Lake City marketing area and it entered the market at a price below the then going prices for respondents' comparable pies. For most of the period involved here its prices were the lowest in the Salt Lake City market. It was, however, challenged by each of the respondents at one time or another and for varying periods. There was ample evidence to show that each of the respondents contributed to what proved to be a deteriorating price structure over the period covered by this suit, and each of the respondents in the course of the ongoing price competition sold frozen pies in the Salt Lake market at prices lower than it sold pies of like grade and quality in other markets considerably closer to its plants. [. . .]

[5] We deal first with petitioner's case against the Pet Milk Company. Pet entered the frozen pie business in 1955, acquired plants in Pennsylvania and California and undertook a large advertising campaign to market its 'Pet-Ritz' brand of frozen pies. Pet's initial emphasis was on quality, but in the face of competition from regional and local companies and in an expanding market where price proved to be a crucial factor, Pet was forced to take steps to reduce the price of its pies to the ultimate consumer.

[6] First, Pet successfully concluded an arrangement with Safeway, which is one of the three largest customers for frozen pies in the Salt Lake market, whereby it would sell frozen pies to Safeway under the latter's own "Bel-air" label at a price significantly lower than it was selling its comparable "Pet-Ritz" brand in the same Salt Lake market and elsewhere. The initial price on "Bel-air" pies was slightly lower than Utah's price for its "Utah" brand of pies at the time, and near the end of the period the "Bel-air" price was comparable to the "Utah" price but higher than Utah's "Frost 'N' Flame" brand. Pet's Safeway business amounted to 22.8%, 12.3%, and 6.3% of the entire Salt Lake City market for the years 1959, 1960, and 1961, respectively, and to 64%, 44%, and 22% of Pet's own Salt Lake City sales for those same years.

[7] Second, it introduced a 20-ounce economy pie under the "Swiss Miss" label and began selling the new pie in the Salt Lake market in August 1960 at prices ranging from $3.25 to $3.30 for the remainder of the period. This pie was at times sold at a lower price in the Salt Lake City market than it was sold in other markets.

[8] Third, Pet became more competitive with respect to the prices for its "Pet-Ritz" proprietary label. For 18 of the relevant 44 months its offering price for Pet-Ritz pies was $4 per dozen or lower, and $3.70 or lower for six of these months. According to the Court of Appeals, in seven of the 44 months Pet's prices in Salt Lake were lower than prices charged in the California markets. This was true although selling in Salt Lake involved a 30- to 35-cent freight cost.

[9] The Court of Appeals first concluded that Pet's price differential on sales to Safeway must be put aside in considering injury to competition because in its view of the evidence the differential had been completely cost justified and because Utah would not in any event have been able to enjoy the Safeway custom. Second, it concluded that the remaining discriminations on "Pet-Ritz" and "Swiss Miss" pies were an insufficient predicate on which the jury could have found a reasonably possible injury either to Utah Pie as a competitive force or to competition generally.

[10] We disagree with the Court of Appeals in several respects. First, there was evidence from which the jury could have found considerably more price discrimination by Pet with respect to "Pet-Ritz" and "Swiss Miss" pies than was considered by the Court of Appeals. In addition to the seven months during which Pet's prices in Salt Lake were lower than prices in the California markets, there was evidence from which the jury could reasonably have found that in 10 additional months the Salt Lake City prices for "Pet-Ritz" pies were discriminatory as compared with sales in western markets other than California. Likewise, with respect to "Swiss Miss" pies, there was evidence in the record from which the jury could have found that in five of the 13 months during which the "Swiss Miss" pies were sold prior to the filing of this suit, prices in Salt Lake City were lower than those charged by Pet in either California or some other western market.

[11] Second, with respect to Pet's Safeway business, the burden of proving cost justification was on Pet and, in our view, reasonable [jurors] could have found that Pet's lower priced, "Bel-air" sales to Safeway were not cost justified in their entirety. Pet introduced cost data for 1961 indicating a cost saving on the Safeway business greater than the price advantage extended to that customer. . . .

[12] With respect to whether Utah would have enjoyed Safeway's business absent the Pet contract with Safeway, it seems clear that whatever the fact is in this regard, it is not determinative of the impact of that contract on competitors other than Utah and on competition generally. There were other companies seeking the Safeway business, including Continental and Carnation, whose pies may have been excluded from the Safeway shelves by what the jury could have found to be discriminatory sales to Safeway. . . . .

[13] Third, the Court of Appeals almost entirely ignored other evidence which provides material support for the jury's conclusion that Pet's behavior satisfied the statutory test regarding competitive injury. This evidence bore on the issue of Pet's predatory intent to injure Utah Pie. As an initial matter, the jury could have concluded that Pet's discriminatory pricing was aimed at Utah Pie; Pet's own management, as early as 1959, identified Utah Pie as an "unfavorable factor," one which "dug holes in our operation" and posed a constant "check" on Pet's performance in the Salt Lake City market. Moreover, Pet candidly admitted that during the period when it was establishing its relationship with Safeway, it sent into Utah Pie's plant an industrial spy to seek information that would be of use to Pet in convincing Safeway that Utah Pie was not worthy of its custom. Pet denied that it ever in fact used what it had learned against Utah Pie in competing for Safeway's business. The parties, however, are not the ultimate judges of credibility. But even giving Pet's view of the incident a measure of weight does not mean the jury was foreclosed from considering the predatory intent underlying Pet's mode of competition. Finally, Pet does not deny that the evidence showed it suffered substantial losses on its frozen pie sales during the greater part of the time involved in this suit, and there was evidence from which the jury could have concluded that the losses Pet sustained in Salt Lake City were greater than those incurred elsewhere. It would not have been an irrational step if the jury concluded that there was a relationship between price and the losses.

[14] It seems clear to us that the jury heard adequate evidence from which it could have concluded that Pet had engaged in predatory tactics in waging competitive warfare in the Salt Lake City market. Coupled with the incidence of price discrimination attributable to Pet, the evidence as a whole established, rather than negated, the reasonable possibility that Pet's behavior produced a lessening of competition proscribed by the Act. [. . .]

[15] Petitioner's case against Continental is not complicated. Continental was a substantial factor in the market in 1957. But its sales of frozen 22-ounce dessert pies, sold under the "Morton" brand, amounted to only 1.3% of the market in 1958, 2.9% in 1959, and 1.8% in 1960. . . .

[16] In late 1960 it worked out a co-packing arrangement in California by which fruit would be processed directly from the trees into the finished pie without large intermediate packing, storing, and shipping expenses. Having improved its position, it attempted to increase its share of the Salt Lake City market by utilizing a local broker and offering short-term price concessions in varying amounts. Its efforts for seven months were not spectacularly successful. Then in June 1961, it took the steps which are the heart of petitioner's complaint against it. Effective for the last two weeks of June it offered its 22-ounce frozen apple pies in the Utah area at $2.85 per dozen. It was then selling the same pies at substantially higher prices in other markets. The Salt Lake City price was less than its direct cost plus an allocation for overhead. Utah's going price at the time for its 24-ounce "Frost 'N' Flame" apple pie sold to Associated Grocers was $3.10 per dozen, and for its "Utah" brand $3.40 per dozen. At its new prices, Continental sold pies to American Grocers in Pocatello, Idaho, and to American Food Stores in Ogden, Utah. Safeway, one of the major buyers in Salt Lake City, also purchased 6,250 dozen, its requirements for about five weeks. Another purchaser ordered 1,000 dozen.

[17] Utah's response was immediate. It reduced its price on all of its apple pies to $2.75 per dozen. Continental refused [its customer] Safeway's request to match Utah's price, but renewed its offer at the same prices effective July 31 for another two-week period. Utah filed suit on September 8, 1961. Continental's total sales of frozen pies increased from 3,350 dozen in 1960 to 18,800 dozen in 1961. Its market share increased from 1.8% in 1960 to 8.3% in 1961. The Court of Appeals concluded that Continental's conduct had had only minimal effect, that it had not injured or weakened Utah Pie as a competitor, that it had not substantially lessened competition and that there was no reasonable possibility that it would do so in the future.

[18] We again differ with the Court of Appeals. Its opinion that Utah was not damaged as a competitive force apparently rested on the fact that Utah's sales volume continued to climb in 1961 and on the court's own factual conclusion that Utah was not deprived of any pie business which it otherwise might have had. But this retrospective assessment fails to note that Continental's discriminatory below-cost price caused Utah Pie to reduce its price to $2.75. The jury was entitled to consider the potential impact of Continental's price reduction absent any responsive price cut by Utah Pie. Price was a major factor in the Salt Lake City market. Safeway, which had been buying Utah brand pies, immediately reacted and purchased a five-week supply of frozen pies from Continental, thereby temporarily foreclosing the proprietary brands of Utah and other firms from the Salt Lake City Safeway market. The jury could rationally have concluded that had Utah not lowered its price, Continental, which repeated its offer once, would have continued it, that Safeway would have continued to buy from Continental and that other buyers, large as well as small, would have followed suit. It could also have reasonably concluded that a competitor who is forced to reduce his price to a new all-time low in a market of declining prices will in time feel the financial pinch and will be a less effective competitive force.

* * *

Cargill, Inc. v. Monfort of Colorado, Inc.
479 U.S. 104 (1986)

Justice Brennan.

[1] Respondent Monfort of Colorado, Inc. (Monfort), the plaintiff below, owns and operates three integrated beef-packing plants, that is, plants for both the slaughter of cattle and the fabrication of beef. . . .

[2] Monfort is the country's fifth-largest beef packer. Petitioner Excel Corporation (Excel), one of the two defendants below, is the second-largest packer. Excel operates five integrated plants and one fabrication plant. It is a wholly owned subsidiary of Cargill, Inc., the other defendant below, a large privately owned corporation with more than 150 subsidiaries in at least 35 countries.

[3] On June 17, 1983, Excel signed an agreement to acquire the third-largest packer in the market, Spencer Beef . . . . Spencer Beef owned two integrated plants and one slaughtering plant. After the acquisition, Excel would still be the second-largest packer, but would command a market share almost equal to that of the largest packer, IBP, Inc. (IBP).

[4] Monfort brought an action . . . to enjoin the prospective merger. Its complaint alleged that the acquisition would violate Section 7 of the Clayton Act because the effect of the proposed acquisition may be substantially to lessen competition or tend to create a monopoly[.] [. . .]

[5] Monfort alleged that after the merger, Excel would attempt to increase its market share at the expense of smaller rivals, such as Monfort. To that end, Monfort claimed, Excel would bid up the price it would pay for cattle, and reduce the price at which it sold boxed beef. Although such a strategy, which Monfort labeled a "price-cost squeeze," would reduce Excel's profits, Excel's parent corporation had the financial reserves to enable Excel to pursue such a strategy. Eventually, according to Monfort, smaller competitors lacking significant reserves and unable to match Excel's prices would be driven from the market; at this point Excel would raise the price of its boxed beef to supracompetitive levels, and would more than recoup the profits it lost during the initial phase. [. . .]

[6] [Monfort claims] that after the merger, Excel would lower its prices to some level at or slightly above its costs in order to compete with other packers for market share. Excel would be in a position to do this because of the multiplant efficiencies its acquisition of Spencer would provide. To remain competitive, Monfort would have to lower its prices; as a result, Monfort would suffer a loss in profitability, but would not be driven out of business. The question is whether Monfort's loss of profits in such circumstances constitutes antitrust injury. [. . .]

[7] . . . We find respondent's proposed construction of § 7 too broad . . . . [T]he antitrust laws do not require the courts to protect small businesses from the loss of profits due to continued competition, but only against the loss of profits from practices forbidden by the antitrust laws. The kind of competition that Monfort alleges here, competition for increased market share, is not activity forbidden by the antitrust laws. It is simply, as petitioners claim, vigorous competition. To hold that the antitrust laws protect competitors from the loss of profits due to such price competition would, in effect, render illegal any decision by a firm to cut prices in order to increase market share. The antitrust laws require no such perverse result, for it is in the interest of competition to permit dominant firms to engage in vigorous competition, including price competition. The logic of [our prior case law] compels the conclusion that the threat of loss of profits due to possible price competition following a merger does not constitute a threat of antitrust injury.

* * *

Olympia Equipment Leasing Co. v. Western Union Telegraph Co.
797 F.2d 370 (7th Cir. 1986)

{Eds.: In the following extract some paragraphs have been broken up to make them easier to read.}

Judge Posner.

[1] The importance of intent in such fields as tort and criminal law makes it natural to suppose that it should play an important role in antitrust law as well, for an antitrust violation is a statutory tort. But there is an insoluble ambiguity about anticompetitive intent that is not encountered in the ordinary tort case. If A strikes B deliberately, we are entitled to infer, first, that A's act was more dangerous than if the blow had been accidental (you are more likely to hurt someone if you are trying to hurt him than if you are trying, however ineptly, to avoid hurting him, as in the typical accident case), and, second, that the cost of avoidance to the injurer would have been less than if the blow had been accidental; indeed, the cost of forbearing to commit an act of deliberate aggression is negative, because the act requires effort. Similar inferences would be possible in antitrust cases if the purpose of antitrust law were to protect the prosperity or solvency (corresponding to the bodily integrity of potential tort victims) of competitors, but it is not. Competition, which is always deliberate, has never been a tort, intentional or otherwise. If firm A through lower prices or a better or more dependable product succeeds in driving competitor B out of business, society is better off, unlike the case where A and B are individuals and A kills B for B's money. In both

cases the "aggressor" seeks to transfer his victim's wealth to himself, but in the first case we applaud the result because society as a whole benefits from the competitive process. . . .

[2] Most businessmen don't like their competitors, or for that matter competition. They want to make as much money as possible and getting a monopoly is one way of making a lot of money. That is fine, however, so long as they do not use methods calculated to make consumers worse off in the long run. Consumers would be worse off if a firm with monopoly power had a duty to extend positive assistance to new entrants, or having extended it voluntarily a duty to continue it indefinitely. The imposition of such a duty would make firms that possessed or might be thought to possess monopoly power, however laudably obtained, timid about relinquishing that power or, having done so, timid about competing with new entrants. The question therefore is not whether [the defendant acted] in order to make money at the expense of [the plaintiff], which of course it did, but whether [the conduct] was an objectively anticompetitive act.

G. Some Further Reading

Jonathan Baker, THE ANTITRUST PARADIGM: RESTORING A COMPETITIVE ECONOMY (2019)

Robert H. Bork, THE ANTITRUST PARADOX: A POLICY AT WAR WITH ITSELF (1978)

Eleanor M. Fox & Daniel A. Crane (eds.), ANTITRUST STORIES (2007)

Eleanor Fox, *The Battle for the Soul of Antitrust*, 75 Cal. L. Rev. 917 (1987)

Herbert J. Hovenkamp, THE ANTITRUST ENTERPRISE: PRINCIPLE AND EXECUTION (2005)

Lina M. Khan & Sandeep Vaheesan, *Market power and inequality: The antitrust counterrevolution and its discontents*, 11 Harv. L. & Pol'y Rev. 235 (2017)

William E. Kovacic & Carl Shapiro, *Antitrust Policy: A Century of Economic and Legal Thinking*, 14 J. Econ. Persp. 43 (2000)

William E. Kovacic, *Failed Expectations: The Troubled Past and Uncertain Future of the Sherman Act as a Tool for Deconcentration*, 74 Iowa L. Rev. 1105 (1989)

Marina Lao, *Ideology Matters in the Antitrust Debate*, 79 Antitrust L.J. 649 (2014)

Robert Pitofsky (ed.), HOW THE CHICAGO SCHOOL OVERSHOT THE MARK: THE EFFECT OF CONSERVATIVE ECONOMIC ANALYSIS ON U.S. ANTITRUST (2008)

Edwin S. Rockefeller, THE ANTITRUST RELIGION (2007)

Hans B. Thorelli, THE FEDERAL ANTITRUST POLICY: THE ORIGINATION OF AN AMERICAN TRADITION (1955)

Gregory J. Werden, THE FOUNDATIONS OF ANTITRUST (2020)

Tim Wu, THE CURSE OF BIGNESS: ANTITRUST IN THE NEW GILDED AGE (2018)

II. ANTITRUST ECONOMICS: A NONTECHNICAL INTRODUCTION

A. Overview

The foundations of antitrust law rest in part on concepts and theories drawn from economics, or informed by economic analysis. This includes not only a set of central ideas like "competition," "monopoly," and "market power," but also propositions about the tendencies of particular practices or circumstances to lead to particular outcomes. For example, antitrust law's central understanding about the tendency of competition to reduce prices and improve quality—and the tendency of practices like price-fixing, or acquisitions of key competitors, to increase prices and reduce quality—comes from what we would today call microeconomic analysis. As a result, some familiarity with basic antitrust *economics* is indispensable for anyone trying to build an understanding of how antitrust *law* operates.

But do not be dismayed or intimidated! You do not need a degree in economics, or anything like it, to be a good antitrust lawyer. In fact, most antitrust lawyers have no formal qualifications in economics. Instead, they rely on a basic understanding of some core economic principles, and they frequently work closely alongside formally trained economists who help illuminate the more complex economic issues presented by an antitrust matter. Both DOJ and the FTC employ many professional economists, and economic experts are retained to consult or testify in many antitrust cases (including public and private investigations and litigations).[124]

This Chapter introduces some economic concepts that underpin antitrust law and practice. Section B provides a short introduction to microeconomics as a means of understanding and analyzing the world. Section C introduces the forces of market supply and demand. Section D presents the idea of perfect competition. In Section E we will meet the concept of monopoly. Section F introduces the related concept of "market power" and some of the conditions in real world markets that may create it. Section G describes the idea of potential competition. Section H introduces the concept of tacit collusion and the related idea of market concentration. Section I brings in buyer-side power, including monopsony and oligopsony. Finally, Section J introduces price discrimination, and Section K offers some thoughts on the relationship between economics and law.

The discipline of economics is, and has always been, very important to antitrust. But it cannot supply us with a full set of clear right answers about what antitrust law should permit or prohibit, or about what set of rules would be socially optimal in an all-things-considered sense. Economics can illuminate and inform some of the hard normative choices that antitrust doctrine raises, and it can help us understand the possible effects of particular practices or rules, but it will still leave us with hard choices and plenty of uncertainty. We all have different prior assumptions about how the world works and how people behave; different beliefs about what is desirable and why; and different views about the relative prevalence or likelihood of particular outcomes in the real world. These and many other things affect our own sense of what antitrust rules should be, our instincts about whether we should label particular practices "anticompetitive" or "procompetitive," and our intuitions about whether it would be better to prohibit or permit those practices. Even (and maybe especially) our sense of what "competition on the merits" *means* is derived from many more sources than just microeconomics textbooks. Economic analysis can make a critically important contribution to our understanding of the hard choices at the heart of antitrust enforcement and policy, but it cannot make those choices for us.

---

[124] The FTC's Bureau of Economics employs roughly 80 economists; the Antitrust Division's Economic Analysis Group includes around 50. *See generally* https://www.ftc.gov/about-ftc/bureaus-offices/bureau-economics/about-bureau-economics; https://www.justice.gov/atr/about-division/economic-analysis-group.

B. The Lens of Microeconomic Analysis

Traditional microeconomic analysis is centrally focused on the question of how individuals face incentives to make particular decisions under conditions of scarcity: that is, in a world of finite resources.

Preferences and rationality. Most microeconomic analysis assumes that people have preferences, and that they act in a way that seems to them to best satisfy those preferences.[125] Preferences are just rankings, from most preferred to least preferred. For example, I prefer having $10 to having $5, and I prefer having $5 to having $1. But preferences need not (and generally do not) relate to quantifiable things. Thus, for example, I might also prefer to take the train for a 100-mile journey rather than drive, with air travel being my least-preferred option. And someone else might have different preferences over means of transportation.

Of course, real people often do not appear to be fully rational. Some economists (and professionals in other disciplines) work to understand when and how people do not think or behave this way.[126] But antitrust analysis generally assumes that they do.[127]

Welfare. The concept of preferences gives us, in turn, the idea of economic *welfare*. We say that a person's welfare is increased when they move from a less preferred state to a more preferred one. Notice that this use of the term "welfare" has nothing to do with what is "best" for the person in any objective sense: the only thing that matters is what that person subjectively prefers. If the person wants more of X, then, all else equal, an increase in that person's amount of X is a welfare improvement for this purpose: even if we, as observers, might personally feel that too much X—or even any X at all—is bad for that person.[128]

In this strict sense, we can generally only talk about increasing or reducing the economic welfare of individuals: if a particular change in the world is preferred by some individuals and disfavored by others, there is no obvious way to determine whether that change would lead to an "overall" increase or reduction in the welfare of society.[129] In economic jargon, this is the problem of "interpersonal comparability": it is not obvious how we can sensibly weigh one person's preference for X over Y against another person's preference for Y over X.[130]

Some analytical methods, such as the Kaldor-Hicks criterion that underlies traditional cost-benefit analysis, attempt to resolve this problem by converting preferences into amounts of money. For example, suppose that you want to plant a tree in your back yard, but I—your neighbor—object, because it will reduce the amount of sunshine that reaches my yard. You might be willing to pay up to $100 to be able to plant the tree; I might be only willing to pay $50 to prevent you from doing so. In a certain sense, then, we might think that the world would be improved if you were allowed to plant the tree: you would receive a benefit that you value at $100, while I would suffer a harm that I value at $50. And you could in principle compensate me from your gains, by paying me any amount between $50 and $100, such that we would both be better off.[131] But this approach raises problems of its own, including the fact that people value dollars, and other resources, less as they have more of them—the so-

---

[125] The "rationality" constraint further provides that these preferences are complete (*i.e.*, cover all the possible alternatives) and transitive (*i.e.*, do not "cycle," such that if I prefer A to B and B to C, I will also prefer A to C). *See generally* Andreu Mas-Colell, Michael D. Whinston & Jerry R. Green, MICROECONOMIC THEORY (1995) Ch. 1.

[126] *See, e.g.*, Amos Tversky & Richard H. Thaler, *Anomalies: Preference Reversals*, 4 J. Econ. Persp. 201 (1990).

[127] *See generally* Christopher R. Leslie, *Rationality Analysis in Antitrust*, 158 U. Pa. L. Rev. 261 (2010). *See also* Symposium, *Behavioral Antitrust*, 1 Comp. Pol'y Int'l (Winter 2019); Amanda P. Reeves & Maurice E. Stucke, *Behavioral Antitrust*, 86 Ind. L.J. 1527 (2011); Avishalom Tor, *Illustrating a Behaviorally Informed Approach to Antitrust Law: The Case of Predatory Pricing*, 18 Antitrust 52 (2003); *but see* Alan Devlin & Michael Jacobs, *The Empty Promise of Behavioral Antitrust*, 37 Harv. J. L. & Pub. Pol'y, 1009 (2013).

[128] *See, e.g.*, FTC, Press Release, FTC Requires Reynolds and Lorillard to Divest Four Cigarette Brands as a Condition of $27.4 Billion Merger (May 26, 2015).

[129] Of course, if a particular change makes at least one person better off, and no-one worse off, we can describe it as an improvement. This is often called a Pareto improvement. *See generally* Lewis Kornhauser, *The Economic Analysis of Law* in STANFORD ENCYCLOPEDIA OF PHILOSOPHY (rev. Jan. 7, 2022) § 6.2.

[130] *See, e.g.*, Paul A. Samuelson, *The Pure Theory of Public Expenditure*, 36 Rev. Econ. & Stat. 387, 387 (1954) ("It is not a 'scientific' task of the economist to 'deduce' the form of [a social welfare] function; this can have as many forms as there are possible ethical views[.]").

[131] This approach underpins the Kaldor-Hicks criterion, which provides that a change is an improvement if the gains to the winners are sufficient to compensate the losses to the losers. *See* Nicholas Kaldor, *Welfare Propositions in Economics and Interpersonal Comparisons of Utility*, 49 Econ. J. 549 (1939).

called "diminishing marginal utility of wealth"—meaning that analysis of this kind may end up favoring the interests of wealthy persons unless we make complex and controversial efforts to try to account for this effect. Moreover, the fact that the gains to the winners might in theory be enough to compensate the losers does not mean that they will *in fact* be so compensated.[132] It's not obvious why a loser should be mollified by the knowledge that it *could in theory have* been compensated from the gains that a winner is now enjoying.

Welfare maximization and profit maximization. Through the lens of microeconomic analysis, then, we see a world of rational persons acting to maximize their welfare. For producers (*i.e.*, entities that supply products and services of any kind), we usually assume that the rationality constraint means that they will aim to maximize their profits, and only their profits. The assumption that producer welfare is equal to profit, and that businesses do not have preferences over other things like social or political goals, is a controversial one, and it touches an active area of scholarship and debate.[133] But much economic analysis, and most standard antitrust economics, generally just assumes that businesses act rationally to maximize their profits.[134]

Of course, consumers—people who buy and use, but do not supply, products and services—do not have profits. But they have preferences, and therefore welfare, all the same. If consumers of a particular product or service are forced to pay more for that product or service, the value they experience above what they have paid—their "consumer surplus"—is reduced. When this happens, then all else being equal their welfare has been reduced. Conversely, a price reduction—again, all else equal—tends to increase the consumer surplus received, and thus welfare.

Note the importance of the "all else equal" assumption when we are talking about prices. Remember that what matters for a welfare analysis is whether the consumer is moving to a more or less preferred state of affairs. A literal decrease in the price number after the dollar sign—that is, the "nominal price" of a product or service—implies a welfare increase only so long as the product or service supplied for that price is not also changing for the worse. To illustrate, suppose I can today obtain a pretty great sandwich from the store for $5. If tomorrow I find that the nominal price of the sandwich has fallen to $4.50, but that the sandwiches are now completely awful, the welfare gain I would receive from a sandwich purchase has probably been reduced, not improved. Alternatively, if the price has gone up to $5.10, but the sandwiches are now world-beating achievements in the field of culinary science, I am probably going to receive a greater welfare benefit from a sandwich purchase as a result. So we often talk about "real price" or "quality-adjusted price" to clarify that what matters in welfare analysis is not just the number on the price sticker but what the buyer is getting for his or her money.

As this suggests, consumer welfare turns on much more than just the price paid for a product or service: quality matters too. If a consumer receives a *better* (that is, more preferred, from their own perspective) product or service for the same nominal price, then that consumer's welfare has been increased. Thus, quality changes can affect consumer welfare even in the absence of any change in price.

But quality can get complicated. Consumers may disagree about whether a qualitative change makes a product better or worse: for example, is it a quality improvement to change an ice cream flavor from lemon to vanilla? (Economists often reserve the word "quality" for something that all buyers agree is better.) This raises complexities that may be absent from discussions about price, as consumers generally do not disagree about whether they prefer higher or lower prices for the same product or service. But even this presumption does not always hold: for some

---

[132] For some thoughtful discussions, *see, e.g.*, Michael A. Livermore & Richard Revesz, REVIVING RATIONALITY: SAVING COST-BENEFIT ANALYSIS FOR THE SAKE OF THE ENVIRONMENT AND OUR HEALTH (2020); Lewis A. Kornhauser, *On Justifying Cost-Benefit Analysis*, 29 J. Leg. Stud. 1037 (2000).

[133] *See, e.g.*, C.F. Camerer & U. Malmendier, *Behavioral economics of organizations* in P. Diamond & H. Vartiainen (eds.), BEHAVIORAL ECONOMICS AND ITS APPLICATIONS (2007); Paul J. H. Schoemaker, *Strategic Decisions In Organizations: Rational And Behavioural Views*, 30 J. Mgmt. Stud. 107 (1993); Eugene F. Fama & Michael C. Jensen, *Separation of Ownership and Control*, 26 J. L. & Econ. 301 (1983); Barry J. Nalebuff & Joseph E. Stiglitz, *Prizes and Incentives Towards a General Theory of Compensation and Competition*, 14 Bell. J. Econ. 21 (1983); Milton Friedman, *A Friedman Doctrine—The Social Responsibility of Business Is to Increase Its Profits*, N.Y. TIMES (Sept. 13, 1970); Richard M. Cyert & James G. March, A BEHAVIORAL THEORY OF THE FIRM (1963); Gary S. Becker, *Irrational Behavior and Economic Theory*, 70 J. Pol. Econ. 1 (1962).

[134] This is a critical assumption, which antitrust analysis uses to predict how particular practices or transactions might change the ability and incentives of market participants to behave in particular ways. *See, e.g.*, United States v. AT&T, Inc., 916 F.3d 1029, 1043–44 (D.C. Cir. 2019). What else could courts and agencies do? *See generally, e.g.*, Christopher R. Leslie, *Rationality Analysis in Antitrust*, 158 U. Pa. L. Rev. 261 (2010); Amanda P. Reeves & Maurice E. Stucke, *Behavioral Antitrust*, 86 Indiana L.J. 1527 (2011).

goods, like champagne, some consumers actually prefer higher rather than lower prices. (These are sometimes called "Veblen goods." And it may be hard to agree on how we should measure quality effects in the real world (how should we measure the quality of word processing software, or of apples, or of fashionable apparel, or of a social networking service?),[135] so we can get bogged down in arguments about whether and how quality has changed, or by how much.[136] But prices can be easier to measure—unless we try to account for "quality-adjusted" rather than nominal price.

What this means in practice is that, when we are trying to measure or predict welfare effects, we may find ourselves tempted—including for reasons of analytical or evidentiary convenience—to focus on price, perhaps to the exclusion of nonprice effects. But we should avoid falling into the trap of assuming that price is all that matters, or even that it matters most. Economic welfare includes everything that matters to persons. Of course, this does not mean—or at least does not *necessarily* mean—that courts and agencies would be well-advised to try to reflect every idiosyncratic preference or prejudice of every market participant in formulating and applying antitrust rules. Among other things, we might not believe they could do so accurately, or predictably, or without undue delay and expense, or without exercising the kind of broad discretion that might make us uncomfortable.

Efficiency. The idea of welfare, and the related idea that maximizing welfare is a good policy objective, underlies another concept you will encounter often in antitrust: "efficiency." This term can have a variety of meanings, but the most important variations are "allocative" and "productive" efficiency. Allocative efficiency is a quality that pertains to a particular distribution of resources: it is improved when resources are distributed to higher-value uses (that is, distributions that improve overall social welfare). Productive efficiency is a quality of a productive process: it is improved when the ratio of output to cost is increased, such that the process produces more output for the same cost, or the same output for less cost (or, of course, more output for less cost!).[137]

These economic concepts—rationality, welfare, profit maximization, and efficiency—are of central importance to modern antitrust analysis.

In particular, as we saw in Chapter I, courts and commentators today often state that the primary goal of antitrust is the promotion of consumer welfare through the efficient operation of markets.[138] (We also saw that that proposition is controversial.[139]) But it is important to appreciate that there is also considerable debate *even among antitrust economists* over what "efficiency" and "consumer welfare" actually mean—or what they should mean for the purposes of antitrust enforcement and policy—and how those things can or should be identified or pursued.

For example, suppose that we could all agree that welfare maximization is the overriding purpose of antitrust, and that we needn't worry about anything else (including the binding authority of past Supreme Court decisions). We might nevertheless disagree about: (1) what practices or rules will actually increase or maximize welfare (including because particular practices may have one effect in the short run but another in the long run); (2) how we should weigh and combine welfare effects on individuals in order to calculate whether a practice should be permitted or prohibited; (3) what tools or heuristics we should use to measure or predict welfare impacts in real antitrust cases; (4) what we should do when we are uncertain about welfare impacts; or (5) whether welfare has actually been improved or reduced in individual cases. We might also disagree about *whose* welfare matters and in what ways.

---

[135] There are of course a variety of ways in which one might try to proxy for quality: one might try to measure purchasers' willingness to pay for particular features, or aspects of their behavior when they are offered a choice, or one might pick some reasonably plausible index for good or bad quality (like the number of crashes that users experience with a particular piece of software). The key point is that there is often real room for argument about which measures are better than others.

[136] This is a common problem in practice. For example, the Bureau of Labor Statistics must grapple with it in determining the CPI. See U.S. Bureau of Labor Statistics, *Frequently Asked Questions about Hedonic Quality Adjustment in the CPI*, https://www.bls.gov/cpi/quality-adjustment/questions-and-answers.htm; U.S. Bureau of Labor Statistics, *Quality Adjustment in the CPI*, https://www.bls.gov/cpi/quality-adjustment/home.htm.

[137] *See generally, e.g.*, Richard O. Zerbe, ECONOMIC EFFICIENCY IN LAW AND ECONOMICS (2001); E.J. Mishan, ECONOMIC EFFICIENCY AND SOCIAL WELFARE (1981).

[138] *See supra* note 4 and accompanying text.

[139] *See supra* notes 4–8 and accompanying text.

(End-consumers? Workers? Trading partners? Everyone, including defendants?) Confusingly, people use the phrase "consumer welfare standard" to encompass a wide variety of views about all these things.[140]

NOTES

1) What are the advantages of microeconomic analysis as a way of understanding the world and the ways in which entities behave?

2) What features of the real world does traditional microeconomic analysis seem to miss or to poorly describe?

3) Does antitrust need a "paradigm," or a consistent way of thinking about how entities make decisions? Does microeconomic analysis meet this need? What else could do so?

4) Do you think it is a problem for antitrust law that most lawyers and judges are not trained in economics? What would be the costs and drawbacks of a requirement of formal qualification in economics for lawyers and judges?

5) How do you feel about the maximization of economic welfare as a normative goal for antitrust? What, if anything, would be a better alternative?

6) "Antitrust law should rely on the same goals and analytical methods as tort and contract law." Do you agree? What are those, exactly?

7) How do you think the U.S. ended up with a consumer welfare standard in antitrust? What would changing the standard concretely involve?

C. Markets, Supply, Demand, and Elasticity

Antitrust law often deals with "markets," and they will play a critical role in many of the topics we will cover in the rest of this book. In this section, we will introduce the concept of markets, and some of the core terms and ideas we will use to talk and think about them.

1. Markets and Substitutes

The foundation of all thinking about markets—and, ultimately, of the entire antitrust project—is the fact that people have demand for products and services: they prefer to receive them, and are willing to pay some amount to have that preference satisfied. Of course, different people have different levels of demand for different things. Thus, I might be willing to pay $4 for a cup of tea but only $2 for a cup of coffee, and you might be willing to pay $5 for a cup of coffee but have no interest in tea at all.

When more than one product or service might meet a particular need or desire, such as our desire for a caffeinated drink in the morning, we may think of them as substitutes. That is, we may compare them and make a choice from among them, in light of whatever might matter to us, including the products' or services' nature, features, quality, price, and perhaps their location. As a result, when many such alternatives exist, suppliers of the products and services will realize that under most realistic circumstances they will generally do better—that is, they will increase their profits—if their product and services are more appealing than the alternatives. The process of vying to make products and services more attractive than rival options is what is often loosely called competition.

Antitrust uses the idea of a "market," and the process of "defining a relevant market," as tools for thinking about this process. This may be different from other uses and meanings of the term "market" with which you are familiar. We can think of a market as an imaginary frame or zone that includes a product or service and the significant alternatives to it (the "supply side" of the market) and the actual and potential buyers of it (the "demand side" of the market). The aim of defining a market is often to understand and describe the demand for a product or service, and the other products or services that those buyers would regard as substitutes for the product or service at issue.

A *substitute* for product or service X is another product or service to which buyers might turn if X became unavailable, or available only on less appealing terms (*e.g.*, at a higher price). When products and services are "homogeneous," the suppliers' products and services are identical and are perfect substitutes for one another, in

---

[140] *See, e.g.*, Jonathan Kanter, *Milton Handler Lecture* (May 18, 2022) ("[C]onsumer welfare is a catch phrase, not a standard.").

that buyers are indifferent about which one they receive. When products and services are "differentiated," they are not identical: thus, some are closer substitutes and others are more distant. For example, if we are defining a market around a particular cola-flavored carbonated soft drink, we might describe other cola-flavored carbonated soft drinks as close substitutes; non-cola-flavored carbonated soft drinks as somewhat substitutable; and non-carbonated soft drinks (like juices) as more distant substitutes.

In general, as we will discuss in the next section, two things usually happen when a supplier increases its price. Fewer people will buy the supplier's product or service; but the supplier will make more profit on each sale. Thus, to determine whether a price increase would be profitable overall, a supplier must weigh the fact that it will make fewer sales against the fact that it will make a greater profit on each sale that it does make. The existence of substitutes for the product or service is a critical factor in this assessment: substitutes give buyers an alternative to which they can turn (or can threaten to turn) in the event that the price of the first product or service rises, or its quality falls. In other words, substitutes exert competitive "pressure" or competitive "discipline."

All else equal, the closer the substitutes that are available to buyers, the stronger the competitive constraint those substitutes exert. If buyers regard Pepsi as very similar to Coke, then even a small increase in the price of Coke will cause many buyers to switch and buy Pepsi instead. As a result, that price increase is less likely to be profitable overall. (If the substitute is truly identical, even a trivial increase in price or diminution in quality will likely cause such switching.[141]) By contrast, if buyers regard Pepsi as very different from Coke, and nothing else is available, then it may be possible to increase the price of Coke substantially before switching makes further increases unprofitable.

A variety of things might affect whether and when one product is a substitute for another from the perspective of consumer demand. These might include, for example: the features and functionalities of the product or service; its aesthetic qualities or branding; the geographic location of the supplier relative to the buyer; the identity and reputation of the supplier; and so on. Economic analysis has no objective theory of when differences "should" matter: whatever matters to buyers affects the assessment of whether products or services are substitutes.

Of course, different buyers might have different views about whether and to what extent one product is substitutable for another. We would then say that demand is "heterogeneous." For example, to some consumers who just want a caffeinated drink, Pepsi may be just as good as Coke. To other consumers who inflexibly drink Coke every day and have no desire to drink anything else, even Pepsi may be unacceptable: it's Coke or nothing.

One final point of terminology when we are talking about markets. Supply chains commonly involve multiple markets, with entities purchasing something in one market and selling into another. For example, an original equipment manufacturer (or "OEM") might buy components from component suppliers and sell finished equipment to retailers. The retailers, likewise, might buy equipment from OEMs and resell to individual consumers. It is usual to talk about markets earlier in the supply chain (like the market for the supply of components, in this example) as being "upstream" and markets later in the chain (like the market for the retail sale of equipment to consumers) as "downstream."

NOTES

1) Is geographic location always important to assessing substitutability? Can you think of two markets in which the location of a supplier seems important to buyers, and two in which it does not?

2) Everyone has idiosyncratic demand for some things. Can you think of three examples where you believe that you personally regard two products or services as closer (or more distant) substitutes for one another than most people do?

3) In each of these examples, do you believe that the availability of the first product or service would cause large numbers of buyers to switch over if the price of the second increased by 5% or 10%?

   a. Brand-name breakfast cereal and supermarket-brand cereal?
   b. Apples and pears?
   c. Coke and Pepsi?
   d. White bread and wheat bread?

---

[141] *But see infra* § II.F. (noting that even physically identical products do not always work this way).

  e. Skim milk and whole milk?

  f. Taxis and ridesharing services?

  g. Planes and trains?

2. Demand, Supply, and Elasticity

Antitrust economics is usually focused on interactions between buyers and sellers. As such, it is helpful to understand some basic propositions about how the behavior of buyers affects the incentives of sellers, and vice versa.

Let's start by thinking about the market demand—that is, the total demand in the market—for a product or service. Holding all else equal, there will almost always be more demand to buy the product or service when it is cheaper, and less demand when it is more expensive: a lower price makes the purchase more attractive because more buyers will find the value of the good to them to be higher than the price they pay. Depending on the nature of the product or service, the additional demand generated by a price reduction may represent new purchasers buying the product or service, the purchase of more units by the same purchasers, or both. This lets us construct a downward-sloping *demand curve*: as market price increases, market demand falls.

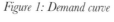

Figure 1: Demand curve

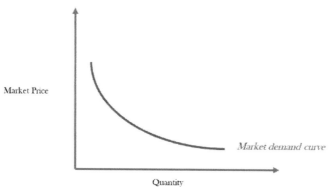

The extent to which a percentage increase in market price triggers a percentage change in market demand is known as the market price elasticity of demand. A higher elasticity of demand means that demand falls off more sharply in reaction to a price increase: in other words, that a particular proportional increase in price will result in a higher proportional decrease in demand. A lower elasticity of demand means that demand falls off more slowly in reaction to a price increase: in other words, that a given proportional increase in price will result in a lower proportional decrease in demand.

It is worth spotting the relationship between elasticity of demand and total revenue available from supply of a product or service. Total revenue—that is, the amount of money generated by sales—is the number of sales multiplied by the sale price. When the market demand is "inelastic," such that the market-price elasticity of demand is less than one, it means that a particular percentage increase in market price would result in a smaller proportional decrease in demand. Thus, a change in market price implemented by all sellers simultaneously (if such a thing could be done and sustained) would result an increase in the total revenue earned by all suppliers (*i.e.*, the number of units sold multiplied by the price of each unit). This might create an incentive for market participants to look for ways to coordinate their conduct, such as a price-fixing cartel. When the market demand is "elastic," such that the market-price elasticity of demand is greater than one, it means that a percentage increase in market price would reduce total revenue earned by all suppliers, as it would result in a greater proportional decrease in the number of units sold. And when market-price elasticity of demand is equal to one, it means that total revenue is being maximized: a percentage change in price will result in an identical and opposite change in demand, and vice versa.

The market price elasticity of demand for a particular product or service depends, among other things, on buyers' views about the available alternatives, given the market price of the product or service. If buyers have access to alternatives that they regard as very nearly as good as the product or service, at the prevailing market price, then they will be very willing to switch in the event of a price increase. If the alternatives are much inferior, then they may be less willing to switch.

For example, suppose that the market price for a PowerZap laptop is $600. If a competing laptop—the PowerPop laptop—is available for about the same price and is roughly as good in almost all respects, then the market price elasticity of demand for the PowerZap may be very high, because even a modest price increase will send consumers running to the PowerPop. But if all the other available laptops are much worse in quality, or much more expensive for the same quality, then even a significant price increase may not reduce sales by much.

As this example suggests, and as you will remember from our discussion above, a change in quality may have a similar effect to a change in price, even if it might be harder to agree about how to measure some dimensions of quality (how would you try to measure "pleasant user experience" or "ease of portability" or even "attractive color" for a laptop? if one laptop has a faster processor and the other has more RAM, which is higher quality overall?).

At any given price point, the portion of demand that is closest to indifference between buying the product or service and not buying it—that is, the portion of demand that will be lost first if the price is increased—is called the "marginal" demand. The portion of demand that will continue to exist even if the price increases is called "inframarginal."

We can also use the language of elasticity to talk about the relationship between *two different* products or services. The relationship between a percentage change in the price of one good and a percentage change in the demand for another good is called the "cross-price elasticity (or just 'cross-elasticity') of demand" from one to the other:

- *Substitutes.* If an increase in the price of one good results in a significant increase in demand for the other good—in technical terms, if there is significant *positive* cross-elasticity of demand from one good with respect to the second—then the two goods are substitutes. In this situation, the higher price on the first good is driving purchasers to demand the other one instead, as an alternative. For example, if the price of pencils were to increase, demand might shift to pens (*i.e.*, demand for pens might increase), suggesting that users regard pens as substitutes for pencils. And if the price of pencils were to fall, then demand for pens would also fall: cheaper pencils would draw consumers away from pens.
- *Complements.* If an increase in the price of one good results in a significant decrease in demand for the other good—a significant *negative* cross-elasticity of demand for one good with respect to the second—then they are complements. In this situation, the higher price on the first good is making the second good less attractive, reflecting the fact that demand for the second good is a function of the availability of the first. For example, if the price of pencils were to increase, demand for pencil erasers might decrease, suggesting that users regard erasers as complements for pencils. And if the price of pencils were to fall, the availability of cheap pencils would fuel demand for pencil erasers.

Now let's think about market supply. Holding all else equal, there will generally be more supply of a product or service as the market price of that product or service increases: the availability of a higher market price makes it more attractive to supply the product or service. Depending on the nature of the product or service, the additional supply generated by a price increase may represent new suppliers selling the product or service, the supply of more units by the same suppliers, or both. This lets us construct an upward-sloping *supply curve:* as price increases, more supply. As the costs of supplying the product or service change, the shape of the supply curve also changes.

We can superimpose the supply curve on the demand curve to see that, for any given price, there will be a certain level of supply and a certain level of demand. And at a particular price point—the so-called "market clearing" price, marked X in the diagram below—supply and demand are equal. We will assume that the costs of producing new units *increases* with quantity, which is true of many but not all markets.

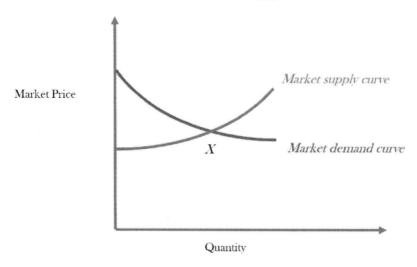

Figure 2: Demand curve and supply curve

As a general rule, market dynamics tend to push quantity and price toward the market-clearing level, at least in the theoretical ideal world in which entry and exit are frictionless (*i.e.*, instantaneous and costless). In particular: when output is below the market-clearing quantity level, demand to buy the good at that price exceeds supply, so there is room for a new entrant to make a profit by entering and selling more output, or for existing suppliers to expand their output. This calls more supply into the market. When output is above the market-clearing quantity level, by contrast, supply exceeds demand, so suppliers cannot profitably sell all their output, and this encourages them to reduce production.

Similarly, when price is above the market clearing level, supply exceeds demand, which creates pressure on suppliers to lower price in order to generate profit from their unsold output. And when price is below the market-clearing level, demand exceeds supply, which makes it profitable for suppliers to increase their price to take advantage of the willingness of purchasers to pay more in order to get the product or service.

The result is that so-called "market forces"—by which we just mean the operation of incentives upon individual market participants—tend to push markets back toward the point at which the amount demanded equals the amount supplied. Indeed, this is part of the classic case for markets: market prices act as signals about market demand, helping to attract resources to the uses in which they are most valued.

At least: that's the theory. Real markets, of course, are much messier, including for reasons we will discuss below.

NOTES

1) Is it really always true that when price increases, demand falls? Can you think of any counterexamples? (One was mentioned earlier: can you think of others?)
2) Is the "market clearing" price necessarily the socially optimal price? If so, why? If not, in what sense if any is it a desirable condition?
3) How much information do you think real businesses have about the shape of the market demand curve? How would they get information of this kind?
4) Without looking ahead to the next section, how do you think a supply curve would change, if at all, if:
    a. the cost of producing each unit were halved (or doubled)?
    b. the fixed cost of being in business were increased (or decreased)?
    c. a major event (*e.g.*, a natural disaster) significantly increased society's need for the product or service?
5) How do you think a demand curve would change, if at all, if:
    a. the cost of producing the product or service were halved (or doubled)?
    b. a complementary product or service were introduced that interoperated in a valuable way with the relevant product or service?
    c. a major event (*e.g.*, a natural disaster) significantly increased society's need for the product or service?

D. Perfect Competition

Imagine a market with a great many sellers, and assume that all the sellers' products or services are identical. Assume that there are no limits on how many units each seller can supply (*i.e.*, no constraints on each seller's capacity), and no costs other than the per-unit cost of making each unit. We will start by assuming that the cost of each unit is a fixed amount and that each firm incurs its costs in the same way.

Real Costs are Complicated!

Despite our simple assumptions, the "costs" of production are usually more complicated than a simple fixed amount for each unit produced. In the real world, businesses incur some costs that vary in light of the number of units produced ("variable costs"), with the cost of producing the next unit known as the "marginal cost." Businesses also usually face some costs that are not incurred in proportion to the volume of output ("fixed costs"), such as the costs of certain facilities and equipment. For now we can assume no fixed costs, but you should be aware that this is a gross oversimplification. Calculating a business's real costs, and allocating them accurately to its various activities, can be tremendously difficult!

In a perfectly competitive market, no supplier can make any money by pricing higher than the competitive price. If a supplier's price is higher than another supplier is offering, potential purchasers will simply go buy from the others instead. (Remember that by assumption all supply is identical.) If prevailing prices are for some reason above the competitive price in a robustly competitive market, each supplier has the incentive to set a fractionally lower price than others are offering in order to win share: each supplier reasons that it is better to drop the price a little, and make a slightly smaller profit margin on more sales, than to make no sale—and thus no profit—at all. Of course, all the suppliers (at least if we assume them all to be rational and possessed of all relevant information) will be doing the same thing! This means that the suppliers will try to outbid each other (or "compete") to offer lower prices. "Competitive pressure"—that is, the struggle to win business by being more attractive to purchasers—thus drives prices down, and profit margins down. As it does so, consumers become progressively better and better off: they are paying less for the same product or service, so they end up with more money in their pocket for other things, as well as receiving the product or service itself.

This process, in which multiple suppliers progressively try to outdo each other by lowering prices, does have a limit: the point at which price cannot be lowered further without the supplier taking a *loss* compared to the next-best use of resources. At the point at which the supplier would do equally well, or better, by not selling the good at all, the supplier will stop lowering price. Thus, the "competitive price" is the price that provides just enough profit margin, above the cost of production, to compensate the suppliers' "opportunity cost" of time and capital: that is, the cost of forgoing the opportunity to use that time and capital in other ways (*e.g.*, investing it elsewhere in the economy for a rate of return). The pressure of competition continually pushes each business toward this point.

When the suppliers in a market are pricing at the competitive point, notice that no individual seller can profitably do anything but the same. If it tries to charge less, the operation of the business will actively lose money. If it tries to charge more, no-one will buy. The supplier in a perfectly competitive market is thus a "price-taker" with no "pricing power," and there is just one price—the competitive one—at which it can make a (slender) profit.

This implies that, in a perfectly competitive market with many suppliers, the *market price* elasticity of demand differs sharply from each supplier's *own-price* elasticity of demand for each supplier. In other words, although there would still be market demand (albeit for a somewhat smaller quantity) if the price of all sellers were to increase *together*, no seller will make the decision to increase price *unilaterally*, because doing so would reduce that seller's sales to zero. Thus, all sellers are forced to price at the competitive price, and only at that price.

Of course, this is just a thought-experiment. In the real world businesses generally do not go the trouble of staying in business for a return that is indistinguishable from that of a passive investment.[142] We will talk below about

---

[142] A business unit with zero *economic* profit in this sense—that is, a business unit that is generating no more profit than the alternative use of those resources—may still have considerable *accounting* profit (*i.e.*, revenue minus expenses of operation).

some of the reasons why real markets do not look like the perfect-competition model. But the key insight for now is that, in imaginary markets that are perfectly competitive, prices are pushed down by competition to a point approaching the economic costs of production. We can reflect this fixed per-unit cost on a demand curve, and we can see how it determines the quantity supplied under competition.

Figure 3: Market price and market demand under competition

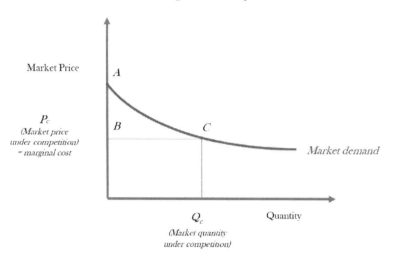

In a perfectly competitive market, with costless entry and expansion by suppliers, the competing suppliers will keep reducing price until market price approaches P_C, with the result that market quantity demanded will approach Q_C.

In a perfectly competitive market like the one we have been describing, purchasers are doing well. They are all paying the same, competitive, price for the product or service, but they all value the product or service more than they value the price in money (otherwise they would just keep their money!). Each purchaser is thus getting a "surplus" value: the most inframarginal purchaser (the one who would be willing to pay the highest price) is getting a lot of surplus value; the marginal purchaser (who is all but indifferent between purchasing and not purchasing at the competitive price) is getting zero surplus. The triangle ABC in Figure 3 represents the total value that purchasers in the market receive above the price paid: the total "consumer surplus." (Having said that, remember what we said earlier about the idea of aggregation across individuals involving some contested moves.)

On the other hand, in a perfectly competitive market, suppliers are much less comfortable: their margins approach zero (or, more accurately, the return available from investment of capital elsewhere). Suppliers who find themselves in this position will try to improve their lot by lowering their cost of production. Thus, in addition to the benefit of pushing prices down toward cost, competition also encourages hungry competitors in search of margin to find ways to lower their costs: that is, to innovate, and to develop more efficient ways to providing the product or service. Other competitors, facing the same incentives, will pursue the same goal. Thus, competition encourages innovation in production.

Lowering costs is typically good for everyone in the market. The result of a reduction in marginal costs is that, for any given price point, the quantity supplied will increase, the market-clearing price will decline, and the market clearing quantity will increase. Conversely, increasing marginal cost will mean that *less* will be supplied for any given price point, and that that market-clearing price will increase.

In sum, we can think of competition—in the everyday sense of rivalry to win the business of purchasers in order to maximize profits—as a force that, among other things, drives each competitor to lower its prices toward its costs, and to lower its costs as far as possible.

Competition also offers a further benefit. Because competitive pressure comes, among other things, from the presence of close substitutes, it creates an incentive for businesses to differentiate their products and services from those of their competitors in ways that buyers value. In other words, the search for profit margin encourages *innovation*: new ways to meet demand. We will discuss product differentiation below.

NOTES

1) Which real-world markets most resemble the perfect competition model?
2) Which real-world markets least resemble the perfect competition model?
3) What tools do producers use to differentiate their products and services?
4) If product differentiation tends to make markets less competitive, does that mean it's a bad or harmful thing?
5) In practice, in most markets, marginal costs generally change with the quantity produced. The nature of this change depends on the nature of the business, but in many markets the marginal costs increase with quantity of output. In others, they decline with quantity of output. In others still, costs may change in different directions as quantity of output increases (*e.g.*, declining up to a certain level of output, and then increasing). Why do you think this is? Can you think of examples?
6) In what sense do all purchasers benefit from the existence of the marginal purchaser?

E. Monopoly

So what happens when we eliminate competition among sellers? We can replace our set of competitive, price-taking sellers with a single monopolist: that is, a lone supplier with no actual or potential rivals. As we will discuss below, this move from competition to monopoly could represent any of a variety of changes in a real market. It could represent the formation of a successful agreement among all the sellers to coordinate their actions (like a price-fixing cartel); it could represent the acquisition, by one seller, of all the others; it could represent the fact that costs decline with scale, such that a larger firm can set prices that a smaller firm cannot match (a so-called "natural monopoly"); or it could represent all but one seller being driven out of the market, perhaps by a superior product, foul play, or government action. But, for now, the means of creating the monopoly is immaterial.

The monopolist is unlike the competitive sellers in one very important respect: it can make a profit by selling above the competitive price. If it does so, it will of course sell fewer units than it would sell at the competitive price: the shape of our demand curve tells us that as price goes up, quantity demanded goes down. But the monopolist will make more profit on each unit sold.

Unlike a competitive seller, the monopolist's own price affects market demand and market price: the market-price demand curve is the same as its own-price demand curve. The result is that the profit-maximizing price for a monopolist—the "monopoly price"—is higher than the profit-maximizing price for a seller in a competitive market, resulting in a lower quantity of units supplied. We can depict this graphically: the move to monopoly results in a higher price and a lower quantity than we saw under perfect competition.

Figure 4: Market price and market demand under competition and monopoly

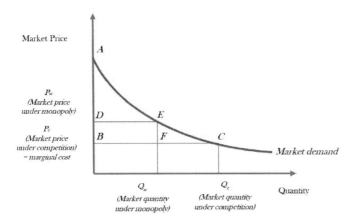

We have already seen that, under perfect competition, suppliers are forced to survive on a profit margin that approaches zero (or, at least, that approaches the rate of return available from other uses of the capital). But the ability to price above cost without competitive discipline means that things are much more pleasant for a monopolist! The area DEFB (*i.e.*, the margin between monopoly price and cost, multiplied by the quantity sold under monopoly) represents the monopolist's total "monopoly profit." But that profit comes at the expense of consumers, who are now worse off. As you will remember, their total surplus at the competitive price is the difference between value of the good to buyers and the price they paid, which, in aggregate, is represented by the area ABC. Under monopoly, consumers' total surplus is now only ADE (which is clearly a smaller area). So they have taken an overall welfare hit, compared to perfect competition, equal to ABC minus ADE.

And here the diagram shows us a helpful fact about the relative values of the quantities we are discussing. We can see from the diagram that the loss sustained by consumers is equal to the area of the shape DECB (*i.e.*, area ABC – area ADE). And we can also see that this harm to consumers is larger than the monopolist's profit DEFB: in fact, the margin of difference is equal to the area of the triangle ECF. We can think of ECF as representing the surplus that would have been enjoyed by consumers who would have bought the product or service at the competitive price, but do not buy it at the monopoly price.

This gives us an absolutely critical insight for antitrust law and policy: the harm suffered by consumers under monopoly outweighs the monopoly profit, leaving society worse off overall compared to a perfectly competitive market. The amount of that overall injury is called the "deadweight loss," and it is equal to the area of triangle ECF in the diagram.

This proposition is central to the standard normative economic case for antitrust. The central objection to monopoly power is not, as such, that consumers (or other purchasers) must pay more: it is that the existence of monopoly, rather than perfect competition, is associated with *social* or overall harm, because the benefit to the monopolist is outweighed by the harm to consumers.[143]

Note, however, that a perfectly competitive market might not be realistically available. If a particular business involves costs that *decline* as output increases ("economies of scale"), then a single monopoly supplier might be able to meet demand more cheaply than would a number of smaller businesses. Indeed, as a result, the smaller firms (with their higher costs) might not be able to compete sustainably with the dominant firm, such that a "natural monopoly" may be the result toward which the market tends to move.[144]

Where does the monopolist price?

We can go one step further and figure out where exactly the monopolist will price. We will continue to assume that every unit sold by the monopolist is priced identically, a constant marginal cost, and no fixed costs.

The monopolist understands that a higher price for its output means that a smaller quantity will be demanded at that price. Each marginal move down the demand curve, starting from the left hand side, will cause a marginal increase in quantity demanded, increasing its total revenue. But with each move downward, this increase in revenue—the marginal revenue from the next sale—will get smaller and smaller, until it reaches the level of marginal cost. The monopolist will not produce the next unit, because it would not be rational to produce a unit for which marginal cost exceeds marginal revenue. So the profit-maximizing price and quantity will be the point at which marginal revenue = marginal cost.

We can see this with an example, with some basic calculus to help us. Suppose that the market demand curve for a widget, setting the relationship between price (P) and quantity (Q), is defined by the function $P = 100 - 10Q$. Suppose also that the marginal cost (MC) of making a widget is constant at \$10. There is a single strict monopolist of widgets, and entry is impossible. Total revenue (TR) at any point is equal to the number of units sold multiplied by the price of each unit (*i.e.*, TR = PQ). Given our demand curve, we know that $TR = PQ = (100 - 10Q)Q = 100Q - 10Q^2$.

Marginal revenue (MR) is the rate of change in total revenue with respect to a marginal change in quantity. Differentiating TR with respect to Q gives us $MR = 100 - 20Q$. And we know that the monopolist will reach its profit-maximizing price when MR = MC, which we have supposed to be 10. If $100 - 20Q = 10$, then $20Q = 90$,

---

[143] *See, e.g.*, Andreu Mas-Colell, Michael D. Whinston & Jerry R. Green, MICROECONOMIC THEORY (1995) § 12.B. at 384–87.

[144] This observation was critical to the development of the theory of utility regulation. *See generally, e.g.*, Morton J. Horwitz, THE TRANSFORMATION OF AMERICAN LAW, 1870–1960: THE CRISIS OF LEGAL ORTHODOXY (1992) Ch. 8; Herbert Hovenkamp, ENTERPRISE AND AMERICAN LAW, 1836–1937 (1991), 142–68.

so Q = 4.5. And if Q = 4.5, then our original demand curve tells us that P = 100 − 10Q = 100 − 10(4.5) = 55. So the monopolist's profit-maximizing price given its costs of $10 per unit, and the shape of our demand curve, is 55, at which it will sell a quantity of 4.5.

We can see this in tabular form too.

Table 1: Where does the monopolist price?

Quantity	Price	Total Revenue (= Quantity x Price)	Total Cost (= Quantity x $10)	Total Profit (= TR − TC)
0.5	95	47.5	5	42.5
1.0	90	90	10	80
1.5	85	127.5	15	112.5
2.0	80	160	20	140
2.5	75	187.5	25	162.5
3.0	70	210	30	180
3.5	65	227.5	35	192.5
4.0	60	240	40	200
4.5	55	247.5	45	202.5
5.0	50	250	50	200

But the emergence of a monopoly is not usually the end of the story. The charging of monopoly prices in the market can act as a signal to others that there are profits to be made in the relevant market. And this profit opportunity may induce others to enter the relevant market and compete with the monopolist. In this way, the existence of monopoly power itself incentivizes greater competition: the higher the monopoly price, the stronger the inducement to enter and compete that calls other suppliers into the market. This idea plays an important part in the observation that markets often have a tendency to "self-correct." However, the strength of this tendency, and the extent to which it can or should be trusted to operate as a cure for the ills of monopoly, are all highly controversial: real markets are imperfect.[145]

In addition, in some settings, the prospect of achieving monopoly power may encourage would-be competitors to radically innovate new ways of meeting demand, rather than pursuing incremental improvements. Sometimes firms may end up driving a "leap" forward in an effort to become the incumbent monopolist in a market that does not yet exist: for example, introducing the car rather than an incrementally better horse-and-carriage; a personal computer rather than an incrementally better typewriter; a smartphone rather than an incrementally better flip phone; and so on.[146]

NOTES

1) Why is it rare for a firm to have literally no competitors (a "strict monopolist")? Can you think of any real examples of strict monopoly?

2) Why isn't the monopoly price infinitely high for a strict monopolist? In other words, if there are literally no competitors, why can't the supplier charge any price it likes, regardless of what the product or service is?

3) Are there reasons to object to monopoly other than the one emphasized in the text?

4) "In a free market society, persons have an inherent right to seek, retain, and enjoy whatever monopoly profits they can get." Do you agree with this statement?

---

[145] The imperfection of real markets has been understood by economists for a long time. *See, e.g.,* Joan Robinson, THE ECONOMICS OF IMPERFECT COMPETITION (1933); Martin Shubik, STRATEGY AND MARKET STRUCTURE: COMPETITION, OLIGOPOLY, AND THE THEORY OF GAMES (1959). For a short, accessible summary of some of the history, *see* Huw Dixon, *A Brief History of Imperfect Competition,* Comp. Pol'y Int'l (Oct. 2021).

[146] *See, e.g.,* Andreas Pyka & Richard R. Nelson, *Schumpeterian Competition and Industrial Dynamics* in Richard R. Nelson (ed.) MODERN EVOLUTIONARY ECONOMICS: AN OVERVIEW (2018); J. Gregory Sidak & David J. Teece, *Dynamic Competition In Antitrust Law,* 5 J. Comp. L. & Econ. 581 (2009); Herbert J. Hovenkamp, *Schumpeterian Competition and Antitrust,* U. Iowa Legal Studies Research Paper No. 08-43 (2008); Jerry Ellig (ed.), DYNAMIC COMPETITION AND PUBLIC POLICY: TECHNOLOGY, INNOVATION, AND ANTITRUST ISSUES (2001); Carl A. Futia, *Schumpeterian Competition,* 94 Q. J. Econ. 675 (1980).

5) "Markets are created by state power to serve us all, underwritten with the coercive power of the state—including the criminal law—and should be subject to whatever rules are necessary to avoid enduring inequalities, including inequalities of opportunity, wealth, or power." Do you agree with this statement?

F. Imperfect Competition and Market Power

A strict monopolist of the kind we just considered—with sole control of production, facing no competition to supply the product or service, and constrained only by the nature of market demand—is a fairly rare sight in a real economy. In practice, we more commonly encounter the cousin of strict monopoly: "market power."

Market power is the ability of an individual supplier to charge a price that is above the competitive level, and it exists in between the clean (but also largely imaginary) worlds of perfect competition and strict monopoly. When the amount of market power is very significant, antitrust lawyers call it "monopoly power," even if the firm is not a strict monopolist, and although this is not a term that economists tend to use.

Lerner Index

One way to measure market power is called the Lerner Index. It is equal to: (price − marginal cost) / price. This yields a value between 0 (when price is equal to marginal cost) and 1 (when marginal cost is zero, so the price is pure profit-margin).[1] This is a helpful tool but it can be hard to calculate, as cost measurement is notoriously difficult. It may also give a misleading impression of a firm's market power: can you think of reasons why this might be so?

So how could a supplier have some pricing power even though it faces some competition? Some of the most important factors include *product differentiation, entry barriers, capacity constraints, imperfect information*, and *transaction costs*.

1. Product differentiation

Real suppliers are not identical, and neither are real purchasers. Products and services are differentiated in a variety of ways, including by brand identity, and purchasers have different preferences. For example, suppose that there are twelve manufacturers of dishwashing liquid, each of which is slightly different. One has a punk-themed brand identity, one has an eco-friendly brand identity, and one is endorsed by a popular sports player. One is slightly better at dealing with food grease; one smells more pleasant; one moisturizes the user's hands. One makes glasses shine a little better; one is gentler for delicate crockery. And so on.

In this example, none of the suppliers of dishwashing liquid are strict monopolists or anything like it. But different consumers will have different preferences over this selection of dishwashing products, for which they are willing to pay a little more: and thus, each of these manufacturers will likely find it profitable to set a price *somewhat* above the pure competitive level, but lower than the strict monopoly point. Somewhat like a monopolist, they must balance the fact that every price increase means a greater margin on each unit but that fewer units will be sold. Of course, this is all a matter of degree: the greater the demand for the special nature of the supplier's product, and the fewer or more dissimilar the alternatives, the more market power the supplier has.

Notice that some of the "differentiation" may involve differences in branding or appearance, rather than physical or chemical differences in the underlying products. If it seems odd to you that consumers would be willing to pay more for something other than an "objective" difference in the product, consider for example the significant price gap between "branded" and "generic" drugs, which generally do not have relevant chemical differences. Consider also the vast premiums paid for designer goods of all kinds by consumers who value the ability to display a famous brand name or logo, even if the goods themselves barely differ from the unbranded alternatives. Nor are consumer preferences set in stone: the vast expenditures on advertising across the economy reflect the role of marketing in helping to shape and form consumer preferences for particular brands. How many ads have you seen that aim to convince you that a particular company, product, or brand is particularly desirable, reliable, trustworthy, or compatible with your values?[147]

Product differentiation is a common feature of the modern economy. The growth and development of modern technology—including technologies relating to the collection and analysis of data on individual consumers—has made it much easier for many businesses to identify customers' preferences and to tailor products and services accordingly.

2. Entry barriers

Real suppliers do not just pop into existence overnight upon learning that there is an infinitesimal profit margin available from the supply of some product or service. In practice, it may take time and money to enter a line of business: facilities must be obtained, employees must be found and hired, suppliers and distributors must be identified and contracts negotiated, and the process of actually providing the product or service may take time and require trial and error to get right. Risks and uncertainties, or the prospect of facing significant "exit costs" if things do not work out, may deter businesses from investing in the first place. Other factors, too, may deter or prevent entry: necessary IP licenses, regulatory permissions from federal, state, or local government, or needed infrastructure may all prove difficult or impossible to obtain. We can think of all these factors individually, at least in a general sense, as "barriers to entry."[148]

As a technical matter, the definition of an "entry barrier" turns out to be more controversial than you might think. The two main competing traditional definitions are: (1) a factor that allows those in the market to raise price above the competitive level without attracting entry; and (2) a cost that would have to be borne by a firm seeking to become active in the market that is not borne by those already present.[149] The first definition includes, but is not limited to, the second. The second, narrower, category includes startup costs like the acquisition of know-how and the one-time costs of obtaining regulatory permissions. The first category also includes a much broader category of cost differentials which advantage incumbents, such as efficiencies of scale and scope, capital requirements, customer brand loyalty, and so on.[150] In practice, the formal labels matter less than our understanding of the various mechanisms by which entry can be impeded or deterred, and our recognition that we might want to use different policy tools to respond to different phenomena that make entry more difficult.

The existence of entry barriers can give incumbents the confidence to increase their prices (or undertake equivalent actions, like lowering their quality) in the knowledge that new entrants will be deterred, hindered, delayed, or completely prevented by entry barriers from entering the market to provide competitive discipline. Obviously, higher barriers will tend to create more pricing power.

Sometimes incumbents may engage in conduct that *increases* entry barriers. For example, incumbents may enter into exclusive dealing arrangements that lock up key suppliers, distributors, or customers; they may extract commitments from trading partners that rivals and entrants will not be granted terms that are as good, or better, than those granted to the incumbent; and they may use or abuse government or regulatory processes to keep competitors out. One important function of antitrust law is to regulate the extent to which, and the ways in which, incumbents with market power can engage in conduct that raises entry barriers or otherwise deters or impedes entry. We will spend plenty of time talking about this in the rest of this book.

---

[147] *See, e.g.*, Anna E. Tuchman, *Advertising and Demand for Addictive Goods: The Effects of E-Cigarette Advertising*, 38 Mktg. Sci. 913 (2019); Gary W. Brester & Ted C. Shroeder, *The Impacts of Brand and Generic Advertising on Meat Demand*, Am. J. Agr. Econ. 969 (1995); Carl Shapiro, *Advertising and Welfare: Comment*, 11 Bell. J. Econ. 749 (1980); James L. Hamilton, *The Demand for Cigarettes: Advertising, the Health Scare, and the Cigarette Advertising Ban*, 54 Rev. Econ. & Stat. 401 (1972).

[148] *See, e.g.*, R. Preston McAfee, Hugo M. Mialon & Michael A. Williams, *What Is a Barrier to Entry?* AEA Papers & Procs. 461 (May 2004); Richard Schmalensee, *Sunk Costs and Antitrust Barriers to Entry*, 94 Am. Econ. Rev. 471 (2004); Harold Demsetz, *Barriers to Entry*, 72 Am. Econ. Rev. 47 (1982); *see generally* George Stigler, THE ORGANIZATION OF INDUSTRY (1968); Joe S. Bain, BARRIERS TO NEW COMPETITION (1956).

[149] Joe S. Bain, BARRIERS TO NEW COMPETITION (1965) 22–23; George Stigler, THE ORGANIZATION OF INDUSTRY (1968) 67.

[150] *See generally, e.g.*, R. Preston McAfee, Hugo M. Mialon & Michael A. Williams, *What Is A Barrier to Entry?*, 94 Am. Econ. Rev. 461 (2004); Harold Demsetz, *Barriers to Entry*, 72 Am. Econ. Rev. 47 (1982).

In addition to traditional entry barriers, special features of certain markets or technologies may favor incumbents in a similar way. For example, "economies of scale" (*i.e.*, cost advantages that arise as a function of the supplier's level of production) may mean that established players who have already achieved a certain level of scale may find it cheaper to meet demand than newcomers do.[151] Similarly, "economies of scope" (*i.e.*, cost advantages that arise from engaging in two or more different productive activities simultaneously) may mean that established players who are active in more than one market may find it cheaper to meet demand than unintegrated single-market competitors.[152] And "network effects" (*i.e.*, benefits to users of a product or service as a function of the number of other people using it, as with a fax machine or a social networking service) may make users reluctant to switch from an incumbent to a new entrant, even if the entrant's product is in some other way superior.[153]

The result of these and similar factors can be to chill the incentive that potential rivals would otherwise have to rush into the market to discipline a price increase. In effect, entry barriers and equivalent phenomena create a shelter from the winds of competition, within which incumbents can enjoy a margin of market power.

However, the presence of these effects does not necessarily mean that something has "gone wrong" in an all-things-considered sense. Economies of scale and scope enable products and services to be provided at lower cost than would be the case if those economies did not exist. Network effects reflected the added value of interconnection with other users. It is important to see that the benefits of lower cost and greater value, and the risks of greater insulation from competition, go hand-in-hand.

3. Capacity constraints

In much the same way that entry barriers can impede or deter new market entry, so too can other factors impede or deter expansion by *existing* market participants. Such factors can include, for example, the costs and delays of upgrading existing facilities or acquiring new ones, as well as difficulties in obtaining critical raw materials, other inputs, licenses, permissions, know-how, or access to distribution infrastructure.

The existence of such capacity constraints may contribute to market power by limiting the ability of existing competitors to discipline price increases or output reductions. For example, if existing rivals could not instantly expand their own output to pick up new customers, the incumbent may be able to implement a significant price increase, at least while competitors work to expand their capacity. And in the meantime, competitors who are unable to serve additional customers may choose to follow the price increase rather than compete aggressively: in other words, capacity constraints may facilitate "oligopoly" dynamics, including through so-called "tacit collusion," a topic we will explore below.

4. Imperfect information and transaction costs

In certain versions of an ideal universe, everyone would always know everything about the world—what suppliers and purchasers are available, how much everything costs and how good it really is, and so on—and it would be instantaneous and effortless to act on that information by switching between trading partners. But in the real world, information is imperfect, and transacting and switching are often costly. These realities can have important implications for competition.

Reliable and accurate information can be hard to find. A supplier or purchaser may not know exactly which potential trading partners are willing and able to deal with it, or on what terms they would be willing and able to do so. They may not know which trading parties can be trusted to provide products and services of the requisite

---

[151] *See, e.g.*, George J. Stigler, *The Economies of Scale*, 1 J. L. & Econ. 54 (1958); Alfred D. Chandler, SCALE AND SCOPE: THE DYNAMICS OF INDUSTRIAL CAPITALISM (1994).

[152] See, e.g., John C. Panzar & Robert D. Willig, *Economies of Scope*, 71 Am. Econ. Rev. 268 (1972); David J. Teece, *Economies of scope and the scope of the enterprise*, 1 J. Econ. Behavior & Org. 223 (1980).

[153] *See, e.g.*, Michael L. Katz & Carl Shapiro, *Systems Competition and Network Effects*, 8 J. Econ. Persp. 93 (1994); Oz Shy, *A Short Survey of Network Economics*, 38 Rev. Indus. Org. 119 (2011).

quality and reliability. And they may not know how far they can trust the information that they do receive, including information about robustness of demand or security of supply.[154]

This means that market participants may, in practice, not avail themselves of more efficient options, or negotiate to more efficient terms, simply because they do not know whether those options or terms are actually available. For example, a purchaser may be willing to pay a supracompetitive price, despite the availability of a more competitive option, because it does not know or believe that the more competitive supplier is available and willing to meet its needs. A supplier may be unwilling to work with the most efficient distributor because it does not know whether that distributor can really be trusted to provide high-quality services of the relevant kind. A consumer may pay over the odds to buy a product or service through a particular platform because the consumer does not realize that the same product or service is available for a better price on an alternative platform. As these examples illustrate, information gaps can work to protect incumbents' market power against competitive pressure.

And just as information is not perfect in real-world markets, neither are transactions instantaneous or costless. It takes time and energy—which may not be available—to negotiate or renegotiate contracts. Parties make investments in specific relationships all the time, and may stand to lose the benefits of those investments if they switch to a "better" competitor. For example, switching among suppliers or distributors might involve spending considerable time and money in evaluating their suitability, working to assess the technical compatibility of the alternative suppliers' products with their needs, negotiating the terms of the commercial relationship, building trust and understanding, and perhaps obtaining new or amended licenses and regulatory permissions. This can all add up to a significant "switching cost." The prospect of that cost may deter market participants from finding, or switching to, even superior competitors.

Consumers can face switching costs too. For example, suppose that you had spent years using a particular kind of consumer electronic device: you had come to rely on that device to keep track of your contacts, to hold records of your messages and other interactions with your friends, to store your photos and videos, and to manage access to other content and files. Even if a "better" device came along, you might be reluctant to switch over if it meant losing your vast store of accumulated value on the incumbent device. The new device might have to be *vastly* better to convince you that it was worth overcoming the "lock-in" effect and leaving your existing investments behind.

Thus, both imperfect information and transaction costs can soften the competitive pressure that attractive alternatives would otherwise exert on incumbents. Just like entry barriers, and just like product differentiation, they can create space between the incumbent and the next-best substitute in which market power can operate.

NOTES

1) Is it possible to ban the possession of substantial market power? Is it desirable?
2) Can you name examples of firms that arguably have some market power due to economies of scale or scope?
3) Can you think of real businesses that enjoyed significant network effects, but nevertheless lost their incumbent position, and were replaced by other firms?
4) Can you think of real businesses that have enjoyed significant network effects for an extended period and have held their incumbent position for a long time? What seems to explain this? What, if anything, do you think will displace those firms?
5) What is the longest-enduring example of significant market power than you can think of?
6) Is the existence of market power in markets for non-necessary products and services (*e.g.*, designer fashion-wear; luxury foods; recreational goods) a problem that society should take seriously?

---

[154] *See generally*, *e.g.*, Michael S. Jacobs, *Market Power Through Imperfect Information: the Staggering Implications of* Eastman Kodak Co. v. Image Technical Services *and a Modest Proposal for Limiting Them*, 52 Md. L. Rev. 336 (1993); Louis Phlips, THE ECONOMICS OF IMPERFECT INFORMATION (1989); Alan Schwartz & Louis L. Wilde, *Intervening in Markets on the Basis of Imperfect Information: A Legal and Economic Analysis*, 127 U. Pa. L. Rev. 630 (1979).

G. The Concerns of Antitrust: Collusion and Exclusion

We noted above that monopoly or market power can emerge in a variety of ways. One way in which it could happen is if one supplier out-competes the others by offering a product that is so much better (or so much cheaper) than those of its rivals that the rivals cannot constrain it. We sometimes think of this as the acquisition of monopoly through "industry" or "competition on the merits." This process, even to the extent that it results in some degree of monopoly power being created for some period of time, is generally regarded as a healthy and necessary feature of life in a free-market society. Indeed, economists often point out that the prospect of gaining monopoly power, and reaping some monopoly profits, is a critical source of the incentive to innovate and invest in the first place, and to develop new products and services that confer value on society.[155]

But other ways of achieving monopoly are less appealing! Antitrust is primarily concerned with protecting against two mechanisms that may lead to monopoly or market power. The first mechanism of harm is *collusion*: if the competitors in a market agree amongst themselves about the prices and other terms they will offer, such that they are making competitive decisions jointly rather than unilaterally, the result can be that the participants act, in at least some respects, like a single monopolist. A group of competitors engaging in naked coordination of this kind is commonly called a cartel.

Successful collusion depends on the group of colluders being able: (1) to coordinate their conduct rather than competing with one another, so they can act in concert (despite the fact that "cheating" on the others by undercutting their price can produce gains, at least in the short term); and (2) to collectively control enough of the market that they exercise market or monopoly power. We will focus on collusion in Chapters IV and V.

The second mechanism of harm is *exclusion*: if a market participant can drive up its rivals' costs, cut off their access to inputs or distribution, or suppress their incentives to compete, monopoly or market power may be acquired or maintained as a result. This could be accomplished in a variety of ways, including by tying up key input suppliers or distributors such that they are available to competitors on less advantageous terms (*e.g.*, higher prices or worse quality), or not at all; by using or abusing regulatory processes to inflict costs on rivals; by engaging in unsustainable "predation" that drives rivals out of the market; or by offering threats or bribes that induce potential rivals to avoid competition.

Successful exclusion depends on being able to hinder enough rivals, by a significant enough degree, to generate market power for the excluding firm. Driving up rivals' costs, or forcing them to reduce their output, can leave the excluder with greater control over price and output. In the extreme case, forcing them all out of the market and precluding entry will leave the excluder as a strict monopolist. (Sometimes a group of colluders may *also* engage in the exclusion of non-participating rivals: for example, cartel members might obtain commitments from key input suppliers not to deal with firms outside the cartel. Why do you think they might do this?) Exclusionary agreements and practices will be a recurrent theme in Chapters VI and VII.

Acquisitions may present the concerns of collusion, exclusion, or both. A horizontal merger with a rival may leave the market more vulnerable to "tacit collusion" (that is, coordination that does not require an actual agreement among the firms, as we will see later in this chapter)—or even express collusion—creating what antitrust calls coordinated effects. Or it may result in the creation of a business that controls enough of the market to hold market power all alone—replicating the effects of collusion between the merging parties—creating what antitrust calls unilateral effects. A vertical merger may leave the merged firm able to exclude rivals by foreclosing their access to inputs or distribution; it may also facilitate explicit or tacit collusion among market participants. To address these concerns, we rely on merger-control laws, as we will see in Chapter VIII.

---

[155] This is a classic justification for the existence of the law of intellectual property, and for property law more generally. *See, e.g.,* Makan Delrahim, *The "New Madison" Approach to Antitrust and Intellectual Property Law* (speech of Mar. 16, 2018), https://www.justice.gov/opa/speech/file/1044316/download; Nancy Gallini & Suzanne Scotchmer, *Intellectual Property: When Is It the Best Incentive System?*, Innovation Pol'y & Econ. 51 (2002); Steven Shavell & Tanguy van Ypersele, *Rewards Versus Intellectual Property Rights*, 44 J. L. & Econ. 525 (2001); Timothy Besley, *Property Rights and Investment Incentives: Theory and Evidence from Ghana*, 103 J. Pol. Econ. 903 (1995); Ejan Mackaay, *Economic Incentives in Markets for Information and Innovation*, 13 Harv. J. L. & Pub. Pol'y 867 (1990); *see also* John Locke, SECOND TREATISE OF GOVERNMENT (1690) Ch. 5.

Second-Order Concerns: Errors, Error Costs, and Decision Theory

Antitrust rules and enforcement practices are not *solely* designed to target harmful collusion and exclusion. They also reflect an effort to minimize the costs and harms of error in the application of antitrust itself. "Decision theory" is the study and analysis of how decisions can best be made with limited information and uncertainty about outcomes, and it has been influential in the development of antitrust rules.[156] Through this lens, courts and scholars often think about the likelihood and harms of "false positives" (*i.e.*, the imposition of liability when the underlying conduct is not of concern) and "false negatives" (*i.e.*, the failure to impose liability when the underlying conduct is, in fact, of concern). They also consider the related effects on incentives: that is, the fear that an overbroad antitrust rule or enforcement practice might deter (or "chill") desirable competition and investment, or the risk that antitrust loopholes will encourage harmful anticompetitive practices.

There is limited evidence about the frequency and magnitudes of these effects in particular contexts or in general, and intuitions vary significantly. For example, many Chicago School scholars argued that false positives in antitrust enforcement were more harmful than false negatives, because the market would erode a monopoly but could not correct government action, and that a robust presumption of non-intervention would therefore be best in most cases.[157] Many post-Chicago scholars argued that courts and agencies have—by overstating the resiliency of markets and the costs of intervention—worried too much about false positives and not enough about false negatives.[158]

H. Potential Competition and Entry

Competitive pressure is exerted not only by businesses already in the market, but also by those who can credibly threaten to enter the market in the event of a price increase. Such competitors are sometimes called "potential" competitors, to distinguish them from actual competitors.

Potential competition works in a very similar way to actual competition. Recall that actual competitors exert competitive pressure on an incumbent through their ability to offer a lower price (or higher quality for the same price), thus winning business if the incumbent tries to charge a price above the competitive level. Potential competition works in the same way, except that the potential competitor is not yet actually active in the market. A potential competitor exerts competitive pressure through the implicit threat to enter in the event that an incumbent tries to raise price.[159]

Suppose that entry into a particular market—say, the market for lemonade—is costless and immediate, such that there are no costs or delays required to get started. And suppose that the competitive price for lemonade is $0.50/cup, and that there is only a single participant currently in the market, selling lemonade for the competitive price.

At first glance, the single lemonade stand looks a strict monopolist. There are no other lemonade suppliers in the market, so it might appear that the lemonade supplier could simply raise its prices to the monopoly point. But now add some potential competitors: potential entrants, peeking out from behind the curtains of the buildings across the street. Right now, those potential entrants are not supplying lemonade. They are, thus, not actual competitors. But if the incumbent tries to raise its prices by any significant margin, they will spot the opportunity to make a profit and will be out on the street in a flash, exerting competitive pressure until the price falls to the competitive

---

[156] *See, e.g.*, Isaac Ehrlich & Richard A. Posner, *An Economic Analysis of Legal Rulemaking*, 3 J. Leg. Stud. 257 (1974).

[157] *See, e.g.*, Frank H. Easterbrook, *The Limits of Antitrust*, 63 Tex. L. Rev. 1 (1984).

[158] *See, e.g.*, Jonathan B. Baker, *Taking the Error out of "Error Cost" Analysis: What's Wrong with Antitrust's Right*, 80 Antitrust L.J. 1 (2015); C. Frederick Beckner III & Steven C. Salop, *Decision Theory and Antitrust Rules*, 67 Antitrust L.J. 41 (1999).

[159] *See generally* William J. Baumol, John C. Panzar & Robert D. Willig, CONTESTABLE MARKETS AND THE THEORY OF INDUSTRY STRUCTURE (1982); William B. Tye, THE THEORY OF CONTESTABLE MARKETS: APPLICATIONS TO REGULATORY AND ANTITRUST PROBLEMS IN THE RAIL INDUSTRY (1990).

level. That threat of potential competition, if the incumbent knows about it, can exert discipline and keep prices down.

There is much we can learn from the lemonade stand example. For one thing, notice the importance of barriers to entry in affecting the pressure exerted by potential entrants. Suppose that, in order to sell lemonade in the street, you need to pay $5 and fill in a lengthy application form. That barrier would likely somewhat deter the potential rivals from entering, and limit the importance of the threat. Maybe the incumbent could increase its price to $0.55, or $0.60, before the rivals felt it was worth coming into the market. A higher entry barrier—say, a $10 or $20 fee, or an obligation to fill out three or ten forms—would create still more market power for the incumbent. The lesson is that the higher the entry barriers, the less the competitive pressure that potential rivals exert. For another thing, notice that the ability of the incumbent to swiftly return to competitive pricing is a powerful deterrent to entry, especially if entry or exit is costly. If the incumbent can instantly drop its price back to the competitive level, reducing the available margin to virtually zero, then the expected profit from entry disappears. After all, why go through the hassle of overcoming an entry barrier, or face the costs of exiting the market in failure, when the incumbent can make the profit margin vanish as soon as you arrive in the market?[160]

NOTES

1) How can we identify a potential competitor in the real world? What kind of evidence could we look at to determine whether a particular business might qualify as a potential competitor?

2) If we are concerned about an incumbent's ability to rapidly lower its prices as a means to deter new market entry, should we introduce rules that require suppliers to stick to posted prices for a minimum time period? Or that prohibit changing prices by more than, say, 10% in a particular time period? What are the advantages and disadvantages of these proposals?

3) If potential competitors are really exerting competitive pressure, shouldn't we describe them as being "in" the market?

4) Suppose that Company X has made a series of public announcements about its readiness and plans to enter Market Y. But, unbeknownst to the rest of the world, Company X has no plans in fact to enter. Is Company X a potential competitor in Market Y? Can it exert competitive discipline on incumbents?

I. Tacit Collusion and Market Concentration

We have so far focused on three main cases; the case of perfect competition, the case of strict monopoly, and the case in which a supplier holds market power short of monopoly. In each case, suppliers have been acting unilaterally, taking the behavior of other market participants as given. But a fourth case is important to antitrust doctrine and policy. In some markets, suppliers may find it profitable to keep an eye on each other and to calibrate their behavior according to what their rivals do. This phenomenon—strategic interdependence—gives rise to what is often called "tacit collusion."

The core insight is simple. In a market with a small number of players that can monitor one another's behavior with some accuracy (sometimes called an "oligopoly" or "oligopolistic market"), each participant might realize that aggressive competition could hurt its overall profits. And so each player may look for ways to cooperate and coordinate—without explicitly colluding, if they want to avoid antitrust trouble—so as to avoid aggressive competition and keep margins high.

Example: Two Service Stations

Consider a very simple example. Suppose a market with only two players and high price transparency: let's say two service stations, North and South, set up across the road from each other, with no other service stations nearby. Each service station posts its gas price prominently in a manner that is visible to the other. Suppose that the strict

---

[160] *See, e.g.*, Robert E. Hall, *Potential Competition, Limit Pricing, and Price Elevation from Exclusionary Conduct*, in ABA Section of Antitrust Law, 1 ISSUES IN COMPETITION LAW AND POLICY (2008); Paul Milgrom & John Roberts, *Limit Pricing and Entry under Incomplete Information: An Equilibrium Analysis*, 50 Econometrica 443 (1982).

competitive price for gas is $1, equal to marginal cost, and that, on Monday morning, both service stations are selling gas for $1.01. At these identical prices, each service station serves 50% of the customers on the road, of which there are 1,000 a day. (Ignore the impact of which way the consumers drive: suppose that it's very easy and safe to turn around, so consumers have an equal choice between the two.) This means each service station is making one cent of profit on 500 consumers per day, for a total of $5 profit each per day.

On Tuesday, suppose that North does something that sounds odd: it *increases* its price by ten cents to $1.11. Of course, if South keeps its price at $1.01, it will clean up: making one cent of profit on all 1000 customers for a daily profit of $10. But South may now start to think: well, North *knows* that if I keep my price at the same level I will clean up, and North isn't crazy. So what is North's game? Well, thinks South, North's strategy would only be profitable for North if I, South, increase my price too. What would that look like? At $1.11, we'd both be making *eleven* cents of profit on every consumer rather than just one. Depending on the overall elasticity of market demand, we are probably losing some consumers: let's say 10% fewer people will buy at $1.11. If we were each serving 50% of that demand, that means we are equally splitting 900 consumers, each of which brings 11 cents of profit, for a total daily profit of $49.50 each. That is a huge improvement over the $5 profit per day we were each making at the competitive price. It is also a huge improvement over the $10 profit per day South would make if it stuck to the competitive price and served every customer that came through. So South thinks, ok, well, let's try it and see how it goes: and increases its price to $1.11 as well.

What happens next depends on a variety of things. You can see that if both North and South stick to their position, each holding steady at $1.11, each of them will make money hand over fist compared to life at the competitive price point. But the situation may be fragile. One morning it may occur to North that if it dropped its price by just one cent, to $1.10, it would immediately pick up 100% of the market and make 9 cents on every customer, taking its profit from $49.50 all the way up to $90. But of course we know what would happen next: South would probably retaliate with a price reduction, and the parties would compete back down to the competitive price. Game theory teaches that, if the parties will face each other indefinitely, each party will do best by demonstrating that it will follow price increases but swiftly punish attempts at discounting.

Notice that the expectation of retaliation is crucial. If either participant thinks it can get away with cutting prices to win more sales without triggering a competitive reaction from the other participant, it will surely do so. So each of them will closely watch the other, and weigh the chances of detection against the benefits of "cheating" on the implicit deal.

Of course, North and South might feel more confident about their chances of keeping prices high if they sat down and explicitly *agreed* that they will price at $1.11, or whatever, for a certain period of time. But this kind of nakedly anticompetitive agreement (a "price fixing" agreement) would be a criminal antitrust violation, so they might well decide to just take their chances in watching one another carefully rather than risk going to prison. As we will see in Chapter IV, simply watching your rivals and setting a price that you think will maximize your profits is not an antitrust violation!

As this example illustrates, the profits of tacit collusion depend on each participant individually refraining from aggressive price competition on the basis that, if it does so, others will also hold off. And in the example we have given—two service stations across the street from one another, with posted prices, identical products, and no other competitors—the oligopolistic equilibrium would probably have a fairly good chance of surviving. Each service station would know that any discounting would likely trigger an immediate and aggressive response by the other, so their incentive to try it in the first place would be limited. In fact, each party might even be tempted to venture an occasional price *increase*, to see whether the other participant would match it and whether they would increase their profits by doing so.

But of course things are often more complicated, and those complications can make it harder to sustain an oligopoly. To see this, we could amend our two-station hypothetical. For example, we could add more players to our hypothetical, so that instead of simply two stations we have seven or fifteen, making it harder for each participant to keep track of all the others. We could eliminate the public posting of prices, so each service station would have to send someone over to visit the others to find out what they were pricing. We could provide for individual and confidential price negotiations (including discounting) with consumers who stop to get gas, so it would be hard or impossible for each station to be sure of what the other was really charging. And we could introduce product differentiation: one service station supplies regular gas; another premium; another diesel; others are located in different locations, making it hard to figure out who is really competing directly with whom, or what prices would amount to "cheating" on the terms of coordination.

These changes all have the same directional effect: they make it harder to sustain coordination. With each such change, each participant will find it harder to be sure that others are sticking to the implicit terms of the bargain. As its confidence falls, each player becomes less certain that the others are not "cheating" on the implicit terms of coordination: and the result that that player's *own* incentive to stick to the higher oligopoly price is eroded, and the incentive to compete rather than coordinate becomes stronger.

As the parable of the service stations demonstrates, the likelihood of coordination—supracompetitive pricing emerging not from the unilateral market power of one supplier, but from the emergence of a tacit agreement to collude—is a function of several different things. Tacit collusive pricing is most likely when[161]:

- the market is *highly concentrated* (*i.e.*, dominated by a small number of companies with large market shares);
- products are *homogeneous*, rather than differentiated, such that it is easy to compare prices to one another and to the terms of tacit coordination;
- it is easy for each participant to *monitor*, with confidence, the terms on which other participants are dealing with purchasers;
- there are *barriers to new market entry*, such that oligopolistic pricing will not simply serve to attract new players into the market;
- there are *capacity constraints and/or barriers to expansion* by existing suppliers, such that each participant knows that the others could not quickly or easily sell more products or services, limiting the potential gains from competition;
- the participants are *symmetrical*, in that their incentives are broadly aligned (*e.g.*, similar levels of vertical integration);
- no participant is pursuing a *different and disruptive business model or revenue strategy* that involves aggressive or low-cost competition (sometimes called a "maverick"); and
- there are credible ways for the participants to "*punish*" those who are caught defecting from the terms of coordination (*e.g.*, the market works in such a way that the other participants could immediately lower their own prices or otherwise inflict punishment on discounters).

One of the most important of these criteria is concentration. A key concept in antitrust, concentration is the extent to which a market is dominated by a small number of companies with large market shares. A highly concentrated market has a few players, each with a large share of the market; an unconcentrated market has many players, each with a small share of the market.

Concentration makes tacit collusion easier to sustain. In a concentrated market, among other things, there are fewer other players to keep an eye on, and each of them—by virtue of its large market share—has more capacity to exert an impact on the market, including to punish those who violate the terms of coordination.

A common way to measure market concentration is a quantitative measure known as the Herfindahl-Hirschman Index ("HHI"). It is easy to calculate an HHI: you calculate the market share of every participant in the market, square each value, and total up the results. The following charts demonstrate how different structures can give rise to different HHIs.

---

[161] Explicitly collusive pricing—that is, price fixing—is also more likely in the presence of these factors.

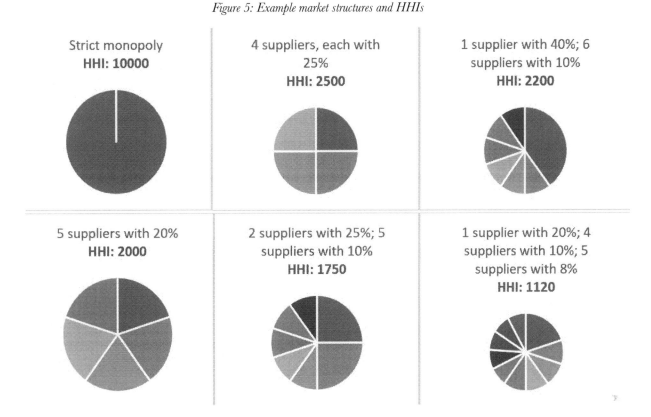

Figure 5: Example market structures and HHIs

As you might expect, different commentators have different views about when we should consider a market "concentrated," or the point at which oligopoly effects are likely to set in.[162] The 2010 Horizontal Merger Guidelines define a market as "moderately concentrated" if the HHI is between 1,500 and 2,500, and as "highly concentrated" if it is above 2,500, which is the HHI of a market with four suppliers each controlling 25% of the market.

Previous merger guidelines drew the line at lower levels of concentration. The 1982, 1984, 1992, and 1997 Guidelines defined a market as "moderately concentrated" if the HHI exceeded 1,000, and "highly concentrated" if the HHI exceeded 1,800. The 1968 Guidelines did not use HHI at all. Rather, they used the "four-firm concentration ratio" (or "CR4"): that is, the combined shares of the four largest firms in a market. It defined a market as "highly concentrated" if the combined shares of the four largest firms amount to "approximately 75% or more." A market with a CR4 of 75 could in theory have an HHI as low as roughly 1,400 (*i.e.*, if the 75% was equally divided among four firms, and the remainder of the market was entirely atomistic), but in practice would likely be rather higher.

HHI is a handy metric because it is often easy to calculate (at least, as long as market shares are easy to calculate), and because it corresponds roughly to something that can matter to competition. But it would be a mistake to think that a change in the HHI inevitably, or even usually, implies a change in price, or that HHI and price have a consistent relationship, even in a single market. As a piece co-authored by a group of former antitrust agency chief economists pointed out, it is unhelpful (and may be actively misleading) to simply measure the relationship between HHI and price in an industry and to use that relationship to try to predict future price effects, in merger analysis in particular:

> [R]egressions of price on the HHI do not predict the competitive effects of mergers and should not be used in merger review. The core of our analysis is that analyses based on regressions of price on the HHI mistake correlation for causation. There are many reasons why the HHI can vary across markets or time periods. Whether the HHI is positively or negatively correlated with price depends on what gives rise to the variation across the markets or periods. . . . [I]f a small

---

[162] *See generally, e.g.,* Volker Nocke & Michael D. Whinston, *Concentration Thresholds for Horizontal Mergers,* 112 Am. Econ. Rev. 1915 (2022).

firm reduces its costs, then both its price and the HHI in its market may decrease, creating a positive correlation between price and the HHI. But if instead a large firm reduces its costs, then its price may decrease and the HHI in its market may increase, creating a negative correlation. Yet whether the large firm or the small firm benefits [by acquiring more market share] from a cost reduction has little bearing on the competitive effects of a merger (which indeed might not involve either firm).[163]

More generally, as we saw in Chapter I, most economists today agree that more concentrated markets are not always less competitive than less concentrated markets.[164] Some markets have a small number of players but appear very competitive; other markets are not highly concentrated but do not seem competitive. In particular, in some markets, competitors are more efficient at higher levels of scale, meaning that competition among a small number of large firms may be more vigorous than competition among a large number of smaller businesses.

NOTES

1) Should we ban concentration beyond a certain HHI threshold? Why or why not?
2) What are the advantages and disadvantages of using HHI to measure the competitive conditions in a market?
3) Suppose that lawmakers have decided to ban "tacit collusion" or oligopoly pricing as described above. Can you draft a statutory prohibition that would do this? And how would you advise Congress on whether to do it?
4) Can you think of three real-world markets that exhibit signs of oligopoly pricing?

J. Buyer Side Power: Monopsony and Oligopsony

So far in this chapter we have focused on market power held individually or collectively by sellers, including in the form of monopoly power, substantial market power, and oligopoly. But buyers can have power too! The term for a buyer-side monopoly is a *monopsony*.[165] In the simplest case, consider a single buyer—a monopsonist—that faces a competitive set of sellers. That buyer knows that the sellers have no alternatives if they want to sell their output: thus, the buyer can force the sellers to accept prices *below* the competitive level (that is, *infracompetitive* prices) because the alternative is to get nothing at all. Of course, a buyer's ability to extract a price below cost is limited by the fact that no-one will stay in business very long at that rate, but an infracompetitive price may be set between the sellers' cost and the competitive price. It may also exploit the reality that even exiting a business may involve some costs—which may be significant—so a supplier may be forced into selling at or below cost for some period, rather than paying those costs of exit.

The antitrust analysis of monopsony power poses a dilemma: aren't low prices good? Well, recall that part of the social value of the market-price mechanism is that, at least in theory, it helps to induce the socially optimal level of supply and demand by nudging market participants toward the market-clearing levels of supply and demand. Setting prices below the competitive level drives supply away from its optimal use.

To see this in action, think about a labor market: consider the set of persons who would be, say, nurses or authors in a perfectly competitive market. Now imagine that wages for nurses and authors were subject to labor monopsony—*i.e.*, there is only one firm hiring nurses, or authors—with the result that wages for these jobs are reduced by 10% below the competitive level. The result is that many of those persons would go and do other things, even if society would most highly value them as nurses or authors. As this example illustrates, an important harm from monopsony is that it leads to the suboptimal allocation of resources across our economy.[166] (This is similar to the concern that is sometimes raised in connection with price caps: the cap dampens the incentive that

---

[163] Nathan Miller et al., *On the Misuse of Regressions of Price on the HHI in Merger Review*, 10 J. Antitrust Enforcement 248 (2021).

[164] *See generally*, *e.g.*, Steven Berry, Martin Gaynor & Fiona Scott Morton, *Do Increasing Markups Matter? Lessons from Empirical Industrial Organization*, 33 J. Econ. Persp. 44 (2019); Leonard W. Weiss, *The Structure-Conduct-Performance Paradigm and Antitrust*, 127 U. Pa. L. Rev. 1104 (1979).

[165] *See generally* Roger D. Blair & Jeffrey L. Harrison, MONOPSONY IN LAW AND ECONOMICS (2010).

[166] *See*, *e.g.*, OECD Background Note, *Monopsony and Buyer Power* (2008) 29 (noting the "misallocation of resources" arising from monopsony).

would otherwise exist for suppliers to move to meet the demand, reducing overall output of the product or service in question.)

Another important harm from monopsony arises in labor markets. Unlike corporations, humans have to live and eat! This means that under extreme conditions a human may be forced to work for very much less than a competitive wage, simply by virtue of the practical need to survive. Here the harm is expressed not just in the inefficient deployment of economic resources across our economy, but in human misery and suffering.

Just as monopsony is the buy-side equivalent of monopoly, "oligopsony" is the label for a buyer-side oligopoly. To imagine this in operation, recall our example from the previous subsection involving two service stations. Now suppose that in addition to advertising gas for sale, the North and South stations were also advertising for labor help, and that they were the only two employers in town. They each post a prominent "help wanted: $20/hour" sign, reflecting the competitive price for certain labor services. But, just as before, if North decided to *decrease* its wage offering, from $20 to $18, South might decide to follow suit rather than compete. The result could be an infracompetitive wage equilibrium which depended on mutually interdependent conduct by both service stations: that is, a labor oligopsony.

NOTES

1) Is monopsony bad? Why or why not?
2) What kind of labor markets might be susceptible to monopsony?
3) Is there any tension between the protection of workers from monopsony and the protection of consumers from monopoly, or are these two goals compatible?
4) If we have an enduring monopsonist, social welfare can under some circumstances be increased if the monopsonist's suppliers are allowed to form a monopoly cartel. (This is the theory of "bilateral monopoly.") When do you think we should rely on this observation to license what would otherwise be price-fixing?[167]

K. Price Discrimination

Throughout the foregoing discussion, we have assumed that every supplier—whether a monopolist, a participant in a competitive market, or something in between—sets one uniform price for all of its own output, and every purchaser pays that price. This means that inframarginal purchasers, who would be willing to pay more than the marginal purchaser for a product or service, benefit from the existence of the marginal purchaser. After all, even a strict monopolist will set the profit-maximizing price in light of marginal demand. But now we will consider what happens if we relax the assumption of equal pricing to all purchasers, by allowing the supplier to engage in price discrimination: that is, charging different prices to different purchasers.

The main consequence of price discrimination, are: (1) to get inelastic purchasers to pay more than elastic ones, and by doing so to give the seller some of the surplus that they would otherwise enjoy; and (2) to allow the seller to sell to those who would buy at prices between the monopoly price and the competitive price.

Of course, if there is no inelastic demand for what the supplier is offering—if no-one is willing to pay any more for it, because of the availability and sufficiency of close substitutes—then price discrimination is impossible. A seller in a perfectly competitive market of homogeneous goods cannot price discriminate: the availability of perfect substitutes means that there *are* no inelastic purchasers to squeeze for any more than the competitive price. But when there is some inelastic demand for the supplier's output, there may be some additional profit to be made from price discrimination.

To successfully execute this strategy, the supplier must find a way to do at least two things: first, it must be able to identify the inelastic purchasers so that they can be targeted for higher prices; second, it must be able to prevent the inelastic purchasers from evading those higher prices and benefiting from the lower prices intended for the

---

[167] *See, e.g.,* Laura M. Alexander, *Countervailing Power: A Comprehensive Assessment of a Persistent but Troubling Idea* (Oct. 15, 2020).

marginal purchasers. One common form of such evasion is "arbitrage" by inelastic purchasers: that is, buying the output from the marginal purchaser who can get it at a lower price and then resell to the inelastic purchaser.

Economists generally talk about three types of price discrimination, known (somewhat unhelpfully) as "degrees" of price discrimination. *First-degree price discrimination* is individually personalized pricing: the supplier knows the identity of each purchaser and sets an individualized price for everyone, which is higher for more inelastic purchasers. This kind of price discrimination is rare in practice, particularly to end-consumers, but may be becoming more feasible as more companies acquire more access to individualized data.

Second-degree price discrimination involves differentiating the supplier's product or service in some way and charging a higher margin on versions that are likely to attract inelastic consumers. This system relies on purchasers to sort themselves into categories by virtue of their own purchasing or consumption choices. First-class and business-class seating on an airplane is a superb example of second-degree price discrimination. Airlines know that most people who choose to buy first- and business-class tickets are less responsive to price (*i.e.*, they are the inelastic purchasers) and so the profit margin on those tickets is much higher than the profit margin on economy-class seating.

This kind of discrimination is sometimes accomplished by charging a higher margin to more intensive users. For example, some users of computer printers are intensive users; others are less so. By offering the printer for a *lower* price than it otherwise would, and offering the replaceable printer cartridges for a *higher* price than it otherwise would, a printer supplier can effectively charge a lower margin on purchases by low-intensity users and a higher margin on purchases by high-intensity users, thus extracting more surplus overall. You can immediately see that this strategy would fail if users could buy the cheap printer and then turn to a third party for cheap printer cartridges. Supplier efforts to stymie this kind of thing, and protect a price-discrimination strategy, can lead to the kind of practices that we will consider in later chapters, such as tying and bundling.

Third-degree price discrimination involves sorting customers into categories that correlate to elasticity, and then charging category-specific prices. Categories corresponding to more inelastic customers can be charged a higher price than categories corresponding to more elastic ones. This strategy can be defeated through arbitrage if customers in the first group can find a way to buy the product or service "through" the customers in the second group. Third degree price discrimination is most likely to be encountered in settings where this kind of strategy can be detected and defeated by the supplier: thus, for example, discounted event tickets for youth or senior purchasers rely on the supplier's ability to make sure those tickets are not being resold to people who do not qualify.

Price discrimination has interesting results. If accomplished perfectly, it allows the supplier to extract more of the surplus from purchasers: it thus transfers welfare from purchasers to the discriminating seller, compared to the world in which discrimination were prohibited, and makes investment in the underlying product or service more attractive to the supplier. It also means that more purchasers can end up buying, compared to the same alternative: the price paid by the most elastic purchasers is lower than the supplier would charge if discrimination were prohibited. Thus, if done perfectly, price discrimination need not result in deadweight losses. However, in the real world, price discrimination can be difficult and costly. Whether the practice is socially beneficial can and does vary in different price discrimination schemes.

Without more, the practice of discriminatory pricing is almost always lawful, but it can affect the application of antitrust rules in some interesting ways. For one thing, as we will see in later chapters, when price discrimination is a realistic possibility—because inelastic purchasers can be identified and targeted in some way—antitrust law may recognize the distinctive vulnerability of those purchasers. In particular, an antitrust market may be defined to include *only* the purchasers that are vulnerable to discriminatory pricing, to the exclusion of purchasers who have better outside options and, as such, do not have to fear especially adverse treatment from a supplier. This is called a "price discrimination market."[168]

For another thing, though, defendants in antitrust cases sometimes also point to price discrimination as a *procompetitive* explanation for particular conduct. In particular, a practice that might have some exclusionary effect on rivals—for example, a "tying" requirement that forces customers of a printer to purchase cartridges from the

---

[168] *See infra* § III.C.3.

same supplier, rather than from a rival manufacturer of cartridges—might be explained as a means of making a price discrimination system work successfully, and thus fully extracting the value of the supplier's existing market power, without increasing the magnitude of that power or making it harder for rivals to compete.

NOTES

1) Should we ban price discrimination? How could we do so?
2) Why should purchasers with idiosyncratic demand for a product or service be specially protected by antitrust?
3) Is the ability to price discriminate a form of market power?
4) Can you identify three examples of price discrimination from your own experience?

L. The Relationship Between Antitrust Economics and Antitrust Law

The relationship between antitrust law and antitrust economics is a complex one. On the one hand, the foundational concepts of antitrust law—competition, monopoly, market power, markets, and so on—are inherently "economic," in that they are part of the subject matter of the field of microeconomic theory and analysis. It is hard to imagine anything that we could recognize as antitrust that would not rely heavily on economic concepts and ideas, or on propositions borrowed from the teachings of economic theory. On the other hand, antitrust law is still *law*. It is made by federal Congressional statute, interpreted by judges, and administered by federal agencies, just like much of the federal regulatory ecosystem.

Antitrust's dual legal-economic character has important implications for the nature of what we call "legal analysis" in this area, and for the shape and direction of the antitrust project more generally. It means that debates among economics, and changes in the economics profession—including the emergence of new ideas and claims, and shifting views about old ones—influence the fabric and operation of antitrust in a variety of ways. We will encounter these dynamics repeatedly throughout the rest of this book. The following extracts offer some brief perspectives on this complex relationship.

Matthew T. Panhans & Reinhard Schumacher, Theory in closer contact with industrial life: American institutional economists on competition theory and policy

17 J. Instit. Econ. 781 (2021)

During the early 20th century . . . the field of economics was broad and diverse in terms of methods of inquiry and ideological underpinnings. . . . One set of economists in this earlier period was the American institutionalists. . . . [They] tended to focus on the role of institutions in shaping incentives and behavior, while also drawing on social psychology to characterize human behavior and pragmatist philosophy to describe their approach to defining problems and methods of investigation. [. . .]

Though institutionalists saw many virtues in market competition, they also questioned the widespread assumptions about the benefits of competition per se. They recognized that modern corporations realized unprecedented efficiencies of scale. Although many economists argued that more competition is always preferable, institutionalists rejected the assumption that unregulated competition leads to economic harmony and stability. For institutionalists, this view rested on unsound theoretical assumptions. In the theory of perfect competition, supply and demand cause prices to rise and fall and arrange industrial matters efficiently. However, [Hamilton wrote,] "As a theory it is a little too beautiful; it looks too much like the textbooks and too little like things in the real world." In reality, Hamilton and other institutionalists argued, demand is fickle and fluctuating, production takes a long time and requires planning under great uncertainty, and overhead has become a dominant expense.

Institutionalists argued, often based on case studies, that competition could have harmful effects. . . . Hamilton argued that each industry had its own circumstances, such that competition provided different degrees of success in different industries. Based on his studies of American industries, especially bituminous coal, Hamilton saw instances where competition could be a disruptive force. [. . .]

What did institutional economists want competition to do for society? Like progressive economists from earlier decades and prominent progressive figures such as Brandeis, institutionalists appealed to a wide range of virtues to justify the importance of effective and vigorous competition policies. And institutionalists championed broader goals for competition than what would later be adopted in the consumer welfare standard in antitrust, which focuses on prices and output. For example, excessive competition could lead to low prices, but would not be desirable if at the expense of industrial stability or when it depressed wages. Institutionalists regarded consumer welfare as important; but they also proposed a much broader and more complex way to measure the consequences of competition, because the public interest is affected by businesses in many ways. [. . .]

The diverse policy proposals [offered by institutionalists] can be broadly categorized into (i) self-control by competing corporations, (ii) control by the various stakeholders, and (iii) direct control by the state. Self-control could be achieved by facilitating the self-regulation of industries, where competitors could agree on industry-wide trade practices and standards. Control could also be exercised by all stakeholders, where it would be important that workers and consumers be involved in the management of a corporation or somehow given a say. Finally, direct control exercised by the state included direct regulations, regulatory agencies, reforming the antitrust system, and other state actions. Institutionalists did not want an overreaching government or a system of central planning. Rather, the main aim of social control by the state was to ensure fair competition where possible and, where not, to avoid the abuse of monopoly powers.

* * *

William E. Kovacic, The Influence of Economics on Antitrust Law
30 Econ. Inquiry 294 (1992)

Economic analysis influences antitrust litigation because the federal antitrust system is unusually permeable. This permeability is the result of . . . important features of the antitrust system. [One such feature] is the wide range of analytical criteria that courts are permitted to consider in resolving antitrust disputes. . . . Outcomes under the Sherman Act depend crucially upon the construction of ambiguous terms such as "conspiracy in restraint of trade" and "monopolize." As [Steven Salop and Lawrence White have noted], the decision to cast the statutes in general terms has given judges substantial discretion to determine litigation outcomes by defining the content of the statutes' operative terms.

In conferring this interpretive role upon the federal courts, Congress has allowed judges to devise standards of conduct at least in part by reference to the likely economic effects of various forms of business behavior. Despite sharp disagreement over the weight Congress meant to accord productive and allocative efficiency as judicial decision-making criteria: few scholars seriously argue that Congress intended that courts treat such concerns as irrelevant. Economists would play a far less important part in antitrust adjudication if Congress had precluded judicial consideration of efficiency in implementing statutory commands. The open-ended language and indeterminate goals of the antitrust statutes allow economists to affect adjudication and rule formulation to a degree unattainable under most other federal regulatory schemes. [. . .]

The relative ease with which new economic concepts can enter the courtroom has major implications for the direction of doctrine and analysis over time. First, the antitrust system's porosity ensures that today's accepted wisdom will face periodic challenges by rival theories that eventually may become the prevailing analytical approaches. Second, owing to the discretion conferred by the antitrust statutes, litigation outcomes in close cases will depend substantially upon the preferences of individual judges. A jurist's receptivity to specific economic arguments will hinge largely upon her tastes, training, and experience. Thus, a president can determine how economics and particular economic views affect antitrust litigation by his choice of judicial nominees. [. . .]

The creation of new economic ideas results from a variety of motivations. One is the economist's ethic of scientific inquiry. [. . .]

. . . A second stimulus to research in antitrust economics is the demand of various antitrust system participants for useful economic ideas. The needs of corporate plaintiffs and defendants, private attorneys, federal enforcement agencies, and state enforcement bodies generate a demand for theories to support favored policy and litigation outcomes. The largest and most prominent part of the demand is for theories that exculpate defendants. This does not mean that the demand for pro-enforcement theories is trivial. [. . .]

. . . From 1945 until the early 1970s, many economists embraced . . . enthusiasm for dispersing market power and preventing further concentration via merger. Carl Kaysen's and Donald Turner's ANTITRUST POLICY (1959), the chief "law and economics" antitrust text of its time, elevated deconcentration to the status of a major antitrust goal in the 1960s and early 1970s. President Johnson's White House Task Force Report on Antitrust Policy (1968) used the Kaysen-Turner proposals to develop its own deconcentration proposal. Task Force members who endorsed the measure included economists . . . and economically astute attorneys . . . . As late as 1971, economists such as Roger Sherman and Robert Tollison backed deconcentration and strict antimerger policies.

The consensus among economists supporting deconcentration crumbled, and scholars such as Meehan and Lamer have extensively recounted the demise of the structure-conduct-performance paradigm that supported attacks on corporate size. However, as [later] Chicago perspectives gained prominence in the late 1970s and the 1980s, the federal enforcement agencies had started an expansive collection of monopolization and shared-monopoly lawsuits that drew upon structuralist economic theories. . . . [Other work has found that the] agencies' commitment of massive resources to deconcentration in the late 1960s and early 1970s would not have occurred without an apparent consensus of support from economists. By the time the deconcentration measures were fully launched, the consensus that inspired them had vanished. [. . .]

Modern adjustments in policy and doctrine are simply the latest signs of how changing economic visions affect the antitrust system. Antitrust law and industrial organization economics have evolved in tandem, with doctrine and enforcement policy lagging behind the formation of a consensus among economists about appropriate liability rules. This process will continue as developments in economic learning, debate among researchers about the proper interpretation of business phenomena, and changes in the political environment move courts and enforcement agencies to modify doctrine and policy. The evolution will be gradual, as the interaction of these elements generally discourages dramatic swings in doctrine.

***

New York v. Deutsche Telekom AG
439 F. Supp. 3d 179 (S.D.N.Y. 2020)

Judge Marrero.

[1] Adjudication of antitrust disputes virtually turns the judge into a fortuneteller. Deciding such cases typically calls for a judicial reading of the future. In particular, it asks the court to predict whether the business arrangement or conduct at issue may substantially lessen competition in a given geographical and product market, thus likely to cause price increases and harm consumers. To aid the courts perform that murky function demands a massive enterprise. In most cases, the litigation consumes years at costs running into millions of dollars. In furtherance of their enterprise, the parties to the dispute retain battalions of the most skilled and highest-paid attorneys in the nation. In turn, the lawyers enlist the services of other professionals—engineers, economists, business executives, academics—all brought into the dispute to render expert opinions regarding the potential procompetitive or anticompetitive effects of the transaction.

[2] The qualifications of litigants' specialists, impressive by the titles they have held and the tomes their CVs fill, can be humbling and intimidating. And those witnesses' authoritative views stated on the stand under oath in open court can leave the lay person wondering whether word so expertly crafted and credentialed can admit room for error or even doubt. Together, counsel and experts amass documentary and testimonial records for trial that can occupy entire storage rooms to capacity. [. . .]

[3] Perhaps most remarkable about antitrust litigation is the blurry product that not infrequently emerges from the parties' huge expenditures and correspondingly exhaustive efforts. Each side, bolstered by the mega records of fact discovery and expert reports it generates, as supplemented by the product of any governmental investigation and resulting action, offers the court evidence the party declares should guide the judge in reaching a compelling and irrefutable decision in the declarant's favor. In fact, however, quite often what the litigants propound sheds little light on a clear path to resolving the dispute. In the final analysis, at the point of sharpest focus and highest clarity and reliability, the adversaries' toil and trouble reduces to imprecise and somewhat suspect aids: competing crystal balls.

[4] . . . [Litigating] parties' costly and conflicting engineering, economic, and scholarly business models, along with the incompatible visions of the competitive future their experts' shades-of-gray forecasts portray, essentially cancel each other out as helpful evidence the Court could comfortably endorse as decidedly affirming one side rather than the other.

[5] The resulting stalemate leaves the Court lacking sufficiently impartial and objective ground on which to rely in basing a sound forecast of the likely competitive effects of a merger. But the expert witnesses' reports and testimony, however, do not constitute the only or even the primary source of support for the Court's assessment of that question. There is another evidentiary foundation more compelling in this Court's assessment than the abstract or hypothetical versions of the relevant market's competitive future that the adversaries and their experts advocate. Conceptually, that underpinning supports a projection of what will happen to competition post-merger that emerges from the evidence in the trial record that the Court heard, admitted through the testimony of fact witnesses, and evaluated with respect to its credibility and the weight it deserves.

[6] How the future manifests itself and brings to pass what it holds is a multifaceted phenomenon that is not necessarily guided by theoretical forces or mathematical models. Instead, causal agents that engender knowing and purposeful human behavior, individual and collective, fundamentally shape that narrative. Confronted by such challenges, courts acting as fact-finders ordinarily turn to traditional judicial methods and guidance more aptly fitted for the task. Specifically, they resort to their own tried and tested version of peering into a crystal ball. Reading what the major players involved in the dispute have credibly said or not said and done or not done, and what they commit to do or not do concerning the merger, the courts are then equipped to interpret whatever formative conduct and decisive events they can reasonably foresee as likely to occur.

[7] For this purpose, however, the courts rely less on the equipoise of mathematical computations, technical data, analytical modeling, and adversarial scientific assumptions that the litigants proffer. Rather, they apply the judge's own skills and frontline experience in weighing, predicting, and judging complex and often conflicting accounts of human conduct, those actions and inactions drawn from the factual evidence. In performing that function, courts employ various behavioral measures that even the most exhaustive and authoritative technical expert study could not adequately capture or gauge as a reliable prognosticator of likely events set in motion fundamentally by business decisions made by various live sources: relevant market competitors, other market participants, public agencies, and even consumers.

M.   Some Further Reading

Elizabeth Popp Berman, THINKING LIKE AN ECONOMIST: HOW EFFICIENCY REPLACED EQUALITY IN U.S. PUBLIC POLICY (2022)

Mark Blaug (ed.), ECONOMIC THEORY IN RETROSPECT (5th ed. 1996)

Paolo Buccirossi (ed.), HANDBOOK OF ANTITRUST ECONOMICS (2008)

Charles River Associates, ANTITRUST ECONOMICS FOR LAWYERS (2021)

Harvey J. Goldscmid, H. Michael Mann & J. Fred Weston, INDUSTRIAL CONCENTRATION: THE NEW LEARNING (1974)

Rebecca Haw, *Adversarial Economics in Antitrust Litigation: Losing Academic Consensus in the Battle of the Experts*, 106 Nw. U. L. Rev. 1261 (2012)

Emma Coleman Jordan & Angela P. Harris, BEYOND RATIONAL CHOICE: ALTERNATIVE PERSPECTIVES ON ECONOMICS (2006)

Louis Kaplow & Steven Shavell, FAIRNESS VERSUS WELFARE (2002)

John E. Kwoka, Jr. & Lawrence J. White (eds.), THE ANTITRUST REVOLUTION: ECONOMICS, COMPETITION, AND POLICY (1999)

Robert J. Larner & James W. Meehan, Jr. (eds.), ECONOMICS AND ANTITRUST POLICY (1989)

John E. Lopatka & William H. Page, *Economic Authority and the Limits of Expertise in Antitrust Cases*, 90 Cornell L. Rev. 617 (2005)

Richard A. Posner, ANTITRUST LAW (2001)

Joseph A. Schumpeter, HISTORY OF ECONOMIC ANALYSIS (1954)

III. MARKET DEFINITION AND MARKET POWER

A. Overview

The idea of a "market," and the related concept of "market power," are among the most important foundations of all antitrust law and practice. Market definition is frequently a dispositive issue in antitrust investigations and litigations of all kinds, and many substantive rules of antitrust law turn on whether market power has been created, augmented, or entrenched. We met some economic fundamentals of markets in Chapter II: in this Chapter, we will turn in some detail to the legal dimensions of markets and market power.

What is a market?

An antitrust "market definition" is an effort to describe or map a competitive environment in which a business supplies or purchases a product or service. As you already know, antitrust law often requires a court or agency to determine whether a practice or transaction will affect competition. To do that, antitrust lawyers often find it helpful to form a rough or working understanding of which products and services will count as "in competition" with one another for the purposes of legal analysis. Market definition can be thought of as a way of drawing a line between those that are "in" and those that are "out" of the sphere of competition for the purposes of antitrust analysis. A market definition is thus a simplification, for analytical purposes, of what is usually a much messier economic reality.

The crucial dynamic underpinning market definition is the insight from microeconomics that one product or service will tend to exercise a competitive constraint on another to the extent that purchasers of the first product or service will regard it as a *substitute* for the second. If Product A is a substitute for Product B, then purchasers can turn (or threaten to turn) to Product A in response to a price increase in Product B, and this fact will tend to limit the ability of Product B's supplier to profitably increase prices.[169] Substitutability can be a complicated matter, as there may be many different substitutes for any given product or service, and different purchasers may regard different alternatives as closer or more distant substitutes for the original product or service, given their own needs and preferences.

We are all used to substituting one product or service for another in everyday life. For example, suppose that you went to the store to buy coffee and found it significantly more expensive than you had expected. In response, you might switch to a substitute by purchasing tea, decaffeinated coffee, or another kind of drink altogether. Or you might be willing to pay the significantly increased price for coffee. Others, of course, would make different choices in your shoes. The higher the price that the store asked for coffee, the more consumers would turn to other things instead: so the fewer units of coffee the store would sell.

This dynamic of substitution underpins a general principle that we saw in Chapter II: as the price of a product or service increases (or as its quality diminishes), different purchasers will substitute away at different price (or quality) levels, and may switch to a variety of products or services when they do. Suppliers accordingly understand that, if they increase their prices, fewer people will buy at the higher price. We saw in Chapter II that traditional microeconomics assumes that suppliers will try to find the pricing point at which these forces lead to the maximization of profits, and antitrust law likewise assumes that they will do so.

A Reminder of Some Technical Terms

As you will remember from Chapter II, those who will substitute more readily are called more "elastic" purchasers, and those who will be the first to substitute are called the "marginal" purchasers. By contrast, those who are willing to pay more than other purchasers for the original product or service before being driven away are more "inelastic"

---

[169] More precisely, substitutability is a one-directional question: the extent to which existing purchasers of Product A may regard Product B as a reasonable alternative for Product A need not be the same—indeed, is usually not the same—as the extent to which existing purchasers of Product B may regard Product A as a substitute for Product B. Can you think of real-world examples?

purchasers, and they constitute the "inframarginal" (*i.e.*, "below the margin") demand for the product or service. The extent to which a percentage change in the supplier's own price will cause a percentage change in demand for its product or service is the supplier's *own-price elasticity of demand*, and it reflects the willingness of purchasers to switch to substitutes in response to such a price increase. A high own-price elasticity of demand means that purchasers are willing and able to switch away to alternatives, suggesting that substitutes are generally pretty close at prevailing prices; a low own-price elasticity of demand indicates that purchasers are unwilling or unable to switch away, suggesting that substitutes are not particularly appealing at prevailing prices. Finally, the extent to which a percentage increase in the price of Product A leads to percentage increase in demand for Product B in particular is called the *cross-price elasticity of demand of B with respect to A*, or just the *cross-elasticity of demand of* B with respect to A. A higher cross-elasticity means that Product B is a closer substitute for Product A: for example, if many consumers would suddenly try to buy tea in response to a small price increase in coffee, but hardly anyone would switch to fruit juice, we can say that tea is a closer substitute for coffee than fruit juice is.

As a matter of economic theory, the universe of substitutes for a particular product or service may be very large if we include very distant substitutes. For example, if the price of coffee were to be significantly increased across the United States, there might be a resulting increase in demand—at least to some extent—for many other drinks, from closer substitutes like tea and energy drinks to more distant substitutes like fruit juices, sodas, and alcoholic drinks.

Antitrust *law* tends, at least for some purposes, to reduce this economic complexity to a more black-and-white legal question: whether a particular product or service is "in" or "out" of a relevant antitrust "market." Of course, there is no such thing in the world as a market: there are only degrees of substitutability from one product or service to another. But the purpose of antitrust market definition is to reduce the complexity of the real world to something that makes it easier for an agency or court to focus on the competitive constraints that matter, while ignoring the rest. Drawing bright lines like this around the most important substitutes makes it possible to speak about things like "market shares," "market concentration," and "the number of competitors in the market."

You may already have guessed that, although the idea of a "market" is a simplification, defining one in practice can be difficult. We can approach this exercise with the help of evidence of many kinds: thus, for example, we might have access to information about "natural experiments" in which a product actually became more expensive or harder to obtain, generating evidence about purchaser substitution in response. Or we might have access to ordinary-course analyses or other documents prepared by market participants, including purchasers and competitors, expressing views about substitution and the scope of competition. We might also be able to call market participants—the relevant suppliers, their competitors, their customers, and their suppliers—to testify, answering questions under oath about how things have worked in the past, or probably would work under certain hypothetical conditions. But not all this information may be available: and, when it is available, it may not all point to the same answer.

Two ways to define a market are particularly important in practice. One way is the "hypothetical monopolist test" and particularly the version of it known as the "SSNIP test" (a "SSNIP" is a "*small but significant non-transitory increase in price*"). This test is essentially a thought experiment. It involves starting with the product or service that we are focused on and adding substitutes one at a time, starting with the closest substitute, until a hypothetical monopolist of *all* included products would find it profitable to increase the price of at least one of those products or services by a significant amount (traditionally, 5–10%) for a non-transitory period of time (traditionally, at least a year). We do this in order to figure out how many of these products or services must come under common control before the supplier has gained the power to inflict economic harm on others. Of course, applying this test with any degree of confidence requires a good deal of information about what real purchasers will do in response to a price increase. It also assumes that everything is currently being supplied at the competitive price rather than a supracompetitive "monopoly" price (can you see why we would get a misleading answer if we tested the profitability of a price increase *above* the monopoly price?).[170]

---

[170] See the discussion of the "Cellophane fallacy" below, § III.B.(a). Clue: is a price increase above a monopoly price *ever* profitable?

Another way to define a market is through the appraisal of qualitative evidence about the relevant products or services, in an effort to identify the relevant similarities or differences that, in light of intuition and market practice, may affect whether different products or services are competing in the same market. As we shall see below, this less formal approach is often associated with the Supreme Court's *Brown Shoe* decision.[171]

In some cases (although not all), geography is a significant consideration in market definition. When transportation is cheap and fast, purchasers may be largely indifferent to the location of a supplier. But in other cases—including most obviously when transportation is expensive, slow, or impossible—purchasers may care about the location of their suppliers, such that a supplier of a particular product or service supplied in a distant location may be inferior, from the purchaser's perspective, to an otherwise-identical product or service that happens to be supplied closer to the purchaser. (In everyday life, we all experience some kinds of demand for which geography appears to matter. For example, if you woke up on a weekend morning and discovered you had run out of milk or cream for your coffee or tea, how far would you be willing to travel to buy more?).

When geography matters, a court or agency often refer to a "geographic market," tracing the outer contour of the market according to the geographic area in which products or services compete. Just like any other dimension of market definition, this is a simplification: suppliers outside the geographic market may in fact exert some constraint.

The Role of Market Definition in an Antitrust Case

A cautionary note! It is important to appreciate right from the outset that market definition is not a mechanical or abstract exercise in an antitrust analysis. You should not think of market definition as a robotic "first step" before identifying and analyzing a theory of harm. (This is a common mistake in law school antitrust exams!) Instead, the role of market definition—and which valid market definition is the "right" or "best" one for an individual case—depends on the nature of the individual theory or story of harm. Let's unpack that a little.

First: many courts have said that a formal market definition is not strictly required as a matter of law in every antitrust case. Liability under the Clayton Act—including Section 7, which governs merger cases, as well as Section 3, which governs certain vertical practices—probably *does* strictly require a market definition. The Clayton Act explicitly refers to a "line of commerce" (a term that is usually understood to mean "market") as the zone in which competition may be harmed, from which courts often infer an obligation to plead and prove a market.[172] But the text of neither Section 1 nor Section 2 of the Sherman Act refers to a market. And under Sections 1 and 2, courts often recognize, at least in theory, that both market (or monopoly) power and the harmful tendency of a challenged practice or transaction can be proved by "direct evidence" without a theoretically pristine market definition.[173]

---

[171] Brown Shoe Co. v. United States, 370 U.S. 294 (1962).

[172] *See, e.g.*, United States v. Bertelsmann S.E., No. 21-2886, at *11 (D.D.C. Nov. 7, 2022) (indicating that market definition is a "necessary predicate" in a Section 7 case). *See generally, e.g.*, James Keyte & Kenneth B. Schwartz, *"Tally Ho!" UPP and the 2010 Horizontal Merger Guidelines*, 77 Antitrust L.J. 587, 594–99 (2011) (arguing that market definition is a statutory requirement under Section 7); Brown Shoe Co. v. United States, 370 U.S. 294, 324 (1962) ("The 'area of effective competition' must be determined by reference to a product market (the 'line of commerce') and a geographic market (the 'section of the country')"). *But see* Herbert Hovenkamp & Carl Shapiro, *Horizontal Mergers, Market Structure, and Burdens of Proof*, 127 Yale LJ. 1996, 2015 (2018) ("The legislative history of Section 7 is not entirely clear on the issue, but more likely than not the two phrases ['line of commerce' and 'section of the country'] were never intended to have so precise a meaning. The phrase 'line of commerce' was in widespread use by both businesspeople and courts to describe a particular 'line' that a seller might sell, often including nonsubstitutable goods").

[173] *See, e.g.*, Ohio v. Am. Express Co., 138 S. Ct. 2274, 2285 n.7 (2018) ("Given that horizontal restraints involve agreements between competitors not to compete in some way, this Court [has] concluded [in such cases] that it did not need to precisely define the relevant market to conclude that these agreements were anticompetitive."); PLS.Com, LLC v. Nat'l Ass'n of Realtors, 32 F.4th 824, 838 (9th Cir. 2022) ("A plaintiff is not required to define a particular market for a per se claim, nor is it required to do so for a rule of reason claim based on evidence of the actual anticompetitive impact of the challenged practice[.]"); Republic Tobacco Co. v. N. Atl. Trading Co., 381 F.3d 717, 736 (7th Cir. 2004) ("[T]here are some circumstances where to establish a violation of antitrust laws it is unnecessary to prove that defendant wielded market power in a properly defined product and geographic market, and may rely instead on direct evidence of anticompetitive effects."); United States v. Microsoft Corp., 253 F.3d 34, 51–52 (D.C. Cir. 2001) (en banc) (confirming viability of direct proof of monopoly power under Section 2); Re/Max Int'l, Inc. v. Realty One, Inc., 173 F.3d 995, 1016 (6th Cir. 1999) (reaffirming viability of direct-effects evidence); In re Intuniv Antitrust Litig., 496 F. Supp. 3d 639, 658 (D. Mass. 2020) ("If the Plaintiffs have actual direct evidence of market power, they need not establish the relevant market."); In re Papa John's Emp. & Franchisee Emp. Antitrust Litig., Case No. 3:18-CV-00825-JHM, 2019 WL 5386484, at *9 (W.D. Ky. Oct. 21,

(There is some disagreement about how exactly this can be done.[174]) In addition, some practices are automatically—i.e., "*per se*"— illegal regardless of their effects, or can be presumed illegal under a "quick look" standard, without a plaintiff being strictly required to define a market at all.[175] We will meet these standards later.[176]

But theory and practice aren't always the same thing! Defining a relevant antitrust market is usually very important in practice, almost invariably expected by judges, and is often the central issue in antitrust investigations and litigations.[177] An effective antitrust case usually requires a fairly clean story about who is in the competitive cast of characters, and who is out, and why: and in many cases, that means a market definition.[178] More generally, agencies and (especially) courts derive practical advantages from working with the relatively clear "in or out" binary of market definition—which make it possible to calculate "market shares" and talk about the "number of market participants" rather than handle all the messy graduations of economic reality. And, as we will see in Chapter VIII, a market definition is a prerequisite for the application of the "structural presumption" thresholds in a merger case, which are a crucial element of many successful merger challenges. And some cases contain language arguably suggesting a stricter market definition requirement.[179] So: for these and other reasons, almost all antitrust cases involve considerable attention to—and often heated disputes over—the market in which competition takes place.

Second: the "right" or "best" market definition in an antitrust case is a function of the particular competitive concern, or theory of harm, that we are exploring. We are usually undertaking an antitrust analysis to figure out whether, say, coordinating with *these particular entities*, or excluding *these particular rivals*, or acquiring *this particular target*, may harm competition by creating, increasing, or entrenching market or monopoly power. The "right" candidate market is the one that best illuminates and tests that concern.

For example, suppose that a defendant operates one of three national chains of office-supply superstores, and that the defendant proposes to acquire one of the other two. When reviewing that merger, the evidence might support the conclusion that the relevant market should be limited to office-supply superstores (*e.g.*, because a hypothetical monopolist of office-supply superstores would be able to profitably implement a significant price increase). But now suppose that, instead of acquiring a rival superstore, the defendant had figured out a way, though exclusionary contracts with upstream suppliers, to cut off *non*-superstores' access to office supplies, thus excluding supermarket chains, mail-order channels, and other sellers as sources of competitive pressure. When analyzing that practice, evidence might support a valid market definition that includes not just superstores but also the victims of exclusion: indeed, cutting off the more distant rivals in this fashion might well increase the defendant's pricing power.[180] Importantly, both the narrower (superstores-only) and the broader (all sellers) markets might be technically valid.

So what does all this mean in practice? It means that antitrust lawyers *start* by identifying a particular theory or story of harm, and *then* define a market that will test that particular competitive concern. "Could this practice or

---

2019) ("In [AmEx] , the Supreme Court indirectly stated that, when dealing with a horizontal restraint that has an adverse effect on competition, a plaintiff need not define the relevant market."); Rio Grande Royalty Co. v. Energy Transfer Partners, L.P., 786 F. Supp. 2d 1190, 1197 (S.D. Tex. 2009) ("A plaintiff, therefore, does not need to define a market if it can support its claim with direct evidence that the defendant controlled prices or excluded the competition.").

[174] For a lucid discussion, *see* Daniel A. Crane, *Market Power Without Market Definition*, 90 Notre Dame L. Rev. 31 (2014).

[175] *See, e.g.*, FTC v. Indiana Fed. of Dentists, 476 U.S. 447, 460–61 (1986).

[176] *See infra* Chapter IV.

[177] Jonathan B. Baker, *Market Definition: An Analytical Overview*, 74 Antitrust L.J. 129, 129, 131 (2007) (noting that "[t]hroughout the history of U.S. antitrust litigation, the outcome of more cases has surely turned on market definition than on any other substantive issue," while "market definition may not be required when market power or anticompetitive effect can be demonstrated directly through means other than inference from the number, size distribution, and other characteristics of firms").

[178] *See* Joshua A. Newberg, *The Narrative Construction of Antitrust*, 12 S. Cal. Interdisc. L.J. 181 (2003).

[179] *See, e.g.*, Spectrum Sports, Inc. v. McQuillan, 506 U.S. 447, 457 (1993) (highlighting the language in Section 2 that refers to "any part of [interstate or international] trade or commerce," and suggesting that "it is beyond doubt that [monopolization] requires proof of market power in a relevant market"); Walker Process Equipment, Inc. v. Food Machinery & Chemical Corp., 382 U.S. 172, 177 (1965) ("To establish [monopolization], it would then be necessary to appraise the exclusionary power of the illegal patent claim in terms of the relevant market for the product involved. Without a definition of that market there is no way to measure [the defendant's] ability to lessen or destroy competition.").

[180] For a helpful discussion, *see, e.g.*, David Glasner & Sean P. Sullivan, *The Logic of Market Definition*, 83 Antitrust L.J. 293, 312 (2020); *see generally* Jonathan B. Baker, *Market Definition: An Analytical Overview*, 74 Antitrust L.J. 129 (2007).

transaction lead to harm, given the availability of substitutes?" is usually the guiding concern. Some complex cases many involve multiple different practices or competitive concerns: and, as a result, multiple different market definitions may be appropriate. Turning all this into a crisp, clean story for a busy generalist judge can be hard. And that's the art of antitrust litigation!

Market definition is the subject of vigorous debate among scholars and commentators, in part because it is so important in litigation, and in part because it involves a simplification of a more complicated reality, with a resulting loss of information.[181] Indeed, some scholars have proposed abandoning the practice of market definition altogether. Louis Kaplow, for example, has prominently argued that the standard methods of market definition are incoherent or circular, and that courts should instead focus on the underlying economic realities.[182] Other scholars, by contrast, have proposed making market definition even *more* central in antitrust cases, including by adopting rules that make metrics like market share or market concentration more important, or even dispositive.[183]

As you read cases and scholarship on market definition, it is worth remembering that the foundation of all market definition, at least in principle, is the *actual* behavior—observed or predicted—of real market participants with real demand for products and services. This can lead to some results that may strike you as odd, and market definitions that may seem surprisingly broad or narrow. If real consumers or other purchasers do in fact care about some feature or dimension of a product or service, then that feature or dimension matters for competition and for antitrust analysis. This means that markets can be defined around preferences that may seem oddly specific or artificial from a distance: say, "luxury fountain pens," "premium and organic natural supermarkets," or "personal social networking."[184] Antitrust takes demand as it finds it, and at least on paper antitrust law takes no view on

---

[181] *See, e.g.*, Robert Pitofsky, *New Definitions of Relevant Market and the Assault on Antitrust*, 90 Colum. L. Rev. 1805, 1807 (1990) ("Unfortunately, no aspect of antitrust enforcement has been handled nearly as badly as market definition. This failure has resulted part because of persistent and unreconciled conflicts of approach in important judicial opinions. It also reflects the fact that the critical issue in relevant market definition—(1) what products are sufficiently close substitutes to compete effectively in each other's market (definition "relevant product market"); (2) what firms are sufficiently proximate to others in spatial terms to compete effectively (definition of "relevant geographic market"); and (3) what substitute sources of supply can diverted promptly and economically to offer effective competition ("supply substitutability")—are all matters of degree that are extremely difficult to measure."); *see also* Christine S. Wilson & Keith Klovers, *Same Rule, Different Result: How the Narrowing of Product Markets Has Altered Substantive Antitrust Rules*, 84 Antitrust L.J. 55, 59 (2021) ("[O]f the 12 product markets defined in Section 7 cases decided by the Supreme Court, half have narrowed over time, with six product markets (used in 12 Supreme Court cases)—banking, beverage containers, energy, footwear, groceries, and spices—narrowing markedly. The remaining six product markets (used in seven Supreme Court cases)—automotive paint, beer, electrical conductor, natural gas, sodium chlorate, and spark plugs—have remained more or less the same. Remarkably, none of the 12 product markets has broadened since then.").

[182] Louis Kaplow, *Market Definition: Impossible and Counterproductive*, 79 Antitrust L.J. 361 (2013).

[183] Tim Wu, THE CURSE OF BIGNESS: ANTITRUST IN THE NEW GILDED AGE (2018) 129.

[184] *See* United States v. Gillette Co., 828 F. Supp. 78, 82 (D.D.C. 1993) ("[P]laintiff has provided ample evidence that fountain pens in the $50 to $400 range effectively do not compete with fountain pens either below or above that range. Plaintiff therefore has met its Clayton Act burden. In contrast to fountain pens with SRPs below $50, the fountain pens here at issue afford their users (as well as those who merely put them in their breast pockets) image, prestige, and status. In accordance with this prestige, manufacturers, retailers, and purchasers of the pens recognize that there is a distinction between these pens, which several of plaintiff's affidavits suggest are priced at approximately $50 and up, and those pens which are priced below this threshold. The evidence suggests that, should the price of a fountain pen costing, for example, $60 be increased in a non-trivial, non-transitory fashion, consumers will nonetheless purchase the now-costlier pen rather than substitute a less expensive, less prestigious model. In other words, there is a low cross-elasticity of demand between these pens and those priced below $50. Similarly, fountain pens priced above $400 also are not interchangeable with pens costing less than $400. Again, there is a threshold beyond which the pens become mere collectors' items or 'jewelry' pieces, and the evidence suggests that consumers will not substitute the $400-and-up pens if prices were to be raised on premium fountain pens."); FTC v. Whole Foods Market, Inc., 548 F.3d 1028, 1037 (D.C. Cir. 2008) ("As the FTC presented its case, success turned on whether there exist core customers, committed to [premium natural and organic supermarkets], for whom one should consider PNOS a relevant market. . . . The district court's error of law led it to ignore FTC evidence that strongly suggested Whole Foods and Wild Oats compete for core consumers within a PNOS market, even if they also compete on individual products for marginal consumers in the broader market."); FTC v. Facebook, Inc., 560 F.Supp.3d 1, 17 (D.D.C. 2021) ("All Plaintiff must do at this stage is provide a plausible explanation as to why users would not switch, even if they technically could, from [personal social networking ("PSN")] services to other services if prompted by a price hike. . . . While the agency certainly could have provided more on that front, the fact that other services are not primarily used for the sort of personal sharing that is the hallmark of a PSN service seems a plausible reason why little switching would occur. Whether due to network effects or the norms around what sort of content is generally posted on different platforms, it is not a stretch to imagine that users are reluctant to share a highly personal milestone on LinkedIn or post a video of their child's first steps to YouTube.").

whether particular preferences are more or less desirable, or worth protecting, than others.[185] It is the real preferences of real consumers, and other market participants, that constitute the foundations of competition, and thus of antitrust itself. Keep this in mind as you read this Chapter!

What is market power?

The idea of market power—and its close cousin "monopoly power," which just means a large amount of market power[186]—is central to antitrust law. A good deal of antitrust analysis aims to determine whether a practice or transaction will create market power, or extend its magnitude or durability.

Unfortunately, it is not always easy to define market power. One of the simplest definitions of market power is the ability to set a profit-maximizing price above the level that would result from a perfectly competitive market. The larger the margin of price above marginal costs, the greater the holder's market power.[187] But it turns out that it would be hard to live with this definition in practice. For one thing, almost every business has some power in this sense. Competition among literally perfect substitutes is very rare in the real world: products are commonly differentiated from one another, and consumers often exhibit brand loyalty—for which they will pay—including when the underlying product or service is identical. As a result, many real-world businesses are able to turn a profit in excess of returns in a perfectly competitive market.[188] Indeed, as Dan Crane points out, "most markets could not function if prices were equated to marginal cost."[189] It also often turns out to be extremely difficult to calculate costs accurately, and to attribute fixed or common costs in a non-arbitrary way to sales of individual products and services, to allow such a margin to be measured with confidence.

Moreover, on this definition it is not obvious that the creation of market power is really a bad thing, even if everything else is held constant. Every software or music company, for example, charges prices far in excess of the marginal cost of supplying a new copy of the software, or a new copy (or stream) of a musical recording. In fact, market power in the sense of margin could represent something that we might think is desirable. A pure efficiency that reduces a business's costs may well have the effect of increasing the business's margin compared to what it was before, while also lowering its profit-maximizing price. But this is usually the kind of thing that we usually think antitrust law—and competition in general—is supposed to encourage, not penalize. Would we want a standard that sees a fall in costs and prices as a problem, simply because margin has increased?

A second common definition focuses on whether a business would increase its profits by *raising* its prices or reducing output.[190] In the most common formulation, market power is present if the business in question would increase its profits if it increased price by implementing a SSNIP (see above) of 5–10%. But the difficulty with this formulation is that it presupposes that the business has not already exercised whatever market power it holds: that is, that it is not currently pricing rationally, contrary to the basic assumption of all antitrust analysis that businesses act rationally to maximize their profits.[191] And if the business is already setting its profit-maximizing price—even if it is a strict monopolist setting a strict monopoly price—then further price increases will not, by definition, be

---

[185] Antitrust's general neutrality among preferences and markets raises some interesting questions—and opportunities for reasonable disagreement!—including about how antitrust treats products and services that some people consider undesirable or harmful (or even that are controlled or prohibited by law), or markets for products and services that might be described as necessary for human life or flourishing. Should antitrust law treat markets for illegal drugs, markets for headache tablets, and markets for lifesaving drugs identically? Should these forms of demand be equal in the eyes of antitrust analysis? Consider also that, while antitrust doctrine may be formally indifferent to the nature and "importance" of a particular market, antitrust *enforcers* may have views of their own about which markets should be prioritized for attention, or for enforcement action.

[186] You may be wondering what it really means to have a "large" amount of market power, how much is enough, and how we could measure it. This question is surprisingly complicated, and we will come back to it in Chapter VII.

[187] As we saw in Chapter II, a metric called the Lerner Index is defined (to summarize and simplify a bit) as margin over price. *See, e.g.*, Kenneth G. Elzinga & David E. Mills, *The Lerner Index of Monopoly Power: Origins and Uses*, 101 Am. Econ. Rev. 558 (2011)

[188] Benjamin Klein & John Shepard Wiley Jr., *Competitive Price Discrimination as an Antitrust Justification for Intellectual Property Refusals to Deal*, 70 Antitrust L.J. 599, 629 (2003) ("Once firms produce unique products, an individual firm's own-price elasticity of demand and profit-maximizing price relative to marginal cost does not tell us the extent of its antitrust market power, that is, its ability to restrict market output and raise market prices above the competitive level.").

[189] Daniel A. Crane, *Market Power without Market Definition*, 90 Notre Dame L. Rev. 31, 57 (2014).

[190] This is a common version. *See, e.g.*, Ohio v. Am. Express Co., 138 S. Ct. 2274, 2288 (2018) ("Market power is the ability to raise price profitably by restricting output.").

[191] *See supra* note 134 and accompanying text.

profitable. In the famous *DuPont* (or "*Cellophane*") case, which dealt with cellophane film and other flexible packaging material, the Supreme Court missed this important point, and failed to spot what many observers consider having been clear monopoly power, because the court found it implausible that DuPont would increase its prices even further.[192] In honor of this case, this error is known as the "*Cellophane* fallacy."

A third practical approach to market power—and one that is often seen in everyday usage—focuses on a firm's "share" of a defined market rather than its existing margins or whether it would be profitable to increase prices. For example, many courts have stated that a high share of a relevant market is a basis to infer market power, if the market is protected by high barriers to entry.[193]

This certainly sounds like it has simplicity going for it. But there are at least three practical problems with this approach. The first problem is that the considerable difficulties and uncertainties involved in defining a market in the first place are present here in full measure: our discussion of market share is only as good as our definition of the underlying relevant market. The second is that it is often not at all obvious how to calculate a market share, even after a market definition has been established: share of units sold or total services provided? Share of dollars? Share of sales? The 2010 Horizontal Merger Guidelines generally favor "actual or projected revenues."[194] What about digital services: share of number of users, or users active during a particular period? Of time spent? Of advertising revenue? Over what time period? What about markets that work through bidding or auctions? And so on.[195] The third problem is that market share is a historical measure, whereas market power analysis is intended to measure present and future power: the ability to inflict harm today or in the foreseeable future. After all, just because a business sold more units than its rivals in the last year, or two years, does not necessarily mean that business is likely to be a dominant presence in the future. In an extreme case, it might even have exited the market.[196]

A fourth definition of market power is satisfied when a supplier can affect *market-wide* output and price by adjusting its own output: if an output reduction would simply shift sales to others, there is no power, but if it would lead to a price increase throughout the relevant market, power is established.[197] This may be more promising, but it suffers from some difficulties we have already seen, including that it requires that we start with a market definition to which the analysis is highly sensitive. Moreover, it is not obvious how to apply this test to differentiated markets in which the prices of some, but not all, other suppliers will likely increase in response to an output reduction.

So, market power is difficult to pin down, beyond the general notion that it means a significant degree of pricing power. So too with monopoly power, which just means a very substantial degree of market power. (Thus, as Einer Elhauge once put it, monopoly power is defined "as requiring a substantial degree of a sort of power that is itself defined to exist only when substantial."[198]) In practice, monopoly power is a demanding bar, as we will see in Chapter VII.

Finally, it is worth noting that power over price need not only result from the dominance of a single supplier: it may also result from a lessening of competition in a market where the participants can sustain a tacit agreement to reduce competition among themselves. As we saw in Chapter II, dynamics of this kind are more likely if, among other things, the market is concentrated and transparent, such that the participants can monitor one another's compliance with the terms of the tacit agreement and punish deviations. However, as we will see below, antitrust

---

[192] United States v. E.I. du Pont de Nemours & Co. ("Cellophane"), 351 U.S. 377 (1956).

[193] *See, e.g.*, *Rebel Oil Co. v. Atl. Richfield Co.*, 51 F.3d 1421, 1438 (9th Cir. 1995) ("ARCO's market share of 44 percent is sufficient as a matter of law to support a finding of market power, if entry barriers are high and competitors are unable to expand their output in response to supracompetitive pricing.").

[194] Horizontal Merger Guidelines (2010) § 5.2.

[195] *See generally, e.g.*, Gregory J. Werden, *Assigning Market Shares*, 70 Antitrust L.J. 67, 67 (2002) (noting that "there always are choices to be made" in calculating market shares, and that "because market shares never come close to telling the whole market power story, the goal in assigning them should be merely to accurately and usefully indicate the relative sizes of competitors in the market").

[196] *See* United States v. General Dynamics Corp., 415 U.S. 486 (1974).

[197] *See, e.g.*, Thomas G. Krattenmaker, Robert H. Lande & Steven C. Salop, *Monopoly Power and Market Power in Antitrust Law*, 76 Geo. L.J. 241, 249 (1987) ("[A] firm or group of firms may raise or maintain price above the competitive level directly by restraining its own output.").

[198] Einer Elhauge, *Defining Better Monopolization Standards*, 56 Stan. L. Rev. 253, 259 (2003).

doctrine does not generally allow the market power of an oligopolistic group to be imputed to any individual participant as a matter of law.

* * *

The rest of this Chapter brings together cases and other materials that illustrate some different facets of these important topics. Section B examines the hypothetical monopolist test—a recurrent feature of market definition—as well as the qualitative analysis exemplified by the Supreme Court's *Brown Shoe* decision. Section C considers some special cases of market definition, including cluster, bundle, price discrimination, and platform markets. Section D examines geographic dimensions of market definition. Section E discusses market power, market share, and entry barriers, and Section F turns to oligopoly.

B. Foundations of Markets: The Hypothetical Monopolist Test and *Brown Shoe*

Market definition, as noted above, is in general terms an effort to identify the important competitive constraints that affect the supply of a particular product or service by offering a reasonable substitute for it. There are a variety of reasons we might do this in an antitrust case. We might do it in order to identify competitive relationships (including to figure out whether the parties to a merger or agreement are, or are not, in competition with one another); to populate the set of all competitors (so we can calculate statistics like market shares and market concentration levels); and/or to work out whether the relevant businesses have, or could obtain, market power through a particular practice or transaction. We might also define a market in order to apply certain rules of substantive antitrust law, like the general (if somewhat fuzzy) rule that, at least in merger cases, competitive harms in a particular market may only be justified by reference to competitive benefits in that same market (*i.e.*, courts may not rely on "out of market" benefits to justify a transaction).[199]

There are two main methodologies for defining a market in an antitrust case. Both are focused on identifying the set of products and services that are a sufficiently close substitute, from the perspective of purchasers, to exert competitive discipline. These are, respectively, the hypothetical monopolist test, and the qualitative assessment associated with *Brown Shoe*. As applied today, these are probably best thought of as alternative approaches for answering the same question: "what substitutes constrain the ability of a supplier, or set of suppliers, to exert market power?" The hypothetical monopolist test approaches this question by considering the profitability of a hypothetical price increase by a sole supplier of a candidate set of products or services; the *Brown Shoe* factors aim to illuminate the question by examining existing features of the market. Let's take a closer look at each.

1. The Hypothetical Monopolist Test

The hypothetical monopolist test ("HMT") is a common tool used by agencies and courts to define markets. It rests on the insight that, when two products or services are close substitutes, they will exhibit significant cross-price elasticity of demand. The core idea of the HMT is that the relevant market should include the products or services that, if brought under common control, would make a significant price increase (5–10%) profitable.[200] A seminal discussion of the HMT is found in Section 4 of the antitrust agencies' Horizontal Merger Guidelines.

Horizontal Merger Guidelines § 4

4. Product Market Definition

---

[199] This is the subject of a thoughtful literature. *See, e.g.*, Laura Alexander & Steven C. Salop, *Antitrust Worker Protections: Rejecting Multi-Market Balancing as a Justification for Anticompetitive Harms to Workers*, 90 U. Chi. L. Rev. 273 (2023); Steven C. Salop, Daniel Francis, Lauren Sillman & Michaela Spero, *Rebuilding Platform Antitrust: Moving On from Ohio v. American Express Co.*, 84 Antitrust L.J. 883 (2022); Gregory J. Werden, *Cross-Market Balancing of Competitive Effects: What Is The Law, and What Should It Be?* 43 J. Corp. L. 119 (2017); Daniel A. Crane, *Balancing Effects Across Markets*, 80 Antitrust L.J. 391 (2015).

[200] For a thoughtful discussion of the challenges and implications of applying the HMT in differentiated markets, *see* James Keyte, *Market Definition and Differentiated Products: The Need for a Workable Standard*, 68 Antitrust L.J. 697 (1995).

[1] When a product sold by one merging firm (Product A) competes against one or more products sold by the other merging firm, the Agencies define a relevant product market around Product A to evaluate the importance of that competition. Such a relevant product market consists of a group of substitute products including Product A. Multiple relevant product markets may thus be identified.

4.1.1 The Hypothetical Monopolist Test

[2] The Agencies employ the hypothetical monopolist test to evaluate whether groups of products in candidate markets are sufficiently broad to constitute relevant antitrust markets. The Agencies use the hypothetical monopolist test to identify a set of products that are reasonably interchangeable with a product sold by one of the merging firms.

[3] The hypothetical monopolist test requires that a product market contain enough substitute products so that it could be subject to post-merger exercise of market power significantly exceeding that existing absent the merger. Specifically, the test requires that a hypothetical profit-maximizing firm, not subject to price regulation, that was the only present and future seller of those products ("hypothetical monopolist") likely would impose at least a small but significant and non-transitory increase in price ("SSNIP") on at least one product in the market, including at least one product sold by one of the merging firms. For the purpose of analyzing this issue, the terms of sale of products outside the candidate market are held constant. The SSNIP is employed solely as a methodological tool for performing the hypothetical monopolist test; it is not a tolerance level for price increases resulting from a merger.

[4] Groups of products may satisfy the hypothetical monopolist test without including the full range of substitutes from which customers choose. The hypothetical monopolist test may identify a group of products as a relevant market even if customers would substitute significantly to products outside that group in response to a price increase.

> *Example 5:* Products A and B are being tested as a candidate market. Each sells for $100, has an incremental cost of $60, and sells 1200 units. For every dollar increase in the price of Product A, for any given price of Product B, Product A loses twenty units of sales to products outside the candidate market and ten units of sales to Product B, and likewise for Product B. Under these conditions, economic analysis shows that a hypothetical profit-maximizing monopolist controlling Products A and B would raise both of their prices by ten percent, to $110. Therefore, Products A and B satisfy the hypothetical monopolist test using a five percent SSNIP, and indeed for any SSNIP size up to ten percent. This is true even though two-thirds of the sales lost by one product when it raises its price are diverted to products outside the relevant market.

[5] When applying the hypothetical monopolist test to define a market around a product offered by one of the merging firms, if the market includes a second product, the Agencies will normally also include a third product if that third product is a closer substitute for the first product than is the second product. The third product is a closer substitute if, in response to a SSNIP on the first product, greater revenues are diverted to the third product than to the second product.

> *Example 6:* In Example 5, suppose that half of the unit sales lost by Product A when it raises its price are diverted to Product C, which also has a price of $100, while one-third are diverted to Product B. Product C is a closer substitute for Product A than is Product B. Thus Product C will normally be included in the relevant market, even though Products A and B together satisfy the hypothetical monopolist test.

[6] The hypothetical monopolist test ensures that markets are not defined too narrowly, but it does not lead to a single relevant market. The Agencies may evaluate a merger in any relevant market satisfying the test, guided by the overarching principle that the purpose of defining the market and measuring market shares is to illuminate the evaluation of competitive effects. Because the relative competitive significance of more distant substitutes is apt to be overstated by their share of sales, when the Agencies rely on market shares and concentration, they usually do so in the smallest relevant market satisfying the hypothetical monopolist test.

Example 7: . . . [I]ncluding cars in [a] market will lead to misleadingly small market shares for motorcycle producers. Unless motorcycles fail the hypothetical monopolist test, the Agencies would not include cars in the market in analyzing [a] motorcycle merger.

4.1.2 Benchmark Prices and SSNIP Size

[7] The Agencies apply the SSNIP starting from prices that would likely prevail absent the merger. If prices are not likely to change absent the merger, these benchmark prices can reasonably be taken to be the prices prevailing prior to the merger. If prices are likely to change absent the merger, e.g., because of innovation or entry, the Agencies may use anticipated future prices as the benchmark for the test. If prices might fall absent the merger due to the breakdown of pre-merger coordination, the Agencies may use those lower prices as the benchmark for the test. In some cases, the techniques employed by the Agencies to implement the hypothetical monopolist test focus on the difference in incentives between pre-merger firms and the hypothetical monopolist and do not require specifying the benchmark prices.

[9] The SSNIP is intended to represent a "small but significant" increase in the prices charged by firms in the candidate market for the value they contribute to the products or services used by customers. This properly directs attention to the effects of price changes commensurate with those that might result from a significant lessening of competition caused by the merger. This methodology is used because normally it is possible to quantify "small but significant" adverse price effects on customers and analyze their likely reactions, not because price effects are more important than non-price effects.

[10] The Agencies most often use a SSNIP of five percent of the price paid by customers for the products or services to which the merging firms contribute value. However, what constitutes a "small but significant" increase in price, commensurate with a significant loss of competition caused by the merger, depends upon the nature of the industry and the merging firms' positions in it, and the Agencies may accordingly use a price increase that is larger or smaller than five percent. Where explicit or implicit prices for the firms' specific contribution to value can be identified with reasonable clarity, the Agencies may base the SSNIP on those prices. [. . .]

4.1.3 Implementing the Hypothetical Monopolist Test

[11] The hypothetical monopolist's incentive to raise prices depends both on the extent to which customers would likely substitute away from the products in the candidate market in response to such a price increase and on the profit margins earned on those products. The profit margin on incremental units is the difference between price and incremental cost on those units. The Agencies often estimate incremental costs, for example using merging parties' documents or data the merging parties use to make business decisions. Incremental cost is measured over the change in output that would be caused by the price increase under consideration.

[12] In considering customers' likely responses to higher prices, the Agencies take into account any reasonably available and reliable evidence, including, but not limited to:

- how customers have shifted purchases in the past in response to relative changes in price or other terms and conditions;
- information from buyers, including surveys, concerning how they would respond to price changes;
- the conduct of industry participants, notably:
    - sellers' business decisions or business documents indicating sellers' informed beliefs concerning how customers would substitute among products in response to relative changes in price;
    - industry participants' behavior in tracking and responding to price changes by some or all rivals;
- objective information about product characteristics and the costs and delays of switching products, especially switching from products in the candidate market to products outside the candidate market;
- the percentage of sales lost by one product in the candidate market, when its price alone rises, that is recaptured by other products in the candidate market, with a higher recapture percentage making a price increase more profitable for the hypothetical monopolist;
- evidence from other industry participants, such as sellers of complementary products;
- legal or regulatory requirements; and

- the influence of downstream competition faced by customers in their output markets.

* * *

As we noted above, a challenge with the application of the HMT in practice is the so-called *Cellophane* fallacy: the problem that arises when the HMT's hypothetical price increase is applied to a monopoly price, and not to the competitive price. Applying the price increase to an existing monopoly price will give a misleadingly broad market definition, because a price increase *on top* of the monopoly price would not be profitable, so the analyst will go looking for a broader market definition and miss the existing, fully exploited, monopoly. Can you see why this might be a particular practical problem in cases where the defendant is accused of maintaining an existing monopoly rather than trying to create a new one through conduct or a transaction?

In the following passage, we can see the Court running afoul of this very fallacy in the case that gave it its name.

United States v. E.I. du Pont de Nemours & Co. ("Cellophane")
351 U.S. 377 (1956)

Justice Reed.

[1] [W]here there are market alternatives that buyers may readily use for their purposes, illegal monopoly does not exist merely because the product said to be monopolized differs from others. If it were not so, only physically identical products would be a part of the market. To accept the Government's argument [that duPont holds monopoly power], we would have to conclude that the manufactures of plain as well as moisture-proof cellophane were monopolists, and so with films such as Pliofilm, foil, glassine, polyethylene, and Saran, for each of these wrapping materials is distinguishable. These were all exhibits in the case. New wrappings appear, generally similar to cellophane, is each a monopoly? What is called for is an appraisal of the "cross-elasticity" of demand in the trade. The varying circumstances of each case determine the result. In considering what is the relevant market for determining the control of price and competition, no more definite rule can be declared than that commodities reasonably interchangeable by consumers for the same purposes make up that part of the trade or commerce, monopolization of which may be illegal. [. . .]

[2] Cellophane differs from other flexible packaging materials. From some it differs more than from others. . . . It may be admitted that cellophane combines the desirable elements of transparency, strength and cheapness more definitely than any of the others. Comparative characteristics have been noted thus:

> Moisture-proof cellophane is highly transparent, tears readily but has high bursting strength, is highly impervious to moisture and gases, and is resistant to grease and oils. Heat sealable, printable, and adapted to use on wrapping machines, it makes an excellent packaging material for both display and protection of commodities. [. . .]

[3] But, despite cellophane's advantages it has to meet competition from other materials in every one of its uses. . . . Food products are the chief outlet, with cigarettes next. The Government makes no challenge to [a finding of fact] that cellophane furnishes less than 7% of wrappings for bakery products, 25% for candy, 32% for snacks, 35% for meats and poultry, 27% for crackers and biscuits, 47% for fresh produce, and 34% for frozen foods. Seventy-five to eighty percent of cigarettes are wrapped in cellophane. Thus, cellophane shares the packaging market with others. The overall result is that cellophane accounts for 17.9% of flexible wrapping materials, measured by the wrapping surface. [. . .]

[4] An element for consideration as to cross-elasticity of demand between products is the responsiveness of the sales of one product to price changes of the other. If a slight decrease in the price of cellophane causes a considerable number of customers of other flexible wrappings to switch to cellophane, it would be an indication that a high cross-elasticity of demand exists between them; that the products compete in the same market. The court below held that the great sensitivity of customers in the flexible packaging markets to price or quality changes prevented du Pont from possessing monopoly control over price. The record sustains these findings.

[5] We conclude that cellophane's interchangeability with the other materials mentioned suffices to make it a part of this flexible packaging material market.

[6] The Government stresses the fact that the variation in price between cellophane and other materials demonstrates they are noncompetitive. As these products are all flexible wrapping materials, it seems reasonable to consider, as was done at the trial, their comparative cost to the consumer in terms of square area. . . . Cellophane costs two or three times as much, surface measure, as its chief competitors for the flexible wrapping market, glassine and greaseproof papers. Other forms of cellulose wrappings and those from other chemical or mineral substances, with the exception of aluminum foil, are more expensive. The uses of these materials . . . are largely to wrap small packages for retail distribution. The wrapping is a relatively small proportion of the entire cost of the article. Different producers need different qualities in wrappings and their need may vary from time to time as their products undergo change. But the necessity for flexible wrappings is the central and unchanging demand. We cannot say that these differences in cost gave du Pont monopoly power over prices in view of the findings of fact on that subject. [. . .]

[7] The facts above considered dispose also of any contention that competitors have been excluded by du Pont from the packaging material market. That market has many producers and there is no proof du Pont ever has possessed power to exclude any of them from the rapidly expanding flexible packaging market. The Government apparently concedes as much, for it states that "lack of power to inhibit entry into this so-called market (*i.e.*, flexible packaging materials), comprising widely disparate products, is no indicium of absence of power to exclude competition in the manufacture and sale of cellophane." The record shows the multiplicity of competitors and the financial strength of some with individual assets running to the hundreds of millions. Indeed, the trial court found that du Pont could not exclude competitors even from the manufacture of cellophane, an immaterial matter if the market is flexible packaging material. Nor can we say that du Pont's profits, while liberal (according to the Government 15.9% net after taxes on the 1937–1947 average), demonstrate the existence of a monopoly without proof of lack of comparable profits during those years in other prosperous industries. Cellophane was a leader over 17%, in the flexible packaging materials market. There is no showing that du Pont's rate of return was greater or less than that of other producers of flexible packaging materials.

[8] The "market" which one must study to determine when a producer has monopoly power will vary with the part of commerce under consideration. The tests are constant. That market is composed of products that have reasonable interchangeability for the purposes for which they are produced—price, use and qualities considered. While the application of the tests remains uncertain, it seems to us that du Pont should not be found to monopolize cellophane when that product has the competition and interchangeability with other wrappings that this record shows. [. . .]

Chief Justice Warren, with whom Justice Black and Justice Douglas join, dissenting.

[9] This case, like many under the Sherman Act, turns upon the proper definition of the market. In defining the market in which du Pont's economic power is to be measured, the majority virtually emasculate s 2 of the Sherman Act. They admit that cellophane combines the desirable elements of transparency, strength and cheapness more definitely than any of a host of other packaging materials. Yet they hold that all of those materials are so indistinguishable from cellophane as to warrant their inclusion in the market. We cannot agree that cellophane . . . is the selfsame product as glassine, greaseproof and vegetable parchment papers, waxed papers, sulphite papers, aluminum foil, cellulose acetate, and Pliofilm and other films.

[10] . . . [C]ellophane has a high bursting strength while glassine's is low; that cellophane's permeability to gases is lower than that of glassine; and that both its transparency and its resistance to grease and oils are greater than glassine's. Similarly, . . . waxed paper's bursting strength is less than cellophane's and that it is highly permeable to gases and offers no resistance whatsoever to grease and oils. With respect to the two other major products held to be close substitutes for cellophane, . . . aluminum foil is actually opaque and has a low bursting strength. And sulphite papers, in addition to being opaque, are highly permeable to both moisture and gases, have no resistance to grease and oils, have a lower bursting strength than cellophane, and are not even heat sealable. Indeed, the majority go further than placing cellophane in the same market with such products. They also include the transparent films, which are more expensive than cellophane. These bear even less resemblance to the lower priced packaging materials than does cellophane. . . .

[11] If the conduct of buyers indicated that glassine, waxed and sulphite papers and aluminum foil were actually the selfsame products as cellophane, the qualitative differences demonstrated by the comparison of physical properties . . . would not be conclusive. But the record provides convincing proof that businessmen did not so regard these products. During the period covered by the complaint (1923–1947) cellophane enjoyed phenomenal growth. Du Pont's 1924 production was 361,249 pounds, which sold for $1,306,662. Its 1947 production was 133,502,858 pounds, which sold for $55,339,626. Yet throughout this period the price of cellophane was far greater than that of glassine, waxed paper or sulphite paper. . . . [I]n 1929 cellophane's price was seven times that of glassine, in 1934, four times, and in 1949 still more than twice glassine's price. [The record] shows that cellophane had a similar price relation to waxed paper and that sulphite paper sold at even less than glassine and waxed paper. We cannot believe that buyers, practical businessmen, would have bought cellophane in increasing amounts over a quarter of a century if close substitutes were available at from one-seventh to one-half cellophane's price. That they did so is testimony to cellophane's distinctiveness.

[12] The inference yielded by the conduct of cellophane buyers is reinforced by the conduct of sellers other than du Pont. . . . Sylvania, the only other cellophane producer, absolutely and immediately followed every du Pont price change, even dating back its price list to the effective date of du Pont's change. Producers of glassine and waxed paper, on the other hand, displayed apparent indifference to du Pont's repeated and substantial price cuts. [Evidence] shows that from 1924 to 1932 du Pont dropped the price of plain cellophane 84%, while the price of glassine remained constant. And during the period 1933—1946 the prices for glassine and waxed paper actually increased in the face of a further 21% decline in the price of cellophane. If shifts of business due to price sensitivity had been substantial, glassine and waxed paper producers who wanted to stay in business would have been compelled by market forces to meet du Pont's price challenge just as Sylvania was. The majority correctly point out that:

> An element for consideration as to cross-elasticity of demand between products is the responsiveness of the sales of one product to price changes of the other. If a slight decrease in the price of cellophane causes a considerable number of customers of other flexible wrappings to switch to cellophane, it would be an indication that a high cross-elasticity of demand exists between them; that the products compete in the same market.

[13] Surely there was more than "a slight decrease in the price of cellophane" during the period covered by the complaint. That producers of glassine and waxed paper remained dominant in the flexible packaging materials market without meeting cellophane's tremendous price cuts convinces us that cellophane was not in effective competition with their products.

[19] Certainly du Pont itself shared our view. From the first, du Pont recognized that it need not concern itself with competition from other packaging materials. For example, when du Pont was contemplating entry into cellophane production, its Development Department reported that glassine "is so inferior that it belongs in an entirely different class and has hardly to be considered as a competitor of cellophane." This was still du Pont's view in 1950 when its survey of competitive prospects wholly omitted reference to glassine, waxed paper or sulphite paper and stated that "Competition for du Pont cellophane will come from competitive cellophane and from non-cellophane films made by us or by others."

[20] Du Pont's every action was directed toward maintaining dominance over cellophane. Its 1923 agreements with La Cellophane, the French concern which first produced commercial cellophane, gave du Pont exclusive North and Central American rights to cellophane's technology, manufacture and sale, and provided, without any limitation in time that all existing and future information pertaining to the cellophane process be considered "secret and confidential," and be held in an exclusive common pool. In its subsequent agreements with foreign licensees, du Pont was careful to preserve its continental market inviolate. In 1929, while it was still the sole domestic producer of cellophane, du Pont won its long struggle to raise the tariff from 25% to 60%, ad valorem, on cellophane imports, substantially foreclosing foreign competition. When Sylvania became the second American cellophane producer the following year and du Pont filed suit [against it] claiming infringement of its moistureproof patents, they settled the suit by entering into a cross-licensing agreement. Under this agreement du Pont obtained the right to exclude third persons from use of any patentable moistureproof invention made during the next 15 years by the sole other domestic cellophane producer, and, by a prohibitive royalty provision, it limited

Sylvania's moistureproof production to approximately 20% of the industry's moistureproof sales. The record shows that du Pont and Sylvania were aware that, by settling the infringement suit, they avoided the possibility that the courts might hold the patent claims invalid and thereby open cellophane manufacture to additional competition. If close substitutes for cellophane had been commercially available, du Pont, an enlightened enterprise, would not have gone to such lengths to control cellophane. [. . .]

[21] . . . The majority approach would apparently enable a monopolist of motion picture exhibition to avoid Sherman Act consequences by showing that motion pictures compete in substantial measure with legitimate theater, television, radio, sporting events and other forms of entertainment. Here, too, shifts of business undoubtedly accompany fluctuations in price and there are market alternatives that buyers may readily use for their purposes. . . . [T]he formula of "reasonable interchangeability," as applied by the majority, appears indistinguishable from the theory of "interindustry competition." The danger in it is that, as demonstrated in this case, it is perfectly compatible with a fully monopolized economy.

[22] The majority hold in effect that, because cellophane meets competition for many end uses, those buyers for other uses who need or want only cellophane are not entitled to the benefits of competition within the cellophane industry. . . . Furthermore, those buyers who have "reasonable alternatives" between cellophane and other products are also entitled to competition within the cellophane industry, for such competition may lead to lower prices and improved quality.

[23] The foregoing analysis of the record shows conclusively that cellophane is the relevant market. Since du Pont has the lion's share of that market, it must have monopoly power[.]

* * *

In brief, and as the dissent suggests, the Court's famous mistake in the quoted passage was to assume that, because duPont had increased its price as far as it was able—that is, to the point where purchasers were switching over to a variety of very different substitutes that had different qualities and were priced very differently—it could not be a monopolist. But what business does *not* increase its price as far as it profitably can? In the process, the Court ignored the evidence that DuPont enjoyed considerable freedom from anything like a close competitive constraint.

2. Brown Shoe Market Definition

The principal alternative methodology to the hypothetical monopolist test is the looser set of qualitative factors associated with the Supreme Court's decision in *Brown Shoe*. In that case, the Court articulated a set of factors which, like the HMT, could be used to help define the zone of reasonably substitutable products or services that would constrain the merged firm.

In the following extract, and in some other cases, the Court uses the term "submarket." Do not be led astray by this confusing term, which crops up from time to time but could probably be banned without doing any harm (and, thus, probably *should* be banned in the interests of clarity). It is best understood to simply mean "market."[201]

---

[201] For a fuller explanation, the term "submarket" is sometimes used in an effort to deal with the following phenomenon. On some definitions, if a market A qualifies as a valid antitrust market, then any larger market including market A will also satisfy it. (This is because, in some formulations of the HMT, the test is satisfied if the hypothetical monopolist could profitably increase the price of *any one* included product or service. Once this test is satisfied, adding additional products or services to the market will result in a market definition that also satisfies the test.) As a result, courts sometimes acknowledge that a valid market definition may contain narrower markets that are themselves also valid, and use the term "submarket" to describe the narrower ones. The possibility of multiple valid markets creates some complexity, particularly in litigation (why do you think this is?), and contributes to the view that the correct market definition should be the *smallest* market that satisfies the HMT. *See, e.g.*, Horizontal Merger Guidelines § 1.11 ("The Agency generally will consider the relevant product market to be the smallest group of products that satisfies this test."). Of course, it may not be obvious how the "smallest" market should be identified.

Brown Shoe Co. v. United States

370 U.S. 294 (1962)

Chief Justice Warren.

[1] The outer boundaries of a product market are determined by the reasonable interchangeability of use or the cross-elasticity of demand between the product itself and substitutes for it. However, within this broad market, well-defined submarkets may exist which, in themselves, constitute product markets for antitrust purposes. The boundaries of such a submarket may be determined by examining such practical indicia as industry or public recognition of the submarket as a separate economic entity, the product's peculiar characteristics and uses, unique production facilities, distinct customers, distinct prices, sensitivity to price changes, and specialized vendors. Because s 7 of the Clayton Act prohibits any merger which may substantially lessen competition "in any line of commerce" . . . , it is necessary to examine the effects of a merger in each such economically significant submarket to determine if there is a reasonable probability that the merger will substantially lessen competition. If such a probability is found to exist, the merger is proscribed.

[2] Applying these considerations to the present case, we conclude that the record supports the District Court's finding that the relevant lines of commerce are men's, women's, and children's shoes. These product lines are recognized by the public; each line is manufactured in separate plants; each has characteristics peculiar to itself rendering it generally noncompetitive with the others; and each is, of course, directed toward a distinct class of customers.

[3] Appellant, however, contends that the District Court's definitions fail to recognize sufficiently "price/quality" and "age/sex" distinctions in shoes. Brown argues that the predominantly medium-priced shoes which it manufactures occupy a product market different from the predominantly low-priced shoes which Kinney sells. But agreement with that argument would be equivalent to holding that medium-priced shoes do not compete with low-priced shoes. We think the District Court properly found the facts to be otherwise. It would be unrealistic to accept Brown's contention that, for example, men's shoes selling below $8.99 are in a different product market from those selling above $9.00.

[4] This is not to say, however, that "price/quality" differences, where they exist, are unimportant in analyzing a merger; they may be of importance in determining the likely effect of a merger. But the boundaries of the relevant market must be drawn with sufficient breadth to include the competing products of each of the merging companies and to recognize competition where, in fact, competition exists. Thus we agree with the District Court that in this case a further division of product lines based on "price/quality" differences would be "unrealistic."

[5] Brown's contention that the District Court's product market definitions should have recognized further "age/sex" distinctions raises a different problem. Brown's sharpest criticism is directed at the District Court's finding that children's shoes constituted a single line of commerce. Brown argues, for example, that "a little boy does not wear a little girl's black patent leather pump" and that "(a) male baby cannot wear a growing boy's shoes." Thus Brown argues that "infants" and "babies" shoes, "misses' and children's" shoes and "youths" and "boys" shoes should each have been considered a separate line of commerce. Assuming, arguendo, that little boys' shoes, for example, do have sufficient peculiar characteristics to constitute one of the markets to be used in analyzing the effects of this merger, we do not think that in this case the District Court was required to employ finer "age/sex" distinctions then those recognized by its classifications of "men's," "women's," and "children's" shoes. Further division does not aid us in analyzing the effects of this merger. Brown manufactures about the same percentage of the Nation's children's shoes (5.8%) as it does of the Nation's youths' and boys' shoes (6.5%), of the Nation's misses' and children's shoes (6.0%) and of the Nation's infants' and babies' shoes (4.9%). Similarly, Kinney sells about the same percentage of the Nation's children's shoes (2%) as it does of the Nation's youths' and boys' shoes (3.1%), of the Nation's misses' and children's shoes (1.9%), and of the Nation's infants' and babies' shoes (1.5%). Appellant can point to no advantage it would enjoy were finer divisions than those chosen by the District Court employed. Brown manufactures significant, comparable quantities of virtually every type of nonrubber men's, women's, and children's shoes, and Kinney sells such quantities of virtually every type of men's, women's, and children's shoes. Thus, whether considered separately or together, the picture of this merger is the same. We, therefore, agree with

the District Court's conclusion that in the setting of this case to subdivide the shoe market further on the basis of "age/sex" distinctions would be "impractical" and "unwarranted."

* * *

In the following extract, the U.S. District Court for the District of Columbia applies a test of this kind to the FTC's alleged market for personal social networking ("PSN services" or just "PSN"), in which Facebook's main social networking service ("Facebook Blue") was active. For the purposes of a motion to dismiss—that is, accepting the complaint's factual allegations as true—the court held that the market definition passed muster, relying on the kind of qualitative information mentioned in *Brown Shoe* itself.

This extract is drawn from the first of two decisions that the district court rendered on a motion to dismiss in the *Facebook* litigation. Later in the same opinion, the court dismissed the complaint on other grounds with leave to amend; the FTC subsequently amended the complaint, and the court denied Facebook's motion to dismiss the amended complaint, allowing the case to proceed into discovery.[202]

FTC v. Facebook, Inc.
560 F. Supp. 3d 1 (D.D.C. 2021)

Judge Boasberg.

[1] The market-definition inquiry in this case is somewhat unusual because, unlike familiar consumer goods like tobacco or office supplies, there is no obvious or universally agreed-upon definition of just what a personal social networking service ["PSN"] is. As a result, to discharge its burden to define the relevant market, the FTC must do two things here. First, it must provide a definition of PSN services (which, obviously, would include at least Facebook Blue). Second, it must further explain whether and why other, non-PSN services available to the public either are or are not reasonably interchangeable substitutes with PSN services. Ultimately, that analysis should demonstrate that Facebook holds a dominant share of a market that includes such substitutes, if any.

[2] On the first point, the agency explains that PSN services are online services that enable and are used by people to maintain personal relationships and share experiences with friends, family, and other personal connections in a shared social space. Such services are allegedly defined, and distinguished, by their having three key elements. First, they are built on a social graph that maps the connections between users and their friends, family, and other personal connections. Second, they include features that many users regularly employ to interact with personal connections and share their personal experiences in a shared virtual social space, including in a one-to-many "broadcast" format. And third, they include features that allow users to find and connect with other users, to make it easier for each user to build and expand their set of personal connections. The social graph also supports this feature by informing the user which new connections might be available based on her existing network.

[3] Having defined PSN services, Plaintiff then alleges that there are in fact no other types of internet services that are adequate substitutes. It buttresses that conclusion by explaining why four different kinds of arguably comparable online services are not reasonably interchangeable with PSN services.

[4] First, specialized social networking services that focus on professional connections (e.g., LinkedIn) are not substitutes because they are designed for and used primarily by professionals for sharing professional content. They therefore would not be used, as PSN services are, to maintain personal relationships and share experiences with friends, family, and other personal connections. The same is true, alleges the FTC, for interest-based social-networking services such as Strava (which relates to physical exercise). The agency also pleads that PSN services are not reasonably interchangeable with services that allow for consuming and sharing video or audio content, such as YouTube, Spotify, Netflix, or Hulu. That is because users of such services mostly consume such content passively or share content created by others (rather than content they have created), and such sharing, where it occurs, is not to the user's network of personal connections but rather to a general and wide audience of unknown users. In such a setting, users do not usually communicate with friends, family, and other personal connections,

---

[202] The second motion-to-dismiss opinion can be found at FTC v. Facebook, Inc., 581 F. Supp. 3d. 34 (D.D.C. 2022).

82

which is the hallmark of a PSN service. Finally, Plaintiff explains that mobile messaging services cannot be substituted for PSN services because the former (i) lack a shared social space for interaction and (ii) do not employ a social graph to facilitate users' finding and friending other users they may know. Zuckerberg himself has colorfully explained one key difference in use that allegedly flows from these disparate features: a PSN service is the digital equivalent of a town square, whereas a mobile messaging service is the digital equivalent of a living room.

[5] According to the FTC, then, the relevant market here thus includes PSN services—such as Facebook Blue, Instagram, and Path—and no other kinds of services. [. . .]

[6] While there are certainly bones that one could pick with the FTC's market-definition allegations, the Court does not find them fatally devoid of meat. [. . .]

[7] Defendant maintains [that] the FTC has neglected to allege any facts regarding the cross-elasticity of demand between PSN services and potential substitutes for it. Cross-elasticity of demand is a measure of the degree to which the rise in the price of one good would tend to create a greater demand for other like goods. It is thus one measure of reasonable interchangeability. There is no authority, however, supporting Facebook's argument that Plaintiff must plead specific facts regarding the price or non-price terms under which PSN-service users would switch (if ever) to alternatives. Instead, at this stage the FTC may permissibly plead that certain factors of both the service at issue and its potential substitutes—e.g., their price, use, and qualities—render them not reasonably interchangeable in the eyes of users. That is what the agency has done here, albeit in a somewhat lean fashion.

[8] Defendant next directly takes aim at the FTC's allegation that users of PSN services would not switch, if prodded by a price increase or quality decrease in a PSN service, to other means of communicating and sharing with their personal connections that lack a "connection-finder" built on the user's social graph (the third leg of the agency's definition of a PSN). That is implausible, Facebook contends, because it is obvious that people also know how to connect and share with family and friends via many other technologies, such as email, messaging, photo-sharing, and video-chats. This argument asks the Court to engage in the sort of deeply fact-intensive inquiry that is improper at this stage. Although open to dispute, the agency's allegation that users view services with and without a social-graph-based connection-finder as fundamentally different and non-interchangeable is at least theoretically rational, and thus hardly facially unsustainable, or untenable on its face. This is therefore not one of the "relatively rare" cases of a glaring deficiency in the market-definition pleadings that renders dismissal at the 12(b)(6) stage appropriate.

[9] Facebook's final fruitless market-definition argument is that the Complaint impermissibly distinguishes PSN services from other possible substitutes based on their primary uses. The company asserts that the question is whether other services can perform the same functions as PSN services, not whether they are primarily used that way. That misstates the law. The analysis looks to both whether two products can be used for the same purpose, and, if so, whether and to what extent purchasers are willing to substitute one for the other. It is for this reason that pen-and-paper do-it-yourself tax prep and assisted tax prep could be outside the market for digital do-it-yourself tax-prep services despite both providing the same basic function[, United States v. H&R Block, Inc., 833 F. Supp. 2d 36, 54 (D.D.C. 2011)], and that Medicare Advantage plans and Original Medicare plans could constitute distinct product markets despite both being capable of providing healthcare insurance to seniors[, United States v. Aetna Inc., 240 F. Supp. 3d 1, 19, 41 (D.D.C. 2017)]. All Plaintiff must do at this stage is provide a plausible explanation as to why users would not switch, even if they technically could, from PSN services to other services if prompted by a price hike. While the agency certainly could have provided more on that front, the fact that other services are not primarily used for the sort of personal sharing that is the hallmark of a PSN service seems a plausible reason why little switching would occur. Whether due to network effects or the norms around what sort of content is generally posted on different platforms, it is not a stretch to imagine that users are reluctant to share a highly personal milestone on LinkedIn or post a video of their child's first steps to YouTube. [. . .]

[10] [T]he Court therefore finds that the Complaint's allegations do enough to make out a plausible market for PSN services[.]

* * *

3. Applying Market Definition Theory

In practice, courts commonly apply both the HMT and the *Brown Shoe* factors together when explaining their conclusions. When doing so, they often must sift through a range of evidence—including econometric and other expert economic evidence, testimony from market participants, and ordinary-course documents—in search of a market definition that best fits the mosaic of evidence and the nature of the competitive concerns at issue. And, as noted above, the market definition must fit the theory of harm too: courts are usually looking for a valid market definition that would capture the risk of harm that might result from *this particular* challenged practice or transaction.

In reaching a bottom-line view about the validity of a candidate market definition, courts often stress their concern to make sure that a market definition in an antitrust case reflects the underlying "commercial realities" of life in the relevant industry. In doing so, they often echo language in another part of the *Brown Shoe* opinion that: "Congress prescribed a pragmatic, factual approach to the definition of the relevant market and not a formal, legalistic one. The . . . market selected must, therefore, both correspond to the commercial realities of the industry and be economically significant."[203]

In some cases, a court's view about these "commercial realities" may lead it to favor lay testimony and documents over expert economic analysis.[204] Thus, for example, in *Swedish Match*—the FTC's successful challenge to the proposed acquisition of one smokeless tobacco supplier, National, by another, Swedish Match—the court held that loose leaf tobacco and moist snuff were not in the same market—but not because of the economic expert evidence!

> The economic evidence in this case . . . is not persuasive. . . . [The FTC's expert] conceded at the hearing that his inference [regarding] the industry-wide elasticity for loose leaf [tobacco] . . . is subjective, follows no objective methodology, and cannot be proven to any statistical significance. . . . [And] [t]he defendant's economics evidence is even less persuasive. . . . [The defendants' expert] issued several different reports, all of which presented new estimates of the elasticity of demand based on new economic models. . . .
>
> [But unlike] the economic analyses, additional evidence of price sensitivity has been presented in this case that is persuasive. The views of Swedish Match and National competitors, statements by loose leaf distributors, and internal documents of Swedish Match and National show that price-based substitution between loose leaf and moist snuff is generally lacking. Swedish Match competitors believe that there is no switching between loose leaf and moist snuff on the basis of price. . . .
>
> Swedish Match and National internal business documents confirm that pricing has little effect on loose leaf demand. . . . National's Chairman . . . stated in a deposition that loose leaf sales cannot be increased by cutting loose leaf prices. Likewise . . . [the] President of Pinkerton Tobacco from 1992 to 1997 and Chief Operating Officer of Swedish Match from 1997 to 1999, testified that Swedish Match could not materially increase loose leaf sales by cutting prices.[205]

But in other cases, a court may conclude that economic expert analysis evidence *is* indeed a reliable guide to those commercial realities—including realities that might not be clear even to a market participant.[206] After all, as the district court judge pointed out in upholding DOJ's challenge to the acquisition by Bazaarvoice (a provider of ecommerce rating and review platforms) of its main competitor PowerReviews, customers don't always have access to the evidence, including data and documents, that inform expert analysis (although the court was talking in that case about effects analysis rather than market definition):

---

[203] Brown Shoe Co. v. United States, 370 U.S. 294, 336–37 (1962).

[204] *See, e.g.*, FTC v. Thomas Jefferson Univ., 505 F. Supp. 3d 522, 553 (E.D. Pa. 2020) ("[T]he Government relies on econometrics and insurer testimony to prove the propriety of its proposed Philadelphia Area market. But it has not shown that the market corresponds with commercial realities and it thus cannot pass the HMT.").

[205] FTC v. Swedish Match, 131 F. Supp. 2d 151, 161–62 (D.D.C. 2000).

[206] *See, e.g.*, FTC v. Advocate Health Care, No. 15 C 11473, 2017 WL 1022015, at *9–10 (N.D. Ill. Mar. 16, 2017) (expressly accepting expert analysis as a guide to "commercial realities").

Bazaarvoice relied heavily on the fact that none of the more than 100 current, former and potential customers who testified in this case believed that the acquisition had harmed or would harm them. The Court finds that the customers were the most credible sources of information on their need for, use of and substitutability of social commerce products, as well as regarding their companies' past responses to price increases. *But customers generally do not engage in a specific analysis of the effects of a merger.* Many of them had given no thought to the effect of the merger or had no opinion. They lacked the same information about the merger presented in court, including from the economic experts. Their testimony on the impact and likely effect of the merger was speculative at best and is entitled to virtually no weight.[207]

In practice, courts tend to look for a conclusion that makes some sense of all the available evidence: including the teachings of the HMT and the qualitative factors associated with *Brown Shoe*. For example, when the Department of Justice challenged H&R Block's acquisition of TaxACT, a central question for the district court was whether the relevant market should include only free DIY tax preparation software, or whether it should also include assisted tax preparation services and/or taxpayers' ability to simply do their own taxes with pen and paper. This issue was a crucial one: a broader market definition would likely have led to a favorable decision for the merging parties; a narrower one was likely to spell doom for the deal. Notice how the district court deploys both hypothetical-monopolist and qualitative reasoning in explaining its conclusion.[208]

United States v. H & R Block, Inc.
833 F.Supp.2d 36 (D.D.C. 2011)

Judge Howell.

[1] Merger analysis begins with defining the relevant product market. Defining the relevant market is critical in an antitrust case because the legality of the proposed merger in question almost always depends upon the market power of the parties involved. Indeed, the relevant market definition is often the key to the ultimate resolution of this type of case because of the relative implications of market power.

[2] The government argues that the relevant market in this case consists of all DDIY [("digital do-it-yourself")] products, but does not include assisted tax preparation or pen-and-paper. Under this view of the market, the acquisition in this case would result in a DDIY market that is dominated by two large players—H & R Block ["HRB"] and Intuit—that together control approximately 90 percent of the market share, with the remaining 10 percent of the market divided amongst a plethora of smaller companies. In contrast, the defendants argue for a broader market that includes all tax preparation methods ("all methods"), comprised of DDIY, assisted, and pen-and-paper. Under this view of the market, the market concentration effects of this acquisition would be much smaller and would not lead to a situation in which two firms control 90 percent of the market. This broader view of the market rests primarily on the premise that providers of all methods of tax preparation compete with each other for the patronage of the same pool of customers—U.S. taxpayers. After carefully considering the evidence and arguments presented by all parties, the Court has concluded that the relevant market in this case is, as the DOJ contends, the market for digital do-it-yourself tax preparation products.

[3] A "relevant product market" is a term of art in antitrust analysis. The Supreme Court has set forth the general rule for defining a relevant product market: "The outer boundaries of a product market are determined by the reasonable interchangeability of use [by consumers] or the cross-elasticity of demand between the product itself and substitutes for it." [*Brown Shoe Co. v. United States*, 370 U.S. 294, 325 (1962).] In other words, courts look at whether two products can be used for the same purpose, and, if so, whether and to what extent purchasers are willing to substitute one for the other.

[4] A broad, overall market may contain smaller markets which themselves constitute product markets for antitrust purposes. [T]he mere fact that a firm may be termed a competitor in the overall marketplace does not necessarily

---

[207] United States v. Bazaarvoice, Inc., No. 13-CV-00133-WHO, 2014 WL 203966, at *61 (N.D. Cal. Jan. 8, 2014) (emphasis added).

[208] For a perspective on the market-definition dimension of the case, *see* Joseph J. Simons & Malcolm B. Coate, United States v. H&R Block: *An Illustration of the DOJ's New But Controversial Approach to Market Definition*, 10 J. Comp. L. & Econ. 543 (2014).

require that it be included in the relevant product market for antitrust purposes. Traditionally, courts have held that the boundaries of a relevant product market within a broader market may be determined by examining such practical indicia as industry or public recognition of the relevant market as a separate economic entity, the product's peculiar characteristics and uses, unique production facilities, distinct customers, distinct prices, sensitivity to price changes, and specialized vendors. These "practical indicia" of market boundaries may be viewed as evidentiary proxies for proof of substitutability and cross-elasticities of supply and demand.

[5] An analytical method often used by courts to define a relevant market is to ask hypothetically whether it would be profitable to have a monopoly over a given set of substitutable products. If so, those products may constitute a relevant market. This approach—sometimes called the "hypothetical monopolist test"—is endorsed by the Horizontal Merger Guidelines issued by the DOJ and Federal Trade Commission. *See* Fed. Trade Comm'n & U.S. Dep't of Justice *Horizontal Merger Guidelines* (2010) (hereinafter, "Merger Guidelines"), § 4.1.1. In the merger context, this inquiry boils down to whether a hypothetical profit-maximizing firm, not subject to price regulation, that was the only present and future seller of those products likely would impose at least a small but significant and non-transitory increase in price ("SSNIP") on at least one product in the market, including at least one product sold by one of the merging firms. The "small but significant and non-transitory increase in price," or SSNIP, is typically assumed to be five percent or more.

[6] Thus, the question here is whether it would be hypothetically useful to have a monopoly over all DDIY tax preparation products because the monopolist could then profitably raise prices for those products by five percent or more; or whether, to the contrary, there would be no reason to monopolize all DDIY tax preparation products because substitution and price competition with other methods of tax preparation would restrain any potential DDIY monopolist from profitably raising prices. In other words, would enough DDIY users switch to the assisted or pen-and-paper methods of tax preparation in response to a five-to-ten percent increase in DDIY prices to make such a price increase unprofitable?

[7] In evaluating the relevant product market here, the Court considers business documents from the defendants and others, the testimony of the fact witnesses, and the analyses of the parties' expert economists. This evidence demonstrates that DDIY is the relevant product market in this case.

1. The Defendants' Documents Show That DDIY Is The Relevant Product Market.

[8] When determining the relevant product market, courts often pay close attention to the defendants' ordinary course of business documents. The government argues that the defendants' ordinary course of business documents in this case "conclusively demonstrate that competition with other [DDIY] firms drive Defendants' pricing decisions, quality improvements, and corporate strategy" for their own DDIY products—thus supporting the government's view of the relevant market. The defendants contend that the government has relied on "select, 'out-of-context' snippets from documents," and that the documents as a whole support the defendants' view that the relevant product market is all methods of tax preparation. The Court finds that the documentary evidence in this case supports the conclusion that DDIY is the relevant product market.

[9] Internal TaxACT documents establish that TaxACT has viewed DDIY offerings by HRB and TurboTax as its primary competitors, that it has tracked their marketing, product offerings, and pricing, and that it has determined its own pricing and business strategy in relation to those companies' DDIY products. Confidential memoranda prepared by TaxACT's investment bankers for potential private equity buyers of TaxACT identify HRB and TurboTax as TaxACT's primary competitors in a DDIY market. These documents also recognize that TaxACT's strategy for competing with Intuit and HRB is to offer a lower price for what it deems a superior product.

[10] While, as defendants point out, parts of these TaxACT documents also discuss the broader tax preparation industry, these documents make clear that TaxACT's own view—and that conveyed by its investment bankers to potential buyers—is that the company primarily competes in a DDIY market against Intuit and HRB and that it develops its pricing and business strategy with that market and those competitors in mind. These documents are strong evidence that DDIY is the relevant product market.

[11] Internal HRB documents also evidence HRB's perception of a discrete DDIY market or market segment. HRB and its outside consultants have tracked its digital competitors' activities, prices, and product offerings. Documents from HRB's DDIY business have also referred to HRB, TaxACT, and TurboTax as the "Big Three" competitors in the DDIY market. Finally, the documents show that, in connection with a proposed acquisition of TaxACT, HRB identified the proposed transaction as a way to grow its digital "market share" and has measured TaxACT's market share in a DDIY market. All of these documents also provide evidence that DDIY is a relevant product market.

[12] The defendants acknowledge that "the merging parties certainly have documents that discuss each other and digital competitors generally, and even reference a digital market and the 'Big Three,'" but contend this evidence is insufficient to prove a market. Rather, the defendants argue that the documents show that the relevant market is all methods of tax preparation, especially in light of documented competition between DDIY providers and assisted providers for the same overall pool of U.S. taxpayers who are potential customers. As discussed below, the Court disagrees and finds that the relevant product market is DDIY products.

2. The Relevant Product Market Does Not Include Assisted Tax Preparation Or Manual Preparation.

[13] It is beyond debate—and conceded by the plaintiff—that all methods of tax preparation are, to some degree, in competition. All tax preparation methods provide taxpayers with a means to perform the task of completing a tax return, but each method is starkly different. Thus, while providers of all tax preparation methods may compete at some level, this does not necessarily require that [they] be included in the relevant product market for antitrust purposes. DDIY tax preparation products differ from manual tax preparation and assisted tax preparation products in a number of meaningful ways. As compared to manual and assisted methods, DDIY products involve different technology, price, convenience level, time investment, mental effort and type of interaction by the consumer. Taken together, these different attributes make the consumer experience of using DDIY products quite distinct from other methods of tax preparation. The question for this court is whether DDIY and other methods of tax preparation are "reasonably interchangeable" so that it would not be profitable to have a monopoly over only DDIY products.

a. Assisted Tax Preparation Is Not In The Relevant Product Market.

[14] Apart from the analysis of their economic expert, the defendants' main argument for inclusion of assisted tax preparation in the relevant market is that DDIY and assisted companies compete for customers. As evidence for this point, the defendants emphasize that Intuit's marketing efforts have targeted HRB's assisted customers. While the evidence does show that companies in the DDIY and assisted markets all generally compete with each other for the same overall pool of potential customers—U.S. taxpayers—that fact does not necessarily mean that DDIY and assisted must be viewed as part of the same relevant product market. DDIY provides customers with tax preparation services through an entirely different method, technology, and user experience than assisted preparation. [. . .]

[15] As Judge Tatel explained in *Whole Foods*[, FTC v. Whole Foods Market, Inc., 548 F.3d 1028, 1048 (D.C. Cir. 2008) (Tatel, J., concurring)]: When the automobile was first invented, competing auto manufacturers obviously took customers primarily from companies selling horses and buggies, not from other auto manufacturers, but that hardly shows that cars and horse-drawn carriages should be treated as the same product market. . . .

[16] The key question for the Court is whether DDIY and assisted products are sufficiently close substitutes to constrain any anticompetitive DDIY pricing after the proposed merger. Evidence of the absence of close price competition between DDIY and assisted products makes clear that the answer to that question is no—and that DDIY is the relevant product market here. Significantly, despite some DDIY efforts to capture tax store customers, none of the major DDIY competitors sets their prices based on consideration of assisted prices. Indeed, there are quite significant price disparities between the average prices of DDIY and assisted products. The average price of TurboTax, the most popular DDIY brand is approximately $55. The average price of HRB's DDIY products is approximately $25. Overall, the DDIY industry average price is $44.13. In contrast, the typical price of an assisted tax return is significantly higher, in the range of $150–200. A 10 percent or even 20 percent price increase in the average price of DDIY would only move the average price up to $48.54 or $52.96, respectively—still substantially

below the average price of assisted tax products. The overall lack of evidence of price competition between DDIY and assisted products supports the conclusion that DDIY is a separate relevant product market for evaluating this transaction, despite the fact that DDIY and assisted firms target their marketing efforts at the same pool of customers.

[17] The defendants point to some evidence that HRB sets prices for certain assisted products to compete with DDIY. These are limited product offerings for which prices appear well below even the 25th percentile price for HRB's assisted products. Relatedly, the defendants' claim that prices for assisted and DDIY products "significantly overlap" is not strongly supported and relies on a comparison of the most limited, low-end assisted products with DDIY products generally. In sum, while defendants' have identified isolated instances in which assisted product offerings are priced lower than the average prices for typical assisted products, they do not and cannot demonstrate that this is generally the case. . . . .

b. Manual Tax Preparation Is Not In The Relevant Product Market.

[18] The defendants also argue that manual tax preparation, or pen-and-paper, should be included in the relevant product market. At the outset, the Court notes that pen-and-paper is not a "product" at all; it is the task of filling out a tax return by oneself without any interactive assistance. Even so, the defendants argue pen-and-paper should be included in the relevant product market because it acts as a "significant competitive constraint" on DDIY. The defendants' argument relies primarily on two factors. First, the defendants cite the results of a 2011 email survey of TaxACT customers. . . . Second, the defendants point to documents and testimony indicating that TaxACT has considered possible diversion to pen-and-paper in setting its prices.

[19] The Court finds that pen-and-paper is not part of the relevant market because it does not believe a sufficient number of consumers would switch to pen-and-paper in response to a small, but significant increase in DDIY prices. The possibility of preparing one's own tax return necessarily constrains the prices of other methods of preparation at some level. For example, if the price of DDIY and assisted products were raised to $1 million per tax return, surely all but the most well-heeled taxpayers would switch to pen-and-paper. Yet, at the more practical price increase levels that trigger antitrust concern—the typical five to ten percent price increase of the SSNIP test—pen-and-paper preparation is unlikely to provide a meaningful restraint for DDIY products, which currently sell for an average price of $44.13.

[20] The government well illustrated the overly broad nature of defendants' proposed relevant market by posing to the defendants' expert the hypothetical question of whether "sitting at home and drinking chicken soup [would be] part of the market for [manufactured] cold remedies?" he defendants' expert responded that the real "question is if the price of cold medicines went up sufficiently, would people turn to chicken soup?" As an initial matter, in contrast to the defendants' expert, the Court doubts that it would ever be legally appropriate to define a relevant product market that included manufactured cold remedies and ordinary chicken soup. This conclusion flows from the deep functional differences between those products. Setting that issue aside, however, a price has increased "sufficiently" to trigger antitrust concern at the level of a five to ten percent small, but significant non-transitory increase in price. Just as chicken soup is unlikely to constrain the price of manufactured cold remedies sufficiently, the Court concludes that a SSNIP in DDIY would not be constrained by people turning to pen-and-paper. First, the share of returns prepared via pen-and-paper has dwindled over the past decade, as the DDIY market has grown. Second, while pen-and-paper filers have been a net source of new customers for DDIY companies, both HRB and {redacted} executives have testified that they do not believe their DDIY products compete closely with pen-and-paper methods. Third, courts in antitrust cases frequently exclude similar "self-supply" substitutes from relevant product markets.

[21] While some diversion from DDIY to manual filing may occur in response to a SSNIP, the Court finds that it would likely be limited and marginal. The functional experience of using a DDIY product is meaningfully different from the self-service task of filling out tax forms independently. Manual completion of a tax return requires different tools, effort, resources, and time investment by a consumer than use of either DDIY or assisted methods. . . .

[22] Inclusion of all possible methods of tax preparation, including pen-and-paper, in the relevant product market also violates the principle that the relevant product market should ordinarily be defined as the smallest product market that will satisfy the hypothetical monopolist test. Indeed, the defendants' inclusion of pen-and-paper in the relevant market ignores at least one obvious, smaller market possibility that they might have proposed—the combined market of all DDIY and assisted tax preparation products. It is hardly plausible that a monopolist of this market—to which the only alternative would be pen-and-paper—could not impose a SSNIP.

[23] The defendants' proposed relevant market of all methods of tax return preparation is so broadly defined that, as the plaintiff's expert testified, there are no conceivable alternatives besides going to jail, fleeing to Canada, or not earning any taxable income. As the plaintiff's expert put it, "if you're talking about the market for all tax preparation, you're talking about a market where, in economist terms, demand is completely [in]elastic. There are no alternatives." In such circumstances, the usual tools of antitrust analysis—such as the hypothetical monopolist test—cease being useful because it is self-evident that a monopolist of all forms of tax preparation, including self-preparation, could impose a small, but significant price increase. Indeed, a monopolist in that situation could essentially name any price since taxpayers would have no alternative but to pay it. As the plaintiff's expert testified, defining a market that broadly negates the entire purpose of defining a relevant market in an antitrust case. . . . The Court agrees with this assessment and finds the defendants' proposed relevant market to be overbroad.

CASENOTE: United States v. Continental Can Co.

373 U.S. 441 (1964)

Today, as we have seen, courts generally approach market definition by identifying particular kinds of demand, such as specific end-uses of a product, and asking which products or services are available to meet that demand.[1] But the courts have not has not always taken such a granular approach. Earlier cases often applied a somewhat looser, broader approach to market definition.[209] In 1964's *Continental Can*, for example, the Supreme Court considered a challenge by the Department of Justice to the acquisition of the third-largest manufacturer of glass containers in the United States by the second-largest manufacturer of metal cans in the United States. The district court had held that the transaction should be analyzed in separate markets for (1) metal containers, (2) glass containers, and (3) beer containers (a market in which both metal and glass containers were competitive), and that, when analyzed in this light, the transaction did not create a reasonable probability of an anticompetitive effect in any market. The Supreme Court reversed.

Majority opinion (Justice White). The Court held that the transaction violated Section 7 in light of evidence that glass and metal containers were in competition for at least some uses. Specifically, the Court held that "the interindustry competition between glass and metal containers is sufficient to warrant treating as a relevant product market the combined glass and metal container industries and all end uses for which they compete." The Court did not include other materials, such as paper and plastic, in this market.

In so holding, the Court relied on evidence of a "general confrontation between metal and glass containers and competition between them for the same end uses which is insistent, continuous, effective and quantity-wise very substantial." The Court noted in broad terms that "[m]etal has replaced glass and glass has replaced metal as the leading container for some important uses; both are used for other purposes; each is trying to expand its share of the market at the expense of the other; and each is attempting to preempt for itself every use for which its product is physically suitable[.]" The Court was unconcerned by evidence that other kinds of containers, such as plastic and paper, also represented additional options for customers for many of the end-uses at issue, and did not clearly separate its analysis of competitive effects by reference to individual kinds of demand for containers.

Dissent (Justice Harlan). In dissent, Justice Harlan called the majority opinion a "travesty of economics" and "an abrupt and unwise departure from established anti-trust [sic] law." The dissent protested that relevant market should have been defined through a more disciplined assessment of *all* substitutes that competed to satisfy

---

[209] *See generally* Christine S. Wilson & Keith Klovers, *Same Rule, Different Result: How the Narrowing of Product Markets Has Altered Substantive Antitrust Rules*, 84 Antitrust L.J. 55 (2021).

particular kinds of demand. Justice Harlan complained that "without support in reason or fact, [the Court] dips into this network of competition and establishes metal and glass containers as a separate 'line of commerce,' leaving entirely out of account all other kinds of containers: plastic, paper, foil and any other materials competing for the same business."

He argued that "the Court is, in effect, laying down a 'per se' rule that mergers between two large companies in related industries are presumptively unlawful under s 7." And "[h]ereafter, however slight (or even nonexistent) the competitive impact of a merger on any actual market, businessmen must rest uneasy lest the Court create some 'market,' in which the merger presumptively dampens competition, out of bits and pieces of real ones. . . . This is said to be recognizing 'meaningful competition where it is found to exist.' It is in fact imagining effects on competition where none has been shown."

Implications. The majority's analysis in *Continental Can* reflects a broader-brush approach to market definition than modern practice would generally support. Today, courts would likely take a more granular approach, along the lines suggested by Justice Harlan.

NOTES

1) What is the value of market definition? Would we be better off without it? What could we do instead? Would it be better or worse to just ask "is it plausible that harm could result from this practice or transaction?"

2) Some writers have suggested that we should rely more heavily on market share thresholds, and/or on concentration statistics that measure the number of participants in a market and their respective shares. For example, Tim Wu has suggested a rule against mergers that reduce the number of competitors in a market to fewer than four.[210] What are the main advantages and disadvantages of moving antitrust further in this direction?

3) Are all rational supplier(s) constrained by other suppliers? How can we tell the difference between constraints from in-market substitutes and constraints from out-of-markets substitutes?

4) What metric do you think the court should have used to determine market share in the Facebook case? Why? Do you think a plaintiff should have to specify which metrics should be used in this way before getting the benefit of the discovery process?

5) The "*Brown Shoe* factors" are somewhat diverse. Do you think some are more important than others? Why? What should "industry and public recognition" mean and how could it be tested?

6) As we noted above, antitrust markets serve multiple functions in antitrust cases. For example, a market definition might provide the basis for identifying market power (*e.g.*, by calculating shares of the defined market); it also usually defines the area of analysis for determining whether adverse "anticompetitive effects" are to be feared; and it also usually defines the area in which benefits can be offered in justification of a harmful transaction or practice (that is, antitrust analysis generally does not allow "out of market" benefits to be considered). Should the same definition be applied for each of these purposes? Why, or why not?[211]

7) The general rule that harms in one market cannot be justified by benefits in another market under the rule of reason (which we will meet in more detail in Chapter IV) means, among other things, that a practice or transaction that is beneficial overall can normally be blocked if it inflicts overall harm in at least one market. What are the strongest arguments in favor of, and against, such a rule? What does it tell us about who antitrust law protects? What alternative rules can you imagine?

C. Special Cases

You will encounter various forms of "special" market definition. In this section, we will briefly meet five common special cases: buyer markets, bundles, clusters, price discrimination markets, and platforms.

---

[210] Tim Wu, THE CURSE OF BIGNESS: ANTITRUST IN THE NEW GILDED AGE (2018) 129.

[211] *See, e.g.,* Daniel Francis & Jay Ezrielev, *Disaggregating Market Definition:* AmEx *and a Plural View of Market Definition*, 98 Neb. L.J. 460, 479 (2019).

1. Buyer Markets

Sometimes we undertake market definition in order to identify competitive constraints on a *purchaser* of products or services, such as an employer (remember, labor is a service!). In such cases, we simply turn the usual analysis on its head, to determine what other purchasers for the products or services in question might, by offering alternatives to suppliers, constrain the purchaser's ability to obtain infracompetitive prices. (You may find it helpful to look back at the discussion of monopsony in Chapter II.)

Horizontal Merger Guidelines § 12

12. Mergers of Competing Buyers

[1] Mergers of competing buyers can enhance market power on the buying side of the market, just as mergers of competing sellers can enhance market power on the selling side of the market. Buyer market power is sometimes called "monopsony power."

[2] To evaluate whether a merger is likely to enhance market power on the buying side of the market, the Agencies employ essentially the [same] framework . . . for evaluating whether a merger is likely to enhance market power on the selling side of the market. In defining relevant markets, the Agencies focus on the alternatives available to sellers in the face of a decrease in the price paid by a hypothetical monopsonist.

[3] Market power on the buying side of the market is not a significant concern if suppliers have numerous attractive outlets for their goods or services. However, when that is not the case, the Agencies may conclude that the merger of competing buyers is likely to lessen competition in a manner harmful to sellers.

[4] The Agencies distinguish between effects on sellers arising from a lessening of competition and effects arising in other ways. A merger that does not enhance market power on the buying side of the market can nevertheless lead to a reduction in prices paid by the merged firm, for example, by reducing transactions costs or allowing the merged firm to take advantage of volume-based discounts. Reduction in prices paid by the merging firms not arising from the enhancement of market power can be significant in the evaluation of efficiencies from a merger[.]

[5] The Agencies do not view a short-run reduction in the quantity purchased as the only, or best, indicator of whether a merger enhances buyer market power. Nor do the Agencies evaluate the competitive effects of mergers between competing buyers strictly, or even primarily, on the basis of effects in the downstream markets in which the merging firms sell.

> *Example 24:* Merging Firms A and B are the only two buyers in the relevant geographic market for an agricultural product. Their merger will enhance buyer power and depress the price paid to farmers for this product, causing a transfer of wealth from farmers to the merged firm and inefficiently reducing supply. These effects can arise even if the merger will not lead to any increase in the price charged by the merged firm for its output.

* * *

Concern with buyer-side market power was the focus of DOJ's 2021 challenge to Penguin Random House's proposed acquisition of Simon & Schuster. DOJ alleged that the transaction would harm competition to purchase publishing rights to highly anticipated books. The government won the battle over market definition—and went on to win the case.

United States v. Bertelsmann SE & CO.

Case No. 1:21-cv-02886 (D.D.C. Nov. 7, 2022)

Judge Pan.

[1] Penguin Random House ("PRH") is by far the largest book publisher in the United States. Owned by Bertelsmann SE & Co. KGaA ("Bertelsmann"), an international media and services company, PRH annually publishes over 2,000 new books in the U.S. and generates nearly $2.5 billion in revenue. Simon & Schuster, Inc.

("S&S"), owned by the media giant Paramount Global (formerly ViacomCBS), is the third-largest publisher in the U.S. S&S publishes about 1,000 new titles yearly and reported over $760 million in net sales in 2020. [. . .]

[2] In November 2021, the Antitrust Division of the United States Department of Justice ("the government") brought this action against PRH, S&S, and their parent companies ("the defendants"), seeking to block the merger of PRH and S&S under Section 7 of the Clayton Act. The government's case sounds in "monopsony," a market condition where a buyer with too much market power can lower prices or otherwise harm sellers. Essentially, the government alleges that the merger will increase market concentration in the publishing industry, which will allow publishing companies to pay certain authors less money for the rights to publish their books. [. . .]

[3] The book industry is dominated by five major publishing houses—PRH, HarperCollins Publishers, S&S, Hachette Book Group, and Macmillan Publishing Group, LLC—which are known as the "Big Five." Together, the Big Five held nearly 60 percent of the market for the sale of trade books in 2021 (i.e., books intended for general readership, as opposed to specialized books like textbooks or manuals). [. . .]

[4] Books begin, of course, with authors. Authors often spend years developing their ideas, conducting research, and refining their manuscripts or proposals before submitting them for publication. A project that is acquired may still take months or years of work before it becomes a completed book that is ready for distribution. To support themselves, authors often rely on "advances" from their publishers. An advance is an upfront payment against the royalties that an author may earn in the future. The advance is the single most important term in a contract for publishing rights because in a large number of cases, it may be the only compensation that the author will receive for their work. Indeed, most authors do not "earn out" their advances, i.e., ultimately earn royalties that exceed the amount of their advances. In addition to the advance, authors care about working with editors who share their vision for the book and who can help them to bring the book into the world. [. . .]

[5] . . . [T]he amount that is paid [by a publisher to an author] is inexorably determined by competition. In an auction, a skillful agent can capitalize on enthusiasm for a book and play bidders off against one another, knowing that a publisher will bid what it needs to buy that book because it only takes one passionate editor at another imprint to win that book away. [. . .]

[6] The government contends that the merger of PRH and S&S would harm competition to acquire the publishing rights to anticipated top-selling books, resulting in lower advances for the authors of such books and less favorable contract terms. The defendants do not dispute that if advances are significantly decreased, some authors will not be able to write, resulting in fewer books being published, less variety in the marketplace of ideas, and an inevitable loss of intellectual and creative output. The defendants vigorously contest, however, whether advances would decrease after the merger: They contend that competition would not be harmed and that advances would actually rise. [. . .]

[7] The government defines the relevant product market as the one for publishing rights to anticipated top-selling books. Anticipated top-selling books are those that are expected to yield significant sales, and for which authors therefore receive higher advances. The government contends that such books have distinctive characteristics, including the need for extra marketing, publicity, and sales support to allow them to reach broader audiences.

[8] The proposed market for anticipated top-selling books is a submarket of the broader publishing market for all trade books. Under the government's monopsony theory, the authors of anticipated top-selling books are "targeted sellers" against whom the merged defendants might lower the prices paid for the authors' wares. See . . . Merger Guidelines § 4.1.4 (If a monopsonist could "profitably target a subset of [sellers] for price [de]creases, the [government] may identify relevant markets defined around those targeted [sellers]."); cf. FTC v. Wilh Wilhelmsen Holding ASA, 341 F. Supp. 3d 27, 46–47 (D.D.C. 2018) ("[A]ntitrust markets can be based on targeted customers"); [FTC v. Sysco Corp., 113 F. Supp. 3d 1, 38–40 (D.D.C. 2015)] (discussing definition of markets based on targeted customers). In the monopsony context, a submarket exists when buyers can profitably cut prices to certain targeted sellers but not to others, in which case regulators may evaluate competitive effects separately by type of seller.

[9] Courts evaluate relevant product markets in the monopsony context in two ways: by considering qualitative, "practical indicia" as described by the Supreme Court in the *Brown Shoe* case; and by examining "supply

substitution" and applying the "hypothetical monopsonist test" . . . . The parties in this case focus their arguments on whether "practical indicia" support the finding of a market to publish anticipated top-selling books. Because the parties choose to fight on the battlefield of "practical indicia," that is where the Court begins its analysis. [. . .]

[10] To identify the books that are anticipated to sell well, the government focuses on the criterion of "distinct pricing": For analytical purposes, it defines anticipated top-selling books as those for which publishers pay an advance of at least $250,000. [. . .]

[11] In the publishing market for anticipated top-selling books, the Big Five publishers hold 91 percent of the market share, while smaller publishers collectively hold only 9 percent. By contrast, in the publishing market for books that earn advances below $250,000, the non-Big Five publishers have a much more substantial market share of 45 percent.

[12] As an initial matter, the government's use of high advances as a proxy for anticipated book sales is logical and supported by market realities. In publishing, advances are correlated with expected sales because books that are expected to sell well receive higher advances. In fact, advance levels are set by using [profit and loss statements ("P&Ls")], and the defining feature of a P&L is the sales estimate. Moreover, industry practices indicate that $250,000 is a reasonable place to draw the line: S&S and two of the three PRH adult divisions require approval from senior publishers or executives for advance offers of $250,000 or more; and *Publishers Marketplace*, a major industry publication, categorizes deals for $250,000 or more as "significant." This evidence is probative of "industry or public recognition" of a distinct category of books that receive advances at or above the $250,000 level.

[13] The defendants take aim at the $250,000 threshold that the government has chosen to bound the market. Most significantly, they argue that the $250,000 threshold is either too high or too low to define a submarket for anticipated top selling books. [. . .]

[14] The defendants' excessive concern over the specific dollar threshold betrays a misunderstanding of why the threshold was chosen. The market that the government seeks to define is the one for anticipated top-selling books, and the $250,000 demarcation was adopted only as an analytical tool to help it group together the books in question. The government's economic expert, Dr. Nicholas Hill, also conducted his analyses at other numerical thresholds (including $150,000, $250,000, $500,000, and $1 million) and observed consistent outcomes at those various high-dollar amounts. Thus, the $250,000 cutoff is merely useful; it is not intended to be a rigid bright line, but rather is helpful for analytical purposes to facilitate the assessment of anticompetitive effects. Accordingly, the Court rejects this argument against the government's defined market.

[15] The Court is unswayed by the defendants' tactic of enumerating other markets or submarkets in which competition would not be harmed by the merger. In addition to proposing submarkets at the $50,000- and $1 million- advance levels, the defendants also declare that the government could not prove anticompetitive effects from the merger in the broad market of publishing rights for all U.S. trade books, or in the downstream market for retail book sales. Those protestations are beside the point because the Clayton Act prohibits mergers that may substantially lessen competition "in *any* line of commerce or in *any* activity affecting commerce." 15 U.S.C. § 18 (emphasis added). Thus, even if alternative submarkets exist at other advance levels, or if there are broader markets that might be analyzed, the viability of such additional markets does not render the one identified by the government unusable.

[16] Ample precedent supports the government's use of a numerical cutoff to identify a submarket. It is common for courts to use seemingly arbitrary criteria to home in on a segment of a broader industry. [. . .]

[17] Aside from distinct pricing, the government argues that the remaining *Brown Shoe* factors demonstrate that there is a relevant submarket for the publishing rights to anticipated top-selling books. The government contends that such books have "peculiar characteristics and uses," in that they require stronger marketing, publicity, and sales support, which allow them to reach a broader audience of readers. In addition, authors of anticipated top-selling books are "distinct sellers," in that they (1) care more about their publishers' reputation and services, which ensure wider distribution of their books; (2) may receive more favorable contract terms than other authors; and (3) face different competitive conditions, as demonstrated by the dominant market share of the Big Five (91%) in

publishing anticipated top sellers. For all those reasons, the government argues, anticipated top-selling books are in a different category from books that are expected to sell relatively few copies, and publishers can target their authors for price decreases.

[18] The defendants, however, insist that all books are in the same market. They argue that books at all advance levels go through an identical editing, marketing, and distribution process; that there is no difference in the personnel who handle such books; that the contracts for all books are negotiated in the same way; and that any special terms in the contracts for some books simply result from an agent's leverage. . . .

[19] The Court has no trouble recognizing that anticipated top-selling books are distinct from the vast majority of books that do not carry the same expectations for success. Obviously, the entire publishing industry is dedicated to selling books; and all editors and publishers naturally are very focused on discovering and acquiring the books that they believe will drive sales. Evidence strongly supports the conclusion that, from the perspective of editors and publishers, not all books are created equal. Beyond advances, contracts for books that are expected to sell well are more likely to include favorable terms like higher royalty rates, higher levels of marketing support, "glam" packages (e.g., for hair, makeup, and wardrobe services), and airfare for authors. Publishers print more of the books they think will do well; circulate more advance copies of such books to reviewers or influencers to create excitement; push for interviews with more media outlets; and schedule book-tour appearances in more locations. Anticipated top-selling books also get more attention from marketing and sales teams. For example, Dr. Hill determined that S&S and PRH spend, on average, under $10,000 on marketing for books with advances under $250,000, and between $40,000 and $90,000 on marketing for books with advances over $250,000[.]

[20] The fact that the Big Five publish 91 percent of anticipated top sellers also supports a finding that the authors of such books have unique needs and preferences. Although smaller publishers can sometimes put out an anticipated top-selling book, it is the Big Five who have the back lists and the marketing, publicity, and sales advantages necessary to consistently provide the high advances and unique services that top-selling authors need. [. . .]

{*Eds.: following its application of the* Brown Shoe *factors, the court turned to the hypothetical monopolist—here monopsonist—test.*}

[21] The traditional way to define a relevant market in the monopsony context would be to examine the commonality and interchangeability of the buyers of a certain good. Indeed, the outer boundaries of a product market are determined by the reasonable interchangeability of use or the cross-elasticity of supply between the product's buyers, in the case of monopsony, and the substitutes for such buyers. Accordingly, the touchstone is supply substitution.

[22] To test the proposed market boundaries, courts commonly turn to the hypothetical monopsonist test. The hypothetical monopsonist test ensures that markets are not defined too narrowly, on the theory that if the test identifies substitute buyers for the product in question, such buyers should be included in the market. The hypothetical monopsonist test assumes that there is only one buyer in the proposed market and asks whether that hypothetical buyer, freed from price regulation, could profitably target a subset of sellers for price decreases. If such a hypothetical monopsonist could profitably impose what economists call a small but significant and non-transitory decrease in price of at least five percent in the proposed market, that indicates the existence of a relevant market. [. . .]

[23] The government's expert, Dr. Hill, estimated what "actual diversions" would be for the defined market, i.e., the percentage of authors who would switch to self-publishing in the face of a small but significant and non-transitory decrease in advances paid for anticipated top-selling books. He found that even if some small number of authors switched to self-publishing, it would be profitable for publishers to decrease advances—that is, the defection of authors in response to the lowered advances would be far less than what would be necessary to make the decrease unprofitable.

[24] The defendants do not dispute that the relevant market of "publishing rights to anticipated top-selling books" passes the hypothetical monopsonist test. [. . .]

2. Bundle and Cluster Markets

There is some confusion and inconsistency in the literature and in court practice regarding the use of the terms "bundle" and "cluster" in market definition.[212] Following the example of Krisha Cerilli and others, we apply the following usage: "bundle" markets are used where purchasers demand a product or service composed of multiple components; "cluster" markets are a shorthand way of analyzing many individual markets at once on the basis that competitive conditions and effects are identical in each one.

Krisha A. Cerilli, Staples/Office Depot: Clarifying Cluster Markets
Comp. Pol'y Int'l (Aug. 2016)

[Certain] cases involve "hundreds if not thousands" of distinct product markets. In [*ProMedica Health System, Inc. v. FTC*, 749 F.3d 559 (6th Cir. 2014)], for instance, which involved a hospital merger, the merging hospitals offered hundreds of distinct medical procedures that were not functionally interchangeable (*e.g.*, chemotherapy is not a substitute for a hip replacement). Each distinct procedure therefore could be assessed as a distinct relevant market. But, as the court observed, it would be administratively burdensome to evaluate each of the hundreds of markets separately.

That is where the cluster market concept arises. *ProMedica* endorsed the concept of aggregating the distinct relevant markets together into a single "cluster" for analytical convenience. Such aggregation is permissible, the court held, when the competitive conditions in the separate markets are similar.

ProMedica is not the first or only case to endorse the concept of a cluster market based on analytical convenience. The concept has origins in the Supreme Court's landmark decision in *Brown Shoe Co. v. United States*. In *Brown Shoe*, the Court first observed that the "outer boundaries" of a relevant product market are determined by evaluating the scope of reasonable substitutes. But the Court then endorsed evaluating the markets for men's, women's and children's shoes together (even though distinct shoe sizes and types were not substitutes) because the competitive conditions for each market were similar. More recently, the cluster market approach has become a common feature of hospital merger cases. [. . .]

In [other cases], distinct product markets [are] not being aggregated for analytical convenience (as in *ProMedica*). Rather, there [is] a single market in which customers purchase[] a bundle or package of goods. *ProMedica* referred to this latter scenario as a "package-deal" approach, and explained that it can arise when customers value the convenience of purchasing certain items together, as a package. Another useful description is that the latter approach represents a bundle market.

a) Bundle Markets

In some cases, market demand is not really for a series of individual components, but for a "bundle" of multiple products and services delivered together. A good example is provided by the monopolization case against Grinnell. Grinnell had engaged in a series of acquisitions and practices that, the Justice Department alleged, had the object and effect of monopolizing a market for a bundle of "central station services": burglar alarm services, fire alarm services, and so on. Crucially, the Court held that these were not distinct markets that could be aggregated for shorthand purposes: they were components of a single integrated market for the entire package or bundle of services.

United States v. Grinnell Corp.
384 U.S. 563 (1966)

Justice Douglas.

[1] In the present case, [Grinnell's control over] 87% of the accredited central station service business leaves no doubt that the congeries of these defendants have monopoly power—power which, as our discussion of the record

---

[212] *See, e.g.*, Sharif Pharmacy, Inc. v. Prime Therapeutics, LLC, 950 F.3d 911, 918 (7th Cir. 2020) (using the terms indiscriminately).

indicates, they did not hesitate to wield—if that business is the relevant market. The only remaining question therefore is, what is the relevant market?

[2] In case of a product it may be of such a character that substitute products must also be considered, as customers may turn to them if there is a slight increase in the price of the main product. That is the teaching of the *du Pont* [*i.e.*, Cellophane] case, viz., that commodities reasonably interchangeable make up that "part" of trade or commerce which s 2 protects against monopoly power.

[3] The District Court treated the entire accredited central station service business as a single market and we think it was justified in so doing. Defendants argue that the different central station services offered are so diverse that they cannot under *du Pont* be lumped together to make up the relevant market. For example, burglar alarm services are not interchangeable with fire alarm services. They further urge that du Pont requires that protective services other than those of the central station variety be included in the market definition.

[4] But there is here a single use, *i.e.*, the protection of property, through a central station that receives signals. It is that service, accredited, that is unique and that competes with all the other forms of property protection. We see no barrier to combining in a single market a number of different products or services where that combination reflects commercial realities. To repeat, there is here a single basic service—the protection of property through use of a central service station—that must be compared with all other forms of property protection. [. . .]

[5] The defendants have not made out a case for fragmentizing the types of services into lesser units.

[6] Burglar alarm service is in a sense different from fire alarm service; from waterflow alarms; and so on. But it would be unrealistic on this record to break down the market into the various kinds of central station protective services that are available. Central station companies recognize that to compete effectively, they must offer all or nearly all types of service. The different forms of accredited central station service are provided from a single office and customers utilize different services in combination. We held in *United States v. Philadelphia Nat. Bank*, 374 U.S. 321, 356 [(1963)] that "the cluster" of services denoted by the term "commercial banking" is "a distinct line of commerce." . . . In our view the lumping together of various kinds of services makes for the appropriate market here as it did in the s 7 case.

[7] There are, to be sure, substitutes for the accredited central station service. But none of them appears to operate on the same level as the central station service so as to meet the interchangeability test of the *du Pont* case. Nonautomatic and automatic local alarm systems appear on this record to have marked differences, not the low degree of differentiation required of substitute services as well as substitute articles.

[8] Watchman service is far more costly and less reliable. Systems that set off an audible alarm at the site of a fire or burglary are cheaper but often less reliable. They may be inoperable without anyone's knowing it. Moreover, there is a risk that the local ringing of an alarm will not attract the needed attention and help. Proprietary systems that a customer purchases and operates are available; but they can be used only by a very large business or by government and are not realistic alternatives for most concerns. There are also protective services connected directly to a municipal police or fire department. But most cities with an accredited central station do not permit direct, connected service for private businesses. These alternate services and devices differ, we are told, in utility, efficiency, reliability, responsiveness, and continuity, and the record sustains that position. And, as noted, insurance companies generally allow a greater reduction in premiums for accredited central station service than for other types of protection.

[9] Defendants earnestly urge that despite these differences, they face competition from these other modes of protection. . . . What defendants overlook is that the high degree of differentiation between central station protection and the other forms means that for many customers, only central station protection will do. Though some customers may be willing to accept higher insurance rates in favor of cheaper forms of protection, others will not be willing or able to risk serious interruption to their businesses, even though covered by insurance, and will thus be unwilling to consider anything but central station protection.

* * *

The bundle market concept is one way of understanding the court's analysis in the first Staples / Office Depot challenge. In 1996, the office superstore Staples attempted to acquire its competitor Office Depot. The merging parties argued to the FTC, and subsequently to the district court, that there was no risk that the merged firm would acquire market power in markets for pens and post-it notes. But the FTC and Judge Hogan took a different view. As the following extract demonstrates, market definition in this case raised a number of complex issues. This extract makes use of the "submarket" concept: again, you can read that word as a synonym for "market."[213]

FTC v. Staples, Inc. (Staples / Office Depot I)
970 F. Supp. 1066 (D.D.C. 1997)

Judge Hogan.

[1] Defendants are both corporations which sell office products—including office supplies, business machines, computers and furniture—through retail stores, commonly described as office supply superstores, as well as through direct mail delivery and contract stationer operations. Staples is the second largest office superstore chain in the United States with approximately 550 retail stores located in 28 states and the District of Columbia, primarily in the Northeast and California. In 1996 Staples' revenues from those stores were approximately $4 billion through all operations. Office Depot, the largest office superstore chain, operates over 500 retail office supply superstores that are located in 38 states and the District of Columbia, primarily in the South and Midwest. Office Depot's 1996 sales were approximately $6.1 billion. OfficeMax, Inc., is the only other office supply superstore firm in the United States. [. . .]

[2] [T]he Commission and the defendants sharply disagree with respect to the appropriate definition of the relevant product market or line of commerce. As with many antitrust cases, the definition of the relevant product market in this case is crucial. In fact, to a great extent, this case hinges on the proper definition of the relevant product market.

[3] The Commission defines the relevant product market as "the sale of consumable office supplies through office superstores," with "consumable" meaning products that consumers buy recurrently, *i.e.*, items which "get used up" or discarded. For example, under the Commission's definition, "consumable office supplies" would not include capital goods such as computers, fax machines, and other business machines or office furniture, but does include such products as paper, pens, file folders, post-it notes, computer disks, and toner cartridges. The defendants characterize the FTC's product market definition as "contrived" with no basis in law or fact, and counter that the appropriate product market within which to assess the likely competitive consequences of a Staples-Office Depot combination is simply the overall sale of office products, of which a combined Staples-Office Depot accounted for 5.5% of total sales in North America in 1996. In addition, the defendants argue that the challenged combination is not likely "substantially to lessen competition" however the product market is defined. After considering the arguments on both sides and all of the evidence in this case and making evaluations of each witness's credibility as well as the weight that the Court should give certain evidence and testimony, the Court finds that the appropriate relevant product market definition in this case is, as the Commission has argued, the sale of consumable office supplies through office supply superstores.

[4] The general rule when determining a relevant product market is that the outer boundaries of a product market are determined by the reasonable interchangeability of use by consumers or the cross-elasticity of demand between the product itself and substitutes for it. Interchangeability of use and cross-elasticity of demand look to the availability of substitute commodities, i.e. whether there are other products offered to consumers which are similar in character or use to the product or products in question, as well as how far buyers will go to substitute one commodity for another. In other words, the general question is whether two products can be used for the same purpose, and if so, whether and to what extent purchasers are willing to substitute one for the other.

[5] Whether there are other products available to consumers which are similar in character or use to the products in question may be termed "functional interchangeability." The consumable office products at issue here are identical whether they are sold by Staples or Office Depot or another seller of office supplies. A legal pad sold by

---

Staples or Office Depot is "functionally interchangeable" with a legal pad sold by Wal-Mart. A post-it note sold by Staples or Office Depot is "functionally interchangeable" with a post-it note sold by Viking or Quill. A computer disk sold by Staples-Office Depot is "functionally interchangeable" with a computer disk sold by CompUSA. No one disputes the functional interchangeability of consumable office supplies. However, as the government has argued, functional interchangeability should not end the Court's analysis. [. . .]

[6] The Court recognizes that it is difficult to overcome the first blush or initial gut reaction of many people to the definition of the relevant product market as the sale of consumable office supplies through office supply superstores. The products in question are undeniably the same no matter who sells them, and no one denies that many different types of retailers sell these products. After all, a combined Staples-Office Depot would only have a 5.5% share of the overall market in consumable office supplies. Therefore, it is logical to conclude that, of course, all these retailers compete, and that if a combined Staples-Office Depot raised prices after the merger, or at least did not lower them as much as they would have as separate companies, that consumers, with such a plethora of options, would shop elsewhere. [. . .]

[7] The [Supreme] Court in *Brown Shoe* provided a series of factors or "practical indicia" for determining whether a submarket exists including "industry or public recognition of the submarket as a separate economic entity, the product's peculiar characteristics and uses, unique production facilities, distinct customers, distinct prices, sensitivity to price changes, and specialized vendors." Since the Court described these factors as "practical indicia" rather than requirements, subsequent cases have found that submarkets can exist even if only some of these factors are present. . . .

[8] . . . [T]he FTC focused on what it termed the "pricing evidence," which the Court finds corresponds with *Brown Shoe*'s "sensitivity to price changes" factor. First, the FTC presented evidence comparing Staples' prices in geographic markets where Staples is the only office superstore, to markets where Staples competes with Office Depot or OfficeMax, or both. Based on the FTC's calculations, in markets where Staples faces no office superstore competition at all, something which was termed a one firm market during the hearing, prices are 13% higher than in three firm markets where it competes with both Office Depot and OfficeMax. The data which underly this conclusion make it compelling evidence. Prices were compared as of January 1997, which, admittedly, only provides data for one specific point in time. However, rather than comparing prices from only a small sampling or "basket" of goods, the FTC used an office supply sample accounting for 90% of Staples' sales and comprised of both price sensitive and non price sensitive items. The FTC presented similar evidence based on Office Depot's prices of a sample of 500 items, also as of January 1997. Similarly, the evidence showed that Office Depot's prices are significantly higher—well over 5% higher, in Depot-only markets than they are in three firm markets.

[9] Other pricing evidence presented by the FTC is less convincing on its own, due to limitations in the underlying data. For example, relatively small samplings or "baskets" of goods may have been used or it may not be clear how many stock keeping units ("SKUs") of supplies were included. For example, the FTC also presented evidence comparing Staples' prices in Staples-only markets with Staples' prices in three-firm markets for four different time periods, August 1994, January 1995, August 1995, and May 1996. The result is startlingly similar to that found in the first two examples. Where Staples does not compete with other office superstores, it charges prices well over 5% higher than where it does so compete. While having the advantage of showing a trend over time, the Court recognizes that this evidence has some problems. These particular calculations were made based on a "basket" or sample of supplies comprised of supplies used by Staples to price check against Office Depot. The number of SKUs in the sample was not provided to the Court, and it appears that the components of the baskets may have changed over time. Therefore, the Court would not give much weight to this evidence standing alone. However, since additional evidence supports the same conclusion, the Court credits this evidence as confirmation of the general pricing trend.

[10] The FTC also pointed to internal Staples documents which present price comparisons between Staples' prices and Office Depot's prices and Staples' prices and OfficeMax's prices within different price zones. The comparisons between Staples and Office Depot were made in August 1994, January 1995, August 1995, and May 1996. Staples' prices were compared with OfficeMax's prices in August 1994, July 1995, and January 1996. For each comparison, Staples calculations were based on a fairly large "basket" or sample of goods, approximately 2000 SKUs containing both price sensitive and non-price sensitive items. Using Staples' data, but organizing it

differently to show which of those zones were one, two, or three firm markets, the FTC showed once again that Staples charges significantly higher prices, more than 5% higher, where it has no office superstore competition than where it competes with the two other superstores.

[11] The FTC offered similar price comparison evidence for Office Depot, comparing Office Depot's prices across Staples' zones. The comparisons were made in August 1994, January 1995, August 1995, and May 1996. Again, a large sample, approximately 2000 SKUs, was considered. The results of this analysis are slightly less favorable to the FTC's position. Price differentials are significantly smaller and there are even a few instances where Office Depot's prices appear to be higher in one of its three firm markets than prices in its two firm markets and at least one point where prices in one of the Depot-only zones were lower than prices in one of the three firm markets. On average, however, this evidence shows that Office Depot's prices are highest in its one firm markets, and lowest in its three firm markets.

[12] This evidence all suggests that office superstore prices are affected primarily by other office superstores and not by non-superstore competitors such as mass merchandisers like Wal–Mart, Kmart, or Target, wholesale clubs such as BJ's, Sam's, and Price Costco, computer or electronic stores such as Computer City and Best Buy, independent retail office supply stores, mail orders firms like Quill and Viking, and contract stationers. Though the FTC did not present the Court with evidence regarding the precise amount of non-superstore competition in each of Staples' and Office Depot's one, two, and three firm markets, it is clear to the Court that these competitors, albeit in different combinations and concentrations, are present in every one of these markets. For example, it is a certainty that the mail order competitors compete in all of the geographic markets at issue in this case. Office products are available through the mail in all 50 states, and have been for approximately 30 years. Despite this mail order competition, however, Staples and Office Depot are still able to charge higher prices in their one firm markets than they do in the two firm markets and the three firm markets without losing a significant number of customers to the mail order firms. [. . .]

[13] The Court has observed that office supply superstores look far different from other sellers of office supplies. Office supply superstores are high volume, discount office supply chain stores averaging in excess of 20,000 square feet, with over 11,000 of those square feet devoted to traditional office supplies, and carrying over 5,000 SKUs of consumable office supplies in addition to computers, office furniture, and other non-consumables. In contrast, stores such as Kmart devote approximately 210 square feet to the sale of approximately 250 SKUs of consumable office supplies. . . .

[14] In addition to the differences in SKU numbers and variety, the superstores are different from many other sellers of office supplies due to the type of customer they target and attract. The superstores' customer base overwhelmingly consists of small businesses with fewer than 20 employees and consumers with home offices. In contrast, mail order customers are typically mid-sized companies with more than 20 employees. Another example is contract stationers who focus on serving customers with more than 100 employees. . . .

[15] It is difficult to fully articulate and explain all of the ways in which superstores are unique. As the plaintiff and defendant requested, the Court viewed some of the various sellers of office supplies located in the Rockville, Maryland area, including Staples, Office Depot, CompUSA, Best Buy, CVS, Kmart, Giant Food, and Wal–Mart. Based on the Court's observations, the Court finds that the unique combination of size, selection, depth and breadth of inventory offered by the superstores distinguishes them from other retailers. Other retailers devote only a fraction of their square footage to office supplies as opposed to Staples or Office Depot. The evidence shows that the typical club, mass merchant, or computer store offers only 210 to 2000 square feet of office supplies, compared to over 11,182 square feet at a typical Staples. This was evident to the Court when visiting the various stores. Superstores are simply different in scale and appearance from the other retailers. No one entering a Wal–Mart would mistake it for an office superstore. No one entering Staples or Office Depot would mistakenly think he or she was in Best Buy or CompUSA. You certainly know an office superstore when you see one. [. . .]

[16] When assessing key trends and making long range plans, Staples and Office Depot focus on the plans of other superstores. In addition, when determining whether to enter a new metropolitan area, both Staples and Office Depot evaluate the extent of office superstore competition in the market and the number of office superstores the market can support. When selecting sites and markets for new store openings, defendants repeatedly refer to

markets without office superstores as "non-competitive," even when the new store is adjacent to or near a warehouse club, consumer electronics store, or a mass merchandiser such as Wal–Mart. In a monthly report entitled "Competitor Store Opening/Closing Report" which Office Depot circulates to its Executive Committee, Office Depot notes all competitor store closings and openings, but the only competitors referred to for its United States stores are Staples and OfficeMax.

b) Cluster Markets

A "cluster market" is really a number of distinct markets, described together for ease of discussion on the basis that competitive conditions and effects in those markets are, in relevant respects, identical.[214]

One commonly encountered cluster market is "the" market for "general acute care" services seen in many hospital cases. When two hospitals merge, the transaction can affect competition in multiple different service lines offered by the two hospitals: gastroenterologic care and orthopedic care, for example. These services do not compete with each other and so fall into separate markets for antitrust purposes. However, when conducting the analysis, it is often the case that many of these markets will involve the same competing hospitals, in the same respective competitive positions, and likely to be affected by the transaction in the same way. As a result, agencies and courts may use the term "general acute care market," or just GAC, as a shorthand for all these individual markets at once. (In fact, the market will usually be general acute care services *to a particular subset of purchasers*, reflecting the difference between commercial payors and government payors.[215])

Here's this concept in action in a hospital merger case.

ProMedica Health Sys., Inc. v. FTC
749 F.3d 559 (6th Cir. 2014)

Judge Kethledge.

[1] Often, the first steps in analyzing a merger's competitive effects are to define the geographic and product markets affected by it. Here, the parties agree that the relevant geographic market is Lucas County. The relevant product market or markets, however, are more difficult. The first principle of market definition is substitutability: a relevant product market must "identify a set of products that are reasonably interchangeable[.]" Horizontal Merger Guidelines § 4.1. Chevrolets and Fords might be interchangeable in this sense, but Chevrolets and Lamborghinis are probably not. The general question is whether two products can be used for the same purpose, and if so, whether and to what extent purchasers are willing to substitute one for the other.

[2] By this measure, each individual medical procedure could give rise to a separate market: if you need your hip replaced, you can't decide to have chemotherapy instead. But nobody advocates that we analyze the effects of this merger upon hundreds if not thousands of markets for individual procedures; instead, the parties agree that we should "cluster" these markets somehow. The parties disagree, however, on the principles that should govern which services are clustered and which are not.

[3] Two theories of clustering are pertinent here. The first—which the FTC advocates and the Commission adopted—is the "administrative-convenience" theory. (A better name might be the "similar-conditions" theory.) This theory holds, in essence, that there is no need to perform separate antitrust analyses for separate product markets when competitive conditions are similar for each. In *Brown Shoe*, for example, the Supreme Court analyzed together the markets for men's, women's, and children's shoes, because the competitive conditions for each of them were similar. [. . .]

[4] Here, the Commission applied this theory to cluster both primary services (but excluding OB [*i.e.*, obstetrical services], for reasons discussed below) and secondary services for purposes of analyzing the merger's competitive

---

[214] *See, e.g.*, Brown Shoe Co. v. United States, 370 U.S. 294, 327–28 (1962) (applying cluster market analysis and refusing to consider competition in narrower categories because, "whether [such categories are] considered separately or together, the picture of this merger is the same").

[215] *See, e.g.*, FTC v. Penn State Hershey Med. Ctr., 838 F.3d 327, 338 (3d Cir. 2016) ("The District Court found, and the parties stipulated, that the relevant product market is general acute care ("GAC") services *sold to commercial payors*.") (emphasis added).

effects. Substantial evidence supports that demarcation. The respective market shares for each of Lucas County's four hospital systems (ProMedica, Mercy, UTMC, St. Luke's) are similar across the range of primary and secondary services. A hospital's market share for shoulder surgery, for example, is similar to its market share for knee replacements. Barriers to entry are likewise similar across primary and secondary services. So are the services' respective geographic markets. Thus, the competitive conditions across the markets for primary and secondary services are similar enough to justify clustering those markets when analyzing the merger's competitive effects.

[5] But the same is not true for OB [*i.e.*, obstetric] services, whose competitive conditions differ in at least two respects from those for other services. First, before the merger, ProMedica's market share for OB services (71.2%) was more than half-again greater than its market share for primary and secondary services (46.8%). And the merger would drive ProMedica's share for OB services even higher, to 80.5%—no small number in this area of the law. Second, and relatedly, before the merger there were only three hospital systems that provided OB services in Lucas County (ProMedica, Mercy, St. Luke's) rather than four; after the merger, there would be only two. (One might also suspect that the geographic market for OB services is smaller than it is for other primary services—one can drive only so far when the baby is on the way—but the record is not clear on that point.) The Commission therefore flagged OB as a separate relevant market for purposes of analyzing the merger's competitive effects. For the reasons just stated, substantial evidence supports that decision. [. . .]

[6] The reference to demand-side considerations in § 4 of the Guidelines concerns the manner in which one defines a relevant market, not the conditions under which one can cluster admittedly different markets when analyzing a merger's competitive effects. The administrative-convenience theory asks a different question (whether the competitive conditions for two markets are similar enough to analyze them together) than the one answered by § 4 of the Guidelines (how one defines an individual market in the first place). . . . . . [. . .]

[7] The relevant markets, for purposes of analyzing the merger's competitive effects, are what the Commission says they are: (1) a cluster market of primary (but not OB) and secondary inpatient services (hereafter, the "GAC market"), and (2) a separate market for OB services.

3. Price-Discrimination Markets

Legal market definition is an exercise in line-drawing: some products or services are "in" the market, while others are "out." But, as we noted above, different buyers may have different perspectives on substitutability. Some customers—the inframarginal ones—might need, or highly value, a specific feature of a product or service, and so cannot turn to products or services that do not have such a feature, while others might not care about that feature at all and so enjoy a much wider range of substitutes.

When the group of inframarginal customers can be easily identified by the merged firm and targeted for some kind of adverse treatment (such as a price increase), then a court or agency might define a market around that group of customers. This is called a "price discrimination" or "targeted customer" market.

Horizontal Merger Guidelines § 4

4.1.4 Product Market Definition with Targeted Customers

[1] If a hypothetical monopolist could profitably target a subset of customers for price increases, the Agencies may identify relevant markets defined around those targeted customers, to whom a hypothetical monopolist would profitably and separately impose at least a SSNIP. Markets to serve targeted customers are also known as price discrimination markets. In practice, the Agencies identify price discrimination markets only where they believe there is a realistic prospect of an adverse competitive effect on a group of targeted customers.

Example 11: Glass containers have many uses. In response to a price increase for glass containers, some users would substitute substantially to plastic or metal containers, but baby food manufacturers would not. If a hypothetical monopolist could price separately and limit arbitrage, baby food manufacturers would be vulnerable to a targeted increase in the price of glass containers. The Agencies could define a distinct market for glass containers used to package baby food.

[2] The Agencies also often consider markets for targeted customers when prices are individually negotiated and suppliers have information about customers that would allow a hypothetical monopolist to identify customers that are likely to pay a higher price for the relevant product. If prices are negotiated individually with customers, the hypothetical monopolist test may suggest relevant markets that are as narrow as individual customers[.] Nonetheless, the Agencies often define markets for groups of targeted customers, i.e., by type of customer, rather than by individual customer. By so doing, the Agencies are able to rely on aggregated market shares that can be more helpful in predicting the competitive effects of the merger.

* * *

This concept is easier to state than it is to apply. In reality, *every* market has some marginal consumers and some inframarginal ones. So courts must often consider whether the inframarginal ones are sufficiently vulnerable— that is, inelastic and identifiable to the supplier—to justify the use of a price-discrimination market.[216]

In the following extract, the D.C. Circuit—faced with a challenge to the acquisition by the Whole Foods supermarket chain of its competitor Wild Oats—wrestles with the question of whether the right market definition is limited to "premium natural and organic supermarkets" or "PNOS." As the court recognizes, price discrimination can occur even when a store cannot literally identify its inframarginal customers as they walk through the door, simply by charging higher margins on the products that those inframarginal customers are focused on buying, and lower margins on the products for which the store faces more competition. (For more on the economics of price discrimination and its different forms, look back at Chapter II.)

FTC v. Whole Foods Market, Inc.
548 F.3d 1028 (D.C. Cir. 2008)

Judge Brown.

[1] A market must include all products reasonably interchangeable by consumers for the same purposes. Whether one product is reasonably interchangeable for another depends not only on the ease and speed with which customers can substitute it and the desirability of doing so, but also on the cost of substitution, which depends most sensitively on the price of the products. A broad market may also contain relevant submarkets which themselves constitute product markets for antitrust purposes. The boundaries of such a submarket may be determined by examining such practical indicia as industry or public recognition of the submarket as a separate economic entity, the product's peculiar characteristics and uses, unique production facilities, distinct customers, distinct prices, sensitivity to price changes, and specialized vendors.

[2] To facilitate this analysis, the Department of Justice and the FTC developed a technique called the SSNIP ("small but significant non-transitory increase in price") test, which both Dr. Murphy and Dr. Scheffman [*i.e.*, the experts retained by the FTC and the merging parties respectively] used. In the SSNIP method, one asks whether a hypothetical monopolist controlling all suppliers in the proposed market could profit from a small price increase. If a small price increase would drive consumers to an alternative product, then that product must be reasonably substitutable for those in the proposed market and must therefore be part of the market, properly defined.

[3] Experts for the two sides disagreed about how to do the SSNIP of the proposed PNOS ["premium natural and organic supermarkets"] market. Dr. Scheffman used a method called critical loss analysis, in which he predicted the loss that would result when marginal customers shifted purchases to conventional supermarkets in response to a SSNIP. He concluded a hypothetical monopolist could not profit from a SSNIP, so that conventional supermarkets must be within the same market as PNOS. In contrast, Dr. Murphy disapproved of critical loss analysis generally, preferring a method called critical diversion that asked how many customers would be diverted to Whole Foods and how many to conventional supermarkets if a nearby Wild Oats closed. Whole Foods's internal planning documents indicated at least a majority of these customers would switch to Whole Foods, thus making the closure profitable for a hypothetical PNOS monopolist. One crucial difference between these approaches was

---

[216] *See, e.g.*, FTC v. Wilh. Wilhelmsen Holding ASA, 341 F. Supp. 3d 27, 51–57 (D.D.C. 2018) (defining market around global fleet customers in light of evidence that they constituted a distinct group with distinct needs and were vulnerable to price discrimination).

that Dr. Scheffman's analysis depended only on the marginal loss of sales, while Dr. Murphy's used the average loss of customers. Dr. Murphy explained that focusing on the average behavior of customers was appropriate because a core of committed customers would continue to shop at PNOS stores despite a SSNIP.

[4] In appropriate circumstances, core customers can be a proper subject of antitrust concern. In particular, when one or a few firms differentiate themselves by offering a particular package of goods or services, it is quite possible for there to be a central group of customers for whom only that package will do. What motivates antitrust concern for such customers is the possibility that fringe competition for individual products within a package may not protect customers who need the whole package from market power exercised by a sole supplier of the package.

[5] Such customers may be captive to the sole supplier, which can then, by means of price discrimination, extract monopoly profits from them while competing for the business of marginal customers. Not that prices that segregate core from marginal consumers are in themselves anticompetitive; such pricing simply indicates the existence of a submarket of core customers, operating in parallel with the broader market but featuring a different demand curve. Sometimes, for some customers a package provides access to certain products or services that would otherwise be unavailable to them. Because the core customers require the whole package, they respond differently to price increases from marginal customers who may obtain portions of the package elsewhere. Of course, core customers may constitute a submarket even without such an extreme difference in demand elasticity. After all, market definition focuses on what products are reasonably substitutable; what is reasonable must ultimately be determined by settled consumer preference.

[6] In short, a core group of particularly dedicated, "distinct customers," paying "distinct prices," may constitute a recognizable submarket, whether they are dedicated because they need a complete cluster of products, because their particular circumstances dictate that a product is the only realistic choice, or because they find a particular product uniquely attractive. For example, [in *FTC v. Staples, Inc.*, 970 F.Supp. 1066, 1078–79 (D.D.C. 1997)] the existence of core customers dedicated to office supply superstores, with their unique combination of size, selection, depth, and breadth of inventory, was an important factor distinguishing that submarket. As always in defining a market, we must take into account the realities of competition. We look to the *Brown Shoe* indicia, among which the economic criteria are primary.

[7] The FTC's evidence delineated a PNOS submarket catering to a core group of customers who have decided that natural and organic is important, [and a] lifestyle of health and ecological sustainability is important. It was undisputed that Whole Foods and Wild Oats provide higher levels of customer service than conventional supermarkets, a unique environment, and a particular focus on the core values these customers espoused. The FTC connected these intangible properties with concrete aspects of the PNOS model, such as a much larger selection of natural and organic products, and a much greater concentration of perishables than conventional supermarkets.

[8] Further, the FTC documented exactly the kind of price discrimination that enables a firm to profit from core customers for whom it is the sole supplier. Dr. Murphy compared the margins of Whole Foods stores in cities where they competed with Wild Oats. He found the presence of a Wild Oats depressed Whole Foods's margins significantly. Notably, while there was no effect on Whole Foods's margins in the product category of "groceries," where Whole Foods and Wild Oats compete on the margins with conventional supermarkets, the effect on margins for perishables was substantial. Confirming this price discrimination, Whole Foods's documents indicated that when it price-checked conventional supermarkets, the focus was overwhelmingly on "dry grocery," rather than on the perishables that were 70% of Whole Foods's business. Thus, in the high-quality perishables on which both Whole Foods and Wild Oats made most of their money, they competed directly with each other, and they competed with supermarkets only on the dry grocery items that were the fringes of their business.

[9] Additionally, the FTC provided direct evidence that PNOS competition had a greater effect than conventional supermarkets on PNOS prices. Dr. Murphy showed the opening of a new Whole Foods in the vicinity of a Wild Oats caused Wild Oats's prices to drop, while entry by non-PNOS stores had no such effect. Similarly, the opening of Earth Fare stores (another PNOS) near Whole Foods stores caused Whole Foods's prices to drop immediately. The price effect continued, while decreasing, until the Earth Fare stores were forced to close.

[10] Finally, evidence of consumer behavior supported the conclusion that PNOS serve a core consumer base. Whole Foods's internal projections, based on market experience, suggested that if a Wild Oats near a Whole Foods were to close, the majority (in some cases nearly all) of its customers would switch to the Whole Foods rather than to conventional supermarkets. Since Whole Foods's prices for perishables are higher than those of conventional supermarkets, such customers must not find shopping at the latter interchangeable with PNOS shopping. They are the core customers. Moreover, market research, including Dr. Scheffman's own studies, indicated 68% of Whole Foods customers are core customers who share the Whole Foods "core values."

[11] Against this conclusion the defendants posed evidence that customers "cross-shop" between PNOS and other stores and that Whole Foods and Wild Oats check the prices of conventional supermarkets. But the fact that PNOS and ordinary supermarkets are direct competitors in some submarkets is not the end of the inquiry. Of course customers cross-shop; PNOS carry comprehensive inventories. The fact that a customer might buy a stick of gum at a supermarket or at a convenience store does not mean there is no definable groceries market. Here, cross-shopping is entirely consistent with the existence of a core group of PNOS customers. Indeed, Dr. Murphy explained that Whole Foods competes actively with conventional supermarkets for dry groceries sales, even though it ignores their prices for high-quality perishables.

[12] In addition, the defendants relied on Dr. Scheffman's conclusion that there is no clearly definable core customer. However, this conclusion was inconsistent with Dr. Scheffman's own report and testimony. Market research had found that customers who shop at Whole Foods because they share the core values it champions constituted at least a majority of its customers. Moreover, Dr. Scheffman acknowledged there are core shoppers who will only buy organic and natural and for that reason go to Whole Foods or Wild Oats. He contended they could be ignored because the numbers are not substantial. Again, Dr. Scheffman's own market data undermined this assertion.

[13] In sum, the district court believed the antitrust laws are addressed only to marginal consumers. This was an error of law, because in some situations core consumers, demanding exclusively a particular product or package of products, distinguish a submarket. The FTC described the core PNOS customers, explained how PNOS cater to these customers, and showed these customers provided the bulk of PNOS's business. The FTC put forward economic evidence—which the district court ignored—showing directly how PNOS discriminate on price between their core and marginal customers, thus treating the former as a distinct market. Therefore, I cannot agree with the district court that the FTC would never be able to prove a PNOS submarket. This is not to say the FTC has in fact proved such a market, which is not necessary at this point. To obtain a preliminary injunction under [15 U.S.C.] § 53(b), the FTC need only show a likelihood of success sufficient . . . to balance any equities that might weigh against the injunction.

Judge Kavanaugh, dissenting.

[14] [T]he record evidence in this case does not show that Whole Foods changed its prices in any significant way in response to exit from an area by Wild Oats. In the four cases where Wild Oats exited and a Whole Foods store remained, there is no evidence in the record that Whole Foods then raised prices. Nor was there any evidence of price increases after Whole Foods took over two Wild Oats stores.

[15] In the absence of any evidence in the record that Whole Foods was able to (or did) set higher prices when Wild Oats exited or was absent, the District Court correctly concluded that Whole Foods competes in a market composed of all supermarkets, meaning that "all supermarkets" is the relevant product market and that the Whole Foods–Wild Oats merger will not substantially lessen competition in that product market.

[16] In addition to the all-but-dispositive price evidence, the District Court identified other factors further demonstrating that the relevant market consists of all supermarkets.

[17] The record shows that Whole Foods makes site selection decisions based on all supermarkets and checks prices against all supermarkets, not only so-called organic supermarkets. . . . The point here is simple: Whole Foods would not examine the locations of and price check conventional grocery stores if it were not a competitor of those stores. Whole Foods does not price check Sports Authority; Whole Foods does price check Safeway.

[18] The record also demonstrates that conventional supermarkets and so-called organic supermarkets are aggressively competing to attract customers from one another. . . . The record shows that Whole Foods has made progress: Most products that Whole Foods sells are not organic. Conversely, conventional supermarkets have shifted towards emphasizing fresh, natural and organic" products. Most of the major chains and others are expanding into private label organic and natural products.

[19] So the dividing line between "organic" and conventional supermarkets has blurred. As the District Court aptly put it, the train has already left the station. The convergence undermines the threshold premise of the FTC's case. This is an industry in transition, and Whole Foods has pioneered a product differentiation that in turn has caused other supermarket chains to update their offerings. These are not separate product markets; this is a market where all supermarkets including so-called organic supermarkets are clawing tooth and nail to differentiate themselves, beat the competition, and make money. [. . .]

[20] In an attempt to save its merger case . . . the FTC cites marginally relevant evidence and advances a scattershot of flawed arguments.

[21] First, the FTC says that so-called organic supermarkets like Whole Foods and Wild Oats constitute their own product market because they are characterized by factors that differentiate them from conventional supermarkets. Those factors include intangible qualities such as customer service and tangible factors such as a focus on perishables.

[22] This argument reflects the key error that permeates the FTC's approach to this case. Those factors demonstrate only product differentiation, and product differentiation does not mean different product markets. [. . .]

[23] The key to distinguishing product differentiation from separate product markets lies in price information. As Professors Areeda and Hovenkamp have stated, differentiated sellers generally compete with one another sufficiently that the prices of one are greatly constrained by the prices of others. . . . To distinguish differentiation from separate product markets, courts thus must ask whether one seller could maximize profit by charging "more than the competitive price without losing too much patronage to other sellers. Here, in other words, could so-called organic supermarkets maximize profit by charging more than a competitive price without losing too much patronage to conventional supermarkets? Based on the evidence regarding Whole Foods's pricing practices, the District Court correctly found that the answer to that question is no. So-called organic supermarkets are engaged in product differentiation; they do not constitute a product market separate from all supermarkets.

[24] Second, the FTC points to internal Whole Foods studies and other evidence showing that if a Wild Oats near a Whole Foods were to close, most of the Wild Oats customers would shift to Whole Foods. But that says nothing about whether Whole Foods could impose a five percent or more price increase and still retain those customers (and its other customers), which is the relevant antitrust question. In other words, the fact that many Wild Oats customers would shift to Whole Foods does not mean that those customers would stay with Whole Foods, as opposed to shifting to conventional supermarkets, if Whole Foods significantly raised its prices. And even if one could infer that all of those former Wild Oats customers would so prefer Whole Foods that they would shop there even in the face of significant price increases, that would not show whether Whole Foods could raise prices without driving out a sufficient number of other customers as to make the price increases unprofitable. In sum, this argument is a diversion from the economic analysis that must be conducted in antitrust cases like this. The District Court properly found that the expert evidence in the record leads to the conclusion that Whole Foods could not profitably impose such a significant price increase.

[25] Third, the FTC cites comments by Whole Foods CEO John Mackey as evidence that Whole Foods perceived Wild Oats to be a unique competitor. Even if Mackey's comments were directed only to Wild Oats, that would not be evidence that Whole Foods and Wild Oats are in their own product market separate from all other supermarkets. It just as readily suggests that Whole Foods and Wild Oats are two supermarkets that have similarly differentiated themselves from the rest of the market, such that Mackey would be especially pleased to see that competitor vanish. Beating the competition from similarly differentiated competitors in a product market is

ordinarily an entirely permissible competitive goal. Saying as much, as Mackey did here, does not mean that the similarly differentiated competitor is the only relevant competition in the marketplace. [. . .]

[26] The bottom line is that, as the District Court found, there is no evidence in the record suggesting that Whole Foods priced differently based on the presence or absence of a Wild Oats store in the area. That is a conspicuous— and all but dispositive—omission in . . . the FTC's case. [. . .]

[27] . . . [T]he Court's decision resuscitates the loose antitrust standards of *Brown Shoe Co. v. United States*, 370 U.S. 294 (1962), the 1960s-era relic. . . . This is a problem because *Brown Shoe*'s brand of free-wheeling antitrust analysis has not stood the test of time.

4. Platform and Zero-Price Markets

In principle, the standard, substitutability-based approach to market definition can be applied to platform markets—that is, markets involving services that connect, or facilitate interactions among, users or groups of users—just like any others. But in *Ohio v. American Express* the Supreme Court signaled a dramatic break with the substitutability principle. In short, American Express provided certain services to cardholders, and certain other services to merchants. Of course, those services were not substitutable for one another: and, thus, ordinarily they would be included in two different markets. But in a blockbuster decision that has been much criticized, the Court held that a *single* market should be defined to embrace both sides of the platform in a single antitrust market, announcing a rule that would apply prospectively to other "transaction platforms." This has left a sharp question about how far this departure from substitutability extends, in a digital economy full of multisided platform businesses.

The case involved a challenge to AmEx's "antisteering" rules, which prohibited merchants that accepted AmEx from nudging or "steering" consumers to use other (*i.e.*, non-AmEx) credit cards, even if those cards charged lower fees to the merchant. The government plaintiffs alleged that the antisteering rules unlawfully harmed price competition by chilling competition among credit cards, in violation of Section 1 of the Sherman Act, and pointed to evidence of increased merchant fees as evidence of harm. The Court set out its market definition analysis in the following terms.

Ohio v. American Express Co.
138 S.Ct. 2274 (2018)

Justice Thomas.

[1] Because legal presumptions that rest on formalistic distinctions rather than actual market realities are generally disfavored in antitrust law, courts usually cannot properly apply the rule of reason without an accurate definition of the relevant market. Without a definition of the market there is no way to measure the defendant's ability to lessen or destroy competition. Thus, the relevant market is defined as the area of effective competition. Typically this is the arena within which significant substitution in consumption or production occurs. But courts should combine different products or services into a single market when that combination reflects commercial realities.

[2] [C]redit-card networks are two-sided platforms. Due to indirect network effects [*i.e.*, the fact that the product becomes more attractive to one category of users (such as merchants) as the number or activity of another category of users (such as cardholding consumers) increases], two-sided platforms cannot raise prices on one side without risking a feedback loop of declining demand. And the fact that two-sided platforms charge one side a price that is below or above cost reflects differences in the two sides' demand elasticity, not market power or anticompetitive pricing. Price increases on one side of the platform likewise do not suggest anticompetitive effects without some evidence that they have increased the overall cost of the platform's services. Thus, courts must include both sides of the platform—merchants and cardholders—when defining the credit-card market.

[3] To be sure, it is not always necessary to consider both sides of a two-sided platform. A market should be treated as one sided when the impacts of indirect network effects and relative pricing in that market are minor. Newspapers that sell advertisements, for example, arguably operate a two-sided platform because the value of an advertisement

increases as more people read the newspaper. But in the newspaper-advertisement market, the indirect network effects operate in only one direction; newspaper readers are largely indifferent to the amount of advertising that a newspaper contains. Because of these weak indirect network effects, the market for newspaper advertising behaves much like a one-sided market and should be analyzed as such.

[4] But two-sided transaction platforms, like the credit-card market, are different. These platforms facilitate a single, simultaneous transaction between participants. For credit cards, the network can sell its services only if a merchant and cardholder both simultaneously choose to use the network. Thus, whenever a credit-card network sells one transaction's worth of card-acceptance services to a merchant it also must sell one transaction's worth of card-payment services to a cardholder. It cannot sell transaction services to either cardholders or merchants individually. To optimize sales, the network must find the balance of pricing that encourages the greatest number of matches between cardholders and merchants.

[5] Because they cannot make a sale unless both sides of the platform simultaneously agree to use their services, two-sided transaction platforms exhibit more pronounced indirect network effects and interconnected pricing and demand. Transaction platforms are thus better understood as supplying only one product—transactions. In the credit-card market, these transactions are jointly consumed by a cardholder, who uses the payment card to make a transaction, and a merchant, who accepts the payment card as a method of payment. Tellingly, credit cards determine their market share by measuring the volume of transactions they have sold.

[6] Evaluating both sides of a two-sided transaction platform is also necessary to accurately assess competition. Only other two-sided platforms can compete with a two-sided platform for transactions. A credit-card company that processed transactions for merchants, but that had no cardholders willing to use its card, could not compete with Amex. Only a company that had both cardholders and merchants willing to use its network could sell transactions and compete in the credit-card market. Similarly, if a merchant accepts the four major credit cards, but a cardholder only uses Visa or Amex, only those two cards can compete for the particular transaction. Thus, competition cannot be accurately assessed by looking at only one side of the platform in isolation.

[7] For all these reasons, in two-sided transaction markets, only one market should be defined. Any other analysis would lead to mistaken inferences of the kind that could chill the very conduct the antitrust laws are designed to protect. Accordingly, we will analyze the two-sided market for credit-card transactions as a whole to determine whether the plaintiffs have shown that Amex's antisteering provisions have anticompetitive effects.

Justice Breyer, with whom Justices Ginsburg, Sotomayor, and Kagan join, dissenting.

[8] [. . .] I recognize that properly defining a market is often a complex business. Once a court has identified the good or service directly restrained … it will sometimes add to the relevant market what economists call "substitutes": other goods or services that are reasonably substitutable for that good or service. The reason that substitutes are included in the relevant market is that they restrain a firm's ability to profitably raise prices, because customers will switch to the substitutes rather than pay the higher prices.

[9] But while the market includes substitutes, it does not include what economists call complements: goods or services that are used together with the restrained product, but that cannot be substituted for that product. An example of complements is gasoline and tires. A driver needs both gasoline and tires to drive, but they are not substitutes for each other, and so the sale price of tires does not check the ability of a gasoline firm (say a gasoline monopolist) to raise the price of gasoline above competitive levels. As a treatise on the subject states: "Grouping complementary goods into the same market" is "economic nonsense," and would "undermine the rationale for the policy against monopolization or collusion in the first place." 2B [Phillip Areeda & Herbert Hovenkamp, ANTITRUST LAW] ¶ 565a, at 431.

[10] Here, the relationship between merchant-related card services and shopper-related card services is primarily that of complements, not substitutes. Like gasoline and tires, both must be purchased for either to have value. Merchants upset about a price increase for merchant-related services cannot avoid that price increase by becoming cardholders, in the way that, say, a buyer of newspaper advertising can switch to television advertising or direct mail in response to a newspaper's advertising price increase. The two categories of services serve fundamentally different purposes. And so, also like gasoline and tires, it is difficult to see any way in which the price of shopper-

related services could act as a check on the card firm's sale price of merchant-related services. If anything, a lower price of shopper-related card services is likely to cause more shoppers to use the card, and increased shopper popularity should make it easier for a card firm to raise prices to merchants, not harder, as would be the case if the services were substitutes. Thus, unless there is something unusual about this case . . . there is no justification for treating shopper-related services and merchant-related services as if they were part of a single market, at least not at step 1 of the rule of reason. [. . .]

[11] Missing from the majority's analysis is any explanation as to why, given the purposes that market definition serves in antitrust law, the fact that a credit-card firm can be said to operate a "two-sided transaction platform" means that its merchant-related and shopper-related services should be combined into a single market. The phrase "two-sided transaction platform" is not one of antitrust art—I can find no case from this Court using those words. The majority defines the phrase as covering a business that "offers different products or services to two different groups who both depend on the platform to intermediate between them," where the business "cannot make a sale to one side of the platform without simultaneously making a sale to the other" side of the platform. I take from that definition that there are four relevant features of such businesses on the majority's account: they (1) offer different products or services, (2) to different groups of customers, (3) whom the "platform" connects, (4) in simultaneous transactions.

[12] What is it about businesses with those four features that the majority thinks justifies a special market-definition approach for them? It cannot be the first two features—that the company sells different products to different groups of customers. Companies that sell multiple products to multiple types of customers are commonplace. A firm might mine for gold, which it refines and sells both to dentists in the form of fillings and to investors in the form of ingots. Or, a firm might drill for both oil and natural gas. Or a firm might make both ignition switches inserted into auto bodies and tires used for cars. I have already explained that, ordinarily, antitrust law will not group the two nonsubstitutable products together for step 1 purposes.

[13] Neither should it normally matter whether a company sells related, or complementary, products, i.e., products which must both be purchased to have any function, such as ignition switches and tires, or cameras and film. It is well established that an antitrust court in such cases looks at the product where the attacked restraint has an anticompetitive effect. The court does not combine the customers for the separate, nonsubstitutable goods and see if "overall" the restraint has a negative effect. That is because, as I have explained, the complementary relationship between the products is irrelevant to the purposes of market-definition.

[14] . . . The relevant question is whether merchant-related and shopper-related services are substitutes, one for the other, so that customers can respond to a price increase for one service by switching to the other service. As I have explained, the two types of services are not substitutes in this way. And so the question remains, just as before: What is it about the economic relationship between merchant-related and shopper-related services that would justify the majority's novel approach to market definition?

[15] What about the last two features—that the company connects the two groups of customers to each other, in simultaneous transactions? That, too, is commonplace. Consider a farmers' market. It brings local farmers and local shoppers together, and transactions will occur only if a farmer and a shopper simultaneously agree to engage in one. Should courts abandon their ordinary step 1 inquiry if several competing farmers' markets in a city agree that only certain kinds of farmers can participate, or if a farmers' market charges a higher fee than its competitors do and prohibits participating farmers from raising their prices to cover it? Why? If farmers' markets are special, what about travel agents that connect airlines and passengers? What about internet retailers, who, in addition to selling their own goods, allow (for a fee) other goods-producers to sell over their networks? Each of those businesses seems to meet the majority's four-prong definition.

[16] Apparently as its justification for applying a special market-definition rule to "two-sided transaction platforms," the majority explains that such platforms "often exhibit" what it calls "indirect network effects." By this, the majority means that sales of merchant-related card services and (different) shopper-related card services are interconnected, in that increased merchant-buyers mean increased shopper-buyers (the more stores in the card's network, the more customers likely to use the card), and vice versa. But this, too, is commonplace. Consider, again, a farmers' market. The more farmers that participate (within physical and esthetic limits), the more

customers the market will likely attract, and vice versa. So too with travel agents: the more airlines whose tickets a travel agent sells, the more potential passengers will likely use that travel agent, and the more potential passengers that use the travel agent, the easier it will likely be to convince airlines to sell through the travel agent. And so forth. Nothing in antitrust law, to my knowledge, suggests that a court, when presented with an agreement that restricts competition in any one of the markets my examples suggest, should abandon traditional market-definition approaches and include in the relevant market services that are complements, not substitutes, of the restrained good.

CASENOTE: United States v. Sabre Corp.
452 F. Supp. 3d 97 (D. Del. 2020) (vacated as moot)

The *AmEx* decision was huge news (by antitrust standards) and has spawned a healthy literature.[217] And it wasn't long until a district court relied on *AmEx*—in the 2020 *Sabre* decision—to reach a surprising conclusion. The *Sabre* decision itself was vacated for mootness, but it stands as an excellent example of how a lower court might understand and apply the central logic of *AmEx*.

In *Sabre*, the court considered DOJ's challenge to a proposed merger between Sabre, a two-sided "global distribution system" ("GDS") platform that connects airlines with travel agents, and Farelogix, a business that supplied IT services to airlines that the airlines used to deal in various ways with travel agents, including to receive and process orders. Unlike Sabre, Farelogix did not deal directly with travel agents: Judge Stark of the U.S. District Court for the District of Delaware had to decide whether and how, after *AmEx*, this fact affected the merger analysis.

The court made extensive findings of fact suggestive of competition between the parties. A "preponderance of the evidence shows that Sabre and Farelogix do view each other as competitors," the court held, "although only in a limited fashion." "The record reflects competition between Sabre's and Farelogix's direct connect solutions for major airlines." Among other things, the parties "competed to provide an NDC direct connect platform" to one customer; "Sabre viewed Farelogix as its 'main competitor' for [another] opportunity." The parties' services also directly overlapped: "Sabre and Farelogix each allow airlines to send their offers to travel agencies, process orders or bookings, and service those orders." And Farelogix identified Sabre as a "key competitor" in order delivery and offer management. Airlines appeared to share this perspective: some airlines considered Sabre's and Farelogix products as "partial substitute[s]" for one another. American Airlines described Farelogix's product as "a low cost substitute for GDSs" like Sabre, while a United employee testified that Farelogix was the "only alternative" to GDSs as a means of reaching U.S. travel agencies. And so on.

And yet, despite concluding that the parties *did* compete with one another in fact, the court held that *AmEx* required the conclusion that they did *not* compete with one another as a matter of law. The court held: "DOJ cannot prevail on its claim as a matter of law. Only other two-sided platforms can compete with a two-sided platform for transactions, and Farelogix is not a two-sided platform, as even DOJ concedes. Even if it is not always necessary to consider both sides of a two-sided transaction platform, it is necessary to do so where, as here, both sides of Sabre's GDS platform facilitate a single, simultaneous transaction between participants. Airlines on one side of Sabre's GDS cannot make a sale to travel agencies on the other side of the GDS unless both sides of the platform simultaneously agree to use Sabre's GDS services. This is a requirement in order for Sabre's GDS to provide its product: transactions." Even if this were not the case, the court added, DOJ had failed to evaluate the other side of the Sabre GDS. DOJ's evidence had focused on the travel-agency side of the Sabre platform, and could not constitute an "accurate assessment of competitive effects" in the absence of airline-side effects evidence as well.

---

[217] *See, e.g.*, Steven C. Salop, Daniel Francis, Lauren Sillman & Michaela Spero, *Rebuilding Platform Antitrust: Moving On from Ohio v. American Express Co.*, 84 Antitrust L.J. 883 (2022); Michael L. Katz & A. Douglas Melamed, *Competition Law as Common Law: American Express and the Evolution of Antitrust*, 168 U. Pa. L. Rev. 2061 (2020); Dennis W. Carlton, *The Anticompetitive Effects of Vertical Most-Favored-Nation Restraints and the Error of American Express*, 2019 Colum. Bus. L. Rev. 93 (2019); Erik Hovenkamp, *Platform Antitrust*, 44 J. Corp. L. 713 (2019); Michael Katz & Jonathan Sallet, *Multisided Platforms and Antitrust Enforcement*, 127 Yale L.J. 2142 (2018).

> This decision was mooted, and subsequently vacated, when the parties abandoned the deal after a challenge from the U.K. competition agency. Do you agree with Judge Stark's reading of *AmEx*?

$* * *$

Platform business models often involve the provision of products or services at zero (or even negative) prices: for example, users may receive email, search, and personal social networking services for free because those platforms are supported by advertising. The existence of such "zero-price" products poses an obvious challenge for SSNIP-based versions of the HMT: how can you assess the impact of a hypothetical 5–10% price increase on a \$0 price?[218] To respond to this problem, some have proposed alternatives, such as the use of a "small but significant non-transitory decrease in quality" ("SSNDQ") test for applying the HMT to such markets.[219] What advantages—and what challenges—would such an approach present? A number of antitrust investigations have concerned competition in zero-price markets: agencies and courts have indicated that the antitrust laws apply fully in such markets despite the lack of a traditional price.[220]

NOTES

1) To what extent do the categories of "special" market definition you have seen—buyer, cluster, bundle, price discrimination, and platform—undermine or qualify the principle of demand-side substitutability as the key to market definition? What, if anything, would be a better key to the concept of market definition?

2) A significant area of antitrust policy attention today is labor monopsony: in particular, whether antitrust enforcement and doctrine have failed to challenge practices and transactions that create or augment buyer-side market power in markets for labor. *See, e.g.*, Eric A. Posner, HOW ANTITRUST FAILED WORKERS (2021). How might you go about defining a labor market? What evidence would you use to prove its scope and the shares of participants?

3) What is the point of using a cluster market definition?

4) The *Sabre* opinion is notable, among other things, for acknowledging that the parties considered each other to be competitors but holding that they were not competitors for the purposes of antitrust law. When and why do you think antitrust courts should defer to the ordinary-course views of market participants, assuming that their documents express a consistent view? When and why do you think that antitrust courts should conclude that they "know better," in a relevant sense, than the market participants do?

5) How would you characterize the *Whole Foods* majority's views of when a price-discrimination market is appropriate? What other kinds of businesses would be able to discriminate in a similar fashion?

6) The price-discrimination market definition rule could, in principle, lead to very small markets. As technological and commercial developments make it easier to personalize terms of dealing with individual customers, price discrimination may be getting easier in some markets. Does this technological change matter for the development of antitrust doctrine?[221]

7) In *AmEx* the Court noted that there are close relationships between activities on the various sides of a platform business, and cited this fact as a reason to deviate from ordinary market-definition principles. But *many* markets are connected by close relationships: for example, markets that are upstream or downstream of one another, or markets for products and services that are complementary. For example, if dinner knives become cheaper, demand for dinner forks will increase. Should we consider applying the *AmEx* approach to other cases of "closely related" markets? What would be the consequences of broadening antitrust markets in this way?

---

[218] *See, e.g.*, John M. Newman, *Antitrust in Zero-Price Markets: Applications*, 94 Wash. U. L. Rev. 49, 64–65 (2016).

[219] Daniel Mandrescu, *The SSNIP Test and Zero-Pricing Strategies: Considerations for Online Platforms*, 2 Eur. Comp. & Reg. L. Rev. 244 (2018); Note by the European Union, *Quality Considerations in the Zero-Price Economy*, https://one.oecd.org/document/DAF/COMP/WD(2018)135/en/pdf (Nov. 28, 2018) ¶ 22.

[220] *See, e.g.*, FTC v. Facebook, Inc., Case No. 20-3590, 2022 WL 103308 (D.D.C. Jan. 11, 2022) (personal social networking services); Statement of Commissioner Ohlhausen, Commissioner Wright, and Commissioner McSweeny Concerning Zillow, Inc./Trulia, Inc., FTC File No. 141-0214 (February 19, 2015) (describing FTC analysis of possible harm on zero-priced side of real estate platform).

[221] *Compare* Jerry A. Hausman, Gregory K. Leonard & Christopher A. Vellturo, *Market Definition Under Price Discrimination*, 64 Antitrust L.J. 367 (1996) (noting some practical problems in achieving price discrimination) *with* Background Note by the OECD Secretariat, *Personalized Pricing in the Digital Era* (Nov. 28, 2018), https://www.justice.gov/atr/page/file/1312741/download (reviewing issues of technology and policy relating to personalized pricing in a digital economy).

D. Geographic Market Definition

In some cases, geography is an important dimension of competition and thus an important aspect of market definition. Some products are difficult, dangerous, or expensive to transport, meaning that purchasers may strongly prefer a local supplier. Likewise, some services may require that the consumer travel to receive them, with the result that a consumer may strongly prefer a local service provider. In such cases, the market may have an important geographic dimension. In other cases, geography may not matter at all.

CASENOTE: United States v. Pabst Brewing Co.
384 U.S. 546 (1966)

A helpful formulation of the basic idea of a geographic market can be found in Justice Harlan's concurrence in *Pabst Brewing*. That case dealt with DOJ's challenge to the consummated acquisition of the eighteenth-largest brewer in the nation, Blatz Brewing, by the tenth-largest, Pabst. In a brief opinion, the Court held the merger was unlawful, referring variously to the merged firm's competitive position: (1) in individual states; (2) in a "three state area" of Wisconsin, Illinois, and Michigan; and (3) in the nation as whole. The Court explained that "[i]n 1957 [*i.e.*, the year before the acquisition] these two companies had combined sales which accounted for 23.95% of the beer sales in Wisconsin, 11.32% of the sales in the three-state area of Wisconsin, Illinois, and Michigan, and 4.49% of the sales throughout the country. . . . the probable effect of the merger on competition in Wisconsin, in the three-state area, and in the entire country was sufficient to show a violation of s 7 in each and all of these three areas."

The *Pabst* majority denied that it was necessary to agonize about which was the "right" frame in which to assess competition. "Congress did not seem to be troubled about the exact spot where competition might be lessened; it simply intended to outlaw mergers which threatened competition in any or all parts of the country."

Justice Harlan concurred in the judgment, but vigorously disagreed with the Court's treatment of geographic market. In so doing, he mapped out a good guide to the kind of approach that courts commonly take today. Any assessment of competitive effects, he argued, "necessarily involves a study of statistics and other evidence bearing upon market shares, market trends, number of competitors and the like. Obviously such figures will vary depending upon what geographic area is chosen as relevant, and the possibilities for 'gerrymandering' are limitless." The rule, he argued, was fairly clear: "[t]he appropriate geographic area in which to examine the effects of an acquisition is an area in which the parties to the merger or acquisition compete, and around which there exist economic barriers that significantly impede the entry of new competitors. Of course . . . no such designation is perfect, for all geographic markets are to some extent interconnected, and over time any barrier may be overcome or may disappear owing to structural or technological changes in the industry, *e.g.*, refrigeration which widened markets for 'perishable' foods."

Applying that test to the facts of the Pabst / Blatz merger, he concluded that the Government had made a satisfactory showing, among other things, that the State of Wisconsin was a relevant geographic market. A series of considerations favored this conclusion. First, both parties were significant competitors in Wisconsin. "[I]ndeed Blatz was the leading seller in Wisconsin and Pabst the fourth largest."

Second, competition in Wisconsin was clearly dominated by local suppliers. "Wisconsin . . . was dominated by substantially the same group of brewers maintaining substantially the same market shares year after year without serious challenge from other brewers operating in other sectors of the country. This picture of local concentration in various regional markets is supported by evidence that brewers are able to sell the same beer in different States for different prices (exclusive of transportation cost). . . . [A]bout 90% of beer sold in Wisconsin comes from breweries located in that State or nearby in Minnesota. . . . To the extent that it is true that local breweries have an advantage in terms of efficiency and thus cost, a significant barrier exists to brewers who wish to sell in Wisconsin but brew their beer in other areas of the country."

Third, Wisconsin-specific investment in marketing and distribution would be necessary for competitive entry into the state. "Beer is not a fungible commodity like wheat; product differentiation is important, and the ordinary

---

consumer is likely to choose a particular brand rather than purchase any beer indiscriminately. . . . [W]ere a brewer from, say, Colorado, interested in entering the Wisconsin market, a great deal of costly preliminary promotional activity would be required before sizable Wisconsin sales could be expected. In addition, the record indicates that beer is sold through distribution networks operating on regional, statewide, and local levels. There are numerous examples in the record of the highly specialized salesmanship needed to induce local retail sellers to carry, display, and advertise new brands of beer." These entry barriers were of significant magnitude: "To enter [Wisconsin] the new entrant must be prepared to incur considerable expense over a substantial period of time[.]"

Fourth, and finally, the regulatory environment was distinctive: "Methods of sales promotion permitted in one State are unlawful in others. State regulations govern labeling, size of containers, alcoholic content of beer, shipping procedures, and credit arrangements with wholesalers. A brewer wishing to enter the Wisconsin market does not merely start transporting beer to Milwaukee; he must comply with these various state requirements, which may differ from those in the States in which he has always dealt."

All this evidence supported the conclusion that Wisconsin was a distinct geographic market. "In terms of antitrust consequences, this means that those already within such a local market can engage in oligopolistic pricing or other practices without a very real threat that brewers operating in other areas could easily, and within a reasonably short time, enter the Wisconsin market as effective competitors of those already entrenched there."

Justice Harlan's approach—not the majority's!—exemplifies the kind of analysis that courts often perform today.

Geography is commonly important in hospital merger cases. (Why do you think this is?) In the following extract, the court considers some challenging aspects of geographic market definition in the FTC's challenge to a proposed hospital merger in Pennsylvania, and explains why an older analytical approach—the Elzinga-Hogarty test—is no longer used to measure the geographic bounds of hospital markets.

FTC v. Penn State Hershey Medical Center
838 F.3d 327 (3d. Cir. 2016)

Judge Fisher.

[1] The relevant geographic market is that area in which a potential buyer may rationally look for the goods or services he seeks. Determined within the specific context of each case, a market's geographic scope must correspond to the commercial realities of the industry being considered and be economically significant. The plaintiff (here, the Government) bears the burden of establishing the relevant geographic market.

[2] A common method employed by courts and the FTC to determine the relevant geographic market is the hypothetical monopolist test. Under the Horizontal Merger Guidelines issued by the U.S. Department of Justice's Antitrust Division and the FTC, if a hypothetical monopolist could impose a small but significant non-transitory increase in price ("SSNIP") in the proposed market, the market is properly defined. If, however, consumers would respond to a SSNIP by purchasing the product from outside the proposed market, thereby making the SSNIP unprofitable, the proposed market definition is too narrow. Important for our purposes, both the Government and the Hospitals agree that this test should govern the instant appeal.

[3] The Government argues, as it did before the District Court, that the relevant geographic market is the "Harrisburg area." More specifically, the four counties encompassing and immediately surrounding Harrisburg, Pennsylvania: Dauphin, Cumberland, Lebanon, and Perry counties.

[4] The District Court rejected the Government's proposed geographic market. It first observed that 43.5% of Hershey's patients—11,260 people—travel to Hershey from outside the four-county area, which "strongly indicate[d] that the FTC had created a geographic market that [was] too narrow because it does not appropriately account for where the Hospitals, particularly Hershey, draw their business." Second, it held that the nineteen hospitals within a sixty-five-minute drive of Harrisburg "would readily offer consumers an alternative" to accepting a SSNIP. . . . The failure to propose the proper relevant geographic market was fatal to the Government's motion, and the District Court denied the preliminary injunction request.

[5] We conclude that the District Court erred in both its formulation and its application of the proper legal test. Although the District Court correctly identified the hypothetical monopolist test, its decision reflects neither the proper formulation nor the correct application of that test. We find three errors in the District Court's analysis. First, by relying almost exclusively on the number of patients that enter the proposed market, the District Court's analysis more closely aligns with a discredited economic theory, not the hypothetical monopolist test. Second, the District Court focused on the likely response of patients to a price increase, completely neglecting any mention of the likely response of insurers. . . . .

i. Formulation of the Legal Test

[6] In formulating the legal standard for the relevant geographic market, the District Court relied primarily on the Eighth Circuit's decision in [*Little Rock Cardiology Clinic PA v. Baptist Health*, 591 F.3d 591 (8th Cir. 2009)]. According to the District Court, to determine the geographic market, a court must apply a two-part test. First, it must determine the market area in which the seller operates, its trade area. Second, it must then determine whether a plaintiff has alleged a geographic market in which only a small percentage of purchasers have alternative suppliers to whom they could practically turn in the event that a defendant supplier's anticompetitive actions result in a price increase. Under the District Court's inquiry, the "end goal" of the relevant geographic market analysis is to delineate a geographic area where, in the medical setting, few patients leave . . . and few patients enter.

[7] This formulation of the relevant geographic market test is inconsistent with the hypothetical monopolist test. Rather, it is one-half of a different test utilized in non-healthcare markets to define the relevant geographic market: the Elzinga–Hogarty test. The Elzinga–Hogarty test consists of two separate measurements: first, the number of customers who come from outside the proposed market to purchase goods and services from inside of it, and, second, the number of customers who reside inside the market but leave that market to purchase goods and services.[222]

[8] The Elzinga–Hogarty test was once the preferred method to analyze the relevant geographic market and was employed by many courts. But subsequent empirical research demonstrated that utilizing patient flow data to determine the relevant geographic market resulted in overbroad markets with respect to hospitals. Professor Elzinga himself testified before the FTC that this method was not an appropriate method to define geographic markets in the hospital sector. [. . .]

[9] As the amici curiae Economics Professors have persuasively demonstrated, patient flow data—such as the 43.5% number emphasized by the District Court—is particularly unhelpful in hospital merger cases because of two problems: the "silent majority fallacy" and the "payor problem." The silent majority fallacy is the false assumption that patients who travel to a distant hospital to obtain care significantly constrain the prices that the closer hospital charges to patients who will not travel to other hospitals. The constraining effect is non-existent because patient decisions are based mostly on non-price factors, such as location or quality of services. This fallacy is particularly salient here, where the District Court relied almost exclusively on the fact that Hershey attracts many patients from outside of the Harrisburg area. In deciding that patients who travel to Hershey would turn to other hospitals outside of Harrisburg if the merger gave rise to higher prices, the District Court did not consider

---

[222] [Editorial note:] The text of the opinion here is not an especially illuminating way to describe the Elzinga-Hogarty test (which you do not need to worry about anyway). But for those wanting a better explanation: "The E-H method usually starts with two measurements. First, an analyst determines the geographic area responsible for a percentage of the sales of the hospital or hospitals in question. Elzinga and Hogarty originally suggested an area responsible for 75 percent of sales, and then later suggested 90 percent for a "strong market" and 75 percent for a "weak market." This area is sometimes called the service area, the draw area, or the catchment area. In the context of health care markets in particular, and in the markets for services more generally, the measure of the service area is referred to as the Little In From Outside (LIFO) measure. Put simply, this means that the hospitals service few patients from outside the service area. The second measurement is the percentage of residents in the service area who obtain their care from hospitals within the area. This is called the Little Out From Inside (LOFI) measure. Again, in the simplest terms, this means that few patients from the service area obtain care outside of the area. The economic presumption is that these static measures are inversely proportional to the number of patients who would switch to hospitals outside the service area in the face of a post-merger price increase. That is, the larger the percentage of patients who leave the proposed market, the larger the number of patients that would switch to hospitals outside the market." H.E. Frech et al., *Elzinga-Hogarty Tests and Alternative Approaches For Market Share Calculations In Hospital Markets*, 71 Antitrust L.J. 921, 926–27 (2004). The test is no longer applied in hospital merger cases for the reasons explained in the text.

that Hershey is a leading academic medical center that provides highly complex medical services. We are skeptical that patients who travel to Hershey for these complex services would turn to other hospitals in the area.

[10] Although the District Court did not employ strict cutoffs to determine whether too many patients enter or leave the proposed market, the silent majority fallacy renders the test employed by the District Court unreliable even in the absence of precise thresholds. In other words, the inadequacy of using patient flow data to determine the geographic market does not depend on whether the District Court used an exact percentage or whether it used a more flexible approach: relying solely on patient flow data is not consistent with the hypothetical monopolist test.

[11] Moreover, even assuming that relying strictly on patient flow data is consistent with the hypothetical monopolist test, the District Court did not consider the other half of the equation: patient outflows. The Government presented undisputed evidence that 91% of patients who live in Harrisburg receive GAC services in the Harrisburg area. Such a high number of patients who do not travel long distances for healthcare supports the Government's contention that GAC services are inherently local and that, in turn, payors would not be able to market a healthcare plan to Harrisburg-area residents that did not include Harrisburg-area hospitals. Although the District Court was not required to cite every piece of evidence it received, or even on which it relied, citing only patient inflows and ignoring patient outflows creates a misleading picture of the relevant geographic market.

ii. Likely Response of Payors

[12] The next problem with utilizing patient flow data—the payor problem—underscores the second error committed by the District Court. By utilizing patient flow data as its primary evidence that the relevant market was too narrow, the District Court failed to properly account for the likely response of insurers in the face of a SSNIP. In fact, it completely neglected any mention of the insurers in the healthcare market. This incorrect focus reflects a misunderstanding of the commercial realities of the healthcare market.

[13] As the FTC and several courts have recognized, the healthcare market is represented by a two-stage model of competition. In the first stage, hospitals compete to be included in an insurance plan's hospital network. In the second stage, hospitals compete to attract individual members of an insurer's plan. Patients are largely insensitive to healthcare prices because they utilize insurance, which covers most of their healthcare costs. Because of this, our analysis must focus, at least in part, on the payors who will feel the impact of any price increase.

[14] The Hospitals argue that there is no fundamental difference between analyzing the likely response of consumers through the patient or the payor perspective. We disagree. Patients are relevant to the analysis, especially to the extent that their behavior affects the relative bargaining positions of insurers and hospitals as they negotiate rates. But patients, in large part, do not feel the impact of price increases. Insurers do. And they are the ones who negotiate directly with the hospitals to determine both reimbursement rates and the hospitals that will be included in their networks.

[15] Imagine that a hospital raised the cost of a procedure from $1,000 to $2,000. The patient who utilizes health insurance will still have the same out-of-pocket costs before and after the price increase. It is the insurer who will bear the immediate impact of that price increase. Not until the insurer passes that cost on to the patient in the form of higher premiums will the patient feel the impact of that price increase. And even then, the cost will be spread among many insured patients; it will not be felt solely by the patient who receives the higher-priced procedure. This is the commercial reality of the healthcare market as it exists today.

[16] Thus, consistent with the mandate to determine the relevant geographic market taking into account the commercial realities of the specific industry involved, when we apply the hypothetical monopolist test, we must also do so through the lens of the insurers: if enough insurers, in the face of a small but significant non-transitory price increase, would avoid the price increase by looking to hospitals outside the proposed geographic market, then the market is too narrow. . . . It was error for the District Court to completely disregard the role that insurers play in the healthcare market.

[17] We do not mean to suggest that, in the healthcare context, considering the effect of a price increase on patients constitutes error standing alone. Patients, of course, are relevant. For instance, an antitrust defendant may be able

to demonstrate that enough patients would buy a health plan marketed to them with no in-network hospital in the proposed geographic market. It would necessarily follow that those patients who purchased the health plan would have to turn to hospitals outside the relevant market (lest they pay significant out-of-pocket costs for an out-of-network hospital). In this scenario, patient response is clearly important, but it is not important with respect to patients' response to the price increase demanded by the post-merger Hospitals. The District Court here did not address this correlated behavior. And although it is possible that this scenario could play out in some healthcare market, to assume that it would in Harrisburg defies the payors' testimony. The payors repeatedly said that they could not successfully market a plan in the Harrisburg area without Hershey and Pinnacle. In fact, one payor that attempted to do just that (with Holy Spirit, a Harrisburg-area hospital, no less) lost half of its membership. That is to say nothing about whether payors would be able to successfully market a plan without any Harrisburg-area hospital, which is the less burdensome question the Government was tasked with answering under the hypothetical monopolist test. [. . .]

[18] Our conclusion that the District Court incorrectly formulated and misapplied the proper standard does not end the inquiry. We must still determine whether the Government has met its burden to properly define the relevant geographic market. We conclude that it has.

[19] The Government presented extensive evidence showing that insurers would have no choice but to accept a price increase from a combined Hershey/Pinnacle in lieu of excluding the Hospitals from their networks. First, two of Central Pennsylvania's largest insurers—Payor A and Payor B—testified that they could not successfully market a network to employers without including at least one of the Hospitals. Payor A's representative stated in his deposition that "[y]ou wouldn't have a whole lot of choice" if Hershey and Pinnacle raised their prices following a merger and there was no price agreement; that "there would be no network without" a combined Hershey and Pinnacle; and that the combined entity would have more bargaining leverage. He estimated that the insurer would lose half of its membership in Dauphin County if they tried to market a plan that excluded Pinnacle and Hershey. [. . .]

[20] The results of one natural experiment also support the insurer's testimony. From 2000 until 2014, Payor E was able to market a viable network in Harrisburg that included only Holy Spirit and Pinnacle but did not include Hershey. In August 2014, Pinnacle terminated its agreement with Payor E. After losing Pinnacle from its network, Payor E negotiated substantial discounts with Holy Spirit and large hospitals in York and Lancaster counties and was able to offer plans at a substantial discount. Despite being priced much lower than its competitors, Payor E lost half its members, who switched to other health plans. Brokers informed the Payor E representative that it no longer had a viable network without Pinnacle, and even in the face of substantial discounts for Payor E's health plan, patients were willing to pay more to other insurers for health plans that included Hershey or Pinnacle. [. . .]

[21] All of the aforementioned evidence answered an even narrower question than the one presented: the Government was not required to show that payors would accept a price increase rather than excluding the merged Hershey/Pinnacle entity from their networks; it was required to show only that payors would accept a price increase rather than excluding all of the hospitals in the Harrisburg area. That is the inquiry under the hypothetical monopolist test. Considering the evidence put forth by the Government, we conclude that the Government has met its burden to properly define the relevant geographic market. It is the four-county Harrisburg area.

E. Market Power, Market Share, and Entry Barriers

As we noted above and in Chapter II, the hallmark of market power is the ability to extract prices or other terms in excess of those that would be available in a competitive market.

There are two main ways to plead and prove market power in an antitrust case. The first is sometimes called "direct proof" of power. Unfortunately—and consistent with our discussion of the ambiguities of market power described above—courts have not always been clear or consistent about what exactly such proof might look like, beyond the general observation that it should connote some kind of power over price and output: namely, clear evidence of the power to profitably increase price above, or reduce output below, competitive levels. But it is hard to spot this in practice: not least because in the real world businesses are usually already maximizing their profits and the "competitive" baseline is hard to calculate. In fact, as Dan Crane has put it in the course of a vigorous criticism of direct-proof mechanisms: "The most commonly repeated maxim—that proof of restricted output and supracompetitive prices establishes market power—is not an analytical criterion at all but merely repeats the definition of market power. It amounts to saying that a plaintiff directly proves market power when she directly proves market power."[223] In *AmEx* the Supreme Court indicated for the first time that this "direct" method of proof might be unavailable in cases involving "vertical" agreements or restraints, although it is not clear why such a limitation would be necessary or desirable.[224]

The second, and much more common, method of proving market power is through so-called "indirect" or "circumstantial" proof. This involves the relative simplicity of a high share of a defined market protected by barriers to entry.[225] What counts as a "high" share has been partly illuminated by litigation: less than thirty percent is generally not enough,[226] although some authorities suggest otherwise[227]; the Ninth Circuit has said that "44 percent is sufficient as a matter of law to support a finding of market power, if entry barriers are high and competitors are unable to expand their output in response to supracompetitive pricing"[228]; sixty percent is surely enough, if supported by other evidence such as entry barriers[229]; and a higher share standing alone might be enough to raise at least a presumption of market power even without other evidence.[230]

Market shares are usually calculated based on the best available evidence of competitive significance in the foreseeable future. In most cases, this will be current sales revenue information, as the HMGs explain.

Horizontal Merger Guidelines § 5

5.2 Market Shares

[1] The Agencies normally calculate market shares for all firms that currently produce products in the relevant market, subject to the availability of data. The Agencies also calculate market shares for other market participants if this can be done to reliably reflect their competitive significance.

[2] Market concentration and market share data are normally based on historical evidence. However, recent or ongoing changes in market conditions may indicate that the current market share of a particular firm either

---

[223] Daniel A. Crane, *Market Power Without Market Definition*, 90 Notre Dame L. Rev. 31, 45 (2014). *See also id.* ("Without guidance from the Supreme Court, lower courts have tried to specify the criteria for a direct evidence approach. The results are a baffling potpourri. Among the criteria identified by courts are: (1) evidence of restricted output and supracompetitive prices; (2) the presence of entry barriers; (3) the exclusion of competition; (4) control over prices; (5) the defendant's ability to engage in price discrimination; (6) 'sustained supranormal profits;' and (7) abrupt changes in practices following the elimination of competitors.").

[224] *See infra* § VI.B. (discussing this aspect of *AmEx*).

[225] *See, e.g.*, Rebel Oil Co. v. Atl. Richfield Co., 51 F.3d 1421, 1434 (9th Cir. 1995) ("To demonstrate market power circumstantially, a plaintiff must: (1) define the relevant market, (2) show that the defendant owns a dominant share of that market, and (3) show that there are significant barriers to entry and show that existing competitors lack the capacity to increase their output in the short run."). The concept of a barrier to entry is surprisingly tricky. For a general working definition, *see, e.g.*, Broadcom Corp. v. Qualcomm Inc., 501 F.3d 297, 307 (3d Cir. 2007) ("Barriers to entry are factors, such as regulatory requirements, high capital costs, or technological obstacles, that prevent new competition from entering a market in response to a monopolist's supracompetitive prices."). For a selection of deeper discussions, *see, e.g.*, Daniel E. Lazaroff, *Entry Barriers and Contemporary Antitrust Litigation*, 7 U.C. Davis Bus. L.J. 1 (2006); R. Preston McAfee, Hugo M. Mialon & Michael A. Williams, *What Is a Barrier to Entry?* AEA Papers & Procs. 461 (May 2004); Richard Schmalensee, *Sunk Costs and Antitrust Barriers to Entry*, 94 Am. Econ. Rev. 471 (2004); Harold Demsetz, *Barriers to Entry*, 72 Am. Econ. Rev. 47 (1982).

[226] *See* Jefferson Par. Hosp. Dist. No. 2 v. Hyde, 466 U.S. 2, 27 (1984) (30% share alone not sufficient); Hardy v. City Optical Inc., 39 F.3d 765, 767 (7th Cir. 1994) (30% is "the minimum market share from which the market power required to be shown at the threshold of a tying case can be inferred"); Grappone, Inc. v. Subaru of New England, Inc., 858 F.2d 792, 797 (1st Cir. 1988) (less than 30% market share precludes finding of significant market power); PSI Repair Servs., Inc. v. Honeywell, Inc., 104 F.3d 811, 818 (6th Cir. 1997) ("A thirty-percent share of the market, standing alone, provides an insufficient basis from which to infer market power.").

[227] United States v. Visa U.S.A., Inc., 163 F. Supp. 2d 322, 341 (S.D.N.Y. 2001) (indicating that MasterCard could hold market power with a 26% share of dollar transactional volume).

[228] Rebel Oil Co. v. Atl. Richfield Co., 51 F.3d 1421, 1438 (9th Cir. 1995).

[229] *See, e.g.*, FTC v. AbbVie Inc, 976 F.3d 327, 371 (3d Cir. 2020) ("A court can infer market power from a market share significantly greater than 55 percent."); In re Visa Check/Mastermoney Antitrust Litig., No. 96-CV-5238 (JG), 2003 WL 1712568, at *4 (E.D.N.Y. Apr. 1, 2003) (holding that "nearly 60 percent" of a market "easily qualifies as 'appreciable economic power'").

[230] Park v. Thomson Corp., No. 05 CIV. 2931 (WHP), 2007 WL 119461, at *8 (S.D.N.Y. Jan. 11, 2007) ("[T]hat Defendants possess an 80-90% market share might, standing alone, permit an inference of market power.").

understates or overstates the firm's future competitive significance. The Agencies consider reasonably predictable effects of recent or ongoing changes in market conditions when calculating and interpreting market share data. For example, if a new technology that is important to long-term competitive viability is available to other firms in the market, but is not available to a particular firm, the Agencies may conclude that that firm's historical market share overstates its future competitive significance. The Agencies may project historical market shares into the foreseeable future when this can be done reliably.

[3] The Agencies measure market shares based on the best available indicator of firms' future competitive significance in the relevant market. This may depend upon the type of competitive effect being considered, and on the availability of data. Typically, annual data are used, but where individual transactions are large and infrequent so annual data may be unrepresentative, the Agencies may measure market shares over a longer period of time.

[4] In most contexts, the Agencies measure each firm's market share based on its actual or projected revenues in the relevant market. Revenues in the relevant market tend to be the best measure of attractiveness to customers, since they reflect the real-world ability of firms to surmount all of the obstacles necessary to offer products on terms and conditions that are attractive to customers. In cases where one unit of a low-priced product can substitute for one unit of a higher-priced product, unit sales may measure competitive significance better than revenues. For example, a new, much less expensive product may have great competitive significance if it substantially erodes the revenues earned by older, higher-priced products, even if it earns relatively few revenues. In cases where customers sign long-term contracts, face switching costs, or tend to re-evaluate their suppliers only occasionally, revenues earned from recently acquired customers may better reflect the competitive significance of suppliers than do total revenues.

[5] In markets for homogeneous products, a firm's competitive significance may derive principally from its ability and incentive to rapidly expand production in the relevant market in response to a price increase or output reduction by others in that market. As a result, a firm's competitive significance may depend upon its level of readily available capacity to serve the relevant market if that capacity is efficient enough to make such expansion profitable. In such markets, capacities or reserves may better reflect the future competitive significance of suppliers than revenues, and the Agencies may calculate market shares using those measures. Market participants that are not current producers may then be assigned positive market shares, but only if a measure of their competitive significance properly comparable to that of current producers is available. When market shares are measured based on firms' readily available capacities, the Agencies do not include capacity that is committed or so profitably employed outside the relevant market, or so high-cost, that it would not likely be used to respond to a SSNIP in the relevant market. [. . .]

[6] When the Agencies define markets serving targeted customers, these same principles are used to measure market shares, as they apply to those customers. In most contexts, each firm's market share is based on its actual or projected revenues from the targeted customers. However, the Agencies may instead measure market shares based on revenues from a broader group of customers if doing so would more accurately reflect the competitive significance of different suppliers in the relevant market. Revenues earned from a broader group of customers may also be used when better data are thereby available.

* * *

In practice, courts may consider both direct and indirect evidence, just as the district court did in the *AmEx* litigation. The trial court's ultimate liability finding in that case was overturned on appeal, but the Supreme Court did not purport to overturn the market power finding (or indeed any of the district court's factual findings). The following extract, drawn from a much longer passage, gives a flavor of the judicial analysis of market power.

United States v. American Exp. Co.

88 F. Supp. 3d 143 (E.D.N.Y. 2015), reversed (on other grounds(?)), 138 S.Ct. 2274 (2018)

Judge Garaufis.

[1] Defined by the Supreme Court as the power to control prices or exclude competition, market power may be proven directly through evidence of specific conduct indicating the defendant's power to control prices or exclude competition, or it may be inferred based on the defendant firm's large share of the relevant market when viewed in the context of the competitive dynamics therein. The Government presents evidence on both points. [. . .]

[2] American Express's percentage share of the network services market is compelling evidence of market power. In reaching this determination, the court remains mindful that data regarding a firm's raw share of the relevant market is probative of market power only after full consideration of the relationship between market share and other relevant market characteristics, including the strength of the competition, the probable development of the industry, the barriers to entry, the nature of the anticompetitive conduct, and the elasticity of consumer demand that characterize this particular market. . . .

[3] Today, American Express is the second largest GPCC [general purpose credit card] card network when measured by charge volume. As of 2013, Amex accounted for 26.4% of general-purpose credit and charge card purchase volume in the United States. It trails only Visa's 45% market share and is larger than both MasterCard (23.3%) and Discover (5.3%). Despite Amex's protestations to the contrary, the proper metric for assigning market shares among the four GPCC networks is the dollar value of the transactions facilitated on those networks. Although other measures of a network's size, such as the number of cards in circulation, the breadth of its merchant acceptance network (whether actual or perceived), and the total number of transactions, will affect that firm's ability to compete in a market characterized by network effects, charge volume is the most direct measure of output in this particular market, and is also the primary determinant of the remuneration networks receive from merchants in exchange for network services. *See* Merger Guidelines § 5.2 ("In most contexts, each firm's market share is based on its actual or projected revenues from the targeted customers."). As a result, in terms of raw percentage share of the relevant market, American Express is larger today than MasterCard was at the time of the *Visa* litigation, when the Second Circuit held that MasterCard possessed market power.

[4] Furthermore, the network services market remains highly concentrated and constrained by high barriers to entry, just as it was in Visa. American Express is one of only four major suppliers of GPCC card network services, and three of the competitors in this market (Visa, American Express, and MasterCard) are significantly larger than the fourth (Discover). The structural susceptibility of this market to an exercise of market power is exacerbated by its inherently high barriers to entry, which further reduce the likelihood that an attempt at anticompetitive conduct would be defeated by new suppliers entering the market. In addition to the sizable setup costs associated with developing the infrastructure and branding necessary to compete in the network services market, any new entrant would also need to overcome what executives from Amex and Discover have termed the "chicken and the egg problem." That is, due to the aforementioned network effects inherent in this platform, a firm attempting entry into the GPCC network market would struggle to convince merchants to join a network without a significant population of cardholders and, in turn, would also struggle to convince cardholders to carry a card associated with a network that is accepted at few merchants. Accordingly, the network services market is not only highly concentrated, but also remarkably static; no firm has entered the GPCC card network services market in the United States since Discover launched its network in 1985. [. . .]

[5] Consequently, American Express's 26.4% share of a highly concentrated market with significant barriers to entry suggests that the firm possesses market power. Yet, Amex's market share alone likely would not suffice to prove market power by a preponderance of the evidence were it not for the amplifying effect of cardholder insistence. [. . .]

[6] American Express's highly insistent or loyal cardholder base is critical to the court's finding of market power in this case. The ability of merchants to resist potential anticompetitive behavior by Amex, including significant price increases, by shifting customers to less expensive credit card networks or other forms of payment is severely impeded by the segment of Amex's cardholder base who insist on paying with their Amex cards and who would

shop elsewhere or spend less if unable to use their cards of choice. In Visa, both the district court and Second Circuit recognized the amplifying effect of cardholder loyalty on Visa's and MasterCard's positions in the market, noting that insistence effectively precluded merchants from dropping acceptance of either Visa or MasterCard credit cards and supported a finding of market power as to both networks. Here, the record developed at trial illustrates a similar dynamic among Defendants' cardholders and merchants, supported not only by merchant testimony on the effect of cardholder insistence, but also by American Express itself, which expressly recognizes, quantifies, and leverages the loyalty of its cardholders in its business dealings with merchants.

[7] Cardholder insistence is derived from a variety of sources. First, and perhaps most importantly, cardholders are incentivized to use their Amex cards by the robust rewards programs offered by the network. Enrollees in American Express's Membership Rewards program, for example, receive points for purchases made with their Amex cards, and may then redeem those points with Amex or one of its redemption partners for merchandise, gift cards, frequent flyer miles, statement credits, or other goods and services. Cardholders who value the ability to earn points, miles, or cash rebates often centralize their spending on their Amex cards to maximize these benefits. Similar "single-homing" behavior is also observed among the approximately 10–20% of Amex cardholders who own or regularly carry only their Amex cards, as well as among those cardholders who consolidate their credit card spending on their American Express cards for other reasons. Amex's industry-leading corporate card program, for instance, drives a significant degree of insistent spending, particularly at those T & E merchants that cater to the needs of business travelers. Indeed, according to one study by American Express, approximately 70% of Corporate Card consumers are subject to some form of "mandation" policy, by which employers require the employee-cardholders to use Amex cards for business expenses.

[8] As in *Visa*, Plaintiffs also have presented merchant testimony illustrating the manner in which cardholder insistence effectively prevents merchants from dropping American Express. While a number of merchant witnesses testified that their companies had never considered terminating acceptance of Amex due to the network's share of the merchants' receipts or a generalized concern that their customers would shop elsewhere if unable to use their American Express cards, others have analyzed the issue in detail and arrived at the same conclusion: The foregone profits associated with losing Amex-insistent customers rendered dropping Amex commercially impractical. Though American Express may be fairly characterized as a discretionary card for consumers when compared to the ubiquity enjoyed by Visa and MasterCard, the degree to which its cardholders insist on using their Amex cards affords the network significant power over merchants, particularly in a market in which merchants' primary recourse when faced with a price increase or similar conduct is an "all-or-nothing" acceptance decision. Defendants' efforts to minimize the significance of cardholder insistence by recasting it as mere "brand loyalty" are unavailing. [. . .]

[9] Finally, the court is unconvinced by Defendants' argument that cardholder insistence cannot be a source of durable market power. Though Defendants are correct that transitory market power is not of particular concern under the federal antitrust laws, the requirement that market power be "durable" speaks to whether a new entrant or other market forces could quickly bring the defendant's exercise of power to an end. The court is aware of no authority that supports Defendants' position that market power is not durable if its maintenance requires continual and replicable investment by the defendant firm. Put simply, American Express cannot avert a finding of market power premised on cardholder insistence merely because that loyalty and its current market share would dissipate if the company were to stop investing in those programs that make its product valuable to cardholders. Of course it would, as would the share of any company that abandoned a core element of a successful business model. Here, the durability of Defendants' power is ensured by the sustained high barriers to entry in the network services market, as evidenced by the lack of any meaningful entry into the market since 1985, and the decades-long persistence of the restraints at issue in this case. [. . .]

[10] Certain of Amex's pricing practices provide direct evidence of the company's market power in the network services market, albeit to varying degrees. [T]he record shows that between 2005 and 2010, American Express repeatedly and profitably raised its discount rates to millions of merchants across the United States as part of its Value Recapture ("VR") initiative without losing a single large merchant and losing relatively few small merchants as a result. Similar evidence of low defection rates among merchants following repeated network price increases

was viewed by the district court in Visa as strong evidence of Visa and MasterCard's market power. The court finds the same is true here. [. . .]

[11] Faced with a declining premium over the all-in rates charged by Visa and MasterCard in the early 2000s . . . American Express executed a series of targeted price increases in certain industry segments between 2005 and 2010, with the stated purpose of better aligning its prices with the value it perceived as being delivered to both cardholders and merchants. Because these Value Recapture initiatives were not paired with offsetting adjustments on the cardholder side of the platform, the resulting increases in merchant pricing are properly viewed as changes to the net price charged across Amex's integrated platform. Given the low rates of merchant defection observed in response to this initiative, which increased prices that were already at or above the competitive level, Value Recapture illustrates Amex's successful exercise of market power.

* * *

Barriers to entry, and to expansion by existing competitors, are a critical element in the indirect proof of market power. As we saw in Chapter II, the economics of entry barriers can raise some complicated questions!

CASENOTE: Rebel Oil Co., Inc. v. Atlantic Richfield Co.
51 F.3d 1421 (9th Cir. 1995)

When assessing market power, courts consider whether the prospect of entry by new rivals, or expansion by existing ones, would defeat any attempt to exert market power. The Ninth Circuit's decision in *Rebel Oil* provides an extended discussion of both entry *and* expansion. That case involved an allegation by plaintiff Rebel Oil, that its competitor Atlantic Richfield Co. ("ARCO") had engaged in "predatory pricing"—a kind of monopolization scheme that we will meet in Chapter VII that involves charging below-cost prices to drive rivals from the market and thus acquiring monopoly power—in markets for retail gasoline. The district court had granted summary judgment to ARCO, on the ground that ARCO had not acquired market power through this scheme, because entry and expansion was sufficiently easy that ARCO would not be able to profitably raise prices above competitive levels. Rebel Oil appealed. The Ninth Circuit evaluated the evidence of barriers to entry and expansion, and affirmed the district court's decision.

Entry or expansion can preclude market power. The court began by noting that "[a] mere showing of substantial or even dominant market share alone cannot establish market power sufficient to carry out a predatory scheme. The plaintiff must show that new rivals are barred from entering the market and show that existing competitors lack the capacity to expand their output to challenge the predator's high price."

Entry analysis. The court defined entry barriers as "additional long-run costs that were not incurred by incumbent firms but must be incurred by new entrants, or factors in the market that deter entry while permitting incumbent firms to earn monopoly returns. The main sources of entry barriers are: (1) legal license requirements; (2) control of an essential or superior resource; (3) entrenched buyer preferences for established brands; (4) capital market evaluations imposing higher capital costs on new entrants; and, in some situations, (5) economies of scale. In evaluating entry barriers, we focus on their ability to constrain not those already in the market, but those who would enter but are prevented from doing so."

On this point, the court held that Rebel Oil had mustered enough evidence that significant entry barriers existed to preclude summary judgment. Among other things, a Nevada law prohibited major oil refiners from entering and operating gasoline stations: only smaller, independent players could enter. Indeed, during the relevant time period, only two new operators had entered, each operating just one station. The court held that, given this evidence, summary judgment for ARCO on the issue of entry was inappropriate.

Expansion analysis. The court next turned to the prospect of expansion: whether rivals could increase output in response to an attempted price increase. "[I]f rivals have idle plants and can quickly respond to any predator's attempt to raise prices above competitive levels, the predator will suffer an immediate loss of market share to competitors. In that instance, the predator does not have market power."

And here the record doomed Rebel Oil's claim. During the relevant period, two of ARCO's competitors had substantially expanded their portfolio of stations (Texaco acquired 40 new stations, and Southland 32). Moreover, both of those firms could easily expand their output to discipline any attempted price increase by ARCO. "Gasoline is produced in Los Angeles refineries, then shipped to Las Vegas via the Cal-Nev pipeline. Competitors do not have to build more gas stations to satisfy customers' wants. They can simply purchase and transport more gasoline via the pipeline."

Rebel Oil protested that rivals like Texaco and Southland would *not* in fact discipline ARCO, because they were co-participants in an oligopolistic market engaged in tacit collusion with ARCO. They would match any price increase, not discipline it. But the court held that, even if this were true, it would not justify a finding that ARCO held market power. Being a member of an oligopoly was not sufficient, as a matter of law, to infer unilateral market power. "We recognize," said the court, "that a gap in the Sherman Act allows oligopolies to slip past its prohibitions, but filling that gap is the concern of Congress, not the judiciary."

The analysis of market power may present particular challenges in an "aftermarket": that is, a market for products or services sold to customers that have already bought a particular primary product. For example, we could speak of an aftermarket for printer cartridges sold to customers that have already bought a particular primary printer, or for repair and maintenance services sold to customers that have already bought particular primary equipment, or for games or other apps sold to customers that have already bought a particular primary smartphone or tablet.

Some complex puzzles can arise when the market for the primary good appears competitive but the aftermarket does not (*e.g.*, because other competitors do not have access to the IP or know-how needed to offer compatible aftermarket products or services). In those circumstances, is it meaningful to speak about "market power" in the aftermarket if consumers can factor aftermarket conditions into their purchasing decisions for the primary product or service, and if that primary market is truly competitive? Is this market power, flowing from freedom from competition, or just the kind of power that any trading party might end up in after making relationship-specific investments?

The leading case dealing with aftermarkets is *Eastman Kodak*, in which the Court controversially held that the concept of monopoly power (itself just a substantial amount of market power) could indeed be applied to aftermarkets. In *Kodak*, as you will see, the primary market was for the supply of "copying and micrographic equipment," and the aftermarket was for the supply of service and parts for such equipment. The Court's decision highlighted some features of consumer behavior in real markets, including transaction costs and information asymmetries, that had not previously played much of an important role in Supreme Court antitrust assessments.[231]

Eastman Kodak Co. v. Image Technical Services, Inc.
504 U.S. 451 (1992)

Justice Blackmun.

[1] Kodak [argues] that even if it concedes monopoly share of the relevant parts market [*i.e.*, the aftermarket], it cannot actually exercise the necessary market power for a Sherman Act violation. This is so, according to Kodak, because competition exists in the equipment market [*i.e.*, the primary market]. Kodak argues that it could not have the ability to raise prices of service and parts above the level that would be charged in a competitive market because any increase in profits from a higher price in the aftermarkets at least would be offset by a corresponding loss in profits from lower equipment sales as consumers began purchasing equipment with more attractive service costs. [. . .]

---

[231] There is a rich literature here. *See, e.g.*, John M. Yun, *App Stores, Aftermarkets & Antitrust*, 53 Ariz. St. L.J. 1283 (2021); David A.J. Goldfine & Kenneth M. Vorrasi, *The Fall of the Kodak Aftermarket Doctrine: Dying A Slow Death in the Lower Courts*, 72 Antitrust L.J. 209 (2004); Paul L. Joskow, *Transaction Cost Economics, Antitrust Rules, and Remedies*, 18 J. L. Econ. & Org. 95 (2002); Carl Shapiro, *Aftermarkets and Consumer Welfare: Making Sense of* Kodak, 62 Antitrust L.J. 483 (1995); Eleanor Fox, Eastman Kodak Company v. Image Technical Services, Inc.—*Information Failure as Soul or Hook?* 62 Antitrust L.J. 759 (1994); Benjamin Klein, *Market Power in Antitrust: Economic Analysis after* Kodak, 3 Sup. Ct. Econ. Rev. 43 (1993).

[2] Kodak contends that there is no need to examine the facts when the issue is market power in the aftermarkets. A legal presumption against a finding of market power is warranted in this situation, according to Kodak, because the existence of market power in the service and parts markets absent power in the equipment market simply makes no economic sense, and the absence of a legal presumption would deter procompetitive behavior. [. . .]

[3] The extent to which one market prevents exploitation of another market depends on the extent to which consumers will change their consumption of one product in response to a price change in another, *i.e.*, the cross-elasticity of demand. Kodak's proposed rule rests on a factual assumption about the cross-elasticity of demand in the equipment and aftermarkets: If Kodak raised its parts or service prices above competitive levels, potential customers would simply stop buying Kodak equipment. Perhaps Kodak would be able to increase short term profits through such a strategy, but at a devastating cost to its long term interests. Kodak argues that the Court should accept, as a matter of law, this basic economic reality, that competition in the equipment market necessarily prevents market power in the aftermarkets.

[4] Even if Kodak could not raise the price of service and parts one cent without losing equipment sales, that fact would not disprove market power in the aftermarkets. The sales of even a monopolist are reduced when it sells goods at a monopoly price, but the higher price more than compensates for the loss in sales. Kodak's claim that charging more for service and parts would be a short-run game, is based on the false dichotomy that there are only two prices that can be charged—a competitive price or a ruinous one. But there could easily be a middle, optimum price at which the increased revenues from the higher priced sales of service and parts would more than compensate for the lower revenues from lost equipment sales. The fact that the equipment market imposes a restraint on prices in the aftermarkets by no means disproves the existence of power in those markets. Thus, contrary to Kodak's assertion, there is no immutable physical law—no "basic economic reality"—insisting that competition in the equipment market cannot coexist with market power in the aftermarkets.

[5] We next consider the more narrowly drawn question: Does Kodak's theory describe actual market behavior so accurately that respondents' assertion of Kodak market power in the aftermarkets, if not impossible, is at least unreasonable?

[6] To review Kodak's theory, it contends that higher service prices will lead to a disastrous drop in equipment sales. Presumably, the theory's corollary is to the effect that low service prices lead to a dramatic increase in equipment sales. According to the theory, one would have expected Kodak to take advantage of lower priced ISO service as an opportunity to expand equipment sales. Instead, Kodak adopted a restrictive sales policy consciously designed to eliminate the lower priced ISO service, an act that would be expected to devastate either Kodak's equipment sales or Kodak's faith in its theory. Yet, according to the record, it has done neither. Service prices have risen for Kodak customers, but there is no evidence or assertion that Kodak equipment sales have dropped.

[7] Kodak and the United States attempt to reconcile Kodak's theory with the contrary actual results by describing a marketing strategy of spreading over time the total cost to the buyer of Kodak equipment. In other words, Kodak could charge subcompetitive prices for equipment and make up the difference with supra–competitive prices for service, resulting in an overall competitive price. This pricing strategy would provide an explanation for the theory's descriptive failings—if Kodak in fact had adopted it. But Kodak never has asserted that it prices its equipment or parts subcompetitively and recoups its profits through service. Instead, it claims that it prices its equipment comparably to its competitors and intends that both its equipment sales and service divisions be profitable. Moreover, this hypothetical pricing strategy is inconsistent with Kodak's policy toward its self-service customers. If Kodak were underpricing its equipment, hoping to lock in customers and recover its losses in the service market, it could not afford to sell customers parts without service. In sum, Kodak's theory does not explain the actual market behavior revealed in the record.

[8] Respondents offer a forceful reason why Kodak's theory, although perhaps intuitively appealing, may not accurately explain the behavior of the primary and derivative markets for complex durable goods: the existence of significant information and switching costs. These costs could create a less responsive connection between service and parts prices and equipment sales.

[9] For the service-market price to affect equipment demand, consumers must inform themselves of the total cost of the "package"—equipment, service, and parts—at the time of purchase; that is, consumers must engage in accurate lifecycle pricing. Lifecycle pricing of complex, durable equipment is difficult and costly. In order to arrive at an accurate price, a consumer must acquire a substantial amount of raw data and undertake sophisticated analysis. The necessary information would include data on price, quality, and availability of products needed to operate, upgrade, or enhance the initial equipment, as well as service and repair costs, including estimates of breakdown frequency, nature of repairs, price of service and parts, length of "downtime," and losses incurred from downtime.

[10] Much of this information is difficult—some of it impossible—to acquire at the time of purchase. During the life of a product, companies may change the service and parts prices, and develop products with more advanced features, a decreased need for repair, or new warranties. In addition, the information is likely to be customer-specific; lifecycle costs will vary from customer to customer with the type of equipment, degrees of equipment use, and costs of down-time.

[11] Kodak acknowledges the cost of information, but suggests, again without evidentiary support, that customer information needs will be satisfied by competitors in the equipment markets. It is a question of fact, however, whether competitors would provide the necessary information. A competitor in the equipment market may not have reliable information about the lifecycle costs of complex equipment it does not service or the needs of customers it does not serve. Even if competitors had the relevant information, it is not clear that their interests would be advanced by providing such information to consumers.

[12] Moreover, even if consumers were capable of acquiring and processing the complex body of information, they may choose not to do so. Acquiring the information is expensive. If the costs of service are small relative to the equipment price, or if consumers are more concerned about equipment capabilities than service costs, they may not find it cost efficient to compile the information. Similarly, some consumers, such as the Federal Government, have purchasing systems that make it difficult to consider the complete cost of the "package" at the time of purchase. State and local governments often treat service as an operating expense and equipment as a capital expense, delegating each to a different department. These governmental entities do not lifecycle price, but rather choose the lowest price in each market.

[13] As Kodak notes, there likely will be some large-volume, sophisticated purchasers who will undertake the comparative studies and insist, in return for their patronage, that Kodak charge them competitive lifecycle prices. Kodak contends that these knowledgeable customers will hold down the package price for all other customers. There are reasons, however, to doubt that sophisticated purchasers will ensure that competitive prices are charged to unsophisticated purchasers, too. As an initial matter, if the number of sophisticated customers is relatively small, the amount of profits to be gained by supracompetitive pricing in the service market could make it profitable to let the knowledgeable consumers take their business elsewhere. More importantly, if a company is able to price discriminate between sophisticated and unsophisticated consumers, the sophisticated will be unable to prevent the exploitation of the uninformed. A seller could easily price discriminate by varying the equipment/parts/service package, developing different warranties, or offering price discounts on different components.

[14] Given the potentially high cost of information and the possibility that a seller may be able to price discriminate between knowledgeable and unsophisticated consumers, it makes little sense to assume, in the absence of any evidentiary support, that equipment-purchasing decisions are based on an accurate assessment of the total cost of equipment, service, and parts over the lifetime of the machine. [. . .]

[15] In sum, there is a question of fact whether information costs and switching costs foil the simple assumption that the equipment and service markets act as pure complements to one another.

[16] We conclude, then, that Kodak has failed to demonstrate that respondents' inference of market power in the service and parts markets is unreasonable, and that, consequently, Kodak is entitled to summary judgment.

NOTES

1) How would you explain to a layperson what market power is? What would you do to look for it in practice: for example, to figure whether your local grocery store holds market power?

2) Bands, sports teams, and movie stars often have fans who do not regard *other* bands, sports teams, and movie stars as reasonable substitutes. Often these fans will pay a significant premium for their favorite. Does this mean that these bands, sports teams, and movie stars all have market or monopoly power?

3) Suppose that you were in charge of figuring out whether a proposed merger between two hospitals would create buyer-side market power in certain labor markets—that is, labor monopsony power—and specifically in markets for the services of: (a) orthopedic surgeons; (b) administrative support staff; and (c) janitors and custodial workers. Concretely and in detail, what would you do to figure out how to define markets (including: what services should be included? what should the geographic scope of the market be?) and to measure market power? How would you estimate the parties' respective market shares? What documents and information would you need, and from whom could you get it?

4) Edwin Rockefeller once wrote that market power "is an imagined power, like witchcraft."[232] Do you agree? How is market power like, or unlike, other kinds of power we encounter in everyday life?

5) Do you think direct proof or indirect proof of market power is more likely to be reliable? Why, and under what conditions?

6) Commentators at the time of *Eastman Kodak* speculated that the decision—and specifically the holding that you can have market power in an aftermarket even if you lack market power in the primary market—would have radical implications for antitrust law. But in practice its impact has been very modest. In today's world of platform ecosystems, in which consumers often pick a platform (say, an iPhone or Android phone, or a Nintendo or Sony games console, or an Apple or Microsoft personal computer) and then face a narrower set of choices for complementary products and services, the ground rules of "aftermarket antitrust" seem to be very important indeed. How do you think the *Kodak* analysis would—or should—map onto today's platform ecosystems? Is each of these companies a monopolist of its own ecosystem, or a competitor in a market for ecosystems?

7) What facts do you think courts should look at to determine whether they should be worried about aftermarket power? Can you identify any industries or markets in which aftermarket power might be a source of concern?

8) Could or should the *Rebel Oil* court have held that, because existing competitors were members of an oligopoly engaging in tacit collusion, expansion was unlikely to constrain any effort by ARCO to exercise market power?

F. Oligopoly and Tacit Collusion

We saw in Chapter II that some markets—particularly but not exclusively those that are concentrated, transparent, and in which participants have symmetrical incentives—are vulnerable to "oligopoly" effects, including "tacit collusion" in particular. The core feature of tacit coordination is that the participants recognize their shared interest in a reduced level of competition, and that each participant eases off its competitive efforts on the tacit understanding that others will do the same. The factors that tend to facilitate such an outcome are described in Chapter II.[233]

Although mere tacit collusion is not illegal, antitrust approaches it with some suspicion. For example, mergers or acquisitions likely to facilitate tacit collusion can be unlawful for that reason.[234] And if the line is crossed from mere tacit collusion to actual conspiracy—that is, if the participants have entered into an *agreement*—then Section 1 of the Sherman Act will have plenty to say about it, and the market power of the participants can be assessed jointly.[235]

---

[232] Edwin Rockefeller, THE ANTITRUST RELIGION (2007) 40.

[233] *See supra* § II.H. (tacit collusion).

[234] *See infra* Chapter VIII.

[235] *See infra* Chapters IV–V.

In the absence of a merger or agreement, antitrust doctrine generally does not permit the pricing power of the oligopolistic whole to be attributed to any individual participant. As Chief Judge Diane Wood of the Seventh Circuit pointed out in 2018, this is something of an anomaly:

> Oligopolies have always posed problems for conventional antitrust law: without something that can be called an agreement, they elude scrutiny under section 1 of the Sherman Act, 15 U.S.C. § 1, and yet no individual firm has enough market power to be subject to Sherman Act section 2, 15 U.S.C. § 2. Tacit collusion is easy in those markets, and firms have little incentive to compete on the basis of price, preferring to share the profits rather than to fight with each other.[236]

As you will recall, the Ninth Circuit said something similar in *Rebel Oil*, rejecting the claim that market power (in that case, monopoly power in the context of a Section 2 claim) could be inferred from the presence of oligopoly in a market:

> Rebel's evidence cannot, as a matter of law, be the basis for inferring market power in its attempted monopolization claim. Although oligopoly pricing cannot be ruled out as a plausible means to recoup predatory losses, oligopoly pricing standing alone does not prove that ARCO has market power, at least not the degree of market power to raise the concerns of the Sherman Act. The fact that competitors may see proper, in the exercise of their own judgment, to follow the prices of another manufacturer, does not establish any suppression of competition or any sinister domination, and does not violate the Sherman Act. The reason for this rule is clear. To pose a threat of monopolization, one firm alone must have the power to control market output and exclude competition. An oligopolist lacks this unilateral power. By definition, oligopolists are interdependent. An oligopolist can increase market price, but only if the others go along.[237]

Of course, it is possible that one or more members of an oligopoly might have unilateral market power in their own right, in light of the factors described above: the point here is only that the existence of an oligopoly does not, without more, provide a legal basis to infer that any individual participant holds market power.[238]

NOTES

1) Should antitrust doctrine prohibit oligopoly or tacit collusion? How? What remedy would we apply to fix it? (We will focus on this problem, among others, in Chapter IV.)

2) Might it be better to treat every participant in an oligopoly as holding market power for the purposes of antitrust doctrine? Why, or why not?

3) The participants in an oligopoly are normally perfectly aware of what is going on, and they may know and intend that higher prices and consumer harm will result from their interdependent behavior. So why should an "agreement" to fix prices be a necessary condition for antitrust liability? And how should we tell when one exists? (We will encounter plenty of law on this question in Chapter IV: for now, think about this as a question of pure principle.) What alternative limiting conditions could you imagine?

G. Some Further Reading

Jonathan B. Baker, *Market Definition: An Analytical Overview*, 74 Antitrust L.J. 129 (2007)

Daniel A. Crane, *Market Power Without Market Definition*, 90 Notre Dame L. Rev. 31 (2014)

Magali Eben, *The Antitrust Market Does Not Exist: Pursuit of Objectivity in a Purposive Process*, 17 J. Comp. L. & Econ. 586 (2021)

---

[236] Kleen Prod. LLC v. Georgia-Pac. LLC, 910 F.3d 927, 931 (7th Cir. 2018).

[237] Rebel Oil Co. v. Atl. Richfield Co., 51 F.3d 1421, 1442–43 (9th Cir. 1995).

[238] *See, e.g.*, Holiday Wholesale Grocery Co. v. Philip Morris Inc., 231 F. Supp. 2d 1253, 1316 (N.D. Ga. 2002) (noting that Philip Morris held individual market power in an oligopolistic market: "The fact that Philip Morris exercised its market power by using its nearly 50% share of the market is not enough to infer that Philip Morris and the remaining Defendants entered into an agreement to fix prices. Moreover, the nature of an oligopoly teaches that when there is a strong market leader, that leader will be the price leader and other market players will often raise prices along with the market leader in order to increase their profit.").

Lapo Filistrucchi, Damien Geradin, Eric Van Damme & Pauline Affeldt, *Market Definition in Two-Sided Markets: Theory and Practice*, 10 J. Comp. L. & Econ. 293 (2014)

David Glasner & Sean P. Sullivan, *The Logic of Market Definition*, 83 Antitrust L.J. 293 (2020)

Pamela Jones Harbour & Tara Isa Koslov, *Section 2 in a Web 2.0 World: An Expanded Vision of Relevant Product Markets*, 76 Antitrust L.J. 769 (2010)

Louis Kaplow, *Market Definition: Impossible and Counterproductive*, 79 Antitrust L.J. 361 (2013)

Thomas G. Krattenmaker, Robert G. Lande & Steven C. Salop, *Monopoly Power and Market Power in Antitrust Law*, 76 Geo. L.J. 241 (1987)

Ioana Marinescu & Eric A. Posner, *A Proposal to Enhance Antitrust Protection Against Labor Market Monopsony*, Roosevelt Institute Working Paper (Dec. 2018)

Steven C. Salop, Daniel Francis, Lauren Sillman & Michaela Spero, *Rebuilding Platform Antitrust: Moving On from Ohio v. American Express Co.*, 84 Antitrust L.J. 883 (2022)

Gregory J. Werden, *The History of Antitrust Market Delineation*, 76 Marquette L. Rev. 123 (1992)

IV. AGREEMENTS

A. Overview

The first pillar of the U.S. antitrust system is the prohibition on anticompetitive agreements in Section 1 of the Sherman Act, 15 U.S.C. § 1. It provides that "[e]very contract, combination in the form of trust or otherwise, or conspiracy, in restraint of trade or commerce among the several States, or with foreign nations, is hereby declared to be illegal[.]"

A violation of Section 1 has two central elements. First, the defendant must have entered into a "contract, combination, or conspiracy"—*i.e.*, an *agreement*. If that agreement is between actual or potential competitors, it is said to be a "horizontal" agreement; if it is between entities at different levels of a supply chain (or between suppliers of complements) it is said to be a "vertical" agreement.[239] Second, the agreement must constitute an *unlawful restraint of trade—i.e.*, it must be unreasonably harmful to competition.

Each of these two elements raises complexities and challenges in practice. The first piece—the definition of an agreement—is notoriously elusive. Courts have struggled *both* to define what an agreement is for the purposes of antitrust law, *and* to specify the circumstances under which the existence of such an agreement can be inferred from the behavior of the relevant firms.

Courts have devised an elaborate framework for evaluating the second piece: that is, whether an agreement unreasonably restrains competition. That framework involves the choice of one of three possible analytical standards, although some courts have emphasized that in practice the analysis more closely resembles a continuum than a three-tier test.[240] The standards differ with respect to the burdens they impose on a plaintiff to show that an agreement is "anticompetitive" (*i.e.*, tends to inflict harm by restricting competition), and with respect to the room they leave for a defendant to show that the agreement has "procompetitive" benefits (*i.e.*, benefits relating to the better satisfaction of market demand). They are:

1. A "per se rule" of automatic illegality for a small set of "nakedly" harmful types of agreement. Certain agreements that are well known to be almost invariably harmful to competition and are unrelated to any procompetitive purpose are "*per se* illegal," regardless of their purpose, circumstances, or effects. This includes practices like agreements to fix prices, rig bids, or divide markets. Once a court concludes that this standard applies, a plaintiff need not show any harmful effects at all, and a defendant has no opportunity to introduce evidence of benefits: if *per se* treatment applies, the plaintiff wins.

2. A "rule of reason" for most other agreements. The default standard of legality for agreements that are not *per se* illegal is called the "rule of reason." That approach measures the anticompetitive harms of the agreement against its procompetitive benefits, and condemns the agreement only when its harmful tendency can be shown to predominate. The rule of reason has been articulated and applied in various different ways by courts. In the most common formulation it is applied as follows: at the first step, the burden is on the plaintiff to establish the anticompetitive effect of the agreement; if this burden is satisfied, at the second step, the burden passes to the defendant to demonstrate its redeeming procompetitive benefits; and if this burden is satisfied, the burden passes back to the plaintiff to establish, at the third step, that the harmful effects outweigh the beneficial ones and/or that

---

[239] An agreement can, therefore, have *both* horizontal and vertical dimensions, if it connects two parties that are at different levels of the same supply chain *and* one of them is a potential entrant into the market in which the other one is active.

[240] *See, e.g.*, California Dental Association v. FTC, 526 U.S. 756, 779 (1999) ("The truth is that our categories of analysis of anticompetitive effect are less fixed than terms like 'per se,' 'quick look,' and 'rule of reason' tend to make them appear. We have recognized, for example, that there is often no bright line separating per se from Rule of Reason analysis, since considerable inquiry into market conditions may be required before the application of any so-called 'per-se' condemnation is justified."); PolyGram Holding, Inc. v. FTC, 416 F.3d 29, 35 (D.C. Cir. 2005) ("It would be somewhat misleading, however, to say the 'quick look' is just a new category of analysis intermediate in complexity between 'per se' condemnation and full-blown 'rule of reason' treatment, for that would suggest the Court has moved from a dichotomy to a trichotomy, when in fact it has backed away from any reliance upon fixed categories and toward a continuum"); NCAA v. Board of Regents of the University of Oklahoma, 468 U.S. 85, 104 n.26 (1984) ("[T]here is often no bright line separating per se from Rule of Reason analysis.").

the claimed procompetitive benefits could be achieved through some less harmful (or "less restrictive") means. (Occasionally the two pieces of step three are separated, creating a four-step framework.) This standard requires a plaintiff to prove that the agreement has actual or likely anticompetitive effects—often a challenging task in practice—and, if it does so, the defendant has a full opportunity to prove that the agreement has countervailing benefits.

3. *"Intermediate" scrutiny for a subset of facially suspicious agreements.* In a fairly small number of cases, courts or agencies apply an intermediate standard sometimes called "quick look" review (or "inherently suspect" review by the FTC), for agreements that present obvious threats to competition give their nature and context, but which are not so nakedly harmful that they make it into the *per se* category. Once a court concludes that this standard applies, the plaintiff may rely on the obviously harmful nature of the agreement to infer anticompetitive harm, but, unlike *per se* analysis, a defendant may offer evidence that, despite appearances, the agreement nevertheless generates sufficient benefits to offset the harms.

In the second half of this chapter, we will set out the three main versions of Section 1's reasonableness test, aiming to understand how the *per se* rule, the rule of reason, and the intermediate-scrutiny test are each applied. In Chapter V, when we discuss horizontal restraints, we will focus more directly on the challenge of figuring out how practices should be classified among the three categories. In Chapter VI, we will see that vertical restraints are almost invariably analyzed under the rule of reason, so the challenge of classification is primarily a matter for horizontal cases.

As you might guess, the choice of standard is often dispositive of the outcome of an antitrust case. The vast majority of agreements are analyzed under the rule of reason, and this has significant implications for the reality of antitrust litigation. For one thing, plaintiffs overwhelmingly lose rule-of-reason cases.[241] For another thing, rule-of-reason litigation is notoriously lengthy and expensive, promising vast discovery costs (particularly for large corporate litigants with many documents), low chances of success for plaintiffs, and long delays for everyone. The Supreme Court has alluded to some of these realities when setting the pleading hurdles for an antitrust claim to clear.[242]

The *per se* rule and the intermediate scrutiny standard are intended, among other things, to make adjudication easier and more efficient, by obviating the need for expensive discovery or detailed analysis when judicial experience shows that a particular kind of agreement is always, or nearly always, unreasonably restrictive in practice.[243] But the efficiency benefits of such a rule can only be realized if plaintiffs can be confident in a *per se* case that they need not *also* develop a discovery record for a full-blown effects-based showing, just in case a judge decides that per se analysis is inappropriate. In practice, courts often decline to apply *per se* scrutiny in all but the very clearest cases: so a plaintiff faces strong incentives to prepare a full rule-of-reason case anyway.[244]

Choosing the Standard v. Applying the Standard

As we will see, judicial opinions often read as if there were a strict separation between a first step of choosing a standard (*i.e.*, *per se*, rule of reason, or intermediate scrutiny) and a second, subsequent, step of applying that standard. And, certainly, that is the way in which an antitrust analysis is often written up by a judge or briefed by a litigant. But that is probably not the best way of understanding what is really going on in the mind of a judge, or an antitrust agency, when working through an analysis. Among other things, in order to figure out what standard

---

[241] Michael A. Carrier, *The Rule of Reason: An Empirical Update for the 21st Century*, 16 Geo. Mason L. Rev. 827, 828 (2009) ("Courts dispose of 97% of [rule of reason] cases at the first stage, on the grounds that there is no anticompetitive effect.").

[242] *See, e.g.*, Bell Atlantic Corp. v. Twombly, 550 U.S. 544, 546 (2007) (noting expense of antitrust discovery in shaping motion-to-dismiss standard).

[243] *See, e.g.*, Broad. Music, Inc. v. Columbia Broad. Sys., Inc., 441 U.S. 1, 19–20 (1979) (key question is "whether the practice facially appears to be one that would always or almost always tend to restrict competition and decrease output, and in what portion of the market, or instead one designed to increase economic efficiency and render markets more, rather than less, competitive.").

[244] *See* Herbert Hovenkamp, THE ANTITRUST ENTERPRISE: PRINCIPLE AND EXECUTION (2005), 115–16; *see, e.g.*, 1-800 Contacts, Inc. v. FTC, 1 F.4th 102, 116–17 (2d Cir. 2021) (declining to apply abbreviated scrutiny); Diaz v. Farley, 215 F.3d 1175, 1182 (10th Cir. 2000) ("Because plaintiffs conceded below that they did not have sufficient evidence to proceed under a theory that defendants' conduct violated the rule of reason, if we find, as the district court did, that the *per se* rule does not apply, the order dismissing plaintiffs' antitrust claims must be affirmed."); *see also* Texaco Inc. v. Dagher, 547 U.S. 1 (2006) (rejecting *per se* claim in the absence of a rule-of-reason theory).

should apply, a court or agency will often need to think about the practice's nature and effects: it's hard to determine that a practice is nakedly anticompetitive without thinking about whether it is linked to any procompetitive benefits!

So it might be helpful to keep in the back of your mind the idea that a court, or an investigating agency, will often really approach a problem by asking two questions: (1) what are the reasons of theory and evidence to fear that a practice will result in anticompetitive harm, and (2) what are the reasons of theory and evidence to expect that a practice will elicit procompetitive benefits (*i.e.*, benefits related to the satisfaction of demand)? If the balance tips very sharply in favor of harm, and the conduct is of a kind that courts have summarily condemned in the past, *per se* condemnation may be in line. If the conduct seems facially very troubling, but the balancing is not so overwhelming (or the conduct is not so familiar) that the court should declare it illegal out of hand—or the practice seems only very distantly related to some legitimate procompetitive collaboration—intermediate scrutiny may be in order. In all other cases, the rule of reason is the default analytical frame for articulating and weighing stories of harm and benefit against one another.

This three-part division has some implications for the scope of criminal antitrust enforcement. For some decades before 2022,[245] criminal enforcement was limited to *per se* violations of Section 1: including price-fixing (including wage-fixing), market division, and bid-rigging.[246] Courts have held that the scope of *per se* illegality is sufficiently clear to satisfy the constitutional "fair notice" requirement for criminal statutes.[247] But in 2022, DOJ expanded its criminal program to cover monopolization, and it remains to be seen whether this presages an expansion of criminal Section 1 enforcement beyond the *per se* category.

The rest of this chapter will focus on Section 1. But it may be helpful to remember that Section 1 exhibits some overlap with Section 2 and Section 7. For example, if a monopolist uses agreements to improperly exclude rivals, those agreements might violate *both* Section 1 and Section 2.[248] Likewise, if a business enters into an agreement to acquire a rival, the merger agreement might violate § 1, while the merger itself could violate § 7 of the Clayton Act.[249] Section 1 also overlaps with Section 3 of the Clayton Act, which is generally understood to provide for modestly elevated scrutiny of certain exclusivity and tying arrangements.[250]

This chapter is the beginning of our survey of the law of agreements. Chapter IV focuses on some issues that are common to the analysis of all agreements, including horizontal agreements (among actual and potential competitors) as well as vertical ones (among entities at different levels of the supply chain, or suppliers of complements). We will focus on three questions. In Section B we will ask when antitrust law considers two entities to be separate, such that they are capable of entering into an agreement that is subject to Section 1. In Section C we will meet antitrust's definition of an "agreement." In Section D we will focus on the three standards of antitrust legality used to appraise the reasonableness of an agreement under Section 1: per se illegality; the rule of reason; and intermediate scrutiny. In Chapter V, we will discuss some specific topics in the study of horizontal restraints on competition, with a focus on figuring out when to apply the different standards of scrutiny. In Chapter VI, we will turn to vertical restraints.

---

[245] Daniel A. Crane, *Criminal Enforcement of Section 2 of the Sherman Act*, 84 Antitrust L.J. 753 (2022).

[246] For a recent DOJ initiative aimed at procurement bid-rigging, *see, e.g.*, Daniel W. Glad, *The Procurement Collusion Strike Force: A Whole-of-Government Approach to Combating a Whole-of-Government Problem* (remarks of Oct. 13, 2021).

[247] *See, e.g.*, United States v. Jindal, No. CV-4:20-CR-00358, 2021 WL 5578687, at *9–10 (E.D. Tex. Nov. 29, 2021) (fair notice that wage-fixing was *per se* illegal); United States v. Miller, 771 F.2d 1219, 1225 (9th Cir. 1985) (fair notice that price-fixing was per se illegal); *see also* Nash v. United States, 229 U.S. 373, 376–78 (1913) ("[T]here is no constitutional difficulty in the way of enforcing the criminal part of the act[.]").

[248] *See, e.g.*, United States v. Microsoft Corp., 253 F.3d 34, 70 (D.C. Cir. 2001) ("In this case, plaintiffs challenged Microsoft's exclusive dealing arrangements . . . under both §§ 1 and 2 of the Sherman Act.").

[249] *See, e.g.*, Complaint, United States v. Booz Allen Hamilton Holding Corp., No. 1:22-cv-01603 (D. Md. filed June 29, 2022) ¶¶ 60–61 ("The merger agreement has sharply reduced incentives for the Defendants to compete vigorously for [a government contract] and therefore constitutes an unreasonable restraint of trade, in violation of Section 1 of the Sherman Act, 15 U.S.C. § 1. Unless enjoined, completion of the merger is likely to substantially lessen competition and tend to create a monopoly in interstate trade and commerce for the [contract], in violation of Section 7 of the Clayton Act, 15 U.S.C. § 18.").

[250] 15 U.S.C. § 14.

B. Contracts, Combinations, and Conspiracies

1. Unilateral v. Joint Action

Before we can have an agreement, we need more than one participant able to agree with one another for the purposes of antitrust analysis. And this is not quite as straightforward as it sounds.

Section 1 of the Sherman Act prohibits "contracts," "combinations," and "conspiracies" in restraint of trade. (Nothing turns on any difference between these three synonyms for "agreement.") But not every instance of literal concerted action constitutes an agreement for the purposes of antitrust analysis. Among other things, concerted action by persons employed by the same corporation, or concerted action between a corporation and its own officers or employees, is not a conspiracy within the meaning of § 1. For example, it is not illegal "price fixing" for two employees of one business—say, a supermarket or bookstore chain—to agree on the prices that they will charge for particular products and services. (That would turn every business into a felonious conspiracy!) So antitrust needs an account of when entities will be treated as separate, such that an agreement may exist between them for the purposes of Section 1.

This issue is often raised in connection with corporate "families." Certainly an agreement within a single corporation (*e.g.*, among employees) is not a conspiracy for the purposes of Section 1.[251] But what about agreements between a corporation and its wholly owned, separately incorporated subsidiaries? These are different *legal* persons: but are they separate for antitrust purposes, such that they are capable of violating Section 1 by entering into an agreement? Or, to put it another way: does antitrust law care whether a corporation implements a practice through an unincorporated division or through a separately incorporated subsidiary?

In *Copperweld* in 1984, the Supreme Court said no, repudiating some earlier understandings that an "intraenterprise" conspiracy of this kind could constitute an unlawful restraint of trade. That case involved private litigation by one business, Independence Tube, against Copperweld and its wholly-owned subsidiary, Regal Tube, on the theory that they had colluded to harm Independence Tube.

Copperweld Corp. v. Independence Tube Corp.
467 U.S. 752 (1984)

Chief Justice Burger.

[1] We granted certiorari to determine whether a parent corporation and its wholly owned subsidiary are legally capable of conspiring with each other under § 1 of the Sherman Act.

[2] The predecessor to petitioner Regal Tube Co. was established in Chicago in 1955 to manufacture structural steel tubing used in heavy equipment, cargo vehicles, and construction. From 1955 to 1968 it remained a wholly owned subsidiary of C.E. Robinson Co. In 1968 Lear Siegler, Inc., purchased Regal Tube Co. and operated it as an unincorporated division. David Grohne, who had previously served as vice president and general manager of Regal, became president of the division after the acquisition.

[3] In 1972 petitioner Copperweld Corp. purchased the Regal division from Lear Siegler; the sale agreement bound Lear Siegler and its subsidiaries not to compete with Regal in the United States for five years. Copperweld then transferred Regal's assets to a newly formed, wholly owned Pennsylvania corporation, petitioner Regal Tube Co. The new subsidiary continued to conduct its manufacturing operations in Chicago but shared Copperweld's corporate headquarters in Pittsburgh.

---

[251] *See, e.g.*, Holter v. Moore & Co., 702 F.2d 854, 855 (10th Cir. 1983) ("Since a corporation has no way of acting except through officers and employees, the officers and employees are part of the same economic unit as the corporation for antitrust purposes. Thus, officers and employees of a corporation are generally incapable of conspiring with the corporation or with each other.") (footnote omitted). For a thoughtful and provocative critical discussion of antitrust's relationship with the corporate form, *see* Sanjukta Paul, *On Firms*, 90 U. Chi. L. Rev. 579 (2023).

[4] Shortly before Copperweld acquired Regal, David Grohne accepted a job as a corporate officer of Lear Siegler. After the acquisition, while continuing to work for Lear Siegler, Grohne set out to establish his own steel tubing business to compete in the same market as Regal. In May 1972 he formed respondent Independence Tube Corp., which soon secured an offer from the Yoder Co. to supply a tubing mill. In December 1972 respondent gave Yoder a purchase order to have a mill ready by the end of December 1973.

[5] When executives at Regal and Copperweld learned of Grohne's plans, they initially hoped that Lear Siegler's noncompetition agreement would thwart the new competitor. Although their lawyer advised them that Grohne was not bound by the agreement, he did suggest that petitioners might obtain an injunction against Grohne's activities if he made use of any technical information or trade secrets belonging to Regal. The legal opinion was given to Regal and Copperweld along with a letter to be sent to anyone with whom Grohne attempted to deal. The letter warned that Copperweld would be "greatly concerned if [Grohne] contemplates entering the structural tube market in competition with Regal Tube" and promised to take "any and all steps which are necessary to protect our rights under the terms of our purchase agreement and to protect the know-how, trade secrets, etc., which we purchased from Lear Siegler." . . .

[6] When Yoder accepted respondent's order for a tubing mill on February 19, 1973, Copperweld sent Yoder one of these letters; two days later Yoder voided its acceptance . . . .

[7] Although the letter to Yoder was [the] most successful effort [by Copperweld and Regal] to discourage those contemplating doing business with [Independence Tube], it was not their only one. Copperweld repeatedly contacted banks that were considering financing [Independence Tube]'s operations. One or both [of Copperweld and Regal] also approached real estate firms that were considering providing plant space to [Independence Tube] and contacted prospective suppliers and customers of the new company.

[8] In 1976 [Independence Tube] filed this action in the District Court against petitioners [*i.e.*, Copperweld and Regal] and Yoder. The jury found that Copperweld and Regal had conspired [with one another] to violate § 1 of the Sherman Act, but that Yoder was not part of the conspiracy. [. . .]

[9] Review of this case calls directly into question whether the coordinated acts of a parent and its wholly owned subsidiary can, in the legal sense contemplated by § 1 of the Sherman Act, constitute a combination or conspiracy. The so-called "intra-enterprise conspiracy" doctrine provides that § 1 liability is not foreclosed merely because a parent and its subsidiary are subject to common ownership. The doctrine derives from declarations in several of this Court's opinions. [. . .]

[10] Petitioners [Copperweld and Regal], joined by the United States as amicus curiae, urge us to repudiate the intra-enterprise conspiracy doctrine. The central criticism is that the doctrine gives undue significance to the fact that a subsidiary is separately incorporated and thereby treats as the concerted activity of two entities what is really unilateral behavior flowing from decisions of a single enterprise. We limit our inquiry to the narrow issue squarely presented: whether a parent and its wholly owned subsidiary are capable of conspiring in violation of § 1 of the Sherman Act. We do not consider under what circumstances, if any, a parent may be liable for conspiring with an affiliated corporation it does not completely own.

[11] The Sherman Act contains a basic distinction between concerted and independent action. The conduct of a single firm is governed by § 2 alone and is unlawful only when it threatens actual monopolization. It is not enough that a single firm appears to "restrain trade" unreasonably, for even a vigorous competitor may leave that impression. . . . In part because it is sometimes difficult to distinguish robust competition from conduct with long-run anti-competitive effects, Congress authorized Sherman Act scrutiny of single firms only when they pose a danger of monopolization. Judging unilateral conduct in this manner reduces the risk that the antitrust laws will dampen the competitive zeal of a single aggressive entrepreneur.

[12] Section 1 of the Sherman Act, in contrast, reaches unreasonable restraints of trade effected by a "contract, combination . . . or conspiracy" between *separate* entities. It does not reach conduct that is "wholly unilateral." Concerted activity subject to § 1 is judged more sternly than unilateral activity under § 2. Certain agreements, such as horizontal price fixing and market allocation, are thought so inherently anticompetitive that each is illegal per se without inquiry into the harm it has actually caused. Other combinations, such as mergers, joint ventures,

and various vertical agreements, hold the promise of increasing a firm's efficiency and enabling it to compete more effectively. Accordingly, such combinations are judged under a rule of reason, an inquiry into market power and market structure designed to assess the combination's actual effect. Whatever form the inquiry takes, however, it is not necessary to prove that concerted activity threatens monopolization.

[13] The reason Congress treated concerted behavior more strictly than unilateral behavior is readily appreciated. Concerted activity inherently is fraught with anticompetitive risk. It deprives the marketplace of the independent centers of decisionmaking that competition assumes and demands. In any conspiracy, two or more entities that previously pursued their own interests separately are combining to act as one for their common benefit. This not only reduces the diverse directions in which economic power is aimed but suddenly increases the economic power moving in one particular direction. Of course, such mergings of resources may well lead to efficiencies that benefit consumers, but their anticompetitive potential is sufficient to warrant scrutiny even in the absence of incipient monopoly.

[14] The distinction between unilateral and concerted conduct is necessary for a proper understanding of the terms "contract, combination . . . or conspiracy" in § 1. Nothing in the literal meaning of those terms excludes coordinated conduct among officers or employees of the same company. But it is perfectly plain that an internal "agreement" to implement a single, unitary firm's policies does not raise the antitrust dangers that § 1 was designed to police. The officers of a single firm are not separate economic actors pursuing separate economic interests, so agreements among them do not suddenly bring together economic power that was previously pursuing divergent goals. Coordination within a firm is as likely to result from an effort to compete as from an effort to stifle competition. In the marketplace, such coordination may be necessary if a business enterprise is to compete effectively. For these reasons, officers or employees of the same firm do not provide the plurality of actors imperative for a § 1 conspiracy.

[15] There is also general agreement that § 1 is not violated by the internally coordinated conduct of a corporation and one of its unincorporated divisions. Although this Court has not previously addressed the question, there can be little doubt that the operations of a corporate enterprise organized into divisions must be judged as the conduct of a single actor. The existence of an unincorporated division reflects no more than a firm's decision to adopt an organizational division of labor. A division within a corporate structure pursues the common interests of the whole rather than interests separate from those of the corporation itself; a business enterprise establishes divisions to further its own interests in the most efficient manner. Because coordination between a corporation and its division does not represent a sudden joining of two independent sources of economic power previously pursuing separate interests, it is not an activity that warrants § 1 scrutiny.

[16] Indeed, a rule that punished coordinated conduct simply because a corporation delegated certain responsibilities to autonomous units might well discourage corporations from creating divisions with their presumed benefits. This would serve no useful antitrust purpose but could well deprive consumers of the efficiencies that decentralized management may bring.

[17] For similar reasons, the coordinated activity of a parent and its wholly owned subsidiary must be viewed as that of a single enterprise for purposes of § 1 of the Sherman Act. A parent and its wholly owned subsidiary have a complete unity of interest. Their objectives are common, not disparate; their general corporate actions are guided or determined not by two separate corporate consciousnesses, but one. They are not unlike a multiple team of horses drawing a vehicle under the control of a single driver. With or without a formal "agreement," the subsidiary acts for the benefit of the parent, its sole shareholder. If a parent and a wholly owned subsidiary do "agree" to a course of action, there is no sudden joining of economic resources that had previously served different interests, and there is no justification for § 1 scrutiny.

[19] Indeed, the very notion of an "agreement" in Sherman Act terms between a parent and a wholly owned subsidiary lacks meaning. A § 1 agreement may be found when the conspirators had a unity of purpose or a common design and understanding, or a meeting of minds in an unlawful arrangement. But in reality a parent and a wholly owned subsidiary always have a unity of purpose or a common design. They share a common purpose whether or not the parent keeps a tight rein over the subsidiary; the parent may assert full control at any moment if the subsidiary fails to act in the parent's best interests.

[20] The intra-enterprise conspiracy doctrine looks to the form of an enterprise's structure and ignores the reality. Antitrust liability should not depend on whether a corporate subunit is organized as an unincorporated division or a wholly owned subsidiary. A corporation has complete power to maintain a wholly owned subsidiary in either form. The economic, legal, or other considerations that lead corporate management to choose one structure over the other are not relevant to whether the enterprise's conduct seriously threatens competition. Rather, a corporation may adopt the subsidiary form of organization for valid management and related purposes . . . . Because there is nothing inherently anticompetitive about a corporation's decision to create a subsidiary, the intra-enterprise conspiracy doctrine imposes grave legal consequences upon organizational distinctions that are of de minimis meaning and effect. [. . .]

[21] The error of treating a corporate division differently from a wholly owned subsidiary is readily seen from the facts of this case. Regal was operated as an unincorporated division of Lear Siegler for four years before it became a wholly owned subsidiary of Copperweld. Nothing in this record indicates any meaningful difference between Regal's operations as a division and its later operations as a separate corporation. Certainly nothing suggests that Regal was a greater threat to competition as a subsidiary of Copperweld than as a division of Lear Siegler. Under either arrangement, Regal might have acted to bar a new competitor from entering the market. In one case it could have relied on economic power from other quarters of the Lear Siegler corporation; instead it drew on the strength of its separately incorporated parent, Copperweld. From the standpoint of the antitrust laws, there is no reason to treat one more harshly than the other. . . .

[22] Any reading of the Sherman Act that remains true to the Act's distinction between unilateral and concerted conduct will necessarily disappoint those who find that distinction arbitrary. It cannot be denied that § 1's focus on concerted behavior leaves a "gap" in the Act's proscription against unreasonable restraints of trade. An unreasonable restraint of trade may be effected not only by two independent firms acting in concert; a single firm may restrain trade to precisely the same extent if it alone possesses the combined market power of those same two firms. Because the Sherman Act does not prohibit unreasonable restraints of trade as such—but only restraints effected by a contract, combination, or conspiracy—it leaves untouched a single firm's anticompetitive conduct (short of threatened monopolization) that may be indistinguishable in economic effect from the conduct of two firms subject to § 1 liability.

[23] We have already noted that Congress left this "gap" for eminently sound reasons. Subjecting a single firm's every action to judicial scrutiny for reasonableness would threaten to discourage the competitive enthusiasm that the antitrust laws seek to promote. Moreover, whatever the wisdom of the distinction, the Act's plain language leaves no doubt that Congress made a purposeful choice to accord different treatment to unilateral and concerted conduct. Had Congress intended to outlaw unreasonable restraints of trade as such, § 1's requirement of a contract, combination, or conspiracy would be superfluous, as would the entirety of § 2. . . .

[24] The appropriate inquiry in this case, therefore, is not whether the coordinated conduct of a parent and its wholly owned subsidiary may ever have anticompetitive effects, as the dissent suggests. Nor is it whether the term "conspiracy" will bear a literal construction that includes parent corporations and their wholly owned subsidiaries. For if these were the proper inquiries, a single firm's conduct would be subject to § 1 scrutiny whenever the coordination of two employees was involved. Such a rule would obliterate the Act's distinction between unilateral and concerted conduct, contrary to the clear intent of Congress as interpreted by the weight of judicial authority. Rather, the appropriate inquiry requires us to explain the logic underlying Congress' decision to exempt unilateral conduct from § 1 scrutiny, and to assess whether that logic similarly excludes the conduct of a parent and its wholly owned subsidiary. Unless we second-guess the judgment of Congress to limit § 1 to concerted conduct, we can only conclude that the coordinated behavior of a parent and its wholly owned subsidiary falls outside the reach of that provision.

[25] Although we recognize that any "gap" the Sherman Act leaves is the sensible result of a purposeful policy decision by Congress, we also note that the size of any such gap is open to serious question. Any anticompetitive activities of corporations and their wholly owned subsidiaries meriting antitrust remedies may be policed adequately without resort to an intra-enterprise conspiracy doctrine. A corporation's initial acquisition of control will always be subject to scrutiny under § 1 of the Sherman Act and § 7 of the Clayton Act. Thereafter, the enterprise is fully subject to § 2 of the Sherman Act and § 5 of the Federal Trade Commission Act. . . .

[26] We hold that Copperweld and its wholly owned subsidiary Regal are incapable of conspiring with each other for purposes of § 1 of the Sherman Act. To the extent that prior decisions of this Court are to the contrary, they are disapproved and overruled. Accordingly, the judgment of the Court of Appeals is reversed. [. . .]

* * *

Copperweld raised as many questions as it answered, not least because it was not entirely clear what definition of "joint conduct" really drove the Court's analysis. Subsequent cases did not clear things up very much. In *Texaco Inc. v. Dagher*, for example, in 2006, the Supreme Court held that when Texaco and Shell formed the "Equilon" joint venture as a home for their retail assets (*i.e.*, service stations and related facilities), it was not price-fixing for the purposes of Section 1 for Equilon to set prices for gasoline, because such price-setting was not joint conduct at all, but rather the unilateral decision of an integrated "legitimate joint venture."[252] A couple of years later, concurring in a prominent Second Circuit decision, then-Judge Sotomayor expressed the fear that price-fixing cartels might evade detection (or at least evade per se condemnation) if they were cleverly labeled as joint ventures.[253]

More guidance was needed. And in 2010 it arrived, in the Supreme Court's *American Needle* decision. That case arose from NFL teams' practice of coordinating their activities for IP licensing through a common agent. When this activity came under antitrust scrutiny, the participants responded that, just like Equilon, the agent was a legitimate joint venture and was entitled to be treated as a single actor for the purposes of joint licensing.[254] The Court disagreed.

American Needle, Inc. v. National Football League
560 U.S. 183 (2010)

Justice Stevens.

[1] "Every contract, combination in the form of a trust or otherwise, or conspiracy, in restraint of trade" is made illegal by § 1 of the Sherman Act. The question whether an arrangement is a contract, combination, or conspiracy is different from and antecedent to the question whether it unreasonably restrains trade. This case raises that antecedent question about the business of the 32 teams in the National Football League (NFL) and a corporate entity that they formed to manage their intellectual property. We conclude that the NFL's licensing activities constitute concerted action that is not categorically beyond the coverage of § 1. The legality of that concerted action must be judged under the Rule of Reason.

[2] . . . [T]he NFL is an unincorporated association that now includes 32 separately owned professional football teams. Each team has its own name, colors, and logo, and owns related intellectual property. . . .

---

[252] Texaco Inc. v. Dagher, 547 U.S. 1, 5–6 (2006) (finding no agreement and explaining: "Texaco and Shell Oil did not compete with one another in the relevant market—namely, the sale of gasoline to service stations in the western United States—but instead participated in that market jointly through their investments in Equilon. In other words, the pricing policy challenged here amounts to little more than price setting by a single entity—albeit within the context of a joint venture—and not a pricing agreement between competing entities with respect to their competing products. Throughout Equilon's existence, Texaco and Shell Oil shared in the profits of Equilon's activities in their role as investors, not competitors. When persons who would otherwise be competitors pool their capital and share the risks of loss as well as the opportunities for profit[,] such joint ventures are regarded as a single firm competing with other sellers in the market.") (internal quotation marks, citations, ellipses, and brackets omitted); *id.* at 8 ("[T]he pricing decisions of a legitimate joint venture do not fall within the narrow category of activity that is *per se* unlawful[.]").

[253] *See* Major League Baseball Properties, Inc. v. Salvino, Inc., 542 F.3d 290, 335–37 (2d Cir. 2008) (Sotomayor, J., concurring) (expressing fear that "competing companies could evade the antitrust laws simply by creating a 'joint venture' to serve as the exclusive seller of their competing products" and stating: "[T]he antitrust laws prohibit two companies A and B, producers of X, from agreeing to set the price of X. Likewise, A and B cannot simply get around this rule by agreeing to set the price of X through a third-party intermediary or "joint venture" if the purpose and effect of that agreement is to raise, depress, fix, peg, or stabilize the price of X.").

[254] *See, e.g.*, Brief for the NFL Respondents, American Needle, Inc. v. NFL, No. 08-661 (filed Nov. 17, 2009), 51 ("Under *Copperweld*, unless its member clubs are independent sources of economic power previously pursuing separate interests, a legitimately formed sports league is ordinarily a single economic entity in the production and promotion of its entertainment product.") (internal quotation marks and citation omitted).

[3] Prior to 1963, the teams made their own arrangements for licensing their intellectual property and marketing trademarked items such as caps and jerseys. In 1963, the teams formed National Football League Properties (NFLP) to develop, license, and market their intellectual property. Most, but not all, of the substantial revenues generated by NFLP have either been given to charity or shared equally among the teams. However, the teams are able to and have at times sought to withdraw from this arrangement.

[4] Between 1963 and 2000, NFLP granted nonexclusive licenses to a number of vendors, permitting them to manufacture and sell apparel bearing team insignias. Petitioner, American Needle, Inc., was one of those licensees. In December 2000, the teams voted to authorize NFLP to grant exclusive licenses, and NFLP granted Reebok International Ltd. an exclusive 10-year license to manufacture and sell trademarked headwear for all 32 teams. It thereafter declined to renew American Needle's nonexclusive license.

[5] American Needle filed this action in the Northern District of Illinois, alleging that the agreements between the NFL, its teams, NFLP, and Reebok violated §§ 1 and 2 of the Sherman Act. In their answer to the complaint, the defendants averred that the teams, the NFL, and NFLP were incapable of conspiring within the meaning of § 1 "because they are a single economic enterprise, at least with respect to the conduct challenged." [T]he District Court granted summary judgment . . . concluding "that in that facet of their operations they have so integrated their operations that they should be deemed a single entity rather than joint ventures cooperating for a common purpose."

[6] The Court of Appeals for the Seventh Circuit affirmed. The panel . . . discounted the significance of potential competition among the teams regarding the use of their intellectual property because the teams "can function only as one source of economic power when collectively producing NFL football . . ." Moreover, "NFL teams share a vital economic interest in collectively promoting NFL football to compete with other forms of entertainment." "It thus follows," the court found, "that only one source of economic power controls the promotion of NFL football," and "it makes little sense to assert that each individual team has the authority, if not the responsibility, to promote the jointly produced NFL football." Recognizing that NFL teams have "licensed their intellectual property collectively" since 1963, the court held that § 1 did not apply. [. . .]

[7] . . . [W]e have only a narrow issue to decide: whether the NFL respondents are capable of engaging in a "contract, combination . . . , or conspiracy" as defined by § 1 of the Sherman Act, or, as we have sometimes phrased it, whether the alleged activity by the NFL respondents must be viewed as that of a single enterprise for purposes of § 1.

[8] The meaning of the term "contract, combination . . . , or conspiracy" is informed by the basic distinction in the Sherman Act between concerted and independent action that distinguishes § 1 of the Sherman Act from § 2. Section 1 applies only to concerted action that restrains trade. Section 2, by contrast, covers both concerted and independent action, but only if that action monopolizes or threatens actual monopolization, a category that is narrower than restraint of trade. Monopoly power may be equally harmful whether it is the product of joint action or individual action.

[9] Congress used this distinction between concerted and independent action to deter anticompetitive conduct and compensate its victims, without chilling vigorous competition through ordinary business operations. The distinction also avoids judicial scrutiny of routine, internal business decisions.

[10] Thus, in § 1 Congress treated concerted behavior more strictly than unilateral behavior. This is so because unlike independent action, concerted activity inherently is fraught with anticompetitive risk insofar as it deprives the marketplace of independent centers of decisionmaking that competition assumes and demands. And because concerted action is discrete and distinct, a limit on such activity leaves untouched a vast amount of business conduct. As a result, there is less risk of deterring a firm's necessary conduct. . . .

[11] We have long held that concerted action under § 1 does not turn simply on whether the parties involved are legally distinct entities. Instead, we have eschewed such formalistic distinctions in favor of a functional consideration of how the parties involved in the alleged anticompetitive conduct actually operate.

[12] As a result, we have repeatedly found instances in which members of a legally single entity violated § 1 when the entity was controlled by a group of competitors and served, in essence, as a vehicle for ongoing concerted activity. In *United States v. Sealy, Inc.*, 388 U.S. 350 (1967), for example, a group of mattress manufacturers operated and controlled Sealy, Inc., a company that licensed the Sealy trademark to the manufacturers, and dictated that each operate within a specific geographic area. The Government alleged that the licensees and Sealy were conspiring in violation of § 1, and we agreed. We explained that we seek the central substance of the situation and therefore we are moved by the identity of the persons who act, rather than the label of their hats. We thus held that Sealy was not a separate entity, but an instrumentality of the individual manufacturers. . . . We have similarly looked past the form of a legally single entity when competitors were part of professional organizations or trade groups.

[13] Conversely, there is not necessarily concerted action simply because more than one legally distinct entity is involved. Although, under a now-defunct doctrine known as the "intraenterprise conspiracy doctrine," we once treated cooperation between legally separate entities as necessarily covered by § 1, we now embark on a more functional analysis. [. . .]

[14] As *Copperweld* exemplifies, substance, not form, should determine whether an entity is capable of conspiring under § 1. This inquiry is sometimes described as asking whether the alleged conspirators are a single entity. That is perhaps a misdescription, however, because the question is not whether the defendant is a legally single entity or has a single name; nor is the question whether the parties involved "seem" like one firm or multiple firms in any metaphysical sense. The key is whether the alleged "contract, combination, or conspiracy" is concerted action—that is, whether it joins together separate decisionmakers. The relevant inquiry, therefore, is whether there is a "contract, combination, or conspiracy" amongst "separate economic actors pursuing separate economic interests," such that the agreement "deprives the marketplace of independent centers of decisionmaking," and therefore of "diversity of entrepreneurial interests," and thus of actual or potential competition. [. . .]

[15] The NFL teams do not possess either the unitary decisionmaking quality or the single aggregation of economic power characteristic of independent action. Each of the teams is a substantial, independently owned, and independently managed business . . . . The teams compete with one another, not only on the playing field, but to attract fans, for gate receipts, and for contracts with managerial and playing personnel.

[16] Directly relevant to this case, the teams compete in the market for intellectual property. To a firm making hats, the Saints and the Colts are two potentially competing suppliers of valuable trademarks. When each NFL team licenses its intellectual property, it is not pursuing the common interests of the whole league but is instead pursuing interests of each corporation itself, teams are acting as separate economic actors pursuing separate economic interests, and each team therefore is a potential independent center of decisionmaking. Decisions by NFL teams to license their separately owned trademarks collectively and to only one vendor are decisions that deprive the marketplace of independent centers of decisionmaking, and therefore of actual or potential competition.

[17] In defense, respondents argue that by forming NFLP, they have formed a single entity, akin to a merger, and market their NFL brands through a single outlet. But it is not dispositive that the teams have organized and own a legally separate entity that centralizes the management of their intellectual property. An ongoing § 1 violation cannot evade § 1 scrutiny simply by giving the ongoing violation a name and label. Perhaps every agreement and combination in restraint of trade could be so labeled.

[18] The NFL respondents may be similar in some sense to a single enterprise that owns several pieces of intellectual property and licenses them jointly, but they are not similar in the relevant functional sense. Although NFL teams have common interests such as promoting the NFL brand, they are still separate, profit-maximizing entities, and their interests in licensing team trademarks are not necessarily aligned. . . .

[19] It may be, as respondents argue, that NFLP has served as the single driver of the teams' promotional vehicle, pursuing the common interests of the whole. But illegal restraints often are in the common interests of the parties to the restraint, at the expense of those who are not parties. It is true, as respondents describe, that they have for

some time marketed their trademarks jointly. But a history of concerted activity does not immunize conduct from § 1 scrutiny. Absence of actual competition may simply be a manifestation of the anticompetitive agreement itself.

[20] Respondents argue that nonetheless, as the Court of Appeals held, they constitute a single entity because without their cooperation, there would be no NFL football. It is true that the clubs that make up a professional sports league are not completely independent economic competitors, as they depend upon a degree of cooperation for economic survival. But the Court of Appeals' reasoning is unpersuasive. The justification for cooperation is not relevant to whether that cooperation is concerted or independent action. . . .

[21] The question whether NFLP decisions can constitute concerted activity covered by § 1 is closer than whether decisions made directly by the 32 teams are covered by § 1. This is so both because NFLP is a separate corporation with its own management and because the record indicates that most of the revenues generated by NFLP are shared by the teams on an equal basis. Nevertheless we think it clear that for the same reasons the 32 teams' conduct is covered by § 1, NFLP's actions also are subject to § 1, at least with regards to its marketing of property owned by the separate teams. NFLP's licensing decisions are made by the 32 potential competitors, and each of them actually owns its share of the jointly managed assets. Apart from their agreement to cooperate in exploiting those assets, including their decisions as the NFLP, there would be nothing to prevent each of the teams from making its own market decisions relating to purchases of apparel and headwear, to the sale of such items, and to the granting of licenses to use its trademarks.

[22] We generally treat agreements within a single firm as independent action on the presumption that the components of the firm will act to maximize the firm's profits. But in rare cases, that presumption does not hold. Agreements made within a firm can constitute concerted action covered by § 1 when the parties to the agreement act on interests separate from those of the firm itself, and the intrafirm agreements may simply be a formalistic shell for ongoing concerted action.

[23] For that reason, decisions by NFLP regarding the teams' separately owned intellectual property constitute concerted action. Thirty-two teams operating independently through the vehicle of NFLP are not like the components of a single firm that act to maximize the firm's profits. The teams remain separately controlled, potential competitors with economic interests that are distinct from NFLP's financial well-being. Unlike typical decisions by corporate shareholders, NFLP licensing decisions effectively require the assent of more than a mere majority of shareholders. And each team's decision reflects not only an interest in NFLP's profits but also an interest in the team's individual profits. The 32 teams capture individual economic benefits separate and apart from NFLP profits as a result of the decisions they make for NFLP. NFLP's decisions thus affect each team's profits from licensing its own intellectual property. . . . In making the relevant licensing decisions, NFLP is therefore "an instrumentality" of the teams.

[24] If the fact that potential competitors shared in profits or losses from a venture meant that the venture was immune from § 1, then any cartel could evade the antitrust laws simply by creating a "joint venture" to serve as the exclusive seller of their competing products. So long as no agreement, other than one made by the cartelists sitting on the board of the joint venture, explicitly listed the prices to be charged, the companies could act as monopolies through the "joint venture." (Indeed, a joint venture with a single management structure is generally a better way to operate a cartel because it decreases the risks of a party to an illegal agreement defecting from that agreement.) However, competitors cannot simply get around antitrust liability by acting through a third-party intermediary or "joint venture."

[25] Football teams that need to cooperate are not trapped by antitrust law. The special characteristics of this industry may provide a justification for many kinds of agreements. The fact that NFL teams share an interest in making the entire league successful and profitable, and that they must cooperate in the production and scheduling of games, provides a perfectly sensible justification for making a host of collective decisions. But the conduct at issue in this case is still concerted activity under the Sherman Act that is subject to § 1 analysis.

NOTES

1) Why, if at all, does antitrust really need a separate entity requirement? What is the value or point, if any, of making this an important issue in antitrust doctrine and a limiting principle of Section 1?

2) Is there a sensible argument that the *Copperweld* majority was wrong about whether a wholly-owned subsidiary and its parent should be capable of entering into a "contract, combination, or conspiracy" as that term is understood in the context of Section 1? Is that, in fact, the law after *American Needle*?

3) The *Copperweld* Court identifies a "gap" between Section 2's coverage of unilateral conduct by current or prospective monopolists, and Section 1's coverage of multi-party conduct. Is this gap a problem? What kind of behavior falls into it?

4) Note that the *Copperweld* Court's holding is a limited one: the Court holds *only* that a parent and its wholly-owned subsidiary cannot conspire. But should the same rule apply to a majority-owned subsidiary?[255] What about a 50%-owned subsidiary? Or a corporate relationship involving less than 50% ownership but rights of veto or management? And what about two corporations not in a parent-subsidiary relationship with one another both owned by a single parent (*i.e.*, corporate "siblings")—can they conspire?[256]

5) Would *American Needle* have come out differently if the teams had simply transferred ownership of their intellectual property to NFLP?

6) In paragraph 15 of the *American Needle* extract, the Court states that the teams are competitors in the market for licensing their intellectual property. Is that statement correct? In what market are the teams competitors to license their IP? Is this an important issue for the purposes of the separate-entities analysis?

7) Suppose that a price-fixing cartel agreed to share its profits and losses. Would that cartel then become a single entity and thus beyond the scope of Section 1? Alternatively: would it become a joint venture that should be analyzed under the rule of reason?

8) With the rise of the gig economy, and some blurring of the lines between "employee" and "independent contractor," does it make sense to apply per se immunity under Section 1 to all employees and no independent contractors? What are the advantages and disadvantages of that approach?

2. Defining and Proving an Agreement

Antitrust courts face the difficult task of sorting between two types of behavior that often are difficult to distinguish from the outside and yet are treated very differently under § 1: agreements, on the one hand, and purely unilateral conduct, on the other. Agreements, of course, are scrutinized under Section 1 for their impact on competition, and may be unlawful or even criminal. Purely unilateral conduct, on the other hand, cannot be challenged or condemned under Section 1. A source of particular difficulty is that businesses may decide to behave in certain ways in light of what rivals (and others) are doing, have done, or seem likely to do in future, all without entering into an "agreement" in the sense that antitrust law understands this term.

A classic example, and a perennial puzzle for antitrust policy, is "conscious parallelism" or "tacit collusion." As we saw in Chapter II, under some circumstances firms may act in mutually interdependent ways (*e.g.*, keeping prices high on the understanding that others will do the same) that may closely replicate the operation of a price-fixing cartel, but without actually agreeing that they will in fact behave in this way. From a legal perspective, if nothing more than parallel conduct is going on, the rivals have not actually agreed, so Section 1 is not implicated.[257]

In light of this reality, and given that businesses commonly adjust their behavior in light of what other market participants do, courts in antitrust cases have struggled to pin down exactly what the concept of agreement really means, or should mean. This is a lawyers' problem rather than an economists' one: antitrust economics generally does not have, or require, a theory of what an agreement is.

[255] *See, e.g.*, Siegel Transfer, Inc. v. Carrier Exp., Inc., 54 F.3d 1125, 1133 (3d Cir. 1995); In re Sulfuric Acid Antitrust Litig., 743 F. Supp. 2d 827, 885 (N.D. Ill. 2010).

[256] *See, e.g.*, Lenox MacLaren Surgical Corp. v. Medtronic, Inc., 847 F.3d 1221, 1233 (10th Cir. 2017); In re Lantus Direct Purchaser Antitrust Litig., No. CV 16-12652-JGD, 2021 WL 8016913, at *3 (D. Mass. June 11, 2021).

[257] Theatre Enterprises v. Paramount Film Distributing Corp., 346 U.S. 537, 541 (1954) ("[T]his Court has never held that proof of parallel business behavior conclusively establishes agreement or, phrased differently, that such behavior itself constitutes a Sherman Act offense.... '[C]onscious parallelism' has not yet read conspiracy out of the Sherman Act entirely."); E.I. du Pont de Nemours & Co. v. FTC, 729 F.2d 128, 139 (2d Cir. 1984) ("The mere existence of an oligopolistic market structure in which a small group of manufacturers engage in consciously parallel pricing of an identical product does not violate the antitrust laws.").

In the landmark *Monsanto* and *Matsushita* cases that follow, the Supreme Court attempted to articulate two different things: (1) the *definition* of an agreement; and (2) what nature and cogency of *evidence* is required to demonstrate that one exists following the close of discovery. Did the Court succeed? And what are the possible alternatives?

Monsanto Co. v. Spray-Rite Service Corp.
465 U.S. 752 (1984)

Justice Powell.

[1] This case presents a question as to the standard of proof required to find a vertical [resale price maintenance agreement (*i.e.*, an agreement between a manufacturer and distributors on the resale price of a product or service), which at the time of this case was *per se* illegal] in violation of Section 1 of the Sherman Act.

[2] Petitioner Monsanto Company manufactures chemical products, including agricultural herbicides. By the late 1960's, the time at issue in this case, its sales accounted for approximately 15% of the corn herbicide market and 3% of the soybean herbicide market. In the corn herbicide market, the market leader commanded a 70% share. In the soybean herbicide market, two other competitors each had between 30% and 40% of the market. Respondent Spray-Rite Service Corporation was engaged in the wholesale distribution of agricultural chemicals from 1955 to 1972. Spray-Rite was essentially a family business, whose owner and president, Donald Yapp, was also its sole salaried salesman. Spray-Rite was a discount operation, buying in large quantities and selling at a low margin.

[3] Spray-Rite was an authorized distributor of Monsanto herbicides from 1957 to 1968. In October 1967, Monsanto announced that it would appoint distributors for one-year terms, and that it would renew distributorships according to several new criteria. Among the criteria were: (i) whether the distributor's primary activity was soliciting sales to retail dealers; (ii) whether the distributor employed trained salesmen capable of educating its customers on the technical aspects of Monsanto's herbicides; and (iii) whether the distributor could be expected "to exploit fully" the market in its geographical area of primary responsibility. Shortly thereafter, Monsanto also introduced a number of incentive programs, such as making cash payments to distributors that sent salesmen to training classes, and providing free deliveries of products to customers within a distributor's area of primary responsibility.

[4] In October 1968, Monsanto declined to renew Spray-Rite's distributorship. At that time, Spray-Rite was the tenth largest out of approximately 100 distributors of Monsanto's primary corn herbicide. Ninety percent of Spray-Rite's sales volume was devoted to herbicide sales, and 16% of its sales were of Monsanto products. After Monsanto's termination, Spray-Rite continued as a herbicide dealer until 1972. It was able to purchase some of Monsanto's products from other distributors, but not as much as it desired or as early in the season as it needed. Monsanto introduced a new corn herbicide in 1969. By 1972, its share of the corn herbicide market had increased to approximately 28%. Its share of the soybean herbicide market had grown to approximately 19%.

[5] Spray-Rite brought this action under Section 1 of the Sherman Act. It alleged that Monsanto and some of its distributors conspired to fix the resale prices of Monsanto herbicides. Its complaint further alleged that Monsanto terminated Spray-Rite's distributorship, adopted compensation programs and shipping policies, and encouraged distributors to boycott Spray-Rite in furtherance of this conspiracy. Monsanto denied the allegations of conspiracy, and asserted that Spray-Rite's distributorship had been terminated because of its failure to hire trained salesmen and promote sales to dealers adequately.

[6] The case was tried to a jury. The District Court instructed the jury that Monsanto's conduct was *per se* unlawful if it was in furtherance of a conspiracy to fix prices. In answers to special interrogatories, the jury found that (i) the termination of Spray-Rite was pursuant to a conspiracy between Monsanto and one or more of its distributors to set resale prices, (ii) the compensation programs, areas of primary responsibility, and/or shipping policies were created by Monsanto pursuant to such a conspiracy, and (iii) Monsanto conspired with one or more distributors to limit Spray-Rite's access to Monsanto herbicides after 1968. The jury awarded $3.5 million in damages, which was trebled to $10.5 million. Only the first of the jury's findings is before us today.

[7] The Court of Appeals for the Seventh Circuit affirmed. It held that there was sufficient evidence to satisfy Spray-Rite's burden of proving a conspiracy to set resale prices. The court stated that "proof of termination following competitor complaints is sufficient to support an inference of concerted action." Canvassing the testimony and exhibits that were before the jury, the court found evidence of numerous complaints from competing Monsanto distributors about Spray-Rite's price-cutting practices. It also noted that there was testimony that a Monsanto official had said that Spray-Rite was terminated because of the price complaints.

[8] In substance, the Court of Appeals held that an antitrust plaintiff can survive a motion for a directed verdict if it shows that a manufacturer terminated a price-cutting distributor in response to or following complaints by other distributors. This view brought the Seventh Circuit into direct conflict with a number of other Courts of Appeals. We granted certiorari to resolve the conflict. We reject the statement by the Court of Appeals for the Seventh Circuit of the standard of proof required to submit a case to the jury in distributor-termination litigation, but affirm the judgment under the standard we announce today.

[9] This Court has drawn two important distinctions that are at the center of this and any other distributor-termination case. First, there is the basic distinction between concerted and independent action—a distinction not always clearly drawn by parties and courts. Section 1 of the Sherman Act requires that there be a "contract, combination or conspiracy" between the manufacturer and other distributors in order to establish a violation. Independent action is not proscribed. A manufacturer of course generally has a right to deal, or refuse to deal, with whomever it likes, as long as it does so independently. *United States v. Colgate & Co.*, 250 U.S. 300, 307 (1919). Under *Colgate*, the manufacturer can announce its resale prices in advance and refuse to deal with those who fail to comply. And a distributor is free to acquiesce in the manufacturer's demand in order to avoid termination.

[10] The second important distinction in distributor-termination cases is that between concerted action to set prices and concerted action on nonprice restrictions. {*Eds: At the time this case was decided, the former were treated as per se illegal and the latter were judged under the rule of reason. Virtually all vertical restraints are now subject to rule of reason analysis. See Chapter VI.*}

[11] While these distinctions in theory are reasonably clear, often they are difficult to apply in practice. In [*Continental T.V., Inc. v. GTE Sylvania Inc.*, 433 U.S. 36 (1977)] we emphasized that the legality of arguably anticompetitive conduct should be judged primarily by its "market impact." But the economic effect of all of the conduct described above—unilateral and concerted vertical price-setting, agreements on price and nonprice restrictions—is in many, but not all, cases similar or identical. And judged from a distance, the conduct of the parties in the various situations can be indistinguishable. For example, the fact that a manufacturer and its distributors are in constant communication about prices and marketing strategy does not alone show that the distributors are not making independent pricing decisions. A manufacturer and its distributors have legitimate reasons to exchange information about the prices and the reception of their products in the market. Moreover, it is precisely in cases in which the manufacturer attempts to further a particular marketing strategy by means of agreements on often costly nonprice restrictions that it will have the most interest in the distributors' resale prices. The manufacturer often will want to ensure that its distributors earn sufficient profit to pay for programs such as hiring and training additional salesmen or demonstrating the technical features of the product, and will want to see that "free-riders" do not interfere. Thus, the manufacturer's strongly felt concern about resale prices does not necessarily mean that it has done more than the *Colgate* doctrine allows.

[12] Nevertheless, it is of considerable importance that independent action by the manufacturer, and concerted action on nonprice restrictions, be distinguished from price-fixing agreements, since under present law the latter are subject to per se treatment and treble damages. On a claim of concerted price-fixing, the antitrust plaintiff must present evidence sufficient to carry its burden of proving that there was such an agreement. If an inference of such an agreement may be drawn from highly ambiguous evidence, there is a considerable danger that the doctrines enunciated in *Sylvania* and *Colgate* will be seriously eroded.

[13] The flaw in the evidentiary standard adopted by the Court of Appeals in this case is that it disregards this danger. Permitting an agreement to be inferred merely from the existence of complaints, or even from the fact that termination came about in response to complaints, could deter or penalize perfectly legitimate conduct. As Monsanto points out, complaints about price-cutters are natural—and from the manufacturer's perspective,

unavoidable—reactions by distributors to the activities of their rivals. Such complaints, particularly where the manufacturer has imposed a costly set of nonprice restrictions, arise in the normal course of business and do not indicate illegal concerted action. Moreover, distributors are an important source of information for manufacturers. In order to assure an efficient distribution system, manufacturers and distributors constantly must coordinate their activities to assure that their product will reach the consumer persuasively and efficiently. To bar a manufacturer from acting solely because the information upon which it acts originated as a price complaint would create an irrational dislocation in the market. In sum, to permit the inference of concerted action on the basis of receiving complaints alone and thus to expose the defendant to treble damage liability would both inhibit management's exercise of independent business judgment and emasculate the terms of the statute.[8]

[14] Thus, something more than evidence of complaints is needed. There must be evidence that tends to exclude the possibility that the manufacturer and nonterminated distributors were acting independently…. [T]he antitrust plaintiff should present direct or circumstantial evidence that reasonably tends to prove that the manufacturer and others had a conscious commitment to a common scheme designed to achieve an unlawful objective.[9]

[15] Applying this standard to the facts of this case, we believe there was sufficient evidence for the jury reasonably to have concluded that Monsanto and some of its distributors were parties to an "agreement" or "conspiracy" to maintain resale prices and terminate price-cutters. In fact there was substantial *direct* evidence of agreements to maintain prices. There was testimony from a Monsanto district manager, for example, that Monsanto on at least two occasions in early 1969, about five months after Spray-Rite was terminated, approached price-cutting distributors and advised that if they did not maintain the suggested resale price, they would not receive adequate supplies of Monsanto's new corn herbicide. When one of the distributors did not assent, this information was referred to the Monsanto regional office, and it complained to the distributor's parent company. There was evidence that the parent instructed its subsidiary to comply, and the distributor informed Monsanto that it would charge the suggested price. Evidence of this kind plainly is relevant and persuasive as to a meeting of minds.[10]

[16] An arguably more ambiguous example is a newsletter from one of the distributors to his dealer-customers. The newsletter is dated October 1, 1968, just four weeks before Spray-Rite was terminated. It was written after a meeting between the author and several Monsanto officials, and discusses Monsanto's efforts to "get the market place in order." The newsletter reviews some of Monsanto's incentive and shipping policies, and then states that in addition "every effort will be made to maintain a minimum market price level." The newsletter relates these efforts as follows:

> In other words, we are assured that Monsanto's company-owned outlets will not retail at less than their suggested retail price to the trade as a whole. Furthermore, those of us on the distributor level are not likely to deviate downward on price to anyone as the idea is implied that doing this possibly could discolor the outlook for continuity as one of the approved distributors during the future upcoming seasons. So, [no-one] interested in the retention of this arrangement is likely to risk being deleted from this customer service opportunity. Also, so far as the national accounts are concerned, they are sure to recognize the desirability of retaining Monsanto's favor on a continuing basis by respecting the wisdom of participating in the suggested program in a manner assuring order on the retail level "playground" throughout the entire country. It is elementary that harmony can only come from following the rules of the game and that in case of dispute, the decision of the umpire is final.

[17] It is reasonable to interpret this newsletter as referring to an agreement or understanding that distributors and retailers would maintain prices, and Monsanto would not undercut those prices on the retail level and would

---

[8] We do not suggest that evidence of complaints has no probative value at all, but only that the burden remains on the antitrust plaintiff to introduce additional evidence sufficient to support a finding of an unlawful contract, combination, or conspiracy.

[9] The concept of "a meeting of the minds" or "a common scheme" in a distributor-termination case includes more than a showing that the distributor conformed to the suggested price. It means as well that evidence must be presented both that the distributor communicated its acquiescence or agreement, and that this was sought by the manufacturer.

[10] In addition, there was circumstantial evidence that Monsanto sought agreement from the distributor to conform to the resale price. The threat to cut off the distributor's supply came during Monsanto's "shipping season" when herbicide was in short supply. The jury could have concluded that Monsanto sought this agreement at a time when it was able to use supply as a lever to force compliance.

terminate competitors who sold at prices below those of complying distributors; these were "the rules of the game."[11]

[18] If, as the courts below reasonably could have found, there was evidence of an agreement with one or more distributors to maintain prices, the remaining question is whether the termination of Spray-Rite was part of or pursuant to that agreement. It would be reasonable to find that it was, since it is necessary for competing distributors contemplating compliance with suggested prices to know that those who do not comply will be terminated. Moreover, there is some circumstantial evidence of such a link. Following the termination, there was a meeting between Spray-Rite's president and a Monsanto official. There was testimony that the first thing the official mentioned was the many complaints Monsanto had received about Spray-Rite's prices.[12] In addition, there was reliable testimony that Monsanto never discussed with Spray-Rite prior to the termination the distributorship criteria that were the alleged basis for the action. By contrast, a former Monsanto salesman for Spray-Rite's area testified that Monsanto representatives on several occasions in 1965–1966 approached Spray-Rite, informed the distributor of complaints from other distributors—including one major and influential one—and requested that prices be maintained. Later that same year, Spray-Rite's president testified, Monsanto officials made explicit threats to terminate Spray-Rite unless it raised its prices.[13]

[19] We conclude that the Court of Appeals applied an incorrect standard to the evidence in this case. The correct standard is that there must be evidence that tends to exclude the possibility of independent action by the manufacturer and distributor. That is, there must be direct or circumstantial evidence that reasonably tends to prove that the manufacturer and others had a conscious commitment to a common scheme designed to achieve an unlawful objective. Under this standard, the evidence in this case created a jury issue as to whether Spray-Rite was terminated pursuant to a price-fixing conspiracy between Monsanto and its distributors. The judgment of the court below is affirmed.

* * *

Matsushita Elec. Industrial Co., Ltd. v. Zenith Radio Corp.
475 U.S. 574 (1986)

Justice Powell.

[1] This case requires that we again consider the standard district courts must apply when deciding whether to grant summary judgment in an antitrust conspiracy case. [. . .]

[2] Petitioners, defendants below, are 21 corporations that manufacture or sell "consumer electronic products" (CEPs)—for the most part, television sets. Petitioners include both Japanese manufacturers of CEPs and American firms, controlled by Japanese parents, that sell the Japanese-manufactured products. Respondents, plaintiffs below, are Zenith Radio Corporation (Zenith) and National Union Electric Corporation (NUE). Zenith is an American firm that manufactures and sells television sets. NUE is the corporate successor to Emerson Radio Company, an American firm that manufactured and sold television sets until 1970, when it withdrew from the market after sustaining substantial losses. Zenith and NUE began this lawsuit in 1974, claiming that petitioners had illegally conspired to drive American firms from the American CEP market. According to respondents, the gist of this conspiracy was a "scheme to raise, fix and maintain artificially *high* prices for television receivers sold by

---

[11] The newsletter also is subject to the interpretation that the distributor was merely describing the likely reaction to unilateral Monsanto pronouncements. But Monsanto itself appears to have construed the flyer as reporting a price-fixing understanding. Six weeks after the newsletter was written, a Monsanto official wrote its author a letter urging him to "correct immediately any misconceptions about Monsanto's marketing policies." The letter disavowed any intent to enter into an agreement on resale prices. The interpretation of these documents and the testimony surrounding them properly was left to the jury.

[12] Monsanto argues that the reference could have been to complaints by Monsanto employees rather than distributors, suggesting that the price controls were merely unilateral action, rather than accession to the demands of the distributors. The choice between two reasonable interpretations of the testimony properly was left for the jury. . . .

[13] The existence of the illegal joint boycott after Spray-Rite's termination, a finding that the Court of Appeals affirmed and that is not before us, is further evidence that Monsanto and its distributors had an understanding that prices would be maintained, and that price-cutters would be terminated. This last, however, is also consistent with termination for other reasons, and is probative only of the ability of Monsanto and its distributors to act in concert.

[petitioners] in Japan and, at the same time, to fix and maintain *low* prices for television receivers exported to and sold in the United States." These "low prices" were allegedly at levels that produced substantial losses for petitioners. The conspiracy allegedly began as early as 1953, and according to respondents was in full operation by sometime in the late 1960's. [. . .]

[3] The District Court [granted] petitioners' motions for summary judgment. In an opinion spanning 217 pages, the court found that the admissible evidence did not raise a genuine issue of material fact as to the existence of the alleged conspiracy. At bottom, the court found, respondents' claims rested on the inferences that could be drawn from petitioners' parallel conduct in the Japanese and American markets, and from the effects of that conduct on petitioners' American competitors. After reviewing the evidence both by category and *in toto*, the court found that any inference of conspiracy was unreasonable, because (i) some portions of the evidence suggested that petitioners conspired in ways that did not injure respondents, and (ii) the evidence that bore directly on the alleged price-cutting conspiracy did not rebut the more plausible inference that petitioners were cutting prices to compete in the American market and not to monopolize it. Summary judgment therefore was granted on respondents' claims under § 1 of the Sherman Act. . . .

[4] The Court of Appeals for the Third Circuit reversed. [. . .]

[5] The court acknowledged that "there are legal limitations upon the inferences which may be drawn from circumstantial evidence," but it found that "the legal problem is different" when "there is direct evidence of concert of action." Here, the court concluded, "there is both direct evidence of certain kinds of concert of action and circumstantial evidence having some tendency to suggest that other kinds of concert of action may have occurred." Thus, the court reasoned, cases concerning the limitations on inferring conspiracy from ambiguous evidence were not dispositive. Turning to the evidence, the court determined that a factfinder reasonably could draw the following conclusions:

1. The Japanese market for CEPs was characterized by oligopolistic behavior, with a small number of producers meeting regularly and exchanging information on price and other matters. This created the opportunity for a stable combination to raise both prices and profits in Japan. American firms could not attack such a combination because the Japanese Government imposed significant barriers to entry.

2. Petitioners had relatively higher fixed costs than their American counterparts, and therefore needed to operate at something approaching full capacity in order to make a profit.

3. Petitioners' plant capacity exceeded the needs of the Japanese market.

4. By formal agreements arranged in cooperation with Japan's Ministry of International Trade and Industry (MITI), petitioners fixed minimum prices for CEPs exported to the American market. The parties refer to these prices as the "check prices," and to the agreements that require them as the "check price agreements."

5. Petitioners agreed to distribute their products in the United States according to a "five company rule": each Japanese producer was permitted to sell only to five American distributors.

6. Petitioners undercut their own check prices by a variety of rebate schemes. Petitioners sought to conceal these rebate schemes both from the United States Customs Service and from MITI [(*i.e.*, the Japanese Ministry of International Trade and Industry)], the former to avoid various customs regulations as well as action under the antidumping laws, and the latter to cover up petitioners' violations of the check-price agreements.

[6] Based on inferences from the foregoing conclusions,[5] the Court of Appeals concluded that a reasonable factfinder could find a conspiracy to depress prices in the American market in order to drive out American competitors, which conspiracy was funded by excess profits obtained in the Japanese market. The court apparently

---

[5] In addition to these inferences, the court noted that there was expert opinion evidence that petitioners' export sales generally were at prices which produced losses, often as high as twenty-five percent on sales. The court did not identify any direct evidence of below-cost pricing; nor did it place particularly heavy reliance on this aspect of the expert evidence.

did not consider whether it was as plausible to conclude that petitioners' price-cutting behavior was independent and not conspiratorial. [. . .]

[7] We granted certiorari to determine . . . whether the Court of Appeals applied the proper standards in evaluating the District Court's decision to grant petitioners' motion for summary judgment. We reverse. . . .

[8] We begin by emphasizing what respondents' claim is *not*. Respondents cannot recover antitrust damages based solely on an alleged cartelization of the Japanese market, because American antitrust laws do not regulate the competitive conditions of other nations' economies. Nor can respondents recover damages for any conspiracy by petitioners to charge higher than competitive prices in the American market. Such conduct would indeed violate the Sherman Act, but it could not injure respondents: as petitioners' competitors, respondents stand to gain from any conspiracy to raise the market price in CEPs. Finally, for the same reason, respondents cannot recover for a conspiracy to impose nonprice restraints that have the effect of either raising market price or limiting output. Such restrictions, though harmful to competition, actually *benefit* competitors by making supracompetitive pricing more attractive. Thus, neither petitioners' alleged supracompetitive pricing in Japan, nor the five-company rule that limited distribution in this country, nor the check prices insofar as they established minimum prices in this country, can by themselves give respondents a cognizable claim against petitioners for antitrust damages. The Court of Appeals therefore erred to the extent that it found evidence of these alleged conspiracies to be "direct evidence" of a conspiracy that injured respondents.

[9] Respondents nevertheless argue that these supposed conspiracies, if not themselves grounds for recovery of antitrust damages, are circumstantial evidence of another conspiracy that *is* cognizable: a conspiracy to monopolize the American market by means of pricing below the market level. The thrust of respondents' argument is that petitioners used their monopoly profits from the Japanese market to fund a concerted campaign to price predatorily and thereby drive respondents and other American manufacturers of CEPs out of business. Once successful, according to respondents, petitioners would cartelize the American CEP market, restricting output and raising prices above the level that fair competition would produce. The resulting monopoly profits, respondents contend, would more than compensate petitioners for the losses they incurred through years of pricing below market level.

[10] The Court of Appeals found that respondents' allegation of a horizontal conspiracy to engage in predatory pricing,[8] if proved,[9] would be a *per se* violation of § 1 of the Sherman Act. Petitioners did not appeal from that conclusion. The issue in this case thus becomes whether respondents adduced sufficient evidence in support of their theory to survive summary judgment. We therefore examine the principles that govern the summary judgment determination.

[11] To survive petitioners' motion for summary judgment, respondents must establish that there is a genuine issue of material fact as to whether petitioners entered into an illegal conspiracy that caused respondents to suffer a cognizable injury. This showing has two components. First, respondents must show more than a conspiracy in violation of the antitrust laws; they must show an injury to them resulting from the illegal conduct. Respondents charge petitioners with a whole host of conspiracies in restraint of trade. Except for the alleged conspiracy to monopolize the American market through predatory pricing, these alleged conspiracies could not have caused respondents to suffer an "antitrust injury," because they actually tended to benefit respondents. Therefore, unless,

---

[8] Throughout this opinion, we refer to the asserted conspiracy as one to price "predatorily." This term has been used chiefly in cases in which a single firm, having a dominant share of the relevant market, cuts its prices in order to force competitors out of the market, or perhaps to deter potential entrants from coming in. In such cases, "predatory pricing" means pricing below some appropriate measure of cost.

There is a good deal of debate, both in the cases and in the law reviews, about what "cost" is relevant in such cases. We need not resolve this debate here, because unlike the cases cited above, this is a Sherman Act § 1 case. For purposes of this case, it is enough to note that respondents have not suffered an antitrust injury unless petitioners conspired to drive respondents out of the relevant markets by (i) pricing below the level necessary to sell their products, or (ii) pricing below some appropriate measure of cost. An agreement without these features would either leave respondents in the same position as would market forces or would actually benefit respondents by raising market prices. Respondents therefore may not complain of conspiracies that, for example, set maximum prices above market levels, or that set minimum prices at *any* level.

[9] We do not consider whether recovery should *ever* be available on a theory such as respondents' when the pricing in question is above some measure of incremental cost. As a practical matter, it may be that only direct evidence of below-cost pricing is sufficient to overcome the strong inference that rational businesses would not enter into conspiracies such as this one.

in context, evidence of these "other" conspiracies raises a genuine issue concerning the existence of a predatory pricing conspiracy, that evidence cannot defeat petitioners' summary judgment motion.

[12] Second, the issue of fact must be "genuine." . . . Where the record taken as a whole could not lead a rational trier of fact to find for the non-moving party, there is no genuine issue for trial.

[13] It follows from these settled principles that if the factual context renders respondents' claim implausible—if the claim is one that simply makes no economic sense—respondents must come forward with more persuasive evidence to support their claim than would otherwise be necessary. . .

[14] Respondents correctly note that on summary judgment the inferences to be drawn from the underlying facts must be viewed in the light most favorable to the party opposing the motion. But antitrust law limits the range of permissible inferences from ambiguous evidence in a § 1 case. Thus, in *Monsanto Co. v. Spray-Rite Service Corp.*, 465 U.S. 752 (1984), we held that conduct as consistent with permissible competition as with illegal conspiracy does not, standing alone, support an inference of antitrust conspiracy. To survive a motion for summary judgment or for a directed verdict, a plaintiff seeking damages for a violation of § 1 must present evidence that tends to exclude the possibility that the alleged conspirators acted independently. Respondents in this case, in other words, must show that the inference of conspiracy is reasonable in light of the competing inferences of independent action or collusive action that could not have harmed respondents. [. . .]

[15] A predatory pricing conspiracy is by nature speculative. Any agreement to price below the competitive level requires the conspirators to forgo profits that free competition would offer them. The forgone profits may be considered an investment in the future. For the investment to be rational, the conspirators must have a reasonable expectation of recovering, in the form of later monopoly profits, more than the losses suffered. As then-Professor Bork, discussing predatory pricing by a single firm, explained:

> Any realistic theory of predation recognizes that the predator as well as his victims will incur losses during the fighting, but such a theory supposes it may be a rational calculation for the predator to view the losses as an investment in future monopoly profits (where rivals are to be killed) or in future undisturbed profits (where rivals are to be disciplined). The future flow of profits, appropriately discounted, must then exceed the present size of the losses.

[Robert H. Bork, THE ANTITRUST PARADOX (1978) 145.]

[16] As this explanation shows, the success of such schemes is inherently uncertain: the short-run loss is definite, but the long-run gain depends on successfully neutralizing the competition. Moreover, it is not enough simply to achieve monopoly power, as monopoly pricing may breed quick entry by new competitors eager to share in the excess profits. The success of any predatory scheme depends on *maintaining* monopoly power for long enough both to recoup the predator's losses and to harvest some additional gain. Absent some assurance that the hoped-for monopoly will materialize, *and* that it can be sustained for a significant period of time, the predator must make a substantial investment with no assurance that it will pay off. For this reason, there is a consensus among commentators that predatory pricing schemes are rarely tried, and even more rarely successful.

[17] These observations apply even to predatory pricing by a *single firm* seeking monopoly power. In this case, respondents allege that a large number of firms have conspired over a period of many years to charge below-market prices in order to stifle competition. Such a conspiracy is incalculably more difficult to execute than an analogous plan undertaken by a single predator. The conspirators must allocate the losses to be sustained during the conspiracy's operation, and must also allocate any gains to be realized from its success. Precisely because success is speculative and depends on a willingness to endure losses for an indefinite period, each conspirator has a strong incentive to cheat, letting its partners suffer the losses necessary to destroy the competition while sharing in any gains if the conspiracy succeeds. The necessary allocation is therefore difficult to accomplish. Yet if conspirators cheat to any substantial extent, the conspiracy must fail, because its success depends on depressing the market price for *all* buyers of CEPs. If there are too few goods at the artificially low price to satisfy demand, the would-be victims of the conspiracy can continue to sell at the "real" market price, and the conspirators suffer losses to little purpose.

[18] Finally, if predatory pricing conspiracies are generally unlikely to occur, they are especially so where, as here, the prospects of attaining monopoly power seem slight. In order to recoup their losses, petitioners must obtain enough market power to set higher than competitive prices, and then must sustain those prices long enough to earn in excess profits what they earlier gave up in below-cost prices. Two decades after their conspiracy is alleged to have commenced, petitioners appear to be far from achieving this goal: the two largest shares of the retail market in television sets are held by RCA and respondent Zenith, not by any of petitioners. Moreover, those shares, which together approximate 40% of sales, did not decline appreciably during the 1970's. Petitioners' collective share rose rapidly during this period, from one-fifth or less of the relevant markets to close to 50%. Neither the District Court nor the Court of Appeals found, however, that petitioners' share presently allows them to charge monopoly prices; to the contrary, respondents contend that the conspiracy is ongoing—that petitioners are still artificially *depressing* the market price in order to drive Zenith out of the market. The data in the record strongly suggest that that goal is yet far distant.

[19] The alleged conspiracy's failure to achieve its ends in the two decades of its asserted operation is strong evidence that the conspiracy does not in fact exist. Since the losses in such a conspiracy accrue before the gains, they must be "repaid" with interest. And because the alleged losses have accrued over the course of two decades, the conspirators could well require a correspondingly long time to recoup. Maintaining supracompetitive prices in turn depends on the continued cooperation of the conspirators, on the inability of other would-be competitors to enter the market, and (not incidentally) on the conspirators' ability to escape antitrust liability for their *minimum* price-fixing cartel.[16] Each of these factors weighs more heavily as the time needed to recoup losses grows. If the losses have been substantial—as would likely be necessary in order to drive out the competition[17]—petitioners would most likely have to sustain their cartel for years simply to break even.

[20] Nor does the possibility that petitioners have obtained supracompetitive profits in the Japanese market change this calculation. Whether or not petitioners have the *means* to sustain substantial losses in this country over a long period of time, they have no *motive* to sustain such losses absent some strong likelihood that the alleged conspiracy in this country will eventually pay off. The courts below found no evidence of any such success, and—as indicated above—the facts actually are to the contrary . . . . More important, there is nothing to suggest any relationship between petitioners' profits in Japan and the amount petitioners could expect to gain from a conspiracy to monopolize the American market. In the absence of any such evidence, the possible existence of supracompetitive profits in Japan simply cannot overcome the economic obstacles to the ultimate success of this alleged predatory conspiracy.[18]

[21] In *Monsanto*, we emphasized that courts should not permit factfinders to infer conspiracies when such inferences are implausible, because the effect of such practices is often to deter procompetitive conduct. Respondents, petitioners' competitors, seek to hold petitioners liable for damages caused by the alleged conspiracy to cut prices. Moreover, they seek to establish this conspiracy indirectly, through evidence of other combinations (such as the check-price agreements and the five company rule) whose natural tendency is to raise prices, and through evidence of rebates and other price-cutting activities that respondents argue tend to prove a combination to suppress prices.[19] But cutting prices in order to increase business often is the very essence of competition. Thus, mistaken inferences in cases such as this one are especially costly, because they chill the very conduct the antitrust laws are designed to protect.

[22] In most cases, this concern must be balanced against the desire that illegal conspiracies be identified and punished. That balance is, however, unusually one-sided in cases such as this one. As we earlier explained,

---

[16] The alleged predatory scheme makes sense only if petitioners can recoup their losses. In light of the large number of firms involved here, petitioners can achieve this only by engaging in some form of price fixing *after* they have succeeded in driving competitors from the market. Such price fixing would, of course, be an independent violation of § 1 of the Sherman Act.

[17] The predators' losses must actually *increase* as the conspiracy nears its objective: the greater the predators' market share, the more products the predators sell; but since every sale brings with it a loss, an increase in market share also means an increase in predatory losses.

[18] The same is true of any supposed excess production capacity that petitioners may have possessed. The existence of plant capacity that exceeds domestic demand does tend to establish the ability to sell products abroad. It does not, however, provide a motive for selling at prices lower than necessary to obtain sales; nor does it explain why petitioners would be willing to *lose* money in the United States market without some reasonable prospect of recouping their investment.

predatory pricing schemes require conspirators to suffer losses in order eventually to realize their illegal gains; moreover, the gains depend on a host of uncertainties, making such schemes more likely to fail than to succeed. These economic realities tend to make predatory pricing conspiracies self-deterring: unlike most other conduct that violates the antitrust laws, failed predatory pricing schemes are costly to the conspirators. Finally, unlike predatory pricing by a single firm, *successful* predatory pricing conspiracies involving a large number of firms can be identified and punished once they succeed, since some form of minimum price-fixing agreement would be necessary in order to reap the benefits of predation. Thus, there is little reason to be concerned that by granting summary judgment in cases where the evidence of conspiracy is speculative or ambiguous, courts will encourage such conspiracies. [. . .]

[23] The Court of Appeals did not take account of the absence of a plausible motive to enter into the alleged predatory pricing conspiracy. It focused instead on whether there was "direct evidence of concert of action." The Court of Appeals erred in two respects: (i) the "direct evidence" on which the court relied had little, if any, relevance to the alleged predatory pricing conspiracy; and (ii) the court failed to consider the absence of a plausible motive to engage in predatory pricing.

[24] The "direct evidence" on which the court relied was evidence of *other* combinations, not of a predatory pricing conspiracy. Evidence that petitioners conspired to raise prices in Japan provides little, if any, support for respondents' claims: a conspiracy to increase profits in one market does not tend to show a conspiracy to sustain losses in another. Evidence that petitioners agreed to fix *minimum* prices (through the check-price agreements) for the American market actually works in petitioners' favor, because it suggests that petitioners were seeking to place a floor under prices rather than to lower them. The same is true of evidence that petitioners agreed to limit the number of distributors of their products in the American market—the so-called five company rule. That practice may have facilitated a horizontal territorial allocation, but its natural effect would be to raise market prices rather than reduce them. Evidence that tends to support any of these collateral conspiracies thus says little, if anything, about the existence of a conspiracy to charge below-market prices in the American market over a period of two decades.

[25] That being the case, the absence of any plausible motive to engage in the conduct charged is highly relevant to whether a "genuine issue for trial" exists within the meaning of Rule 56(e). Lack of motive bears on the range of permissible conclusions that might be drawn from ambiguous evidence: if petitioners had no rational economic motive to conspire, and if their conduct is consistent with other, equally plausible explanations, the conduct does not give rise to an inference of conspiracy. Here, the conduct in question consists largely of (i) pricing at levels that succeeded in taking business away from respondents, and (ii) arrangements that may have limited petitioners' ability to compete with each other (and thus kept prices from going even lower). This conduct suggests either that petitioners behaved competitively, or that petitioners conspired to *raise* prices. Neither possibility is consistent with an agreement among 21 companies to price below-market levels. Moreover, the predatory pricing scheme that this conduct is said to prove is one that makes no practical sense: it calls for petitioners to destroy companies larger and better established than themselves, a goal that remains far distant more than two decades after the conspiracy's birth. Even had they succeeded in obtaining their monopoly, there is nothing in the record to suggest that they could recover the losses they would need to sustain along the way. In sum, in light of the absence of any rational motive to conspire, neither petitioners' pricing practices, nor their conduct in the Japanese market, nor their agreements respecting prices and distribution in the American market, suffice to create a "genuine issue for trial."[21]

[26] On remand, the Court of Appeals is free to consider whether there is other evidence that is sufficiently unambiguous to permit a trier of fact to find that petitioners conspired to price predatorily for two decades despite the absence of any apparent motive to do so. The evidence must tend to exclude the possibility that petitioners underpriced respondents to compete for business rather than to implement an economically senseless conspiracy.

---

[21] We do not imply that, if petitioners had had a plausible reason to conspire, ambiguous conduct could suffice to create a triable issue of conspiracy. Our decision in *Monsanto Co. v. Spray-Rite Service Corp.*, 465 U.S. 752 (1984), establishes that conduct that is as consistent with permissible competition as with illegal conspiracy does not, without more, support even an inference of conspiracy.

In the absence of such evidence, there is no "genuine issue for trial" under Rule 56(e), and petitioners are entitled to have summary judgment reinstated. [. . .]

[27] The decision of the Court of Appeals is reversed, and the case is remanded for further proceedings consistent with this opinion.

Justice White, with whom Justice Brennan, Justice Blackmun, and Justice Stevens join, dissenting.

[28] In defining what respondents must show in order to recover, the Court makes assumptions that invade the factfinder's province. The Court states with very little discussion that respondents can recover under § 1 of the Sherman Act only if they prove that "petitioners conspired to drive respondents out of the relevant markets by (i) pricing below the level necessary to sell their products, or (ii) pricing below some appropriate measure of cost." This statement is premised on the assumption that "[a]n agreement without these features would either leave respondents in the same position as would market forces or would actually benefit respondents by raising market prices." In making this assumption, the Court ignores the contrary conclusions of respondents' expert DePodwin, whose report in very relevant part was erroneously excluded by the District Court.

[29] The DePodwin Report, on which the Court of Appeals relied along with other material, indicates that respondents were harmed in two ways that are independent of whether petitioners priced their products below the level necessary to sell their products or some appropriate measure of cost. First, the Report explains that the price-raising scheme in Japan resulted in lower consumption of petitioners' goods in that country and the exporting of more of petitioners' goods to this country than would have occurred had prices in Japan been at the competitive level. Increasing exports to this country resulted in depressed prices here, which harmed respondents. Second, the DePodwin Report indicates that petitioners exchanged confidential proprietary information and entered into agreements such as the five company rule with the goal of avoiding intragroup competition in the United States market. The Report explains that petitioners' restrictions on intragroup competition caused respondents to lose business that they would not have lost had petitioners competed with one another.

[30] The DePodwin Report alone creates a genuine factual issue regarding the harm to respondents caused by Japanese cartelization and by agreements restricting competition among petitioners in this country. No doubt the Court prefers its own economic theorizing to Dr. DePodwin's, but that is not a reason to deny the factfinder an opportunity to consider Dr. DePodwin's views on how petitioners' alleged collusion harmed respondents. [. . .]

[31] In reversing the Third Circuit's judgment, the Court identifies two alleged errors: "(i) [T]he 'direct evidence' on which the [Court of Appeals] relied had little, if any, relevance to the alleged predatory pricing conspiracy; and (ii) the court failed to consider the absence of a plausible motive to engage in predatory pricing." The Court's position is without substance.

[32] The first claim of error is that the Third Circuit treated evidence regarding price fixing in Japan and the so-called five company rule and check prices as "'direct evidence' of a conspiracy that injured respondents." The passage from the Third Circuit's opinion in which the Court locates this alleged error makes what I consider to be a quite simple and correct observation, namely, that this case is distinguishable from traditional "conscious parallelism" cases, in that there is direct evidence of concert of action among petitioners. The Third Circuit did not, as the Court implies, jump unthinkingly from this observation to the conclusion that evidence regarding the five company rule could support a finding of antitrust injury to respondents. The Third Circuit twice specifically noted that horizontal agreements allocating customers, though illegal, do not ordinarily injure competitors of the agreeing parties. However, after reviewing evidence of cartel activity in Japan, collusive establishment of dumping prices in this country, and long-term, below-cost sales, the Third Circuit held that a factfinder could reasonably conclude that the five company rule was not a simple price-raising device:

> [A] factfinder might reasonably infer that the allocation of customers in the United States, combined with price-fixing in Japan, was intended to permit concentration of the effects of dumping upon American competitors while eliminating competition among the Japanese manufacturers in either market.

I see nothing erroneous in this reasoning.

[33] The Court's second charge of error is that the Third Circuit was not sufficiently skeptical of respondents' allegation that petitioners engaged in predatory pricing conspiracy. But the Third Circuit is not required to engage in academic discussions about predation; it is required to decide whether respondents' evidence creates a genuine issue of material fact. The Third Circuit did its job, and remanding the case so that it can do the same job again is simply pointless.

[34] The Third Circuit indicated that it considers respondents' evidence sufficient to create a genuine factual issue regarding long-term, below-cost sales by petitioners. The Court tries to whittle away at this conclusion by suggesting that the "expert opinion evidence of below-cost pricing has little probative value in comparison with the economic factors that suggest that such conduct is irrational." But the question is not whether the Court finds respondents' experts persuasive, or prefers the District Court's analysis; it is whether, viewing the evidence in the light most favorable to respondents, a jury or other factfinder could reasonably conclude that petitioners engaged in long-term, below-cost sales. I agree with the Third Circuit that the answer to this question is "yes."

* * *

It has long been clear that a plaintiff in a conspiracy case need not plead or prove the existence of a "formal" or "explicit" agreement to prevail.[258] Among other things, it is probably not realistic to expect plaintiffs to have access to information about what is likely, if they are right, to be a secret illegal agreement! As a result, a critical issue in antitrust litigation is what kind of allegations and evidence might be necessary at each stage of a litigation to support the inference that the parties reached an actual agreement. And, as *Matsushita* illustrates, courts weigh the factual evidence that such an agreement may have been reached—documents, testimony, and so on—in light of economic theory about whether the purported agreement would in fact have been rational for the participants.

Inferring Conspiracy: Interstate Circuit *and the Role of "Plus Factors"*

Interstate Circuit v. United States, 306 U.S. 208 (1939)

One famous early case in which conspiracy was inferred without direct evidence of the existence and terms of an agreement was *Interstate Circuit* (1939).[259] In that case, two affiliated movie cinema chains in Texas ("Interstate") wrote to eight movie distributors to request that they each commit to maintaining a minimum admission price for the showing of certain of their movies in all subsequent cinema runs after the first, and that they each commit that those movies would never be shown as part of a double feature. The purpose of the request was to protect Interstate's first-run showings of movies from low-price competition from subsequent-run showings elsewhere. Most of the distributors effectively acquiesced, imposing the restrictions on other cinemas in the relevant cities. DOJ challenged the practice under Section 1 as a conspiracy that included a horizontal agreement among the distributors, despite the lack of direct evidence of communications among them to that effect.

The Supreme Court held that an agreement among the distributors could be inferred from the "course of conduct" in which they had engaged. The Court pointed out that each distributor knew that no one distributor could profitably have imposed the conditions unless all did so. "[F]rom the beginning each of the distributors knew that the proposals were under consideration by the others," and that "without substantially unanimous action . . . there was risk of a substantial loss of . . . business . . . but that with it there was the prospect of increased profits. There was, therefore, strong motive for concerted action [among the distributors], full advantage of which was taken by Interstate . . . in presenting [its] demands to all in a single document." "It taxes credulity to believe that the several distributors would, in the circumstances, have accepted and put into operation with substantial unanimity such far-reaching changes in their business methods without some understanding that all were to join, and we reject as beyond the range of probability that it was the result of mere chance." Finally, the Court noted that the distributors declined to offer testimony from any "officer or agent of a distributors who knew, or was in a position to know, whether in fact an agreement had been reached[.]" This choice was "itself persuasive," given that the record otherwise supported the inference of conspiracy: in fact, it was "evidence of the most convincing character." In

---

[258] American Tobacco Co. v. United States, 328 U.S. 781, 809 (1946); United States v. Paramount Pictures, Inc., 334 U.S. 131, 142 (1948).

[259] Interstate Circuit v. United States, 306 U.S. 208 (1939).

sum: the observed behavior of the distributors was itself evidence from which a hidden agreement could be inferred, as it would have been implausible for the distributors to behave as they did without having previously entered into one.

Finally, in the alternative, the Court noted that it would also have been enough for DOJ merely to show that each defendant had knowingly joined an existing concerted scheme knowing that "concerted action was contemplated and invited." After all, "[e]ach distributor was advised that the others were asked to participate; each knew that cooperation was essential to successful operation of the plan. . . . Acceptance by competitors, without previous agreement, of an invitation to participate in a plan [to restrain trade] is sufficient to establish [a] conspiracy[.]"

Today, courts and commentators often refer to a set of "plus factors" that, in addition to parallel conduct, can support the inference of an agreement among businesses by tending to exclude the hypothesis of independent action.[260] Such plus factors are identified variously by courts and commentators, but can include among other things: (1) the existence of a common motive to conspire; (2) conduct that would appear to be against the participants' economic self-interest in the absence of an agreement; (3) the existence of government antitrust investigations or enforcement action; (4) uniform increases in prices or reductions in output, particularly when demand, prices, and profits are high and with excess capacity; (5) extensive interfirm communications, especially with respect to price and/or output; (6) market structures and conditions (including concentration, high barriers to entry, and product homogeneity) that would make cartelization profitable; (7) stable market shares despite rising prices and excess capacity; (8) mechanisms of distributing profits to participants; and (9) joint conduct to exclude rivals.[261]

Monsanto and *Matsushita* each dealt, in part, with the question of what evidence a plaintiff must develop in discovery in order to reach a trial before a factfinder: *i.e.*, the summary judgment standard under Rule 56. But, in practice, the motion-to-dismiss standard under Rule 12 is at least as important to antitrust litigation, because it is the gatekeeper to the (notoriously expensive and lengthy) antitrust discovery process. What must a plaintiff allege in an antitrust complaint in order to be given access to the tools of factfinding?

The leading modern case on antitrust pleading standards at the motion-to-dismiss stage is 2007's *Twombly* decision, which re-set the standard that *all* complaints—antitrust and non-antitrust alike—must satisfy to withstand a challenge under Rule 12(b)(6) for failure to state claim.[262] Before *Twombly*, a complaint would proceed to discovery "unless it appears beyond doubt that the plaintiff can prove no set of facts in support of his claim which would entitle him to relief."[263] *Twombly* materially raised the bar of factual detail and specificity a complaint alleging an "agreement" under Section 1 must clear to survive dismissal.

Bell Atlantic Corp. v. Twombly
550 U.S. 544 (2007)

Justice Souter.

[1] Liability under § 1 of the Sherman Act requires a contract, combination, or conspiracy, in restraint of trade or commerce. The question in this putative class action is whether a § 1 complaint can survive a motion to dismiss when it alleges that major telecommunications providers engaged in certain parallel conduct unfavorable to

[260] *See generally* Christopher R. Leslie, *The Probative Synergy of Plus Factors in Price-Fixing Litigation*, 115 Nw. U. L. Rev. 1581 (2021); William E. Kovacic, Robert C. Marshall, Leslie M. Marx & Halbert L. White, *Plus Factors and Agreement in Antitrust Law*, 110 Mich. L.Rev. 393 (2011).
[261] *See, e.g.* Valspar Corp. v. E.I. Du Pont De Nemours & Co., 873 F.3d 185, 193 (3d Cir. 2017); Gelboim v. Bank of Am. Corp., 823 F.3d 759, 781 (2d Cir. 2016); In re Musical Instruments & Equip. Antitrust Litig., 798 F.3d 1186, 1194 (9th Cir. 2015); Hyland v. HomeServices of Am., Inc., 771 F.3d 310, 320 (6th Cir. 2014); Mayor & City Council of Baltimore, Md. v. Citigroup, Inc., 709 F.3d 129, 136 (2d Cir. 2013); Williamson Oil Co. v. Philip Morris USA, 346 F.3d 1287, 1301 (11th Cir. 2003); City of Tuscaloosa v. Harcros Chemicals, Inc., 158 F.3d 548, 572 (11th Cir. 1998); In re Coordinated Pretrial Proc. in Petroleum Prods. Antitrust Litig., 906 F.2d 432, 446–47 (9th Cir. 1990) *see also* note 260 and works cited therein.
[262] *See* Ashcroft v. Iqbal, 556 U.S. 662, 684 (2009) (confirming that *Twombly* is not confined to antitrust cases).
[263] Conley v. Gibson, 355 U.S. 41, 45–46 (1957).

competition, absent some factual context suggesting agreement, as distinct from identical, independent action. We hold that such a complaint should be dismissed.

[2] The upshot of the 1984 divestiture of the American Telephone & Telegraph Company's (AT & T) local telephone business was a system of regional service monopolies (variously called "Regional Bell Operating Companies," "Baby Bells," or "Incumbent Local Exchange Carriers" (ILECs)), and a separate, competitive market for long-distance service from which the ILECs were excluded. More than a decade later, Congress withdrew approval of the ILECs' monopolies by enacting the Telecommunications Act of 1996 (1996 Act), which fundamentally restructured local telephone markets and subjected ILECs to a host of duties intended to facilitate market entry. In recompense, the 1996 Act set conditions for authorizing ILECs to enter the long-distance market.

[3] Central to the new scheme was each ILEC's obligation to share its network with competitors, which came to be known as "competitive local exchange carriers" (CLECs). A CLEC could make use of an ILEC's network in any of three ways: by (1) purchasing local telephone services at wholesale rates for resale to end users, (2) leasing elements of the ILEC's network on an unbundled basis, or (3) interconnecting its own facilities with the ILEC's network. Owing to the considerable expense and effort required to make unbundled network elements available to rivals at wholesale prices, the ILECs vigorously litigated the scope of the sharing obligation imposed by the 1996 Act, with the result that the Federal Communications Commission (FCC) three times revised its regulations to narrow the range of network elements to be shared with the CLECs.

[4] Respondents William Twombly and Lawrence Marcus (hereinafter plaintiffs) represent a putative class consisting of all subscribers of local telephone and/or high speed internet services from February 8, 1996 to present. In this action against petitioners, a group of ILECs, plaintiffs seek treble damages and declaratory and injunctive relief for claimed violations of § 1 of the Sherman Act. . . .

[5] The complaint alleges that the ILECs conspired to restrain trade in two ways, each supposedly inflating charges for local telephone and high-speed Internet services. Plaintiffs say, first, that the ILECs "engaged in parallel conduct" in their respective service areas to inhibit the growth of upstart CLECs. Their actions allegedly included making unfair agreements with the CLECs for access to ILEC networks, providing inferior connections to the networks, overcharging, and billing in ways designed to sabotage the CLECs' relations with their own customers. According to the complaint, the ILECs' compelling common motivation to thwart the CLECs' competitive efforts naturally led them to form a conspiracy; had any one ILEC not sought to prevent CLECs from competing effectively, the resulting greater competitive inroads into that ILEC's territory would have revealed the degree to which competitive entry by CLECs would have been successful in the other territories in the absence of such conduct.

[6] Second, the complaint charges agreements by the ILECs to refrain from competing against one another. These are to be inferred from the ILECs' common failure meaningfully to pursue attractive business opportunities in contiguous markets where they possessed substantial competitive advantages, and from a statement of Richard Notebaert, chief executive officer (CEO) of the ILEC Qwest, that competing in the territory of another ILEC "might be a good way to turn a quick dollar but that doesn't make it right."

[7] The complaint couches its ultimate allegations this way:

> In the absence of any meaningful competition between the [ILECs] in one another's markets, and in light of the parallel course of conduct that each engaged in to prevent competition from CLECs within their respective local telephone and/or high speed internet services markets and the other facts and market circumstances alleged above, Plaintiffs allege upon information and belief that [the ILECs] have entered into a contract, combination or conspiracy to prevent competitive entry in their respective local telephone and/or high speed internet services markets and have agreed not to compete with one another and otherwise allocated customers and markets to one another.

[8] The United States District Court for the Southern District of New York dismissed the complaint for failure to state a claim upon which relief can be granted. . . . The District Court found plaintiffs' allegations of parallel ILEC actions to discourage competition inadequate because the behavior of each ILEC in resisting the incursion of CLECs is fully explained by the ILEC's own interests in defending its individual territory. As to the ILECs'

supposed agreement against competing with each other, the District Court found that the complaint does not allege facts suggesting that refraining from competing in other territories as CLECs was contrary to the ILECs' apparent economic interests, and consequently does not raise an inference that the ILECs' actions were the result of a conspiracy.

[9] The Court of Appeals for the Second Circuit reversed, holding that the District Court tested the complaint by the wrong standard. It held that plus factors are not *required* to be pleaded to permit an antitrust claim based on parallel conduct to survive dismissal. Although the Court of Appeals took the view that plaintiffs must plead facts that include conspiracy among the realm of "plausible" possibilities in order to survive a motion to dismiss, it then said that to rule that allegations of parallel anticompetitive conduct fail to support a plausible conspiracy claim, a court would have to conclude that there is no set of facts that would permit a plaintiff to demonstrate that the particular parallelism asserted was the product of collusion rather than coincidence.

[10] We granted certiorari to address the proper standard for pleading an antitrust conspiracy through allegations of parallel conduct, and now reverse.

[11] Because § 1 of the Sherman Act does not prohibit all unreasonable restraints of trade but only restraints effected by a contract, combination, or conspiracy, the crucial question is whether the challenged anticompetitive conduct stems from independent decision or from an agreement, tacit or express. While a showing of parallel business behavior is admissible circumstantial evidence from which the fact finder may infer agreement, it falls short of conclusively establishing agreement or itself constituting a Sherman Act offense. Even "conscious parallelism," a common reaction of firms in a concentrated market that recognize their shared economic interests and their interdependence with respect to price and output decisions[,] is not in itself unlawful.

[12] The inadequacy of showing parallel conduct or interdependence, without more, mirrors the ambiguity of the behavior: consistent with conspiracy, but just as much in line with a wide swath of rational and competitive business strategy unilaterally prompted by common perceptions of the market. Accordingly, we have previously hedged against false inferences from identical behavior at a number of points in the trial sequence. An antitrust conspiracy plaintiff with evidence showing nothing beyond parallel conduct is not entitled to a directed verdict . . . ; proof of a § 1 conspiracy must include evidence tending to exclude the possibility of independent action, see *Monsanto Co. v. Spray–Rite Service Corp.*, 465 U.S. 752 (1984); and at the summary judgment stage a § 1 plaintiff's offer of conspiracy evidence must tend to rule out the possibility that the defendants were acting independently, see *Matsushita Elec. Industrial Co. v. Zenith Radio Corp.*, 475 U.S. 574 (1986).

[13] This case presents the antecedent question of what a plaintiff must plead in order to state a claim under § 1 of the Sherman Act [and thus avoid dismissal under Rule 12(b)(6)]. Federal Rule of Civil Procedure 8(a)(2) requires only "a short and plain statement of the claim showing that the pleader is entitled to relief," in order to "give the defendant fair notice of what the claim is and the grounds upon which it rests." While a complaint attacked by a Rule 12(b)(6) motion to dismiss does not need detailed factual allegations, a plaintiff's obligation to provide the "grounds" of his "entitlement to relief" requires more than labels and conclusions, and a formulaic recitation of the elements of a cause of action will not do. Factual allegations must be enough to raise a right to relief above the speculative level, on the assumption that all the allegations in the complaint are true (even if doubtful in fact).

[14] In applying these general standards to a § 1 claim, we hold that stating such a claim requires a complaint with enough factual matter (taken as true) to suggest that an agreement was made. Asking for plausible grounds to infer an agreement does not impose a probability requirement at the pleading stage; it simply calls for enough fact to raise a reasonable expectation that discovery will reveal evidence of illegal agreement.[4] And, of course, a well-pleaded complaint may proceed even if it strikes a savvy judge that actual proof of those facts is improbable, and

---

[4] Commentators have offered several examples of parallel conduct allegations that would state a § 1 claim under this standard. *See, e.g.*, 6 Areeda & Hovenkamp ¶ 1425, at 167–185 (discussing "parallel behavior that would probably not result from chance, coincidence, independent responses to common stimuli, or mere interdependence unaided by an advance understanding among the parties"); Blechman, *Conscious Parallelism, Signalling and Facilitating Devices: The Problem of Tacit Collusion Under the Antitrust Laws*, 24 N.Y.L. S. L.Rev. 881, 899 (1979) (describing "conduct [that] indicates the sort of restricted freedom of action and sense of obligation that one generally associates with agreement"). The parties in this case agree that complex and historically unprecedented changes in pricing structure made at the very same time by multiple competitors, and made for no other discernible reason, would support a plausible inference of conspiracy.

that a recovery is very remote and unlikely. In identifying facts that are suggestive enough to render a § 1 conspiracy plausible, we have the benefit of the prior rulings and considered views of leading commentators . . . that lawful parallel conduct fails to bespeak unlawful agreement. It makes sense to say, therefore, that an allegation of parallel conduct and a bare assertion of conspiracy will not suffice. Without more, parallel conduct does not suggest conspiracy, and a conclusory allegation of agreement at some unidentified point does not supply facts adequate to show illegality. Hence, when allegations of parallel conduct are set out in order to make a § 1 claim, they must be placed in a context that raises a suggestion of a preceding agreement, not merely parallel conduct that could just as well be independent action.

[15] The need at the pleading stage for allegations plausibly suggesting (not merely consistent with) agreement reflects the threshold requirement of Rule 8(a)(2) that the "plain statement" possess enough heft to "show that the pleader is entitled to relief." A statement of parallel conduct, even conduct consciously undertaken, needs some setting suggesting the agreement necessary to make out a § 1 claim; without that further circumstance pointing toward a meeting of the minds, an account of a defendant's commercial efforts stays in neutral territory. An allegation of parallel conduct is thus much like a naked assertion of conspiracy in a § 1 complaint: it gets the complaint close to stating a claim, but without some further factual enhancement it stops short of the line between possibility and plausibility of entitlement to relief.

[16] We alluded to the practical significance of the Rule 8 entitlement requirement in Dura Pharmaceuticals, Inc. v. Broudo, 544 U.S. 336 (2005), when we explained that something beyond the mere possibility of loss causation must be alleged, lest a plaintiff with a largely groundless claim be allowed to take up the time of a number of other people, with the right to do so representing an in terrorem increment of the settlement value. . . .

[17] Thus, it is one thing to be cautious before dismissing an antitrust complaint in advance of discovery, but quite another to forget that proceeding to antitrust discovery can be expensive. As we indicated over 20 years ago . . . a district court must retain the power to insist upon some specificity in pleading before allowing a potentially massive factual controversy to proceed. . . .

[18] It is no answer to say that a claim just shy of a plausible entitlement to relief can, if groundless, be weeded out early in the discovery process through careful case management, given the common lament that the success of judicial supervision in checking discovery abuse has been on the modest side. And it is self-evident that the problem of discovery abuse cannot be solved by careful scrutiny of evidence at the summary judgment stage, much less lucid instructions to juries; the threat of discovery expense will push cost-conscious defendants to settle even anemic cases before reaching those proceedings. Probably, then, it is only by taking care to require allegations that reach the level suggesting conspiracy that we can hope to avoid the potentially enormous expense of discovery in cases with no reasonably founded hope that the discovery process will reveal relevant evidence to support a § 1 claim. [. . .]

[19] When we look for plausibility in this complaint, we agree with the District Court that plaintiffs' claim of conspiracy in restraint of trade comes up short. To begin with, the complaint leaves no doubt that plaintiffs rest their § 1 claim on descriptions of parallel conduct and not on any independent allegation of actual agreement among the ILECs. Although in form a few stray statements speak directly of agreement, on fair reading these are merely legal conclusions resting on the prior allegations. Thus, the complaint first takes account of the alleged "absence of any meaningful competition between the ILECs in one another's markets," "the parallel course of conduct that each ILEC engaged in to prevent competition from CLECs," "and the other facts and market circumstances alleged [earlier]"; "in light of" these, the complaint concludes "that the ILECs have entered into a contract, combination or conspiracy to prevent competitive entry into their markets and have agreed not to compete with one another." The nub of the complaint, then, is the ILECs' parallel behavior, consisting of steps to keep the CLECs out and manifest disinterest in becoming CLECs themselves, and its sufficiency turns on the suggestions raised by this conduct when viewed in light of common economic experience.

[20] We think that nothing contained in the complaint invests either the action or inaction alleged with a plausible suggestion of conspiracy. As to the ILECs' supposed agreement to disobey the 1996 Act and thwart the CLECs' attempts to compete, we agree with the District Court that nothing in the complaint intimates that the resistance to the upstarts was anything more than the natural, unilateral reaction of each ILEC intent on keeping its regional

dominance. The 1996 Act did more than just subject the ILECs to competition; it obliged them to subsidize their competitors with their own equipment at wholesale rates. The economic incentive to resist was powerful, but resisting competition is routine market conduct, and even if the ILECs flouted the 1996 Act in all the ways the plaintiffs allege, there is no reason to infer that the companies had agreed among themselves to do what was only natural anyway; so natural, in fact, that if alleging parallel decisions to resist competition were enough to imply an antitrust conspiracy, pleading a § 1 violation against almost any group of competing businesses would be a sure thing.

[21] The complaint makes its closest pass at a predicate for conspiracy with the claim that collusion was necessary because success by even one CLEC in an ILEC's territory "would have revealed the degree to which competitive entry by CLECs would have been successful in the other territories." But, its logic aside, this general premise still fails to answer the point that there was just no need for joint encouragement to resist the 1996 Act; as the District Court said, "each ILEC has reason to want to avoid dealing with CLECs" and "each ILEC would attempt to keep CLECs out, regardless of the actions of the other ILECs."

[22] Plaintiffs' second conspiracy theory rests on the competitive reticence among the ILECs themselves in the wake of the 1996 Act, which was supposedly passed in the hope that the large incumbent local monopoly companies . . . might attack their neighbors' service areas, as they are the best situated to do so. Contrary to hope, the ILECs declined to enter each other's service territories in any significant way, and the local telephone and high-speed Internet market remains highly compartmentalized geographically, with minimal competition. Based on this state of affairs, and perceiving the ILECs to be blessed with "especially attractive business opportunities" in surrounding markets dominated by other ILECs, the plaintiffs assert that the ILECs' parallel conduct was "strongly suggestive of conspiracy."

[23] But it was not suggestive of conspiracy, not if history teaches anything. In a traditionally unregulated industry with low barriers to entry, sparse competition among large firms dominating separate geographical segments of the market could very well signify illegal agreement, but here we have an obvious alternative explanation. In the decade preceding the 1996 Act and well before that, monopoly was the norm in telecommunications, not the exception. The ILECs were born in that world, doubtless liked the world the way it was, and surely knew the adage about him who lives by the sword. Hence, a natural explanation for the noncompetition alleged is that the former Government-sanctioned monopolists were sitting tight, expecting their neighbors to do the same thing.

[24] In fact, the complaint itself gives reasons to believe that the ILECs would see their best interests in keeping to their old turf. Although the complaint says generally that the ILECs passed up especially attractive business opportunities by declining to compete as CLECs against other ILECs, it does not allege that competition as CLECs was potentially any more lucrative than other opportunities being pursued by the ILECs during the same period, and the complaint is replete with indications that any CLEC faced nearly insurmountable barriers to profitability owing to the ILECs' flagrant resistance to the network sharing requirements of the 1996 Act. Not only that, but even without a monopolistic tradition and the peculiar difficulty of mandating shared networks, firms do not expand without limit and none of them enters every market that an outside observer might regard as profitable, or even a small portion of such markets. The upshot is that Congress may have expected some ILECs to become CLECs in the legacy territories of other ILECs, but the disappointment does not make conspiracy plausible. We agree with the District Court's assessment that antitrust conspiracy was not suggested by the facts adduced under either theory of the complaint, which thus fails to state a valid § 1 claim. [. . .]

[25] . . .[W]e do not require heightened fact pleading of specifics, but only enough facts to state a claim to relief that is plausible on its face. Because the plaintiffs here have not nudged their claims across the line from conceivable to plausible, their complaint must be dismissed..

Justice Stevens, with whom Justice Ginsburg joins except as to Part IV {*Eds.: Part IV is not excerpted here*}, dissenting.

[26] In the first paragraph of its 23-page opinion the Court states that the question to be decided is whether allegations that "major telecommunications providers engaged in certain parallel conduct unfavorable to competition" suffice to state a violation of § 1 of the Sherman Act. The answer to that question has been settled

for more than 50 years. If that were indeed the issue, a summary reversal . . . would adequately resolve this case. . . . [P]arallel conduct is circumstantial evidence admissible on the issue of conspiracy, but it is not itself illegal.

[27] Thus, this is a case in which there is no dispute about the substantive law. If the defendants acted independently, their conduct was perfectly lawful. If, however, that conduct is the product of a horizontal agreement among potential competitors, it was unlawful. The plaintiffs have alleged such an agreement and, because the complaint was dismissed in advance of answer, the allegation has not even been denied. Why, then, does the case not proceed? Does a judicial opinion that the charge is not "plausible" provide a legally acceptable reason for dismissing the complaint? I think not. [. . .]

[28] . . . [A] judge ruling on a defendant's motion to dismiss a complaint must accept as true all of the factual allegations contained in the complaint. But . . . the majority permits immediate dismissal based on the assurances of company lawyers that nothing untoward was afoot. The Court embraces the argument of those lawyers that there is no reason to infer that the companies had agreed among themselves to do what was only natural anyway; that there was just no need for joint encouragement to resist the 1996 Act; and that the natural explanation for the noncompetition alleged is that the former Government-sanctioned monopolists were sitting tight, expecting their neighbors to do the same thing.

[29] The Court and petitioners' legal team are no doubt correct that the parallel conduct alleged is consistent with the absence of any contract, combination, or conspiracy. But that conduct is also entirely consistent with the *presence* of the illegal agreement alleged in the complaint. And the charge that petitioners agreed not to compete with one another is not just one of a few stray statements; it is an allegation describing unlawful conduct. As such, the Federal Rules of Civil Procedure, our longstanding precedent, and sound practice mandate that the District Court at least require some sort of response from petitioners before dismissing the case.

[30] Two practical concerns presumably explain the Court's dramatic departure from settled procedural law. Private antitrust litigation can be enormously expensive, and there is a risk that jurors may mistakenly conclude that evidence of parallel conduct has proved that the parties acted pursuant to an agreement when they in fact merely made similar independent decisions. Those concerns merit careful case management, including strict control of discovery, careful scrutiny of evidence at the summary judgment stage, and lucid instructions to juries; they do not, however, justify the dismissal of an adequately pleaded complaint without even requiring the defendants to file answers denying a charge that they in fact engaged in collective decisionmaking. More importantly, they do not justify an interpretation of Federal Rule of Civil Procedure 12(b)(6) that seems to be driven by the majority's appraisal of the plausibility of the ultimate factual allegation rather than its legal sufficiency. [. . .]

[31] This case is a poor vehicle for the Court's new pleading rule, for we have observed that in antitrust cases, where the proof is largely in the hands of the alleged conspirators, dismissals prior to giving the plaintiff ample opportunity for discovery should be granted very sparingly. [. . .]

[32] The Court does not suggest that an agreement to do what the plaintiffs allege would be permissible under the antitrust laws. Nor does the Court hold that these plaintiffs have failed to allege an injury entitling them to sue for damages under those laws. Rather, the theory on which the Court permits dismissal is that, so far as the Federal Rules are concerned, no agreement has been alleged at all. This is a mind-boggling conclusion.

[33] As the Court explains, prior to the enactment of the Telecommunications Act of 1996 the law prohibited the defendants from competing with each other. The new statute was enacted to replace a monopolistic market with a competitive one. The Act did not merely require the regional monopolists to take affirmative steps to facilitate entry to new competitors; it also permitted the existing firms to compete with each other and to expand their operations into previously forbidden territory. Each of the defendants decided not to take the latter step. That was obviously an extremely important business decision, and I am willing to presume that each company acted entirely independently in reaching that decision. I am even willing to entertain the majority's belief that any agreement among the companies was unlikely. But the plaintiffs allege in three places in their complaint, that the ILECs did in fact agree both to prevent competitors from entering into their local markets and to forgo competition with

each other. And as the Court recognizes, at the motion to dismiss stage, a judge assumes "that all the allegations in the complaint are true (even if doubtful in fact)."

[34] The majority circumvents this obvious obstacle to dismissal by pretending that it does not exist. The Court admits that "in form a few stray statements in the complaint speak directly of agreement," but disregards those allegations by saying that "on fair reading these are merely legal conclusions resting on the prior allegations" of parallel conduct. The Court's dichotomy between factual allegations and "legal conclusions" is the stuff of a bygone era. That distinction was a defining feature of code pleading, but was conspicuously abolished when the Federal Rules were enacted in 1938.

[35] Even if I were inclined to accept the Court's anachronistic dichotomy and ignore the complaint's actual allegations, I would dispute the Court's suggestion that any inference of agreement from petitioners' parallel conduct is "implausible." . . . Respondents' complaint points not only to petitioners' numerous opportunities to meet with each other, but also to [ILEC CEO Richard] Notebaert's curious statement that encroaching on a fellow incumbent's territory "might be a good way to turn a quick dollar but that doesn't make it right." What did he mean by that? One possible (indeed plausible) inference is that he meant that while it would be in his company's economic self-interest to compete with its brethren, he had agreed with his competitors not to do so. . . .

[36] Perhaps Notebaert meant instead that competition would be sensible in the short term but not in the long run. That's what his lawyers tell us anyway. But I would think that no one would know better what Notebaert meant than Notebaert himself. Instead of permitting respondents to ask Notebaert, however, the Court looks to other quotes from that and other articles and decides that what he meant was that entering new markets as a competitive local exchange carrier would not be a "sustainable economic model." . . . But . . . the District Court was required at this stage of the proceedings to construe Notebaert's ambiguous statement in the plaintiffs' favor. The inference the statement supports—that simultaneous decisions by ILECs not even to attempt to poach customers from one another once the law authorized them to do so were the product of an agreement—sits comfortably within the realm of possibility. That is all the Rules require. [. . .]

[37] I fear that the unfortunate result of the majority's new pleading rule will be to invite lawyers' debates over economic theory to conclusively resolve antitrust suits in the absence of any evidence. It is no surprise that the antitrust defense bar—among whom "lament" as to inadequate judicial supervision of discovery is most common—should lobby for this state of affairs. But we must recall that their primary responsibility is to win cases for their clients, not to improve law administration for the public. As we did in our prior decisions, we should have instructed them that their remedy was to seek to amend the Federal Rules—not our interpretation of them. [. . .]

[38] Accordingly, I respectfully dissent.

* * *

So how does a court apply these rules in practice? A famous illustration-in-two-acts is found in the *In re Text Messaging Antitrust Litigation* saga, which gave Judge Richard Posner not one but two opportunities to pronounce on whether the plaintiffs had provided a basis from which an unlawful price-fixing agreement could be inferred. In December 2010, he held that the plaintiffs in that case had alleged enough in a complaint to make the inference of a price-fixing conspiracy among AT & T, Verizon, Sprint, and T–Mobile "plausible," and thus to clear the threshold established in *Twombly* for surviving a motion to dismiss. The litigation accordingly rumbled on. But in April 2015, he held that the plaintiffs had not mustered enough evidence in discovery to survive summary judgment.

In re Text Messaging Antitrust Litigation
630 F.3d 622 (7th Cir. 2010)

Judge Posner.

[1] A class action suit that has been consolidated for pretrial proceedings in the district court in Chicago charges the defendants with conspiring to fix prices of text messaging services in violation of federal antitrust law. [. . .]

[2] The complaint in *Twombly* alleged that the regional telephone companies that were the successors to the Bell Operating Companies which AT & T had been forced to divest in settlement of the government's antitrust suit against it were engaged in "parallel behavior." Bluntly, they were not competing. But section 1 of the Sherman Act, under which the suit had been brought, does not require sellers to compete; it just forbids their agreeing or conspiring not to compete. So as the Court pointed out, a complaint that merely alleges parallel behavior alleges facts that are equally consistent with an inference that the defendants are conspiring and an inference that the conditions of their market have enabled them to avoid competing without having to agree not to compete. The core allegations of the complaint in *Twombly* were simply that

> In the absence of any meaningful competition between the defendants in one another's markets, and in light of the parallel course of conduct that each engaged in to prevent competition from other carriers within their respective local telephone and/or high speed internet services markets and the other facts and market circumstances alleged above, Plaintiffs allege upon information and belief that the defendants have entered into a contract, combination or conspiracy to prevent competitive entry in their respective local telephone and/or high speed internet services markets and have agreed not to compete with one another and otherwise allocated customers and markets to one another.

[3] Our defendants contend that in this case too the complaint alleges merely that they are not competing. But we agree with the district judge that the complaint alleges a conspiracy with sufficient plausibility to satisfy the pleading standard of *Twombly*. It is true as the defendants contend that the differences between the first amended complaint, which the judge dismissed, and the second, which he refused to dismiss, are slight; but if his refusal to dismiss the second complaint is properly described as a reconsideration of his ruling on the first, so what? Judges are permitted to reconsider their rulings in the course of a litigation.

[4] The second amended complaint alleges a mixture of parallel behaviors, details of industry structure, and industry practices, that facilitate collusion. There is nothing incongruous about such a mixture. If parties agree to fix prices, one expects that as a result they will not compete in price—that's the purpose of price fixing. Parallel behavior of a sort anomalous in a competitive market is thus a symptom of price fixing, though standing alone it is not proof of it; and an industry structure that facilitates collusion constitutes supporting evidence of collusion. An accusation that the thousands of children who set up makeshift lemonade stands all over the country on hot summer days were fixing prices would be laughed out of court because the retail sale of lemonade from lemonade stands constitutes so dispersed and heterogeneous and uncommercial a market as to make a nationwide conspiracy of the sellers utterly implausible. But the complaint in this case alleges that the four defendants sell 90 percent of U.S. text messaging services, and it would not be difficult for such a small group to agree on prices and to be able to detect "cheating" (underselling the agreed price by a member of the group) without having to create elaborate mechanisms, such as an exclusive sales agency, that could not escape discovery by the antitrust authorities.

[5] Of note is the allegation in the complaint that the defendants belonged to a trade association and exchanged price information directly at association meetings. This allegation identifies a practice, not illegal in itself, that facilitates price fixing that would be difficult for the authorities to detect. The complaint further alleges that the defendants, along with two other large sellers of text messaging services, constituted and met with each other in an elite "leadership council" within the association—and the leadership council's stated mission was to urge its members to substitute "co-opetition" for competition.

[6] The complaint also alleges that in the face of steeply falling costs, the defendants increased their prices. This is anomalous behavior because falling costs increase a seller's profit margin at the existing price, motivating him, in the absence of agreement, to reduce his price slightly in order to take business from his competitors, and certainly not to increase his price. And there is more: there is an allegation that all at once the defendants changed their pricing structures, which were heterogeneous and complex, to a uniform pricing structure, and then simultaneously jacked up their prices by a third. The change in the industry's pricing structure was so rapid, the complaint suggests, that it could not have been accomplished without agreement on the details of the new structure, the timing of its adoption, and the specific uniform price increase that would ensue on its adoption.

[7] A footnote in *Twombly* had described the type of evidence that enables parallel conduct to be interpreted as collusive: "Commentators have offered several examples of parallel conduct allegations that would state a

Sherman Act § 1 claim under this standard[,] namely, parallel behavior that would probably not result from chance, coincidence, independent responses to common stimuli, or mere interdependence unaided by an advance understanding among the parties; conduct that indicates the sort of restricted freedom of action and sense of obligation that one generally associates with agreement. The parties in this case agree that complex and historically unprecedented changes in pricing structure made at the very same time by multiple competitors, and made for no other discernible reason would support a plausible inference of conspiracy." That is the kind of "parallel plus" behavior alleged in this case.

[8] What is missing, as the defendants point out, is the smoking gun in a price-fixing case: direct evidence, which would usually take the form of an admission by an employee of one of the conspirators, that officials of the defendants had met and agreed explicitly on the terms of a conspiracy to raise price. The second amended complaint does allege that the defendants agreed to uniformly charge an unprecedented common per-unit price of ten cents for text messaging services, but does not allege direct evidence of such an agreement; the allegation is an inference from circumstantial evidence. Direct evidence of conspiracy is not a sine qua non, however. Circumstantial evidence can establish an antitrust conspiracy. We need not decide whether the circumstantial evidence that we have summarized is sufficient to compel an inference of conspiracy; the case is just at the complaint stage and the test for whether to dismiss a case at that stage turns on the complaint's "plausibility."

[9] The [Supreme] Court [has said] that the plausibility standard is not akin to a probability requirement, but it asks for more than a sheer possibility that a defendant has acted unlawfully. This is a little unclear because plausibility, probability, and possibility overlap. Probability runs the gamut from a zero likelihood to a certainty. What is impossible has a zero likelihood of occurring and what is plausible has a moderately high likelihood of occurring. The fact that the allegations undergirding a claim could be true is no longer enough to save a complaint from being dismissed; the complaint must establish a nonnegligible probability that the claim is valid; but the probability need not be as great as such terms as "preponderance of the evidence" connote.

[10] The plaintiffs have conducted no discovery. Discovery may reveal the smoking gun or bring to light additional circumstantial evidence that further tilts the balance in favor of liability. All that we conclude at this early stage in the litigation is that the district judge was right to rule that the second amended complaint provides a sufficiently plausible case of price fixing to warrant allowing the plaintiffs to proceed to discovery.

* * *

In re Text Messaging Antitrust Litigation
782 F.3d 867 (7th Cir. 2015)

Judge Posner.

[1] This class action antitrust suit is before us for the second time. More than four years ago we granted the defendants' petition to take an interlocutory appeal . . . from the district judge's refusal to dismiss the complaint for failure to state a claim. But we upheld the judge's ruling. Three years of discovery ensued, culminating in the district judge's grant of the defendants' motion for summary judgment, followed by entry of final judgment dismissing the suit, precipitating this appeal by the plaintiffs.

[2] The suit is on behalf of customers of text messaging—the sending of brief electronic messages between two or more mobile phones or other devices, over telephone systems (usually wireless systems), mobile communications systems, or the Internet. (The most common method of text messaging today is to type the message into a cellphone, which transmits it instantaneously over a telephone or other communications network to a similar device.) Text messaging is thus an alternative both to email and to telephone calls. The principal defendants are four wireless network providers—AT & T, Verizon, Sprint, and T–Mobile—and a trade association, The Wireless Association, to which those companies belong. The suit claims that the defendants, in violation of section 1 of the Sherman Act, conspired with each other to increase one kind of price for text messaging service—price per use (PPU), each "use" being a message, separately priced. This was the original method of pricing text messaging; we'll see that it has largely given way to other methods, but it still has some customers and they are the plaintiffs and the members of the plaintiff class.

[3] The defendants' unsuccessful motion to dismiss the complaint—the motion the denial of which we reviewed and upheld in the first appeal—invoked *Bell Atlantic Corp. v. Twombly*, 550 U.S. 544 (2007), which requires a complaint to pass a test of "plausibility" in order to avoid dismissal. The reason for this requirement is to spare defendants the burden of a costly defense against charges likely to prove in the end to have no merit. We decided that the plaintiffs' second amended complaint passed the test[.] [. . .]

[4] In short, we pointed to the small number of leading firms in the text messaging market, which would facilitate concealment of an agreement to fix prices; to the alleged exchanges of price information, orchestrated by the firms' trade association; to the seeming anomaly of a price increase in the face of falling costs; and to the allegation of a sudden simplification of pricing structures followed very quickly by uniform price increases.

[5] With dismissal of the complaint refused and the suit thus alive in the district court, the focus of the lawsuit changed to pretrial discovery by the plaintiffs, which in turn focused on the alleged price exchange through the trade association and the sudden change in pricing structure followed by uniform price increases. Other factors mentioned in our first opinion—the small number of firms, and price increases in the face of falling costs—were conceded to be present but could not be thought dispositive. It is true that if a small number of competitors dominates a market, they will find it safer and easier to fix prices than if there are many competitors of more or less equal size. For the fewer the conspirators, the lower the cost of negotiation and the likelihood of defection; and provided that the fringe of competitive firms is unable to expand output sufficiently to drive the price back down to the competitive level, the leading firms can fix prices without worrying about competition from the fringe. But the other side of this coin is that the fewer the firms, the easier it is for them to engage in "follow the leader" pricing ("conscious parallelism," as lawyers call it, "tacit collusion" as economists prefer to call it)—which means coordinating their pricing without an actual agreement to do so. As for the apparent anomaly of competitors' raising prices in the face of falling costs, that is indeed evidence that they are not competing in the sense of trying to take sales from each other. However, this may be not because they've agreed not to compete but because all of them have determined independently that they may be better off with a higher price. That higher price, moreover—the consequence of parallel but independent decisions to raise prices—may generate even greater profits (compared to competitive pricing) if costs are falling, provided that consumers do not have attractive alternatives.

[6] Important too is the condition of entry. If few firms can or want to enter the relevant market, a higher price generating higher profits will not be undone by the output of new entrants. Indeed, prospective entrants may be deterred from entering by realization that their entry might lead simply to a drastic fall in prices that would deny them the profits from having entered. And that drastic fall could well be the result of parallel but independent pricing decisions by the incumbent firms, rather than of agreement.

[7] The challenge to the plaintiffs in discovery was thus to find evidence that the defendants had colluded expressly—that is, had explicitly agreed to raise prices—rather than tacitly ("follow the leader" or "consciously parallel" pricing). The focus of the plaintiffs' discovery was on the information exchange orchestrated by the trade association, the change in the defendants' pricing structures and the defendants' ensuing price hikes, and the possible existence of the smoking gun—and let's begin there, for the plaintiffs think they have found it, and they have made it the centerpiece—indeed, virtually the entirety—of their argument.

[8] Their supposed smoking gun is a pair of emails from an executive of T-Mobile named Adrian Hurditch to another executive of the firm, Lisa Roddy. Hurditch was not a senior executive but he was involved in the pricing of T-Mobile's products, including its text messaging service. The first of the two emails to Roddy, sent in May 2008, said "Gotta tell you but my gut says raising messaging pricing again is nothing more than a price gouge on consumers. I would guess that consumer advocates groups are going to come after us at some point. It's not like we've had an increase in the cost to carry message to justify this or a drop in our subscription SOC rates? I know the other guys are doing it but that doesn't mean we have to follow." ("SOC" is an acronym for "system on a chip," a common component of cellphones.) The second email, sent in September 2008 in the wake of a congressional investigation of alleged price gouging by the defendants, said that "at the end of the day we know there is no higher cost associated with messaging. The move [the latest price increase by T-Mobile] was colusive [sic] and opportunistic." The misspelled "collusive" is the heart of the plaintiffs' case.

[9] It is apparent from the emails that Hurditch disagreed with his firm's policy of raising the price of its text messaging service. (The price increase, however, was limited to the PPU segment of the service; we'll see that this is an important qualification.) But that is all that is apparent. In emphasizing the word "col[l]usive"—and in arguing in their opening brief that "Hurditch's statement that the price increases were collusive is thus dispositive. Hurditch's statement is a party admission and a co-conspirator statement"—the plaintiffs' counsel demonstrate a failure to understand the fundamental distinction between express and tacit collusion. Express collusion violates antitrust law; tacit collusion does not. There is nothing to suggest that Hurditch was referring to (or accusing his company of) express collusion. In fact the first email rather clearly refers to tacit collusion; for if Hurditch had thought that his company had agreed with its competitors to raise prices he wouldn't have said "I know the other guys are doing it but that doesn't mean we have to follow" (emphasis added). They would have to follow, or at least they would be under great pressure to follow, if they had agreed to follow.

[10] As for the word "opportunistic" in the second email, this is a reference to the remark in the first email that T-Mobile and its competitors were seizing an opportunity to gouge consumers—and in a highly concentrated market, seizing such an opportunity need not imply express collusion.

[11] Consider the last sentence in the second, the "colusive," email: "Clearly get why but it doesn't surprise me why public entities and consumer advocacy groups are starting to groan." This accords with another of Hurditch's emails, in which he predicted that the price increase would cause "bad PR [public relations]." Those concerns would be present whether the collusion among the carriers was tacit or express.

[12] Nothing in any of Hurditch's emails suggests that he believed there was a conspiracy among the carriers. There isn't even evidence that he had ever communicated on any subject with any employee of any of the other defendants. The reference to "the other guys" was not to employees of any of them but to the defendants themselves—the companies, whose PPU prices were public knowledge.

[13] The plaintiffs make much of the fact that Hurditch asked Roddy to delete several emails in the chain that culminated in the "colusive" email. But that is consistent with his not wanting to be detected by his superiors criticizing their management of the company. The plaintiffs argue that, no, the reason for the deletion was to destroy emails that would have shown that T-Mobile was conspiring with the other carriers. If this were true, the plaintiffs would be entitled to have a jury instructed that it could consider the deletion of the emails to be evidence (not conclusive of course) of the defendants' (or at least of T-Mobile's) guilt. But remember that there is no evidence that Hurditch was involved in, or had heard about, any conspiracy, and there is as we've just seen an equally plausible reason for the deletion of the emails in question. There's nothing unusual about sending an intemperate email, regretting sending it, and asking the recipient to delete it. And abusing one's corporate superiors—readily discernible even in Hurditch's emails that were not deleted—is beyond intemperate; it is career-endangering, often career-ending. Hurditch and Roddy acknowledged in their depositions that at least one of the deleted emails had criticized T-Mobile's senior management in "emotional" terms. Furthermore, if T-Mobile destroyed emails that would have revealed a conspiracy with its competitors, why didn't it destroy the "smoking gun" email—the "colusive" email?

[14] Even if the district judge should have allowed a jury to draw an adverse inference from the destruction of the emails, this could not have carried the day for the plaintiffs or even gotten them a trial. T-Mobile's Record Retention Guidelines indicate that Hurditch and Roddy had no obligation to retain their correspondence, because the guidelines state that employees need not retain "routine letters and notes that require no acknowledgment or follow-up" as distinct from "letters of general inquiry and replies that complete a cycle of correspondence." Hurditch's emails to Roddy were not inquiries; they were gripes and worries. Nor can a subordinate employee's destruction of a document, even if in violation of company policy, be automatically equated to a bad-faith act by the company.

[15] The problems with the plaintiff's case go beyond the inconclusiveness of the "colusive" email on which their briefs dwell at such length. The point that they have particular difficulty accepting is that the Sherman Act imposes no duty on firms to compete vigorously, or for that matter at all, in price. This troubles some antitrust experts, such as Harvard Law School Professor Louis Kaplow, whose book COMPETITION POLICY AND PRICE FIXING (2013) argues that tacit collusion should be deemed a violation of the Sherman Act. That of course is not the law,

and probably shouldn't be. A seller must decide on a price; and if tacit collusion is forbidden, how does a seller in a market in which conditions (such as few sellers, many buyers, and a homogeneous product, which may preclude nonprice competition) favor convergence by the sellers on a joint profit-maximizing price without their actually agreeing to charge that price, decide what price to charge? If the seller charges the profit-maximizing price (and its "competitors" do so as well), and tacit collusion is illegal, it is in trouble. But how is it to avoid getting into trouble? Would it have to adopt cost-plus pricing and prove that its price just covered its costs (where cost includes a "reasonable return" to invested capital)? Such a requirement would convert antitrust law into a scheme resembling public utility price regulation, now largely abolished.

[16] And might not entry into concentrated markets be deterred because an entrant who, having successfully entered such a market, charged the prevailing market price would be a tacit colluder and could be prosecuted as such, if tacit collusion were deemed to violate the Sherman Act? What could be more perverse than an antitrust doctrine that discouraged new entry into highly concentrated markets? Prices might fall if the new entrant's output increased the market's total output, but then again it might not fall; the existing firms in the market might reduce their output in order to prevent the output of the new entrant from depressing the market price. If as a result the new entrant found itself charging the same price as the incumbent firms, it would be tacitly colluding with them and likewise even if it set its price below that of those firms in order to maximize its profit from entry yet above the price that would prevail were there no tacit collusion.

[17] Further illustrating the danger of the law's treating tacit collusion as if it were express collusion, suppose that the firms in an oligopolistic market don't try to sell to each other's sleepers, "sleepers" being a term for a seller's customers who out of indolence or ignorance don't shop but instead are loyal to whichever seller they've been accustomed to buy from. Each firm may be reluctant to "awaken" any of the other firms' sleepers by offering them discounts, fearing retaliation. To avoid punishment under antitrust law for such forbearance (which would be a form of tacit collusion, aimed at keeping prices high), would firms be required to raid each other's sleepers? It is one thing to prohibit competitors from agreeing not to compete; it is another to order them to compete. How is a court to decide how vigorously they must compete in order to avoid being found to have tacitly colluded in violation of antitrust law? Such liability would, to repeat, give antitrust agencies a public-utility style regulatory role.

[18] Or consider the case, of which the present one may be an exemplar, in which there are four competitors and one raises its price and the others follow suit. Maybe they do that because they think the first firm—the price leader—has insights into market demand that they lack. Maybe they're afraid that though their sales will increase if they don't follow the leader up the price ladder, the increase in their sales will induce the leader to reduce his price, resulting in increased sales by him at the expense of any firm that had refused to increase its price. Or the firms might fear that the price leader had raised his price in order to finance product improvements that would enable him to hold on to his existing customers—and win over customers of the other firms. If any of these reflections persuaded the other firms—without any communication with the leader—to raise their prices, there would be no conspiracy, but merely tacit collusion, which to repeat is not illegal despite the urging of Professor Kaplow and others.

[19] Competitors in concentrated markets watch each other like hawks. Think of what happens in the airline industry, where costs are to a significant degree a function of fuel prices, when those prices rise. Suppose one airline thinks of and implements a method for raising its profit margin that it expects will have a less negative impact on ticket sales than an increase in ticket prices—such as a checked-bag fee or a reservation-change fee or a reduction in meals or an increase in the number of miles one needs in order to earn a free ticket. The airline's competitors will monitor carefully the effects of the airline's response to the higher fuel prices afflicting the industry and may well decide to copy the response should the responder's response turn out to have increased its profits.

[20] The collusion alleged by the plaintiffs spanned the period 2005 to 2008 (the year the suit was filed), and we must consider closely the evolution of the text messaging market in that period. Text messaging (a descendant of the old telex service) started in the 1990s and started slowly. In 2005, 81 billion text messages were sent in the United States, which sounds like a lot; in fact it was peanuts—for by 2008 the number had risen to a trillion and by 2011 to 2.3 trillion. One reason for the rapid increase was the advent and increasing popularity of volume-discounted text messaging plans. These plans entitled the buyer to send a large number of messages (often an

unlimited number) at a fixed monthly price that made each message sent very cheap to the sender. We'll call these plans "bundles," and ignore the fact that often a text messaging bundle includes services in addition to text messaging, such as voice and video messaging. The pricing of text messaging bundles (for example charging a fixed monthly rate for unlimited messaging) largely replaced the original method of pricing text messages, which had been price per use (PPU), that is, price per individual message, not per month or per some fixed number of messages. Once text messaging bundles became popular, the PPU market shrunk to the relative handful of people who send text messages infrequently. The collusion alleged in this case is limited to that market.

[21] In 2005 the price per use was very low—as low as 2 cents, though more commonly 5 cents. But between then and late 2008 all four defendant companies, in a series of steps (10 steps in all for the four companies), raised each of their PPUs to 20 cents. The increase attracted congressional concern and an investigation by the Justice Department's antitrust division, but neither legislative nor prosecutorial action resulted—only the series of class actions suits consolidated in 2009 in the suit before us.

[22] The popularity of text messaging bundles took a big bite out of the PPU market. The consumers left in that market were as we said those who sent very few messages. The total cost to such users was very low. Each defendant company made, so far as appears, an independent judgment that PPU usage per customer was on average so low that the customer would not balk at, if he would even notice, an occasional increase of a few cents per message. Suppose a grandparent living in Florida sends one text message a week to his grandchild in Illinois at a cost of 5 cents a message. That adds up to roughly 4 messages a month, for a total of 20 cents. The text messaging service now doubles the price, to 10 cents a message. The monthly charge is now 40 cents. Is the customer likely to balk? When in 2006 Sprint raised its PPU from 10 cents to 15 cents, it estimated that the average result would be an increase of 74 cents a month in the cost of the service for the vast majority of its PPU customers. Neither in our hypothetical example nor in Sprint's real-world analysis is a competing carrier likely to spend money advertising that its PPU price is 5 cents lower than what the competition is charging.

[23] Our earlier discussion of "sleepers" is relevant here. As heavy users of text messaging switched from PPU to bundles, the PPU market was left with the dwindling band of consumers whose use of text messaging was too limited to motivate them to switch to bundles or to complain about small increases in price per message. And they certainly weren't going to undergo the hassle of switching companies just because they would be paying a few dollars a year more for text messaging. This is no more than a plausible interpretation of the motive for and character of the price increases of which the plaintiffs complain, but the burden of establishing a prima facie case of explicit collusion was on the plaintiffs, and as the district judge found in his excellent opinion they failed to carry the burden.

[24] Granted, the defendants overstate their case in some respects. They point out that each company conducted independent evaluations of the profitability of raising their PPUs, but one would expect such "independent" evaluations even if the firms were expressly colluding, as the "independent" evaluations would disguise what they were doing. The firms contend unnecessarily that the evaluations showed that the contemplated price increases would be profitable even if none of the other three carriers raised its PPU. That is overkill because it is not a violation of antitrust law for a firm to raise its price, counting on its competitors to do likewise (but without any communication with them on the subject) and fearing the consequences if they do not. In fact AT & T held back on raising its PPU for several months, fearing that Sprint's increase would have a bad effect on public opinion, and raised its own price only when the bad effect did not materialize.

[25] The plaintiffs point out that the existence of express collusion can sometimes be inferred from circumstantial evidence, and they claim that they produced such evidence, along with Hurditch's emails, which they term direct evidence of such collusion—which, as we know, they are not. Circumstantial evidence of such collusion might be a decline in the market shares of the leading firms in a market, for their agreeing among themselves to charge a high fixed price might have caused fringe firms and new entrants to increase output and thus take sales from the leading firms. Circumstantial evidence might be inflexibility of the market leaders' market shares over time, suggesting a possible agreement among them not to alter prices, since such an alteration would tend to cause market shares to change. Or one might see a surge in nonprice competition, a form of competition outside the scope of the cartel agreement and therefore a possible substitute for price competition. Other evidence of express collusion might be a high elasticity of demand (meaning that a small change in price would cause a substantial

change in quantity demanded), for this might indicate that the sellers had agreed not to cut prices even though it would be to the advantage of each individual seller to do so until the market price fell to a level at which the added quantity sold did not offset the price decrease.

[26] The problem is that these phenomena are consistent with tacit as well as express collusion; their absence would tend to negate both, but their presence would not point unerringly to express collusion. And anyway these aren't the types of circumstantial evidence on which the plaintiffs rely. Rather they argue that had any one of the four carriers not raised its price, the others would have experienced costly consumer "churn" (the trade's term for losing customers to a competitor), and therefore all four dared raise their prices only because they had agreed to act in concert. For that would minimize churn—PPU customers would have no place to turn for a lower price. There is, however, a six-fold weakness to this suggested evidence of express collusion:

[27] First, a rational profit-maximizing seller does not care about the number of customers it has but about its total revenues relative to its total costs. If the seller loses a third of its customers because it has doubled its price, it's ahead of the game because twice two-thirds is greater than one ($4/3 > 3/3$).

[28] Second, in any case of tacit collusion the colluders risk churn, because no one would have committed to adhere to the collusive price. And yet tacit collusion appears to be common, each tacit colluder reckoning that in all likelihood the others will see the advantages of hanging together rather than hanging separately.

[29] Third, the four defendants in this case did not move in lockstep. For months on end there were price differences in their services. For example, during most of the entire period at issue (2005 to 2008) T–Mobile's PPU was 5 cents below Sprint's. To eliminate all risk of churn the defendants would have had to agree to raise their prices simultaneously, and they did not.

[30] Fourth, while there was some churn, this does not imply that each defendant had decided to raise its price so high as to drive away droves of customers had the other defendants not followed suit. T–Mobile, for example, appears not to have gained a significant number of customers from charging less for PPU service than Sprint. (As one internal T–Mobile email puts it, "we should seriously consider raising our pay per message rate. [F]or having the lowest messaging rates on the planet, we are not necessarily receiving a more favorable share of the market. I'm thinking we can move to 10c[ents] with little erosive concerns.") One reason is that, as noted earlier, while 5 cents can make a large percentage difference in this market, it is such a small absolute amount of money that it may make no difference to most consumers, especially when a nickel or a dime or 20 cents is multiplied by a very small number of monthly messages. More important, as a customer's monthly messaging increases, and also the price per message (as was happening during this period), the alternative of a text messaging bundle plan becomes more attractive. A company that stands to lose some PPU customers because of a price increase may be confident that they will not abandon the company for another but instead sign on to the company's text messaging bundle plan. Put differently, there is no evidence that PPU pricing is a major determinant of consumers' choice of carrier.

[31] Fifth, the period during which the carriers were raising their prices was also the period in which text messaging caught on with the consuming public and surged in volume. Many PPU customers would have found that they were text messaging more, and the more one text messages the more attractive the alternative of a bundle plan. The defendants wanted their PPU customers to switch to bundles; as an internal T–Mobile email in the plaintiffs' appendix explains, "the average cost to serve an 'Unlimited SMS' [i.e., a bundled short-message service at a fixed price regardless of the number of messages, "short message" referring to a simple text message, rather than a message having voice or video content] customer paying $9.99 [per month] is $1.90 per month and [we make] a profit of $8.09 per sub[scriber]."

[32] And sixth, if the carriers were going to agree to fix prices, they wouldn't have fixed their PPU prices; why risk suit or prosecution for fixing such prices when the PPU market was generating such a slight—and shrinking—part of the carriers' overall revenues? The possible gains would be more than offset by the inevitable legal risks. Furthermore, since an agreement to fix prices in the PPU market would have left the carriers free to cut prices on the bulk of their business (for they are not accused of fixing bundle prices), the slight gains from fixing PPU prices would be negated by increased competition in the carriers' other markets. [. . .]

[33] It remains to consider the claim that the trade association of which the defendants were members, The Wireless Association (it has a confusing acronym—CTIA, reflecting the original name of the association, which was Cellular Telephone Industries Association), and a component of the association called the Wireless Internet Caucus of CTIA, were forums in which officers of the defendants met and conspired to raise PPU prices. Officers of some of the defendants attended meetings both of the association and of its caucus, but representatives of companies not alleged to be part of the conspiracy frequently were present at these meetings, and one of the plaintiffs' expert witnesses admitted that in the presence of non-conspirators "the probability of collusion would go away." Still, opportunities for senior leaders of the defendants to meet privately in these officers' retreats abounded. And an executive of one of the defendants (AT & T) told the president of the association that "we all try not to surprise each other" and "if any of us are about to do something major we all tend to give the group a heads up"—"plus we all learn valuable info from each other." This evidence would be more compelling if the immediate sequel to any of these meetings had been a simultaneous or near-simultaneous price increase by the defendants. Instead there were substantial lags. And as there is no evidence of what information was exchanged at these meetings, there is no basis for an inference that they were using the meetings to plot prices increases.

[34] This and other circumstantial evidence that the plaintiffs cite are almost an afterthought. They have staked almost their all on Hurditch's emails—the name "Hurditch" recurs more than 160 times in the plaintiffs' opening and reply briefs. It's a mystery to us that the plaintiffs have placed such weight on those emails, thereby wasting space in their briefs that might have been better used. The plaintiffs greatly exaggerate the significance of the emails, but apart from the emails the circumstantial evidence that they cite provides insufficient support for the charge of express collusion.

[35] It is of course difficult to prove illegal collusion without witnesses to an agreement. And there are no such witnesses in this case. We can, moreover, without suspecting illegal collusion, expect competing firms to keep close track of each other's pricing and other market behavior and often to find it in their self-interest to imitate that behavior rather than try to undermine it—the latter being a risky strategy, prone to invite retaliation. The plaintiffs have presented circumstantial evidence consistent with an inference of collusion, but that evidence is equally consistent with independent parallel behavior.

[36] We hope this opinion will help lawyers understand the risks of invoking "collusion" without being precise about what they mean. Tacit collusion, also known as conscious parallelism, does not violate section 1 of the Sherman Act. Collusion is illegal only when based on agreement. Agreement can be proved by circumstantial evidence, and the plaintiffs were permitted to conduct and did conduct full pretrial discovery of such evidence. Yet their search failed to find sufficient evidence of express collusion to make a prima facie case. The district court had therefore no alternative to granting summary judgment in favor of the defendants.

* * *

NOTES

1) Are "agreements" invariably more stable or more harmful than parallel practices? What is the point of the "agreement" requirement?

2) *Monsanto* can be read to emphasize three different key elements in the definition of an agreement: first, "evidence that tends to exclude the possibility that the [parties] were acting independently" (paragraph 14); second, "conscious commitment to a common scheme" (paragraph 14); and, third, "evidence . . . that the distributor communicated its acquiescence or agreement, and that this was sought by the manufacturer" (footnote 9). Are these three elements equally important? Do *Matushita* and *Twombly* suggest a definition of agreement that is consistent with, or different from, this view?

3) Does tacit collusion of the kind described in Chapter II—in which parties monitor each other and set their conduct accordingly—meet the *Monsanto* standard for an agreement?

4) In *Monsanto*, at paragraph 9, the Court emphasized that a manufacturer can have, and announce, a unilateral policy of selling only to dealers that comply with its stated resale prices, *without* the result being considered joint action. And at paragraph 11, the Court added that "the fact that a manufacturer and its distributors are in constant communication about prices and marketing strategy does not alone show that the distributors are

not making independent pricing decisions." Given this understanding why exactly were Monsanto's actions not unilateral?

5) Look back at paragraphs 15 and 16 of the *Monsanto* extract. How, if at all, does the evidence described here support the inference of agreement rather than unilateral conduct?

6) The allegations in *Matsushita* were unusual—the plaintiff alleged that the defendants conspired to set prices *below* cost, whereas most price-fixing conspiracies seek to raise prices. Predatory pricing conspiracies, which involve agreements to depress prices, are less obviously harmful to consumers (at least absent the likely prospect of later monopolization and recoupment) than conspiracies to raise prices, which raises the prospect that perhaps *Matsushita's* demanding standard of proof might have been reserved for unusual (and thus perhaps less plausible) conspiracies like the one alleged in that case. And yet many courts have applied the demanding *Matsushita* standard to standard price-raising conspiracies as well, requiring plaintiff to produce evidence which "tends to exclude the possibility" of unilateral conduct.[264] A few courts, however, have taken a more subtle approach, interpreting the *Matsushita* standard to require a court to assess the inherent economic plausibility of the plaintiff's theory of harm, with a less demanding proof requirement for theories that are easier to believe. The Second Circuit has articulated that view concisely:

> *Matsushita*, then, stands for the proposition that substantive "antitrust law limits the range of permissible inferences" that may be drawn from ambiguous evidence. It further holds that the range of inferences that may be draw from such evidence depends on the plausibility of the plaintiff's theory. Thus, where a plaintiff's theory of recovery is implausible, it takes "strong direct or circumstantial evidence" to satisfy Matsushita's "tends to exclude" standard. By contrast, broader inferences are permitted, and the "tends to exclude" standard is more easily satisfied, when the conspiracy is economically sensible for the alleged conspirators to undertake and the challenged activities could not reasonably be perceived as procompetitive. [C]f. Eastman Kodak Co. v. Image Technical Servs., Inc., 504 U.S. 451, 468 (1992) ("Matsushita demands only that the nonmoving party's inferences be reasonable in order to reach the jury, a requirement that was not invented, but merely articulated, in that decision.").[265]

Which view of *Matsushita*—unitary standard for proving agreement or sliding scale depending on the plausibility of the allegations—do you think is most useful? Most consistent with the *Matsushita* opinion itself? Most administrable by courts? Does *Twombly's* treatment of *Matsushita* illuminate this issue at all?

7) Is the economic plausibility of a theory of harm a question of law or fact? When is it appropriate for determination on summary judgment, as the Court did in *Matsushita* itself? How does a court know what is, and is not, economically plausible?[266]

8) Do you agree with the following statement: "At bottom, *Twombly* applies a long-held principle in antitrust law to the pleading stage: parallel conduct, standing alone, does not establish the required agreement because it is equally consistent with lawful conduct."[267]

9) Is *Twombly* consistent with the "notice pleading" standard adopted by the Federal Rules of Civil Procedure? (A notice pleading standard does not require a plaintiff to plead facts supporting its claims, but rather only factual allegations sufficient to put the defendant on notice of the nature of those claims.) Can you think of reasons why the Court may have believed that notice pleading is the wrong standard for antitrust claims alleging agreements?

10) What exactly is the nature of the disagreement between the majority and the dissent in *Twombly*? Is it about the pleading standard that applies? Or do the majority and dissent agree on the pleading standard but disagree regarding whether Twombly has satisfied it?

11) Twombly's complaint alleged that the ILECs had *agreed not to compete*. The Court held that the complaint failed because it did not allege facts that, if taken as true, sufficiently supported an inference that the ILECs were acting pursuant to an agreement, rather than engaging in parallel but independent conduct that made sense for each of them individually. Why do you think the Court took the route of arguably raising pleading

---

[264] *See, e.g.*, Blomkest Fertilizer, Inc. v. Potash Corp. of Sasketchewan, Inc., 203 F.3d 1028, 1032 (8th Cir. 2000) (joining majority of circuits applying *Matsushita* broadly in both horizontal and vertical price-fixing cases).

[265] In re Publication Paper Antitrust Litig., 690 F.3d 51, 63 (2d Cir. 2012).

[266] *See generally* Herbert Hovenkamp, THE ANTITRUST ENTERPRISE: PRINCIPLE AND EXECUTION (2005) Ch. 4.

[267] SD3, LLC v. Black & Decker (U.S.) Inc., 801 F.3d 412, 424 (4th Cir. 2015), *as amended on reh'g in part* (Oct. 29, 2015).

standards, rather than relying on courts' discretionary powers to manage litigation? For example, courts in antitrust cases could order narrow (and expedited) discovery on facts relevant to the existence of an agreement, and could grant a defendant's motion for summary judgment if such evidence is not forthcoming. Would it have been better to simply encourage lower courts to take that approach?

12) Calibrating the motion-to-dismiss standard for an antitrust case is a tricky business. Consider first the position of the plaintiff: at the motion to dismiss stage, the plaintiff has not yet had the opportunity to use discovery tools that would give access to documents and information in the possession, custody, or control of the defendant (and any co-conspirators). And, of course, agreements not to compete are generally not public: all that may be publicly visible is the conduct of the participants, which may be as consistent with parallelism as with agreement. But now consider the position of the defendant: antitrust discovery is incredibly expensive, and trading partners and rivals have real incentives to file speculative claims. Weighing these factors, does *Twombly* set the bar in the right place?

C. Evaluating Reasonableness: Per Se, Rule of Reason, and Intermediate Scrutiny

When an agreement exists, Section 1 analysis requires the application of one of three substantive legal standards to determine whether it unreasonably restrains competition. As noted above, these are:

(1) a standard of *per se*, or automatic, illegality for a narrow category of highly troubling agreements, such as price-fixing, bid-rigging, and market-allocation agreements;

(2) a "rule of reason"—the default standard for most agreements, including all vertical agreements and any horizontal agreement with a plausible procompetitive purpose or effect—which provides that an agreement is illegal if its harmful tendencies can be shown to outweigh its beneficial tendencies; and

(3) an intermediate standard of review (usually called "quick look") for a small set of agreements that are facially troubling but which could nevertheless be justified by sufficient evidence of competitive benefit.

In the rest of this chapter we will focus on understanding *how* each rule applies. When we turn to horizontal restraints in the next Chapter, we will take up the task of figuring out when a court may choose to apply one rather than the other.

The three standards are nowhere to be found on the face of Section 1, which just states that "[e]very contract, combination in the form of trust or otherwise, or conspiracy, in restraint of trade or commerce among the several States, or with foreign nations, is hereby declared to be illegal[.]"[268] Instead, they were developed by courts.

In *Trans-Missouri Freight* in 1897—a case involving price-fixing among railroads—the Supreme Court took a strikingly literal approach to the meaning of the word "every" in Section 1, according to which every restraint of trade was automatically illegal:

> When . . . the body of an act pronounces as illegal every contract or combination in restraint of trade or commerce among the several states, etc., the plain and ordinary meaning of such language is not limited to that kind of contract alone with is in unreasonable restraint of trade, but all contracts are included in such language, and no exception or limitation can be added without placing in the act that which has been omitted by Congress.[269]

Justice Edward Douglass White dissented in *Trans-Missouri Freight*, laying out what would later become the standard interpretation of Section 1: that it prohibits only *unreasonable* restraints of trade.[270] And nearly a decade and a half

---

[268] 15 U.S.C. § 1.

[269] United States v. Trans-Missouri Freight Ass'n, 166 U.S. 290, 328 (1897). *See also* N. Sec. Co. v. United States, 193 U.S. 197, 331 (1904).

[270] United States v. Trans-Missouri Freight Ass'n, 166 U.S. 290, 328–29 (1897) (White, J., dissenting).

later, the Court would adopt that view in an opinion written by then-Chief-Justice White in the iconic case of *Standard Oil* in 1911:[271]

> [Section 1] necessarily called for the exercise of judgment which required that some standard should be resorted to for the purpose of determining whether the prohibitions contained in the statute had or had not in any given case been violated. Thus not specifying but indubitably contemplating and requiring a standard, it follows that it was intended that *the standard of reason* which had been applied at the common law and in this country in dealing with subjects of the character embraced by the statute, *was intended to be the measure used for the purpose of determining whether in a given case a particular act had or had not brought about the wrong against which the statute provided.*[272]

As we shall see, the new focus on reasonableness—established in *Standard Oil* and confirmed in *American Tobacco*,[273] both in 1911—raised plenty of complexities. A foundational early effort to formulate a principled approach to reasonableness can be traced to an even earlier case: the opinion of (then-Sixth Circuit Judge) William Taft in *Addyston Pipe*.[274] Judge Taft separated restraints into two categories. First were those "where the sole object of both parties in making the contract as expressed therein is merely to restrain competition, and enhance or maintain prices."[275] These restraints would be condemned in all cases. "[I]t would seem," Judge Taft wrote, "that there was nothing to justify or excuse the restraint, that it would necessarily have a tendency to monopoly, and therefore would be void."[276] The second category involved restraints Judge Taft labeled "ancillary" (meaning, broadly, "secondary to and supportive of"): *i.e.*, restraints supporting a primary, and legitimate, purpose.[277] For example, consider a joint venture agreement between a car-maker and a battery company that provided that the car-maker would not work with another battery company on an electric car project during the life of the joint venture. Such a restraint might be necessary to permit the underlying, socially valuable joint venture to move forward: if, for example, the battery company was worried about the car-maker taking valuable knowledge about battery technology it had gained through the joint venture and giving that information to a rival battery company. Ancillary restraints, Taft argued, should be permitted if they were "reasonable"—*i.e.*, when they were crucial to the viability of a legitimate arrangement and no broader than necessary to facilitate that arrangement.[278]

In one important passage, Taft pointed out that it had long been understood that sometimes a "restraint" was necessary if a procompetitive purpose (such as the sale of a business) was to be achieved at all:

> After a time it became apparent to the people and the courts that it was in the interest of trade that certain covenants in restraint of trade should be enforced. It was of importance, as an incentive to industry and honest dealing in trade, that, after a man had built up a business with an extensive good will, he should be able to sell his business and good will to the best advantage, and he could not do so unless he could bind himself by an enforceable contract not to engage in the same business in such a way as to prevent injury to that which he was about to sell. It was equally for the good of the public and trade, when partners dissolved, and one took the business, or they divided the business, that each partner might bind himself not to do anything in trade thereafter which would derogate from his grant of the interest conveyed to his former partner. Again, when two men became partners in a business, although their union might reduce competition, this effect was only an incident to the main purpose of a union of their capital, enterprise, and energy to carry on a successful business, and one useful to the community. Restrictions in the articles of partnership upon the business activity of the members, with a view of securing their entire effort in the common enterprise, were, of course, only ancillary to the main end of the union, and were to be encouraged. Again, when one in business sold property with which the buyer might set up a rival business, it was certainly reasonable that the seller

---

[271] Standard Oil Co. v. United States, 221 U.S. 1 (1911).

[272] Standard Oil Co. v. United States, 221 U.S. 1, 60 (1911) (emphasis added).

[273] Standard Oil Co. v. United States, 221 U.S. 1, 60 (1911); United States v. American Tobacco Co., 221 U.S. 106, 181 (1911) (re-affirming *Standard Oil* and noting that "it remains only to determine whether they establish that the acts, contracts, agreements, combinations, etc., which were assailed, were of such an unusual and wrongful character as to [render them illegal]").

[274] United States v. Addyston Pipe & Steel Co., 85 F. 271 (6th Cir. 1898), *modified and affirmed*, 175 U.S. 211 (1896).

[275] *Id.* at 282-83.

[276] *Id.* at 283.

[277] *Id.* at 282.

[278] *Id.* at 290–91.

should be able to restrain the buyer from doing him an injury which, but for the sale, the buyer would be unable to inflict. This was not reducing competition, but was only securing the seller against an increase of competition of his own creating. Such an exception was necessary to promote the free purchase and sale of property. Again, it was of importance that business men and professional men should have every motive to employ the ablest assistants, and to instruct them thoroughly; but they would naturally be reluctant to do so unless such assistants were able to bind themselves not to set up a rival business in the vicinity after learning the details and secrets of the business of their employers. [279]

Taft's core idea—that courts should distinguish among restraints by reference to whether they were related to a procompetitive purpose, carefully analyzing those that *were* so related, and automatically condemning those that were *not*—was immensely influential. But this has turned out to be easier to state than to do! Distinguishing among those categories, and figuring out what "careful analysis" should look like for agreements that are not automatically illegal, has challenged courts, scholars, and businesses for many decades.

1. Per Se Illegality

The rule of *per se* or automatic illegality applies to a small number of horizontal agreements that have been established, by judicial experience, to be always or almost always harmful to competition. Classic examples include agreements to fix prices, limit output, divide markets, or rig bids.

The Court expressed this point clearly in *Trenton Potteries* in 1927. That case involved a challenge to an alleged scheme to fix prices by suppliers of "sanitary pottery" for use in bathrooms and lavatories. The trial court had instructed the jurors that they could find the agreement illegal regardless of whether the prices actually fixed were unreasonably high. The Supreme Court agreed, distinguishing its own earlier rule-of-reason decision in *Chicago Board of Trade* and emphasizing the distinctively anticompetitive character of price-fixing agreements.

United States v. Trenton Potteries Co.

273 U.S. 392 (1927)

Justice Stone.

[1] Respondents, 20 individuals and 23 corporations, were convicted in the District Court for Southern New York of violating the Sherman Anti-Trust Law. The indictment was in two counts. The first charged a combination to fix and maintain uniform prices for the sale of sanitary pottery, in restraint of interstate commerce; the second, a combination to restrain interstate commerce by limiting sales of pottery to a special group known to respondents as "legitimate jobbers."

[2] Respondents, engaged in the manufacture or distribution of 82 per cent of the vitreous pottery fixtures produced in the United States for use in bathrooms and lavatories, were members of a trade organization known as the Sanitary Potters' Association. Twelve of the corporate respondents had their factories and chief places of business in New Jersey, one was located in California, and the others were situated in Illinois, Michigan, West Virginia, Indiana, Ohio, and Pennsylvania. Many of them sold and delivered their product within the Southern district of New York, and some maintained sales offices and agents there.

[3] There is no contention here that the verdict was not supported by sufficient evidence that respondents, controlling some 82 per cent of the business of manufacturing and distributing in the United States vitreous pottery of the type described, combined to fix prices and to limit sales in interstate commerce to jobbers. [. . .]

[4] That only those restraints upon interstate commerce which are unreasonable are prohibited by the Sherman Law was the rule laid down by the opinions of this court in the *Standard Oil* and *Tobacco* Cases. But it does not follow that agreements to fix or maintain prices are reasonable restraints and therefore permitted by the statute, merely because the prices themselves are reasonable. Reasonableness is not a concept of definite and unchanging content. Its meaning necessarily varies in the different fields of the law, because it is used as a convenient summary

---

[279] *Id.* at 280–81.

of the dominant considerations which control in the application of legal doctrines. Our view of what is a reasonable restraint of commerce is controlled by the recognized purpose of the Sherman Law itself. Whether this type of restraint is reasonable or not must be judged in part at least, in the light of its effect on competition, for, whatever difference of opinion there may be among economists as to the social and economic desirability of an unrestrained competitive system, it cannot be doubted that the Sherman Law and the judicial decisions interpreting it are based upon the assumption that the public interest is best protected from the evils of monopoly and price control by the maintenance of competition. . . .

[5] The aim and result of every price-fixing agreement, if effective, is the elimination of one form of competition. The power to fix prices, whether reasonably exercised or not, involves power to control the market and to fix arbitrary and unreasonable prices. The reasonable price fixed today may through economic and business changes become the unreasonable price of to-morrow. Once established, it may be maintained unchanged because of the absence of competition secured by the agreement for a price reasonable when fixed. Agreements which create such potential power may well be held to be in themselves unreasonable or unlawful restraints, without the necessity of minute inquiry whether a particular price is reasonable or unreasonable as fixed and without placing on the government in enforcing the Sherman Law the burden of ascertaining from day to day whether it has become unreasonable through the mere variation of economic conditions. Moreover, in the absence of express legislation requiring it, we should hesitate to adopt a construction making the difference between legal and illegal conduct in the field of business relations depend upon so uncertain a test as whether prices are reasonable—a determination which can be satisfactorily made only after a complete survey of our economic organization and a choice between rival philosophies. [. . .]

[6] Cases in both the federal and state courts[1] have generally proceeded on a like assumption, and in the second circuit the view maintained below that the reasonableness or unreasonableness of the prices fixed must be submitted to the jury has apparently been abandoned. [. . .]

[7] Whether the prices actually agreed upon were reasonable or unreasonable was immaterial in the circumstances charged in the indictment and necessarily found by the verdict.

* * *

Despite the clarity of this language, *Trenton Potteries* did not quite settle the question. In subsequent cases, the Court appeared to take a more indulgent approach to practices that looked an awful lot like naked price fixing. For example, in the infamous 1933 *Appalachian Coals* case, the Court upheld the legality of an "exclusive selling arrangement," including fixed prices, among coal producers representing 73% of all output in Appalachia.[280] The *per se* illegality of price-fixing cartels would not be confirmed beyond all doubt until *Socony-Vacuum* in 1940.

---

[1] The illegality of such agreements has commonly been assumed without consideration of the reasonableness of the price levels established. Loder v. Jayne (C. C.) 142 F. 1010; Crafe v. McConoughy, 79 Ill. 346, 22 Am. Rep. 171; Vulcan Powder Co. v. Hercules Powder Co., 96 Cal. 510, 31 P. 581, 31 Am. St. Rep. 242; Johnson v. People. 72 Colo. 218, 210 P. 843; People v. Amanna, 203 App. Div. 548, 196 N. Y. S. 606. See Trenton Potteries Co. v. Oliphant, 58 N. J. Eq. 507, 521, 43 A. 723, 46 L. R. A. 255, 78 Am. St. Rep. 612; Beechley v. Mulville, 102 Iowa, 602, 608, 70 N. W. 107, 71 N. W. 428, 63 Am. St. Rep. 479; People v. Milk Exchange, 145 N. Y. 267, 39 N. E. 1062, 27 L. R. A. 437, 45 Am. St. Rep. 609 (purchase prices). In many of these cases price-fixing was accompanied by other factors contributing to the illegality. Upon the precise question, there has been diversity of view. People v. Sheldon, 139 N. Y. 251, 34 N. E. 785, 23 L. R. A. 221, 36 Am. St. Rep. 690; State v. Eastern Coal Co., 29 R. I. 254, 256, 265, 70 A. 1, 132 Am. St. Rep. 817, 17 Ann. Cas. 96; Pope, Legal Aspect of Monopoly, 20 Harvard Law Rev. 167, 178; Watkins, Change in Trust Policy, 35 Harvard Law Rev. 815, 821-823 (reasonableness of prices immaterial). Contra: Cade & Sons v. Daly (1910) 1 Ir. Ch. 306; Central Shade Roller Co. v. Cushman, 143 Mass. 353, 9 N. E. 629; Skrainka v. Scharringhausen, 8 Mo. App. 522; Dueber Watch Case Mfg. Co. v. Howard Watch Co. (C. C.) 55 F. 851.

[280] *See* Appalachian Coals v. United States, 288 U.S. 344, 360-61 (1933) ("The mere fact that the parties to an agreement eliminate competition between themselves is not enough to condemn it. 'The legality of an agreement or regulation cannot be determined by so simple a test, as whether it restrains competition. . . . The question of the application of the statute is one of intent and effect, and is not to be determined by arbitrary assumptions. It is therefore necessary in this instance to consider the economic conditions peculiar to the coal industry, the practices which have obtained, the nature of defendant's plan of making sales, the reasons which led to its adoption, and the probable consequences of the carrying out of that plan in relation to market prices and other matters affecting the public interest in interstate commerce in bituminous coal."). The decision is almost universally abhorred. But for a supportive take, *see* Sheldon Kimmel, *How and Why the Per Se Rule Against Price-Fixing Went Wrong*, 19 Sup. Ct. Econ. Rev. 245 (2011).

CASENOTE: United States v. Socony-Vacuum Oil Co.

310 U.S. 150 (1940)

The story of *Socony-Vacuum* is an intricate one.[281] The defendants in that case were major oil refiners operating in the U.S. Midwest. These major refiners were vertically integrated—each owning oil wells, refineries, storage facilities, and gas stations. Starting in the mid-1920s, the U.S. petroleum industry experienced a period of "overproduction," resulting in sharply falling oil and gasoline prices. Some states responded by setting production caps, but these attempts failed as a number of companies continued to produce both oil and gasoline in excess of the amount permitted under the caps—so-called "hot oil" from which illegal "hot gasoline" was refined.

Smaller independent refiners who complied with the production caps suffered the most from the production of hot oil. The smaller independent refiners lacked substantial storage capacity, and so were forced to sell the gasoline they produced at a "distress" price reduced by competition from hot gasoline. Under authority granted by the National Industrial Recovery Act of 1933 ("NIRA"), the President promulgated a "code of fair competition" for the petroleum industry which forbade shipments of hot oil. Oil and gasoline prices rose as a result. But the Supreme Court soon held that the industry codes promulgated under NIRA represented an unconstitutional delegation of legislative authority.[282] So the problem returned.

In the aftermath of the Court's decision, a group of oil refiners took matters into their own hands and devised a strategy to raise prices. They agreed that certain of the major refiners would purchase gasoline directly from the independents at what they jointly "recommended" as "fair market" prices, thereby removing a substantial quantity of low-priced gasoline from the market. A committee produced a monthly list pairing each major refiner with a "dancing partner"—*i.e.*, an independent from which it would purchase excess gasoline that month.

The federal government charged the oil refiners with violating Section 1, alleging that they had conspired through the "dancing partners" arrangement to fix the spot market price for gasoline, and thereby to raise the price at which defendants sold gasoline. The result was higher prices for gasoline. The trial court instructed the jury that an agreement made for the purpose of raising prices could result in civil liability under Section 1, without regard to whether the price was reasonable or whether the agreement was likely to be effective in raising prices. However, the court instructed the jury that *criminal* liability under Section 1 required them to find beyond a reasonable doubt that the rise in gasoline retail prices was caused by the agreement and not solely by some other factor or factors. The jury convicted. But the Court of Appeals reversed, holding that the jury should not have been instructed that the agreement was illegal per se. Instead, the appellate court concluded, liability depended on showing that the agreement had in fact unreasonably restrained trade. The court remanded for a new trial to determine the competitive effects of the agreement. The government appealed to the Supreme Court—where it prevailed.

Today, Justice Douglas's opinion for the Supreme Court is a classic authority for the automatic or *per se* illegality of price-fixing and other naked restraints on competition. And indeed much of the opinion sets out that view. "[F]or over forty years," the Court stated, "this Court has consistently and without deviation adhered to the principle that price-fixing agreements are unlawful per se under the Sherman Act and that no showing of so-called competitive abuses or evils which those agreements were designed to eliminate or alleviate may be interposed as a defense."

The Court specifically rejected the idea that courts should inquire into whether fixed prices were actually reasonable. "Ruinous competition, financial disaster, evils of price cutting and the like appear throughout our history as ostensible justifications for price-fixing. If the so-called competitive abuses were to be appraised here, the reasonableness of prices would necessarily become an issue in every price-fixing case. In that event the Sherman Act would soon be emasculated; its philosophy would be supplanted by one which is wholly alien to a system of free competition; it would not be the charter of freedom which its framers intended." Indeed, "[t]hose who fixed reasonable prices today would perpetuate unreasonable prices tomorrow, since those prices would not

---

[281] Dan Crane, characteristically, tells it well. Daniel Crane, *The Story of United States v. Socony-Vacuum: Hot Oil and Antitrust in the Two New Deals* in Eleanor M. Fox & Daniel A. Crane (eds.) ANTITRUST STORIES (2007).

[282] Panama Ref. Co. v. Ryan, 293 U.S. 388, 405 (1935).

be subject to continuous administrative supervision and readjustment in light of changed conditions." Congress had taken this whole issue out of the judiciary's hands: "Congress has not left with us the determination of whether or not particular price-fixing schemes are wise or unwise, healthy or destructive. It has not permitted the age-old cry of ruinous competition and competitive evils to be a defense to price-fixing conspiracies. It has no more allowed genuine or fancied competitive abuses as a legal justification for such schemes than it has the good intentions of the members of the combination. If such a shift is to be made, it must be done by the Congress."

"Price fixing" for this purpose simply meant agreeing on price or on some scheme to replace or distort price competition. "[P]rices are fixed within the meaning of the *Trenton Potteries* case if the range within which purchases or sales will be made is agreed upon, if the prices paid or charged are to be at a certain level or on ascending or descending scales, if they are to be uniform, or if by various formulae they are related to the market prices. They are fixed because they are agreed upon. And the fact that, as here, they are fixed at the fair going market price is immaterial."

So far, so clear, right? Price-fixing is always illegal, end of story. And certainly: that is the proposition for which *Socony* is cited today, and it has been confirmed by countless cases since as one of antitrust's most important commandments. But a modern reader of the *Socony* opinion itself may be surprised to find much language that suggests a narrower rule condemning price-fixing only when the participants hold a degree of market power. For example, at some points the Court's opinion implies that an effect of some kind on prices is required: "Any combination which tampers with price structures is engaged in an unlawful activity. Even though the members of the price-fixing group were in no position to control the market, *to the extent that they raised, lowered, or stabilized prices* they would be directly interfering with the free play of market forces. The Act places all such schemes beyond the pale and protects that vital part of our economy against any degree of interference." (Emphasis added.) And: "So far as cause and effect are concerned it is sufficient in this type of case if the buying programs of the combination *resulted in a price rise and market stability which but for them would not have happened.*" (Emphasis added.)

At another point, the Court was even more explicit: "Under the Sherman Act a combination formed for the purpose *and with the effect* of raising, depressing, fixing, pegging, or stabilizing the price of a commodity in interstate or foreign commerce is illegal per se. Where the machinery for price-fixing is an agreement on the prices to be charged or paid for the commodity in the interstate or foreign channels of trade, the power to fix prices exists if the combination has control of a substantial part of the commerce in that commodity. Where the means for price-fixing are purchases or sales of the commodity in a market operation or, as here, purchases of a part of the supply of the commodity for the purpose of keeping it from having a depressive effect on the markets, such power may be found to exist though the combination does not control a substantial part of the commodity. In such a case that power may be established if as a result of market conditions, the resources available to the combinations, the timing and the strategic placement of orders and the like, effective means are at hand to accomplish the desired objective.. But there may be effective influence over the market though the group in question does not control it. . . . Proof that a combination was formed for the purpose of fixing prices *and that it caused them to be fixed or contributed to that result* is proof of the completion of a price-fixing conspiracy under s 1 of the Act. The indictment in this case charged that this combination had that purpose and effect. And there was abundant evidence to support it. Hence the existence of power on the part of members of the combination to fix prices was but a conclusion from the finding that the buying programs caused or contributed to the rise and stability of prices."

The closest thing the Court offers to a resolution of this tension is tucked away in footnote 59 of the opinion. The Court noted there that an actual impact on price in the Midwest was necessary to establish jurisdiction in the district court. But this did not mean "that both a purpose and a power to fix prices are necessary for the establishment of a conspiracy under s 1 of the Sherman Act. . . . [I]t is well established that a person may be guilty of conspiring, although incapable of committing the objective offense. And it is likewise well settled that conspiracies under the Sherman Act are not dependent on any overt act other than the act of conspiring. . . . In view of these considerations a conspiracy to fix prices violates s 1 of the Act though no overt act is shown, though it is not established that the conspirators had the means available for accomplishment of their objective, and though the conspiracy embraced but a part of the interstate or foreign commerce in the commodity. . . . Whatever economic justification particular price-fixing agreements may be thought to have, the law does not permit an inquiry into their reasonableness. They are all banned because of their actual or potential threat to the central nervous system of the economy."

So the modern reading of *Socony*—as an authority for Section 1's flat *per se* ban on price-fixing and other naked restraints, regardless of power or effects—probably remains the best way to make sense of this convoluted opinion!

NOTES

1) Does it make sense to apply a *per se* rule without regard to the parties' market share or market power?

2) Think for a moment about the context of the *Socony* litigation. Under the auspices of the NIRA, the federal government had, in substance, tried to bring about the same disciplining of prices that the defendants, following the Supreme Court's invalidation of the federal government's industry codes, later sought to achieve through their private "dancing partner" arrangement. Does it make sense to condemn as unlawful the parties' cooperative achievement of the same ends—higher prices—that the government had attempted to pursue?

3) "*Socony-Vacuum* cannot stand for the proposition that price-fixing cartels are per se unlawful, as the case involved neither agreements on sales nor the fixing of any actual prices." Do you agree?

4) What, if anything, does *Socony-Vacuum* add to *Trenton Potteries*?

2. The Rule of Reason

The rule of reason is the default, and most common, analytical standard under Section 1. It applies to all vertical agreements, even those relating to price,[283] and to the vast majority of horizontal agreements also. And remarkably—even after more than a century of rule of reason litigation—there is still some confusion about what exactly rule-of-reason analysis entails, with multiple formulations in common use, and real controversy regarding their application.

Happily, however, there is significant consensus about the fundamentals. A series of basic steps have traditionally been at the core of rule of reason analysis.[284] At step one, a plaintiff must discharge an affirmative burden to show that the challenged restraint has an "anticompetitive effect." This centrally means that the plaintiff must show that the restraint in question tends to harm competition. There are two main ways to make this showing: "directly," by proof that the restraint has caused or likely will cause some outcome consistent with competitive harm (such as increased prices, reduced output, lower quality, reduced innovation, and so on), or "indirectly," by *both* a showing that the participants hold market power in a defined antitrust market protected by barriers to entry *and* a showing that the restraint is of a kind that, by its nature and context, is liable to harm competition.[285] Courts often state that, in the absence of market power—however proved—restraints cannot cause competitive harm.[286]

If the plaintiff can discharge this burden, the analysis moves to step two. At step two, the burden flips to the defendant to show that, despite the restraint's *prima facie* anticompetitive effect, the restraint generates offsetting procompetitive benefits. Procompetitive benefits include things like lower prices, improved efficiency, higher quality, additional innovation, and so on. If the defendant can discharge this burden, which different courts have described in different terms, the analysis moves to step three.

At step three, the burden returns to the plaintiff to show that the restraint is harmful notwithstanding what the defendant has offered at step two. Depending on the formulation, this might involve showing that the harms

---

[283] *See* Chapter VI.

[284] Ohio v. American Express Co., 138 S.Ct. 2274, 2284 (2018).

[285] Ohio v. American Express Co., 138 S.Ct. 2274, 2284 (2018) (describing direct and indirect methods of proof). *See also, e.g.*, PLS.Com, LLC v. Nat'l Ass'n of Realtors, 32 F.4th 824, 834 (9th Cir. 2022) (same); MacDermid Printing Sols. LLC v. Cortron Corp., 833 F.3d 172, 184–87 (2d Cir. 2016) (analyzing direct and indirect evidence); Tops Markets, Inc. v. Quality Markets, Inc., 142 F.3d 90 (2d Cir. 1998) (articulating indirect standard).

[286] *See, e.g.*, Viamedia, Inc. v. Comcast Corp., 951 F.3d 429, 452 (7th Cir. 2020) ("A firm's market power is important because, without it, a firm will have little to no ability to distort or harm competition, no matter how great its desire to do so, even when engaging in conduct that in different circumstances might be perceived as anticompetitive."); Kaufman v. Time Warner, 836 F.3d 137, 143 (2d Cir. 2016) ("[W]ithout market power, there is little risk of anticompetitive harm from the seller's tie-in."); Jacobs v. Tempur-Pedic Int'l, Inc., 626 F.3d 1327, 1340 (11th Cir. 2010) (noting that "a showing of market power is necessary, but not sufficient, to establish potential harm to competition").

outweigh the benefits, through a "balancing" analysis, or that the claimed benefits could be achieved by means that would be less harmful to competition, or both (resulting in what is sometimes described as a *four*-step process).[287]

This all sounds simple enough: plaintiff must show harm, then defendant must show benefit, and finally plaintiff must discharge the ultimate burden of persuading the factfinder that the agreement should be condemned overall. But there are many nuances, open questions, and puzzles in the law of the rule of reason. Some of the most important include:

- At step one, how can a plaintiff show an affirmative case of harm to competition?
    - *Must plaintiffs quantify effects on outcomes of the competitive process?* Some courts seem to expect or even require that a plaintiff establish harm to competition by showing actual measurable impacts on outcomes of competition, like higher prices or reduced output.[288] But, in principle, it seems clear that plaintiffs ought to be able to discharge the burden by showing strong reasons of theory to expect that a restraint will tend to cause harm, combined with evidence that the theory is a good fit for the litigated facts, even if the particular ways in which that harm may be expressed are not yet clear or cannot be measured with precision. This is the central logic of the "indirect proof" avenue. In markets where it is difficult to measure price and other outcomes of competition (like quality or output), requiring quantified impact on outcomes may cause courts to deny meritorious claims. On the other hand, inferring harm too readily from ambiguous evidence may deter or punish beneficial competition. Cases where the theory of harm is that prices would, but for the challenged conduct, have *fallen*—for example, because the challenged agreement deterred or prevented entry—are doubly tricky: when should courts be willing to infer harm from the *absence* of a change in prices?
    - *How far can evidence of a price increase get a plaintiff?* One might think that a price increase is the clearest of all kinds of evidence of harm. Many courts have said so.[289] But some courts have suggested that an increase in nominal price is not enough even to discharge a prima facie burden, and that a plaintiff must—at least to some extent—affirmatively disprove that the price increase is not a function of procompetitive effects like increased quality or demand.[290] It is not

---

[287] *See, e.g.*, Buccaneer Energy (USA) Inc. v. Gunnison Energy Corp., 846 F.3d 1297, 1310 (10th Cir. 2017); Apani Sw., Inc. v. Coca-Cola Enterprises, Inc., 300 F.3d 620, 627 (5th Cir. 2002); Nat'l Bancard Corp. (NaBanco) v. VISA U.S.A., Inc., 779 F.2d 592, 603 (11th Cir. 1986).

[288] *See, e.g.*, MacDermid Printing Sols. LLC v. Cortron Corp., 833 F.3d 172, 183 (2d Cir. 2016).

[289] *See, e.g.*, In re Suboxone Antitrust Litig., No. 13-MD-2445, 2022 WL 3588024, at *20 (E.D. Pa. Aug. 22, 2022) ("Plaintiffs have presented evidence that this conduct resulted in the market paying artificially high prices for Suboxone tablets."); FTC v. Shkreli, No. 20-CV-00706, 2022 WL 135026, at *42 (S.D.N.Y. Jan. 14, 2022) ("Under § 1, the Plaintiffs may show the existence of anticompetitive effects from restraints on trade through direct evidence of increased prices in the relevant market, which they have done."); In re Digital Music Antitrust Litig., 812 F. Supp. 2d 390, 401 (S.D.N.Y. 2011) (price increase in digital music constituted antitrust injury in a case challenging alleged price-fixing).

[290] *See, e.g.*, Ohio v. American Express Co., 138 S.Ct. 2274, 2288–89 (2018) (evidence of increased prices to merchants did not discharge plaintiffs' obligation to show anticompetitive effect in platform market); 1-800 Contacts, Inc. v. Fed. Trade Comm'n, 1 F.4th 102, 118 (2d Cir. 2021) ("When an antitrust plaintiff advances an antitrust claim based on direct evidence in the form of increased prices, the question is whether it can show an actual anticompetitive change in prices after the restraint was implemented. . . . The government could not make that showing because it did not conduct an empirical analysis of the Challenged Agreements' effect on the price of contact lenses in the online market for contacts. The evidence offered by the government is theoretical and anecdotal; it is not 'direct.'"); Jacobs v. Tempur-Pedic Int'l, Inc., 626 F.3d 1327, 1339 (11th Cir. 2010) ("Higher prices alone are not the "epitome" of anticompetitive harm (as Jacobs claims). . . . By 'anticompetitive,' the law means that a given practice both harms allocative efficiency *and* could raise the prices of goods above competitive levels or diminish their quality. . . . Here, beyond the bald statement that consumers lost hundreds of millions of dollars, there is nothing establishing the competitive level above which [the defendant's] allegedly anticompetitive conduct artificially raised prices."); OJ Com. LLC v. KidKraft LP, No. 19-60341-CIV, 2021 WL 1348412, at *4 (S.D. Fla. Mar. 31, 2021) (granting summary judgment for defendants under Sections 1 and 2 for, among other things, failure to show harm to competition, and stating: "Sure, Plaintiffs assert that KidKraft did in fact raise the price of its wooden play kitchens in 2017 and in 2018. However, higher prices alone are not the epitome of anticompetitive harm. Rather, consumer welfare, understood in the sense of allocative efficiency, is the animating concern of the Sherman Act.") (internal quotation marks and brackets omitted); *see also* E.W. French & Sons, Inc. v. Gen. Portland Inc., 885 F.2d 1392, 1404 (9th Cir. 1989) (Farris, J., concurring) ("The ultimate issue in a rule of reason case is whether a challenged practice will produce adverse effects on price or output. . . . The only direct way to answer that question is to introduce evidence of actual price increases or reductions in output after the challenged practice. But even if a plaintiff is lucky enough to gather such evidence, he will face the momentous task of proving that the observed price or output effects were not attributable to any one of an infinite number of independent causes:

obvious how this kind of prove-the-negative can effectively be done, or when it is enough to simply point to an increase in nominal prices.

- At step two, how can a defendant show offsetting benefits?

  o *Must the defendant merely "assert" a benefit or must it do more?* It is not clear just what a defendant must do at step two of the rule of reason: is it enough for a defendant to simply assert a benefit? Identify one that is theoretically plausible in principle and could reasonably be imputed to the challenged practice? Show that a claimed benefit has *some* kind of factual grounding in the actual purpose or actual effect of the measure, without needing to prove the magnitude of actual benefit? Or show that the restraint *actually* promoted the benefit and it was sufficient in magnitude to offset the harms? Some Section 1 cases suggest that the benefit must be in some sense "sufficient": what does this mean?[291] Other cases do not allude to such a test.[292]

  o *What kind of benefits count?* Certainly a core set of procompetitive benefits are beyond dispute: lower prices, higher quality, greater output, faster or more valuable innovation, greater choice and variety, and so on.[293] But the outer bounds of this zone of "procompetitive justification" are not quite clear. Defendants often argue (often with some basis!) that some challenged restraint or other is designed to protect the benefit of their investments from "free riding," and ultimately to safeguard their incentive to innovate and compete by protecting their profits from the activity. But *any* restraint that a rational defendant chooses to impose will likely have the effect of increasing its profits, and thus of increasing its incentives to invest in its competitive activities. To put it another way, *all* antitrust violations are profitable! But the "procompetitive justification" criterion is surely more demanding than this, even if its boundaries are not fully clear.[294] So when is profit-protection, or "incentivizing investment," a cognizable benefit?

  o *What about "out of market" benefits?* It is not entirely clear whether benefits must be in the same market as the harms in order to be cognizable under the rule of reason.[295] Merger law, at least, generally supports the proposition that harms in one market can only be offset by benefits in the

---

exhaustion of raw materials, increases in labor costs, increases in the price of substitute goods, tax hikes, etc. Situations will arise where a plaintiff is able to meet this burden. . . . But doubtless those occasions will be rare.").

[291] *See, e.g.*, In re Se. Milk Antitrust Litig., 739 F.3d 262, 272 (6th Cir. 2014) ("[T]he burden then shifts to the defendant to produce evidence that the restraint in question has procompetitive effects that are sufficient to justify the otherwise anticompetitive injuries.") (cleaned up); Law v. Nat'l Collegiate Athletic Ass'n, 134 F.3d 1010, 1024 (10th Cir. 1998) ("[T]he NCAA did not establish evidence of sufficient procompetitive benefits[.]"); United States v. Brown Univ. in Providence in State of R.I., 5 F.3d 658, 669 (3d Cir. 1993) (under the Section 1 rule of reason "the burden shifts to the defendant to show that the challenged conduct promotes a sufficiently pro-competitive objective"); Paschall v. Kansas City Star Co., 727 F.2d 692, 702 (8th Cir. 1984) ("The optimum monopoly price theory is useful in ascertaining whether such procompetitive effects are sufficient to counteract the anticompetitive effects of removing potential competition from the market so that in the end there are no unreasonable anticompetitive effects.").

[292] *See, e.g.*, In re Loestrin 24 Fe Antitrust Litig., 261 F. Supp. 3d 307, 329 (D.R.I. 2017).

[293] *See, e.g.*, Leegin Creative Leather Prod., Inc. v. PSKS, Inc., 551 U.S. 877, 890 (2007) (procompetitive benefits included facilitation of investment in services and "more options" for consumers); Nat'l Collegiate Athletic Ass'n v. Bd. of Regents of Univ. of Oklahoma, 468 U.S. 85, 102 (1984) (increased "consumer choice" procompetitive); Cont'l T. V., Inc. v. GTE Sylvania Inc., 433 U.S. 36, 54 (1977) (procompetitive benefits included more efficient distribution and the avoidance of free-riding that imperiled dealer investment); Law v. Nat'l Collegiate Athletic Ass'n, 134 F.3d 1010, 1023 (10th Cir. 1998) (noting that "increasing output, creating operating efficiencies, making a new product available, enhancing product or service quality, and widening consumer choice have been accepted by courts as justifications for otherwise anticompetitive agreements"); In re Dealer Mgmt. Sys. Antitrust Litig., 362 F. Supp. 3d 477, 493 (N.D. Ill. 2019) (procompetitive benefits include "increasing allocative efficiency" and "preventing free-riding").

[294] *See, e.g.*, Viamedia, Inc. v. Comcast Corp., 951 F.3d 429, 479 (7th Cir. 2020) ("Any claimed benefits from [the challenged] conduct must be procompetitive and not simply the result of eliminating competition."); United States v. Microsoft Corp., 253 F.3d 34 (D.C. Cir. 2001) (en banc) ("Microsoft's only explanation for its exclusive dealing is that it wants to keep developers focused upon its APIs—which is to say, it wants to preserve its power in the operating system market. That is not an unlawful end, but neither is it a procompetitive justification for the specific means here in question, namely exclusive dealing contracts[.]"); Law v. Nat'l Collegiate Athletic Ass'n, 134 F.3d 1010, 1023 (10th Cir. 1998) (noting that "mere profitability" is not without more procompetitive); see also, e.g., United States v. Arnold, Schwinn & Co., 388 U.S. 365, 375 (1967) ("[E]very restrictive practice is designed to augment the profit and competitive position of its participants."). *But see, e.g.*, Image Tech. Servs., Inc. v. Eastman Kodak Co., 125 F.3d 1195, 1219 (9th Cir. 1997) ("Kodak may assert that its desire to profit from its intellectual property rights justifies its conduct, and the jury should presume that this justification is legitimately procompetitive.").

[295] *See generally, e.g.*, Laura Alexander & Steven C. Salop, *Antitrust Worker Protections: Rejecting Multi-Market Balancing as a Justification for Anticompetitive Harms to Workers*, 90 U. Chi. L. Rev. 273 (2023); Steven C. Salop, Daniel Francis, Lauren Sillman & Michaela Spero, *Rebuilding Platform Antitrust: Moving On from* Ohio v. American Express Co., 84 Antitrust L.J. 883 (2022); Gregory J. Werden, *Cross-Market Balancing of Competitive Effects: What Is The Law, and What Should It Be?* 43 J. Corp. L. 119 (2017); Daniel A. Crane, *Balancing Effects Across Markets*, 80 Antitrust L.J. 391 (2015).

same market.[296] But the position under Section 1 is not so clear. There is some language in the Court's decision in *Topco* (a case discussed more fully in Chapter V) that is sometimes cited for the proposition that out-of-market benefits are not cognizable in conduct cases.[297] On the other hand, in two recent cases that we will meet later in this Chapter—*Alston* and *AmEx*—the Court appeared to implicitly accept that benefits to one group could justify harms to another.[298] But neither case actually held that "out of market" benefits are cognizable under Section 1: in *Alston* the issue was not raised by the parties, and in *AmEx* the Court deviated from regular market definition principles such that the benefits and harms were included in the same antitrust market. So the question remains open.[299]

- At step three, how can a plaintiff discharge its overall burden?

  o *Can courts ever "balance"?* Courts often say that the rule of reason involves balancing the anticompetitive effects of a restraint against its procompetitive benefits. But this may be very hard in practice. Suppose that the evidence shows that a restraint will have four effects: (1) it is highly likely to increase short term prices for all consumers; (2) it is moderately likely to increase product quality that some but not all consumers value; (3) there is some chance that it will promote game-changing innovation; and (4) it is somewhat likely to lead to a reduction in prices over the long term. How is a court supposed to "balance" these factors (including short term against long term, static effects against dynamic effects, price against quality, some consumers against others)?[300] And if courts cannot really balance in any meaningfully rigorous way—or when they cannot—what should they do instead? (As we note below, in recent cases the Court has not mentioned balancing at all.)

  o *What is the "less restrictive alternative" test?* It is all very well to say, as courts often do, that a plaintiff can discharge its burden at the third stage by showing that the defendant's claimed benefits could be achieved with a less restrictive alternative ("LRA").[301] This principle is the subject of a robust literature.[302] But what exactly does it involve? Must a plaintiff show that such an alternative *would in fact* be adopted if the challenged restraint were prohibited?[303] If the parties would not in fact adopt the less restrictive alternative, why is it relevant? If multiple such alternatives exist, must a plaintiff investigate—with fact and expert discovery—the relative competitive impact, and the actual likelihood, of each possible alternative? Courts emphasize that it is not enough to identify a mere theoretical alternative: so how far can a plaintiff be reasonably expected to go? The Court in *Alston* said that "antitrust law does not require businesses to use anything like the least restrictive means of achieving legitimate business purposes. . . . [C]ourts should not second-guess degrees of reasonable necessity so that the

---

[296] The traditional citation is United States v. Philadelphia Nat. Bank, 374 U.S. 321, 371 (1963). *See infra* § VIII.D.1.

[297] United States v. Topco Associates, 405 U.S. 596, 611 (1972) (stating, in the context of interbrand v. intrabrand competition in supermarket "white label" goods: "If a decision is to be made to sacrifice competition in one portion of the economy for greater competition in another portion this too is a decision that must be made by Congress and not by private forces or by the courts. Private forces are too keenly aware of their own interests in making such decisions and courts are ill-equipped and ill-situated for such decisionmaking.").

[298] Ohio v. American Express Co., 138 S.Ct. 2274 (2018); National Collegiate Athletic Association v. Alston, 141 S.Ct. 2141 (2021).

[299] *See, e.g.*, United States v. Topco Associates, 405 U.S. 596, 611 (1972); Paladin Assocs. Inc. v. Montana Power Co., 328 F.3d 1145, 1157 n.11 (9th Cir. 2003) (noting but not resolving the issue); Steven C. Salop, Daniel Francis, Lauren Sillman & Michaela Spero, *Rebuilding Platform Antitrust: Moving On from Ohio v. American Express Co.*, 84 Antitrust L.J. 883 (2022); Gregory J. Werden, *Cross-Market Balancing of Competitive Effects: What Is the Law, and What Should It Be?* 43 J. Comp. L. 119 (2017); Jonathan B. Baker, THE ANTITRUST PARADIGM (2019) 191.

[300] For a very thoughtful discussion, *see* Rebecca Haw Allensworth, *The Commensurability Myth in Antitrust*, 69 Vand. L. Rev. 1 (2016).

[301] *See, e.g.*, 1-800 Contacts, Inc. v. FTC, 1 F.4th 102, 114 (2d Cir. 2021); Impax Labs., Inc. v. FTC, 994 F.3d 484, 492 (5th Cir. 2021); Los Angeles Mem'l Coliseum Comm'n v. Nat'l Football League, 726 F.2d 1381, 1396 (9th Cir. 1984).

[302] *See, e.g.*, C. Scott Hemphill, *Less Restrictive Alternatives in Antitrust Law*, 1216 Colum. L. Rev. 927 (2016); Gabriel A. Feldman, *The Misuse of the Less Restrictive Alternative Inquiry in Rule of Reason Analysis*, 58 Am. U. L. Rev. 561 (2009); Michael A. Carrier, *The Real Rule of Reason: Bridging the Disconnect*, B.Y.U. L. Rev. 1265, 1336–38 (1999).

[303] *Compare* Horizontal Merger Guidelines § 10 ("The Agencies credit only those efficiencies likely to be accomplished with the proposed merger *and unlikely to be accomplished in the absence of either the proposed merger or another means having comparable anticompetitive effects*.") (emphasis added).

lawfulness of conduct turns upon judgments of degrees of efficiency."[304] In saying this, how much latitude did the Court mean to give defendants?

Courts and commentators express the rule of reason in different ways. In its most recent formulations, for example, the Supreme Court has entirely omitted any reference to balancing in step three:

> [T]he plaintiff has the initial burden to prove that the challenged restraint has a substantial anticompetitive effect. Should the plaintiff carry that burden, the burden then shifts to the defendant to show a procompetitive rationale for the restraint. If the defendant can make that showing, the burden shifts back to the plaintiff to demonstrate that the procompetitive efficiencies could be reasonably achieved through less anticompetitive means.[305]

Lower courts have expressed the rule-of-reason framework in different ways. Consider the following formulations:

- The Second Circuit has held that at step one the plaintiff must show that "[the] defendant's challenged behavior can have an adverse effect on competition in the relevant market"; at step two the defendant must "demonstrate the procompetitive effects of the challenged restraint"; at step three the plaintiff must "show that these legitimate competitive benefits could have been achieved through less restrictive means."[306]

- The Third Circuit has held that at step one the plaintiff must show that "the alleged combination or agreement produced adverse, anti-competitive effects within the relevant product and geographic markets" (noting that because direct proof is "often impossible," a showing of "market power" may also be sufficient); at step two the defendant must "show that the challenged conduct promotes a sufficiently pro-competitive objective"; at step three the plaintiff "must demonstrate that the restraint is not reasonably necessary to achieve the stated objective."[307]

- The Fifth Circuit has held that at step one the plaintiff must "show anticompetitive effects" (including by effects on outcomes like price or by elimination of "competition"); at step two the defendant must "demonstrate that the restraint produced procompetitive benefits"; at step three, the plaintiff may "demonstrate that any procompetitive effects could be achieved through less anticompetitive means"; and at step four "if the [plaintiff] fails to demonstrate a less restrictive alternative way to achieve the procompetitive benefits, the court must balance the anticompetitive and procompetitive effects of the restraint."[308]

- The Ninth Circuit has held that at step one, "the plaintiff has the initial burden to prove that the challenged restraint has a substantial anticompetitive effect that harms consumers in the relevant market" (either directly or indirectly); at step two, the defendant must "show a procompetitive rationale for the restraint"; at step three, "the plaintiff [must] demonstrate that the procompetitive efficiencies could be reasonably achieved through less anticompetitive means."[309]

- The Tenth Circuit has held that at step one, the plaintiff must show "that an agreement had a substantially adverse effect on competition" (by showing that an elevated-scrutiny standard applies, that the agreement adversely affected competitive outcomes like price, or that the defendant held market power in a relevant antitrust market); at step two, the defendant must "come forward with evidence of the procompetitive virtues of the alleged wrongful conduct"; at step three, "the plaintiff then must prove that the challenged conduct is not reasonably necessary to achieve the legitimate objectives or that those objectives can be achieved in a substantially less restrictive manner"; and "[u]ltimately, if these steps are met, the harms and benefits must be weighed against each other in order to judge whether the challenged behavior is, on balance, reasonable."[310]

---

[304] National Collegiate Athletic Association v. Alston, 141 S.Ct. 2141, 2161 (2021).

[305] National Collegiate Athletic Association v. Alston, 141 S.Ct. 2141, 2160 (2021); *see also* Ohio v. American Express Co., 138 S.Ct. 2274, 2284 (2018).

[306] N. Am. Soccer League, LLC v. United States Soccer Fed'n, Inc., 883 F.3d 32, 42 (2d Cir. 2018)

[307] King Drug Co. of Florence v. Smithkline Beecham Corp., 791 F.3d 388, 412 (3d Cir. 2015).

[308] Impax Lab'ys, Inc. v. FTC, 994 F.3d 484, 492–93 (5th Cir. 2021).

[309] PLS.Com, LLC v. Nat'l Ass'n of Realtors, 32 F.4th 824, 834 (9th Cir. 2022).

[310] Buccaneer Energy (USA) Inc. v. Gunnison Energy Corp., 846 F.3d 1297, 1310 (10th Cir. 2017).

As we have noted, some recent decisions show a tendency to minimize or downplay the analytical importance of balancing in rule of reason cases. A leading scholar of the rule of reason, Michael Carrier, has criticized this development, arguing that, among other things:

> [T]he omission of balancing is not consistent with courts' application of the rule of reason. Since the dawn of the modern rule of reason in 1977 in *Sylvania*, courts have uniformly explained that the final step of the antitrust analysis involves balancing anticompetitive and procompetitive effects. Even the courts that describe a three-stage analysis often follow that with a discussion of the "ultimate" balancing stage. To simply remove the balancing step is not justified based on history.

> [And] removal is not consistent with the policies underlying the rule of reason. Central to this framework is a court's consideration of a restraint's anticompetitive and procompetitive effects. It is hard to see how this can be done without, at some point, having the chance to directly consider the two.[311]

As noted above, the very concept of "balancing" is fraught with complexity in antitrust analysis: not least because it is very far from clear how to weigh a short-term effect against a long-term one, a static price effect against a dynamic innovation effect, or what underlying or metric courts actually use to figure out a "net" effect on competition.

Rebecca Haw Allensworth, The Commensurability Myth in Antitrust
69 Vand. L. Rev. 1 (2016)

At its heart, antitrust law believes it is exceptional. Unlike most areas of regulation where rules must trade off costs and benefits different in kind, antitrust claims to pursue one single goal: competition. Courts often endorse the idea that the values traded off in competition regulation-the procompetitive effects and the anticompetitive effects-are commensurate. For example, courts frequently characterize Sherman Act § 1 as condemning restraints on trade having a "net" anticompetitive effect, and condoning those whose effects sum to a neutral or procompetitive effect. This supposedly unitary goal of antitrust-to facilitate competition-allows the law to appear to avoid the murky, value-laden compromises struck by other areas of regulation.

But antitrust law is not exceptional. Even within the now-dominant paradigm that antitrust pursues only economic goals, value judgments are unavoidable. What are typically offered in antitrust cases as procompetitive and anticompetitive effects are rarely two sides of the same coin, and there is no such monolithic thing as "competition" that is furthered or impeded by competitor conduct. In fact, competition-whether defined as a process or as a set of outcomes associated with competitive markets-is multifaceted. Antitrust law often must trade off one kind of competition for another, or one salutary effect of competition (such as price, quality or innovation) for another. And in so doing, antitrust courts must make judgments between different and incommensurate values. [. . .]

The absence of attention to the fact that procompetitive and anticompetitive effects, as they are presented in an antitrust suit, are usually incommensurate, and the absence of debate about how to trade them off means that antitrust law is under-theorized. Rhetoric of commensurability in antitrust has made it unpopular for judges to acknowledge the use of value judgments in deciding antitrust cases.

This has pushed important debates about those values into the subtext of antitrust opinions rather than allowing for the full and open discussion that they merit. It has also led to a set of doctrines that courts use to avoid the appearance of judgment, which distort antitrust litigation usually in favor of defendants. These evasive maneuvers have made a mess out of questions such as when the burden of production shifts from plaintiff to defendant, which arguments require empirical proof or a rigorously defined market, and what kinds of procompetitive justifications are categorically illegitimate. [. . .]

Judges, just like consumers, can and do make judgments between these incommensurate values and so, in the philosophical sense, make them commensurate again. The commensurability myth is that those choices, because

---

[311] Michael A. Carrier, *The Four-Step Rule of Reason*, ANTITRUST (Spring 2019), 50-54.

they aim to maximize a seemingly unitary goal, such as consumer welfare or competition, can be made without reliance on contested (at best) or idiosyncratic (at worst) value judgments.

* * *

In practice, balancing is seldom the critical stage in an antitrust litigation. The overwhelming majority of rule-of-reason claims are lost by the plaintiff at step one, with the court concluding that the plaintiff has failed to establish a *prima facie* anticompetitive effect. In the following extract, Carrier summarizes the findings of his empirical investigation of rule-of-reason litigation.

Michael A. Carrier, Rule of Reason: An Empirical Update for the 21st Century
16 Geo. Mason L. Rev. 827 (2009)

A decade ago [*i.e.*, in 1999, in Michael A. Carrier, *The Real Rule of Reason: Bridging the Disconnect*, 1999 B.Y.U. L. Rev. 1265 (1999)], I showed that the rule of reason is far less amorphous than commonly believed. After reviewing all 495 rule of reason cases from 1977 to 1999, I showed that courts actually followed a burden-shifting approach.

In the first stage, the plaintiff must show a significant anticompetitive effect. The plaintiff's failure to make such a showing led to the courts' dismissal of 84% of the cases. In the second stage, the defendant must demonstrate a legitimate procompetitive justification; its failure to do so led to invalidation of the restraint in 3% of the cases.

If the defendant satisfies this burden, the plaintiff can show that the restraint is not reasonably necessary or that the defendant's objectives could be achieved by less restrictive alternatives. At most, 1% of the cases were dismissed because the plaintiff made this showing. Only after the completion of these three stages does the court balance anticompetitive and procompetitive effects. Balancing occurred in 4% of the cases.

A decade has passed. This Article updates my 1999 study. It concludes that the burden-shifting trend has continued and, in fact, has increased. Courts dispose of 97% of cases at the first stage, on the grounds that there is no anticompetitive effect. They balance in only 2% of cases. [. . .]

This survey is based on a Westlaw search of all federal cases decided between February 2, 1999, and May 5, 2009. I located the cases by searching broadly for all rule of reason cases: "DA(aft 2/2/1999) & antitrust & (Rule +2 Reason)." [. . .]

My survey includes instances in which a court entered a final judgment in an antitrust dispute that it decided (at least in part) under the rule of reason. Nearly all of the included cases involve courts' grants of summary judgment and motions to dismiss. These observations apply only to the antitrust issues of a case; the continued vitality of non-antitrust claims does not affect the inclusion of the case in the survey.

The survey does not include cases that have not reached an ultimate determination, such as denials of summary judgment or motions to dismiss. It also does not cover grants or denials of preliminary injunctions unaccompanied by final findings.

* * *

One of the most famous rule-of-reason cases in the history of antitrust is the 1918 decision in *Chicago Board of Trade*, in which Justice Brandeis wrote the opinion for the Court. This was the first Supreme Court case in which the rule of reason—which had in principle been introduced seven years earlier in *Standard Oil*—actually saved a restraint from condemnation by the Court. As you read the case, ask how well it maps onto the modern analysis described above. What factors is the Court applying to distinguish between "procompetitive" and "anticompetitive" restraints? And how much help is the Court's guidance, really?

Board of Trade of City of Chicago v. United States
246 U.S. 231 (1918)

Justice Brandeis.

[1] Chicago is the leading grain market in the world. . . . The standard forms of trading are: (a) Spot sales; that is, sales of grain already in Chicago in railroad cars or elevators for immediate delivery by order on carrier or transfer of warehouse receipt. (b) Future sales; that is, agreements for delivery later in the current or in some future month. (c) Sales "to arrive"; that is, agreements to deliver on arrival grain which is already in transit to Chicago or is to be shipped there within a time specified. On every business day sessions of the Board are held at which all bids and sales are publicly made. Spot sales and future sales are made at the regular sessions of the Board from 9:30 a.m. to 1:15 p.m., except on Saturdays, when the session closes at 12 [p.]m. Special sessions, termed the "call," are held immediately after the close of the regular session, at which sales "to arrive" are made. These sessions are not limited as to duration, but last usually about half an hour. At all these sessions transactions are between members only; but they may trade either for themselves or on behalf of others. Members may also trade privately with one another at any place, either during the sessions or after, and they may trade with nonmembers at any time except on the premises occupied by the Board.

[2] Purchases of grain "to arrive" are made largely from country dealers and farmers throughout the whole territory tributary to Chicago. . . . The purchases are sometimes the result of bids to individual country dealers made by telegraph or telephone either during the sessions or after; but most purchases are made by the sending out from Chicago by the afternoon mails to hundreds of country dealers, offers to buy at the prices named, any number of carloads, subject to acceptance before 9:30 a.m. on the next business day.

[3] In 1906 the Board adopted what is known as the "call" rule. By it members were prohibited from purchasing or offering to purchase, during the period between the close of the call and the opening of the session on the next business day, any wheat, corn, oats or rye "to arrive" at a price other than the closing bid at the call. The call was over, with rare exceptions, by 2 o'clock. The change effected was this: Before the adoption of the rule, members fixed their bids throughout the day at such prices as they respectively saw fit; after the adoption of the rule, the bids had to be fixed at the day's closing bid on the call until the opening of the next session.

[4] In 1913 the United States filed . . . this suit against the Board and its executive officers and directors, to enjoin the enforcement of the call rule, alleging it to be in violation of the [Sherman Act]. The defendants admitted the adoption and enforcement of the call rule, and averred that its purpose was not to prevent competition or to control prices, but to promote the convenience of members by restricting their hours of business and to break up a monopoly in that branch of the grain trade acquired by four or five warehousemen in Chicago. On motion of the government the allegations concerning the purpose of establishing the regulation were stricken from the record . . . and a decree was entered which declared that defendants became parties to a combination or conspiracy to restrain interstate and foreign trade and commerce by adopting, acting upon and enforcing the call rule; and enjoined them from acting upon the same or from adopting or acting upon any similar rule. . . .

[5] The government proved the existence of the rule and described its application and the change in business practice involved. It made no attempt to show that the rule was designed to or that it had the effect of limiting the amount of grain shipped to Chicago; or of retarding or accelerating shipment; or of raising or depressing prices; or of discriminating against any part of the public; or that it resulted in hardship to any one. The case was rested upon the bald proposition, that a rule or agreement by which men occupying positions of strength in any branch of trade, fixed prices at which they would buy or sell during an important part of the business day, is an illegal restraint of trade under the Anti-Trust Law. But the legality of an agreement or regulation cannot be determined by so simple a test, as whether it restrains competition. Every agreement concerning trade, every regulation of trade, restrains. To bind, to restrain, is of their very essence. The true test of legality is whether the restraint imposed is such as merely regulates and perhaps thereby promotes competition or whether it is such as may suppress or even destroy competition. To determine that question the court must ordinarily consider the facts peculiar to the business to which the restraint is applied; its condition before and after the restraint was imposed; the nature of the restraint and its effect, actual or probable. The history of the restraint, the evil believed to exist,

the reason for adopting the particular remedy, the purpose or end sought to be attained, are all relevant facts. This is not because a good intention will save an otherwise objectionable regulation or the reverse; but because knowledge of intent may help the court to interpret facts and to predict consequences. The District Court erred, therefore, in striking from the answer allegations concerning the history and purpose of the call rule and in later excluding evidence on that subject. But the evidence admitted makes it clear that the rule was a reasonable regulation of business consistent with the provisions of the Anti-Trust Law.

[6] First. The nature of the rule: The restriction was upon the period of price-making. It required members to desist from further price-making after the close of the call until 9:30 a.m. the next business day; but there was no restriction upon the sending out of bids after close of the call. Thus it required members who desired to buy grain "to arrive" to make up their minds before the close of the call how much they were willing to pay during the interval before the next session of the Board. The rule made it to their interest to attend the call; and if they did not fill their wants by purchases there, to make the final bid high enough to enable them to purchase from country dealers.

[7] Second. The scope of the rule: It is restricted in operation to grain "to arrive." It applies only to a small part of the grain shipped from day to day to Chicago, and to an even smaller part of the day's sales; members were left free to purchase grain already in Chicago from any one at any price throughout the day. It applies only during a small part of the business day; members were left free to purchase during the sessions of the Board grain "to arrive," at any price, from members anywhere and from nonmembers anywhere except on the premises of the Board. It applied only to grain shipped to Chicago; members were left free to purchase at any price throughout the day from either members or non-members, grain "to arrive" at any other market. Country dealers and farmers had available in practically every part of the territory called tributary to Chicago some other market for grain "to arrive." . . .

[8] Third. The effects of the rule: As it applies to only a small part of the grain shipped to Chicago and to that only during a part of the business day and does not apply at all to grain shipped to other markets, the rule had no appreciable effect on general market prices; nor did it materially affect the total volume of grain coming to Chicago. But within the narrow limits of its operation the rule helped to improve market conditions thus:

(a) It created a public market for grain "to arrive." Before its adoption, bids were made privately. Men had to buy and sell without adequate knowledge of actual market conditions. This was disadvantageous to all concerned, but particularly so to country dealers and farmers.

(b) It brought into the regular market hours of the Board sessions, more of the trading in grain "to arrive."

(c) It brought buyers and sellers into more direct relations; because on the call they gathered together for a free and open interchange of bids and offers.

(d) It distributed the business in grain "to arrive" among a far larger number of Chicago receivers and commission merchants than had been the case there before.

(e) It increased the number of country dealers engaging in this branch of the business; supplied them more regularly with bids from Chicago; and also increased the number of bids received by them from competing markets.

(f) It eliminated risks necessarily incident to a private market, and thus enabled country dealers to do business on a smaller margin. In that way the rule made it possible for them to pay more to farmers without raising the price to consumers.

(g) It enabled country dealers to sell some grain to arrive which they would otherwise have been obliged either to ship to Chicago commission merchants or to sell for "future delivery."

(h) It enabled those grain merchants of Chicago who sell to millers and exporters, to trade on a smaller margin and by paying more for grain or selling it for less, to make the Chicago market more attractive for both shippers and buyers of grain.

(i) Incidentally it facilitated trading "to arrive" by enabling those engaged in these transactions to fulfill their contracts by tendering grain arriving at Chicago on any railroad, whereas formerly shipments had to be made over the particular railroad designated by the buyer . . . .

[9] Every Board of Trade and nearly every trade organization imposes some restraint upon the conduct of business by its members. Those relating to the hours in which business may be done are common; and they make a special appeal where, as here, they tend to shorten the working day or, at least, limit the period of most exacting activity. The decree of the District Court is reversed with directions to dismiss the bill.

* * *

An important limitation on rule-of-reason analysis is the proposition that only "procompetitive" justifications may be advanced in defense of a restraint. Other "good reasons" unrelated to the promotion of competition are not cognizable. This principle was of central importance in *Professional Engineers*, when the Court declined an invitation to welcome professional ethical concerns into the realm of admissible justifications.

National Society of Professional Engineers v. United States
435 U.S. 679 (1978)

Justice Stevens.

[1] This is a civil antitrust case brought by the United States to nullify an association's canon of ethics prohibiting competitive bidding by its members. The question is whether the canon may be justified under the Sherman Act, because it was adopted by members of a learned profession for the purpose of minimizing the risk that competition would produce inferior engineering work endangering the public safety. The District Court rejected this justification without making any findings on the likelihood that competition would produce the dire consequences foreseen by the association. The Court of Appeals affirmed. We granted certiorari to decide whether the District Court should have considered the factual basis for the proffered justification before rejecting it. Because we are satisfied that the asserted defense rests on a fundamental misunderstanding of the Rule of Reason frequently applied in antitrust litigation, we affirm. . . .

[2] The National Society of Professional Engineers (Society) was organized in 1935 to deal with the nontechnical aspects of engineering practice, including the promotion of the professional, social, and economic interests of its members. Its present membership of 69,000 resides throughout the United States and in some foreign countries. Approximately 12,000 members are consulting engineers who offer their services to governmental, industrial, and private clients. Some Society members are principals or chief executive officers of some of the largest engineering firms in the country.

[3] The charges of a consulting engineer may be computed in different ways. He may charge the client a percentage of the cost of the project, may set his fee at his actual cost plus overhead plus a reasonable profit, may charge fixed rates per hour for different types of work, may perform an assignment for a specific sum, or he may combine one or more of these approaches. Suggested fee schedules for particular types of services in certain areas have been promulgated from time to time by various local societies. This case does not, however, involve any claim that the National Society has tried to fix specific fees, or even a specific method of calculating fees. It involves a charge that the members of the Society have unlawfully agreed to refuse to negotiate or even to discuss the question of fees until after a prospective client has selected the engineer for a particular project. Evidence of this agreement is found in § 11(c) of the Society's Code of Ethics, adopted in July 1964.

[4] That section, which remained in effect at the time of trial, provided: "Section 11 — The Engineer will not compete unfairly with another engineer by attempting to obtain employment or advancement or professional engagements by competitive bidding . . . . "c. He shall not solicit or submit engineering proposals on the basis of competitive bidding. Competitive bidding for professional engineering services is defined as the formal or informal submission, or receipt, of verbal or written estimates of cost or proposals in terms of dollars, man days of work required, percentage of construction cost, or any other measure of compensation whereby the prospective client may compare engineering services on a price basis prior to the time that one engineer, or one engineering

organization, has been selected for negotiations. The disclosure of recommended fee schedules prepared by various engineering societies is not considered to constitute competitive bidding. An Engineer requested to submit a fee proposal or bid prior to the selection of an engineer or firm subject to the negotiation of a satisfactory contract, shall attempt to have the procedure changed to conform to ethical practices, but if not successful he shall withdraw from consideration for the proposed work. These principles shall be applied by the Engineer in obtaining the services of other professions."

[5] The District Court found that the Society's Board of Ethical Review has uniformly interpreted the "ethical rules against competitive bidding for engineering services as prohibiting the submission of any form of price information to a prospective customer which would enable that customer to make a price comparison on engineering services." If the client requires that such information be provided, then § 11(c) imposes an obligation upon the engineering firm to withdraw from consideration for that job. The Society's Code of Ethics thus "prohibits engineers from both soliciting and submitting such price information," and seeks to preserve the profession's "traditional" method of selecting professional engineers. Under the traditional method, the client initially selects an engineer on the basis of background and reputation, not price.

[6] In addition to § 11(c) of the Society's Code of Ethics, the Society's Board of Directors has adopted various "Professional Policy" statements. Policy statement 10-F was issued to "make it clear beyond all doubt" that the Society opposed competitive bidding for all engineering projects. This policy statement was replaced in 1972 by Policy 10-G which permits price quotations for certain types of engineering work—in particular, research and development projects.

[7] Although the Society argues that it has never "enforced" its ban on competitive bidding, the District Court specifically found that the record supports a finding that NSPE and its members actively pursue a course of policing adherence to the competitive bid ban through direct and indirect communication with members and prospective clients. This finding has not been challenged as clearly erroneous.

[8] Having been selected, the engineer may then, in accordance with the Society's canons of ethics, negotiate a satisfactory fee arrangement with the client. If the negotiations are unsuccessful, then the client may withdraw his selection and approach a new engineer.

[9] In 1972 the Government filed its complaint against the Society alleging that members had agreed to abide by canons of ethics prohibiting the submission of competitive bids for engineering services and that, in consequence, price competition among the members had been suppressed and customers had been deprived of the benefits of free and open competition. The complaint prayed for an injunction terminating the unlawful agreement.

[10] In its answer the Society admitted the essential facts alleged by the Government and pleaded a series of affirmative defenses, only one of which remains in issue. In that defense, the Society averred that the standard set out in the Code of Ethics was reasonable because competition among professional engineers was contrary to the public interest. It was averred that it would be cheaper and easier for an engineer to design and specify inefficient and unnecessarily expensive structures and methods of construction. Accordingly, competitive pressure to offer engineering services at the lowest possible price would adversely affect the quality of engineering. Moreover, the practice of awarding engineering contracts to the lowest bidder, regardless of quality, would be dangerous to the public health, safety, and welfare. For these reasons, the Society claimed that its Code of Ethics was not an unreasonable restraint of interstate trade or commerce. [. . .]

[11] The District Court made detailed findings about the engineering profession, the Society, its members' participation in interstate commerce, the history of the ban on competitive bidding, and certain incidents in which the ban appears to have been violated or enforced. The District Court did not, however, make any finding on the question whether, or to what extent, competition had led to inferior engineering work which, in turn, had adversely affected the public health, safety, or welfare. That inquiry was considered unnecessary because the court was convinced that the ethical prohibition against competitive bidding was "on its face a tampering with the price structure of engineering fees in violation of § 1 of the Sherman Act."

[12] Although it modified the injunction entered by the District Court, the Court of Appeals affirmed its conclusion that the agreement was unlawful on its face and therefore "illegal without regard to claimed or possible benefits." [. . .]

[13]. . . [P]etitioner argues that its attempt to preserve the profession's traditional method of setting fees for engineering services is a reasonable method of forestalling the public harm which might be produced by unrestrained competitive bidding. To evaluate this argument it is necessary to identify the contours of the Rule of Reason and to discuss its application to the kind of justification asserted by petitioner. [. . .]

[14] One problem presented by the language of § 1 of the Sherman Act is that it cannot mean what it says. The statute says that "every" contract that restrains trade is unlawful. But, as Mr. Justice Brandeis perceptively noted, restraint is the very essence of every contract; read literally, § 1 would outlaw the entire body of private contract law. Yet it is that body of law that establishes the enforceability of commercial agreements and enables competitive markets—indeed, a competitive economy—to function effectively. [. . .]

[15] Congress . . . did not intend the text of the Sherman Act to delineate the full meaning of the statute or its application in concrete situations. The legislative history makes it perfectly clear that it expected the courts to give shape to the statute's broad mandate by drawing on common-law tradition. The Rule of Reason, with its origins in common-law precedents long antedating the Sherman Act, has served that purpose. It has been used to give the Act both flexibility and definition, and its central principle of antitrust analysis has remained constant. Contrary to its name, the Rule does not open the field of antitrust inquiry to any argument in favor of a challenged restraint that may fall within the realm of reason. Instead, it focuses directly on the challenged restraint's impact on competitive conditions. [. . .]

[16] Price is the central nervous system of the economy, and an agreement that interferes with the setting of price by free market forces is illegal on its face. In this case we are presented with an agreement among competitors to refuse to discuss prices with potential customers until after negotiations have resulted in the initial selection of an engineer. While this is not price fixing as such, no elaborate industry analysis is required to demonstrate the anticompetitive character of such an agreement. It operates as an absolute ban on competitive bidding, applying with equal force to both complicated and simple projects and to both inexperienced and sophisticated customers. As the District Court found, the ban impedes the ordinary give and take of the market place, and substantially deprives the customer of the ability to utilize and compare prices in selecting engineering services. On its face, this agreement restrains trade within the meaning of § 1 of the Sherman Act.

[17] The Society's affirmative defense confirms rather than refutes the anticompetitive purpose and effect of its agreement. The Society argues that the restraint is justified because bidding on engineering services is inherently imprecise, would lead to deceptively low bids, and would thereby tempt individual engineers to do inferior work with consequent risk to public safety and health. The logic of this argument rests on the assumption that the agreement will tend to maintain the price level; if it had no such effect, it would not serve its intended purpose. The Society nonetheless invokes the Rule of Reason, arguing that its restraint on price competition ultimately inures to the public benefit by preventing the production of inferior work and by insuring ethical behavior. [T]his Court has never accepted such an argument. [. . .]

[18] It may be, as petitioner argues, that competition tends to force prices down and that an inexpensive item may be inferior to one that is more costly. There is some risk, therefore, that competition will cause some suppliers to market a defective product. Similarly, competitive bidding for engineering projects may be inherently imprecise and incapable of taking into account all the variables which will be involved in the actual performance of the project. Based on these considerations, a purchaser might conclude that his interest in quality—which may embrace the safety of the end product—outweighs the advantages of achieving cost savings by pitting one competitor against another. Or an individual vendor might independently refrain from price negotiation until he has satisfied himself that he fully understands the scope of his customers' needs. These decisions might be reasonable; indeed, petitioner has provided ample documentation for that thesis. But these are not reasons that satisfy the Rule; nor are such individual decisions subject to antitrust attack. [. . .]

[19] The Sherman Act does not require competitive bidding; it prohibits unreasonable restraints on competition. Petitioner's ban on competitive bidding prevents all customers from making price comparisons in the initial selection of an engineer, and imposes the Society's views of the costs and benefits of competition on the entire marketplace. It is this restraint that must be justified under the Rule of Reason, and petitioner's attempt to do so on the basis of the potential threat that competition poses to the public safety and the ethics of its profession is nothing less than a frontal assault on the basic policy of the Sherman Act. [. . .]

[20] The Sherman Act reflects a legislative judgment that ultimately competition will produce not only lower prices, but also better goods and services. The heart of our national economic policy long has been faith in the value of competition. The assumption that competition is the best method of allocating resources in a free market recognizes that all elements of a bargain—quality, service, safety, and durability—and not just the immediate cost, are favorably affected by the free opportunity to select among alternative offers. Even assuming occasional exceptions to the presumed consequences of competition, the statutory policy precludes inquiry into the question whether competition is good or bad.

[21] The fact that engineers are often involved in large-scale projects significantly affecting the public safety does not alter our analysis. Exceptions to the Sherman Act for potentially dangerous goods and services would be tantamount to a repeal of the statute. In our complex economy the number of items that may cause serious harm is almost endless—automobiles, drugs, foods, aircraft components, heavy equipment, and countless others, cause serious harm to individuals or to the public at large if defectively made. The judiciary cannot indirectly protect the public against this harm by conferring monopoly privileges on the manufacturers. [. . .]

[22] In sum, the Rule of Reason does not support a defense based on the assumption that competition itself is unreasonable. [. . .]

* * *

The Supreme Court's two most recent applications of the rule of reason have concerned very different practices. In *American Express* (2018) the Court considered a rule, adopted by the American Express credit card system, that prevented merchants from "steering" consumers to other credit cards (*e.g.*, encouraging them to use cards that charge merchants lower fees). In that case, very controversially, the Court held that the government plaintiffs had failed to discharge their burden at step one of the rule of reason, despite a lengthy trial record that established that the antisteering rules had driven merchant fees up. *AmEx* sharply presented the question of what constitutes a market-wide anticompetitive effect, and what factors courts may consider when evaluating the sufficiency of a plaintiff's showing. For context, you might find it helpful to look back at the discussion of AmEx's market-definition holding in Chapter III.[312] And in *Alston* (2021) the Court condemned some of the NCAA's limitations on certain forms of compensation to student athletes. By contrast with *AmEx*, anticompetitive effect was relatively straightforward in *Alston* (although the case concerned competition qua *purchasers of labor*, so rather than supracompetitive prices the evidence of harm focused on infracompetitive wages): the *Alston* decision helpfully ventilated the concept of a procompetitive justification.

CASENOTE: Ohio v. American Express Co.

138 S.Ct. 2274 (2018)

As you will remember from Chapter III, *AmEx* dealt with the imposition by American Express of "antisteering" rules that prevented merchants from nudging customers to other credit cards, even if they charged lower merchant fees. As we saw, the Court held that a single market should be defined to include both sides of the credit-card platform: services to merchants *and* those to cardholders. But *AmEx* is also notable for its application of the rule of reason. In the district court, the plaintiffs had won after a lengthy trial. By the time the appeal reached the Supreme Court, the plaintiffs had opted to proceed only on their direct-evidence case, relying on evidence that the antisteering rules had led to an increase in merchant fees.

---

[312] *See supra* § III.C.4.

The Court set out the rule of reason in terms that omitted any reference to step-three balancing of anticompetitive and procompetitive effects. And it held that plaintiffs had failed at step one: they had not shown *prima facie* harm. "[T]he plaintiffs' argument about merchant fees wrongly focuses on only one side of the two-sided credit-card market. . . . [T]he product that credit-card companies sell is transactions, not services to merchants, and the competitive effects of a restraint on transactions cannot be judged by looking at merchants alone."

So, what would have been enough? Well, the Court explained, "[t]o demonstrate anticompetitive effects on the two-sided credit-card market as a whole, the plaintiffs must prove that Amex's antisteering provisions increased the cost of credit-card transactions above a competitive level, reduced the number of credit-card transactions, or otherwise stifled competition in the credit-card market." But, on this record, the plaintiffs had "failed to offer any reliable measure of Amex's transaction price or profit margins."

The Court preferred alternative, procompetitive explanations for the higher prices: "Amex's increased merchant fees reflect increases in the value of its services and the cost of its transactions, not an ability to charge above a competitive price. . . . Amex uses its higher merchant fees to offer its cardholders a more robust rewards program, which is necessary to maintain cardholder loyalty and encourage the level of spending that makes Amex valuable to merchants." And the Court was moved by evidence that "[t]he output of credit-card transactions grew dramatically from 2008 to 2013, increasing 30%. Where output is expanding at the same time prices are increasing, rising prices are equally consistent with growing product demand."

Finally, in an apparent evaluation of "indirect" evidence of competitive harm, the Court stated that "there is nothing inherently anticompetitive about Amex's antisteering provisions. These agreements actually stem negative externalities in the credit-card market and promote interbrand competition. When merchants steer cardholders away from Amex at the point of sale, it undermines the cardholder's expectation of "welcome acceptance"—the promise of a frictionless transaction."

There are at least two ways to read *AmEx*'s application of the rule of reason. One is a narrow, almost traditional one: a plaintiff cannot discharge its obligation at step one by simply pointing to a nominal increase in price paid by a subset of customers in the relevant market. Step one requires a showing of *market-wide* effects. Thus, for example, at step one a plaintiff cannot succeed by showing only that customers wearing blue hats paid more: for that tells us nothing about whether the challenged practice is harmful overall. (Remember that merchants were only a subset of customers in the relevant market, given the inclusion of cardholders as well.)

The other reading is much more radical. On this view, the Court indicated that plaintiffs can be required, after producing evidence of harm in the form of a demonstrated price increase, to *disprove the possibility of a benign or procompetitive explanation for the price increase*—as part of their affirmative case! This appears to violate the principle that redeeming benefits (such as the procompetitive effects of improved service or more valuable rewards, or the stimulation of demand) must be proved by a defendant, not disproved by a plaintiff at step one.

Time will tell which reading of *AmEx* becomes the authoritative one.

Justice Breyer's dissent charted a very different course. In articulating the core rule-of-reason framework, he gave lukewarm endorsement to balancing, noting that a plaintiff may "perhaps" prevail at step three by showing "that the legitimate objective does not outweigh the harm that competition will suffer, *i.e.*, that the agreement 'on balance' remains unreasonable." He pointed out that market definition is normally unnecessary when a plaintiff has offered direct evidence of anticompetitive effects, such as increased prices. And he protested that the majority had analyzed American Express's claimed justifications at step one of the rule of the reason, rather than step two, and moreover completely ignored an extensive district court record concluding that no such justifications had been proved at trial!

National Collegiate Athletic Association v. Alston
141 S.Ct. 2141 (2021)

Justice Gorsuch.

[1] In the Sherman Act, Congress tasked courts with enforcing a policy of competition on the belief that market forces "yield the best allocation" of the Nation's resources. The plaintiffs before us brought this lawsuit alleging that the National Collegiate Athletic Association (NCAA) and certain of its member institutions violated this policy by agreeing to restrict the compensation colleges and universities may offer the student-athletes who play for their teams. After amassing a vast record and conducting an exhaustive trial, the district court . . . refused to disturb the NCAA's rules limiting undergraduate athletic scholarships and other compensation related to athletic performance. At the same time, the court struck down NCAA rules limiting the education-related benefits schools may offer student-athletes—such as rules that prohibit schools from offering graduate or vocational school scholarships. Before us, the student-athletes do not challenge the district court's judgment. But the NCAA does. In essence, it seeks immunity from the normal operation of the antitrust laws and argues, in any event, that the district court should have approved all of its existing restraints. [. . .]

[2] The plaintiffs are current and former student-athletes in men's Division I . . . football and men's and women's Division I basketball. They filed a class action against the NCAA and 11 Division I conferences (for simplicity's sake, we refer to the defendants collectively as the NCAA). The student-athletes challenged the "current, interconnected set of NCAA rules that limit the compensation they may receive in exchange for their athletic services." Specifically, they alleged that the NCAA's rules violate § 1 of the Sherman Act, which prohibits contracts, combinations, or conspiracies in restraint of trade or commerce. [. . .]

[3] . . . This Court has long recognized that in view of the common law and the law in this country when the Sherman Act was passed, the phrase "restraint of trade" is best read to mean "undue restraint." Determining whether a restraint is undue for purposes of the Sherman Act presumptively calls for what we have described as a rule of reason analysis. That manner of analysis generally requires a court to conduct a fact-specific assessment of market power and market structure to assess a challenged restraint's actual effect on competition. Always, the goal is to distinguish between restraints with anticompetitive effect that are harmful to the consumer and restraints stimulating competition that are in the consumer's best interest.

[4] In applying the rule of reason, the district court began by observing that the NCAA enjoys "near complete dominance of, and exercises monopsony power in, the relevant market"—which it defined as the market for "athletic services in men's and women's Division I basketball and . . . football, wherein each class member participates in his or her sport-specific market." The "most talented athletes are concentrated" in the "markets for Division I basketball and . . . football." There are no "viable substitutes," as the "NCAA's Division I essentially *is* the relevant market for elite college football and basketball." In short, the NCAA and its member schools have the "power to restrain student-athlete compensation in any way and at any time they wish, without any meaningful risk of diminishing their market dominance."

[5] The district court then proceeded to find that the NCAA's compensation limits "produce significant anticompetitive effects in the relevant market." Though member schools compete fiercely in recruiting student-athletes, the NCAA uses its monopsony power to "cap artificially the compensation offered to recruits." In a market without the challenged restraints, the district court found, "competition among schools would increase in terms of the compensation they would offer to recruits, and student-athlete compensation would be higher as a result. "Student-athletes would receive offers that would more closely match the value of their athletic services." . . .

[6] The district court next considered the NCAA's procompetitive justifications for its restraints. The NCAA suggested that its restrictions help increase output in college sports and maintain a competitive balance among teams. But the district court rejected those justifications, and the NCAA does not pursue them here. The NCAA's only remaining defense was that its rules preserve amateurism, which in turn widens consumer choice by providing a unique product—amateur college sports as distinct from professional sports. Admittedly, this asserted benefit accrues to consumers in the NCAA's seller-side consumer market rather than to student-athletes whose

compensation the NCAA fixes in its buyer-side labor market. But, the NCAA argued, the district court needed to assess its restraints in the labor market in light of their procompetitive benefits in the consumer market—and the district court agreed to do so.

[7] Turning to that task, the court observed that the NCAA's conception of amateurism has changed steadily over the years. The court noted that the NCAA "nowhere defines the nature of the amateurism they claim consumers insist upon." [. . .]

[8] Nor did the district court find much evidence to support the NCAA's contention that its compensation restrictions play a role in consumer demand. As the court put it, the evidence failed "to establish that the challenged compensation rules, in and of themselves, have any direct connection to consumer demand . . . ." At the same time, however, the district court did find that one particular aspect of the NCAA's compensation limits "may have some effect in preserving consumer demand." Specifically, the court found that rules aimed at ensuring "student-athletes do not receive unlimited payments unrelated to education" could play some role in product differentiation with professional sports and thus help sustain consumer demand for college athletics.

[9] The court next required the student-athletes to show that "substantially less restrictive alternative rules" existed that "would achieve the same procompetitive effect as the challenged set of rules." . . . The court rejected the student-athletes' challenge to NCAA rules that limit athletic scholarships to the full cost of attendance and that restrict compensation and benefits unrelated to education. These may be price-fixing agreements, but the court found them to be reasonable in light of the possibility that "professional-level cash payments could blur the distinction between college sports and professional sports and thereby negatively affect consumer demand."

[10] The court reached a different conclusion for caps on education-related benefits—such as rules that limit scholarships for graduate or vocational school, payments for academic tutoring, or paid posteligibility internships. On no account, the court found, could such education-related benefits be "confused with a professional athlete's salary." If anything, they "emphasize that the recipients are students." Enjoining the NCAA's restrictions on these forms of compensation alone, the court concluded, would be substantially less restrictive than the NCAA's current rules and yet fully capable of preserving consumer demand for college sports. [. . .]

[11] . . . [The Ninth Circuit] affirmed in full, explaining its view that the district court struck the right balance in crafting a remedy that both prevents anticompetitive harm to Student-Athletes while serving the procompetitive purpose of preserving the popularity of college sports.

[12] Unsatisfied with this result, the NCAA asks us to reverse to the extent the lower courts sided with the student-athletes. . . .

[13] . . . [S]ome of the issues most frequently debated in antitrust litigation are uncontested. The parties do not challenge the district court's definition of the relevant market. They do not contest that the NCAA enjoys monopoly (or, as it's called on the buyer side, monopsony) control in that labor market—such that it is capable of depressing wages below competitive levels and restricting the quantity of student-athlete labor. Nor does the NCAA dispute that its member schools compete fiercely for student-athletes but remain subject to NCAA-issued-and-enforced limits on what compensation they can offer. Put simply, this suit involves admitted horizontal price fixing in a market where the defendants exercise monopoly control.

[14] Other significant matters are taken as given here too. No one disputes that the NCAA's restrictions *in fact* decrease the compensation that student-athletes receive compared to what a competitive market would yield. No one questions either that decreases in compensation also depress participation by student-athletes in the relevant labor market—so that price and quantity are both suppressed.

[15] Meanwhile, the student-athletes do not question that the NCAA may permissibly seek to justify its restraints in the labor market by pointing to procompetitive effects they produce in the consumer market. Some *amici* argue that "competition in input markets is incommensurable with competition in output markets," and that a court should not "trade off " sacrificing a legally cognizable interest in competition in one market to better promote competition in a different one; review should instead be limited to the particular market in which antitrust plaintiffs have asserted their injury. But the parties before us do not pursue this line. [. . .]

[16] While the NCAA devotes most of its energy to resisting the rule of reason in its usual form, the league lodges some objections to the district court's application of it as well.

[17] When describing the rule of reason, this Court has sometimes spoken of a three-step, burden-shifting framework as a means for distinguishing between restraints with anticompetitive effect that are harmful to the consumer and restraints stimulating competition that are in the consumer's best interest. [Ohio v. American Express Co., 585 U. S. __, 138 S.Ct. 2274, 2284 (2018)]. As we have described it, the plaintiff has the initial burden to prove that the challenged restraint has a substantial anticompetitive effect. Should the plaintiff carry that burden, the burden then shifts to the defendant to show a procompetitive rationale for the restraint. If the defendant can make that showing, the burden shifts back to the plaintiff to demonstrate that the procompetitive efficiencies could be reasonably achieved through less anticompetitive means. [. . .]

[18] In the proceedings below, the district court followed circuit precedent to apply a multistep framework closely akin to *American Express*'s. As its first step, the district court required the student-athletes to show that the challenged restraints produce significant anticompetitive effects in the relevant market. .... As we have seen, based on a voluminous record, the district court held that the student-athletes had shown the NCAA enjoys the power to set wages in the market for student-athletes' labor—and that the NCAA has exercised that power in ways that have produced significant anticompetitive effects. Perhaps even more notably, the NCAA did not meaningfully dispute this conclusion.

[19] [T]he district court proceeded to the second step, asking whether the NCAA could muster a procompetitive rationale for its restraints. This is where the NCAA claims error first crept in. On its account, the district court examined the challenged rules at different levels of generality. At the first step of its inquiry, the court asked whether the NCAA's entire package of compensation restrictions has substantial anticompetitive effects *collectively*. Yet, at the second step, the NCAA says the district court required it to show that each of its distinct rules limiting student-athlete compensation has procompetitive benefits *individually*. The NCAA says this mismatch had the result of effectively—and erroneously—requiring it to prove that each rule is the least restrictive means of achieving the procompetitive purpose of differentiating college sports and preserving demand for them.

[20] We agree with the NCAA's premise that antitrust law does not require businesses to use anything like the least restrictive means of achieving legitimate business purposes. To the contrary, courts should not second-guess degrees of reasonable necessity so that the lawfulness of conduct turns upon judgments of degrees of efficiency. [. . .]

[21] While we agree with the NCAA's legal premise, we cannot say the same for its factual one. Yes, at the first step of its inquiry, the district court held that the student-athletes had met their burden of showing the NCAA's restraints collectively bear an anticompetitive effect. And, given that, yes, at step two the NCAA had to show only that those same rules collectively yield a procompetitive benefit. The trouble for the NCAA, though, is not the level of generality. It is the fact that the district court found unpersuasive much of its proffered evidence. Recall that the court found the NCAA failed to establish that the challenged compensation rules have any direct connection to consumer demand.

[22] To be sure, there is a wrinkle here. While finding the NCAA had failed to establish that its rules collectively sustain consumer demand, the court did find that some of those rules may have procompetitive effects to the extent they prohibit compensation unrelated to education, akin to salaries seen in professional sports leagues. The court then proceeded to what corresponds to the third step of the *American Express* framework, where it required the student-athletes to show that there are substantially less restrictive alternative rules that would achieve the same procompetitive effect as the challenged set of rules. And there, of course, the district court held that the student-athletes partially succeeded—they were able to show that the NCAA could achieve the procompetitive benefits it had established with substantially less restrictive restraints on education-related benefits.

[23] Even acknowledging this wrinkle, we see nothing about the district court's analysis that offends the legal principles the NCAA invokes. The court's judgment ultimately turned on the key question at the third step: whether the student-athletes could prove that substantially less restrictive alternative rules existed to achieve the same procompetitive benefits the NCAA had proven at the second step. Of course, deficiencies in the NCAA's

proof of procompetitive benefits at the second step influenced the analysis at the third. But that is only because, however framed and at whichever step, anticompetitive restraints of trade may wind up flunking the rule of reason to the extent the evidence shows that substantially less restrictive means exist to achieve any proven procompetitive benefits.

[24] Simply put, the district court nowhere—expressly or effectively—required the NCAA to show that its rules constituted the *least* restrictive means of preserving consumer demand. Rather, it was only after finding the NCAA's restraints patently and inexplicably stricter than is necessary to achieve the procompetitive benefits the league had demonstrated that the district court proceeded to declare a violation of the Sherman Act. That demanding standard hardly presages a future filled with judicial micromanagement of legitimate business decisions. [. . .]

[25] Finally, the NCAA attacks as indefensible the lower courts' holding that substantially less restrictive alternatives exist capable of delivering the same procompetitive benefits as its current rules. The NCAA claims, too, that the district court's injunction threatens to micromanage its business.

[26] Once more, we broadly agree with the legal principles the NCAA invokes. As we have discussed, antitrust courts must give wide berth to business judgments before finding liability. Similar considerations apply when it comes to the remedy. Judges must be sensitive to the possibility that the continuing supervision of a highly detailed decree could wind up impairing rather than enhancing competition. . . .

[27] Once again, though, we think the district court honored these principles. The court enjoined only restraints on education-related benefits—such as those limiting scholarships for graduate school, payments for tutoring, and the like. The court did so, moreover, only after finding that relaxing these restrictions would not blur the distinction between college and professional sports and thus impair demand—and only after finding that this course represented a significantly (not marginally) less restrictive means of achieving the same procompetitive benefits as the NCAA's current rules.

[28] Even with respect to education-related benefits, the district court extended the NCAA considerable leeway. As we have seen, the court provided that the NCAA could develop its own definition of benefits that relate to education and seek modification of the court's injunction to reflect that definition. The court explained that the NCAA and its members could agree on rules regulating how conferences and schools go about providing these education-related benefits. The court said that the NCAA and its members could continue fixing education-related cash awards, too—so long as those limits are never lower than the limit on awards for athletic performance. And the court emphasized that its injunction applies only to the NCAA and multiconference agreements; individual conferences remain free to reimpose every single enjoined restraint tomorrow—or more restrictive ones still. [. . .]

Affirmed.

Justice Kavanaugh, concurring.

[29] [T]his case involves only a narrow subset of the NCAA's compensation rules—namely, the rules restricting the *education-related* benefits that student athletes may receive, such as post-eligibility scholarships at graduate or vocational schools. The rest of the NCAA's compensation rules are not at issue here and therefore remain on the books. Those remaining compensation rules generally restrict student athletes from receiving compensation or benefits from their colleges for playing sports. And those rules have also historically restricted student athletes from receiving money from endorsement deals and the like.

[30] I add this concurring opinion to underscore that the NCAA's remaining compensation rules also raise serious questions under the antitrust laws. Three points warrant emphasis.

[31] *First*, the Court does not address the legality of the NCAA's remaining compensation rules. As the Court says, the student-athletes do not renew their across-the-board challenge to the NCAA's compensation restrictions. Accordingly, we do not pass on the rules that remain in place or the district court's judgment upholding them. Our review is confined to those restrictions now enjoined.

[32] *Second*, although the Court does not weigh in on the ultimate legality of the NCAA's remaining compensation rules, the Court's decision establishes how any such rules should be analyzed going forward. After today's decision, the NCAA's remaining compensation rules should receive ordinary "rule of reason" scrutiny under the antitrust laws. . . . And the Court stresses that the NCAA is not otherwise entitled to an exemption from the antitrust laws. . . .

[33] *Third*, there are serious questions whether the NCAA's remaining compensation rules can pass muster under ordinary rule of reason scrutiny. Under the rule of reason, the NCAA must supply a legally valid procompetitive justification for its remaining compensation rules. As I see it, however, the NCAA may lack such a justification.

[34] The NCAA acknowledges that it controls the market for college athletes. The NCAA concedes that its compensation rules set the price of student athlete labor at a below-market rate. And the NCAA recognizes that student athletes currently have no meaningful ability to negotiate with the NCAA over the compensation rules.

[35] The NCAA nonetheless asserts that its compensation rules are procompetitive because those rules help define the product of college sports. Specifically, the NCAA says that colleges may decline to pay student athletes because the defining feature of college sports, according to the NCAA, is that the student athletes are not paid.

[36] In my view, that argument is circular and unpersuasive. . . . The NCAA's business model would be flatly illegal in almost any other industry in America. All of the restaurants in a region cannot come together to cut cooks' wages on the theory that "customers prefer" to eat food from low-paid cooks. Law firms cannot conspire to cabin lawyers' salaries in the name of providing legal services out of a "love of the law." Hospitals cannot agree to cap nurses' income in order to create a "purer" form of helping the sick. News organizations cannot join forces to curtail pay to reporters to preserve a "tradition" of public-minded journalism. Movie studios cannot collude to slash benefits to camera crews to kindle a "spirit of amateurism" in Hollywood.

[37] Price-fixing labor is price-fixing labor. And price-fixing labor is ordinarily a textbook antitrust problem because it extinguishes the free market in which individuals can otherwise obtain fair compensation for their work. Businesses like the NCAA cannot avoid the consequences of price-fixing labor by incorporating price-fixed labor into the definition of the product. Or to put it in more doctrinal terms, a monopsony cannot launder its price-fixing of labor by calling it product definition.

[38] The bottom line is that the NCAA and its member colleges are suppressing the pay of student athletes who collectively generate billions of dollars in revenues for colleges every year. Those enormous sums of money flow to seemingly everyone except the student athletes. College presidents, athletic directors, coaches, conference commissioners, and NCAA executives take in six- and seven-figure salaries. Colleges build lavish new facilities. But the student athletes who generate the revenues, many of whom are African American and from lower-income backgrounds, end up with little or nothing. [. . .]

[39] . . . [T]raditions alone cannot justify the NCAA's decision to build a massive money-raising enterprise on the backs of student athletes who are not fairly compensated. Nowhere else in America can businesses get away with agreeing not to pay their workers a fair market rate on the theory that their product is defined by not paying their workers a fair market rate. And under ordinary principles of antitrust law, it is not evident why college sports should be any different. The NCAA is not above the law.

NOTES

1) Did the Court apply the same rule of reason in *Chicago Board of Trade*, *AmEx* and *Alston*?

2) The Court in *Chicago Board of Trade* says the legality of the restraint in that case must be judged according to whether it encourages or impedes competition. Why is the restraint at issue in this case analyzed differently than the restraint in *Socony-Vacuum*? What is the difference between the two restraints that leads the Supreme Court to treat the restraint in *Socony-Vacuum* as per se illegal, while inquiring more carefully into the competitive effects of the restraint in *Chicago Board of Trade*? Is the Court right to analyze the two restraints so differently?

3) Isn't the restraint at issue in *Chicago Board of Trade* nakedly anticompetitive: specifically, isn't it best understood as an agreement to refrain from price competition during long periods of the day? If not, why not?

4) In *Chicago Board of Trade*, do you find the Court's account of the procompetitive effects of the restraint to be convincing? What do you think motivated the Board to impose the "call" rule?

5) The Court in *Chicago Board of Trade* mentioned that rules or practices of a broadly similar kind were "common." Assuming that that statement was correct, should it matter? Should courts consider whether a particular practice is common as a factor in favor of its legality?

6) Why did the Court in *Professional Engineers* apply the rule of reason rather than the per se rule? Was the restraint not a form of price-fixing, if the only purported justification was not cognizable?

7) On the other hand: why was the purpose of the restraint in *Professional Engineers* not a procompetitive one? Could it have been characterized as such?

8) In *AmEx*, the Court emphasized that credit card utilization was generally increasing. Why and how does this matter to an assessment of the effects of the challenged antisteering rules?

9) The *AmEx* opinion can be understood to have three striking features: first, its approach to market definition (specifically: including in the same market services that are not substitutes for one another); second, its approach to the plaintiff's affirmative burden in showing *prima facie* harm (specifically: holding that an increase in nominal price to merchants was not sufficient to establish harm to competition[313]); and, third, its implicit holding that (possible) benefits to cardholders in that case justified harms to merchants, despite the norm that harms to one group must be justified by reference to benefits to the same group.

10) Do you agree with Justice Kavanaugh's suggestion in *Alston* that the remainder of the NCAA's compensation rules are likely to fail once subjected to rule of reason analysis? Do you agree with him that the NCAA's purported justification that those rules help define the product that college sports offer—*i.e.*, amateur athletic competition—is "circular and unpersuasive"?

11) Can "amateurism" be a procompetitive justification?

12) Both *AmEx* and *Alston* seem to implicitly accept the idea that procompetitive benefits are relevant, and can be redeeming, even if the benefits accrue to different persons from those who are harmed (merchants v. cardholders; athletes v. consumers). Do you agree with that approach? What are its advantages and disadvantages?[314]

3. Intermediate Scrutiny

Finally, a small number of agreements are not quite familiar and nakedly harmful enough to warrant *per se* condemnation, but are facially suspicious enough to warrant so-called "quick look" analysis. Such agreements trigger what amounts to a defeasible presumption of anticompetitive effect. The Supreme Court has indicated that this approach applies only to agreements that are so obviously harmful that even "an observer with even a rudimentary understanding of economics could conclude that the arrangements in question would have an anticompetitive effect on customers and markets" such that "the great likelihood of anticompetitive effects can easily be ascertained."[315]

These agreements are not *per se* illegal—a defendant can still introduce evidence of justification—but they allow the plaintiff to discharge its own affirmative burden by pointing to the fact that the agreement is obviously harmful, rather than through a detailed showing of anticompetitive effects of the kind required at step one of the rule of reason. (However, as you may remember from earlier, a plaintiff who fears that a court may disagree with its proposed choice of standard may feel compelled to develop such a full-court-press showing anyway.[316])

There is plenty of debate about how intermediate scrutiny does and should work, and courts and commentators express a wide variety of views about how the nature of an agreement should affect the standard against which it is measured under Section 1. In particular, it is not quite clear that the intermediate scrutiny standard is very different in kind from the rule of reason. After all, the regular rule of reason includes plenty of room to consider

---

[313] In fact, despite the Supreme Court's description of the record, the district court below had found—in factual findings that the Supreme Court did not purport to disturb—that the antisteering rules had caused overall harm to consumers as well as merchants, and that the claimed procompetitive justifications were pretextual. *See* United States v. Am. Express Co., 88 F. Supp. 3d. 143, 150, 208, 215, 225–38 (E.D.N.Y. 2015).

[314] *See supra* notes 295 to 299 and accompanying text (out of market benefits under Section 1).

[315] California Dental Ass'n v. FTC, 526 U.S. 756, 770 (1999) (collecting cases).

[316] *See supra* note 244 and accompanying text.

the facially anticompetitive nature of an agreement: indeed, some courts have indicated that the rule of reason can sometimes be applied in a "twinkling of an eye," which sounds very much like a "quick look" review.[317] Likewise, the FTC considers some kinds of agreement to be "inherently suspect,"[318] which amounts to a synonym for quick look analysis.[319] As you see the quick-look standard in action, ask yourself whether and how it differs from standard rule-of-reason analysis.

A landmark precedent in quick-look review is the Supreme Court's 1984 opinion in *Board of Regents of the University of Oklahoma*, a major antitrust lawsuit brought against the National Collegiate Athletic Association ("NCAA").

Since its inception in 1905, the NCAA has played an important role in the regulation of amateur collegiate sports. (It has also made considerable contributions over the years to antitrust doctrine.[320]) At issue in the *Board of Regents* litigation was the NCAA's plan for television broadcasts of the football games played by its "Division I" schools. The NCAA licensed to each of two television networks, ABC and CBS, the right to telecast 14 live games (or "exposures") per year. Each network was authorized by the agreement to negotiate directly with NCAA member schools for the right to televise their games. Each network agreed to pay a "minimum aggregate compensation" to NCAA members totaling approximately $132 million over four years, but the agreement did not establish a formula determining compensation for any particular telecast. Instead, the NCAA set a recommended fee for each telecast. The fee was higher for national telecasts, as opposed to regional telecasts or telecasts involving teams outside of Division I, but the fee did not vary with the size of the viewing audience. The networks did not compete for games they both wished to televise, but rather took turns choosing games so that over time they would share in the most desirable telecasts. The bidding network submitted the sole bid to the schools involved in a particular exposure at the price the NCAA had recommended.

The NCAA plan also regulated how the networks selected which games they would telecast. During each 2-year period covered by the plan, the networks were required to telecast games involving at least 82 different schools. No school could appear more than six times, or more than four times nationally, with the appearances to be divided equally between ABC and CBS.

The NCAA stated that its objective was to "reduce, insofar as possible, the adverse effects of live television upon football game attendance and, in turn, upon the athletic and related educational programs dependent upon the proceeds therefrom; to spread football television participation among as many colleges as practicable; to reflect properly the image of universities as educational institutions; to promote college football through the use of television, to advance the overall interests of intercollegiate athletics, and to provide college football television to the public to the extent compatible with these other objectives."

Finally, and crucially: the NCAA required member schools to televise football games *only* in accordance with the plan. Independent television deals were prohibited.

The member schools of the College Football Association (CFA)—a group of NCAA member schools with major football programs—received a contract offer from NBC that provided for appearances and revenue in excess of what the NCAA plan permitted. The NCAA responded by threatening to punish any CFA member that televised games under the NBC contract. That punishment, the NCAA stated, would extend to the school's entire sports program: not just its football activities. In 1981, CFA members filed an antitrust lawsuit challenging the NCAA's plan. As we will see, the Supreme Court concluded that the plan violated Section 1.

---

[317] NCAA v. Alston, 141 S. Ct. 2141, 2155 (2021); NCAA v. Bd. of Regents of Univ. of Oklahoma, 468 U.S. 85, 110 n.39 (1984).

[318] *See* In The Matter Of Polygram Holding, Inc., 136 F.T.C. 310 (F.T.C. 2003).

[319] *See* 1-800 Contacts, Inc. v. FTC, 1 F.4th 102 (2d Cir. 2021); N. Tex. Specialty Physicians v. FTC, 528 F.3d 346 (5th Cir. 2008).

[320] *See, e.g.*, NCAA v. Alston, 141 S. Ct. 2141 (2021); NCAA v. Board of Regents of the University of Oklahoma, 468 U.S. 85 (1984); O'Bannon v. NCAA, 802 F.3d 1049 (9th Cir. 2015).

NCAA v. Board of Regents of the University of Oklahoma

468 U.S. 85 (1984)

Justice Stevens.

[1] There can be no doubt that the challenged practices of the NCAA constitute a "restraint of trade" in the sense that they limit members' freedom to negotiate and enter into their own television contracts. In that sense, however, every contract is a restraint of trade, and as we have repeatedly recognized, the Sherman Act was intended to prohibit only unreasonable restraints of trade.

[2] It is also undeniable that these practices share characteristics of restraints we have previously held unreasonable. The NCAA is an association of schools which compete against each other to attract television revenues, not to mention fans and athletes. As the District Court found, the policies of the NCAA with respect to television rights are ultimately controlled by the vote of member institutions. By participating in an association which prevents member institutions from competing against each other on the basis of price or kind of television rights that can be offered to broadcasters, the NCAA member institutions have created a horizontal restraint—an agreement among competitors on the way in which they will compete with one another. A restraint of this type has often been held to be unreasonable as a matter of law. Because it places a ceiling on the number of games member institutions may televise, the horizontal agreement places an artificial limit on the quantity of televised football that is available to broadcasters and consumers. By restraining the quantity of television rights available for sale, the challenged practices create a limitation on output; our cases have held that such limitations are unreasonable restraints of trade. Moreover, the District Court found that the minimum aggregate price in fact operates to preclude any price negotiation between broadcasters and institutions, thereby constituting horizontal price fixing, perhaps the paradigm of an unreasonable restraint of trade.

[3] Horizontal price fixing and output limitation are ordinarily condemned as a matter of law under an "illegal per se" approach because the probability that these practices are anticompetitive is so high; a per se rule is applied when the practice facially appears to be one that would always or almost always tend to restrict competition and decrease output. In such circumstances a restraint is presumed unreasonable without inquiry into the particular market context in which it is found. Nevertheless, we have decided that it would be inappropriate to apply a per se rule to this case. This decision is not based on a lack of judicial experience with this type of arrangement,[21] on the fact that the NCAA is organized as a nonprofit entity,[22] or on our respect for the NCAA's historic role in the preservation and encouragement of intercollegiate amateur athletics.[23] Rather, what is critical is that this case involves an industry in which horizontal restraints on competition are essential if the product is to be available at all.

[4] . . . What the NCAA and its member institutions market in this case is competition itself—contests between competing institutions. Of course, this would be completely ineffective if there were no rules on which the competitors agreed to create and define the competition to be marketed. A myriad of rules affecting such matters as the size of the field, the number of players on a team, and the extent to which physical violence is to be encouraged or proscribed, all must be agreed upon, and all restrain the manner in which institutions compete. Moreover, the NCAA seeks to market a particular brand of football—college football. The identification of this "product" with an academic tradition differentiates college football from and makes it more popular than professional sports to which it might otherwise be comparable, such as, for example, minor league baseball. In order to preserve the character and quality of the "product," athletes must not be paid, must be required to attend

---

[21] While judicial inexperience with a particular arrangement counsels against extending the reach of per se rules, the likelihood that horizontal price and output restrictions are anticompetitive is generally sufficient to justify application of the per se rule without inquiry into the special characteristics of a particular industry.

[22] There is no doubt that the sweeping language of § 1 applies to nonprofit entities, and in the past we have imposed antitrust liability on nonprofit entities which have engaged in anticompetitive conduct. Moreover, the economic significance of the NCAA's nonprofit character is questionable at best. Since the District Court found that the NCAA and its member institutions are in fact organized to maximize revenues, it is unclear why petitioner is less likely to restrict output in order to raise revenues above those that could be realized in a competitive market than would be a for-profit entity. Petitioner does not rely on its nonprofit character as a basis for reversal.

[23] While as the guardian of an important American tradition, the NCAA's motives must be accorded a respectful presumption of validity, it is nevertheless well settled that good motives will not validate an otherwise anticompetitive practice.

class, and the like. And the integrity of the "product" cannot be preserved except by mutual agreement; if an institution adopted such restrictions unilaterally, its effectiveness as a competitor on the playing field might soon be destroyed. Thus, the NCAA plays a vital role in enabling college football to preserve its character, and as a result enables a product to be marketed which might otherwise be unavailable. In performing this role, its actions widen consumer choice—not only the choices available to sports fans but also those available to athletes—and hence can be viewed as procompetitive.

[5] [Broadcast Music, Inc. v. Columbia Broadcasting System, Inc., 441 U.S. 1 (1979)] squarely holds that a joint selling arrangement may be so efficient that it will increase sellers' aggregate output and thus be procompetitive. Similarly, as we indicated in [*Sylvania*], a restraint in a limited aspect of a market may actually enhance marketwide competition. Respondents concede that the great majority of the NCAA's regulations enhance competition among member institutions. Thus, despite the fact that this case involves restraints on the ability of member institutions to compete in terms of price and output, a fair evaluation of their competitive character requires consideration of the NCAA's justifications for the restraints.

[6] Our analysis of this case under the Rule of Reason, of course, does not change the ultimate focus of our inquiry. Both per se rules and the Rule of Reason are employed to form a judgment about the competitive significance of the restraint. A conclusion that a restraint of trade is unreasonable may be based either (1) on the nature or character of the contracts, or (2) on surrounding circumstances giving rise to the inference or presumption that they were intended to restrain trade and enhance prices. Under either branch of the test, the inquiry is confined to a consideration of impact on competitive conditions.

[7] Per se rules are invoked when surrounding circumstances make the likelihood of anticompetitive conduct so great as to render unjustified further examination of the challenged conduct. But whether the ultimate finding is the product of a presumption or actual market analysis, the essential inquiry remains the same—whether or not the challenged restraint enhances competition. . . .[26]

[8] Because it restrains price and output, the NCAA's television plan has a significant potential for anticompetitive effects. The findings of the District Court indicate that this potential has been realized. The District Court found that if member institutions were free to sell television rights, many more games would be shown on television, and that the NCAA's output restriction has the effect of raising the price the networks pay for television rights. Moreover, the court found that by fixing a price for television rights to all games, the NCAA creates a price structure that is unresponsive to viewer demand and unrelated to the prices that would prevail in a competitive market. And, of course, since as a practical matter all member institutions need NCAA approval, members have no real choice but to adhere to the NCAA's television controls.

[9] The anticompetitive consequences of this arrangement are apparent. Individual competitors lose their freedom to compete. Price is higher and output lower than they would otherwise be, and both are unresponsive to consumer preference. This latter point is perhaps the most significant, since Congress designed the Sherman Act as a consumer welfare prescription. A restraint that has the effect of reducing the importance of consumer preference in setting price and output is not consistent with this fundamental goal of antitrust law. Restrictions on price and output are the paradigmatic examples of restraints of trade that the Sherman Act was intended to prohibit. At the same time, the television plan eliminates competitors from the market, since only those broadcasters able to bid on television rights covering the entire NCAA can compete. Thus, as the District Court found, many telecasts that would occur in a competitive market are foreclosed by the NCAA's plan.

[10] Petitioner argues, however, that its television plan can have no significant anticompetitive effect since the record indicates that it has no market power—no ability to alter the interaction of supply and demand in the market. We must reject this argument for two reasons, one legal, one factual.

---

[26] Indeed, there is often no bright line separating per se from Rule of Reason analysis. Per se rules may require considerable inquiry into market conditions before the evidence justifies a presumption of anticompetitive conduct. For example, while the Court has spoken of a "per se" rule against tying arrangements, it has also recognized that tying may have procompetitive justifications that make it inappropriate to condemn without considerable market analysis.

[11] As a matter of law, the absence of proof of market power does not justify a naked restriction on price or output. To the contrary, when there is an agreement not to compete in terms of price or output, no elaborate industry analysis is required to demonstrate the anticompetitive character of such an agreement. Petitioner does not quarrel with the District Court's finding that price and output are not responsive to demand. Thus the plan is inconsistent with the Sherman Act's command that price and supply be responsive to consumer preference. We have never required proof of market power in such a case. This naked restraint on price and output requires some competitive justification even in the absence of a detailed market analysis.

[12] As a factual matter, it is evident that petitioner does possess market power. The District Court employed the correct test for determining whether college football broadcasts constitute a separate market—whether there are other products that are reasonably substitutable for televised NCAA football games. . . . It found that intercollegiate football telecasts generate an audience uniquely attractive to advertisers and that competitors are unable to offer programming that can attract a similar audience. These findings amply support its conclusion that the NCAA possesses market power. Indeed, the District Court's subsidiary finding that advertisers will pay a premium price per viewer to reach audiences watching college football because of their demographic characteristics is vivid evidence of the uniqueness of this product. . . . It inexorably follows that if college football broadcasts be defined as a separate market—and we are convinced they are—then the NCAA's complete control over those broadcasts provides a solid basis for the District Court's conclusion that the NCAA possesses market power with respect to those broadcasts. . . .

[13] Thus, the NCAA television plan on its face constitutes a restraint upon the operation of a free market, and the findings of the District Court establish that it has operated to raise prices and reduce output. Under the Rule of Reason, these hallmarks of anticompetitive behavior place upon petitioner a heavy burden of establishing an affirmative defense which competitively justifies this apparent deviation from the operations of a free market. We turn now to the NCAA's proffered justifications.

[14] Relying on [Broadcast Music, Inc. v. Columbia Broadcasting System, Inc., 441 U.S. 1 (1979)], petitioner argues that its television plan constitutes a cooperative "joint venture" which assists in the marketing of broadcast rights and hence is procompetitive. While joint ventures have no immunity from the antitrust laws, as *Broadcast Music* indicates, a joint selling arrangement may make possible a new product by reaping otherwise unattainable efficiencies. The essential contribution made by the NCAA's arrangement is to define the number of games that may be televised, to establish the price for each exposure, and to define the basic terms of each contract between the network and a home team. The NCAA does not, however, act as a selling agent for any school or for any conference of schools. The selection of individual games, and the negotiation of particular agreements, are matters left to the networks and the individual schools. Thus, the effect of the network plan is not to eliminate individual sales of broadcasts, since these still occur, albeit subject to fixed prices and output limitations. Unlike *Broadcast Music*'s blanket license covering broadcast rights to a large number of individual compositions, here the same rights are still sold on an individual basis, only in a non-competitive market.

[15] The District Court did not find that the NCAA's television plan produced any procompetitive efficiencies which enhanced the competitiveness of college football television rights; to the contrary it concluded that NCAA football could be marketed just as effectively without the television plan. There is therefore no predicate in the findings for petitioner's efficiency justification. Indeed, petitioner's argument is refuted by the District Court's finding concerning price and output. If the NCAA's television plan produced procompetitive efficiencies, the plan would increase output and reduce the price of televised games. The District Court's contrary findings accordingly undermine petitioner's position. In light of these findings, it cannot be said that the agreement on price is necessary to market the product at all. In *Broadcast Music*, the availability of a package product that no individual could offer enhanced the total volume of music that was sold. Unlike this case, there was no limit of any kind placed on the volume that might be sold in the entire market and each individual remained free to sell his own music without restraint. Here production has been limited, not enhanced. No individual school is free to televise its own games without restraint. The NCAA's efficiency justification is not supported by the record.

[16] Neither is the NCAA's television plan necessary to enable the NCAA to penetrate the market through an attractive package sale. Since broadcasting rights to college football constitute a unique product for which there is no ready substitute, there is no need for collective action in order to enable the product to compete against its

nonexistent competitors. This is borne out by the District Court's finding that the NCAA's television plan reduces the volume of television rights sold.

[17] Throughout the history of its regulation of intercollegiate football telecasts, the NCAA has indicated its concern with protecting live attendance. This concern, it should be noted, is not with protecting live attendance at games which are shown on television; that type of interest is not at issue in this case. Rather, the concern is that fan interest in a televised game may adversely affect ticket sales for games that will not appear on television.

[18] Although . . . studies in the 1950's provided some support for the thesis that live attendance would suffer if unlimited television were permitted, the District Court found that there was no evidence to support that theory in today's market. Moreover . . . the television plan has evolved in a manner inconsistent with its original design to protect gate attendance. Under the current plan, games are shown on television during all hours that college football games are played. The plan simply does not protect live attendance by ensuring that games will not be shown on television at the same time as live events.

[19] There is, however, a more fundamental reason for rejecting this defense. The NCAA's argument that its television plan is necessary to protect live attendance is not based on a desire to maintain the integrity of college football as a distinct and attractive product, but rather on a fear that the product will not prove sufficiently attractive to draw live attendance when faced with competition from televised games. At bottom the NCAA's position is that ticket sales for most college games are unable to compete in a free market. The television plan protects ticket sales by limiting output—just as any monopolist increases revenues by reducing output. By seeking to insulate live ticket sales from the full spectrum of competition because of its assumption that the product itself is insufficiently attractive to consumers, petitioner forwards a justification that is inconsistent with the basic policy of the Sherman Act. The Rule of Reason does not support a defense based on the assumption that competition itself is unreasonable.

[20] Petitioner argues that the interest in maintaining a competitive balance among amateur athletic teams is legitimate and important and that it justifies the regulations challenged in this case. We agree with the first part of the argument but not the second.

[21] Our decision not to apply a per se rule to this case rests in large part on our recognition that a certain degree of cooperation is necessary if the type of competition that petitioner and its member institutions seek to market is to be preserved. It is reasonable to assume that most of the regulatory controls of the NCAA are justifiable means of fostering competition among amateur athletic teams and therefore procompetitive because they enhance public interest in intercollegiate athletics. The specific restraints on football telecasts that are challenged in this case do not, however, fit into the same mold as do rules defining the conditions of the contest, the eligibility of participants, or the manner in which members of a joint enterprise shall share the responsibilities and the benefits of the total venture.

[22] The NCAA does not claim that its television plan has equalized or is intended to equalize competition within any one league. The plan is nationwide in scope and there is no single league or tournament in which all college football teams complete. There is no evidence of any intent to equalize the strength of teams in Division I–A with those in Division II or Division III, and not even a colorable basis for giving colleges that have no football program at all a voice in the management of the revenues generated by the football programs at other schools. The interest in maintaining a competitive balance that is asserted by the NCAA as a justification for regulating all television of intercollegiate football is not related to any neutral standard or to any readily identifiable group of competitors.

[23] The television plan is not even arguably tailored to serve such an interest. . . . The plan simply imposes a restriction on one source of revenue that is more important to some colleges than to others. There is no evidence that this restriction produces any greater measure of equality throughout the NCAA than would a restriction on alumni donations, tuition rates, or any other revenue-producing activity. At the same time . . . the NCAA imposes a variety of other restrictions designed to preserve amateurism which are much better tailored to the goal of competitive balance than is the television plan, and which are "clearly sufficient" to preserve competitive balance to the extent it is within the NCAA's power to do so. . . . No other NCAA sport employs a similar plan, and in

particular the court found that in the most closely analogous sport, college basketball, competitive balance has been maintained without resort to a restrictive television plan.

[24] Perhaps the most important reason for rejecting the argument that the interest in competitive balance is served by the television plan is the District Court's unambiguous and well-supported finding that many more games would be televised in a free market than under the NCAA plan. The hypothesis that legitimates the maintenance of competitive balance as a procompetitive justification under the Rule of Reason is that equal competition will maximize consumer demand for the product. The finding that consumption will materially increase if the controls are removed is a compelling demonstration that they do not in fact serve any such legitimate purpose. [. . .]

Affirmed.

* * *

The FTC has its own version of an abbreviated quick look analysis, known as the "inherently suspect" standard.[321] A seminal statement of that standard is found in the FTC's *PolyGram* litigation, which involved an agreement among music distributors to refrain from advertising products that competed with an album that they were distributing jointly.

The FTC's "Inherently Suspect" Standard and the PolyGram Litigation

In the Matter of PolyGram Holding, Inc., 136 F.T.C. 310 (2003); PolyGram Holding, Inc. v. FTC, 416 F.3d 29 (D.C. Cir. 2005)

The FTC has its own version of an abbreviated quick look analysis, which it calls the "inherently suspect" standard. A seminal statement of that standard is found in *PolyGram*. That case involved a joint venture between two music distributors: PolyGram and Warner. Each had previously distributed one album by the "Three Tenors" (Luciano Pavarotti, Plácido Domingo, and José Carreras) at a previous World Cup: PolyGram distributed the album for World Cup 1990 in Italy and Warner did so for World Cup 1994 in the United States. The two distributors subsequently cooperated to jointly distribute a third album for World Cup 1998. When they did so, the distributors also agreed that each of them would restrict promotion of their own Three Tenors albums.

The FTC challenged this agreement, and the Commission held—in a unanimous opinion by Chairman Muris—that no detailed proof of anticompetitive effects was necessary because the agreement was "inherently suspect." In a close echo of the Supreme Court's quick-look framework, the Commission stated: "A plaintiff may avoid full rule of reason analysis, including the pleading and proof of market power, if it demonstrates that the conduct at issue is inherently suspect owing to its likely tendency to suppress competition. Such conduct ordinarily encompasses behavior that past judicial experience and current economic learning have shown to warrant summary condemnation."

If this showing is made, the Commission explained, then "the defendant can avoid summary condemnation only by advancing a legitimate justification for those practices. Such justifications may consist of plausible reasons why practices that are competitively suspect as a general matter may not be expected to have adverse consequences in the context of the particular market in question; or they may consist of reasons why the practices are likely to have beneficial effects for consumers." Only if the defendant can point to "cognizable" (*i.e.*, procompetitive) justifications which are "plausible" (*i.e.*, "cannot be rejected without extensive factual inquiry") must a plaintiff take the longer road by making a more detailed showing of harm.

After losing before the Commission, PolyGram appealed to the D.C. Circuit. Writing for the Court of Appeals, Chief Judge Douglas Ginsburg—a prominent antitrust expert—upheld the Commission's decision. Identifying the FTC's "inherently suspect" standard with the Supreme Court's quick-look framework, the court confirmed that

---

[321] *See, e.g.*, North Texas Specialty Physicians v. FTC, 528 F.3d 346, 360–61 (5th Cir. 2008) ("The 'inherently suspect' paradigm . . . is a "quick-look" rule-of-reason analysis.").

liability without proof of "actual anticompetitive effect" was appropriate for "restraints that judicial experience and economic learning have shown to be likely to harm consumers." In other words, if, "based on economic learning and the experience of the market, it is obvious that a restraint of trade likely impairs competition, then the restraint is presumed unlawful." This analysis, the court held, was appropriate in cases involving a "close family resemblance between the suspect practice and another practice that already stands convicted in the court of consumer welfare."

Applying that rule, Chief Judge Ginsburg agreed that the agreement between PolyGram and Warner was indeed inherently suspect and thus could be condemned without detailed proof of harm. The mere fact of some procompetitive cooperation was not a license to eliminate existing rivalry. After all, he explained: even if General Motors entered a joint venture with a rival to produce an SUV, "an agreement to restrain prices and advertising on existing SUVs" would not for that reason be lawful. "And it simply does not matter whether the new SUV would have been profitable absent the restraint; if the only way a new product can profitably be introduced is to restrain the legitimate competition of older products, then one must seriously wonder whether consumers are genuinely benefitted by the new product."

NOTES

1) Does quick-look analysis involve a different standard from rule-of-reason analysis, or is it just a particular application of the rule of reason in which anticompetitive effect can be inferred from the nature and context of the restraint?

2) Is the FTC's inherently-suspect standard in *Polygram*, as understood by the D.C. Circuit, the same standard as the one applied by the Supreme Court in *Board of Regents*?

3) In *Board of Regents*, at paragraphs 11 and 13 of the extract, the Court described the core principle in intermediate-scrutiny cases. Why did the Court call the restraint "naked," given that the joint enterprise of football competition was (presumably) a legitimate and procompetitive one? What feature, or features, of the joint practice triggered the elevated scrutiny in this case? Can you imagine a variation that would deserve full rule-of-reason analysis?

4) The Court in *Board of Regents* described the defendant's justification burden as a "heavy" one. Does the Court's treatment of justifications seem more skeptical, or more demanding, than in the standard rule of reason cases you read above?

5) What lessons does *Board of Regents* teach about what counts as a "procompetitive" justification? Could you give a coherent case for including in that category the goals that the Court considers and rejects?

6) The majority in *Board of Regents* acknowledges that the NCAA's television plan fixes prices and restricts output (i.e., it limits the number of televised games). Isn't that tantamount to admitting that the television plan is equivalent to price fixing? If so, why did the Court not simply apply per se analysis?

7) In footnote 26 of *Board of Regents*, the Court says that "there is often no bright line separating *per se* from Rule of Reason analysis." Is that right? Should it be?

8) Why did the Court go out of its way in footnote 23 of *Board of Regents* to say that, "as the guardian of an important American tradition, the NCAA's motives must be accorded a respectful presumption of validity"? What other businesses, if any, should enjoy this presumption and what is its legal effect?

D. Some Further Reading

Rebecca Haw Allensworth, *The Commensurability Myth in Antitrust*, 69 Vand. L. Rev. 1 (2016)

Daniel A. Crane, *Rules Versus Standards in Antitrust Adjudication*, 64 Wash. & Lee L. Rev. 49 (2007)

Rocco J. De Grasse, Maricopa County *and the Problem of Per Se Characterization in Horizontal Price Fixing Cases*, 18 Val. U. L. Rev. 1007 (1984)

Herbert Hovenkamp, *The Rule of Reason*, 70 Fla. L. Rev. 81 (2018)

Sheldon Kimmel, *How and Why the Per Se Rule Against Price- Fixing Went Wrong*, 19 Sup. Ct. Econ. Rev. 1 (2011)

William E. Kovacic, *The Future Adaptation of the Per Se Rule of Illegality in U.S. Antitrust Law*, Col. Bus. L. Rev. 33 (2021)

Alan J. Meese, *In Praise of All or Nothing Dichotomous Categories: Why Antitrust Law Should Reject the Quick Look*, 104 Geo. L.J. 835 (2016)

Sanjukta Paul, *Antitrust as Allocator of Coordination Rights*, 67 U.C.L.A. L. Rev. 4 (2020)

Donald F. Turner, *The Definition of Agreement under the Sherman Act: Conscious Parallelism and Refusals to Deal*, 75 Harv. L. Rev. 655 (1962)

V. HORIZONTAL RESTRAINTS

A. Overview

Antitrust analysis generally divides agreements, and provisions in them that may restrain competition, into two categories: "horizontal" restraints among actual or potential competitors, and "vertical" restraints among parties at different levels of the same supply chain or suppliers of complements. Of these, horizontal restraints are much more likely to raise competitive concerns: businesses generally have more good reasons to enter into agreements with their trading partners than they do with their competitors! We will consider horizontal restraints in this chapter, and will turn to vertical restraints in Chapter VI.

The category of horizontal restraints includes a very broad spectrum of agreements and practices. At the most troubling end of this spectrum we find hardcore cartelization and equivalent practices, including price fixing, market allocation, and bid-rigging. As we saw in Chapter IV, a small set of nakedly anticompetitive practices are *per se* illegal in civil litigation: these may be subject to criminal punishment too. DOJ seeks and obtains extradition, criminal fines, and terms of imprisonment for conduct in this category. The classic formulation of the competitive concern with such agreements is that they harm competition—increasing prices and reducing output, quality, and innovation—but offer no redeeming public benefit in the vast majority of cases, making a flat ban appropriate and efficient. The imposition of criminal penalties, among other things, reflects an effort to offset the difficulties of detecting such agreements, which are typically kept secret by the participants. DOJ also operates a criminal "leniency" program, which provides businesses with significant protection from criminal and civil enforcement in exchange for informing on cartel activity and cooperating with prosecutors. We will turn to criminal enforcement (briefly) in Chapter XI.

Outside the zone of hardcore antitrust violations, horizontal practices and restraints may take almost any form, and may present almost any level of concern under the antitrust laws, from very mild to very considerable. These agreements come in all shapes and size, but you may encounter some or all of the following:

- **Standard-setting activities.** Groups of businesses, including competitors, may participate in so-called "standard setting" or "standards development" activities in order to establish technical and commercial standards for certain kinds of activity. This process may involve some government participation or it may be wholly private. There are countless standard setting organizations, large and small, in the national and global economy that design, promulgate, review, and amend standards for markets of all kinds.[322] Possible competitive concerns include worries that standard-setting may become a cloak for collusion (*e.g.*, competitors fixing prices or dividing markets) or a tool for exclusion (*e.g.*, manipulation, deception, or distortion of the standard setting process in a manner that may exclude competition, and wrongfully create or maintain market power). But standard setting can also offer tremendous procompetitive benefits, including the opportunity to spur innovation and investment in areas where the lack of a focal point might otherwise act as a deterrent, as well as the opportunity to promote valuable forms of interoperability.[323] Congress recognized the procompetitive benefits of standard setting in the Standards Development Organization Act of 2004, protecting participants from the threat of *per se* liability.[324] Standard setting activities are analyzed under the rule of reason. We will return to standard-setting in Chapter X.
- **Joint buying or selling arrangements.** Competing firms may aim to coordinate their selling or buying activities: for example, through a group purchasing organization. Such arrangements, even among competitors, may be benign, such as when they do not involve participants that individually or

---

[322] *See generally, e.g.*, Maureen K. Ohlhausen, *The Elusive Role of Competition In The Standard-Setting Antitrust Debate*, 20 Stan. Tech. L. Rev. 93 (2017); Mark A. Lemley, *Intellectual Property Rights and Standard-Setting Organizations*, 90 Calif. L. Rev. 1889 (2002)

[323] *See, e.g.*, Deborah Platt Majoras, *Recognizing the Procompetitive Potential of Royalty Discussions in Standard Setting* (remarks of Sept. 23, 2005).

[324] 15 U.S.C. § 4301 *et seq.* The Act excludes from its protection from per se liability exchanges of competitively sensitive information, market allocation, and price fixing. *Id.* at § 4301(c).

collectively hold market power, enable the participants to access efficiencies of scope and scale that would otherwise be unavailable, and are structured to avoid or minimize coordination on terms of dealing. But the potential competitive concerns are obvious: after all, a cartel is a form of "joint selling arrangement," and conduct that involves coordination with competitors on terms of trading raises evident hazards. Joint buying or selling may invite *per se* condemnation when it lacks arguable procompetitive benefits in the form of some economic integration among the participants, and particularly if the participants hold market power. Courts and agencies tend to apply the rule of reason to less nakedly harmful versions of such practices.

- **"Joint ventures."** You will often hear the term "joint venture" in the study of Section 1. This phrase is a vague catchall. It encompasses everything from informal and short-term projects of cooperation among separate businesses to the creation or merger of co-owned incorporated businesses[325]—and everything in between. Some joint ventures involve mergers or acquisitions that are subject to Section 7 of the Clayton Act. But any joint venture that involves an agreement is also subject to review under Section 1 of the Sherman Act, and in this chapter our focus will be on Section 1 analysis. Joint ventures are analyzed in a manner reflecting their economic structure and operation: in some cases, courts have condemned as *per se* illegal conduct that would be fairly described as a plausible joint venture,[326] in other cases, joint ventures are recognized as plainly procompetitive under the rule of reason.[327] However, in most modern cases, a venture will be analyzed under the rule of reason rather than the *per se* rule if it is reasonably related to the achievement of a procompetitive purpose.[328] You may remember from Chapter IV that an economically integrated joint venture may be a single enterprise for the purposes of antitrust analysis of its decisions, taking it outside the scope of Section 1, but the creation of the enterprise itself usually remains an agreement subject to antitrust challenge under Section 1.[329]

- **Trade associations and information sharing.** Antitrust lawyers often love to quote Adam Smith's aphoristic warning about trade associations.[330] But trade association activity is by no means all bad. It is ubiquitous in the economy, and it invariably involves competitors' employees meeting with one another, communicating about matters of interest, and undertaking joint projects. Certainly, this kind of contact can lead to illegal conduct like price-fixing, particularly when participants are imprudent (or poorly counseled!). But it can also lead to conduct that may violate the rule of reason (*e.g.*, anticompetitive sharing of competitively sensitive information), as well as plenty of conduct that is clearly procompetitive and lawful (*e.g.*, joint analysis of market conditions in a manner that does not harm competition and may improve it). Antitrust lawyers often play an important role in helping participants in trade associations stay on the right side of the line—and in dealing with the consequences if they do not!

- **Agreements involving IP.** Sometimes IP licenses or other agreements may involve actual or potential rivals. Licensing negotiations, a license agreement, or a settlement of an infringement claim may all have implications for competition between the parties. We will consider IP issues, and these concerns, in Chapter X.

Analytically, the appraisal of horizontal restraints typically involves two critical stages: first, determining the standard of legality that will govern the agreement (*per se* illegal, full rule of reason, or intermediate scrutiny such as "quick look"); second, applying that standard to determine whether the agreement is an unreasonable restraint.

---

[325] *See, e.g.*, Analysis of Agreement Containing Consent Order to Aid Public Comment, In the Matter of The Boeing Company, Lockheed Martin Corporation, and United Launch Alliance, FTC File No. 051-0165 (Oct. 3, 2006) (incorporated joint venture between Boeing and Lockheed Martin to offer space launch services).

[326] *See, e.g.*, United States v. Topco Associates, 405 U.S. 596 (1972) (cooperative buying and selling arrangement *per se* illegal); United States v. Sealy, Inc., 388 U.S. 350 (1967) (cooperative marketing and selling venture was *per se* illegal).

[327] *See, e.g.*, Toscano v. PGA Tour, Inc., 201 F. Supp. 2d 1106, 1123 (E.D. Cal. 2002).

[328] *See, e.g.*, Med. Ctr. at Elizabeth Place, LLC v. Atrium Health Sys., 922 F.3d 713, 728 (6th Cir. 2019) ("If the record in this case reveals a plausible way in which the challenged restraints contribute to the procompetitive efficiencies of the joint venture, then "the possibility of countervailing procompetitive effects" is not remote and per se treatment is improper.").

[329] *See supra* § IV.B.1.

[330] Adam Smith, 1 THE WEALTH OF NATIONS (1776) ("People of the same trade seldom meet together, even for merriment and diversion, but the conversation ends in a conspiracy against the public, or in some contrivance to raise prices.").

The antitrust agencies have issued a set of guidelines for competitor collaborations that provide some helpful guidance regarding the analysis of horizontal cooperation. Although these guidelines are not binding on courts, they helpfully summarize the ways in which agencies and courts tend to approach such practices, and are sometimes cited by courts in adjudicating such cases.[331] They also shed some helpful light on the agencies' views about the application of Section 1 to horizontal practices more generally.

U.S. Department of Justice and FTC, Antitrust Guidelines for Collaborations Among Competitors (2000)

Section 2: General Principles For Evaluating Agreements Among Competitors

2.1 Potential Procompetitive Benefits

[1] The Agencies recognize that consumers may benefit from competitor collaborations in a variety of ways. For example, a competitor collaboration may enable participants to offer goods or services that are cheaper, more valuable to consumers, or brought to market faster than would be possible absent the collaboration. A collaboration may allow its participants to better use existing assets, or may provide incentives for them to make output-enhancing investments that would not occur absent the collaboration. The potential efficiencies from competitor collaborations may be achieved through a variety of contractual arrangements including joint ventures, trade or professional associations, licensing arrangements, or strategic alliances.

[2] Efficiency gains from competitor collaborations often stem from combinations of different capabilities or resources. For example, one participant may have special technical expertise that usefully complements another participant's manufacturing process, allowing the latter participant to lower its production cost or improve the quality of its product. In other instances, a collaboration may facilitate the attainment of scale or scope economies beyond the reach of any single participant. For example, two firms may be able to combine their research or marketing activities to lower their cost of bringing their products to market, or reduce the time needed to develop and begin commercial sales of new products. Consumers may benefit from these collaborations as the participants are able to lower prices, improve quality, or bring new products to market faster.

2.2 Potential Anticompetitive Harms

[3] Competitor collaborations may harm competition and consumers by increasing the ability or incentive profitably to raise price above or reduce output, quality, service, or innovation below what likely would prevail in the absence of the relevant agreement. Such effects may arise through a variety of mechanisms. Among other things, agreements may limit independent decision making or combine the control of or financial interests in production, key assets, or decisions regarding price, output, or other competitively sensitive variables, or may otherwise reduce the participants' ability or incentive to compete independently.

[4] Competitor collaborations also may facilitate explicit or tacit collusion through facilitating practices such as the exchange or disclosure of competitively sensitive information or through increased market concentration. Such collusion may involve the relevant market in which the collaboration operates or another market in which the participants in the collaboration are actual or potential competitors.

2.3 Analysis of the Overall Collaboration and the Agreements of Which It Consists

[5] A competitor collaboration comprises a set of one or more agreements, other than merger agreements, between or among competitors to engage in economic activity, and the economic activity resulting therefrom. In general, the Agencies assess the competitive effects of the overall collaboration and any individual agreement or set of agreements within the collaboration that may harm competition. For purposes of these Guidelines, the phrase "relevant agreement" refers to whichever of these three—the overall collaboration, an individual agreement, or a set of agreements—the evaluating Agency is assessing. Two or more agreements are assessed together if their

---

[331] *See, e.g.*, Impax Labs., Inc. v. FTC, 994 F.3d 484, 496 (5th Cir. 2021); Viamedia, Inc. v. Comcast Corp., 951 F.3d 429, 478 (7th Cir. 2020); Med. Ctr. at Elizabeth Place, LLC v. Atrium Health Sys., 922 F.3d 713, 726 (6th Cir. 2019).

procompetitive benefits or anticompetitive harms are so intertwined that they cannot meaningfully be isolated and attributed to any individual agreement. . . .

2.4 Competitive Effects Are Assessed as of the Time of Possible Harm to Competition

[6] The competitive effects of a relevant agreement may change over time, depending on changes in circumstances such as internal reorganization, adoption of new agreements as part of the collaboration, addition or departure of participants, new market conditions, or changes in market share. The Agencies assess the competitive effects of a relevant agreement as of the time of possible harm to competition, whether at formation of the collaboration or at a later time, as appropriate. . . . However, an assessment after a collaboration has been formed is sensitive to the reasonable expectations of participants whose significant sunk cost investments in reliance on the relevant agreement were made before it became anticompetitive.

Section 3: Analytical Framework For Evaluating Agreements Among Competitors

3.1 Introduction

[7] Section 3 sets forth the analytical framework that the Agencies use to evaluate the competitive effects of a competitor collaboration and the agreements of which it consists. Certain types of agreements are so likely to be harmful to competition and to have no significant benefits that they do not warrant the time and expense required for particularized inquiry into their effects. Once identified, such agreements are challenged as per se illegal.

[8] Agreements not challenged as per se illegal are analyzed under the rule of reason. Rule of reason analysis focuses on the state of competition with, as compared to without, the relevant agreement. Under the rule of reason, the central question is whether the relevant agreement likely harms competition by increasing the ability or incentive profitably to raise price above or reduce output, quality, service, or innovation below what likely would prevail in the absence of the relevant agreement. Given the great variety of competitor collaborations, rule of reason analysis entails a flexible inquiry and varies in focus and detail depending on the nature of the agreement and market circumstances. Rule of reason analysis focuses on only those factors, and undertakes only the degree of factual inquiry, necessary to assess accurately the overall competitive effect of the relevant agreement.

3.2 Agreements Challenged as Per Se Illegal

[9] Agreements of a type that always or almost always tends to raise price or reduce output are per se illegal. The Agencies challenge such agreements, once identified, as per se illegal. Typically these are agreements not to compete on price or output. Types of agreements that have been held per se illegal include agreements among competitors to fix prices or output, rig bids, or share or divide markets by allocating customers, suppliers, territories or lines of commerce. The courts conclusively presume such agreements, once identified, to be illegal, without inquiring into their claimed business purposes, anticompetitive harms, procompetitive benefits, or overall competitive effects. The Department of Justice prosecutes participants in hard-core cartel agreements criminally.

[10] If, however, participants in an efficiency-enhancing integration of economic activity enter into an agreement that is reasonably related to the integration and reasonably necessary to achieve its procompetitive benefits, the Agencies analyze the agreement under the rule of reason, even if it is of a type that might otherwise be considered per se illegal. . . . In an efficiency enhancing integration, participants collaborate to perform or cause to be performed (by a joint venture entity created by the collaboration or by one or more participants or by a third party acting on behalf of other participants) one or more business functions, such as production, distribution, marketing, purchasing or R&D, and thereby benefit, or potentially benefit, consumers by expanding output, reducing price, or enhancing quality, service, or innovation. Participants in an efficiency-enhancing integration typically combine, by contract or otherwise, significant capital, technology, or other complementary assets to achieve procompetitive benefits that the participants could not achieve separately. The mere coordination of decisions on price, output, customers, territories, and the like is not integration, and cost savings without integration are not a basis for avoiding per se condemnation. The integration must be of a type that plausibly would generate procompetitive benefits cognizable under the [agencies' approach to] efficiencies analysis . . . . Such procompetitive benefits may enhance the participants' ability or incentives to compete and thus may offset an agreement's anticompetitive tendencies. . . .

[11] An agreement may be "reasonably necessary" without being essential. However, if the participants could achieve an equivalent or comparable efficiency-enhancing integration through practical, significantly less restrictive means, then the Agencies conclude that the agreement is not reasonably necessary. In making this assessment, except in unusual circumstances, the Agencies consider whether practical, significantly less restrictive means were reasonably available when the agreement was entered into, but do not search for a theoretically less restrictive alternative that was not practical given the business realities.

[12] Before accepting a claim that an agreement is reasonably necessary to achieve procompetitive benefits from an integration of economic activity, the Agencies undertake a limited factual inquiry to evaluate the claim. Such an inquiry may reveal that efficiencies from an agreement that are possible in theory are not plausible in the context of the particular collaboration. Some claims such as those premised on the notion that competition itself is unreasonable – are insufficient as a matter of law, and others may be implausible on their face. In any case, labeling an arrangement a "joint venture" will not protect what is merely a device to raise price or restrict output; the nature of the conduct, not its designation, is determinative.

3.3 Agreements Analyzed under the Rule of Reason

[13] Agreements not challenged as per se illegal are analyzed under the rule of reason to determine their overall competitive effect. Rule of reason analysis focuses on the state of competition with, as compared to without, the relevant agreement. The central question is whether the relevant agreement likely harms competition by increasing the ability or incentive profitably to raise price above or reduce output, quality, service, or innovation below what likely would prevail in the absence of the relevant agreement.

[14] Rule of reason analysis entails a flexible inquiry and varies in focus and detail depending on the nature of the agreement and market circumstances. The Agencies focus on only those factors, and undertake only that factual inquiry, necessary to make a sound determination of the overall competitive effect of the relevant agreement. Ordinarily, however, no one factor is dispositive in the analysis.

[15] Under the rule of reason, the Agencies' analysis begins with an examination of the nature of the relevant agreement, since the nature of the agreement determines the types of anticompetitive harms that may be of concern. As part of this examination, the Agencies ask about the business purpose of the agreement and examine whether the agreement, if already in operation, has caused anticompetitive harm. If the nature of the agreement and the absence of market power[26] together demonstrate the absence of anticompetitive harm, the Agencies do not challenge the agreement. . . . Alternatively, where the likelihood of anticompetitive harm is evident from the nature of the agreement, or anticompetitive harm has resulted from an agreement already in operation, then, absent overriding benefits that could offset the anticompetitive harm, the Agencies challenge such agreements without a detailed market analysis.

[16] If the initial examination of the nature of the agreement indicates possible competitive concerns, but the agreement is not one that would be challenged without a detailed market analysis, the Agencies analyze the agreement in greater depth. The Agencies typically define relevant markets and calculate market shares and concentration as an initial step in assessing whether the agreement may create or increase market power or facilitate its exercise and thus poses risks to competition. The Agencies examine factors relevant to the extent to which the participants and the collaboration have the ability and incentive to compete independently, such as whether an agreement is exclusive or non-exclusive and its duration. The Agencies also evaluate whether entry would be timely, likely, and sufficient to deter or counteract any anticompetitive harms. In addition, the Agencies assess any other market circumstances that may foster or impede anticompetitive harms.

[17] If the examination of these factors indicates no potential for anticompetitive harm, the Agencies end the investigation without considering procompetitive benefits. If investigation indicates anticompetitive harm, the

---

[26] That market power is absent may be determined without defining a relevant market. For example, if no market power is likely under any plausible market definition, it does not matter which one is correct. Alternatively, easy entry may indicate an absence of market power.

Agencies examine whether the relevant agreement is reasonably necessary to achieve procompetitive benefits that likely would offset anticompetitive harms.

3.31 Nature of the Relevant Agreement: Business Purpose, Operation in the Marketplace and Possible Competitive Concerns

[18] The nature of the agreement is relevant to whether it may cause anticompetitive harm. For example, by limiting independent decision making or combining control over or financial interests in production, key assets, or decisions on price, output, or other competitively sensitive variables, an agreement may create or increase market power or facilitate its exercise by the collaboration, its participants, or both. An agreement to limit independent decision making or to combine control or financial interests may reduce the ability or incentive to compete independently. An agreement also may increase the likelihood of an exercise of market power by facilitating explicit or tacit collusion, either through facilitating practices such as an exchange of competitively sensitive information or through increased market concentration.

[19] In examining the nature of the relevant agreement, the Agencies take into account inferences about business purposes for the agreement that can be drawn from objective facts. The Agencies also consider evidence of the subjective intent of the participants to the extent that it sheds light on competitive effects. The Agencies do not undertake a full analysis of procompetitive benefits . . . , however, unless an anticompetitive harm appears likely. The Agencies also examine whether an agreement already in operation has caused anticompetitive harm. Anticompetitive harm may be observed, for example, if a competitor collaboration successfully mandates new, anticompetitive conduct or successfully eliminates procompetitive pre-collaboration conduct, such as withholding services that were desired by consumers when offered in a competitive market. If anticompetitive harm is found, examination of market power ordinarily is not required. In some cases, however, a determination of anticompetitive harm may be informed by consideration of market power.

* * *

In the rest of this chapter, we will explore some issues specific to the classification and evaluation of horizontal restraints. In Section B we will encounter some *per se* unlawful restraints that go beyond simple price-fixing cartels, including wage-fixing agreements, bid-rigging practices, hub-and-spoke conspiracies, and group boycotts. In Section C we will focus on the border between the *per se* rule and the rule of reason, and investigate how courts and agencies classify horizontal restraints on that boundary. In Section D we will focus on the border between rule of reason and intermediate (or "quick look") scrutiny, and the standards that courts have applied to determine when a horizontal restraint merits elevated skepticism rather than open-minded rule-of-reason review.

B. *Per Se* Unlawful Collusion—Beyond Price Fixing

The classic case of *per se* illegality is the simple price-fixing cartel, as we saw in Chapter IV.[332] Although the *per se* zone is fairly narrow, it covers more than just literal price fixing, as the extract from the Competitor Collaboration Guidelines above suggests. Any naked coordination on terms of dealing among competitors—*i.e.*, coordination unrelated to a genuine procompetitive purpose or an economic integration among the participants—may invite *per se* treatment by courts. This may include coordination among buyers as well as among sellers; coordination on output and quality as well as on price; and agreements to divide markets or rig bids.

1. Price Fixing, Buyers' Cartels, and Wage Fixing

The naked price-fixing cartel is the clearest imaginable violation of the antitrust laws. The core insight underpinning a cartel is that, if the participants can collectively exercise market power by coordinating to raise prices or reduce output, without attracting entry or expansion, it may be possible to move market supply and demand toward monopoly levels and to split the resulting monopoly profits. In order to achieve this goal, a cartel must coordinate the pricing and output decisions of its members to avoid "cheating" (*i.e.*, individual cartelists lowering their own price or increasing their own output in an effort to win share), and must have some reason to

---

[332] *See, e.g.*, United States v. Trenton Potteries Co., 273 U.S. 392 (1927); *see generally supra* § IV.C.1.

believe that other actors—including existing competitors and potential entrants—will not be able to defeat the cartel by expanding their capacity and/or lowering their price.

But antitrust doctrine punishes cartel agreements—and all "naked" agreements not to compete—regardless of their success or economic effects. As we saw in the previous chapter, the underlying idea is that naked collusion (that is, collusion not related to any procompetitive purpose) is so reliably harmful that the socially optimal rule is a flat ban. (Procompetitive justifications for a particular cartel are as irrelevant in criminal cases as in civil ones.[333]) Even this ban, however, is subject to a small number of narrow exceptions and immunities—such as the immunity for labor unions—that we will discuss in Chapter IX.

This rule of automatic illegality places tremendous load on two distinctions in the law of Section 1. The first is the distinction between the treatment of price-fixing "cartels," which are *per se* illegal and criminally prosecuted, and the treatment of tacit collusion without an agreement, which is *per se* legal. That distinction turns on whether there is an *agreement* among the parties to coordinate their conduct: and, as we saw in Chapter IV, defining and proving an agreement can be harder than it sounds. But the distinction is utterly critical. In the 1980s, the FTC tried to work around Section 1's agreement criterion by leaning on the broad language of Section 5 of the FTC Act, which prohibits "unfair methods of competition," to challenge tacit collusion. But the Second Circuit shot the effort down, re-affirming the rule that "[t]he mere existence of an oligopolistic market structure in which a small group of manufacturers engage in consciously parallel pricing of an identical product does not violate the antitrust laws."[334] (The FTC has been successful, however, in establishing the principle that a unilateral *invitation* to fix price violates Section 5.[335] Why do you think this effort has been successful when challenges to tacit collusion have not been? We will talk more about Section 5 of the FTC Act in Chapter XI.)

The second is the distinction between "naked" collusion, which is unrelated to any procompetitive purpose, and coordination that is related (or "ancillary") to a broader procompetitive purpose or economic integration among the participants. This distinction—usually dated to then-Judge Taft's decision in *Addyston Pipe*[336]—turns on whether the parties are merely eliminating competition between themselves in some way, or by contrast are attempting to pursue some broader procompetitive enterprise. As we saw in Chapter IV, agreements in the first category are *per se* illegal while those in the second are judged under the rule of reason. Figuring out whether an activity should be treated as an illegal cartel or as a legitimate joint endeavor has often challenged the courts: we will meet some of these cases in Section C below.

The hardcore cartels that are often described as the "supreme evil" of antitrust involve both an agreement and a resulting naked restraint on competition.[337] Examples in recent memory include:

- **Auto parts.** A "supercartel" involving dozens of overlapping price-fixing and bid-rigging agreements, a vast network of auto-parts cartels was the subject of intensive prosecution by multiple international antitrust enforcers over about a decade from 2008 onward, resulting in the imposition of billions of dollars in penalties and fines, charges against dozens of companies, and indictments of many executives.[338]

---

[333] *See, e.g.*, United States v. Aiyer, 33 F.4th 97 (2d Cir. 2022) (holding that it "would have been legal error" to consider claimed procompetitive justifications for price-fixing, "absent a properly asserted exception to the *per se* rule").

[334] E.I. du Pont de Nemours & Co. v. FTC, 729 F.2d 128, 139 (2d Cir. 1984).

[335] *See, e.g.*, Analysis to Aid Public Comment, In the Matter of Fortiline, LLC, File No. 151-0000 (F.T.C. Aug. 9, 2016); Analysis to Aid Public Comment, In the Matter of U-Haul Int'l, Inc., File No. 081-0157 (F.T.C. June 9, 2010).

[336] United States v. Addyston Pipe & Steel Co., 85 F. 271, 282–84 (6th Cir. 1898) (distinguishing restrictive agreements that have "no main lawful purpose" and of which "the sole object is to restrain trade" from those that are "merely ancillary to the main purpose of a lawful contract, and necessary to protect the covenantee in the full enjoyment of the legitimate fruits of the contract, or to protect him from the dangers of an unjust use of those fruits by the other party").

[337] Verizon Communications Inc. v. Law Offices of Curtis V. Trinko, LLP, 540 U.S. 398, 408 (2004).

[338] John M. Connor, *Twilight of Prosecutions of the Global Auto-Parts Cartels*, American Antitrust Institute Working Paper (July 17, 2019); Sharis A. Pozen, U.S. Dept. of Justice, *Briefing on Department's Enforcement Action in Auto Parts Industry* (remarks of Jan. 30, 2012).

- **Capacitors.** A major cartel of electrolytic capacitor manufacturers that operated between 1998 and 2012 has been the subject of significant penalties (amounting to hundreds of millions of dollars, in addition to U.S. criminal sanctions) in Europe and the United States.[339]
- **Lysine.** In a rare overlap between the world of antitrust and the world of Matt Damon, the blockbuster detection and prosecution of the lysine cartel is the subject of the 2009 movie *The Informant*, based on Kurt Eichenwald's book of the same name. The cartel, which involved suppliers of lysine, an additive to animal feed, included participants in the United States, Japan, and Korea, and led to prison time for multiple executives.[340] It is regarded as a watershed moment in modern cartel policy, and kicked off an era of increased criminal antitrust enforcement.

The following remarks of a senior DOJ official give a window into the life of the lysine cartel.

Scott D. Hammond, Caught in the Act: Inside an International Cartel
(Remarks of Oct. 18, 2005)

[1] Today you will experience the sensation of being a fly on the wall, watching as a crime is being committed. Actually, to be precise, you will be looking through the lens of a hidden camera, and the view is not from the wall but rather from a lamp tucked away in the corner of the room. However, the effect is still the same—these tapes will put you in the smoke-filled rooms with the members of an international price-fixing cartel as they formulate, agree upon, attempt to conceal, and carry out their conspiracy.

[2] The undercover audio and video tapes that you will see today were recorded by U.S. Federal Bureau of Investigation (FBI) agents with the help of a cooperating witness. The tapes capture an international cartel in the act of fixing prices and carving up the worldwide market for the feed additive, lysine, a product used by farmers around the world. Worldwide sales of lysine were over $600 million annually. The tapes reveal how the world's major lysine producers were able to secretly meet at trade association meetings around the world and agree on the exact tonnage each of them would produce and sell the next year, and then fix the price of it down to the penny in the United States and countries around the world, effective the very next day.

[3] One of the characteristics we see over and over again in international cartels is the brazen or lawless nature of the conspiracies. By that, I refer to the contempt and disregard that the members of the cartel typically have for antitrust laws and enforcement. I think this is a good place to begin because we are sometimes asked by defense counsel to treat a certain member of a cartel more favorably because he/she resides in a country where cartel activity is treated differently than it is in the United States. The fundamental problem with this argument is that it is our experience, without exception, that the conspirators are fully aware that they are violating the law in the United States and elsewhere, and their only concern is avoiding detection. The international cartels that we have cracked have not involved international business persons who for cultural, linguistic, or some other innocent reason find themselves mistakenly engaged in a violation of U.S. antitrust laws. Rather, the cartels that we have prosecuted criminally have invariably involved hard core cartel activity—price-fixing, bid-rigging, and market and customer-allocation agreements. The conspirators have discussed the criminal nature of their agreements; they have discussed the need to avoid detection by antitrust enforcers in the United States and abroad; and they have gone to great lengths to cover-up their actions—such as using code names with one another, meeting in secret venues around the world, creating false "covers"—i.e. facially legal justifications—for their meetings, using home phone numbers to contact one another, and giving explicit instructions to destroy any evidence of the conspiracy. Moreover, the cartels typically involve senior executives at firms—executives who have received extensive antitrust compliance counseling, and who often have significant responsibilities in the firm's antitrust compliance programs.

[4] The first tape segment captures this lawlessness and the contempt that the members of the cartel have for law enforcement and their victims. The meeting that you are about to see was attended by executives from the world's

---

[339] European Commission, Press Release, Antitrust: Commission fines eight producers of capacitors €254 million for participating in cartel (Mar. 21, 2018); U.S. Dept. of Justice, Press Release, Leading Electrolytic Capacitor Manufacturer Ordered to Pay $60 Million Criminal Fine for Price Fixing (Oct. 3, 2018).

[340] *See, e.g.*, Kurt Eichenwald, *The Tale of the Secret Tapes*, N.Y. TIMES (Nov. 16, 1997); U.S. Dept. of Justice, Press Release, Former Top ADM Executives, Japanese Executive, Indicted in Lysine Price Fixing Conspiracy (Dec. 3, 1996).

five dominant lysine producers. As you will see in this tape, the cartel members took steps to conceal their meeting, including staggering their arrival and departure times for the meeting so as not to arouse suspicion by having the entire group enter and leave the room at the same time. The members of the cartel had to be careful because the meeting coincided with the largest poultry industry trade association convention, so all of their customers were in town for the trade show. But, as you will see, the lysine executives laughed at the thought of being observed by their customers or by law enforcement. The videotaped recording of this meeting shows that, as the meeting begins, there are some empty seats around the table because of the staggered arrival times. The cartel members are captured on tape jokingly discussing who will fill those empty seats. One cartel member offered that one empty chair was for Tyson Foods, the largest purchaser of lysine in the United States, and that another chair was for ConAgra Foods, also a large U.S. customer. Another cartel member mocked, ironically, that one chair was for the FBI, and a third cartel executive added that the remaining chairs were for the Federal Trade Commission.

{*Eds.: a transcript of the clip played here is available at https://www.justice.gov/atr/tab-1-cartel-members-show-disdain-customers-and-antitrust-enforcement.*}

[5] The knock at the door heard at the very end of this tape segment, in fact, was an FBI agent, disguised as a hotel employee returning to the cooperating witness the briefcase containing a hidden audio recorder he had mistakenly left in the hotel restaurant. [. . .]

[6] While cartel members know full well that their conduct is illegal under the antitrust laws of many countries, they often have a particular fear of detection and prosecution by U.S. antitrust authorities resulting in jail sentences. Shortly after this investigation became public in 1995 and cartel members realized that the FBI might be watching, we learned from cooperating defendants in several investigations that the cartels changed their practices in order to avoid having meetings or calls in the United States and tried, where possible, to exclude the participation of U.S. personnel in the conspiracies. These same cartels continued to target U.S. businesses and consumers, but the meetings, the calls, the documents, and the participants largely resided safely overseas, or so they thought. This next segment demonstrates the initial reluctance of one of the foreign cartel members in the lysine conspiracy to conduct cartel activity in the United States for fear of detection. The conversation is between an ADM executive, who also was a cooperating witness, and an executive at the Japanese firm, Ajinomoto. They are discussing the location for the next cartel meeting. As you will hear, the Ajinomoto executive is clearly reluctant to have a cartel meeting in Hawaii, but ultimately agrees to consider it because Hawaii is a convenient location for everyone and because of the lure of the golf courses located near the meeting site. The Ajinomoto executive's reluctance was well founded, as the meeting was video taped by the FBI and became a critical piece of evidence in the prosecution of the lysine conspirators.

{*Eds.: a transcript of the clip played here is available at https://www.justice.gov/atr/tab-2-foreign-co-conspirator-expresses-reluctance-meet-united-states.*}

[7] Another characteristic of international cartels is that they frequently use trade associations as a means of providing "cover" for their cartel activities. In order to avoid arousing suspicion about the meetings they attended, the lysine conspirators actually created an amino acid working group or subcommittee of the European Feed Additives Association, a legitimate trade group. The sole purpose of the new subcommittee was to provide a false, but facially legitimate, explanation as to why they were meeting. [. . .]

{*Eds.: a transcript of the clip played here is available at https://www.justice.gov/atr/tab-3-cartel-members-use-trade-association-cover-conspiracy-meetings.*}

[8] Many cartels recognize that price-fixing schemes are more effective if the cartel also allocates sales volume among the firms. For example, the lysine, vitamin, graphite electrode, and citric acid cartels prosecuted by the Division all utilized volume-allocation agreements in conjunction with their price-fixing agreements. Cartel members typically meet to determine how much each producer has sold during the preceding year and to calculate the total market size. Next, the cartel members estimate the market growth for the upcoming year and allocate that growth among themselves. The volume-allocation agreement then becomes the basis for (1) an annual "budget" for the cartel, (2) a reporting and auditing function, and (3) a compensation scheme—three more common characteristics of international cartels.

[9] In this next tape segment, you will see the lysine cartel members divide up the world's lysine market. The meeting was attended by two high-ranking ADM executives. Representing all of the Japanese and Korean cartel members were two senior executives from Ajinomoto. Earlier in the meeting, the cartel members had determined how much each producer had sold in the prior year. Then, they used those figures to determine the total market size. Next, they estimated what they believed the sales growth would be in the coming year. All of these figures were written down on the easel board by one of the cartel members. On the tape, you'll see them decide how they are going to allocate that sales growth among the five cartel members. As you will hear, the growth in the market is estimated to be 14,000 tons, and the question posed by the senior ADM executive is: how do we divide this market growth? [. . .]

[10] Another common feature of international cartels is the use of a compensation scheme to discourage cheating. The compensation scheme used by the lysine cartel worked as follows. Any firm that had sold more than its allocated or budgeted share of the market at the end of the calendar year would compensate the firm or firms that were under budget by purchasing that quantity of lysine from any under-budget firms. This compensation agreement reduced the incentive to cheat on the sales volume-allocation agreement by selling additional product, which, of course, also reduced the incentive to cheat on the price-fixing agreement by lowering the price on the volume allocated to each conspirator firm.

[11] In this next segment, one of the lysine conspirators from ADM explains the importance of a compensation scheme to the cartel and gives the other cartel members a motivational speech that has to be one of the best pieces of evidence ever obtained in a cartel investigation. {*Eds.: this speech can be found here https://www.justice.gov/atr/tab-6-co-conspirator-explains-how-end-year-compensation-scheme-eliminates-incentive-cheat-cartel .*} [. . .]

[12] These tapes demonstrate the awesome power of cartels to rip-off businesses and consumers. Unbeknownst to their customers, five executives sitting in a hotel room can raise and fix prices around the world effective the very next day. International cartels, like the one involving vitamins, can operate profitably for a decade or more wholly undetected. The fact is that the obstacles to cracking cartels are huge. These are sophisticated, premeditated crimes committed by highly-educated individuals in absolute secrecy. In most cases, there will be no smoking guns left around and no cameras hidden in the lamps to capture the moment. Today's workshop will examine effective strategies for fighting cartels, but their successful deployment in a particular jurisdiction depends in large part on how seriously the jurisdiction views the threat posed by cartels to its economy. I hope that viewing these tapes has set the stage for today's program by making the case that hardcore cartel offenses deserve to be treated as crimes and that, wherever possible, competition authorities and public prosecutors must work closely together to prosecute these harmful offenses.

[13] The three U.S. executives representing ADM at the meetings—defendants Andreas, Wilson, and Whitacre—were convicted by a jury of violating the Sherman Antitrust Act and were sentenced to lengthy terms of imprisonment. The investigation also resulted in the conviction of all of the world's major lysine producers -- including one U.S. company, two Japanese companies, and two Korean companies. All of the producers pled guilty before trial and received substantial fines, including what was then a record-breaking $100 million fine imposed on ADM. Two Japanese executives and a Korean executive also agreed to plead guilty and cooperate after the search warrants were executed in the investigation, and they paid heavy individual fines. The lysine investigation eventually led the Division to evidence that exposed additional worldwide cartels operating in other chemical markets, including citric acid, sodium gluconate, sodium erythorbate, and maltol. In all, 10 companies and 11 individuals from 7 different countries were convicted and paid over $225 million in criminal fines (in the United States alone) as a result of the these five inter-connected investigations.

* * *

The classic cartel, like the lysine cartel itself, involves sellers of a product or service. But a cartel of buyers that agree on purchase prices is every bit as unlawful as a cartel of sellers that agree on sale prices.[341] And in the absence

---

[341] *See, e.g.*, Mandeville Island Farms v. American Crystal Sugar Co., 334 U.S. 219, 235 (1948) ("It is clear that the agreement is the sort of combination condemned by the Act, even though the price-fixing was by purchasers, and the persons specially injured under the treble damage claim are sellers, not customers or consumers."); Vogel v. Am. Soc. of Appraisers, 744 F.2d 598, 601 (7th Cir.

of an applicable antitrust exemption, the rule against naked collusion applies just as strongly in labor markets as in any others.[342] Putting these two propositions together suggests that wage-fixing by employers, like price-fixing by suppliers, is *per se* illegal.

In 2021 DOJ put this proposition to the test, prosecuting employers of physical therapy professionals for fixing wages. Although the defendants were ultimately acquitted of violating the law, the district court emphatically confirmed the *per se* illegality of wage fixing in the following passage.

United States v. Jindal
Case No. 4:20-CR-358, 2021 WL 5578687 (E.D. Tex. Nov. 29, 2021)

Judge Mazzant.

[1] For over 100 years, the Supreme Court has consistently held that price-fixing agreements are unlawful *per se* under the Sherman Act. In fact, the Supreme Court has stated that no antitrust offense is more pernicious than price fixing. Defendants do not dispute that the Supreme Court has designated price fixing as a per se Sherman Act violation. But Defendants do dispute that the Indictment in-fact alleges a price-fixing agreement.

[2] The core of Defendants' argument is that the Indictment does not allege a price-fixing agreement because it at most alleges an agreement to fix wages. . . . Defendants argue that the Indictment does not allege any agreement to fix prices because wages do not fall within the definition of price fixing, which is defined as fixing the price of a. commodity. Further, according to Defendants, merely substituting the word "prices" for "wages" does not transform the factual allegations from alleging a wage-fixing agreement to alleging a price-fixing agreement. But Defendants' narrow view of horizontal price-fixing agreements reveals the flaw in their arguments.

[3] The scope of conduct found to constitute horizontal price-fixing agreements warranting application of the per se rule is broad. For example, courts have applied the per se rule to price-fixing agreements: 1) establishing minimum prices, 2) setting maximum prices, 3) fixing credit terms, 4) setting fee schedules, 5) purchasing surplus product to keep it off the market, 6) refusing to advertise prices, and 7) excluding purchasers unless they increased the price they paid for a service. Thus, contrary to Defendants' argument, "price fixing" has not been limited to conduct that literally directly fixes the price of a commodity. Instead, as the above cases and many more have recognized, the definition of horizontal price-fixing agreements cuts broadly. As such, any naked agreement among competitors—whether by sellers or buyers—that fixes components that affect price meets the definition of a horizontal price-fixing agreement.

[4] The Court recognizes that the facts of this case do not present those typical of a price-fixing agreement. For example, the classic horizontal price-fixing scheme involves an agreement among sellers to fix the prices of goods they sell. But just because the typical price-fixing conspiracy involves certain hallmarks does not mean that other less prevalent forms of price-fixing agreements are not likewise unlawful. Indeed, Courts have not limited price-fixing conspiracies to agreements concerning the purchase and sale of goods but have found them to cover the purchase and sale of services. More importantly, courts have also not only found price-fixing agreements among sellers, but also among buyers. In sum, price-fixing agreements come in many forms and include agreements among competing buyers of services.

[5] The Supreme Court has made clear that the Sherman Act applies equally to all industries and markets—to sellers and buyers, to goods and services, and consequently to buyers of services—otherwise known as employers in the labor market. . . . .

[6] With these principles in mind, the Court turns to the Indictment to determine if it alleges a price-fixing agreement that is per se illegal. The Indictment alleges that Jindal, Rodgers, and co-conspirators knowingly entered into and engaged in a conspiracy to suppress competition by agreeing to fix prices by lowering the pay rates to [physical therapists and physical therapy assistants ("PTs" and "PTAs")]. The Indictment thus alleges a

---

1984) ("[B]uyer cartels, the object of which is to force the prices that suppliers charge the members of the cartel below the competitive level, are illegal per se."); Nat'l Macaroni Mfrs. Ass'n v. FTC, 345 F.2d 421 (7th Cir. 1965).

[342] *See infra* Chapter X (describing labor exemptions).

naked price-fixing conspiracy among buyers in the labor market to fix the pay rates of the PTs and PTAs. As such, the Indictment describes a price-fixing conspiracy that is per se unlawful. . . . Accordingly, the Indictment sufficiently alleges a price-fixing conspiracy that warrants the per se rule.

[7] Defendants do not dispute that price-fixing agreements are per se illegal; they do, however, challenge how the Government labeled the offense and whether the charged conduct constitutes a per se offense. But, contrary to Defendants' argument, whether the Indictment refers to the "pay rates" of the PTs and PTAs as "prices" or "wages" does not affect the outcome. The antitrust laws fully apply to the labor markets, and price-fixing agreements among buyers—like therapist staffing companies—are prohibited by the Sherman Act. At bottom, the alleged agreement between Defendants and co-conspirators had the purpose and effect of fixing the pay rates of the PTs and PTAs—the price of labor.

[8] When the price of labor is lowered, or wages are suppressed, fewer people take jobs, which always or almost always tend[s] to restrict competition and decrease output. This type of agreement is plainly anticompetitive and has no purpose except stifling competition. [. . .]

[9] The Indictment charges Defendants with price fixing. For more than 100 years, courts have repeatedly held price fixing as per se illegal under the Sherman Act. Thus, Defendants could not have had any reasonable doubt that any price-fixing agreement was per se illegal. Defendants do not dispute this conclusion and instead insist that the novel construction of the statute to construe wage fixing as per se unlawful fails to give fair warning of the prohibited conduct. But this argument relies on the same semantical arguments this Court already rejected.

[10] Regardless of whether the Indictment characterizes Defendants' conduct as wage fixing or price fixing, the Sherman Act, in conjunction with the decades of case law, made it reasonably clear that Defendants' conduct was unlawful. Indeed, most criminal statutes deal with untold and unforeseen variations in factual situations, so no more than a reasonable degree of certainty can be demanded. Belaboring the point discussed in Part I, the Supreme Court has long recognized that price-fixing agreements come in many forms. And the Supreme Court has long recognized that § 1 categorically prohibits per se unlawful restraints across all markets and industries— including restraints on the buyer side and in the labor market. Thus, decades of precedent gave Defendants more than sufficient notice that agreements among competitors to fix the price of labor are per se illegal. Moreover, the numerous district court decisions holding that agreements to fix the compensation of employees are per se unlawful reinforce this conclusion. At a minimum, these decisions foreclose Defendants' argument because it cannot be said that no prior judicial decision has fairly disclosed Defendants' conduct to be within the scope of the Sherman Act.

[11] Moreover, the holding today is not a "novel" construction of the Sherman Act—it comports with previous broad interpretations of the Act and is a logical application of precedent. Similarly, that no court has found that purported wage-fixing agreements constitute criminal conduct under the Sherman Act does not mean that Defendants' did not have fair notice. Rather, the lack of criminal judicial decisions only indicates Defendants' unlucky status as the first two individuals that the Government has prosecuted for this type of conduct before.

[12] But, to find unfair notice whenever a court specified new types of acts to which a criminal statute applied would stifle courts' ability to interpret and fairly apply criminal statutes. Rather, . . . lack of prior court interpretations fundamentally similar to the case in question does not create unfair notice. Instead, so long as the prior decisions gave reasonable warning that the conduct was unlawful, then fair notice was satisfied. And, here, decades of judicial interpretations gave Defendants more than reasonably clear notice that their conduct was unlawful.

[13] [E]ven accepting Defendants' argument that their conduct was not literally price fixing, Defendants were still on notice that their conduct was perilously close to a line that subjected them to criminal prosecution. Thus, Defendants received fair notice that their conduct was illegal.

NOTES

1) Suppose that you organize a group of consumers to boycott a store whose prices you feel are too high, or whose products are not safe enough. Is that a *per se* illegal—and potentially criminal—violation of Section 1?

2) As we saw in Chapter II, a buyers' cartel that exercises monopsony power can reduce purchase prices to infracompetitive levels, which in turn reduces output in the upstream market. But it might also lower the costs of the cartel participants, including in ways that might be passed on (at least to some extent) to consumers. Does this fact suggest that *per se* treatment is inappropriate?

3) Do you think a buyers' cartel should be treated more leniently if it is facing sellers with market or monopoly power, or who may be themselves engaging in unlawful conduct?

4) In 2010, DOJ settled with six tech companies for agreeing not to approach each others' employees with job offers.[343] What standard should apply to such an agreement in litigation? Why do you think DOJ settled?

5) Why do you think the prosecution of wage-fixing cartels has not been a prominent theme in the history of antitrust enforcement?

2. Bid Rigging and Market Division

The *per se* rule is not limited to literal fixing of sale and purchase prices. Naked agreements among competitors to simply refrain from competition with one another are equally unlawful. Two common ways in which this might be done are through the division or allocation of markets (in which the participants effectively agree to stay out of each other's way) and through the rigging of bids (in which the participants collusively pre-bake the operation and outcome of a competitive tender or bidding process). Such practices are *per se* illegal, just like the simple fixing of sale and purchase prices, and may be the subject of criminal enforcement attention.

In *Palmer*, for example, rather than fixing their prices, two bar-review prep service providers simply agreed to stay out of each other's geographic markets. The Supreme Court was not impressed. (Why do you think the trade name license was not enough to transmute the market-division agreement into a procompetitive collaboration?)

Palmer v. BRG of Georgia, Inc.
498 U.S. 46 (1990)

Per Curiam.

[1] In preparation for the 1985 Georgia Bar Examination, petitioners contracted to take a bar review course offered by respondent BRG of Georgia, Inc. (BRG). In this litigation, they contend that the price of BRG's course was enhanced by reason of an unlawful agreement between BRG and respondent Harcourt Brace Jovanovich Legal and Professional Publications (HBJ), the Nation's largest provider of bar review materials and lecture services. The central issue is whether the 1980 agreement between respondents violated § 1 of the Sherman Act.[. . .]

[2] HBJ began offering a Georgia bar review course on a limited basis in 1976, and was in direct, and often intense, competition with BRG during the period from 1977–1979. BRG and HBJ were the two main providers of bar review courses in Georgia during this time period. In early 1980, they entered into an agreement that gave BRG an exclusive license to market HBJ's material in Georgia and to use its trade name "Bar/Bri." The parties agreed that HBJ would not compete with BRG in Georgia and that BRG would not compete with HBJ outside of Georgia. Under the agreement, HBJ received $100 per student enrolled by BRG and 40% of all revenues over $350. Immediately after the 1980 agreement, the price of BRG's course was increased from $150 to over $400.

[3] The 1980 agreement contained two provisions, one called a "Covenant Not to Compete" and the other called "Other Ventures." The former required HBJ not to "directly or indirectly own, manage, operate, join, invest, control, or participate in or be connected as an officer, employee, partner, director, independent contractor or otherwise with any business which is operating or participating in the preparation of candidates for the Georgia State Bar Examination." The latter required BRG not to compete against HBJ in states in which HBJ currently operated outside the state of Georgia.

---

[343] U.S. Dept. of Justice, Press Release, Justice Department Requires Six High Tech Companies to Stop Entering into Anticompetitive Employee Solicitation Agreements (Sept. 24, 2010).

[4] On petitioners' motion for partial summary judgment as to the § 1 counts in the complaint and respondents' motion for summary judgment, the District Court held that the agreement was lawful. The United States Court of Appeals for the Eleventh Circuit, with one judge dissenting, agreed with the District Court that *per se* unlawful horizontal price fixing required an explicit agreement on prices to be charged or that one party have the right to be consulted about the other's prices. The Court of Appeals also agreed with the District Court that to prove a *per se* violation under a geographic market allocation theory, petitioners had to show that respondents had subdivided some relevant market in which they had previously competed. The Court of Appeals denied a petition for rehearing en banc that had been supported by the United States.

[5] In dissent, Judge Clark explained that, in his view, HBJ and BRG were capable of engaging in *per se* horizontal restraints because they had competed against each other, and then had joined forces. He believed the District Court's analysis was flawed because it had failed to recognize that the agreements could be price-fixing agreements even without explicit reference to price, and because it had failed to recognize that allocation, rather than subdivision, of markets could also constitute a *per se* antitrust violation.

[6] The United States, as *amicus curiae*, had urged the court to adopt the views of the dissent.

[7] In United States v. Socony-Vacuum Oil Co., 310 U.S. 150 (1940), we held that an agreement among competitors to engage in a program of buying surplus gasoline on the spot market in order to prevent prices from falling sharply was unlawful, even though there was no direct agreement on the actual prices to be maintained. We explained that [u]nder the Sherman Act, a combination formed for the purpose and with the effect of raising, depressing, fixing, pegging, or stabilizing the price of a commodity in interstate or foreign commerce is illegal *per se*.

[8] The revenue-sharing formula in the 1980 agreement between BRG and HBJ, coupled with the price increase that took place immediately after the parties agreed to cease competing with each other in 1980, indicates that this agreement was "formed for the purpose and with the effect of raising" the price of the bar review course. It was, therefore, plainly incorrect for the District Court to enter summary judgment in respondents' favor. Moreover, it is equally clear that the District Court and the Court of Appeals erred when they assumed that an allocation of markets or submarkets by competitors is not unlawful unless the market in which the two previously competed is divided between them.

[9] In United States v. Topco Associates, Inc., 405 U.S. 596 (1972), we held that agreements between competitors to allocate territories to minimize competition are illegal:

> One of the classic examples of a *per se* violation of § 1 is an agreement between competitors at the same level of the market structure to allocate territories in order to minimize competition. . . . This Court has reiterated time and time again that horizontal territorial limitations . . . are naked restraints of trade with no purpose except stifling of competition. Such limitations are *per se* violations of the Sherman Act.

[10] The defendants in *Topco* had never competed in the same market, but had simply agreed to allocate markets. Here, HBJ and BRG had previously competed in the Georgia market; under their allocation agreement, BRG received that market, while HBJ received the remainder of the United States. Each agreed not to compete in the other's territories. Such agreements are anticompetitive regardless of whether the parties split a market within which both do business or whether they merely reserve one market for one and another for the other. Thus, the 1980 agreement between HBJ and BRG was unlawful on its face.

* * *

Just like market allocation, the collusive rigging of a competitive bidding process is a *per se* illegal activity. This might be done in a variety of ways: for example, competitors might agree to "rotate" the role of bidding to avoid head-to-head competition, or might just fix the prices at which bids will be submitted, to create the appearance of competition without the reality.[344] In 1992, for example, the Fifth Circuit upheld criminal verdicts against a group of pipe distributors for participating in a cartel run by one of their customers: the customer would win client contracts on a "cost-plus" basis, and then run a rigged "bidding" process among the distributors, passing on the inflated cost to the customer and sharing the overcharge.[345] "[D]efendants cannot escape the per se rule," the court held, "simply because their conspiracy depended upon the participation of a 'middle-man,' even if that middleman conceptualized the conspiracy, orchestrated it by bringing the distributors together . . . , and collected most of the booty."[346]

NOTES

1) *Palmer* emphasizes that *per se* liability neither requires an explicit agreement on price, nor (in the context of a market allocation agreement) that the parties must have previously been competitors in the market they are sub-dividing. Do these understandings of the *per se* rule make sense? Why do you think the *Palmer* Court made these points?'

2) In *Palmer* the parties had entered into an exclusive license. So why was their activity considered nakedly anticompetitive, rather than a procompetitive joint economic investment in the Bar/Bri brand? Isn't this the kind of joint economic activity that the rule of reason is intended to evaluate? Or is that the wrong way to think about what was going on in *Palmer*?

3. Group Boycotts

Agreements among competitors to refrain from dealing with trading partners—"group boycotts," or "concerted refusals to deal"—are often described as *per se* illegal. But this rule is a controversial one, and the Supreme Court has sheepishly conceded that its application is particularly confusing.[347] In this section we will meet a trinity of famous Supreme Court boycott cases: *Klor's* (1959), *Northwest Stationers* (1985), and *Superior Court Trial Lawyers* (1990). In the first and third, the Supreme Court applied the *per se* rule; in the second, the Court applied the rule of reason.

As you read, think about the wide variety of contexts in which competitors might jointly refuse to deal with others. In the first two cases, the group boycott takes place in a purely commercial setting: in *Klor's*, the plaintiff alleges (perhaps implausibly) that suppliers have agreed to boycott a disfavored retailer; in *Northwest Stationers*, the plaintiff complains of being excluded from a joint buying group. But in the third case, the group boycott is not purely commercial—it involves lawyers agreeing not to represent indigent criminal defendants until the local government raised the wage for doing so: it could fairly be described as an effort to ensure that indigent defendants receive competent counsel in criminal cases.

Read together, do the opinions provide a compelling case for applying the *per se* rule to a subset of group boycotts? Is the treatment of group boycotts rational and consistent?

---

[344] *See, e.g.*, United States v. Romer, 148 F.3d 359, 363 (4th Cir. 1998) ("Appellants are real estate speculators who, together with others, participated in a conspiracy to limit bidding competition at certain public foreclosure auctions in Fairfax County, Virginia. The purpose of the conspiracy was to hold down the price of auctioned properties by agreeing not to bid against one another at auctions—an activity commonly known as "bid-rigging." During an auction, most members of the conspiracy would refrain from bidding, while one designated member would bid on and receive the property at a much-reduced price. Following the auction, members of the conspiracy would hold a private auction amongst themselves, at which point they would discuss the price they each would have bid for the property. The person with the highest bid would be given the deed, and the conspirators would divide amongst themselves the money saved by artificially holding down the price of the property."). *See also, e.g.*, United States v. Heffernan, 43 F.3d 1144 (7th Cir. 1994) (considering the application of federal sentencing guidelines to "bid rigging" in comparison to other forms of naked collusion).

[345] United States v. All Star Industries, 962 F.2d 465 (5th Cir. 1992).

[346] United States v. All Star Industries, 962 F.2d 465, 473 (5th Cir. 1992).

[347] *See* Northwest Wholesale Stationers, Inc. v. Pacific Stationery and Printing Co., 472 U.S. 284, 294 (1985) ("Exactly what types of activity fall within the forbidden category is, however, far from certain. There is more confusion about the scope and operation of the per se rule against group boycotts than in reference to any other aspect of the per se doctrine.") (internal quotation marks and citation omitted).

CASENOTE: Klor's v. Broadway-Hale Stores

359 U.S. 207 (1959)

Klor's is probably the most famous (or infamous?) decision applying the *per se* rule to a group boycott. Klor's was a retailer of televisions, refrigerators, and other appliances on Mission Street in San Francisco: Broadway-Hale, a chain of department stores, owned a store next door. Klor's alleged that Broadway-Hale had conspired with a number of appliance manufacturers to cut off Klor's from access to appliances, and that this violated Section 1 (and 2!) of the Sherman Act. In other words, Klor's argued that manufacturers were boycotting Klor's at Broadway-Hale's request.

The district court granted summary judgment for Broadway-Hale, among other reasons because the challenged conduct had no discernible effect on competition: that is, no impact on the overall availability, price, output, quality, or variety of appliances. In fact, the very same appliances were widely available elsewhere on the same street. The district court noted that "a member of the public desiring to purchase an appliance and strolling down Mission Street for a span of but 11 blocks, of which [Klor's] is approximately in the center, would pass the shops of 43 retailers, selling the specific items and brands referred to in the complaint." Klor's appealed to the Ninth Circuit, which affirmed the district court. In doing so, the court of appeals emphasized that "[t]he purpose of the antitrust statutes is to protect the public from the harm which follows from concerted or monopolistic conduct designed to acquire control of a market," and had concluded that there was no evidence that the decision by manufacturers to sell to Broadway-Hale instead of Klor's had caused such public harm. Indeed, the court noted, even Klor's seemed to have plenty of alternatives: "there are numerous brands of appliances to which plaintiff was not denied access and which compete favorably with those he was denied."

But the Supreme Court reversed. Writing for the Court, Justice Black framed the central issue as whether "a group of powerful businessmen may act in concert to deprive a single merchant, like Klor, of the goods he needs to compete effectively." Noting that some forms of conduct are *per se* illegal, the Court held that "[g]roup boycotts, or concerted refusals by traders to deal with other traders, have long been held to be in the forbidden category. They have not been saved by allegations that they were reasonable in the specific circumstances, nor by a failure to show that they fixed or regulated prices, parcelled out or limited production, or brought about a deterioration in quality. Even when they operated to lower prices or temporarily to stimulate competition they were banned." He continued: "This is not a case of a single trader refusing to deal with another, nor even of a manufacturer and a dealer agreeing to an exclusive distributorship. Alleged in this complaint is a wide combination consisting of manufacturers, distributors and a retailer. This combination takes from Klor's its freedom to buy appliances in an open competitive market and drives it out of business as a dealer in the defendants' products." Thus, summary judgment for Broadway-Hale was inappropriate.

Klor's stands as a landmark authority for the proposition that group boycotts among competitors can, at least sometimes, be illegal *per se*. Later cases like *Northwest Stationers* and *Superior Court Trial Lawyers* have struggled to articulate the bounds of this *per se* rule. But *Klor's* remains a puzzling and frustrating case. Most importantly, there did not seem to be any reason to infer a horizontal agreement among manufacturers: or even to think that one was particularly plausible. At most, what seems to have happened is that a department store asked its suppliers not to sell literally identical appliances to the store literally next door, even though those very same appliances were broadly available from other stores on the same street. That, of course, would be a series of vertical agreements between Broadway-Hale and its suppliers, with no common action among competitors, and with no suggestion that these vertical agreements created market power or generated anticompetitive effects. Nor does there seem to be any reason to think the manufacturers would have needed or wanted to agree with one another to cut off Klor's.

In sum: *Klor's* leaves us with the knowledge that some group boycotts are illegal *per se*—and the sense that if the same facts came before the Court today they would probably not be considered a group boycott at all.

Northwest Wholesale Stationers, Inc. v. Pacific Stationery and Printing Co.

472 U.S. 284 (1985)

Justice Brennan.

[1] This case requires that we decide whether a per se violation of § 1 of the Sherman Act, 15 U.S.C. § 1, occurs when a cooperative buying agency comprising various retailers expels a member without providing any procedural means for challenging the expulsion. The case also raises broader questions as to when per se antitrust analysis is appropriately applied to joint activity that is susceptible of being characterized as a concerted refusal to deal. [. . .]

[2] Petitioner Northwest Wholesale Stationers is a purchasing cooperative made up of approximately 100 office supply retailers in the Pacific Northwest States. The cooperative acts as the primary wholesaler for the retailers. Retailers that are not members of the cooperative can purchase wholesale supplies from Northwest at the same price as members. At the end of each year, however, Northwest distributes its profits to members in the form of a percentage rebate on purchases. Members therefore effectively purchase supplies at a price significantly lower than do nonmembers. Northwest also provides certain warehousing facilities. The cooperative arrangement thus permits the participating retailers to achieve economies of scale in purchasing and warehousing that would otherwise be unavailable to them. In fiscal 1978 Northwest had $5.8 million in sales.

[3] Respondent Pacific Stationery & Printing Co. sells office supplies at both the retail and wholesale levels. Its total sales in fiscal 1978 were approximately $7.6 million; the record does not indicate what percentage of revenue is attributable to retail and what percentage is attributable to wholesale. Pacific became a member of Northwest in 1958. In 1974 Northwest amended its bylaws to prohibit members from engaging in both retail and wholesale operations. A grandfather clause preserved Pacific's membership rights. In 1977 ownership of a controlling share of the stock of Pacific changed hands, and the new owners did not officially bring this change to the attention of the directors of Northwest. This failure to notify apparently violated another of Northwest's bylaws.

[4] In 1978 the membership of Northwest voted to expel Pacific. Most factual matters relevant to the expulsion are in dispute. No explanation for the expulsion was advanced at the time, and Pacific was given neither notice, a hearing, nor any other opportunity to challenge the decision. Pacific argues that the expulsion resulted from Pacific's decision to maintain a wholesale operation. Northwest contends that the expulsion resulted from Pacific's failure to notify the cooperative members of the change in stock ownership. The minutes of the meeting of Northwest's directors do not definitively indicate the motive for the expulsion. It is undisputed that Pacific received approximately $10,000 in rebates from Northwest in 1978, Pacific's last year of membership. Beyond a possible inference of loss from this fact, however, the record is devoid of allegations indicating the nature and extent of competitive injury the expulsion caused Pacific to suffer.

[5] Pacific brought suit in 1980 in the United States District Court for the District of Oregon alleging a violation of § 1 of the Sherman Act. The gravamen of the action was that Northwest's expulsion of Pacific from the cooperative without procedural protections was a group boycott that limited Pacific's ability to compete and should be considered per se violative of § 1. On cross-motions for summary judgment the District Court rejected application of the per se rule and held instead that rule-of-reason analysis should govern the case. Finding no anticompetitive effect on the basis of the record as presented, the court granted summary judgment for Northwest.

[6] The Court of Appeals for the Ninth Circuit reversed, holding that the uncontroverted facts of this case support a finding of per se liability. The court reasoned that the cooperative's expulsion of Pacific was an anticompetitive concerted refusal to deal with Pacific on equal footing, which would be a per se violation of § 1 in the absence of any specific legislative mandate for self-regulation sanctioning the expulsion. [. . .]

[7] This Court has long held that certain concerted refusals to deal or group boycotts are so likely to restrict competition without any offsetting efficiency gains that they should be condemned as per se violations of § 1 of the Sherman Act. The question presented in this case is whether Northwest's decision to expel Pacific should fall within this category of activity that is conclusively presumed to be anticompetitive. The Court of Appeals held that the exclusion of Pacific from the cooperative should conclusively be presumed unreasonable on the ground that Northwest provided no procedural protections to Pacific. Even if the lack of procedural protections does not justify

a conclusive presumption of predominantly anticompetitive effect, the mere act of expulsion of a competitor from a wholesale cooperative might be argued to be sufficiently likely to have such effects under the present circumstances and therefore to justify application of the per se rule. [. . .]

[8] This case . . . turns . . . on whether the decision to expel Pacific is properly viewed as a group boycott or concerted refusal to deal mandating per se invalidation. Group boycotts are often listed among the classes of economic activity that merit per se invalidation under § 1. Exactly what types of activity fall within the forbidden category is, however, far from certain. There is more confusion about the scope and operation of the per se rule against group boycotts than in reference to any other aspect of the per se doctrine. Some care is therefore necessary in defining the category of concerted refusals to deal that mandate per se condemnation.

[9] Cases to which this Court has applied the per se approach have generally involved joint efforts by a firm or firms to disadvantage competitors by either directly denying or persuading or coercing suppliers or customers to deny relationships the competitors need in the competitive struggle. In these cases, the boycott often cut off access to a supply, facility, or market necessary to enable the boycotted firm to compete, and frequently the boycotting firms possessed a dominant position in the relevant market. In addition, the practices were generally not justified by plausible arguments that they were intended to enhance overall efficiency and make markets more competitive. Under such circumstances the likelihood of anticompetitive effects is clear and the possibility of countervailing procompetitive effects is remote.

[10] Although a concerted refusal to deal need not necessarily possess all of these traits to merit per se treatment, not every cooperative activity involving a restraint or exclusion will share with the per se forbidden boycotts the likelihood of predominantly anticompetitive consequences. For example, we recognized last Term in *National Collegiate Athletic Assn. v. Board of Regents of University of Oklahoma* [468 U.S. 85 (1984)] that per se treatment of the NCAA's restrictions on the marketing of televised college football was inappropriate—despite the obvious restraint on output—because the "case involves an industry in which horizontal restraints on competition are essential if the product is to be available at all."

[11] Wholesale purchasing cooperatives such as Northwest are not a form of concerted activity characteristically likely to result in predominantly anticompetitive effects. Rather, such cooperative arrangements would seem to be designed to increase economic efficiency and render markets more, rather than less, competitive. The arrangement permits the participating retailers to achieve economies of scale in both the purchase and warehousing of wholesale supplies, and also ensures ready access to a stock of goods that might otherwise be unavailable on short notice. The cost savings and order-filling guarantees enable smaller retailers to reduce prices and maintain their retail stock so as to compete more effectively with larger retailers.

[12] Pacific, of course, does not object to the existence of the cooperative arrangement, but rather raises an antitrust challenge to Northwest's decision to bar Pacific from continued membership. It is therefore the action of expulsion that must be evaluated to determine whether per se treatment is appropriate. The act of expulsion from a wholesale cooperative does not necessarily imply anticompetitive animus and thereby raise a probability of anticompetitive effect. Wholesale purchasing cooperatives must establish and enforce reasonable rules in order to function effectively. Disclosure rules, such as the one on which Northwest relies, may well provide the cooperative with a needed means for monitoring the creditworthiness of its members. Nor would the expulsion characteristically be likely to result in predominantly anticompetitive effects, at least in the type of situation this case presents. Unless the cooperative possesses market power or exclusive access to an element essential to effective competition, the conclusion that expulsion is virtually always likely to have an anticompetitive effect is not warranted. Absent such a showing with respect to a cooperative buying arrangement, courts should apply a rule-of-reason analysis. At no time has Pacific made a threshold showing that these structural characteristics are present in this case.

[13] The District Court appears to have followed the correct path of analysis—recognizing that not all concerted refusals to deal should be accorded per se treatment and deciding this one should not. The foregoing discussion suggests, however, that a satisfactory threshold determination whether anticompetitive effects would be likely might require a more detailed factual picture of market structure than the District Court had before it. Nonetheless, in our judgment the District Court's rejection of per se analysis in this case was correct. A plaintiff

seeking application of the per se rule must present a threshold case that the challenged activity falls into a category likely to have predominantly anticompetitive effects. The mere allegation of a concerted refusal to deal does not suffice because not all concerted refusals to deal are predominantly anticompetitive. When the plaintiff challenges expulsion from a joint buying cooperative, some showing must be made that the cooperative possesses market power or unique access to a business element necessary for effective competition. Focusing on the argument that the lack of procedural safeguards required per se liability, Pacific did not allege any such facts. Because the Court of Appeals applied an erroneous per se analysis in this case, the court never evaluated the District Court's rule-of-reason analysis rejecting Pacific's claim. A remand is therefore appropriate for the limited purpose of permitting appellate review of that determination.

[14] The per se rule is a valid and useful tool of antitrust policy and enforcement. It does not denigrate the per se approach to suggest care in application. In this case, the Court of Appeals failed to exercise the requisite care and applied per se analysis inappropriately. The judgment of the Court of Appeals is therefore reversed, and the case is remanded for further proceedings consistent with this opinion.

* * *

In the following extract, Justice Stevens' opinion for the Court refers to the doctrine that conduct is immune from antitrust liability if it involves constitutionally protected petitioning of government. This principle, often called the "*Noerr-Pennington*" doctrine (after the decisions in *Eastern Railroad Presidents Conference* v. *Noerr Motor Freight, Inc.*, 365 U.S. 127 (1961) and *United Mine Workers of America v. Pennington*, 381 U.S. 657 (1965)), will be on our menu in Chapter IX. For now, all you need to know to make sense of the following is that the doctrine exists!

FTC v. Superior Court Trial Lawyers Ass'n
493 U.S. 411 (1990)

Justice Stevens.

[1] Pursuant to a well-publicized plan, a group of lawyers agreed not to represent indigent criminal defendants in the District of Columbia Superior Court until the District of Columbia government increased the lawyers' compensation. The questions presented are whether the lawyers' concerted conduct violated § 5 of the Federal Trade Commission Act and, if so, whether it was nevertheless protected by the First Amendment to the Constitution.

[2] The burden of providing competent counsel to indigent defendants in the District of Columbia is substantial. During 1982, court-appointed counsel represented the defendant in approximately 25,000 cases. In the most serious felony cases, representation was generally provided by full-time employees of the District's Public Defender System (PDS). Less serious felony and misdemeanor cases constituted about 85 percent of the total caseload. In these cases, lawyers in private practice were appointed and compensated pursuant to the District of Columbia Criminal Justice Act (CJA).

[3] Although over 1,200 lawyers have registered for CJA appointments, relatively few actually apply for such work on a regular basis. In 1982, most appointments went to approximately 100 lawyers who are described as "CJA regulars." These lawyers derive almost all of their income from representing indigents. In 1982, the total fees paid to CJA lawyers amounted to $4,579,572.

[4] In 1974, the District created a Joint Committee on Judicial Administration with authority to establish rates of compensation for CJA lawyers not exceeding the rates established by the federal Criminal Justice Act of 1964. After 1970, the federal Act provided for fees of $30 per hour for court time and $20 per hour for out-of-court time. These rates accordingly capped the rates payable to the District's CJA lawyers, and could not be exceeded absent amendment to either the federal statute or the District Code.

[5] Bar organizations began as early as 1975 to express concern about the low fees paid to CJA lawyers. Beginning in 1982, respondents, the Superior Court Trial Lawyers Association (SCTLA) and its officers, and other bar groups sought to persuade the District to increase CJA rates to at least $35 per hour. Despite what appeared to be uniform

support for the bill, it did not pass. It is also true, however, that nothing in the record indicates that the low fees caused any actual shortage of CJA lawyers or denied effective representation to defendants.

[6] In early August 1983, in a meeting with officers of SCTLA, the Mayor expressed his sympathy but firmly indicated that no money was available to fund an increase. The events giving rise to this litigation then ensued.

[7] At an SCTLA meeting, the CJA lawyers voted to form a "strike committee." The eight members of that committee promptly met and informally agreed "that the only viable way of getting an increase in fees was to stop signing up to take new CJA appointments, and that the boycott should aim for a $45 out-of-court and $55 in-court rate schedule."

[8] On August 11, 1983, about 100 CJA lawyers met and resolved not to accept any new cases after September 6 if legislation providing for an increase in their fees had not passed by that date. Immediately following the meeting, they prepared (and most of them signed) a petition stating:

> We, the undersigned private criminal lawyers practicing in the Superior Court of the District of Columbia, agree that unless we are granted a substantial increase in our hourly rate we will cease accepting new appointments under the Criminal Justice Act.

[9] On September 6, 1983, about 90 percent of the CJA regulars refused to accept any new assignments. Thereafter, SCTLA arranged a series of events to attract the attention of the news media and to obtain additional support. These events were well publicized and did engender favorable editorial comment, but the Administrative Law Judge (ALJ) found that "there is no credible evidence that the District's eventual capitulation to the demands of the CJA lawyers was made in response to public pressure, or, for that matter, that this publicity campaign actually engendered any significant measure of public pressure."

[10] As the participating CJA lawyers had anticipated, their refusal to take new assignments had a severe impact on the District's criminal justice system. The massive flow of new cases did not abate, and the need for prompt investigation and preparation did not ease. . . . The overall response of the uptown lawyers to the PDS call for help was feeble, reflecting their universal distaste for criminal law, their special aversion for compelled indigency representation, the near epidemic siege of self-doubt about their ability to handle cases in this field, and their underlying support for the demands of the CJA lawyers. . . .

[11] Within 10 days, the key figures in the District's criminal justice system "became convinced that the system was on the brink of collapse because of the refusal of CJA lawyers to take on new cases." On September 15, they hand-delivered a letter to the Mayor describing why the situation was expected to "reach a crisis point" by early the next week and urging the immediate enactment of a bill increasing all CJA rates to $35 per hour. The Mayor promptly met with members of the strike committee and offered to support an immediate temporary increase to the $35 level as well as a subsequent permanent increase to $45 an hour for out-of-court time and $55 for in-court time.

[12] At noon on September 19, 1983, over 100 CJA lawyers attended an SCTLA meeting and voted to accept the $35 offer and end the boycott. The city council's Judiciary Committee convened at 2 o'clock that afternoon. The committee recommended legislation increasing CJA fees to $35, and the council unanimously passed the bill on September 20. On September 21, the CJA regulars began to accept new assignments and the crisis subsided.

[13] The Federal Trade Commission (FTC) filed a complaint against SCTLA and four of its officers (respondents) alleging that they had "entered into an agreement among themselves and with other lawyers to restrain trade by refusing to compete for or accept new appointments under the CJA program beginning on September 6, 1983, unless and until the District of Columbia increased the fees offered under the CJA program." The complaint alleged that virtually all of the attorneys who regularly compete for or accept new appointments under the CJA program had joined the agreement. The FTC characterized respondents' conduct as "a conspiracy to fix prices and to conduct a boycott" and concluded that they were engaged in "unfair methods of competition in violation of Section 5 of the Federal Trade Commission Act." {*Eds.: The FTC's complaint was filed in "Part 3" administrative proceedings, before an Administrative Law Judge ("ALJ") at the Federal Trade Commission, who heard the arguments of the FTC's "complaint counsel" and of the defendants. The FTC's unique statutory power to file antitrust enforcement actions in administrative court is discussed in more detail in Chapter XI below.*}

[14] After a 3-week hearing, the ALJ found that the facts alleged in the complaint had been proved, and rejected each of respondents' three legal defenses — that the boycott was adequately justified by the public interest in obtaining better legal representation for indigent defendants; that as a method of petitioning for legislative change it was exempt from the antitrust laws under our decision in *Eastern Railroad Presidents Conference* v. *Noerr Motor Freight, Inc.*, 365 U.S. 127 (1961); and that it was a form of political action protected by the First Amendment under our decision in *NAACP* v. *Claiborne Hardware Co.*, 458 U.S. 886 (1982). The ALJ nevertheless concluded that the complaint should be dismissed because the District officials, who presumably represented the victim of the boycott, recognized that its net effect was beneficial. The increase in fees would attract more CJA lawyers, enabling them to reduce their caseloads and provide better representation for their clients. "I see no point," he concluded, "in striving resolutely for an antitrust triumph in this sensitive area when the particular case can be disposed of on a more pragmatic basis—there was no harm done."

[15] The ALJ's pragmatic moderation found no favor with the FTC. Like the ALJ, the FTC rejected each of respondents' defenses. It held that their "coercive, concerted refusal to deal" had the "purpose and effect of raising prices" and was illegal *per se*. Unlike the ALJ, the FTC refused to conclude that the boycott was harmless, noting that the "boycott forced the city government to increase the CJA fees from a level that had been sufficient to obtain an adequate supply of CJA lawyers to a level satisfactory to the respondents. The city must, as a result of the boycott, spend an additional $4 million to $5 million a year to obtain legal services for indigents. We find that these are substantial anticompetitive effects resulting from the respondents' conduct." Finally, the FTC determined that the record did not support the ALJ's conclusion that the District supported the boycott. The FTC also held that such support would not in any event excuse respondents' antitrust violations. Accordingly, it entered a cease-and-desist order "to prohibit the respondents from initiating another boycott . . . whenever they become dissatisfied with the results or pace of the city's legislative process."

[16] The Court of Appeals vacated the FTC order and remanded for a determination whether respondents possessed "significant market power." The court began its analysis by recognizing that absent any special First Amendment protection, the boycott "constituted a classic restraint of trade within the meaning of Section 1 of the Sherman Act." The Court of Appeals was not persuaded by respondents' reliance on *Claiborne Hardware* or *Noerr*, or by their argument that the boycott was justified because it was designed to improve the quality of representation for indigent defendants. It concluded, however, that "the SCTLA boycott did contain an element of expression warranting First Amendment protection." It noted that boycotts have historically been used as a dramatic means of expression and that respondents intended to convey a political message to the public at large. It therefore concluded that under *United States* v. *O'Brien*, 391 U.S. 367 (1968), a restriction on this form of expression could not be justified unless it is no greater than is essential to an important governmental interest. This test, the court reasoned, could not be satisfied by the application of an otherwise appropriate *per se* rule, but instead required the enforcement agency to "prove rather than presume that the evil against which the Sherman Act is directed looms in the conduct it condemns."

[17] Because of our concern about the implications of the Court of Appeals' unique holding, we granted the FTC's petition for certiorari as well as respondents' cross-petition.

[18] We consider first the cross-petition, which contends that respondents' boycott is outside the scope of the Sherman Act or is immunized from antitrust regulation by the First Amendment. We then turn to the FTC's petition.

[19] Reasonable lawyers may differ about the wisdom of this enforcement proceeding . . . . Respondents' boycott may well have served a cause that was worthwhile and unpopular. We may assume that the pre-boycott rates were unreasonably low, and that the increase has produced better legal representation for indigent defendants. Moreover, given that neither indigent criminal defendants nor the lawyers who represent them command any special appeal with the electorate, we may also assume that without the boycott there would have been no increase in District CJA fees at least until the Congress amended the federal statute. These assumptions do not control the case, for it is not our task to pass upon the social utility or political wisdom of price-fixing agreements.

[20] As the ALJ, the FTC, and the Court of Appeals all agreed, respondents' boycott "constituted a classic restraint of trade within the meaning of Section 1 of the Sherman Act." As such, it also violated the prohibition against

unfair methods of competition in § 5 of the FTC Act. Prior to the boycott CJA lawyers were in competition with one another, each deciding independently whether and how often to offer to provide services to the District at CJA rates. The agreement among the CJA lawyers was designed to obtain higher prices for their services and was implemented by a concerted refusal to serve an important customer in the market for legal services and, indeed, the only customer in the market for the particular services that CJA regulars offered. This constriction of supply is the essence of price-fixing, whether it be accomplished by agreeing upon a price, which will decrease the quantity demanded, or by agreeing upon an output, which will increase the price offered. The horizontal arrangement among these competitors was unquestionably a naked restraint on price and output.

[21] It is, of course, true that the city purchases respondents' services because it has a constitutional duty to provide representation to indigent defendants. It is likewise true that the quality of representation may improve when rates are increased. Yet neither of these facts is an acceptable justification for an otherwise unlawful restraint of trade. As we have remarked before, the "Sherman Act reflects a legislative judgment that ultimately competition will produce not only lower prices, but also better goods and services." *National Society of Professional Engineers* v. *United States*, 435 U.S. 679, 695 (1978) . . . .

[22] The social justifications proffered for respondents' restraint of trade thus do not make it any less unlawful. The statutory policy underlying the Sherman Act "precludes inquiry into the question whether competition is good or bad." . . . .

[23] Our decision in *Noerr* in no way detracts from this conclusion. In *Noerr*, we "considered whether the Sherman Act prohibited a publicity campaign waged by railroads" and "designed to foster the adoption of laws destructive of the trucking business, to create an atmosphere of distaste for truckers among the general public, and to impair the relationships existing between truckers and their customers." Interpreting the Sherman Act in the light of the First Amendment's Petition Clause, the Court noted that "at least insofar as the railroads' campaign was directed toward obtaining governmental action, its legality was not at all affected by any anticompetitive purpose it may have had."

[24] It of course remains true that "no violation of the Act can be predicated upon mere attempts to influence the passage or enforcement of laws," even if the defendants' sole purpose is to impose a restraint upon the trade of their competitors. But in the *Noerr* case the alleged restraint of trade was the intended *consequence* of public action; in this case the boycott was the *means* by which respondents sought to obtain favorable legislation. The restraint of trade that was implemented while the boycott lasted would have had precisely the same anticompetitive consequences during that period even if no legislation had been enacted. In *Noerr*, the desired legislation would have created the restraint on the truckers' competition; in this case the emergency legislative response to the boycott put an end to the restraint. [. . .]

[25] SCTLA argues that if its conduct would otherwise be prohibited by the Sherman Act and the Federal Trade Commission Act, it is nonetheless protected by the First Amendment rights recognized in *NAACP v. Claiborne Hardware Co.*, 458 U.S. 886 (1982). That case arose after black citizens boycotted white merchants in Claiborne County, Mississippi. The white merchants sued under state law to recover losses from the boycott. We found that the "right of the States to regulate economic activity could not justify a complete prohibition against a nonviolent, politically motivated boycott designed to force governmental and economic change and to effectuate rights guaranteed by the Constitution itself." We accordingly held that "the nonviolent elements of petitioners' activities are entitled to the protection of the First Amendment."

[26] SCTLA contends that because it, like the boycotters in *Claiborne Hardware*, sought to vindicate constitutional rights, it should enjoy a similar First Amendment protection. It is, of course, clear that the association's efforts to publicize the boycott, to explain the merits of its cause, and to lobby District officials to enact favorable legislation—like similar activities in *Claiborne Hardware*—were activities that were fully protected by the First Amendment. But nothing in the FTC's order would curtail such activities, and nothing in the FTC's reasoning condemned any of those activities.

[27] The activity that the FTC order prohibits is a concerted refusal by CJA lawyers to accept any further assignments until they receive an increase in their compensation; the undenied objective of their boycott was an

economic advantage for those who agreed to participate. It is true that the *Claiborne Hardware* case also involved a boycott. That boycott, however, differs in a decisive respect. Those who joined the *Claiborne Hardware* boycott sought no special advantage for themselves. They were black citizens in Port Gibson, Mississippi, who had been the victims of political, social, and economic discrimination for many years. They sought only the equal respect and equal treatment to which they were constitutionally entitled. They struggled "to change a social order that had consistently treated them as second class citizens." As we observed, the campaign was not intended "to destroy legitimate competition." Equality and freedom are preconditions of the free market, and not commodities to be haggled over within it.

[28] The same cannot be said of attorney's fees. As we recently pointed out, our reasoning in *Claiborne Hardware* is not applicable to a boycott conducted by business competitors who "stand to profit financially from a lessening of competition in the boycotted market." No matter how altruistic the motives of respondents may have been, it is undisputed that their immediate objective was to increase the price that they would be paid for their services. Such an economic boycott is well within the category that was expressly distinguished in the *Claiborne Hardware* opinion itself. [. . .]

[29] In any event, however, we cannot accept the Court of Appeals' characterization of this boycott or the antitrust laws. Every concerted refusal to do business with a potential customer or supplier has an expressive component. At one level, the competitors must exchange their views about their objectives and the means of obtaining them. The most blatant, naked price-fixing agreement is a product of communication, but that is surely not a reason for viewing it with special solicitude. [. . .]

[30] In sum, there is thus nothing unique about the "expressive component" of respondents' boycott. A rule that requires courts to apply the antitrust laws "prudently and with sensitivity" whenever an economic boycott has an "expressive component" would create a gaping hole in the fabric of those laws. Respondents' boycott thus has no special characteristics meriting an exemption from the *per se* rules of antitrust law. [. . .]

[31] The judgment of the Court of Appeals is accordingly reversed insofar as that court held the *per se* rules inapplicable to the lawyers' boycott. The case is remanded for further proceedings consistent with this opinion.

* * *

When Is a Boycott *Per Se* Illegal?

In thinking about the tangled law of group boycotts, it may be helpful to think of two categories of case in which *per se* condemnation may be appropriate. The first category includes naked agreements among groups of competitors not to deal with trading partners (*e.g.*, customers) *except* on certain terms, such as at a supracompetitive price. This kind of boycott is just another way of thinking about naked collusion: every cartel works in this way! The second category includes naked agreements among groups of competitors not to deal with trading partners that deal with rivals of the group. This kind of boycott amounts to a cartel attempting to cut off its rivals by inducing exclusivity from its trading partners. *Superior Court Trial Lawyers* is an example of an agreement in the first category. The second category appears to be the kind of thing the *Northwest Stationers* Court had in mind at paragraph 9 of the extract above. The first category involves collusion on terms of dealing; the second involves collusion to exclude non-participant rivals of the colluders. Both are generally *per se* illegal.

In a variation on the first category, we could imagine a group of competitors agreeing to restrict output in some way other than by a simple price increase. For example, competitors might agree to restrict their use of retail or other distribution channels—"boycotting" certain, perhaps discounting, sellers—especially in partnership with, or at the request of, a single downstream retailer or distributor that held, or hoped to acquire, downstream market power. That was the kind of agreement alleged in *Klor's* (although it is not clear why such an agreement was plausible in that case, given the ample other channels that remained open and the lack of reason to believe that Broadway-Hale had any chance of gaining market power). And, as we will see later in the chapter, something similar was alleged in the FTC's case against Toys R Us and in the DOJ's case against Apple and the e-book publishers.

NOTES

1) Under what circumstances is a group boycott *per se* illegal? When should it be? Do you agree with the Court's characterization in FTC v. Indiana Federation of Dentists, 476 U.S. 447, 458 (1986), that in group boycott cases "the *per se* approach has generally been limited to cases in which firms with market power boycott suppliers or customers in order to discourage them from doing business with a competitor"? Would that be a good rule?

2) Does *Northwest Stationers* hold that the existence of a possible procompetitive justification for a boycott means that the *per se* rule does not apply? If so, does that mean that there is no *per se* rule in the first place?

3) Could the collective enterprise in *Superior Court Trial Lawyers* have been described as a procompetitive one? Should it matter that the lawyers were not otherwise economically integrated outside the scope of their boycott?

4) What seems to have been going on to prompt the complaint in *Klor's*? Do you think that the allegations described by the Court would pass muster under *Twombly* today?

5) Was the Court in *Klor's* correct to find a "monopolistic tendency" in the practice in question? In what market?

6) In general, do you think the category of group boycotts (or "concerted refusals to deal") less threatening, equally threatening, or more threatening to competition than other forms of *per se* illegal conduct?

7) What kind of remedy do you think is likely to be sensible and effective in a group boycott case?

8) Do you agree that the two-part typology in the breakout box above is a helpful way to divide the cases? Is there another way to think about group boycotts that makes better sense of the cases?

9) How should courts analyze a boycott motivated by ESG concerns?

4. Hub and Spoke Conspiracies

Sometimes a horizontal agreement is implemented through a set of vertical interactions, in what is known as a "hub and spoke conspiracy." In a traditional horizontal conspiracy, of course, the competitors directly agree on price: for example, competing retailers might get together and fix prices or other terms of dealing. In a hub-and-spoke conspiracy, however, the conspirators (the "spokes") do not directly coordinate with one another: instead, the means of coordination is through parallel agreements with a central facilitator (the "hub"), which acts as a go-between and facilitates a conscious commitment to a common scheme among the spokes.

This is an important analytical insight, because it means that under some circumstances courts will pierce through the fact that interactions seem to be formally vertical, in order to conclude that the agreement in question was "really" horizontal. This, in turn, may result in the applicability of the *per se* rule.

Two famous antitrust cases illustrate how this can work in practice. In *Toys R Us*, a downstream retailer, unhappy with competition from "warehouse club" stores, served as an intermediary to facilitate an agreement among various toy manufacturers, each of whom was willing to restrict sales to the discounting warehouse stores on the condition that other manufacturers did the same. In *Apple*, competing e-book publishers, unhappy with competitive pressure resulting from aggressive discounting by Amazon, entered into parallel vertical agreements with Apple regarding the terms on which their respective e-books could be distributed, as part of an implicit agreement to switch to a higher-priced sale model.

In both cases, the court held, the relevant agreement was *horizontal* in substance and that *per se* treatment was appropriate, even though a noncompetitor served as an intermediary. The court also held that the noncompetitor hub was liable on the same terms with as the participating direct competitors.

Note that the *Toys R Us* case also touches on an issue we discussed in Chapter IV: the nature and cogency of evidence required before an agreement can be inferred. Why might this be a particularly complex issue in hub-and-spoke cases? The *Toys R Us* court draws a thoughtful parallel to the facts of *Interstate Circuit*, a case summarized in Chapter IV.[348]

---

[348] *See supra* § IV.B.2.

Toys "R" Us, Inc. v. FTC
221 F.3d 928 (7th Cir. 2000)

Judge Wood.

[1] What happened in this case, according to the Commission, was fairly simple. For a long time, [Toys R Us, a/k/a] TRU had enjoyed a strong position at the low price end for toy sales, because its only competition came from traditional toy stores who could not or did not wish to meet its prices, or from general discounters like Wal-Mart or K-Mart, which could not offer anything like the variety of items TRU had and whose prices were not too far off TRU's mark.

[2] The advent of the warehouse clubs changed all that. They were a retail innovation of the late 1970s: the first one opened in 1976, and by 1992 there were some 600 individual club stores around the country. Rather than earning all of their money from their mark-up on products, the clubs sell only to their members, and they charge a modest annual membership fee, often about $30. As the word "warehouse" in the name suggests, the clubs emphasize price competition over service amenities. Nevertheless, the Commission found that the clubs seek to offer name-brand merchandise, including toys. During the late 1980s and early 1990s, warehouse clubs selected and purchased from the toy manufacturers' full array of products, just like everyone else. In some instances they bought specialized packs assembled for the "club" trade, but they normally preferred stocking conventional products so that their customers could readily compare the price of an item at the club against the price of the same item at a competing store.

[3] To the extent this strategy was successful, however, TRU did not welcome it. By 1989, its senior executives were concerned that the clubs were a threat to TRU's low-price image and, more importantly, to its profits. A little legwork revealed that as of that year the clubs carried approximately 120–240 items in direct competition with TRU, priced as much as 25 to 30% below TRU's own price levels.

[4] TRU put its President of Merchandising, a Mr. Goddu, to work to see what could be done. The response Goddu and other TRU executives formulated to beat back the challenge from the clubs began with TRU's decision to contact some of its suppliers, including toy manufacturing heavyweights Mattel, Hasbro, and Fisher Price. At the Toy Fair in 1992 (a major event at which the next Christmas season's orders are placed), Goddu informed the manufacturers of a new TRU policy, which was reflected in a memo of January 29, 1992. The policy set forth the following conditions and privileges for TRU:

• The clubs could have no new or promoted product unless they carried the entire line.

• All specials and exclusives to be sold to the clubs had to be shown first to TRU to see if TRU wanted the item.

• Old and basic product had to be in special packs.

• Clearance and closeout items were permissible provided that TRU was given the first opportunity to buy the product.

• There would be no discussion about prices.

[5] TRU was careful to meet individually with each of its suppliers to explain its new policy. Afterwards, it then asked each one what it intended to do. Negotiations between TRU and the manufacturers followed, as a result of which each manufacturer eventually agreed that it would sell to the clubs only highly differentiated products (either unique individual items or combo packs) that were not offered to anything but a club (and thus of course not to TRU). As the Commission put it, "[t]hrough its announced policy and the related agreements discussed below, TRU sought to eliminate the competitive threat the clubs posed by denying them merchandise, forcing the clubs' customers to buy products they did not want, and frustrating customers' ability to make direct price comparisons of club prices and TRU prices."

[6] The agreements between TRU and the various manufacturers were, of course, vertical agreements, because they ran individually from the supplier/manufacturer to the purchaser/retailer. The Commission found that TRU

reached about 10 of these agreements. After the agreements were concluded, TRU then supervised and enforced each toy company's compliance with its commitment.

[7] But TRU was not content to stop with vertical agreements. Instead, the Commission found, it decided to go further. It worked for over a year and a half to put the vertical agreements in place, but the biggest hindrance TRU had to overcome was the major toy companies' reluctance to give up a new, fast-growing, and profitable channel of distribution. The manufacturers were also concerned that any of their rivals who broke ranks and sold to the clubs might gain sales at their expense, given the widespread and increasing popularity of the club format. To address this problem, the Commission found, TRU orchestrated a horizontal agreement among its key suppliers to boycott the clubs. The evidence on which the Commission relied showed that, at a minimum, Mattel, Hasbro, Fisher Price, Tyco, Little Tikes, Today's Kids, and Tiger Electronics agreed to join in the boycott on the condition that their competitors would do the same.

[8] The Commission first noted that internal documents from the manufacturers revealed that they were trying to expand, not to restrict, the number of their major retail outlets and to reduce their dependence on TRU. They were specifically interested in cultivating a relationship with the warehouse clubs and increasing sales there. Thus, the sudden adoption of measures under which they decreased sales to the clubs ran against their independent economic self-interest. Second, the Commission cited evidence that the manufacturers were unwilling to limit sales to the clubs without assurances that their competitors would do likewise. Goddu himself testified that TRU communicated the message "I'll stop if they stop" from manufacturer to competing manufacturer. He specifically mentioned having such conversations with Mattel and Hasbro, and he said more generally "We communicated to our vendors that we were communicating with all our key suppliers, and we did that I believe at Toy Fair 1992. We made a point to tell each of the vendors that we spoke to that we would be talking to our other key suppliers."

[9] Evidence from the manufacturers corroborated Goddu's account. A Mattel executive said that it would not sell the clubs the same items it was selling to TRU, and that this decision was "based on the fact that competition would do the same." A Hasbro executive said much the same thing: "because our competitors had agreed not to sell loaded [that is, promoted] product to the clubs, that we would go along with this." TRU went so far as to assure individual manufacturers that no one would be singled out.

[10] Once the special warehouse club policy (or, in the Commission's more pejorative language, boycott) was underway, TRU served as the central clearinghouse for complaints about breaches in the agreement. The Commission gave numerous examples of this conduct in its opinion.

[11] Last, the Commission found that TRU's policies had bite. In the year before the boycott began, the clubs' share of all toy sales in the United States grew from 1.5% in 1991 to 1.9% in 1992. After the boycott took hold, that percentage slipped back by 1995 to 1.4%. Local numbers were more impressive. Costco, for example, experienced overall growth on sales of all products during the period 1991 to 1993 of 25%. Its toy sales increased during same period by 51%. But, after the boycott took hold in 1993, its toy sales decreased by 1.6% even while its overall sales were still growing by 19.5%. The evidence indicated that this was because TRU had succeeded in cutting off its access to the popular toys it needed. In 1989, over 90% of the Mattel toys Costco and other clubs purchased were regular (i.e. easily comparable) items, but by 1993 that percentage was zero. Once again, the Commission's opinion is chock full of similar statistics.

[12] The Commission also considered the question whether TRU might have been trying to protect itself against free riding, at least with respect to its vertical agreements. It acknowledged that TRU provided several services that might be important to consumers, including advertising, carrying an inventory of goods early in the year, and supporting a full line of products. Nevertheless, it found that the manufacturers compensated TRU directly for advertising toys, storing toys made early in the year, and stocking a broad line of each manufacturer's toys under one roof. A 1993 TRU memorandum confirms that advertising is manufacturer-funded and is "essentially free." In 1994, TRU's net cost of advertising was a tiny 0.02% of sales, or $750,000, out of a total of $199 million it spent on advertising that year. As the Commission saw it, "advertising was a service the toy manufacturers provided for TRU and not the other way around." TRU records also showed that manufacturers routinely paid TRU credits for warehousing services, and that they compensated it for full line stocking. In short, the Commission found, there was no evidence that club competition without comparable services threatened to drive TRU services

out of the market or to harm customers. Manufacturers paid each retailer directly for the services they wanted the retailer to furnish.

[13] Based on this record, the Commission drew three central conclusions of law: (1) the TRU-led manufacturer boycott of the warehouse clubs was illegal per se under the rule enunciated in *Northwest Wholesale Stationers, Inc. v. Pacific Stationery & Printing Co.*, 472 U.S. 284 (1985); (2) the boycott was illegal under a full rule of reason analysis because its anticompetitive effects "clearly outweighed any possible business justification"; and (3) the vertical agreements between TRU and the individual toy manufacturers, "entered into seriatim with clear anticompetitive effect, violate section 1 of the Sherman Act." These antitrust violations in turn were enough to prove a violation of FTC Act § 5, which for present purposes tracks the prohibitions of the Sherman and Clayton Acts. [. . .]

[14] As TRU correctly points out, the critical question here is whether substantial evidence supported the Commission's finding that there was a horizontal agreement among the toy manufacturers, with TRU in the center as the ringmaster, to boycott . . . warehouse clubs [which competed with TRU in selling toys]. It acknowledges that such an agreement may be proved by either direct or circumstantial evidence . . . . When circumstantial evidence is used, there must be some evidence that tends to exclude the possibility that the alleged conspirators acted independently. This does not mean, however, that the Commission had to exclude all possibility that the manufacturers acted independently. . . . [T]hat would amount to an absurd and legally unfounded burden to prove with 100% certainty that an antitrust violation occurred. The test states only that there must be some evidence which, if believed, would support a finding of concerted behavior. In the context of an appeal from the Commission, the question is whether substantial evidence supports its conclusion that it is more likely than not that the manufacturers acted collusively.

[15] In TRU's opinion, this record shows nothing more than a series of separate, similar vertical agreements between itself and various toy manufacturers. It believes that each manufacturer in its independent self-interest had an incentive to limit sales to the clubs, because TRU's policy provided strong unilateral incentives for the manufacturer to reduce its sales to the clubs. Why gain a few sales at the clubs, it asks, when it would have much more to gain by maintaining a good relationship with the 100-pound gorilla of the industry, TRU, and make far more sales?

[16] We do not disagree that there was some evidence in the record that would bear TRU's interpretation. But that is not the standard we apply when we review decisions of the Federal Trade Commission. Instead, we apply the substantial evidence test . . . .

[17] The Commission's theory, stripped to its essentials, is that this case is a modern equivalent of the old *Interstate Circuit* decision [*i.e.*, Interstate Circuit, Inc. v. United States, 306 US 208 (1939)]. {*Eds.: As noted above, this case is summarized in Chapter IV.*} That case too involved actors at two levels of the distribution chain, distributors of motion pictures and exhibitors. Interstate Circuit was one of the exhibitors; it had a stranglehold on the exhibition of movies in a number of Texas cities. The antitrust violation occurred when Interstate's manager, O'Donnell, sent an identical letter to the eight branch managers of the distributor companies, with each letter naming all eight as addressees, in which he asked them to comply with two demands: a minimum price for first-run theaters, and a policy against double features at night. The trial court there drew an inference of agreement from the nature of the proposals, from the manner in which they were made, from the substantial unanimity of action taken, and from the lack of evidence of a benign motive; the Supreme Court affirmed. The new policies represented a radical shift from the industry's prior business practices, and the Court rejected as beyond the range of probability that such unanimity of action was explainable only by chance.

[18] The Commission is right. Indeed, as it argues in its brief, the TRU case if anything presents a more compelling case for inferring horizontal agreement than did *Interstate Circuit*, because not only was the manufacturers' decision to stop dealing with the warehouse clubs an abrupt shift from the past, and not only is it suspicious for a manufacturer to deprive itself of a profitable sales outlet, but the record here included the direct evidence of communications that was missing in *Interstate Circuit*. Just as in *Interstate Circuit*, TRU tries to avoid this result by hypothesizing independent motives. If there were no evidence in the record tending to support concerted behavior, then we agree that *Matsushita* would require a ruling in TRU's favor. But there is. The evidence showed that the companies wanted to diversify from TRU, not to become more dependent upon it; it showed that each

manufacturer was afraid to curb its sales to the warehouse clubs alone, because it was afraid its rivals would cheat and gain a special advantage in that popular new market niche. The Commission was not required to disbelieve the testimony of the different toy company executives and TRU itself to the effect that the only condition on which each toy manufacturer would agree to TRU's demands was if it could be sure its competitors were doing the same thing.

[19] That is a horizontal agreement. . . . [I]t has nothing to do with enhancing efficiencies of distribution from the manufacturer's point of view. The typical story of a legitimate vertical transaction would have the manufacturer going to TRU and asking it to be the exclusive carrier of the manufacturer's goods; in exchange for that exclusivity, the manufacturer would hope to receive more effective promotion of its goods, and TRU would have a large enough profit margin to do the job well. But not all manufacturers think that exclusive dealing arrangements will maximize their profits. Some think, and are entitled to think, that using the greatest number of retailers possible is a better strategy. These manufacturers were in effect being asked by TRU to reduce their output (especially of the popular toys), and as is classically true in such cartels, they were willing to do so only if TRU could protect them against cheaters.

[20] *Northwest Stationers* also demonstrates why the facts the Commission found support its conclusion that the essence of the agreement network TRU supervised was horizontal. There the Court described the cases that had condemned boycotts as "per se" illegal as those involving joint efforts by a firm or firms to disadvantage competitors by either directly denying or persuading or coercing suppliers or customers to deny relationships the competitors need in the competitive struggle. The boycotters had to have some market power, though the Court did not suggest that the level had to be as high as it would require in a case under Sherman Act § 2. Here, TRU was trying to disadvantage the warehouse clubs, its competitors, by coercing suppliers to deny the clubs the products they needed. It accomplished this goal by inducing the suppliers to collude, rather than to compete independently for shelf space in the different toy retail stores.

* * *

United States v. Apple, Inc.
791 F.3d 290 (2d Cir. 2015)

Judge Livingston.

{*Eds.: Amazon, which operated an e-commerce website, sold e-books for use on its Kindle e-reader that were published by (among others) the "Big Six" book publishers: Hachette, HarperCollins, Penguin, RandomHouse, Macmillan, and Simon & Schuster. These e-books were sold through a "wholesale" model: the publisher set a "wholesale price" that Amazon paid to the publisher for each e-book sold to a consumer. Publishers charged a higher wholesale prices for new releases and New York Times bestsellers, reflecting their higher print book prices for those desirable titles. But Amazon refused to charge a premium to its customers for these books: it set the retail price at the low point of $9.99—near, or even below, the wholesale price of those e-books. This strategy caused the publishers concern, as the court explains.*}

[1] [T]op executives in the Big Six [book publishers: *i.e.*, Hachette, HarperCollins, Penguin, RandomHouse, Macmillan, and Simon & Schuster] saw Amazon's $9.99 pricing strategy as a threat to their established way of doing business. . . . In the short term, these members of the Big Six thought that Amazon's lower-priced ebooks would make it more difficult for them to sell hardcover copies of new releases, which were often priced, as the district court noted, at thirty dollars or more, as well as New York Times bestsellers. Further down the road, the publishers feared that consumers would become accustomed to the uniform $9.99 price point for these ebooks, permanently driving down the price they could charge for print versions of the books. Moreover, if Amazon became powerful enough, it could demand lower wholesale prices from the Big Six or allow authors to publish directly with Amazon, cutting out the publishers entirely. As Hachette's [CEO] put it, the idea of the "wretched $9.99 price point becoming a de facto standard" for ebooks "sickened" him. [. . .]

[2] [Apple, which was planning to enter the market for ebook retail by introducing the iBookstore,] learned that the publishers feared that Amazon's pricing model could change their industry, that several publishers had engaged in simultaneous windowing efforts to thwart Amazon, and that the industry as a whole was in a state of

turmoil. "Apple understood," as the district court put it, "that the Publishers wanted to pressure Amazon to raise the $9.99 price point for e-books, that the Publishers were searching for ways to do that, and that they were willing to coordinate their efforts to achieve that goal." [. . .]

[3] [Apple felt that it would be unable to negotiate wholesale prices that were low enough to allow it to compete with Amazon. Accordingly, Apple proposed the "agency" model to publishers, pursuant to which] the publisher sets the price that consumers will pay for each ebook. Then, rather than the retailer paying the publisher for each ebook that it sells, the publisher pays the retailer a fixed percentage of each sale. In essence, the retailer receives a commission for distributing the publisher's ebooks. Under the system Apple devised, publishers would have the freedom to set ebook prices in the iBookstore, and would keep 70% of each sale. The remaining 30% would go to Apple as a commission.

[4] This switch to an agency model obviated Apple's concerns about negotiating wholesale prices with the Big Six while ensuring that Apple profited on every sale. It did not, however, solve all of the company's problems. Because the agency model handed the publishers control over pricing, it created the risk that the Big Six would sell ebooks in the iBookstore at far higher prices than Kindle's $9.99 offering. If the prices were too high, Apple could be left with a brand new marketplace brimming with titles, but devoid of customers.

[5] To solve this pricing problem, [Apple] initially devised two strategies. First, they realized that they could maintain "realistic prices" by establishing price caps for different types of books. Of course, these caps would need to be higher than Amazon's $9.99 price point, or Apple would face the same difficult price negotiations that it sought to avoid by switching away from the wholesale model. But at this point Apple was not content to open its iBookstore offering prices higher than the competition. For as the district court found, if the Publisher Defendants wanted to end Amazon's $9.99 pricing, Apple similarly desired that there be no price competition at the retail level.

[6] Apple next concluded, then, as the district court found, that to ensure that the iBookstore would be competitive at higher prices, Apple needed to eliminate all retail price competition. Thus, rather than simply agreeing to price caps above Amazon's $9.99 price point, Apple created a second requirement: publishers must switch all of their other ebook retailers—including Amazon—to an agency pricing model. The result would be that Apple would not need to compete with Amazon on price, and publishers would be able to eliminate Amazon's $9.99 pricing. Or, as Cue would later describe the plan to executives at Simon & Schuster, Macmillan, and Random House, the plan solved the Amazon issue by allowing the publishers to wrest control over pricing from Amazon.

[7] On January 4 and 5, Apple sent essentially identical emails to each member of the Big Six to explain its agency model proposal. Each email described the commission split between Apple and the publishers and recommended three price caps: $14.99 for hardcover books with list prices above $35; $12.99 for hardcover books with list prices below $35; and $9.99 for all other trade books. The emails also explained that, to sell ebooks at realistic prices all other resellers of new titles need to be in [the] agency model" as well. Or, as [Apple] told [the CEO of Simon & Schuster], "all publishers" would need to move "all retailers" to an agency model. [. . .]

[8] [Rather than explicitly insert contractual clauses that obliged publishers to change their contractual relationships with other retailers such as Amazon, Apple] devised an alternative to explicitly requiring publishers to switch other retailers to agency. This alternative involved the use of a "most-favored nation" clause ("MFN Clause" or "MFN"). In general, an MFN Clause is a contractual provision that requires one party to give the other the best terms that it makes available to any competitor. In the context of Apple's negotiations, the MFN Clause mandated that, "if, for any particular New Release in hardcover format, the Customer Price in the iBookstore at any time is or becomes higher than a customer price offered by any other reseller, then the Publisher shall designate a new, lower Customer Price in the iBookstore to meet such lower customer price." Put differently, the MFN would require the publisher to offer any ebook in Apple's iBookstore for no more than what the same ebook was offered elsewhere, such as from Amazon.

[9] On January 11, Apple sent each of the Big Six a proposed eBook Agency Distribution Agreement (the "Contracts"). As described in the January 4 and 5 emails, these Contracts would split the proceeds from each ebook sale between the publisher and Apple, with the publisher receiving 70%, and would set price caps on ebooks

at $14.99, $12.99, and $9.99 depending on the book's hardcover price. But unlike the initial emails, the Contracts contained MFN Clauses in place of the requirement that publishers move all other retailers to an agency model. Apple then assured each member of the Big Six that it was being offered the same terms as the others.

[10] The Big Six understood the economic incentives that the MFN Clause created. Suppose a new hardcover release sells at a list price of $25, and a wholesale price of $12.50. With Amazon, the publishers had been receiving the wholesale price (or a slightly lower digital wholesale price) for every ebook copy of the volume sold on Kindle, even if Amazon ultimately sold the ebook for less than that wholesale price. Under Apple's initial agency model—with price caps but no MFN Clause—the publishers already stood to make less money per ebook with Apple. Because Apple capped the ebook price of a $25 hardcover at $12.99 and took 30% of that price, publishers could only expect to make $8.75 per sale. But what the publishers sacrificed in short-term revenue, they hoped to gain in long-term stability by acquiring more control over pricing and, accordingly, the ability to protect their hardcover sales.

[11] The MFN Clause changed the situation by making it imperative, not merely desirable, that the publishers wrest control over pricing from ebook retailers generally. Under the MFN, if Amazon stayed at a wholesale model and continued to sell ebooks at $9.99, the publishers would be forced to sell in the iBookstore, too, at that same $9.99 price point. The result would be the worst of both worlds: lower short-term revenue and no control over pricing. The publishers recognized that, as a practical matter, this meant that the MFN Clause would force them to move Amazon to an agency relationship. As [the CEO of Simon & Schuster] put it, her company would need to move all its other ebook retailers to agency unless we wanted to make even less money in this growing market. This situation also gave each of the publishers a stake in Apple's quest to have a critical mass of publishers join the iBookstore because, "while no one Publisher could effect an industry-wide shift in prices or change the public's perception of a book's value, if they moved together they could."

[12] Apple understood this dynamic as well. As the district court found, Apple did not change its thinking when it replaced the explicit requirement that the publishers move other retailers to an agency model with the MFN. Indeed, in the following weeks, Apple assiduously worked to make sure that the shift to agency occurred. But Apple also understood that . . . "any decent MFN forces the model" away from wholesale and to agency. Or as the district court found, the MFN protected Apple from retail price competition as it punished a Publisher if it failed to impose agency terms on other e-tailers.

[13] Thus, the terms of the negotiation between Apple and the publishers became clear: Apple wanted quick and successful entry into the ebook market and to eliminate retail price competition with Amazon. In exchange, it offered the publishers an opportunity to confront Amazon as one of an organized group united in an effort to eradicate the $9.99 price point. Both sides needed a critical mass of publishers to achieve their goals. The MFN played a pivotal role in this quid pro quo by stiffening the spines of the publishers to ensure that they would demand new terms from Amazon, and protecting Apple from retail price competition. [. . .]

[14] By the January 27 iPad launch, five of the Big Six—Hachette, HarperCollins, Macmillan, Penguin, and Simon & Schuster—had agreed to participate in the iBookstore. The lone holdout, Random House, did not join because its executives believed it would fare better under a wholesale pricing model and were unwilling to make a complete switch to agency pricing. [. . .]

[15] Apple portrays its Contracts with the Publisher Defendants as, at worst, "unwittingly facilitat[ing]" their joint conduct. All Apple did, it claims, was attempt to enter the market on profitable terms by offering contractual provisions—an agency model, the MFN Clause, and tiered price caps—which ensured the company a small profit on each ebook sale and insulated it from retail price competition. This had the effect of raising prices because it created an incentive for the Publisher Defendants to demand that Amazon adopt an agency model and to seize control over consumer-facing ebook prices industry-wide. But although Apple knew that its contractual terms would entice the Publisher Defendants (who wanted to do away with Amazon's $9.99 pricing) to seek control over prices from Amazon and other ebook retailers, Apple's success in capitalizing on the Publisher Defendants' preexisting incentives, it contends, does not suggest that it joined a conspiracy among the Publisher Defendants to raise prices. In sum, Apple's basic argument is that because its Contracts with the Publisher Defendants were fully

consistent with its independent business interests, those agreements provide only "ambiguous" evidence of a § 1 conspiracy, and the district court therefore erred under Matsushita and Monsanto in inferring such a conspiracy.

[16] We disagree. At the start, Apple's benign portrayal of its Contracts with the Publisher Defendants is not persuasive—not because those Contracts themselves were independently unlawful, but because, in context, they provide strong evidence that Apple consciously orchestrated a conspiracy among the Publisher Defendants. As explained below, and as the district court concluded, Apple understood that its proposed Contracts were attractive to the Publisher Defendants only if they collectively shifted their relationships with Amazon to an agency model—which Apple knew would result in higher consumer-facing ebook prices. In addition to these Contracts, moreover, ample additional evidence identified by the district court established both that the Publisher Defendants' shifting to an agency model with Amazon was the result of express collusion among them and that Apple consciously played a key role in organizing that collusion. The district court did not err in concluding that Apple was more than an innocent bystander.

[17] Apple offered each Big Six publisher a proposed Contract that would be attractive only if the publishers acted collectively. Under Apple's proposed agency model, the publishers stood to make less money per sale than under their wholesale agreements with Amazon, but the Publisher Defendants were willing to stomach this loss because the model allowed them to sell new releases and bestsellers for more than $9.99. Because of the MFN Clause, however, each new release and bestseller sold in the iBookstore would cost only $9.99 as long as Amazon continued to sell ebooks at that price. So in order to receive the perceived benefit of Apple's proposed Contracts, the Publisher Defendants had to switch Amazon to an agency model as well—something no individual publisher had sufficient leverage to do on its own. Thus, each Publisher Defendant would be able to accomplish the shift to agency—and therefore have an incentive to sign Apple's proposed Contracts—only if it acted in tandem with its competitors. By the very act of signing a Contract with Apple containing an MFN Clause, then, each of the Publisher Defendants signaled a clear commitment to move against Amazon, thereby facilitating their collective action. As the district court explained, the MFNs "stiffened the spines" of the Publisher Defendants.

[18] As a sophisticated negotiator, Apple was fully aware that its proposed Contracts would entice a critical mass of publishers only if these publishers perceived an opportunity collectively to shift Amazon to agency. In fact, this was the very purpose of the MFN, which Apple's [employee] devised as an elegant alternative to a provision that would have explicitly required the publishers to adopt an agency model with other retailers. As [another Apple employee] put it, the MFN "force[d] the model" from wholesale to agency. Indeed, the MFN's capacity for forcing collective action by the publishers was precisely what enabled [CEO Steve] Jobs to predict with confidence that "the price will be the same" on the iBookstore and the Kindle when he announced the launch of the iPad—the same, Jobs said, because the publishers would make Amazon "sign agency contract[s]" by threatening to withhold their ebooks. Apple was also fully aware that once the Publisher Defendants seized control over consumer-facing ebook prices, those prices would rise. It knew from the outset that the publishers hated Amazon's $9.99 price point, and it put price caps in its agreements because it specifically anticipated that once the publishers gained control over prices, they would push them higher than $9.99, higher than Apple itself deemed "realistic."

[19] On appeal, Apple nonetheless defends the Contracts that it proposed to the publishers as an "aikido move" that shrewdly leveraged market conditions to its own advantage. "Aikido move" or not, the attractiveness of Apple's offer to the Publisher Defendants hinged on whether it could successfully help organize them to force Amazon to an agency model and then to use their newfound collective control to raise ebook prices. The Supreme Court has defined an agreement for Sherman Act § 1 purposes as a conscious commitment to a common scheme designed to achieve an unlawful objective. Plainly, this use of the promise of higher prices as a bargaining chip to induce the Publisher Defendants to participate in the iBookstore constituted a conscious commitment to the goal of raising ebook prices. "Antitrust law has never required identical motives among conspirators" when their independent reasons for joining together lead to collusive action. Put differently, "independent reasons" can also be "interdependent," and the fact that Apple's conduct was in its own economic interest in no way undermines the inference that it entered an agreement to raise ebook prices.

[20] Nor was the Publisher Defendants' joint action against Amazon a result of parallel decisionmaking. As we have explained, conduct resulting solely from competitors' independent business decisions—and not from any "agreement"—is not unlawful under § 1 of the Sherman Act, even if it is anticompetitive. But to generate a

permissible inference of agreement, a plaintiff need only present sufficient evidence that such agreement conclude that it was not equally likely that the near-simultaneous signing of Apple's Contracts by multiple publishers—which led to all of the Publisher Defendants moving against Amazon—resulted from the parties' independent decisions, as opposed to a meeting of the minds. That the Publisher Defendants were in constant communication regarding their negotiations with both Apple and Amazon can hardly be disputed. Indeed, Apple never seriously argues that the Publisher Defendants were not acting in concert.

[21] Even so, Apple claims, it cannot have organized the conspiracy among the Publisher Defendants if it merely unwittingly facilitated their joint conduct. But this argument founders—and dramatically so—on the factual findings of the district court. As the district court explained, Apple's Contracts with the publishers must be considered in the context of the entire record. Even if Apple was unaware of the extent of the Publisher Defendants' coordination when it first approached them, its subsequent communications with them as negotiations progressed show that Apple consciously played a key role in organizing their express collusion. From the outset, [Apple] told the publishers that Apple would launch its iBookstore only if a sufficient number of them agreed to participate and that each publisher would receive identical terms, assuring them that a critical mass of major publishers would be prepared to move against Amazon. Later on, [Apple] kept the publishers updated about how many of their peers signed Apple's Contracts, and reminded them that it was offering "the best chance for publishers to challenge the 9.99 price point" before it became "cemented" in "consumer expectations." When time ran short, Apple coordinated phone calls between the publishers who had agreed and those who remained on the fence. As Cue said at trial, Apple endeavored to "assure the publishers that they weren't going to be alone, so that Apple would take the fear away of the Amazon retribution that they were all afraid of." [. . .]

[22] In short, we have no difficulty on this record rejecting Apple's argument that the district court erred in concluding that Apple conspired with the Publisher Defendants to eliminate retail price competition and to raise e-book prices. . . . .

[23] By agreeing to orchestrate a horizontal price-fixing conspiracy, Apple committed itself to achieving that unlawful objective: namely, collusion with and among the Publisher Defendants to set ebook prices. This type of agreement, moreover, is a restraint that would always or almost always tend to restrict competition and decrease output.

[24] The response, raised by Apple . . . that Apple engaged in "vertical conduct" that is unfit for per se condemnation therefore misconstrues the Sherman Act analysis. It is the type of restraint Apple agreed to impose that determines whether the per se rule or the rule of reason is appropriate. These rules are means of evaluating whether a restraint is unreasonable, not the reasonableness of a particular defendant's role in the scheme.

[25] Consistent with this principle, the Supreme Court and our Sister Circuits have held all participants in "hub-and-spoke" conspiracies liable when the objective of the conspiracy was a per se unreasonable restraint of trade. In *Klor's, Inc. v. Broadway–Hale Stores, Inc.*, for example, the Supreme Court considered whether a prominent retailer of electronic appliances could be held liable under § 1 of the Sherman Act for fostering an agreement with and among its distributors to have those companies boycott a competing retailer. The Court characterized this arrangement as a "group boycott" supported by a wide combination consisting of manufacturers, distributors and a retailer. It then decided that, if the combination were proved at trial, holding the retailer liable would be appropriate because group boycotts, or concerted refusals by traders to deal with other traders, are per se unreasonable restraints of trade. [. . .]

[26] Because the reasonableness of a restraint turns on its anticompetitive effects, and not the identity of each actor who participates in imposing it, Apple and the dissent's observation that the Supreme Court has refused to apply the *per se* rule to certain vertical agreements is inapposite. The rule of reason is unquestionably appropriate to analyze an agreement between a manufacturer and its distributors to, for instance, limit the price at which the distributors sell the manufacturer's goods or the locations at which they sell them. These vertical restrictions are widely used in our free market economy, can enhance interbrand competition, and do not inevitably have a pernicious effect on competition. But the relevant agreement in restraint of trade in this case is not Apple's vertical Contracts with the Publisher Defendants (which might well, if challenged, have to be evaluated under the rule of reason); it is the horizontal agreement that Apple organized among the Publisher Defendants to raise ebook prices.

As explained below, horizontal agreements with the purpose and effect of raising prices are per se unreasonable because they pose a threat to the central nervous system of the economy; that threat is just as significant when a vertical market participant organizes the conspiracy. Indeed, as the dissent notes, the Publisher Defendants' coordination to fix prices is uncontested on appeal. The competitive effects of that same restraint are no different merely because a different conspirator is the defendant. [. . .]

[27] In short, the relevant "agreement in restraint of trade" in this case is the price-fixing conspiracy identified by the district court, not Apple's vertical contracts with the Publisher Defendants. How the law might treat Apple's vertical agreements in the absence of a finding that Apple agreed to create the horizontal restraint is irrelevant. Instead, the question is whether the vertical organizer of a horizontal conspiracy designed to raise prices has agreed to a restraint that is any less anticompetitive than its co-conspirators, and can therefore escape per se liability. We think not.

NOTES

1) Could Toys R Us have unilaterally announced that it would not deal with any manufacturer that was selling to warehouse clubs? If so, why was the conduct described above challenged and punished?

2) Do you agree with the Second Circuit that Apple organized a horizontal conspiracy? Or did Apple, understanding each publisher's incentives, simply act in ways designed to facilitate each publisher's unilateral decisionmaking in ways that benefited Apple? What rule or principle are you using to differentiate between those two characterizations: and what evidence in the case is critical to your view?

3) Think back to the discussion in Chapter IV on the definition of agreement. Is it fair to say that the horizontal competitors in *Toys R Us* and *Apple* satisfied that definition while participants in tacit collusion do not?

4) Was there a procompetitive justification for the conduct in either of these hub-and-spoke cases?

C. What Is Naked Collusion? The *Per Se* / Rule of Reason Boundary

When is "literal" price fixing not "antitrust" price fixing? This is one of the recurrent riddles in the string of Supreme Court cases that attempt to define the border between *per se* illegal conduct and practices that merit rule of reason analysis.

Of course, some forms of literal "price fixing" do not even get onto the radar of antitrust analysis. Some are not regarded as joint conduct at all: for example, as we saw in Chapter IV, employees and subsidiaries wholly within the bounds of the firm coordinate on price and output all the time without any suggestion of antitrust scrutiny.[349] Other forms of price fixing are specially protected by antitrust exemptions, as we shall see in Chapter X, including collective wage bargaining by unions.

But other practices that come under antitrust scrutiny may raise serious questions about whether it is appropriate to treat the behavior in question as naked collusion and apply *per se* condemnation. In this section we will meet several of these "edge cases." The unifying theme in these cases is that there is a serious question about whether what is going on should be characterized as naked collusion among competitors—that is, conduct equivalent to a price-fixing cartel—or alternatively as a collaborative effort among competitors to do something that could be procompetitive, even if it involves reducing or eliminating competition between the participants.

1. Joint Ventures and Joint Products

The antitrust analysis of cooperative ventures among rivals to find new ways to meet demand has changed significantly over the last 60 years. We begin with *Sealy* and *Topco*, two somewhat infamous older decisions that condemn as *per se* illegal practices that would almost certainly be analyzed under the rule of reason today. In *Sealy* the court held that a group of mattress manufacturers violated the Sherman Act when they jointly developed and

---

[349] Sanjukta Paul has called this the "firm exception" to a general rule against coordination. Sanjukta Paul, *Fissuring and the Firm Exception*, 82 L. & Contemp. Probs. 65 (2019); Sanjukta Paul, *On Firms*, 90 U. Chi. L. Rev. 579 (2023).

offered "Sealy" label mattresses, because the participants had divided territories amongst themselves for the purposes of the jointly-offered Sealy mattresses only. In *Topco*, the Court condemned as *per se* illegal a cooperative enterprise between smaller supermarkets that aimed to facilitate more vigorous competition with larger rivals, involving restrictions on their dealings with the jointly-branded private label goods.

CASENOTE: United States v. Sealy, Inc.
388 U.S. 350 (1967)

In *Sealy* DOJ challenged an arrangement between manufacturers of mattresses and other bedding products that permitted smaller, regional manufacturers to build national brand recognition. The arrangement involved Sealy granting licenses to make "Sealy" products to a series of manufacturer-licensees, each of which had the exclusive right to make and sell products under the Sealy name and trademark in a particular territory. The prices of the Sealy mattresses were set collectively. The arrangement did *not* involve any limitation or agreement on each manufacturer-licensee's ability to make, sell, or price products that were not branded with the Sealy name.

Writing for the Court, Justice Fortas called this venture "flagrant and pervasive price-fixing, in obvious violation of the law." Arguments that the venture actually promoted competition were irrelevant, given the coordination on price: "It is argued . . . that a number of small grocers might allocate territory among themselves on an exclusive basis as incident to the use of a common name and common advertisements, and that this sort of venture should be welcomed in the interests of competition, and should not be condemned as per se unlawful. But condemnation of appellee's territorial arrangements certainly does not require us to go so far as to condemn that quite different situation, whatever might be the result if it were presented to us for decision. For here, the arrangements for territorial limitations are part of 'an aggregation of trade restraints' including unlawful price-fixing and policing. Within settled doctrine, they are unlawful under s 1 of the Sherman Act without the necessity for an inquiry in each particular case as to their business or economic justification, their impact in the marketplace, or their reasonableness."

Justice Harlan dissented, but he did not argue that Sealy's project was a horizontal collaboration for which rule of reason treatment was appropriate. Instead, he argued that the arrangement was fundamentally vertical, as it was grounded in the relationships between Sealy (the licensor) and the individual manufacturer-licensees. This, he argued, was crucial: "[V]ertical restraints—that is, limitations imposed by a manufacturer on its own dealers . . . or by a licensor on his licensees—may have independent and valid business justifications. The person imposing the restraint cannot necessarily be said to be acting for anticompetitive purposes. Quite to the contrary, he can be expected to be acting to enhance the competitive position of his product vis-a-vis other brands." And vertical restraints may represent "the only practicable means a small company has for breaking into or staying in business." As such, they should be "tested by the rule of reason."

United States v. Topco Associates
405 U.S. 596 (1972)

Justice Marshall.

[1] The United States brought this action for injunctive relief against alleged violation by Topco Associates, Inc. (Topco), of § 1 of the Sherman Act . . . . Following a trial on the merits, the United States District Court for the Northern District of Illinois entered judgment for Topco, and the United States appealed directly to this Court pursuant to § 2 of the Expediting Act. We noted probable jurisdiction, and we now reverse the judgment of the District Court.

[2] Topco is a cooperative association of approximately 25 small and medium-sized regional supermarket chains that operate stores in some 33 States. Each of the member chains operates independently; there is no pooling of earnings, profits, capital, management, or advertising resources. No grocery business is conducted under the Topco name. Its basic function is to serve as a purchasing agent for its members. In this capacity, it procures and distributes to the members more than 1,000 different food and related nonfood items, most of which are distributed

under brand names owned by Topco. The association does not itself own any manufacturing, processing, or warehousing facilities, and the items that it procures for members are usually shipped directly from the packer or manufacturer to the members. Payment is made either to Topco or directly to the manufacturer at a cost that is virtually the same for the members as for Topco itself.

[3] All of the stock in Topco is owned by the members, with the common stock, the only stock having voting rights, being equally distributed. The board of directors, which controls the operation of the association, is drawn from the members and is normally composed of high-ranking executive officers of member chains. It is the board that elects the association's officers and appoints committee members, and it is from the board that the principal executive officers of Topco must be drawn. Restrictions on the alienation of stock and the procedure for selecting all important officials of the association from within the ranks of its members give the members complete and unfettered control over the operations of the association.

[4] Topco was founded in the 1940's by a group of small, local grocery chains, independently owned and operated, that desired to cooperate to obtain high quality merchandise under private labels in order to compete more effectively with larger national and regional chains. . . . By 1964, Topco's members had combined retail sales of more than $2 billion; by 1967, their sales totaled more than $2.3 billion, a figure exceeded by only three national grocery chains.

[5] Members of the association vary in the degree of market share that they possess in their respective areas. The range is from 1.5% to 16%, with the average being approximately 6%. While it is difficult to compare these figures with the market shares of larger regional and national chains because of the absence in the record of accurate statistics for these chains, there is much evidence in the record that Topco members are frequently in as strong a competitive position in their respective areas as any other chain. The strength of this competitive position is due, in some measure, to the success of Topco-brand products. Although only 10% of the total goods sold by Topco members bear the association's brand names, the profit on these goods is substantial and their very existence has improved the competitive potential of Topco members with respect to other large and powerful chains.

[6] It is apparent that from meager beginnings approximately a quarter of a century ago, Topco has developed into a purchasing association wholly owned and operated by member chains, which possess much economic muscle, individually as well as cooperatively. [. . .]

[7] The United States charged that, beginning at least as early as 1960 and continuing up to the time that the complaint was filed, Topco had combined and conspired with its members to violate § 1 in two respects. First, the Government alleged that there existed:

> a continuing agreement, understanding and concert of action among the co-conspirator member firms acting through Topco, the substantial terms of which have been and are that each co-conspirator member firm will sell Topco-controlled brands only within the marketing territory allocated to it, and will refrain from selling Topco-controlled brands outside such marketing territory.

[8] The division of marketing territories to which the complaint refers consists of a number of practices by the association.

[9] Article IX, § 2, of the Topco bylaws establishes three categories of territorial licenses that members may secure from the association:

(a) *Exclusive* — An exclusive territory is one in which the member is licensed to sell all products bearing specified trademarks of the Association, to the exclusion of all other persons.

(b) *Non-exclusive* — A non-exclusive territory is one in which a member is licensed to sell all products bearing specified trademarks of the Association, but not to the exclusion of others who may also be licensed to sell products bearing the same trademarks of the Association in the same territory.

(c) *Coextensive* — A coextensive territory is one in which two (2) or more members are licensed to sell all products bearing specified trademarks of the Association to the exclusion of all other persons. . . .

[10] When applying for membership, a chain must designate the type of license that it desires. Membership must first be approved by the board of directors, and thereafter by an affirmative vote of 75% of the association's members. If, however, the member whose operations are closest to those of the applicant, or any member whose operations are located within 100 miles of the applicant, votes against approval, an affirmative vote of 85% of the members is required for approval. Because, as indicated by the record, members cooperate in accommodating each other's wishes, the procedure for approval provides, in essence, that members have a veto of sorts over actual or potential competition in the territorial areas in which they are concerned.

[11] Following approval, each new member signs an agreement with Topco designating the territory in which that member may sell Topco-brand products. No member may sell these products outside the territory in which it is licensed. Most licenses are exclusive, and even those denominated "coextensive" or "non-exclusive" prove to be *de facto* exclusive. Exclusive territorial areas are often allocated to members who do no actual business in those areas on the theory that they may wish to expand at some indefinite future time and that expansion would likely be in the direction of the allocated territory. When combined with each member's veto power over new members, provisions for exclusivity work effectively to insulate members from competition in Topco-brand goods. Should a member violate its license agreement and sell in areas other than those in which it is licensed, its membership can be terminated under Art. IV, §§ 2(a) and 2(b) of the bylaws. Once a territory is classified as exclusive, either formally or *de facto*, it is extremely unlikely that the classification will ever be changed.

[12] The Government maintains that this scheme of dividing markets violates the Sherman Act because it operates to prohibit competition in Topco-brand products among grocery chains engaged in retail operations. The Government also makes a subsidiary challenge to Topco's practices regarding licensing members to sell at wholesale. Under the bylaws, members are not permitted to sell any products supplied by the association at wholesale, whether trademarked or not, without first applying for and receiving special permission from the association to do so. Before permission is granted, other licenses (usually retailers), whose interests may potentially be affected by wholesale operations, are consulted as to their wishes in the matter. If permission is obtained, the member must agree to restrict the sale of Topco products to a specific geographic area and to sell under any conditions imposed by the association. Permission to wholesale has often been sought by members, only to be denied by the association. The Government contends that this amounts not only to a territorial restriction violative of the Sherman Act, but also to a restriction on customers that in itself is violative of the Act.

[13] From the inception of this lawsuit, Topco accepted as true most of the Government's allegations regarding territorial divisions and restrictions on wholesaling, although it differed greatly with the Government on the conclusions, both factual and legal, to be drawn from these facts.

[14] Topco's answer to the complaint is illustrative of its posture in the District Court and before this Court:

> Private label merchandising is a way of economic life in the food retailing industry, and exclusivity is the essence of a private label program; without exclusivity, a private label would not be private. Each national and large regional chain has its own exclusive private label products in addition to the nationally advertised brands which all chains sell. Each such chain relies upon the exclusivity of its own private label line to differentiate its private label products from those of its competitors and to attract and retain the repeat business and loyalty of consumers. Smaller retail grocery stores and chains are unable to compete effectively with the national and large regional chains without also offering their own exclusive private label products. [. . .]

> The only feasible method by which Topco can procure private label products and assure the exclusivity thereof is through trademark licenses specifying the territory in which each member may sell such trademarked products.

[15] Topco essentially maintains that it needs territorial divisions to compete with larger chains; that the association could not exist if the territorial divisions were anything but exclusive; and that by restricting competition in the sale of Topco-brand goods, the association actually increases competition by enabling its members to compete successfully with larger regional and national chains.

[16] The District Court, considering all these things relevant to its decision, agreed with Topco. It recognized that the panoply of restraints that Topco imposed on its members worked to prevent competition in Topco-brand products, but concluded that

> whatever anti-competitive effect these practices may have on competition in the sale of Topco private label brands is far outweighed by the increased ability of Topco members to compete both with the national chains and other supermarkets operating in their respective territories.

[17] The court held that Topco's practices were procompetitive and, therefore, consistent with the purposes of the antitrust laws. But we conclude that the District Court used an improper analysis in reaching its result. [. . .]

[18] We think that it is clear that the restraint in this case is a horizontal one, and, therefore, a *per se* violation of § 1. The District Court failed to make any determination as to whether there were *per se* horizontal territorial restraints in this case and simply applied a rule of reason in reaching its conclusions that the restraints were not illegal. In so doing, the District Court erred. *United States* v. *Sealy, Inc.*, [388 U.S. 350 (1967)] is, in fact, on all fours with this case. Sealy licensed manufacturers of mattresses and bedding to make and sell products using the Sealy trademark. Like Topco, Sealy was a corporation owned almost entirely by its licensees, who elected the Board of Directors and controlled the business. Just as in this case, Sealy agreed with the licensees not to license other manufacturers or sellers to sell Sealy-brand products in a designated territory in exchange for the promise of the licensee who sold in that territory not to expand its sales beyond the area demarcated by Sealy. The Court held that this was a horizontal territorial restraint, which was *per se* violative of the Sherman Act.[9]

[19] Whether or not we would decide this case the same way under the rule of reason used by the District Court is irrelevant to the issue before us. The fact is that courts are of limited utility in examining difficult economic problems.[10] Our inability to weigh, in any meaningful sense, destruction of competition in one sector of the economy against promotion of competition in another sector is one important reason we have formulated *per se* rules.

[20] In applying these rigid rules, the Court has consistently rejected the notion that naked restraints of trade are to be tolerated because they are well intended or because they are allegedly developed to increase competition.

[21] Antitrust laws in general, and the Sherman Act in particular, are the Magna Carta of free enterprise. They are as important to the preservation of economic freedom and our free-enterprise system as the Bill of Rights is to the protection of our fundamental personal freedoms. And the freedom guaranteed each and every business, no matter how small, is the freedom to compete—to assert with vigor, imagination, devotion, and ingenuity whatever economic muscle it can muster. Implicit in such freedom is the notion that it cannot be foreclosed with respect to one sector of the economy because certain private citizens or groups believe that such foreclosure might promote greater competition in a more important sector of the economy.

[22] The District Court determined that by limiting the freedom of its individual members to compete with each other, Topco was doing a greater good by fostering competition between members and other large supermarket chains. But, the fallacy in this is that Topco has no authority under the Sherman Act to determine the respective values of competition in various sectors of the economy. On the contrary, the Sherman Act gives to each Topco member and to each prospective member the right to ascertain for itself whether or not competition with other supermarket chains is more desirable than competition in the sale of Topco-brand products. Without territorial restrictions, Topco members may indeed "cut each other's throats." But, we have never found this possibility sufficient to warrant condoning horizontal restraints of trade. [. . .]

---

[9] It is true that in *Sealy* the Court dealt with price fixing as well as territorial restrictions. To the extent that *Sealy* casts doubt on whether horizontal territorial limitations, unaccompanied by price fixing, are *per se* violations of the Sherman Act, we remove that doubt today.

[10] There has been much recent commentary on the wisdom of *per se* rules. Without the *per se* rules, businessmen would be left with little to aid them in predicting in any particular case what courts will find to be legal and illegal under the Sherman Act. Should Congress ultimately determine that predictability is unimportant in this area of the law, it can, of course, make *per se* rules inapplicable in some or all cases, and leave courts free to ramble through the wilds of economic theory in order to maintain a flexible approach.

[23] There have been tremendous departures from the notion of a free-enterprise system as it was originally conceived in this country. These departures have been the product of congressional action and the will of the people. If a decision is to be made to sacrifice competition in one portion of the economy for greater competition in another portion, this too is a decision that must be made by Congress and not by private forces or by the courts. Private forces are too keenly aware of their own interests in making such decisions and courts are ill-equipped and ill-situated for such decisionmaking. To analyze, interpret, and evaluate the myriad of competing interests and the endless data that would surely be brought to bear on such decisions, and to make the delicate judgment on the relative values to society of competitive areas of the economy, the judgment of the elected representatives of the people is required.

[24] Just as the territorial restrictions on retailing Topco-brand products must fall, so must the territorial restrictions on wholesaling. The considerations are the same, and the Sherman Act requires identical results.

[25] We also strike down Topco's other restrictions on the right of its members to wholesale goods. These restrictions amount to regulation of the customers to whom members of Topco may sell Topco-brand goods. Like territorial restrictions, limitations on customers are intended to limit intra-brand competition and to promote inter-brand competition. For the reasons previously discussed, the arena in which Topco members compete must be left to their unfettered choice absent a contrary congressional determination.

[26] We reverse the judgment of the District Court and remand the case for entry of an appropriate decree.

Justice Blackmun, concurring in the result.

[27] The conclusion the Court reaches has its anomalous aspects, for surely, as the District Court's findings make clear, today's decision in the Government's favor will tend to stultify Topco members' competition with the great and larger chains. The bigs, therefore, should find it easier to get bigger and, as a consequence, reality seems at odds with the public interest. The per se rule, however, now appears to be so firmly established by the Court that, at this late date, I could not oppose it. Relief, if any is to be forthcoming, apparently must be by way of legislation.

Chief Justice Burger, dissenting.

[28] This case does not involve restraints on interbrand competition or an allocation of markets by an association with monopoly or near-monopoly control of the sources of supply of one or more varieties of staple goods. Rather, we have here an agreement among several small grocery chains to join in a cooperative endeavor that, in my view, has an unquestionably lawful principal purpose; in pursuit of that purpose they have mutually agreed to certain minimal ancillary restraints that are fully reasonable in view of the principal purpose and that have never before today been held by this Court to be *per se* violations of the Sherman Act.

[29] In joining in this cooperative endeavor, these small chains did not agree to the restraints here at issue in order to make it possible for them to exploit an already established line of products through noncompetitive pricing. There was no such thing as a Topco line of products until this cooperative was formed. The restraints to which the cooperative's members have agreed deal only with the marketing of the products in the Topco line, and the only function of those restraints is to permit each member chain to establish, within its own geographical area and through its own local advertising and marketing efforts, a local consumer awareness of the trademarked family of products as that member's "private label" line. The goal sought was the enhancement of the individual members' abilities to compete, albeit to a modest degree, with the large national chains which had been successfully marketing private-label lines for several years. The sole reason for a cooperative endeavor was to make economically feasible such things as quality control, large quantity purchases at bulk prices, the development of attractively printed labels, and the ability to offer a number of different lines of trademarked products. All these things, of course, are feasible for the large national chains operating individually, but they are beyond the reach of the small operators proceeding alone.

[30] After a careful review of the economic considerations bearing upon this case, the District Court determined that "the relief which the government here seeks would not increase competition in Topco private label brands"; on the contrary, such relief "would substantially diminish competition in the supermarket field." This Court has not today determined, on the basis of an examination of the underlying economic realities, that the District Court's

conclusions are incorrect. Rather, the majority holds that the District Court had no business examining Topco's practices under the "rule of reason"; it should not have sought to determine whether Topco's practices did in fact restrain trade or commerce within the meaning of § 1 of the Sherman Act; it should have found no more than that those practices involve a "horizontal division of markets" and are, by that very fact, *per se* violations of the Act.

[31] I do not believe that our prior decisions justify the result reached by the majority. Nor do I believe that a new *per se* rule should be established in disposing of this case, for the judicial convenience and ready predictability that are made possible by *per se* rules are not such overriding considerations in antitrust law as to justify their promulgation without careful prior consideration of the relevant economic realities in the light of the basic policy and goals of the Sherman Act. [. . .]

[32] I cannot agree with the Court's description of *Sealy* as being "on all fours with this case." *Sealy* does support the proposition that the restraints on the Topco licensees are horizontally imposed. Beyond that, however, *Sealy* is hardly controlling here. The territorial restrictions in *Sealy* were found by this Court to be so intimately a part of an unlawful price-fixing and policing scheme that the two arrangements fell together:

> [T]his unlawful resale price-fixing activity refutes appellee's claim that the territorial restraints
> were mere incidents of a lawful program of trademark licensing. The territorial restraints were
> a part of the unlawful price-fixing and policing.

[33] [. . .] The foregoing analysis . . . indicates to me that the Court is not merely following prior holdings; on the contrary, it is establishing a new *per se* rule. In the face of the District Court's well supported findings that the effects of such a rule in this case will be adverse to the public welfare, the Court lays down that rule without regard to the impact that the condemned practices may have on competition. In doing so, the Court virtually invites Congress to undertake to determine that impact. I question whether the Court is fulfilling the role assigned to it under the statute when it declines to make this determination; in any event, if the Court is unwilling on this record to assess the economic impact, it surely should not proceed to make a new rule to govern the economic activity. [. . .]

[34] In formulating a new *per se* rule today, the Court does not tell us what "pernicious effect on competition" the practices here outlawed are perceived to have; nor does it attempt to show that those practices "lack . . . any redeeming virtue." Rather, it emphasizes only the importance of predictability, asserting that "courts are of limited utility in examining difficult economic problems" and have not yet been left free by Congress to "ramble through the wilds of economic theory in order to maintain a flexible approach."

[35] With all respect, I believe that there are two basic fallacies in the Court's approach here. First, while I would not characterize our role under the Sherman Act as one of "rambling through the wilds," it is indeed one that requires our "examination of difficult economic problems." We can undoubtedly ease our task, but we should not abdicate that role by formulation of *per se* rules with no justification other than the enhancement of predictability and the reduction of judicial investigation. Second, from the general proposition that *per se* rules play a necessary role in antitrust law, it does not follow that the particular *per se* rule promulgated today is an appropriate one. Although it might well be desirable in a proper case for this Court to formulate a *per se* rule dealing with horizontal territorial limitations, it would not necessarily be appropriate for such a rule to amount to a blanket prohibition against all such limitations. More specifically, it is far from clear to me why such a rule should cover those division-of-market agreements that involve no price fixing and which are concerned only with trademarked products that are not in a monopoly or near-monopoly position with respect to competing brands. The instant case presents such an agreement; I would not decide it upon the basis of a *per se* rule.

[36] The District Court specifically found that the horizontal restraints involved here tend positively to promote competition in the supermarket field and to produce lower costs for the consumer. The Court seems implicitly to accept this determination, but says that the Sherman Act does not give Topco the authority to determine for itself "whether or not competition with other supermarket chains is more desirable than competition in the sale of Topco-brand products." But the majority overlooks a further specific determination of the District Court, namely, that the invalidation of the restraints here at issue "would not increase competition in Topco private label brands." Indeed, the District Court seemed to believe that it would, on the contrary, lead to the likely demise of those brands in time. And the evidence before the District Court would appear to justify that conclusion.

[37] There is no national demand for Topco brands, nor has there ever been any national advertising of those brands. It would be impracticable for Topco, with its limited financial resources, to convert itself into a national brand distributor in competition with distributors of existing national brands. Furthermore, without the right to grant exclusive licenses, it could not attract and hold new members as replacements for those of its present members who, following the pattern of the past, eventually grow sufficiently in size to be able to leave the cooperative organization and develop their own individual private-label brands. Moreover, Topco's present members, once today's decision has had its full impact over the course of time, will have no more reason to promote Topco products through local advertising and merchandising efforts than they will have such reason to promote any other generally available brands.

[38] The issues presented by the antitrust cases reaching this Court are rarely simple to resolve under the rule of reason; they do indeed frequently require us to make difficult economic determinations. We should not for that reason alone, however, be overly zealous in formulating new *per se* rules, for an excess of zeal in that regard is both contrary to the policy of the Sherman Act and detrimental to the welfare of consumers generally. Indeed, the economic effect of the new rule laid down by the Court today seems clear: unless Congress intervenes, grocery staples marketed under private-label brands with their lower consumer prices will soon be available only to those who patronize the large national chains.

* * *

We now turn to two more modern landmarks on the boundary between the *per se* rule and the rule of reason: *Broadcast Music Inc.* (often just "*BMI*") and *Maricopa County*. *BMI* was a watershed case, and arguably it marked the repudiation of the formalism on display in *Sealy* and *Topco*. In *BMI*, the Court declined to condemn as per se illegal an activity that, it recognized, involved "literal" price fixing. *BMI* established that coordination among competitors to create a new product or service that would not otherwise be available, without restricting the participants' freedom to compete individually, should be judged under the rule of reason, not the *per se* rule. In *Maricopa County*, by contrast, the Court went the other way, condemning as *per se* illegal joint activity among competitors that one might have thought plausibly related to a procompetitive activity.[350]

Broadcast Music, Inc. v. Columbia Broadcasting System, Inc.
441 U.S. 1 (1979)

Justice White.

[1] This case involves an action under the antitrust and copyright laws brought by respondent Columbia Broadcasting System, Inc. (CBS), against petitioners, American Society of Composers, Authors and Publishers (ASCAP) and Broadcast Music, Inc. (BMI), and their members and affiliates. The basic question presented is whether the issuance by ASCAP and BMI to CBS of blanket licenses to copyrighted musical compositions at fees negotiated by them is price fixing *per se* unlawful under the antitrust laws. [. . .]

[2] CBS operates one of three national commercial television networks, supplying programs to approximately 200 affiliated stations and telecasting approximately 7,500 network programs per year. Many, but not all, of these programs make use of copyrighted music recorded on the soundtrack. CBS also owns television and radio stations in various cities. [. . .]

[3] Since 1897, the copyright laws have vested in the owner of a copyrighted musical composition the exclusive right to perform the work publicly for profit, but the legal right is not self-enforcing. In 1914, Victor Herbert and a handful of other composers organized ASCAP because those who performed copyrighted music for profit were so numerous and widespread, and most performances so fleeting, that as a practical matter it was impossible for the many individual copyright owners to negotiate with and license the users and to detect unauthorized uses. ASCAP was organized as a clearing-house for copyright owners and users to solve these problems associated with the licensing of music. As ASCAP operates today, its 22,000 members grant it nonexclusive rights to license

---

[350] *See, e.g.*, Rocco J. De Grasse, Maricopa County *and the Problem of Per Se Characterization in Horizontal Price Fixing Cases*, 18 Val. U. L. Rev. 1007 (1984); *but see, e.g.*, Keith B. Leffler, Arizona v. Maricopa County Medical Society: *Maximum-Price Agreements in Markets with Insured Buyers*, 2 Sup. Ct. Econ. Rev. 187 (1983) (supporting per se condemnation).

nondramatic performances of their works, and ASCAP issues licenses and distributes royalties to copyright owners in accordance with a schedule reflecting the nature and amount of the use of their music and other factors.

[4] BMI, a nonprofit corporation owned by members of the broadcasting industry, was organized in 1939, is affiliated with or represents some 10,000 publishing companies and 20,000 authors and composers, and operates in much the same manner as ASCAP. Almost every domestic copyrighted composition is in the repertory either of ASCAP, with a total of three million compositions, or of BMI, with one million.

[5] Both organizations operate primarily through blanket licenses, which give the licensees the right to perform any and all of the compositions owned by the members or affiliates as often as the licensees desire for a stated term. Fees for blanket licenses are ordinarily a percentage of total revenues or a flat dollar amount, and do not directly depend on the amount or type of music used. Radio and television broadcasters are the largest users of music, and almost all of them hold blanket licenses from both ASCAP and BMI. Until this litigation, CBS held blanket licenses from both organizations for its television network on a continuous basis since the late 1940's and had never attempted to secure any other form of license from either ASCAP[5] or any of its members.

[6] The complaint filed by CBS charged various violations of the Sherman Act and the copyright laws. CBS argued that ASCAP and BMI are unlawful monopolies and that the blanket license is illegal price fixing, an unlawful tying arrangement, a concerted refusal to deal, and a misuse of copyrights. The District Court, though denying summary judgment to certain defendants, ruled that the practice did not fall within the *per se* rule. After an 8-week trial, limited to the issue of liability, the court dismissed the complaint, rejecting again the claim that the blanket license was price fixing and a *per se* violation of § 1 of the Sherman Act, and holding that since direct negotiation with individual copyright owners is available and feasible there is no undue restraint of trade, illegal tying, misuse of copyrights, or monopolization.

[7] Though agreeing with the District Court's factfinding and not disturbing its legal conclusions on the other antitrust theories of liability, the Court of Appeals held that the blanket license issued to television networks was a form of price fixing illegal *per se* under the Sherman Act. This conclusion, without more, settled the issue of liability under the Sherman Act, established copyright misuse, and required reversal of the District Court's judgment, as well as a remand to consider the appropriate remedy.

[8] [. . .] Because we disagree with the Court of Appeals' conclusions with respect to the *per se* illegality of the blanket license, we reverse its judgment and remand the cause for further appropriate proceedings.

[9] In construing and applying the Sherman Act's ban against contracts, conspiracies, and combinations in restraint of trade, the Court has held that certain agreements or practices are so plainly anticompetitive and so often lack . . . any redeeming virtue , that they are conclusively presumed illegal without further examination under the rule of reason generally applied in Sherman Act cases. This *per se* rule is a valid and useful tool of antitrust policy and enforcement. And agreements among competitors to fix prices on their individual goods or services are among those concerted activities that the Court has held to be within the *per se* category. But easy labels do not always supply ready answers.

[10] To the Court of Appeals and CBS, the blanket license involves "price fixing" in the literal sense: the composers and publishing houses have joined together into an organization that sets its price for the blanket license it sells. But this is not a question simply of determining whether two or more potential competitors have literally "fixed" a "price." As generally used in the antitrust field, "price fixing" is a shorthand way of describing certain categories of business behavior to which the *per se* rule has been held applicable. The Court of Appeals' literal approach does not alone establish that this particular practice is one of those types or that it is "plainly anticompetitive" and very likely without "redeeming virtue." Literalness is overly simplistic and often overbroad. When two partners set the price of their goods or services they are literally "price fixing," but they are not *per se* in violation of the Sherman Act. Thus, it is necessary to characterize the challenged conduct as falling within or without that category of behavior to which we apply the label "*per se* price fixing." That will often, but not always, be a simple matter.

---

[5] Unless the context indicates otherwise, references to ASCAP alone in this opinion usually apply to BMI as well. . . .

[11] Consequently, as we recognized in *United States v. Topco Associates, Inc.*, 405 U.S. 596, 607–608 (1972), "[i]t is only after considerable experience with certain business relationships that courts classify them as *per se* violations . . . ." We have never examined a practice like this one before; indeed, the Court of Appeals recognized that in dealing with performing rights in the music industry we confront conditions both in copyright law and in antitrust law which are *sui generis*. And though there has been rather intensive antitrust scrutiny of ASCAP and its blanket licenses, that experience hardly counsels that we should outlaw the blanket license as a *per se* restraint of trade. [. . .]

[12] [The Department of Justice sued ASCAP in 1941, alleging that the blanket license was anticompetitive. That litigation resulted in settlement and a consent decree, which was modified in 1950.] Under the amended decree . . .members may grant ASCAP only nonexclusive rights to license their works for public performance. Members, therefore, retain the rights individually to license public performances, along with the rights to license the use of their compositions for other purposes. ASCAP itself is forbidden to grant any license to perform one or more specified compositions in the ASCAP repertory unless both the user and the owner have requested it in writing to do so. ASCAP is required to grant to any user making written application a nonexclusive license to perform all ASCAP compositions either for a period of time or on a per-program basis. ASCAP may not insist on the blanket license, and the fee for the per-program license, which is to be based on the revenues for the program on which ASCAP music is played, must offer the applicant a genuine economic choice between the per-program license and the more common blanket license. If ASCAP and a putative licensee are unable to agree on a fee within 60 days, the applicant may apply to the District Court for a determination of a reasonable fee, with ASCAP having the burden of proving reasonableness.

[13] The 1950 decree, as amended from time to time, continues in effect, and the blanket license continues to be the primary instrument through which ASCAP conducts its business under the decree. The courts have twice construed the decree not to require ASCAP to issue licenses for selected portions of its repertory. It also remains true that the decree guarantees the legal availability of direct licensing of performance rights by ASCAP members; and the District Court found, and in this respect the Court of Appeals agreed, that there are no practical impediments preventing direct dealing by the television networks if they so desire. Historically, they have not done so. Since 1946, CBS and other television networks have taken blanket licenses from ASCAP and BMI. It was not until this suit arose that the CBS network demanded any other kind of license.

[14] Of course, a consent judgment, even one entered at the behest of the Antitrust Division, does not immunize the defendant from liability for actions, including those contemplated by the decree, that violate the rights of nonparties. But it cannot be ignored that the Federal Executive and Judiciary have carefully scrutinized ASCAP and the challenged conduct, have imposed restrictions on various of ASCAP's practices, and, by the terms of the decree, stand ready to provide further consideration, supervision, and perhaps invalidation of asserted anticompetitive practices. In these circumstances, we have a unique indicator that the challenged practice may have redeeming competitive virtues and that the search for those values is not almost sure to be in vain. Thus, although CBS is not bound by the Antitrust Division's actions, the decree is a fact of economic and legal life in this industry, and the Court of Appeals should not have ignored it completely in analyzing the practice. That fact alone might not remove a naked price-fixing scheme from the ambit of the *per se* rule, but... here we are uncertain whether the practice on its face has the effect, or could have been spurred by the purpose, of restraining competition among the individual composers. [. . .]

[15] Finally, we note that Congress itself, in the new Copyright Act, has chosen to employ the blanket license and similar practices. Congress created a compulsory blanket license for secondary transmissions by cable television systems and provided that "[n]otwithstanding any provisions of the antitrust laws, . . . any claimants may agree among themselves as to the proportionate division of compulsory licensing fees among them, may lump their claims together and file them jointly or as a single claim, or may designate a common agent to receive payment on their behalf." 17 U.S.C. App. § 111(d)(5)(A). And the newly created compulsory license for the use of copyrighted compositions in jukeboxes is also a blanket license, which is payable to the performing-rights societies such as ASCAP unless an individual copyright holder can prove his entitlement to a share. § 116(c)(4). Moreover, in requiring noncommercial broadcasters to pay for their use of copyrighted music, Congress again provided that "[n]otwithstanding any provision of the antitrust laws" copyright owners "may designate common agents to

negotiate, agree to, pay, or receive payments." § 118(b). Though these provisions are not directly controlling, they do reflect an opinion that the blanket license, and ASCAP, are economically beneficial in at least some circumstances. [. . .]

[16] As a preliminary matter, we are mindful that the Court of Appeals' holding would appear to be quite difficult to contain. If, as the court held, there is a *per se* antitrust violation whenever ASCAP issues a blanket license to a television network for a single fee, why would it not also be automatically illegal for ASCAP to negotiate and issue blanket licenses to individual radio or television stations or to other users who perform copyrighted music for profit? Likewise, if the present network licenses issued through ASCAP on behalf of its members are *per se* violations, why would it not be equally illegal for the members to authorize ASCAP to issue licenses establishing various categories of uses that a network might have for copyrighted music and setting a standard fee for each described use?

[17] Although the Court of Appeals apparently thought the blanket license could be saved in some or even many applications, it seems to us that the *per se* rule does not accommodate itself to such flexibility and that the observations of the Court of Appeals with respect to remedy tend to impeach the *per se* basis for the holding of liability.[27]

[18] CBS would prefer that ASCAP be authorized, indeed directed, to make all its compositions available at standard per-use rates within negotiated categories of use. But if this in itself or in conjunction with blanket licensing constitutes illegal price fixing by copyright owners, CBS urges that an injunction issue forbidding ASCAP to issue any blanket license or to negotiate any fee except on behalf of an individual member for the use of his own copyrighted work or works. Thus, we are called upon to determine that blanket licensing is unlawful across the board. We are quite sure, however, that the *per se* rule does not require any such holding. [. . .]

[19] In the first place, the line of commerce allegedly being restrained, the performing rights to copyrighted music, exists at all only because of the copyright laws. Those who would use copyrighted music in public performances must secure consent from the copyright owner or be liable at least for the statutory damages for each infringement and, if the conduct is willful and for the purpose of financial gain, to criminal penalties. Furthermore, nothing in the Copyright Act of 1976 indicates in the slightest that Congress intended to weaken the rights of copyright owners to control the public performance of musical compositions. Quite the contrary is true. Although the copyright laws confer no rights on copyright owners to fix prices among themselves or otherwise to violate the antitrust laws, we would not expect that any market arrangements reasonably necessary to effectuate the rights that are granted would be deemed a *per se* violation of the Sherman Act. Otherwise, the commerce anticipated by the Copyright Act and protected against restraint by the Sherman Act would not exist at all or would exist only as a pale reminder of what Congress envisioned.[32]

[20] More generally, in characterizing this conduct under the *per se* rule,[33] our inquiry must focus on whether the effect and, here because it tends to show effect, the purpose of the practice are to threaten the proper operation of

---

[27] The Court of Appeals would apparently not outlaw the blanket license across the board but would permit it in various circumstances where it is deemed necessary or sufficiently desirable. It did not even enjoin blanket licensing with the television networks, the relief it realized would normally follow a finding of *per se* illegality of the license in that context. Instead, as requested by CBS, it remanded to the District Court to require ASCAP to offer in addition to blanket licensing some competitive form of per-use licensing. But per-use licensing by ASCAP, as recognized in the consent decrees, might be even more susceptible to the *per se* rule than blanket licensing.

The rationale for this unusual relief in a *per se* case was that "[t]he blanket license is not simply a 'naked restraint' ineluctably doomed to extinction." To the contrary, the Court of Appeals found that the blanket license might well "serve a market need" for some. This, it seems to us, is not the *per se* approach, which does not yield so readily to circumstances, but in effect is a rather bobtailed application of the rule of reason, bobtailed in the sense that it is unaccompanied by the necessary analysis demonstrating why the particular licensing system is an undue competitive restraint.

[32] Because a musical composition can be "consumed" by many different people at the same time and without the creator's knowledge, the "owner" has no real way to demand reimbursement for the use of his property except through the copyright laws *and* an effective way to enforce those legal rights. It takes an organization of rather large size to monitor most or all uses and to deal with users on behalf of the composers. Moreover, it is inefficient to have too many such organizations duplicating each other's monitoring of use.

[33] The scrutiny occasionally required must not merely subsume the burdensome analysis required under the rule of reason, or else we should apply the rule of reason from the start. That is why the *per se* rule is not employed until after considerable experience with the type of challenged restraint.

our predominantly free-market economy—that is, whether the practice facially appears to be one that would always or almost always tend to restrict competition and decrease output, and in what portion of the market, or instead one designed to increase economic efficiency and render markets more, rather than less, competitive.

[21] The blanket license, as we see it, is not a naked restraint of trade with no purpose except stifling of competition, but rather accompanies the integration of sales, monitoring, and enforcement against unauthorized copyright use. As we have already indicated, ASCAP and the blanket license developed together out of the practical situation in the marketplace: thousands of users, thousands of copyright owners, and millions of compositions. Most users want unplanned, rapid, and indemnified access to any and all of the repertory of compositions, and the owners want a reliable method of collecting for the use of their copyrights. Individual sales transactions in this industry are quite expensive, as would be individual monitoring and enforcement, especially in light of the resources of single composers. Indeed, as both the Court of Appeals and CBS recognize, the costs are prohibitive for licenses with individual radio stations, nightclubs, and restaurants, and it was in that milieu that the blanket license arose.

[22] A middleman with a blanket license was an obvious necessity if the thousands of individual negotiations, a virtual impossibility, were to be avoided. Also, individual fees for the use of individual compositions would presuppose an intricate schedule of fees and uses, as well as a difficult and expensive reporting problem for the user and policing task for the copyright owner. Historically, the market for public-performance rights organized itself largely around the single-fee blanket license, which gave unlimited access to the repertory and reliable protection against infringement. When ASCAP's major and user-created competitor, BMI, came on the scene, it also turned to the blanket license.

[23] With the advent of radio and television networks, market conditions changed, and the necessity for and advantages of a blanket license for those users may be far less obvious than is the case when the potential users are individual television or radio stations, or the thousands of other individuals and organizations performing copyrighted compositions in public. But even for television network licenses, ASCAP reduces costs absolutely by creating a blanket license that is sold only a few, instead of thousands, of times, and that obviates the need for closely monitoring the networks to see that they do not use more than they pay for. ASCAP also provides the necessary resources for blanket sales and enforcement, resources unavailable to the vast majority of composers and publishing houses. Moreover, a bulk license of some type is a necessary consequence of the integration necessary to achieve these efficiencies, and a necessary consequence of an aggregate license is that its price must be established.

[24] This substantial lowering of costs, which is of course potentially beneficial to both sellers and buyers, differentiates the blanket license from individual use licenses. The blanket license is composed of the individual compositions plus the aggregating service. Here, the whole is truly greater than the sum of its parts; it is, to some extent, a different product. The blanket license has certain unique characteristics: It allows the licensee immediate use of covered compositions, without the delay of prior individual negotiations and great flexibility in the choice of musical material. Many consumers clearly prefer the characteristics and cost advantages of this marketable package, and even small-performing rights societies that have occasionally arisen to compete with ASCAP and BMI have offered blanket licenses. Thus, to the extent the blanket license is a different product, ASCAP is not really a joint sales agency offering the individual goods of many sellers, but is a separate seller offering its blanket license, of which the individual compositions are raw material.[40] ASCAP, in short, made a market in which individual composers are inherently unable to compete fully effectively.

[25] Finally, we have some doubt—enough to counsel against application of the *per se* rule—about the extent to which this practice threatens the "central nervous system of the economy," *United States v. Socony-Vacuum Oil Co.*, 310 U.S. 150, 226 n.59 (1940), that is, competitive pricing as the free market's means of allocating resources. Not all arrangements among actual or potential competitors that have an impact on price are *per se* violations of the Sherman Act or even unreasonable restraints. Mergers among competitors eliminate competition, including price competition, but they are not *per se* illegal, and many of them withstand attack under any existing antitrust standard. Joint ventures and other cooperative arrangements are also not usually unlawful, at least not as price-fixing schemes, where the agreement on price is necessary to market the product at all.

[26] Here, the blanket-license fee is not set by competition among individual copyright owners, and it is a fee for the use of any of the compositions covered by the license. But the blanket license cannot be wholly equated with a simple horizontal arrangement among competitors. ASCAP does set the price for its blanket license, but that license is quite different from anything any individual owner could issue. The individual composers and authors have neither agreed not to sell individually in any other market nor use the blanket license to mask price fixing in such other markets. Moreover, the substantial restraints placed on ASCAP and its members by the consent decree must not be ignored. The District Court found that there was no legal, practical, or conspiratorial impediment to CBS's obtaining individual licenses; CBS, in short, had a real choice.

[27] With this background in mind, which plainly enough indicates that over the years, and in the face of available alternatives, the blanket license has provided an acceptable mechanism for at least a large part of the market for the performing rights to copyrighted musical compositions, we cannot agree that it should automatically be declared illegal in all of its many manifestations. Rather, when attacked, it should be subjected to a more discriminating examination under the rule of reason. It may not ultimately survive that attack, but that is not the issue before us today.

[28] As we have noted, the enigmatic remarks of the Court of Appeals with respect to remedy appear to have departed from the court's strict, *per se* approach and to have invited a more careful analysis. But this left the general import of its judgment that the licensing practices of ASCAP and BMI under the consent decree are *per se* violations of the Sherman Act. We reverse that judgment . . . and remand for further proceedings to consider any unresolved issues that CBS may have properly brought to the Court of Appeals. Of course, this will include an assessment under the rule of reason of the blanket license as employed in the television industry, if that issue was preserved by CBS in the Court of Appeals. [. . .]

Justice Stevens, dissenting.

[29] The Court holds that ASCAP's blanket license is not a species of price fixing categorically forbidden by the Sherman Act. I agree with that holding. The Court remands the cases to the Court of Appeals, leaving open the question whether the blanket license as employed by ASCAP and BMI is unlawful under a rule-of-reason inquiry. I think that question is properly before us now and should be answered affirmatively.

[30] There is ample precedent for affirmance of the judgment of the Court of Appeals on a ground that differs from its rationale, provided of course that we do not modify its judgment. In this litigation, the judgment of the Court of Appeals was not that blanket licenses may never be offered by ASCAP and BMI. Rather, its judgment directed the District Court to fashion relief requiring them to offer additional forms of license as well. Even though that judgment may not be consistent with its stated conclusion that the blanket license is "illegal *per se*" as a kind of price fixing, it is entirely consistent with a conclusion that petitioners' exclusive all-or-nothing blanket-license policy violates the rule of reason.

[31] The Court of Appeals may well so decide on remand. In my judgment, however, a remand is not necessary. The record before this Court is a full one, reflecting extensive discovery and eight weeks of trial. The District Court's findings of fact are thorough and well supported. They clearly reveal that the challenged policy does have a significant adverse impact on competition. I would therefore affirm the judgment of the Court of Appeals. [. . .]

[32] The market for music at issue here is wholly dominated by ASCAP-issued blanket licenses. Virtually every domestic copyrighted composition is in the repertoire of either ASCAP or BMI. And again, virtually without exception, the only means that has been used to secure authority to perform such compositions is the blanket license.

[33] The blanket all-or-nothing license is patently discriminatory. The user purchases full access to ASCAP's entire repertoire, even though his needs could be satisfied by a far more limited selection. The price he pays for this access is unrelated either to the quantity or the quality of the music he actually uses, or, indeed, to what he would probably use in a competitive system. Rather, in this unique all-or-nothing system, the price is based on a percentage of the user's advertising revenues, a measure that reflects the customer's ability to pay but is totally unrelated to factors—such as the cost, quality, or quantity of the product—that normally affect price in a competitive market. The ASCAP system requires users to buy more music than they want at a price which, while

not beyond their ability to pay and perhaps not even beyond what is "reasonable" for the access they are getting, may well be far higher than what they would choose to spend for music in a competitive system. It is a classic example of economic discrimination.

[34] The record plainly establishes that there is no price competition between separate musical compositions. Under a blanket license, it is no more expensive for a network to play the most popular current hit in prime time than it is to use an unknown composition as background music in a soap opera. Because the cost to the user is unaffected by the amount used on any program or on all programs, the user has no incentive to economize by, for example, substituting what would otherwise be less expensive songs for established favorites or by reducing the quantity of music used on a program. The blanket license thereby tends to encourage the use of more music, and also of a larger share of what is really more valuable music, than would be expected in a competitive system characterized by separate licenses. And since revenues are passed on to composers on a basis reflecting the character and frequency of the use of their music, the tendency is to increase the rewards of the established composers at the expense of those less well known. Perhaps the prospect is in any event unlikely, but the blanket license does not present a new songwriter with any opportunity to try to break into the market by offering his product for sale at an unusually low price. The absence of that opportunity, however unlikely it may be, is characteristic of a cartelized rather than a competitive market.

[35] The current state of the market cannot be explained on the ground that it could not operate competitively, or that issuance of more limited—and thus less restrictive—licenses by ASCAP is not feasible. The District Court's findings disclose no reason why music-performing rights could not be negotiated on a per-composition or per-use basis, either with the composer or publisher directly or with an agent such as ASCAP. In fact, ASCAP now compensates composers and publishers on precisely those bases. If distributions of royalties can be calculated on a per-use and per-composition basis, it is difficult to see why royalties could not also be collected in the same way. Moreover, the record also shows that where ASCAP's blanket-license scheme does not govern, competitive markets do. A competitive market for "synch" rights exists, and after the use of blanket licenses in the motion picture industry was discontinued, such a market promptly developed in that industry. In sum, the record demonstrates that the market at issue here is one that could be highly competitive, but is not competitive at all. [. . .]

[36] More basically, ASCAP's underlying argument that CBS must be viewed as having acted with complete freedom in choosing the blanket license is not supported by the District Court's findings. The District Court did not find that CBS could cancel its blanket license "tomorrow" and continue to use music in its programming and compete with the other networks. Nor did the District Court find that such a course was without any risk or expense. Rather, the District Court's finding was that within a year, during which it would continue to pay some millions of dollars for its annual blanket license, CBS would be able to develop the needed machinery and enter into the necessary contracts. In other words, although the barriers to direct dealing by CBS as an alternative to paying for a blanket license are real and significant, they are not insurmountable.

[37] Far from establishing ASCAP's immunity from liability, these District Court findings, in my judgment, confirm the illegality of its conduct. Neither CBS nor any other user has been willing to assume the costs and risks associated with an attempt to purchase music on a competitive basis. The fact that an attempt by CBS to break down the ASCAP monopoly might well succeed does not preclude the conclusion that smaller and less powerful buyers are totally foreclosed from a competitive market. [. . .]

[38] Antitrust policy requires that great aggregations of economic power be closely scrutinized. That duty is especially important when the aggregation is composed of statutory monopoly privileges. Our cases have repeatedly stressed the need to limit the privileges conferred by patent and copyright strictly to the scope of the statutory grant. The record in this case plainly discloses that the limits have been exceeded and that ASCAP and BMI exercise monopoly powers that far exceed the sum of the privileges of the individual copyright holders. Indeed, ASCAP itself argues that its blanket license constitutes a product that is significantly different from the sum of its component parts. I agree with that premise, but I conclude that the aggregate is a monopolistic restraint of trade proscribed by the Sherman Act.

CASENOTE: Arizona v. Maricopa County Medical Society

457 U.S. 332 (1982)

BMI marked a profound inflection point in the history of antitrust's approach to horizontal restraints: a shift away from the formal severity of *Sealy* and *Topco*'s reaction to coordination among rivals, toward a more cautious, more granular, effects-based approach. But *BMI* did not spell the end of the *per se* rule, or even its application to conduct that was clearly more complicated than simple price fixing or market division. *Maricopa County*—decided in 1982, just three years after *BMI* came down—stands as a reminder that, even post-*BMI*, the *per se* rule may be applied to conduct of some complexity.

The case concerned the activities of the Maricopa Foundation for Medical Care and the Pima Foundation for Medical Care ("Foundations"), two nonprofits that had been created in order to provide an alternative to existing healthcare models. Under the traditional models, a patient either: (1) obtains insurance coverage from an insurer for customary and reasonable medical expenses, and then obtains treatment from a provider, with the reasonable costs borne by the insurer and any excess being borne by the insured patient themselves (the traditional fee-for-service model); or (2) pays a fixed regular amount to a group of healthcare providers, in exchange for the provision of medical care, with the provider group bearing the risk that costs of care will exceed the insured's payments (the health maintenance organization or "HMO" model).

The Foundations were designed to provide a new model of payment for healthcare by offering something distinctive to doctors, insurers, and patients:

- Doctors were offered the opportunity to participate in the model, and thus receive the business of covered patients and the benefits of swift payment, in exchange for committing to accept a schedule of maximum fees (set by a vote of the member physicians) as full payment for their services, subject to the Foundations' determination that the care was necessary and appropriate. Participating doctors were free to charge anything they liked to patients not covered by the model, and were also free to charge *less* than the maximum fee to covered patients.

- Insurers were offered the opportunity to participate in the model, and thus receive the business of covered patients, the benefit of guaranteed low prices from doctors, and the benefits of the Foundations' technical assessment of the necessity and appropriateness of care, in exchange for allowing the Foundations to write checks that drew directly on their accounts to pay doctors swiftly for providing necessary and appropriate care.

- Patients were offered the opportunity to participate in the model, and thus receive efficient care—as well as freedom from the threat that they will be made to bear the burden of excess medical expenses—in exchange for their premiums. Patients were free to go to nonparticipating doctors to obtain care: if they did so, they would be covered up to the scheduled amount for the service received, but would be personally on the hook for any excess.

The Foundations were a success. About 70% of the medical practitioners in Maricopa County, Arizona, joined the Maricopa Foundation, and about 400 doctors joined the Pima Foundation. And the maximum-fee schedules seemed to compare favorably to market rates for service: around 90% of the physicians in Maricopa County billed at or above the fee rates set by the Maricopa Foundation.

But then things hit a snag: Arizona sued the Foundations (and the Maricopa County Medical Society) under Section 1 for price-fixing. Arizona moved for summary judgment on the issue of liability, which the district court and court of appeals both declined to grant. But the Supreme Court granted cert and, in an opinion by Justice Stevens for a four-Justice majority (with two recusals), granted Arizona's motion.

The Court began by acknowledging that the evidence on the competitive effects of the Foundations' new model—and particularly the fee schedules—was mixed. Arizona argued that the schedules tended to stabilize and increase prices, while the Foundations argued that they tended to limit and reduce prices. As Arizona was the summary judgment movant, the Court acknowledged accepted the Foundations' interpretation.

But this benefit of the doubt did not save the Foundations! The Court sternly reiterated the *per se* illegality of all agreements to fix prices, even agreements to fix maximum prices. And here, the Court continued, that rule "is violated by a price restraint that tends to provide the same economic rewards to all practitioners regardless of their skill, their experience, their training, or their willingness to employ innovative and difficult procedures in individual cases. Such a restraint also may discourage entry into the market and may deter experimentation and new developments by individual entrepreneurs. It may be a masquerade for an agreement to fix uniform prices, or it may in the future take on that character." The fact that the Court had "little antitrust experience in the health care industry" would not change that conclusion. Indeed, the whole point of the rule was to avoid "an incredibly complicated and prolonged economic investigation into the entire history of the industry involved . . . an inquiry so often wholly fruitless when undertaken."

The Foundations had argued that *per se* condemnation was inappropriate because the collaboration here had procompetitive benefits, and specifically that it made it possible to "provide consumers of health care with a uniquely desirable form of insurance coverage that could not otherwise exist." The Foundations specifically emphasized the value of offering patients "a choice of doctors, complete insurance coverage, and lower premiums," compared to existing models of healthcare coverage. But the Court was not impressed. The first two items could be obtained in other ways. And while a maximum fee schedule was probably necessary in order to secure (the potential for) lower prices and an assurance of complete coverage, "it is not necessary that the doctors do the price fixing": after all, insurers could set their own maximum-price schedules rather than having competing doctors do so jointly. "[N]othing in the record," the Court concluded, "even arguably supports the conclusion that this type of insurance program could not function if the fee schedules were set in a different way."

Despite the summary-judgment posture, the Court seemed to credit Arizona's interpretation of the evidence of the interaction of the model's positive and negative effects. "[T]here is no reason to believe that any savings that might accrue from this arrangement would be sufficiently great to affect the competitiveness of these kinds of insurance plans. It is *entirely possible* that the potential or actual power of the foundations to dictate the terms of such insurance plans may more than offset the theoretical efficiencies upon which the respondents' defense ultimately rests." (Emphasis added.)

Nor did the Court's recent *BMI* decision save the day for the Foundations. *BMI*, the Court explained, involved the joint creation of a product that would not otherwise have been available. By contrast, the doctors' cooperation here "does not permit them to sell any different product. Their combination has merely permitted them to sell their services to certain customers at fixed prices and arguably to affect the prevailing market price of medical care."

In closing, the Court nodded at possible alternative models that might have earned more favorable treatment. "The foundations are not analogous to partnerships or other joint arrangements in which persons who would otherwise be competitors pool their capital and share the risks of loss as well as the opportunities for profit. . . . The agreement under attack is an agreement among hundreds of competing doctors concerning the price at which each will offer his own services to a substantial number of consumers. . . . If a clinic offered complete medical coverage for a flat fee, the cooperating doctors would have the type of partnership arrangement in which a price-fixing agreement among the doctors would be perfectly proper. But the fee agreements disclosed by the record in this case are among independent competing entrepreneurs. They fit squarely into the horizontal price-fixing mold." Liability followed.

Justice Powell, joined by two other members of the Court, dissented. The Foundations, he argued, offered a "comparatively new method of providing insured medical services at predetermined maximum costs. . . . [T]he plan seems to be in the public interest." Moreover, given the summary-judgment posture, the Foundations were entitled to the benefit of all reasonable inferences from the record. And here, that compelled the assumption that the Foundations' model had limited doctors' fees, helped insurers to assess risk more accurately, and saved patients and payers money.

He pointed out that the Foundations did not prohibit or deter what would amount to cheating on the supposed cartel: physicians and insurers retained freedom to deal on whatever terms they liked outside of the scope of the collaboration. Even more telling was the fact that seven insurers—the payers for care, with every incentive to keep costs down rather than drive them up—had voluntarily chosen to invite the doctors to jointly establish appropriate maximum prices. This suggested that the collaboration's true effect was indeed to keep prices down rather than drive them up.

The blanket license in *BMI* was a close parallel to the enterprise here. "Each involved competitors and resulted in co-operative pricing. Each arrangement also was prompted by the need for better service to the consumers. And each arrangement apparently makes possible a new product by reaping otherwise unattainable efficiencies."

In condemning the collaboration, Justice Powell concluded, the Court had "[lost] sight of the basic purposes of the Sherman Act. . . . [T]he antitrust laws are a consumer welfare prescription. In its rush to condemn a novel plan about which it knows very little, the Court suggests that this end is achieved only by invalidating activities that may have some potential for harm. But the little that the record does show about the effect of the plan suggests that it is a means of providing medical services that in fact benefits rather than injures persons who need them." To label this enterprise "price fixing" and condemn it out of hand was to ignore the reality that a complex economy often produces complex arrangements that merited a closer look. "It is unwise for the Court, in a case as novel and important as this one, to make a final judgment in the absence of a complete record and where mandatory inferences create critical issues of fact."

NOTES

1) Did *Broadcast Music* repudiate *Sealy* and *Topco*? And did *Maricopa County* in turn cut back on *Broadcast Music*? Or is there a consistent principle that explains all four cases?

2) Can you articulate why the Court in *Broadcast Music* applied the rule of reason rather than the *per se* rule? Do you agree with the Court that the system of blanket licensing of musical compositions is procompetitive? What about Justice Stevens' point that the same competitive benefits can be obtained without an "all-or-nothing" system of blanket licensing?

3) ASCAP and BMI remain under antitrust consent decrees to this day; in fact, in 2021, the Antitrust Division decided to leave the consent decrees in place without modification. But the apparent stability may be deceiving. During the most recent DOJ review of the consent decrees, the Division learned that ASCAP and BMI (as well as smaller "performance rights organization" competitors SESAC and GMR) are engaging in so-called "fractional licensing"—i.e., instead of licensing the full rights to each composition in their portfolio, for compositions with more than one owner the PROs license only the *share* of copyright ownership that belongs to the copyright owner or owners that license through that PRO. The result is that for many popular musical compositions, a licensee must license from multiple PROs in order to clear rights for the composition. And this means that, at least for these compositions, the PROs are not competitors, but rather, complements. As one of us has recently written:

> The music publishing industry is dominated by three major publishers, but there is a competitive fringe featuring a very large number of smaller publishers. Significantly, ownership of musical compositions is often fragmented among two or more authors, who may be represented by multiple publishers (representation which changes with some frequency as publishers are acquired, or pieces of a publisher's catalog are sold off), and the data that is available to licensees regarding who owns what is very poor. Now imagine that the streaming services, instead of licensing public performance of musical compositions from a few PROs (two of which are subject to non-discrimination requirements), must license directly from literally hundreds of music publishing companies. The opportunities for licensor collusion, holdout and strategic behavior would multiply. And the streaming services would almost inevitably face a wave of copyright infringement lawsuits claiming that the services' direct licenses do not cover all of the copyright ownership shares in some large number of compositions. Perhaps not surprisingly, the streaming services, well aware of the difficulties direct licensing would create for their businesses, expressed relief when the DOJ rebuffed the request to permit partial withdrawal.

> Nor would I bet that a Division guided by neo-Brandeisians will move in the coming years to terminate or sunset the consent decrees in favor of an unregulated licensing market. It's more likely that neo-Brandeisians among the Division leadership would conclude that the PROs practice of fractional licensing suggests that the existing consent decrees aren't strong enough. And I think that it's possible that the neo-Brandeisians may go even further. They may conclude

that the decrees should be dissolved and new price fixing litigation instituted against the PROs; not just ASCAP and BMI, but the up-and-coming rival PROs SESAC and Global Music Rights (GMR) as well. After all, if ASCAP and BMI are price-fixing vehicles, then SESAC and GMR, which work according to the same basic structure, are too.

If I'm right, then the neo-Brandeisians' end-game might be to use the enormous leverage from the prospect of a new price-fixing lawsuit to negotiate new decrees that apply to all of the PROs. Decrees that strengthen the anti-discrimination provisions of the current decrees, that specifically bar partial withdrawal, that mandate 100% licensing. And that subject all of the PROs to rate court determinations.[351]

4) Were the doctors in *Maricopa County* cooperating to offer a lower-cost healthcare solution in competition with existing options? If so, why was their conduct unlawful? If not, why is that characterization inapt?

5) In both *Topco* and *Maricopa County*, the majority and dissenting opinions disagree on whether the restraints incident to the competitor collaborations in those cases were socially beneficial. Does that disagreement suggest anything about the wisdom of *per se* rules in the context of competitor collaborations?

6) The DOJ/FTC Competitor Collaboration Guidelines state that "[i]f . . . participants in an efficiency-enhancing integration of economic activity enter into an agreement that is reasonably related to the integration and reasonably necessary to achieve its procompetitive benefits, the Agencies analyze the agreement under the rule of reason, even if it is of a type that might otherwise be considered per se illegal." In light of the cases you have just read—or whichever of them you think is still good law—what does it mean for a restraint to be "reasonably necessary" to the collaboration? Does this mean that the collaboration would be profitable only with the restraint? Does it mean that the collaboration would be *significantly more* profitable with the restraint? Something else?

2. Joint Facilitating Practices and Information Exchange

As we noted at the beginning of this chapter, competitors across the economy engage in a wide variety of joint practices, from the very benign to the extremely suspicious, leaving agencies and courts to try to separate the harmful ones from the beneficial ones. One long, and sometimes tangled, strand of cases under Section 1 deals with so-called "facilitating practices": that is, practices that may not constitute outright collusion but might have the effect of making collusive-like outcomes much more likely. Such practices may be themselves concerted or unilateral. Unilateral facilitating practices—that is, practices adopted independently by market participants in an effort to make tacit collusion easier—fall outside Section 1, for want of an agreement. In Chapter XI we will see that efforts to tackle them using Section 5 of the FTC Act (which contains a broader prohibition on "unfair methods of competition") have also not generally been successful.[352] But an agreement, express or implied, to do something that may soften competition invites scrutiny under Section 1.

A particularly prominent genre of joint facilitating practice that is clearly subject to evaluation under Section 1 involves the concerted exchange of information among rivals. Information-sharing practices can range from barely disguised cartels to deeply ambiguous activities with genuine procompetitive benefits.

Cases of this kind usually raise either (or both) of two distinct questions under Section 1. The first is whether such practices furnish a basis for inferring an implicit agreement to fix prices or divide markets among competitors: that is, whether they constitute "plus factors" in addition to parallelism from which agreement can be inferred.[353] The second is whether a particular agreement to exchange information is, itself, anticompetitive and a violation of Section 1.

In approaching the second question, courts and agencies recognize that rivals may agree to exchange information with one another for a variety of purposes, and with a variety of effects. On the procompetitive side, information-sharing may promote participants' ability to accurately and efficiently assess current and future market conditions. For example, businesses may be better able to meet demand—now or in future—if they know that a new

---

[351] Christopher Jon Sprigman, *What Does Antitrust's Revival Mean for Copyright?: The 50ᵗʰ Annual Brace Memorial Lecture of the Copyright Society of the USA*, 68 J. of the Copyright Soc'y 401, 422-423 (2021) (internal citations and notes removed).

[352] *See infra* § XI.B.2.(a).

[353] *See generally supra* § IV.2. (inference of conspiracy from parallelism and the role of "plus factors").

distribution channel has opened up, or that a supply shortage is coming for a key input, or that demand is likely to spike in a few months' time, or that a new technology will soon become available in a complementary market. In some circumstances, likewise, having accurate information about what my rivals are up to might help facilitate more aggressive competition: perhaps by helping me spot opportunities to satisfy demand more efficiently, borrow strategies to lower my own costs, or win a key customer.

On the anticompetitive side, though, the sharing of information among rivals may also tend to soften, restrict, and even eliminate competition. If I have up-to-date and accurate information about my rivals' current and/or anticipated future prices, this may significantly help me to sustain tacit collusion with them. (As noted above, if my rivals and I are agreeing to exchange such information, that exchange might well be part of an implicit underlying agreement to actually fix prices.) But competitive harm can result from the exchange of information short of current or future price information. More insight into my rivals' costs, margins, customers, capacity, stock-on-hand, and so on, may make me better able to anticipate their reactions in ways that make tacit collusion possible, or more successful.

The Supreme Court's Information-Exchange Jurisprudence

On a number of occasions, the Court has applied Section 1 to information exchanges among rivals, and its approach has changed over time. In its earlier jurisprudence, and particularly a trio of cases in the 1920s, the Court mingled *per se* style language with rule-of-reason-like attention to evidence; it was not until the 1970s that the Court finally clarified that the rule of reason applies to most information-sharing agreements.

In a well-known early case, *American Column* (1921), the Court considered the "Open Competition Plan" operated by the American Hardwood Manufacturers Association.[354] The Plan involved 365 hardwood mill owners, together representing about a third of the national hardwood production of the United States. Under the Plan, each member was required (among other things) to: (1) make a daily report to the Association of all sales and shipments and their terms, including the identity of each customer; (2) make monthly reports of all production and stock on hand; and (3) to file price lists at the beginning of each month and update them immediately with any changes. The Court noted that that the participants had entered into no "definite agreement" to fix or limit production or prices, but noted that "it would be very difficult to devise a more minute disclosure of everything connected with one's business than . . . this Plan."

The *American Column* Court had little difficulty in holding that the Plan violated Section 1. Noting that the Plan's reports to its members, and the discussions at the Association's meetings, were suffused with repeated warnings about "overproduction" and heavy hints about "the proper course [for market participants] to pursue"—and given the testimonials of delighted members about how the Plan had helped to increase prices—the Court found it clear that "the united action of the large and influential membership of dealers contributed greatly to [an] extraordinary price increase." "Genuine competitors," the Court pointed out, "do not make daily, weekly, and monthly reports of the minutest details of their business of their rivals[.]" The Plan was "an old evil in a new dress and with a new name." In condemning the Plan, the Court did not quite make clear whether it was applying a *per se* rule of illegality or a rule-of-reason-style approach: some of the language reaches very broadly, but the court's attention to effects evidence suggests a granular analysis. Justice Holmes wrote a dissenting opinion, finding antitrust condemnation of information exchange "surprising in a country of free speech that affects to regard education and knowledge as desirable." Justice Brandeis also dissented, protesting that the Plan involved neither coercion nor actual uniformity in prices, but rather was an effort to "permit a multitude of small rivals to co-operate . . . in order to protect themselves and the public from the chaos and havoc wrought in their trade by ignorance."

The Court's follow-up decision in *American Linseed* (1923) concerned the operation of the "Armstrong Bureau of Related Industries."[355] The Bureau provided a contract service to 12 linseed "crushers"—manufacturers of linseed oil, together accounting for a "very large part" of national linseed oil consumption—pursuant to which each

---

[354] American Column & Lumber Co. v. United States, 257 U.S. 377 (1921).

[355] United States v. American Linseed Oil Co., 262 U.S. 371 (1923).

crusher would commit to report all sales, quotations, and deliveries of linseed (on pain of forfeiting a significant bond deposited with the Bureau) and attend monthly in-person meetings to discuss market conditions. The Court had little difficulty in concluding that "[t]he obvious policy—indeed, the declared purpose—of the arrangement was to submerge the competition . . . among the subscribers." The "necessary tendency" and "manifest purpose" of participation in the scheme was the suppression of competition, and it was clearly unlawful. The Court drew a sharp distinction between unilateral information-sharing, on the one hand, and joint activities like the work of the Bureau on the other: "In the absence of a purpose to monopolize, *or the compulsion that results from contract or agreement*, the individual certainly may exercise great freedom; but concerted action . . . presents a wholly different problem, and is forbidden when the necessary tendency is to destroy . . . competition[.]" (Emphasis added.)

Maple Flooring (1925) presented a closer call.[356] In that case, 22 sellers and shippers of maple, beech, and birch flooring, mostly based in Michigan, Minnesota, and Wisconsin, had formed the Maple Flooring Manufacturers' Association. The Association's activities included the computation and distribution to members of: (1) average cost information for all "dimensions and grades" of flooring, (2) freight rates from Cadillac, MI, to many destinations throughout the United States; and (3) sales, price, and stock-on-hand information *in anonymized form only* (*i.e.,* revealing no specific information about any identifiable member). No agreement on production or prices was alleged or proved, nor was there any "direct proof" that the association's activities had increased prices. In fact, there was "undisputed evidence that the prices of members were fair and reasonable and that they were usually lower than the prices of nonmembers[.]" The Section 1 challenge was aimed at "the plan of the association itself," on the theory that it was unlawful "regardless of its actual operation and effect so far as price maintenance is concerned." DOJ argued that the joint activity, by its nature, necessarily would tend to keep prices near the reported cost levels.

The *Maple Flooring* Court agreed in principle with DOJ that the exchange of cost information among members, when combined with a calculated freight rate, *could* be the basis for inferring an actual underlying agreement to fix prices. But here the evidence did not support such an inference. The mere transmission of information alone was not invariably harmful: "Competition does not become less free merely because the conduct of commercial operations becomes more intelligent through the free distribution of knowledge," noted the Court: "[i]t was not the purpose or intent of the [Sherman Act] to inhibit the intelligent conduct of business operations[.]" The sharing of market information did not become unlawful "merely because the ultimate result of their efforts may be to stabilize prices or limit production *merely through a better understanding of economic laws and a more general ability to conform to them.*" (Emphasis added.) The costs of production and transportation were "legitimate subjects of inquiry and knowledge." Thus, while in some cases, information exchange "may be the basis of agreement or concerted action to lessen production arbitrarily or to raise prices," as it was in *American Column* and *American Linseed*, here—"in the absence of proof of such agreement or concerted action having been actually reached or actually attempted"— there was no basis to infer illegality or any harm to competition.

In *Container Corp.* (1969), by contrast, the Court needed barely a thousand words to condemn an agreement among manufacturers of corrugated containers—collectively representing 90% of all shipments from the Southeastern United States—to inform one another of the most recent price each had charged or quoted.[357] The effect of that practice appeared, unsurprisingly, to have had the effect "of keeping prices within a fairly narrow ambit." With capacity exceeding demand, and with market entry "easy," prices had been falling and, as a result of the challenged practice, appeared to have been "stabilized[,] though at a downward level." Condemning the practice as a violation of Section 1, the Court pointed out that the practice had had an "anticompetitive effect": it had resulted in the "limitation or reduction" of price competition, by stabilizing prices that were generally declining: and the Sherman Act prohibited "[stabilizing prices as well as raising them[.]" The Court (somewhat pointedly, given Justice Fortas's concurring opinion) did not make clear whether it was applying *per se* or rule-of-reason scrutiny.

In a concurring opinion, Justice Fortas expressly argued that the *per se* rule should not be applied to an agreement to exchange information. Proof of anticompetitive effect, under the rule of reason, was necessary: the mere "[t]heoretical probability" of competitive harm was not in his view enough to make the exchange of price

---

[356] Maple Flooring Mfrs. Ass'n v. United States, 268 U.S. 563 (1925).

[357] United States v. Container Corp. of America, 393 U.S. 333 (1969).

information "so akin to price-fixing. . . as to deserve the per se classification. But, here, he concluded that such proof was available: the record indicated that the practice "did in fact substantially limit the amount of price competition." Justice Marshall's dissenting opinion (joined by two other members of the Court) also took the view that this was a rule-of-reason case: but denied that there was evidence of harm in the record! "On the contrary," he argued, "the evidence establishes that the information . . . was actually employed for the purpose of engaging in active price competition."

Finally, two cases in the 1970s made clear that when the target of Section 1 analysis is the information-sharing agreement, rather than an inferred underlying conspiracy to fix prices, the rule of reason generally applies. In *Citizens and Southern*—citing among other things to Justice Fortas' concurrence in *Container Corp.*—the Supreme Court directly stated that "the dissemination of price information is not itself a *per se* violation of the Sherman Act."[358] And in a footnote in *U.S. Gypsum*, the Court set up the frame for modern antitrust analysis of information sharing among rivals: "The exchange of price data and other information among competitors does not invariably have anticompetitive effects; indeed such practices can in certain circumstances increase economic efficiency and render markets more, rather than less, competitive. . . . [S]uch exchanges of information do not constitute a per se violation of the Sherman Act. A number of factors including most prominently the structure of the industry involved and the nature of the information exchanged are generally considered in divining the procompetitive or anticompetitive effects of this type of interseller communication. Exchanges of current price information, of course, have the greatest potential for generating anticompetitive effects and although not per se unlawful have consistently been held to violate the Sherman Act."[359]

So what do courts actually do today in the shadow of these decisions, when confronted with a complaint alleging that information sharing has harmed competition? Modern analysis is exemplified by then-Judge Sotomayor's 2001 opinion for the Second Circuit in *Todd*. Confronted with a detailed allegation that several major oil companies had agreed to exchange information in a manner that tended to suppress their wages for certain employees, and mindful of the *Gypsum* footnote described above, the court of appeals set out a crisp framework for the rule-of-reason analysis of information sharing.

Todd v. Exxon Corp.
275 F.3d 191 (2d Cir. 2001)

Judge Sotomayor.

[1] Plaintiff brought this action against fourteen major companies in the integrated oil and petrochemical industry, collectively accounting for 80–90% of the industry's revenues and employing approximately the same percentage of the industry's workforce. On behalf of herself and all other similarly situated current and former Exxon employees (the putative class), plaintiff alleges that defendants violated § 1 of the Sherman Act by regularly sharing detailed information regarding compensation paid to nonunion managerial, professional, and technical ("MPT") employees and using this information in setting the salaries of these employees at artificially low levels. Plaintiff seeks money damages and equitable relief pursuant to § 1 of the Sherman Act.

[2] Accepting the allegations in the complaint as true, as we must on this motion to dismiss, the facts of this case are as follows. Defendants instituted a system whereby they periodically conducted surveys comparing past and current MPT salary information and participated in regular meetings at which current and future salary budgets were discussed. The data exchanges were also accompanied by assurances that the information would be used in setting the salaries of MPT employees. Defendants' "Job Match Survey" created a common denominator to facilitate the comparison of MPT salaries. The survey used certain jobs at defendant Chevron as benchmarks. The other defendants would submit detailed information regarding the jobs at their companies that were most comparable to the Chevron benchmark jobs so that they could be matched. The survey compared the responsibilities and compensation packages offered by defendants for certain jobs and job types against those of the benchmark positions at Chevron. This survey was coordinated by defendants Unocal and Chevron. Chevron

---

[358] United States v. Citizens and Southern Nat. Bank, 422 U.S. 86, 113 (1975).
[359] United States v. U.S. Gypsum Co., 438 U.S. 422, 441 n.16 (1978).

and Unocal each would meet with half of the other companies involved to develop matches to the benchmarks, and then would gather the information before submitting it to a third-party consultant, Towers Perrin. Towers Perrin compiled the information, then analyzed, refined, and distributed it to the defendants on diskettes and in the form of hard copies.

[3] Defendants' "Job Family Survey" provided the most current account of the compensation being paid in the industry. Each company submitted information on salaries actually paid in thirty different categories of jobs, or "job families," classified according to the nature of the work. . . .

[4] . . . [E]ach company was entitled to receive subsets of Job Family Survey data, consisting of salary information from as few as three companies at a time. Plaintiff alleges that Exxon used these subsets to compare its own salaries with those of six particular competitors, referred to as the "Six Majors." [. . .]

[5] Plaintiff contends that defendants' arrangement violated § 1 of the Sherman Act. According to the complaint, these violations had the purpose and effect of depressing MPT salaries paid by defendants. [. . .]

[6] Section 1 of the Sherman Act prohibits "[e]very contract, combination in the form of trust or otherwise, or conspiracy, in restraint of trade or commerce among the several States, or with foreign nations." Traditional "hard-core" price fixing remains per se unlawful . . . . If the plaintiff in this case could allege that defendants actually formed an agreement to fix MPT salaries, this per se rule would likely apply. Furthermore, even in the absence of direct "smoking gun" evidence, a horizontal price-fixing agreement may be inferred on the basis of conscious parallelism, when such interdependent conduct is accompanied by circumstantial evidence and plus factors such as defendants' use of facilitating practices. Information exchange is an example of a facilitating practice that can help support an inference of a price-fixing agreement.

[7] There is a closely related but analytically distinct type of claim, also based on § 1 of the Sherman Act, where the violation lies in the information exchange itself—as opposed to merely using the information exchange as evidence upon which to infer a price-fixing agreement. This exchange of information is not illegal per se, but can be found unlawful under a rule of reason analysis. [. . .]

[8] As plaintiff does not allege an actual agreement among defendants to fix salaries, we analyze plaintiff's complaint solely as to whether it alleges unlawful information exchange pursuant to this rule of reason. [. . .]

[9] The traditional horizontal conspiracy case involves an agreement among sellers with the purpose of raising prices to supracompetitive levels. The Sherman Act, however, also applies to abuse of market power on the buyer side—often taking the form of monopsony or oligopsony. Plaintiff is correct to point out that a horizontal conspiracy among buyers to stifle competition is as unlawful as one among sellers. [. . .]

[10] Plaintiff claims that MPT employees accumulate industry-specific knowledge that renders them more valuable to employers in the oil and petrochemical industry than to employers in other industries. . . . It is consistent with common sense and empirical research that employees' industry-specific experience may cause them to suffer a pay cut if forced to switch industries. [. . .]

[11] [P]laintiff is simply alleging that a slight decrease in salary by a hypothetical oligopsonist cartel in the oil/petrochemical industry would not cause MPT employees to leave the industry because they would have difficulty finding compensation fully reflecting the value of their experience elsewhere. At trial, plaintiff would have to prove this theory with economic evidence regarding the cross-industrial elasticity of MPT employees. [. . .]

[12] In sum, plaintiff's complaint alleges a plausible product market. [. . .]

[13] Market power defined as a percentage market share . . . is not the only way to demonstrate defendants' ability to depress salaries. . . .

[14] In this Circuit, a threshold showing of market share is not a prerequisite for bringing a § 1 claim. If a plaintiff can show an actual adverse effect on competition, such as reduced output, we do not require a further showing of market power. If, for example, the plaintiff in this case could prove that (1) defendants engaged in information exchanges that would be deemed anticompetitive . . . and (2) such activities did in fact have an anticompetitive

effect on the market for MPT labor in the oil and petrochemical industry, we would not deny relief on the basis of market share figures. [. . .]

[15] The Supreme Court [has] explained that one of the two most prominent factors in the rule of reason analysis of a data exchange is the structure of the industry involved. Therefore, once the relevant market is defined, a court must analyze the structure of that market to determine whether it is susceptible to the exercise of market power through tacit coordination. As the district court explained, susceptible markets tend to be highly concentrated— that is, oligopolistic—and to have fungible products subject to inelastic demand. [. . .]

[16] The Supreme Court has found that data exchange can be unlawful despite a relatively large number of sellers. In [United States v. Container Corp. of America, 393 U.S. 333 (1969)], the Court used the oft-cited language that the industry was dominated by relatively few sellers. But in fact, the defendants in *Container Corp.* were eighteen firms controlling 90% of the market, defined as the sale of cardboard cartons in the Southeast. The Court nonetheless found the market sufficiently concentrated to support the finding of a violation. It is fairly clear that the reason the Court reached its holding despite the multiplicity of sellers was the specific anticompetitive characteristics of the information exchange. Given that the market concentration in this case is not radically different from that in *Container Corp.*, and given that concentration is part of a rule of reason inquiry that also emphasizes the nature of the information exchanged, we do not think that fourteen companies sharing an 80– 90% market share is so unconcentrated as to warrant a Rule 12(b)(6) dismissal where the nature of the exchanges appears anticompetitive. We also find it unsurprising that data exchange cases may involve a number of participants that begins to push the boundaries of oligopoly. These players are *most* in need of such data exchange arrangements in order to facilitate price coordination; a very small handful of firms in a more highly concentrated market may be less likely to require the kind of sophisticated data dissemination alleged in this case. [. . .]

[17] The inquiry [into fungibility] is one part of the question of whether the market is susceptible to the exercise of market power though tacit coordination. Fungibility is relevant on this point because it is less realistic for a cartel to establish and police a price conspiracy where it is difficult to compare the products being sold. . . .

[18] The question in this case is whether jobs at the various oil and petrochemical companies were comparable, or fungible enough so that the defendants could have used the exchanged information as part of a tacit conspiracy to depress salaries. [. . .]

[19] Plaintiff's complaint alleges in detail the sophisticated techniques defendants used to achieve a common denominator with respect to the compensation paid to their MPT employees. Defendants developed the Job Match Survey because they realized it was not functionally efficient simply to know what each others' employees were being paid unless they were able to horizontally match the various job classifications. . . .

[20] Plaintiff is thus on solid ground when she argues that defendants made their own employees' positions "fungible" for comparison purposes with those of their competitors. [. . .]

[21] Alongside the structure of the industry involved, the other major factor for courts to consider in a data exchange case is the nature of the information exchanged. There are certain well-established criteria used to help ascertain the anticompetitive potential of information exchanges. As part of the analysis, a court should consider, broadly speaking, whether it was of the sort in *American Column & Lumber Co. v. United States* or of that in *Maple Flooring Manufacturers Ass'n v. United States*. Applying the relevant criteria reveals anticompetitive potential in this case.

[22] The first factor to consider is the time frame of the data. The Supreme Court has made clear that exchanges of current price information, of course, have the greatest potential for generating anti-competitive effects and although not per se unlawful have consistently been held to violate the Sherman Act. The exchange of past price data is greatly preferred because current data have greater potential to affect future prices and facilitate price conspiracies. By the same reasoning, exchanges of future price information are considered especially anticompetitive.

[23] Plaintiff's complaint alleges that defendants exchanged past and current salary information, as well as future salary budget information. . . .

[24] In addition to the time frame, another factor courts look to is the specificity of the information. Price exchanges that identify particular parties, transactions, and prices are seen as potentially anticompetitive because they may be used to police a secret or tacit conspiracy to stabilize prices. Courts prefer that information be aggregated in the form of industry averages, thus avoiding transactional specificity.

[25] Two aspects of the information exchange at issue are problematic in this regard. First, although the salary information was aggregated and distributed by a third-party consulting firm, companies participating in the Job Family Survey received compensation data broken down to subsets consisting of as few as three competitors. . . . Second, at their meetings defendants discussed current and future salary budgets, including company-specific information, such that all participants learn[ed] where each other participant [was] going with its salary budget for the upcoming year or, if a participant's salary year had only recently begun, for that new year.

[26] Another important factor to consider in evaluating an information exchange is whether the data are made publicly available. Public dissemination is a primary way for data exchange to realize its procompetitive potential. . . .

[27] In the instant case, dissemination of the information to the employees could have helped mitigate any anticompetitive effects of the exchange and possibly enhanced market efficiency by making employees more sensitive to salary increases. No such dissemination occurred, however. The information was not disclosed to the public nor to the employees whose salaries were the subject of the exchange. [. . .]

[28] In sum, the "nature of the information exchanged" weighs against the motion to dismiss. The characteristics of the data exchange in this case are precisely those that arouse suspicion of anticompetitive activity under the rule of reason.

[29] An antitrust plaintiff must allege not only cognizable harm to herself, but an adverse effect on competition market-wide. . . [I]nformation exchange is not always anticompetitive and can enhance competition by making competitors more sensitive to each other's price changes, enhancing rivalry among them.

[30] The complaint in this case, however, points to anticompetitive effects the exchanges have had on MPT salaries market-wide, most particularly with respect to Exxon. Plaintiff specifically alleges that salary levels across the integrated oil and petrochemical industry have been artificially depressed because the information exchange has reduced competitive incentives. Moreover, Exxon has supposedly used the information . . . to reduce its salaries 4.1% between 1987 and 1994 in comparison to the Six Majors and to reduce its [relative salary index] in relation to the competition [by an amount quantified in the complaint]. . . . In her claim for relief, plaintiff again alleges that she received compensation materially below what she would have received in an uncontaminated marketplace.

[31] . . . [Although the defendants' salaries had been increasing year-on-year,] [t]he fact that Exxon increased its salaries each year would not defeat an allegation that those increases were lower than they would have been but for a conspiracy to stabilize prices. We understand the complaint as alleging a market where Exxon's salaries and those of the Six Majors continue to increase, but where the difference grows gradually smaller—a portrait of market stabilization. [. . .]

[32] For the reasons stated, we vacate the district court's grant of defendants' Rule 12(b)(6) motion to dismiss and remand for proceedings consistent with this opinion.

NOTES

1) In practice, information exchange among competitors—through trade and professional associations, trade publications, or informal contacts—is very common. Why do you think this is?

2) Justice Holmes, dissenting in *American Column*, objected that "I should have supposed that the Sherman Act did not set itself against knowledge—did not aim at a transitory cheapness unprofitable to the community as a whole because not corresponding to the actual conditions of the country." Does he have a point? Should the exchange of true factual information about current or past events be *per se* legal?

3) What do you make of the following proposition? "It should be *per se* illegal for competitors to privately exchange information about anything to do with their businesses. They don't need to do it, and a *per se* rule

would make things clearer for businesses and more competitive for everyone. If they really must talk about 'market conditions,' nothing is lost and much is gained by making them do it in public."

4) Imagine you were asked to give one paragraph of advice to non-lawyer sales employees attending their first trade association meeting. They know nothing about the Sherman Act, antitrust, or microeconomics, and they ask you for clear, straightforward advice so they know what is off-limits. What do you tell them?

D. What Is "Inherently Suspect"? The Quick Look / Rule of Reason Boundary

As we saw in Chapter IV, courts have recognized that some restraints may be presumed to have an anticompetitive effect by reason of their nature. In *Board of Regents*, as you have already seen, the Court expressed the core principle in terms like the following:

> As a matter of law, the absence of proof of market power does not justify a naked restriction on price or output. To the contrary, when there is an agreement not to compete in terms of price or output, no elaborate industry analysis is required to demonstrate the anticompetitive character of such an agreement. Petitioner does not quarrel with the District Court's finding that price and output are not responsive to demand. Thus the plan is inconsistent with the Sherman Act's command that price and supply be responsive to consumer preference. We have never required proof of market power in such a case. This naked restraint on price and output requires some competitive justification even in the absence of a detailed market analysis. [. . .]
>
> [T]he NCAA television plan [at issue in *Board of Regents*] on its face constitutes a restraint upon the operation of a free market, and the findings of the District Court establish that it has operated to raise prices and reduce output. Under the Rule of Reason, these hallmarks of anticompetitive behavior place upon petitioner a heavy burden of establishing an affirmative defense which competitively justifies this apparent deviation from the operations of a free market.[360]

But the existence of this standard raises an obvious question: when, exactly, does joint conduct warrant this kind of treatment? The question is critical, given the high proportion of rule-of-reason cases that fail at step one. Quick look treatment—or equivalent standards like the FTC's "inherently suspect" classification—allows a plaintiff to satisfy this obligation by reference to the nature of the conduct, with the burden then shifting immediately to the defendant to produce procompetitive benefits.

Board of Regents was decided in 1984. Two years later, the concept of quick-look review was developed and reinforced in *Indiana Federation of Dentists*.

FTC v. Indiana Federation of Dentists
476 U.S. 447 (1986)

{Eds.: In the following extract, some paragraphs have been broken up to make them easier to read.}

Justice White.

[1] Since the 1970's, dental health insurers . . . have attempted to contain the cost of dental treatment by, among other devices, limiting payment of benefits to the cost of the "least expensive yet adequate treatment" suitable to the needs of individual patients. Implementation of such cost-containment measures, known as "alternative benefits" plans, requires evaluation by the insurer of the diagnosis and recommendation of the treating dentist, either in advance of or following the provision of care. In order to carry out such evaluation, insurers frequently request dentists to submit, along with insurance claim forms requesting payment of benefits, any dental x rays that have been used by the dentist in examining the patient as well as other information concerning their diagnoses and treatment recommendations. . . . On the basis of the materials available, supplemented where appropriate by

---

[360] NCAA v. Board of Regents of the University of Oklahoma, 468 U.S. 85 (1984).

further diagnostic aids, [a] dental consultant may recommend that the insurer approve a claim, deny it, or pay only for a less expensive course of treatment.

[2] Such review of diagnostic and treatment decisions has been viewed by some dentists as a threat to their professional independence and economic well-being. In the early 1970's, the Indiana Dental Association, a professional organization comprising some 85% of practicing dentists in the State of Indiana, initiated an aggressive effort to hinder insurers' efforts to implement alternative benefits plans by enlisting member dentists to pledge not to submit x rays in conjunction with claim forms. The Association's efforts met considerable success: large numbers of dentists signed the pledge, and insurers operating in Indiana found it difficult to obtain compliance with their requests for x rays and accordingly had to choose either to employ more expensive means of making alternative benefits determinations (for example, visiting the office of the treating dentist or conducting an independent oral examination) or to abandon such efforts altogether.

[3] By the mid-1970's, fears of possible antitrust liability had dampened the Association's enthusiasm for opposing the submission of x rays to insurers. In 1979, the Association and a number of its constituent societies consented to a Federal Trade Commission order requiring them to cease and desist from further efforts to prevent member dentists from submitting x rays. Not all Indiana dentists were content to leave the matter of submitting x rays to the individual dentist. In 1976, a group of such dentists formed the Indiana Federation of Dentists, respondent in this case, in order to continue to pursue the Association's policy of resisting insurers' requests for x rays. The Federation, which styled itself a "union" in the belief that this label would stave off antitrust liability, immediately promulgated a "work rule" forbidding its members to submit x rays to dental insurers in conjunction with claim forms. Although the Federation's membership was small, numbering less than 100, its members were highly concentrated in and around three Indiana communities: Anderson, Lafayette, and Fort Wayne. The Federation succeeded in enlisting nearly 100% of the dental specialists in the Anderson area, and approximately 67% of the dentists in and around Lafayette. In the areas of its strength, the Federation was successful in continuing to enforce the Association's prior policy of refusal to submit x rays to dental insurers.

[4] In 1978, the Federal Trade Commission issued a complaint against the Federation [alleging that the practice violated the antitrust laws.] . . . The Commission found that the Federation had conspired both with the Indiana Dental Association and with its own members to withhold cooperation with dental insurers' requests for x rays; that absent such a restraint, competition among dentists for patients would have tended to lead dentists to compete with respect to their policies in dealing with patients' insurers; and that in those areas where the Federation's membership was strong, the Federation's policy had had the actual effect of eliminating such competition among dentists and preventing insurers from obtaining access to x rays in the desired manner. These findings of anticompetitive effect, the Commission concluded, were sufficient to establish that the restraint was unreasonable even absent proof that the Federation's policy had resulted in higher costs to the insurers and patients than would have occurred had the x rays been provided. Further, the Commission rejected the Federation's argument that its policy of withholding x rays was reasonable because the provision of x rays might lead the insurers to make inaccurate determinations of the proper level of care and thus injure the health of the insured patients: the Commission found no evidence that use of x rays by insurance companies in evaluating claims would result in inadequate dental care. . . .

[5] The Federation sought judicial review of the Commission's order in the United States Court of Appeals for the Seventh Circuit, which vacated the order on the ground that it was not supported by substantial evidence. [. . .]

[6] . . . [T]he sole basis of the FTC's finding of an unfair method of competition was the Commission's conclusion that the Federation's collective decision to withhold x rays from insurers was an unreasonable and conspiratorial restraint of trade in violation of § 1 of the Sherman Act. Accordingly, the legal question before us is whether the Commission's factual findings, if supported by evidence, make out a violation of Sherman Act § 1. [. . .]

[7] Under our precedents, a restraint may be adjudged unreasonable either because it fits within a class of restraints that has been held to be "per se" unreasonable, or because it violates what has come to be known as the "Rule of Reason," under which the test of legality is whether the restraint imposed is such as merely regulates and perhaps thereby promotes competition or whether it is such as may suppress or even destroy competition.

[8] The policy of the Federation with respect to its members' dealings with third-party insurers resembles practices that have been labeled "group boycotts": the policy constitutes a concerted refusal to deal on particular terms with patients covered by group dental insurance. Although this Court has in the past stated that group boycotts are unlawful per se, we decline to resolve this case by forcing the Federation's policy into the "boycott" pigeonhole and invoking the per se rule. As we observed last Term in Northwest Wholesale Stationers, Inc. v. Pacific Stationery & Printing Co., 472 U.S. 284 (1985), the category of restraints classed as group boycotts is not to be expanded indiscriminately, and the per se approach has generally been limited to cases in which firms with market power boycott suppliers or customers in order to discourage them from doing business with a competitor—a situation obviously not present here. Moreover, we have been slow to condemn rules adopted by professional associations as unreasonable per se, and, in general, to extend per se analysis to restraints imposed in the context of business relationships where the economic impact of certain practices is not immediately obvious. Thus, as did the FTC, we evaluate the restraint at issue in this case under the Rule of Reason rather than a rule of per se illegality.

[9] Application of the Rule of Reason to these facts is not a matter of any great difficulty. The Federation's policy takes the form of a horizontal agreement among the participating dentists to withhold from their customers a particular service that they desire—the forwarding of x rays to insurance companies along with claim forms. While this is not price fixing as such, no elaborate industry analysis is required to demonstrate the anticompetitive character of such an agreement. A refusal to compete with respect to the package of services offered to customers, no less than a refusal to compete with respect to the price term of an agreement, impairs the ability of the market to advance social welfare by ensuring the provision of desired goods and services to consumers at a price approximating the marginal cost of providing them. Absent some countervailing procompetitive virtue—such as, for example, the creation of efficiencies in the operation of a market or the provision of goods and services—such an agreement limiting consumer choice by impeding the ordinary give and take of the market place, cannot be sustained under the Rule of Reason. No credible argument has been advanced for the proposition that making it more costly for the insurers and patients who are the dentists' customers to obtain information needed for evaluating the dentists' diagnoses has any such procompetitive effect.

[10] The Federation advances three principal arguments for the proposition that, notwithstanding its lack of competitive virtue, the Federation's policy of withholding x rays should not be deemed an unreasonable restraint of trade. First, . . . the Federation suggests that in the absence of specific findings by the Commission concerning the definition of the market in which the Federation allegedly restrained trade and the power of the Federation's members in that market, the conclusion that the Federation unreasonably restrained trade is erroneous as a matter of law, regardless of whether the challenged practices might be impermissibly anticompetitive if engaged in by persons who together possessed power in a specifically defined market.

[11] This contention, however, runs counter to the Court's holding in *National Collegiate Athletic Assn. v. Board of Regents of Univ. of Okla.* [468 U.S. 85 (1984)], that as a matter of law, the absence of proof of market power does not justify a naked restriction on price or output, and that such a restriction requires some competitive justification even in the absence of a detailed market analysis. Moreover, even if the restriction imposed by the Federation is not sufficiently naked to call this principle into play, the Commission's failure to engage in detailed market analysis is not fatal to its finding of a violation of the Rule of Reason. The Commission found that in two localities in the State of Indiana (the Anderson and Lafayette areas), Federation dentists constituted heavy majorities of the practicing dentists and that as a result of the efforts of the Federation, insurers in those areas were, over a period of years, actually unable to obtain compliance with their requests for submission of x rays. Since the purpose of the inquiries into market definition and market power is to determine whether an arrangement has the potential for genuine adverse effects on competition, proof of actual detrimental effects, such as a reduction of output, can obviate the need for an inquiry into market power, which is but a surrogate for detrimental effects. In this case, we conclude that the finding of actual, sustained adverse effects on competition in those areas where IFD dentists predominated, viewed in light of the reality that markets for dental services tend to be relatively localized, is legally sufficient to support a finding that the challenged restraint was unreasonable even in the absence of elaborate market analysis.

[12] Second, the Federation ... argues that a holding that its policy of withholding x rays constituted an unreasonable restraint of trade is precluded by the Commission's failure to make any finding that the policy resulted in the provision of dental services that were more costly than those that the patients and their insurers would have chosen were they able to evaluate x rays in conjunction with claim forms. This argument, too, is unpersuasive. Although it is true that the goal of the insurers in seeking submission of x rays for use in their review of benefits claims was to minimize costs by choosing the least expensive adequate course of dental treatment, a showing that this goal was actually achieved through the means chosen is not an essential step in establishing that the dentists' attempt to thwart its achievement by collectively refusing to supply the requested information was an unreasonable restraint of trade. A concerted and effective effort to withhold (or make more costly) information desired by consumers for the purpose of determining whether a particular purchase is cost justified is likely enough to disrupt the proper functioning of the price-setting mechanism of the market that it may be condemned even absent proof that it resulted in higher prices or, as here, the purchase of higher priced services, than would occur in its absence. Moreover, even if the desired information were in fact completely useless to the insurers and their patients in making an informed choice regarding the least costly adequate course of treatment—or, to put it another way, if the costs of evaluating the information were far greater than the cost savings resulting from its use—the Federation would still not be justified in deciding on behalf of its members' customers that they did not need the information: presumably, if that were the case, the discipline of the market would itself soon result in the insurers' abandoning their requests for x rays. The Federation is not entitled to pre-empt the working of the market by deciding for itself that its customers do not need that which they demand.

[13] Third, the Federation complains that the Commission erred in failing to consider, as relevant to its Rule of Reason analysis, noncompetitive "quality of care" justifications for the prohibition on provision of x rays to insurers in conjunction with claim forms. . . . The gist of the claim is that x rays, standing alone, are not adequate bases for diagnosis of dental problems or for the formulation of an acceptable course of treatment. Accordingly, if insurance companies are permitted to determine whether they will pay a claim for dental treatment on the basis of x rays as opposed to a full examination of all the diagnostic aids available to the examining dentist, there is a danger that they will erroneously decline to pay for treatment that is in fact in the interest of the patient, and that the patient will as a result be deprived of fully adequate care.

[14] The Federation's argument is flawed both legally and factually. The premise of the argument is that, far from having no effect on the cost of dental services chosen by patients and their insurers, the provision of x rays will have too great an impact: it will lead to the reduction of costs through the selection of inadequate treatment. Precisely such a justification for withholding information from customers was rejected as illegitimate in the *National Society of Professional Engineers* case. The argument is, in essence, that an unrestrained market in which consumers are given access to the information they believe to be relevant to their choices will lead them to make unwise and even dangerous choices. Such an argument amounts to nothing less than a frontal assault on the basic policy of the Sherman Act. Moreover, there is no particular reason to believe that the provision of information will be more harmful to consumers in the market for dental services than in other markets. Insurers deciding what level of care to pay for are not themselves the recipients of those services, but it is by no means clear that they lack incentives to consider the welfare of the patient as well as the minimization of costs. They are themselves in competition for the patronage of the patients—or, in most cases, the unions or businesses that contract on their behalf for group insurance coverage—and must satisfy their potential customers not only that they will provide coverage at a reasonable cost, but also that that coverage will be adequate to meet their customers' dental needs. There is thus no more reason to expect dental insurance companies to sacrifice quality in return for cost savings than to believe this of consumers in, say, the market for engineering services. Accordingly, if noncompetitive quality-of-service justifications are inadmissible to justify the denial of information to consumers in the latter market, there is little reason to credit such justifications here.

[15] In any event, the Commission did not, as the Federation suggests, refuse even to consider the quality-of-care justification for the withholding of x rays. Rather, the Commission held that the Federation had failed to introduce sufficient evidence to establish such a justification[.] [. . .]

[16] The factual findings of the Commission regarding the effect of the Federation's policy of withholding x rays are supported by substantial evidence, and those findings are sufficient as a matter of law to establish a violation of § 1 of the Sherman Act . . . .

* * *

In *California Dental*, the Supreme Court held that the Ninth Circuit and the FTC had been wrong to conclude that advertising restraints adopted by dental practitioners in California were sufficiently suspicious to warrant quick-look scrutiny. Do you agree?

California Dental Association v. FTC

526 U.S. 756 (1999)

Justice Souter.

[1] There are two issues in this case: whether the jurisdiction of the Federal Trade Commission extends to the California Dental Association (CDA), a nonprofit professional association {*Eds: we have excised this portion of the decision: it is enough to know that the FTC's power to enforce the antitrust laws through Section 5 of the FTC does not extend to nonprofit entities.*[361]}, and whether a "quick look" sufficed to justify finding that certain advertising restrictions adopted by the CDA violated the antitrust laws. We hold that the Commission's jurisdiction under the Federal Trade Commission Act (FTC Act) extends to an association that, like the CDA, provides substantial economic benefit to its for-profit members, but that where, as here, any anticompetitive effects of given restraints are far from intuitively obvious, the rule of reason demands a more thorough enquiry into the consequences of those restraints than the Court of Appeals performed.

[2] The CDA is a voluntary nonprofit association of local dental societies to which some 19,000 dentists belong, including about three-quarters of those practicing in the State. The CDA is exempt from federal income tax . . . , although it has for-profit subsidiaries that give its members advantageous access to various sorts of insurance, including liability coverage, and to financing for their real estate, equipment, cars, and patients' bills. The CDA lobbies and litigates in its members' interests, and conducts marketing and public relations campaigns for their benefit.

[3] The dentists who belong to the CDA through these associations agree to abide by a Code of Ethics (Code) including the following . . . :

> Although any dentist may advertise, no dentist shall advertise or solicit patients in any form of communication in a manner that is false or misleading in any material respect. In order to properly serve the public, dentists should represent themselves in a manner that contributes to the esteem of the public. Dentists should not misrepresent their training and competence in any way that would be false or misleading in any material respect.

[4] The CDA has issued a number of advisory opinions interpreting this section, and through separate advertising guidelines intended to help members comply with the Code and with state law the CDA has advised its dentists of disclosures they must make under state law when engaging in discount advertising. [. . .]

{Eds: The CDA's advertising guidelines directed that any advertisement offering a discount must specify the dollar amount of the non-discounted fee, the amount and duration of the discount, and any conditions or restrictions. CDA advisory opinions stated that any price advertising "shall be exact, without omissions, and shall make each service clearly identifiable, without the use of such phrases as 'as low as.'" CDA advisory opinions also prohibited quality claims, stating that such claims "are not susceptible to measurement or verification" and hence "are likely to be false or misleading." Local dental societies enforced the Code, including CDA guidelines and advisory opinions interpreting the Code. Applicants for CDA membership who violated the advertising restrictions could be denied membership. CDA members who violated the advertising restrictions faced suspension or expulsion from CDA.}

---

[361] *See infra* Chapter XI.

[5] The Commission brought a complaint against the CDA, alleging that it applied its guidelines so as to restrict truthful, nondeceptive advertising, and so violated § 5 of the FTC Act The complaint alleged that the CDA had unreasonably restricted two types of advertising: price advertising, particularly discounted fees, and advertising relating to the quality of dental services. An Administrative Law Judge (ALJ) held the Commission to have jurisdiction over the CDA. . . . He found that, although there had been no proof that the CDA exerted market power, no such proof was required to establish an antitrust violation . . . since the CDA had unreasonably prevented members and potential members from using truthful, nondeceptive advertising, all to the detriment of both dentists and consumers of dental services. He accordingly found a violation of § 5 of the FTC Act.

[6] The Commission adopted the factual findings of the ALJ except for his conclusion that the CDA lacked market power, with which the Commission disagreed. The Commission treated the CDA's restrictions on discount advertising as illegal *per se*. In the alternative, the Commission held the price advertising (as well as the nonprice) restrictions to be violations of the Sherman and FTC Acts under an abbreviated rule-of-reason analysis. . . .

[7] The Court of Appeals for the Ninth Circuit affirmed, sustaining the Commission's assertion of jurisdiction over the CDA and its ultimate conclusion on the merits. The court thought it error for the Commission to have applied *per se* analysis to the price advertising restrictions, finding analysis under the rule of reason required for all the restrictions. But the Court of Appeals went on to explain that the Commission had properly applied an abbreviated, or "quick look," rule of reason analysis designed for restraints that are not per se unlawful but are sufficiently anticompetitive on their face that they do not require a full-blown rule of reason inquiry. [. . .]

[8] The Court of Appeals treated as distinct questions the sufficiency of the analysis of anticompetitive effects and the substantiality of the evidence supporting the Commission's conclusions. Because we decide that the Court of Appeals erred when it held as a matter of law that quick-look analysis was appropriate . . . we do not reach the question of the substantiality of the evidence supporting the Commission's conclusion.

[9] In *National Collegiate Athletic Assn. v. Board of Regents of Univ. of Okla.*, 468 U.S. 85 (1984), we held that a "naked restraint on price and output requires some competitive justification even in the absence of a detailed market analysis." Elsewhere, we held that no elaborate industry analysis is required to demonstrate the anticompetitive character of horizontal agreements among competitors to refuse to discuss prices, *National Soc. of Professional Engineers v. United States*, 435 U.S. 679, 692 (1978), or to withhold a particular desired service, *FTC v. Indiana Federation of Dentists*, 476 U.S. 447, 459 (1986). In each of these cases, which have formed the basis for what has come to be called abbreviated or "quick-look" analysis under the rule of reason, an observer with even a rudimentary understanding of economics could conclude that the arrangements in question would have an anticompetitive effect on customers and markets. In *National Collegiate Athletic Assn.*, the league's television plan expressly limited output (the number of games that could be televised) and fixed a minimum price. In *National Soc. of Professional Engineers*, the restraint was an absolute ban on competitive bidding. In *Indiana Federation of Dentists*, the restraint was a horizontal agreement among the participating dentists to withhold from their customers a particular service that they desire. As in such cases, quick-look analysis carries the day when the great likelihood of anticompetitive effects can easily be ascertained.

[10] The case before us, however, fails to present a situation in which the likelihood of anticompetitive effects is comparably obvious. Even on Justice Breyer's view that bars on truthful and verifiable price and quality advertising are *prima facie* anticompetitive, and place the burden of procompetitive justification on those who agree to adopt them, the very issue at the threshold of this case is whether professional price and quality advertising is sufficiently verifiable in theory and in fact to fall within such a general rule. Ultimately our disagreement with Justice Breyer turns on our different responses to this issue. Whereas he accepts . . . that the restrictions here were like restrictions on advertisement of price and quality generally, it seems to us that the CDA's advertising restrictions might plausibly be thought to have a net procompetitive effect, or possibly no effect at all on competition. The restrictions on both discount and nondiscount advertising are, at least on their face, designed to avoid false or deceptive advertising in a market characterized by striking disparities between the information available to the professional and the patient. In a market for professional services, in which advertising is relatively rare and the comparability of service packages not easily established, the difficulty for customers or potential competitors to get and verify information about the price and availability of services magnifies the dangers to competition associated with misleading advertising. What is more, the quality of professional services tends to resist either calibration or

monitoring by individual patients or clients, partly because of the specialized knowledge required to evaluate the services, and partly because of the difficulty in determining whether, and the degree to which, an outcome is attributable to the quality of services (like a poor job of tooth filling) or to something else (like a very tough walnut). Patients' attachments to particular professionals, the rationality of which is difficult to assess, complicate the picture even further. The existence of such significant challenges to informed decisionmaking by the customer for professional services immediately suggests that advertising restrictions arguably protecting patients from misleading or irrelevant advertising call for more than cursory treatment as obviously comparable to classic horizontal agreements to limit output or price competition.

[11] The explanation proffered by the Court of Appeals for the likely anticompetitive effect of the CDA's restrictions on discount advertising began with the unexceptionable statements that "price advertising is fundamental to price competition," and that "[r]estrictions on the ability to advertise prices normally make it more difficult for consumers to find a lower price and for dentists to compete on the basis of price." The court then acknowledged that, according to the CDA, the restrictions nonetheless furthered the "legitimate, indeed procompetitive, goal of preventing false and misleading price advertising." The Court of Appeals might, at this juncture, have recognized that the restrictions at issue here are very far from a total ban on price or discount advertising, and might have considered the possibility that the particular restrictions on professional advertising could have different effects from those "normally" found in the commercial world, even to the point of promoting competition by reducing the occurrence of unverifiable and misleading across-the-board discount advertising. Instead, the Court of Appeals confined itself to the brief assertion that the "CDA's disclosure requirements appear to prohibit across-the-board discounts because it is simply infeasible to disclose all of the information that is required," followed by the observation that "the record provides no evidence that the rule has in fact led to increased disclosure and transparency of dental pricing."

[12] But these observations brush over the professional context and describe no anticompetitive effects. Assuming that the record in fact supports the conclusion that the CDA disclosure rules essentially bar advertisement of across-the-board discounts, it does not obviously follow that such a ban would have a net anticompetitive effect here. Whether advertisements that announced discounts for, say, first-time customers, would be less effective at conveying information relevant to competition if they listed the original and discounted prices for checkups, X-rays, and fillings, than they would be if they simply specified a percentage discount across the board, seems to us a question susceptible to empirical but not *a priori* analysis. In a suspicious world, the discipline of specific example may well be a necessary condition of plausibility for professional claims that for all practical purposes defy comparison shopping. It is also possible in principle that, even if across-the-board discount advertisements were more effective in drawing customers in the short run, the recurrence of some measure of intentional or accidental misstatement due to the breadth of their claims might leak out over time to make potential patients skeptical of any such across-the-board advertising, so undercutting the method's effectiveness. It might be, too, that across-the-board discount advertisements would continue to attract business indefinitely, but might work precisely because they were misleading customers, and thus just because their effect would be anticompetitive, not procompetitive. Put another way, the CDA's rule appears to reflect the prediction that any costs to competition associated with the elimination of across-the-board advertising will be outweighed by gains to consumer information (and hence competition) created by discount advertising that is exact, accurate, and more easily verifiable (at least by regulators). As a matter of economics this view may or may not be correct, but it is not implausible, and neither a court nor the Commission may initially dismiss it as presumptively wrong.

[13] In theory, it is true, the Court of Appeals neither ruled out the plausibility of some procompetitive support for the CDA's requirements nor foreclosed the utility of an evidentiary discussion on the point. The court indirectly acknowledged the plausibility of procompetitive justifications for the CDA's position when it stated that "the record provides no evidence that the rule has in fact led to increased disclosure and transparency of dental pricing[.]" But because petitioner alone would have had the incentive to introduce such evidence, the statement sounds as though the Court of Appeals may have thought it was justified without further analysis to shift a burden to the CDA to adduce hard evidence of the procompetitive nature of its policy; the court's aversion to empirical evidence at the moment of this implicit burden shifting underscores the leniency of its enquiry into evidence of the restrictions' anticompetitive effects.

[14] The Court of Appeals was comparably tolerant in accepting the sufficiency of abbreviated rule-of-reason analysis as to the nonprice advertising restrictions. The court began with the argument that "[t]hese restrictions are in effect a form of output limitation, as they restrict the supply of information about individual dentists' services." Although this sentence does indeed appear as cited, it is puzzling, given that the relevant output for antitrust purposes here is presumably not information or advertising, but dental services themselves. The question is not whether the universe of possible advertisements has been limited (as assuredly it has), but whether the limitation on advertisements obviously tends to limit the total delivery of dental services. The court came closest to addressing this latter question when it went on to assert that limiting advertisements regarding quality and safety "prevents dentists from fully describing the package of services they offer," adding that "[t]he restrictions may also affect output more directly, as quality and comfort advertising may induce some customers to obtain nonemergency care when they might not otherwise do so." This suggestion about output is also puzzling. If quality advertising actually induces some patients to obtain more care than they would in its absence, then restricting such advertising would reduce the demand for dental services, not the supply; and it is of course the producers' supply of a good in relation to demand that is normally relevant in determining whether a producer-imposed output limitation has the anticompetitive effect of artificially raising prices.

[15] Although the Court of Appeals acknowledged the CDA's view that "claims about quality are inherently unverifiable and therefore misleading," it responded that this concern "does not justify banning all quality claims without regard to whether they are, in fact, false or misleading." As a result, the court said, "the restriction is a sufficiently naked restraint on output to justify quick look analysis." The court assumed, in these words, that some dental quality claims may escape justifiable censure, because they are both verifiable and true. But its implicit assumption fails to explain why it gave no weight to the countervailing, and at least equally plausible, suggestion that restricting difficult-to-verify claims about quality or patient comfort would have a procompetitive effect by preventing misleading or false claims that distort the market. It is, indeed, entirely possible to understand the CDA's restrictions on unverifiable quality and comfort advertising as nothing more than a procompetitive ban on puffery.

[16] The point is not that the CDA's restrictions necessarily have the procompetitive effect claimed by the CDA; it is possible that banning quality claims might have no effect at all on competitiveness if, for example, many dentists made very much the same sort of claims. And it is also of course possible that the restrictions might in the final analysis be anticompetitive. The point, rather, is that the plausibility of competing claims about the effects of the professional advertising restrictions rules out the indulgently abbreviated review to which the Commission's order was treated. The obvious anticompetitive effect that triggers abbreviated analysis has not been shown. [. . .]

[17] Saying here that the Court of Appeals's conclusion at least required a more extended examination of the possible factual underpinnings than it received is not, of course, necessarily to call for the fullest market analysis. Although we have said that a challenge to a naked restraint on price and output need not be supported by a detailed market analysis in order to require some competitive justification, it does not follow that every case attacking a less obviously anticompetitive restraint (like this one) is a candidate for plenary market examination. The truth is that our categories of analysis of anticompetitive effect are less fixed than terms like "*per se*," "quick look," and "rule of reason" tend to make them appear. We have recognized, for example, that there is often no bright line separating *per se* from Rule of Reason analysis, since considerable inquiry into market conditions may be required before the application of any so-called "*per se*" condemnation is justified. . . . What is required . . . is an enquiry meet for the case, looking to the circumstances, details, and logic of a restraint. The object is to see whether the experience of the market has been so clear, or necessarily will be, that a confident conclusion about the principal tendency of a restriction will follow from a quick (or at least quicker) look, in place of a more sedulous one. And of course what we see may vary over time, if rule-of-reason analyses in case after case reach identical conclusions. For now, at least, a less quick look was required for the initial assessment of the tendency of these professional advertising restrictions. Because the Court of Appeals did not scrutinize the assumption of relative anticompetitive tendencies, we vacate the judgment and remand the case for a fuller consideration of the issue.

Justice Breyer, with whom Justice Stevens, Justice Kennedy, and Justice Ginsburg join, concurring in part and dissenting in part.

[18] . . . [I]n a rule of reason antitrust case the quality of proof required should vary with the circumstances, . . . what is required is an enquiry meet for the case, and that the object is a confident conclusion about the principal tendency of a restriction. But I do not agree that the Court has properly applied those unobjectionable principles here. In my view, a traditional application of the rule of reason to the facts as found by the Commission requires affirming the Commission-just as the Court of Appeals did below.

[19] The Commission's conclusion is lawful if its factual findings, insofar as they are supported by substantial evidence, make out a violation of Sherman Act § 1. To determine whether that is so, I would not simply ask whether the restraints at issue are anticompetitive overall. Rather, like the Court of Appeals (and the Commission), I would break that question down into four classical, subsidiary antitrust questions: (1) What is the specific restraint at issue? (2) What are its likely anticompetitive effects? (3) Are there offsetting procompetitive justifications? (4) Do the parties have sufficient market power to make a difference?

[20] The most important question is the first: What are the specific restraints at issue? [. . .]

[21] The Court of Appeals referred explicitly to some of the evidence that it found adequate to support the Commission's conclusions. It pointed out, for example, that the Dental Association's advisory opinions and guidelines indicate that descriptions of prices as "reasonable" or "low" do not comply with the Association's rule; that in "numerous cases" the Association advised members of objections to special offers, senior citizen discounts, and new patient discounts, apparently without regard to their truth; and that one advisory opinion expressly states that claims as to the quality of services are inherently likely to be false or misleading, all without any particular consideration of whether such statements were true or false.

[22] The Commission itself had before it far more evidence. It referred to instances in which the Association, without regard for the truthfulness of the statements at issue, recommended denial of membership to dentists wishing to advertise, for example, "reasonable fees quoted in advance," "major savings," or "making teeth cleaning inexpensive." It referred to testimony that "across-the-board discount advertising in literal compliance with the requirements 'would probably take two pages in the telephone book' and '[n]obody is going to really advertise in that fashion.'" And it pointed to many instances in which the Dental Association suppressed such advertising claims as "we guarantee all dental work for 1 year," "latest in cosmetic dentistry," and "gentle dentistry in a caring environment."

[23] Do each of the three restrictions mentioned have the potential for genuine adverse effects on competition? I should have thought that the anticompetitive tendencies of the three restrictions were obvious. An agreement not to advertise that a fee is reasonable, that service is inexpensive, or that a customer will receive a discount makes it more difficult for a dentist to inform customers that he charges a lower price. If the customer does not know about a lower price, he will find it more difficult to buy lower price service. That fact, in turn, makes it less likely that a dentist will obtain more customers by offering lower prices. And that likelihood means that dentists will prove less likely to offer lower prices. But why should I have to spell out the obvious? To restrain truthful advertising about lower prices is likely to restrict competition in respect to price-the central nervous system of the economy. The Commission thought this fact sufficient to hold (in the alternative) that the price advertising restrictions were unlawful *per se*. [C]f. *Socony-Vacuum* (finding agreement among competitors to buy "spot-market oil" unlawful *per se* because of its tendency to restrict price competition). For present purposes, I need not decide whether the Commission was right in applying a *per se* rule. I need only assume a rule of reason applies, and note the serious anticompetitive tendencies of the price advertising restraints.

[24] The restrictions on the advertising of service quality also have serious anticompetitive tendencies. This is not a case of "mere puffing," as the FTC recognized . . . [S]ome parents may . . . want to know that a particular dentist makes a point of "gentle care." Others may want to know about 1-year dental work guarantees. To restrict that kind of service quality advertisement is to restrict competition over the quality of service itself, for, unless consumers know, they may not purchase, and dentists may not compete to supply that which will make little difference to the demand for their services. That, at any rate, is the theory of the Sherman Act. And it is rather late in the day for anyone to deny the significant anticompetitive tendencies of an agreement that restricts competition in any legitimate respect, let alone one that inhibits customers from learning about the quality of a dentist's service. [. . .]

[25] The FTC found that the price advertising restrictions amounted to a naked attempt to eliminate price competition. It found that the service quality advertising restrictions deprive consumers of information they value and of healthy competition for their patronage. It added that the anticompetitive nature of these restrictions was plain. The Court of Appeals agreed. I do not believe it possible to deny the anticompetitive tendencies I have mentioned.

[26] We must also ask whether, despite their anticompetitive tendencies, these restrictions might be justified by other procompetitive tendencies or redeeming virtues. This is a closer question—at least in theory. The Dental Association argues that the three relevant restrictions are inextricably tied to a legitimate Association effort to restrict false or misleading advertising. The Association, the argument goes, had to prevent dentists from engaging in the kind of truthful, nondeceptive advertising that it banned in order effectively to stop dentists from making unverifiable claims about price or service quality, which claims would mislead the consumer.

[27] The problem with this or any similar argument is an empirical one. Notwithstanding its theoretical plausibility, the record does not bear out such a claim. The Commission, which is expert in the area of false and misleading advertising, was uncertain whether petitioner had even *made* the claim. It characterized petitioner's efficiencies argument as rooted in the (unproved) factual assertion that its ethical rule "challenges *only* advertising that is false or misleading." Regardless, the Court of Appeals wrote, in respect to the price restrictions, that "the record provides no evidence that the rule has in fact led to increased disclosure and transparency of dental pricing." With respect to quality advertising, the Commission stressed that the Association "offered no convincing argument, let alone evidence, that consumers of dental services have been, or are likely to be, harmed by the broad categories of advertising it restricts." Nor did the Court of Appeals think that the Association's unsubstantiated contention that claims about quality are inherently unverifiable and therefore misleading could justify banning all quality claims without regard to whether they are, in fact, false or misleading. [. . .]

[28] The upshot, in my view, is that the Court of Appeals, applying ordinary antitrust principles, reached an unexceptional conclusion. It is the same legal conclusion that this Court itself reached in *Indiana Federation*—a much closer case than this one. There the Court found that an agreement by dentists not to submit dental X rays to insurers violated the rule of reason. The anticompetitive tendency of that agreement was to reduce competition among dentists in respect to their willingness to submit X rays to insurers—a matter in respect to which consumers are relatively indifferent, as compared to advertising of price discounts and service quality, the matters at issue here. The redeeming virtue in *Indiana Federation* was the alleged undesirability of having insurers consider a range of matters when deciding whether treatment was justified—a virtue no less plausible, and no less proved, than the virtue offered here. The "power" of the dentists to enforce their agreement was no greater than that at issue here (control of 75% to 90% of the relevant markets). It is difficult to see how the two cases can be reconciled.

CASENOTE: The *1-800 Contacts* Litigation

In the Matter of 1-800 Contacts, Inc., 2018 WL 6078349 (F.T.C. 2018); 1-800 Contacts, Inc. v. FTC, 1 F.4th 102 (2d Cir. 2021)

In a more recent effort to apply quick-look analysis, the FTC was again knocked back. *1-800 Contacts* was an e-commerce case, in which the defendant contact lens retailer, 1-800 Contacts, discovered that its competitors were buying search advertising—that is, ad space alongside search engine results—that would be displayed when a user typed in "1-800 contacts" into the search bar. 1-800 Contacts sued these competitors on the theory that buying search advertising for this keyword was a form of trademark infringement. 1-800 Contacts then settled those infringement claims in agreements that included a commitment by each party to refrain from bidding on keywords including one another's trademarks and internet URLs in future.

The Commission, in an opinion by Chairman Simons, held that the restraints were inherently suspect and unlawful. Quoting *PolyGram*, the Commission noted that "[i]nherently suspect conduct ordinarily encompasses behavior that past judicial experience and current economic learning have shown to warrant summary condemnation." And the settlements here met that standard: they "are, in essence, agreements between horizontal competitors to restrict the information provided by advertising to consumers when they search for 1-800 Contacts' trademark terms and URLs; consumers could have used that withheld information to compare and evaluate the prices and other features of competing online sellers. Ultimately, the effect of the advertising restrictions is to make information enabling consumer comparisons more difficult and costly to obtain." The Commission emphasized the importance of online search, and online search advertising, as a forum for competition, as "the advertising is presented to a consumer at a time when the consumer is more likely to be looking to buy." It followed from this that "[b]ecause the Challenged Agreements restrict the ability of lower cost online sellers to show their ads to consumers, it is easy to see how an observer with even a rudimentary understanding of economics could conclude that the arrangements in question would have an anticompetitive effect on customers and markets."

Commissioner Phillips dissented, emphasizing that "[t]he per se and inherently suspect standards are exceptional and their application is reserved for the most patently anticompetitive restraints." Unlike previous cases dealing with broad bans or limits on advertising, he argued, the trademark settlements in this case were of narrow application ("[t]hey do not restrict the content of advertisements that 1-800 Contacts or the counterparties can run in innumerable contexts, including in response to search queries.") and were related to a procompetitive justification (the protection of trademarks, a "competing federal policy"). He identified the Second Circuit's *Clorox* decision—Clorox Co. v. Sterling Winthrop, Inc., 117 F.3d 50 (2d Cir. 1997)—as support for the proposition that trademark settlements that limited competition should be analyzed under the full-blown rule of reason, not under an abbreviated approach.

On appeal, the Second Circuit agreed with Commissioner Phillips. "[I]f an arrangement might plausibly be thought to have a net procompetitive effect, or possibly no effect at all on competition," the court explained, "more than a quick look is required." And the presence of a trademark interest here was decisive. "[T]he restraints at issue here could plausibly be thought to have a net procompetitive effect because they are derived from trademark settlement agreements. . . . As the [settlements] restrict the parties from running advertisements on [1-800-Contacts'] trademarked terms, they directly implicate trademark policy." Full rule of reason scrutiny was appropriate, and the Commission's record could not support liability on such a theory.

NOTES

1) Now that you have read *Board of Regents* (Chapter IV), *IFD*, and *California Dental*, what is the best way to understand the circumstances under which courts will apply a "quick look" analysis? Does the Second Circuit's opinion in *1-800-Contacts* add anything to understanding, or merely apply it?

2) Given that quick-look review is really a way of discharging the plaintiff's burden at step one of a rule of reason analysis, to what extent are they really different rules at all?

E. Some Further Reading

Edward D. Cavanagh, *Whatever Happened to Quick Look?*, 26 U. Miami Bus. L. Rev. 39 (2017)

John M. Connor & Darren Bush, *How to Block Cartel Formation and Price Fixing: Using Extraterritorial Application of the Antitrust Laws as a Deterrence Mechanism*, 112 Dick. L. Rev. 813 (2008)

Vivek Ghosal & D. Daniel Sokol, *The Evolution of U.S. Cartel Enforcement*, 57 J. L. & Econ. S51 (2014)

Eric H. Grush & Claire M. Korenblit, American Needle *and a "Positive" Quick Look Approach in Challenges to Joint Ventures*, 25 Antitrust 55 (2011)

Herbert Hovenkamp & Christopher R. Leslie, *The Firm as Cartel Manager*, 64 Vand. L. Rev. 811 (2011)

Louis Kaplow, COMPETITION POLICY AND PRICE FIXING (2013)

Sanjukta Paul, *On Firms*, 90 U. Chi. L. Rev. 579 (2023)

Richard A. Posner, *Review of Kaplow, COMPETITION POLICY AND PRICE FIXING*, 79 Antitrust L.J. 761 (2014)

Maurice E. Stucke, *Does the Rule of Reason Violate the Rule of Law?*, 42 U.C. Davis L. Rev. 1375 (2009)

Gregory J. Werden, *Economic Evidence on The Existence of Collusion*, 71 Antitrust L.J. 719 (2004)

VI. VERTICAL RESTRAINTS

A. Overview

"Vertical" restraints are restrictive provisions in agreements between entities at different levels of the supply chain, like those between a manufacturer and a retailer, or between a component supplier and an original equipment manufacturer. They are more common, and less likely to be harmful under most circumstances, than horizontal restraints. After all, most companies have more reasons (at least, more good and procompetitive reasons) to enter into agreements with their trading partners than with their competitors!

But this does not mean that vertical agreements are invariably benign. On the contrary, the imposition of restrictive obligations on one's trading partners can be a powerful means of excluding rivals or even facilitating collusion. In this chapter we will focus on some of the ways in which this may occur.

Anticompetitive vertical restraints were among the concerns raised during the early years of the Sherman Act. Practices that attracted attention and scrutiny included: exclusivity commitments that prohibited trading partners of one party from dealing with that party's competitors; "tying" agreements that committed the buyer of a primary product or service to buy a secondary product or service as well; so-called "vertical price-fixing" agreements between a manufacturer and a retailer regarding downstream retail prices (what we would now call "resale price maintenance," or just "RPM"); most-favored-nation ("MFN") agreements, which guaranteed that the beneficiary would receive terms at least as preferable as those offered to its rivals; agreements which guaranteed "discriminatory" preferred treatment from a trading partner (what we would now call "MFN-plus" agreements); and a variety of other vertical practices. For example, the famous *Standard Oil* decision of 1911 concerned, among (many) other things, allegations that Standard Oil had obtained "[r]ebates, preferences, and other discriminatory practices" from railroads.[362]

Vertical restraints may threaten competition in a variety of ways. In some cases, a vertical restraint may enable a business with market power to weaken or exclude competition by raising the costs of its rivals. For example, if a monopolist locked up key suppliers or distributors to exclusive deals, competitors might be forced to switch over to higher-priced, lower-quality alternatives that would weaken their ability to compete with the monopolist. In extreme cases, with no workable alternatives at all, rivals might be forced out of the market entirely. In other cases, vertical restraints may soften horizontal competition by facilitating coordination among competitors: for example, competitors aiming to generate or facilitate tacit collusion might introduce parallel vertical restraints (such as MFN commitments to customers, which we will discuss below) as a way of committing to rivals that they will not engage in aggressive discounting.[363] Vertical restraints may also diminish "intrabrand" competition among distributors of a single product, although as we will see that has become a secondary concern in modern law.

At certain times in the history of antitrust, judicial treatment of vertical restraints has been strongly influenced by concerns about exploitation of power asymmetries, the domination of a weaker party by a stronger, and discrimination (in the sense of dissimilar treatment of trading partners). In particular, a number of earlier cases dealing with vertical restraints expressed a consistent concern that the freedom and independence of trading partners, including small businesses, ought not be fettered by an obligation imposed by a more powerful trading partner. This theme is exemplified by a passage in the district court's opinion in the 1951 *Richfield Oil* case:

> Richfield cannot, by creating the relationship of landlord and tenant, long and anciently known
> to our law, with all the responsibilities that such relationship imposes on the transferee, restrain

---

[362] Standard Oil Co. of New Jersey v. United States, 221 U.S. 1, 42–43 (1911).

[363] Jonathan B. Baker & Judith A. Chevalier, *The Competitive Consequences of Most-Favored-Nation Provisions*, 27 Antitrust 20, 22–23 (Spring 2013) ("The most immediate and direct significance of an MFN for the seller, and the source of competitive harms from facilitating coordination and dampening competition, is to raise the seller's cost of cutting price to buyers other than the buyer that is the beneficiary of the MFN. . . . To see why a tax on price-cutting facilitates coordination, suppose that coordinated conduct in this industry is inhibited by suppliers' incentives to cheat—that is, deterring cheating is the 'cartel problem' the bottle makers have to solve to make coordination possible or more effective. A bottle maker that adopts an MFN with some or all customers helps the industry solve that problem by tying its own hands.").

trade through that outlet by imposing illegitimate oral contacts which restrict the transferee to the handling of Richfield's products or Richfield's sponsored products. . . . It follows that the . . . operators are, by the instrument of their creation, independent business men, as that concept is understood in anti-trust law, and that the imposition on them by oral agreements of restrictive conditions limiting their dealings to Richfield products and Richfield sponsored . . . products, and denying access to other dealers in petroleum and accessories to these stations, and, through them, to the public, is violative of both Section 1 of the Sherman Anti-Trust law and Section 3 of the Clayton Act.[364]

This theme is embroidered throughout earlier vertical cases.[365] But these concerns are no longer prominent in the adjudication of vertical Sherman Act cases: since the 1970s, courts have focused antitrust analysis on the creation and maintenance of market power, rather than on its exploitation or on discrimination as such.[366] (Concern with discriminatory treatment of small businesses also played a central role in motivating the enactment of the Robinson-Patman Act of 1936.[367])

Partly as a function of these concerns, vertical restraints in a number of categories—including minimum RPM, maximum RPM, and tying agreements—were *per se* illegal for much of the 20th century, just as price-fixing agreements are today.[368]

Today, most antitrust economists believe that, under some circumstances, certain vertical restraints can cause significant harm by enabling entities with significant market power to exclude rivals, or by promoting or facilitating collusion or coordination.[369] But most would also agree that in many circumstances vertical restraints can be helpful rather than harmful to competition and consumers, including in ways that the early critics of vertical restraints did not always appreciate. A series of academic contributions in the 1950s, 1960s, and 1970s articulated some reasons why courts should pause before automatically condemning broad categories of vertical restraints.[370]

---

[364] *See, e.g.*, United States v. Richfield Oil Corp., 99 F. Supp. 280, 293–94 (S.D. Cal. 1951). For a contemporaneous perspective, *see also* Thomas E. Kauper, *The "Warren Court" and the Antitrust Laws: of Economics, Populism, and Cynicism*, 67 Mich. L. Rev. 325, 332 (1968) ("Apparently uncertain about the effect of such vertical arrangements upon concentration in the market and not confident that in all cases such effects can be determined on a case-by-case basis, the Court has proceeded with a method of analysis placing primary emphasis on equality of opportunity, free access to markets by competing sellers, and complete freedom of choice by buyers. If it can be proved that the challenged practice is likely to increase concentration or create high barriers to entry, so much the better. But in any event, the practice may be condemned as an unwarranted limitation on buyer and/or seller opportunities.").

[365] *See, e.g.*, Continental T.V., Inc. v. GTE Sylvania Inc., 433 U.S. 36, 66–67 (1977) (White, J., concurring in the judgment) ("[I]ndependent businessmen should have the freedom to dispose of the goods they own as they see fit."); United States v. Arnold, Schwinn & Co., 388 U.S. 365, 378–79 (1967) (holding that remedy should ensure "freedom of distributors to dispose of the [defendant's] products, which they have bought from [the defendant], where and to whomever they choose," and stating that "[u]nder the Sherman Act, it is unreasonable without more for a manufacturer to seek to restrict and confine areas or persons with whom an article may be traded after the manufacturer has parted with dominion over it"); Dr. Miles Medical Co. v. John D. Park & Sons Co., 220 U.S. 373, 407–08 (1911) (noting the "freedom of trade on the part of dealers who own what they sell"); GTE Sylvania Inc. v. Continental T.V., Inc., 537 F.2d 980, 1019–29 (9th Cir. 1976) (Browning, J., dissenting) (extended and detailed discussion of the "statutory policy [under the Sherman Act] of protecting the independence of individual business units").

[366] For early harbingers, *see, e.g.*, Albrecht v. Herald Co., 390 U.S. 145, 158 (1968) (Harlan. J., dissenting) ("It has long been recognized that one of the objectives of the Sherman Act was to preserve, for social rather than economic reasons, a high degree of independence, multiplicity, and variety in the economic system. Recognition of this objective does not, however, require this Court to hold that every commercial act that fetters the freedom of some trader is a proper subject for a per se rule in the sense that it has no adequate provable justification."); Dr. Miles Medical Co. v. John D. Park & Sons Co., 220 U.S. 373, 412 (1911) (Holmes, J., dissenting) ("[I]t seems to me that the point of most profitable returns marks the equilibrium of social desires, and determines the fair price in the only sense in which I can find meaning in those words. The Dr. Miles Medical Company knows better than we do what will enable it to do the best business. . . . I cannot believe that in the long run the public will profit by this court permitting knaves to cut reasonable prices for some ulterior purpose of their own, and thus to impair, if not to destroy, the production and sale of articles which it is assumed to be desirable that the public should be able to get.").

[367] We touched briefly on the Robinson-Patman Act in Chapter I.

[368] *See, e.g.*, Dr. Miles Medical Co. v. John D. Park & Sons Co., 220 U.S. 373 (1911) (minimum RPM illegal), *overruled by* Leegin Creative Leather Products, Inc. v. PSKS, Inc., 551 U.S. 877 (2007).

[369] *See, e.g.*, Dennis W. Carlton & Ralph A. Winter, *Vertical Most-Favored-Nation Restraints and Credit Card No-Surcharge Rules*, 61 J. L. & Econ. 215 (2018); Claudia M. Landeo, *Exclusionary Vertical Restraints and Antitrust: Experimental Law and Economics Contributions* in Kathryn Zeiler & Joshua Teitelbaum (eds.), THE RESEARCH HANDBOOK ON BEHAVIORAL LAW AND ECONOMICS (2015); Steven C. Salop, *Economic Analysis of Exclusionary Vertical Conduct: Where Chicago Has Overshot the Mark* in Robert Pitofsky (ed.) HOW THE CHICAGO SCHOOL OVERSHOT THE MARK: THE EFFECT OF CONSERVATIVE ECONOMIC ANALYSIS ON U.S. ANTITRUST (2008).

[370] *See, e.g.*, Lester G. Telser, *Why Should Manufacturers Want Fair Trade?* 3 J. L. & Econ. 86 (1960) (resale price maintenance); Ward S. Bowman Jr., *Tying Arrangements and the Leverage Problem*, 67 Yale L.J. 19 (1957); Aaron Director & Edward H. Levi, *Law and the Future: Trade Regulation*, 51 Nw. U. L. Rev. 281, 290 (1956) (single monopoly profit theorem, briefly stated).

Today, there is a rich and thoughtful literature on the economics of vertical restraints, much of which emphasizes the importance of understanding specific markets, practices, and circumstances in judging their effects.[371]

The Idea of Free Riding

One important way in which some vertical restraints can help to promote competition is by deterring "free riding." This is a recurrent idea in discussion of vertical restraints. The core point is that businesses may be deterred from investing in the supply or improvement of a product or service if their rivals are able to appropriate the benefits of those investments: and, conversely, that businesses may invest more fully in competition if they are allowed to protect their investments from appropriation by competitors. And one way in which they may do so is through vertical contracts.[372]

To make this more concrete with an example, suppose that a device OEM (original equipment manufacturer: a company that makes devices) wants to introduce a valuable new feature into its device, and in order to do this it must cooperate closely with some upstream component manufacturers. Suppose that the OEM knows that developing the new feature will involve a major investment of money and resources in R&D, and will involve sharing the fruits of that R&D activity—and perhaps other proprietary information—with the component manufacturers. Now, if the component suppliers are then free to share the benefits of the investment with other, competing OEMs, then the original OEM's investment might end up subsidizing its direct competitors, giving rivals the benefit of the expensive R&D without any of the costs. And the OEM knows all this in advance, when it is deciding whether, and how much, to invest. Its reluctance to subsidize rivals may discourage investment. But if the OEM can require, as a precondition of participation in the project, a period of exclusivity in which the component suppliers will not work with rivals in particular ways, the OEM's incentive to undertake and invest in this project can be preserved. Conversely, if the exclusivity commitment is impossible (*e.g.*, because it is forbidden by the antitrust laws), the incentive will be reduced, leading to less investment and innovation. A valuable new feature may never be developed.

Of course, the fact that "free riding" may threaten or soften investment incentives does not mean that a free-riding concern is, or should be, a hall pass for any conceivable form of restriction. For one thing, free riding may not be a serious concern in a particular case[373]; for another, the mere existence of a directional free-riding threat does not mean that a restraint designed to block it is actually net-beneficial to consumers![374] In the example above, for example, it is not at all clear whether the harm from exclusivity will outweigh the benefits from the extra innovation and investment. It is also worth remembering that "free riding"—that is, the receipt of unpriced benefits from the investments of others—is ubiquitous in the economy, including through competition's core mechanic of

---

[371] *See, e.g.*, Patrick Rey & Thibaud Vergé, *Economics of Vertical Restraints* in Paolo Buccirossi (ed.), HANDBOOK OF ANTITRUST ECONOMICS (2008); Daniel P. O'Brien, *The Antitrust Treatment of Vertical Restraints: Beyond the Possibility Theorems* in Konkurrensverket (Swedish Competition Authority), THE PROS AND CONS OF VERTICAL RESTRAINTS (2008); B. Douglas Bernheim & Michael D. Whinston, *Exclusive Dealing*, 106 J. Pol. Econ. 64 (1998).

[372] *See, e.g.*, Ward S. Bowman, *The Prerequisites and Effects of Resale Price Maintenance*, 22 U. Chi. L. Rev. 825, 835 (1955) (RPM as a response to free riding concerns).

[373] *See, e.g.*, Warren S. Grimes, *The Sylvania Free Rider Justification for Downstream-Power Vertical Restraints: Truth or Invitation for Pretext?* in Robert Pitofsky (ed.), HOW THE CHICAGO SCHOOL OVERSHOT THE MARK: THE EFFECT OF CONSERVATIVE ECONOMIC ANALYSIS ON U.S. ANTITRUST (2008); *see also* Toys "R" Us, Inc. v. FTC, 221 F.3d 928, 933 (7th Cir. 2000) ("The Commission also considered the question whether [Toys R Us ("TRU")] might have been trying to protect itself against free riding, at least with respect to its vertical agreements. . . . Nevertheless, it found that the manufacturers compensated TRU directly for advertising toys, storing toys made early in the year, and stocking a broad line of each manufacturer's toys under one roof. A 1993 TRU memorandum confirms that advertising is manufacturer-funded and is 'essentially free.'").

[374] *See, e.g.*, Gregory T. Gundlach, Joseph P. Cannon & Kenneth C. Manning, *Free riding and resale price maintenance: Insights from marketing research and practice*, 55 Antitrust Bull. 381 (2010); George A. Hay, *The Free Rider Rationale and Vertical Restraints Analysis Reconsidered*, 56 Antitrust L.J. 27 (1987).

competitive imitation.[375] The world would not necessarily be better, all things considered, if all free riding were prohibited![376]

A central feature of vertical-restraint law is the distinction between "interbrand" restraints (that is, in the classic form, restraints imposed by a producer on trading partners' ability to deal in the products of *other* manufacturers) and "intrabrand" restraints (that is, restraints imposed by a producer on the distribution of its *own* product as part of a distribution strategy). As we will see, in general, pure intrabrand restraints are of little or no concern in modern law: as Eleanor Fox has put it, "firms have no duty to create or tolerate competition in their own product, and if they impose territorial restraints in the course of distributing their product, those restraints are presumed to be efficient for the firm and efficient or at least neutral for competition and consumers."[377] We will consider intrabrand and interbrand restraints separately below.

In recent decades, the law of vertical restraints has generally moved away from *per se* bans on vertical restraints and toward rule-of-reason assessment. As we will see in the rest of the chapter, the rule of reason is now the norm. The *per se* rule against the use of exclusive distribution territories was eliminated in the 1970s (after having been introduced in the 1960s); the *per se* rule against RPM was eliminated in two steps in 1997 and 2007 (for agreements on maximum and minimum price respectively); the *per se* rule against tying has not *quite* been formally eliminated but in practice something approaching a rule-of-reason assessment is the norm today; and the analysis of exclusive dealing generally requires a thoughtful examination of the circumstances, and the effects of the restraint on competition. Thus, today, with an asterisk for tying arrangements, no vertical restraints are *per se* illegal.

Antitrust's turn away from *per se* bans on certain vertical practices has attracted some controversy, particularly in light of the difficulty that plaintiffs often face in mounting a rule of reason case (see Chapter IV). Today, at the broadest level, we can think of three general schools of thought on vertical restraints: first, a general "Chicago School" style view that vertical restraints should be *per se* legal or nearly so; second, a view that we should return to the broad-brush bans of earlier decades rather than mire the courts in difficult effects analyses; and, third, a view (reflecting, for the most part, current law) that vertical restraints can generate both significant benefits and significant harms, and that courts should navigate on a case-by-case basis, with a focus on harm to interbrand competition.

The following extracts briefly illustrate these perspectives. We start with Judge Frank Easterbrook—one of the leading figures of antitrust's Chicago Revolution—proposing *per se* legality for what he calls "distribution restraints."[378]

Frank Easterbrook, Vertical Arrangements and the Rule of Reason
53 Antitrust L.J. 135 (1984)

I want to make a point as simple as it is controversial. No practice a manufacturer uses to distribute its products should be a subject of serious antitrust attention. It should make no difference whether the manufacturer prescribes territories, customers, quality standards, or prices for its dealers. It should make no difference whether the manufacturer "ties" products together in a bundle, employs full-line forcing or exclusivity clauses, or uses "reciprocity." It should make no difference whether the restrictions are set by contract or by manufacturers' ownership of the retail outlets, the most "extreme" form of control. They are all the same.

This is not a radical proposal. Most of these practices, which I lump under the term "restricted dealing," are in common use. All of them except the prescription of prices and tying are dealt with under a highly deferential

---

[375] *See, e.g.*, Brett M. Frischmann & Mark A. Lemley, *Spillovers*, 1207 Colum. L. Rev. 25 (2007); Wendy J. Gordon, *On Owning Information: Intellectual Property and the Restitutionary Impulse*, 78 Va. L. Rev. 149 (1992). *See generally* Philippe Fontaine, *Free Riding*, J. Hist. Econ. Thought 359 (2015); Orly Lobel, TALENT WANTS TO BE FREE: WHY WE SHOULD LEARN TO LOVE LEAKS, RAIDS, AND FREE RIDING (2013); Richard Tuck, FREE RIDING (2008).

[376] *See* Kal Raustiala & Christopher Sprigman, THE KNOCKOFF ECONOMY: HOW IMITATION SPARKS INNOVATION (2012).

[377] Eleanor M. Fox, *Parallel Imports, The Intrabrand/Interbrand Competition Paradigm, and the Hidden Gap Between Intellectual Property Law and Antitrust*, 25 Fordham Int'l L.J. 982, 982 (2002).

[378] A similar view can be found in Richard A. Posner, *The Next Step in the Antitrust Treatment of Restricted Distribution: Per Se Legality*, 48 U. Chi. L. Rev. 6 (1981).

standard of review and are lawful except in the rarest of cases. The treatment of prices and tying is an anomaly that should be brought in line with the treatment of vertical integration and other restrictions on distribution.

If restricted dealing arises out of a cartel among dealers or manufacturers, by all means let us prosecute. Cartels are unlawful per se and should remain so. But restricted dealing is not often used by cartels, and most restricted dealing is just a way by which one manufacturer competes with others. Our economy has many ways of assembling and distributing products. The more routes to market, the broader the consumers' choice. The broader their choice, the better off they are. Cartels restrict rather than increase the range of choice. We should welcome restricted dealing as a benefit to consumers and not lump it with cartels, with which it has nothing in common.

. . . [M]ost forms of restricted dealing could be anticompetitive in one manifestation or another. But so too could the charging of low prices or the opening of new plants. There are limits on the ability of courts to sort the beneficial from the deleterious manifestations of these practices, and most of the time it is better not to try than to try and fail. [. . .]

Why . . . would cooperative agreements in the chain of distribution be subject to antitrust scrutiny? The usual argument for prohibition is that restricted dealing is "like" a cartel in the sense that firms agree on price (or quality, or place of distribution). True enough. But one can find such agreements inside every firm too. The fact that two practices have such a feature in common is just the beginning of analysis. This holds, too, for the subsidiary rationale used to attack ties, exclusive distribution and reciprocity: that these "extend" a monopoly from one market to another. Perhaps they do. But they can do this only if there is a monopoly to start with, and even then there will be difficult questions about whether the "extension" is profitable to the firm or harmful to consumers. One must look further.

Before going on, I want to dispatch a line of argument one hears too often in political discourse. It is that restricted dealing, and especially resale price maintenance, is bad because it enables manufacturers to jack up the retail price of its products. So it does. Resale price maintenance is no different in this respect from other restrictions (for example, if there are fewer dealers, each can charge more).

So what? If Russell Stover wants its chocolates to sell for $20 per pound, it can achieve this easily enough. It may raise the wholesale prices. It may improve or change the product's quality or style, so that it tastes better than Godiva. The observation that these things influence retail prices is not even interesting as an antitrust concern. Every manufacturer may sell what it wants and charge what the traffic will bear. Other manufacturers, perhaps using less chocolate per pound or employing more efficient manufacturing, may sell different goods and charge less. This is competition. Consumers will choose. The question is whether restricted dealing affects price in an anticompetitive way. If manufacturers may affect retail prices by changing wholesale prices or quality, why may they not affect prices through restricted dealing?

The argument must be that restricted dealing can facilitate a real cartel, such as an agreement among manufacturers or dealers to charge an elevated price. One of the cartel arguments might run like this: Dealers— say, druggists—in some city collude to drive up the price of toothpaste. Each dealer is worried that the others will "cheat," that is, that other dealers will reduce the price in order to make additional sales at the expense of these adhering to the fixed price. So the dealers conscript the manufacturers to help them out. The manufacturers set a fixed resale price and penalize dealers that sell at a lower price.

The argument that restricted dealing is a way of enforcing a dealers' cartel conceals substantial problems. First, the industry must be one in which the dealers can form a cartel. But when will this be? Most retail markets have free entry, and retailing is about as close to an atomistic market as you can get. There is a drug store on every other corner. There are so many retailers (and potential retailers) of toothpaste and other consumer goods that the firms could not form or sustain a cartel with or without the aid of manufacturers.

As for the manufacturers: Why go along? What's in it for them? A manufacturer that helps dealers form a cartel is doing itself in. It will sell less, and dealers will get the monopoly profits. Manufacturers could be 'paid' in higher wholesale prices for cooperating, but that would increase the incentives of dealers not to join the cartel—to cheat by buying the product at a lower price and selling on a lower margin. If significant numbers of dealers cheat, bye-bye cartel.

It won't do to get just one manufacturer of toothpaste to adopt restricted dealing. All or almost all must do so. If there are holdouts, noncooperating dealers can sell the holdouts' products for less. That would destroy the cartel. Yet why would all manufacturers want to go along? It pays one or more to hold out. Dealers could conscript all manufacturers only when the conditions of a manufacturers' cartel existed.

Things are just as bad if the manufacturers make slightly different products. One manufacturer may hang back by setting the cartel price, but changing what it supplies for the price. It may put more paste in the tube, or use a formula that requires less paste per brushing. Differentiated products spoil the use of restricted dealing to enforce a cartel.

Then there is a problem of verification. Why are manufacturers any better at policing prices than fellow dealers are? The cheating dealer can't attract extra business without advertising its lower prices. Then its fellow conspirators learn in the same way manufacturers do. They could enforce the deal themselves. The extra enforcement from the cutoff by the manufacturer may be too late, or too little.

So the dealers' cartel explanation won't amount to much unless there are (1) few dealers; (2) few manufacturers; (3) homogeneous products; and (4) easy policing. If we see many dealers and many manufacturers, we can exclude the cartel possibility. And if we see some manufacturers using restricted dealing while others do not, or if we see substantially differentiated products, we can exclude the cartel hypothesis no matter how many or few dealers and manufacturers there are.

The conditions for restricted dealing to be a useful part of a dealer's cartel just do not exist very often. (I could show the same for the use of restricted dealing as part of a manufacturers' cartel, but that is unnecessary. The argument proceeds in the same way.) We do not condemn business practices under the antitrust laws unless they are anticompetitive in a given case or are so likely to be anticompetitive that detailed investigation is unnecessary. Because the conditions under which restricted dealing is anticompetitive are so rare, automatic condemnation would pick up far too many procompetitive examples to be worthwhile.

Why Would Trading Partners Ever Accept Anticompetitive Restraints?

The prospect of harmful vertical restraints presents an economic puzzle that was prominently emphasized by Chicago School writers in the 70s and 80s. If a particular vertical restraint—let's say, an exclusivity commitment made by distributors or suppliers to a trading partner with market power—is truly harmful to competition, why would the distributors or suppliers ever agree to it, thus making their own lives worse by contributing to market power? Isn't it more likely—the argument goes—that if a distributor or supplier accepts a restraint, it's because the parties have figured out that the restraint is part of an overall efficient arrangement?[379]

Subsequent writers have identified some answers to this question. One of the most prominent responses focuses on the existence of a "collective action problem"—that is, a situation involving multiple participants, in which the unilateral self-interested act of each participant leads to an outcome that is overall worse for everyone.[380] In the context of vertical restraints, a collective action problem can show up in something like the following way.

Suppose that there is a manufacturer with monopoly power, and four distributors of identical size and scale in competition with one another downstream. The manufacturer fears competitive entry from a potential entrant. It offers its distributors a deal: commit to deal with me exclusively and I will give you a 10% discount. Each distributor now thinks: well, if the potential entrant manages to enter the market, I could get a competitive price that's even lower than the discounted deal that the monopolist is offering me.

But the distributor will then try to figure out whether the rival will be able to successfully enter, including whether the entrant would be competitively viable with the business of just one distributor. If the business of one distributor would be enough to support the entrant, then each distributor would know that it could unilaterally make sure the

---

[379] *See, e.g.*, Robert H. Bork, The Antitrust Paradox: A Policy At War With Itself (1978) 309 ("A seller who wants exclusivity must give the buyer something for it. If he gives a lower price, the reason must be that the seller expects the arrangement to create efficiencies that justify the lower price."). In addition, individual firms may be bought off with a share of monopoly profits.

[380] *See, e.g.*, Eric B. Rasmusen, J. Mark Ramseyer, John S. Wiley Jr., *Naked Exclusion*, 81 Am. Econ. Rev. 1137 (1991).

rival entered successfully. This would give each distributor the confidence to decline the monopolist's offer of a discount in exchange for exclusivity: the scheme would fail.

But if the entrant needed the business of *two or three* distributors to make its entry successful, things could work out very differently. Each distributor knows that if it declines the monopolist's offer and bets on working with the entrant instead, it cannot alone guarantee that the entrant will be successful: and if entry does not in fact take place the distributor that turned down the monopolist will get hammered by its competitors who did take the 10% discount. Thus, each distributor will unilaterally take the deal from the monopolist, even if all the distributors collectively would be better off if they did not. This is the collective action dynamic that helps to explain why trading partners might agree to deals that end up making things worse for them.

A clever monopolist can exploit this collective-action dynamic more effectively: for example, by asking for long-term exclusivity commitments that come up for renewal at staggered intervals, so that whenever any individual distributor faces the question, all its rivals are locked into exclusivity and are unavailable to help support competitive entry or expansion.

At the other end of the spectrum from the "Chicago School" view that vertical practices—or at least broad categories of such practices—should be left entirely alone by courts, the Open Markets Institute and other groups and individuals petitioned the FTC in July 2020 to ban certain vertical restraints entirely.[381] Note that where the Easterbrook extract above focused primarily on "intrabrand" distribution restraints; the petition extract presented below is aimed at vertical agreements with some interbrand effects.

Petition for Rulemaking to Prohibit Exclusionary Contracts by Open Markets Institute et al.

(F.T.C., filed July 21, 2020)

Vertical restraints are an instrument by which corporations can control less powerful economic actors. Through contract and contract-like arrangements, a powerful manufacturer can restrict the autonomy of a distributor, limiting its freedom to select trading partners and the terms on which it sells its goods. For instance, under exclusive dealing, a manufacturer can bar its distributors from handling the products of manufacturing rivals and prohibit suppliers from selling inputs to competing manufacturers. McDonald's founder Ray Kroc described, and indeed boasted, about how McDonald's controlled franchisees through contract, stating "the only way we can positively know what these [franchisees] are doing what they are supposed to do is to give them no alternative whatsoever. You can't give them an inch." Through vertical restraints, firms can vertically integrate in effect, and often shed legal responsibilities that come with traditional vertical integration through ownership and control. Historically, the Supreme Court, in interpreting the antitrust laws, limited firms' ability to dominate trading partners using vertical restraints.

The Court in [*Richfield Oil Corp v. United States*, 343 U.S. 922 (1952), *aff'g United States v. Richfield Oil Corp.*, 99 F. Supp. 280 (S.D. Cal. 1951)] held certain contract and contract-like agreements as per se illegal on the grounds that they interfere with business autonomy. {*Eds.: note that the Supreme Court in this case summarily affirmed the decision of the district court: in this paragraph the petition is quoting the district court, not the Supreme Court.*} The Court noted the general independence of businesses bound by these restraints, stating that these proprietors "in the performance of a particular contract, or in the conduct of his business, acts chiefly for himself and for his own benefit and profit, and not others and the benefit and profit of others." Vertical restraints that "exercised de facto control over these 'independent business men'" contravened antitrust law, which Congress enacted to secure "equality of opportunity." The Court subsequently affirmed the purpose of antitrust law as standing "against coercion of non-employees by vertical supply contract" in [*Simpson v. Union Oil Co. of Cal.*, 377 U.S. 13 (1964)]. The Court emphasized how the contractual agreements shift the risk and liability from the dominant firm to the subordinated firm. These agreements, in attempting to establish resale price maintenance, deprived "independent dealers of the

---

[381] For a discussion of the FTC's rulemaking power, *see infra* Chapter XI.

exercise of free judgment whether to become consignees at all, or remain consignees, and, in any event, to sell at competitive prices." [. . .]

. . . [Court decisions] from the 1940s through the 1960s were rooted in an economic framework expressed in the legislative history of the antitrust laws. The drafters of the Sherman Act drew from existing common law frameworks around fair trade, economic and vocational liberty, and economic governance by workers and small firms. Denizens of 19th century America believed that a just distribution of control over one's own work would secure economic liberty and political liberty for all without fear of domination. [. . .]

Given the real evidence of harm from certain exclusionary contracts and the specious justifications presented in their favor, the FTC should ban exclusivity with customers, distributors, or suppliers that results in substantial market foreclosure as per se illegal under the FTC Act. The present rule of reason governing exclusive dealing by all firms is infirm on multiple grounds. Through rulemaking, the FTC should hold that such exclusivity is an unfair method of competition. The substantial foreclosure test is consistent with the rule announced by the Supreme Court in [*Standard Oil Co. of California v. United States*, 337 U.S. 293 (1949)] (hereafter "*Standard Stations*"), a case concerning Section 3 of the Clayton Act. To offer guidance, the FTC should articulate what "substantial foreclosure" means and define it in relation to:

1) The power of the firm or firms using exclusivity,

2) The fraction of customers, distributors, or suppliers bound by exclusivity, or

3) The significance of the customers, distributors, or suppliers bound by exclusivity.

This rule would clarify the law on exclusive arrangements, encouraging dominant firms to compete on the merits and allowing most firms to use exclusivity in their contracts.

While enforcers can and have successfully challenged exclusive arrangements under the rule of reason, this prevailing legal standard has multiple deficiencies. First, the rule of reason, with its fact-intensive inquiry, is a poor analytical fit for exclusionary contracts by dominant firms. The harms from exclusionary contracting and related practices are real and documented whereas the justifications are of especially limited relevance to dominant firms. Accordingly, antitrust law should heavily restrict the practice. Second, the rule of reason, by placing most of the legal burdens on the plaintiff, requires the government and other enforcers to devote excessive time and resources to developing and litigating a case. Because of these burdens, an antitrust lawsuit under the rule of reason is extraordinarily difficult to prosecute and win. Indeed, the record suggests that the rule of reason approximates a standard of practical legality. In practice, the rule of reason means that dominant firms can use exclusionary and other unfair competitive practices without the fear of significant legal consequences.

Third, even as the rule of reason frees large corporations with sophisticated counsel to engage in exclusionary contracting, it offers little guidance to risk-averse businesses that cannot spend substantial sums on outside counsel. While it offers some markers on when exclusive dealing may violate the Sherman Act, the rule of reason does not provide prospective clarity to a firm that wants to use exclusivity for beneficial or innocuous ends. [. . .]

Drawing on *Standard Stations*, the FTC should hold that exclusive arrangements that result in substantial foreclosure of customers, distributors, or suppliers are per se illegal under the FTC Act. [. . .]

Substantial foreclosure should be satisfied through one of three ways. First, a firm with a share of 30% or more of a relevant market and that uses exclusivity with all its customers, distributors, or suppliers of an essential input engages in substantial foreclosure ("dominance test"). [. . .]

Second, a firm that uses exclusivity with customers, distributors, or suppliers of a particular input together accounting for 30% or more of their relevant market engages in substantial foreclosure ("quantitative foreclosure test"). [. . .]

Third, a firm that ties up the top three or more customers, distributors or suppliers in a concentrated market through exclusivity engages in substantial foreclosure ("qualitative foreclosure test").

* * *

Other perspectives reject both *per se* legality and *per se* illegality, and embrace rule-of-reason weighing for vertical restraints. The following extract is a good example. In it, Steve Salop explains why exclusivity agreements can present serious competitive concerns (despite arguments that competition for exclusive-partner status will usually provide enough competitive discipline) as well as the possibility of meaningful benefit.

Steven C. Salop, The Raising Rivals' Cost Foreclosure Paradigm, Conditional Pricing Practices, and the Flawed Incremental Price-Cost Test
81 Antitrust L.J. 371 (2017)

Exclusive dealing, conditional pricing practices, and other exclusionary conduct can raise entrants' or existing rivals' costs by "input foreclosure," that is, by materially raising their costs or eliminating their efficient access to critical inputs. These inputs can involve manufacturing inputs, such as raw materials, intellectual property, or distribution. Distribution can be understood as an input, and raising rivals' costs of distribution can weaken their ability to serve the entire customer base and their ability and incentives to expand. For example, by excluding its rivals' access to an efficient distribution system or other input, a monopolist can reduce the rivals' ability to induce downward pricing pressure and so can permit the monopolist to maintain its monopoly power in the face of entry. [. . .]

The substantiality of input foreclosure is demonstrated most accurately by the resulting impact on the competitors' costs and output, not by the simple fraction of input suppliers that are affected. Input foreclosure can be so severe that the foreclosed rivals will exit from the market or be deterred from attempting entry. But even if a rival can cover its costs and remain viable, it will be a weaker and less efficient competitor if its distribution or other input costs are higher. A competitor will have the incentive to raise its prices and/or restrict its output when its marginal costs are increased, even if it earns enough revenue to cover its costs or even to reach minimum efficient scale.

Thus, input foreclosure is substantial if it substantially increases rivals' costs or constrains their output or ability to expand. Similar results occur if the foreclosure reduces rivals' product quality. Some commentators inappropriately focus solely on whether the foreclosure will prevent entrants or small competitors from reaching "minimum efficient scale" (MES), the output level where a firm's average costs bottom out. Others inappropriately limit their concerns solely to whether the foreclosure will prevent rivals from reaching "minimum viable scale" (MVS), the output level where a firm can turn a profit at current prices and thus survive. This narrowing of concerns is artificial and leads to false negatives and underdeterrence. The conditions under which foreclosure can reduce competition are not limited to a failure to achieve MES or MVS.

Even if a viable rival is able to reach the MES output level, its costs may be significantly raised by exclusionary conduct if it has to pay more for distribution or other inputs or if it has to use a more costly input or distribution method. In that sense, its costs also will not be truly minimized, regardless of scale. For example, even if direct distribution is feasible or substitute distributors exist, higher costs from the foreclosure will reduce efficiency and the rival's competitive impact. Similarly, even if a rival's output exceeds MVS and the competitor remains viable, bearing higher costs from the foreclosure will reduce its efficiency and the competitive constraint it provides. . . . In both cases, the excluding firm may gain the power to raise or maintain supracompetitive prices as a result. [. . .]

Customer foreclosure focuses on the impact of losing efficient access to customers, including distributor customers. Customer foreclosure by a monopolist can injure competitors and harm competition in several distinct ways. First, in the most extreme scenario, the customer base of an entrant or small rival may be limited to such a degree that it is unable to earn sufficient revenue to cover its costs and remain viable in the market. If anticipated sales likely would fall below this "minimum viable scale (MVS)," an entrant would lack an incentive to enter and an existing competitor would have the incentive to exit. Second, the entrant or competitor may remain viable, but customer foreclosure may limit its output to a low level and constrain its ability and incentive to expand profitably, by reducing its capacity or by raising its effective costs of expansion. This impact can occur even if the rival can achieve the MVS or MES output level. Third, such customer foreclosure may permit the rival to remain in the market, but may relegate it to a niche position at a low output level, where it will provide less of a constraint on the pricing of the excluding firm(s), again, even if it reaches MES. For example, a monopolist may have the incentive to maintain monopoly prices while ceding a small market share to the entrant. Or, the monopolist may reduce prices, but only to a limited extent because the constrained competitor will not pose a significant threat, or will pose less of a threat. Consumers clearly are harmed by this foreclosure that maintains higher prices. Fourth, by reducing the competitor's likely potential customer base, customer foreclosure may reduce the rival's incentives to invest and innovate over time. This can harm consumers directly. It also can weaken the monopolist's own incentives to innovate. [. . .]

The fact that one or more competitors are injured by input or customer foreclosure does not necessarily mean that market or monopoly power will be achieved or consumers will be harmed. Consumer harm may be prevented by the existence of and continued competition from a sufficient number of non-excluded competitors . . . . These other competitors might prevent the excluding firm or firms from achieving, enhancing or maintaining market (or monopoly) power. This outcome can occur if sufficient other rivals are not foreclosed from the critical input, the remaining rivals are not at a cost disadvantage, and the remaining competitors do not coordinate prices. . . . Consumer harm requires power over price, that is, the power to raise or maintain supracompetitive prices, as well as raising rivals' costs. [. . .]

Exclusive dealing and other exclusionary conduct can have procompetitive motivations and cognizable beneficial effects. The courts have long recognized the potential for cognizable efficiency benefits from conduct that forecloses rivals. In cases where there are both significant and probable harms and cognizable benefits, the two effects must be compared in order to estimate the overall, net effects on consumer welfare and the competitive process. This comparison would involve both the probability and magnitude of the opposing effects.

The efficiencies can involve a variety of mechanisms. For example, in nonmonopoly markets, buyers sometimes can use exclusives to induce more price competition among their suppliers. Exclusives potentially can reduce risk by assuring a buyer with a guaranteed source of inputs or a seller with a guaranteed outlet for its products. Exclusives can provide incentives for improved products, better service, and increased promotion. When there is competition among a number of relatively equal competitors each with its own exclusives, and no coordination, then exclusives also are on balance less likely to cause harm to competition, as opposed to exclusives adopted by a monopolist facing a new entrant.

Exclusivity by monopolists could also be procompetitive by preventing free riding. For example, a new entrant manufacturer might free ride on the advertising by the monopolist, if the retailer carries both brands and the monopolist's advertising drives consumers to the retailer . . . . A dishonest retailer might even attempt to employ bait-and-switch tactics, if selling the entrant's brand is more profitable. If a software applications developer intends to port its application to multiple platforms, it may sacrifice quality by programming for the lowest common denominator, rather than using all the capabilities of the monopoly platform.

When exclusivity is instituted by a monopolist against all of its competitors, there is a greater likelihood that the harms dominate the benefits because there is no other competition to protect consumers. The claimed efficiencies also may not be cognizable. For example, bold claims of increased "dealer loyalty" may amount to nothing more than creation of barriers to entry that maintain monopoly prices, rather than leading to product or service improvements that increase total market output and benefit consumers. Thus, it is important to analyze the efficiency claims on a case-by-case basis, taking market structure into account, rather than assuming their existence.

* * *

As the diversity of these views may suggest, the evidence of the effects of vertical restraints is mixed, complex, and evolving.

Francine Lafontaine & Margaret Slade, Exclusive Contracts and Vertical Restraints: Empirical Evidence & Public Policy

in Paolo Buccirossi (ed.), HANDBOOK OF ANTITRUST ECONOMICS (2008)

There is perhaps no aspect of competition policy that is as controversial or has been as inconsistent over time and across jurisdictions as policy towards restraints between upstream firms and their downstream retailers. [. . .]

In such an ambiguous legal and theoretical environment, the need for an overall empirical assessment seems particularly pressing[.] [. . .]

In most western economies, a large fraction of retail sales through independent retailers is subject to some form of exclusive–dealing clauses. For example, in the U.S., that fraction is over one third. [. . .]

[A] typical succession-of-monopoly problem arises when an upstream monopolist sells an input to a downstream firm at a price above marginal cost. If the downstream firm also has market power, it is well known that it will choose a price that is higher, and a quantity that is lower, than the price and quantity that would maximize joint profits. {*Eds: This is called "double marginalization": the upstream margin and the downstream margin, together, are greater than the profit-maximizing margin that would result from a single seller.*} [. . .]

To overcome the double–marginalization problem and reduce retail prices, franchisors might want to use some form of vertical restraint. Maximum resale prices is an obvious candidate. Alternatively, franchisors could use a minimum quantity requirement or eliminate royalties on sales altogether and replace them with higher franchise fees. The latter solution corresponds to the standard two-part tariff used in traditional franchising. Finally, a manufacturer who controls the number of stores that sell her product could eliminate the double-marginalization problem by increasing outlet density and thus the intensity of intrabrand competition. When double marginalization is an issue, the imposition of vertical restraints will not only increase the overall efficiency of the vertical structure but also lead to lower prices for customers. Thus restraints are usually welfare enhancing when used to solve the successive-monopoly problem. [. . .]

Manufacturers who invest in improving retail outlets, promoting retail products, or training outlet managers might worry that dealers will free ride on those investments. For example, dealers might encourage customers who visit their store to switch to a competing brand that has a lower price—thereby making the sale easier—or that has a higher retail margin—thereby making the sale privately more profitable. Exclusive dealing resolves this problem by making it impossible for the dealer to propose an alternative brand to his customers. In such a context, exclusive dealing is a mechanism that enables manufacturers to protect their investments against potential dealer opportunism. Furthermore, in its absence, potentially profitable investments might not be undertaken. [. . .]

A number of authors have shown that vertical restraints such as tying, exclusive dealing and refusals to deal can be used by manufacturers to enforce price-discrimination schemes. . . . [T]he welfare implications of vertical restraints in this context, as for price discrimination generally, are ambiguous, as are the expected effects on observed quantities. [. . .]

The arguments that explain how certain types of vertical restraints can facilitate dealer cartels or monopoly power are straightforward. In particular, a manufacturer that imposes a minimum price for her product can help a dealer cartel enforce the monopoly price. Similarly, exclusive territories, if they are large enough, can insulate retailers from competition by eliminating nearby competitors as well as preventing entry. The main issue that these arguments raise, however, is why manufacturers would find it in their own best interest to impose such restraints. If upstream firms have no market power, they will be indifferent to the imposition of restraints and might agree to adopt them to satisfy dealers. However, brand differentiation and the use of trademarks usually confer some market power on upstream firms. [. . .]

The main worry of antitrust authorities in the U.S. and the E.U. when it comes to vertical restraints is the possibility that their use will foreclose entry by competitors at some level of the vertical chain. In the context of relationships involving a retailer, such as the ones that we are concerned with here, a manufacturer that establishes an exclusive retail network (*i.e.*, exclusive dealing) that involves most retailers, might prevent her competitors from gaining access to customers at a reasonable cost, if at all. This in turn could prevent entry of potential competitors or perhaps even lead to rivals exiting the upstream industry. This argument requires that entry into retailing be costly due to, for example, economies of scale or a scarcity of good locations.

Exclusive dealing, which has sometimes been referred to as vertical integration by contract, is the form of restraint for which foreclosure arguments are most frequently made. In addition, [under appropriate circumstances] tying can foreclose entry of firms in the tied goods industry.

In the end, if vertical restraints are used to lessen competition at some level of the vertical structure through foreclosing or disadvantaging rivals, prices to consumers should be higher and quantities sold smaller than they would be in the absence of such restraints. [. . .]

[The authors' examination of empirical work conducted to date on the effects of vertical restraints] highlights how very few studies there really are . . . . One can contrast this paucity with the very large number of theoretical articles that have been written on the subject as well as the multiplicity of retail and service industries that have used the restraints. [. . .]

Given the small number of available studies, it is difficult to make definitive claims about robust empirical regularities. . . . Nevertheless, the results are quite striking. Indeed, . . . in all but three cases [the authors identified], privately imposed vertical restraints benefit consumers or at least do not harm them. [. . .]

In general . . . the empirical evidence leads one to conclude that consumer well being tends to be congruent with manufacturer profits, at least with respect to the voluntary adoption of vertical restraints. When the government intervenes and forces firms to adopt (or discontinue the use of) vertical restraints, in contrast, it tends to make consumers worse off. Moreover, this is true even when the pressure for the intervention comes from consumers themselves. When the pressure comes from downstream firms, intervention tends to lead to dealer entrenchment and the inability of manufacturers to use restraints as incentive devices.

* * *

Vertical restraints constitute agreements between economically distinct entities—that is, conscious commitments to a common scheme[382]—and can, accordingly, be challenged under Section 1 of the Sherman Act. Section 1 will be the focus of our discussion in this chapter.

However, when a party to an anticompetitive vertical agreement holds monopoly power, the use of vertical restraints that tend to expand or maintain that power may also (or instead) be challenged under Section 2. Courts often apply similar or identical analysis under the two provisions when both apply.[383] So there is some overlap between the practices described in this chapter and those addressed in Chapter VII on monopolization.

But it is worth keeping an eye on the difference between cases in which an *agreement* is the cause of the competitive harm and those in which the source of harm is a unilateral *policy* by a monopolist rather than an agreement. For example, tying cases—which a supplier makes a first ("ty<u>ing</u>") product available only subject to a commitment that the purchaser will buy a second ("ti<u>ed</u>") product as well—are often challenged under Section 1. This is appropriate if the obligation to buy the tied product is grounded in an agreement. But some tying cases involve the essentially unilateral practice of a seller in deciding not to supply a tying product unless the tied product is purchased as well: and a unilateral practice of this kind is not an agreement. Likewise, in some exclusivity cases, the source of the relevant economic effect is an agreement that imposes a prohibition on, or penalty for, dealing with rivals, making Section 1 applicable. In other exclusivity cases, however, the supplier simply operates a unilateral policy of dealing only with those that do not deal with its rivals, which would fall outside of Section 1 but may implicate Section 2.[384] Keep this distinction in the back of your mind as you encounter vertical-restraint cases: remember that unilateral policies can be challenged under Section 2, while Section 1 is focused on agreements.[385]

The rest of this chapter offers a tour of the antitrust assessment of vertical restraints. Section B describes a unifying feature of most theories of harm: the requirement of market power. Section C considers a common class of vertical restraints: "intrabrand" distribution restrictions such as those imposed by a manufacturer on the sale of its

---

[382] Monsanto Co. v. Spray-Rite Service Corp., 465 U.S. 752, 764 (1984). *See generally supra* § IV.B. (definition of agreement)

[383] *But see, e.g.*, United States v. Microsoft Corp., 253 F.3d 34, 70 (D.C. Cir. 2001) (en banc) (discussing differences between Section 1 and Section 2 analysis of exclusive dealing, and suggesting that liability might result under Section 2 at a lower level of foreclosure— that is, a lower level of impact upon the market—than would be required in a Section 1 case).

[384] *See, e.g.*, Lorain Journal Co. v. United States, 342 U.S. 143 (1951).

[385] *See, e.g.*, Roland Machinery Co. v. Dresser Industries, Inc., 749 F.2d 380 (7th Cir. 1984) ("One mind is not enough for a meeting of minds. The fact that Dresser was hostile to dealers who would not live and die by its product . . . and acted on its hostility by canceling a dealer who did the thing to which it was hostile, does not establish an agreement, but if anything the opposite: a failure to agree on a point critical to one of the parties.").

products. Section D turns to exclusivity commitments: perhaps the paradigm example of a vertical restraint. Sections E and F discuss tying and bundling. Section G considers "most favored nation" or "MFN" agreements.

B. The Role of Market Power

It is generally agreed that vertical restraints are unlikely to be harmful to competition unless the participants hold some degree of market power. This is because, in the absence of market power, by definition, the participants do not have the ability to affect overall competitive conditions. A business in a competitive market that tries to impose an exclusionary restraint may soon find that its trading partners simply choose to work with alternatives.[386]

For example, suppose that a small input supplier in a competitive upstream input market and a small device manufacturer in a competitive downstream device market enter into reciprocal exclusivity commitments that preclude each from dealing with competitors of the other. If reasonable alternatives to both participants are available in the market, harmful effects are unlikely: supply relationships might simply be realigned, as other market participants find new trading partners, but overall output and welfare will probably not be impaired, and consumers will not be harmed.

As you will remember from Chapter III, market power can normally be proven in either of two ways: directly (that is, by evidence of actual anticompetitive effects on competitive conditions or market outcomes like price and output) or indirectly (that is, by evidence of high shares in a defined market protected by barriers to entry).[387] But the Supreme Court has recently suggested, in a footnote in the 2018 *AmEx* decision, that plaintiffs in vertical cases may be limited to indirect proof of market power.[388]

The meaning of this controversial footnote is not entirely clear. On the one hand, it could be read narrowly to simply underscore the basic reality that a plaintiff in an antitrust case must at least provide a rough or directional sketch of the relevant zone of competition. On this view, it would not foreclose the avenue of direct proof of market power through a showing of anticompetitive effects, even in vertical cases, and would not require that a plaintiff furnish a technically pristine market definition. On the other hand, it could be read more strictly to impose a requirement that a plaintiff cannot show market power through direct proof, and must instead plead and prove a legally sufficient market definition in every vertical case. But you can judge for yourself! Here is the footnote, followed by an extract criticizing it.[389]

Ohio v. American Express Co.
138 S.Ct. 2274 (2018)

Justice Thomas.

[1] The plaintiffs argue that we need not define the relevant market in this case because they have offered actual evidence of adverse effects on competition—namely, increased merchant fees. We disagree. The cases that the plaintiffs cite for this proposition evaluated whether horizontal restraints had an adverse effect on competition. *See Indiana Federation of Dentists*, 476 U.S. 447, 450–451, 459 (1986) (agreement between competing dentists not to share X rays with insurance companies); *Catalano, Inc. v. Target Sales, Inc.*, 446 U.S. 643, 644–645, 650 (1980) (agreement among competing wholesalers not to compete on extending credit to retailers). Given that horizontal restraints involve agreements between competitors not to compete in some way, this Court concluded that it did not need

---

[386] *See, e.g.*, Daniel A. Crane, *Market Power Without Market Definition*, 90 Notre Dame L. Rev. 31 (2014) ("Market power is an indispensable element in all antitrust cases except for those arising under the Sherman Act's rule of per se illegality."); Muenster Butane, Inc. v. Stewart Co., 651 F.2d 292, 298 (5th Cir. 1981) ("A requirement that plaintiff prove market power in this case would have saved the litigants and the courts much expense. Stewart . . . had no market power in Gainesville. The market was highly competitive. Whatever vertical restraints Stewart imposed on its dealers, their effect could not have been to raise the price consumers paid for television sets.").

[387] *See supra* § III.E.

[388] Ohio v. Am. Express Co., 138 S. Ct. 2274, 2285 n.7 (2018).

[389] *See also, e.g.*, Herbert Hovenkamp, *Platforms and the Rule of Reason: The* American Express *Case*, 2019 Colum. Bus. L. Rev. 35, 46–53 (2019) (assuming the broad reading and criticizing it as "economically incoherent" and "regressive," and noting that the issue "was never briefed").

to precisely define the relevant market to conclude that these agreements were anticompetitive. But vertical restraints are different. *See Arizona v. Maricopa County Medical Soc.*, 457 U.S. 332, 348, n. 18 (1982); *Leegin Creative Leather Products, Inc. v. PSKS, Inc.*, 551 U.S. 877, 888 (2007). Vertical restraints often pose no risk to competition unless the entity imposing them has market power, which cannot be evaluated unless the Court first defines the relevant market. *See id.*, at 898 (noting that a vertical restraint "may not be a serious concern unless the relevant entity has market power"); Easterbrook, Vertical Arrangements and the Rule of Reason, 53 Antitrust L.J. 135, 160 (1984) ("[T]he possibly anticompetitive manifestations of vertical arrangements can occur only if there is market power").

* * *

Steven C. Salop, Daniel Francis, Lauren Sillman, & Michaela Spero, Rebuilding Platform Antitrust: Moving On from Ohio v. American Express
84 Antitrust L.J. 883 (2022)

The strangest of the *Amex* Court's errors was its insistence on a formal market definition and market share evidence to establish market power [in vertical cases]. It has long been hornbook law that this is not a necessary component of modern antitrust analysis, and much modern antitrust scholarship encourages courts and agencies to move beyond the strictures of market definition where it is possible to do so.

As the district court correctly pointed out, plaintiffs have long had two avenues to satisfy their burden to demonstrate anticompetitive effects under the first step of the rule of reason in both vertical and horizontal cases. Plaintiffs may either (1) provide direct evidence of anticompetitive effects, or (2) provide circumstantial (or indirect) evidence consisting of (i) demonstrated market power, and (ii) additional indicia that the conduct is likely to harm competition.

Market definition can play an important role in an indirect evidence case because one way to demonstrate market power is to show that the defendant has a substantial share in a relevant market. But market definition is an analytical step designed to screen for the ability to inflict harm—that is, market power—and it is widely recognized that direct evidence of actual anticompetitive effects makes it unnecessary to prove such power indirectly. Accordingly, courts have long held that direct evidence of anticompetitive effects necessarily implies the existence of sufficient market power to cause such effects.

Before *Amex*, the Supreme Court itself had expressly recognized this principle. In *Indiana Federation of Dentists*, a challenge to a decision by a dentists' professional organization to restrict insurers' access to dental x-rays, the Court held that "the finding of actual, sustained adverse effects on competition" obviated the need for formal market definition. But the *Amex* Court limited *Indiana Federation of Dentists* to horizontal cases, and held that formal market definition is indispensable in vertical cases. "Vertical restraints," the majority explained, "often pose no risk to competition unless the entity imposing them has market power, *which cannot be evaluated unless the Court first defines the relevant market.*" For this proposition, the Court cited its decision in *Leegin Creative Leather Products, Inc. v. PSKS, Inc.*, as well as Judge Easterbrook's article, *Vertical Arrangements and the Rule of Reason.*

But these sources simply noted the importance of evaluating market power. They did not endorse a requirement of formal market definition. In fact, Judge Easterbrook's article specifically stated that "[a]n inquiry into market power does *not* entail the definition of a 'market,' a subject that has bedeviled the law of mergers. Market definition is just a tool in the investigation of market power." Indeed, direct evidence is normally considered more reliable than circumstantial evidence based on market shares.

Nor did the argument make economic sense. The Court's central claim—that a critical difference exists between horizontal and vertical cases, in that vertical restraints do not present any risk to competition unless the entity imposing them has market power—is no difference at all. Horizontal restraints also do not present any risk to competition unless the participants collectively enjoy market power. Moreover, direct evidence of market power has often been used by courts of appeals in vertical cases. And the Supreme Court has never required a heightened burden of proof of harm, even for intrabrand vertical restraints. *Amex* involved a restraint that directly reduced interbrand competition, a category of agreement widely understood to present competitive dangers.

Ultimately, the market-definition requirement was an unforced error. The point of the rule of reason is to allow for careful and neutral examination of evidence and theory specific to a challenged restraint. While antitrust cases litigated under the rule of reason are already famously challenging for plaintiffs, if the Court was determined to make them harder still, it could have done so directly by expressly imposing an elevated burden of proof, such as "clear and convincing evidence" or "clear showing."

* * *

The meaning of this notorious footnote on proof of market power in vertical cases—like much else in the *AmEx* opinion—will be left for future courts and writers (and law students!). That process has already begun. In *Chase Manufacturing v. Johns Manville Corp.*, 2022 WL 522345 (D. Colo. Feb. 22, 2022), a tying case, the district court said: "The Rule of Reason offers two ways to show that a restraint on trade has an unreasonable effect on competition: either through direct evidence of such harm or through indirect evidence from which such harm may be inferred. Plaintiff relies on the direct evidence option. *Am. Express* does not foreclose that approach as a matter of law." *Id.* at *9. How would you explain and defend this reading of the *AmEx* footnote?

C. "Intrabrand" Distribution Restraints

It is common for a business that supplies a product or service through other market participants (like retailers or distributors) to enter into agreements with other participants in the distribution system that restrict how its own product or service is sold. Restraints of this kind—imposed by a manufacturer of a product, or an entity in an economically analogous position on the distribution of its own product—are known generally as "intrabrand" (*i.e.*, within-a-brand) restraints. A good example might be rules established by a television manufacturer for the distribution of its own televisions (perhaps including rules about who will be entitled to sell the televisions, how they can be displayed or sold, and at what prices).

Such "intrabrand" restraints can be contrasted with "interbrand" restraints that affect competition among the output of different suppliers (such as rules prohibiting a retailer from selling competing televisions, or limiting the conditions on which it may do so).[390] In modern law these categories are analyzed through very different lenses. In particular, courts and agencies generally consider intrabrand restraints much less likely to harm competition, as they generally reflect a manufacturer (or other upstream supplier) voluntarily limiting its *own* output without impairing rivals' ability or incentive to reach the market. Interbrand restraints, on the other hand, include cases in which a manufacturer uses its own market power to exclude or impair rivals' access to inputs or distribution in ways that may raise sharper competitive concerns.

In this Section we will focus on intrabrand restraints. For many years, antitrust law divided intrabrand restraints into "nonprice" restraints and "price" restraints, with somewhat different standards applying to each at different times. Today, as we will see, the law of both nonprice and price restraints has shifted from *per se* prohibitions to a fairly lenient rule-of-reason approach. The law has not adopted the *per se* legality standard for distribution restraints that, as you have already seen, some Chicago School writers favored, but it has gone a long way in that direction.[391]

1. Nonprice Restraints: Territorial Restrictions

Suppliers commonly impose nonprice restrictions on how their products or services are distributed. For example, a consumer goods manufacturer might decide to have just one authorized distributor, or a limited number of such distributors, in each geographic region, or for each kind of product; similarly, a franchisor might decide to limit the number of franchisees in a particular area, or even grant that status exclusively to one franchisee. Suppliers may also establish rules for how and when their products and services are distributed.

---

[390] For a thoughtful overview of the relationship between antitrust and distribution, *see generally* Herbert Hovenkamp, THE ANTITRUST ENTERPRISE: PRINCIPLE AND EXECUTION (2005) Ch. 8.

[391] Frank Easterbrook, *Vertical Arrangements and the Rule of Reason*, 53 Antitrust L.J. 135 (1984); Richard A. Posner, *The Next Step in the Antitrust Treatment of Restricted Distribution: Per Se Legality*, 48 U. Chi. L. Rev. 6 (1981).

There are a number of reasons why distribution restraints might be beneficial. For example, a manufacturer might want to make sure that its products or services are sold only through channels associated with a sufficient level of prestige, or that provide a particular type of consumer experience, to preserve the value of its brand or the quality and consistency of what buyers receive. Alternatively, a manufacturer might want its retail or distribution outlets to provide specific costly services to customers or consumers—like showrooming, customer advice, or repair—and vertical restraints may be necessary to make this work given free-riding concerns.

To illustrate, suppose that in a world of *unrestricted* distribution Retailer A had invested in providing these services in connection with the sale of Manufacturer X's goods, while Retailer B did not provide such services. By avoiding the costs of the services, Retailer B would be able to offer the manufacturer's product to consumers at a lower price. As a result, rational consumers would likely avail themselves of the services at Retailer A—for example, by examining the products at a showroom—and then buy the product from Retailer B at a lower price. This "free riding" by B on A's investments might be an unsustainable situation for Retailer A and could lead to the cessation of the services. If the free riding were sufficiently destructive, *no* retailer would end up providing the consumer services, and overall demand for the product would suffer.[392]

The manufacturer can protect against this concern through the application of nonprice restraints: for example, by giving each retailer an exclusive sales territory in which it will enjoy the full benefit of its own investments,[393] or by simply setting rules for the services retailers must provide and terminating their distribution contract (or imposing lesser penalties) if they fail to do so.[394]

Before the emergence of the modern rule in the 1970s, the Court had struggled with a rule of evaluation for restraints that limited distributors to exclusive sales areas. The leading pre-modern case was *Schwinn*, which had held that such restraints were *per se* illegal if the distributor had bought the goods from the manufacturer and was reselling them, and subject to the rule of reason if the distributor was selling them as an agent, without having taken title.[395] The *Schwinn* Court explained that conclusion in the following terms:

> Under the Sherman Act, it is unreasonable without more for a manufacturer to seek to restrict and confine areas or persons with whom an article may be traded after the manufacturer has parted with dominion over it. Such restraints are so obviously destructive of competition that their mere existence is enough. If the manufacturer parts with dominion over his product or transfers risk of loss to another, he may not reserve control over its destiny or the conditions of its resale. To permit this would sanction franchising and confinement of distribution as the ordinary instead of the unusual method which may be permissible in an appropriate and impelling competitive setting, since most merchandise is distributed by means of purchase and sale. On the other hand . . . we are not prepared to introduce the inflexibility which a *per se* rule might bring if it were applied to prohibit all vertical restrictions of territory and all franchising, in the sense of designating specified distributors and retailers as the chosen instruments through which the manufacturer, retaining ownership of the goods, will distribute them to the public. Such a rule might severely hamper smaller enterprises resorting to reasonable methods of meeting the competition of giants and of merchandising through independent dealers, and it might sharply accelerate the trend towards vertical integration of the distribution process. But to allow this freedom where the manufacturer has parted with dominion over the goods—the usual marketing situation—would violate the ancient rule against restraints on alienation and open the door to exclusivity of outlets and limitation of territory further than prudence permits.[396]

---

[392] *See supra* § VI.A.

[393] For an early recognition, *see* Richard E. Day, *Exclusive Territorial Arrangements under the Antitrust Laws—A Reappraisal*, 40 N.C. L. Rev. 223, 266–27 (1962).

[394] See Robert L. Steiner, *Manufacturers' Promotional Allowances, Free Riders and Vertical Restraints*, Antitrust Bull. 383 (1991).

[395] The Court had previously indicated a rule-of-reason approach to nonprice restraints unconnected to resale price maintenance. *See* White Motor Co. v. United States, 372 U.S. 253, 261 (1963) ("This is the first case involving a territorial restriction in a vertical arrangement; and we know too little of the actual impact of both that restriction and the one respecting customers to reach a conclusion on the bare bones of the documentary evidence before us.").

[396] United States v. Arnold, Schwinn & Co., 388 U.S. 365 (1967), *overruled by* Continental T.V., Inc. v. GTE Sylvania Inc., 433 U.S. 36 (1977).

Note the resonance with the earlier idea, mentioned above, that the autonomy of an "independent" trading partner was a matter of specific concern to the antitrust law of vertical restraints.[397]

But *Schwinn* did not last. It was overruled ten years later in the seminal modern case on the legality of nonprice distribution restraints: *GTE Sylvania*. In that case, the Court was invited to reconsider whether a distributor who buys and resells goods, and one who distributes on some other basis (*e.g.*, consignment), should really be treated so dissimilarly. The Court held, overruling *Schwinn*, that nonprice distribution restraints should be assessed under the rule of reason. In so holding, the Court placed considerable emphasis on the distinction between "interbrand" and "intrabrand" competition, and stated that the latter was a matter of secondary concern to federal antitrust law.

GTE Sylvania (1977) was a turning point for the law of vertical restraints, just as *BMI* (1979) was a turning point in the law of horizontal collaborations between competitors. As you read *Sylvania*, notice how Justice Powell's opinion for the Court focuses on economic welfare effects: and contrast it with Justice White's concurrence in the judgment, which captures the older themes of liberty and independence. You will also see—at paragraph 5 and footnote 19 of the extract—the critical embrace of interbrand competition as the "primary concern" of antitrust law. Following this extract, you will find a passage from Judge Browning's dissent in the Ninth Circuit below, which drew heavily on these older themes to argue that the restraints should have been *per se* unlawful. Judge Browning's dissent is a striking example of the older freedom-based approach to vertical restraints: and it touches interestingly on some broader themes, including the weighing of incommensurate harms and benefits and the judicial capacity to balance economic effects with confidence. Together, the opinions show the turn in vertical restraint law—and antitrust more generally—that *Sylvania* symbolizes.

Continental T.V., Inc. v. GTE Sylvania Inc.
433 U.S. 36 (1977)

Justice Powell.

[1] Respondent GTE Sylvania Inc. (Sylvania) manufactures and sells television sets through its Home Entertainment Products Division. Prior to 1962, like most other television manufacturers, Sylvania sold its televisions to independent or company-owned distributors who in turn resold to a large and diverse group of retailers. Prompted by a decline in its market share to a relatively insignificant 1% to 2% of national television sales, Sylvania conducted an intensive reassessment of its marketing strategy, and in 1962 adopted the franchise plan challenged here. Sylvania phased out its wholesale distributors and began to sell its televisions directly to a smaller and more select group of franchised retailers. An acknowledged purpose of the change was to decrease the number of competing Sylvania retailers in the hope of attracting the more aggressive and competent retailers thought necessary to the improvement of the company's market position. To this end, Sylvania limited the number of franchises granted for any given area and required each franchisee to sell his Sylvania products only from the location or locations at which he was franchised. A franchise did not constitute an exclusive territory, and Sylvania retained sole discretion to increase the number of retailers in an area in light of the success or failure of existing retailers in developing their market. The revised marketing strategy appears to have been successful during the period at issue here, for by 1965 Sylvania's share of national television sales had increased to approximately 5%, and the company ranked as the Nation's eighth largest manufacturer of color television sets.

[2] This suit is the result of the rupture of a franchiser-franchisee relationship that had previously prospered under the revised Sylvania plan. Dissatisfied with its sales in the city of San Francisco, Sylvania decided in the spring of 1965 to franchise Young Brothers, an established San Francisco retailer of televisions, as an additional San Francisco retailer. The proposed location of the new franchise was approximately a mile from a retail outlet operated by petitioner Continental T. V., Inc. (Continental), one of the most successful Sylvania franchisees. Continental protested that the location of the new franchise violated Sylvania's marketing policy, but Sylvania persisted in its plans. Continental then canceled a large Sylvania order and placed a large order with Phillips, one of Sylvania's competitors.

---

[397] *See supra* note 364 and accompanying text.

[3] During this same period, Continental expressed a desire to open a store in Sacramento, Cal., a desire Sylvania attributed at least in part to Continental's displeasure over the Young Brothers decision. Sylvania believed that the Sacramento market was adequately served by the existing Sylvania retailers and denied the request. In the face of this denial, Continental advised Sylvania in early September 1965, that it was in the process of moving Sylvania merchandise from its San Jose, Cal., warehouse to a new retail location that it had leased in Sacramento. Two weeks later, allegedly for unrelated reasons, Sylvania's credit department reduced Continental's credit line from $300,000 to $50,000. In response to the reduction in credit and the generally deteriorating relations with Sylvania, Continental withheld all payments owed to John P. Maguire & Co., Inc. (Maguire), the finance company that handled the credit arrangements between Sylvania and its retailers. Shortly thereafter, Sylvania terminated Continental's franchises, and Maguire filed this diversity action in the United States District Court for the Northern District of California seeking recovery of money owed and of secured merchandise held by Continental.

[4] The antitrust issues before us originated in cross-claims brought by Continental against Sylvania [after Maguire's suit against Continental]. Most important for our purposes was the claim that Sylvania had violated s1 of the Sherman Act by entering into and enforcing franchise agreements that prohibited the sale of Sylvania products other than from specified locations. [. . .]

[5] The market impact of vertical restrictions is complex because of their potential for a simultaneous reduction of intrabrand competition and stimulation of interbrand competition.[19] Significantly, the Court in *Schwinn* did not distinguish among the challenged restrictions on the basis of their individual potential for intrabrand harm or interbrand benefit. Restrictions that completely eliminated intrabrand competition among Schwinn distributors were analyzed no differently from those that merely moderated intrabrand competition among retailers. The pivotal factor was the passage of title: All restrictions were held to be per se illegal where title had passed, and all were evaluated and sustained under the rule of reason where it had not. The location restriction at issue here would be subject to the same pattern of analysis under *Schwinn*.

[6] Vertical restrictions reduce intrabrand competition by limiting the number of sellers of a particular product competing for the business of a given group of buyers. Location restrictions have this effect because of practical constraints on the effective marketing area of retail outlets. Although intrabrand competition may be reduced, the ability of retailers to exploit the resulting market may be limited both by the ability of consumers to travel to other franchised locations and, perhaps more importantly, to purchase the competing products of other manufacturers. None of these key variables, however, is affected by the form of the transaction by which a manufacturer conveys his products to the retailers.

[7] Vertical restrictions promote interbrand competition by allowing the manufacturer to achieve certain efficiencies in the distribution of his products. These "redeeming virtues" are implicit in every decision sustaining vertical restrictions under the rule of reason. Economists have identified a number of ways in which manufacturers can use such restrictions to compete more effectively against other manufacturers.[23] For example, new manufacturers and manufacturers entering new markets can use the restrictions in order to induce competent and aggressive retailers to make the kind of investment of capital and labor that is often required in the distribution of products unknown to the consumer. Established manufacturers can use them to induce retailers to engage in promotional activities or to provide service and repair facilities necessary to the efficient marketing of their products. Service and repair are vital for many products, such as automobiles and major household appliances. The availability and quality of such services affect a manufacturer's goodwill and the competitiveness of his product. Because of market imperfections such as the so-called "free rider" effect, these services might not be

---

[19] Interbrand competition is the competition among the manufacturers of the same generic product television sets in this case and is the primary concern of antitrust law. The extreme example of a deficiency of interbrand competition is monopoly, where there is only one manufacturer. In contrast, intrabrand competition is the competition between the distributors wholesale or retail of the product of a particular manufacturer.

[23] Marketing efficiency is not the only legitimate reason for a manufacturer's desire to exert control over the manner in which his products are sold and serviced. As a result of statutory and common-law developments, society increasingly demands that manufacturers assume direct responsibility for the safety and quality of their products. For example, at the federal level, apart from more specialized requirements, manufacturers of consumer products have safety responsibilities under the Consumer Product Safety Act, and obligations for warranties under the Consumer Product Warranties Act. Similar obligations are imposed by state law. The legitimacy of these concerns has been recognized in cases involving vertical restrictions.

provided by retailers in a purely competitive situation, despite the fact that each retailer's benefit would be greater if all provided the services than if none did.

[8] Economists also have argued that manufacturers have an economic interest in maintaining as much intrabrand competition as is consistent with the efficient distribution of their products. Although the view that the manufacturer's interest necessarily corresponds with that of the public is not universally shared, even the leading critic of vertical restrictions concedes that *Schwinn*'s distinction between sale and nonsale transactions is essentially unrelated to any relevant economic impact. Indeed, to the extent that the form of the transaction is related to interbrand benefits, the Court's distinction is inconsistent with its articulated concern for the ability of smaller firms to compete effectively with larger ones. Capital requirements and administrative expenses may prevent smaller firms from using the exception for nonsale transactions.

[9] We conclude that the distinction drawn in *Schwinn* between sale and nonsale transactions is not sufficient to justify the application of a per se rule in one situation and a rule of reason in the other. The question remains whether the *per se* rule stated in *Schwinn* should be expanded to include non-sale transactions or abandoned in favor of a return to the rule of reason. We have found no persuasive support for expanding the *per se* rule. As noted above, the *Schwinn* Court recognized the undesirability of prohibiting all vertical restrictions of territory and all franchising. And even Continental does not urge us to hold that all such restrictions are *per se* illegal.

[10] We revert to the standard articulated in [earlier cases] for determining whether vertical restrictions must be conclusively presumed to be unreasonable and therefore illegal without elaborate inquiry as to the precise harm they have caused or the business excuse for their use. Such restrictions, in varying forms, are widely used in our free market economy. As indicated above, there is substantial scholarly and judicial authority supporting their economic utility. There is relatively little authority to the contrary. Certainly, there has been no showing in this case, either generally or with respect to Sylvania's agreements, that vertical restrictions have or are likely to have a "pernicious effect on competition" or that they "lack . . . any redeeming virtue." Accordingly, we conclude that the *per se* rule stated in *Schwinn* must be overruled. In so holding we do not foreclose the possibility that particular applications of vertical restrictions might justify *per se* prohibition . . . . But we do make clear that departure from the rule-of-reason standard must be based upon demonstrable economic effect rather than as in *Schwinn* upon formalistic line drawing.

[11] In sum, we conclude that the appropriate decision is to return to the rule of reason that governed vertical restrictions prior to *Schwinn*. When anticompetitive effects are shown to result from particular vertical restrictions they can be adequately policed under the rule of reason, the standard traditionally applied for the majority of anticompetitive practices challenged under s 1 of the Act.

Justice White, concurring in the judgment.

[12] I have . . . substantial misgivings about the approach the majority takes to overruling *Schwinn*. The reason for the distinction in *Schwinn* between sale and nonsale transactions was not, as the majority would have it, the Court's effort to accommodate the perceived intrabrand harm and interbrand benefit of vertical restrictions, the reason was rather, as Judge Browning argued in dissent below, the notion in many of our cases involving vertical restraints that independent businessmen should have the freedom to dispose of the goods they own as they see fit. Thus the first case cited by the Court in *Schwinn* for the proposition that restraints upon alienation are beyond the power of the manufacturer to impose upon its vendees and are violations of s 1 of the Sherman Act, was this Court's seminal decision holding, a series of resale-price-maintenance agreements per se illegal. *Dr. Miles Medical Co. v. John D. Park & Sons Co.*, 220 U.S. 373, (1911). In *Dr. Miles* the Court stated that a general restraint upon alienation is ordinarily invalid, citing Coke on Littleton, and emphasized that the case involved agreements restricting the freedom of trade on the part of dealers who own what they sell. . . .

[13] This concern for the freedom of the businessman to dispose of his own goods as he sees fit is most probably the explanation for two subsequent cases in which the Court allowed manufacturers to achieve economic results similar to that in *Dr. Miles* where they did not impose restrictions on dealers who had purchased their products [*i.e.*, United States v. Colgate & Co., 250 U.S. 300 (1919) and United States v. General Electric Co., 272 U.S. 476 (1926)].

[14] After summarily rejecting this concern, reflected in our interpretations of the Sherman Act, for the autonomy of independent businessmen, the majority not surprisingly finds no justification for *Schwinn*'s distinction between sale and nonsale transactions because the distinction is essentially unrelated to any relevant economic impact. But while according some weight to the businessman's interest in controlling the terms on which he trades in his own goods may be anathema to those who view the Sherman Act as directed solely to economic efficiency, this principle is without question more deeply embedded in our cases than the notions of "free rider" effects and distributional efficiencies borrowed by the majority from the new economics of vertical relationships. Perhaps the Court is right in partially abandoning this principle and in judging the instant nonprice vertical restraints solely by their "relevant economic impact"; but the precedents which reflect this principle should not be so lightly rejected by the Court. The rationale of *Schwinn* is no doubt difficult to discern from the opinion, and it may be wrong; it is not, however, the aberration the majority makes it out to be here.

***

GTE Sylvania Inc. v. Continental T.V., Inc.
537 F.2d 980 (9th Cir. 1976)

Judge Browning, dissenting.

[1] Sylvania's conduct toward Continental thwarted an important purpose of the Sherman Act. Legislative history and Supreme Court decisions establish that a principal objective of the Sherman Act was to protect the right of independent business entities to make their own competitive decisions, free of coercion, collusion, or exclusionary practices.

[2] Congress' general purpose in passing the Sherman Act was to limit and restrain accumulated economic power, represented by the trusts, and to restore and preserve a system of free competitive enterprise. The congressional debates reflect a concern not only with the consumer interest in price, quality, and quantity of goods and services, but also with society's interest in the protection of the independent businessman, for reasons of social and political as well as economic policy.[1]

[3] The Supreme Court has implemented the statutory policy of protecting the independence of individual business units in a series of decisions banning resale price maintenance agreements. These cases are particularly relevant here for, like territorial restraints, resale price maintenance is justified by manufacturers as necessary to enable them to control intrabrand competition by independent dealers in the interest of effective interbrand competition. Indeed, 'any argument that can be made on behalf of exclusive territories can also be made on behalf of resale price maintenance.'

[4] In the first resale price maintenance decision, Dr. Miles Medical Co. v. John D. Park & Sons Co., 220 U.S. 373 (1911), contracts between a manufacturer and its dealers setting minimum retail prices at which the product could be sold were held illegal in part because they created a restraint upon alienation, which the Court described as restricting the freedom of trade on the part of dealers who own what they sell. The Court concluded that after Dr. Miles sold its product at prices satisfactory to itself, the public is entitled to whatever advantage may be derived from competition in the subsequent traffic. [. . .]

[5] The same theme of protecting the right of independent business entities to compete runs through Supreme Court decisions holding group boycotts illegal per se. . . . .

---

[1] If the majority's statement that "the legislative intent underlying the Sherman Act had as its goal the promotion of consumer welfare" is meant to exclude other purposes, it is refuted by the legislative history referred to in the authorities cited herein. Even assuming that some contemporary economists might maintain that in a given case consumer interests might be better served by eliminating competition between independent businessmen, [t]here is little evidence that Sherman and the others had any idea of imposing an economist's model of competition on American industry. They did not consult economists of the time; and if they had done so, they would have found little support for any such course. In striking contrast to the views of the Congress, economists of the late 1800's considered "trusts" and other combinations to be a natural evolutionary advance, and monopolies to be both inevitable and potentially beneficial. Considering the level of economic thought prevailing in 1890, it is inconceivable that Congress passed the Sherman Act out of an exclusive preoccupation with the idea that prices should always equal marginal costs.

Antitrust | Francis & Sprigman | Chapter VI

[6] In many other contexts, the Supreme Court has rested decisions upon the premise that protection of the freedom to compete of separate business entities is an important objective of the Sherman Act. In Silver v. New York Stock Exchange, 373 U.S. 341 (1963), for example, the Court reasoned that the antitrust laws are an appropriate check upon anticompetitive conduct of market exchanges, since the antitrust laws serve, among other things, to protect competitive freedom, i.e., the freedom of individual business units to compete unhindered by the group action of others. A combination between General Motors and some of its dealers to eliminate sales through "discount houses" was held per se illegal . . . because it served to eliminate a class of competitors by terminating business dealings between them and a minority of Chevrolet dealers and to deprive franchised dealers of their freedom to deal through discounters if they so choose. . . . .

[7] From the holdings and rationale of these and other Supreme Court decisions, it seems clear that the protection of individual traders from unnecessary restrictions upon their freedom of action is a significant independent objective of antitrust policy. As a commentator recently put it, "The most important of the social policy objectives found in the Court's antitrust decisions are the concepts of business independence and freedom of business opportunity." In Judge Hand's well-known words [in United States v. Aluminum Co. of America, 148 F.2d 416, 427 (2d Cir. 1945)], Congress was not "actuated by economic motives alone. It is possible, because of its indirect social or moral effect, to prefer a system of small producers, each dependent for his success upon his own skill and character, to one in which the great mass of those engaged must accept the directions of a few. These considerations, which we have suggested as possible purposes of the Act, we think the decisions prove to have been in fact its purposes." [. . .]

[8] Despite the majority's contention that a *per se* rule is appropriate only if the restraint "lacks any redeeming virtue," the Supreme Court's holding in *Schwinn* and *Topco* that a restriction upon the territory in which independent traders may resell is per se illegal did not depend upon a conclusion that this restraint has no affirmative value. On the contrary, the Supreme Court recognized that in some circumstances a territorial restraint may promote competition. The Court held that such a restraint is nonetheless per se illegal when imposed upon independent business entities (1) because such a restraint is "obviously destructive" of competition among independent dealers, and (2) because it is not an appropriate judicial function to strike a public interest balance between the certain loss of competition among independent dealers and a possible gain of competition at some other point in the marketing process. [. . .]

[9] The Supreme Court has held that it is not an appropriate judicial function to weigh the loss of intrabrand competition against an alleged gain in interbrand competition in determining whether the Sherman Act has been violated for two related reasons. The first is that courts are ill-equipped to resolve the complex economic problems involved in deciding in a given case whether elimination of intrabrand competition among dealers through territorial restrictions in fact produced compensating gains in interbrand competition among producers. As the Court said in United States v. Topco Associates, Inc., 405 U.S. 596, 609–10 (1972):

> The fact is that courts are of limited utility in examining difficult economic problems. Our inability to weigh, in any meaningful sense, destruction of competition in one sector of the economy against promotion of competition in another is one important reason we have formulated per se rules.

[10] [. . .] The majority frankly acknowledges "that, as a matter of economic theory, there is a sharp divergence of opinion as to the alleged procompetitive effect of vertical territorial restrictions," but regards this disagreement as a reason for submitting the question of the legality of such restraints to the fact-finding judge or jury. The majority's view of the judicial function is at odds with *Schwinn*, *Topco*, and the traditions and precedent on which they rest. It is also an invitation to a fruitless enterprise.

[11] Sylvania's own expert witness, Professor Lee E. Preston, testified that in the present state of economic analysis it is not possible to determine the effect that changes in marketing practices at one level of a market will have at other levels. [. . .]

[12] A judge or jury should not be expected to determine whether Sylvania's locations practice contributed to Sylvania's success in interbrand competition when Sylvania's expert witness was unable to do so. Because the interbrand effects of Sylvania's locations practice cannot be measured, a decision as to whether the net effect of

the practice was procompetitive would be sheer guesswork. Finally, as has been shown, even if a net gain in purely economic terms could be established, such restraints could not be sustained consistent with Schwinn, Topco, and the purpose of the Sherman Act to maintain the competitive freedom of independent business units.

[13] The second reason given by the Supreme Court in *Topco* in support of its holding that courts are unsuitable for the task of deciding whether intrabrand competition among independent dealers should be sacrificed to promote interbrand competition among producers, is that the question is one of public policy properly determined by Congress. The Court said:

> If a decision is to be made to sacrifice competition in one portion of the economy for greater competition in another portion, this too is a decision that must be made by Congress and not by private forces or by the courts. Private forces are too keenly aware of their own interests in making such decisions and courts are ill-equipped and ill-situated for such decisionmaking. To analyze, interpret, and evaluate the myriad of competing interests and the endless data that would surely be brought to bear on such decisions, and to make the delicate judgment on the relative values to society of competitive areas of the economy, the judgment of the elected representatives of the people is required.

[14] A judicial tradition, dating at least from Judge Taft's opinion in *Addyston Pipe* in 1898, bars the courts from weighing conflicting economic predictions to determine the public interest in antitrust litigation. Even when applying the rule of reason, the courts have not inquired whether on some ultimate reckoning of social or economic debits or credits the conduct may be deemed beneficial. A value choice of such magnitude is beyond the ordinary limits of judicial competence.

[15] This tradition is founded, as the Supreme Court said in *Topco*, both upon the inadequacy of the judicial process to deal with such disputes, and upon a conviction that questions of economic policy are for legislative rather than judicial determination. The courts have shown that they can get at the facts of agreement and restrictive intent but cannot find a truly justiciable issue in the choice between rival economic predictions. [. . .]

2. Price Restraints: Resale Price Maintenance

For a long time it was *per se* unlawful for a manufacturer and a retailer of a particular product to agree on the price, or minimum price, at which the product would be sold. This rule against "vertical price fixing" was established by the Supreme Court in the 1911 *Dr. Miles* decision, and lasted almost a century until it was overruled in 2007.[398] Indeed, some early discussions of price-fixing often do not distinguish clearly between "horizontal" and "vertical" price-fixing.[399]

In *Dr. Miles*, the Court considered the legality of an agreement between a manufacturer of medicines and the retailers through which they were sold to the public, which established retail prices for the medicines. The Court concluded that "fixing of prices" of this kind was illegal, regardless of the "advantages which the participants expect to derive" from the agreements. Justice Holmes dissented. As you read these extracts, keep an eye out for the freedom / welfare tension we have seen in the history of the law of nonprice intrabrand restraints.

Dr. Miles Medical Co. v. John D. Park & Sons Co.
220 U.S. 373 (1911)

Justice Hughes.

---

[398] Congress intervened to exempt certain retail RPM agreements from antitrust scrutiny in the Miller-Tydings Act of 1937 and the McGuire Act of 1952; these efforts were repealed in 1976. *See generally* Note, *Resale Price Maintenance and the McGuire Act*, 27 St. J. L. Rev. 379 (1953); David F. Shores, *Vertical Price-Fixing and the Contract Conundrum: Beyond* Monsanto, 54 Fordham L. Rev. 377, 379–80 (1985).

[399] *See, e.g.*, United States v. Bausch & Lomb Optical Co., 321 U.S. 707, 719–720 (1944) (stating, in a resale price maintenance case: "[T]he retail license provisions binding dealers to sell at locally prevailing prices and only to the public constitute illegal restraints. Our former decisions compel this conclusion. Price fixing, reasonable or unreasonable, is unlawful per se.") (internal quotation marks omitted); *see also* John C. Peppin, *Price-Fixing Agreements under the Sherman Anti-Trust Law*, 28 Calif. L. Rev. 297, 300 (1940) (noting that in light of recent case law a resale price maintenance agreement could be treated identically to a horizontal cartel).

[1] [We now consider] whether the complainant . . . is entitled to maintain the restrictions [on price] by virtue of the fact that they relate to products of its own manufacture.

[2] The basis of the argument appears to be that, as the manufacturer may make and sell, or not, as he chooses, he may affix conditions as to the use of the article or as to the prices at which purchasers may dispose of it. The propriety of the restraint is sought to be derived from the liberty of the producer.

[3] But because a manufacturer is not bound to make or sell, it does not follow in case of sales actually made he may impose upon purchasers every sort of restriction. Thus, a general restraint upon alienation is ordinarily invalid. The right of alienation is one of the essential incidents of a right of general property in movables, and restraints upon alienation have been generally regarded as obnoxious to public policy, which is best subserved by great freedom of traffic in such things as pass from hand to hand. . . .

[4] Nor can the manufacturer by rule and notice, in the absence of contract or statutory right, even though the restriction be known to purchasers, fix prices for future sales. It has been held by this court that no such privilege exists under the copyright statutes, although the owner of the copyright has the sole right to vend copies of the copyrighted production. . . . It will hardly be contended, with respect to such a matter, that the manufacturer of an article of commerce not protected by any statutory grant is in any better case. Whatever right the manufacturer may have to project his control beyond his own sales must depend not upon an inherent power incident to production and original ownership, but upon agreement.

[5] With respect to contracts in restraint of trade, the earlier doctrine of the common law has been substantially modified in adaptation to modern conditions. But the public interest is still the first consideration. To sustain the restraint, it must be found to be reasonable both with respect to the public and to the parties, and that it is limited to what is fairly necessary, in the circumstances of the particular case, for the protection of the covenantee. Otherwise restraints of trade are void as against public policy. [. . .]

[6] The present case is not analogous to that of a sale of good will, or of an interest in a business, or of the grant of a right to use a process of manufacture. The complainant has not parted with any interest in its business or instrumentalities of production. It has conferred no right by virtue of which purchasers of its products may compete with it. It retains complete control over the business in which it is engaged, manufacturing what it pleases and fixing such prices for its own sales as it may desire. Nor are we dealing with a single transaction, conceivably unrelated to the public interest. The agreements are designed to maintain prices after the complainant has parted with the title to the articles, and to prevent competition among those who trade in them.

[7] The bill asserts the importance of a standard retail price, and alleges generally that confusion and damage have resulted from sales at less than the prices fixed. But the advantage of established retail prices primarily concerns the dealers. The enlarged profits which would result from adherence to the established rates would go to them, and not to the complainant. It is through the inability of the favored dealers to realize these profits, on account of the described competition, that the complainant works out its alleged injury. If there be an advantage to the manufacturer in the maintenance of fixed retail prices, the question remains whether it is one which he is entitled to secure by agreements restricting the freedom of trade on the part of dealers who own what they sell. As to this, the complainant can fare no better with its plan of identical contracts than could the dealers themselves if they formed a combination and endeavored to establish the same restrictions, and thus to achieve the same result, by agreement with each other. If the immediate advantage they would thus obtain would not be sufficient to sustain such a direct agreement, the asserted ulterior benefit to the complainant cannot be regarded as sufficient to support its system.

[8] But agreements or combinations between dealers, having for their sole purpose the destruction of competition and the fixing of prices, are injurious to the public interest and void. They are not saved by the advantages which the participants expect to derive from the enhanced price to the consumer.

[9] The complainant's plan falls within the principle which condemns contracts of this class. It, in effect, creates a combination for the prohibited purposes. No distinction can properly be made by reason of the particular character of the commodity in question. It is not entitled to special privilege or immunity. It is an article of commerce, and the rules concerning the freedom of trade must be held to apply to it. Nor does the fact that the

margin of freedom is reduced by the control of production make the protection of what remains, in such a case, a negligible matter. And where commodities have passed into the channels of trade and are owned by dealers, the validity of agreements to prevent competition and to maintain prices is not to be determined by the circumstance whether they were produced by several manufacturers or by one, or whether they were previously owned by one or by many. The complainant having sold its product at prices satisfactory to itself, the public is entitled to whatever advantage may be derived from competition in the subsequent traffic.

Justice Holmes, dissenting.

[10] [. . .] The sale to the retailers is made by the plaintiff, and the only question is whether the law forbids a purchaser to contract with his vendor that he will not sell below a certain price. This is the important question in this case. I suppose that in the case of a single object, such as a painting or a statute, the right of the artist to make such a stipulation hardly would be denied. In other words, I suppose that the reason why the contract is held bad is that it is part of a scheme embracing other similar contracts, each of which applies to a number of similar things, with the object of fixing a general market price. This reason seems to me inadequate in the case before the court. In the first place, by a slight change in the form of the contract the plaintiff can accomplish the result in a way that would be beyond successful attack. if it should make the retail dealers also agents in law as well as in name, and retain the title until the goods left their hands, 1 cannot conceive that even the present enthusiasm for regulating the prices to be charged by other people would deny that the owner was acting within his rights. It seems to me that this consideration by itself ought to give us pause.

[11] But I go farther. There is no statute covering the case; there is no body of precedent that, by ineluctable logic, requires the conclusion to which the court has come. The conclusion is reached by extending a certain conception of public policy to a new sphere. On such matters we are in perilous country. I think that at least it is safe to say that the most enlightened judicial policy is to let people manage their own business in their own way, unless the ground for interference is very clear. What, then, is the ground upon which we interfere in the present case? Of course, it is not the interest of the producer. No one, I judge, cares for that. It hardly can be the interest of subordinate vendors, as there seems to be no particular reason for preferring them to the originator and first vendor of the product. Perhaps it may be assumed to be the interest of the consumers and the public. On that point I confess that I am in a minority as to larger issues than are concerned here. I think that we greatly exaggerate the value and importance to the public of competition in the production or distribution of an article (here it is only distribution) as fixing a fair price. What really fixes that is the competition of conflicting desires. We, none of us, can have as much as we want of all the things that we want. Therefore, we have to choose. As soon as the price of something that we want goes above the point at which we are willing to give up other things to have that, we cease to buy it and buy something else. Of course, I am speaking of things that we can get along without. There may be necessaries that sooner or later must be dealt with like short rations in a shipwreck, but they are not Dr. Miles's medicines. With regard to things like the latter, it seems to me that the point of most profitable returns marks the equilibrium of social desires, and determines the fair price in the only sense in which I can find meaning in those words. The Dr. Miles Medical Company knows better than we do what will enable it to do the best business. We must assume its retail price to be reasonable, for it is so alleged and the case is here on demurrer; so I see nothing to warrant my assuming that the public will not be served best by the company being allowed to carry out its plan. I cannot believe that in the long run the public will profit by this court permitting knaves to cut reasonable prices for some ulterior purpose of their own, and thus to impair, if not to destroy, the production and sale of articles which it is assumed to be desirable that the public should be able to get.

* * *

The *per se* rule established in *Dr. Miles* against the fixing of a minimum resale price was criticized as "judicial legislation" by no less an authority than Louis Brandeis.

Louis D. Brandeis, Competition That Kills

Harper's Weekly (Nov. 15, 1913)

When a court decides a case upon grounds of public policy, the judges become, in effect, legislators. The question then involved is no longer one for lawyers only. It seems fitting, therefore, to inquire whether this judicial legislation is sound—whether the common trade practice of maintaining the price of trade-marked articles has been justly condemned. And when making that inquiry we may well bear in mind this admonition of Sir George Jessel, a very wise English judge:

> If there is one thing which more than any other public policy requires, it is that men of full age and competent understanding shall have the utmost liberty of contracting, and that their contracts, when entered into freely and voluntarily, shall be held sacred, and shall be enforced by courts of justice. Therefore, you have this paramount public policy to consider, that you are not lightly to interfere with this freedom of contract.

The Supreme Court says that a contract by which a producer binds a retailer to maintain the established selling price of his trade-marked product is void; because it prevents competition between retailers of the article and restrains trade.

Such a contract does, in a way, limit competition; but no man is bound to compete with himself. And when the same trade-marked article is sold in the same market by one dealer at a less price than by another, the producer, in effect, competes with himself. To avoid such competition, the producer of a trade-marked article often sells it to but a single dealer in a city or town; or he establishes an exclusive sales agency. No one has questioned the legal right of an independent producer to create such exclusive outlets for his product. But if exclusive selling agencies are legal, why should the individual manufacturer of a trade-marked article be prevented from establishing a marketing system under which his several agencies for distribution will sell at the same price? There is no difference, in substance, between an agent who retails the article and a dealer who retails it.

For many business concerns the policy of maintaining a standard price for a standard article is simple. The village baker readily maintained the quality and price of his product, by sale and delivery over his own counter. The great Standard Oil monopoly maintains quality and price (when it desires so to do) by selling throughout the world to the retailer or the consumer from its own tank-wagons. But for most producers the jobber and the retailer are the necessary means of distribution—as necessary as the railroad, the express or the parcel post. The Standard Oil Company can, without entering into contracts with dealers, maintain the price through its dominant power. Shall the law discriminate against the lesser concerns which have not that power, and deny them the legal right to contract with dealers to accomplish a like result? For in order to insure to the small producer the ability to maintain the price of his product, the law must afford him contract protection, when he deals through the middleman.

But the Supreme Court says that a contract which prevents a dealer of trade-marked articles from cutting the established selling price, restrains trade. In a sense every contract restrains trade; for after one has entered into a contract, he is not as free in trading as he was before he bound himself. But the right to bind one's self is essential to trade development. And it is not every contract in restraint of trade, but only contracts unreasonably in restraint of trade, which are invalid. Whether a contract does unreasonably restrain trade is not to be determined by abstract reasoning. Facts only can be safely relied upon to teach us whether a trade practice is consistent with the general welfare. And abundant experience establishes that the one-price system, which marks so important an advance in the ethics of trade, has also greatly increased the efficiency of merchandising, not only for the producer, but for the dealer and the consumer as well.

* * *

The criticism of antitrust's tough line on RPM resulted in legislative efforts to soften the rigor of the rule. The Miller-Tydings Act of 1937 and the McGuire Act of 1952 allowed state governments to authorize resale price maintenance, enduring until the Consumer Goods Pricing Act of 1975.[400]

Notwithstanding the criticism, the rule endured for a long time. And in *Albrecht* in 1968—which imposed liability on a newspaper publisher that set a maximum price for its newspaper carriers to avoid them overcharging customers—the Court's skepticism of price restraints reached an all-time-high, with the holding that the *per se* rule

---

[400] For contemporary perspectives, *see, e.g.*, Note, *Resale Price Maintenance: The Miller-Tydings Enabling Act*, 51 Harv. L. Rev. 336 (1937); Note, *Resale Price Maintenance and the McGuire Act*, 27 St. J. L. Rev. 379 (1953).

against RPM flatly forbids fixing a *maximum* resale price. From that point on, the *per se* rule against RPM came under steadily increasing pressure. Perhaps appropriately enough, the retreat started with maximum RPM.

The Law of Maximum RPM

Albrecht v. Herald Co., 390 U.S. 145 (1968); State Oil Co. v. Khan, 522 U.S. 3 (1997)

In 1968, the Court held in *Albrecht* that it was *per se* illegal for an upstream firm to agree a *maximum* resale price with its distributors. In that case, a newspaper publisher, Herald, had set a maximum price for its newspapers, to prevent its carriers overcharging customers. One carrier, Albrecht, violated the policy, and so Herald engaged an alternative carrier that was willing to abide by it. Albrecht sued under Section 1, and won in the Supreme Court.

The Court, in an opinion by Justice White, was unmoved by the argument that setting *maximum* prices was unlikely to cause competitive harm: "Maximum prices may be fixed too low for the dealer to furnish services essential to the value which goods have for the consumer or to furnish services and conveniences which consumers desire and for which they are willing to pay. Maximum price fixing may channel distribution through a few large or specifically advantaged dealers who otherwise would be subject to significant nonprice competition. Moreover, if the actual price charged under a maximum price scheme is nearly always the fixed maximum price, which is increasingly likely as the maximum price approaches the actual cost of the dealer, the scheme tends to acquire all the attributes of an arrangement fixing minimum prices." *Per se* illegality was the result.

Dissenting in *Albrecht*, Justice Harlan argued that a manufacturer's choice of distribution method was essentially a unilateral policy decision—there was no meaningful "conspiracy" between Herald and the new carrier—and that Herald had every incentive to set rules that maximized distribution of its newspapers and that best served its customers.

But the rule against maximum RPM did not last. In *Atlantic Richfield* in 1990, the Court rejected an antitrust suit brought by a competitor on the theory that maximum RPM had led to a price that was unfairly low, and in doing so it implicitly recognized that low prices were a procompetitive benefit of the maximum RPM policies in that case.[401] And in 1997, in *Khan*, the *per se* ban on maximum RPM was explicitly overruled.

Justice O'Connor's opinion for the Court in *Khan* closely echoes the themes of *GTE Sylvania* 20 years before, and particularly Sylvania's turn from dealer freedom to consumer welfare. Adjudicating a challenge to an RPM policy imposed by a gasoline supplier on gas stations, the Court emphasized the primacy of consumers and competition: "Low prices . . . benefit consumers regardless of how those prices are set, and so long as they are above predatory levels, they do not threaten competition." The older rule against maximum RPM, set out in *Albrecht*, "was grounded in the fear that maximum price fixing by suppliers could interfere with dealer freedom." But that concern would no longer govern. "[A]lthough vertical maximum price fixing might limit the viability of inefficient dealers, that consequence is not necessarily harmful to competition and consumers." The *Khan* Court did acknowledge the risk that maximum RPM could be used as a mask for minimum RPM (which was to remain *per se* illegal for another decade): but that concern could be examined under the rubric of the rule of reason. The upshot: "We conclude that *Albrecht* should be overruled."

Finally, the *per se* rule against minimum price fixing gave way also, in the Court's 2007 *Leegin* decision which established that all vertical distribution restraints, nonprice and price alike, should be analyzed under the rule of reason. Leegin—a leather-goods manufacturer that had operated a minimum RPM policy—found *amicus* support

---

[401] Atlantic Richfield Co. v. USA Petroleum Co., 495 U.S. 328, 345–46 (1990) ("A competitor is not injured by the *anticompetitive* effects of vertical, maximum price-fixing . . . and does not have any incentive to vindicate the legitimate interests of a rival's dealer. A competitor will not bring suit to protect the dealer against a maximum price that is set too low, inasmuch as the competitor would *benefit* from such a situation. Instead, a competitor will be motivated to bring suit only when the vertical restraint promotes interbrand competition between the competitor and the dealer subject to the restraint. In short, a competitor will be injured and hence motivated to sue only when a vertical, maximum-price-fixing arrangement has a *procompetitive* impact on the market. Therefore, providing the competitor a cause of action would not protect the rights of dealers and consumers under the antitrust laws.") (emphasis in original).

not only from the Justice Department and Federal Trade Commission,[402] but also from a group of economists, who argued that the time had come to abandon the last remaining *per se* rule for vertical restraints.

Brief of Amici Curiae Economists in Support of Petitioner, Leegin Creative Leather Prods., Inc. v. PSKS, Inc.
Case No. 06-480 (filed Jan. 22, 2007)

[T]he manufacturer that uses minimum RPM can enhance interbrand competition by causing resellers to provide additional services that will increase the product's competitiveness against other products and increase sales of the product. Thus, even where minimum RPM raises the price charged by a given retailer, that does not mean that there is necessarily an anticompetitive effect. [. . .]

One objection to minimum RPM that had some traction historically is that it might be used to facilitate a cartel at the manufacturer level. There is no reason to believe, however, that this occurs frequently, or that a per se rule is needed to address any cases in which it does occur.

Most cartels do not involve manipulation or control of downstream resale prices, but minimum RPM has been proposed as one means by which a cartel can dissuade cheating by its members, which have incentives to reduce prices slightly and thereby gain market share. Cartel members seeking to prevent "cheating" on their agreement ideally would observe each other's prices directly. Market circumstances or prudence, however, may preclude that from happening. As an alternative, manufacturers might agree to impose RPM agreements on their dealers, so that any reduction in price by a manufacturer could not be passed on to the consumer by the retailer, but would enrich only the retailer. With no benefit to consumers, demand for the product would not increase, and the would-be "cheat" would not benefit from its reduced prices.

There are reasons to believe that this type of use of minimum RPM would not be very common.

First, this situation could arise only where manufacturers had agreed to a criminal cartel and where market conditions made such a cartel practical. Thus, it would not apply where a manufacturer is law-abiding or where the number of competing manufacturers, the ease of entry, or other market circumstances rendered a successful cartel implausible.

Second, it would not apply where compliance with a conspiracy can be monitored without RPM. It is noteworthy that minimum RPM has not been generally reported as an enforcement mechanism in the major price-fixing cartels that the Department of Justice has prosecuted in the past decade.

Third, there is no empirical evidence that minimum RPM is used with any frequency in this manner. To the contrary, the empirical evidence that does exist suggests that such use of minimum RPM is not common. In 1991, Pauline Ippolito of the Federal Trade Commission reported a study of the frequency with which both manufacturer cartels and retailer cartels (discussed below) were alleged in the 153 reported minimum RPM cases from 1976 to 1982. Ippolito found that only 5.9 percent of the cases involved allegations of horizontal manufacturer price fixing in addition to RPM. She concluded, on this basis, there is little evidence to support the hypothesis that the RPM law primarily deters collusion or that collusion is the primary reason for the use of RPM. [. . .]

It also has been suggested that minimum RPM could be used to facilitate reseller cartels. Retailers that sought to form a cartel could induce manufacturers to implement minimum RPM agreements and thereby become the cartel's enforcement mechanism.

For many of the reasons mentioned above with respect to manufacturer conspiracies, the use of minimum RPM to enforce dealer cartels is not likely to be very common. Such a situation would require a retail market with high barriers to entry, because manufacturers would otherwise sell through non-colluding, lower-margin dealers.

---

[402] Brief for the United States as Amicus Curiae Supporting Petitioner, Leegin Creative Leather Products, Inc. v. PSKS, Inc., Case No. 06-480 (filed Jan. 22, 2007), 6 ("*Dr. Miles* should be overruled, and . . . RPM should be evaluated under the same rule-of-reason standard that applies to other vertical agreements.").

Cartelization is also an unlikely motive in markets where only one or few competitors implement RPM programs because otherwise consumers could switch to brands not encumbered by collusive retail margins. Moreover, because dealers often can observe each other's prices directly, participation by suppliers in such a cartel through minimum RPM agreements is unlikely to be necessary.

In addition, the manufacturer—a key element in these agreements—receives no benefit from a dealer cartel, but on the contrary, suffers diminished sales. Therefore, manufacturers generally lack incentives to cooperate in furthering a dealer cartel. [. . .]

In the theoretical literature, it is essentially undisputed that minimum RPM can have procompetitive effects and that under a variety of market conditions it is unlikely to have anticompetitive effects. The disagreement in the literature relates principally to the relative frequency with which procompetitive and anticompetitive effects are likely to ensue. The critical issue is the boundaries of that dispute. Some believe that minimum RPM is almost always benign and thus should basically be ignored by antitrust law except when it is part of a cartel case. Others believe that RPM has been demonstrated to be anticompetitive in some cases and thus merits serious antitrust consideration. The position absent from the literature is that minimum RPM is most often, much less almost invariably, anticompetitive. Thus, the economics literature provides no support for the application of a per se rule.

* * *

The Court took the hint and embraced the rule of reason, marking the end of *per se* treatment of vertical restraints.

Leegin Creative Leather Products, Inc. v. PSKS, Inc.
551 U.S. 877 (2007)

Justice Kennedy.

[1] Petitioner, Leegin Creative Leather Products, Inc. (Leegin), designs, manufactures, and distributes leather goods and accessories. In 1991, Leegin began to sell belts under the brand name "Brighton." The Brighton brand has now expanded into a variety of women's fashion accessories. It is sold across the United States in over 5,000 retail establishments, for the most part independent, small boutiques and specialty stores. Leegin's president, Jerry Kohl, also has an interest in about 70 stores that sell Brighton products. Leegin asserts that, at least for its products, small retailers treat customers better, provide customers more services, and make their shopping experience more satisfactory than do larger, often impersonal retailers. . . . .

[2] Respondent, PSKS, Inc. (PSKS), operates Kay's Kloset, a women's apparel store in Lewisville, Texas. Kay's Kloset buys from about 75 different manufacturers and at one time sold the Brighton brand. It first started purchasing Brighton goods from Leegin in 1995. Once it began selling the brand, the store promoted Brighton. . . . .

[3] In 1997, Leegin instituted the "Brighton Retail Pricing and Promotion Policy." Following the policy, Leegin refused to sell to retailers that discounted Brighton goods below suggested prices. The policy contained an exception for products not selling well that the retailer did not plan on reordering. In the letter to retailers establishing the policy, Leegin stated:

> In this age of mega stores like Macy's, Bloomingdales, May Co. and others, consumers are perplexed by promises of product quality and support of product which we believe is lacking in these large stores. Consumers are further confused by the ever popular sale, sale, sale, etc.

> We, at Leegin, choose to break away from the pack by selling [at] specialty stores; specialty stores that can offer the customer great quality merchandise, superb service, and support the Brighton product 365 days a year on a consistent basis.

> We realize that half the equation is Leegin producing great Brighton product and the other half is you, our retailer, creating great looking stores selling our products in a quality manner.

[4] Leegin adopted the policy to give its retailers sufficient margins to provide customers the service central to its distribution strategy. It also expressed concern that discounting harmed Brighton's brand image and reputation. [. . .]

[5] In December 2002, Leegin discovered Kay's Kloset had been marking down Brighton's entire line by 20 percent. Kay's Kloset contended it placed Brighton products on sale to compete with nearby retailers who also were undercutting Leegin's suggested prices. Leegin, nonetheless, requested that Kay's Kloset cease discounting. Its request refused, Leegin stopped selling to the store. The loss of the Brighton brand had a considerable negative impact on the store's revenue from sales.

[6] PSKS sued Leegin in the United States District Court for the Eastern District of Texas. It alleged, among other claims, that Leegin had violated the antitrust laws by entering into agreements with retailers to charge only those prices fixed by Leegin. [. . .]

[7] Though each side of the debate can find sources to support its position, it suffices to say here that economics literature is replete with procompetitive justifications for a manufacturer's use of resale price maintenance. *See, e.g.*, Brief for Economists as Amici Curiae 16 ("In the theoretical literature, it is essentially undisputed that minimum [resale price maintenance] can have procompetitive effects and that under a variety of market conditions it is unlikely to have anticompetitive effects"); Brief for United States as Amicus Curiae 9 ("[T]here is a widespread consensus that permitting a manufacturer to control the price at which its goods are sold may promote interbrand competition and consumer welfare in a variety of ways"); ABA Section of Antitrust Law, ANTITRUST LAW AND ECONOMICS OF PRODUCT DISTRIBUTION 76 (2006) ("[T]he bulk of the economic literature on [resale price maintenance] suggests that [it] is more likely to be used to enhance efficiency than for anticompetitive purposes"). Even those more skeptical of resale price maintenance acknowledge it can have procompetitive effects.

[8] The few recent studies documenting the competitive effects of resale price maintenance also cast doubt on the conclusion that the practice meets the criteria for a *per se* rule.

[9] The justifications for vertical price restraints are similar to those for other vertical restraints. Minimum resale price maintenance can stimulate interbrand competition—the competition among manufacturers selling different brands of the same type of product—by reducing intrabrand competition—the competition among retailers selling the same brand. The promotion of interbrand competition is important because the primary purpose of the antitrust laws is to protect this type of competition. A single manufacturer's use of vertical price restraints tends to eliminate intrabrand price competition; this in turn encourages retailers to invest in tangible or intangible services or promotional efforts that aid the manufacturer's position as against rival manufacturers. Resale price maintenance also has the potential to give consumers more options so that they can choose among low-price, low-service brands; high-price, high-service brands; and brands that fall in between.

[10] Absent vertical price restraints, the retail services that enhance interbrand competition might be underprovided. This is because discounting retailers can free ride on retailers who furnish services and then capture some of the increased demand those services generate. Consumers might learn, for example, about the benefits of a manufacturer's product from a retailer that invests in fine showrooms, offers product demonstrations, or hires and trains knowledgeable employees. Or consumers might decide to buy the product because they see it in a retail establishment that has a reputation for selling high-quality merchandise. If the consumer can then buy the product from a retailer that discounts because it has not spent capital providing services or developing a quality reputation, the high-service retailer will lose sales to the discounter, forcing it to cut back its services to a level lower than consumers would otherwise prefer. Minimum resale price maintenance alleviates the problem because it prevents the discounter from undercutting the service provider. With price competition decreased, the manufacturer's retailers compete among themselves over services.

[11] Resale price maintenance, in addition, can increase interbrand competition by facilitating market entry for new firms and brands. New manufacturers and manufacturers entering new markets can use the restrictions in order to induce competent and aggressive retailers to make the kind of investment of capital and labor that is often required in the distribution of products unknown to the consumer. New products and new brands are essential to

a dynamic economy, and if markets can be penetrated by using resale price maintenance there is a procompetitive effect.

[12] Resale price maintenance can also increase interbrand competition by encouraging retailer services that would not be provided even absent free riding. It may be difficult and inefficient for a manufacturer to make and enforce a contract with a retailer specifying the different services the retailer must perform. Offering the retailer a guaranteed margin and threatening termination if it does not live up to expectations may be the most efficient way to expand the manufacturer's market share by inducing the retailer's performance and allowing it to use its own initiative and experience in providing valuable services. [. . .]

[13] While vertical agreements setting minimum resale prices can have procompetitive justifications, they may have anticompetitive effects in other cases; and unlawful price fixing, designed solely to obtain monopoly profits, is an ever–present temptation. Resale price maintenance may, for example, facilitate a manufacturer cartel. An unlawful cartel will seek to discover if some manufacturers are undercutting the cartel's fixed prices. Resale price maintenance could assist the cartel in identifying price-cutting manufacturers who benefit from the lower prices they offer. Resale price maintenance, furthermore, could discourage a manufacturer from cutting prices to retailers with the concomitant benefit of cheaper prices to consumers.

[14] Vertical price restraints also might be used to organize cartels at the retailer level. A group of retailers might collude to fix prices to consumers and then compel a manufacturer to aid the unlawful arrangement with resale price maintenance. In that instance the manufacturer does not establish the practice to stimulate services or to promote its brand but to give inefficient retailers higher profits. Retailers with better distribution systems and lower cost structures would be prevented from charging lower prices by the agreement. Historical examples suggest this possibility is a legitimate concern.

[15] A horizontal cartel among competing manufacturers or competing retailers that decreases output or reduces competition in order to increase price is, and ought to be, per se unlawful. To the extent a vertical agreement setting minimum resale prices is entered upon to facilitate either type of cartel, it, too, would need to be held unlawful under the rule of reason. This type of agreement may also be useful evidence for a plaintiff attempting to prove the existence of a horizontal cartel.

[16] Resale price maintenance, furthermore, can be abused by a powerful manufacturer or retailer. A dominant retailer, for example, might request resale price maintenance to forestall innovation in distribution that decreases costs. A manufacturer might consider it has little choice but to accommodate the retailer's demands for vertical price restraints if the manufacturer believes it needs access to the retailer's distribution network. A manufacturer with market power, by comparison, might use resale price maintenance to give retailers an incentive not to sell the products of smaller rivals or new entrants. As should be evident, the potential anticompetitive consequences of vertical price restraints must not be ignored or underestimated. [. . .]

[17] Notwithstanding the risks of unlawful conduct, it cannot be stated with any degree of confidence that resale price maintenance always or almost always tend[s] to restrict competition and decrease output. Vertical agreements establishing minimum resale prices can have either procompetitive or anticompetitive effects, depending upon the circumstances in which they are formed. And although the empirical evidence on the topic is limited, it does not suggest efficient uses of the agreements are infrequent or hypothetical. As the rule would proscribe a significant amount of procompetitive conduct, these agreements appear ill suited for per se condemnation.

[18] Respondent contends, nonetheless, that vertical price restraints should be per se unlawful because of the administrative convenience of *per se* rules. That argument suggests *per se* illegality is the rule rather than the exception. This misinterprets our antitrust law. *Per se* rules may decrease administrative costs, but that is only part of the equation. Those rules can be counterproductive. They can increase the total cost of the antitrust system by prohibiting procompetitive conduct the antitrust laws should encourage. They also may increase litigation costs by promoting frivolous suits against legitimate practices. The Court has thus explained that administrative advantages are not sufficient in themselves to justify the creation of *per se* rules, and has relegated their use to restraints that are manifestly anticompetitive. Were the Court now to conclude that vertical price restraints should

be *per se* illegal based on administrative costs, we would undermine, if not overrule, the traditional demanding standards for adopting per se rules. Any possible reduction in administrative costs cannot alone justify the Dr. Miles rule.

[19] Respondent also argues the *per se* rule is justified because a vertical price restraint can lead to higher prices for the manufacturer's goods. *See also* [T. Overstreet, RESALE PRICE MAINTENANCE: ECONOMIC THEORIES AND EMPIRICAL EVIDENCE (1983)] 160 (noting that "price surveys indicate that [resale price maintenance] in most cases increased the prices of products sold"). Respondent is mistaken in relying on pricing effects absent a further showing of anticompetitive conduct. *Cf. id.*, at 106 (explaining that price surveys "do not necessarily tell us anything conclusive about the welfare effects of [resale price maintenance] because the results are generally consistent with both procompetitive and anticompetitive theories"). For, as has been indicated already, the antitrust laws are designed primarily to protect interbrand competition, from which lower prices can later result. The Court, moreover, has evaluated other vertical restraints under the rule of reason even though prices can be increased in the course of promoting procompetitive effects. And resale price maintenance may reduce prices if manufacturers have resorted to costlier alternatives of controlling resale prices that are not per se unlawful.

[20] Respondent's argument, furthermore, overlooks that, in general, the interests of manufacturers and consumers are aligned with respect to retailer profit margins. The difference between the price a manufacturer charges retailers and the price retailers charge consumers represents part of the manufacturer's cost of distribution, which, like any other cost, the manufacturer usually desires to minimize. A manufacturer has no incentive to overcompensate retailers with unjustified margins. The retailers, not the manufacturer, gain from higher retail prices. The manufacturer often loses; interbrand competition reduces its competitiveness and market share because consumers will substitute a different brand of the same product. As a general matter, therefore, a single manufacturer will desire to set minimum resale prices only if the increase in demand resulting from enhanced service will more than offset a negative impact on demand of a higher retail price.

[21] The implications of respondent's position are far reaching. Many decisions a manufacturer makes and carries out through concerted action can lead to higher prices. A manufacturer might, for example, contract with different suppliers to obtain better inputs that improve product quality. Or it might hire an advertising agency to promote awareness of its goods. Yet no one would think these actions violate the Sherman Act because they lead to higher prices. The antitrust laws do not require manufacturers to produce generic goods that consumers do not know about or want. The manufacturer strives to improve its product quality or to promote its brand because it believes this conduct will lead to increased demand despite higher prices. The same can hold true for resale price maintenance.

[22] Resale price maintenance, it is true, does have economic dangers. If the rule of reason were to apply to vertical price restraints, courts would have to be diligent in eliminating their anticompetitive uses from the market. This is a realistic objective, and certain factors are relevant to the inquiry. For example, the number of manufacturers that make use of the practice in a given industry can provide important instruction. When only a few manufacturers lacking market power adopt the practice, there is little likelihood it is facilitating a manufacturer cartel, for a cartel then can be undercut by rival manufacturers. Likewise, a retailer cartel is unlikely when only a single manufacturer in a competitive market uses resale price maintenance. Interbrand competition would divert consumers to lower priced substitutes and eliminate any gains to retailers from their price-fixing agreement over a single brand. Resale price maintenance should be subject to more careful scrutiny, by contrast, if many competing manufacturers adopt the practice.

[23] The source of the restraint may also be an important consideration. If there is evidence retailers were the impetus for a vertical price restraint, there is a greater likelihood that the restraint facilitates a retailer cartel or supports a dominant, inefficient retailer. If, by contrast, a manufacturer adopted the policy independent of retailer pressure, the restraint is less likely to promote anticompetitive conduct. A manufacturer also has an incentive to protest inefficient retailer-induced price restraints because they can harm its competitive position. [. . .]

[24] The rule of reason is designed and used to eliminate anticompetitive transactions from the market. This standard principle applies to vertical price restraints. A party alleging injury from a vertical agreement setting minimum resale prices will have, as a general matter, the information and resources available to show the existence

of the agreement and its scope of operation. As courts gain experience considering the effects of these restraints by applying the rule of reason over the course of decisions, they can establish the litigation structure to ensure the rule operates to eliminate anticompetitive restraints from the market and to provide more guidance to businesses. Courts can, for example, devise rules over time for offering proof, or even presumptions where justified, to make the rule of reason a fair and efficient way to prohibit anticompetitive restraints and to promote procompetitive ones. [. . .]

[25] For these reasons the Court's decision in *Dr. Miles Medical Co. v. John D. Park & Sons Co.*, 220 U.S. 373 (1911), is now overruled. Vertical price restraints are to be judged according to the rule of reason.

Justice Breyer, dissenting, joined by Justices Stevens, Souter, and Ginsburg.

[26] On the one hand, agreements setting minimum resale prices may have serious anticompetitive consequences. In respect to dealers: Resale price maintenance agreements, rather like horizontal price agreements, can diminish or eliminate price competition among dealers of a single brand or (if practiced generally by manufacturers) among multibrand dealers. In doing so, they can prevent dealers from offering customers the lower prices that many customers prefer; they can prevent dealers from responding to changes in demand, say, falling demand, by cutting prices; they can encourage dealers to substitute service, for price, competition, thereby threatening wastefully to attract too many resources into that portion of the industry; they can inhibit expansion by more efficient dealers whose lower prices might otherwise attract more customers, stifling the development of new, more efficient modes of retailing; and so forth.

[27] In respect to producers: Resale price maintenance agreements can help to reinforce the competition-inhibiting behavior of firms in concentrated industries. In such industries firms may tacitly collude, i.e., observe each other's pricing behavior, each understanding that price cutting by one firm is likely to trigger price competition by all. Where that is so, resale price maintenance can make it easier for each producer to identify (by observing retail markets) when a competitor has begun to cut prices. And a producer who cuts wholesale prices without lowering the minimum resale price will stand to gain little, if anything, in increased profits, because the dealer will be unable to stimulate increased consumer demand by passing along the producer's price cut to consumers. In either case, resale price maintenance agreements will tend to prevent price competition from "breaking out"; and they will thereby tend to stabilize producer prices. [. . .]

[28] On the other hand, those favoring resale price maintenance have long argued that resale price maintenance agreements can provide important consumer benefits. The majority lists two: First, such agreements can facilitate new entry. For example, a newly entering producer wishing to build a product name might be able to convince dealers to help it do so—if, but only if, the producer can assure those dealers that they will later recoup their investment. Without resale price maintenance, late-entering dealers might take advantage of the earlier investment and, through price competition, drive prices down to the point where the early dealers cannot recover what they spent. By assuring the initial dealers that such later price competition will not occur, resale price maintenance can encourage them to carry the new product, thereby helping the new producer succeed. The result might be increased competition at the producer level, i.e., greater inter-brand competition, that brings with it net consumer benefits.

[29] Second, without resale price maintenance a producer might find its efforts to sell a product undermined by what resale price maintenance advocates call "free riding." . . . .

[30] The upshot is, as many economists suggest, sometimes resale price maintenance can prove harmful; sometimes it can bring benefits. But before concluding that courts should consequently apply a rule of reason, I would ask such questions as, how often are harms or benefits likely to occur? How easy is it to separate the beneficial sheep from the antitrust goats?

[31] Economic discussion, such as the studies the Court relies upon, can help provide answers to these questions, and in doing so, economics can, and should, inform antitrust law. But antitrust law cannot, and should not, precisely replicate economists' (sometimes conflicting) views. That is because law, unlike economics, is an administrative system the effects of which depend upon the content of rules and precedents only as they are applied by judges and juries in courts and by lawyers advising their clients. And that fact means that courts will often bring

their own administrative judgment to bear, sometimes applying rules of per se unlawfulness to business practices even when those practices sometimes produce benefits. [. . .]

[32] How easily can courts identify instances in which the benefits are likely to outweigh potential harms? My own answer is, not very easily. For one thing, it is often difficult to identify who—producer or dealer—is the moving force behind any given resale price maintenance agreement. Suppose, for example, several large multibrand retailers all sell resale-price-maintained products. Suppose further that small producers set retail prices because they fear that, otherwise, the large retailers will favor (say, by allocating better shelf space) the goods of other producers who practice resale price maintenance. Who "initiated" this practice, the retailers hoping for considerable insulation from retail competition, or the producers, who simply seek to deal best with the circumstances they find? For another thing, as I just said, it is difficult to determine just when, and where, the "free riding" problem is serious enough to warrant legal protection.

[33] I recognize that scholars have sought to develop checklists and sets of questions that will help courts separate instances where anticompetitive harms are more likely from instances where only benefits are likely to be found. But applying these criteria in court is often easier said than done. The Court's invitation to consider the existence of "market power," for example, invites lengthy time-consuming argument among competing experts, as they seek to apply abstract, highly technical, criteria to often ill-defined markets. And resale price maintenance cases, unlike a major merger or monopoly case, are likely to prove numerous and involve only private parties. One cannot fairly expect judges and juries in such cases to apply complex economic criteria without making a considerable number of mistakes, which themselves may impose serious costs.

[34] Are there special advantages to a bright-line rule? Without such a rule, it is often unfair, and consequently impractical, for enforcement officials to bring criminal proceedings. And since enforcement resources are limited, that loss may tempt some producers or dealers to enter into agreements that are, on balance, anticompetitive.

[35] Given the uncertainties that surround key items in the overall balance sheet, particularly in respect to the "administrative" questions, I can concede to the majority that the problem is difficult. And, if forced to decide now, at most I might agree that the per se rule should be slightly modified to allow an exception for the more easily identifiable and temporary condition of new entry. But I am not now forced to decide this question. The question before us is not what should be the rule, starting from scratch. We here must decide whether to change a clear and simple price-related antitrust rule that the courts have applied for nearly a century. [. . .]

[36] . . . I do not believe that the majority has shown new or changed conditions sufficient to warrant overruling a decision of such long standing [as *Dr. Miles*]. All ordinary stare decisis considerations indicate the contrary. For these reasons, with respect, I dissent.

* * *

Leegin—and the correct judicial and economic treatment of resale price maintenance—continues to be a subject of lively debate.[403] (Note that RPM continues to be *per se* illegal under the laws of certain states.[404])

NOTES

1) What is a "brand" in the sense used in *Sylvania* and *Leegin*, and why is competition between, rather than within, brands the primary concern of antitrust law? What alternatives to this approach are plausible?[405] (And can intrabrand restraints ever have interbrand effects?[406])

---

[403] *See, e.g.*, William S. Comanor & David Salant, *Resale Price Maintenance Post* Leegin: *A Model of RPM Incentives*, 50 Rev. Ind. Org. 169 (2017); Gregory T. Gundlach, *Resale Price Maintenance: A Review and Call for Research*, American Antitrust Institute Working Paper (Apr. 17, 2014); Gregory T. Gundlach, *Overview and contents of the special issue: Antitrust analysis of resale price maintenance after* Leegin, 55 Antitrust Bull. 1 (2010); Richard M. Brunell, *Overruling* Dr. Miles: *The Supreme Trade Commission in Action*, 52 Antitrust Bull. 475 (2007).

[404] *See, e.g.*, Alsheikh v. Superior Court, No. B249822, 2013 WL 5530508, at *3 (Cal. App. 2 Dist. Oct. 7, 2013); MD. CODE ANN., COM. LAW § 11-204(b) (defining any "contract, combination, or conspiracy that establishes a minimum price below which a retailer, wholesaler, or distributor may not sell a commodity or service" to be an unreasonable restraint of trade or commerce).

[405] *See generally, e.g.*, Stephen Martin & John T. Scott, GTE Sylvania *and Interbrand Competition as the Primary Concern of Antitrust Law*, 51 Rev. Ind. Org. 217 (2017).

[406] *See, e.g.*, William S. Comanor & Patrick Rey, *Vertical Restraints and the Market Power of Large Distributors*, 17 Rev. Indus. Org. 135 (2000) (identifying one mechanism through which intrabrand restraints could play a role in suppressing interbrand competition).

2) What treatment of intrabrand competition is implied by the cases above: is it relevant but secondary, or completely irrelevant? What factors should lead a court to place greater importance on intrabrand competition in a particular case?

3) *"GTE Sylvania*, read with *Topco* and *Sealy*, implies that if retail markets are divided by a manufacturer, courts should apply a lenient rule of reason; but if the same thing is done by retailers, it's per se illegal." Do you agree with this characterization?

4) What is most persuasive in Judge Browning's dissent in the Ninth Circuit in *Sylvania*? What is least persuasive?

5) The shift from *Schwinn* to *GTE Sylvania* seems to reflect the view that antitrust law should treat agreements between manufacturers and resellers, and agreements between manufacturers and their sales agents, identically. Are there circumstances under which you think this difference should affect antitrust analysis: that is, are there things that manufacturers should be able to agree with trading partners in one of these categories but not the other?

6) Some suppliers do not distribute their products or services through third parties at all: instead, they do it themselves, through "closed" vertically integrated distribution systems. One reason that they might choose to do this is if antitrust law would create a liability risk if they tried to implement their desired distribution method through restrictive contracts with trading partners. Should antitrust law favor or disfavor the use of closed systems, rather than the kind of open systems at issue in *Schwinn* and *GTE Sylvania*? Would your answer change if we were talking about digital ecosystems rather than traditional consumer goods?[407]

7) Should it be *per se* legal for a manufacturer to establish single exclusive authorized distributors, selling at specified prices, in each geographic area? If so, how can *less* restrictive systems plausibly be unlawful? If not, couldn't the manufacturer simply accomplish the same thing by making itself the only distributor of its products?

8) To the extent that manufacturers (or courts) may be worried about "free riding" by some retailers on the efforts of others, would it make a difference if retailers could:
   a. charge consumers directly for the services?
   b. be bound by contract with a manufacturer to provide such services in exchange for specific compensation?

9) Resale price maintenance is often observed for products that do not seem to require any retailer services at all, including "pet food, vitamins, shampoo, men's underwear," and so on.[408] Why do you think this is?

10) Suppose that Manufacturer X has operated an unrestricted distribution system for some years, but over time one or two retailers have become leaders in each state. Following a retailers' conference, these leading retailers jointly recommend that Manufacturer X grant them each exclusive territorial status in their respective states, including provisions that prevent them from selling into each other's territories, and phase out supply to other retailers. The leading retailers do not tell Manufacturer X that they were also motivated by concern that competition among them is hurting their pricing and profits, and that they would do better if they could divide the national market into cosy exclusive territories. Manufacturer X analyzes the proposal, agrees that it would improve demand and output, and implements it.
   a. What standard of review should apply to the agreement: *per se* or rule of reason? If the latter, under what circumstances would it be unlawful?
   b. Would it affect your answer if the retailers had informally agreed, before Manufacturer X adopted the proposal, that they would do their best to respect the terms of the proposal while waiting for Manufacturer X's decision?

11) Is the modern approach to distribution restraints better or worse for consumers than the previous, per se-based approach? What informs your belief?

12) What was lost or sacrificed when the law of vertical restraints made the turn in *Sylvania*? What was gained? Was it worth the trade?

---

[407] *See, e.g.*, Daniel A. Crane, *Ecosystem Competition and the Antitrust Laws*, 98 Neb. L. Rev. 412 (2019); Autorité de la Concurrence & Competition & Markets Authority, THE ECONOMICS OF OPEN AND CLOSED SYSTEMS (Dec. 2014); Hanno F. Kaiser, *Are "Closed Systems" an Antitrust Problem?*, 7 Comp. Pol'y Int'l 91 (2011).

[408] Marina Lao, *Free Riding: An Overstated, and Unconvincing, Explanation for Resale Price Maintenance*, in Robert Pitofsky (ed.) HOW THE CHICAGO SCHOOL OVERSHOT THE MARK: THE EFFECT OF CONSERVATIVE ECONOMIC ANALYSIS ON U.S. ANTITRUST (2008) 201.

D. Exclusivity

Perhaps the most obvious form of vertical restraint on interbrand competition is the exclusivity agreement: that is, a commitment given by an upstream or downstream firm (say, an input supplier or a distributor) that it will refrain from dealing with the competitors of its trading partner.

The possible threat to competition from such agreements is fairly clear. If a dominant firm extracts an exclusivity commitment from the supplier of a critical input, or from a key distributor, then its market power may be protected and enhanced through the imposition of higher costs on rivals. The primary concern is usually that rivals may not have access to enough of the input or distribution capacity, or may be restricted inputs or distribution of insufficient quality: the effect is often described as "raising rivals' costs" (or just "RRC").[409] (Some courts have indicated that, if an exclusivity agreement is imposed by a seller, only the seller imposing the condition—not buyers that accept it—will be liable.[410]) On the other hand, as we will see below, exclusive agreements may play an important role in achieving a variety of beneficial goals, including supporting investments of various kinds. They may be analyzed under Section 1 of the Sherman Act or Section 3 of the Clayton Act.

Clayton Act Section 3

You may remember from Chapter I that, in 1914, the Clayton Act introduced some conduct prohibitions intended to reinforce the Sherman Act. One of these is Section 3 of the Clayton Act, 15 U.S.C. § 14. It provides in relevant part: "It shall be unlawful for any person engaged in commerce, in the course of such commerce, to lease or make a sale or contract for sale of goods . . . or other commodities, whether patented or unpatented, for use, consumption, or resale within the United States or any Territory thereof or the District of Columbia . . . or fix a price charged therefor, or discount from, or rebate upon, such price, on the condition, agreement, or understanding that the lessee or purchaser thereof shall not use or deal in the goods . . . or other commodities of a competitor or competitors of the lessor or seller, where the effect of such lease, sale, or contract for sale or such condition, agreement, or understanding may be to substantially lessen competition or tend to create a monopoly in any line of commerce." On its face, this applies to the use of exclusivity; it has also been interpreted to cover tying as well.[411]

Section 3 exhibits some interesting differences from Section 1. For one thing, Section 3 does not on its face state that an agreement is required—a "condition" is enough—although courts generally appear to require an agreement.[412] For another thing, Section 3 is limited to commodities: thus, exclusivity and tying in services fall

---

[409] *See*, seminally, Thomas G. Krattenmaker & Steven C. Salop, *Anticompetitive Exclusion: Raising Rivals' Costs to Achieve Power over Price*, 96 Yale L.J. 209, 211 (1986).

[410] *See, e.g.*, Genetic Sys. Corp. v. Abbott Labs., 691 F. Supp. 407, 414 (D.D.C. 1988) ("Though few courts have ever addressed the issue, plaintiff has not pointed to any case where a court found a purchaser liable for an exclusive dealing contract, and it appears from the plain language of the statute, the relevant legislative history, and the observations of commentators that Section 3 does not impose liability on purchasers for exclusive dealing contracts. . . . This conclusion, drawn from the clear import of the statutory language, is also consistent with the fundamental antitrust concept that the alleged sins of sellers should not be visited on buyers because of the risk of chilling competition. . . . plaintiff has cited no case where a purchaser has been considered a proper defendant in an exclusive dealing contract case under Section 3 of the Clayton Act or Section 1 of the Sherman Act."); Truck-Lite Co., LLC v. Grote Indus., Inc., No. 18-CV-599, 2021 WL 8322467, at *15 (W.D.N.Y. Sept. 17, 2021) ("The language of [Section 3 of the Clayton Act] defines liability in terms of a person who makes a sale or contracts for sale and nowhere provides for liability of the buyer."); Marion Healthcare, LLC v. S. Illinois Healthcare, No. 12-CV-871, 2015 WL 3466585, at *5 (S.D. Ill. May 29, 2015) (applying the no-liability-for-buyers rule under Section 1 of the Sherman Act even when the buyer was alleged to have aggressively promoted the imposition of exclusivity); *see also* McGuire v. Columbia Broad. Sys., Inc., 399 F.2d 902, 906 (9th Cir. 1968) ("General Foods is not the seller, and consequently no cause of action is created against it.").

[411] *See, e.g.*, IBM Corp. v. United States, 298 U.S. 131, 135 (1936).

[412] Insulate SB, Inc. v. Advanced Finishing Sys., Inc., 797 F.3d 538, 543 (8th Cir. 2015); Roland Mach. Co. v. Dresser Indus., Inc., 749 F.2d 380 (7th Cir. 1984); SolarCity Corp. v. Salt River Project Agric. Improvement, No. CV-15-00374, 2015 WL 6503439, at *10 (D. Ariz. Oct. 27, 2015).

outside Section 3. [413] And, for a third thing, Section 3 provides only for the liability of a seller, not a buyer: thus, it would not apply to a buyer who agreed only to purchase from sellers that did not supply its rivals.[414]

Today, Section 3 is often construed consistently with the Sherman Act,[415] despite the fact that Congressional intent appears to have been to set up a somewhat more demanding standard,[416] and some cases imply that liability is a little easier to establish under Section 3, when that provision applies, than under Section 1.[417] In practice, courts today very seldom make much hay out of the difference between Section 1 and Section 3.

The legal standard against which exclusivity agreements are evaluated has changed over time. Perhaps the seminal pre-modern case is *Standard Stations* in 1949.[418] In *Standard Stations*, the Court held that—although exclusivity commitments offered the possibility of some benefits to competition—illegality could be inferred, at least under Section 3, from the mere fact that exclusivity had been used by the "major competitor" defendant with independent service stations that represented 16% of the retail outlets, and accounted for just 6.7% of all gasoline sales, in a multistate "Western Area."[419] In doing so, the Court held that the relevant arrangements could fairly be described as violating a prohibition on exclusivity that forecloses a "substantial share of the line of commerce affected."[420]

The notion of "substantial foreclosure" has survived and is foundational to the modern law of exclusivity, although the application of it in *Standard Stations* no longer represents the law. Today, "substantial foreclosure" means something like "material impairment of access to relevant input or distribution, sufficient to impose a burden on actual or potential rivals and threaten harm to competition."[421] Courts assess foreclosure in a variety of ways, and in doing so often evaluate the proportion of the input or distribution market that has been denied to rivals.[422]

The leading Supreme Court case on exclusivity agreements, and on the concept of substantial foreclosure, is *Tampa Electric*.[423] That case was decided under Section 3 of the Clayton Act, but has subsequently been accepted as a touchstone for the analysis of exclusivity under the Sherman Act as well. In that case, the Court held that an

---

[413] Sheridan v. Marathon Petroleum Co. LLC, 530 F.3d 590, 592 (7th Cir. 2008) ("The tying arrangement is challenged under section 1 of the Sherman Act rather than section 3 of the Clayton Act because the things alleged to be tied—the franchise and the processing service—are services rather than commodities."); Chelson v. Oregonian Pub. Co., 715 F.2d 1368, 1372 (9th Cir. 1983) (holding that Section 3 applied because "[t]he agreement between the dealers and Oregonian provides that the dealers purchase the newspapers, which are goods, from Oregonian and resell them to readers").

[414] Genetic Sys. Corp. v. Abbott Labs., 691 F. Supp. 407, 414 (D.D.C. 1988).

[415] Sheridan v. Marathon Petroleum Co. LLC, 530 F.3d 590, 592 (7th Cir. 2008) ("Though some old cases say otherwise, the standards for adjudicating tying under the two statutes are now recognized to be the same."); Roland Machinery Co. v. Dresser Industries, Inc., 749 F.2d 380, 393 (7th Cir. 1984) (exclusivity now analyzed under the rule of reason under Section 1 and Section 3); *see also* Dos Santos v. Columbus-Cuneo-Cabrini Med. Ctr., 684 F.2d 1346, 1352 n. 11 (7th Cir. 1982) ("*Tampa Electric* is applicable to Sherman Act section 1 cases even though it was decided under section 3 of the Clayton Act[.]").

[416] *See, e.g.*, Standard Oil Co. of California v. United States, 337 U.S. 293, 312 (1949) ("It seems hardly likely that, having with one hand set up an express prohibition against a practice thought to be beyond the reach of the Sherman Act, Congress meant, with the other hand, to reestablish the necessity of meeting the same tests of detriment to the public interest as that Act had been interpreted as requiring.").

[417] *See, e.g.*, CDC Techs., Inc. v. IDEXX Labs., Inc., 186 F.3d 74, 79 (2d Cir. 1999) ("The conclusion that a contract does not violate § 3 of the Clayton Act ordinarily implies the conclusion that the contract does not violate the Sherman Act.") (citation omitted); Barr Labs., Inc. v. Abbott Labs., 978 F.2d 98, 110 (3d Cir. 1992) ("more rigorous standards of section 3 of the Clayton Act"); Twin City Sportservice, Inc. v. Charles O. Finley & Co., 676 F.2d 1291, 1304 n.9 (9th Cir.1982) ("[A] greater showing of anticompetitive effect is required to establish a Sherman Act violation than a section 3 Clayton Act violation in exclusive-dealing cases.").

[418] *See, e.g.*, Standard Oil Co. of California v. United States, 337 U.S. 293 (1949).

[419] Standard Oil Co. of California v. United States, 337 U.S. 293, 295 (1949).

[420] Standard Oil Co. of California v. United States, 337 U.S. 293, 314(1949).

[421] For a thoughtful discussion, *see* Joshua D. Wright & Alexander Krzepicki, *Rethinking Foreclosure Analysis in Antitrust Law: From Standard Stations to Google*, Concurrentialiste (Dec. 17, 2020), https://www.networklawreview.org/wright-krzepicki-foreclosure/.

[422] *See, e.g.*, United States v. Microsoft Corp., 253 F.3d 34, 70 (D.C. Cir. 2001) (en banc) (contract must foreclosure "roughly 40% or 50% share" of the market to violate Section 1). Calculating this share can raise some complexities. *See, e.g.*, Joshua D. Wright, *Moving Beyond Naïve Foreclosure Analysis*, 19 Geo. Mason L. Rev. 1163, 1165 (2012) (proposing "assessing the foreclosure attributable to the defendant's conduct as a result of the business practice at issue by comparing foreclosure under the restraint as observed with a "but-for" analysis of the share of the input market the defendant would occupy in the absence of such an agreement").

[423] Tampa Elec. Co. v. Nashville Coal Co., 365 U.S. 320 (1961). The earlier *Standard Stations* case had emphasized the centrality of the amount of foreclosure resulting from a challenged practice. *Standard Oil Co. of California v. United States*, 337 U.S. 293, 314 (1949) (holding that condemnation under Section 3 of the Clayton Act requires "proof that competition has been foreclosed in a substantial share of the line of commerce affected").

exclusivity agreement could not violate the law when it concerned only a marginal share of the market for coal, an important input in the market for power generation: something more—substantial foreclosure—was required.

Tampa Elec. Co. v. Nashville Coal Co.
365 U.S. 320 (1961)

Justice Clark.

[1] Petitioner Tampa Electric Company is a public utility located in Tampa, Florida. It produces and sells electric energy to a service area, including the city . . . . In 1955 Tampa Electric decided to expand its facilities by the construction of an additional generating plant to be comprised ultimately of six generating units, and to be known as the Francis J. Gannon Station. . . . Accordingly, it contracted with the respondents[, Nashville Coal Co.,] to furnish the expected coal requirements for the units. The agreement, dated May 23, 1955, embraced Tampa Electric's "total requirements of fuel . . . for the operation of its first two units to be installed at the Gannon Station . . . ," for a period of 20 years. The contract further provided that "if during the first 10 years of the term . . . the Buyer constructs additional units (at Gannon) in which coal is used as the fuel, it shall give the Seller notice thereof two years prior to the completion of such unit or units and upon completion of same the fuel requirements thereof shall be added to this contract." . . . .

[2] In April 1957, soon before the first coal was actually to be delivered and after Tampa Electric, in order to equip its first two Gannon units for the use of coal, had expended some $3,000,000 more than the cost of constructing oil-burning units, and after respondents had expended approximately $7,500,000 readying themselves to perform the contract, the latter advised petitioner that the contract was illegal under the antitrust laws, would therefore not be performed, and no coal would be delivered. This turn of events required Tampa Electric to look elsewhere for its coal requirements. . . . .

[3] The record indicates that the total consumption of coal in peninsular Florida, as of 1958, aside from Gannon Station, was approximately 700,000 tons annually. It further shows that there were some 700 coal suppliers in the producing area where respondents operated, and that Tampa Electric's anticipated maximum requirements at Gannon Station, i.e., 2,250 tons annually, would approximate 1% of the total coal of the same type produced and marketed from respondents' producing area.

[4] Petitioner brought this suit in the District Court . . . for a declaration that its contract with respondents was valid, and for enforcement according to its terms. In addition to its Clayton Act defense, respondents contended that the contract violated both ss 1 and 2 of the Sherman Act which, it claimed, likewise precluded its enforcement. [. . .]

[5] In practical application, even though a contract is found to be an exclusive-dealing arrangement, it does not violate the section unless the court believes it probable that performance of the contract will foreclose competition in a substantial share of the line of commerce affected. Following the guidelines of earlier decisions, certain considerations must be taken. First, the line of commerce, i.e., the type of goods, wares, or merchandise, etc., involved must be determined, where it is in controversy, on the basis of the facts peculiar to the case. Second, the area of effective competition in the known line of commerce must be charted by careful selection of the market area in which the seller operates, and to which the purchaser can practically turn for supplies. In short, the threatened foreclosure of competition must be in relation to the market affected. [. . .]

[6] Third, and last, the competition foreclosed by the contract must be found to constitute a substantial share of the relevant market. That is to say, the opportunities for other traders to enter into or remain in that market must be significantly limited as was pointed out in *Standard Oil Co. v. United States*[, 337 U.S. 293 (1949)]. There the impact of the requirements contracts was studied in the setting of the large number of gasoline stations—5,937 or 16% of the retail outlets in the relevant market—and the large number of contracts, over 8,000, together with the great volume of products involved. This combination dictated a finding that Standard's use of the contracts created just such a potential clog on competition as it was the purpose of s 3 [of the Clayton Act] to remove where, as there, the affected proportion of retail sales was substantial. . . . [I]n *United States v. Columbia Steel Co.*[, 334 U.S. 495

(1948)], substantiality was judged on a comparative basis, *i.e.*, Consolidated's use of rolled steel was "a small part" when weighed against the total volume of that product in the relevant market.

[7] To determine substantiality in a given case, it is necessary to weigh the probable effect of the contract on the relevant area of effective competition, taking into account the relative strength of the parties, the proportionate volume of commerce involved in relation to the total volume of commerce in the relevant market area, and the probable immediate and future effects which pre-emption of that share of the market might have on effective competition therein. It follows that a mere showing that the contract itself involves a substantial number of dollars is ordinarily of little consequence. [. . .]

[8] It is urged that the present contract pre-empts competition to the extent of purchases worth perhaps $128,000,000, and that this is, of course, not insignificant or insubstantial. While $128,000,000 is a considerable sum of money, even in these days, the dollar volume, by itself, is not the test, as we have already pointed out.

[9] The remaining determination, therefore, is whether the pre-emption of competition to the extent of the tonnage involved tends to substantially foreclose competition in the relevant coal market. We think not. That market sees an annual trade in excess of 250,000,000 tons of coal and over a billion dollars—multiplied by 20 years it runs into astronomical figures. There is here neither a seller with a dominant position in the market . . . ; nor myriad outlets with substantial sales volume, coupled with an industry-wide practice of relying upon exclusive contracts . . .; nor a plainly restrictive tying arrangement . . . . On the contrary, we seem to have only that type of contract which may well be of economic advantage to buyers as well as to sellers. In the case of the buyer it may assure supply, while on the part of the seller it may make possible the substantial reduction of selling expenses, give protection against price fluctuations, and offer the possibility of a predictable market. The 20-year period of the contract is singled out as the principal vice, but at least in the case of public utilities the assurance of a steady and ample supply of fuel is necessary in the public interest. Otherwise consumers are left unprotected against service failures owing to shutdowns; and increasingly unjustified costs might result in more burdensome rate structures eventually to be reflected in the consumer's bill. The compelling validity of such considerations has been recognized fully in the natural gas public utility field. This is not to say that utilities are immunized from Clayton Act proscriptions, but merely that, in judging the term of a requirements contract in relation to the substantiality of the foreclosure of competition, particularized considerations of the parties' operations are not irrelevant. In weighing the various factors, we have decided that in the competitive bituminous coal marketing area involved here the contract sued upon does not tend to foreclose a substantial volume of competition.

[10] We need not discuss the respondents' further contention that the contract also violates s 1 and s 2 of the Sherman Act, for if it does not fall within the broader proscription of s 3 of the Clayton Act it follows that it is not forbidden by those of the former.

Incentivizing, Rather than Strictly Requiring, Exclusivity: The Surescripts Litigation

FTC v. Surescripts, LLC, 424 F. Supp. 3d 92 (D.D.C. 2020)

In an exclusivity case, as we have noted, the source of the harm to competition is usually the impairment ("foreclosure") of rivals' access to inputs or distribution, and the resulting reduction in their ability to exert competitive discipline on a market participant with market or monopoly power.[424] Sometimes the relevant impairment may involve a formal contractual commitment that leaves suppliers or distributors "locked in" for a long period of time. But harm to competition can arise without anything of the kind (and even with no contract at all, as in the case of unilateral conditional-dealing policies, as we will see in Chapter VII).[425] Importantly, an equivalent effect—"de facto exclusivity"—can often be created by simply offering preferential terms, such as low prices, as an incentive for exclusive trading. And, just as with traditional exclusivity, this can be structured either as an agreement between the parties (*e.g.*, a contract providing for a sale price X for a period in which the trading partner deals exclusively with the defendant and a, higher, sale price Y for during other periods) or simply from a

---

[424] *See supra* note 409 and accompanying text.

[425] *See, e.g.*, Lorain Journal Co. v. United States, 342 U.S. 143 (1951).

unilateral conditional-dealing policy of offering better terms to partners that do not deal with rivals.[426] (Of course, the latter would be vulnerable to challenge under Section 2 but not Section 1.)

The FTC's lawsuit against the e-prescribing platform Surescripts illustrates de facto exclusivity in action. Surescripts operated a market-leading platform that connected insurers to healthcare providers, and healthcare providers to pharmacies. The FTC's enforcement action—which was brought under Section 2, rather than Section 1, although the distinction is immaterial for present purposes—involved a challenge to the use of contractual "loyalty pricing" by Surescripts. In particular, the FTC's complaint alleged that "[b]eginning in mid-2009, Surescripts devised a scheme to include 'loyalty' provisions in contracts with customers on both sides of the routing and eligibility markets, which conditioned discounts or payments on actual or de facto exclusivity [with Surescripts]." In order to qualify for a loyalty discount under this scheme, the FTC alleged, "a customer must be exclusive to Surescripts," and "[t]o be considered exclusive, Surescripts requires that a pharmacy and PTV customer route 100% of its transactions through and only through the Surescripts network." The FTC alleged that Surescripts' executives "repeatedly admitted that Surescripts's web of exclusive contracts quashed any competitive threat."

Surescripts moved to dismiss the complaint. Among other things, it emphasized that its loyalty programs "are entirely optional and thus do not necessarily constitute exclusive contracts." But Judge Bates of the U.S. District Court for the District of Columbia was not persuaded: "[A] contract need not contain specific agreements not to use the services of a competitor as long as the practical effect is to prevent such use. The FTC alleges that the threat of increased prices had the practical effect of preventing customers from working with other e-prescribing platforms, since doing so would trigger the massive penalty provisions in their contracts with Surescripts and cost routing and eligibility customers millions of dollars through increased prices . . . [T]he test of whether a monopolist forecloses competition is not total foreclosure, but whether the challenged practices bar a substantial number of rivals or severely restrict the market's ambit. Here, the government has pleaded facts demonstrating such substantial foreclosure." In other words, it was enough that the agreements strongly *incentivized* exclusivity, even if they did not literally require it.

Surescripts tried a different tack, arguing that "the FTC failed to plead sufficient facts showing that Surescripts's business practices foreclosed market competition to a 'substantial' degree," on the basis that "exclusive dealing is illegal only if the arrangement 'substantially' weakens competition, and . . . its contracts, even if facially exclusive, were easily terminable, of short duration, and therefore presumptively lawful." But this, too, failed to move the court. "Even if the contracts were short term and easily terminable," the court pointed out, "the FTC argues that their exclusive terms, when combined with the nature of the two relevant markets and Surescripts's dominant monopoly position, had the effect of foreclosing large parts of both markets and harming competition." In so doing, the court implicitly underscored the importance of economic substance, rather than legal form: even short-term, easily-terminated agreements can strongly incentivize exclusivity and harm competition.

Despite the potential for competitive harm under particular circumstances, exclusivity agreements are fairly common in the economy, and are often used by businesses that lack market or monopoly power.[427] As long ago as *Standard Stations* (1949) the Court acknowledged the possible benefits of exclusive agreements:

> In the case of the buyer, they may assure supply, afford protection against rises in price, enable long-term planning on the basis of known costs, and obviate the expense and risk of storage in the quantity necessary for a commodity having a fluctuating demand. From the seller's point of view, requirements contracts may make possible the substantial reduction of selling expenses, give protection against price fluctuations, and—of particular advantage to a newcomer to the

---

[426] *See, e.g.*, Roland Machinery Co. v. Dresser Industries, Inc., 749 F.2d 380 (7th Cir. 1984) ("One mind is not enough for a meeting of minds. The fact that Dresser was hostile to dealers who would not live and die by its product . . . and acted on its hostility by canceling a dealer who did the thing to which it was hostile, does not establish an agreement, but if anything the opposite: a failure to agree on a point critical to one of the parties.").

[427] Francine Lafontaine & Margaret Slade, *Exclusive Contracts and Vertical Restraints: Empirical Evidence and Public Policy* in Paolo Buccirossi (ed.), HANDBOOK OF ANTITRUST ECONOMICS (2008) 392 ("In most western economies, a large fraction of retail sales through independent retailers is subject to some form of exclusive–dealing clauses. For example, in the U.S., that fraction is over one third.").

field to whom it is important to know what capital expenditures are justified—offer the possibility of a predictable market.[428]

Indeed, exclusive agreements may play a critical role in making certain kinds of investment and cooperation possible, as the following extracts point out.

In *Roland Machinery*, the plaintiff, Roland, was a distributor of construction equipment that was cut off by a manufacturer, Dresser, when it started distributing a second line of equipment manufactured by Dresser's competitor, Komatsu. Roland sued under Section 3 of the Clayton Act, alleging that Dresser's termination was pursuant to an unlawful implicit exclusive agreement between Dresser and Roland. The trial court below was persuaded to grant a preliminary injunction which prevented Dresser from cutting Roland off during the litigation. On appeal, the Seventh Circuit was much less enthusiastic. In the article extract that follows the extract from *Roland Machinery*, Benjamin Klein and Andres Lerner set out some circumstances under which exclusivity may play a role in protecting against free riding.

Roland Mach. Co. v. Dresser Indus., Inc.
749 F.2d 380 (7th Cir. 1984)

Judge Posner.

[1] Roland Machinery Company, a substantial dealer . . . in construction equipment and related items, serving a 45-county area in central Illinois, was for many years the area's exclusive distributor of International Harvester's line of construction equipment. International Harvester got into serious financial trouble and in 1982 sold its construction-equipment division to Dresser Industries. Dresser promptly signed a dealership agreement with Roland. The agreement provided that it could be terminated by either party, without cause, on 90 days' notice. It did not contain an exclusive-dealing clause (that is, a clause forbidding the dealer to sell any competing manufacturer's construction equipment). Eight months after signing the agreement Roland signed a similar agreement with Komatsu, a Japanese manufacturer of construction equipment. Several months after discovering that Roland had done this, Dresser gave notice that it would exercise its contract right to terminate its dealership agreement with Roland without cause. Roland brought this suit shortly before the end of the 90-day notice period, charging that Dresser had violated section 3 of the Clayton Act and other provisions of federal and state law. The district judge granted Roland a preliminary injunction based solely on the section 3 charges, and Dresser has appealed . . . . None of Roland's other charges is before us on this appeal.

[2] At the hearing on Roland's motion for preliminary injunction, Dresser presented evidence that it had cut off Roland because it was afraid that Roland intended to phase out the Dresser line and become an exclusive Komatsu dealer, and because it believed that as long as Roland (a well-established firm) remained a Dresser dealer, no other dealer in the area would be willing to handle Dresser equipment, as this would mean competing with Roland. The usual practice in the industry is for dealers not to carry competing lines, and Dresser presented evidence that this makes for more aggressive promotion of each line. Roland, however, presented evidence that it had no intention of phasing out Dresser equipment, that it was terminated because the dealership contract contained what Roland at argument called a "secret" term requiring Roland to deal exclusively in Dresser equipment, and that the sudden termination would bankrupt it or at least cause it serious loss. But it seems that only about 50 percent of Roland's revenues are derived directly or indirectly from Dresser equipment, and only about 10 percent from selling new Dresser equipment (the other 40 percent coming from renting and servicing equipment, and from selling parts); and Dresser argues that Roland could survive simply by promoting Komatsu equipment aggressively—which it intended to do anyway. [. . .]

[3] On the probable merits of Roland's section 3 claim, the judge found that while Dresser's contract with Roland contained no exclusive-dealing requirement, Roland has adequately shown that an implied exclusive dealing arrangement existed between itself and Dresser. [. . .]

---

[428] Standard Oil Co. of California v. United States, 337 U.S. 293, 306–07 (1949).

[4] In order to prevail on its section 3 claim, Roland will have to show both that there was an agreement, though not necessarily an explicit agreement, between it and Dresser that it not carry a line of construction equipment competitive with Dresser's, and that the agreement was likely to have a substantial though not necessarily an immediate anticompetitive effect. Regarding the first of these required showings, the record of the preliminary-injunction proceeding contains no evidence that either Roland or any other Dresser dealer agreed with Dresser not to carry a competing manufacturer's line. Nothing in the dealership agreement even hints at a requirement of exclusive dealing, and the fact that after signing the agreement with Dresser, Roland applied for a Komatsu dealership is evidence that Roland itself did not think it had made an implied commitment to exclusive dealing. True, Dresser prefers exclusive dealers—so much so as to be willing to terminate its only dealer in a large marketing area. The district judge believed that evidence of this preference, coupled with the absence of any reason for Dresser's having terminated Roland other than Roland's having taken on an additional line of construction equipment, established a prima facie case of agreement. But an agreement requires a meeting of minds, and there is no evidence that Roland ever thought itself bound to carry only the Dresser line. Indeed, at argument Roland disclaimed any knowledge of what it describes as the implied exclusive-dealing term in the contract; it called it a "secret" term, echoing the district judge's description of exclusive dealing as something "in the mind of" Dresser. One mind is not enough for a meeting of minds. The fact that Dresser was hostile to dealers who would not live and die by its product (as the district judge put it), and acted on its hostility by canceling a dealer who did the thing to which it was hostile, does not establish an agreement, but if anything the opposite: a failure to agree on a point critical to one of the parties.

[5] Actually, it is not important whether Dresser's antipathy to nonexclusive dealing was secret. Assume that Dresser made clear to Roland and its other dealers that it wanted only exclusive dealers and would exercise its contract right to terminate, immediately and without cause, any dealer who took on a competing line. The mere announcement of such a policy, and the carrying out of it by canceling Roland or any other noncomplying dealer, would not establish an agreement. . . .

[6] Dresser's preference for exclusive dealers, its efforts to find out whether its dealers were exclusive dealers, and its terminating Roland when it found out that Roland no longer was its exclusive dealer do not support an inference both that the distributor communicated its acquiescence or agreement to exclusive dealing and that this was sought by the manufacturer. But even if Roland can prove at trial that there was an exclusive-dealing agreement, it will have grave difficulty—we infer from this record—in proving that the agreement is anticompetitive. The objection to exclusive-dealing agreements is that they deny outlets to a competitor during the term of the agreement. At one time it was thought that this effect alone would condemn exclusive-dealing agreements under section 3 of the Clayton Act, provided that the agreements covered a large fraction of the market. Although the Supreme Court has not decided an exclusive-dealing case in many years, it now appears most unlikely that such agreements, whether challenged under section 3 of the Clayton Act or section 1 of the Sherman Act, will be judged by the simple and strict test of [earlier law]. They will be judged under the Rule of Reason, and thus condemned only if found to restrain trade unreasonably.

[7] The exclusion of competitors is cause for antitrust concern only if it impairs the health of the competitive process itself. Hence a plaintiff must prove two things to show that an exclusive-dealing agreement is unreasonable. First, he must prove that it is likely to keep at least one significant competitor of the defendant from doing business in a relevant market. If there is no exclusion of a significant competitor, the agreement cannot possibly harm competition. Second, he must prove that the probable (not certain) effect of the exclusion will be to raise prices above (and therefore reduce output below) the competitive level, or otherwise injure competition; he must show in other words that the anticompetitive effects (if any) of the exclusion outweigh any benefits to competition from it.

[8] Roland has as yet made very little effort to establish either of these two things. On the present record it appears that Komatsu cannot be kept out of the central Illinois market even if every manufacturer of construction equipment prefers exclusive dealers and will cancel any dealer who switches to the Komatsu line. Komatsu is the second largest manufacturer of construction equipment in the world. Its total sales of such equipment are four times as great as Dresser's. Already it is a major factor in the U.S. construction-equipment market; in some items it outsells Dresser. The nationwide practice of exclusive dealing has not kept Komatsu from becoming a major

factor in the U.S. market, apparently in a short period of time. The reason is evident. Since dealership agreements in this industry are terminable by either party on short notice, Komatsu, to obtain its own exclusive dealer in some area, has only to offer a better deal to some other manufacturer's dealer in the area. It need not fear being sued for interference with contract; Roland would not be breaking its contract with Dresser if it gave Dresser the heave-ho, provided it gave 90 days' notice. Maybe if Roland had known that it would be cut off by Dresser as soon as it was, it would have demanded some guarantees from Komatsu to tide it over the period of transition when Komatsu was not yet as well established a name in central Illinois as Dresser (though Dresser itself was in a sense new to the market); and probably Komatsu would have given Roland these guarantees to get a foothold in the central Illinois market. The likeliest consequence of our dissolving the preliminary injunction would be to accelerate Komatsu's efforts to promote its brand through the Roland dealership.

[9] Admittedly this analysis may exaggerate the smoothness with which the competitive process operates. Knowing that it cannot move gradually into central Illinois by persuading dealers to carry its line as a second line, Komatsu may expand more slowly than it would otherwise have done, and at somewhat higher cost. And since the national market in construction equipment appears to be highly concentrated (although the record is scanty in this regard, particularly in its omission of any data on foreign sales, which may conceivably be part of the U.S. market, properly defined), any impediments to new competition may harm consumers by keeping prices at noncompetitive levels—though whether the industry at present is or is not highly competitive must be a matter of conjecture on this record. But with all this conceded we still cannot agree that Roland has shown a substantial anticompetitive effect, actual or potential, from the alleged exclusive-dealing agreement, when we reflect on Komatsu's strength and on the fact that neither Dresser nor, it appears, any other manufacturer has long-term exclusive-dealing contracts. Exclusive-dealing contracts terminable in less than a year are presumptively lawful under section 3. This one was terminable in 90 days. Finally, Komatsu undoubtedly has the resources to establish its own dealership in central Illinois, if it cannot lure away someone else's dealer despite the lack of long-term contracts binding dealers to their existing suppliers.

[10] The calculus of competitive effect must . . . include some consideration of the possible competitive benefits of exclusive dealing in this industry. Competition is the allocation of resources in which economic welfare (consumer welfare, to oversimplify slightly) is maximized; it is not rivalry per se, or a particular form of rivalry, or some minimum number of competitors. If, as Dresser argues, exclusive dealing leads dealers to promote each manufacturer's brand more vigorously than would be the case under nonexclusive dealing, the quality-adjusted price to the consumer (where quality includes the information and other services that dealers render to their customers) may be lower with exclusive dealing than without, even though a collateral effect of exclusive dealing is to slow the pace at which new brands, such as Komatsu, are introduced. The evidence on this point is slim. But it is at least plausible that Dresser, having if we may judge from its operation in central Illinois only one dealer in a large territory, would want that dealer to devote his efforts entirely to selling Dresser's brand. A dealer who expresses his willingness to carry only one manufacturer's brand of a particular product indicates his commitment to pushing that brand; he doesn't have divided loyalties. If the dealer carries several brands, his stake in the success of each is reduced. Suppose, though there is contrary evidence in the record, that Roland intended to promote Dresser and Komatsu products with equal vigor. It is still the case that if Roland failed to promote Dresser vigorously, it would have Komatsu to fall back on—but Dresser might suffer a drastic decline in the central Illinois market, all of its eggs being in the Roland basket. Exclusive dealing may also enable a manufacturer to prevent dealers from taking a free ride on his efforts (for example, efforts in the form of national advertising) to promote his brand. The dealer who carried competing brands as well might switch customers to a lower-priced substitute on which he got a higher margin, thus defeating the manufacturer's effort to recover the costs of his promotional expenditures by charging the dealer a higher price.

[11] Therefore, even if, in signing on with Komatsu, Roland did not intend to discontinue its sales of the Dresser line eventually and in the meantime to begin phasing Dresser out, Dresser still has a plausible argument that an exclusive dealer would promote its line more effectively than a nonexclusive dealer, and by doing so would increase competition in the market for construction equipment. The argument is no more than plausible; it is supported by very little evidence; it may be wrong. But when we consider how tenuous is the evidence that exclusive dealing in this market will exclude or even significantly retard Komatsu—how tenuous even is the inference that there was

an exclusive-dealing agreement—even weak evidence of competitive gains from exclusive dealing must reinforce our conclusion that Roland has failed to show that it is more likely than not to prevail at the trial on the merits.

[12] It should go without saying that although we have concluded that the district judge should not have granted Roland's motion for a preliminary injunction, our discussion of the probable merits of Roland's antitrust claim is tentative. We do not exclude the possibility that on the fuller record made in the trial on the merits Roland will succeed in establishing its claim.

***

Benjamin Klein & Andres V. Lerner, The Expanded Economics of Free-Riding: How Exclusive Dealing Prevents Free-Riding and Creates Undivided Loyalty
74 Antitrust L.J. 473 (2007)

Dealers often have an insufficient incentive to supply the quantity of brand-specific promotion that maximizes manufacturer profitability because they earn less profit than the manufacturer on their promotional efforts. This is because the manufacturer's profit margin on the incremental sales induced by dealer promotion often is significantly greater than the dealer's incremental profit margin and because the manufacturer's quantity increase from brand-specific dealer promotion is significantly greater than the dealer's quantity increase. These differential quantity effects are a consequence of the fact that brand-specific dealer promotion primarily shifts consumer purchases to the promoted brand from other brands without causing consumers to shift their purchases between dealers. In these circumstances dealers will find it in their independent economic interests to supply less brand-specific promotion than is desired by a manufacturer, creating an incentive for manufacturers to compensate dealers for providing increased promotion of their products. [. . .]

Because dealers are supplying more brand-specific promotion under these arrangements than they would otherwise independently find profitable to supply, dealers can increase their short-run profits (before manufacturer detection and termination) by not providing the increased promotion they have been paid to supply. Dealers may profit in three economically distinct ways, each of which can usefully be described as dealer free-riding on the manufacturer because in all three cases dealers are taking advantage of the way in which the manufacturer is compensating dealers for increased promotion. The first type of dealer free-riding, which is the focus of standard economic and antitrust analysis of exclusive dealing, involves a dealer taking advantage of manufacturer-provided promotional investments, such as dealer sales training or display fixtures. These investments are supplied to dealers free of charge as a way for the manufacturer to subsidize brand-specific dealer promotion. Free-riding dealers then use these investments to sell alternative products on which they can earn greater profit. This form of dealer free-riding is clearly prevented with exclusive dealing since the dealer is prohibited from selling alternative products. Although this is a valid economic rationale for exclusive dealing, we demonstrate that this is not the only or most common form of free-riding that may be mitigated by exclusive dealing.

Whether or not a manufacturer supplies dealers with investments that the dealers can use to sell rival products, a second type of potential dealer free-riding exists when manufacturers pay dealers for supplying increased promotion. Dealers then have an economic incentive to use their promotional efforts purchased by the manufacturer to switch consumers to other products upon which they can earn greater profit. This dealer free-riding problem is shown to exist because dealer promotion compensation arrangements, such as exclusive territories, often pay dealers as a function of all their sales, not solely the incremental sales induced by the additional dealer promotion the manufacturer has purchased. Therefore, when a dealer uses its extra promotional efforts to sell another brand, it continues to receive most of the manufacturer's compensation for providing additional promotion while not promoting the manufacturer's products. Exclusive dealing can be used to prevent this second type of free-riding in the same way it prevents the first type of free-riding, by preventing dealers from using their promotional efforts that have been paid for by the manufacturer to sell alternative brands.

. . . [A] third form of potential dealer free-riding exists which may be mitigated by exclusive dealing. Rather than a dealer using manufacturer-supplied promotional investments or manufacturer paid-for dealer promotional efforts to promote the sale of other brands, a dealer may free-ride on the manufacturer merely by failing to supply the level of promotion for which the manufacturer has paid. Since dealers often are compensated for supplying additional promotion on the basis of all their sales, including sales the dealer would make even if it did not provide the additional promotional efforts it has been paid for, dealers have an incentive not to supply the additional promotion and continue to collect most of the manufacturer's compensation. Exclusive dealing is shown to mitigate this third type of free-riding by creating dealers with "undivided loyalty" that have an increased independent economic incentive to more actively promote the manufacturer's products. [. . .]

The expanded economic analysis of exclusive dealing presented in this article does not mean that exclusive dealing is always benign. In particular, the additional procompetitive efficiencies of exclusive dealing we describe may be outweighed in specific cases by potential anticompetitive effects of the exclusive dealing contract in foreclosing rivals. What it does mean, however, is that, because of the expanded legitimate procompetitive justifications that may be offered for exclusive dealing, balancing procompetitive efficiencies against potential anticompetitive effects will be required in many more exclusive dealing cases than previously believed.

* * *

NOTES

1) Who sued whom in *Tampa Electric* and why? What was the story of harm from exclusivity at issue? What do you think motivated the suit?

2) In appropriate circumstances, exclusive agreements can be challenged under Section 1 of the Sherman Act, Section 2 of the Sherman Act, and Section 3 of the Clayton Act. These three provisions have different language, histories, and purposes. When they apply to a common practice (like an exclusivity agreement obtained by a monopolist pertaining to the sale of a commodity), should the same analytical standard be applied across all three provisions?

3) The court in *Surescripts* said that "a contract need not contain specific agreements not to use the services of a competitor as long as the practical effect is to prevent such use." Suppose that a market participant with market power placed such a large order with an input supplier that, in practice, fulfilling the order would mean saying no to the participant's rivals. Under what circumstances, if any, should that order be analyzed as an exclusivity agreement? Would it affect your answer if:

   a. the business with market power genuinely needed the full amount of the order and had no idea whether it would impair the supplier's ability to sell to rivals?

   b. the business with market power did not strictly need the full amount of the order, but genuinely thought it prudent to build up a surplus, and also knew that the order would make it impossible to fully serve rivals?

   c. the business with market power had no real clue how much it needed, or what the impact would be on rivals, but placed the large order generally hoping that it would have the result of ensuring adequate supply for itself and insufficient supply for rivals?

4) Many businesses reward loyal customers with better terms. Suppose that a client asks you for general guidance on when a loyalty discount violates the antitrust laws. What would you say?

5) Should "coercion" be relevant to the assessment of the legality of an exclusive deal? If so, on what definition, and why?[429]

6) What does "free riding" mean in antitrust analysis, in your own words? Could "prevention of free riding" cover all occasions on which a monopolist prevents a competitor from doing something that would reduce the profitability of the monopoly?

7) In *Roland Machinery* Judge Posner said that, for an exclusivity agreement to be illegal, it must "keep at least one significant competitor of the defendant from doing business in a relevant market." Is that formulation an accurate statement of the "substantial foreclosure" test, or is it substantially more demanding? Can you imagine circumstances in which an agreement could harmfully and substantially foreclose competition without driving a rival out of the market?

---

[429] *See generally, e.g.,* Jean Wegmen Burns, *The New Role of Coercion in Antitrust*, 60 Fordham L. Rev. 379 (1991); Mark R. Patterson, *Coercion, Deception, and Other Demand-Increasing Practices in Antitrust Law*, 66 Antitrust L.J. 1 (1997).

E. Tying

Tying involves selling a product or service that customers desire (the "tying" product or service) only on the condition that the customers *also* purchase another product or service (the "tied" product or service). The core competitive concern in a tying case is that market power in the market for the tying product will be used to suppress demand for rivals' products in the tied market, and that competitive harm may result (*e.g.*, because tied-market rivals are unable to maintain viable scale).

It may immediately occur to you that there are many reasons why suppliers, as well as their trading partners, might find it efficient to sell and buy products and services together. Consumers often want to buy complete products—cars, computers, board games, pizzas, and so on—rather than to source and assemble individual components themselves: and suppliers very often would not find it commercially reasonable to sell individual components instead of integrated products. Indeed, it is central to the value proposition of products like smartphones and operating systems that they provide a broad array of functionalities to consumers right "out of the box," without requiring consumers to independently research and obtain specific solutions for a variety of needs. It is certainly a good thing, overall, that smartphone manufacturers can integrate a telephone, a digital camera, email software, and other products and services and supply them to consumers together. Any sensible tying law must, therefore, take account of these and similar benefits.

Like exclusivity, tying cases can often be brought under Section 1 or under Section 2. They may also be brought under Section 3 of the Clayton Act, as the Supreme Court has held.[430] And just as with exclusivity, it may be necessary to distinguish between the competitive effects of a tying agreement (for example, a contract in which the customer commits to purchase the tied product only from the seller) and the effects of a seller's unilateral conditional-dealing policy (for example, a seller's unilateral policy of refusing to supply the tying product or service to anyone who buys the tied product or service from a rival).

The law of tying under Section 1 is a little peculiar. Among other things, as a matter of black-letter law, tying can be *per se* illegal. Indeed, this was the basic rule for many years.[431] In 1949 the Supreme Court put its name to the proposition that "tying arrangements service hardly any purpose beyond the suppression of competition,"[432] and in 1969 the Court condemned under the *per se* rule a home-builder that was offering credit on favorable terms to those who bought its houses.[433]

But for many decades courts have realized that a *per se* rule against tying—taken seriously and applied regardless of whether competitive harm was likely, and regardless of whether the tie would generate procompetitive benefits—would make very little economic, legal, or practical sense. As a result, today, courts vacillate somewhat between applying a very strained version of a *per se* rule, according to which *per se* scrutiny applies if certain preconditions are met, and applying something that amounts to the rule of reason. The usual preconditions for *per se* condemnation include: (1) the existence of economically separate products or services; (2) market power in the tying product market; (3) actual conditioning; (4) evidence—required by some, but not all, lower courts[434]—of

---

[430] *See* Int'l Bus. Machines Corp. v. United States, 298 U.S. 131, 135 (1936).

[431] Int'l Salt Co. v. United States, 332 U.S. 392, 396 (1947) (analyzing tying clause and stating that "it is unreasonable, per se, to foreclose competitors from any substantial market,"), *abrogated by* Illinois Tool Works Inc. v. Indep. Ink, Inc., 547 U.S. 28 (2006).

[432] Standard Oil Co. of California v. United States, 337 U.S. 293, 305 (1949). *See also* Brown Shoe Co. v. United States, 370 U.S. 294, 330 (1962) (noting that tying is "inherently anticompetitive").

[433] Fortner Enterprises, Inc. v. U.S. Steel Corp., 394 U.S. 495, 498 (1969) ("Our cases have made clear that, at least when certain prerequisites are met, arrangements of this kind are illegal in and of themselves, and no specific showing of unreasonable competitive effect is required").

[434] *Compare, e.g.*, In re Cox Enterprises, Inc., 871 F.3d 1093, 1107 (10th Cir. 2017) ("[P]laintiffs alleging per se unlawful tying arrangements must do more to meet the foreclosure element than point to a dollar amount. . . . They must show that the alleged tying arrangement had the potential to or actually did injure competition."); *id.* at 1100 ("[E]ven if tying plaintiffs show that a tie affected a substantial dollar volume of sales, they must still show that the tie meets *Jefferson Parish*'s threshold requirements to trigger the per se rule. In other words, the tying arrangement must be the type of tie that could potentially harm competition in the tied-product market. . . . [T]hough the per se rule against tying doesn't require an exhaustive analysis into a tie's anticompetitive effects in the tied product market, the rule can be coherent only if tying is defined by reference to the economic effect of the arrangement."); Kaufman v. Time Warner, 836 F.3d 137, 141 (2d Cir. 2016) (requiring "anticompetitive effects in the tied market"); Wells Real Est., Inc. v. Greater Lowell Bd. of Realtors, 850 F.2d 803, 815 & n.11 (1st Cir. 1988) ("The tying claim must fail absent

actual or potential harm to competition in the tied product market (making this, at least in some courts, a "*per se*" standard that approaches the rule of reason); and (5) the existence of a "not insubstantial" volume of interstate commerce affected by the tie.[435]

In practice, courts also often find a way to consider procompetitive benefits of ties, whether explicitly or implicitly: in the *Microsoft* case, for example, the D.C. Circuit simply held that "the rule of reason, rather than per se analysis, should govern the legality of tying arrangements involving platform software products," given the novelty of software markets and the fact that "simplistic application of per se tying rules carries a serious risk of harm."[436] The *Microsoft* court explained its thinking in the following terms, when analyzing the integration of an internet browser into an operating system and the allegation that this constituted an unlawful "technological tie":

> There is no doubt that it is far too late in the history of our antitrust jurisprudence to question the proposition that *certain* tying arrangements pose an unacceptable risk of stifling competition and therefore are unreasonable per se. But there are strong reasons to doubt that the integration of additional software functionality into [a computer operating system] falls among these arrangements. Applying *per se* analysis to such an amalgamation creates undue risks of error and of deterring welfare-enhancing innovation.
>
> The Supreme Court has warned that it is only after considerable experience with certain business relationships that courts classify them as per se violations. Yet the sort of tying arrangement attacked here is unlike any the Supreme Court has considered. . . .
>
> In none of these cases was the tied good physically and technologically integrated with the tying good. Nor did the defendants ever argue that their tie improved the value of the tying product to users and to makers of complementary goods. In those cases where the defendant claimed that use of the tied good made the tying good more valuable to users, the Court ruled that the same result could be achieved via quality standards for substitutes of the tied good. Here Microsoft argues that [Internet Explorer ("IE")] and [the Windows operating system] are an integrated physical product and that the bundling of IE [technologies] with Windows makes the latter a better applications platform for third-party software. It is unclear how the benefits from IE [technologies] could be achieved by quality standards for different browser manufacturers. We do not pass judgment on Microsoft's claims regarding the benefits from integration of its [technologies]. We merely note that these and other novel, purported efficiencies suggest that judicial experience provides little basis for believing that, because of their pernicious effect on competition and lack of any redeeming virtue, a software firm's decisions to sell multiple functionalities as a package should be conclusively presumed to be unreasonable and therefore illegal without elaborate inquiry as to the precise harm they have caused or the business excuse for their use.[437]

---

any proof of anti-competitive effects in the market for the tied product" and stating: "This is not to say that a plaintiff necessarily must prove the actual scope of anti-competitive effects in the market—the per se rule eliminates such a requirement. But the plaintiff must make some minimal showing of real or potential foreclosed commerce caused by the tie, if only as a matter of practical inferential common sense."); Amey, Inc. v. Gulf Abstract & Title, Inc., 758 F.2d 1486, 1503 (11th Cir. 1985) (requiring "anticompetitive effects in the tied market") *with* Suture Express, Inc. v. Owens & Minor Distribution, Inc., 851 F.3d 1029, 1037 (10th Cir. 2017) ("The four elements of a per se tying violation are: (1) two separate products are involved; (2) the sale or agreement to sell one product is conditioned on the purchase of the other; (3) the seller has sufficient economic power in the tying product market to enable it to restrain trade in the tied product market; and (4) a "not insubstantial" amount of interstate commerce in the tied product is affected."). *See also* Reifert v. S. Cent. Wisconsin MLS Corp., 450 F.3d 312, 317 (7th Cir. 2006) (stating the elements of a *per se* claim without listing anticompetitive effects in the tied market, but quoting with approval language from *Wells Real Estate* including "The tying claim must fail absent any proof of anti-competitive effects in the market for the tied product.").

[435] *See, e.g.*, Jefferson Parish Hosp. Dist. No 2 v. Hyde, 466 U.S. 2, 9–18 (1984); In re: Cox Enterprises, Inc., 871 F.3d 1093, 1098 (10th Cir. 2017); Wells Real Est., Inc. v. Greater Lowell Bd. of Realtors, 850 F.2d 803, 815 (1st Cir. 1988); Coniglio v. Highwood Servs., Inc., 495 F.2d 1286, 1291 (2d Cir. 1974); Driskill v. Dallas Cowboys Football Club, Inc., 498 F.2d 321, 323 (5th Cir. 1974). *See also* Illinois Tool Works Inc. v. Independent Ink, Inc., 547 U.S. 28, 46 (2006) (market power).

[436] United States v. Microsoft Corp., 253 F.3d 34, 84 (D.C. Cir. 2001) (en banc).

[437] *See* United States v. Microsoft Corp., 253 F.3d 34, 90–91 (D.C. Cir. 2001) (en banc). *See also id.* at 95 ("Because [Microsoft's argument about the benefits of technological tying] applies with distinct force when the tying product is platform software, we have no present basis for finding the per se rule inapplicable to software markets generally. Nor should we be interpreted as setting a precedent for switching to the rule of reason every time a court identifies an efficiency justification for a tying arrangement. Our reading of the record suggests merely that integration of new functionality into platform software is a common practice and that wooden application of *per se* rules in this litigation may cast a cloud over platform innovation in the market for PCs, network computers and information appliances.").

The Supreme Court has also hinted on more than one occasion at its support for assessing procompetitive benefits when evaluating the legality of tying arrangements.[438] The Supreme Court has also explicitly noted that, if a *per se* claim cannot be established, a plaintiff has the option of attempting to plead and prove a case under the rule of reason.[439] In light of all this, it may not surprise you to learn that courts have resorted to a range of devices to avoid holding that *per se* condemnation is warranted in an individual tying case.[440]

In sum: the "*per se* rule against tying" actually amounts to something very much like the rule of reason, and it is not obvious why it is helpful to preserve the illusion of a real difference at the cost of wasted energy in pleading and adjudication.

The leading modern tying case is *Jefferson Parish*. The case dealt with a tie between healthcare services provided at a Louisiana hospital and anesthesiology services provided by a firm in a special relationship with the hospital. Justice O'Connor's concurrence in the judgment, for herself and three other members of the Court—which sets out criteria for the analysis of a tying claim under the rule of reason and proposes a candid recognition that the *per se* rule has been abandoned—has been at least as influential as Justice Stevens' opinion for the Court, which refused to abandon at least the rhetoric of *per se* illegality but indicated that special preconditions would govern the rule's application in tying cases.

Jefferson Parish Hosp. Dist. No. 2 v. Hyde
466 U.S. 2 (1984)

Justice Stevens.

[1] We must decide whether the [contract challenged in this case] gives rise to a per se violation of § 1 of the Sherman Act because every patient undergoing surgery at the [East Jefferson Hospital] must use the services of one firm of anesthesiologists [Roux and Associates], and, if not, whether the contract is nevertheless illegal because it unreasonably restrains competition among anesthesiologists. [. . .]

[2] It is far too late in the history of our antitrust jurisprudence to question the proposition that certain tying arrangements pose an unacceptable risk of stifling competition and therefore are unreasonable "per se." The rule was first enunciated in *International Salt Co. v. United States*, 332 U.S. 392, 396 (1947), and has been endorsed by this Court many times since. The rule also reflects congressional policies underlying the antitrust laws. In enacting § 3 of the Clayton Act, 15 U.S.C. § 14, Congress expressed great concern about the anticompetitive character of tying arrangements. While this case does not arise under the Clayton Act, the congressional finding made therein concerning the competitive consequences of tying is illuminating, and must be respected.

[3] It is clear, however, that every refusal to sell two products separately cannot be said to restrain competition. If each of the products may be purchased separately in a competitive market, one seller's decision to sell the two in a single package imposes no unreasonable restraint on either market, particularly if competing suppliers are free to sell either the entire package or its several parts. For example, we have written that if one of a dozen food stores in a community were to refuse to sell flour unless the buyer also took sugar it would hardly tend to restrain competition if its competitors were ready and able to sell flour by itself. Buyers often find package sales attractive;

---

[438] *See* Nat'l Collegiate Athletic Ass'n v. Bd. of Regents of Univ. of Oklahoma, 468 U.S. 85, 104 n.26 (1984) ([T]ying may have procompetitive justifications that make it inappropriate to condemn without considerable market analysis."); Eastman Kodak Co. v. Image Tech. Servs., Inc., 504 U.S. 451, 478–79 (1992) ("It is undisputed that competition is enhanced when a firm is able to offer various marketing options, including bundling of support and maintenance service with the sale of equipment. *Nor do such actions run afoul of the antitrust laws. . . .*") (emphasis added).

[439] Jefferson Parish Hosp. Dist. No. 2 v. Hyde, 466 U.S. 2, 29 (1984) ("In order to prevail in the absence of per se liability, respondent has the burden of proving that the [tying] contract violated the Sherman Act because it unreasonably restrained competition. That burden necessarily involves an inquiry into the actual effect of the exclusive contract on competition among anesthesiologists.").

[440] *See, e.g.,* Suture Exp., Inc. v. Cardinal Health 200, LLC, 963 F. Supp. 2d 1212, 1220 (D. Kan. 2013) (declining to apply *per se* rule because, among other things, the tie in question involved "vertical arrangements, and [are] therefore less likely to be a per se violation"—what tie does not involve a vertical arrangement?—and because market power allegations were insufficient to support *per se* liability, although apparently they were not insufficient to support a rule-of-reason analysis). *See also* Illinois Tool Works Inc. v. Independent Ink, Inc., 547 U.S. 28, 35 (2006) ("Over the years . . . this Court's strong disapproval of tying arrangements has substantially diminished.").

a seller's decision to offer such packages can merely be an attempt to compete effectively—conduct that is entirely consistent with the Sherman Act.

[4] Our cases have concluded that the essential characteristic of an invalid tying arrangement lies in the seller's exploitation of its control over the tying product to force the buyer into the purchase of a tied product that the buyer either did not want at all, or might have preferred to purchase elsewhere on different terms. When such "forcing" is present, competition on the merits in the market for the tied item is restrained and the Sherman Act is violated. [. . .]

[5] Accordingly, we have condemned tying arrangements when the seller has some special ability—usually called "market power"—to force a purchaser to do something that he would not do in a competitive market. [. . .]

[6] *Per se* condemnation—condemnation without inquiry into actual market conditions—is only appropriate if the existence of forcing is probable. Thus, application of the *per se* rule focuses on the probability of anticompetitive consequences. Of course, as a threshold matter there must be a substantial potential for impact on competition in order to justify *per se* condemnation. If only a single purchaser were "forced" with respect to the purchase of a tied item, the resultant impact on competition would not be sufficient to warrant the concern of antitrust law. It is for this reason that we have refused to condemn tying arrangements unless a substantial volume of commerce is foreclosed thereby. Similarly, when a purchaser is "forced" to buy a product he would not have otherwise bought even from another seller in the tied product market, there can be no adverse impact on competition because no portion of the market which would otherwise have been available to other sellers has been foreclosed. [. . .]

[7] When . . . the seller does not have either the degree or the kind of market power that enables him to force customers to purchase a second, unwanted product in order to obtain the tying product, an antitrust violation can be established only by evidence of an unreasonable restraint on competition in the relevant market. [. . .]

[8] . . . [A] tying arrangement cannot exist unless two separate product markets have been linked.

[9] The requirement that two distinguishable product markets be involved follows from the underlying rationale of the rule against tying. The definitional question depends on whether the arrangement may have the type of competitive consequences addressed by the rule. The answer to the question whether petitioners have utilized a tying arrangement must be based on whether there is a possibility that the economic effect of the arrangement is that condemned by the rule against tying—that petitioners have foreclosed competition on the merits in a product market distinct from the market for the tying item. Thus, in this case no tying arrangement can exist unless there is a sufficient demand for the purchase of anesthesiological services separate from hospital services to identify a distinct product market in which it is efficient to offer anesthesiological services separately from hospital services.

[10] Unquestionably, the anesthesiological component of the package offered by the hospital could be provided separately and could be selected either by the individual patient or by one of the patient's doctors if the hospital did not insist on including anesthesiological services in the package it offers to its customers. As a matter of actual practice, anesthesiological services are billed separately from the hospital services petitioners provide. There was ample and uncontroverted testimony that patients or surgeons often request specific anesthesiologists to come to a hospital and provide anesthesia, and that the choice of an individual anesthesiologist separate from the choice of a hospital is particularly frequent in respondent's specialty, obstetric anesthesiology. The District Court found that the provision of anesthesia services is a medical service separate from the other services provided by the hospital. The Court of Appeals agreed with this finding, and went on to observe that an anesthesiologist is normally selected by the surgeon, rather than the patient, based on familiarity gained through a working relationship. Obviously, the surgeons who practice at East Jefferson Hospital do not gain familiarity with any anesthesiologists other than Roux and Associates. The record amply supports the conclusion that consumers differentiate between anesthesiological services and the other hospital services provided by petitioners. [. . .]

[11] The question remains whether this arrangement involves the use of market power to force patients to buy services they would not otherwise purchase. Respondent's only basis for invoking the per se rule against tying and thereby avoiding analysis of actual market conditions is by relying on the preference of persons residing in Jefferson Parish to go to East Jefferson, the closest hospital. A preference of this kind, however, is not necessarily probative of significant market power.

[12] Seventy per cent of the patients residing in Jefferson Parish enter hospitals other than East Jefferson. Thus East Jefferson's "dominance" over persons residing in Jefferson Parish is far from overwhelming. The fact that a substantial majority of the parish's residents elect not to enter East Jefferson means that the geographic data does not establish the kind of dominant market position that obviates the need for further inquiry into actual competitive conditions. The Court of Appeals acknowledged as much; it recognized that East Jefferson's market share alone was insufficient as a basis to infer market power, and buttressed its conclusion by relying on "market imperfections" that permit petitioners to charge noncompetitive prices for hospital services: the prevalence of third party payment for health care costs reduces price competition, and a lack of adequate information renders consumers unable to evaluate the quality of the medical care provided by competing hospitals. While these factors may generate "market power" in some abstract sense, they do not generate the kind of market power that justifies condemnation of tying. [. . .]

[13] The record therefore does not provide a basis for applying the per se rule against tying to this arrangement. [. . .]

[14] In order to prevail in the absence of per se liability, respondent has the burden of proving that the [relevant] contract violated the Sherman Act because it unreasonably restrained competition. That burden necessarily involves an inquiry into the actual effect of the exclusive contract on competition among anesthesiologists. This competition takes place in a market that has not been defined. The market is not necessarily the same as the market in which hospitals compete in offering services to patients; it may encompass competition among anesthesiologists for exclusive contracts such as the . . . contract [at issue in this case] and might be statewide or merely local. There is, however, insufficient evidence in this record to provide a basis for finding that the [present] contract, as it actually operates in the market, has unreasonably restrained competition. The record sheds little light on how this arrangement affected consumer demand for separate arrangements with a specific anesthesiologist. The evidence indicates that some surgeons and patients preferred respondent's services to those of [the anesthesiologist designated by the hospital], but there is no evidence that any patient who was sophisticated enough to know the difference between two anesthesiologists was not also able to go to a hospital that would provide him with the anesthesiologist of his choice.

Justice O'Connor, with whom Chief Justice Burger, Justice Powell, and Justice Rehnquist join, concurring in the judgment.

[15] Some of our earlier cases did indeed declare that tying arrangements serve hardly any purpose beyond the suppression of competition. However, this declaration was not taken literally even by the cases that purported to rely upon it. In practice, a tie has been illegal only if the seller is shown to have sufficient economic power with respect to the tying product to appreciably restrain free competition in the market for the tied product. Without control or dominance over the tying product, the seller could not use the tying product as an effectual weapon to pressure buyers into taking the tied item, so that any restraint of trade would be insignificant. The Court has never been willing to say of tying arrangements, as it has of price-fixing, division of markets and other agreements subject to per se analysis, that they are always illegal, without proof of market power or anticompetitive effect.

[16] The "per se" doctrine in tying cases has thus always required an elaborate inquiry into the economic effects of the tying arrangement. As a result, tying doctrine incurs the costs of a rule of reason approach without achieving its benefits: the doctrine calls for the extensive and time-consuming economic analysis characteristic of the rule of reason, but then may be interpreted to prohibit arrangements that economic analysis would show to be beneficial. Moreover, the per se label in the tying context has generated more confusion than coherent law because it appears to invite lower courts to omit the analysis of economic circumstances of the tie that has always been a necessary element of tying analysis.

[17] The time has therefore come to abandon the "per se" label and refocus the inquiry on the adverse economic effects, and the potential economic benefits, that the tie may have. The law of tie-ins will thus be brought into accord with the law applicable to all other allegedly anticompetitive economic arrangements, except those few horizontal or quasi-horizontal restraints that can be said to have no economic justification whatsoever. This change will rationalize rather than abandon tie-in doctrine as it is already applied. [. . .]

[18] Tying may be economically harmful primarily in the rare cases where power in the market for the tying product is used to create additional market power in the market for the tied product. The antitrust law is properly concerned with tying when, for example, the flour monopolist threatens to use its market power to acquire additional power in the sugar market, perhaps by driving out competing sellers of sugar, or by making it more difficult for new sellers to enter the sugar market. But such extension of market power is unlikely, or poses no threat of economic harm, unless the two markets in question and the nature of the two products tied satisfy three threshold criteria.

[19] First, the seller must have power in the tying product market. Absent such power tying cannot conceivably have any adverse impact in the tied-product market, and can be only pro-competitive in the tying product market. If the seller of flour has no market power over flour, it will gain none by insisting that its buyers take some sugar as well.

[20] Second, there must be a substantial threat that the tying seller will acquire market power in the tied-product market. No such threat exists if the tied-product market is occupied by many stable sellers who are not likely to be driven out by the tying, or if entry barriers in the tied product market are low. If, for example, there is an active and vibrant market for sugar—one with numerous sellers and buyers who do not deal in flour—the flour monopolist's tying of sugar to flour need not be declared unlawful. If, on the other hand, the tying arrangement is likely to erect significant barriers to entry into the tied-product market, the tie remains suspect.

[21] Third, there must be a coherent economic basis for treating the tying and tied products as distinct. All but the simplest products can be broken down into two or more components that are "tied together" in the final sale. Unless it is to be illegal to sell cars with engines or cameras with lenses, this analysis must be guided by some limiting principle. For products to be treated as distinct, the tied product must, at a minimum, be one that some consumers might wish to purchase separately without also purchasing the tying product. When the tied product has no use other than in conjunction with the tying product, a seller of the tying product can acquire no additional market power by selling the two products together. If sugar is useless to consumers except when used with flour, the flour seller's market power is projected into the sugar market whether or not the two products are actually sold together; the flour seller can exploit what market power it has over flour with or without the tie. The flour seller will therefore have little incentive to monopolize the sugar market unless it can produce and distribute sugar more cheaply than other sugar sellers. And in this unusual case, where flour is monopolized and sugar is useful only when used with flour, consumers will suffer no further economic injury by the monopolization of the sugar market.

[22] Even when the tied product does have a use separate from the tying product, it makes little sense to label a package as two products without also considering the economic justifications for the sale of the package as a unit. When the economic advantages of joint packaging are substantial the package is not appropriately viewed as two products, and that should be the end of the tying inquiry. The lower courts largely have adopted this approach.

[23] These three conditions—market power in the tying product, a substantial threat of market power in the tied product, and a coherent economic basis for treating the products as distinct—are only threshold requirements. Under the rule of reason a tie-in may prove acceptable even when all three are met. Tie-ins may entail economic benefits as well as economic harms, and if the threshold requirements are met these benefits should enter the rule-of-reason balance. [. . .]

[24] The ultimate decision whether a tie-in is illegal under the antitrust laws should depend upon the demonstrated economic effects of the challenged agreement. It may, for example, be entirely innocuous that the seller exploits its control over the tying product to "force" the buyer to purchase the tied product. For when the seller exerts market power only in the tying product market, it makes no difference to him or his customers whether he exploits that power by raising the price of the tying product or by "forcing" customers to buy a tied product. On the other hand, tying may make the provision of packages of goods and services more efficient. A tie-in should be condemned only when its anticompetitive impact outweighs its contribution to efficiency.

* * *

In practice, the separate-products test can often be decisive, but it can be hard to apply: particularly in cases alleging that the technological integration of digital products and services constitutes an objectionable tie. This was the dispositive issue in the district court's analysis of Epic Games' challenge to Apple's requirement that apps distributed in the iOS App Store must use Apple's own In-App Payments ("IAP") solution.

CASENOTE: Epic Games, Inc. v. Apple Inc.
559 F. Supp. 3d 898 (N.D. Cal. 2021)

One of the highest-profile tying cases of recent years involved a challenge by Epic Games, the developer of the blockbuster video game Fortnite, to some of the conditions imposed by Apple as a condition of participation in the iOS ecosystem. One claim involved the allegation that Apple's requirement that an app sold on iOS must use Apple's in-app payment ("IAP") system. Epic challenged this obligation as an unlawful tie in violation of Section 1: on this theory, the iOS app distribution platform was the tying product, and IAP was the tied product.

Judge Gonzales-Rogers began with a formulation of the *per se* rule against tying. "For a tying claim to suffer *per se* condemnation, a plaintiff must prove: (1) that the defendant tied together the sale of two distinct products or services; (2) that the defendant possesses enough economic power in the tying product market to coerce its customers into purchasing the tied product; and (3) that the tying arrangement affects a not insubstantial volume of commerce in the tied product market."

But the judge declined to say whether the per se rule or the rule of reason should apply to Apple's alleged tie. "Epic Games' claim fails under either framework because a tying claim cannot be sustained where the alleged good is not a separate and distinct product. . . . [But] IAP is not a product." Instead, "IAP is but one component of the full suite of services offered by iOS and the App Store." It "is not bought or sold but it is integrated into the iOS devices." The court declined to disaggregate the two-side App Store platform into separate services "to create artificially two products," just as it would decline to disaggregate a car from the tires with which it was sold.

The judge noted that Epic had not presented any evidence that "demand exists for IAP as a standalone product." By contrast , the record showed that "[p]ayment processing is simply an input into the larger bundle of services provided by the IAP system. While there may be a market for payment processing, that fact is irrelevant as IAP is not just payment processing." As a result, "whether analyzed as an integrated functionality or from the perspective of consumer demand, IAP is not a separate product from iOS app distribution. Thus, Epic Games . . . fails to show the existence of an illegal tie under Section 1."

The case is on appeal to the Ninth Circuit.

---

* * *

The Single Monopoly Profit Theorem

In cases and commentary dealing with tying and related practices, you will certainly encounter references to the "single monopoly profit theorem." This is the proposition that, under certain circumstances, only a fixed amount of profit can be extracted from a particular degree of market or monopoly power in a given market. As a result, when the theorem applies, certain practices that might be thought anticompetitive involving the use of market power in one market to increase market share in another market—like tying—do not increase the level of market power or the profits to be derived from it. In other words, there is only a "single monopoly profit" to be extracted— and in most circumstances it is probably already being extracted by the monopolist. And it follows that if a business is engaging in that practice, it must be profitable for other reasons than the generation of additional market power: as a result, a natural inference may be that it is profitable because it generates efficiencies.[441]

---

[441] Ward S. Bowman Jr., *Tying Arrangements and the Leverage Problem*, 67 Yale L.J. 19, 23 (1957) ("Where fixed proportions are involved, no revenue can be derived from setting a higher price for the tied product which could not have been made by setting the optimum price for the tying product. The imposition of a tie-in under these circumstances determines the identity of the seller, but the amount of the tied product actually sold will not differ at all from that which could be sold if the optimum price for the tying product were set. Another monopoly is not created. The seller has only established a new method of exercising his already existing monopoly in the regulated product. Leverage, therefore, does not exist when the proportions of the two products are fixed."); *see also* Aaron Director & Edward H. Levi, *Law and the Future: Trade Regulation*, 51 Nw. U. L. Rev. 281, 290 (1956).

We can see the point more clearly with a somewhat simplified numerical example (which will ignore several complexities but illustrate the core principle). Suppose that there is a market for cups and a market for saucers. They are strict complements in fixed proportions: people only use cups with saucers, only use saucers with cups, and the ratio is always 1:1. Each cup and each saucer costs $1 to make and the monopoly price for each cup and saucer is $3. A monopolist in both markets would charge $6 for a cup+saucer set and make $4 of profit per set in total on, say, 1,000 set sales. (In other words, the revenue-maximizing price for a cup+saucer set is $6, of which $4 is profit.)

Suppose we make the saucer market perfectly competitive rather than monopolized. The price of saucers then goes down to the cost of $1 per saucer. But every saucer customer still needs one cup per saucer: a saucer alone is no good. The cup monopolist knows that demand is really for cup+saucer sets, and that the revenue-maximizing price for each set is $6. So the cup monopolist now charges $5 for each cup, of which $4 per cup is profit. The effective cup+saucer set price is now $6 (just as it was with a monopolist of both in the previous paragraph), and the total quantity sold of cups and saucers is just the same as it was with a single monopolist of both. And the cup monopolist makes the same profit ($4 per cup, 1,000 cups sold) as the monopolist in both cups and saucers would be making.

The point is that if underlying demand is for cup+saucer sets, then there is a fixed amount of maximum revenue, and thus of maximum profit, to be generated from monopoly sales of that set (a "single monopoly profit," if you will). A monopolist of any necessary component of that set can extract some amount up to that single monopoly profit: a monopolist of cups with a competitive saucer market cannot increase its profits any further by tying cups to saucers. So if we see that going on—the idea goes—it is probably because it is cheaper to supply them together or because there is a customer preference to buy them together. And those are *procompetitive* and proconsumer reasons to tie.

It is important to understand that the single monopoly profit theorem applies only when some restrictive criteria are met. Among other things, it applies only when the products or services supplied in the two markets are strict complements consumed in fixed proportions (*e.g.*, one cup is always used with one saucer), and when the competitiveness of both markets are fixed. Let's look at some of the most important assumptions.

Assumption 1: strict complements consumed in fixed proportions. If the products are used in varying proportions by users depending on their price elasticity (*e.g.*, if more price-inelastic users purchase more games per console, or more razor blades per handle), then tying can help to measure usage and increase the monopolist's profits. In particular, shifting margin from the tying product (*e.g.*, games console or razor handle) to the tied product (*e.g.*, games or razor blades) can operate like second-degree price discrimination: less elastic users are charged a higher margin than more elastic ones, because they purchase more of the high-margin tied product.[442] In this case the tie may replicate an effect that the defendant could generate by engaging in price discrimination in the tying market alone. In other words, it would lead to an increase in profits. In light of the ambiguity of price discrimination, reasonable minds can disagree about whether the ability to extract surplus in this way through effective price discrimination should be seen as an efficiency, a harm, or a neutral consequence.

Separately, and importantly, if the products are not strict complements, such that there is some demand for the tied product without the tying product, the monopolist may generate additional profits by monopolizing the tied product market (*e.g.*, by driving rivals below viable scale through the tie).[443]

---

[442] Ward S. Bowman Jr., *Tying Arrangements and the Leverage Problem*, 67 Yale L.J. 19, 23 (1957).

[443] Michael D. Whinston, *Tying, Foreclosure, and Exclusion*, 80 Am. Econ. Rev. 837, 850 (1990); Steven C. Salop, *Economic Analysis of Exclusionary Vertical Conduct: Where Chicago Has Overshot the Mark* in Robert Pitofsky (ed.) HOW THE CHICAGO SCHOOL OVERSHOT THE MARK: THE EFFECT OF CONSERVATIVE ECONOMIC ANALYSIS ON U.S. ANTITRUST (2008) ("Suppose, however, that some consumers do not buy the tying product and only buy the tied product. Those consumers would continue to benefit from tied-market competition. In contrast, if the monopolist engages in tying and drives out of the market all the independent producers of the tied product, then it would be in the position to exercise market power or even to monopolize the tying product. This anticompetitive theory requires an assumption that the tied-product market involves sufficient economies of scale that there would be an insufficient number of viable firms to maintain intense competition, if those firms were restricted to selling solely to consumers who purchased only the tied product market. Or, the number of competitors could fall to the point where tacit coordination is dangerously likely to succeed.").

Assumption 2: tied market not vulnerable to competitive harm. If the market for the tied product is vulnerable to market power (*e.g.*, because costs decrease with scale), a tie could increase the monopolist's overall level of market power. For example, suppose that tying the monopolist's razor handles to razor blades would mean that rivals would be deprived of crucial scale economies and would not remain competitive. The result could be that they would exit from the market for blades and would face increased barriers to re-entry, leaving the monopolist with a second monopoly in blades in addition to the handle monopoly.[444]

Assumption 3: tied market not an entry path to the tying market. If the market for the tied product is an important competitive on-ramp for entry into the tying market, a tie could increase the monopolist's overall level of market power by blocking the path. For example, suppose that it is generally difficult to enter the market for personal social networking services, because of powerful network effects (*i.e.*, a social network is more valuable when other people are already using the service). But suppose that one way in which it might be possible to enter such a market profitably is to build a large user base in an adjacent product or service, like mobile messaging services, and then to spin out additional social-networking features to those users. Under such circumstances, a monopolist of personal social networking might find it profitable to tie its social network to a mobile messaging app, to make it harder for a potential social networking competitor to use the messaging market as a staging ground to attack the networking monopoly.[445] Such a tie could increase the monopolist's overall pricing power by entrenching its social-network monopoly.[446] Likewise, if the tie may have the effect of requiring a would-be entrant into the tying market to also enter the tied market—that is, forcing "two-level entry"—it may serve to protect the monopoly in the tying market and thus increase market power. (A tie may also help the tier to evade rate regulation: can you see why?)

NOTES

1) Look back at the history of the law of resale price maintenance. Is it really "far too late in the history of our antitrust jurisprudence to question the proposition that certain tying arrangements pose an unacceptable risk of stifling competition and therefore are unreasonable 'per se'"? Why? How can we tell when it is too late to change a rule?

2) Justice Stevens's opinion for the Court in *Jefferson Parish* appears to distinguish between "abstract" market power, on the one hand, and the kind of market power that matters for antitrust analysis of tying arrangements, on the other. What do you make of that distinction, in general and in light of the specific factors enumerated in the opinion?

3) What is the purpose of the separate products test?

4) In *Jefferson Parish* itself, the tied service was provided by a third party, not by the hospital that provided the tying service. Should this have affected the analysis?

5) Can you think of two or three tying practices, from the real world, that would satisfy the conditions for the single monopoly profit theorem to apply, and two or three that would not?

---

[444] Barry Nalebuff, *Exclusionary Bundling*, 50 Antitrust Bull. 321, 325 (2005) ("If entry is costly, then rivals may not reappear after exiting, especially if they anticipate that the [defendant] can repeatedly drive them out via a costless cross-subsidy."); Einer Elhauge, *Tying, Bundled Discounts, and the Death of the Single Monopoly Profit Theory*, 123 Harv. L. Rev. 397, 413 (2009) ("If there are costs to entering the tied market, tying can profitably deter entry by an equally efficient rival by foreclosing enough of the tied market to make entry profits lower than entry costs. Likewise, if there are fixed costs to operating in the tied market, tying can cause equally efficient rivals in the tied market to exit (or deter their entry) and thus enable the tying firm to obtain a monopoly in the tied market. Other articles generalize the point to show that foreclosing a market can create anticompetitive effects by depriving rivals of network effects or economies of scale, scope, distribution, supply, research, or learning. If foreclosure decreases rival efficiency in any of those ways, it will worsen the market options available to buyers and lessen the constraint on the tying firm's market power in the tied market, thus enabling it to raise prices in the tied market even though rivals are not completely eliminated.").

[445] *See, e.g.*, First Amended Complaint, FTC v. Facebook, Inc., Case No. 1:20-cv-03590 (D.D.C. filed Aug. 19, 2021).

[446] Barry Nalebuff, *Exclusionary Bundling*, 50 Antitrust Bull. 321, 325 (2005) ("The elimination of B rivals may help protect the A monopoly. If potential entrants into the A market need a good B to make their package whole, they will now be at a disadvantage as the competitive complements market will have disappeared. It might also be possible that the A monopolist will gain power in the B market."); Steven C. Salop, *Economic Analysis of Exclusionary Vertical Conduct: Where Chicago Has Overshot the Mark* in Robert Pitofsky (ed.) HOW THE CHICAGO SCHOOL OVERSHOT THE MARK: THE EFFECT OF CONSERVATIVE ECONOMIC ANALYSIS ON U.S. ANTITRUST (2008) ("Suppose that [a] PC monopolist engages in tying of the media player and succeeds in monopolizing the media player as well. In this situation, entrants into PC operating systems would be forced to produce media player software too. In principle, this could raise barriers to entry into operating systems.").

6) In cases where tying allows a defendant to measure inelasticity, and thus to permit a form of price discrimination, it may allow a defendant to extract the profits that it could otherwise able to reap by just setting discriminatory prices for the tying product. When this is true, is it correct that, as a result, the tying practice is not harmful to competition: just allowing the defendant to extract the benefit of its existing and unchanged market power?

7) In the (in)famous *Windows Media Player* case, the European Commission prosecuted Microsoft for supplying Windows Media Player for free with Windows. It obtained a remedy requiring Microsoft to make an alternative version of Windows—"Windows N"—available without Windows Media Player, but permitted Microsoft to set the same price for that version. (Spoiler alert: it did not sell well.[447]) Was this a bad case for the Commission to have brought? A good case with a bad remedy? Or a good case with a good remedy?

F. Bundling

Bundling is closely related to tying. Like tying, it involves the application of a condition that allows market power in one market to be used to affect a second market. But, where tying requires the imposition of a requirement to purchase multiple products or services as a condition for buying one of them, bundling involves offering discounts for purchasing multiple different products or services together in a "bundle." In the paradigm case of bundling, a seller with market power in one product offers a discount on that product to customers that also buy another product or service from the seller. The core competitive concern is that the inability of unintegrated rivals—even equally or more efficient ones—to match the discounts may tend to support the creation or maintenance of market power in the second market.

For example, suppose that a company sells chemicals A, B, and C, each of which is in a separate market. The company is a monopolist of A and B, but the market for C is competitive. The company offers its customers a discount: any customer that buys A, B, *and* C together will get a discount of 20% on the bundle. Unintegrated rivals, which only offer C, may be unable to match that deep discount, even if they are more efficient producers of C: the integrated firm can make a profit on the overall bundle while the unintegrated firm could not profitably set an attractive price for C. Given the deeper discount offered by the integrated firm, customers are likely to agree to take the bundle.[448] As a result, the unintegrated rivals may be deprived of minimum viable scale and may be forced to exit the market, leaving the company with a monopoly in all three products and the ability to charge monopoly prices.

It may be helpful to see this with a numerical example. Suppose that units of A, B, and C each cost $9 to make. The competitive price of each is $10; the monopoly price of each is $15. Without bundling, the monopolist will sell A and B for $15 (setting aside additional factors like Cournot complement pricing) and the monopolist and its unintegrated rivals will all sell C at $10. With bundling, the monopolist can offer a substantial discount on the bundle without taking a loss, offering its customers a total discount of as much as $12 ($15+$15+$10 = $40; $40–$12 = $28), while still making $1 of profit on the bundle as a whole. But unintegrated rivals, selling only C, cannot get close to this: any discount of more than $1 from the competitive price of $10 will take them below their own costs. As a result, all else equal, the monopolist of A and B could comfortably offer a bundled discount sufficient to displace rivals' share in the market for C. If there are barriers to re-entering the market, the result could be that the monopolist of A and B acquires a third monopoly of C as well.

As with tying, there are many reasons why bundled discounts may be—and usually are—good rather than bad. All else equal, of course, low prices are great for consumers and for overall welfare. Bundled discounts may represent economies of scope (*i.e.*, supply-side cost savings arising from the simultaneous supply of different products or services), and/or (if the bundled products are complements) so-called Cournot complement pricing

---

[447] *See, e.g.*, Nicholas Economides & Ioannis Lianos, *A Critical Appraisal of Remedies In The E.U. Microsoft Cases*, 2 Colum. Bus. L. Rev. 346, 385 (2010) ("The two versions of Windows were sold in the E.U. at the same price and practically no OEM bought and adopted Windows-N. Thus, the remedy imposed by the Commission had no noticeable effect in the marketplace.").

[448] *See generally* Barry Nalebuff, *Exclusionary Bundling*, 50 Antitrust Bull. 321 (2005).

(the fact that the profit-maximizing pricing for two complementary products is lower than the total of the profit-maximizing prices for supplying each separately[449]).

And, as with tying, bundled pricing may result from an agreement between trading partners or from a unilateral conditional dealing policy of the seller: as such, bundles may be challenged under Section 1 or Section 2. But the leading cases—the Ninth Circuit's decision in *PeaceHealth* and the Third Circuit's decision in *LePage's*—establish a circuit split for the standard of legality. Both *PeaceHealth* and *LePage's* were decided under Section 2 alone. And unlike tying, bundling does not implicate a possible rule of *per se* illegality under Section 1.

As a result, Section 2 law is much more important to the analysis of bundling: so we will reserve our fuller discussion for Chapter VII.[450] We mention it here only to introduce the concept, and in light of bundling's close relationship with tying.

G. "Most Favored Nation" Agreements

A most favored nation agreement or clause—universally known as an "MFN" agreement—is a promise to treat a benefited party at least as well as that party's competitors. A simple MFN clause would provide, for example, that an input supplier will provide to its downstream customer inputs on terms no less favorable than the terms on which the input is available to the customer's rivals. It thus reassures the benefited party that competitors will not get a better deal from the bound party.

MFNs are complex creatures. On the one hand, they sound at first blush like a good and fair idea (nondiscriminatory treatment certainly sounds like a good idea), and they can support and promote competition, including by ensuring that the benefits of low prices or favorable terms are shared. On the other hand, however, MFNs can prevent trading partners, like input suppliers or distributors, from offering better terms to induce rivals to enter or expand in competition with incumbent monopolists, and they make it more expensive for the bound party to offer discounts (because such discounts must be shared with the beneficiaries of any MFNs). Thus, MFNs can be imposed by dominant firms to prevent rivals from making inroads by negotiating more favorable deals with input suppliers and distributors. When applied by a monopolist, an MFN may be challenged under Section 2 as well as, or instead of, Section 1.

MFNs can also be used by suppliers in oligopolistic markets to support and facilitate supracompetitive pricing by the participants in the oligopoly. Suppose that four participants in an oligopoly are currently enjoying the benefits of their legally independent but implicitly coordinated supracompetitive pricing, but they each fear that the others will cheat on the implicit terms of coordination by offering discounts. The public use of MFN clauses by each participant in dealings with customers can serve as a commitment mechanism, as it would make it more expensive for any one oligopolist to discount to any individual customer (because the MFN agreements would require that discount to be shared with all its customers, such that discounting would take a larger bite out of its profits). If all oligopolists introduce MFNs in parallel, supracompetitive pricing will be easier to maintain and the oligopoly will be more resilient.[451]

A variation of the MFN clause, called an "MFN-plus," provides that the trading partner will be treated *better* than its rivals: for example, such a clause might provide that the beneficiary will receive prices that are 10% lower than its competitors. These agreements, which effectively require trading partners to impose a surcharge on sales to rivals, generally pose much higher risks to competition and welfare.[452]

---

[449] To see this intuitively, consider that an integrated seller of complements A and B considering whether to lower the price of complement A will not only be induced to do so the prospect of additional sales of A (which would be enjoyed by any unintegrated sellers of A), but also by the prospect of additional demand for complement B resulting from those additional sales. *See* Richard J. Gilbert & Michael L. Katz, *An Economist's Guide to* U.S. v. Microsoft, 15 J. Econ. Perspectives 25 (2001).

[450] *See infra* § VII.G.4.

[451] *See, e.g.*, Jonathan B. Baker & Judith A. Chevalier, *The Competitive Consequences of Most-Favored-Nation Provisions*, 27 Antitrust 20, 22–23 (Spring 2013).

[452] This appears to have been a primary target of the Robinson-Patman Act, contrary to the subsequent enforcement of that statute. For discussion, *see* Herbert Hovenkamp, THE ANTITRUST ENTERPRISE: PRINCIPLE AND EXECUTION (2005) 196.

CASENOTE: United States v. Apple, Inc.

791 F.3d 290 (2d Cir. 2015)

MFNs played a critical role in the *Apple* e-books case you will remember from Chapter V. As you may recall, in that case Apple facilitated a hub-and-spoke conspiracy to increase retail prices.

The scheme challenged in that case was, in part, a response to the fact that publishers had become dissatisfied with the pre-existing "wholesale" model of e-book sales through Amazon. Under that model, publishers sold e-books to Amazon at a wholesale price, which Amazon then sold to consumers at a retail price that Amazon independently determined. This retail price chosen by Amazon was often very low, even for the most desirable bestsellers. Publishers feared that these low retail prices would condition consumers to expect lower prices for e-books in future and erode the value of the value. But no individual publisher had the commercial clout to risk their e-books becoming unavailable on Amazon. Without the ability to coordinate directly among the publishers for joint negotiation—which of course would be a flagrant Section 1 violation—the publishers lacked an obvious way to change the status quo.

Along came Apple, a new entrant in e-book retail, with an idea. Apple would sell books on an "agency" model and remit 70% of the proceeds back to the publisher. The publisher, not Apple, would set the retail price: up to $14.99, $12.99, or $9.99 depending on the hardcopy price. The jewel in the crown of this plan was an MFN clause in Apple's agreement with each publisher. Each publisher would set an Apple price *no higher* than that e-book was selling elsewhere.

As the Second Circuit emphasized, the contribution of the MFN to the effectiveness of the scheme was profound. A publisher that signed and accepted such an obligation would have no commercially reasonable alternative to moving Amazon over to the same agency model set by Apple. If Amazon retained the ability to independently set low prices—prices that the publishers would then be forced by the MFN to apply to Apple sales as well—the consequences would be unsustainable. As a result, the MFN "played a pivotal role . . . by stiffening the spines of the publishers to ensure that they would demand new terms from Amazon, and protecting Apple from retail price competition." In effect, accepting the MFN amounted to accepting a penalty for continuing to tolerate Amazon's discounting: and, thus, a highly credible commitment to change it.

As we saw in Chapter V, Apple served as the intermediary to make sure that each publisher knew when other publishers signed up to the arrangement. In so doing, it helped establish a common understanding built on a shared commitment to end Amazon's discounting and move to a higher-priced model for e-book sales.

MFNs were again front and center in the DOJ's complaint in its suit against Blue Cross Blue Shield of Michigan, which was dismissed when Michigan banned health care provider MFNs by statute.[453]

Complaint, United States v. Blue Cross Blue Shield of Michigan

Case No. 2:10-cv-15155 (filed E.D. Mich. Oct. 18, 2010)

I. NATURE OF THIS ACTION

1. Blue Cross is by far the largest provider of commercial health insurance in Michigan and has been for many years. Blue Cross competes with for-profit and nonprofit health insurers. Blue Cross' commercial health insurance policies cover more than three million Michigan residents, more than 60% of the commercially insured population. Blue Cross insures more than nine times as many Michigan residents as its next largest commercial health insurance competitor. Blue Cross had revenues in excess of $10 billion in 2009. Blue Cross has market power in the sale of commercial health insurance in each of the relevant geographic markets alleged below.

---

[453] U.S. Dept. of Justice, Press Release, Justice Department Files Motion to Dismiss Antitrust Lawsuit Against Blue Cross Blue Shield of Michigan After Michigan Passes Law to Prohibit Health Insurers from Using [MFN] Clauses in Provider Contracts (Mar. 25, 2013).

2. Blue Cross is also the largest non-governmental purchaser of health care services, including hospital services, in Michigan. As part of its provision of health insurance, Blue Cross purchases hospital services on behalf of its insureds from all 131 general acute care hospitals in the state. Blue Cross purchased more than $4 billion in hospital services in 2007.

3. Over the past several years, Blue Cross has sought to include MFNs (sometimes called "most favored pricing," "most favored discount," or "parity" clauses) in many of its contracts with hospitals. Blue Cross currently has agreements containing MFNs or similar clauses with at least 70 of Michigan's 131 general acute care hospitals. These 70 hospitals operate more than 40% of Michigan's acute care hospital beds. Unless enjoined, Blue Cross is likely to enter into MFNs with additional Michigan hospitals.

4. Blue Cross generally enters into two types of MFNs, which require a hospital to provide hospital services to Blue Cross' competitors either at higher prices than Blue Cross pays or at prices no less than Blue Cross pays. Both types of MFNs inhibit competition:

> (A) "MFN-plus." Blue Cross' existing MFNs include agreements with 22 hospitals that require the hospital to charge some or all other commercial insurers more than the hospital charges Blue Cross, typically by a specified percentage differential. These hospitals include major hospitals and hospital systems, and all of the major hospitals in some communities. These 22 hospitals operate approximately 45% of Michigan's tertiary care hospital beds. (A tertiary care hospital provides a full range of basic and sophisticated diagnostic and treatment services, including many specialized services.) Blue Cross' MFN-plus clauses require that some hospitals charge Blue Cross' competitors as much as 40% more than they charge Blue Cross. Two hospital contracts with MFN-plus clauses also prohibit giving Blue Cross' competitors better discounts than they currently receive during the life of the Blue Cross contracts. Blue Cross' MFN-plus clauses guarantee that Blue Cross' competitors cannot obtain hospital services at prices comparable to the prices Blue Cross pays, which limits other health insurers' ability to compete with Blue Cross. Blue Cross has sought and, on most occasions, obtained MFN-plus clauses when hospitals have sought significant rate increases.

> (B) "Equal-to MFNs." Blue Cross has entered into agreements containing MFNs with more than 40 small, community hospitals, which typically are the only hospitals in their communities, requiring the hospitals to charge other commercial health insurers at least as much as they charge Blue Cross. Under these agreements, Blue Cross agreed to pay more to community hospitals, which Blue Cross refers to as "Peer Group 5" hospitals, raising Blue Cross' own costs and its customers' costs, in exchange for the equal-to MFN. A community hospital that declines to enter into these agreements would be paid approximately 16% less by Blue Cross than if it accepts the MFN. Blue Cross has also entered into equal-to MFNs with some larger hospitals.

5. Blue Cross has sought and obtained MFNs in many hospital contracts in exchange for increases in the prices it pays for the hospitals' services. In these instances, Blue Cross has purchased protection from competition by causing hospitals to raise the minimum prices they can charge to Blue Cross' competitors, but in doing so has also increased its own costs. Blue Cross has not sought or used MFNs to lower its own cost of obtaining hospital services.

6. Blue Cross' MFNs have caused many hospitals to (1) raise prices to Blue Cross' competitors by substantial amounts, or (2) demand prices that are too high to allow competitors to compete, effectively excluding them from the market. By denying Blue Cross' competitors access to competitive hospital contracts, the MFNs have deterred or prevented competitive entry and expansion in health insurance markets in Michigan, and likely increased prices for health insurance sold by Blue Cross and its competitors and prices for hospital services paid by insureds and self-insured employers, in violation of Section 1 of the Sherman Act, 15 U.S.C. § 1, and Section 2 of the Michigan Antitrust Reform Act, MCL 445.772.

[. . .]

VI. BLUE CROSS' MFNs AND THEIR ANTICOMPETITIVE EFFECTS

A. The MFNs and their Terms

36. Since at least 2007, Blue Cross has sought to include MFNs or similar clauses in many of its agreements with Michigan hospitals. In some contracts, Blue Cross requires the hospital to contract with any other commercial insurer at rates at least as high as the hospital contracts with Blue Cross - an equal-to MFN. In others, Blue Cross demands even more and requires the hospital to contract with other insurers at rates higher than those paid by Blue Cross, typically by a specified percentage differential - an MFN-plus. Some Blue Cross MFNs contain very limited exceptions, most notably an exception for commercial health insurers with a de minimis presence, as discussed in paragraph 47 below.

37. Blue Cross currently has MFNs in its contracts with more than half of Michigan's general acute care hospitals. Very few hospitals have refused Blue Cross' demands for an MFN. Other hospitals' contracts have not been renegotiated in recent years, but Blue Cross is likely to seek MFNs when its contracts with those hospitals come up for renegotiation, especially if the hospital requests a price increase.

38. Most of Blue Cross' MFNs require the hospital to "attest" or "certify" annually to Blue Cross that the hospital is complying with the MFN, and they often give Blue Cross the right to audit compliance. Insurers pay hospitals under different formulas…. These varying payment methodologies can cause uncertainty for a hospital comparing Blue Cross' effective payment rates with anticipated payment rates from different insurers. Therefore, a hospital seeking to avoid a payment reduction by Blue Cross - generally its largest commercial payer - sometimes contracts with Blue Cross' competitors at prices even higher than the MFN requires, to avoid being penalized if Blue Cross audits the hospital's compliance with the MFN.

39. Blue Cross' agreements with at least 22 Michigan hospitals contain MFN-plus clauses. These hospitals are among the most important providers of hospital services in their respective areas. . . .

40. In 2007, Blue Cross entered into a "Participating Hospital Agreement" ("PHA") containing an equal-to MFN with each of more than 40 hospitals it classifies as "Peer Group 5" hospitals: small, rural community hospitals, which are often the only hospital in their communities. Under that agreement, Blue Cross committed to pay more to those community hospitals that agreed to charge all other commercial insurers rates that would be at least as high as those paid by Blue Cross. Any community hospital that failed to attest compliance with the MFN would be penalized by payments from Blue Cross at least 16% less than if it complied with the MFN.

B. Anticompetitive Effects of Blue Cross' MFNs

41. Blue Cross' existing MFNs, and the additional MFNs that Blue Cross is likely to seek to include in future agreements with Michigan hospitals, have unreasonably lessened competition and are likely to continue to lessen competition by:

> a. Maintaining a significant differential between Blue Cross' hospital costs and its rivals' costs at important hospitals, which prevents those rivals from lowering their hospital costs and becoming more significant competitive constraints to Blue Cross;

> b. Raising hospital costs to Blue Cross' competitors, which likely reduces those competitors' ability to compete against Blue Cross;

> c. Establishing a price floor below which important hospitals would not be willing to sell hospital services to other commercial health insurers and thereby deterring cost competition among commercial health insurers;

> d. Raising the price floor for hospital services to all commercial health insurers and, as a result, likely raising the prices for commercial health insurance charged by Blue Cross and its competitors; and

> e. Limiting the ability of other health insurers to compete with Blue Cross by raising barriers to entry and expansion, discouraging entry, likely raising the price of commercial health insurance, and preserving Blue Cross' leading market position.

42. Blue Cross often receives substantially better discounts for hospital services than other commercial health insurers receive. Blue Cross knows that its discounts provide a competitive advantage against other health insurers.

Blue Cross noted in April 2009 that its "medical cost advantage, delivered primarily through its facility [i.e., hospital] discounts, is its largest source of competitive advantage," and earlier stated that its advantages in hospital discounts "have been a major factor in its success in the marketplace."

43. In recent years, Blue Cross became concerned that competition from other insurers was eroding its hospital discount advantage - as it was. Blue Cross therefore sought to preserve its discount advantage by obtaining MFN-plus clauses, with the "expectation . . . that we would not have any slippage in our differential from what we experience today." In other words, rather than seeking lower prices from hospitals, Blue Cross negotiated MFN-plus clauses to maintain its discount differential and prevent potential competitors from obtaining hospital services at prices close to Blue Cross' prices and thereby becoming more significant competitive constraints on Blue Cross. During negotiations in 2008 with one hospital in Grand Rapids, Blue Cross wrote that "we need to make sure they [the hospital] get a price increase from Priority if we are going to increase their rates."

44. In most cases, Blue Cross obtained an MFN from a hospital by agreeing to increase its payments to the hospital. Blue Cross has sought and, on most occasions, obtained MFN-plus clauses when hospitals have sought significant rate increases. Blue Cross also agreed to increase rates to Peer Group 5 hospitals as part of the Peer Group 5 PHA, which included an equal-to MFN. Had a hospital not agreed to an MFN, Blue Cross likely would not have agreed to pay the higher rates sought by the hospital. Thus, the likely effect of the MFN has been to raise the prices of hospital services paid by both Blue Cross and its competitors, and by self-insured employers, and to increase health insurance prices charged by Blue Cross and its competitors.

45. Blue Cross' MFNs have resulted and are likely to continue to result in these anticompetitive effects in each of the relevant markets because they effectively create a large financial penalty for hospitals that do not accept them. Blue Cross patients are a significant portion of these hospitals' business, and Blue Cross patients typically are more profitable than Medicare and Medicaid patients, the hospitals' other most significant sources of business. A hospital that would otherwise contract with a competing insurer at lower prices than it charges Blue Cross would have to lower its prices to Blue Cross pursuant to the MFN if it sought to maintain or offer lower prices in contracts with other commercial insurers. The resulting financial penalty discourages a hospital with a Blue Cross MFN from lowering prices to health insurers competing with Blue Cross. Blue Cross' MFNs have caused hospitals to raise prices charged to other commercial health insurers, rather than lower prices to Blue Cross.

46. Prior to Blue Cross' obtaining MFNs, some hospitals gave greater discounts to some other commercial health insurers than they gave to Blue Cross. Without Blue Cross' MFNs, some hospitals had an incentive to offer lower prices to other insurers seeking to enter or expand in the hospital's service area and increase competition in the sale of commercial health insurance. [. . .]

48. Blue Cross' use of MFNs has caused anticompetitive effects in the markets for commercial health insurance in the geographic markets discussed below, among others. Hospitals in these markets have raised prices to some commercial health insurers, and declined to contract with other commercial health insurers at competitive prices. As a result, commercial health insurers that likely would have entered local markets to compete with Blue Cross have not done so, or have competed less effectively than they would have without the MFNs. Blue Cross' MFNs therefore have helped Blue Cross maintain its market power in those markets. The actual anticompetitive effects alleged below illustrate the types of competitive harm that have occurred and are likely to occur where Blue Cross obtains MFNs from hospitals throughout Michigan.

* * *

Steven C. Salop & Fiona Scott Morton, Developing an Administrable MFN Enforcement Policy

27 Antitrust 15 (2013)

[M]ost-favored-nation contractual provisions (MFNs) can lead to either procompetitive benefits or anticompetitive harms. MFNs can be procompetitive by enabling new products and thereby enhancing competition. For instance, MFNs can be used to prevent opportunism in situations where one of the parties makes relationship-specific investments in order to create a new product or improve an existing product or service. MFNs also can be used by a firm to deter rent-seeking delays and hold out problems in instances where important market information such as demand, value, or costs would be discovered after some contracts are signed. In these circumstances, the MFN also may enable the parties to create or improve a product, where in its absence they would face too much risk and might choose not to. [. . .]

The anticompetitive effects of MFNs can be either collusive or exclusionary. MFNs can facilitate coordination or dampen oligopoly competition by making it impossible to offer selective discounts or prevent secret discounts. MFNs can soften price competition and thereby allow firms to charge higher prices than they otherwise would. These are harmful collusive effects. MFNs also can have exclusionary effects by raising the costs of rivals or entrants that attempt to compete by negotiating lower prices from suppliers of critical inputs, or by pioneering a different business model. [. . .]

[T]he following conditions suggest that MFNs are less likely to raise antitrust concerns:

- [a] Received only by smaller buyers: MFNs received only by small buyers comprising a small share of the market are likely to cause a smaller increase in seller price levels, perhaps additionally because the largest buyers may have sufficient bargaining power to prevent such price increases.
- [b] Provided to buyers (all of which are small) by smaller sellers that lack market power: MFNs offered by such sellers are unlikely to cause an increase in bargaining power or raise barriers to entry that would lead to consumer harm. Exceptions to this condition occur when a power buyer obtains MFNs from numerous small sellers or where the MFNs facilitate coordination among the small sellers.
- [c] Unconcentrated markets: Where neither the input market nor the output market are concentrated, coordination is less likely to be concern, even if there are MFNs. However, where only one of the markets is unconcentrated, the MFNs can raise barriers to entry or can facilitate coordination.
- [d] Input with close substitutes: Where inputs subject to MFNs have close substitutes, non-recipients can avoid being placed at a significant competitive disadvantage by purchasing a substitute input instead.
- [e] As part of long-term contract with locked-in or sunk assets: In this situation, MFNs may be a device for allocating cost and demand risk or for avoiding the potential for expropriation of efficient investment.
- [f] In exchange for significant investment, particularly by initial customer or technology sponsor: Providing an MFN can avoid delays and facilitate the launch of network effects by ensuring that an initial sponsoring buyer will not suffer a price disadvantage relative to other buyers that wait.
- [g] Input has uncertain value for innovative new product, with resulting potential for delays and holdout problems: Similar benefits of MFNs can occur when the value of the input is unclear and early buyers fear being locked into long-term contracts at prices that do not reflect market values.
- [h] As part of the settlement of one in a series a number of law suits brought against the provider: An MFN can be used to avoid holding out by plaintiffs hoping for a better settlement if they wait.

In contrast, the following conditions suggest that MFNs are more likely to raise competitive concerns, ceteris paribus. We do not intend these conditions to comprise irrebuttable presumptions. These concerns could well be offset by beneficial effects. Instead, these conditions suggest the need for further analysis of benefits and harms by counsel and the antitrust agencies:

- [a] Jointly adopted by horizontal agreement: Antitrust is generally suspicious of horizontal agreements involving price because they are more likely to have anticompetitive effects and are presumed less likely to be efficiency enhancing.
- [b] Provided by large sellers with market power: If a seller has market power, there is a greater concern that its MFN could have an anticompetitive purpose and effect.
- [c] Received by largest buyers: Similarly, if MFNs are received by the largest buyers, they are more likely to lead to higher prices paid by rivals than they are to generate lower prices paid by the buyers who receive the MFNs.
- [d] Multiple MFNs with high market coverage: The broader the coverage of MFNs, the more likely they are to have price effects downstream. This conclusion comes with the caveat, however, that highly efficient MFNs are more likely to gain large coverage.

- [e] Highly significant input: An MFN for an input that comprises just a trivial share of the buyers' cost is unlikely to generate substantial cost effects, whereas an MFN for a highly significant input can have that effect. Significant cost effects can both affect prices and impact entry and innovation.

- [f] Airtight MFN with audit rights and penalties for noncompliance: If an MFN is easily evaded by the seller granting it, it is less likely to constrain the seller's prices to other buyer and, therefore, less likely to have anticompetitive effects.

- [g] Retroactive MFN, perhaps with penalties: Retroactive MFNs can create larger disincentives for price discounts, particularly where there are penalties in addition to having to match the discounted price, thereby making price competition less likely.

- [h] MFN-plus provisions: MFN-plus provisions promise the recipient a strictly lower price than what is paid by rivals. As a result, even if the recipient pays a higher input price, the profits earned from its resulting cost-advantage may more than offset the adverse impact of the higher input price. This term is more likely lead to consumer harm.

- [i] Obtained by a leading buyer in response to new entry by a low cost, innovative competitor: This timing raises concerns that the purpose and likely effect of the MFN is to raise the cost and reduce the procompetitive impact of the new entrant.

- [j] Obtained by a leading buyer in exchange for an agreement by that buyer to deal exclusively with a leading seller: This timing and connection to an exclusive dealing agreement raises concerns that the MFN and exclusive dealing have the purpose and likely effect of raising barriers to competition at both levels of the market.

- [k] Only claimed rationale is that the buyer is more concerned about the price it pays relative to other competitors, not the absolute level of the price paid: A firm's competitive advantage and profits often are related more to the relative price it pays for inputs than the absolute price level. Where this occurs, a buyer may be willing to pay a higher input price in exchange for retaining a cost advantage, a condition that is more likely to lead to less price competition and consumer harm. Thus, it raises suspicions of anticompetitive purpose.

- [l] Only claimed rationale is that the largest buyer "deserves" the lowest price: The largest buyer sometimes (but not always) has the bargaining power to negotiate the lowest input price. But, entrants or smaller buyers sometimes have the ability to negotiate lower prices, and when they do, consumers may benefit from the increased competition. Where it occurs, the largest buyer's possibly greater bargaining power does not necessarily translate into consumer benefits or create an antitrust "right." Indeed, if the largest buyer would get the lowest price anyway, it does not need an MFN. This rationale might well be considered "non-cognizable" justification under the Sherman Act.

As noted above, this checklist is not intended to be a substitute for a full competitive effects analysis. That analysis would evaluate the likely benefits and harms from the implementation of MFNs in the particular market in order to predict the likely net effect on consumers. The impacts on price, quality, and innovation are the ultimate determinants of benefits and harms.

NOTES

1) Can you think of a good reason a firm might want an MFN-plus for procompetitive reasons? If not: should they be *per se* illegal? (Criminal, even?)

2) Suppose that a business with market power was willing to make investments in a trading partner (*e.g.*, to help them cover their costs or stay in business), but was worried about subsidizing competitors. Could an MFN help convince the business to make those investments?[454]

   a. Is the fear of "subsidizing competitors" unusual? Does contributing to the profitability of a trading partner *always* mean subsidizing rivals to some extent? Should a business be able to refuse to do so?

---

[454] *See, e.g.*, BCBS's Motion to Dismiss, United States v. BCBS of Michigan, Case No. 2:10-cv-14155, 2010 WL 5134814, *2 (E.D. Mich. filed Dec. 17, 2010) ("Blue Cross's MFNs help it fulfill its statutory obligations by ensuring that Blue Cross is not required to pay more than its fair share of hospital costs.").

3) Do the competitive dangers of MFN provisions suggest that legislators and agencies should be cautious about creating nondiscrimination obligations? When might a statutory or regulatory nondiscrimination obligation be a desirable tool? When might it be harmful?

4) Would you advise a state or federal legislator to ban (some or all) MFNs? Under what circumstances? Take a shot at writing a statutory provision performing this function.

H. Some Further Reading

Jonathan Baker & Fiona Scott Morton, *Antitrust Enforcement Against Platform MFNs*, 127 Yale L.J. 2176 (2018)

Aaron Director & Edward H. Levi, *Law and the Future: Trade Regulation*, 51 Nw. U. L. Rev. 281 (1956)

John J. Flynn & James F. Ponsoldt, *Legal Reasoning and the Jurisprudence of Vertical Restraints: The Limitations of Neoclassical Economic Analysis in the Resolution of Antitrust Disputes*, 62 N.Y.U. L. Rev. 1125 (1987)

C. Scott Hemphill, *Posner on Vertical Restraints*, 86 U. Chi. L. Rev. 1057 (2019)

Konkurrensverket [Swedish Competition Authority], THE PROS AND CONS OF VERTICAL RESTRAINTS (2008)

Jonathan M. Jacobson, *Exclusive Dealing, "Foreclosure," And Consumer Harm*, 70 Antitrust L.J. 311 (2002)

Claudia M. Landeo, *Exclusionary Vertical Restraints and Antitrust: Experimental Law and Economics Contributions* in Kathryn Zeiler & Joshua Teitelbaum (eds.), THE RESEARCH HANDBOOK ON BEHAVIORAL LAW AND ECONOMICS (2015)

Marina Lao, *Free Riding: An Overstated, and Unconvincing, Explanation for Resale Price Maintenance*, in Robert Pitofsky (ed.) HOW THE CHICAGO SCHOOL OVERSHOT THE MARK: THE EFFECT OF CONSERVATIVE ECONOMIC ANALYSIS ON U.S. ANTITRUST (2008)

Michael J. Meurer, *Vertical Restraints and Intellectual Property Law: Beyond Antitrust*, 87 Minn. L. Rev. 1871 (2003)

Daniel P. O'Brien, *The Economics of Vertical Restraints in Digital Markets* in Global Antitrust Institute, REPORT ON THE DIGITAL ECONOMY (2020)

Open Markets Institute, WHAT DO FRANCHISEES DO? VERTICAL RESTRAINTS AS WORKPLACE FISSURING AND LABOR DISCIPLINE DEVICES (2021)

Rudolph J. Peritz, *A Genealogy of Vertical Restraints Doctrine*, 40 Hastings L.J. 511 (1989)

Patrick Rey & Thibaud Vergé, *Economics of Vertical Restraints* in Paolo Buccirossi (ed.), HANDBOOK OF ANTITRUST ECONOMICS (2008)

D. Daniel Sokol, *The Transformation of Vertical Restraints: Per Se Illegality, The Rule Of Reason, And Per Se Legality*, 79 Antitrust L.J. 1003 (2014)

VII. MONOPOLIZATION

A. Overview

The second, and perhaps the most enigmatic, of antitrust's three great pillars is the monopolization offense, which prohibits some unilateral conduct by monopolists and near-monopolists that may harm competition. Section 2 of the Sherman Act, 15 U.S.C. § 2, prohibits monopolization, attempted monopolization, and conspiracy to monopolize:

> Every person who shall monopolize, or attempt to monopolize, or combine or conspire with any other person or persons, to monopolize any part of the trade or commerce among the several States, or with foreign nations, shall be deemed guilty of a felony, and, on conviction thereof, shall be punished by fine not exceeding $100,000,000 if a corporation, or, if any other person, $1,000,000, or by imprisonment not exceeding 10 years, or by both said punishments, in the discretion of the court.

This of course places a great deal of weight on one of the thorniest questions in all of antitrust law: what exactly does it mean to "monopolize"? And how is it different from aggressive competition, which antitrust is supposed to encourage, even—and perhaps especially—from monopolists?

The Supreme Court has said that monopolization has just two elements: (1) monopoly power; and (2) "anticompetitive conduct."[455] Monopoly power is fairly straightforward. But it is much harder to figure out what the conduct element requires. Sometimes courts describe it as a requirement of "predatory" or "exclusionary" behavior, or just something *other* than "competition on the merits."[456] But the parade of synonyms is little help in practice.

Happily, there is broad agreement about some fundamentals of Section 2 law. First, the prohibition applies to firms that hold or acquire monopoly power (and, for the attempt offense, those who have a dangerous probability of attaining it through the challenged conduct). Second, monopolization centrally involves either the acquisition or the maintenance—meaning the increase or entrenchment—of monopoly power. Thus, the monopolization offense generally does not prohibit conduct unless it increases the magnitude or durability of monopoly power, even if that conduct harms consumers or rivals and even if it exploits existing monopoly power.[457] For example, merely charging high prices that reflect monopoly power does not constitute monopolization. Third, the prohibition does not cover *all*, or even most, conduct that leads to the acquisition or maintenance of monopoly power: there are plenty of lawful ways to attain, keep, or increase monopoly power. In particular, courts routinely emphasize that Section 2 does not prohibit conduct that is variously described as "industry," "honest competition," "innovation," and so on, which is often contrasted with behavior labeled "predatory," "exclusionary," and "anticompetitive."[458] But the resulting line between lawful competition and unlawful monopolization has always been complex, blurry, and controversial.[459]

---

[455] Verizon Communications Inc. v. Law Offices of Curtis V. Trinko, LLP, 540 U.S. 398 (2004).

[456] *See, e.g.*, Coalition for ICANN Transparency, Inc. v. VeriSign, Inc., 611 F.3d 495, 506 (9th Cir. 2010) ("illegitimate predatory practices"); Superior Prod. P'ship v. Gordon Auto Body Parts Co., 784 F.3d 311, 318 (6th Cir. 2015) ("anti-competitive or exclusionary means"); Stearns Airport Equip. Co. v. FMC Corp., 170 F.3d 518, 522 (5th Cir. 1999) ("means other than the competition on the merits").

[457] *See* Verizon Communications Inc. v. Law Offices of Curtis V. Trinko, LLP, 540 U.S. 398, 407 (2004).

[458] *See, e.g.*, United States v. Grinnell Corp., 384 U.S. 563, 570-71 (1966) (monopolization offense is concerned with "the willful acquisition or maintenance of [monopoly] power as distinguished from growth or development as a consequence of a superior product, business acumen, or historic accident"); Mercatus Grp., LLC v. Lake Forest Hosp., 641 F.3d 834, 854 (7th Cir. 2011) ("After all, many kinds of conduct may prevent or discourage a potential competitor from entering a particular market. Federal antitrust laws are implicated only when that conduct is predatory or unjustifiable.").

[459] *See, e.g.*, Thomas A. Lambert, *Defining Unreasonably Exclusionary Conduct: The "Exclusion of a Competitive Rival" Approach*, 92 N.C. L. Rev. 1175, 1177 (2014) (noting that the "problem with Section 2" is that "nobody knows what it means"); Einer Elhauge, *Defining Better Monopolization Standards*, 56 Stan. L. Rev. 253, 342 (2003) (suggesting that "[i]t is time . . . to acknowledge that the emperor has no clothes," and that monopolization doctrine is a "barrage of conclusory labels"); Herbert Hovenkamp, *Exclusion and the Sherman Act*,

Whether there are truly principles common to all monopolization cases, and what those principles might be, remains unclear. There is a flourishing scholarly literature offering theories of monopolization that purport to explain current law, outline desirable reforms, or both. These theories differ widely. For example, some commentators and courts indicate that monopolization law should prohibit only those practices that make "no economic sense" but for their tendency to drive out rivals and contribute to monopoly[460]; others claim that courts should assess whether an individual practice can be shown to be actually harmful, overall, to consumers[461]; others think Section 2 should condemn only conduct that would be capable of excluding an "equally efficient competitor" from the market (to avoid antitrust becoming a tool to protect less effective rivals from the rigors of competition)[462]; while still others propose that monopolization law should be reframed into a series of bright-line rules to avoid bogging courts and agencies down in difficult factual assessments.[463] Former AAG Hew Pate once called the search for a general monopolization framework a hunt for a "Holy Grail" of antitrust.[464]

Partly as a result of this indeterminacy, and partly for fear that monopolization law will end up discouraging monopolists from competing aggressively, modern courts are often reluctant to impose liability under Section 2, above all in cases involving novel practices, unusual markets, or new technologies.[465] Agencies and plaintiffs, in turn, may be deterred by the uncertain prospects of success from even filing a Section 2 case in the first place. This is a serious concern, and suggests that it would be valuable to clarify monopolization law. Nevertheless, claims of agency inaction are often overstated: the agencies, and the FTC in particular, have a long record of bringing monopolization cases, including in high-technology markets.[466]

Although no general theory of monopolization has won broad acceptance, there is somewhat greater clarity about the legal standards that apply to some specific subsets of practices (such as exclusivity, tying, and predatory pricing) that fall within the broader definition of monopolization. Such practices are governed by a set of more specific doctrinal frameworks: thus, for example, we have a set of rules for tying claims, a set of rules for predatory pricing claims, and so on. So, although we are still waiting for a Grand Unified Theory of Monopolization to win universal acceptance, we have a pretty good working sense of the standards that govern familiar types of monopolization.

Today, monopolization law faces several sharp questions. These include:

- **Digital markets and platform ecosystems.** Section 2 is center stage in debates about antitrust's response to the problems of digital monopoly. How, for example, should monopolization law apply to conduct by digital platform businesses that excludes competition on their own platforms? Many platforms face a choice between a "closed" business model, in which third parties are not permitted to offer products and services that interoperate with the platform, and an "open" business model, in which third parties are permitted to offer some such services. Does monopolization law give businesses a right to compete— at all or on particular terms—against monopolists on their own platforms? If so, will antitrust law encourage businesses to fully close their platforms? Is that a good thing? "Closed systems" have existed for a long time in other settings (*e.g.*, healthcare systems): are digital ecosystems special?

---

72 U. Chi. L. Rev. 147, 147–48 (2005) ("Notwithstanding a century of litigation, the scope and meaning of exclusionary conduct under the Sherman Act remain poorly defined. No generalized formulation of unilateral or multilateral exclusionary conduct enjoys anything approaching universal acceptance.").

[460] *See, e.g.*, Gregory J. Werden, *Identifying Exclusionary Conduct Under Section 2: The "No Economic Sense" Test*, 73 Antitrust L.J. 413 (2006); In re Adderall XR Antitrust Litig., 754 F.3d 128, 133 (2d Cir. 2014).

[461] *See, e.g.*, Steven C. Salop & Craig Romaine, *Preserving Monopoly: Economic Analysis, Legal Standards, and* Microsoft, 7 Geo. Mason L. Rev. 617, 652 (1999).

[462] Richard A. Posner, ANTITRUST LAW (2001) 43.

[463] Open Markets Institute, *Restoring Antimonopoly Through Bright-Line Rules*, PROMARKET (Apr. 26, 2019), https://www.promarket.org/2019/04/26/restoring-antimonopoly-through-bright-line-rules/; Zephyr Teachout, BREAK 'EM UP: RECOVERING OUR FREEDOM FROM BIG AG, BIG TECH, AND BIG MONEY (2020) 214 (FTC should "lay out very particular clear, bright-line rules—like speed limits—against certain kinds of "vertical" behavior").

[464] R. Hewitt Pate, *The Common Law Approach and Improving Standards for Analyzing Single Firm Conduct* (Oct. 23, 2003).

[465] *See, e.g.*, FTC v. Qualcomm Inc., 969 F.3d 974, 990–91 (9th Cir. 2020).

[466] *See* Daniel Francis, *Making Sense of Monopolization*, 84 Antitrust L.J. 779, Appx. A (2022) (collecting more than 30 selected monopolization cases filed post-*Microsoft*). *Compare, e.g.*, Carl Shapiro, *Antitrust in a Time of Populism*, 61 Int'l J. Indus. Org. 714, 742–43 (2018) ("[M]any observers appear frustrated that the DOJ and the FTC have brought very few Sherman Act Section 2 monopolization cases over the past 25 years.").

- **The antitrust / IP interface.** How should monopolization law interact with intellectual property law? In particular, when should antitrust liability be imposed for conduct involving the use and enforcement of IP rights, or of claimed IP rights?[467] (We will explore some of these themes in detail in Chapter X.)

- **Is the bar too high?** For a long time, courts have been explicitly concerned with the dangers of too much monopolization enforcement.[468] Has this led the law astray: in particular, do courts today impose unrealistically demanding conditions in monopolization cases? Do they require unnecessarily clear or convincing evidence of actual effects on outcomes of the competitive process, such as price or quality?

- **What about unfamiliar conduct?** How should courts approach conduct falling outside the familiar categories of concern (exclusive dealing, tying, and so on)? What legal criteria should apply to the assessment of practices that appear to increase or shore up monopoly but that do not neatly fall into established doctrinal categories? Should courts be skeptical of practices that appear to them to be non-standard, or should they err in favor of tolerating novel practices unless and until their harmful tendencies are clear?

- **Monopsony and monopsonization.** As we have already seen, antitrust is equally concerned with monopoly power on the buy-side of a market ("monopsony power").[469] It follows that Section 2 provides a basis to prohibit and remedy "monopsonization"—conduct that improperly creates or augments monopsony power—as well as traditional seller-side monopolization. But this concern has not been particularly visible in Section 2 enforcement practice or case law, nor heavily studied by academic writers. Where, and how, might agencies and courts find troubling monopsonization out in the world? How, if at all, should monopsonization doctrine differ from traditional monopolization law?

- **Criminal prosecution.** As we've seen, the Sherman Act makes monopolization a *felony*, punishable by criminal fines and up to 10 years of imprisonment. But modern practice confined criminal prosecution to *per se* violations of Section 1 until 2022, when DOJ launched a series of criminal monopolization prosecutions.[470] Is this desirable? What is the proper role for criminal enforcement of Section 2?

This chapter will give only a brief overview of this deeply complex area of law. In Section B we will consider the foundation-stone of monopolization doctrine: monopoly power. In Section C we will examine some of the common threads that appear to unite all monopolization cases: exclusion of rivals; contribution to monopoly power; the monopolist's freedom of competitive action; and the analysis of procompetitive justifications. In Section D, we will consider some of the most important recognized categories of monopolization: exclusivity, tying, and so on. Finally, in Section E, we will briefly encounter the attempt and conspiracy variations on the core monopolization offense.

---

[467] As we will see in Chapter X there are many perspectives on the right way to define this interface. *See, e.g.*, Robin Feldman, *Patent and Antitrust: Different Shades of Meaning*, 13 Va. J.L. & Tech. 1, 18–20 (2008); Makan Delrahim, *The "New Madison" Approach to Antitrust and Intellectual Property Law* (speech of Mar. 16, 2018), https://www.justice.gov/opa/speech/file/1044316/download; Daniel Francis, *Making Sense of Monopolization*, 84 Antitrust L.J. 779 (2022); Herbert Hovenkamp, Mark D. Janis, Mark A. Lemley, Christopher R. Leslie & Michael A. Carrier, 1 IP AND ANTITRUST: AN ANALYSIS OF ANTITRUST PRINCIPLES APPLIED TO INTELLECTUAL PROPERTY LAW (2020).

[468] *See, e.g.*, United States v. Aluminum Co. of Am., 148 F.2d 416, 430 (2d Cir. 1945) (Hand., J.) ("The successful competitor, having been urged to compete, must not be turned upon when he wins."); Verizon Communications Inc. v. Law Offices of Curtis V. Trinko, LLP, 540 U.S. 398, 414 (2004) (under Section 2 "[m]istaken inferences and the resulting false condemnations are especially costly, because they chill the very conduct the antitrust laws are designed to protect"). *See also* Robert H. Bork, THE ANTITRUST PARADOX: A POLICY AT WAR WITH ITSELF (1978) 157 ("The real danger for the law is less that predation will be missed than that normal competitive behavior will be wrongly classified as predatory and suppressed.").

[469] *See supra* § III.E.

[470] *See* Press Release, U.S. Department of Justice, Executive Pleads Guilty to Criminal Attempted Monopolization (Oct. 31, 2022); Press Release, U.S. Department of Justice, Criminal Charges Unsealed Against 12 Individuals in Wide-Ranging Scheme to Monopolize Transmigrante Industry and Extort Competitors Near U.S.-Mexico Border (Dec. 6, 2022). For earlier signals, *see* Richard A. Powers, *Effective Antitrust Enforcement: The Future Is Now* (remarks of June 3, 2022); *see also* Jonathan Kanter, *Remarks at 2022 Spring Enforcers Summit* (Apr. 4, 2022). *See also* Daniel A. Crane, *Criminal Enforcement of Section 2 of the Sherman Act*, 84 Antitrust L.J. 753 (2022); D. Daniel Sokol, *Reinvigorating Criminal Antitrust?*, 60 Wm. & Mary L. Rev. 1545 (2019); Spencer W. Waller, *The Incoherence of Punishment in Antitrust*, 78 Chi.-Kent L. Rev. 207 (2003). For older cases, *see* United States v. Dunham Concrete Prods., Crim. No. 1842 (E.D. La. 1969); United States v. United Fruit Co., 11 Trade Reg. Rep. (CCH) ¶ 45,063, at 52,528 (July 16, 1963); United States v. Gen. Motors Corp., 11 Trade Reg. Rep. (CCH) ¶ 45,061, at 52,424 (Apr. 12, 1961).

B. Monopoly Power

It is elementary that the first element of the monopolization offense is the possession of monopoly power.[471] Monopoly power is something like market power,[472] but it is greater in magnitude. It thus amounts to something like very substantial market power, although it is certainly not limited to "strict monopoly" involving only a single seller. But, as Einer Elhauge explains in the following extract, this is a harder concept to pin down than we might think. You may remember some of these concerns from our discussion of the law of market power in Chapter III.

Einer Elhauge, Defining Better Monopolization Standards
56 Stan. L. Rev. 253 (2003)[473]

The Court defines "monopoly power" as "the power to control prices or exclude competition." This definition raises a problem because the standard economic definition of any "market power" is a power to raise prices over the competitive level. Given this, doesn't all market power necessarily give a defendant "control" over its prices and thus make it a monopolist? Apparently not, because the Court has stressed: "Monopoly power under § 2 requires, of course, something greater than market power under § 1." But then, just what is the difference?

To an economist, the distinction is theoretically puzzling: A firm either enjoys a downward-sloping demand curve or it doesn't. But courts and regulators sensibly recoil from that conclusion because it would make antitrust far too sweeping given that, in our brand-differentiated world, just about every producer has a brand name that enables it to enjoy a downward-sloping demand curve and thus has some pricing discretion. This is a problem that has only gotten worse over time, as we have moved from an economy that tends to focus on mass-produced, homogeneous commodities to an economy that focuses on providing not only brand-differentiated products but services and experiences that inevitably enjoy some pricing discretion. Likewise, the price discrimination normally taken to evidence market power is so ubiquitous that it would indicate market power exists everywhere. The logical purity of the economist's test thus must be rejected, for it would disable the monopoly power element from serving its intended function of limiting antitrust challenges against unilateral conduct to a subset of cases where the potential harm to markets is gravest.

The usual reaction is to cut down on this excessive potential sweep by defining monopoly power to be a "significant" or "substantial" degree of market power. But this raises three problems. The first is rather predictable: This approach is vague about how much power it takes to cross this line of "substantiality." The second problem is more comical. To avoid excessive sweep even under § 1, market power itself is normally defined as not just any ability to raise prices above competitive levels but an ability to raise prices "substantially" over those levels. We are thus left with a standard that defines itself as requiring a substantial degree of a sort of power that is itself defined to exist only when substantial. This builds vagueness upon vagueness. It reminds me of the story of the flat-earth adherent who insisted the earth rested on the back of a giant turtle, and when asked what held up the turtle, answered that from then on, "it's turtles all the way down." Substantial turtles, one supposes.

The third problem is more serious: This standard fails even to define which variable is having its "substantiality" judged. One could imagine . . . deciding the monopoly power issue based directly on whether a particular firm's individual demand curve has an elasticity lower than some defined number X, or on whether it has the ability to raise prices more than Y percent over the competitive level, with less demanding Xs and Ys being used to define market power. But while considering such issues, courts generally seem moved more by market shares, with the classic formulation being that 90% is certainly enough, 33% is certainly not, and 60–64% is close to the line. Nor is the market share approach supported by only precedent and the statutory language referring to a "monopoly," for a pure firm-specific demand elasticity approach that ignored market share would create problems by sweeping in firms with brands that enjoy considerable pricing discretion but compete vigorously with other brands. It would also cause legal rules to vary from day to day with shifts in demand, costs, or rival abilities, and would subject

---

[471] *See, e.g.*, United States v. Grinnell Corp., 384 U.S. 563, 570 (1966).

[472] *See supra* §§ II.F (economics of market power) and III.E (law of market power)

[473] {*Eds.: A full version of this work previously appeared in the Stanford Law Review at the citation above. When possible and appropriate, please cite to that version.*}

different firms that engage in the same anticompetitive conduct to acquire the same high market share to different rules depending on the degree of demand elasticity in their industry. On the other hand, a market share test is problematic because high market shares may not indicate much ability to raise prices over competitive levels, which is the economic injury of concern. We are thus left uncertain about just what to do when our inferences from market share conflict with those from firm-specific demand elasticity. [. . .]

[But] at least we all have a sense of what sort of evidence moves us closer to a conclusion of monopoly power: More market share or more discretion over prices makes it more likely a firm has monopoly power. Sometimes these two standards diverge, but it is not the case that the sort of evidence that affirmatively supports a monopoly power conclusion under one standard actually cuts against that conclusion under the other standard. And often the same sort of evidence supports a monopoly power conclusion under either standard. While we may not know how many lost hairs it takes to become bald, and have some conflict in beliefs about what precisely constitutes a hair, most of the time that variation in belief does not matter much because the same sorts of things are judged a hair under either belief.

{*Eds: later in the article, Elhauge proposes a working definition: a market share of 50% and the "ability to either influence marketwide prices or impose significant marketwide foreclosure that impairs rival efficiency."*}

* * *

Monopoly power—like market power, as you will remember from Chapter III—can be shown through "direct evidence," like evidence of actual control over prices and output levels in the relevant market, and/or through "indirect evidence," usually in the form of a high share of a defined relevant market protected by barriers to entry.[474]

In practice, as you might expect, market share is often an important starting point for inquiries into monopoly power (just as with market power). A seminal statement of the relationship between market share and monopoly is found in *Alcoa*, a 1945 decision of the Second Circuit.

CASENOTE: United States v. Aluminum Co. of America
148 F.2d 416 (2d Cir. 2015)

Alcoa concerned a challenge by the Department of Justice to a variety of practices used by the Aluminum Company of America ("Alcoa"), an industrial powerhouse of the mid-20th century that still exists today. (We will talk briefly about the challenged practices later in this chapter.[475] For now, as our focus is on the question of monopoly power, it is enough to know that DOJ challenged a range of conduct, including acquisitions, buying-up of important inputs, and other behavior.) In an unusual feature of the case, so many Supreme Court Justices were recused that a quorum could not be formed. So the case was referred by the Supreme Court to the Second Circuit, where Judge Learned Hand wrote an opinion that has become a landmark in the history of monopolization.[476]

Before considering whether Alcoa's conduct had violated Section 2, Judge Hand was required first to figure out whether Alcoa held monopoly power in the market for aluminum. It was easy enough to measure aluminum output, but two complexities presented themselves: first, whether the market share calculations should include Alcoa's production of aluminum for the use of its own downstream businesses, rather than for sale on the open market; and, second, whether the ability of some customers to use "secondary" (*i.e.*, recycled) aluminum rather than "virgin" (*i.e.*, new) aluminum ingot should be considered as an independent source of competition in the market. It was not clear whether there was any physical difference between virgin and secondary aluminum: certainly the plaintiff had not proven any such difference, although some customers declined to use secondary.

---

[474] *See, e.g.*, Optronic Techs., Inc. v. Ningbo Sunny Elec. Co., 20 F.4th 466, 484 (9th Cir. 2021); Mylan Pharms. Inc. v. Warner Chilcott Pub. Ltd. Co., 838 F.3d 421, 434–38 (3d Cir. 2016); McWane, Inc. v. FTC, 783 F.3d 814, 830 (11th Cir. 2015); United States v. Microsoft Corp., 253 F.3d 34, 51–52 (D.C. Cir. 2001) (en banc).

[475] *See infra* § VII.C.3.

[476] For some context regarding the Alcoa case ("antitrust's closest equivalent to an epic poem"), *see* Marc Winerman & William E. Kovacic, *Learned Hand, "Alcoa," And The Reluctant Application Of The Sherman Act*, 79 Antitrust L.J. 295 (2013).

In approaching the analysis, Judge Hand articulated a meaning of "monopoly power" that has passed into antitrust scripture: "[Ninety percent] is enough to constitute a monopoly; it is doubtful whether sixty or sixty-four percent would be enough; and certainly thirty-three per cent is not." This rough guidance about the inference of monopoly power from market share is still cited with approval by courts.[477] (Indeed, it is probably the only holding of the case that is routinely invoked or relied upon by courts and litigants today! Much of the court's analysis of conduct has been overtaken by time and subsequent case law.)

On the first issue, Judge Hand concluded that Alcoa's production of aluminum ingot for internal use *should* count toward its share of the market for aluminum. That production, he pointed out, "necessarily had a direct effect on the ingot market," by reducing the demand for aluminum from other sources.[478] As a result, Alcoa's market share should reflect all of its production, whether Alcoa chose to sell it on the open market or not.

On the second issue, Judge Hand declined to treat the availability of recycled "secondary" aluminum as an independent "competitor" when calculating market shares. The fact that some customers might use their aluminum again, or sell it to others who would, did not change the identity or relative strength of the suppliers of fresh aluminum to the market. "Alcoa always knew that the future supply of ingot would be made up in part of what it produced at the time, and, if it was as far-sighted as it proclaims itself, that consideration must have had its share in determining how much to produce. . . . The competition of secondary [aluminum] must therefore be disregarded, as soon as we consider the position of Alcoa over a period of years; it was as much within Alcoa's control as was the production of the 'virgin' [aluminum] from which it had been derived."

Alcoa was an unusual (and complicated!) case in many ways. One was that it involved an assessment of competition between a product and a kind of recycled or second-hand supply of that same product. Would you have included secondary aluminum in the same market as virgin? Can you think of other markets or industries where "second-hand" products might be an important constraint on new production? Why do you think Judge Hand indicated that the extent of substitutability differed from one use to the next, but did not measure monopoly power within individual use-specific product markets?[479]

In some cases, monopoly power is easily shown; in others, it is harder. Digital markets can pose particular challenges: not just in proving monopoly power after discovery but even in pleading it in a complaint in terms that will survive dismissal under Rule 12(b)(6). In some such markets it may be very hard to identify something that could plausibly be used as a market share—market shares are not legally necessary for a plaintiff, but they sure do help! A central issue in the disposition of the FTC's first antitrust complaint against Facebook was whether the FTC had adequately alleged that Facebook held monopoly power in a market for personal social networking ("PSN") services. The case involved a Section 2 challenge to Facebook's acquisition of competitive threats and its use of "platform policies" that were applied to the social network's dealings with app developers.

FTC v. Facebook, Inc.
Case No. 20-3590, 2021 WL 2643627 (D.D.C. June 28, 2021)

Judge Boasberg.

[1] Begin with the linchpin of this Opinion: whether the FTC has plausibly alleged, as it must, that Facebook exercises monopoly power. As explained by the Circuit in *Microsoft*, monopoly power is the power to control prices or exclude competition, such that a firm is a monopolist if it can profitably raise prices substantially above the competitive level. Where a plaintiff can provide direct proof that a firm has in fact profitably done so, the existence of monopoly power is clear. Because such proof is rare, however, plaintiffs and courts usually search for indirect or circumstantial evidence of monopoly power by inferring it from a firm's possession of a dominant share of a

---

[477] *See, e.g.*, Spirit Airlines, Inc. v. Nw. Airlines, Inc., 431 F.3d 917, 935 (6th Cir. 2005); Syufy Enterprises v. Am. Multicinema, Inc., 793 F.2d 990, 995 (9th Cir. 1986); City of Mt. Pleasant, Iowa v. Associated Elec. Co-op., Inc., 838 F.2d 268, 279 (8th Cir. 1988); In re Pool Prod. Distribution Mkt. Antitrust Litig., 940 F. Supp. 367, 382 (E.D. La. 2013); Emigra Grp., LLC v. Fragomen, Del Rey, Bernsen & Loewy, LLP, 612 F. Supp. 2d 330, 368 n.156 (S.D.N.Y. 2009).

[478] This may remind you of some of the logic in Wickard v. Filburn, 317 U.S. 111 (1942), which was decided just a few years earlier.

[479] *Compare, e.g.*, FTC v. RAG-Stiftung, 436 F. Supp. 3d 278, 303 (D.D.C. 2020) (defining product markets around specific end uses).

relevant market. . . . Because market power is meaningful only if it is durable, a plaintiff proceeding by the indirect method of providing a relevant market and share thereof must also show that there are barriers to entry into that market.

[2] Although the FTC briefly suggests in its Opposition that it can offer direct proof of market power . . . it spends nearly its entire brief arguing why it has sufficiently pleaded indirect proof—viz., that Facebook has a dominant share of a relevant product and geographic market (the United States market for Personal Social Networking [("PSN")] Services) protected by entry barriers. Because the agency thus makes no real direct-proof argument, the Court will analyze the Complaint's market-power allegations using the indirect framework. Again, that framework first requires the plaintiff to establish the relevant market in which the defendant firm allegedly has monopoly power. . . . It then demands that a plaintiff establish that the defendant has a dominant share of that market protected by entry barriers. . . . As the Court explains below, it is the market-share step that trips up the FTC here. [. . .]

[3] Off the bat, there is ample authority that the FTC's bare assertions would be too conclusory to plausibly establish market power in any context. It is hard to imagine a market-share allegation that is much more conclusory than the FTC's here.

[4] Even accepting that merely alleging market share "in excess of 60%" might sometimes be acceptable, it cannot suffice in this context, where Plaintiff does not even allege what it is measuring. Indeed, in its Opposition the FTC expressly contends that it need not specify which metrics or method it used to calculate Facebook's market share. In a case involving a more typical goods market, perhaps the Court might be able to reasonably infer how Plaintiff arrived at its calculations—e.g., by proportion of total revenue or of units sold. See U.S. Dep't of Justice & FTC, Horizontal Merger Guidelines § 5.2 (2010) (suggesting these to be the typical methods). As the above market-definition analysis underscores, however, the market at issue here is unusual in a number of ways, including that the products therein are not sold for a price, meaning that PSN services earn no direct revenue from users. The Court is thus unable to understand exactly what the agency's "60%-plus" figure is even referring to, let alone able to infer the underlying facts that might substantiate it.

[5] Rather than undergirding any inference of market power, Plaintiff's allegations make it even less clear what the agency might be measuring. The overall revenues earned by PSN services cannot be the right metric for measuring market share here, as those revenues are all earned in a separate market—viz., the market for advertising. Percent of daily users or monthly users of PSN services—metrics the Complaint mentions offhandedly—are not much better, as they might significantly overstate or understate any one firm's market share depending on the various proportions of users who have accounts on multiple services, not to mention how often users visit each service and for how long.

[6] What about the share of total time spent by users on PSN services? Plaintiff says nothing about that metric in its Complaint. And although it seems tenable at first glance, that metric may also be of limited utility. That is because at least some of the features offered by a Facebook or Instagram or Path are not, seemingly, part of those firms' PSN-services offerings as defined by the FTC; time spent on those apps or websites, accordingly, is not necessarily time spent on a PSN service. The Commission, for instance, expressly alleges that social-networking services based on interest-based connections such as Strava are not, by its definition, PSN services. That definition of what is in the market, perhaps counterintuitively to Facebook users, would mean that time a user spends engaging with specific interest-based Facebook pages or groups may not qualify as time spent on a PSN service. The same problem arises when a user passively consumes online video on a PSN service. To the extent that, say, Instagram users spend their time on the site or app watching a comedy routine posted by the official page of a famous comedian, are they spending time on a PSN service? If not, as the Complaint suggests is the case, then time spent "on Facebook" or "on Instagram" bears an uncertain relationship to the actual metric that would be relevant: time spent using their PSN services in particular. Put another way, the uncertainty left open by the Complaint as to exactly which features of Facebook, Instagram, et al. do and do not constitute part of their PSN services, while not necessarily rendering the alleged PSN-services market implausible, compounds the trouble created by the FTC's vaguer-still allegations regarding Facebook's share of that market.

[7] Nor do the difficulties stop there. Readers may well have noticed that the discussion to this point has consistently referred to Instagram and Facebook as examples of PSN services. That is because, outside of Path, Myspace, and Friendster, all of which seem to be long defunct or quite small, Plaintiff's Complaint does not identify any other providers of PSN services. Yet the FTC is apparently unwilling to allege that Facebook has ever (pre- or post-Instagram acquisition) had something like 85% or even 75% market share; instead it hedges by offering only that the number is somewhere north of 60%. The question naturally arises: which firms make up the remaining 30–40%? Although Plaintiff is correct that it is not required to identify every alleged competitor in its pleadings, its choice to identify essentially none is striking. Especially when combined with its refusal to offer any clue as to how it calculated its noncommittal market-share number, the Court cannot see how the Commission has nudged its market power claims across the line from conceivable to plausible. Its complaint must therefore be dismissed.

[8] The Court's decision here does not rest on some pleading technicality or arcane feature of antitrust law. Rather, the existence of market power is at the heart of any monopolization claim. As the Supreme Court explained in [*Bell Atlantic Corp. v. Twombly*, 550 U.S. 544 (2007)], itself an antitrust case, [a] district court must retain the power to insist upon some specificity in pleading before allowing a potentially massive factual controversy to proceed. Here, this Court must exercise that power. The FTC's Complaint says almost nothing concrete on the key question of how much power Facebook actually had, and still has, in a properly defined antitrust product market. It is almost as if the agency expects the Court to simply nod to the conventional wisdom that Facebook is a monopolist. After all, no one who hears the title of the 2010 film "The Social Network" wonders which company it is about. Yet, whatever it may mean to the public, "monopoly power" is a term of art under federal law with a precise economic meaning: the power to profitably raise prices or exclude competition in a properly defined market. To merely allege that a defendant firm has somewhere over 60% share of an unusual, nonintuitive product market— the confines of which are only somewhat fleshed out and the players within which remain almost entirely unspecified—is not enough. The FTC has therefore fallen short of its pleading burden.

[9] That said, because it believes that the agency may be able to cure these deficiencies by repleading, the Court will dismiss without prejudice only the Complaint, not the entire case, leaving Plaintiff free to amend [its] pleading and continue the litigation. Whether and how the agency chooses to do so is up to it.

* * *

The FTC took the hint and bulked up the complaint's monopoly-power allegations, as the next extract shows.

FTC v. Facebook, Inc.

Case No. 20-3590, 2022 WL 103308 (D.D.C. Jan. 11, 2022)

Judge Boasberg.

[1] [T]he Court now addresses what has thus far been the FTC's Achilles' heel: sufficiently alleging Facebook's market dominance. In the last go-round, the Commission alleged only that Facebook has maintained a dominant share of the U.S. personal social networking market (in excess of 60%) since 2011, and that no other social network of comparable scale exists in the United States. The Court concluded that such bare allegations—which do not even provide an estimated actual figure or range for Facebook's market share at any point over the past ten years— ultimately fall short of plausibly establishing that Facebook holds market power. Because it was conceivable that the agency may be able to cure these deficiencies by repleading, however, the Court dismissed the Complaint without prejudice, leaving Plaintiff free to amend its pleading and continue the litigation.

[2] The FTC has now done precisely that, adding substantial new allegations about the contours of Facebook's market share. Most notably, the Amended Complaint alleges far more detailed facts to support its claim that Facebook has today, and has maintained since 2011, a dominant share of the relevant market for U.S. personal social networking services. Specifically, the Amended Complaint includes allegations regarding Facebook's market share of daily average users (DAUs) and monthly average users (MAUs) of [personal social networking ("PSN")] services in the United States, as well as its share of users' average time spent on PSN services. For instance, the FTC alleges that, based on an analysis of data maintained by Comscore, a commercially-available data source,

Facebook's share of DAUs of apps providing personal social networking services in the United States has exceeded 70% since 2016 and was at least as high in 2011. Indeed, the Amended Complaint alleges that, from September 2016 through December 2020, Facebook's share of DAUs among apps providing personal social networking services in the United States averaged 80% per month for smartphones, 86% per month in tablets, and 98% per month for desktop computers, and that Facebook's share of DAUs has not dropped below 70% in any month on any device-type. The combined shares of other PSN providers, meanwhile—which the FTC identifies as including Snapchat, Google+, Myspace, Path, MeWe, Orkut, and Friendster—did not exceed 30% on any device type during any month in this period.

[3] The agency's allegations concerning MAUs tell the same story. Again relying on Comscore data, the FTC alleges that Facebook's share of MAUs of apps providing personal social networking services in the United States has exceeded 65% since 2012 and was at least as high in 2011. Similarly, the combined shares of other providers did not exceed 32% on either device type, mobile or desktop, in any month during the period of September 2012 to December 2020. Plaintiff's allegations concerning Facebook's share of the time spent by users of apps providing personal social networking services in the United States are also in accord with the DAU and MAU data. In fact, the FTC alleges that Facebook's share of users' time spent on such services has exceeded 80% since 2012 and was at least as high in 2011.

[4] The Amended Complaint also adequately alleges that the three metrics offered to measure market share—DAUs, MAUs, and time spent—are appropriate indicators. The FTC explains, consistent with common sense, that a personal social networking service's attractiveness to users, and therefore its competitive significance, is related to its number of users and to how intensively its users engage with the service. Significantly, the Amended Complaint alleges that Facebook itself uses these metrics to assess its performance, as well as that of rival PSN services. Indeed, in the ordinary course of business, Facebook's executives and investors, rival personal social networking providers, and industry observers have assessed the performance of Facebook Blue, Instagram, and other personal social networking providers using measures of active user base and how much people use the services—with DAUs, MAUs, and the amount time spent by users on the service being common units of measure. For instance, Facebook's internal presentations assessing the performance of Facebook Blue and Instagram focus on time spent per month, MAUs, and DAUs, and the company relies on these same metrics to assess its rivals' competitive significance.

[5] The FTC similarly alleges that other firms offering PSN services cite these metrics. Snapchat, for example, regularly compares its performance with that of Instagram by observing the firms' MAUs, DAUs, and time spent metrics. Relatedly, the FTC also alleges that commercial data sources track the usage of online services within the United States using metrics such as MAUs, DAUs, and time spent.

[6] Considering these new allegations and granting Plaintiff the benefit of all inferences that can be derived from the facts alleged, means that the Amended Complaint contains sufficient factual matter, accepted as true, to state a claim to relief that is plausible on its face. In stark contrast with its predecessor, this Complaint provides reinforcing, specific allegations that all point toward the same conclusion: Facebook has maintained a dominant market share during the relevant time period. Accepting the market definition (which Defendant does) and the truth of Plaintiff's market-share allegations (which the Court must at this stage), Facebook's market share comfortably exceeds the levels that courts ordinarily find sufficient to establish monopoly power.

NOTES

1) What is the difference between market power and monopoly power? Would we do better to eliminate the distinction altogether? How could we do so?
2) What does it mean to talk as Elhauge does about a firm having "more discretion over prices"? Don't all businesses have a profit-maximizing price, such that all other prices would be less profitable?
3) How does antitrust's conception of "monopoly power" differ from the everyday public usage of that term? Would it be an improvement to use the everyday meaning instead?
4) Do you think that, in practice, the managers of businesses generally know whether or not their business holds monopoly power in the antitrust sense? Does this matter for antitrust law or policy?

5) As we have seen, the court gave some famous guidance in *Alcoa* about the relationship between market share and monopoly power, often cited by courts today. But how do you think the *Alcoa* court calculated or determined that "[ninety percent] is enough to constitute a monopoly; it is doubtful whether sixty or sixty-four percent would be enough; and certainly thirty-three per cent is not"? Where did this come from?

6) How would you measure market share in social networking? Does Facebook's share of monthly and daily active users, and of time spent on the platform, illuminate the kind of power that antitrust's concept of monopoly is designed to capture? Why, or why not? What other information or materials would you consider probative or helpful, and why?

7) Some markets for content are highly differentiated. How would you go about figuring out whether a content publisher—say, a book publisher or a music publisher—had monopoly power in the antitrust sense?

8) What does "monopoly power" mean in a market in which the product or service is provided to a user for free? Is the concept helpful or important in such markets? Why, or why not?

9) Suppose that every brand of some product (say, clothing, music, or candy) has a small percentage of customers who are fanatically loyal to the brand and will pay vastly in excess of the competitive price for it. Is each of those brands a monopolist in a price-discrimination market? (The economics and law of price-discrimination markets are covered in Chapters II and III respectively.). What facts would affect your answer?

10) Suppose that a firm is the only supplier of a particular product or service, but that its prices are limited by law at what the government (correctly) considers to be a roughly competitive level. Does that firm hold monopoly power in the antitrust sense, such that Section 2 would govern its conduct?

C. The Conduct Element: Are There Any Common Principles?

So we know that Section 2 applies to monopolists. But what, exactly, does Section 2 tell a monopolist that it may not *do*? What counts as "exclusionary," "anticompetitive," or "predatory" conduct? Or, to put it another way, what counts as "competition on the merits"? As we will see in the next section, we have pretty good micro-rules for analyzing exclusivity, tying, and so on: but are there any common principles that apply across Section 2? Can we understand the micro-rules as reflecting or implementing some deeper underlying themes?

In this Section we will focus on four "big picture" themes or ideas that characterize many monopolization cases and which might be understood to underpin the micro-rules for individual practices: (1) a violation of Section 2 requires "exclusion" of one or more rivals (that is, impairment of their ability or incentive to compete); (2) a violation requires that the exclusion be sufficiently likely to make a contribution to the defendant's monopoly power; (3) some practices (like above-cost discounting, or an unconditional refusal to deal) are treated much more indulgently than other practices; and (4) courts are willing to consider procompetitive justifications for conduct that would otherwise constitute monopolization, even if the rules for analyzing justifications are less than perfectly clear.

We will take these four themes in turn, before turning in the next section to specific categories of exclusionary practice. Keep in mind that this is just one way of thinking about the common threads or themes that unify Section 2. There are plenty of other ways of understanding what monopolization law does, or should do.

1. Exclusion

The first, and perhaps the clearest, of the unifying themes in monopolization law is that, in order to violate Section 2, the monopolist's conduct must in some way suppress the ability or incentive of rivals to compete. In other words, it must tend to "exclude." This can be, and usually is, accomplished in a way that we might call "indirect": that is, by changing the incentives of trading partners (like input suppliers, distributors, or customers) in a way that increases competitors' costs. For example, signing key trading partners up to deal with the monopolist exclusively, or on preferred terms, can drive up rivals' costs and reduce competitive pressure on the monopolist. In rarer cases, exclusion can be accomplished in a way that we might call "direct": that is, operating immediately on the excluded firms, such as by offering threats or benefits to induce actual or potential rivals to avoid competition,[480] by purchasing them, or even by directly damaging their competitive assets.[481] (The terms "direct" and "indirect" do not appear in the cases: they are used here to illustrate a difference between two categories of exclusion.)

A simple example of indirect exclusion is found in the Third Circuit's *Dentsply* decision. In that case, the defendant monopolist obtained exclusive control over dental dealers—the best and most cost-effective method of distributing dental products to the customers (dental laboratories)—leaving rivals to make do with markedly inferior alternatives. The court imposed monopolization liability.

United States v. Dentsply Intern., Inc.
399 F.3d 181 (3d Cir. 2005)

Judge Weis.

[1] . . . Dentsply has long dominated the [prefabricated artificial teeth] industry consisting of 12–13 manufacturers and enjoys a 75%—80% market share on a revenue basis, 67% on a unit basis, and is about 15 times larger than its next closest competitor.

[2] For more than fifteen years, Dentsply has operated under a policy that discouraged its dealers from adding competitors' teeth to their lines of products. In 1993, Dentsply adopted "Dealer Criterion 6." It provides that in order to effectively promote Dentsply–York products, authorized dealers "may not add further [(*i.e.*, competitors')] tooth lines to their product offering." Dentsply operates on a purchase order basis with its distributors and, therefore, the relationship is essentially terminable at will. Dealer Criterion 6 was enforced against dealers with the exception of those who had carried competing products before 1993 and were "grandfathered" for sales of those products. Dentsply rebuffed attempts by those particular distributors to expand their lines of competing products beyond the grandfathered ones. [. . .]

[3] Dealers have been dissatisfied with Dealer Criterion 6, but, at least in the recent past, none of them have given up the popular Dentsply teeth to take on a competitive line. [. . .]

[4] The reality is that over a period of years, because of Dentsply's domination of dealers, direct sales have not been a practical alternative for most manufacturers. It has not been so much the competitors' less than enthusiastic efforts at competition that produced paltry results, as it is the blocking of access to the key dealers. This is the part of the real market that is denied to the rivals.

[5] The apparent lack of aggressiveness by competitors is not a matter of apathy, but a reflection of the effectiveness of Dentsply's exclusionary policy. Although its rivals could theoretically convince a dealer to buy their products and drop Dentsply's line, that has not occurred. [. . .]

[6] The realities of the artificial tooth market were candidly expressed by two former managerial employees of Dentsply when they explained their rules of engagement. One testified that Dealer Criterion 6 was designed to "block competitive distribution points." He continued, "Do not allow competition to achieve toeholds in dealers; tie up dealers; do not 'free up' key players."

[7] Another former manager said:

> You don't want your competition with your distributors, you don't want to give the distributors an opportunity to sell a competitive product. And you don't want to give your end user, the customer, meaning a laboratory and/or a dentist, a choice. He has to buy Dentsply teeth. That's the only thing that's available. The only place you can get it is through the distributor and the only one that the distributor is selling is Dentsply teeth. That's your objective.

These are clear expressions of a plan to maintain monopolistic power.

---

[480] *See, e.g.*, FTC v. Actavis, Inc., 570 U.S. 136 (2013) ("pay for delay").
[481] *See, e.g.*, Conwood Co., L.P. v. U.S. Tobacco Co., 290 F.3d 768 (6th Cir. 2002).

[8] The District Court detailed some ten separate incidents in which Dentsply required agreement by new as well as long-standing dealers not to handle competitors' teeth. For example, when the DLDS firm [(a dealer)] considered adding two other tooth lines because of customers' demand, Dentsply threatened to sever access not only to its teeth, but to other dental products as well. DLDS yielded to that pressure. The termination of Trinity Dental, which had previously sold Dentsply products other than teeth, was a similar instance. When Trinity wanted to add teeth to its line for the first time and chose a competitor, Dentsply refused to supply other dental products. [. . .]

[9] The evidence demonstrated conclusively that Dentsply had supremacy over the dealer network and it was at that crucial point in the distribution chain that monopoly power over the market for artificial teeth was established. The reality in this case is that the firm that ties up the key dealers rules the market. [. . .]

[10] The factual pattern here is quite similar to that in LePage's, Inc. v. 3M, 324 F.3d 141 (3d Cir. 2003). There, a manufacturer of transparent tape locked up high volume distribution channels by means of substantial discounts on a range of its other products. We concluded that the use of exclusive dealing and bundled rebates to the detriment of the rival manufacturer violated Section 2. Similarly, in [United States v. Microsoft, 253 F.3d 34 (D.C. Cir. 2001)], the Court of Appeals for the D.C. Circuit concluded that, through the use of exclusive contracts with key dealers, a manufacturer foreclosed competitors from a substantial percentage of the available opportunities for product distribution.

[11] The evidence in this case demonstrates that for a considerable time, through the use of Dealer Criterion 6 Dentsply has been able to exclude competitors from the dealers' network, a narrow, but heavily traveled channel to the dental laboratories. [. . .]

[12] Assessing anti-competitive effect is important in evaluating a challenge to a violation of Section 2. Under that Section of the Sherman Act, it is not necessary that all competition be removed from the market. The test is not total foreclosure, but whether the challenged practices bar a substantial number of rivals or severely restrict the market's ambit. [. . .]

[13] By ensuring that the key dealers offer Dentsply teeth either as the only or dominant choice, Dealer Criterion 6 has a significant effect in preserving Dentsply's monopoly. It helps keep sales of competing teeth below the critical level necessary for any rival to pose a real threat to Dentsply's market share. As such, Dealer Criterion 6 is a solid pillar of harm to competition. [. . .]

[14] For a great number of dental laboratories, the dealer is the preferred source for artificial teeth. . . . [L]aboratories are driven by the realities of the marketplace to buy far more heavily from dealers than manufacturers. This may be largely attributed to the beneficial services, credit function, economies of scale and convenience that dealers provide to laboratories, benefits which are otherwise unavailable to them when they buy direct.

[15] The record is replete with evidence of benefits provided by dealers. For example, they provide laboratories the benefit of "one stop-shopping" and extensive credit services. Because dealers typically carry the products of multiple manufacturers, a laboratory can order, with a single phone call to a dealer, products from multiple sources. Without dealers, in most instances laboratories would have to place individual calls to each manufacturer, expend the time, and pay multiple shipping charges to fill the same orders. [. . .]

[16] Buying through dealers also enables laboratories to take advantage of obtaining discounts. Because they engage in price competition to gain laboratories' business, dealers often discount manufacturers' suggested laboratory price for artificial teeth. There is no finding on this record that manufacturers offer similar discounts. [. . .]

[17] Dealers also provide benefits to manufacturers, perhaps the most obvious of which is efficiency of scale. Using select high-volume dealers, as opposed to directly selling to hundreds if not thousands of laboratories, greatly reduces the manufacturer's distribution costs and credit risks. Dentsply, for example, currently sells to twenty three dealers. If it were instead to sell directly to individual laboratories, Dentsply would incur significantly higher transaction costs, extension of credit burdens, and credit risks. [. . .]

[18] The benefits that dealers provide manufacturers help make dealers the preferred distribution channels—in effect, the "gateways"—to the artificial teeth market. Nonetheless, the District Court found that selling direct is a "viable" method of distributing artificial teeth. But we are convinced that it is "viable" only in the sense that it is "possible," not that it is practical or feasible in the market as it exists and functions. [. . .]

[19] It is true that Dentsply's competitors can sell directly to the dental laboratories and an insignificant number do. The undeniable reality, however, is that dealers have a controlling degree of access to the laboratories. The long-entrenched Dentsply dealer network with its ties to the laboratories makes it impracticable for a manufacturer to rely on direct distribution to the laboratories in any significant amount.

[20] That some manufacturers resort to direct sales and are even able to stay in business by selling directly is insufficient proof that direct selling is an effective means of competition. The proper inquiry is not whether direct sales enable a competitor to "survive" but rather whether direct selling "poses a real threat" to defendant's monopoly. The minuscule 5% and 3% market shares eked out by direct-selling manufacturers Ivoclar and Vita, Dentsply's "primary competitors," reveal that direct selling poses little threat to Dentsply.

[21] Although the parties to the sales transactions consider the exclusionary arrangements to be agreements, they are technically only a series of independent sales. Dentsply sells teeth to the dealers on an individual transaction basis and essentially the arrangement is "at-will." Nevertheless, the economic elements involved—the large share of the market held by Dentsply and its conduct excluding competing manufacturers—realistically make the arrangements here as effective as those in written contracts.

[22] . . . Dealer Criterion 6 created a strong economic incentive for dealers to reject competing lines in favor of Dentsply's teeth.

Theories of Exclusion

As we saw in evaluating vertical restraints in Chapter VI, there are many ways to "exclude" rivals by suppressing their ability or incentive to compete. These may include, for example:

Foreclosure. Perhaps the classic method of exclusion is foreclosure: that is, cutting rivals off from access to inputs, distribution, or customers in a manner that reduces those rivals' ability/incentive to compete. This comes in several flavors:

Input foreclosure. If a monopolist can limit rivals to higher-cost or lower-quality inputs, those rivals may find it harder, or impossible, to exert competitive pressure on the monopolist. As a result, the monopolist may obtain increased power.

Complement foreclosure. If a monopolist can limit the access of rivals' customers to complements for rivals' inputs, the value of rivals' products will be reduced—and so too the competitive pressure on the monopolist. Increased power may be the result.

Distribution foreclosure. The same tactic can work just as well with distribution infrastructure as with inputs. If a monopolist can make it more expensive or difficult for rivals to reach consumers, by forcing them to switch to inferior mechanisms of distribution, the result may be a reduction in competitive pressure on the monopolist.

Customer foreclosure. In a slight variation on distribution foreclosure, a monopolist may engage in conduct that deprives rivals of access to a sufficient customer base to maintain competitive viability (for example, scale economies). For example, through tying or bundling, a monopolist may cause customers to switch over to the monopolist's products—even if rivals offer a superior product—and as a consequence rivals may lose scale economies and be forced from the market.

Predation. Predation is a play in two acts. In the first stage, a monopolist may charge unsustainably low prices that rivals cannot match, driving them out of a market protected by entry barriers. In the second stage, the successful monopolist enjoys more power over price and output following the exits of its rivals, and raises prices to recoup the losses incurred during the predation scheme. Courts tend to be cautious to condemn predation not because exclusion is implausible, but in light of the costs and risks of punishing or deterring low prices.

Buying off and buying up. Monopolists can also suppress rivals by targeting their *incentives* to compete: for example, by acquiring them or by paying them (or otherwise compensating them) to stay out of the market or to delay their entry. (We will meet the so called pay-for-delay practice when we consider IP and pharmaceutical competition in Chapter X.)

Other exclusion. In theory, anything else that limits rivals' ability or incentives to compete might be capable of constituting exclusion for the purposes of Section 2, including abuses of process (like sham litigation and fraudulently obtaining intellectual property), and even some torts & deception. (Of course, exclusion alone is not enough to establish illegality.)

The most famous academic article on exclusion is probably the pathbreaking piece by Steve Salop and Tom Krattenmaker on "raising rivals' costs." Among other things, the article explores different ways in which a monopolist can drive input costs up. As Salop and Krattenmaker explain, a monopolist might leave rivals with inputs that are too expensive, insufficient in quality, or vulnerable to oligopoly or cartelization.

Thomas G. Krattenmaker and Steven C. Salop, Anticompetitive Exclusion: Raising Rivals' Costs to Achieve Power Over Price
96 Yale L.J. 209 (1989)

We present an antitrust theory that explains how a wide variety of exclusionary restraints can, under fairly strict conditions, create or enhance market power. We also offer guidelines to assist enforcement agencies and courts in developing reliable, objective, administrable tests to indicate when such anticompetitive results are probable and, therefore, which specific conditions should be present before the arrangement is condemned.

To summarize, a firm may gain the ability to raise price by contracting with input suppliers for the suppliers' agreements not to deal with the purchasing firm's competitors on equal terms. We call these agreements "exclusionary rights contracts." Under certain conditions, such contracts for exclusionary rights can have the effect of raising rivals' costs by restraining the supply of inputs available to rivals, thereby giving the purchaser power to raise prices in its output market. Courts should inquire whether the firm that purchases an exclusionary rights agreement thereby places its competitors at such a cost disadvantage that the purchaser can then exercise monopoly power by raising its price. [. . .]

We can identify four distinct methods by which an exclusionary rights contract can raise the costs of the purchaser's rivals. With all these methods, the agreement raises rivals' costs by "foreclosure": more precisely, by restricting the supply available to rivals of a key input without similarly restricting the amount available to satisfy the purchaser's demand. Two of these methods succeed by restricting rivals' supply directly. They are techniques of direct foreclosure. The others induce suppliers to restrict output in response to incentives created by the exclusionary rights agreement. They are methods of facilitating tacit or express collusion that lead to foreclosed or restricted supply. [. . .]

The simplest and most obvious method by which foreclosure of supply can raise rivals' costs is the purchaser's obtaining exclusionary rights from all (or a sufficient number of) the lowest-cost suppliers, where those suppliers determine the input's market price. Competitors of the purchaser experience a cost increase as they necessarily shift to higher cost suppliers or less efficient inputs.

Antitrust literati know this as the "Bottleneck" or "essential facilities" problem. This Bottleneck method is precisely the technique employed collectively by a group of vertically integrated firms in the *Terminal Railroad* case. In that case, a group of railroad operators obtained an important input: the only railroad bridges across the Mississippi River at St. Louis. The railroad operators also obtained a promise from the bridge owners (here, the railroad operators themselves) that the bridges could be made available to other, non-owner, railroads on discriminatory terms. Excluded railroads could avoid this risk only by building their own bridges or ferries. [. . .]

Foreclosure also can raise rivals' costs when the purchaser acquires an exclusionary right over a representative portion of the supply, withholding that portion from rivals and thereby driving up the market price for the remainder of the input still available to rivals. Antitrust lingo often dubs this method a "supply squeeze" or "quantitative foreclosure," because the emphasis is not on the unique quality of the input foreclosed, but rather is on the sheer amount. We call it the Real Foreclosure technique to denote that the purchaser gains actual, effective control of the inputs to restrict potential supply and to raise price.

In a leading monopoly case, Alcoa was accused of having employed this Real Foreclosure tactic on two separate occasions. First, when Alcoa's patents on the manufacture of aluminum expired after the turn of the century, Alcoa maintained its monopoly in part by obtaining promises from some electrical utilities not to supply power to any other aluminum manufacturer. The price of electricity to Alcoa's potential rivals would increase as they bid for the remaining scarce supply. The right acquired was a naked exclusionary right; Alcoa apparently did not purchase any electricity from these utilities. Alcoa also involved a more controversial type of Real Foreclosure. Judge Learned Hand concluded that, wholly apart from its covenants with electrical utilities, Alcoa had illegally maintained its monopoly by repeatedly expanding its capacity before demand for aluminum increased. One interpretation of this charge against Alcoa is that it used a variant of the Real Foreclosure technique that we denote as Overbuying. Alcoa's excess accumulation of scarce inputs, notably bauxite, left potential new aluminum manufacturers facing the prospect that their bids would significantly drive up the prices of the remaining available inputs. By overbuying bauxite, Alcoa raised its rivals' costs of producing aluminum. [. . .]

Under certain conditions, exclusionary vertical restraints also can facilitate pricing coordination that enriches suppliers while raising the cost of the purchaser's competitors. The suppliers who inflict these harms may or may not participate in the vertical restraint. [. . .]

There are two variants of this collusive method, one involving discrimination against rivals and the other involving refusal to deal. We denominate both as the Cartel Ringmaster technique because the purchaser, in effect, orchestrates cartel-like discriminatory input pricing against its rivals. The purchaser provides a more efficient organizing, profit-sharing, and policing mechanism than the suppliers could generate themselves.

In the first type of case, a firm purchasing a vertical restraint may, as part of the agreement, induce a number of its suppliers to deal with the purchaser's rivals only on terms disadvantageous to those rivals. Antitrust lore sometimes describes this as a "price squeeze," although this term is most commonly employed when the selling and buying firms practicing the restraint are merged. [. . .]

Cartel Ringmaster also may involve outright refusals to deal with rivals by a number of suppliers. In this case, the suppliers also can gain by sharing directly in the increased profits of the purchaser or by extracting some of its gains by raising the purchaser's input costs.

Cartel Ringmaster is somewhat different from the other techniques analyzed here because it has a greater horizontal aspect. Its profitability may not depend on the purchaser's gaining power over price in the market in which it sells and sharing the resulting profit with restrained suppliers. Instead, it is possible that the suppliers themselves may gain sufficient benefits from charging a higher monopoly price for their input, irrespective of any additional benefits obtained by the purchaser from competing against higher cost rivals. Indeed, in extreme cases, they may profit enough to be able to compensate the purchaser for its role as organizer of the collusive scheme. Moreover, by embedding the collusive agreement in a vertical contract that raises input prices, it is easier to prevent cheating and to redistribute the collusive gains. The purchaser can monitor the agreement and, absent antitrust strictures, enforce it. Given this difference, it may be unnecessary for courts to require proof of power over price before finding an antitrust violation in this case, where the suppliers' conduct is essentially horizontal, that is, where it is profitable to suppliers irrespective of any payments made to them by the purchaser. [. . .]

Finally, a vertical restraint can effectively alter the industry structure confronting the purchaser's competitors and thereby significantly increase the probability that the remaining unrestrained suppliers can successfully collude, expressly or tacitly, to raise price. We denominate this the Frankenstein Monster technique, because through this method the purchaser of an exclusionary rights contract creates and turns loose upon its rivals an industry structure likely to generate a price increase. As an extreme example, suppose a manufacturer signs exclusive dealing contracts with all but one retailer. Assuming that there are entry barriers, the one remaining retailer can then monopolize trade with the manufacturer's rivals. That retailer is the Frankenstein Monster. Similarly, by purchasing exclusionary rights from the most likely potential entrants, the purchaser might also use the

Frankenstein Monster technique to facilitate collusion among established input suppliers by eliminating or reducing the threat of entry. Unlike the Cartel Ringmaster technique, when a purchaser employs the Frankenstein Monster tactic, its rivals' cost increase is inflicted by suppliers that are not parties to the exclusionary rights agreement.

NOTES

1) Most of the examples above deal with impairing the *ability* of competitors to compete with the monopolist: but what about conduct that impairs only the *incentive* to compete, while leaving intact rivals' ability to do so? What kinds of conduct would, or might, be included in this category? Should antitrust treat impact on ability and impact on incentive similarly or differently? What, in economic analysis, is the difference?

2) When a monopolist engages in conduct that make it costlier or harder for a rival to deal with a key input supplier, or a key distributor, the rival's incentive to create or sponsor alternatives is increased. This can result in *more* competition among suppliers or distributors. Is this a good reason to be cautious in imposing Section 2 liability? Under what circumstances is this argument stronger or weaker?

3) What is the difference between wrongful exclusion and merely losing out in the competitive struggle? To put it another way: what's the difference between competing successfully and wrongfully excluding your rivals?

4) Should courts and agencies focus on whether a company has actually been driven out of the market, rather than on whether its ability or incentive to compete have been impaired?

5) Is a rival "excluded" for the purposes of monopolization law if:

> a) a monopolist buys the best or cheapest inputs or distribution, such that rivals are left with inferior alternatives? (Assume no exclusivity commitments or other restraints: the monopolist just offers the best price for the inputs or distribution in a spot market.)

> b) a monopolist makes misleading claims about the inferiority of the rival's product, and, by doing so, seems to influence some actual and potential customers?

> c) a monopolist makes misleading claims about the superiority and desirability of its own product, and, by doing so, seems to influence some actual and potential customers?

> d) a monopolist refuses to give a rival a free benefit (*e.g.*, free or subsidized access to its infrastructure and resources)?

> e) a monopolist refuses to sell to a rival on the terms that it would sell to a non-rival?

> f) a monopolist fraudulently avoids paying taxes, or minimum wages to its employees, thus deriving a significant cost advantage over rivals?

> g) a monopolist recruits away key employees from a rival by offering them better salaries, knowing that the rival may struggle to navigate an important period in the industry without their help?

6) Should courts worry about subjective intentions in assessing whether exclusion has taken place? In particular, should the law evaluate:

> a) the intentions of the monopolist (*e.g.*, by asking whether the alleged exclusion was intentional, incidental to another purpose, or entirely unforeseen), or

> b) the intentions of the "excluded" firm (*e.g.*, by asking whether the rival actually intended to exert serious competitive pressure on the monopolist)?

2. Contribution to Monopoly

The exclusion that is challenged in a monopolization case must make a contribution of some kind to the acquisition or maintenance of the defendant's monopoly power. Excluding an entirely irrelevant rival, or a company that will surely not become a competitor of the monopolist, almost certainly cannot violate Section 2. Nor can conduct that will exclude rivals only in a market in which the defendant is not present.[482]

In some cases, the existence of a causal relationship between the conduct and a contribution to monopoly will be very clear. For example, if a monopolist blows up the factory of its single major competitor, in a market where entry takes many years and a vast amount of capital, leaving the monopolist without any active rivals at all, the necessary contribution will probably not be hard to establish.

But if things are more complicated—and they usually are—then the threshold becomes much more important. For example, what if a monopolist acquires an upstart competitor that is rapidly gaining momentum and share, but before it becomes clear that the competitor is likely to take a bite out of the monopolist's market position? Or what if the monopolist somehow eliminates multiple small entrants or startups, each of which had a modest chance of becoming a serious competitive threat?

The starting point is that *some* contribution is necessary: there must be a reason to think that the challenged practice or transaction will or could lead to more, or more durable, monopoly power. Conduct that merely *exploits* existing monopoly power, without increasing or reinforcing it, does not violate Section 2. The seminal modern statement of this point came in *Trinko*:

> The mere possession of monopoly power, and the concomitant charging of monopoly prices, is not only not unlawful; it is an important element of the free-market system. The opportunity to charge monopoly prices—at least for a short period—is what attracts "business acumen" in the first place; it induces risk taking that produces innovation and economic growth. To safeguard the incentive to innovate, the possession of monopoly power will not be found unlawful unless it is accompanied by an element of anticompetitive conduct.[483]

So the conduct must contribute to monopoly power: but *how much* contribution is enough—both in terms of magnitude and in terms of confidence that the conduct will matter at all? And what evidence can we trust to figure this out?

The leading modern case is the 2001 decision of the *en banc* D.C. Circuit in *Microsoft*. This decision—which followed a high-profile and lengthy (76-day!) trial in D.C. district court—is sufficiently central to modern antitrust, and to modern Section 2 law in particular, that it is worth familiarizing yourself with the case in some detail.

The *Microsoft* Case: Background

The famous *Microsoft* case dealt primarily with Microsoft's efforts to protect its monopoly in the computer operating system ("OS") market from incipient threats.[484] In the federal government's telling, what happened was something like the following. Microsoft had perceived that its monopoly in PC operating systems (which it held through its "Windows" OS) was protected by the fact that third-party software developers wrote applications and other software that depended on Windows, and would not run on rival operating systems. As long as this remained true, would-be entrants and rivals would face a chicken-and-egg problem: there would be little demand for their operating systems without a thriving ecosystem of compatible software; but there was little reason for software developers to invest in creating such software until there was consumer demand for those other operating systems.

But by the mid-1990s, this barrier to effective competition appeared to be under some threat from the emergence of so-called "middleware" products like Netscape's Navigator internet browser and Sun's Java libraries and related technologies. These middleware products were not themselves operating systems—they ran "on top" of Windows or another operating system—but they provided resources and interfaces to support third-party applications and software. In other words, both independently and together, they represented the threat that a cross-OS operating

---

[482] *See, e.g.*, Discon, Inc. v. NYNEX Corp., 93 F.3d 1055, 1062 (2d Cir. 1996) ("[I]t is axiomatic that a firm cannot monopolize a market in which it does not compete."), *vacated on other grounds*, 525 U.S. 128 (1998).

[483] Verizon Communications Inc. v. Law Offices of Curtis V. Trinko, LLP, 540 U.S. 398, 407 (2004). *See also* NYNEX Corp. v. Discon, Inc., 525 U.S. 128 (1998).

[484] United States v. Microsoft Corp., 253 F.3d 34 (D.C. Cir. 2001). Microsoft had previously been the subject of federal antitrust attention. *See* United States v. Microsoft Corp., 56 F.3d 1448 (D.C. Cir. 1995); United States v. Microsoft Corp., 147 F.3d 935 (D.C. Cir. 1998).

environment built on middleware could emerge, capable of running on a number of operating systems, for which software developers could start writing applications. If this happened, Microsoft's operating-system rivals would no longer face the chicken-and-egg problem: Netscape and Sun would have effectively solved the problem by stimulating the development of compatible software.

This prospect was (at the time) a fairly distant future possibility—but it's worth noting that it has to a significant extent come true. Internet browsers, for example, are middleware on which a suite of web-based applications (including Google's portfolio of productivity applications) run that compete with Microsoft's Windows Office productivity software. Microsoft itself offers cloud versions of its Office productivity software that can run in a browser on non-Windows operating systems. But at the time of the litigation against Microsoft, it was far from certain that middleware would take on a platform role, and the lowering of the barrier to entry that protected the dominance of Microsoft's OS might not have materialized at all. Navigator and Java might not have gained sufficient traction, or might not have been able to support a vibrant ecosystem of software that could, in turn, lower barriers to entry in operating systems. Or rivals might simply have been unable or unwilling to invest in taking on Windows in the OS market. Nevertheless, Microsoft's executives saw the threat on the horizon, and decided to do something about it.

Microsoft engaged in multiple complementary strategies designed to forestall the middleware threat. The company directed four strategies at Netscape Navigator:

> (1) entering into exclusive licenses with PC computer manufacturers ("original equipment manufacturers" or "OEMs") that required preinstalling Microsoft's own web browser, Internet Explorer, on new PCs, and ensuring that it was prominently presented to users (thus deterring OEMs from installing a second browser, like Navigator, that would perform the same function and (Microsoft claimed) confuse users[485]), while limiting the changes that an OEM could make to a PC that could have the effect of promoting rival browsers;

> (2) technologically "tying" the Internet Explorer browser to Windows, by making it an irremovable part of the operating system (thus forcing OEMs to train their support staff to answer questions about it, and in turn deterring them from incurring that same investment for rival browsers);

> (3) entering into various arrangements with all leading internet service providers ("ISPs") for sole preferential promotion (ISP promotion being a key distribution channel for consumer software), and obtaining commitments that the service providers would limit their distribution of rival browsers; and

> (4) entering into various arrangements with other third parties, including Apple as well as independent software vendors, that guaranteed Internet Explorer default-browser status on much third-party software and on Mac OS devices, while ensuring that other browsers would not be installed on the desktops of Mac computers.

Microsoft also targeted Sun's Java technologies with four main practices:

> (1) designing its own "Java virtual machine"—essentially a system that translated between Java and the operating system—that was incompatible with Sun's virtual machine (note that the D.C. Circuit would later conclude that this was *not* an anticompetitive practice[486]);

> (2) entering into various arrangements with independent software vendors requiring that Microsoft's Java virtual machine be the default virtual machine in the software they developed (affecting a "substantial portion of the field" for virtual machine distribution);

> (3) providing Java developers with certain tools, as well as its own Java virtual machine, and deceiving the developers into believing that applications made using those tools would be cross-platform, when in fact they would run only on Windows; and

---

[485] At this time, preinstallation by an OEM—so that the software is already installed on the computer when the user starts it up for the first time—was a critical method of distribution for software. Direct download as a means of purchasing software was not widespread until much later, after high-speed internet access became more widely available.

[486] United States v. Microsoft Corp., 253 F.3d 34, 74–75 (D.C. Cir. 2001).

(4) offering benefits to Intel, a key chip-maker, conditioned on Intel terminating its assistance to Sun in developing Sun's Java technologies.

The ensuing litigation raised a wide range of challenging questions under Section 2—including the principles guiding its application to dynamic technology markets—and terminated in a lengthy *en banc* decision of the D.C. Circuit that has become a landmark of modern antitrust jurisprudence and a subject of extensive commentary.[487]

One of the decision's most important facets was its treatment of causation: specifically, the causal link between Microsoft's conduct, aimed at Java and Navigator, and the maintenance of its monopoly in the operating-system market. This was a particularly tricky issue in *Microsoft* because neither Netscape Navigator nor Sun's Java products were actually competing with Microsoft's operating system. Microsoft wasn't trying to take out an existing rival: rather, Microsoft was trying to suppress the threat that middleware could evolve in a way that would stimulate software development that would, in turn, lower the barriers to entry into the operating system market. As such, it would have been extremely challenging to show that, but for Microsoft's conduct, the threat feared by the company—the emergence of a cross-platform ecosystem of apps and the subsequent entry of operating system competitors—would actually have been more likely than not to materialize. This illustrates a general problem in monopolization cases: how confident should a court be that it can predict what would have happened had the defendant not acted (sometimes called the "counterfactual world" or the "but-for world"[488] (*i.e.*, the world that would exist *but for* the defendant's conduct))?

To see how the *Microsoft* court approached this issue, first read the district court's findings of fact regarding the nature and strength of the threat posed by Navigator and Java, and then the court of appeals' discussion of causation.

Findings of Fact, United States v. Microsoft Corp.
84 F. Supp. 2d 9 (D.D.C. 1999)

Judge Jackson.[489]

[1] Middleware technologies . . . have the potential to weaken the applications barrier to entry. Microsoft was apprehensive that the APIs exposed by middleware technologies would attract so much developer interest, and would become so numerous and varied, that there would arise a substantial and growing number of full-featured applications that relied largely, or even wholly, on middleware APIs. The applications relying largely on middleware APIs would potentially be relatively easy to port from one operating system to another. The applications relying exclusively on middleware APIs would run, as written, on any operating system hosting the requisite middleware. So the more popular middleware became and the more APIs it exposed, the more the positive feedback loop that sustains the applications barrier to entry would dissipate. Microsoft was concerned with middleware as a category of software; each type of middleware contributed to the threat posed by the entire category. At the same time, Microsoft focused its antipathy on two incarnations of middleware that, working together, had the potential to weaken the applications barrier severely without the assistance of any other middleware. These were Netscape's Web browser and Sun's implementation of the Java technologies. [. . .]

[2] Netscape Navigator possesses three key middleware attributes that endow it with the potential to diminish the applications barrier to entry. First, in contrast to non-Microsoft, Intel-compatible PC operating systems, which few users would want to use on the same PC systems that carry their copies of Windows, a browser can gain widespread use based on its value as a complement to Windows. Second, because Navigator exposes a set (albeit

---

[487] *See, e.g.*, Andrew I. Gavil & Harry First, THE MICROSOFT ANTITRUST CASES: COMPETITION POLICY FOR THE TWENTY-FIRST CENTURY (2014); William H. Page & John E. Lopatka, THE MICROSOFT CASE: ANTITRUST, HIGH TECHNOLOGY, AND CONSUMER WELFARE (2009); Stan J. Liebowitz & Stephen E. Margolis, WINNERS, LOSERS & MICROSOFT: COMPETITION AND ANTITRUST IN HIGH TECHNOLOGY (1999).

[488] This term will appear again when we discuss merger law in Chapter VIII.

[489] Judge Thomas Penfield Jackson's role in presiding over the *Microsoft* trial became a focus of intense attention and controversy when it emerged that he had been giving interviews to journalists during the proceedings that gave rise to a strong appearance of partiality: the *en banc* D.C. Circuit disqualified him from hearing the case on remand, describing his ethical violations as "deliberate, repeated, egregious, and flagrant," but did not conclude that his findings were tainted by bias. *See* United States v. Microsoft Corp., 253 F.3d 34, 107–18 (D.C. Cir. 2001).

a limited one) of APIs, it can serve as a platform for other software used by consumers. A browser product is particularly well positioned to serve as a platform for network-centric applications that run in association with Web pages. Finally, Navigator has been ported to more than fifteen different operating systems. Thus, if a developer writes an application that relies solely on the APIs exposed by Navigator, that application will, without any porting, run on many different operating systems.

[3] Adding to Navigator's potential to weaken the applications barrier to entry is the fact that the Internet has become both a major inducement for consumers to buy PCs for the first time and a major occupier of the time and attention of current PC users. For any firm looking to turn its browser product into an applications platform such to rival Windows, the intense consumer interest in all things Internet-related is a great boon.

[4] Microsoft knew in the fall of 1994 that Netscape was developing versions of a Web browser to run on different operating systems. It did not yet know, however, that Netscape would employ Navigator to generate revenue directly, much less that the product would evolve in such a way as to threaten Microsoft. In fact, in late December 1994, Netscape's chairman and chief executive officer ("CEO"), Jim Clark, told a Microsoft executive that the focus of Netscape's business would be applications running on servers and that Netscape did not intend to succeed at Microsoft's expense.

[5] As soon as Netscape released Navigator on December 15, 1994, the product began to enjoy dramatic acceptance by the public; shortly after its release, consumers were already using Navigator far more than any other browser product. This alarmed Microsoft, which feared that Navigator's enthusiastic reception could embolden Netscape to develop Navigator into an alternative platform for applications development. In late May 1995, Bill Gates, the chairman and CEO of Microsoft, sent a memorandum entitled "The Internet Tidal Wave" to Microsoft's executives describing Netscape as a "new competitor 'born' on the Internet." He warned his colleagues within Microsoft that Netscape was "pursuing a multi-platform strategy where they move the key API into the client to commoditize the underlying operating system." By the late spring of 1995, the executives responsible for setting Microsoft's corporate strategy were deeply concerned that Netscape was moving its business in a direction that could diminish the applications barrier to entry. [. . .]

[6] The term "Java" refers to four interlocking elements. First, there is a Java programming language with which developers can write applications. Second, there is a set of programs written in Java that expose APIs on which developers writing in Java can rely. These programs are called the "Java class libraries." The third element is the Java compiler, which translates the code written by the developer into Java "bytecode." Finally, there are programs called "Java virtual machines," or "JVMs," which translate Java bytecode into instructions comprehensible to the underlying operating system. If the Java class libraries and a JVM are present on a PC system, the system is said to carry a "Java runtime environment."

[7] The inventors of Java at Sun Microsystems intended the technology to enable applications written in the Java language to run on a variety of platforms with minimal porting. A program written in Java and relying only on APIs exposed by the Java class libraries will run on any PC system containing a JVM that has itself been ported to the resident operating system. Therefore, Java developers need to port their applications only to the extent that those applications rely directly on the APIs exposed by a particular operating system. The more an application written in Java relies on APIs exposed by the Java class libraries, the less work its developer will need to do to port the application to different operating systems. The easier it is for developers to port their applications to different operating systems, the more applications will be written for operating systems other than Windows. To date, the Java class libraries do not expose enough APIs to support the development of full-featured applications that will run well on multiple operating systems without the need for porting; however, they do allow relatively simple, network-centric applications to be written cross-platform. It is Sun's ultimate ambition to expand the class libraries to such an extent that many full-featured, end-user-oriented applications will be written cross-platform. The closer Sun gets to this goal of "write once, run anywhere," the more the applications barrier to entry will erode.

[8] Sun announced in May 1995 that it had developed the Java programming language. Mid-level executives at Microsoft began to express concern about Sun's Java vision in the fall of that year, and by late spring of 1996, senior Microsoft executives were deeply worried about the potential of Sun's Java technologies to diminish the applications barrier to entry.

[9] Sun's strategy could only succeed if a Java runtime environment that complied with Sun's standards found its way onto PC systems running Windows. Sun could not count on Microsoft to ship with Windows an implementation of the Java runtime environment that threatened the applications barrier to entry. Fortunately for Sun, Netscape agreed in May 1995 to include a copy of Sun's Java runtime environment with every copy of Navigator, and Navigator quickly became the principal vehicle by which Sun placed copies of its Java runtime environment on the PC systems of Windows users.

[10] The combined efforts of Netscape and Sun threatened to hasten the demise of the applications barrier to entry, opening the way for non-Microsoft operating systems to emerge as acceptable substitutes for Windows. By stimulating the development of network-centric Java applications accessible to users through browser products, the collaboration of Netscape and Sun also heralded the day when vendors of information appliances and network computers could present users with viable alternatives to PCs themselves. Nevertheless, these middleware technologies have a long way to go before they might imperil the applications barrier to entry. Windows 98 exposes nearly ten thousand APIs, whereas the combined APIs of Navigator and the Java class libraries, together representing the greatest hope for proponents of middleware, total less than a thousand. Decision-makers at Microsoft are apprehensive of potential as well as present threats, though, and in 1995 the implications of the symbiosis between Navigator and Sun's Java implementation were not lost on executives at Microsoft, who viewed Netscape's cooperation with Sun as a further reason to dread the increasing use of Navigator. [. . .]

[11] Although they have been the most prominent, Netscape's Navigator and Sun's Java implementation are not the only manifestations of middleware that Microsoft has perceived as having the potential to weaken the applications barrier to entry. Starting in 1994, Microsoft exhibited considerable concern over the software product Notes, distributed first by Lotus and then by IBM. Microsoft worried about Notes for several reasons: It presented a graphical interface that was common across multiple operating systems; it also exposed a set of APIs to developers; and, like Navigator, it served as a distribution vehicle for Sun's Java runtime environment. Then in 1995, Microsoft reacted with alarm to Intel's Native Signal Processing software, which interacted with the microprocessor independently of the operating system and exposed APIs directly to developers of multimedia content. Finally, in 1997 Microsoft noted the dangers of Apple's and RealNetworks' multimedia playback technologies, which ran on several platforms (including the Mac OS and Windows) and similarly exposed APIs to content developers. Microsoft feared all of these technologies because they facilitated the development of user-oriented software that would be indifferent to the identity of the underlying operating system.

* * *

Now see how the D.C. Circuit handled these findings on appeal.

United States v. Microsoft Corp.
253 F.3d 34 (D.C. Cir. 2001) (en banc)

Per curiam.

[1] Microsoft urges this court to reverse on the monopoly maintenance claim, because plaintiffs never established a causal link between Microsoft's anticompetitive conduct, in particular its foreclosure of Netscape's and Java's distribution channels, and the maintenance of Microsoft's operating system monopoly. . . . According to Microsoft, the District Court cannot simultaneously find that middleware is not a reasonable substitute and that Microsoft's exclusionary conduct contributed to the maintenance of monopoly power in the operating system market. Microsoft claims that the first finding depended on the court's view that middleware does not pose a serious threat to Windows . . . while the second finding required the court to find that Navigator and Java would have developed into serious enough cross-platform threats to erode the applications barrier to entry. We disagree.

[2] Microsoft points to no case, and we can find none, standing for the proposition that, as to § 2 liability in an equitable enforcement action, plaintiffs must present direct proof that a defendant's continued monopoly power is precisely attributable to its anticompetitive conduct. As its lone authority, Microsoft cites the following passage from Professor Areeda's antitrust treatise: "The plaintiff has the burden of pleading, introducing evidence, and

presumably proving by a preponderance of the evidence that reprehensible behavior has contributed significantly to the maintenance of the monopoly."

[3] But, with respect to actions seeking injunctive relief, the authors of that treatise also recognize the need for courts to infer causation from the fact that a defendant has engaged in anticompetitive conduct that reasonably appears capable of making a significant contribution to maintaining monopoly power. To require that § 2 liability turn on a plaintiff's ability or inability to reconstruct the hypothetical marketplace absent a defendant's anticompetitive conduct would only encourage monopolists to take more and earlier anticompetitive action.

[4] We may infer causation when exclusionary conduct is aimed at producers of nascent competitive technologies as well as when it is aimed at producers of established substitutes. Admittedly, in the former case there is added uncertainty, inasmuch as nascent threats are merely potential substitutes. But the underlying proof problem is the same—neither plaintiffs nor the court can confidently reconstruct a product's hypothetical technological development in a world absent the defendant's exclusionary conduct. To some degree, the defendant is made to suffer the uncertain consequences of its own undesirable conduct.

[5] Given this rather edentulous test for causation, the question in this case is not whether Java or Navigator would actually have developed into viable platform substitutes, but (1) whether as a general matter the exclusion of nascent threats is the type of conduct that is reasonably capable of contributing significantly to a defendant's continued monopoly power and (2) whether Java and Navigator reasonably constituted nascent threats at the time Microsoft engaged in the anticompetitive conduct at issue. As to the first, suffice it to say that it would be inimical to the purpose of the Sherman Act to allow monopolists free reign to squash nascent, albeit unproven, competitors at will—particularly in industries marked by rapid technological advance and frequent paradigm shifts. As to the second, the District Court made ample findings that both Navigator and Java showed potential as middleware platform threats. Counsel for Microsoft admitted as much at oral argument.

[6] Microsoft's concerns over causation have more purchase in connection with the appropriate remedy issue, i.e., whether the court should impose a structural remedy or merely enjoin the offensive conduct at issue. As we point out later in this opinion, divestiture is a remedy that is imposed only with great caution, in part because its long-term efficacy is rarely certain. Absent some measure of confidence that there has been an actual loss to competition that needs to be restored, wisdom counsels against adopting radical structural relief. But these queries go to questions of remedy, not liability. In short, causation affords Microsoft no defense to liability for its unlawful actions undertaken to maintain its monopoly in the operating system market.

* * *

There is considerable controversy over the meaning and scope of this holding. Some have read it as authority for a flexible (*i.e.*, relaxed) test of causation in monopolization cases.[490] They emphasize that the "reasonably capable of making a substantial contribution" test is well grounded in cases long preceding *Microsoft*.[491] Others argue that it is confined to a narrow subset of monopolization cases, such as practices lacking procompetitive justifications, or circumstances where an "anticompetitive effect" of some kind has already been shown.[492]

---

[490] *See, e.g.*, D. Bruce Hoffman, *Antitrust in the Digital Economy: A Snapshot of FTC Issues* (May 2019) ("[The *Microsoft* causation standard] has two important implications. One is that given that Section 2 arises only in the exceptional case of actual monopoly power . . . this slightly reduced causation burden should not be viewed with alarm. Second, as the D.C. Circuit explained, a different view would reward monopolists for taking more aggressive anticompetitive steps earlier, and, perversely, would result in the most effective and egregious monopolists—those with longstanding monopolies, who successfully extinguish all competitive threats in their incipiency—being least vulnerable to challenge."); Daniel Francis, *Making Sense of Monopolization*, 84 Antitrust L.J. 779, 807–11 (2022).

[491] *See, e.g.*, Barry Wright Corp. v. ITT Grinnell Corp., 724 F.2d 227, 230 (1st Cir. 1983); S. Pac. Commc'ns Co. v. Am. Tel. & Tel. Co., 740 F.2d 980, 999 n.19 (D.C. Cir. 1984); C.E. Servs., Inc. v. Control Data Corp., 759 F.2d 1241, 1247 n.7 (5th Cir. 1985); Instructional Sys. Dev. Corp. v. Aetna Cas. & Sur. Co., Case No. 82-2105, 1986 WL 30775, at *7 (10th Cir. Mar. 31, 1986), *modified on reh'g*, 817 F.2d 639 (10th Cir. 1987).

[492] Timothy J. Muris & Jonathan E. Nuechterlein, *First Principles for Review of Long-Consummated Mergers*, 5 Criterion J. on Innovation 29, 35, 39–40 (2020) (arguing, among other things, that "even where Microsoft's plaintiff-friendly standard of causation is relevant at all, it is relevant only to liability but not to remedy"); Douglas Ginsburg & Koren Wong-Ervin, *Challenging Consummated Mergers Under Section 2*, Comp. Pol'y Int'l (May 2020) 4 ("[T]he Microsoft court's more lenient "reasonably capable" standard applies by its terms

Setting aside the question of causation, multiple Section 2 cases indicate that there is a difference between creating or extending monopoly power (which can violate Section 2), and merely removing or reducing constraints on the exercise of that power (which cannot). This can be an elusive distinction.

NYNEX Corp. v. Discon, Inc.

525 U.S. 128 (1998)

Justice Breyer.

[1] Discon, Inc., the respondent, sold removal services used by New York Telephone Company, a firm supplying local telephone service in much of New York State and parts of Connecticut. New York Telephone is a subsidiary of NYNEX Corporation. NYNEX also owns Materiel Enterprises Company, a purchasing entity that bought removal services for New York Telephone. Discon, in a lengthy detailed complaint, alleged that the NYNEX defendants . . . engaged in unfair, improper, and anticompetitive activities in order to hurt Discon and to benefit Discon's . . . competitor, AT & T Technologies . . . . The Federal District Court dismissed Discon's complaint for failure to state a claim. The Court of Appeals for the Second Circuit affirmed that dismissal with an exception, and that exception is before us for consideration.

[2] The Second Circuit focused on one of Discon's specific claims, a claim that Materiel Enterprises had switched its purchases from Discon to Discon's competitor, AT & T Technologies, as part of an attempt to defraud local telephone service customers by hoodwinking regulators. According to Discon, Materiel Enterprises would pay AT & T Technologies more than Discon would have charged for similar removal services. It did so because it could pass the higher prices on to New York Telephone, which in turn could pass those prices on to telephone consumers in the form of higher regulatory-agency-approved telephone service charges. At the end of the year, Materiel Enterprises would receive a special rebate from AT & T Technologies, which Materiel Enterprises would share with its parent, NYNEX. Discon added that it refused to participate in this fraudulent scheme, with the result that Materiel Enterprises would not buy from Discon, and Discon went out of business.

[3] These allegations, the Second Circuit said, state a cause of action under § 1 of the Sherman Act [for a group boycott.] . . . For somewhat similar reasons the Second Circuit believed the complaint stated a valid claim of conspiracy to monopolize under § 2 of the Sherman Act. [. . .]

[4] We concede Discon's claim that the petitioners' behavior hurt consumers by raising telephone service rates. But that consumer injury naturally flowed not so much from a less competitive market for removal services, as from the exercise of market power that is *lawfully* in the hands of a monopolist, namely, New York Telephone, combined with a deception worked upon the regulatory agency that prevented the agency from controlling New York Telephone's exercise of its monopoly power. [. . .]

[5] The Court of Appeals . . . upheld the complaint's charge of a conspiracy to monopolize in violation of § 2 of the Sherman Act . . . on the understanding that the conspiracy in question consisted of the very same purchasing practices that we have previously discussed. Unless those agreements harmed the competitive process, they did not amount to a conspiracy to monopolize. We do not see, on the basis of the facts alleged, how Discon could succeed on this claim without prevailing on its § 1 claim. Given our conclusion that Discon has not alleged a § 1 per se violation, we think it prudent to vacate this portion of the Court of Appeals' decision and allow the court to reconsider its finding of a § 2 claim.

* * *

NYNEX has come to stand for the idea that gaining the ability to charge a higher price—for example, by evading a price cap or by manipulating a regulatory scheme—does not amount to an increase in monopoly power unless it reflects increased freedom from competition. For example, in *Rambus*—a case we will meet in detail in Chapter X—Rambus, a participant in a standard-setting organization, had deceptively concealed its IP rights, which were then incorporated into an industry standard, giving Rambus monopoly power. The FTC alleged that but for

---

only to exclusionary conduct lacking any procompetitive justification . . . only when anticompetitive effects are shown . . . does the "reasonably capable of" causation standard apply to allegations that exclusionary conduct killed a nascent threat.").

Rambus's deception, the organization would either have incorporated a different technology or imposed a price cap (a prohibition on charging more than a reasonable and non-discriminatory ("RAND") royalty) on Rambus. Relying on *NYNEX*, the D.C. Circuit held that the deception would not have violated Section 2 if its only effect was to avoid a pricing limitation:

> Under [one of the FTC's two alternative legal theories, the standard-setting organization] lost only an opportunity to secure a RAND commitment from Rambus. But loss of such a commitment is not a harm to competition from alternative technologies in the relevant markets. Indeed, had [the organization] limited Rambus to reasonable royalties and required it to provide licenses on a nondiscriminatory basis, we would expect less competition from alternative technologies, not more; high prices and constrained output tend to attract competitors, not to repel them.

> Scholars in the field have urged that if nondisclosure to [a standard-setting organization] enables a participant to obtain higher royalties than would otherwise have been attainable, the overcharge can properly constitute competitive harm attributable to the nondisclosure, as the overcharge will distort competition in the downstream market. The contention that price-raising deception has downstream effects is surely correct, but that consequence was equally surely true in *NYNEX* (though perhaps on a smaller scale) and equally obvious to the Court. The Commission makes the related contention that because the ability to profitably restrict output and set supracompetitive prices is the *sine qua non* of monopoly power, any conduct that permits a monopolist to avoid constraints on the exercise of that power must be anticompetitive. But again, as in *NYNEX*, an otherwise lawful monopolist's end-run around price constraints, even when deceptive or fraudulent, does not alone present a harm to competition in the monopolized market.

> Thus, if [the standard-setting organization], in the world that would have existed but for Rambus's deception, would have standardized the very same technologies, Rambus's alleged deception cannot be said to have had an effect on competition in violation of the antitrust laws; [the organization's] loss of an opportunity to seek favorable licensing terms is not as such an antitrust harm. Yet the Commission did not reject this as being a possible—perhaps even the more probable—effect of Rambus's conduct. We hold, therefore, that the Commission failed to demonstrate that Rambus's conduct was exclusionary, and thus to establish its claim that Rambus unlawfully monopolized the relevant markets.[493]

NOTES

1) Suppose that you have been asked to advise a company with a 40% share of a relevant market for steel production. The company has asked you to determine whether a proposed exclusive deal would contribute to monopoly power. Concretely, what documents and information would you want to examine, and what analysis would you want to conduct, to figure out the answer? What if the company supplied free email services rather than steel? What about nursing services across the Pacific Northwest and West Coast?

2) Imagine that every year, exactly ten new startups appear in a market for some digital product or service. Today, that market is dominated by a monopolist with a market share of 90%. But each startup has a 5% chance of completely displacing the monopolist. How many of those startups should the monopolist be able to buy, or otherwise exclude, each year without creating a prohibited contribution to monopoly for the purposes of Section 2—and why is that the right number? (Do not worry about other legal tests: just focus on contribution to monopoly power. And assume that the 5% chance of competitive success is known with perfect accuracy by the court and by all market participants.)

a) What if each startup had a 1% chance of displacing the monopolist? Or a 10% chance?

b) Suppose that the monopolist had in fact managed to purchase more than the prohibited number of startups before the litigation was filed. How would you determine which ones should be sold off as a remedy?[494]

---

[493] Rambus Inc. v. FTC, 522 F.3d 456, 466–67 (D.C. Cir. 2008). *See also infra* § X.D.1.

[494] We will talk about merger remedies in Chapter VIII.

3) How far should agencies and courts rely on the subjective assessment of market participants, when gauging how much difference some practice or transaction has made or is likely to make to monopoly power? What if the monopolist, the target, and other market participants disagree: whose assessment is likely to be most helpful, and why? What if ordinary-course documents express one view, but executives tell a different story in deposition under oath?

4) When, how, and why should we insist that plaintiffs show a price increase in order to establish a contribution to monopoly power? Can you imagine circumstances under which a business gains greater monopoly power but does not increase its prices?

5) How could we see the effects of an increase in monopoly power in a zero-price market? Could we quantify such effects?

6) Do you agree with the holding in *NYNEX*?

7) What kinds of labor markets, or groups of employees, do you think might be vulnerable to labor monopsonization?

3. Freedom of Action and Refusal to Deal: When Is Excluding Rivals OK?

Not all conduct that makes life harder for rivals and contributes to monopoly is unlawful: in fact, much such conduct is not only legal but actually desirable overall. Most obviously, improving a product makes it harder for rivals to survive. So does finding a way to lower costs or improve operational efficiency. Winning contracts and bids generally comes at the expense of rivals. In fact, most things that we would think of as "desirable competition" involve harm to competitors, including the impairment of opportunities and loss of profits.

Thus, even monopolists enjoy considerable freedom to compete on the merits and to make competitive decisions, including if rivals suffer as a result. But: how much freedom? When does sharp-elbowed competition become unlawful monopolization? This is an immensely difficult question and there is a great deal of disagreement about what the answer should be.

There is an old strand of thinking in monopolization law that certain kinds of conduct can be thought of as "fair competition" and are not a basis for antitrust liability *regardless of their effects*: that is, even if exclusion, monopoly power, and consumer harm follow.[495] The Court seems to have been getting at something like this when it tried to summarize the conduct element of the monopolization offense in *Grinnell*—but the Court buried the idea in a passage that becomes more confusing the more closely you read it:

> The offense of monopoly under s 2 of the Sherman Act has two elements: (1) the possession of monopoly power in the relevant market and (2) the *willful acquisition or maintenance of that power as distinguished from growth or development as a consequence of a superior product, business acumen, or historic accident*. We shall see that this second ingredient presents no major problem here, as what was done in building the empire was done plainly and explicitly for a single purpose.[496]

Read element (2) carefully. Can you see why it may be unhelpful to contrast "the willful acquisition or maintenance of monopoly power" with "growth or development as a consequence of a superior product, business acumen, or historic accident"? For example: are there cases that might fall into *both* categories? And what business does not knowingly pursue market or monopoly power, even if it does so solely through innovation?

In any event: the idea that certain kinds of behavior not be haunted by the threat of monopolization liability—or at least that courts should be particularly reluctant to impose liability for certain types of behavior—has a long pedigree in monopolization's history. For example, on the day that the Sherman Act passed the Senate (April 8,

---

[495] *See, e.g.*, Mark S. Popofsky, *Defining Exclusionary Conduct: Section 2, The Rule of Reason, and the Unifying Principle Underlying Antitrust Rules*, 73 Antitrust L.J. 435, 442 (2006).

[496] United States v. Grinnell Corp., 384 U.S. 563, 570–71 (1966) (emphasis added).

1890), the senators were explicitly reassured that someone who does "[no]thing but compete" need not fear antitrust liability, even if a monopoly resulted from his or her "skill and energy":

> Mr. KENNA. Suppose a citizen of Kentucky is dealing in shorthorn cattle and by virtue of his superior skill in that particular product it turns out that be is the only one in the United States to whom an order comes from Mexico for cattle of that stock for a considerable period, so that be is conceded to have a monopoly of that trade with Mexico; is it intended by the committee that the bill shall make that man a culprit?

> Mr. EDMUNDS. It is not intended by it and the bill does not do it. Anybody who knows the meaning of the word "monopoly," as the courts apply it, would not apply it to such a person at all; and I am sure my friend must understand that.

> Mr. KENNA. [. . .] [H]ere is a provision in the bill which, if plain English means anything in the courts or elsewhere, provides a penalty for such conduct on the part of any citizen of this country engaged in the commonest and most legitimate callings of the country, who happens by his skill and energy to command an innocent and legitimate monopoly of a business.

> Mr. EDMUNDS. It does not do anything of the kind, because in the case stated the gentleman has not any monopoly at all. He has not bought off his adversaries. He has not got the possession of all the horned cattle in the United State. He has not done anything but compete with his adversaries in trade, if he had any, to furnish the commodity for the lowest price. So I assure my friend he need not be disturbed upon that subject.[497]

There are many different ways in which monopolization law could reflect the concern to allow "competition" or "industry" even if it leads to the acquisition or maintenance of monopoly power. One way to understand the shape of monopolization law is to posit a "privilege" or "safe harbor": a zone of competitive conduct within which courts will be particularly reluctant to impose liability under Section 2, as some have suggested.[498] Something like this may help to explain antitrust's response to certain kinds of core competitive decisions, including those relating to pricing decisions.[499] A second approach would be to provide, as some other writers suggest, that a monopolist's conduct must be in some sense "bad"—perhaps we could say "anticompetitive" if we had some specific meaning in mind for that term—before it can violate Section 2.[500] For example, some global theories of Section 2 propose that courts should examine whether the specific conduct challenged is overall harmful to consumers, or whether it lacks any "legitimate" business purpose or rational economic basis.[501] A third approach could involve something more intricately structured than a unitary "goodness" or "badness" test: for example, we might attempt to define zones of both *per se* illegality and *per se* legality.[502] Another approach might be to focus analytical attention on the subjective intention of the monopolist, although a rule of this kind could raise some serious challenges.[503] In this area, among others, it is very hard to identify clear lines of consistency that unite the Court's many and varied Section 2 cases.

There are a number of areas in which courts appear to foreclose, or at least strongly disfavor, the possibility of liability under Section 2 for conduct by a monopolist even when it excludes rivals and contributes to monopoly.[504] These include:

---

[497] 21 Cong. Rec. 3151–52 (Apr. 8, 1890).

[498] *See, e.g.*, Mark S. Popofsky, *Defining Exclusionary Conduct: Section 2, The Rule of Reason, and the Unifying Principle Underlying Antitrust Rules*, 73 Antitrust L.J. 435 (2006); Daniel Francis, *Making Sense of Monopolization*, 84 Antitrust L.J. 779 (2022).

[499] *See, e.g.*, Brooke Group Ltd. v. Brown & Williamson Tobacco Corp., 509 U.S. 209 (1993).

[500] *See, e.g.*, Timothy J. Muris, *The FTC and the Law of Monopolization*, 67(3) Antitrust L.J. 693, 695 (2003).

[501] *See, e.g.*, Gregory J. Werden, Iden*tifying Exclusionary Conduct Under Section 2: The "No Economic Sense" Test*, 73 Antitrust L.J. 413 (2006) (no economic sense); Steven C. Salop & Craig Romaine, *Preserving Monopoly: Economic Analysis, Legal Standards, and Microsoft*, 7 Geo. Mason L. Rev. 617, 652 (1999) (overall harm).

[502] *See, e.g.*, Einer Elhauge, *Defining Better Monopolization Standards*, 56 Stan. L. Rev. 253, 315 (2003) (proposing that conduct should be "per se legal if its exclusionary effect on rivals depends on enhancing the defendant's efficiency," but "per se illegal if its exclusionary effect on rivals will enhance monopoly power regardless of any improvement in defendant efficiency").

[503] *See, e.g.*, Marina Lao, *Reclaiming a Role for Intent Evidence in Monopolization Analysis*, 54 Am. U. L. Rev. 151 (2004).

[504] *See also, e.g.*, Viamedia, Inc. v. Comcast Corporation, 951 F.3d 429, 452 (7th Cir. 2020) (no liability for "innovation resulting in superior products, the introduction of efficiencies reflecting superior business acumen, or even the luck of a firm that unwittingly stumbles into a monopoly position").

- **Unconditional refusals to deal.** If a plaintiff's theory of harm is simply that it was excluded by the fact that a monopolist won't sell to it—or won't sell to it at desired prices or terms—then it will be hard or impossible to establish antitrust liability. As we will see below, the dominant modern view is that a monopolist can almost never be liable under Section 2 for refusing to sell a product or service to a new customer: refusal-to-deal liability is often thought to be limited to a termination of a previous profitable course of dealing (or perhaps other forms of short-run profit sacrifice) for purely anticompetitive reasons. The Court has said that "[t]he freedom to switch suppliers lies close to the heart of the competitive process that the antitrust laws seek to encourage."[505] Later in this section we will meet the "essential facilities" doctrine, which may very modestly qualify this position: at least in theory.[506]

- **Unconditional above-cost discounting.** If a plaintiff's theory of harm is simply that it was excluded by a monopolist's unconditional above-cost discounting—even if precisely calibrated to exclude entry— liability seems foreclosed under existing law.[507]

- **Mere introduction of a new product or mere withdrawal of an old one.** If a plaintiff's theory of harm is simply that a new product was introduced with which it cannot compete, or that a product was withdrawn from the market, liability seems foreclosed or at least very unlikely.[508] (In Chapter X we will meet the practice of "product hopping" in which these principles come under some pressure.[509])

- **Product "design changes" or "improvements"?** Some courts and commentators have suggested that changes in design should be immune or nearly immune from antitrust attack, at least where there is a plausible claim that the change is an improvement.[510]

- **Advertising.** Courts have held that Section 2 should be particularly slow to punish advertising, even when it may affect competition and protect monopoly. In *Ayerst*, for example, the Second Circuit articulated a special presumption that misleading advertising has no more than a *de minimis* effect on competition.[511] Other courts have erected similarly stiff barriers to claims of this kind.[512]

The difficulty in defining the scope of a monopolist's "competitive freedom" is presented with unusual sharpness by antitrust's tangled law on "refusals to deal": that is, cases where a competitor wants to deal with a monopolist in some way (*e.g.*, to interoperate with it, or to purchase products or supplies from it) and the monopolist says no. On the one hand, courts repeatedly warn that there is no general duty to deal with rivals, and emphasize the freedom of all enterprises—even monopolists—to choose to whom they will sell.[513] And there are certainly very good reasons to encourage businesses to develop their own facilities rather than encouraging them to rely on the efforts of their competitors. If a rival firm has the option of simply relying on the monopolist's investment, it may be much less likely to invest in its own competitive alternative. On the other hand, refusals to deal can function as an enforcement mechanism for various complementary anticompetitive strategies, and the Supreme Court has indicated that a failure or refusal to deal can, sometimes, lead to antitrust liability. How can these principles be reconciled?

---

[505] NYNEX Corp. v. Discon, Inc., 525 U.S. 128, 137 (1998).

[506] *See infra* notes 517–521 and accompanying text.

[507] *See infra* § VII.D.3.

[508] *See, e.g.*, New York ex rel. Schneiderman v. Actavis PLC, 787 F.3d 638, 653–54 (2d Cir. 2015) ("[N]either product withdrawal nor product improvement alone is anticompetitive."); *see also* In re Asacol Antitrust Litig., 233 F. Supp. 3d 247, 268 (D. Mass. 2017); In re Suboxone (Buprenorphine Hydrochloride & Naloxone) Antitrust Litig., 64 F. Supp. 3d 665, 682 (E.D. Pa. 2014); Steamfitters Loc. Union No. 420 Welfare Fund v. Philip Morris, Inc., 171 F.3d 912, 925 n.7 (3d Cir. 1999).

[509] *See infra* § X.B.3.

[510] *See, e.g.*, Allied Orthopedic Appliances Inc. v. Tyco Health Care Grp. LP, 592 F.3d 991, 999–1000 (9th Cir. 2010) (describing as uncontroversial the proposition that "product improvement by itself does not violate Section 2, even if it is performed by a monopolist and harms competitors as a result"); Herbert Hovenkamp, *Exclusion and the Sherman Act*, 72 U. Chi. L. Rev. 147, 158 (2005) ("Innovation is anticompetitive only in the very rare situation when the innovator knew in advance that the product would not be an improvement but that it would serve to make a rival's technology (typically a complement to the innovated product) incompatible with the dominant technology.").

[511] National Ass'n of Pharmaceutical Mfrs., Inc. v. Ayerst Labs., 850 F.2d 904, 916 (2d Cir. 1988).

[512] *See, e.g.*, Lenox MacLaren Surgical Corp. v. Medtronic, Inc., 762 F.3d 1114, 1127 (10th Cir. 2014); Am. Pro. Testing Serv., Inc. v. Harcourt Brace Jovanovich Legal & Pro. Publications, Inc., 108 F.3d 1147, 1152 (9th Cir. 1997); Am. Council of Certified Podiatric Physicians & Surgeons v. Am. Bd. of Podiatric Surgery, Inc., 323 F.3d 366, 371 (6th Cir. 2003).

[513] The classic citation is United States v. Colgate & Co., 250 U.S. 300, 307 (1919).

Colgate and the Right to Choose Your Trading Partners

United States v. Colgate & Co., 250 U.S. 300 (1919)

Colgate is a short, early decision that has come to stand for a basic proposition of refusal-to-deal law. In that case, the Court reviewed a "rather vague and general" allegation that Colgate—a manufacturer of "soap and toilet articles"—had terminated dealers that had failed to respect Colgate's proposed retail prices. The Court pointed out that no resale price maintenance agreement (see Chapter VI) had been alleged: this was unilateral action. In a famous passage, the Court indicated that—at least absent a forbidden purpose—a business had a right to pick its own trading partners. Thus, as there was no RPM *agreement*, Colgate would not be liable for merely cutting off businesses that did not respect its retail price schedules.

The relevant passage provides: "The purpose of the Sherman Act is to prohibit monopolies, contracts and combinations which probably would unduly interfere with the free exercise of their rights by those engaged, or who wish to engage, in trade and commerce—in a word to preserve the right of freedom to trade. In the absence of any purpose to create or maintain a monopoly, the act does not restrict the long recognized right of trader or manufacturer engaged in an entirely private business, freely to exercise his own independent discretion as to parties with whom he will deal; and, of course, he may announce in advance the circumstances under which he will refuse to sell. The trader or manufacturer, on the other hand, carries on an entirely private business, and can sell to whom he pleases. A retail dealer has the unquestioned right to stop dealing with a wholesaler for reasons sufficient to himself, and may do so because he thinks such dealer is acting unfairly in trying to undermine his trade." What do you make of the language "[i]n the absence of any purpose to create or maintain a monopoly"?

Today, the leading Supreme Court cases on unconditional refusals to deal are *Aspen Skiing* (in which the Court imposed antitrust liability for a ski company's withdrawal from a joint ticket arrangement with its smaller competitor) and *Trinko* (in which the Court declined to impose antitrust liability for Verizon's failure to supply interconnection services to a smaller rival). These are controversial cases and they excite strong feelings! *Trinko* has acquired symbolic status as an emblem of the modern Court's hesitation to impose liability in monopolization cases.[514] *Aspen Skiing*—described in *Trinko* as "at or near the outer bounds of Section 2"—has been criticized with equal vigor from the other direction.[515]

As you read the extracts, ask yourself: are they in tension? Or do they coherently define a border between lawful and unlawful refusals to deal? Does *Trinko* leave room for refusal-to-deal liability beyond *Aspen Skiing*'s facts?

Aspen Skiing Co. v. Aspen Highlands Skiing Corp.
472 U.S. 585 (1985)

Justice Stevens.

[1] Aspen is a destination ski resort with a reputation for super powder, a wide range of runs, and an active night life, including some of the best restaurants in North America. Between 1945 and 1960, private investors independently developed three major facilities for downhill skiing: Aspen Mountain (Ajax), Aspen Highlands (Highlands), and Buttermilk. A fourth mountain, Snowmass, opened in 1967. [. . .]

---

[514] *See, e.g.*, Spencer Weber Waller, *Microsoft and* Trinko: *A Tale of Two Courts*, 2006 Utah L. Rev. 741, 742 (2006) ("Justice Scalia's opinion [in *Trinko*] is wrong on the law, wrong on the facts, wrong as a matter of procedure, wrong as a matter of economics, wrong as a matter of institutional competencies, and a poor contrast with the way Section 2 legal standards have been articulated by courts in antitrust cases since the passage of the Sherman Act"); *see also id.* at 741–42 ("Sometimes there is an opinion that it so profoundly wrong that Mary McCarthy's famous quote about Lillian Hellman comes to mind: '[E]very word she writes is a lie, including *and* and *the*.' *Trinko* is such an opinion.").

[515] *See, e.g.*, Michael Jacobs, *Introduction: Hail or Farewell? The* Aspen *Case 20 Years Later*, 73 Antitrust L.J. 59, 63– (2005) (articulating criticisms of *Aspen*'s "oddities and inexplicable failures"—including a "fundamental mistake" regarding market definition, a "rather remarkable and utterly incorrect" conclusion regarding price effects, a "circular" justification analysis, and "economically perverse" implications—and concluding that the case is an "anomaly" that "did little to clarify the meaning of Section 2 and much to obscure it").

[2] Between 1958 and 1964, three independent companies operated Ajax, Highlands, and Buttermilk. In the early years, each company offered its own day or half-day tickets for use of its mountain. In 1962, however, the three competitors also introduced an interchangeable ticket. The 6-day, all-Aspen ticket provided convenience to the vast majority of skiers who visited the resort for weekly periods, but preferred to remain flexible about what mountain they might ski each day during the visit. It also emphasized the unusual variety in ski mountains available in Aspen.

[3] As initially designed, the all-Aspen ticket program consisted of booklets containing six coupons, each redeemable for a daily lift ticket at Ajax, Highlands, or Buttermilk. . . . The revenues from the sale of the 3-area coupon books were distributed in accordance with the number of coupons collected at each mountain.

[4] In 1964, Buttermilk was purchased by Ski Co., but the interchangeable ticket program continued. In most seasons after it acquired Buttermilk, Ski Co. offered 2-area, 6- or 7-day tickets featuring Ajax and Buttermilk in competition with the 3-area, 6-coupon booklet. Although it sold briskly, the all-Aspen ticket did not sell as well as Ski Co.'s multiarea ticket until Ski Co. opened Snowmass in 1967. Thereafter, the all-Aspen coupon booklet began to outsell Ski Co.'s ticket featuring only its mountains. [. . .]

[5] In the 1970's the management of Ski Co. increasingly expressed their dislike for the all-Aspen ticket. They complained that a coupon method of monitoring usage was administratively cumbersome. They doubted the accuracy of the survey and decried the appearance, deportment, and attitude of the college students who were conducting it. In addition, Ski Co.'s president had expressed the view that the 4-area ticket was siphoning off revenues that could be recaptured by Ski Co. if the ticket was discontinued. In fact, Ski Co. had reinstated its 3-area, 6-day ticket during the 1977-1978 season, but that ticket had been outsold by the 4-area, 6-day ticket nearly two to one.

[6] In March 1978, the Ski Co. management recommended to the board of directors that the 4-area ticket be discontinued for the 1978-1979 season. The board decided to offer Highlands a 4-area ticket provided that Highlands would agree to receive a 12.5% fixed percentage of the revenue-considerably below Highlands' historical average based on usage. Later in the 1978-1979 season, a member of Ski Co.'s board of directors candidly informed a Highlands official that he had advocated making Highlands an offer that it could not accept.

[7] Finding the proposal unacceptable, Highlands suggested a distribution of the revenues based on usage to be monitored by coupons, electronic counting, or random sample surveys. If Ski Co. was concerned about who was to conduct the survey, Highlands proposed to hire disinterested ticket counters at its own expense—"somebody like Price Waterhouse"—to count or survey usage of the 4-area ticket at Highlands. Ski Co. refused to consider any counterproposals, and Highlands finally rejected the offer of the fixed percentage.

[8] As far as Ski Co. was concerned, the all-Aspen ticket was dead. In its place Ski Co. offered the 3-area, 6-day ticket featuring only its mountains. In an effort to promote this ticket, Ski Co. embarked on a national advertising campaign that strongly implied to people who were unfamiliar with Aspen that Ajax, Buttermilk, and Snowmass were the only ski mountains in the area. For example, Ski Co. had a sign changed in the Aspen Airways waiting room at Stapleton Airport in Denver. The old sign had a picture of the four mountains in Aspen touting "Four Big Mountains" whereas the new sign retained the picture but referred only to three. [. . .]

[9] In this Court, Ski Co. contends that even a firm with monopoly power has no duty to engage in joint marketing with a competitor, that a violation of § 2 cannot be established without evidence of substantial exclusionary conduct, and that none of its activities can be characterized as exclusionary. It also contends that the Court of Appeals incorrectly relied on the "essential facilities" doctrine and that an "anticompetitive intent" does not transform nonexclusionary conduct into monopolization. In response, Highlands submits that, given the evidence in the record, it is not necessary to rely on the "essential facilities" doctrine in order to affirm the judgment.

[10] The central message of the Sherman Act is that a business entity must find new customers and higher profits through internal expansion—that is, by competing successfully rather than by arranging treaties with its competitors. Ski Co., therefore, is surely correct in submitting that even a firm with monopoly power has no general duty to engage in a joint marketing program with a competitor. Ski Co. is quite wrong, however, in

suggesting that the judgment in this case rests on any such proposition of law. For the trial court unambiguously instructed the jury that a firm possessing monopoly power has no duty to cooperate with its business rivals.

[11] The absence of an unqualified duty to cooperate does not mean that every time a firm declines to participate in a particular cooperative venture, that decision may not have evidentiary significance, or that it may not give rise to liability in certain circumstances. The absence of a duty to transact business with another firm is, in some respects, merely the counterpart of the independent businessman's cherished right to select his customers and his associates. The high value that we have placed on the right to refuse to deal with other firms does not mean that the right is unqualified.

[12] In *Lorain Journal Co. v. United States*, 342 U.S. 143 (1951), we squarely held that this right was not unqualified. Between 1933 and 1948 the publisher of the Lorain Journal, a newspaper, was the only local business disseminating news and advertising in that Ohio town. In 1948, a small radio station was established in a nearby community. In an effort to destroy its small competitor, and thereby regain its "pre-1948 substantial monopoly over the mass dissemination of all news and advertising," the Journal refused to sell advertising to persons that patronized the radio station.

[13] In holding that this conduct violated § 2 of the Sherman Act, the Court dispatched the same argument raised by the monopolist here:

> The publisher claims a right as a private business concern to select its customers and to refuse to accept advertisements from whomever it pleases. We do not dispute that general right. But the word "right" is one of the most deceptive of pitfalls; it is so easy to slip from a qualified meaning in the premise to an unqualified one in the conclusion. Most rights are qualified. The right claimed by the publisher is neither absolute nor exempt from regulation. Its exercise as a purposeful means of monopolizing interstate commerce is prohibited by the Sherman Act. The operator of the radio station, equally with the publisher of the newspaper, is entitled to the protection of that Act. In the absence of any purpose to create or maintain a monopoly, the act does not restrict the long recognized right of trader or manufacturer engaged in an entirely private business, freely to exercise his own independent discretion as to parties with whom he will deal.

[14] The Court approved the entry of an injunction ordering the Journal to print the advertisements of the customers of its small competitor.

[15] In *Lorain Journal*, the violation of § 2 was an attempt to monopolize, rather than monopolization, but the question of intent is relevant to both offenses. In the former case it is necessary to prove a specific intent to accomplish the forbidden objective—as Judge Hand explained, an intent which goes beyond the mere intent to do the act. In the latter case evidence of intent is merely relevant to the question whether the challenged conduct is fairly characterized as "exclusionary" or "anticompetitive"—to use the words in the trial court's instructions— or "predatory," to use a word that scholars seem to favor. Whichever label is used, there is agreement on the proposition that no monopolist monopolizes unconscious of what he is doing. As Judge Bork stated more recently: "Improper exclusion (exclusion not the result of superior efficiency) is always deliberately intended."

[16] The qualification on the right of a monopolist to deal with whom he pleases is not so narrow that it encompasses no more than the circumstances of *Lorain Journal*. In the actual case that we must decide, the monopolist did not merely reject a novel offer to participate in a cooperative venture that had been proposed by a competitor. Rather, the monopolist elected to make an important change in a pattern of distribution that had originated in a competitive market and had persisted for several years. The all-Aspen, 6-day ticket with revenues allocated on the basis of usage was first developed when three independent companies operated three different ski mountains in the Aspen area. It continued to provide a desirable option for skiers when the market was enlarged to include four mountains, and when the character of the market was changed by Ski Co.'s acquisition of monopoly power. Moreover, since the record discloses that interchangeable tickets are used in other multimountain areas which apparently are competitive, it seems appropriate to infer that such tickets satisfy consumer demand in free competitive markets.

[17] Ski Co.'s decision to terminate the all-Aspen ticket was thus a decision by a monopolist to make an important change in the character of the market. Such a decision is not necessarily anticompetitive, and Ski Co. contends that neither its decision, nor the conduct in which it engaged to implement that decision, can fairly be characterized as exclusionary in this case. It recognizes, however, that as the case is presented to us, we must interpret the entire record in the light most favorable to Highlands and give to it the benefit of all inferences which the evidence fairly supports, even though contrary inferences might reasonably be drawn.

[18] Moreover, we must assume that the jury followed the court's instructions. The jury must, therefore, have drawn a distinction between practices which tend to exclude or restrict competition on the one hand, and the success of a business which reflects only a superior product, a well-run business, or luck, on the other. Since the jury was unambiguously instructed that Ski Co.'s refusal to deal with Highlands does not violate Section 2 if valid business reasons exist for that refusal, we must assume that the jury concluded that there were no valid business reasons for the refusal. The question then is whether that conclusion finds support in the record. [. . .]

[19] The question whether Ski Co.'s conduct may properly be characterized as exclusionary cannot be answered by simply considering its effect on Highlands. In addition, it is relevant to consider its impact on consumers and whether it has impaired competition in an unnecessarily restrictive way. If a firm has been attempting to exclude rivals on some basis other than efficiency, it is fair to characterize its behavior as predatory. It is, accordingly, appropriate to examine the effect of the challenged pattern of conduct on consumers, on Ski Co.'s smaller rival, and on Ski Co. itself. [. . .]

[20] The average Aspen visitor is a well-educated, relatively affluent, experienced skier who has skied a number of times in the past. Over 80% of the skiers visiting the resort each year have been there before-40% of these repeat visitors have skied Aspen at least five times. Over the years, they developed a strong demand for the 6-day, all-Aspen ticket in its various refinements. Most experienced skiers quite logically prefer to purchase their tickets at once for the whole period that they will spend at the resort; they can then spend more time on the slopes and enjoying après-ski amenities and less time standing in ticket lines. The 4-area attribute of the ticket allowed the skier to purchase his 6-day ticket in advance while reserving the right to decide in his own time and for his own reasons which mountain he would ski on each day. It provided convenience and flexibility, and expanded the vistas and the number of challenging runs available to him during the week's vacation.

[21] While the 3-area, 6-day ticket offered by Ski Co. possessed some of these attributes, the evidence supports a conclusion that consumers were adversely affected by the elimination of the 4-area ticket. In the first place, the actual record of competition between a 3-area ticket and the all-Aspen ticket in the years after 1967 indicated that skiers demonstrably preferred four mountains to three. Highlands' expert marketing witness testified that many of the skiers who come to Aspen want to ski the four mountains, and the abolition of the 4-area pass made it more difficult to satisfy that ambition. A consumer survey undertaken in the 1979-1980 season indicated that 53.7% of the respondents wanted to ski Highlands, but would not; 39.9% said that they would not be skiing at the mountain of their choice because their ticket would not permit it.

[22] Expert testimony and anecdotal evidence supported these statistical measures of consumer preference. A major wholesale tour operator asserted that he would not even consider marketing a 3-area ticket if a 4-area ticket were available. During the 1977-1978 and 1978-1979 seasons, people with Ski Co.'s 3-area ticket came to Highlands on a very regular basis and attempted to board the lifts or join the ski school. Highlands officials were left to explain to angry skiers that they could only ski at Highlands or join its ski school by paying for a 1-day lift ticket. Even for the affluent, this was an irritating situation because it left the skier the option of either wasting 1 day of the 6-day, 3-area pass or obtaining a refund which could take all morning and entailed the forfeit of the 6-day discount. An active officer in the Atlanta Ski Club testified that the elimination of the 4-area pass "infuriated" him. [. . .]

[23] The adverse impact of Ski Co.'s pattern of conduct on Highlands is not disputed in this Court. Expert testimony described the extent of its pecuniary injury. The evidence concerning its attempt to develop a substitute product either by buying Ski Co.'s daily tickets in bulk, or by marketing its own Adventure Pack, demonstrates that it tried to protect itself from the loss of its share of the patrons of the all-Aspen ticket. The development of a new distribution system for providing the experience that skiers had learned to expect in Aspen proved to be

prohibitively expensive. As a result, Highlands' share of the relevant market steadily declined after the 4-area ticket was terminated. The size of the damages award also confirms the substantial character of the effect of Ski Co.'s conduct upon Highlands.

[24] Perhaps most significant, however, is the evidence relating to Ski Co. itself, for Ski Co. did not persuade the jury that its conduct was justified by any normal business purpose. Ski Co. was apparently willing to forgo daily ticket sales both to skiers who sought to exchange the coupons contained in Highlands' Adventure Pack, and to those who would have purchased Ski Co. daily lift tickets from Highlands if Highlands had been permitted to purchase them in bulk. The jury may well have concluded that Ski Co. elected to forgo these short-run benefits because it was more interested in reducing competition in the Aspen market over the long run by harming its smaller competitor.

[25] That conclusion is strongly supported by Ski Co.'s failure to offer any efficiency justification whatever for its pattern of conduct. In defending the decision to terminate the jointly offered ticket, Ski Co. claimed that usage could not be properly monitored. The evidence, however, established that Ski Co. itself monitored the use of the 3-area passes based on a count taken by lift operators, and distributed the revenues among its mountains on that basis. Ski Co. contended that coupons were administratively cumbersome, and that the survey takers had been disruptive and their work inaccurate. Coupons, however, were no more burdensome than the credit cards accepted at Ski Co. ticket windows. Moreover, in other markets Ski Co. itself participated in interchangeable lift tickets using coupons. As for the survey, its own manager testified that the problems were much overemphasized by Ski Co. officials, and were mostly resolved as they arose. Ski Co.'s explanation for the rejection of Highlands' offer to hire-at its own expense-a reputable national accounting firm to audit usage of the 4-area tickets at Highlands' mountain, was that there was no way to "control" the audit.

[26] In the end, Ski Co. was pressed to justify its pattern of conduct on a desire to disassociate itself from-what it considered the inferior skiing services offered at Highlands. The all-Aspen ticket based on usage, however, allowed consumers to make their own choice on these matters of quality. Ski Co.'s purported concern for the relative quality of Highlands' product was supported in the record by little more than vague insinuations, and was sharply contested by numerous witnesses. Moreover, Ski Co. admitted that it was willing to associate with what it considered to be inferior products in other markets.

[27] Although Ski Co.'s pattern of conduct may not have been as bold, relentless, and predatory as the publisher's actions in *Lorain Journal*, the record in this case comfortably supports an inference that the monopolist made a deliberate effort to discourage its customers from doing business with its smaller rival. The sale of its 3-area, 6-day ticket, particularly when it was discounted below the daily ticket price, deterred the ticket holders from skiing at Highlands. The refusal to accept the Adventure Pack coupons in exchange for daily tickets was apparently motivated entirely by a decision to avoid providing any benefit to Highlands even though accepting the coupons would have entailed no cost to Ski Co. itself, would have provided it with immediate benefits, and would have satisfied its potential customers. Thus the evidence supports an inference that Ski Co. was not motivated by efficiency concerns and that it was willing to sacrifice short-run benefits and consumer goodwill in exchange for a perceived long-run impact on its smaller rival.

[28] Because we are satisfied that the evidence in the record, construed most favorably in support of Highlands' position, is adequate to support the verdict under the instructions given by the trial court, the judgment of the Court of Appeals is

Affirmed.

* * *

The meaning, basis, and scope of *Aspen Skiing* were all at issue twenty years later when *Trinko* came before the Court. As we noted above, *Trinko* has come to symbolize a modern, somewhat conservative approach to the imposition of liability for monopolization, which emphasizes the relative freedom of a monopolist, and the value of allowing sharp-elbowed behavior in the marketplace, as well as the difficulties of imposing and supervising forced-sharing obligations under the antitrust laws. It is, at least in tone and emphasis, and perhaps in substance too, a long way from *Aspen Skiing*.[516]

Verizon Communications Inc. v. Law Offices of Curtis V. Trinko, LLP

540 U.S. 398 (2004)

Justice Scalia.

[1] The Telecommunications Act of 1996 imposes certain duties upon incumbent local telephone companies in order to facilitate market entry by competitors, and establishes a complex regime for monitoring and enforcement. In this case we consider whether a complaint alleging breach of the incumbent's duty under the 1996 Act to share its network with competitors states a claim under § 2 of the Sherman Act.

[2] Petitioner Verizon Communications Inc. is the incumbent local exchange carrier (LEC) serving New York State. . . . Central to the scheme of the Act is the incumbent LEC's obligation under 47 U.S.C. § 251(c) to share its network with competitors, including provision of access to individual elements of the network on an "unbundled" basis. New entrants, so-called competitive LECs, resell these unbundled network elements (UNEs), recombined with each other or with elements belonging to the LECs. [. . .]

[3] Part of Verizon's UNE obligation under § 251(c)(3) is the provision of access to operations support systems (OSS), a set of systems used by incumbent LECs to provide services to customers and ensure quality. . . .

[4] In late 1999, competitive LECs complained to regulators that many orders were going unfilled, in violation of Verizon's obligation to provide access to OSS functions. The [New York Public Service Commission ("PSC")] and [Federal Communications Commission ("FCC")] opened parallel investigations, which led to a series of orders by the PSC and a consent decree with the FCC. . . .

[5] Respondent Law Offices of Curtis V. Trinko, LLP, a New York City law firm, was a local telephone service customer of AT & T. . . . [Its] complaint . . . alleged that Verizon had filled rivals' orders on a discriminatory basis as part of an anticompetitive scheme to discourage customers from becoming or remaining customers of competitive LECs, thus impeding the competitive LECs' ability to enter and compete in the market for local telephone service. According to the complaint, Verizon has filled orders of competitive LEC customers after filling those for its own local phone service, has failed to fill in a timely manner, or not at all, a substantial number of orders for competitive LEC customers, and has systematically failed to inform competitive LECs of the status of their customers' orders. . . . It asserted that the result of Verizon's improper behavior with respect to providing access to its local loop was to deter potential customers of rivals from switching. The complaint sought damages and injunctive relief for violation of § 2 of the Sherman Act . . . .

[6] To decide this case, we must first determine what effect (if any) the 1996 Act has upon the application of traditional antitrust principles. The Act imposes a large number of duties upon incumbent LECs—above and beyond those basic responsibilities it imposes upon all carriers . . . . Under the sharing duties of § 251(c), incumbent LECs are required to offer [various] kinds of access. Already noted, and perhaps most intrusive, is the duty to offer access to UNEs on just, reasonable, and nondiscriminatory terms, a phrase that the FCC has interpreted to mean a price reflecting long-run incremental cost. A rival can interconnect its own facilities with those of the incumbent LEC, or it can simply purchase services at wholesale from the incumbent and resell them to consumers.

[7] That Congress created these duties, however, does not automatically lead to the conclusion that they can be enforced by means of an antitrust claim. Indeed, a detailed regulatory scheme such as that created by the 1996 Act ordinarily raises the question whether the regulated entities are not shielded from antitrust scrutiny altogether by the doctrine of implied immunity. In some respects the enforcement scheme set up by the 1996 Act is a good

---

[516] *See, e.g.*, Eleanor M. Fox, *Is There Life In* Aspen *After* Trinko? 73 Antitrust L.J. 153 (2005) ("While in theory *Aspen* is not overruled, *Trinko* has, at least, opened wide the door to argument in every Section 2 case that the starting point is skepticism about Section 2 based on fear that courts will condemn ambiguous conduct that is in fact efficient.").

candidate for implication of antitrust immunity, to avoid the real possibility of judgments conflicting with the agency's regulatory scheme that might be voiced by courts exercising jurisdiction under the antitrust laws.

[8] Congress, however, precluded that interpretation. Section 601(b)(1) of the 1996 Act is an antitrust-specific saving clause providing that "nothing in this Act or the amendments made by this Act shall be construed to modify, impair, or supersede the applicability of any of the antitrust laws." This bars a finding of implied immunity. . . .

[9] But just as the 1996 Act preserves claims that satisfy existing antitrust standards, it does not create new claims that go beyond existing antitrust standards; that would be equally inconsistent with the saving clause's mandate that nothing in the Act "modify, impair, or supersede the applicability" of the antitrust laws. . . .

[10] The complaint alleges that Verizon denied interconnection services to rivals in order to limit entry. If that allegation states an antitrust claim at all, it does so under § 2 of the Sherman Act, 15 U.S.C. § 2, which declares that a firm shall not "monopolize" or "attempt to monopolize." It is settled law that this offense requires, in addition to the possession of monopoly power in the relevant market, the willful acquisition or maintenance of that power as distinguished from growth or development as a consequence of a superior product, business acumen, or historic accident. The mere possession of monopoly power, and the concomitant charging of monopoly prices, is not only not unlawful; it is an important element of the free-market system. The opportunity to charge monopoly prices—at least for a short period—is what attracts "business acumen" in the first place; it induces risk taking that produces innovation and economic growth. To safeguard the incentive to innovate, the possession of monopoly power will not be found unlawful unless it is accompanied by an element of anticompetitive *conduct*.

[11] Firms may acquire monopoly power by establishing an infrastructure that renders them uniquely suited to serve their customers. Compelling such firms to share the source of their advantage is in some tension with the underlying purpose of antitrust law, since it may lessen the incentive for the monopolist, the rival, or both to invest in those economically beneficial facilities. Enforced sharing also requires antitrust courts to act as central planners, identifying the proper price, quantity, and other terms of dealing—a role for which they are ill suited. Moreover, compelling negotiation between competitors may facilitate the supreme evil of antitrust: collusion. Thus, as a general matter, the Sherman Act does not restrict the long recognized right of a trader or manufacturer engaged in an entirely private business, freely to exercise his own independent discretion as to parties with whom he will deal.

[12] However, the high value that we have placed on the right to refuse to deal with other firms does not mean that the right is unqualified. Under certain circumstances, a refusal to cooperate with rivals can constitute anticompetitive conduct and violate § 2. We have been very cautious in recognizing such exceptions, because of the uncertain virtue of forced sharing and the difficulty of identifying and remedying anticompetitive conduct by a single firm. The question before us today is whether the allegations of respondent's complaint fit within existing exceptions or provide a basis, under traditional antitrust principles, for recognizing a new one.

[13] The leading case for § 2 liability based on refusal to cooperate with a rival, and the case upon which respondent understandably places greatest reliance, is *Aspen Skiing*. The Aspen ski area consisted of four mountain areas. The defendant, who owned three of those areas, and the plaintiff, who owned the fourth, had cooperated for years in the issuance of a joint, multiple-day, all-area ski ticket. After repeatedly demanding an increased share of the proceeds, the defendant canceled the joint ticket. The plaintiff, concerned that skiers would bypass its mountain without some joint offering, tried a variety of increasingly desperate measures to re-create the joint ticket, even to the point of in effect offering to buy the defendant's tickets at retail price. The defendant refused even that. We upheld a jury verdict for the plaintiff, reasoning that the jury may well have concluded that the defendant elected to forgo these short-run benefits because it was more interested in reducing competition over the long run by harming its smaller competitor.

[14] *Aspen Skiing* is at or near the outer boundary of § 2 liability. The Court there found significance in the defendant's decision to cease participation in a cooperative venture. The unilateral termination of a voluntary (and thus presumably profitable) course of dealing suggested a willingness to forsake short-term profits to achieve an anticompetitive end. Similarly, the defendant's unwillingness to renew the ticket even if compensated at retail price revealed a distinctly anticompetitive bent.

[15] The refusal to deal alleged in the present case does not fit within the limited exception recognized in *Aspen Skiing*. The complaint does not allege that Verizon voluntarily engaged in a course of dealing with its rivals, or would ever have done so absent statutory compulsion. Here, therefore, the defendant's prior conduct sheds no light upon the motivation of its refusal to deal—upon whether its regulatory lapses were prompted not by competitive zeal but by anticompetitive malice. The contrast between the cases is heightened by the difference in pricing behavior. In *Aspen Skiing*, the defendant turned down a proposal to sell at its own retail price, suggesting a calculation that its future monopoly retail price would be higher. Verizon's reluctance to interconnect at the cost-based rate of compensation . . . tells us nothing about dreams of monopoly.

[16] The specific nature of what the [Telecommunications Act of 1996] compels makes this case different from *Aspen Skiing* in a more fundamental way. In *Aspen Skiing*, what the defendant refused to provide to its competitor was a product that it already sold at retail—to oversimplify slightly, lift tickets representing a bundle of services to skiers. Similarly, in *Otter Tail Power Co. v. United States*, [410 U.S. 366 (1973)], another case relied upon by respondent, the defendant was already in the business of providing a service to certain customers (power transmission over its network), and refused to provide the same service to certain other customers. In the present case, by contrast, the services allegedly withheld are not otherwise marketed or available to the public. The sharing obligation imposed by the 1996 Act created something brand new—the wholesale market for leasing network elements. The unbundled elements offered pursuant to [the 1996 Act] exist only deep within the bowels of Verizon; they are brought out on compulsion of the 1996 Act and offered not to consumers but to rivals, and at considerable expense and effort. New systems must be designed and implemented simply to make that access possible—indeed, it is the failure of one of those systems that prompted the present complaint.

[17] We conclude that Verizon's alleged insufficient assistance in the provision of service to rivals is not a recognized antitrust claim under this Court's existing refusal-to-deal precedents. This conclusion would be unchanged even if we considered to be established law the "essential facilities" doctrine crafted by some lower courts, under which the Court of Appeals concluded respondent's allegations might state a claim. . . . We have never recognized such a doctrine, and we find no need either to recognize it or to repudiate it here. It suffices for present purposes to note that the indispensable requirement for invoking the doctrine is the unavailability of access to the "essential facilities"; where access exists, the doctrine serves no purpose. Thus, it is said that essential facility claims should be denied where a state or federal agency has effective power to compel sharing and to regulate its scope and terms. Respondent believes that the existence of sharing duties under the 1996 Act supports its case. We think the opposite: The 1996 Act's extensive provision for access makes it unnecessary to impose a judicial doctrine of forced access. To the extent respondent's "essential facilities" argument is distinct from its general § 2 argument, we reject it. [. . .]

[18] Finally, we do not believe that traditional antitrust principles justify adding the present case to the few existing exceptions from the proposition that there is no duty to aid competitors. Antitrust analysis must always be attuned to the particular structure and circumstances of the industry at issue. Part of that attention to economic context is an awareness of the significance of regulation. As we have noted, careful account must be taken of the pervasive federal and state regulation characteristic of the industry. . . . .

[19] One factor of particular importance is the existence of a regulatory structure designed to deter and remedy anticompetitive harm. Where such a structure exists, the additional benefit to competition provided by antitrust enforcement will tend to be small, and it will be less plausible that the antitrust laws contemplate such additional scrutiny. Where, by contrast, there is nothing built into the regulatory scheme which performs the antitrust function, the benefits of antitrust are worth its sometimes considerable disadvantages. Just as regulatory context may in other cases serve as a basis for implied immunity, it may also be a consideration in deciding whether to recognize an expansion of the contours of § 2. [. . .]

[20] Against the slight benefits of antitrust intervention here, we must weigh a realistic assessment of its costs. Under the best of circumstances, applying the requirements of § 2 can be difficult because the means of illicit exclusion, like the means of legitimate competition, are myriad. Mistaken inferences and the resulting false condemnations are especially costly, because they chill the very conduct the antitrust laws are designed to protect. The cost of false positives counsels against an undue expansion of § 2 liability. One false-positive risk is that an incumbent LEC's failure to provide a service with sufficient alacrity might have nothing to do with exclusion.

Allegations of violations of [duties under the Telecommunications Act] are difficult for antitrust courts to evaluate, not only because they are highly technical, but also because they are likely to be extremely numerous, given the incessant, complex, and constantly changing interaction of competitive and incumbent LECs implementing the sharing and interconnection obligations. Amici States have filed a brief asserting that competitive LECs are threatened with death by a thousand cuts, the identification of which would surely be a daunting task for a generalist antitrust court. Judicial oversight under the Sherman Act would seem destined to distort investment and lead to a new layer of interminable litigation, atop the variety of litigation routes already available to and actively pursued by [competitors].

[21] Even if the problem of false positives did not exist, conduct consisting of anticompetitive violations of [the 1996 Act] may be, as we have concluded with respect to above-cost predatory pricing schemes, beyond the practical ability of a judicial tribunal to control. Effective remediation of violations of regulatory sharing requirements will ordinarily require continuing supervision of a highly detailed decree. We think that Professor Areeda got it exactly right: No court should impose a duty to deal that it cannot explain or adequately and reasonably supervise. The problem should be deemed irremediable by antitrust law when compulsory access requires the court to assume the day-to-day controls characteristic of a regulatory agency. In this case, respondent has requested an equitable decree to preliminarily and permanently enjoin Verizon from providing access to the local loop market to rivals on terms and conditions that are not as favorable as those that Verizon enjoys. An antitrust court is unlikely to be an effective day-to-day enforcer of these detailed sharing obligations.

The Essential Facilities Doctrine

Although—as Justice Scalia noted in paragraph 8 of the *Trinko* extract above—the Supreme Court has never endorsed the theory,[517] many lower courts have acknowledged or indicated the existence of an "essential facilities" doctrine.[518]

In principle, this doctrine requires a monopolist in possession of a strictly necessary facility to offer to share it with rivals. But this broad-sounding rule is very limited in practice. Among other things, it applies only to strictly necessary facilities or assets, when no alternative is available and where the plaintiff cannot duplicate them, and this requirement is construed sternly.[519] Moreover, in order to be really effective, an essential-facilities doctrine requires courts to specify or at least police the terms of access—price, terms, and so on—in ways that courts tend to be reluctant to do.[520] Perhaps unsurprisingly, then, courts are *exceptionally* reluctant to actually apply the doctrine to compel sharing: in fact, they virtually never do so.[521] However, despite the Supreme Court's evident skepticism,

---

[517] *But see* Otter Tail Power Co. v. United States, 410 U.S. 366 (1973).

[518] *See, e.g.*, Kerwin v. Casino, 802 F. App'x 723, 727 (3d Cir. 2020); Buccaneer Energy (USA) Inc. v. Gunnison Energy Corp., 846 F.3d 1297, 1310 (10th Cir. 2017); Aerotec Int'l, Inc. v. Honeywell Int'l, Inc., 836 F.3d 1171, 1185 (9th Cir. 2016); MetroNet Servs. Corp. v. Qwest Corp., 383 F.3d 1124, 1128–29 (9th Cir. 2004); Twin Labs., Inc. v. Weider Health & Fitness, 900 F.2d 566, 568–69 (2d Cir. 1990); Fishman v. Wirtz, 807 F.2d 520, 539 (7th Cir. 1986); MCI Commc'ns Corp. v. Am. Tel. & Tel. Co., 708 F.2d 1081, 1132 (7th Cir. 1983); Hecht v. Pro-Football, Inc., 570 F.2d 982, 992 (D.C. Cir. 1977). *See also, e.g.*, Robert Pitofsky, Donna Patterson, & Jonathan Hooks, *The Essential Facilities Doctrine Under United States Antitrust Law*, 70 Antitrust L.J. 443 (2002); Nikolas Guggenberger, *The Essential Facilities Doctrine in the Digital Economy: Dispelling Persistent Myths*, 23 Yale J.L. & Tech. 301 (2021); *Antitrust Chronicle: Essential Digital Facilities*, Comp. Pol'y Intl. (Spring 2023) (symposium).

[519] *See, e.g.*, MetroNet Servs. Corp. v. Qwest Corp., 383 F.3d 1124, 1129–30 (9th Cir. 2004) ("The doctrine makes a facility that is essential to competition in a given market available to competitors so that they may compete in that market. A facility is 'essential' only if it is otherwise unavailable and cannot be reasonably or practically replicated. The doctrine does not guarantee competitors access to the essential facility in the most profitable manner.") (internal quotation marks and citation omitted); Epic Games, Inc. v. Apple Inc., 559 F. Supp. 3d 898, 1051 (N.D. Cal. 2021) ("This doctrine does not require distribution in the manner preferred by the competitor, here native apps. The availability of these other avenues of distribution, even if they are not the preferred or ideal methods, is dispositive of Epic Games' claim. The doctrine does not demand an ideal or preferred standard.").

[520] *See, e.g.*, Blue Cross & Blue Shield United of Wisconsin v. Marshfield Clinic, 881 F. Supp. 1309, 1320–21 (W.D. Wis. 1994) ("A denial of access on reasonable terms may be sufficient to satisfy the essential facilities doctrine; a complete denial of access may not be necessary."); Robert Pitofsky, Donna Patterson, & Jonathan Hooks, *The Essential Facilities Doctrine Under United States Antitrust Law*, 70 Antitrust L.J. 443, 448 n.21 (2002).

[521] *But see, e.g.*, MCI Commc'ns Corp. v. Am. Tel. & Tel. Co., 708 F.2d 1081, 1133 (7th Cir. 1983) ("[T]he evidence supports the jury's determination that AT & T denied the essential facilities, the interconnections for FX and CCSA service, when they could have been feasibly provided.").

the doctrine retains at least theoretical viability among the lower courts, and the threat of liability may affect the behavior of some monopolists in the real world, including their willingness to negotiate with rivals over access.

In the wake of *Trinko*, courts have generally taken a narrow view of the scope of *Aspen Skiing* and of liability for refusal to deal.[522]

Refusal to Deal after Trinko

Viamedia, Inc. v. Comcast Corporation, 951 F.3d 429 (7th Cir. 2020); Novell, Inc. v. Microsoft Corp., 731 F.3d 1064 (10th Cir. 2013)

After *Trinko*, courts have struggled to define the narrow zone in which a monopolist will be liable for a refusal to deal. Two contrasting decisions from the Seventh and Tenth Circuits provide prominent illustrations of how appellate courts have navigated the terrain.

Novell dealt with allegations by Novell—the creator of the WordPerfect word processor application—that Microsoft had violated Section 2 by cutting off WordPerfect's access to certain functions on Microsoft's Windows operating system. Specifically, Novell alleged that Microsoft feared that WordPerfect could offer rival operating systems a promising unintegrated complement, and thus encourage such rivals to enter and compete against Windows in the operating system market. To eliminate this threat, the theory went, Microsoft cut off the access that third-party applications like WordPerfect had previously enjoyed to certain software interfaces ("namespace extensions") on Windows.

The Tenth Circuit, in an opinion by then-Judge Gorsuch, affirmed the dismissal of the claim. "In earlier days, some courts suggested that a monopolist must lend smaller rivals a helping hand." But "[t]he Supreme Court and this one . . . have long and emphatically rejected this approach, realizing that the proper focus of section 2 isn't on protecting competitors but on protecting the process of competition, with the interests of consumers, not competitors, in mind. Forcing monopolists to hold an umbrella over inefficient competitors might make rivals happy but it usually leaves consumers paying more for less." The court indicated that the touchstone for monopolization liability was "whether, based on the evidence and experience derived from past cases, the conduct at issue before us has little or no value beyond the capacity to protect the monopolist's market power—bearing in mind the risk of false positives (and negatives) any determination on the question of liability might invite, and the limits on the administrative capacities of courts to police market terms and transactions."

To prevail on a refusal-to-deal claim in the Tenth Circuit, the court held, a plaintiff must show: (1) "a preexisting voluntary and presumably profitable course of dealing between the monopolist and rival"; and (2) discontinuation of that course of dealing that "suggest[s] a willingness to forsake short-term profits to achieve an anti-competitive end." Satisfying this test requires "proof not just that the monopolist decided to forsake short-term profits. Just as in predatory pricing cases, we also require a showing that the monopolist's refusal to deal was part of a larger anticompetitive enterprise, such as (again) seeking to drive a rival from the market or discipline it for daring to compete on price. Put simply, the monopolist's conduct must be irrational but for its anticompetitive effect." The Tenth Circuit held that when analyzing whether Microsoft had forsaken profits, what mattered was the total profits from selling both Windows and Microsoft Office, not just foregone profits on Windows from making Windows a less useful product. And Novell had not shown such a sacrifice.

Seven years later, the plaintiff in *Viamedia* had somewhat better luck in the Seventh Circuit. In that case, Comcast held monopoly power in two markets: a market for "interconnect" services ("cooperative selling arrangements for

---

[522] *See, e.g.*, Novell, Inc. v. Microsoft Corp., 731 F.3d 1064, 1074–76 (10th Cir. 2013) (refusal to deal claim requires "preexisting voluntary and presumably profitable course of dealing between the monopolist and rival" and "willingness to forsake short-term profits"); FTC v. Qualcomm Inc., 969 F.3d 974, 993–94 (9th Cir. 2020) (claim requires termination of a voluntary and profitable course of dealing, sacrifice of short-run profits, and product or service that the defendant sells to similarly situated buyers); Covad Communications Co. v. Bell Atlantic Corp., 398 F.3d 666 (D.C. Cir. 2005) (plaintiff must prove refusal caused defendant "short-term economic loss"). *See also, e.g.*, In re Elevator Antitrust Litig., 502 F.3d 47, 53 (2d Cir. 2007) (noting "[t]he limited nature of this exception to the right of refusal to deal" after *Trinko*). *But see, e.g.*, Michael A. Carrier, *Sharing, Samples, and Generics: An Antitrust Framework*, 103 Cornell L. Rev. 1, 51–53 (2017) (collecting authority for liability without a prior course of dealing).

advertising through an 'Interconnect' that enables providers of retail cable television services to sell advertising targeted efficiently at regional audiences") and a market for "advertising representation" services ("services for retail cable television providers [that] assist those providers with the sale and delivery of national, regional, and local advertising"). The theory of harm was that Comcast used its interconnect monopoly to give cable TV businesses a choice: buy advertising representation services from Comcast or be cut off from interconnect services. Viamedia, an advertising representation competitor, sued for monopolization.

The Seventh Circuit reversed the district court's dismissal of the case. In doing so, it denied that *Aspen Skiing* provided a straitjacket for claims premised on a refusal to deal: "The *Aspen Skiing* factors help case-by-case assessments of whether a challenged refusal to deal is indeed anticompetitive, even though no factor is always decisive by itself." And "because the factors as a whole provide a window into likely harm to competition, a court should start with the *Aspen Skiing* factors in determining whether a refusal to deal is unlawful." The court held that Viamedia had stated a claim that was at least as strong as that in *Aspen Skiing* itself, given the relationship between the two markets: "unlike in *Aspen Skiing*, where the ultimate customers were skiers who did not compete against the defendant ski resort, Comcast's refusal to deal with Viamedia has left its MVPD customers in these markets no practical choice but to turn over their ad sales business, along with their sensitive business information and a large percentage of their ad revenue, to their dominant MVPD competitor."

Critically, the court declined to accept Comcast's protestations that its refusal to deal might have promoted its own efficiency. The court expressed pointed skepticism of the idea that liability under Section 2 required a showing that the refusal was economically irrational; rather, an assessment of "procompetitive benefits and anticompetitive harms is necessary to answer the ultimate question of whether competition was harmed." In a footnote, the court indicated that a balancing test of some kind might be applied to condemn certain refusals when the harm very significantly outweighed the efficiency gain. But "[e]ven if an allegation that a defendant's conduct was irrational but for its anticompetitive effect were necessary, Viamedia has plausibly alleged just that."

As *Novell* and *Viamedia* illustrate, some courts regard a profit sacrifice or some kind of irrationality as the sole remaining avenue for a refusal-to-deal claim, while others recognize the theoretical viability of other avenues. Today, *Novell* represents the more common view among courts.[523] At the time of writing, no plaintiff in a refusal-to-deal case seems to have won a final judgment since *Trinko*.[524]

As you ponder the interaction of the modern landmarks of *Aspen Skiing* and *Trinko*, it is worth keeping in mind that antitrust was not always so solicitous of the monopolist's freedom to do "nothing but compete."

CASENOTE: United States v. Aluminum Co. of America
148 F.2d 416 (2d Cir. 2015)

As you will remember, *Alcoa* dealt with a monopolization suit against Aluminum Co. of America ("Alcoa"): the Supreme Court lacked a quorum and the case was heard by the Second Circuit. The plaintiff alleged, among other things, that Alcoa had violated Section 2 through a range of conduct, including predatory overbuying of bauxite (an ore from which aluminum is created) and water power, various acquisitions, and various practices relating to downstream markets for "fabricated goods," including a so-called "price squeeze" of competing "sheet rollers."

The court's specific findings with respect to these practices are not of great importance today, having been overtaken by subsequent developments in the law. For example, the court ultimately condemned Alcoa's price squeeze—*i.e.*, Alcoa charged a high price for ingot, which is an input to sheet rolling, and a low price for sheet rolling itself, so that competing rollers could not profitably compete—although today that practice is *per se* lawful. *See* Pacific Bell Telephone Co. v. Linkline Communications, Inc., 555 U.S. 438 (2009).

---

[523] *See, e.g.*, OJ Com., LLC v. KidKraft, Inc., 34 F.4th 1232, 1245 (11th Cir. 2022); St. Luke's Hosp. v. ProMedica Health Sys., Inc., 8 F.4th 479, 486 (6th Cir. 2021); New York v. Facebook, Inc., 549 F. Supp. 3d 6, 25–28 (D.D.C. 2021).

[524] *See* Erik Hovenkamp, *The Antitrust Duty to Deal in the Age of Big Tech*, 131 Yale L.J. 1483, 1497 n.71 (2022).

Of some more interest, at least as a matter of antitrust history, are Judge Hand's broad-brush comments about the line between aggressive competition and monopolization. For example, Judge Hand used the terms "exclusion" and "monopolization" in terms that differ sharply from most modern usage:

- "Nothing compelled [Alcoa] to keep doubling and redoubling its capacity before others entered the field. It insists that it never excluded competitors; but we can think of no more effective exclusion than progressively to embrace each new opportunity as it opened, and to face every newcomer with new capacity already geared into a great organization, having the advantage of experience, trade connections and the elite of personnel. Only in case we interpret 'exclusion' as limited to maneuvers not honestly industrial, but actuated solely by a desire to prevent competition, can such a course, indefatigably pursued, be deemed not 'exclusionary.' So to limit it would in our judgment emasculate the Act; would permit just such consolidations as it was designed to prevent."

- "Alcoa meant to keep, and did keep, that complete and exclusive hold upon the ingot market with which it started. That was to 'monopolize' that market, however innocently it otherwise proceeded."

Alcoa is also intriguing, through modern eyes, for its treatment of subjective intent. Early in the opinion, Judge Hand indicated that monopolization liability does not depend on any question of intent other than "intent to bring about the forbidden act." It is not necessary, for example, that the specific means of monopolization be themselves independently unlawful.

However, when reviewing the individual allegations against Alcoa, Judge Hand appeared to pay close attention to matters of intention. In some places, he appeared to suggest that a monopolist acted lawfully when it was motivated by something like legitimate competitive purposes. For example, in discussing the allegations of overbuying, the court indicated that the decisive question was "whether, when 'Alcoa' bought up the bauxite deposits, it really supposed that they would be useful in the future," and whether the purchasing of water power was "for the purpose of preventing competition." Likewise, in reviewing Alcoa's acquisitions, Judge Hand appeared to focus on the company's own reasons for the acquisitions, rather than their positive and negative effects on competition. Only when the court turned to consider Alcoa's conduct directed to markets for fabricated goods did the focus more directly shift to whether the challenged practices "served to make Alcoa's legal position as to the ingot industry less vulnerable than it would otherwise have been." The price squeeze was condemned on that basis under Section 2.

There are many ways to read the *Alcoa* opinion today. Among other things, it represents a mingling of older and newer views about the morality of competitive practices and the legal concept of monopolization itself. It can be seen as a boundary stone between a monopolization offense built on a theory of bad purposes and one based on competitive effects.

NOTES

1) Note that *Aspen Skiing, Trinko, Novell, Viamedia,* and so on deal with <u>unconditional</u> refusals to deal, where the harm arises from the defendant's failure to supply something to the plaintiff. After we meet exclusivity and tying, we will think about the relationship between these refusal-to-deal cases and "conditional dealing."[525]

2) Some courts suggest that a refusal to deal violates Section 2 if a plaintiff can show: (1) that the defendant has terminated a preexisting voluntary (and therefore presumably profitable) course of dealing; (2) the defendant supplies the product or service to other non-competitor purchasers; and (3) that the termination suggests a willingness to sacrifice short-term profits for anticompetitive purposes.[526] Is this a suitable reconciliation of *Aspen Skiing* and *Trinko*? What is the point of the second criterion? For some critical discussion of the profit-sacrifice test, *see* Steven C. Salop, *Exclusionary Conduct, Effect on Consumers, and the Flawed Profit-Sacrifice Standard,* 73 Antitrust L.J. 311 (2006).

3) What is a "superior product"? What practices, if any, that would otherwise violate Section 2, should be protected because they represent product superiority? What about "business acumen"?

---

[525] *See infra* note 554 and accompanying text.

[526] *See, e.g.,* FTC v. Qualcomm Inc., 969 F.3d 974, 993–94 (9th Cir. 2020); FTC v. Facebook, Inc., 560 F.Supp.3d 1, 23–24 (D.D.C. 2021).

4) Courts do not often use the language of "privilege" or "safe harbor." Are there other ways of capturing the concept that monopolization treats some practices more leniently than others? For example:

    a. Could, or should, the law apply a sliding scale that subjects conduct to increasingly demanding scrutiny based on its likelihood to harm competition? What facts or factors should determine where conduct appears on that scale?[527]

    b. Could we define a category of "bad conduct" into which unlawful monopolization would fall? What could that look like?

5) Was the "joint ticket" arrangement in *Aspen Skiing* procompetitive or anticompetitive? How did it differ from a price-fixing arrangement?

6) In *Trinko*, the Court emphasized the complexities of enforcing a remedy that requires one business to sell to another. How hard do you think this is in practice? Are the difficulties different from those that attend other antitrust remedies? Could you imagine other enforcement mechanisms or approaches that might help allay these difficulties? Does a court need to define "fair terms" in order to impose liability for refusal to deal?

7) When and how do you think remedial complexities should influence the shape of substantive liability rules?

8) In cases like *Aspen Skiing*, should courts treat cases in which a monopolist terminates a deal with a rival differently from cases in which a monopolist simply declines to enter into such a deal? How would it change monopolist's incentives if an ongoing duty to deal could result from a decision to deal?

9) One of us has written: "[The *Grinnell*] definition makes no sense: virtually every business seeks to win share from competitors—it willfully seeks monopoly—including through superior products and business acumen. No one thinks that 'willfulness' in chasing monopoly is bad or rare. Every monopolization defendant claims that its conduct facilitates 'superior' operation. And if the use of 'acumen' is exculpatory, then what remains? The first half of the Court's binary is not necessarily bad, the second part is not necessarily good, and they are in no real tension."[528] Do you agree?

10) How important is it that a monopolist be able to accurately predict in advance whether a particular practice will be held to be unlawful monopolization?

11) In *Alcoa*, what if anything was objectionable about Alcoa's decision to "embrace each new opportunity as it opened, and to face every newcomer with new capacity already geared into a great organization, having the advantage of experience, trade connections and the elite of personnel"?

12) What do you make of the following argument? "The Supreme Court tells us in *Trinko* that monopolists very rarely have a duty to deal. And if it's not unlawful to refuse to deal, then surely it's not (or shouldn't be) unlawful to deal on conditions like exclusivity, product tying, etc., because those things are by definition lesser included rights in the right to refuse to deal."

13) There was no dissent in *Trinko*: does this surprise you? Justices Stevens, Souter, and Thomas concurred in the judgment, on the ground that AT&T, not its own customer, would have been the proper plaintiff. What might a dissent in *Trinko* have looked like?

4. Justification and the Microsoft Burden-Shifting Framework

Courts and commentators broadly agree that Section 2 requires courts to entertain arguments and evidence that purportedly exclusionary conduct is, in fact, justified by one or more procompetitive goals. Unfortunately, there is considerable confusion and contradiction regarding the relevant legal standard.

A frequently cited justification test for monopolization in modern law is found in *Microsoft*. It provides that a justification assessment should be applied in substantially the same form as Section 1's rule of reason; *i.e.*, in the form of a burden-shifting regime. First, a plaintiff must prove a *prima facie* case of harm; second, a defendant must establish the existence of a nonprextual justification; third, the burden of proof reverts to the plaintiff to establish

---

[527] *See, e.g.*, Mark S. Popofsky, *Section 2, Safe Harbors, and the Rule of Reason*, 15 Geo. Mason L. Rev. 1265 (2008).

[528] Daniel Francis, *Making Sense of Monopolization*, 84 Antitrust L.J. 779 (2022).

that on "balance," the harmful tendencies of the relevant practice or transaction exceed the beneficial ones.[529] The relevant language provides as follows:

> From a century of case law on monopolization under § 2 . . . several principles . . . emerge. First, to be condemned as exclusionary, a monopolist's act must have an "anticompetitive effect." That is, it must harm the competitive process and thereby harm consumers. In contrast, harm to one or more competitors will not suffice. The Sherman Act directs itself not against conduct which is competitive, even severely so, but against conduct which unfairly tends to destroy competition itself.

> Second, the plaintiff, on whom the burden of proof of course rests . . . must demonstrate that the monopolist's conduct indeed has the requisite anticompetitive effect. In a case brought by a private plaintiff, the plaintiff must show that its injury is of the type that the statute was intended to forestall[.] [N]o less in a case brought by the Government, it must demonstrate that the monopolist's conduct harmed competition, not just a competitor.

> Third, if a plaintiff successfully establishes a prima facie case under § 2 by demonstrating anticompetitive effect, then the monopolist may proffer a "procompetitive justification" for its conduct. . . . If the monopolist asserts a procompetitive justification—a nonpretextual claim that its conduct is indeed a form of competition on the merits because it involves, for example, greater efficiency or enhanced consumer appeal—then the burden shifts back to the plaintiff to rebut that claim. . . . .

> Fourth, if the monopolist's procompetitive justification stands unrebutted, then the plaintiff must demonstrate that the anticompetitive harm of the conduct outweighs the procompetitive benefit. In cases arising under § 1 of the Sherman Act, the courts routinely apply a similar balancing approach under the rubric of the rule of reason. The source of the rule of reason is Standard Oil Co. v. United States, 221 U.S. 1 . . . (1911), in which the Supreme Court used that term to describe the proper inquiry under both sections of the Act.

> Finally, in considering whether the monopolist's conduct on balance harms competition and is therefore condemned as exclusionary for purposes of § 2, our focus is upon the effect of that conduct, not upon the intent behind it. Evidence of the intent behind the conduct of a monopolist is relevant only to the extent it helps us understand the likely effect of the monopolist's conduct.[530]

There is a lot of detail and structure here. But there are important questions that remain open. First, can the defendant discharge its burden at step two by merely "proffer[ing]" or "asserting" a nonpretextual procompetitive purpose, as the language in *Microsoft* arguably suggests? Other parts of the *Microsoft* opinion suggest that the defendant's burden is more onerous than a mere assertion.[531] Or must the defendant make an evidentiary showing of some kind (*e.g.*, about the effect or purpose of the challenged practice or transaction): and if so, what is required, and how much?

Second, in what sense must a benefit be "nonpretextual"? Some courts, citing *Microsoft*, have suggested that the defendant's obligation is to "assert" or "proffer" a nonpretextual claimed procompetitive benefit.[532] Is this an objective test: that is, must a defendant prove significant actual procompetitive benefits (*i.e.*, "objectively

---

[529] *See, e.g.*, FTC v. Qualcomm Inc., 969 F.3d 974, 991–92 (9th Cir. 2020) (indicating that, "[r]egardless of whether the alleged antitrust violation involves concerted anticompetitive conduct under § 1 or independent anticompetitive conduct under § 2, the three-part burden-shifting test under the rule of reason is essentially the same," and stating that "[i]f, in reviewing an alleged Sherman Act violation, a court finds that the conduct in question is not anticompetitive under § 1, the court need not separately analyze the conduct under § 2"); *see also, e.g.*, BRFHH Shreveport, LLC v. Willis Knighton Med. Ctr., 176 F. Supp. 3d 606, 623 (W.D. La. 2016) ("Though the Fifth Circuit has not explicitly accepted or rejected the Microsoft framework, it previously has suggested that some type of burden-shifting framework is appropriate for analyzing section 2 claims."). *But see, e.g.*, United States v. Microsoft Corp., 253 F.3d 34, 70 (D.C. Cir. 2001) ("[A] monopolist's use of exclusive contracts, in certain circumstances, may give rise to a § 2 violation even though the contracts foreclose less than the roughly 40% or 50% share usually required in order to establish a § 1 violation.").

[530] United States v. Microsoft Corp., 253 F.3d 34, 58–59 (D.C. Cir. 2001).

[531] *See* United States v. Microsoft Corp., 253 F.3d 34, 66 (D.C. Cir. 2001) (rejecting a claimed procompetitive justification for failure to "specif[y]" or "substantiate[ ]" some "general claims" of procompetitive benefit).

[532] *See, e.g.*, FTC v. Qualcomm Inc., 969 F.3d 974, 991 (9th Cir. 2020); Viamedia, Inc. v. Comcast Corp., 951 F.3d 429, 463 (7th Cir. 2020); New York ex rel. Schneiderman v. Actavis PLC, 787 F.3d 638, 652 (2d Cir. 2015).

nonpretextual")? Or is it a subjective one, requiring that defendants prove that, regardless of how things in fact turned out, the conduct was motivated (at least in part?) by a subjective purpose to pursue a procompetitive goal rather than anticompetitive ones? What *is* a "procompetitive" goal for this purpose? Surely the defendant need not have had the subjective purpose of improving consumer welfare: so what is the test?

Third, can it really be right that it falls to the plaintiff to measure the procompetitive effects of a claimed justification, given that many procompetitive benefits relate to the efficiency of the defendant's own operation, such that the defendant is uniquely well placed to develop that information?

The formulation in *Microsoft* does not reflect the last word, nor really a settled, worked-out consensus, on the analysis of procompetitive justifications under Section 2. Other cases and scholarly contributions support approaches that are both more and less demanding for plaintiffs. For example, some cases suggest that the mere existence of a legitimate business purpose could be exculpatory, regardless of the balance of benefits and harms.[533] The Third Circuit has used a formulation requiring that a benefit must be not just procompetitive but *"sufficiently procompetitive,"* suggesting that a defendant has some obligation to show that the claimed beneficial effects are sufficient in magnitude.[534] Moreover, a number of courts have indicated that a "less restrictive alternative" test applies under Section 2: a plaintiff may rebut a claimed procompetitive benefit by showing that a less restrictive alternative—that is, a genuinely practicable means of obtaining the relevant benefit with significantly less harm— was available to the defendant, such that the practice in question was "unnecessarily restrictive."[535] It is also not quite clear whether justifications should be measured against the same standards for different kinds of monopolization: for example, courts in refusal-to-deal cases commonly require only that a defendant demonstrate a legitimate business purpose, or that the conduct was economically rational aside from any exclusionary effects, which seems to reflect a relatively low bar for defendants in such cases.[536]

---

[533] *See, e.g.*, Mercatus Grp., LLC v. Lake Forest Hosp., 641 F.3d 834, 856 (7th Cir. 2011) ("[W]e conclude that the [defendant] Hospital's conduct can be considered predatory only if its promises were made not to compete in the market, but only to unfairly stymie unwanted competition. That might be the case if, for example, it could be shown that the Hospital's promises were made with no intent of ever being kept, or if the Hospital's promises were broken only after the Hospital realized that [the plaintiff's] competitive threat had passed."); Imaging Ctr., Inc. v. W. Maryland Health Sys., Inc., 158 F. App'x 413, 421 (4th Cir. 2005) (suggesting that a "valid business reason " or "concern for efficiency" may be exculpatory under Section 2); Tech. Res. Servs., Inc. v. Dornier Med. Sys., Inc., 134 F.3d 1458, 1466 (11th Cir. 1998) ("A defendant can escape § 2 liability if the defendant's actions can be explained by legitimate business justifications."); Illinois ex rel. Burris v. Panhandle E. Pipe Line Co., 935 F.2d 1469, 1481–82 (7th Cir. 1991) ("When courts consider the 'intent' of a firm charged with monopolization, they look not to whether the firm intended to achieve or maintain a monopoly, but to whether the underlying purpose of the firm's conduct was to enable the firm to compete more effectively. Did the firm engage in the challenged conduct for a legitimate business reason? Or was the firm's conduct designed solely to insulate the firm from competitive pressure? Intent is relevant, then, because intent determines "whether the challenged conduct is fairly characterized as 'exclusionary' or 'anticompetitive.' . . . Conduct that tends to exclude competitors may . . . survive antitrust scrutiny if the exclusion is the product of a normal business purpose, for the presence of a legitimate business justification reduces the likelihood that the conduct will produce undesirable effects on the competitive process.") (citations omitted).

[534] *See, e.g.*, United States v. Dentsply Intern., Inc., 399 F.3d 181 (3d Cir. 2005) ("The Government, having demonstrated harm to competition, the burden shifts to Dentsply to show that Dealer Criterion 6 promotes a sufficiently pro-competitive objective.").

[535] *See, e.g.*, Retractable Techs., Inc. v. Becton Dickinson & Co., 842 F.3d 883, 891–92 (5th Cir. 2016); Cascade Health Sols. v. PeaceHealth, 515 F.3d 883, 894 (9th Cir. 2008); LePage's Inc. v. 3M, 324 F.3d 141, 167 (3d Cir. 2003) (en banc) (jury instruction); Trans Sport, Inc. v. Starter Sportswear, Inc., 964 F.2d 186, 188–89 (2d Cir. 1992). *See also* Aspen Skiing Co. v. Aspen Highlands Skiing Corp., 472 U.S. 585, 605 (1985) ("The question whether Ski Co.'s conduct may properly be characterized as exclusionary cannot be answered by simply considering its effect on Highlands. In addition, it is relevant to consider its impact on consumers and whether it has impaired competition in an unnecessarily restrictive way.").

[536] *See, e.g.*, Morris Commc'ns Corp. v. PGA Tour, Inc., 364 F.3d 1288, 1295 (11th Cir. 2004) ("Even a company with monopoly power has no general duty to cooperate with its business rivals and may refuse to deal with them if valid business reasons exist for such refusal."); *see also* FTC v. Qualcomm Inc., 969 F.3d 974 (9th Cir. 2020) (refusal to deal unlawful only if "the only conceivable rationale or purpose" is anticompetitive). *But see* Viamedia, Inc. v. Comcast Corporation, 951 F.3d 429, 461 n.13 (7th Cir. 2020) ("[I]t has been observed that although the "no economic sense" test offers good insights into when aggressive actions by a single firm go too far, it can lead to erroneous results unless one also seeks to balance gains to the monopolist against losses to consumers, rivals, or others. Otherwise we could arrive at absurd outcomes: Theoretically, an act might benefit the defendant very slightly while doing considerable harm to the rest of the economy, and it would be lawful. It is possible the test could be adapted to meet these criticisms, given that a court should not consider any gain from eliminating competition, but—in any event—the no economic sense test was not intended to displace all other approaches. Rather, it is likely to be most useful as one part of a sufficient condition: If challenged conduct has a tendency to eliminate competition and would make no economic sense but for that tendency, the conduct is exclusionary. Areeda and Hovenkamp also suggest a broader approach, in which harm wholly disproportionate to the valid business justification can also support a refusal-to-deal-claim.") (internal quotation marks, brackets, and citations omitted).

In *McWane*, the FTC considered procompetitive justifications for an exclusive-dealing scheme operated by a supplier of pipe fittings, which had excluded Star, McWane's competitor. In particular—as we will see in more detail later in this chapter—McWane, a nearly-strict monopolist of certain kinds of pipe fittings, had required its dealers to deal with it exclusively on pain of losing access to valuable rebates and supply of product. This exclusivity scheme was very effective, and seriously hindered Star's efforts to erode McWane's monopoly. McWane attempted, unsuccessfully, to justify its use of exclusivity by asserting some procompetitive justifications for its conduct. The FTC's rejection of those justifications was subsequently endorsed by the Eleventh Circuit on appeal.[537] What test is the Commission applying?

In the Matter of McWane, Inc.

2014-1 Trade Cas. (CCH) ¶ 78670, 2014 WL 556261 (F.T.C. Jan. 30, 2014)

Chairwoman Ramirez.

[1] Complaint Counsel has demonstrated harm to competition here, shifting the burden to McWane to show that the challenged conduct promotes a sufficiently pro-competitive objective. Cognizable justifications are typically those that reduce cost, increase output or improve product quality, service, or innovation.

[2] McWane offers two justifications for its conduct. It argues first that it engaged in exclusive dealing to preserve sales in order to generate sufficient volume to operate its last domestic foundry. While preserving sales volume to continue to operate a foundry may have been a significant business objective, it is not a cognizable procompetitive justification for antitrust purposes. As the ALJ recognized, McWane's sales goal provides benefits for McWane, but Respondent has proffered no explanation as to how its Full Support Program benefits consumers.

[3] Significantly, the measures that McWane took to preserve its sales volume were not the type of steps, such as a price reduction, that typically promote consumer welfare by increasing overall market output. Indeed, McWane considered the impact of lowering its domestic fittings pricing "to defend [its] near 100% share position," but ultimately determined that lowering pricing would hurt margins. Instead, the sales gained for production by McWane's exclusive-dealing arrangement were sales taken from Star by virtue of the increased costs imposed by the Full Support Program. That is, McWane's sales did not result from lower prices, improved service or quality, or other consumer benefits; instead, McWane's sales stemmed from anticompetitive reductions in Star's output. Sales so gained are not cognizable as procompetitive justifications.

[4] Furthermore, contemporaneous evidence belies McWane's contention that its exclusive dealing policies were motivated by a desire to gain volume in order to preserve operations at McWane's domestic foundry. Although that justification shows up in testimony from McWane witnesses, McWane's contemporaneous planning documents from 2009 demonstrate that the objectives were almost exclusively to maintain domestic prices and profitability, deny Star critical mass, and prevent Star from becoming an effective competitor.

[5] McWane also argues that the Full Support Program prevents customers from cherry-picking the highest selling items from Star and persuades them to support McWane's full line of domestic fittings. Here too McWane fails to identify the benefit to consumers.

[6] In support of McWane's claim, its expert, Dr. Normann, explains that a full-line manufacturer incurs the costs of producing all fitting types and is able to bear these costs because it captures the benefit of scale economies arising from production of the most common fittings. According to Dr. Normann, a manufacturer that produces only the common fittings could avoid the cost of producing a full line and consequently could sell the common fittings at lower prices. If distributors were able to source from multiple manufacturers, he reasons, they would buy the common fittings from the limited supplier (at lower prices) and turn to the full-line supplier for less common products only, which could lead to the collapse of the full-line seller.

[7] This argument is unpersuasive. If a limited supplier undersells a full-line supplier for more common products, there is no reason in principle why the full-line supplier could not compete for that business by lowering its price

---

[537] McWane, Inc. v. FTC, 783 F.3d 814, 840–42 (11th Cir. 2015).

for those products and increasing its price for the less common products. McWane offers no reason why supply would not be forthcoming to meet demand at a higher price, and we cannot conclude that consumers are necessarily worse off because less common fittings are sold for higher prices, when simultaneously, more common fittings are sold at lower prices. Even if selective entry by the full-line supplier's rivals led to the collapse of the full-line seller, that itself would not constitute a harm to the market (as opposed to harm to a single firm). Courts have long rejected claims that because of the special characteristics of a particular industry, monopolistic arrangements will better promote trade and commerce than competition, concluding instead that the Sherman Act reflects a legislative judgment that ultimately competition will produce the best results. McWane's claim is not consonant with this core judgment of the Sherman Act, and it is inconsistent with the basic objectives of Section 2.

* * *

In *Eastman Kodak*, a case you may remember from our discussion of aftermarkets in Chapter III, the defendant was accused of monopolizing the aftermarket for service of its equipment, by operating a tying scheme. In particular, Kodak would only sell parts to customers if they agreed not to buy service from independent third parties. Kodak raised several justifications for its conduct. The matter was raised to the Court on the defendant's motion for summary judgment: the Court concluded that the applicability of the defenses would be a matter for a factfinder. In the process, the Court shed some light on what counts as a "procompetitive" justification.

Eastman Kodak Co. v. Image Technical Services, Inc.
504 U.S. 451 (1992)

Justice Blackmun.

[1] [Plaintiffs] have presented evidence that Kodak took exclusionary action to maintain its parts monopoly and used its control over parts to strengthen its monopoly share of the Kodak service market. Liability turns, then, on whether valid business reasons can explain Kodak's actions. Kodak contends that it has three valid business justifications for its actions: (1) to promote interbrand equipment competition by allowing Kodak to stress the quality of its service; (2) to improve asset management by reducing Kodak's inventory costs; and (3) to prevent [independent service organizations ("ISOs")] from free-riding on Kodak's capital investment in equipment, parts and service. Factual questions exist, however, about the validity and sufficiency of each claimed justification, making summary judgment inappropriate.

[2] Kodak first asserts that by preventing customers from using ISO's, it can best maintain high quality service for its sophisticated equipment and avoid being blamed for an equipment malfunction, even if the problem is the result of improper diagnosis, maintenance or repair by an ISO. Respondents have offered evidence that ISO's provide quality service and are preferred by some Kodak equipment owners. This is sufficient to raise a genuine issue of fact.

[3] Moreover, there are other reasons to question Kodak's proffered motive of commitment to quality service; its quality justification appears inconsistent with its thesis that consumers are knowledgeable enough to lifecycle price [(*i.e.*, choose equipment in light of knowledge of aftermarket prices for parts and services)], and its self-service policy. Kodak claims the exclusive-service contract is warranted because customers would otherwise blame Kodak equipment for breakdowns resulting from inferior ISO service. Thus, Kodak simultaneously claims that its customers are sophisticated enough to make complex and subtle lifecycle-pricing decisions, and yet too obtuse to distinguish which breakdowns are due to bad equipment and which are due to bad service. Kodak has failed to offer any reason why informational sophistication should be present in one circumstance and absent in the other. In addition, because self-service customers are just as likely as others to blame Kodak equipment for breakdowns resulting from (their own) inferior service, Kodak's willingness to allow self-service casts doubt on its quality claim. In sum, we agree with the Court of Appeals that respondents have presented evidence from which a reasonable trier of fact could conclude that Kodak's first reason is pretextual.

[4] There is also a triable issue of fact on Kodak's second justification—controlling inventory costs. As respondents argue, Kodak's actions appear inconsistent with any need to control inventory costs. Presumably, the inventory of parts needed to repair Kodak machines turns only on breakdown rates, and those rates should be the same whether

Kodak or ISO's perform the repair. More importantly, the justification fails to explain respondents' evidence that Kodak forced [original equipment manufacturers ("OEMs")], equipment owners, and parts brokers not to sell parts to ISO's, actions that would have no effect on Kodak's inventory costs.

[5] Nor does Kodak's final justification entitle it to summary judgment on respondents' § 2 claim. Kodak claims that its policies prevent ISO's from exploiting the investment Kodak has made in product development, manufacturing and equipment sales in order to take away Kodak's service revenues. Kodak does not dispute that respondents invest substantially in the service market, with training of repair workers and investment in parts inventory. Instead, according to Kodak, the ISO's are free-riding because they have failed to enter the equipment and parts markets. This understanding of free-riding has no support in our case law. To the contrary, as the Court of Appeals noted, one of the evils proscribed by the antitrust laws is the creation of entry barriers to potential competitors by requiring them to enter two markets simultaneously.

[6] None of Kodak's asserted business justifications, then, are sufficient to prove that Kodak is entitled to a judgment as a matter of law on respondents' § 2 claim.

[7] In the end, of course, Kodak's arguments may prove to be correct. It may be that its parts, service, and equipment are components of one unified market, or that the equipment market does discipline the aftermarkets so that all three are priced competitively overall, or that any anti-competitive effects of Kodak's behavior are outweighed by its competitive effects. But we cannot reach these conclusions as a matter of law on a record this sparse. Accordingly, the judgment of the Court of Appeals denying summary judgment is affirmed.

* * *

The nature of the rule, and the question of what exactly the defendant's burden is, is of crucial importance in practice, as Daniel Francis argues in the following extract.

Daniel Francis, Making Sense of Monopolization
84 Antitrust L.J. 779 (2022)

The treatment of justification is a notoriously tangled area of Section 2 law. I will argue here—in [an] . . . explicitly normative register—for a simple rule that reflects the settled welfarist turn in modern antitrust law, as well as the post-Sherman Act recognition that "monopolization" may not always be harmful to consumers, without undermining the structure [of the monopolization offense].

The existence of a justification test is implied by a set of basic ideas: that antitrust rules, including Section 2, should be understood to prohibit practices and transactions by reason of their tendency to cause harm; that, all else equal, it is desirable for antitrust rules to avoid prohibiting or punishing conduct that is beneficial; and that, in some cases, even conduct that falls outside the competitive privilege, and contributes to monopoly by excluding rivals, may nevertheless be beneficial overall. It follows from these three premises that it may be desirable for antitrust doctrine, including Section 2 doctrine, to make room for some kind of case-by-case appraisal of the merits and harms of the individual practice or transaction at issue.

The most appealing version of the substantive justification standard is something like the following. When a factfinder is confident that a practice or transaction is overall beneficial for consumers—in an economic welfare sense across the foreseeable future—it ought not be condemned. That principle is consistent with the core aim of the antitrust enterprise, and the deepest commitment of modern doctrine, that antitrust should leave market participants better, not worse, off. This assessment turns on the overall tendency of the practice or transaction, compared with the most likely but-for alternative and judged *ex ante*: in the interests of good incentives, conduct that *ex ante* appeared overall beneficial for consumers, but turned out in practice to be harmful, ought not be condemned. Benefits that would have been achieved by less restrictive means [if the challenged practice were prohibited] are not cognizable.

Justification is an affirmative defense, and the burden of persuasion lies with the defendant, after the plaintiff has established a prima facie case . . . . This approach rejects the notion, given currency by *Microsoft*, that a defendant need only identify a directional or categorical benefit (and perhaps produce a little evidence) in order to force a plaintiff to prove overall net harmful effects: effectively, to *disprove* the possibility that benefits might outstrip harms.

To endorse this means rejecting some alternatives that others have favored. It cannot be enough simply to have a "legitimate" purpose: we long ago abandoned any effort to distinguish among subjective intentions to prosper at rivals' expense, and it would obviously harm predictability to treat identical practices or transactions differently by reason of subjective occurrent thoughts. Nor can we immunize conduct with a marginal efficiency gain, regardless of the harm: many forms of monopolization often have an efficiency benefit of some kind, even alongside greater harm. We can also rule out benefits enjoyed as a citizen rather than as a consumer or worker, like social equity or national security, which threaten to create a politicized free-for-all.

The allocation of burden of proof to the defendant is critical. *Microsoft* contains some language suggesting that a defendant need only "assert" a non-pretextual benefit to flip the burden back to the plaintiff to show that the procompetitive benefit is actually outweighed by outcome harms. This language or its equivalent has often been repeated . . . . But there are compelling reasons to reject this approach, and require a defendant to show not just the existence of a justification, but its sufficiency. Indeed, it is not at all clear that in *Microsoft* itself the court regarded "assertion" as enough to discharge the defendant's burden.

First, the Supreme Court has (at least arguably) said so, in a neglected aspect of the most recent of its Section 2 cases to turn, on a full trial record, on justification. In *Aspen Skiing*, the defendant monopolist ski resort operator had terminated a profitable cooperative joint-ticketing enterprise with the plaintiff ski resort, and when sued for monopolization the defendant raised defenses of "legitimate business justifications." These were—despite the Court's odd language—efficiency justifications of the usual kind: that "usage [of the joint ticket] could not be properly monitored," including because it was "cumbersome" to do so, and that the plaintiff was offering "inferior skiing services" from which the defendant was trying to protect its brand. The record appears to have been murky. But the Court affirmed on the ground that "[the defendant] *did not persuade the jury that its conduct was justified* by any normal business purpose." Some post-*Microsoft* courts have made the same point.

Second, our framework implies that the prima facie monopolization offense does not depend upon injury to the end results of competition, such as price, quality, or output. There is no point at all in having a flexible causation standard short of a but-for test if a plaintiff must show actual but-for effects on outcomes. This approach captures the intent of the Sherman Act legislators, who . . . focused on processual concerns like exclusion and contribution to monopoly. There is no suggestion that they, or courts, expected plaintiffs to show that competitive outcomes like prices had *actually* been driven to unreasonable levels. . . . .

Third, it is consistent with the use of the "affirmative defense" category elsewhere in the law. Affirmative defenses are those that suggest some [additional] reason, apart from simple denial of the basic offense, why there is no right of recovery, particularly when the relevant facts and evidence are within the defendant's knowledge or reach. The burden of proving such defenses is routinely placed on defendants, even in criminal cases.

That shoe fits well here. A defendant usually has enormous advantages in access to relevant evidence: justifications typically relate to an improvement in the efficiency of the defendant's own operations, leaving a defendant uniquely placed to prove the nature and magnitude of that effect. It strains reason to require a plaintiff to *disprove* them, either out of the gate or after a defendant has simply cried "free riding," brandished an email or two, and ridden off into the sunset, leaving a plaintiff to try to calculate and balance relative magnitudes.

But the *Microsoft* formulation, taken literally, threatens such a result in almost every real case. A defendant can almost always "assert" a directional efficiency justification, not least because the term "free riding" can be applied to almost any example of a competitor profitably doing something that the monopolist could prevent or appropriate. *Any* act of monopolization—however flagrant—has *at least* the effect of increasing incentives to invest in the underlying monopoly, by making that monopoly more profitable. So in practice a plaintiff ends up forced to disprove the possibility of net benefit in virtually every case.

Fourth, pragmatic considerations point the same way. We are concerned here with cases in which a plaintiff has already established [a prima facie case of monopolization], and a defendant has named a countervailing beneficial effect, but not proven that the good effects outweigh the bad ones. The problem bites when the evidence of respective magnitudes is inconclusive: if the defendant's burden is of production only, it wins; if it is one of persuasion, the plaintiff wins. This situation is most likely to occur in markets like digital ones, in which competitive futures are least predictable, and in which innovation and product change are key dimensions of competition. Tolerating conduct amounting to prima-facie monopolization when we are least certain it is worth the trade seems to have things backwards.

D. Specific Exclusionary Practices

The vagueness in monopolization's conceptual core is somewhat offset by greater specificity and clarity in the law of specific *forms* of the offense. For example, we have already discussed antitrust treatment of unconditional refusals to deal earlier in this chapter.[538] More than a century of jurisprudence has given us a taxonomy of other practices— including exclusive dealing, tying, predatory pricing, and so on—and a set of more specific doctrinal tests that apply to these forms of behavior. As you consider these practices and their respective analytical frames, consider whether and to what extent they can be seen as consistent with one another, with a "grand theory" of monopolization, or with the common themes considered in the previous section.

1. Exclusivity

In a traditional exclusivity case, a monopolist obtains or induces an exclusive relationship of some kind with a key trading partner, disadvantaging rivals who must then make do with a second-best option. By driving up competitors' costs, the monopolist softens their ability to exert competitive constraint.[539] The crucial question in a Section 2 exclusivity case, just as under Section 1, is usually whether the exclusive agreement "substantially forecloses" access to inputs, distribution, customers, or complements. And when a monopolist excludes rivals through substantial foreclosure that is reasonably capable of making a significant contribution to monopoly power, without sufficient procompetitive justification, liability typically follows.

Unlike Section 1, no agreement is required to violate Section 2. A monopolist can therefore violate Section by inducing exclusivity through the application of a unilateral conditional-dealing policy (*e.g.*, "I will only sell to trading partners that do not deal with my rivals.").[540] And—because the assessment of exclusivity turns on economic substance, not on legal formalities—practices that result in or induce exclusivity can violate Section 2 even in the absence of a formal or literal requirement that input suppliers or distributors must completely refrain from dealing with rivals.

Exclusivity can violate Section 2 even if there are some literal alternatives to the foreclosed supply, so long as those alternatives do not constitute reasonable alternatives (a rival does not have an antitrust right to its favorite or most preferred kind of supply. Thus, in *Dentsply*, as we saw above, the excluded rivals had the option of selling directly to their dental-lab customers rather than using the dealers who had been incentivized to deal exclusively with Dentsply: Dentsply was nevertheless held liable for monopolization, in light of the fact that direct selling was much less effective.[541]

Likewise, exclusivity can also violate Section 2 even if rivals are not wholly denied access to the relevant trading partners, so long as the supply that *is* foreclosed to them is sufficiently critical, by comparison with the available alternatives, to make enough of a difference to competition. Consigning rivals to supply that is significantly inferior quality, more expensive, less effective, or otherwise disadvantageous can be an effective mechanism of exclusion. For example, in the *Microsoft* case, some of the challenged practices involved inducing trading partners to assign Microsoft's internet browser a valuable default status, rather than literally preventing any dealings with third

---

[538] *See supra* § VII.C.3.

[539] Thomas G. Krattenmaker & Steven C. Salop, *Anticompetitive Exclusion: Raising Rivals' Costs to Achieve Power over Price*, 96 Yale L.J. 209 (1986).

[540] *See, e.g.*, Roland Machinery Co. v. Dresser Industries, Inc., 749 F.2d 380 (7th Cir. 1984) ("One mind is not enough for a meeting of minds. The fact that Dresser was hostile to dealers who would not live and die by its product . . . and acted on its hostility by canceling a dealer who did the thing to which it was hostile, does not establish an agreement, but if anything the opposite: a failure to agree on a point critical to one of the parties.").

[541] United States v. Dentsply Intl., Inc., 399 F.3d 181, 191–93 (3d Cir. 2005).

parties: can you see why and how this could have an effect equivalent to exclusivity?[542] (Do default statuses always have this effect?)

Finally—and no less importantly—a practice can constitute "exclusivity" for the purposes of the antitrust laws even if there is no contract or agreement that actually commits the relevant third party to dealing exclusively. It is enough, under Section 2, that exclusive dealing is incentivized by the monopolist's behavior.[543] For example, unilaterally offering a pricing schedule that provides more attractive "loyalty" pricing for customers that do not deal with rivals can violate Section 2. (Indeed, you may remember that the *Surescripts* litigation was brought under Section 2 and involved such pricing.[544])

But despite all this, exclusivity is not always, or even usually, unlawful. Exclusive deals are widespread in the economy, and courts have recognized a wide range of economic benefits that exclusive commercial relationships can create or protect. As we have already seen, one prominent justification in exclusivity cases is protection against "free riding": the economic phenomenon that occurs when the benefits of an investment are involuntarily shared with third parties. Thus, in cases where a defendant would be deterred from making a particular beneficial investment by a risk that the fruits of the investment would be appropriated in some way by a competitor, a court may consider whether exclusivity might be playing an important role in solving that problem and making the investment possible. However, the scope of the "free riding defense" is a matter of real controversy and criticism.[545]

As you will remember from Chapter VI, the modern law of exclusive dealing begins with *Tampa Electric*, a case decided under Section 3 of the Clayton Act, but which has been understood to guide the Sherman Act on exclusive dealing as well.[546] *Tampa* stands in particular for the proposition that a plaintiff in an exclusive dealing case must prove "substantial foreclosure" in a relevant market. As *Tampa* demonstrates—and like certain other practices such as tying—exclusive dealing can be challenged under multiple provisions, including Section 1 of the Sherman Act; Section 2 of the Sherman Act; and Section 3 of the Clayton Act. As we saw in Chapter VI, Section 3 is a specialized provision that provides, in principle, a slightly elevated level of scrutiny for exclusivity and tying arrangements involving the sale of goods, but in practice is very close to Section 1 in content and effect.[547]

A classic case of Section 2 exclusivity—maybe *the* classic Section 2 exclusivity case[548]—is *Lorain Journal*. In that case the Supreme Court considered a dominant newspaper that faced competition, as a seller of advertising space, from the developing radio industry. In order to keep radio rivals at bay, Lorain Journal refused to accept advertising from any company that was also buying advertising space on the radio. The Court had no hesitation in imposing liability.

---

[542] *See* United States v. Microsoft Corp., 253 F.3d 34, 65 (D.C. Cir. 2001) ("[T]he District Court found that Microsoft designed Windows 98 so that using Navigator on Windows 98 would have unpleasant consequences for users by, in some circumstances, overriding the user's choice of a browser other than IE as his or her default browser. Plaintiffs argue that this override harms the competitive process by deterring consumers from using a browser other than IE even though they might prefer to do so, thereby reducing rival browsers' usage share and, hence, the ability of rival browsers to draw developer attention away from the APIs exposed by Windows. Microsoft does not deny, of course, that overriding the user's preference prevents some people from using other browsers. Because the override reduces rivals' usage share and protects Microsoft's monopoly, it too is anticompetitive.") (internal quotation marks and citations omitted). *See also* United States v. Google, Case No 1:20-cv-3010 (D.D.C. filed Oct. 20, 2020) ¶ 3 ("For a general search engine, by far the most effective means of distribution is to be the preset default general search engine for mobile and computer search access points. Even where users can change the default, they rarely do. This leaves the preset default general search engine with de facto exclusivity. As Google itself has recognized, this is particularly true on mobile devices, where defaults are especially sticky.").

[543] *See, e.g.*, Lorain Journal Co. v. United States, 342 U.S. 143, 155 (1951); United States v. Microsoft Corp., 253 F.3d 34, 77 (D.C. Cir. 2001); McWane, Inc. v. FTC, 783 F.3d 814, 833–35 (11th Cir. 2015); FTC v. Surescripts, LLC, 424 F.Supp.3d 92, 101–02 (2020).

[544] *See supra* § VI.D.

[545] *See supra* Chapter VI (discussing the relationship between free riding concerns and vertical restraints).

[546] *See, e.g.*, Dos Santos v. Columbus-Cuneo-Cabrini Med. Ctr., 684 F.2d 1346, 1352 n. 11 (7th Cir. 1982) ("*Tampa Electric* is applicable to Sherman Act section 1 cases even though it was decided under section 3 of the Clayton Act[.]").

[547] *See supra* notes 411 to 417 and accompanying text.

[548] *Lorain Journal*'s status as a landmark authority across the political spectrum is buttressed by an endorsement from a prominent monopolization skeptic: Robert Bork's comment that the result "seem[s] clearly correct." Robert H. Bork, THE ANTITRUST PARADOX: A POLICY AT WAR WITH ITSELF (1978) 344–46. *See also* Leon B. Greenfield, *Afterwords:* Lorain Journal *and the Antitrust Legacy of Robert Bork*, 79 Antitrust L.J. 1047 (2014).

Lorain Journal Co. v. United States
342 U.S. 143 (1951)

Justice Burton.

[1] From 1933 to 1948 [Lorain Journal Co.] enjoyed a substantial monopoly in Lorain of the mass dissemination of news and advertising, both of a local and national character. However, in 1948 the Elyria-Lorain Broadcasting Company, a corporation independent of the publisher, was licensed by the Federal Communications Commission to establish and operate in Elyria, Ohio, eight miles south of Lorain, a radio station whose call letters, WEOL, stand for Elyria, Oberlin and Lorain. [. . .]

[2] [The Journal] knew that a substantial number of Journal advertisers wished to use the facilities of the radio station as well. For some of them . . . advertising in the Journal was essential for the promotion of their sales in Lorain County. [The court below] found that at all times since WEOL commenced broadcasting, [Lorain Journal] had executed a plan conceived to eliminate the threat of competition from the station. Under this plan the publisher refused to accept local advertisements in the Journal from any Lorain County advertiser who advertised or who appellants believed to be about to advertise over WEOL. The court found expressly that the purpose and intent of this procedure was to destroy the broadcasting company.

[3] The court [below] characterized all this as "bold, relentless, and predatory commercial behavior." To carry out appellants' plan, the publisher monitored WEOL programs to determine the identity of the station's local Lorain advertisers. Those using the station's facilities had their contracts with the publisher terminated and were able to renew them only after ceasing to advertise through WEOL. The program was effective. Numerous Lorain County merchants testified that, as a result of the publisher's policy, they either ceased or abandoned their plans to advertise over WEOL. [. . .]

[4] The conduct complained of was an attempt to monopolize interstate commerce. It consisted of the publisher's practice of refusing to accept local Lorain advertising from parties using WEOL for local advertising. Because of the Journal's complete daily newspaper monopoly of local advertising in Lorain and its practically indispensable coverage of 99% of the Lorain families, this practice forced numerous advertisers to refrain from using WEOL for local advertising. That result not only reduced the number of customers available to WEOL in the field of local Lorain advertising and strengthened the Journal's monopoly in that field, but more significantly tended to destroy and eliminate WEOL altogether. Attainment of that sought-for elimination would automatically restore to the publisher of the Journal its substantial monopoly in Lorain of the mass dissemination of all news and advertising, interstate and national, as well as local. It would deprive not merely Lorain but Elyria and all surrounding communities of their only nearby radio station. [. . .]

[5] The publisher claims a right as a private business concern to select its customers and to refuse to accept advertisement from whomever it pleases. We do not dispute that general right. But the word "right" is one of the most deceptive of pitfalls; it is so easy to slip from a qualified meaning in the premise to an unqualified one in the conclusion. Most rights are qualified. The right claimed by the publisher is neither absolute nor exempt from regulation. Its exercise in a purposeful means of monopolizing interstate commerce is prohibited by the Sherman Act. The operator of the radio station, equally with the publisher of the newspaper, is entitled to the protection of that Act.

* * *

A similar arrangement was at work in *Dentsply*, in which the Third Circuit noted that exclusivity was the result of a conditional-dealing practice, not an agreement:

> Although the parties to the sales transactions consider the exclusionary arrangements to be agreements, they are technically only a series of independent sales. Dentsply sells teeth to the dealers on an individual transaction basis and essentially the arrangement is "at-will." Nevertheless, the economic elements involved—the large share of the market held by Dentsply

and its conduct excluding competing manufacturers—realistically make the arrangements here as effective as those in written contracts.[549]

When an agreement does exist, does it matter whether exclusivity is challenged under Section 1 or Section 2? The answer is: it might! One of the (relatively few) explicit discussions of the differences between Section 1 and Section 2 exclusivity claims is found in *Microsoft*. The plaintiffs had challenged Microsoft's use of exclusivity agreements with certain internet access providers ("IAPs") under both Sections 1 and 2, on the theory that these agreements foreclosed Netscape's opportunities for browser distribution. The district court had concluded that the plaintiffs could not prevail on their Section 1 claim unless the agreements fully excluded Netscape from roughly 40% of the browser market, and that the agreements had not in fact done so. Nevertheless, the district court held that the same exclusive agreements could nevertheless violate Section 2. On appeal, Microsoft protested to the D.C. Circuit that the same standard of legality should apply under Section 1 and Section 2. Rejecting that view, the court of appeals indicated that an exclusivity agreement could violate Section 2 at a lower level of foreclosure than Section 1 would require:

> On appeal Microsoft argues that courts have applied the same standard to alleged exclusive dealing agreements under both Section 1 and Section 2, and it argues that the District Court's holding of no liability under § 1 necessarily precludes holding it liable under § 2. The District Court appears to have based its holding with respect to § 1 upon a "total exclusion test" rather than the 40% standard drawn from the caselaw. Even assuming the holding is correct, however, we nonetheless reject Microsoft's contention.
>
> The basic prudential concerns relevant to §§ 1 and 2 are admittedly the same: exclusive contracts are commonplace—particularly in the field of distribution—in our competitive, market economy, and imposing upon a firm with market power the risk of an antitrust suit every time it enters into such a contract, no matter how small the effect, would create an unacceptable and unjustified burden upon any such firm. At the same time, however, we agree with plaintiffs that a monopolist's use of exclusive contracts, in certain circumstances, may give rise to a § 2 violation even though the contracts foreclose less than the roughly 40% or 50% share usually required in order to establish a § 1 violation.[550]

When a monopolist is involved, Section 2's thresholds are in some respects more plaintiff-friendly than those of Section 1: including the lack of an agreement requirement, the *Microsoft* court's lower foreclosure threshold for Section 2, and perhaps also the flexible "reasonably capable" causal test for contribution to monopoly. It is therefore unsurprising that some plaintiffs choose to bring their exclusive-dealing cases only under Section 2. *McWane* is a good example of such a case. (*Dentsply*, discussed above, is another.) In *McWane*, the Eleventh Circuit gave a fine tour of monopolization analysis, including the workings of an exclusion analysis, the operation of the substantial foreclosure test, and the flexible threshold for the assessment of causal contribution to monopoly power.

McWane, Inc. v. FTC
783 F.3d 814 (11th Cir. 2015)

Judge Marcus.

[1] This antitrust case involves allegedly anticompetitive conduct in the ductile iron pipe fittings ("DIPF") market by McWane, Inc., a family-run company headquartered in Birmingham, Alabama. In 2009, following the passage of federal legislation that provided a large infusion of money for waterworks projects that required domestic pipe fittings, Star Pipe Products entered the domestic fittings market. In response, McWane, the dominant producer of domestic pipe fittings, announced to its distributors that (with limited exceptions) unless they bought all of their domestic fittings from McWane, they would lose their rebates and be cut off from purchases for 12 weeks. The Federal Trade Commission ("FTC") investigated and brought an enforcement action under Section 5 of the Federal Trade Commission Act. The Administrative Law Judge ("ALJ"), after a two-month trial, and then a divided Commission, found that McWane's actions constituted an illegal exclusive dealing policy used to maintain McWane's monopoly power in the domestic fittings market. The Commission issued an order directing McWane

[549] United States v. Dentsply Intl., Inc., 399 F.3d 181 (3d Cir. 2005).
[550] United States v. Microsoft Corp., 253 F.3d 34, 70 (D.C. Cir. 2001) (en banc).

to stop requiring exclusivity from distributors. McWane appealed, challenging nearly every aspect of the Commission's ruling. [. . .]

[2] In response to Star's forthcoming entry into the domestic DIPF market, McWane implemented its "Full Support Program" in order to protect [its] domestic brands and market position. This program was announced in a September 22, 2009 letter to distributors. McWane informed customers that if they did not fully support McWane branded products for their domestic fitting and accessory requirements, they may forgo participation in any unpaid rebates they had accrued for domestic fittings and accessories or shipment of their domestic fitting and accessory orders of McWane products for up to 12 weeks. In other words, distributors who bought domestic fittings from other companies (such as Star) might lose their rebates or be cut off from purchasing McWane's domestic fittings for up to three months. [. . .]

[3] Internal documents reveal that McWane's express purpose was to raise Star's costs and impede it from becoming a viable competitor. McWane executive Richard Tatman wrote, "We need to make sure that they [Star] don't reach any critical market mass that will allow them to continue to invest and receive a profitable return." In another document, he observed that "any competitor" seeking to enter the domestic fittings market could face "significant blocking issues" if they are not a "full line" domestic supplier. In yet another, McWane employees described the nascent Full Support Program as a strategy to "force distribution to pick their horse," which would "force Star to absorb the costs associated with having a more full line before they can secure major distribution." Mr. Tatman was concerned about the "erosion of domestic pricing if Star emerges as a legitimate competitor," and another McWane executive wrote that his "chief concern is that the domestic market might get creamed from a pricing standpoint" should Star become a "domestic supplier."

[4] Initially, the Full Support Program was enforced as threatened. Thus, for example, when the Tulsa, Oklahoma branch of distributor Hajoca Corporation purchased Star domestic fittings, McWane cut off sales of its domestic fittings to all Hajoca branches and withheld its rebates. Other distributors testified to abiding by the Full Support Program in order to avoid the devastating result of being cut off from all McWane domestic fittings. For example, following the announcement of the Full Support Program, the country's two largest waterworks distributors, HD Supply (with approximately a 28–35% share of the distribution market) and Ferguson (with approximately 25%), prohibited their branches from purchasing domestic fittings from Star unless the purchases fell into one of the Full Support Program exceptions, and even canceled pending orders for domestic fittings that they had placed with Star. . . .

[5] Despite McWane's Full Support Program, Star entered the domestic fittings market and made sales to various distributors. From 2006 until Star's entry in 2009, McWane was the only manufacturer of domestic fittings, with 100% of the market for domestic-only projects. By 2010, Star had gained approximately 5% of the domestic fittings market, while McWane captured the remaining 95%. Star grew to just under 10% market share in 2011, leaving the remaining 90% for McWane, and Star was "on pace, at the time of trial, to have its best year ever for [d]omestic [f]ittings sales in 2012." The Commission noted that "many distributors made purchases under the exceptions allowed by the Full Support Program," but that Star's sales in total "were small compared to the overall size of the market." Star estimated that if the Full Support Program had not been in place, its sales would have been greater by a multiple of 2.5 in 2010 and by a multiple of three in 2011. [. . .]

[6] Substantial foreclosure continues to be a requirement for exclusive dealing to run afoul of the antitrust statutes. Foreclosure occurs when the opportunities for other traders to enter into or remain in the market are significantly limited by the exclusive dealing arrangements. Traditionally a foreclosure percentage of at least 40% has been a threshold for liability in exclusive dealing cases. However, some courts have found that a lesser degree of foreclosure is required when the defendant is a monopolist.

[7] In this case, both the Commission and the ALJ found that the Full Support Program foreclosed Star from a substantial share of the market. Although the Commission did not quantify a percentage, it did note that the two largest distributors, who together controlled approximately 50–60% of distribution, prohibited their branches from purchasing from Star (except through the Full Support Program exceptions) following the announcement of the Full Support Program. Indeed, [one customer,] HD Supply went so far as to cancel pending orders for domestic fittings that it had placed with Star. . . . Although the Commission did not place an exact number on the

percentage foreclosed, it found that the Full Support Program tied up the key dealers and that the foreclosure was substantial and problematic.

[8] These factual findings are all consistent with the ALJ's determinations, and all pass our deferential review. Nevertheless, McWane challenges the Commission's conclusion by arguing that Star's entry and growth in the market demonstrate that, as a matter of law, the Full Support Program did not cause substantial foreclosure. As before, when McWane raised a substantially similar claim to rebut the Commission's finding of monopoly power, this argument is ultimately unpersuasive. The test is not total foreclosure, but whether the challenged practices bar a substantial number of rivals or severely restrict the market's ambit. Our sister circuits have found monopolists liable for anticompetitive conduct where, as here, the targeted rival gained market share—but less than it likely would have absent the conduct. As noted above, exclusive dealing measures that slow a rival's expansion can still produce consumer injury. Given the ample evidence in the record that the Full Support Program significantly contributed to key dealers freezing out Star, the Commission's foreclosure determination is supported by substantial evidence and sufficient as a matter of law. [. . .]

[9] Having concluded that the Commission's finding of substantial foreclosure is supported by substantial evidence, we turn to the remainder of the Commission's evidence that McWane's Full Support Program injured competition. The record contains both direct and indirect evidence that the Full Support Program harmed competition. The Commission relied on both, and taken together they are more than sufficient to meet the government's burden. The Commission found that McWane's program deprived its rivals of distribution sufficient to achieve efficient scale, thereby raising costs and slowing or preventing effective entry. It found that the Full Support Program made it infeasible for distributors to drop the monopolist McWane and switch to Star. This, the Commission found, deprived Star of the revenue needed to purchase its own domestic foundry, forcing it to rely on inefficient outsourcing arrangements and preventing it from providing meaningful price competition with McWane.

[10] Perhaps the Commission's most powerful evidence of anticompetitive harm was direct pricing evidence. It noted that McWane's prices and profit margins for domestic fittings were notably higher than prices for imported fittings, which faced greater competition. Thus, these prices appeared to be supracompetitive. Yet in states where Star entered as a competitor, notably there was no effect on McWane's prices. Indeed, soon after Star entered the market, McWane raised prices and increased its gross profits—despite its flat production costs and its own internal projections that Star's unencumbered entry into the market would cause prices to fall. Since McWane was an incumbent monopolist already charging supracompetitive prices (as demonstrated by the difference in price and profit margin between domestic and imported fittings), evidence that McWane's prices did not fall is consistent with a reasonable inference that the Full Support Program significantly contributed to maintaining McWane's monopoly power.

[11] McWane claims, however, that the government did not adequately prove that the Full Support Program was responsible for this price behavior. But as we've noted, McWane demands too high a bar for causation. While it is true that there could have been other causes for the price behavior, the government need not demonstrate that the Full Support Program was the sole cause—only that the program reasonably appeared to be a significant contribution to maintaining McWane's monopoly power. Moreover, under our deferential standard of review, the mere fact that two inconsistent conclusions could be drawn from the record does not prevent the Commission's finding from being supported by substantial evidence. [. . .]

[12] We also consider it significant that alternative channels of distribution were unavailable to Star. In cases where exclusive dealing arrangements tie up distributors in a market, courts will often consider whether alternative channels of distribution exist. If firms can use other means of distribution, or sell directly to consumers, then it is less likely that their foreclosure from distributors will harm competition. . . .

[13] Finally, the clear anticompetitive intent behind the Full Support Program also supports the inference that it harmed competition. Anticompetitive intent alone, no matter how virulent, is insufficient to give rise to an antitrust violation. But, as this Court has said, evidence of intent is highly probative not because a good intention will save an otherwise objectionable regulation or the reverse; but because knowledge of intent may help the court to interpret facts and to predict consequences. For a monopolization charge, intent is relevant to the question whether

the challenged conduct is fairly characterized as exclusionary or anticompetitive. There is agreement on the proposition that no monopolist monopolizes unconscious of what he is doing.

[14] In this case, the evidence of anticompetitive intent is particularly powerful. Testimony from McWane executives leaves little doubt that the Full Support Program was a deliberate plan to prevent Star from reaching any critical market mass that will allow them to continue to invest and receive a profitable return by forcing Star to absorb the costs associated with having a more full line before they can secure major distribution. Indeed, the plan was implemented as a reaction to concerns about the erosion of domestic pricing if Star emerges as a legitimate competitor. Although such intent alone is not illegal, it could reasonably help the Commission draw the inference that the witnessed price behavior was the (intended) result of the Full Support Program.

[15] Not all of the evidence adduced in this case uniformly points against McWane. For example, as we've previously noted, Star was not completely excluded from the domestic fittings market; it was able to enter and grow despite the presence of the Full Support Program. However, it is still perfectly plausible to conclude on this record that Star's growth was meaningfully (and deliberately) slowed and its development into a rival that could constrain McWane's monopoly power was stunted. Also, the Full Support Program was not a binding contract of a lengthy duration. As noted above, these characteristics do not render the program presumptively lawful, but they also do not point in the FTC's favor as an indirect indicator of anticompetitive harm. Nevertheless, the direct and indirect evidence of anticompetitive harm is more than sufficient to pass our deferential review. Again, the Commission's conclusion that the Full Support Program harmed competition is supported by substantial evidence and sound as a matter of law. [. . .]

[16] Having established that the defendant's conduct harmed competition, the burden shifts to the defendant to offer procompetitive justifications for its conduct.

NOTES

1) What is substantial foreclosure?
   a. Does it relate to one of the basic concerns of monopolization we described above: monopoly power, exclusion, contribution to monopoly, and so on, or is it something else?
   b. Should courts apply a quantitative test or a qualitative test to determine whether it is present, and what should that test be?
   c. Should the analysis differ depending on whether Section 1 or Section 2 is at issue?
2) What kind of practice could constitute a "de facto" exclusive? Is there a sense in which every sale of a product is to some extent "exclusive"? In what circumstances should courts apply the exclusivity framework to agreements that do not literally prohibit suppliers or distributors from dealing with a monopolist's competitors?
3) Digital products and services often have "default" options so that users don't have to manually select an option each time: for example, computer or device operating systems commonly have default internet browsers, search engines, email programs, and so on. When and how do you think the designation of a default could work like an exclusivity agreement? What would "substantial foreclosure" mean in this context and how could it be measured? What remedy would be appropriate?
4) As we saw in Chapter VI, a common justification for exclusive dealing is protection against free riding on the defendant's investments. Does that justification sound with equal, lesser, or greater force when the defendant is a monopolist?

2. Tying

As we saw in Chapter VI, tying is the practice of making access to one product or service (such as a printer) conditional on customers' purchase of another product or service (such as a printer cartridge). The first product or service—the one that consumers want to buy (here, the printer)—is called the "tying" product or service. The second one—the one that the defendant insists they buy (here, the cartridge)—is called the "tied" product or service. Where this is done through an agreement, it may be challenged under Section 1 (or under Section 3 of the Clayton Act[551]); when it is done by a monopolist—regardless of whether an agreement is involved—it may be challenged under Section 2. In practice tying cases are often brought under multiple provisions.

The competitive concern in a Section 2 tying case is that, when a defendant has monopoly power in a market for the tying product, the induced purchase of the tied product or service will exclude competition in the market for that (tied) product or service and create or extend monopoly in that second market: for example, by driving competitors below minimum viable scale. The successful tying monopolist might thus be able to turn one monopoly into two.

The difference in legal standards between Section 1 and Section 2 is not entirely clear, but the main points of differentiation—apart from the agreement requirement—appear to be: (1) the existence of a (qualified and limited) *per se* rule under Section 1; (2) Section 2's requirement of monopoly power (or a dangerous probability thereof), which is more demanding than Section 1's market power requirement; (3) Section 2's more flexible threshold for the causal relationship between the conduct and a contribution to an outcome of the competitive process (*i.e.*, the acquisition or maintenance of monopoly power); and perhaps also (4) a lower threshold under Section 2—by analogy with exclusive-dealing law—for foreclosure of access to customers.[552]

Moreover, just as with exclusivity, Section 2 is often a more natural fit for a tying claim than Section 1. Recall that Section 1 needs an *agreement*: a mutual commitment to a common scheme. But tying claims—like exclusive dealing claims—often arise from a mere conditional dealing policy: that is, the seller simply will not sell to a trading partner unless the trading partner buys the tied product or service. No agreement is required to make tying work in that fashion.

Perhaps the most prominent discussion of tying under Section 2 is that in *Microsoft*. The tying at issue in that case involved not a formal condition of purchasing a separate product, but rather so-called "technological tying": the integration through technological means of what might otherwise be separate products. The tying claim involved integrating the Internet Explorer browser into Windows, making it an irremovable part of the operating system. We will review an excerpt from the district court's findings of fact, along with the treatment of the issue by the D.C. Circuit. You may remember from the discussion in Chapter VI that the court of appeals held that, under Section 1, the technological tying practice should be analyzed under the rule of reason, not the per se rule[553]; here our focus will be on the heart of the court's Section 2 analysis.

Findings of Fact, United States v. Microsoft Corp.

84 F. Supp. 2d 9 (D.D.C. 1999)

Judge Jackson.

[1] . . . Microsoft placed many of the routines that are used by Internet Explorer . . . into the same files that support [general Windows functionality]. Microsoft's primary motivation for this action was to ensure that the deletion of any file containing browsing-specific routines would also delete vital operating system routines and thus cripple Windows 95. Although some of the code that provided Web browsing could still be removed, without disabling the operating system, by entering individual files and selectively deleting routines used only for Web browsing, licensees of Microsoft software were, and are, contractually prohibited from reverse engineering, decompiling, or disassembling any software files. Even if this were not so, it is prohibitively difficult for anyone who does not have access to the original, human-readable source code to change the placement of routines into files, or otherwise to alter the internal configuration of software files, while still preserving the software's overall functionality.

[2] Microsoft's technical personnel implemented [the] "Windows integration" strategy in two [further] ways. First, they did not provide users with the ability to uninstall Internet Explorer from Windows 98. The omission of a browser removal function was particularly conspicuous given that Windows 98 did give users the ability to uninstall

---

[551] *See* Int'l Bus. Machines Corp. v. United States, 298 U.S. 131, 135 (1936).

[552] *See* United States v. Microsoft Corp. 253 F.3d 34, 70 (D.C. Cir. 2001) ("[A] monopolist's use of exclusive contracts, in certain circumstances, may give rise to a § 2 violation even though the contracts foreclose less than the roughly 40% or 50% share usually required in order to establish a § 1 violation.").

[553] *See supra* § VI.E.

numerous features other than Internet Explorer—features that Microsoft also held out as being integrated into Windows 98. Microsoft took this action despite specific requests from Gateway that Microsoft provide a way to uninstall Internet Explorer 4.0 from Windows 98.

[3] The second way in which Microsoft's engineers implemented [the] strategy was to make Windows 98 override the user's choice of default browser in certain circumstances. As shipped to users, Windows 98 has Internet Explorer configured as the default browser. While Windows 98 does provide the user with the ability to choose a different default browser, it does not treat this choice as the "default browser" within the ordinary meaning of the term. Specifically, when a user chooses a browser other than Internet Explorer as the default, Windows 98 nevertheless requires the user to employ Internet Explorer in numerous situations that, from the user's perspective, are entirely unexpected. As a consequence, users who choose a browser other than Internet Explorer as their default face considerable uncertainty and confusion in the ordinary course of using Windows 98.

[4] Microsoft's refusal to respect the user's choice of default browser fulfilled Brad Chase's 1995 promise to make the use of any browser other than Internet Explorer on Windows "a jolting experience." By increasing the likelihood that using Navigator on Windows 98 would have unpleasant consequences for users, Microsoft further diminished the inclination of OEMs to pre-install Navigator onto Windows. The decision to override the user's selection of non-Microsoft software as the default browser also directly disinclined Windows 98 consumers to use Navigator as their default browser, and it harmed those Windows 98 consumers who nevertheless used Navigator.

* * *

United States v. Microsoft Corp.
253 F.3d 34 (D.C. Cir. 2001)

Per curiam.

[1] [I]n late 1995 or early 1996, Microsoft set out to bind [Internet Explorer ("IE")] more tightly to Windows 95 as a technical matter.

[2] Technologically binding IE to Windows, the District Court found, both prevented OEMs from pre-installing other browsers and deterred consumers from using them. In particular, having the IE software code as an irremovable part of Windows meant that pre-installing a second browser would increase an OEM's product testing costs, because an OEM must test and train its support staff to answer calls related to every software product preinstalled on the machine; moreover, pre-installing a browser in addition to IE would to many OEMs be a questionable use of the scarce and valuable space on a PC's hard drive.

[3] Although the District Court, in its Conclusions of Law, broadly condemned Microsoft's decision to bind Internet Explorer to Windows with technological shackles its findings of fact in support of that conclusion center upon three specific actions Microsoft took to weld IE to Windows: excluding IE from the "Add/Remove Programs" utility; designing Windows so as in certain circumstances to override the user's choice of a default browser other than IE; and commingling code related to browsing and other code in the same files, so that any attempt to delete the files containing IE would, at the same time, cripple the operating system. As with the license restrictions, we consider first whether the suspect actions had an anticompetitive effect, and then whether Microsoft has provided a procompetitive justification for them. [. . .]

[4] As a general rule, courts are properly very skeptical about claims that competition has been harmed by a dominant firm's product design changes. In a competitive market, firms routinely innovate in the hope of appealing to consumers, sometimes in the process making their products incompatible with those of rivals; the imposition of liability when a monopolist does the same thing will inevitably deter a certain amount of innovation. This is all the more true in a market, such as this one, in which the product itself is rapidly changing. Judicial deference to product innovation, however, does not mean that a monopolist's product design decisions are per se lawful.

[5] The District Court first condemned as anticompetitive Microsoft's decision to exclude IE from the "Add/Remove Programs" utility in Windows 98. Microsoft had included IE in the Add/Remove Programs utility

in Windows 95, but when it modified Windows 95 to produce Windows 98, it took IE out of the Add/Remove Programs utility. This change reduces the usage share of rival browsers not by making Microsoft's own browser more attractive to consumers but, rather, by discouraging OEMs from distributing rival products. Because Microsoft's conduct, through something other than competition on the merits, has the effect of significantly reducing usage of rivals' products and hence protecting its own operating system monopoly, it is anticompetitive; we defer for the moment the question whether It is nonetheless justified.

[6] Second, the District Court found that Microsoft designed Windows 98 so that using Navigator on Windows 98 would have unpleasant consequences for users by, in some circumstances, overriding the user's choice of a browser other than IE as his or her default browser. Plaintiffs argue that this override harms the competitive process by deterring consumers from using a browser other than IE even though they might prefer to do so, thereby reducing rival browsers' usage share and, hence, the ability of rival browsers to draw developer attention away from the APIs exposed by Windows. Microsoft does not deny, of course, that overriding the user's preference prevents some people from using other browsers. Because the override reduces rivals' usage share and protects Microsoft's monopoly, it too is anticompetitive.

[7] Finally, the District Court condemned Microsoft's decision to bind IE to Windows 98 by placing code specific to Web browsing in the same files as code that provided operating system functions. Putting code supplying browsing functionality into a file with code supplying operating system functionality ensures that the deletion of any file containing browsing-specific routines would also delete vital operating system routines and thus cripple Windows. As noted above, preventing an OEM from removing IE deters it from installing a second browser because doing so increases the OEM's product testing and support costs; by contrast, had OEMs been able to remove IE, they might have chosen to pre-install Navigator alone.

[8] Microsoft denies, as a factual matter, that it commingled browsing and non-browsing code, and it maintains the District Court's findings to the contrary are clearly erroneous. According to Microsoft, its expert testified without contradiction that the very same code in Windows 98 that provides Web browsing functionality also performs essential operating system functions—not code in the same files, but the very same software code.

[9] Microsoft's expert did not testify to that effect "without contradiction," however. A Government expert, Glenn Weadock, testified that Microsoft designed IE so that some of the code that it uses co-resides in the same library files as other code needed for Windows. Another Government expert likewise testified that one library file, SHDOCVW.DLL, is really a bundle of separate functions. It contains some functions that have to do specifically with Web browsing, and it contains some general user interface functions as well. One of Microsoft's own documents suggests as much.

[10] In view of the contradictory testimony in the record, some of which supports the District Court's finding that Microsoft commingled browsing and non-browsing code, we cannot conclude that the finding was clearly erroneous. Accordingly, we reject Microsoft's argument that we should vacate [the district court's relevant finding of fact] as it relates to the commingling of code, and we conclude that such commingling has an anticompetitive effect; as noted above, the commingling deters OEMs from pre-installing rival browsers, thereby reducing the rivals' usage share and, hence, developers' interest in rivals' APIs as an alternative to the API set exposed by Microsoft's operating system. [. . .]

[11] Microsoft proffers no justification for two of the three challenged actions that it took in integrating IE into Windows—excluding IE from the Add/Remove Programs utility and commingling browser and operating system code. Although Microsoft does make some general claims regarding the benefits of integrating the browser and the operating system, it neither specifies nor substantiates those claims. Nor does it argue that either excluding IE from the Add/Remove Programs utility or commingling code achieves any integrative benefit. Plaintiffs plainly made out a prima facie case of harm to competition in the operating system market by demonstrating that Microsoft's actions increased its browser usage share and thus protected its operating system monopoly from a middleware threat and, for its part, Microsoft failed to meet its burden of showing that its conduct serves a purpose other than protecting its operating system monopoly. Accordingly, we hold that Microsoft's exclusion of IE from the Add/Remove Programs utility and its commingling of browser and operating system code constitute exclusionary conduct, in violation of § 2.

[12] As for the other challenged act that Microsoft took in integrating IE into Windows—causing Windows to override the user's choice of a default browser in certain circumstances—Microsoft argues that it has "valid technical reasons." Specifically, Microsoft claims that it was necessary to design Windows to override the user's preferences when he or she invokes one of a few out of the nearly 30 means of accessing the Internet. According to Microsoft:

> The Windows 98 Help system and Windows Update feature depend on ActiveX controls not supported by Navigator, and the now-discontinued Channel Bar utilized Microsoft's Channel Definition Format, which Navigator also did not support. Lastly, Windows 98 does not invoke Navigator if a user accesses the Internet through "My Computer" or "Windows Explorer" because doing so would defeat one of the purposes of those features—enabling users to move seamlessly from local storage devices to the Web in the same browsing window.

[13] The plaintiff bears the burden not only of rebutting a proffered justification but also of demonstrating that the anticompetitive effect of the challenged action outweighs it. In the District Court, plaintiffs appear to have done neither, let alone both; in any event, upon appeal, plaintiffs offer no rebuttal whatsoever. Accordingly, Microsoft may not be held liable for this aspect of its product design.

Conditional Dealing or Refusal to Deal?

FTC v. Facebook, Inc., 560 F. Supp. 3d 1 (D.D.C. 2021)

Exclusivity and tying (as well as bundling, which we will meet later in this chapter) can be manifested in a similar fashion. A defendant with market power may announce a conditional-dealing policy, pursuant to which a desired product or service will be available, or available on preferred terms, to trading partners *only if they comply with a condition* that may harm competition. This condition could involve refraining from dealing with rivals (exclusivity), purchasing a tied product or service (tying), or purchasing all components of a bundle (bundling). We might therefore call all these forms of "conditional dealing."

In these cases, when there is harm to competition it comes primarily from the effect of the announced condition on behavior, not from the punishment that the monopolist applies or exacts if the trading partner will not play ball. It's the impact of the threat / bribe on incentives, not impact of an actual refusal, that harms competition. *Lorain Journal* and *Dentsply* are good examples.[554]

The relationship between conditional dealing and refusal-to-deal is not always clear. In the FTC's 2020 monopolization case against Facebook, the FTC had alleged that Facebook's "platform policies" made access to its valuable APIs conditional upon its trading partners' refraining from either competing directly or working with Facebook's rivals, and that the announcement of this condition suppressed the incentives of actual and potential rivals to compete.

But the court disagreed. First, the court held that the policies did not violate existing refusal-to-deal law under *Trinko*. And then it went on to hold: "Plaintiff [*i.e.*, the FTC] gets no further by maintaining that Facebook's policies also violated antitrust rules against what they call 'conditional dealing.' As an initial matter, the FTC is wrong to argue that a monopolist violates that so-called doctrine whenever it 'induces trading partners or other firms not to compete with it by conditioning access to some resource of the monopolist. . . . [S]uch a broadly formulated rule would cover refusals to deal with competitors, thus contradicting [other cases]—such refusals can always be reframed as offers to deal only on the condition that the third party refrains from competing."

The court went on: "To the extent any scholarly commentary uses the term 'conditional dealing' . . . the phrase generally refers to actions such as tying or exclusive dealing. The key fact distinguishing such conduct from a standard refusal to deal is that it is not unilateral, but instead involves some assay by the monopolist into the marketplace that interferes with the relationship between rivals and third parties. Tying, for instance, occurs when a firm requires third parties to purchase a bundle of goods rather than just the ones they really want, thereby leveraging the monopolist's power in the 'tying' product market to harm its competitors (who lose access to

---

[554] *See supra* § VII.D.1.

customers) in the 'tied' product market. Exclusive dealing is similar: it refers to a monopolist's conditioning the sale of a product on the buyer's agreement not to deal with its competitors. Again, these 'conditional dealing' schemes are thus categorically different from unilateral conduct that involves only the monopolist's competitors, such as its refusal to deal with them. The distinction is critical, as antitrust law is far more tolerant of unilateral behavior."

NOTES

1) Car dealers don't sell components like tires and steering wheels, or cars without them. You have to buy the whole car. Is this tying? Should it be illegal?

2) Under what circumstances do you think tying is most, and least, harmful to competition?

3) Should we have different rules for tying in "high technology" markets? If so, what should those rules be? If not, what's the strongest case for doing so and why is it wrong? (What is a "high technology" market anyway?)

4) Can you think of circumstances under which there might be good reasons for a business insisting that a consumer must use only its own complementary product (say, an app with a device, or repair services with an item of equipment)? What are those reasons? Could they be accommodated without a tying arrangement?

5) If a monopolist designs one of its products to work particularly well with another of its products, is that—or should it be—a "tie" in the antitrust sense? What if a monopolist makes a design choice in the knowledge that this design choice will impede interoperability with rivals' products?

6) If the operator of a digital ecosystem wants to invoke "security" as justification for a tie, what kind of information or evidence should be needed to establish the defense? *Compare, e.g.*, *Epic Games, Inc. v. Apple Inc.*, __ F.Supp.3d __, 2021 WL 4128925 (N.D. Cal. Sept. 10, 2021).

7) Suppliers of devices or operating systems often include apps and software as well, for no additional cost. Is this tying? Under what circumstances should it be unlawful?

8) The interaction of tying law and refusal-to-deal law raises some oddities. Suppose that Windows had come with an app store, from which all software (including browsers) had to be obtained. Then suppose that Microsoft had not engaged in any traditional tying to get third parties to use Internet Explorer; instead, it simply refused to let Netscape or any other rival browsers into its app store. This has the same economic effects as Microsoft's tie, but it transforms the case into a pure refusal to deal. Thus, it would completely change the legal analysis--the court would focus on profit sacrifice and prior dealing, rather than ordinary tying/foreclosure analysis. Does that make sense? (Thanks to Erik Hovenkamp for this excellent question and hypothetical!)

3. Pricing Practices: Predation and Price Squeezes

We now turn to the most basic of all competitive decisions: choices about pricing. Alongside the right to refuse to deal, the right to set a price—even if in some sense too high for purchasers' comfort, or too low for competitors'—is strongly protected in modern antitrust law.

Contrary to what is sometimes popularly supposed, antitrust law does not condemn the mere charging of unconditional *high* prices: indeed, charging high prices makes entry easier and more attractive for competitors.[555] But in limited circumstances it does discipline the charging of *low* prices. This is the law of "predatory pricing." The core concern is that a monopolist may charge prices that are so low that its competitors cannot survive, are forced out, and then face barriers to re-entry, leading to an increase in monopoly power. (Why do the barriers to re-entry matter? In particular: can you see why there would be no contribution to monopoly power if there were no such barriers?) The basic theory of harm is thus a play in two acts: at time 1, the monopolist charges an unsustainably low price, driving rivals out past barriers to re-entry; at time 2, the monopolist enjoys increased (or protected) monopoly power which allows it to recoup its losses.

As you might expect, antitrust treads very carefully when it comes to punishing low prices: antitrust law is supposed to be encouraging firms to set attractive low prices to win business from their rivals, not punishing them for doing

---

[555] The European Union takes a different approach. *See, e.g.*, Case C-177/16, Autortiesību un komunicēšanās konsultāciju aģentūra/Latvijas Autoru apvienība v. Konkurences padome, ECLI:EU:C:2017:689, ¶¶ 35–38.

so, or deterring them from offering a "too good" price. Thus, as Dan Crane has pointed out: "Predatory pricing is a paradoxical offense. Although antitrust law values low prices and abhors high ones, the "predator" stands accused of charging too low of a price—of doing too much of a good thing. Society considers predation socially harmful because the artificially low prices of today drive out competitors and allow the high prices of tomorrow.[556]

It is worth distinguishing clearly between the economic logic of predation and the economic logic of foreclosure that we see in most exclusivity and tying cases.[557] In the following extract, Steve Salop summarizes the difference between the two kinds of competitive concern.

Steven C. Salop, The Raising Rivals' Cost Foreclosure Paradigm, Conditional Pricing Practices, and the Flawed Incremental Price-Cost Test

81 Antitrust L.J. 371 (2017)

The two general paradigms of exclusionary conduct—predatory pricing and [raising rivals' costs ("RRC")] foreclosure—focus on different aspects of exclusionary conduct and take very different views of the relevant antitrust risks. In order to understand the law and economics of exclusionary conduct, and CPPs in particular, it is necessary to distinguish between these two paradigms.

Predatory pricing is one paradigmatic type of exclusionary conduct. In the simplest rendition, predatory pricing involves an across-the-board reduction in prices intended to permit a deep-pocket defendant to win a war of attrition against a less well-financed entrant or small competitor. The reduction in prices during the predatory phase of a predatory pricing strategy involves short-term profit-sacrifice or actual losses by the predator. These losses then might be recovered by supracompetitive prices during the recoupment period after the entrant exits from the market or is disciplined to raise price. Predatory pricing is a risky investment in exclusion because the predator sacrifices profits in the short-run but may be unable to recoup them in the long run. The predator may blink first in light of the fact that its profit-sacrifice (relative to more accommodative pricing) exceeds the losses borne by the entrant, as a result of the predator's higher market share. The entrant may merely reduce its output to conserve resources and wait out the attack. The entrant also may obtain the necessary financing to withstand the attack for a significant period of time and eliminate the credibility of further predatory pricing threats. Either way, the entrant may not exit. And, even if the entrant does exit, subsequent re-entry by either the entrant or competition from others may prevent the predator from recouping its profit sacrifice or losses. This reasoning led the Court in *Matsushita* to conclude that "predatory pricing schemes are rarely tried and even more rarely successful."

The impact on consumer welfare from such "deep-pocket" predatory pricing also is unclear, according to the paradigm. Consumers benefit from the lower prices during the predatory phase. These benefits potentially could exceed the harms suffered by consumers during the recoupment phase, particularly if the predatory pricing period continues for a long time. Moreover, there may never be a recoupment phase. Failed predatory pricing is a gift to consumers. [. . .]

The modern approach to foreclosure embodied in the RRC foreclosure paradigm is very different. The RRC foreclosure paradigm generally describes exclusionary conduct that totally or partially "forecloses" competitors from access either to critical inputs or customers, with the effect of causing them to raise their prices or reduce their output, thereby allowing the excluding firm to profit by setting a supracompetitive output price, with the effect of harming consumers. A rule of reason analysis, which is commonly applied to exclusivity arrangements and other exclusionary conduct with its burden-shifting test, is entirely consistent with the RRC foreclosure paradigm

---

[556] Daniel A. Crane, *The Paradox of Predatory Pricing*, 91 Cornell L. Rev. 1, 2–3 (2005).

[557] For some broader discussions of the economics of predation, *see generally*, *e.g.*, David Beanko, Ulrigh Doraszelski, & Yaroslav Kryukov, *The Economics of Predation: What Drives Pricing When There Is Learning-by-Doing?* 104 Am. Econ. Rev. 868 (2014); Jonathan B. Baker, *Predatory Pricing after* Brooke Group: *An Economic Perspective*, 62 Antitrust L.J. 585 (1994); Joseph F. Bradley & George A. Hay, *Predatory Pricing: Competing Economic Theories and The Evolution of Legal Standards*, 66 Cornell L. Rev. 738 (1981); Janusz A. Ordover & Robert D. Willig, *An Economic Definition of Predation: Pricing and Product Innovation*, 91 Yale L.J. 8 (1981).

. . . RRC foreclosure conduct is more likely to be attempted and more likely to harm consumers than is predatory pricing. [. . .]

There are several reasons for these heightened concerns. First, unlike the paradigmatic view of predatory pricing, successful RRC foreclosure does not require a risky investment or losses during an initial period that may only be recouped with some probability at some later point in the future. Instead, recoupment often occurs simultaneously with RRC conduct. Thus, it is more likely to succeed, which also means that it is more likely to be attempted.

Second, unlike predatory pricing, successful RRC conduct does not require the exit of rivals, or even the permanent reduction in competitors' production capacity. If the marginal costs of established competitors are raised, those competitors will have the incentive to raise their prices and reduce their output, even if they remain viable. This also means that RRC conduct is more likely to succeed, and therefore, is more likely to be attempted.

Third, unlike paradigmatic predatory pricing, RRC foreclosure conduct is not necessarily more costly to the monopolist than it is to the excluded rivals.

* * *

The leading case on price predation is the Court's decision in *Brooke Group*. The complaint in that case alleged that the cigarette market was dominated by a cozy oligopoly of six firms (R.J. Reynolds, Philip Morris, American Brands, Lorillard, Brooke Group (previously, and in the extract below, "Liggett"), and Brown & Williamson), until—unhappy with declining demand—Liggett disrupted the market by introducing a low-price "generic" cigarette. Brown & Williamson responded with its own aggressively priced generic cigarette, which, following a price war, it offered for sale at below-cost prices. Liggett alleged that the point of B&W's strategy was to punish Liggett's effort at disruptive competition, in an effort to restore discipline and preserve the supracompetitive oligopoly profits that B&W (and the other oligopolists) had previously enjoyed. Liggett prevailed at a jury trial; B&W moved for judgment notwithstanding the verdict. The case was presented under the Robinson-Patman Act, but the Court has since explained that its reasoning governs the treatment of predatory pricing under Section 2.[558]

Brooke Group Ltd. v. Brown & Williamson Tobacco Corp.
509 U.S. 209 (1993)

Justice Kennedy.

[1] [There are two prerequisites for recovery for predatory pricing.] First, a plaintiff seeking to establish competitive injury resulting from a rival's low prices must prove that the prices complained of are below an appropriate measure of its rival's costs. Although [the Court's previous decisions] reserved as a formal matter the question whether recovery should ever be available when the pricing in question is above some measure of incremental cost, the reasoning in both opinions suggests that only below-cost prices should suffice, and we have rejected elsewhere the notion that above-cost prices that are below general market levels or the costs of a firm's competitors inflict injury to competition cognizable under the antitrust laws. Low prices benefit consumers regardless of how those prices are set, and so long as they are above predatory levels, they do not threaten competition. We have adhered to this principle regardless of the type of antitrust claim involved. As a general rule, the exclusionary effect of prices above a relevant measure of cost either reflects the lower cost structure of the alleged predator, and so represents competition on the merits, or is beyond the practical ability of a judicial tribunal to control without courting intolerable risks of chilling legitimate price-cutting. To hold that the antitrust laws protect competitors from the loss of profits due to such price competition would, in effect, render illegal any decision by a firm to cut prices in order to increase market share. The antitrust laws require no such perverse result.

[2] Even in an oligopolistic market, when a firm drops its prices to a competitive level to demonstrate to a maverick the unprofitability of straying from the group, it would be illogical to condemn the price cut: The antitrust laws

---

[558] Weyerhaeuser Co. v. Ross-Simmons Hardwood Lumber Co., 549 U.S. 312, 318 n.1 (2007); Brooke Group Ltd. v. Brown & Williamson Tobacco Corp., 509 U.S. 209, 222 (1993) ("[W]hether [a] claim alleges predatory pricing under § 2 of the Sherman Act or primary-line price discrimination under the Robinson–Patman Act, two prerequisites to recovery remain the same").

then would be an obstacle to the chain of events most conducive to a breakdown of oligopoly pricing and the onset of competition. Even if the ultimate effect of the cut is to induce or reestablish supracompetitive pricing, discouraging a price cut and forcing firms to maintain supracompetitive prices, thus depriving consumers of the benefits of lower prices in the interim, does not constitute sound antitrust policy.

[3] The second prerequisite to holding a competitor liable under the antitrust laws for charging low prices is a demonstration that the competitor had a reasonable prospect, or, under § 2 of the Sherman Act, a dangerous probability, of recouping its investment in below-cost prices. For the investment to be rational, the [predator] must have a reasonable expectation of recovering, in the form of later monopoly profits, more than the losses suffered. Recoupment is the ultimate object of an unlawful predatory pricing scheme; it is the means by which a predator profits from predation. Without it, predatory pricing produces lower aggregate prices in the market, and consumer welfare is enhanced. Although unsuccessful predatory pricing may encourage some inefficient substitution toward the product being sold at less than its cost, unsuccessful predation is in general a boon to consumers.

[4] That below-cost pricing may impose painful losses on its target is of no moment to the antitrust laws if competition is not injured: It is axiomatic that the antitrust laws were passed for the protection of competition, not competitors. . . . Even an act of pure malice by one business competitor against another does not, without more, state a claim under the federal antitrust laws; those laws do not create a federal law of unfair competition or purport to afford remedies for all torts committed by or against persons engaged in interstate commerce.

[5] For recoupment to occur, below-cost pricing must be capable, as a threshold matter, of producing the intended effects on the firm's rivals, whether driving them from the market, or, as was alleged to be the goal here, causing them to raise their prices to supracompetitive levels within a disciplined oligopoly. This requires an understanding of the extent and duration of the alleged predation, the relative financial strength of the predator and its intended victim, and their respective incentives and will. The inquiry is whether, given the aggregate losses caused by the below-cost pricing, the intended target would likely succumb.

[6] If circumstances indicate that below-cost pricing could likely produce its intended effect on the target, there is still the further question whether it would likely injure competition in the relevant market. The plaintiff must demonstrate that there is a likelihood that the predatory scheme alleged would cause a rise in prices above a competitive level that would be sufficient to compensate for the amounts expended on the predation, including the time value of the money invested in it. As we have observed on a prior occasion, in order to recoup their losses, predators must obtain enough market power to set higher than competitive prices, and then must sustain those prices long enough to earn in excess profits what they earlier gave up in below-cost prices.

[7] Evidence of below-cost pricing is not alone sufficient to permit an inference of probable recoupment and injury to competition. Determining whether recoupment of predatory losses is likely requires an estimate of the cost of the alleged predation and a close analysis of both the scheme alleged by the plaintiff and the structure and conditions of the relevant market. If market circumstances or deficiencies in proof would bar a reasonable jury from finding that the scheme alleged would likely result in sustained supracompetitive pricing, the plaintiff's case has failed. In certain situations—for example, where the market is highly diffuse and competitive, or where new entry is easy, or the defendant lacks adequate excess capacity to absorb the market shares of his rivals and cannot quickly create or purchase new capacity—summary disposition of the case is appropriate.

[8] These prerequisites to recovery are not easy to establish, but they are not artificial obstacles to recovery; rather, they are essential components of real market injury. As we have said in the Sherman Act context, predatory pricing schemes are rarely tried, and even more rarely successful, and the costs of an erroneous finding of liability are high. The mechanism by which a firm engages in predatory pricing—lowering prices—is the same mechanism by which a firm stimulates competition; because cutting prices in order to increase business often is the very essence of competition; mistaken inferences are especially costly, because they chill the very conduct the antitrust laws are designed to protect. It would be ironic indeed if the standards for predatory pricing liability were so low that antitrust suits themselves became a tool for keeping prices high. [. . .]

[9] In this case, the price and output data do not support a reasonable inference that Brown & Williamson and the other cigarette companies elevated prices above a competitive level for generic cigarettes. Supracompetitive

pricing entails a restriction in output. In the present setting, in which output expanded at a rapid rate following Brown & Williamson's alleged predation, output in the generic segment can only have been restricted in the sense that it expanded at a slower rate than it would have absent Brown & Williamson's intervention. Such a counterfactual proposition is difficult to prove in the best of circumstances; here, the record evidence does not permit a reasonable inference that output would have been greater without Brown & Williamson's entry into the generic segment.

[10] Following Brown & Williamson's entry, the rate at which generic cigarettes were capturing market share did not slow; indeed, the average rate of growth doubled. During the four years from 1980 to 1984 in which Liggett was alone in the generic segment, the segment gained market share at an average rate of 1% of the overall market per year, from 0.4% in 1980 to slightly more than 4% of the cigarette market in 1984. In the next five years, following the alleged predation, the generic segment expanded from 4% to more than 15% of the domestic cigarette market, or greater than 2% per year.

[11] While this evidence tends to show that Brown & Williamson's participation in the economy segment did not restrict output, it is not dispositive. One could speculate, for example, that the rate of segment growth would have tripled, instead of doubled, without Brown & Williamson's alleged predation. But there is no concrete evidence of this. Indeed, the only industry projection in the record estimating what the segment's growth would have been without Brown & Williamson's entry supports the opposite inference. In 1984, Brown & Williamson forecast in an important planning document that the economy segment would account for 10% of the total cigarette market by 1988 if it did not enter the segment. In fact, in 1988, after what Liggett alleges was a sustained and dangerous anticompetitive campaign by Brown & Williamson, the generic segment accounted for over 12% of the total market. Thus the segment's output expanded more robustly than Brown & Williamson had estimated it would had Brown & Williamson never entered.

[12] Brown & Williamson did note in 1985, a year after introducing its black and whites, that its presence within the generic segment appears to have resulted in a slowing in the segment's growth rate. But this statement was made in early 1985, when Liggett itself contends the below-cost pricing was still in effect and before any anticompetitive contraction in output is alleged to have occurred. Whatever it may mean, this statement has little value in evaluating the competitive implications of Brown & Williamson's later conduct, which was alleged to provide the basis for recouping predatory losses.

[13] In arguing that Brown & Williamson was able to exert market power and raise generic prices above a competitive level in the generic category through tacit price coordination with the other cigarette manufacturers, Liggett places its principal reliance on direct evidence of price behavior. This evidence demonstrates that the list prices on all cigarettes, generic and branded alike, rose to a significant degree during the late 1980's. From 1986 to 1989, list prices on both generic and branded cigarettes increased twice a year by similar amounts. Liggett's economic expert testified that these price increases outpaced increases in costs, taxes, and promotional expenditures. The list prices of generics, moreover, rose at a faster rate than the prices of branded cigarettes, thus narrowing the list price differential between branded and generic products. Liggett argues that this would permit a reasonable jury to find that Brown & Williamson succeeded in bringing about oligopolistic price coordination and supracompetitive prices in the generic category sufficient to slow its growth, thereby preserving supracompetitive branded profits and recouping its predatory losses.

[14] A reasonable jury, however, could not have drawn the inferences Liggett proposes. All of Liggett's data are based upon the list prices of various categories of cigarettes. Yet the jury had before it undisputed evidence that during the period in question, list prices were not the actual prices paid by consumers. As the market became unsettled in the mid–1980's, the cigarette companies invested substantial sums in promotional schemes, including coupons, stickers, and giveaways, that reduced the actual cost of cigarettes to consumers below list prices. This promotional activity accelerated as the decade progressed. Many wholesalers also passed portions of their volume rebates on to the consumer, which had the effect of further undermining the significance of the retail list prices. Especially in an oligopoly setting, in which price competition is most likely to take place through less observable and less regulable means than list prices, it would be unreasonable to draw conclusions about the existence of tacit coordination or supracompetitive pricing from data that reflect only list prices. [. . .]

[15] . . . [A]n inference of supracompetitive pricing would be particularly anomalous in this case, as the very party alleged to have been coerced into pricing through oligopolistic coordination denied that such coordination existed: Liggett's own officers and directors consistently denied that they or other firms in the industry priced their cigarettes through tacit collusion or reaped supracompetitive profits. Liggett seeks to explain away this testimony by arguing that its officers and directors are businesspeople who do not ascribe the same meaning to words like "competitive" and "collusion" that an economist would. This explanation is entitled to little, if any, weight. As the District Court found:

> This argument was considered at the summary judgment stage since these executives gave basically the same testimony at their depositions. The court allowed the case to go to trial in part because the Liggett executives were not economists and in part because of affidavits from the Liggett executives stating that they were confused by the questions asked by Brown & Williamson lawyers and did not mean to contradict the testimony of their economic expert Burnett. However, at trial, despite having consulted extensively with Burnett and having had adequate time to familiarize themselves with concepts such as tacit collusion, oligopoly, and monopoly profits, these Liggett executives again contradicted Burnett's theory.

[. . .]

[16] Not only does the evidence fail to show actual supracompetitive pricing in the generic segment, it also does not demonstrate its likelihood. At the time Brown & Williamson entered the generic segment, the cigarette industry as a whole faced declining demand and possessed substantial excess capacity. These circumstances tend to break down patterns of oligopoly pricing and produce price competition. The only means by which Brown & Williamson is alleged to have established oligopoly pricing in the face of these unusual competitive pressures is through tacit price coordination with the other cigarette firms.

[17] Yet the situation facing the cigarette companies in the 1980's would have made such tacit coordination unmanageable. Tacit coordination is facilitated by a stable market environment, fungible products, and a small number of variables upon which the firms seeking to coordinate their pricing may focus. Uncertainty is an oligopoly's greatest enemy. By 1984, however, the cigarette market was in an obvious state of flux. The introduction of generic cigarettes in 1980 represented the first serious price competition in the cigarette market since the 1930's. This development was bound to unsettle previous expectations and patterns of market conduct and to reduce the cigarette firms' ability to predict each other's behavior.

[18] The larger number of product types and pricing variables also decreased the probability of effective parallel pricing. When Brown & Williamson entered the economy segment in 1984, the segment included Value–25s, black and whites, and branded generics. With respect to each product, the net price in the market was determined not only by list prices, but also by a wide variety of discounts and promotions to consumers and by rebates to wholesalers. In order to coordinate in an effective manner and eliminate price competition, the cigarette companies would have been required, without communicating, to establish parallel practices with respect to each of these variables, many of which, like consumer stickers or coupons, were difficult to monitor. . . . .

[19] In addition, [competitor] R.J. Reynolds had incentives that, in some respects, ran counter to those of the other cigarette companies. It is implausible that without a shared interest in retarding the growth of the economy segment, Brown & Williamson and its fellow oligopolists could have engaged in parallel pricing and raised generic prices above a competitive level. Coordination will not be possible when any significant firm chooses, for any reason, to go it alone. It is undisputed—indeed it was conceded by Liggett's expert—that R.J. Reynolds acted without regard to the supposed benefits of oligopolistic coordination when it repriced Doral at generic levels in the spring of 1984 and that the natural and probable consequence of its entry into the generic segment was procompetitive. Indeed, Reynolds' apparent objective in entering the segment was to capture a significant amount of volume in order to regain its number one sales position in the cigarette industry from Philip Morris. There is no evidence that R.J. Reynolds accomplished this goal during the period relevant to this case, or that its commitment to achieving that goal changed. Indeed, R.J. Reynolds refused to follow Brown & Williamson's attempt to raise generic prices in June 1985. The jury thus had before it undisputed evidence that contradicts the suggestion that the major cigarette companies shared a goal of limiting the growth of the economy segment; one of the industry's two major players concededly entered the segment to expand volume and compete.

[20] Even if all the cigarette companies were willing to participate in a scheme to restrain the growth of the generic segment, they would not have been able to coordinate their actions and raise prices above a competitive level unless they understood that Brown & Williamson's entry into the segment was not a genuine effort to compete with Liggett. If even one other firm misinterpreted Brown & Williamson's entry as an effort to expand share, a chain reaction of competitive responses would almost certainly have resulted, and oligopoly discipline would have broken down, perhaps irretrievably. . . . [. . .]

[21] Finally, although some of Brown & Williamson's corporate planning documents speak of a desire to slow the growth of the segment, no objective evidence of its conduct permits a reasonable inference that it had any real prospect of doing so through anticompetitive means. It is undisputed that when Brown & Williamson introduced its generic cigarettes, it offered them to a thousand wholesalers who had never before purchased generic cigarettes. The inevitable effect of this marketing effort was to expand the segment, as the new wholesalers recruited retail outlets to carry generic cigarettes. Even with respect to wholesalers already carrying generics, Brown & Williamson's unprecedented volume rebates had a similar expansionary effect. Unlike many branded cigarettes, generics came with no sales guarantee to the wholesaler; any unsold stock represented pure loss to the wholesaler. By providing substantial incentives for wholesalers to place large orders, Brown & Williamson created strong pressure for them to sell more generic cigarettes. In addition, as we have already observed, many wholesalers passed portions of the rebates about which Liggett complains on to consumers, thus dropping the retail price of generics and further stimulating demand. Brown & Williamson provided a further, direct stimulus, through some $10 million it spent during the period of alleged predation placing discount stickers on its generic cartons to reduce prices to the ultimate consumer. In light of these uncontested facts about Brown & Williamson's conduct, it is not reasonable to conclude that Brown & Williamson threatened in a serious way to restrict output, raise prices above a competitive level, and artificially slow the growth of the economy segment of the national cigarette market. [. . .]

[22] We understand that the chain of reasoning by which we have concluded that Brown & Williamson is entitled to judgment as a matter of law is demanding. But a reasonable jury is presumed to know and understand the law, the facts of the case, and the realities of the market. We hold that the evidence cannot support a finding that Brown & Williamson's alleged scheme was likely to result in oligopolistic price coordination and sustained supracompetitive pricing in the generic segment of the national cigarette market. Without this, Brown & Williamson had no reasonable prospect of recouping its predatory losses and could not inflict the injury to competition the antitrust laws prohibit.

Justice Stevens, joined by Justice White and Justice Blackmun, dissenting.

[23] After 115 days of trial, during which it considered 2,884 exhibits, 85 deposition excerpts, and testimony from 23 live witnesses, the jury deliberated for nine days and then returned a verdict finding that B & W engaged in price discrimination with a reasonable possibility of injuring competition. The Court's contrary conclusion rests on a hodgepodge of legal, factual, and economic propositions that are insufficient, alone or together, to overcome the jury's assessment of the evidence. [. . .]

[24] As a matter of fact, the Court emphasizes the growth in the generic segment following B & W's entry. As the Court notes, generics' expansion to over 12% of the total market by 1988 exceeds B & W's own forecast that the segment would grow to only about 10%, assuming no entry by B & W. What these figures do not do, however, is answer the relevant question: whether the prices of generic cigarettes during the late 1980's were competitive or supracompetitive.

[25] On this point, there is ample, uncontradicted evidence that the list prices on generic cigarettes, as well as the prices on branded cigarettes, rose regularly and significantly during the late 1980's, in a fashion remarkably similar to the price change patterns that characterized the industry in the 1970's when supracompetitive, oligopolistic pricing admittedly prevailed. Given its knowledge of the industry's history of parallel pricing, I think the jury plainly was entitled to draw an inference that these increased prices were supracompetitive. [. . .]

[26] As a matter of economics, the Court reminds us that price cutting is generally pro-competitive, and hence a boon to consumers. This is true, however, only so long as reduced prices do not fall below cost, as the cases cited by the majority make clear. When a predator deliberately engages in below-cost pricing targeted at a particular

competitor over a sustained period of time, then price cutting raises a credible inference that harm to competition is likely to ensue. None of our cases disputes that proposition.

[27] Also as a matter of economics, the Court insists that a predatory pricing program in an oligopoly is unlikely to succeed absent actual conspiracy. Though it has rejected a somewhat stronger version of this proposition as a rule of decision, the Court comes back to the same economic theory, relying on the supposition that an anticompetitive minuet is most difficult to compose and to perform, even for a disciplined oligopoly. I would suppose, however, that the professional performers who had danced the minuet for 40 to 50 years would be better able to predict whether their favorite partners would follow them in the future than would an outsider, who might not know the difference between Haydn and Mozart. In any event, the jury was surely entitled to infer that at the time of the price war itself, B & W reasonably believed that it could signal its intentions to its fellow oligopolists, assuring their continued cooperation.

[28] Perhaps the Court's most significant error is the assumption that seems to pervade much of the final sections of its opinion: that Liggett had the burden of proving either the actuality of supracompetitive pricing, or the actuality of tacit collusion. In my opinion, the jury was entitled to infer from the succession of price increases after 1985—when the prices for branded and generic cigarettes increased every six months from $33.15 and $19.75, respectively, to $46.15 and $33.75—that B & W's below-cost pricing actually produced supracompetitive prices, with the help of tacit collusion among the players. But even if that were not so clear, the jury would surely be entitled to infer that B & W's predatory plan, in which it invested millions of dollars for the purpose of achieving an admittedly anticompetitive result, carried a "reasonable possibility" of injuring competition.

* * *

Brooke Group thus establishes a high bar for predation claims.[559] The Court confirmed that a similar analysis applies to claims of "predatory overbuying"—that is, the practice of overpaying for inputs and distribution so that competitors are excluded—in *Weyerhauser*.[560]

You may notice that the Court's jurisprudence on unconditional pricing decisions somewhat resembles its jurisprudence on refusal to deal: in both groups of cases, the respect for a monopolist's freedom of action is close to its height, and the Court's concern to avoid interfering with ordinary commercial activities is very clear.[561]

The two streams—refusal to deal and predatory pricing—collided in *Linkline*, the Court's seminal decision on "price squeeze" theories of harm. In a price squeeze, a vertically integrated monopolist charges a high price in an upstream market to its downstream rivals, and sets a low downstream price with which those rivals cannot compete. The competitive concern is that unintegrated rivals cannot compete in the downstream market. But, as the Court pointed out in *Linkline*, if the high upstream price is not illegal, why should antitrust challenge be triggered by the additional fact of low-price supply in that downstream market? There is a healthy literature on price-squeeze claims.[562]

Pacific Bell Telephone Co. v. Linkline Communications, Inc.

555 U.S. 438 (2009)

Chief Justice Roberts.

---

[559] For some discussion of how that bar might be cleared in practice, *see* C. Scott Hemphill & Philip J. Weiser, *Beyond* Brooke Group*: Bringing Reality to the Law of Predatory Pricing*, 127 Yale L.J. 2048 (2018).

[560] Weyerhaeuser Co. v. Ross-Simmons Hardwood Lumber Co., Inc., 549 U.S. 312 (2007) ("The first prong of Brooke Group's test requires little adaptation for the predatory-bidding context. A plaintiff must prove that the alleged predatory bidding led to below-cost pricing of the predator's outputs. That is, the predator's bidding on the buy side must have caused the cost of the relevant output to rise above the revenues generated in the sale of those outputs. . . . A predatory-bidding plaintiff also must prove that the defendant has a dangerous probability of recouping the losses incurred in bidding up input prices through the exercise of monopsony power."). *See also, e.g.*, Steven C. Salop, *Anticompetitive Overbuying by Power Buyers*, 72 Antitrust L.J. 669, 672 (2005).

[561] *See supra* § VII.C.3.

[562] *See, e.g.*, Steven C. Salop, *Refusals to Deal and Price Squeezes by an Unregulated, Vertically Integrated Monopolist*, 76 Antitrust L.J. No. 709 (2010); Erik N. Hovenkamp & Herbert Hovenkamp, *The Viability of Antitrust Price Squeeze Claims*, 51 Ariz. L. Rev. 273 (2009); J. Gregory Sidak, *Abolishing the Price Squeeze as a Theory of Antitrust Liability*, 4 J. Comp. L. & Econ. 279 (2008).

[1] This case involves the market for digital subscriber line (DSL) service, which is a method of connecting to the Internet at high speeds over telephone lines. AT & T owns much of the infrastructure and facilities needed to provide DSL service in California. In particular, AT & T controls most of what is known as the "last mile"—the lines that connect homes and businesses to the telephone network. Competing DSL providers must generally obtain access to AT & T's facilities in order to serve their customers. [. . .]

[2] The plaintiffs are four independent Internet service providers (ISPs) that compete with AT & T in the retail DSL market. Plaintiffs do not own all the facilities needed to supply their customers with this service. They instead lease DSL transport service from AT & T pursuant to the merger conditions described above. AT & T thus participates in the DSL market at both the wholesale and retail levels; it provides plaintiffs and other independent ISPs with wholesale DSL transport service, and it also sells DSL service directly to consumers at retail.

[3] In July 2003, the plaintiffs brought suit in District Court, alleging that AT & T violated § 2 of the Sherman Act, by monopolizing the DSL market in California. The complaint alleges that AT & T refused to deal with the plaintiffs, denied the plaintiffs access to essential facilities, and engaged in a "price squeeze." Specifically, plaintiffs contend that AT & T squeezed their profit margins by setting a high wholesale price for DSL transport and a low retail price for DSL Internet service. This maneuver allegedly excluded and unreasonably impeded competition, thus allowing AT & T to preserve and maintain its monopoly control of DSL access to the Internet. [. . .]

[3] The challenge here focuses on retail prices—where there is no predatory pricing—and the terms of dealing—where there is no duty to deal. Plaintiffs' price-squeeze claims challenge a different type of unilateral conduct in which a firm "squeezes" the profit margins of its competitors. This requires the defendant to be operating in two markets, a wholesale ("upstream") market and a retail ("downstream") market. A firm with market power in the upstream market can squeeze its downstream competitors by raising the wholesale price of inputs while cutting its own retail prices. This will raise competitors' costs (because they will have to pay more for their inputs) and lower their revenues (because they will have to match the dominant firm's low retail price). Price-squeeze plaintiffs assert that defendants must leave them a "fair" or "adequate" margin between the wholesale price and the retail price. In this case, we consider whether a plaintiff can state a price-squeeze claim when the defendant has no obligation under the antitrust laws to deal with the plaintiff at wholesale. [. . .]

[4] A straightforward application of our recent decision in *Trinko* forecloses any challenge to AT & T's wholesale prices. In *Trinko*, Verizon was required by statute to lease its network elements to competing firms at wholesale rates. The plaintiff—a customer of one of Verizon's rivals—asserted that Verizon denied its competitors access to interconnection support services, making it difficult for those competitors to fill their customers' orders. The complaint alleged that this conduct in the upstream market violated § 2 of the Sherman Act by impeding the ability of independent carriers to compete in the downstream market for local telephone service.

[5] We held that the plaintiff's claims were not actionable under § 2. Given that Verizon had no antitrust duty to deal with its rivals at all, we concluded that Verizon's alleged insufficient assistance in the provision of service to rivals did not violate the Sherman Act. *Trinko* thus makes clear that if a firm has no antitrust duty to deal with its competitors at wholesale, it certainly has no duty to deal under terms and conditions that the rivals find commercially advantageous.

[6] In this case, as in *Trinko*, the defendant has no antitrust duty to deal with its rivals at wholesale; any such duty arises only from FCC regulations, not from the Sherman Act. There is no meaningful distinction between the "insufficient assistance" claims we rejected in *Trinko* and the plaintiffs' price-squeeze claims in the instant case. The *Trinko* plaintiff challenged the quality of Verizon's interconnection service, while this case involves a challenge to AT&T's pricing structure. But for antitrust purposes, there is no reason to distinguish between price and nonprice components of a transaction. The nub of the complaint in both *Trinko* and this case is identical—the plaintiffs alleged that the defendants (upstream monopolists) abused their power in the wholesale market to prevent rival firms from competing effectively in the retail market. *Trinko* holds that such claims are not cognizable under the Sherman Act in the absence of an antitrust duty to deal.

[7] The District Court and the Court of Appeals did not regard *Trinko* as controlling because that case did not directly address price-squeeze claims. This is technically true, but the reasoning of *Trinko* applies with equal force

to price-squeeze claims. AT & T could have squeezed its competitors' profits just as effectively by providing poor-quality interconnection service to the plaintiffs, as Verizon allegedly did in *Trinko*. But a firm with no duty to deal in the wholesale market has no obligation to deal under terms and conditions favorable to its competitors. If AT & T had simply stopped providing DSL transport service to the plaintiffs, it would not have run afoul of the Sherman Act. Under these circumstances, AT & T was not required to offer this service at the wholesale prices the plaintiffs would have preferred.

[8] The other component of a price-squeeze claim is the assertion that the defendant's retail prices are "too low." Here too plaintiffs' claims find no support in our existing antitrust doctrine.

[9] Cutting prices in order to increase business often is the very essence of competition. In cases seeking to impose antitrust liability for prices that are too low, mistaken inferences are especially costly, because they chill the very conduct the antitrust laws are designed to protect. To avoid chilling aggressive price competition, we have carefully limited the circumstances under which plaintiffs can state a Sherman Act claim by alleging that prices are too low. Specifically, to prevail on a predatory pricing claim, a plaintiff must demonstrate that: (1) the prices complained of are below an appropriate measure of its rival's costs; and (2) there is a dangerous probability that the defendant will be able to recoup its investment in below-cost prices. Low prices benefit consumers regardless of how those prices are set, and so long as they are above predatory levels, they do not threaten competition.

[10] In the complaint at issue in this interlocutory appeal, there is no allegation that AT & T's conduct met either of the *Brooke Group* requirements. Recognizing a price-squeeze claim where the defendant's retail price remains above cost would invite the precise harm we sought to avoid in *Brooke Group*: Firms might raise their retail prices or refrain from aggressive price competition to avoid potential antitrust liability.

[11] Plaintiffs' price-squeeze claim, looking to the relation between retail and wholesale prices, is thus nothing more than an amalgamation of a meritless claim at the retail level and a meritless claim at the wholesale level. If there is no duty to deal at the wholesale level and no predatory pricing at the retail level, then a firm is certainly not required to price both of these services in a manner that preserves its rivals' profit margins. [. . .]

[11] Institutional concerns also counsel against recognition of such claims. We have repeatedly emphasized the importance of clear rules in antitrust law. Courts are ill suited to act as central planners, identifying the proper price, quantity, and other terms of dealing. No court should impose a duty to deal that it cannot explain or adequately and reasonably supervise. The problem should be deemed irremediable by antitrust law when compulsory access requires the court to assume the day-to-day controls characteristic of a regulatory agency.

[12] It is difficult enough for courts to identify and remedy an alleged anticompetitive practice at one level, such as predatory pricing in retail markets or a violation of the duty-to-deal doctrine at the wholesale level. Recognizing price-squeeze claims would require courts simultaneously to police both the wholesale and retail prices to ensure that rival firms are not being squeezed. And courts would be aiming at a moving target, since it is the interaction between these two prices that may result in a squeeze.

[13] Perhaps most troubling, firms that seek to avoid price-squeeze liability will have no safe harbor for their pricing practices. At least in the predatory pricing context, firms know they will not incur liability as long as their retail prices are above cost. No such guidance is available for price-squeeze claims.

[14] The most commonly articulated standard for price squeezes is that the defendant must leave its rivals a "fair" or "adequate" margin between the wholesale price and the retail price. One of our colleagues has highlighted the flaws of this test in Socratic fashion:

> How is a judge or jury to determine a "fair price?" Is it the price charged by other suppliers of the primary product? None exist. Is it the price that competition "would have set" were the primary level not monopolized? How can the court determine this price without examining costs and demands, indeed without acting like a rate-setting regulatory agency, the rate-setting proceedings of which often last for several years? Further, how is the court to decide the proper size of the price "gap?" Must it be large enough for all independent competing firms to make a "living profit," no matter how inefficient they may be? And how should the court respond when costs or demands change over time, as they inevitably will? [. . .]

[Concord v. Boston Edison Co., 915 F.2d 17, 25 (1st Cir. 1990) (Breyer, J.).]

[15] Amici assert that there are circumstances in which price squeezes may harm competition. For example, they assert that price squeezes may raise entry barriers that fortify the upstream monopolist's position; they also contend that price squeezes may impair nonprice competition and innovation in the downstream market by driving independent firms out of business.

[16] The problem, however, is that amici have not identified any independent competitive harm caused by price squeezes above and beyond the harm that would result from a duty-to-deal violation at the wholesale level or predatory pricing at the retail level. To the extent a monopolist violates one of these doctrines, the plaintiffs have a remedy under existing law. We do not need to endorse a new theory of liability to prevent such harm.

NOTES

1) What are the dangers of an unduly lax predation standard? What about an unduly aggressive one?

2) How likely should "recoupment" be before courts impose liability? What evidence should we look for to determine whether it is sufficiently likely?[563]

3) Some writers have suggested that predatory pricing might be taking place in certain digital markets.[564] In what digital markets do you think there is a risk of predation, and how should we test for it? Should we have different standards for digital predation: if so, what should these be and why?

4) In *Linkline* the Court concluded that if, the upstream refusal to deal is lawful and the downstream low price is lawful, then the combination—a price squeeze—must also be lawful. Do you agree that this conclusion is necessary? Can the combination of two practices, each in themselves lawful, ever create an antitrust violation? What risks and goals do you think the Court had in mind in articulating this rule? What would the consequences of a rule against price squeezes be?

5) Does a price squeeze result in an increase in market power?

6) Is the cost-based standard for predatory pricing the right one? What are the most plausible alternatives? What should we do in cases where costs are difficult to calculate?

4. Bundling

Bundling is closely related to tying. Where tying involves conditioning the sale of one (tying) product or service on the buyer agreeing also to purchase another (tied) product or service, bundling involves offering a price discount on doing so. Competitive concerns can arise when an integrated seller (*i.e.*, a seller that offers product A *and* product B) uses a bundled discount to exclude unintegrated rivals (*i.e.*, a seller that offers only A or only B) in a way that contributes to the acquisition or maintenance of monopoly power.[565]

Antitrust courts and commentators often talk about two kinds of bundling. "Fixed" or "pure" bundling involves selling two products *only* in the form of a bundle: this is usually just tying by another name. The distinctive economics of bundling come into play with "mixed" bundling: that is, when products are available for separate purchase, but a discount is offered for purchasing them together.

The Power of Bundling

The economics of exclusionary bundling are best seen with a simple example. Suppose that firms X and Y both produce dinner forks, and that Y is more efficient: Y has costs of $2.50 for a dinner fork; X has costs of $3.00 to produce an identical fork. But suppose that X also holds market power in a market for dinner knives, with costs of $2.50 for each knife and a profit-maximizing monopoly price of $4.00. Assume further that anyone who needs a fork needs a knife. If all sales are individual and unbundled, and assuming no constraints on the capacity of either

---

[563] *See generally*, *e.g.*, Louis Kaplow, *Recoupment and Predatory Pricing Analysis*, 10 J. Leg. Analysis 46 (2018).

[564] *See*, *e.g.*, Lina M. Khan, *Amazon's Antitrust Paradox*, 126 Yale L.J. 710 (2017).

[565] For general discussion, *see*, *e.g.*, Roger D. Blair & Thomas Knight, *Bundled Discounts, Loyalty Discounts and Antitrust Policy*, 16 Rutgers Bus. L. Rev. 123 (2020); Einer Elhauge, *Tying, Bundled Discounts, and the Death of the Single Monopoly Profit Theory*, 123 Harv. L. Rev. 397 (2009); Herbert Hovenkamp, *Discounts and Exclusions*, 2006 Utah L. Rev. 841 (2006); Barry Nalebuff, *Exclusionary Bundling*, 50 Antitrust Bull. 321 (2005).

X or Y, consumers will likely buy forks from Y and knives from X. X will likely not be able to compete effectively in the market for forks.

But now suppose that X offers consumers a knife-and-fork bundle for a total price of $6.00, or a knife alone for $4.00. From the point of view of any individual consumer who needs a knife, the opportunity to get a fork as well for an additional $2.00—rather than the $2.50 that Y would charge—may be irresistible.

Notice that Y, despite its significantly superior efficiency in fork production, can't afford to meet a price of $2.00 for a fork given its costs of $2.50. The result is that X still makes money on every sale—with a total bundled sale price of $6.00 above costs of $5.50—but Y is completely driven out of the market. If re-entry into the fork market is difficult, X can end up holding monopoly power in the fork market, with the power to raise its prices significantly after Y has exited.

These numbers are fairly extreme for the sake of illustration: in practice, X would realize that it may only need to offer the bundle for $6.49 to exclude Y, as being cheaper by a penny is still cheaper assuming identical products.[566] As with tying, the products need not be complements for the conduct to have the relevant harmful effect, though in practice they often are.[567]

But the law moves with caution in condemning bundled discounts, for reasons similar to those we encountered in discussing predatory pricing. Competition is valued, in significant part, for its power to bring lower prices. Moreover, low bundled prices may reflect a variety of good things, including economies of scope (*i.e.*, supply-side savings from supplying multiple different products or services) and demand-side complementarities (*i.e.*, the fact that the profit-maximizing price for a set of complements is lower than the total of the profit-maximizing prices for each complement separately). Undue skepticism of package deals would harm consumers and punish businesses for offering good deals.

The antitrust analysis of mixed bundling is the subject of a prominent circuit split between the Third and Ninth Circuits. We start with the Third Circuit's decision in *LePage's*.

LePage's Inc. v. 3M
324 F.3d 141 (3d Cir. 2003) (en banc)

Judge Sloviter.

[1] 3M, which manufactures Scotch tape for home and office use, dominated the United States transparent tape market with a market share above 90% until the early 1990s. It has conceded that it has a monopoly in that market. LePage's, founded in 1876, has sold a variety of office products and, around 1980, decided to sell "second brand" and private label transparent tape, i.e., tape sold under the retailer's name rather than under the name of the manufacturer. By 1992, LePage's sold 88% of private label tape sales in the United States, which represented but a small portion of the transparent tape market. Private label tape sold at a lower price to the retailer and the customer than branded tape.

[2] Distribution patterns and consumer acceptance accounted for a shift of some tape sales from branded tape to private label tape. With the rapid growth of office superstores, such as Staples and Office Depot, and mass merchandisers, such as Wal-Mart and Kmart, distribution patterns for second brand and private label tape changed as many of the large retailers wanted to use their "brand names" to sell stationery products, including transparent tape. 3M also entered the private label business during the early 1990s and sold its own second brand under the name "Highland."

---

[566] In the real world, brand loyalty and other forms of product differentiation would make things more complicated: we are stylizing for the sake of illustration.

[567] Complementarity is particularly likely in these cases because the conduct is likely to harm competition in the secondary (*i.e.*, knife) market in proportion to the extent to which customers in that market are also customers in the primary market with a need for the primary good. In other words, if most fork customers don't care about buying knives, then the ability to offer a discount on the price of a knife isn't likely to move many customers to buy a fork they don't prefer.

[3] LePage's claims that, in response to the growth of this competitive market, 3M engaged in a series of related, anticompetitive acts aimed at restricting the availability of lower-priced transparent tape to consumers. It also claims that 3M devised programs that prevented LePage's and the other domestic company in the business, Tesa Tuck, Inc., from gaining or maintaining large volume sales and that 3M maintained its monopoly by stifling growth of private label tape and by coordinating efforts aimed at large distributors to keep retail prices for Scotch tape high. LePage's claims that it barely was surviving at the time of trial and that it suffered large operating losses from 1996 through 1999.

[4] LePage's brought this antitrust action asserting that 3M used its monopoly over its Scotch tape brand to gain a competitive advantage in the private label tape portion of the transparent tape market in the United States through the use of 3M's multi-tiered "bundled rebate" structure, which offered higher rebates when customers purchased products in a number of 3M's different product lines. LePage's also alleges that 3M offered to some of LePage's customers large lump-sum cash payments, promotional allowances and other cash incentives to encourage them to enter into exclusive dealing arrangements with 3M.

[5] LePage's asserted claims for unlawful agreements in restraint of trade under § 1 of the Sherman Act, monopolization and attempted monopolization under § 2 of the Sherman Act, and exclusive dealing under § 3 of the Clayton Act. After a nine week trial, the jury returned its verdict for LePage's on both its monopolization and attempted monopolization claims under § 2 of the Sherman Act, and assessed damages of $22,828,899 on each. It found in 3M's favor on LePage's claims under § 1 of the Sherman Act and § 3 of the Clayton Act. 3M filed its motions for judgment as a matter of law and for a new trial, arguing that its rebate and discount programs and the other conduct of which LePage's complained did not constitute the basis for a valid antitrust claim as a matter of law and that, in any event, the court's charge to the jury was insufficiently specific and LePage's damages proof was speculative. The District Court granted 3M's motion for judgment as a matter of law on LePage's "attempted maintenance of monopoly power" claim but denied 3M's motion for judgment as a matter of law in all other respects and denied its motion for new trial. The Court subsequently entered a judgment for trebled damages of $68,486,697 to which interest was to be added. LePage's filed a cross appeal on the District Court's judgment dismissing its attempted maintenance of monopoly power claim.

[6] On appeal, the panel of this court before which this case was originally argued reversed the District Court's judgment on LePage's § 2 claim by a divided vote. This court granted LePage's motion for rehearing en banc and, pursuant to its practice, vacated the panel opinion. The appeal was then orally argued before the court en banc. [. . .]

[7] [W]e must evaluate 3M's contention that it was entitled to judgment as a matter of law on the basis of the decision in [*Brooke Group Ltd. v. Brown & Williamson Tobacco Corp.*, 509 U.S. 209 . . . (1993).] {*Eds.: in other words, 3M argued that the legality of a bundle should be analyzed under the predatory-pricing standard, by asking whether any component of the bundle is being supplied at a below-cost price.*} [. . .]

[8] Assuming arguendo that *Brooke Group* should be read for the proposition that a company's pricing action is legal if its prices are not below its costs, nothing in the decision suggests that its discussion of the issue is applicable to a monopolist with its unconstrained market power. Moreover, LePage's, unlike the plaintiff in *Brooke Group*, does not make a predatory pricing claim. 3M is a monopolist; a monopolist is not free to take certain actions that a company in a competitive (or even oligopolistic) market may take, because there is no market constraint on a monopolist's behavior.

[9] Nothing in any of the Supreme Court's opinions in the decade since the *Brooke Group* decision suggested that the opinion overturned decades of Supreme Court precedent that evaluated a monopolist's liability under § 2 by examining its exclusionary, *i.e.*, predatory, conduct. *Brooke Group* has been cited only four times by the Supreme Court, three times in cases that were not even antitrust cases for propositions patently inapplicable here. . . . [N]othing that the Supreme Court has written since *Brooke Group* dilutes the Court's consistent holdings that a monopolist will be found to violate § 2 of the Sherman Act if it engages in exclusionary or predatory conduct without a valid business justification.

[10] In considering LePage's conduct that led to the jury's ultimate verdict, we note that the jury had before it evidence of the full panoply of 3M's exclusionary conduct, including both the exclusive dealing arrangements and the bundled rebates which could reasonably have been viewed as effectuating exclusive dealing arrangements because of the way in which they were structured.

[11] Through a program denominated Executive Growth Fund ("EGF") and thereafter Partnership Growth Fund ("PGF"), 3M offered many of LePage's major customers substantial rebates to induce them to eliminate or reduce their purchases of tape from LePage's. Rather than competing by offering volume discounts which are concededly legal and often reflect cost savings, 3M's rebate programs offered discounts to certain customers conditioned on purchases spanning six of 3M's diverse product lines. The product lines covered by the rebate program were: Health Care Products, Home Care Products, Home Improvement Products, Stationery Products (including transparent tape), Retail Auto Products, and Leisure Time. In addition to bundling the rebates, both of 3M's rebate programs set customer-specific target growth rates in each product line. The size of the rebate was linked to the number of product lines in which targets were met, and the number of targets met by the buyer determined the rebate it would receive on all of its purchases. If a customer failed to meet the target for any one product, its failure would cause it to lose the rebate across the line. This created a substantial incentive for each customer to meet the targets across all product lines to maximize its rebates.

[12] The rebates were considerable, not "modest" as 3M states. For example, Kmart, which had constituted 10% of LePage's business, received $926,287 in 1997, Sealed App. at 2980, and in 1996 Wal–Mart received more than $1.5 million, Sam's Club received $666,620, and Target received $482,001. Just as significant as the amounts received is the powerful incentive they provided to customers to purchase 3M tape rather than LePage's in order not to forego the maximum rebate 3M offered. The penalty would have been $264,000 for Sam's Club, $450,000 for Kmart, and $200,000 to $310,000 for American Stores.

[13] 3M does not deny that it offered these programs although it gives different reasons for the discounts to each customer. Instead it argues that they were no more exclusive than procompetitive lawful discount programs. And, as it responds to each of LePage's allegations, it returns to its central premise that it is not unlawful to lower one's prices so long as they remain above cost.

[14] However, one of the leading treatises discussing the inherent anticompetitive effect of bundled rebates, even if they are priced above cost, notes that the great majority of bundled rebate programs yield aggregate prices above cost. Rather than analogizing them to predatory pricing, they are best compared with tying, whose foreclosure effects are similar. Indeed, the package discount is often a close analogy.

[15] The treatise then discusses the anticompetitive effect as follows:

> The anticompetitive feature of package discounting is the strong incentive it gives buyers to take increasing amounts or even all of a product in order to take advantage of a discount aggregated across multiple products. In the anticompetitive case, which we presume is in the minority, the defendant rewards the customer for buying its product B rather than the plaintiff's B, not because defendant's B is better or even cheaper. Rather, the customer buys the defendant's B in order to receive a greater discount on A, which the plaintiff does not produce. In that case the rival can compete in B only by giving the customer a price that compensates it for the foregone A discount.

[16] The authors then conclude:

> Depending on the number of products that are aggregated and the customer's relative purchases of each, even an equally efficient rival may find it impossible to compensate for lost discounts on products that it does not produce.

[Phillip E. Areeda & Herbert Hovenkamp, ANTITRUST LAW ¶ 794 (2002) 83–84.]

[17] The principal anticompetitive effect of bundled rebates as offered by 3M is that when offered by a monopolist they may foreclose portions of the market to a potential competitor who does not manufacture an equally diverse group of products and who therefore cannot make a comparable offer. We recognized this in our decision in *SmithKline Corp. v. Eli Lilly & Co.*, 575 F.2d 1056 (3d Cir. 1978), where we held that conduct substantially identical

to 3M's was anticompetitive and sustained the finding of a violation of § 2. . . . The defendant in *SmithKline*, Eli Lilly & Company, the pharmaceutical manufacturer, sold three of its cephalosporins to hospitals under the trade names Kefzol, Keflin and Keflex. Cephalosporins are broad spectrum antibiotics that were at that time indispensable to hospital pharmacies. Lilly had a monopoly on both Keflin and Keflex because of its patents. However, those drugs faced competition from the generic drug cefazolin which Lilly sold under the trade name Kefzol and which plaintiff SmithKline sold under the trade name Ancef.

[18] Lilly's profits on the patented Keflin were far higher than those it received from its sales of Kefzol where its pricing was constrained by the existence of SmithKline. To preserve its market position in Keflin and discourage sales of Ancef and even of its own Kefzol, Lilly instituted a rebate program that provided a 3% bonus rebate for hospitals that purchased specified quantities of any three of Lilly's five cephalosporins. SmithKline brought a § 2 monopolization claim, alleging that Lilly used these multi-line volume rebates to maintain its monopoly over the hospital market for cephalosporins.

[19] The district court . . . found that Lilly's pricing policy violated § 2. We affirmed by a unanimous decision. Although customers were not forced to select which cephalosporins they purchased from Lilly, we recognized that the effect of the rebate program was to induce hospitals to conjoin their purchases of Kefzol with Keflin and Keflex, Lilly's leading sellers. As we stated, although eligibility for the 3% bonus rebate was based on the purchase of specified quantities of any three of Lilly's cephalosporins, in reality it meant the combined purchases of Kefzol and the leading sellers, Keflin and Keflex. The gravamen of Lilly's § 2 violation was that Lilly linked a product on which it faced competition with products on which it faced no competition.

[20] The effect of the 3% bundled rebate was magnified by the volume of Lilly products sold, so that in order to offer a rebate of the same net dollar amount as Lilly's, SmithKline had to offer purchasers of Ancef rebates of some 16% to hospitals of average size, and 35% to larger volume hospitals. Lilly's rebate structure combining Kefzol with Keflin and Keflex insulated Kefzol from true price competition with its competitor Ancef.

[21] LePage's private-label and second-tier tapes are, as Kefzol and Ancef were in relation to Keflin, less expensive but otherwise of similar quality to Scotch-brand tape. Indeed, before 3M instituted its rebate program, LePage's had begun to enjoy a small but rapidly expanding toehold in the transparent tape market. 3M's incentive was thus the same as Lilly's in SmithKline: to preserve the market position of Scotch-brand tape by discouraging widespread acceptance of the cheaper, but substantially similar, tape produced by LePage's.

[22] 3M bundled its rebates for Scotch-brand tape with other products it sold in much the same way that Lilly bundled its rebates for Kefzol with Keflin and Keflex. In both cases, the bundled rebates reflected an exploitation of the seller's monopoly power. Just as cephalosporins were carried in virtually every general hospital in the country [in *SmithKline*], the evidence in this case shows that Scotch-brand tape is indispensable to any retailer in the transparent tape market.

[23] Our analysis of § 2 of the Sherman Act in *SmithKline* is instructive here where the facts are comparable. Speaking through Judge Aldisert, we said:

> With Lilly's cephalosporins subject to no serious price competition from other sellers, with the barriers to entering the market substantial, and with the prospects of new competition extremely uncertain, we are confronted with a factual complex in which Lilly has the awesome power of a monopolist. Although it enjoyed the status of a legal monopolist when it was engaged in the manufacture and sale of its original patented products, that status changed when it instituted its bundled rebate program. The goal of that plan was to associate Lilly's legal monopolistic practices with an illegal activity that directly affected the price, supply, and demand of Kefzol and Ancef. Were it not for the bundled rebate program, the price, supply, and demand of Kefzol and Ancef would have been determined by the economic laws of a competitive market. Lilly's bundled rebate program blatantly revised those economic laws and made Lilly a transgressor under § 2 of the Sherman Act.

[24] The effect of 3M's rebates were even more powerfully magnified than those in *SmithKline* because 3M's rebates required purchases bridging 3M's extensive product lines. In some cases, these magnified rebates to a particular customer were as much as half of LePage's entire prior tape sales to that customer. For example, LePage's sales to

Sam's Club in 1993 totaled $1,078,484, while 3M's 1996 rebate to Sam's Club was $666,620. Similarly, LePage's 1992 sales to Kmart were $2,482,756; 3M's 1997 rebate to Kmart was $926,287. The jury could reasonably find that 3M used its monopoly in transparent tape, backed by its considerable catalog of products, to squeeze out LePage's. 3M's conduct was at least as anticompetitive as the conduct which this court held violated § 2 in *SmithKline*.

* * *

LePage's is half of the circuit-split story; the other half of the circuit split (and indeed the majority approach) is the approach mapped out by the Ninth Circuit in *PeaceHealth*.

Cascade Health Solutions v. PeaceHealth
515 F.3d 883 (9th Cir. 2008)

[1] McKenzie–Willamette Hospital ("McKenzie") filed a complaint in the district court against PeaceHealth asserting seven claims for relief. [. . .]

[2] In Lane County, PeaceHealth operates three hospitals while McKenzie operates one. McKenzie's sole endeavor is McKenzie–Willamette Hospital, a 114–bed hospital that offers primary and secondary acute care in Springfield, Oregon. McKenzie does not provide tertiary care. In the time period leading up to and including this litigation, McKenzie had been suffering financial losses, and, as a result, merged with Triad Hospitals, Inc. so that it could add tertiary services to its menu of care. {*Eds: Following this merger, McKenzie was renamed Cascade Health.*}

[3] The largest of PeaceHealth's three facilities is Sacred Heart Hospital, a 432–bed operation that offers primary, secondary, and tertiary care in Eugene, Oregon. PeaceHealth also operates Peace Harbor Hospital, a 21–bed hospital in Florence, Oregon and Cottage Grove Hospital, an 11–bed hospital in Cottage Grove, Oregon. In Lane County, PeaceHealth has a 90% market share of tertiary neonatal services, a 93% market share of tertiary cardiovascular services, and a roughly 75% market share of primary and secondary care services. [. . .]

[4] On McKenzie's monopolization and attempted monopolization claims, McKenzie's primary theory was that PeaceHealth engaged in anticompetitive conduct by offering insurers "bundled" or "package" discounts. McKenzie asserted that PeaceHealth offered insurers discounts of 35% to 40% on tertiary services if the insurers made PeaceHealth their sole preferred provider for all services—primary, secondary, and tertiary. McKenzie introduced evidence of a few specific instances of PeaceHealth's bundled discounting practices. [. . .]

[5] [B]undled discounts, while potentially procompetitive by offering bargains to consumers, can also pose the threat of anticompetitive impact by excluding less diversified but more efficient producers. These considerations put into focus this problem: How are we to discern where antitrust law draws the line between bundled discounts that are procompetitive and part of the normal rough-and-tumble of our competitive economy and bundled discounts, offered by firms holding or on the verge of gaining monopoly power in the relevant market, that harm competition and are thus proscribed by § 2 of the Sherman Act? [. . .]

[6] In this case, the district court used *LePage's* to formulate its jury instruction. Specifically, the district court instructed the jury that

> plaintiff . . . contends that defendant has bundled price discounts for its primary, secondary, and tertiary acute care products and that doing so is anticompetitive. Bundled pricing occurs when price discounts are offered for purchasing an entire line of services exclusively from one supplier. Bundled price discounts may be anti-competitive if they are offered by a monopolist and substantially foreclose portions of the market to a competitor who does not provide an equally diverse group of services and who therefore cannot make a comparable offer.

[7] As 3M did in *LePage's*, PeaceHealth argues that the jury instruction incorrectly stated the law because it allowed the jury to find that a defendant with monopoly power (or, in the case of an attempted monopolization claim, a dangerous probability of achieving monopoly power) engaged in exclusionary conduct by simply offering a bundled discount that its competitor could not match. The instruction did not require the jury to consider whether the defendant priced below cost. *LePage's*, PeaceHealth asserts, was wrongly decided because it allows the jury to

conclude, from the structure of the market alone, that a competitor has been anticompetitively excluded from the market. We generally review jury instructions for abuse of discretion, but we review de novo whether jury instructions correctly stated the law.

[8] As the bipartisan Antitrust Modernization Commission ("AMC") recently noted, the fundamental problem with the *LePage's* standard is that it does not consider whether the bundled discounts constitute competition on the merits, but simply concludes that all bundled discounts offered by a monopolist are anticompetitive with respect to its competitors who do not manufacture an equally diverse product line. Antitrust Modernization Comm'n, REPORT AND RECOMMENDATIONS (2007) 97 [hereinafter AMC Report]. The *LePage's* standard, the AMC noted, asks the jury to consider whether the plaintiff has been excluded from the market, but does not require the jury to consider whether the plaintiff was at least as efficient of a producer as the defendant. Thus, the *LePage's* standard could protect a less efficient competitor at the expense of consumer welfare. As Judge Greenberg explained in his *LePage's* dissent, the Third Circuit's standard risks curtailing price competition and a method of pricing beneficial to customers because the bundled rebates effectively lowered the seller's costs.

[9] The AMC also lamented that *LePage's* "offers no clear standards by which firms can assess whether their bundled rebates are likely to pass antitrust muster." The Commission noted that efficiencies, and not schemes to acquire or maintain monopoly power, likely explain the use of bundled discounts because many firms without market power offer them. The AMC thus proposed a three-part test that it believed would protect procompetitive bundled discounts from antitrust scrutiny. The AMC proposed that:

> Courts should adopt a three-part test to determine whether bundled discounts or rebates violate Section 2 of the Sherman Act. To prove a violation of Section 2, a plaintiff should be required to show each one of the following elements (as well as other elements of a Section 2 claim): (1) after allocating all discounts and rebates attributable to the entire bundle of products to the competitive product, the defendant sold the competitive product below its incremental cost for the competitive product; (2) the defendant is likely to recoup these short-term losses; and (3) the bundled discount or rebate program has had or is likely to have an adverse effect on competition.

[10] We must decide whether we should follow *LePage's* or whether we should part ways with the Third Circuit by adopting a cost-based standard to apply in bundled discounting cases. [. . .]

[11] [T]he Supreme Court has forcefully suggested that we should not condemn prices that are above some measure of incremental cost. In *Brooke Group*, the Court held that a plaintiff seeking to establish competitive injury resulting from a rival's low prices must prove that the prices complained of are below an appropriate measure of its rival's costs. In the course of rejecting the plaintiff's argument that a predatory pricing plaintiff need not prove below-cost pricing, the Court wrote that it has "rejected the notion that above-cost prices that are below general market levels or the costs of a firm's competitors inflict injury to competition cognizable under the antitrust laws. . . . The Court went on to emphasize that "[l]ow prices benefit consumers regardless of how those prices are set, and so long as they are above predatory levels, they do not threaten competition." The Court also noted the broad application of the principle that only below-cost prices are anticompetitive, stating that "[w]e have adhered to this principle regardless of the type of antitrust claim involved." As a general rule, the Court concluded, the exclusionary effect of prices above a relevant measure of cost either reflects the lower cost structure of the alleged predator, and so represents competition on the merits, or is beyond the practical ability of a judicial tribunal to control without courting intolerable risks of chilling legitimate price-cutting. [. . .]

[12] Of course, in neither *Brooke Group* nor *Weyerhaeuser* did the Court go so far as to hold that in every case in which a plaintiff challenges low prices as exclusionary conduct the plaintiff must prove that those prices were below cost. But the Court's opinions strongly suggest that, in the normal case, above-cost pricing will not be considered exclusionary conduct for antitrust purposes, and the Court's reasoning poses a strong caution against condemning bundled discounts that result in prices above a relevant measure of costs.

[13] The Supreme Court's long and consistent adherence to the principle that the antitrust laws protect the process of competition, and not the pursuits of any particular competitor, reinforce our conclusion of caution concerning bundled discounts that result in prices above an appropriate measure of costs. . . . . [. . .]

[14] One of the challenges of interpreting and enforcing the amorphous prohibitions of §§ 1 and 2 of the Sherman Act is ensuring that the antitrust laws do not punish economic behavior that benefits consumers and will not cause long-run injury to the competitive process. A bundled discount, however else it might be viewed, is a price discount on a collection of goods. The Supreme Court has undoubtedly shown a solicitude for price competition. In *Weyerhaeuser*, Justice Thomas, writing for the Court, reminded us that, in *Brooke Group*, the Court had cautioned that the costs of erroneous findings of predatory-pricing liability were quite high because the mechanism by which a firm engages in predatory pricing—lowering prices—is the same mechanism by which a firm stimulates competition, and therefore, mistaken findings of liability would chill the very conduct the antitrust laws are designed to protect.

[15] Given the endemic nature of bundled discounts in many spheres of normal economic activity, we decline to endorse the Third Circuit's definition of when bundled discounts constitute the exclusionary conduct proscribed by § 2 of the Sherman Act. Instead, we think the course safer for consumers and our competitive economy to hold that bundled discounts may not be considered exclusionary conduct within the meaning of § 2 of the Sherman Act unless the discounts resemble the behavior that the Supreme Court in *Brooke Group* identified as predatory. Accordingly, we hold that the exclusionary conduct element of a claim arising under § 2 of the Sherman Act cannot be satisfied by reference to bundled discounts unless the discounts result in prices that are below an appropriate measure of the defendant's costs. [. . .]

[16] The next question we must address is how we define the appropriate measure of the defendant's costs in bundled discounting cases and how we determine whether discounted prices fall below that mark. Defining the appropriate measure of costs in a bundled discounting case is more complex than in a single product case. In a single product case, we may simply ask whether the defendant has priced its product below its incremental cost of producing that product because a rival that produces the same product as efficiently as the defendant should be able to match any price at or above the defendant's cost. However, as we discussed above, a defendant offering a bundled discount, without pricing below cost either the individual products in the bundle or the bundle as a whole, can, in some cases, exclude a rival who produces one of the products in the bundle equally or more efficiently than the defendant. Thus, simply asking whether the defendant's prices are below its incremental costs might fail to alert us to bundled discounts that threaten the exclusion of equally efficient rivals. Nonetheless, we are mindful that, in single product pricing cases, the Supreme Court has not adopted rules condemning prices above a seller's incremental costs. With these considerations in mind, we assess the rules the parties and amici propose for us to use in bundled discounting cases to determine the appropriate measure of a defendant's costs and whether a defendant has priced below that level.

[17] PeaceHealth and some amici urge us to adopt a rule they term the "aggregate discount" rule. This rule condemns bundled discounts as anticompetitive only in the narrow cases in which the discounted price of the entire bundle does not exceed the bundling firm's incremental cost to produce the entire bundle. PeaceHealth and amici argue that support for such a rule can be found in the Supreme Court's single product predation cases—*Brooke Group* and *Weyerhaeuser*.

[18] We are not persuaded that those cases require us to adopt an aggregate discount rule in multi-product discounting cases. As we discussed above, bundled discounts present one potential threat to consumer welfare that single product discounts do not: A competitor who produces fewer products than the defendant but produces the competitive product at or below the defendant's cost to produce that product may nevertheless be excluded from the market because the competitor cannot match the discount the defendant offers over its numerous product lines. This possibility exists even when the defendant's prices are above cost for each individual product and for the bundle as a whole. Under a discount aggregation rule, anticompetitive bundled discounting schemes that harm competition may too easily escape liability.

[19] Additionally, as commentators have pointed out, *Brooke Group*'s safe harbor for above-cost discounting in the single product discount context is not based on a theory that above-cost pricing strategies can never be anticompetitive, but rather on a cost-benefit rejection of a more nuanced rule. . . . That is, the safe harbor rests on the premise that any consumer benefit created by a rule that permits inquiry into above-cost, single-product discounts, but allows judicial condemnation of those deemed legitimately exclusionary, would likely be outweighed by the consumer harm occasioned by overdeterring nonexclusionary discounts. So, in adopting an appropriate

cost-based test for bundled discounting cases, we should not adopt an aggregate discount rule without inquiring whether a rule exists that is more likely to identify anticompetitive bundled discounting practices while at the same time resulting in little harm to competition. [. . .]

[20] [A]s our cost-based rule, we adopt what amici refer to as a "discount attribution" standard. Under this standard, the full amount of the discounts given by the defendant on the bundle are allocated to the competitive product or products. If the resulting price of the competitive product or products is below the defendant's incremental cost to produce them, the trier of fact may find that the bundled discount is exclusionary for the purpose of § 2. This standard makes the defendant's bundled discounts legal unless the discounts have the potential to exclude a hypothetical equally efficient producer of the competitive product.[15] [. . .]

[21] The discount attribution standard provides clear guidance for sellers that engage in bundled discounting practices. A seller can easily ascertain its own prices and costs of production and calculate whether its discounting practices run afoul of the rule we have outlined. . . . [U]nder the discount attribution standard a bundled discounter need not fret over and predict or determine its rivals' cost structure.

[22] We are aware that liability under the discount attribution standard has the potential to sweep more broadly than under the aggregate discount rule . . . . However, there is limited judicial experience with bundled discounts, and academic inquiry into the competitive effects of bundled discounts is only beginning. By comparison, the Supreme Court's decision in *Brooke Group* . . . marked the culmination of nearly twenty years of scholarly and judicial analysis of the feasibility and competitive effects of single product predatory pricing schemes. The cost-based standard we adopt will allow courts the experience they need to divine the prevalence and competitive effects of bundled discounts and will allow these difficult issues to further percolate in the lower courts. As the Solicitor General noted in his amicus brief urging the denial of certiorari in *LePage's*:

> There is insufficient experience with bundled discounts to this point to make a firm judgment about the relative prevalence of exclusionary versus procompetitive bundled discounts. Relative to the practice of predatory pricing analyzed in *Brooke Group*, there is less knowledge on which to assess whether, or to what extent, the legal approach to a monopolist's allegedly exclusionary bundled discounts should be driven by a strong concern for false positives and low risk of false negatives. Further empirical development may shed light on that question.

[23] Pending further judicial and academic inquiry into the prevalence of anticompetitive bundled discounts, we think it preferable to allow plaintiffs to challenge bundled discounts if those plaintiffs can prove a defendant's bundled discounts would have excluded an equally efficient competitor.

[24] To summarize, the primary anticompetitive danger posed by a multi-product bundled discount is that such a discount can exclude a rival is who is equally efficient at producing the competitive product simply because the rival does not sell as many products as the bundled discounter. Thus, a plaintiff who challenges a package discount as anticompetitive must prove that, when the full amount of the discounts given by the defendant is allocated to the competitive product or products, the resulting price of the competitive product or products is below the defendant's incremental cost to produce them. This requirement ensures that the only bundled discounts

---

[15] [An example] illustrates how the discount attribution standard condemns discounts that could not be matched by an equally or more efficient producer of the competitive product. . . . [T]he example involves A, a firm that makes both shampoo and conditioner. A's incremental cost of shampoo is $1.50 and A's incremental cost of conditioner is $2.50. A prices shampoo at $3 and conditioner at $5, if purchased separately. However, if purchased as a bundle, A prices shampoo at $2.25 and conditioner at $3. Purchased separately from A, the total price of one unit of shampoo and one unit of conditioner is $8. However, with the bundled discount, a customer can purchase both products from A for $5.25, a discount of $2.75 off the separate prices, but at a price that is still above A's variable cost of producing the bundle. Applying the discount attribution rule to the example, we subtract the entire discount on the package of products, $2.75, from the separate per unit price of the competitive product, shampoo, $3. The resulting effective price of shampoo is thus $0.25, meaning that, if a customer must purchase conditioner from A at the separate price of $5, a rival who produces only shampoo must sell the shampoo for $0.25 to make customers indifferent between A's bundle and the separate purchase of conditioner from A and shampoo from the hypothetical rival. A's pricing scheme thus has the effect of excluding any potential rival who would produce only shampoo, and would produce it at an incremental cost above $0.25. However, as we noted above, A's incremental cost of producing shampoo is $1.50. Thus, A's pricing practices exclude potential competitors that could produce shampoo more efficiently than A (i.e., at an incremental cost of less than $1.50). A's discount could thus be considered exclusionary under our rule, supporting Sherman Act § 2 liability if the other elements were proved.

condemned as exclusionary are those that would exclude an equally efficient producer of the competitive product or products. [. . .]

[25] . . . [T]he relevant inquiry is not whether PeaceHealth's pricing practices forced McKenzie to price below cost, but whether PeaceHealth priced its own services below an appropriate measure of its cost, as we have defined that concept using the discount attribution rule. In this case, we cannot conclude that the error in the jury instructions was harmless. We vacate the judgment entered in McKenzie's favor and remand for further proceedings consistent with our opinion.

NOTES

1) The *PeaceHealth* price-cost test is a demanding one for plaintiffs. (Why do you think it is hard for the plaintiff to prove the various quantitative measures on which that test depends?) Is this justified as a policy matter by the dangers of deterring healthy competition? Is it compelled as a legal matter by *Brooke Group*?
2) Can you discern the rule that the court was applying in *LePage*'s to distinguish between lawful and unlawful bundles?
3) Do you think bundling should be approached through the lens of foreclosure (as in tying or exclusivity cases) or predation (as in predatory-pricing cases)?

5. Torts, Misrepresentations, and Abuse of Process

Although it would be easy to think of monopolization as defined by its familiar, shoebox-like categories—exclusive dealing, tying, predatory pricing, and so on—this would be a mistake. There is no formal limit to the types and varieties of conduct that can, in principle, constitute monopolization.[568]

Among other things, this means that there is some overlap between monopolization and traditional torts, when committed by monopolists and sufficiently threatening to competition. Excluding rivals by smashing up their factories or display cases, for example, can violate Section 2 where it is sufficiently connected to the acquisition or maintenance of monopoly power. So too, under the right circumstances, can misrepresentations![569]

Torts and Misrepresentation

Conwood Co., L.P. v. U.S. Tobacco Co., 290 F.3d 768 (6th Cir. 2002); National Ass'n of Pharmaceutical Mfrs., Inc. v. Ayerst Labs., 850 F.2d 904 (2d Cir. 1988)

The overlap between Section 2 and the broader realm of business torts has been explored in a number of cases. In *Conwood*, a supplier of chewing tobacco (Conwood) sued its competitor (U.S. Tobacco Corp. or "USTC") for monopolization. Conwood alleged that USTC had misused its role as a "category manager" or "category captain"—in which capacity retailers asked for its help in arranging in-store displays of chewing tobacco, including not just those of USTC but also those of rival brands[570]—through a variety of practices, including the literal removal and destruction of Conwood's product display racks. USTC argued, among other things, that the conduct amounted to "isolated sporadic torts" and could not form the basis for antitrust liability.

But the Sixth Circuit disagreed. "Isolated tortious activity alone does not constitute exclusionary conduct for purposes of a § 2 violation, absent a significant and more than a temporary effect on competition, and not merely on a competitor or customer. Business torts will be violative of § 2 only in rare gross cases. [But] this is not to say that tortious conduct may never violate the antitrust laws. Moreover, merely because a particular practice might

---

568 *See, e.g.*, United States v. Microsoft Corp., 253 F.3d 34, 58 (D.C. Cir. 2001) ("[T]he means of illicit exclusion . . . are myriad."); Caribbean Broad. Sys., Ltd. v. Cable & Wireless PLC, 148 F.3d 1080, 1087 (D.C. Cir. 1998) (anticompetitive conduct comes "in too many different forms" for exhaustive definition).

569 *See, e.g.*, Lenox MacLaren Surgical Corp. v. Medtronic, Inc., 762 F.3d 1114, 1127 (10th Cir. 2014); Am. Pro. Testing Serv., Inc. v. Harcourt Brace Jovanovich Legal & Pro. Publications, Inc., 108 F.3d 1147, 1152 (9th Cir. 1997); Am. Council of Certified Podiatric Physicians & Surgeons v. Am. Bd. of Podiatric Surgery, Inc., 323 F.3d 366, 371 (6th Cir. 2003); National Ass'n of Pharmaceutical Mfrs., Inc. v. Ayerst Labs., 850 F.2d 904 (2d Cir. 1988). For a thoughtful discussion of liability for false advertising, *see* Michael A. Carrier & Rebecca Tushnet, *An Antitrust Framework for False Advertising*, 106 Iowa L. Rev. 1841 (2021).

570 This may strike you as an odd-sounding practice, but it is common. *See, e.g.*, Bradley J. Lorden, *Category Management: The Antitrust Implications in the United States and Europe*, 23 Loyola Consumer L. Rev. 541 (2011).

be actionable under tort law does not preclude an action under the antitrust laws as well. Anticompetitive conduct can come in too many different forms, and is too dependent upon context, for any court or commentator ever to have enumerated all the varieties."[571]

Monopolists can even run afoul of Section 2 through exclusionary deception. In *Ayerst*, the Second Circuit confirmed that under certain circumstances a business might monopolize through deceptive advertising, but indicated that courts should apply "a presumption that the effect on competition of such a practice was de minimis." The court noted that: "while there is no redeeming virtue in deception, there is a social cost in litigation over it. Thus, because the likelihood of a significant impact upon the opportunities of rivals is so small in most observed instances—and because the prevalence of arguably improper utterance is so great—the courts would be wise to regard misrepresentations as presumptively de minimis for § 2 purposes." The court quoted, with apparent approval, the views of Professors Areeda and Turner that such a presumption could be overcome by a showing that the statements were (1) clearly false, (2) clearly material, (3) clearly likely to induce reasonable reliance, (4) made to buyers without knowledge of the subject matter, (5) continued for prolonged periods, and (6) not readily susceptible of neutralization or other offset by rivals.

In *Ayerst* itself, the plaintiff, Zenith, had alleged that the defendant, Ayerst, had unlawfully monopolized by distributing to customers a false and misleading letter that falsely claimed that the plaintiff's product was inferior to the defendant's. Noting that the Food and Drug Administration ("FDA") had already concluded that the letter in question was false and misleading, and that the plaintiff might be able to prove that the letter could not readily have been neutralized or corrected, the Second Circuit concluded that the plaintiff should be allowed to move ahead to discovery.

Under certain circumstances, too, the misuse of government and regulatory processes, or similar processes like those of private standard-setting organizations ("SSOs"), can constitute monopolization. But—as with refusal-to-deal cases and pricing cases—courts are often particularly reluctant to interfere with recourse to the machinery of government. Indeed, there are some sharp constitutional and other concerns with doing so.[572] For now, it is enough to know that conduct that involves petitioning any branch of the government—including the judiciary, administrative agencies, and so on—is constitutionally protected, and you have to clear a high bar to face antitrust trouble for doing so.

The classic abuse-of-process case is *Walker Process*, in which the defendant was alleged to have obtained a patent by fraud on the Patent Office. The Court confirmed that, at least in principle, monopolization liability was available in such cases. Of course, there are lots of other ways to misuse regulatory and similar processes. These include, for example, "sham litigation" (*i.e.*, litigation filed for the sole purpose of driving up a competitor's costs through the expenses and difficulties of defending the litigation),[573] as well as abuse of private standard-setting organizations (*i.e.*, misusing or abusing quasi-regulatory processes to exclude competitors).[574]

A key consideration in this area is "*Noerr-Pennington* immunity," which provides defendants with robust immunity for most conduct that involves petitioning the government (including the executive, judicial, and legislative branches). We will meet this immunity, and others, in Chapter IX.

Walker Process Equipment Inc v Food Machinery & Chemical Corp.
382 U.S. 172 (1965)

Justice Clark.

---

[571] Conwood Co., L.P. v. U.S. Tobacco Co., 290 F.3d 768 (6th Cir. 2002).

[572] *See infra* § IX.B. (discussing the *Noerr-Pennington* doctrine).

[573] *See, e.g.*, FTC v. AbbVie Inc., 976 F.3d 327, 346 (3d Cir. 2020); Professional Real Estate Investors, Inc. v. Columbia Pictures Industries, Inc., 508 U.S. 49, 60–61 (1993); *see also* California Motor Transp. Co. v. Trucking Unlimited, 404 U.S. 508 (1972).

[574] *See, e.g.*, Allied Tube & Conduit Corp. v. Indian Head, Inc., 486 U.S. 492 (1988); Radiant Burners, Inc. v. Peoples Gas Co., 364 U.S. 656 (1961).

[1] The question before us is whether the maintenance and enforcement of a patent obtained by fraud on the Patent Office may be the basis of an action under s 2 of the Sherman Act,1 and therefore subject to a treble damage claim by an injured party under s 4 of the Clayton Act. The respondent, Food Machinery, & Chemical Corp. (hereafter Food Machinery), filed this suit for infringement of its patent No. 2,328,655 covering knee-action swing diffusers used in aeration equipment for sewage treatment systems. Petitioner, Walker Process Equipment, Inc. (hereafter Walker), denied the infringement and counterclaimed for a declaratory judgment that the patent was invalid. After discovery, Food Machinery moved to dismiss its complaint with prejudice because the patent had expired. Walker then amended its counterclaim to charge that Food Machinery had illegally monopolized interstate and foreign commerce by fraudulently and in bad faith obtaining and maintaining its patent well knowing that it had no basis for a patent. It alleged fraud on the basis that Food Machinery had sworn before the Patent Office that it neither knew nor believed that its invention had been in public use in the United States for more than one year prior to filing its patent application when, in fact, Food Machinery was a party to prior use within such time. The counterclaim further asserted that the existence of the patent had deprived Walker of business that it would have otherwise enjoyed. Walker prayed that Food Machinery's conduct be declared a violation of the antitrust laws and sought recovery of treble damages.

[2] The District Court granted Food Machinery's motion and dismissed its infringement complaint along with Walker's amended counterclaim, without leave to amend and with prejudice. The Court of Appeals for the Seventh Circuit affirmed. We granted certiorari. We have concluded that the enforcement of a patent procured by fraud on the Patent Office may be violative of s 2 of the Sherman Act provided the other elements necessary to a s 2 case are present. In such event the treble damage provisions of s 4 of the Clayton Act would be available to an injured party. [. . .]

[3] Both Walker and the United States, which appears as amicus curiae, argue that if Food Machinery obtained its patent by fraud and thereafter used the patent to exclude Walker from the market through "threats of suit" and prosecution of this infringement suit, such proof would establish a prima facie violation of s 2 of the Sherman Act. On the other hand, Food Machinery says that a patent monopoly and a Sherman Act monopolization cannot be equated; the removal of the protection of a patent grant because of fraudulent procurement does not automatically result in a s 2 offense. Both lower courts seem to have concluded that proof of fraudulent procurement may be used to bar recovery for infringement, . . . but not to establish invalidity. As the Court of Appeals expressed the proposition, only the government may annul or set aside a patent. It went on to state that no case had decided, or hinted that fraud on the Patent Office may be turned to use in an original affirmative action, instead of as an equitable defense. Since Walker admits that its anti-trust theory depends on its ability to prove fraud on the Patent Office, it follows that Walker's second amended counterclaim failed to state a claim upon which relief could be granted. [. . .]

[4] Walker's counterclaim alleged that Food Machinery obtained the patent by knowingly and willfully misrepresenting facts to the Patent Office. Proof of this assertion would be sufficient to strip Food Machinery of its exemption from the antitrust laws. By the same token, Food Machinery's good faith would furnish a complete defense. This includes an honest mistake as to the effect of prior installation upon patentability—so-called 'technical fraud.'

[5] To establish monopolization or attempt to monopolize a part of trade or commerce under s 2 of the Sherman Act, it would then be necessary to appraise the exclusionary power of the illegal patent claim in terms of the relevant market for the product involved. Without a definition of that market there is no way to measure Food Machinery's ability to lessen or destroy competition. It may be that the device—knee-action swing diffusers—used in sewage treatment systems does not comprise a relevant market. There may be effective substitutes for the device which do not infringe the patent. This is a matter of proof, as is the amount of damages suffered by Walker.

[6] As respondent points out, Walker has not clearly articulated its claim. It appears to be based on a concept of per se illegality under s 2 of the Sherman Act. But in these circumstances, the issue is premature. . . . [T]he area of per se illegality is carefully limited. We are reluctant to extend it on the bare pleadings and absent examination of market effect and economic consequences.

[7] However, even though the per se claim fails at this stage of litigation, we believe that the case should be remanded for Walker to clarify the asserted violations of s 2 and to offer proof thereon. The trial court dismissed its suit not because Walker failed to allege the relevant market, the dominance of the patented device therein, and the injurious consequences to Walker of the patent's enforcement, but rather on the ground that the United States alone may "annul or set aside" a patent for fraud in procurement. The trial court has not analyzed any economic data. Indeed, no such proof has yet been offered because of the disposition below. In view of these considerations, as well as the novelty of the claim asserted and the paucity of guidelines available in the decided cases, this deficiency cannot be deemed crucial. Fairness requires that on remand Walker have the opportunity to make its s 2 claims more specific, to prove the alleged fraud, and to establish the necessary elements of the asserted s 2 violation.

Justice Harlan, concurring.

[8] We hold today that a treble-damage action for monopolization which, but for the existence of a patent, would be violative of s 2 of the Sherman Act may be maintained under s 4 of the Clayton Act if two conditions are satisfied: (1) the relevant patent is shown to have been procured by knowing and willful fraud practiced by the defendant on the Patent Office or, if the defendant was not the original patent applicant, he had been enforcing the patent with knowledge of the fraudulent manner in which it was obtained; and (2) all the elements otherwise necessary to establish a s 2 monopolization charge are proved. Conversely, such a private cause of action would not be made out if the plaintiff: (1) showed no more than invalidity of the patent arising, for example, from a judicial finding of 'obviousness,' or from other factors sometimes compendiously referred to as 'technical fraud'; or (2) showed fraudulent procurement, but no knowledge thereof by the defendant; or (3) failed to prove the elements of a s 2 charge even though he has established actual fraud in the procurement of the patent and the defendant's knowledge of that fraud.

[9] It is well also to recognize the rationale underlying this decision, aimed of course at achieving a suitable accommodation in this area between the differing policies of the patent and antitrust laws. To hold, as we do, that private suits may be instituted under s 4 of the Clayton Act to recover damages for Sherman Act monopolization knowingly practiced under the guise of a patent procured by deliberate fraud, cannot well be thought to impinge upon the policy of the patent laws to encourage inventions and their disclosure. Hence, as to this class of improper patent monopolies, antitrust remedies should be allowed room for full play. On the other hand, to hold, as we do not, that private antitrust suits might also reach monopolies practiced under patents that for one reason or another may turn out to be voidable under one or more of the numerous technicalities attending the issuance of a patent, might well chill the disclosure of inventions through the obtaining of a patent because of fear of the vexations or punitive consequences of treble-damage suits. Hence, this private antitrust remedy should not be deemed available to reach s 2 monopolies carried on under a nonfraudulently procured patent.

NOTES

1) When a court considers whether to impose monopolization liability for a particular act, should it matter whether that act also constitutes a tort? What about conduct that constitutes a breach of contract? IP infringement? A crime?
2) Do you think courts and agencies should be particularly skeptical of monopolization claims premised on misrepresentation, compared to other monopolization claims? Why?
3) How, if at all, should monopolization law constrain advertising by a monopolist? Are there any special policy concerns in so doing?
4) Should subjective intent matter more in monopolization-by-tort cases than in other cases?
5) When, if ever, should misleading omissions give rise to antitrust liability? Are there circumstances where supplying a product or service involves an implicit representation about the product's safety, legality, etc.?

E. Attempt and Conspiracy

Section 2 also prohibits attempts and conspiracies to monopolize. Of these, the most important in practice is the attempt offense, as—among other things—conspiracies to monopolize tend to fall within the ambit of Section 1.[575] The leading case on attempt is *Spectrum Sports*.

Spectrum Sports, Inc. v. McQuillan
506 U.S. 447 (1993)

Justice White.

[1] While § 1 of the Sherman Act forbids contracts or conspiracies in restraint of trade or commerce, § 2 addresses the actions of single firms that monopolize or attempt to monopolize, as well as conspiracies and combinations to monopolize. Section 2 does not define the elements of the offense of attempted monopolization. Nor is there much guidance to be had in the scant legislative history of that provision, which was added late in the legislative process. The legislative history does indicate that much of the interpretation of the necessarily broad principles of the Act was to be left for the courts in particular cases.

[2] This Court first addressed the meaning of attempt to monopolize under § 2 in *Swift & Co. v. United States*, 196 U.S. 375 (1905). The Court's opinion, written by Justice Holmes, contained the following passage:

> Where acts are not sufficient in themselves to produce a result which the law seeks to prevent— for instance, the monopoly—but require further acts in addition to the mere forces of nature to bring that result to pass, an intent to bring it to pass is necessary in order to produce a dangerous probability that it will happen. But when that intent and the consequent dangerous probability exist, this statute, like many others and like the common law in some cases, directs itself against that dangerous probability as well as against the completed result.

[3] The Court went on to explain, however, that not every act done with intent to produce an unlawful result constitutes an attempt. It is a question of proximity and degree. *Swift* thus indicated that intent is necessary, but alone is not sufficient, to establish the dangerous probability of success that is the object of § 2's prohibition of attempts.

[4] The Court's decisions since *Swift* have reflected the view that the plaintiff charging attempted monopolization must prove a dangerous probability of actual monopolization, which has generally required a definition of the relevant market and examination of market power. In *Walker Process Equipment, Inc. v. Food Machinery & Chemical Corp.*, 382 U.S. 172, 177 (1965), we found that enforcement of a fraudulently obtained patent claim could violate the Sherman Act. We stated that, to establish monopolization or attempt to monopolize under § 2 of the Sherman Act, it would be necessary to appraise the exclusionary power of the illegal patent claim in terms of the relevant market for the product involved. The reason was that without a definition of that market there is no way to measure the defendant's ability to lessen or destroy competition.

[5] Similarly, this Court reaffirmed in *Copperweld Corp. v. Independence Tube Corp.*, 467 U.S. 752 (1984), that Congress authorized Sherman Act scrutiny of single firms only when they pose a danger of monopolization. Judging unilateral conduct in this manner reduces the risk that the antitrust laws will dampen the competitive zeal of a single aggressive entrepreneur. Thus, the conduct of a single firm, governed by § 2, is unlawful only when it threatens actual monopolization.

[6] The Courts of Appeals other than the Ninth Circuit have followed this approach. Consistent with our cases, it is generally required that to demonstrate attempted monopolization a plaintiff must prove (1) that the defendant has engaged in predatory or anticompetitive conduct with (2) a specific intent to monopolize and (3) a dangerous probability of achieving monopoly power. In order to determine whether there is a dangerous probability of

---

[575] *See, e.g.*, NYNEX Corp. v. Discon, Inc., 525 U.S. 128, 132 (1998) (overlapping Section 1 and conspiracy-to-monopolize theories).

monopolization, courts have found it necessary to consider the relevant market and the defendant's ability to lessen or destroy competition in that market.

[7] [T]he Court of Appeals in this case reaffirmed its prior holdings {*Eds.: those earlier holdings took a more expansive view of liability, based on the Ninth Circuit's earlier opinion in* Lessig v. Tidewater Oil Co., *327 F.2d 459 (9th Cir. 1964)*}; indeed, it did not mention either this Court's decisions discussed above or the many decisions of other Courts of Appeals reaching contrary results. Respondents urge us to affirm the decision below. We are not at all inclined, however, to embrace [a more expansive] interpretation of § 2, for there is little, if any, support for it in the statute or the case law, and the notion that proof of unfair or predatory conduct alone is sufficient to make out the offense of attempted monopolization is contrary to the purpose and policy of the Sherman Act. [. . .]

[8] In support of its determination that an inference of dangerous probability was permissible from a showing of intent, the *Lessig* opinion cited, and added emphasis to, this Court's reference in its opinion in *Swift* to "intent and the consequent dangerous probability." But any question whether dangerous probability of success requires proof of more than intent alone should have been removed by the subsequent passage in *Swift* which stated that "not every act that may be done with intent to produce an unlawful result constitutes an attempt. It is a question of proximity and degree."[. . .]

[9] It is also our view that *Lessig* and later Ninth Circuit decisions refining and applying it are inconsistent with the policy of the Sherman Act. The purpose of the Act is not to protect businesses from the working of the market; it is to protect the public from the failure of the market. The law directs itself not against conduct which is competitive, even severely so, but against conduct which unfairly tends to destroy competition itself. It does so not out of solicitude for private concerns but out of concern for the public interest. Thus, this Court and other courts have been careful to avoid constructions of § 2 which might chill competition, rather than foster it. It is sometimes difficult to distinguish robust competition from conduct with long-term anticompetitive effects; moreover, single-firm activity is unlike concerted activity covered by § 1, which inherently is fraught with anticompetitive risk. For these reasons, § 2 makes the conduct of a single firm unlawful only when it actually monopolizes or dangerously threatens to do so. The concern that § 2 might be applied so as to further anticompetitive ends is plainly not met by inquiring only whether the defendant has engaged in "unfair" or "predatory" tactics. Such conduct may be sufficient to prove the necessary intent to monopolize, which is something more than an intent to compete vigorously, but demonstrating the dangerous probability of monopolization in an attempt case also requires inquiry into the relevant product and geographic market and the defendant's economic power in that market. [. . .]

[10] We hold that petitioners may not be liable for attempted monopolization under § 2 of the Sherman Act absent proof of a dangerous probability that they would monopolize a particular market and specific intent to monopolize. In this case, the trial instructions allowed the jury to infer specific intent and dangerous probability of success from the defendants' predatory conduct, without any proof of the relevant market or of a realistic probability that the defendants could achieve monopoly power in that market. In this respect, the instructions misconstrued § 2, as did the Court of Appeals in affirming the judgment of the District Court. Since the affirmance of the § 2 judgment against petitioners rested solely on the legally erroneous conclusion that petitioners had attempted to monopolize in violation of § 2 and since the jury's verdict did not negate the possibility that the § 2 verdict rested on the attempt to monopolize ground alone, the judgment of the Court of Appeals is reversed, and the case is remanded for further proceedings consistent with this opinion.

NOTES

1) How would you characterize the purpose of the attempted-monopolization offense?
2) What should *Spectrum Sports'* "dangerous probability" standard mean in percentage terms? Why?
3) Why do we need a conspiracy-to-monopolize offense, given the existence of Section 1? What conspiracy to monopolize would not also be an anticompetitive restraint of trade?
4) Under what circumstances, if any, should a monopolist be held liable for attempted monopolization if—with the sole purpose and intention of defending and increasing its monopoly—it:
   a. actually acquires a startup that the monopolist wrongly believes is a serious threat to its monopoly?

    b. unsuccessfully invites a key supplier to enter into an exclusive contract that would lock out the monopolist's competitors?

    c. destroys a wax model of its only competitor's sole factory in the earnest (but false) belief that this will destroy the factory? or

    d. acquires (or raises the costs of) a rival under circumstances where it is plausible, but not likely, that the effect may have been to augment monopoly power?

5) Does—or should—Section 2 prohibit an attempt (or invitation) to conspire to monopolize? What would that look like?

6) Why should specific intent to monopolize be a requirement for attempts to monopolize but not for monopolization itself? Can you think of cases involving anticompetitive conduct where a plaintiff would not be able to show the required specific intent?

F. Some Further Reading

Phillip Areeda, *Essential Facilities: An Epithet in Need of Limiting Principles*, 58 Antitrust L.J. 841 (1990)

Michael Carrier & Rebecca Tushnet, *An Antitrust Framework for False Advertising*, 106 Iowa L. Rev. 1841 (2021).

Einer Elhauge, *Defining Better Monopolization Standards*, 56 Stan. L. Rev. 253 (2003)

Eleanor M. Fox, *Is There Life In* Aspen *After* Trinko?, 73 Antitrust L.J. 153 (2005)

Daniel A. Crane, *Criminal Enforcement of Section 2 of the Sherman Act*, 84 Antitrust L.J. 753 (2022)

Daniel Francis, *Making Sense of Monopolization*, 84 Antitrust L.J. 779 (2022)

Erik Hovenkamp, *The Antitrust Duty to Deal in the Age of Big Tech*, 131 Yale L.J. 1483 (2022)

Herbert Hovenkamp, *Exclusion and the Sherman Act*, 72 U. Chi. L. Rev. 147 (2005)

Thomas G. Krattenmaker & Steven C. Salop, *Anticompetitive Exclusion: Raising Rivals' Costs to Achieve Power over Price*, 96 Yale L.J. 209 (1986)

Thomas A. Lambert, *Defining Unreasonably Exclusionary Conduct: The "Exclusion of a Competitive Rival" Approach*, 92 N.C. L. Rev. 1175 (2014)

Marina Lao, *Reclaiming a Role for Intent Evidence in Monopolization Analysis*, 54 Am. U. L. Rev. 151 (2004)

Marina Lao, *No-Fault Digital Platform Monopolization*, 61 Wm. & Mary L. Rev. 755 (2020)

Douglas Melamed, *Exclusive Dealing Agreements and Other Exclusionary Conduct—Are There Unifying Principles*, 73 Antitrust L.J. 375 (2006)

Mark S. Popofsky, *Defining Exclusionary Conduct: Section 2, The Rule of Reason, and the Unifying Principle Underlying Antitrust Rules*, 73 Antitrust L.J. 435 (2006)

Sandeep Vaheesan, *The Morality of Monopolization Law*, 63 Wm. & Mary L. Rev. Online (2022)

Gregory J. Werden, *Identifying Exclusionary Conduct Under Section 2: The "No Economic Sense" Test*, 73 Antitrust L.J. 413 (2006)

VIII. Mergers and Acquisitions

A. Overview

The third of antitrust's three great pillars—alongside the rule against agreements in restraint of trade and the rule against monopolization—is the prohibition of anticompetitive mergers and acquisitions. The enforcement of this prohibition, often known as "merger control," constitutes a huge part of the day-to-day work of the antitrust agencies (and of many antitrust lawyers!).

The basic legal standard for mergers and acquisitions is found in Section 7 of the Clayton Act, 15 U.S.C. § 18:

> No person engaged in commerce or in any activity affecting commerce shall acquire, directly or indirectly, the whole or any part of the stock or other share capital and no person subject to the jurisdiction of the Federal Trade Commission shall acquire the whole or any part of the assets of another person engaged also in commerce or in any activity affecting commerce, where in any line of commerce or in any activity affecting commerce in any section of the country, the effect of such acquisition may be substantially to lessen competition, or to tend to create a monopoly.

As we saw in Chapter I, the Clayton Act was enacted in 1914 to reinforce the Sherman Act. Section 7 of the Clayton Act was directly aimed at mergers and acquisitions, and it was amended in 1950 to close some loopholes created by the earlier statutory language.[576] And while the Clayton Act is today the primary statute under which merger challenges are litigated, it did not displace the applicability of the Sherman Act to transactions. Thus, an agreement to merge with, or acquire, another firm can constitute a restraint of trade in violation of Section 1 of the Sherman Act, and an anticompetitive acquisition by a monopolist can constitute monopolization in violation of Section 2.[577]

To determine whether a proposed or completed ("consummated" or "closed") merger violates Section 7, courts and agencies start by evaluating the economic relationship between the merging parties (usually just the "parties"). Theories of competitive concern can generally be described as either "horizontal" theories, relating to a relationship of actual or potential competition between the parties, or "vertical" theories, relating to the fact that the parties are actually or potentially active at different levels of the same supply chain, or are suppliers of complements. Some mergers present neither horizontal nor vertical concerns: for example, a shoe manufacturer merging with a supplier of fruit. Those mergers—which are sometimes known as "conglomerate" deals—usually do not raise competitive concerns, although they might be concerning for other reasons.[578] And some mergers

---

[576] The Celler-Kefauver Amendments of 1950 clarified, among other things, that Section 7 is not only focused on competition "between" the parties (and thus can address vertical concerns), and that it applies to asset transactions, rather than only stock transactions. (Can you see why the "asset loophole" was a serious problem?) For some history and context, *see, e.g.*, M.A. Adelman, *The Antimerger Act, 1950–60*, 51 Am. Econ. Rev. 236, 236 (1961); Milton Handler & Stanley D. Robinson, *A Decade of Administration of the Celler-Kefauver Antimerger Act*, 61 Colum. L. Rev. 629 (1961); Note, *Section 7 of the Clayton Act: A Legislative History*, 52 Colum. L. Rev. 766 (1952).

[577] *See, e.g.*, United States v. Grinnell Corp., 384 U.S. 563 (1966) (analyzing acquisitions under Section 2); Complaint, United States v. Booz Allen Hamilton Holding Corp., Case No. 1:22-cv-01603 (D. Md. filed June 29, 2022) (challenging proposed merger as a violation of Section 7 and the merger agreement as a violation of Section 1).

[578] Some scholars have pointed out that such transactions may raise concerns on other grounds: for example, by making a company so large that it acquires great political influence, or by threatening national security when it would place key industries under the control of non-U.S. actors. But in the modern era courts and antitrust agencies have generally not regarded these concerns as a matter for antitrust analysis, with some very specific exceptions. For a cross-section of discussion from various periods in this transition, *see, e.g.*, OECD, Note by the United States, *Conglomerate Effects of Mergers*, DAF/COMP/WD(2020)7 (June 2020); Thomas B. Leary, *Antitrust Scrutiny of a Pure Conglomerate Merger: The* Ovation *Case*, ANTITRUST (Summer 2009) 74; Eleanor M. Fox, *GE/Honeywell: The U.S. Merger that Europe Stopped—A Story of the Politics of Convergence* in Eleanor M. Fox & Daniel A. Crane (eds.), ANTITRUST STORIES (2007); Deputy Asst. Att'y Gen. William J. Kolasky, U.S. Dept. of Justice Antitrust Division, *Conglomerate Mergers and Range Effects: It's A Long Way from Chicago to Brussels* (speech of November 9, 2001); Donna E. Patterson & Carl Shapiro, *Transatlantic Divergence in* GE/Honeywell: *Causes and Lessons*, ANTITRUST (Fall 2001) 18; Michael Pertshuk & Kenneth M. Davidson, *What's Wrong With Conglomerate Mergers?* 48 Fordham L. Rev. 1 (1979); Joseph P. Bauer, *Challenging Conglomerate Mergers Under Section 7 of the Clayton Act: Today 's Law and Tomorrow's Legislation*, 68 B.U.L. Rev. 199 (1978); Donald F. Turner, *Conglomerate Mergers and Section 7 of the Clayton Act*, 78 Harv. L. Rev. 1313 (1965). *See also* Robert H. Lande & Sandeep Vaheesan, *Preventing the Curse of Bigness Through*

present both horizontal *and* vertical concerns: for example, if the parties are active at different levels of the chain but one is also a potential entrant into the other's market.

Horizontal merger analysis is usually motivated by either, or both, of two basic concerns. The first concern is that the loss of head-to-head competition between the parties will, by creating or increasing market power, allow the merged firm to unilaterally increase its own prices, or to inflict some equivalent form of harm such as reduced quality, generating so-called "unilateral anticompetitive effects." (The effects are "unilateral" in that the merged firm will have the ability and incentive to inflict harm without having to anticipate the behavior of, or coordinate with, other market participants.) The second concern is that by changing the structure of the market, and particularly by increasing its concentration (*i.e.*, leaving a smaller number of competitively significant firms controlling more of the market), the merger may encourage or facilitate tacit (or even explicit) collusion among the remaining participants, generating so-called "coordinated anticompetitive effects." The concepts of concentration and tacit collusion are described in more detail in Chapter II.

Vertical mergers can raise competitive concerns too. The primary concern here is usually "foreclosure": the prospect that the merged firm might have the ability and incentive to limit rivals' access to important inputs, distribution, or complements in ways that would harm competition overall. Another concern is that a vertical merger might give the merged firm access to confidential information about its competitors (such as capacity constraints or input costs) that could lead to a reduction in the intensity of competition by diminishing rivals' incentives to compete. A third concern is that a vertical merger could increase the likelihood of coordination between the participants in a market (just as in a horizontal case). A vertical merger could do this, for example, by increasing market participants' symmetry—that is, the extent to which their incentives are similar—or by changing the incentives of a business that has previously been a particularly vigorous and disruptive competitor. A merger involving sellers of complements may also create the ability and incentive to foreclose rivals through bundling or tying, though this theme is not prominent in modern enforcement practice.

As a class, horizontal mergers are more likely to raise competitive concerns than are vertical deals, for two main reasons. The first is that there is by definition at least some competition between the parties before a horizontal deal, which the merger eliminates by putting both parties under common ownership. The second is that vertical transactions, unlike horizontal ones, often bring benefits, including reductions in the transaction costs of dealing between downstream and upstream divisions (because it is typically less costly to coordinate within a firm than between firms) that can lead to lower prices. Some of these are cost savings that we associate broadly with "the theory of the firm."[579] In addition, a vertical merger may generate beneficial incentive effects that arise from the imperative to maximize profits across the integrated company rather than at each stage of the process individually.[580] However, this can be overstated. Not all horizontal mergers are harmful, and not all vertical mergers are benign. There is some controversy today over whether agencies and scholars have historically been too quick to assume that vertical transactions are beneficial overall, and that those benefits are shared with consumers. The empirical evidence is limited and ambiguous.[581]

Horizontal mergers have often been litigated—including by the federal agencies, by State AGs, and by private plaintiffs—and as a result there is a healthy jurisprudence of merger law that fleshes out the circumstances under which a merger will be unlawful. But these are overwhelmingly lower-court decisions: the Supreme Court has not rendered a substantive merger decision since 1975.[582] Vertical mergers, by contrast, have been litigated less often in the modern era. Below, we will explore some of the reasons for this disparity, and some of the resulting criticisms.

Conglomerate Merger Legislation, 52 Ariz. St. L. J. 75 (2020). Other legal processes, like CFIUS review, regulate mergers on non-competition grounds. *See generally* Chapter I (discussing visions of the goals of antitrust).

[579] R.H. Coase, *The Nature of the Firm*, 4 Economica 386 (1937).

[580] *See infra* § VIII.D.2 (discussing the elimination of double marginalization).

[581] *See, e.g.*, Marissa Beck & Fiona Scott Morton, *Evaluating the Evidence on Vertical Mergers*, 59 Rev. Indus. Org. 273 (2021); James C. Cooper, Luke M. Froeb, Dan O'Brien, & Michael G. Vita, *Vertical Antitrust Policy as a Problem of Inference*, 23 Int'l J. Indus. Org. 639 (2005); Francine Lafontaine & Margaret Slade, *Vertical Integration and Firm Boundaries: The Evidence*, 45 J. Econ. Lit. 629 (2007); Timothy Bresnahan and Jonathan Levin, *Vertical Integration and Market Structure* in Robert Gibbons & John Roberts (eds.) THE HANDBOOK OF ORGANIZATIONAL ECONOMICS (2013); Paul L. Joskow, *Vertical Integration*, in Claude Ménard & Mary M. Shirley (eds.), HANDBOOK OF NEW INSTITUTIONAL ECONOMICS (2008).

[582] *See* United States v. Citizens and Southern Nat'l Bank, 422 U.S. 86 (1975).

Most litigated merger cases focus on effects on competition among sellers. But, at least in principle, merger law equally protects competition among purchasers, including purchasers of labor.[583] Thus, a merger that has the effect of reducing competition among purchasers of products or services—*i.e.*, a merger that tends to create a *monopsony*—can be unlawful, even in the absence of sell-side effects.[584] In 2022, the Department of Justice successfully challenged a high-profile proposed merger between publishers Penguin Random House and Simon & Schuster on just such a theory.[585]

*

Merger control is an unusual component of antitrust in several ways. First, in practice, most sizeable mergers are usually analyzed *ex ante*—that is, before the merger is consummated—thanks to the Hart-Scott-Rodino ("HSR") Act, which requires prior notification of many proposed mergers and acquisitions to the agencies before closing, so that the agencies have an opportunity to analyze the transaction, and challenge it if appropriate. Thus, whereas most Sherman Act challenges to anticompetitive conduct typically involve challenges to past or ongoing actions by a defendant, and usually require a court to decide whether those actions do or did in fact harm competition, merger challenges most commonly require a court to *predict* whether a proposed merger or acquisition will harm competition if it goes ahead. Merger cases can involve sharp clashes of view between opposing economic or industry experts with different predictions of how the transaction will affect competition, or between economic expert evidence and lay testimony and documents. Different courts will form different views about the best guide to the relevant "commercial realities."[586] The *ex ante* footing of much merger review and merger litigation often means a heavy emphasis on certain kinds of evidence: predictive tools (such as economic modeling), the internal documents of merging parties, and the expectations of customers, suppliers, and competitors.

This prospective focus reveals a difficult puzzle in Section 7 law: what exactly Congress meant when it prohibited transactions of which the effect "may be" substantially to lessen competition, or to tend to create a monopoly. The Court emphasized in *Brown Shoe* that Congress chose the phrase "*may be*" in order to capture incipient harms to competition, and that "probability" of harm was the correct threshold.[587] Some modern courts and the HMGs have focused on whether harm is "probable," while other courts have used language suggesting a lower threshold.[588] Courts have directly expressed frustration with the lack of clarity around the meaning of the "may

---

[583] *See, e.g.*, C. Scott Hemphill & Nancy L. Rose, *Mergers that Harm Sellers*, 127 Yale L.J. 2078 (2018).

[584] *See, e.g.*, United States v. Pennzoil Co., 252 F. Supp. 962, 985 (W.D. Pa. 1965) ("[T]he merger of Pennzoil and Kendall will substantially lessen competition in the purchase of Penn Grade crude in the Penn Grade crude producing area."). *See also, e.g.*, Statement of the FTC Chairman Regarding Announcement that Aveanna Healthcare and Maxim Healthcare Services Have Terminated Their Acquisition Agreement (Jan. 30, 2020) (noting that both patients *and nurses* would continue to benefit from competition following the abandonment of the proposed transaction).

[585] Complaint, United States v. Bertelsmann SE & Co., Case No. 1:21-cv-02886 (D.D.C. filed Nov. 2, 2021).

[586] *See, e.g.*, FTC v. Thomas Jefferson Univ., 505 F. Supp. 3d 522, 553 (E.D. Pa. 2020) ("[T]he Government relies on econometrics and insurer testimony to prove the propriety of its proposed Philadelphia Area market. But it has not shown that the market corresponds with commercial realities and it thus cannot pass the HMT."); United States v. AT&T Inc., 310 F. Supp. 3d 161, 222 (D.D.C. 2018) ("[The] opinion by Professor Shapiro runs contrary to all of the real-world testimony during the trial from those who have actually negotiated on behalf of vertically integrated companies."); FTC v. Swedish Match, 131 F. Supp. 2d 151, 161–62 (D.D.C. 2000) (rejecting economic expert evidence provided by both plaintiff and defendants, and relying instead on lay testimony and documents for market definition analysis).

[587] Brown Shoe Co. v. United States, 370 U.S. 294, 317–18 (1962) ("[A] keystone in the erection of a barrier to what Congress saw was the rising tide of economic concentration, was its provision of authority for arresting mergers at a time when the trend to a lessening of competition in a line of commerce was still in its incipiency. Congress saw the process of concentration in American business as a dynamic force; it sought to assure the Federal Trade Commission and the courts the power to brake this force at its outset and before it gathered momentum."); *id.* at 323 & n.39 (indicating that "Congress used the words 'may be substantially to lessen competition' (emphasis supplied), to indicate that its concern was with probabilities, not certainties . . . Mergers with a probable anticompetitive effect were to be proscribed by this Act," and quoting a Senate Report indicating that the language "may be" "would not apply to the mere possibility but only to the reasonable probability of the [proscribed] effect"). *See also* Doha Mekki, *Remarks at Mercatus Center Second Annual Antitrust Forum* (Jan. 26, 2023) ("Congress prohibited any merger whose effect 'may be'—and those words, 'may be,' are critical—substantially to lessen competition. Does that mean we prohibit more mergers than we would need to if we had a crystal ball that perfectly predicted the future? Of course. There is nothing radical about that approach. That was Congress's design.").

[588] *See, e.g.*, HMGs § 1 ("Most merger analysis is necessarily predictive, requiring an assessment of what will likely happen if a merger proceeds as compared to what will likely happen if it does not."); United States v. AT&T, Inc., 916 F.3d 1029, 1038 (D.C. Cir. 2019) (noting the government's burden "of showing that the proposed merger *is likely* to increase [the merged firm's] bargaining leverage"); United States v. Baker Hughes Inc., 908 F.2d 981, 984 (D.C. Cir. 1990) ("Section 7 involves probabilities, not certainties or

be" standard, and its interaction with the plaintiff's obligation to prove liability on a preponderance of the evidence.[589] Adding to the puzzle, the independent meaning of the phrase "tend to create a monopoly" remains very far from clear.[590] At least in principle—and setting aside the question of whether the "tend to create a monopoly" language might create room for new law—some courts seem to understand Section 7 to provide that a merger that is 51% likely to cause a "substantial"[591] lessening of competition is (absent defenses) unlawful, while a merger that is 49% likely to cause a much greater harm to competition is not unlawful.[592] As we shall see below, this approach has been criticized.

Despite the focus on prediction during an HSR review, Section 7 is equally applicable to consummated deals. Thus, an agency or a private plaintiff can sue to unwind—that is, break up—a deal that has already closed, even if that transaction was notified to the agencies pursuant to HSR.[593] (There is some controversy over whether and when such *ex post* challenges represent wise policy: we will talk about this when we examine the HSR process in Chapter XI.)

A second distinctive feature of merger control law is the central role of agency guidelines, which are not binding law but which have considerable practical influence. While agency guidelines are occasionally a focus of attention in conduct cases,[594] they are virtually always front and center in merger analysis. In particular, the Horizontal Merger Guidelines ("HMGs") (first issued in 1968 and revised in 1982, 1984, 1992, 1997, and 2010) play a central role in modern merger practice: including in the agencies' own evaluation of whether to challenge a proposed transaction, and in the courts' adjudication of merger cases, where the Guidelines are often cited as persuasive

---

possibilities."); Hospital Corp. of America v. FTC, 807 F.2d 1381 (7th Cir. 1986) ("Section 7 does not require proof that a merger or other acquisition has caused higher prices in the affected market. All that is necessary is that the merger create an appreciable danger of such consequences in the future"); Yamaha Motor Co., Ltd. v. FTC, 657 F.2d 971, 977 (8th Cir. 1981) ("[W]ould Yamaha, absent the joint venture, probably have entered the U.S. outboard-motor market independently, and would this new entry probably have increased competition more than the joint venture did? We stress the word 'probably' in this formulation of the issue, because the question under Section 7 is not whether competition was actually lessened, but whether it 'may be' lessened substantially."); United States v. H&R Block, Inc., 833 F.Supp.2d 36 (D.D.C. 2011) (quoting authorities stating that a plaintiff must show a merger is "reasonably likely to cause anticompetitive effects," that this is a matter of "probabilities, not certainties," and that an "appreciable danger" of effects suffices); FTC v. Steris Corp., 133 F.Supp.3d 962, 966 (N.D. Ohio 2015) ("The FTC asserts that the acquisition of an actual potential competitor violates Section 7 if (1) the relevant market is highly concentrated, (2) the competitor "probably" would have entered the market, (3) its entry would have had pro-competitive effects, and (4) there are few other firms that can enter effectively. . . . [T]he Court directed counsel to focus their attention at the hearing on the second prong of the actual potential entrant doctrine, i.e., whether, absent the acquisition, the evidence shows that Synergy probably would have entered the U.S. contract sterilization market by building one or more x-ray facilities within a reasonable period of time."). Daniel A. Crane, *Antitrust Antitextualism*, 96 Notre Dame L. Rev. 1205, 1242–55 (2021); Richard M. Steuer, *Incipiency*, 31 Loyola Consumer L. Rev. 155 (2019).

[589] *See, e.g.*, United States v. Bertelsmann SE & Co. KGaA, Case No. CV-21-2886, 2022 WL 16748157, at *10 n.15 (D.D.C. Nov. 7, 2022) ("In *United States v. AT&T, Inc.*, the D.C. Circuit described the Section 7 standard of proof as follows: The government must show that the proposed merger is likely to substantially lessen competition, which encompasses a concept of reasonable probability. The parties dispute the meaning of this language. The defendants argue that *AT&T* requires the government to prove that a merger is likely to cause substantial harm to competition, not only that harm may occur. The government points to *AT&T*'s explanation that this standard encompasses a concept of reasonable probability, arguing that *AT&T* requires something less than what the defendants propose [and specifically an "appreciable danger" standard]. The root of these competing formulations may be uncertainty over how the government's preponderance-of-the-evidence burden interacts with Section 7's already probabilistic standard; combined, the two standards require the government to prove by a preponderance of the evidence that the effect of a challenged merger or acquisition may be substantially to lessen competition. Like the district court in *AT&T*, this Court need not further toil over discerning or articulating the daylight, if any, between 'appreciable danger,' 'probable,' 'reasonably probable,' and 'likely' as used in the Section 7 context. The selection of any of the competing permutations is not outcome-determinative in this case.") (cleaned up).

[590] *See, e.g.*, Jonathan Kanter, Asst. Att'y Gen., U.S. Dept. of Justice Antitrust Division, *Remarks to the New York State Bar Association Antitrust Section* (Jan. 24, 2022) ("The second prong [of Section 7]—["]or tend to create a monopoly["]—has often been given less emphasis. No longer: we intend to remain faithful to the plain language of the Clayton Act."); Rebecca Kelly Slaughter, *Storming the Concentration Castle: Antitrust Lessons from* The Princess Bride (remarks of Mar. 31, 2022).

[591] Brown Shoe Co. v. United States, 370 U.S. 294, 321 (1962) (noting that Congress provided "no definite quantitative or qualitative tests by which enforcement agencies could gauge the effects of a given merger to determine whether it may 'substantially' lessen competition or tend toward monopoly").

[592] *See, e.g.*, FTC v. Steris Corp., 133 F. Supp. 3d 962, 966 (N.D. Ohio 2015).

[593] 18 U.S.C. § 18a(i)(1) (HSR does not bar subsequent action); FTC v. Facebook, Inc., 581 F. Supp. 3d 34, 57 (D.D.C. 2022).

[594] However, such guidelines do exist. *See, e.g.*, U.S. Dept. of Justice & FTC, ANTITRUST GUIDELINES FOR THE LICENSING OF INTELLECTUAL PROPERTY (January 2017); U.S. Dept. of Justice Antitrust Division & FTC, ANTITRUST GUIDANCE FOR HUMAN RESOURCE PROFESSIONALS (October 2016); U.S. Dept. of Justice & FTC, ANTITRUST GUIDELINES FOR COLLABORATIONS AMONG COMPETITORS (April 2000).

authority by litigants and courts.[595] The HMGs have been criticized on various grounds, including by those who think that they are too aggressive and those who think they are too lax.[596] Vertical Merger Guidelines were issued in 2020, along with a Vertical Merger Commentary, replacing Section 4 of the 1984 Merger Guidelines which addressed vertical theories. The FTC (but not DOJ) withdrew from these in 2021.[597]

This chapter is intended to introduce some of the central issues, and a sprinkling of the key cases, in merger analysis. It will necessarily be a brief overview: merger control is a vast topic. We will proceed as follows. In Section B we will look at some central themes in horizontal merger analysis, including the role of the HMGs and the main theories of competitive harm. In Section C we will venture into the realm of vertical mergers, examining the main theories of harm and some core economic principles. In Section D we will consider some important defenses specific to merger cases, including the role of efficiencies as well as the so-called "failing firm" defense. (We will meet some more defenses and immunities that may apply to mergers in Chapter IX.) In Section E we will briefly meet merger remedies.

NOTES

1) Businesses undertake mergers and acquisitions for many different reasons. How many can you think of?

2) Sometimes mergers and acquisitions—or, conversely divestitures or "sell-offs"—are a centerpiece of a change in corporate strategy. Can you identify examples from your everyday experience?

3) In light of what you already know about Sections 1 and 2, was the Clayton Act's separate merger-control provision really necessary? Could Sections 1 and 2 have done an adequate job of policing transactions?

4) Should we have a "conduct review" process for proposed business conduct under Sections 1 and 2?

B. Horizontal Mergers

Horizontal mergers—that is, mergers between, or acquisitions of, actual or potential competitors[598]—have been a core concern of antitrust law for a long time. Indeed, some of the earliest antitrust cases dealt with what we would now call corporate concentrations: a term that embraces mergers (unions between two entities) and acquisitions (the purchasing of one "target" entity by a "parent" entity), as well as certain kinds of joint ventures.[599] In this section we will examine the basic framework through which courts approach the assessment of horizontal mergers.

1. The Merger Guidelines and the Structural Presumption

Merger law, just like the rest of antitrust law, is elaborated and developed through judicial interpretation of Congressional statutes. But because many of the most significant merger challenges are brought not by private plaintiffs but by government enforcers, and particularly the federal agencies,[600] the analytical approach taken by the expert agency staff is immensely influential in practice. And the agencies explain their analytical approach,

---

[595] *See generally* Daniel Francis, *Revisiting The Merger Guidelines: Protecting An Enforcement Asset*, Comp. Pol'y Int'l (Nov. 2022).

[596] For two very different collections of recent comments on the merger guidelines, *see generally*, *e.g.*, Joseph Farrell & Carl Shapiro, *The 2010 Horizontal Merger Guidelines After 10 Years*, 58 Rev. Indus. Org. 1 (2021) (introducing special issue of the Review of Industrial Organization dedicated to the 2010 HMGs); All Comments, *Request for Information on Merger Enforcement*, Regulations.Gov, https://www.regulations.gov/docket/FTC-2022-0003/comments.

[597] *See, e.g.*, FTC, Press Release, [FTC] Withdraws Vertical Merger Guidelines and Commentary (Sept. 15, 2021).

[598] For a refresher on the concept of "potential competition," *see* Chapter II. Some joint ventures—that is, cooperative projects between entities—may also involve mergers or acquisitions. U.S. Dept. of Justice & FTC, ANTITRUST GUIDELINES FOR COLLABORATIONS AMONG COMPETITORS (April 2000) 5 ("The Agencies treat a competitor collaboration as a horizontal merger in a relevant market and analyze the collaboration pursuant to the Horizontal Merger Guidelines if appropriate, which ordinarily is when: (a) the participants are competitors in that relevant market; (b) the formation of the collaboration involves an efficiency-enhancing integration of economic activity in the relevant market; (c) the integration eliminates all competition among the participants in the relevant market; and (d) the collaboration does not terminate within a sufficiently limited period by its own specific and express terms.").

[599] For some early cases, *see, e.g.*, N. Sec. Co. v. United States, 193 U.S. 197 (1904); United States v. Am. Tobacco Co., 221 U.S. 106 (1911); United States v. E.I. Du Pont De Nemours & Co., 188 F. 127, 129 (C.C.D. Del. 1911); United States v. Union Pac. R. Co., 226 U.S. 61 (1912); United States v. U.S. Steel Corp., 251 U.S. 417 (1920).

[600] *But see* Kevin Hahm, Ryan Phair, Carter Simpson & Jack Martin, *Recent Private Merger Challenges: Anomaly or Harbinger?* 35 ANTITRUST 90 (Summer 2021) (emphasizing importance of private merger litigation).

which is informed by the underlying law, in public Merger Guidelines. The Horizontal Merger Guidelines are used routinely by agency staff and private attorneys to guide their analytical work, and are often cited by courts as persuasive authority.[601] (Recent proposals to revise the merger guidelines have raised some sharp questions about the extent to which the guidelines should attempt to guide the development of the law, reflect its current state, and/or merely state agency analytical practices.[602])

In broad terms, the HMGs imply a "roadmap" of key questions for a merger case: (1) threshold classification of whether the merger is horizontal, vertical, or otherwise; (2) definition of one or more relevant markets; (3) calculation of market shares and market concentration in the relevant market(s); (4) analysis of unilateral and/or coordinated anticompetitive effects; (5) analysis of countervailing power that might operate to discipline any anticompetitive effects; (6) analysis of whether new entry into the market, or expansion by existing competitors, may provide additional competitive pressure that could discipline the merged firm and prevent competitive harm; (7) determination of whether the merger would result in procompetitive efficiencies that may eliminate concerns; and finally (8) the assessment of defenses, including but not limited to the so-called "failing firm" defense. This is not a rigid framework, and not every step is necessary in every case. But it is a good outline of the key issues on which, in practice, agencies focus when analyzing a merger, and on which courts focus when adjudicating a merger case.

In practice, the starting point in the determination of whether a horizontal merger will violate Section 7 is the application of the so-called "structural presumption," after a market has been defined. This is the principle that mergers that significantly increase market concentration—the extent to which that market is dominated by a few large firms—may be presumed to be anticompetitive, such that the burden of proof shifts to the defendant to rebut the *prima facie* case that the structural change establishes. (For a refresher on the concept of market "concentration," look back at Chapter II.)

The structural presumption is grounded in a landmark Supreme Court merger case: *Philadelphia National Bank* (colloquially just "*PNB*"), in which the Court endorsed the inference of competitive harm from an increase in concentration.

United States v. Philadelphia Nat. Bank
374 U.S. 321 (1963)

Justice Brennan.

[1] The Philadelphia National Bank and Girard Trust Corn Exchange Bank are, respectively, the second and third largest of the 42 commercial banks with head offices in the Philadelphia metropolitan area, which consists of the City of Philadelphia and its three contiguous counties in Pennsylvania. The home county of both banks is the city itself; Pennsylvania law, however, permits branching into the counties contiguous to the home county, and both banks have offices throughout the four-county area. PNB, a national bank, has assets of over $1,000,000,000, making it (as of 1959) the twenty-first largest bank in the Nation. Girard a state bank is a member of the FRS and is insured by the FDIC; it has assets of about $750,000,000. Were the proposed merger to be consummated, the resulting bank would be the largest in the four-county area, with (approximately) 36% of the area banks' total assets, 36% of deposits, and 34% of net loans. It and the second largest (First Pennsylvania Bank and Trust Company, now the largest) would have between them 59% of the total assets, 58% of deposits, and 58% of the

---

[601] For a great historical overview, *see* Hillary Greene, *Guideline Institutionalization: The Role of Merger Guidelines in Antitrust Discourse*, 48 Wm. & Mary L. Rev. 771 (2006). *See also, e.g.*, FTC v. Hackensack Meridian Health, Inc., 30 F.4th 160, 167 (3d Cir. 2022) ("We begin our analysis with the Merger Guidelines."); Steves & Sons, Inc. v. JELD-WEN, Inc., 988 F.3d 690, 704 (4th Cir. 2021) ("While courts aren't bound by the Guidelines, they're a helpful tool, in view of the many years of thoughtful analysis they represent, for analyzing mergers.") (internal quotation marks, citation, and ellipses omitted); FTC v. Sanford Health, 926 F.3d 959, 964 (8th Cir. 2019) (quoting HMGs); United States v. AT&T, Inc., 916 F.3d 1029, 1032 (D.C. Cir. 2019) (citing then-operative vertical merger guidance).

[602] *See, e.g.*, Daniel Francis, *Revisiting the Merger Guidelines: Protecting an Enforcement Asset*, Comp. Pol'y Int'l (Nov. 2022); James Keyte, *New Merger Guidelines: Are the Agencies on a Collision Course with Case Law?* ANTITRUST (Fall 2021) 49; K. Sabeel Rahman & Lina Khan, *Restoring Competition in the U.S. Economy*, in Nell Abernathy, Mike Konczal & Kathryn Milani, UNTAMED: HOW TO CHECK CORPORATE FINANCIAL, AND MONOPOLY POWER (June 2016) 18.

net loans, while after the merger the four largest banks in the area would have 78% of total assets, 77% of deposits, and 78% of net loans.

[2] The present size of both PNB and Girard is in part the result of mergers. Indeed, the trend toward concentration is noticeable in the Philadelphia area generally, in which the number of commercial banks has declined from 108 in 1947 to the present 42. Since 1950, PNB has acquired nine formerly independent banks and Girard six; and these acquisitions have accounted for 59% and 85% of the respective banks' asset growth during the period, 63% and 91% of their deposit growth, and 12% and 37% of their loan growth. During this period, the seven largest banks in the area increased their combined share of the area's total commercial bank resources from about 61% to about 90%.

[3] In November 1960 the boards of directors of the two banks approved a proposed agreement for their consolidation under the PNB charter. . . . Such a consolidation is authorized, subject to the approval of the Comptroller of the Currency, by [12 U.S.C. § 2157.] But under the Bank Merger Act of 1960, [12 U.S.C. § 1828(c)], the Comptroller may not give his approval until he has received reports from the other two banking agencies and the Attorney General respecting the probable effects of the proposed transaction on competition. All three reports advised that the proposed merger would have substantial anticompetitive effects in the Philadelphia metropolitan area. However, on February 24, 1961, the Comptroller approved the merger. . . . [H]e reasoned that "since there will remain an adequate number of alternative sources of banking service in Philadelphia, and in view of the beneficial effects of this consolidation upon international and national competition it was concluded that the over-all effect upon competition would not be unfavorable." He also stated that the consolidated bank "would be far better able to serve the convenience and needs of its community by being of material assistance to its city and state in their efforts to attract new industry and to retain existing industry." The day after the Comptroller approved the merger, the United States commenced the present action. No steps have been taken to consummate the merger pending the outcome of this litigation.

[4] The Government's case in the District Court relied chiefly on statistical evidence bearing upon market structure and on testimony by economists and bankers to the effect that, notwithstanding the intensive governmental regulation of banking, there was a substantial area for the free play of competitive forces; that concentration of commercial banking, which the proposed merger would increase, was inimical to that free play; that the principal anticompetitive effect of the merger would be felt in the area in which the banks had their offices, thus making the four-county metropolitan area the relevant geographical market; and that commercial banking was the relevant product market. The defendants, in addition to offering contrary evidence on these points, attempted to show business justifications for the merger. They conceded that both banks were economically strong and had sound management, but offered the testimony of bankers to show that the resulting bank, with its greater prestige and increased lending limit, would be better able to compete with large out-of-state (particularly New York) banks, would attract new business to Philadelphia, and in general would promote the economic development of the metropolitan area.[10]

[5] Upon this record, the District Court held that: . . . even assuming that s 7 is applicable and that the four-county area is the relevant market, there is no reasonable probability that competition among commercial banks in the area will be substantially lessened as the result of the merger; . . . since the merger does not violate s 7 of the Clayton Act, a fortiori it does not violate s 1 of the Sherman Act; [and] the merger will benefit the Philadelphia metropolitan area economically. [. . .]

[6] We think that the four-County Philadelphia metropolitan area, which state law apparently recognizes as a meaningful banking community in allowing Philadelphia banks to branch within it, and which would seem roughly to delineate the area in which bank customers that are neither very large nor very small find it practical to do their banking business, is a more appropriate "section of the country" in which to appraise the instant merger than any larger or smaller or different area. We are helped to this conclusion by the fact that the three federal banking

---

[10] There was evidence that Philadelphia, although it ranks fourth or fifth among the Nation's urban areas in terms of general commercial activity, ranks only ninth in terms of the size of its largest bank, and that some large business firms which have their head offices in Philadelphia must seek elsewhere to satisfy their banking needs because of the inadequate lending limits of Philadelphia's banks . . . .

agencies regard the area in which banks have their offices as an "area of effective competition." Not only did the FDIC and FRB, in the reports they submitted to the Comptroller of the Currency in connection with appellees' application for permission to merge, so hold, but the Comptroller, in his statement approving the merger, agreed: "With respect to the effect upon competition, there are three separate levels and effective areas of competition involved. These are the national level for national accounts, the regional or sectional area, and the local area of the City of Philadelphia and the immediately surrounding area."

[7] Having determined the relevant market, we come to the ultimate question under s 7: whether the effect of the merger "may be substantially to lessen competition" in the relevant market. Clearly, this is not the kind of question which is susceptible of a ready and precise answer in most cases. It requires not merely an appraisal of the immediate impact of the merger upon competition, but a prediction of its impact upon competitive conditions in the future; this is what is meant when it is said that the amended s 7 was intended to arrest anticompetitive tendencies in their incipiency. Such a prediction is sound only if it is based upon a firm understanding of the structure of the relevant market; yet the relevant economic data are both complex and elusive. And unless businessmen can assess the legal consequences of a merger with some confidence, sound business planning is retarded. So also, we must be alert to the danger of subverting congressional intent by permitting a too-broad economic investigation. And so in any case in which it is possible, without doing violence to the congressional objective embodied in s 7, to simplify the test of illegality, the courts ought to do so in the interest of sound and practical judicial administration. This is such a case.

[8] We noted in *Brown Shoe Co.* that the dominant theme pervading congressional consideration of the 1950 amendments (to s 7) was a fear of what was considered to be a rising tide of economic concentration in the American economy. This intense congressional concern with the trend toward concentration warrants dispensing, in certain cases, with elaborate proof of market structure, market behavior, or probable anticompetitive effects. Specifically, we think that a merger which produces a firm controlling an undue percentage share of the relevant market, and results in a significant increase in the concentration of firms in that market is so inherently likely to lessen competition substantially that it must be enjoined in the absence of evidence clearly showing that the merger is not likely to have such anticompetitive effects.

[9] Such a test lightens the burden of proving illegality only with respect to mergers whose size makes them inherently suspect in light of Congress' design in s 7 to prevent undue concentration. Furthermore, the test is fully consonant with economic theory. That competition is likely to be greatest when there are many sellers, none of which has any significant market share, is common ground among most economists, and was undoubtedly a premise of congressional reasoning about the antimerger statute.

[10] The merger of appellees will result in a single bank's controlling at least 30% of the commercial banking business in the four-county Philadelphia metropolitan area. Without attempting to specify the smallest market share which would still be considered to threaten undue concentration, we are clear that 30% presents that threat. Further, whereas presently the two largest banks in the area (First Pennsylvania and PNB) control between them approximately 44% of the area's commercial banking business, the two largest after the merger (PNB-Girard and First Pennsylvania) will control 59%. Plainly, we think, this increase of more than 33% in concentration must be regarded as significant.

[11] Our conclusion that these percentages raise an inference that the effect of the contemplated merger of appellees may be substantially to lessen competition is not an arbitrary one, although neither the terms of s 7 nor the legislative history suggests that any particular percentage share was deemed critical. The House Report states that the tests of illegality under amended s 7 "are intended to be similar to those which the courts have applied in interpreting the same language as used in other sections of the Clayton Act." Accordingly, we have relied upon decisions under these other sections in applying s 7. In *Standard Oil Co. of Cal. & Standard Stations v. United States*, [337 U.S. 293 (1949)], this Court held violative of s 3 of the Clayton Act exclusive contracts whereby the defendant company, which accounted for 23% of the sales in the relevant market and, together with six other firms, accounted for 65% of such sales, maintained control over outlets through which approximately 7% of the sales were made. In *Federal Trade Comm'n v. Motion Picture Adv. Serv. Co.*, [344 U.S. 392 (1953)], we held unlawful, under s 1 of the Sherman Act and s 5 of the Federal Trade Commission Act, rather than under s 3 of the Clayton Act, exclusive arrangements whereby the four major firms in the industry had foreclosed 75% of the relevant market;

the respondent's market share, evidently, was 20%. In the instant case, by way of comparison, the four largest banks after the merger will foreclose 78% of the relevant market. . . . Doubtless these cases turned to some extent upon whether by the nature of the market there is room for newcomers. . . . But they remain highly suggestive in the present context, for as we noted in *Brown Shoe Co.*, integration by merger is more suspect than integration by contract, because of the greater permanence of the former. The market share and market concentration figures in the contract-integration cases, taken together with scholarly opinion . . . support, we believe, the inference we draw in the instant case from the figures disclosed by the record.

[12] There is nothing in the record of this case to rebut the inherently anticompetitive tendency manifested by these percentages. There was, to be sure, testimony by bank officers to the effect that competition among banks in Philadelphia was vigorous and would continue to be vigorous after the merger. We think, however, that the District Court's reliance on such evidence was misplaced. This lay evidence on so complex an economic-legal problem as the substantiality of the effect of this merger upon competition was entitled to little weight, in view of the witnesses' failure to give concrete reasons for their conclusions.

[13] Of equally little value, we think, are the assurances offered by appellees' witnesses that customers dissatisfied with the services of the resulting bank may readily turn to the 40 other banks in the Philadelphia area. In every case short of outright monopoly, the disgruntled customer has alternatives; even in tightly oligopolistic markets, there may be small firms operating. A fundamental purpose of amending s 7 was to arrest the trend toward concentration, the tendency to monopoly, before the consumer's alternatives disappeared through merger, and that purpose would be ill-served if the law stayed its hand until 10, or 20, or 30 more Philadelphia banks were absorbed. This is not a fanciful eventuality, in view of the strong trend toward mergers evident in the area; and we might note also that entry of new competitors into the banking field is far from easy.

* * *

Note the decisive move in paragraph 8 of the extract: "a merger which produces a firm controlling an undue percentage share of the relevant market, and results in a significant increase in the concentration of firms in that market is so inherently likely to lessen competition substantially that it must be enjoined in the absence of evidence clearly showing that the merger is not likely to have such anticompetitive effects."

In reading this, it may be helpful to recall from Chapter II that the Court's observation in paragraph 9 of the *PNB* extract that "competition is likely to be greatest when there are many sellers, none of which has any significant market share" is actually more controversial than it sounds. The relationship between concentration and competition is the subject of a rich literature: in some cases, more concentration can indeed mean that tacit collusion will be the outcome; in others, an increase in market concentration is compatible with intense competition. Indeed, as you may remember from Chapter I, at the time that *PNB* was decided, much antitrust economics was heavily influenced by the "structuralist" or "structure-conduct-performance" perspective, a set of views which centrally held that concentration in a market strongly implied harm to competition.[603] That view eventually lost ground to evidence that the relationship between competition and concentration was more complex, and that a more concentrated market did not necessarily indicate competitive trouble as opposed to, for example, the effects of certain kinds of efficiencies and economies.[604] Today, some are calling for a return to more structuralist perspectives.[605]

But even if economists no longer broadly agree that the fact of a concentrated market means that something is amiss, they generally do agree that a horizontal merger that will significantly increase market concentration will

---

[603] *See supra* § I.E.3. (discussing the mid-20th century ascendancy of structuralism).

[604] *See, e.g.*, Leonard W. Weiss, *Structure-Conduct-Performance Paradigm and Antitrust*, 127 U. Pa. L. Rev. 1104 (1979). *But see, e.g.*, Richard Schmalensee, *Inter-Industry Studies of Structure and Performance*, in Richard Schmalensee & Robert D. Willig (eds.), 2 HANDBOOK OF INDUSTRIAL ORGANIZATION (1989) 976 (noting relationship between concentration and prices).

[605] *See, e.g.*, K. Sabeel Rahman & Lina Khan, *Restoring Competition in the U.S. Economy*, in Nell Abernathy, Mike Konczal & Kathryn Milani, UNTAMED: HOW TO CHECK CORPORATE FINANCIAL, AND MONOPOLY POWER (June 2016) 20 (proposing that the next Administration should "reassert the centrality of market structure to competition analysis—namely, the idea that how a market is structured directly implicates its competitiveness. A mainstay of antitrust thinking for much of the last century, this foundational idea has since fallen into disuse.").

often be harmful, justifying a structural presumption of illegality.[606] (Even this, however, is not uncontroversial.[607]) As an article co-authored by 25 academic former chief economists from the FTC and DOJ recently put it:

> Economists widely agree that, absent sufficient efficiencies or other offsetting factors, mergers that increase concentration substantially are likely to be anticompetitive. The reason is that economic theory indicates that competition among firms leads to lower prices. The joint profit of any two competitors is higher if they both raise price, yet neither would do so unilaterally because it would simply lose sales to the competitor. A merger between competitors aligns incentives such that price increases or output restrictions can be implemented profitably, to the detriment of consumers and (often) total welfare.

> Economic theory also indicates that the magnitude of these adverse price effects tends to be larger, holding everything else equal, the larger is the increase in concentration caused by the merger."[608]

Of course, *PNB* did not explain at what level of concentration, or increase in concentration, the presumption of illegality would apply. Today, the presumption is fleshed out and specified in the HMGs.[609] The presumption centrally relies on the Herfindahl-Hirschman Index ("HHI") measure of concentration. (If you need a refresher, look back at Chapter II.)

Horizontal Merger Guidelines § 5

5.3 Market Concentration

[1] Market concentration is often one useful indicator of likely competitive effects of a merger. In evaluating market concentration, the Agencies consider both the post-merger level of market concentration and the change in concentration resulting from a merger. Market shares may not fully reflect the competitive significance of firms in the market or the impact of a merger. They are used in conjunction with other evidence of competitive effects.

[2] In analyzing mergers between an incumbent and a recent or potential entrant, to the extent the Agencies use the change in concentration to evaluate competitive effects, they will do so using projected market shares. A merger between an incumbent and a potential entrant can raise significant competitive concerns. The lessening of competition resulting from such a merger is more likely to be substantial, the larger is the market share of the incumbent, the greater is the competitive significance of the potential entrant, and the greater is the competitive threat posed by this potential entrant relative to others.

[3] The Agencies give more weight to market concentration when market shares have been stable over time, especially in the face of historical changes in relative prices or costs. If a firm has retained its market share even after its price has increased relative to those of its rivals, that firm already faces limited competitive constraints, making it less likely that its remaining rivals will replace the competition lost if one of that firm's important rivals is eliminated due to a merger. By contrast, even a highly concentrated market can be very competitive if market

---

[606] See, e.g., Herbert J. Hovenkamp & Carl Shapiro, Horizontal Mergers, Market Structure, and Burdens of Proof, 127 Yale L.J. 1996, 2001 (2018); John Kwoka, The Structural Presumption and The Safe Harbor in Merger Review: False Positives or Unwarranted Concerns? 81 Antitrust L.J. 837 (2017) (discussing theoretical and empirical foundations).

[607] *See, e.g.*, Louis Kaplow, *Replacing the Structural Presumption*, 84 Antitrust L.J. 565, 566 (2022) ("[T]he structural presumption is fundamentally flawed because of its own internal illogic, its sharp conflict with the economic analysis of anticompetitive effects, and the unintelligibility of its associated legal framework. The structural presumption's failure even as a preliminary screening device a fortiori renders it unsound as a basis for actual decision-making. It is therefore necessary to replace the structural presumption—and dangerous to extend and enshrine it as currently proposed."); Douglas H. Ginsburg & Joshua D. Wright, Philadelphia National Bank: *Bad Economics, Bad Law, Good Riddance*, 80 Antitrust L.J. 377, 380 (2015) ("The point is not that 30 percent is an outdated threshold above which to presume adverse effects upon competition; rather, it is that market structure is an inappropriate starting point for the analysis of likely competitive effects. Market structure and competitive effects are not systematically correlated."); ABA Section of Antitrust Law, *Comments, HMG Revision Project* (June 4, 2010) 4 ("[T]he Section urges the Agencies to remove the presumption of illegality keyed to the level and increase in the HHI. The presumption does not reflect how the Agencies conduct investigations, is not theoretically warranted, and could be misinterpreted by other countries thereby undercutting international efforts to promulgate solid merger analysis principles."); *see also* John Harkrider, *Proving Anticompetitive Impact: Moving Past Merger Guidelines Presumptions*, 2005 Colum. Bus. L. Rev. 317 (2005).

[608] Nathan Miller et al., *On The Misuse of Regressions of Price on the HHI in Merger Review*, 10 J. Antitrust Enforcement 248 (2021).

[609] The Court did, however, hold that a merger to 30% share triggered concerns, as some subsequent courts have emphasized. *See, e.g.*, FTC v. Swedish Match, 131 F. Supp. 2d 151, 166 (D.D.C. 2000) ("In *Philadelphia National Bank*, the Court specifically held that a post-merger market share of thirty percent triggers the presumption.").

shares fluctuate substantially over short periods of time in response to changes in competitive offerings. However, if competition by one of the merging firms has significantly contributed to these fluctuations, perhaps because it has acted as a maverick, the Agencies will consider whether the merger will enhance market power by combining that firm with one of its significant rivals.

[4] The Agencies may measure market concentration using the number of significant competitors in the market. This measure is most useful when there is a gap in market share between significant competitors and smaller rivals or when it is difficult to measure revenues in the relevant market. The Agencies also may consider the combined market share of the merging firms as an indicator of the extent to which others in the market may not be able readily to replace competition between the merging firms that is lost through the merger.

[5] The Agencies often calculate the Herfindahl-Hirschman Index ("HHI") of market concentration. The HHI is calculated by summing the squares of the individual firms' market shares, and thus gives proportionately greater weight to the larger market shares. When using the HHI, the Agencies consider both the post-merger level of the HHI and the increase in the HHI resulting from the merger. The increase in the HHI is equal to twice the product of the market shares of the merging firms.

[6] Based on their experience, the Agencies generally classify markets into three types:

a)   Unconcentrated Markets: HHI below 1500
b)   Moderately Concentrated Markets: HHI between 1500 and 2500
c)   Highly Concentrated Markets: HHI above 2500

[7] The Agencies employ the following general standards for the relevant markets they have defined:

- *Small Change in Concentration:* Mergers involving an increase in the HHI of less than 100 points are unlikely to have adverse competitive effects and ordinarily require no further analysis.
- *Unconcentrated Markets:* Mergers resulting in unconcentrated markets are unlikely to have adverse competitive effects and ordinarily require no further analysis.
- *Moderately Concentrated Markets:* Mergers resulting in moderately concentrated markets that involve an increase in the HHI of more than 100 points potentially raise significant competitive concerns and often warrant scrutiny.
- *Highly Concentrated Markets:* Mergers resulting in highly concentrated markets that involve an increase in the HHI of between 100 points and 200 points potentially raise significant competitive concerns and often warrant scrutiny. Mergers resulting in highly concentrated markets that involve an increase in the HHI of more than 200 points will be presumed to be likely to enhance market power. The presumption may be rebutted by persuasive evidence showing that the merger is unlikely to enhance market power.

[8] The purpose of these thresholds is not to provide a rigid screen to separate competitively benign mergers from anticompetitive ones, although high levels of concentration do raise concerns. Rather, they provide one way to identify some mergers unlikely to raise competitive concerns and some others for which it is particularly important to examine whether other competitive factors confirm, reinforce, or counteract the potentially harmful effects of increased concentration. The higher the post-merger HHI and the increase in the HHI, the greater are the Agencies' potential competitive concerns and the greater is the likelihood that the Agencies will request additional information to conduct their analysis.

* * *

Previous merger guidelines drew the structural-presumption line at lower levels of concentration:

- The 1968 Guidelines, issued by DOJ alone, stated the concentration test as follows:
  - if the sum of the shares of the four largest firms in the market (the "four-firm concentration ratio" or "CR4") was 75% or more, DOJ would "ordinarily challenge" transactions between: (a) an acquiring firm of share >4% and an acquired firm of >4%; (b) an acquiring firm of >10% and an acquired firm of >2%; or (c) an acquiring firm of share >15% and an acquired firm of >1%;

- o if the sum of the shares of the four largest firms in the market (the "four-firm concentration ratio" or "CR4") was less than 75%, DOJ would "ordinarily challenge" transactions between: (a) an acquiring firm of share >5% and an acquired firm of >5%; (b) an acquiring firm of share >10% and an acquired firm of >4%; (c) an acquiring firm of share >15% and an acquired firm of >3%; (d) an acquiring firm of share >20% and an acquired firm of >2%; and (e) an acquiring firm of share >25% and an acquired firm of >1%; and
  - o if a market showed a "significant trend toward increased concentration," defined as a situation in which "the aggregate market share of any grouping of the largest firms in the market from the two largest to the eight largest has increased by approximately 7% or more of the market over a period of time extending from any base year 5-10 years prior to the merger," DOJ would "ordinarily challenge any acquisition, by any firm in a grouping of such largest firms showing the requisite increase in market share, of any firm whose market share amounts to approximately 2% or more.
- The 1982 Guidelines, issued by DOJ alone,[610] introduced the hypothetical monopolist test into the Guidelines.[611] They switched from CR4 to HHI and stated:
  - o if the post-merger HHI was below 1000, DOJ would be "unlikely" to challenge the transaction;
  - o if the post-merger HHI was between 1000 and 1800, DOJ would be "unlikely" to challenge the merger if the transaction increased the HHI by less than 100 points, but "more likely than not" to challenge the merger if the transaction increased the HHI by more than 100 points; and
  - o if the post-merger HHI was above 1800, DOJ would be "unlikely" to challenge the merger if the transaction increased the HHI by less than 50 points, would review other factors if the transaction increased the HHI by between 50 and 100 points, but would be "likely" to challenge the merger if the transaction increased the HHI by more than 100 points.
- The 1984 Guidelines retained the 1982 concentration thresholds.
- The 1992 Guidelines were issued jointly by DOJ and the FTC,[612] and stated:
  - o if the post-merger HHI was below 1000, the transaction would be "unlikely" to have adverse effects;
  - o if the post-merger HHI was between 1000 and 1800, a transaction that increased the HHI by less than 100 points would be "unlikely" to have adverse effects, and a transaction that increased the HHI by more than 100 points would "potentially raise significant competitive concerns" based on other factors;
  - o if the post-merger HHI was above 1800, a transaction that increased the HHI by less than 50 points would be "unlikely" to have adverse effects, a transaction that increased the HHI by more than 50 points would "potentially raise significant competitive concerns" based on other factors, and a transaction that increased the HHI by more than 100 points would be presumed "likely to create or enhance market power or facilitate its exercise," with such presumption rebuttable by a showing that other factors make this concern unlikely.

  (Note the transition in the 1992 guidelines from a statement of enforcement intentions to an analytical presumption about economic effects!)
- The 1997 Guidelines retained the 1992 concentration thresholds.
- The 2010 Guidelines raised the concentration thresholds,[613] and stated:

---

[610] For contemporaneous perspectives, *see* William F. Baxter, *New Merger Guidelines: A Justice Department Perspective*, 51 Antitrust L.J. 287 (1982); William F. Smith, *Changing Enforcement Policy*, 51 Antitrust L.J. 95 (1982); Thomas J. Campbell, *New Merger Guidelines: A Federal Trade Commission Perspective*, 51 Antitrust L.J. 295, 297 (1982); Donald I. Baker & William Blumenthal, *The 1982 Guidelines and Preexisting Law*, 71 Calif. L. Rev. 311 (1983).

[611] For commentary on this change and its aftermath, *see* Barry C. Harris & Joseph J. Simons, *Focusing Market Definition: How Much Substitution Is Necessary?*, 12 Research in L. & Econ. 207 (1989); Joseph J. Simons & Michael A. Williams, *The Renaissance of Market Definition*, Antitrust Bull. 799 (1993).

[612] For contemporaneous perspectives, *see* Charles A. James, *Overview of the 1992 Horizontal Merger Guidelines*, 61 Antitrust L.J. 447 (1993); Thomas B. Leary, *The Essential Stability of Merger Policy in the United States*, 70 Antitrust L.J. 105 (2002) (including 1997 revisions).

[613] For contemporaneous perspectives, *see* Christine A. Varney, *An Update on the Review of the Merger Guidelines*, Remarks for the Horizontal Merger Guidelines Review Project's Final Workshop (Jan. 26, 2010); Dennis W. Carlton, *Revising the Horizontal Merger Guidelines*, 6 J. Comp. L. & Econ. 619 (2010).

- o if the transaction increased the HHI by less than 100 points, it would be "unlikely" to have adverse effects;
- o if the post-merger HHI was below 1500, the transaction would be "unlikely" to have adverse effects;
- o if the post-merger HHI was between 1500 and 2500, a transaction that increased the HHI by more than 100 points would "potentially raise significant competitive concerns and often warrant scrutiny";
- o if the post-merger HHI was above 2500, a transaction that increased the HHI by between 100 and 200 points would "potentially raise significant competitive concerns and often warrant scrutiny," and a transaction that increased the HHI by more than 200 points would be presumed "likely to enhance market power," with such presumption rebuttable by "persuasive evidence" showing that the merger is unlikely to enhance market power.

"Delta HHIs"

The so-called "delta HHI"--that is, the *increase* in HHI resulting from a proposed transaction—is very important in merger analysis. As you can see from the HMG extract above, if a transaction results in a post-merger HHI above 2,500 and a "delta HHI" above 200, it will be *presumed* likely to enhance market power. This is a critical threshold in practice.

A hot tip: if you want to calculate the delta HHI resulting from a transaction without calculating full HHIs for the market as a whole—either because you don't want to go through the trouble of that calculation or because you don't have share data for other market participants—you can still do so. *The delta HHI is equal to twice the product of the premerger market shares of the two merging firms.* (Bonus points for proving this algebraically.)

The presumption, once established, can be rebutted by other evidence.[614] Such evidence, for example, could involve a showing that the market shares are poorly correlated to the parties' real competitive position, or that harm is unlikely in light of evidence regarding entry by new firms, expansion by existing ones, or efficiencies arising from the transaction.[615]

The seminal modern case on the operation of the structural presumption in merger litigation is the D.C. Circuit's 1990 decision in *Baker Hughes*.[616] In that case, then-Judge Clarence Thomas, joined by then-Judge Ruth Bader Ginsburg, laid out the burden-shifting framework that guides modern merger analysis. In the process, he reviewed the changes in merger adjudication since the 1960s, and highlighted the disconnect between the Court's early merger cases (including decisions like *Von's Grocery* and *Pabst Brewing*) and the approach that had emerged by 1990, which still prevails today.

United States v. Baker Hughes Inc.
908 F.2d 981 (D.C. Cir. 1990)

Judge Thomas.

[1] Appellee Oy Tampella AB, a Finnish corporation, through its subsidiary Tamrock AG, manufactures and sells hardrock hydraulic underground drilling rigs ("HHUDRs") in the United States and throughout the world.

---

[614] *See, e.g.*, United States v. General Dynamics Corp., 415 U.S. 486 (1974); United States v. Baker Hughes Inc., 908 F.2d 981 (D.C. Cir. 1990). For some thoughtful discussions of the status and function of the presumption's operation, *see* Sean P. Sullivan, *What Structural Presumption?: Reuniting Evidence and Economics on the Role of Market Concentration in Horizontal Merger Analysis*, 42 J. Corp. L. 403 (2016); Steven C. Salop, *The Evolution and Vitality of Merger Presumptions: A Decision-Theoretic Approach*, 80 Antitrust L.J. 269 (2015).

[615] Herbert J. Hovenkamp & Carl Shapiro, *Horizontal Mergers, Market Structure, and Burdens of Proof*, 127 Yale L.J. 1996, 1997 (2018) ("Generally, [parties rebut the presumption] by making one of three showings: first, that the proposed market is poorly defined or that market shares exaggerate the merger's anticompetitive potential; second, that entry into the market will discipline any price increase; or third, that the merger produces offsetting efficiencies sufficient to keep prices at premerger levels or otherwise counteract any anticompetitive effects").

[616] For another influential case in which the structural presumption was central (but in which, unlike *Baker Hughes*, the government plaintiff prevailed largely on the basis of structural evidence), *see* FTC v. H.J. Heinz Co., 246 F.3d 708 (D.C. Cir. 2001).

Appellee Baker Hughes Inc., a corporation based in Houston, Texas, owned a French subsidiary, Eimco Secoma, S.A. (Secoma), that was similarly involved in the HHUDR industry. In 1989, Tamrock proposed to acquire Secoma.

[2] The United States challenged the proposed acquisition, charging that it would substantially lessen competition in the United States HHUDR market in violation of section 7 of the Clayton Act, 15 U.S.C. § 18. In December 1989, the government sought and obtained a temporary restraining order blocking the transaction. In February 1990, the district court held a bench trial and issued a decision rejecting the government's request for a permanent injunction and dismissing the section 7 claim. The government immediately appealed to this court, requesting expedited proceedings and an injunction pending appeal. We granted the motion for expedited briefing and argument, but denied the motion for an injunction pending appeal. The appellees consummated the acquisition shortly thereafter.

[3] The basic outline of a section 7 horizontal acquisition case is familiar. By showing that a transaction will lead to undue concentration in the market for a particular product in a particular geographic area, the government establishes a presumption that the transaction will substantially lessen competition. The burden of producing evidence to rebut this presumption then shifts to the defendant. If the defendant successfully rebuts the presumption, the burden of producing additional evidence of anticompetitive effect shifts to the government, and merges with the ultimate burden of persuasion, which remains with the government at all times. [. . .]

[4] By presenting statistics showing that combining the market shares of Tamrock and Secoma would significantly increase concentration in the already highly concentrated United States HHUDR market, the government established a prima facie case of anticompetitive effect.[3] The district court, however, found sufficient evidence that the merger would not substantially lessen competition to conclude that the defendants had rebutted this prima facie case. The government did not produce any additional evidence showing a probability of substantially lessened competition, and thus failed to carry its ultimate burden of persuasion.

[5] In this appeal, the government assails the court's conclusion that the defendants rebutted the prima facie case. Doubtless aware that this court will set aside the district court's findings of fact only if they are clearly erroneous, the government frames the issue as a pure question of law, which we review de novo. The government's key contention is that the district court, which did not expressly state the legal standard that it applied in its analysis of rebuttal evidence, failed to apply a sufficiently stringent standard. The government argues that, as a matter of law, section 7 defendants can rebut a prima facie case only by a clear showing that entry into the market by competitors would be quick and effective. Because the district court failed to apply this standard, the government submits, the court erred in concluding that the proposed acquisition would not substantially lessen future competition in the United States HHUDR market.

[6] We find no merit in the legal standard propounded by the government. It is devoid of support in the statute, in the case law, and in the government's own Merger Guidelines. Moreover, it is flawed on its merits in three fundamental respects. First, it assumes that ease of entry by competitors is the only consideration relevant to a section 7 defendant's rebuttal. Second, it requires that a defendant who seeks to show ease of entry bear the onerous burden of proving that entry will be "quick and effective." Finally, by stating that the defendant can rebut a prima facie case only by a clear showing, the standard in effect shifts the government's ultimate burden of persuasion to the defendant. Although the district court in this case did not expressly set forth a legal standard when it evaluated the defendants' rebuttal, we have carefully reviewed the court's thorough analysis of competitive conditions in the United States HHUDR market, and we are satisfied that the court effectively applied a standard faithful to section 7. Concluding that the court applied this legal standard to factual findings that are not clearly

---

[3] From 1986 through 1988, Tamrock had an average 40.8% share of the United States HHUDR market, while Secoma's share averaged 17.5%. In 1988 alone, the two firms enjoyed a combined share of 76% of the market. (The district court inaccurately calculated this figure as 66%.) The acquisition thus has brought about a dramatic increase in the Herfindahl-Hirschman Index (HHI)—a yardstick of concentration—for this market. The Department of Justice's Merger Guidelines characterize as "highly concentrated" any market in which the HHI exceeds 1800. This acquisition has increased the HHI in this market from 2878 to 4303.

erroneous, we affirm the court's denial of a permanent injunction and its dismissal of the government's section 7 claim. [. . .]

[7] It is a foundation of section 7 doctrine, disputed by no authority cited by the government, that evidence on a variety of factors can rebut a prima facie case. These factors include, but are not limited to, the absence of significant entry barriers in the relevant market. In this appeal, however, the government inexplicably imbues the entry factor with talismanic significance. If, to successfully rebut a prima facie case, a defendant must show that entry by competitors will be quick and effective, then other factors bearing on future competitiveness are all but irrelevant. The district court in this case considered at least two factors in addition to entry: the misleading nature of the statistics underlying the government's prima facie case and the sophistication of HHUDR consumers. These non-entry factors provide compelling support for the court's holding that Tamrock's acquisition of Secoma was not likely to lessen competition substantially. We have concluded that the court's consideration of these factors was crucial, and that the government's fixation on ease of entry is misplaced.

[8] Section 7 involves probabilities, not certainties or possibilities. The Supreme Court has adopted a totality-of-the-circumstances approach to the statute, weighing a variety of factors to determine the effects of particular transactions on competition. That the government can establish a prima facie case through evidence on only one factor, market concentration, does not negate the breadth of this analysis. Evidence of market concentration simply provides a convenient starting point for a broader inquiry into future competitiveness; the Supreme Court has never indicated that a defendant seeking to rebut a prima facie case is restricted to producing evidence of ease of entry. Indeed, in numerous cases, defendants have relied entirely on non-entry factors in successfully rebutting a prima facie case. [. . .]

[9] The district court's analysis of this case is fully consonant with precedent and logic. The court reviewed the evidence proffered by the defendants as part of its overall assessment of future competitiveness in the United States HHUDR market. As noted above, the court gave particular weight to two non-entry factors: the flawed underpinnings of the government's prima facie case and the sophistication of HHUDR consumers. The court's consideration of these factors was not only appropriate, but imperative, because in this case these factors significantly affected the probability that the acquisition would have anticompetitive effects.

[10] With respect to the first factor, the statistical basis of the prima facie case, the court accepted the defendants' argument that the government's statistics were misleading. Because the United States HHUDR market is minuscule, market share statistics are volatile and shifting, and easily skewed. In 1986, for instance, only 22 HHUDRs were sold in the United States. In 1987, the number rose to 43, and in 1988 it fell to 38. Every HHUDR sold during this period, thus, increased the seller's market share by two to five percent. A contract to provide multiple HHUDRs could catapult a firm from last to first place. The district court found that, in this unusual market, at any given point in time an individual seller's future competitive strength may not be accurately reflected. While acknowledging that the HHUDR market would be highly concentrated after Tamrock acquired Secoma, the court found that such concentration in and of itself would not doom competition. High concentration has long been the norm in this market. For example, only four firms sold HHUDRs in the United States between 1986 and 1989. Nor is concentration surprising where, as here, a product is esoteric and its market small. Indeed, the trial judge found that concentration has existed for some time in the United States HHUDR market but there is no proof of overpricing, excessive profit or any decline in quality, service or diminishing innovation.

[11] The second non-entry factor that the district court considered was the sophistication of HHUDR consumers. HHUDRs currently cost hundreds of thousands of dollars, and orders can exceed $1 million. These products are hardly trinkets sold to small consumers who may possess imperfect information and limited bargaining power. HHUDR buyers closely examine available options and typically insist on receiving multiple, confidential bids for each order. This sophistication, the court found, was likely to promote competition even in a highly concentrated market. Id. at 11.

[12] The government has not provided us with any reason to suppose that these findings of fact are unsupported in the record or clearly erroneous. We thus accept them as correct. These findings provide considerable support for the district court's conclusion that the defendants successfully rebutted the government's prima facie case.

Because the defendants also provided compelling evidence on ease of entry into this market, we need not decide whether these findings, without more, are sufficient to rebut the government's prima facie case. [. . .]

[13] The district court in this case discussed a number of considerations that led it to conclude that entry barriers to the United States HHUDR market were not high enough to impede future entry should Tamrock's acquisition of Secoma lead to supracompetitive pricing. First, the court noted that at least two companies, Cannon and Ingersoll-Rand, had entered the United States HHUDR market in 1989, and were poised for future expansion. Second, the court stressed that a number of firms competing in Canada and other countries had not penetrated the United States market, but could be expected to do so if Tamrock's acquisition of Secoma led to higher prices. Because the market is small, it is inexpensive to develop a separate sales and service network in the United States. Third, these firms would exert competitive pressure on the United States HHUDR market even if they never actually entered the market. Finally, the court noted that there had been tremendous turnover in the United States HHUDR market in the 1980s. Secoma, for example, did not sell a single HHUDR in the United States in 1983 or 1984, but then lowered its price and improved its service, becoming market leader by 1989. Secoma's growth suggests that competitors not only can, but probably will, enter or expand if this acquisition leads to higher prices. The district court, to be sure, also found some facts suggesting difficulty of entry, but these findings do not negate its ultimate finding to the contrary. [. . .]

[14] The government argues that the court erred by failing to require the defendants to make a "clear" showing. The relevant precedents, however, suggest that this formulation overstates the defendants' burden. We conclude that a "clear" showing is unnecessary, and we are satisfied that the district court required the defendants to produce sufficient evidence.

[15] The government's "clear showing" language is by no means unsupported in the case law. In the mid-1960s, the Supreme Court construed section 7 to prohibit virtually any horizontal merger or acquisition. At the time, the Court envisioned an ideal market as one composed of many small competitors, each enjoying only a small market share; the more closely a given market approximated this ideal, the more competitive it was presumed to be.

[16] This perspective animated a series of decisions in which the Court stated that a section 7 defendant's market share measures its market power, that statistics alone establish a prima facie case, and that a defendant carries a heavy burden in seeking to rebut the presumption established by such a prima facie case. The Court most clearly articulated this approach in *Philadelphia Bank*:

> Th[e] intense congressional concern with the trend toward concentration [underlying section 7] warrants dispensing, in certain cases, with elaborate proof of market structure, market behavior, or probable anticompetitive effects. Specifically, we think that a merger which produces a firm controlling an undue percentage share of the relevant market, and results in a significant increase in the concentration of firms in that market, is so inherently likely to lessen competition substantially that it must be enjoined in the absence of evidence clearly showing that the merger is not likely to have such anticompetitive effects.

[17] *Philadelphia Bank* involved a proposed merger that would have created a bank commanding over 30% of a highly concentrated market. While acknowledging that the banks could in principle rebut the government's prima facie case, the Court found unpersuasive the banks' evidence challenging the alleged anticompetitive effect of the merger.

[18] In *United States v. Von's Grocery Co.*, [384 U.S. 270 (1966)], the Court further emphasized the weight of a defendant's burden. Despite evidence that a post-merger company had only a 7.5% share of the Los Angeles retail grocery market, the Court, citing anticompetitive "trends" in that market, ordered the merger undone. The Court summarily dismissed the defendants' contention that the post-merger market was highly competitive. . . . Noting that the market was marked at the same time by both a continuous decline in the number of small businesses and a large number of mergers, the *Von's Grocery* Court predicted that, if the merger were not undone, the market "would slowly but inevitably gravitate from a market of many small competitors to one dominated by one or a few giants, and competition would thereby be destroyed."

[19] Although the Supreme Court has not overruled these section 7 precedents, it has cut them back sharply. In [*United States v. General Dynamics*, 415 U.S. 486 (1974)], the Court affirmed a district court determination that, by

presenting evidence that undermined the government's statistics, section 7 defendants had successfully rebutted a prima facie case. In so holding, the Court did not expressly reaffirm or disavow *Philadelphia Bank*'s statement that a company must "clearly" show that a transaction is not likely to have substantial anticompetitive effects. The Court simply held that the district court was justified, based on all the evidence, in finding that no substantial lessening of competition occurred or was threatened by the acquisition.

[20] *General Dynamics* began a line of decisions differing markedly in emphasis from the Court's antitrust cases of the 1960s. Instead of accepting a firm's market share as virtually conclusive proof of its market power, the Court carefully analyzed defendants' rebuttal evidence. These cases discarded *Philadelphia Bank*'s insistence that a defendant "clearly" disprove anticompetitive effect, and instead described the rebuttal burden simply in terms of a "showing." Without overruling *Philadelphia Bank*, then, the Supreme Court has at the very least lightened the evidentiary burden on a section 7 defendant.

[21] In the aftermath of *General Dynamics* and its progeny, a defendant seeking to rebut a presumption of anticompetitive effect must show that the prima facie case inaccurately predicts the relevant transaction's probable effect on future competition. The more compelling the prima facie case, the more evidence the defendant must present to rebut it successfully. A defendant can make the required showing by affirmatively showing why a given transaction is unlikely to substantially lessen competition, or by discrediting the data underlying the initial presumption in the government's favor.

[22] By focusing on the future, section 7 gives a court the uncertain task of assessing probabilities. In this setting, allocation of the burdens of proof assumes particular importance. By shifting the burden of producing evidence, present law allows both sides to make competing predictions about a transaction's effects. If the burden of production imposed on a defendant is unduly onerous, the distinction between that burden and the ultimate burden of persuasion—always an elusive distinction in practice—disintegrates completely. A defendant required to produce evidence "clearly" disproving future anticompetitive effects must essentially persuade the trier of fact on the ultimate issue in the case—whether a transaction is likely to lessen competition substantially. Absent express instructions to the contrary, we are loath to depart from settled principles and impose such a heavy burden.

[23] Imposing a heavy burden of production on a defendant would be particularly anomalous where, as here, it is easy to establish a prima facie case. The government, after all, can carry its initial burden of production simply by presenting market concentration statistics. To allow the government virtually to rest its case at that point, leaving the defendant to prove the core of the dispute, would grossly inflate the role of statistics in actions brought under section 7. The Herfindahl–Hirschman Index cannot guarantee litigation victories. Requiring a "clear showing" in this setting would move far toward forcing a defendant to rebut a probability with a certainty.

[24] The appellees in this case presented the district court with considerable evidence regarding the United States HHUDR market. The court credited the evidence concerning the sophistication of HHUDR consumers and the insignificance of entry barriers, as well as the argument that the statistics underlying the government's prima facie case were misleading. This evidence amply justified the court's conclusion that the prima facie case inaccurately depicted the probable anticompetitive effect of Tamrock's acquisition of Secoma. Because the government did not produce sufficient evidence to overcome this successful rebuttal, the district court concluded that it is not likely that the acquisition will substantially lessen competition in the United States either immediately or long-term. The government has given us no reason to reverse that conclusion.

[25] For the foregoing reasons, the judgment of the district court is

Affirmed.

The Shape of a Merger Case: The Burden-Shifting Framework

After *Baker Hughes*, the rough shape of a merger case can be thought of as follows.

Plaintiff's affirmative case. First, a plaintiff must demonstrate an affirmative or *prima facie* case of illegality. This is most readily done by showing that the structural presumption is satisfied, but plaintiffs almost invariably adduce other evidence suggestive of competitive harm at this stage too (supporting a coordinated-effects theory, unilateral-effects theory, or both). Note that, while the core logic of the structural presumption is a close fit with coordinated-effects theories, it can be used to discharge the plaintiff's affirmative burden in pure unilateral-effects cases too.[617]

Defendant's rebuttal case. Second, the defendant can present a rebuttal case, including evidence tending to undermine the applicability or force of the structural presumption; evidence suggesting that the theory or theories of harm are misfounded; evidence that entry or expansion, or the countervailing power of trading partners, will preclude competitive concerns; or other evidence of any kind tending to indicate that the merger will not be anticompetitive. (This may include evidence related to efficiencies to the extent that they tend to exclude the possibility of competitive harm.) The weight of the defendant's rebuttal burden is a function of the strength of the plaintiff's affirmative case: a more compelling *prima facie* case requires a more persuasive rebuttal.

Analysis of defenses in the strict sense. The defendant may also present any defenses in the strict sense, such as the "failing firm" defense, or those grounded in other doctrines like the "state action" defense that we will meet in Chapter IX.

Finally, the plaintiff has the ultimate burden of persuading a factfinder that the transaction is unlawful.

NOTES

1) In light of what you can tell from the decision, does *PNB* involve a merger that would raise concerns today?

2) Why was the *PNB* Court so dismissive of customer testimony?

3) The court in *Baker Hughes* indicated that it is "easy to establish a prima facie case" by "presenting concentration statistics," and that as a result a prima facie case built on concentration should be relatively easy to rebut. How would you defend that view? How would you criticize it?

4) Why is a merger that significantly increases market concentration presumed to be anticompetitive? Should the strength of this presumption vary from one market to another?

5) How do you think the antitrust agencies determined the concentration levels at which the structural presumption would apply? Why do you think the presumptions have changed over time?

6) Are the guidelines binding on courts? What is the source of their authority? Are they binding on agencies?

7) Most agency merger litigations are in practice brought at concentration levels materially above the structural presumption.[618] Why do you think this is? Does it imply a problem: and, if so, what is it?

8) What would you want to know, or evaluate, in order to determine whether the structural presumptions are set at the "right" level? What values or concerns should be weighed in determining what the "right" level is?

9) Should the presumption be made irrebuttable?

10) Jonathan Baker and Carl Shapiro have written that, in the years between *Philadelphia National Bank* and *Baker Hughes*, "the emphasis in merger enforcement has shifted . . . from proving market concentration to telling a convincing story of how the merger will actually lead to a reduction in competition. Put simply, market definition and market shares have become far less important relative to proof of competitive effects."[619] Assuming that this is correct, do you think it is a good or bad development?

2. Competitive Effects Theories in Horizontal Merger Cases

A horizontal merger may give rise to competitive concerns in at least two ways: by creating "unilateral" competitive effects through the reduction of competition between the parties, or by creating "coordinated" competitive effects through facilitating tacit (or explicit) collusion among the market participants.

---

[617] *See, e.g.*, ProMedica Health System, Inc. v. FTC, 749 F.3d 559, 570 (6th Cir. 2014).

[618] For some related data and discussion, *see* John Kwoka, *The Structural Presumption and The Safe Harbor in Merger Review: False Positives or Unwarranted Concerns?* 81 Antitrust L.J. 837, 867–71 (2017); Malcolm B. Coate, *Benchmarking the Upward Pricing Pressure Model with Federal Trade Commission Evidence*, 7 J. Comp. L. & Econ. 825, 834 tbl. 2 (2011).

[619] Jonathan B. Baker & Carl Shapiro, *Reinvigorating Horizontal Merger Enforcement*, in Robert Pitofsky (ed.) HOW CHICAGO SCHOOL OVERSHOT THE MARK: THE EFFECT OF CONSERVATIVE ECONOMIC ANALYSIS ON U.S. ANTITRUST (2008) 238.

a) Unilateral Effects Theories

"Unilateral" anticompetitive effects arise when, as a result of the loss of head-to-head competition between the two parties to a horizontal merger, the merged firm can "unilaterally" raise its prices, lower quality or output, or otherwise change its behavior in harmful ways as a result of the lost competitive pressure. This kind of harm, which was explicitly described in the merger guidelines for the first time in 1992, is a central concern when the parties are particularly close competitors in a market with differentiated products or services before the transaction.[620] In principle, unilateral-effects analysis is not dependent on the bounds of a relevant market definition, as the focus is on direct competitive interactions between the parties, but as noted above in practice market definition is enormously important in virtually every merger case, including because Section 7 speaks of a "line of commerce."[621]

Horizontal Merger Guidelines § 6

6. Unilateral Effects

[1] The elimination of competition between two firms that results from their merger may alone constitute a substantial lessening of competition. Such unilateral effects are most apparent in a merger to monopoly in a relevant market, but are by no means limited to that case. Whether cognizable efficiencies resulting from the merger are likely to reduce or reverse adverse unilateral effects is addressed in Section 10.

[2] Several common types of unilateral effects are discussed in this section. Section 6.1 discusses unilateral price effects in markets with differentiated products. Section 6.2 discusses unilateral effects in markets where sellers negotiate with buyers or prices are determined through auctions. Section 6.3 discusses unilateral effects relating to reductions in output or capacity in markets for relatively homogeneous products. Section 6.4 discusses unilateral effects arising from diminished innovation or reduced product variety. These effects do not exhaust the types of possible unilateral effects; for example, exclusionary unilateral effects also can arise.

[3] A merger may result in different unilateral effects along different dimensions of competition. For example, a merger may increase prices in the short term but not raise longer-term concerns about innovation, either because rivals will provide sufficient innovation competition or because the merger will generate cognizable research and development efficiencies. {Eds.: efficiencies are discussed in Section 10 of the HMGs, and below at § VIII.D.1.}

6.1 Pricing of Differentiated Products

[4] In differentiated product industries, some products can be very close substitutes and compete strongly with each other, while other products are more distant substitutes and compete less strongly. For example, one high-end product may compete much more directly with another high-end product than with any low-end product.

[5] A merger between firms selling differentiated products may diminish competition by enabling the merged firm to profit by unilaterally raising the price of one or both products above the pre-merger level. Some of the sales lost due to the price rise will merely be diverted to the product of the merger partner and, depending on relative margins, capturing such sales loss through merger may make the price increase profitable even though it would not have been profitable prior to the merger.

[6] The extent of direct competition between the products sold by the merging parties is central to the evaluation of unilateral price effects. Unilateral price effects are greater, the more the buyers of products sold by one merging firm consider products sold by the other merging firm to be their next choice. The Agencies consider any reasonably available and reliable information to evaluate the extent of direct competition between the products sold by the merging firms. This includes documentary and testimonial evidence, win/loss reports and evidence from discount approval processes, customer switching patterns, and customer surveys. The types of evidence relied

---

[620] *See generally* Gregory Werden & Luke Froeb, *Unilateral Competitive Effects of Horizontal Mergers*, in Paolo Buccirossi (ed.), HANDBOOK OF ANTITRUST ECONOMICS (2007); Jonathan B. Baker, *Unilateral Competitive Effects Theories in Merger Analysis*, ANTITRUST (Spring 1997) 21.

[621] *See, e.g.*, Herbert J. Hovenkamp & Carl Shapiro, *Horizontal Mergers, Market Structure, and Burdens of Proof*, 127 Yale L.J. 1996, 2015 (2018) ("Economic analysis of unilateral effects can proceed without defining a relevant market, although there is some question about whether such analysis is permitted by the statute.")

on often overlap substantially with the types of evidence of customer substitution relevant to the hypothetical monopolist test. See Section 4.1.1.

[7] Substantial unilateral price elevation post-merger for a product formerly sold by one of the merging firms normally requires that a significant fraction of the customers purchasing that product view products formerly sold by the other merging firm as their next-best choice. However, unless pre-merger margins between price and incremental cost are low, that significant fraction need not approach a majority. For this purpose, incremental cost is measured over the change in output that would be caused by the price change considered. A merger may produce significant unilateral effects for a given product even though many more sales are diverted to products sold by non-merging firms than to products previously sold by the merger partner. [. . .]

[8] In some cases, the Agencies may seek to quantify the extent of direct competition between a product sold by one merging firm and a second product sold by the other merging firm by estimating the diversion ratio from the first product to the second product. The diversion ratio is the fraction of unit sales lost by the first product due to an increase in its price that would be diverted to the second product. Diversion ratios between products sold by one merging firm and products sold by the other merging firm can be very informative for assessing unilateral price effects, with higher diversion ratios indicating a greater likelihood of such effects. Diversion ratios between products sold by merging firms and those sold by non-merging firms have at most secondary predictive value.

[9] Adverse unilateral price effects can arise when the merger gives the merged entity an incentive to raise the price of a product previously sold by one merging firm and thereby divert sales to products previously sold by the other merging firm, boosting the profits on the latter products. Taking as given other prices and product offerings, that boost to profits is equal to the value to the merged firm of the sales diverted to those products. The value of sales diverted to a product is equal to the number of units diverted to that product multiplied by the margin between price and incremental cost on that product. In some cases, where sufficient information is available, the Agencies assess the value of diverted sales, which can serve as an indicator of the upward pricing pressure on the first product resulting from the merger. Diagnosing unilateral price effects based on the value of diverted sales need not rely on market definition or the calculation of market shares and concentration. The Agencies rely much more on the value of diverted sales than on the level of the HHI for diagnosing unilateral price effects in markets with differentiated products. If the value of diverted sales is proportionately small, significant unilateral price effects are unlikely.

[10] Where sufficient data are available, the Agencies may construct economic models designed to quantify the unilateral price effects resulting from the merger. These models often include independent price responses by non-merging firms. They also can incorporate merger-specific efficiencies. These merger simulation methods need not rely on market definition. The Agencies do not treat merger simulation evidence as conclusive in itself, and they place more weight on whether their merger simulations consistently predict substantial price increases than on the precise prediction of any single simulation.

[11] A merger is unlikely to generate substantial unilateral price increases if non-merging parties offer very close substitutes for the products offered by the merging firms. In some cases, non-merging firms may be able to reposition their products to offer close substitutes for the products offered by the merging firms. Repositioning is a supply-side response that is evaluated much like entry, with consideration given to timeliness, likelihood, and sufficiency. See Section 9. The Agencies consider whether repositioning would be sufficient to deter or counteract what otherwise would be significant anticompetitive unilateral effects from a differentiated products merger.

6.2 Bargaining and Auctions

[12] In many industries, especially those involving intermediate goods and services, buyers and sellers negotiate to determine prices and other terms of trade. In that process, buyers commonly negotiate with more than one seller, and may play sellers off against one another. Some highly structured forms of such competition are known as auctions. Negotiations often combine aspects of an auction with aspects of one-on-one negotiation, although pure auctions are sometimes used in government procurement and elsewhere.

[13] A merger between two competing sellers prevents buyers from playing those sellers off against each other in negotiations. This alone can significantly enhance the ability and incentive of the merged entity to obtain a result

more favorable to it, and less favorable to the buyer, than the merging firms would have offered separately absent the merger. The Agencies analyze unilateral effects of this type using similar approaches to those described in Section 6.1.

[14] Anticompetitive unilateral effects in these settings are likely in proportion to the frequency or probability with which, prior to the merger, one of the merging sellers had been the runner-up when the other won the business. These effects also are likely to be greater, the greater advantage the runner-up merging firm has over other suppliers in meeting customers' needs. These effects also tend to be greater, the more profitable were the pre-merger winning bids. All of these factors are likely to be small if there are many equally placed bidders. [. . .]

6.3 Capacity and Output for Homogeneous Products

[15] In markets involving relatively undifferentiated products, the Agencies may evaluate whether the merged firm will find it profitable unilaterally to suppress output and elevate the market price. A firm may leave capacity idle, refrain from building or obtaining capacity that would have been obtained absent the merger, or eliminate pre-existing production capabilities. A firm may also divert the use of capacity away from one relevant market and into another so as to raise the price in the former market. The competitive analyses of these alternative modes of output suppression may differ.

[16] A unilateral output suppression strategy is more likely to be profitable when (1) the merged firm's market share is relatively high; (2) the share of the merged firm's output already committed for sale at prices unaffected by the output suppression is relatively low; (3) the margin on the suppressed output is relatively low; (4) the supply responses of rivals are relatively small; and (5) the market elasticity of demand is relatively low. [. . .]

[17] In some cases, a merger between a firm with a substantial share of the sales in the market and a firm with significant excess capacity to serve that market can make an output suppression strategy profitable. This can occur even if the firm with the excess capacity has a relatively small share of sales, if that firm's ability to expand, and thus keep price from rising, has been making an output suppression strategy unprofitable for the firm with the larger market share.

6.4 Innovation and Product Variety

[18] Competition often spurs firms to innovate. The Agencies may consider whether a merger is likely to diminish innovation competition by encouraging the merged firm to curtail its innovative efforts below the level that would prevail in the absence of the merger. That curtailment of innovation could take the form of reduced incentive to continue with an existing product-development effort or reduced incentive to initiate development of new products.

[19] The first of these effects is most likely to occur if at least one of the merging firms is engaging in efforts to introduce new products that would capture substantial revenues from the other merging firm. The second, longer-run effect is most likely to occur if at least one of the merging firms has capabilities that are likely to lead it to develop new products in the future that would capture substantial revenues from the other merging firm. The Agencies therefore also consider whether a merger will diminish innovation competition by combining two of a very small number of firms with the strongest capabilities to successfully innovate in a specific direction.

[20] The Agencies evaluate the extent to which successful innovation by one merging firm is likely to take sales from the other, and the extent to which post-merger incentives for future innovation will be lower than those that would prevail in the absence of the merger. The Agencies also consider whether the merger is likely to enable innovation that would not otherwise take place, by bringing together complementary capabilities that cannot be otherwise combined or for some other merger-specific reason. See Section 10.

[21] The Agencies also consider whether a merger is likely to give the merged firm an incentive to cease offering one of the relevant products sold by the merging parties. Reductions in variety following a merger may or may not be anticompetitive. Mergers can lead to the efficient consolidation of products when variety offers little in value to customers. In other cases, a merger may increase variety by encouraging the merged firm to reposition its products to be more differentiated from one another.

[22] If the merged firm would withdraw a product that a significant number of customers strongly prefer to those products that would remain available, this can constitute a harm to customers over and above any effects on the price or quality of any given product. If there is evidence of such an effect, the Agencies may inquire whether the reduction in variety is largely due to a loss of competitive incentives attributable to the merger. An anticompetitive incentive to eliminate a product as a result of the merger is greater and more likely, the larger is the share of profits from that product coming at the expense of profits from products sold by the merger partner. Where a merger substantially reduces competition by bringing two close substitute products under common ownership, and one of those products is eliminated, the merger will often also lead to a price increase on the remaining product, but that is not a necessary condition for anticompetitive effect.

Analytical Methods for Mergers: Diversions, UPP, and Merger Simulation

Economists use a variety of tools to assess the strength of competition between merging parties and to predict effects caused by the merger.[622] As a lawyer, you will not be expected to be a master of intricate econometrics! But it may be helpful to have a basic sense of the nature and function of some of the tools that are commonly used to think in an organized way about unilateral effects. Each of the tools described here is best thought of, and used, as one form of evidence and analysis among many.[623]

Diversion Ratios

The HMG extract above mentions "diversion ratios", which are often used as one measure of the intensity of head-to-head competition between two firms. These are important in practice, so it is worth making sure you have absorbed the idea.[624] As the HMGs explain, a diversion ratio is measured from one firm to another: thus, in merger between Firm A and Firm B we might calculate a diversion ratio from A to B, and separately calculate the diversion ratio from B to A. The diversion ratio from A to B is the proportion of customers who, when switching away from A, do or would turn to B.

For example, suppose that we were considering a merger between two supermarkets: SuperStore (a general supermarket) and BakeryFirst (a supermarket that particularly focused on high-end baked goods), in an area where there were two other supermarkets: GeneralStores and OKStuff. The diversion ratio from SuperStore to BakeryFirst would be the proportion of users switching away from SuperStore (because it increased its prices, reduced its opening hours, closed altogether, etc.) who turned to BakeryFirst. Thus, if X% of customers (or customer dollars) switching away from SuperStore would go to BakeryFirst rather than GeneralStores or OKStuff, or rather than not purchasing at all, the diversion ratio from SuperStore to BakeryFirst would be X%.

Note that diversions may be "asymmetrical": the ratio from A to B may be very different from the ratio from B to A. In the example above, suppose that BakeryFirst is an expensive store with a great baked-goods selection but limited offerings in other areas, and that it therefore attracts customers who prefer higher-priced, higher-quality baked goods, and who care a bit less about other product lines. Suppose also that BakeryFirst and SuperStore were geographically close to one another, with GeneralStores and OKStuff located somewhat further away, and that BakeryFirst was the only supermarket that focused on high-quality baked goods to the exclusion of other things.

Under those circumstances, we could imagine that the diversions from BakeryFirst to SuperStore might be fairly high (because customers who cannot shop at BakeryFirst—and who will therefore have to shop at a generalist supermarket—probably prefer a nearby store to one located further away), while diversions from SuperStore to BakeryFirst might be much lower (because SuperStore's existing customers may not want to shop at a more

[622] *See, e.g.*, Nathan H. Miller & Gloria Sheu, *Quantitative Methods for Evaluating the Unilateral Effects of Mergers*, 58 Rev. Indus. Org. 143 (2021); Gregory J. Werden, *Unilateral Competitive Effects of Horizontal Mergers I: Basic Concepts and Models*, in ABA Section of Antitrust Law, 2 ISSUES IN COMPETITION LAW AND POLICY (2008).

[623] *See, e.g.*, Carl Shapiro, *The 2010 Horizontal Merger Guidelines: From Hedgehog to Fox in Forty Years*, 77 Antitrust L.J. 49 (2010).

[624] *See, e.g.*, FTC v. Swedish Match, 131 F. Supp. 2d 151, 169 (D.D.C. 2000) ("High margins and high diversion ratios support large price increases, a tenet endorsed by most economists.").

expensive, bakery-focused store, and might prefer to travel a bit further to reach a similarly generalized supermarket).

As this example illustrates, diversions can be a helpful data point in building an overall picture of the shape of head-to-head competition between two firms, particularly when there is some product and/or geographic differentiation in the market. Of course, diversions can be difficult to calculate: in some cases, there may be actual evidence of how customers actually responded in the past when one party has experienced a price increase, output reduction, or service interruption, allowing diversions to be measured directly. In other cases, sources like customer surveys, customer testimony, win/loss records, or qualitative industry evidence may help to illuminate substitution practices. In still other cases, diversion ratios might have to be inferred, including from market shares. The analytical value of diversion ratios in such cases may be rather small, particularly in differentiated markets. (Can you see why?)

The Concept of Upward Pricing Pressure and GUPPIs

Diversion ratios are a key input into the calculation of "upward pricing pressure" ("UPP") arising from a proposed transaction, which is mentioned in the Guidelines extract above.[625] The core idea is fairly simple. When a merger combines two competing firms, it changes the effects of a price increase on the profit derived from the firm's separate products or services. Before the merger, a price increase means fewer sales of the product or service in question, but higher margins on the sales that are made at the higher price. A merger with a competing firm changes things a little because some of those lost sales will be lost to the *other* merging party: meaning that the "lost" sale is in fact "recaptured" by the merged firm. As a result, a price increase that would not have been profitable before the merger (because of lost sales) may be profitable for the merged firm (because some of the lost sales are recouped by the merging firm). We can thus think of a merger between competitors as creating "upward pressure" on prices. Of course, if the merger *also* generates efficiencies (which we will discuss later in this chapter), those efficiencies will create some *downward* pressure on prices. The balance of the two effects will determine the direction in which the merger will affect prices.

Sometimes lawyers and economists will use the "Gross Upward Pricing Pressure Index" ("GUPPI") to get a raw sense of how much upward pressure a merger might create (before allowing for countervailing efficiencies, reactions of other market participants, resulting entry, repositioning by other suppliers, impact on prices of other products supplied by the firms, innovation effects, or anything else). In a merger between the supplier of product 1 and the supplier of product 2, the GUPPI on product 1 can be calculated in a simple way by multiplying (the diversion ratio from product 1 to product 2) by (the percentage profit margin on product 2) and then by (the price of product 2 divided by the price of product 1). (Note that GUPPI calculation can get much more complicated, but this is the core idea!) In this illustration, the GUPPI is higher when the diversion ratio from product 1 to product 2 is higher (because more lost sales are recouped), when the profit margin on product 2 is high (because the recouped sales on product 2 are valuable), and when the price of product 2 relative to product 1 is high (because the recouped sales on product 2 are valuable relative to the lost sales on product 1).

It is important to understand the GUPPI is a crude measure that does not—and does not attempt to—estimate the *actual* impact a merger will have on prices. The other factors mentioned above, like efficiencies and reactions of market participants, are frequently very important indeed. But it is one way of getting a sense of a transaction's capacity to inflict certain kinds of static price harms. It is also a helpful way of establishing the amount by which the merger would need to reduce the firm's marginal costs in order to have the overall effect of reducing prices (the so-called "CMCR" or compensating marginal cost reduction).

Merger Simulation

The Guidelines also mention "merger simulation." Merger simulation involves creating an economic model of a market, based on information about market demand and market supply, in an effort to predict the competitive conditions that may result from the transaction.

---

[625] For a seminal contribution to this tool, *see* J. Farrell & C. Shapiro, *Antitrust Evaluation of Horizontal Mergers: An Economic Alternative to Market Definition*, 10 B.E. J. of Theoretical Econ. (2010).

Accurate merger simulation is usually a demanding exercise, requiring granular information about the market. Its utility is, among other things, a function of the quality of the inputs—including the quality of data and the accuracy of models—and a function of the aptness of particular economic modeling tools to reflect the way the relevant industries and markets actually work.

(i) Beyond the Presumption: Staples II, Baby Foods, and Oracle/PeopleSoft

In practice, building a strong merger case almost invariably requires more than just an impressive structural case built on high market shares. This is for at least three reasons. First, there often is no single "correct" way to calculate a market share, so parties often argue over how this should be done, and parties' market-share arguments may be subject to some plausible criticism and doubt. Second, courts generally expect (and often require) robust qualitative support from some combination of: (1) economic expert evidence; (2) customers who are willing to credibly testify that they anticipate adverse effects from the merger; and (3) ordinary-course documents showing the parties' competitive significance. Third, in a unilateral effects case in particular, the structural presumption is a very imperfect proxy for the core story of harm. The structural presumption is based on market-wide statistics; the unilateral theory of harm zooms in on the competitive interactions between the parties.

Staples / Office Depot II—the second successful FTC effort to block the acquisition of Office Depot by Staples[626]— showcases *both* the difficulties of calculating a market share *and* the importance of the three main types of qualitative evidence. It also underscores the value, to a plaintiff in a merger trial, of the parties' internal documents![627]

After the *Staples* extract, we will take a briefer look at the district court's thorough analysis of unilateral effects in the DOJ's challenge to the H&R Block / TaxAct transaction. As in *Staples*, the court's conclusion was buttressed by multiple alternative forms of evidence, including some of the forms of analysis described above.

FTC v. Staples, Inc. ("Staples / Office Depot II")
190 F. Supp. 3d 100 (D.D.C. 2016)

Judge Sullivan.

[1] There is overwhelming evidence in this case that large [business-to-business, or "B-to-B"] customers constitute a market that Defendants could target for price increases if they are allowed to merge. Significantly, Defendants themselves used the proposed merger to pressure B-to-B customers to lock in prices based on the expectation that they would lose negotiating leverage if the merger were approved. See, e.g., PX05236 (ODP) at 001 ("This offer is time sensitive. If and when the purchase of OfficeDepot is approved, Staples will have no reason to make this offer."); PX05249 (ODP) at 001 ("[The merger] will remove, your ability to evaluate your program with two competitors. There will only be one."); PX05514 (ODP) at 003 ("Today, the FTC announced 45 days for its final decision. You still have time! You would be able to leverage the competition, gain an agreement that is grandfathered in and drive down expenses!").

[2] Having concluded that Plaintiffs have carried their burden of establishing that the sale and distribution of consumable office supplies to large B-to-B customers in the United States is the relevant market, the Court now turns to an analysis of the likely effects of the proposed merger on competition within the relevant market. If the FTC can make a prima facie showing that the acquisition in this case will result in a significant market share and an undue increase in concentration in the relevant market, then a presumption is established that the merger will substantially lessen competition. The burden is on the government to show that the merger would produce a firm

---

[626] The quest continued. *See* Lauren Hirsch, *Staples returns to Office Depot with a $1 billion offer for its consumer business*, N.Y. TIMES (June 4, 2021), https://www.nytimes.com/2021/06/04/business/staples-office-depot-deal.html; Ben Unglesbee, *After much mulling, Office Depot owner rejects both sale and split*, RETAIL DIVE (June 22, 2022), https://www.retaildive.com/news/after-much-mulling-office-depot-owner-rejects-sale-and-split/625844/.

[627] For another case in which extensive qualitative evidence played a key role, look at the Department of Justice's challenge to Bazaarvoice/PowerReviews. DOJ assembled a compelling deck, linked here, filled with internal documents in support of their successful effort to block the deal.

controlling an undue percentage share of the relevant market that would result in a significant increase in the concentration of firms in that market.

[3] The Plaintiffs can establish their prima facie case by showing that the merger will result in an increase in market concentration above certain levels. Market concentration is a function of the number of firms in a market and their respective market shares. The Herfindahl-Hirschmann Index ("HHI") is a tool used by economists to measure changes in market concentration. Merger Guidelines § 5.3. HHI is calculated by "summing the squares of the individual firms' market shares," a calculation that "gives proportionately greater weight to the larger market shares." = An HHI above 2,500 is considered "highly concentrated"; a market with an HHI between 1,500 and 2,500 is considered "moderately concentrated"; and a market with an HHI below 1,500 is considered "unconcentrated". A merger that results in a highly concentrated market that involves an increase of 200 points will be presumed to be likely to enhance market power.

Concentration in the sale and distribution of consumable office supplies to large B-to-B customers

[4] Dr. Shapiro estimated Defendants' market shares by using data collected from Fortune 100 companies. During the data collecting process, 81 of the Fortune 100 companies responded with enough detail to be used in Dr. Shapiro's sample. The critical data provided by the companies was fiscal year 2014 information on: (1) their overall spend on consumable office supplies; (2) the amount spent on consumable office supplies from Staples; and (3) the amount spent on consumable office supplies from OfficeDepot. Some Fortune 100 companies have an established primary vendor relationship with Staples or OfficeDepot. For example, Staples has 100 percent of the market share relating to [redacted text]'s spend on consumable office supplies and OfficeDepot has 100 percent of the market share relating to [redacted text]'s spend on consumable office supplies. Other Fortune 100 customers purchase office supplies from a mix of vendors. For example, Staples accounted for twenty-seven percent of [redacted text]'s spend on consumable office supplies in 2014 and OfficeDepot accounted for twenty-one percent.

[5] Defendants' market share of the Fortune 100 sample as a whole is striking: Staples captures 47.3 percent and OfficeDepot captures 31.6 percent, for a total of 79 percent market share. The pre-merger HHI is already highly concentrated in this market, resting at 3,270. Put another way, Staples and OfficeDepot currently operate in the relevant market as a duopoly with a competitive fringe. If allowed to merge, the HHI would increase nearly 3,000 points, from 3,270 to 6,265. This market structure would constitute one dominant firm with a competitive fringe. Staples' proposed acquisition of OfficeDepot is therefore presumptively illegal because the HHI increases more than 200 points and the post-merger HHI is greater than 2,500.

[6] Defendants make several arguments in opposition to Dr. Shapiro's market share methodology and calculation. Defendants argue that: . . . the Fortune 100 sample overstates Defendants' actual market share; . . . and (3) Dr. Shapiro underestimates leakage, inflating Defendants' market shares. However, despite significant time spent cross-examining Dr. Shapiro with regard to his methodology, Defendants produced no expert evidence during the hearing to rebut that methodology. Moreover, it is significant that Defendants' final 100-page brief devotes only seven paragraphs to challenging Dr. Shapiro's market share calculations.

[7] Defendants' first argument in opposition to Dr. Shapiro's focus on the Fortune 100 is that his failure to take a sample of the other approximate 1100 companies in the relevant market is error because it results in dramatically inflated market shares. Dr. Shapiro conceded that the data he analyzed is imperfect because it does not include all large B-to-B customers. However, Dr. Shapiro was confident that there is no reason to believe the market shares are biased when it comes to estimating the market shares of Staples and OfficeDepot. To test whether his analysis of the Fortune 100 might have overstated Defendants' market shares because the Fortune 100 companies are especially large, Dr. Shapiro measured the market share of the top half of his sample separate from the bottom half. The range of spending on consumable office supplies among the companies analyzed in Dr. Shapiro's analysis is vast: from less than $200,000 per year on the low end, to more than $33 million per year on the high end. The combined market share for Defendants is seventy-nine percent among the top half of the Fortune 100 and eighty-nine percent among the bottom half.. Thus, Dr. Shapiro states that he is confident that the market shares for Staple[s] and OfficeDepot reported in Exhibit 5B are not overstated.

[8] Defendants' second challenge relating to the Fortune 100 sample focuses on the fact that only eighty-one of the 100 companies responded with enough data to be included in Dr. Shapiro's analysis. Defendants argue that the nineteen omitted are the most likely to purchase supplies from vendors other than Staples and OfficeDepot. Defendants highlight Costco as an example, a company that charges each department with procuring its own office supplies, whether from Costco or other vendors. The fact that Costco is able to purchase office supplies from Costco itself makes that company's procurement of office supplies an anomaly. Because Defendants did not present a case, they do not provide the Court with an analysis of the nineteen Fortune 100 companies excluded from Dr. Shapiro's analysis to show that their exclusion skewed Defendants' market shares in a way favorable to Plaintiffs. Antitrust economists rely on data from third parties through surveys, and therefore the measure of market shares is normally imperfect. . . . For all of these reasons, and in view of the absence of expert testimony offered by the Defendants, the Court is persuaded that Dr. Shapiro's analysis of the Fortune 100 represents a reasonable and reliable approximation of the Defendants' market share. [. . .]

[9] Finally, Defendants contend that Dr. Shapiro did not adequately account for "leakage" in his market share analysis. Leakage refers to unreported discretionary employee purchases of office supplies. Dr. Shapiro requested an estimate of leakage from the Fortune 100. Of the eighty-one companies included in his market-share analysis, twenty-six reported on leakage. Twelve of the twenty-six indicated that leakage spend was de minimis or immaterial. In these cases, Dr. Shapiro assumed that one percent of the companies' spend on office supplies was leakage.

[10] Testimony from fact witnesses during the hearing made it clear that even the largest companies in the world are either not concerned enough about leakage to track it or do not have a reliable way of tracking it. These same companies have tremendous incentive to ensure that their employees spend on contract. Purchases made by employees online or from a brick and mortar store are [redacted text] to [redacted text] percent higher than the contract price paid by large companies. Most companies with a primary-vendor contract have an official policy that requires employees to purchase office supplies through the contract. Best Buy produced a video to educate employees about the benefits of buying on contract.

[11] For all of these reasons, the Court is confident that Dr. Shapiro accounted for any impact leakage has on Defendants' market shares in this case.

[15] Plaintiffs have met their burden of showing that the merger would result in undue concentration in the relevant market of the sale and distribution of consumable office supplies to large B-to-B customers in the United States. The relevant HHI would increase nearly 3,000 points, from 3270 to 6265. These HHI numbers far exceed the 200 point increase and post-merger concentration level of 2500 necessary to entitle Plaintiffs to a presumption that the merger is illegal. The Court rejects Defendants' arguments in opposition to Dr. Shapiro's market analysis for the reasons discussed in detail . . . supra. Nevertheless, to strengthen their prima facie case, Plaintiffs presented additional evidence of harm, which the Court analyzes next.

Plaintiffs' evidence of additional harm

[16] Sole reliance on HHI calculations cannot guarantee litigation victories. Plaintiffs therefore highlight additional evidence, including bidding data ("bid data"), ordinary course documents, and fact-witness testimony. This additional evidence substantiates Plaintiffs' claim that this merger, if consummated, would result in a lessening of competition.

[17] Mergers that eliminate head-to-head competition between close competitors often result in a lessening of competition. Plaintiffs' evidence supports the conclusion that Defendants compete head-to-head for large B-to-B customers.

1. Bidding Data

[18] Dr. Shapiro analyzed five sets of bid data including: (1) Defendants' win-loss data; (2) data on Defendants' top wins and top losses; and (3) Fortune 100 bid data. Defendants often bid against each other for large B-to-B contracts.

[19] The bid data also shows that Defendants win large B-to-B customer bids more frequently than other bidders. The B-to-B contract market accounts for approximately thirty-five percent of Defendants' sales. According to Dr. Shapiro, the sale of consumable office supplies accounts for about [redacted text] percent of Defendants' B-to-B customer revenues. Staples CEO Mr. Sargent describes the B-to-B contract business as a "cornerstone" of Staples' business. In fact, seventy-eight percent of OfficeDepot bid losses are to Staples. Similarly, eighty-one percent of Staples' bid losses were to OfficeDepot. Defendants compete aggressively for the others' business, exemplified by Staples' 2014 "Operation Take Share," a campaign that sought to capture some of OfficeDepot's market share.

2. Ordinary Course Documents

[20] Defendants' own documents created in the ordinary course of their business show that Defendants view themselves as the most viable office supply vendors for large businesses in the United States. See, e.g. PX04082 (SPLS) at 029 ("[T]here are only two real choices for them. Us or Them."); PX04042 (SPLS) at 024; PX05311 (ODP) at 001. Not surprisingly, Defendants view themselves as each other's fiercest competition. See, e.g., PX04322 (SPLS) at 001 (identifying only OfficeDepot as "Key Competitor[ ]"); PX04414 (SPLS) at 008 ("For core office supplies we often compare ourselves to our most direct competitor, ODP"); PX05229 (ODP) at 149 (stating that Staples is OfficeDepot's "[t]oughest and most aggressively priced national competitor.").

[21] Defendants consistently compete head-to-head with each other to win large B-to-B contracts. For example, in early 2015, HPG began negotiations with Staples. Staples' initial price reduction was retracted until OfficeDepot was invited to bid. Pitting Defendants against each other, HPG received substantial price concessions from both. In November 2014, Staples increased its up-front payment to [redacted text] to $[redacted text] to prevent [redacted text] from switching to OfficeDepot. In March 2014, [redacted text] engaged the Defendants in multiple rounds of bidding. Ultimately, OfficeDepot could not meet the six percent core list savings necessary to win the contract from Staples.

3. Fact Witness Testimony

[22] Large B-to-B customers view Defendants as their best option for nationwide sale and delivery of consumable office supplies. See e.g. Hrg Tr. 225:25-226:5 (AEP: "Q: And after OfficeDepot and Staples, what's the—what's the next best option after that? A: Then we're in trouble. We don't have a good—I don't think we have a good option after that."); 1205:17-20 (Best Buy "Q: So today Best Buy has a contract with OfficeDepot. Who does Best Buy consider to be its next best option for general office supplies and copy paper? A: Staples."); 1938:14-1939:18 (HPG "There's two nationally capable office supply vendors, from our perspective. One is Staples and one is Depot. And they control, roughly—when I say control, they own 80 percent of the market in terms of revenue."); 361:2-21, 373:9-15; 492:3-7 (McDonalds' noting its consideration of Staples and OfficeDepot, but ultimately did not invite Staples to submit an RFP because the company was able to "recognize immediate savings" by not going through an expensive bid process.); 1018:1-13 (Select Medical, a company that contracts with OfficeDepot, testified that it has concerns about the merger going through because "I believe it's important to have that competition to be able to properly service our national footprint, our national presence, and to also be able to provide the best possible pricing."). This testimony shows that absent OfficeDepot, large B-to-B customers would lose tremendous leverage and likely have to pay higher prices for consumable office supplies.

[23] This additional evidence strengthens Plaintiffs' claim that harm will result in the form of loss of competition if Staples is permitted to acquire OfficeDepot.

CASENOTE: United States v. H & R Block, Inc.

833 F. Supp. 2d 36 (D.D.C. 2011)

You may remember *H & R Block*—DOJ's challenge to the proposed acquisition of TaxACT by H & R Block ("HRB")—from Chapter III, where we considered some of the market definition challenges. In that case, DOJ advanced both unilateral and coordinated effects theories, and triggered the structural presumption by showing that the deal would increase HHI by around 400, resulting in a post-acquisition HHI of almost 4700(!).

The court began its analysis by explaining that unilateral anticompetitive effects arise "if the acquiring firm will have the incentive to raise prices or reduce quality after the acquisition, independent of competitive responses from other firms." The court quoted a framework from an earlier case, FTC v. CCC Holdings, Inc., 605 F. Supp. 2d 26, 68 (D.D.C. 2009): "Unilateral effects in a differentiated product market are likely to be profitable under the following conditions: (1) the products must be differentiated; (2) the products controlled by the merging firms must be close substitutes, i.e., a substantial number of the customers of one firm would turn to the other in response to a price increase; (3) other products must be sufficiently different from the products offered by the merging firms that a merger would make a small but significant and non-transitory price increase profitable for the merging firm; and (4) repositioning [by existing competitors to defeat anticompetitive effects] must be unlikely."

DOJ's unilateral case rested on considerable evidence of head-to-head competition between HRB and TaxACT. This included evidence that "HRB has lowered its [digital do-it-yourself] DDIY prices to better compete with free online products, the category pioneered by TaxACT, and has directly considered TaxACT's prices in setting its own prices. HRB has also determined the nature of its free offerings in response to competitive activity from TaxACT. The government also points to HRB documents that appear to acknowledge that TaxACT has put downward pressure on HRB's pricing ability." The court concluded that "[f]rom all of this evidence, and the additional evidence discussed in this opinion, it is clear that HRB and TaxACT are head-to-head competitors."

DOJ's position was supported by economic expert analysis. DOJ's expert had calculated that, if customer diversions were proportional to market share, diversions from HRB to TaxACT would be at least 14% and those from TaxACT to HRB would be at least 12%. Considering the parties' respective profit margins, DOJ's merger simulations suggested that the merged firm would increase TaxACT's price by 10.5–12.2% and HRB's price by 2.2–2.5%. Defendants raised various objections to these simulations (including the inputs to the economics model as well as to the model itself).

In response, the court emphasized that, while the government's quantitative analysis was necessarily imprecise, it was a helpful data point among others: "The Court finds that the merger simulation model used by the government's expert is an imprecise tool, but nonetheless has some probative value in predicting the likelihood of a potential price increase after the merger. The results of the merger simulation tend to confirm the Court's conclusions based upon the documents, testimony, and other evidence in this case that HRB and TaxACT are head-to-head competitors, that TaxACT's competition has constrained HRB's pricing, and that, post-merger, overall prices in the DDIY products of the merged firms are likely to increase to the detriment of the American taxpayer."

The merging parties offered some additional arguments in an effort to rebut DOJ's case: a couple of these are particularly important. First, the parties pointed to the fact that TaxACT had promised to maintain its current prices for three years as a guarantee against harm from the deal. But the court closed the door firmly on this kind of good-behavior remedy. "[T]his type of guarantee cannot rebut a likelihood of anticompetitive effects in this case. Even if TaxACT's list price remains the same, the merged firm could accomplish what amounts to a price increase through other means. For example, instead of raising TaxACT's prices, it could limit the functionality of TaxACT's products, reserving special features or innovations for higher priced, HRB-branded products. The merged firm could also limit the availability of TaxACT to consumers by marketing it more selectively and less vigorously."

Second, the parties pointed to evidence suggesting that a third player—the market leader, Intuit, which offered the popular TurboTax product—was a closer competitor to each of the merging parties than the other party. But the court was again unmoved, given the evidence of direct competition between HRB and TaxACT on both pricing and features: "[t]he fact that Intuit may be the closest competitor for both HRB and TaxACT also does not necessarily prevent a finding of unilateral effects for this merger."

Staples / Office Depot II and *H&R Block* demonstrate some ways in which additional evidence can reinforce the structural presumption. But in other cases, it can work the other way: additional evidence can *undermine* the structural presumption and allay competitive concerns. *Baker Hughes*, discussed above, was just such a case. *General*

Dynamics, which we will meet later in this chapter, was another.[628] A more recent example was the state AGs' challenge to the *Sprint / T-Mobile* merger: in that case, a combination of efficiencies evidence, a remedy negotiated by the DOJ (which the state AG plaintiffs did not accept as sufficient), and a "flailing firm" argument operated to defeat the presumption. We will talk about efficiencies and flailing firms later in this chapter, and will consider remedies below, as well as in Chapters XI and XII.

In general, consistent with the teachings of *Baker Hughes*, the stronger the structural case gets—that is, the higher the post-merger concentration HHI measure and the higher the increase in concentration caused by the deal (the so-called "delta HHI")—the less additional evidence courts or agencies will require from a plaintiff.[629] In *Heinz*, as we will see in a moment, the structural case seems to have stood virtually alone to discharge the plaintiff's burden.

Merger cases, like virtually all antitrust cases, are heavily driven by their own contexts and circumstances. This means that merger investigations and litigations are evidence-driven, discovery-heavy affairs, as agencies and courts work to understand the workings of competition in each relevant market. A merger can give rise to unilateral anticompetitive effects: even if neither party is the market leader; even if other firms are also close competitors of the merging parties; and even if the competition between the parties occurs higher up the distribution chain than the level at which end-consumers make their purchases. All three of these factors were at issue in the *Heinz* case (colloquially, the "Baby Foods" litigation). In *Heinz*, the merging parties—Heinz and Beech-Nut—were #2 and #3 in the market but, due to supermarket retailing practices, they were very seldom competing side-by-side on the same shelf. Instead they competed for the so-called "second position" on the supermarket shelf, alongside the market leader, Gerber, which was carried virtually everywhere. The district court denied the FTC's motion for a preliminary injunction to block the deal during an administrative challenge.[630] But, as the D.C. Circuit concluded on appeal, the deal was still unlawful, given the brands' robust competition to get onto the supermarket shelf in the first place.[631]

FTC v. H.J. Heinz Co.
246 F.3d 708 (D.C. Cir. 2001)

Judge Henderson.

[1] Four million infants in the United States consume 80 million cases of jarred baby food annually, representing a domestic market of $865 million to $1 billion. The baby food market is dominated by three firms, Gerber Products Company, Heinz and Beech-Nut. Gerber, the industry leader, enjoys a 65 per cent market share while Heinz and Beech-Nut come in second and third, with a 17.4 per cent and a 15.4 per cent share respectively. The district court found that Gerber enjoys unparalleled brand recognition with a brand loyalty greater than any other product sold in the United States. Gerber's products are found in over 90 per cent of all American supermarkets.

[2] By contrast, Heinz is sold in approximately 40 per cent of all supermarkets. Its sales are nationwide but concentrated in northern New England, the Southeast and Deep South and the Midwest. Despite its second-place domestic market share, Heinz is the largest producer of baby food in the world with $1 billion in sales worldwide. Its domestic baby food products with annual net sales of $103 million are manufactured at its Pittsburgh, Pennsylvania plant, which was updated in 1991 at a cost of $120 million. The plant operates at 40 per cent of its production capacity and produces 12 million cases of baby food annually. Its baby food line includes about 130 SKUs (stock keeping units), that is, product varieties (e.g., strained carrots, apple sauce, etc.). Heinz lacks Gerber's brand recognition; it markets itself as a "value brand" with a shelf price several cents below Gerber's.

[3] Beech-Nut has a market share (15.4%) comparable to that of Heinz (17.4%), with $138.7 million in annual sales of baby food, of which 72 per cent is jarred baby food. Its jarred baby food line consists of 128 SKUs. Beech–

---

[628] *See infra* § VIII.D.3.

[629] *See, e.g.*, United States v. Anthem, Inc., 855 F.3d 345, 349–50 (D.C. Cir. 2017) ("The more compelling the prima facie case, the more evidence the defendant must present to rebut it successfully, but because the burden of persuasion ultimately lies with the plaintiff, the burden to rebut must not be unduly onerous.") (internal quotation marks omitted).

[630] FTC v. H.J. Heinz Co., 116 F.Supp.2d 190 (D.D.C. 2000).

[631] For a similar transaction that abandoned after an FTC challenge, *see* Complaint, In the matter of Post Holdings, Inc., FTC Dkt. No. 9388 (filed Dec. 19, 2019).

Nut manufactures all of its baby food in Canajoharie, New York at a manufacturing plant that was built in 1907 and began manufacturing baby food in 1931. Beech–Nut maintains price parity with Gerber, selling at about one penny less. It markets its product as a premium brand. Consumers generally view its product as comparable in quality to Gerber's. Id. Beech-Nut is carried in approximately 45 per cent of all grocery stores. Although its sales are nationwide, they are concentrated in New York, New Jersey, California and Florida.

[4] At the wholesale level Heinz and Beech-Nut both make lump-sum payments called "fixed trade spending" (also known as "slotting fees" or "pay-to-stay" arrangements) to grocery stores to obtain shelf placement. Gerber, with its strong name recognition and brand loyalty, does not make such pay-to-stay payments. The other type of wholesale trade spending is "variable trade spending," which typically consists of manufacturers' discounts and allowances to supermarkets to create retail price differentials that entice the consumer to purchase their product instead of a competitor's.

a. Prima Facie Case

[5] Merger law rests upon the theory that, where rivals are few, firms will be able to coordinate their behavior, either by overt collusion or implicit understanding, in order to restrict output and achieve profits above competitive levels. Increases in concentration above certain levels are thought to raise a likelihood of interdependent anticompetitive conduct. Market concentration, or the lack thereof, is often measured by the Herfindahl-Hirschmann Index (HHI).

[6] Sufficiently large HHI figures establish the FTC's prima facie case that a merger is anti-competitive. The district court found that the pre-merger HHI score for the baby food industry is 4775—indicative of a highly concentrated industry. The merger of Heinz and Beech-Nut will increase the HHI by 510 points. This creates, by a wide margin, a presumption that the merger will lessen competition in the domestic jarred baby food market. Here, the FTC's market concentration statistics are bolstered by the indisputable fact that the merger will eliminate competition between the two merging parties at the wholesale level, where they are currently the only competitors for what the district court described as the second position on the supermarket shelves. Heinz's own documents recognize the wholesale competition and anticipate that the merger will end it. Indeed, those documents disclose that Heinz considered three options to end the vigorous wholesale competition with Beech-Nut: two involved innovative measures while the third entailed the acquisition of Beech-Nut. Heinz chose the third, and least pro-competitive, of the options.

[7] Finally, the anticompetitive effect of the merger is further enhanced by high barriers to market entry. The district court found that there had been no significant entries in the baby food market in decades and that new entry was difficult and improbable. This finding largely eliminates the possibility that the reduced competition caused by the merger will be ameliorated by new competition from outsiders and further strengthens the FTC's case.

[8] As far as we can determine, no court has ever approved a merger to duopoly under similar circumstances.

b. Rebuttal Arguments

[9] [. . .] The appellees first contend, and the district court agreed, that Heinz and Beech-Nut do not really compete against each other at the retail level. Consumers do not regard the products of the two companies as substitutes, the appellees claim, and generally only one of the two brands is available on any given store's shelves. Hence, they argue, there is little competitive loss from the merger.

[10] This argument has a number of flaws which render clearly erroneous the court's finding that Heinz and Beech-Nut have not engaged in significant pre-merger competition. First, in accepting the appellees' argument that Heinz and Beech–Nut do not compete, the district court failed to address the record evidence that the two do in fact price against each other, and that, where both are present in the same areas, they depress each other's prices as well as those of Gerber even though they are virtually never all found in the same store. This evidence undermines the district court's factual finding.

[11] Second, the district court's finding is inconsistent with its conclusion that there is a single, national market for jarred baby food in the United States. The Supreme Court has explained that "[t]he outer boundaries of a product

market are determined by the reasonable interchangeability of use [by consumers] or the cross-elasticity of demand between the product itself and substitutes for it." *Brown Shoe*, 370 U.S. at 325. The definition of product market thus focuses solely on demand substitution factors, i.e., that consumers regard the products as substitutes. By defining the relevant product market generically as jarred baby food, the district court concluded that in areas where Heinz's and Beech-Nut's products are both sold, consumers will switch between them in response to a small but significant and nontransitory increase in price (SSNIP). The district court never explained this inherent inconsistency in its logic nor could counsel for the appellees explain it at oral argument.

[12] Third, and perhaps most important, the court's conclusion concerning pre-merger competition does not take into account the indisputable fact that the merger will eliminate competition at the wholesale level between the only two competitors for the "second shelf" position. Competition between Heinz and Beech-Nut to gain accounts at the wholesale level is fierce with each contest concluding in a winner-take-all result. The district court regarded this loss of competition as irrelevant because the FTC did not establish to its satisfaction that wholesale competition ultimately benefitted consumers through lower retail prices. The district court concluded that fixed trade spending did not affect consumer prices and that the FTC's assertion that the proposed merger will affect variable trade spending levels and consumer prices is at best, inconclusive. Although the court noted the FTC's examples of consumer benefit through couponing initiatives, the court held that it was impossible to conclude with any certainty that the consumer benefit from such couponing initiatives would be lost in the merger.

[13] In rejecting the FTC's argument regarding the loss of wholesale competition, the court committed two legal errors. First, as the appellees conceded at oral argument, no court has ever held that a reduction in competition for wholesale purchasers is not relevant unless the plaintiff can prove impact at the consumer level. Second, it is, in any event, not the FTC's burden to prove such an impact with "certainty." To the contrary, the antitrust laws assume that a retailer faced with an increase in the cost of one of its inventory items will try so far as competition allows to pass that cost on to its customers in the form of a higher price for its product. Section 7 is, after all, concerned with probabilities, not certainties.

* * *

Although a unilateral effects case presupposes that meaningful competition would occur between the parties absent the transaction, merger enforcement does *not* depend on the conclusion that the parties are literally one another's closest or nearest competitors.

Stephen Mohr, The closest competitor is not the only competitor
FTC Competition Matters Blog (Dec. 9, 2019)

More and more, merging parties argue that their merger does not raise competition concerns because they are not each other's closest competitors. Parties have advanced this argument even in markets where there will be only two or three remaining firms post-transaction, including the merged firm. This argument is not new, and it often misunderstands merger analysis.

For any merger involving direct competitors—firms that are actively bidding against one another or vying for the same customers—the key question is whether the elimination of competition between the merging parties increases opportunities for anticompetitive unilateral or coordinated conduct in the post-merger market. While removal of the closest competitor likely eliminates the most significant source of competitive pressure on the merging firm, the Bureau's analysis does not end merely because the merging parties are not each other's most intense rivals. Instead, the Bureau routinely examines mergers that do not involve the two closest competitors in a market because a merger that removes a close (though not closest) competitor also may have a significant effect on the competitive dynamics in the post-merger market—that is, it too may "substantially lessen competition" in violation of Section 7. This is consistent with the discussion in the Horizontal Merger Guidelines § 6.1 regarding competition between differentiated products, and is especially true if the acquired firm plays the role of a disruptor or innovator in the market. These firms often punch above their weight, having an out-sized impact on market dynamics despite a small market share.

For more recent real world guidance, merging parties need look no further than two of the Commission's recent merger challenges: *In re CDK Global, Inc. (CDK)* and *In re Otto Bock HealthCare North America, Inc. (Otto Bock)*. Last year, the Commission challenged the proposed merger of CDK and Auto/Mate, providers of dealer management systems for car dealerships. As the Commission stated in its Complaint, CDK and Reynolds & Reynolds were the two dominant players in the U.S. market, while Auto/Mate was an "innovative, disruptive challenger" that engaged in aggressive pricing. Although Auto/Mate was far from being CDK's closest competitor, the Commission nonetheless determined that Auto/Mate was poised to become an even stronger competitive threat in the future and that existing, current competition between the parties understated the most likely anticompetitive effects of this transaction. After the Commission issued a complaint and authorized staff to seek a PI, the parties abandoned their transaction.

Even more illuminating is this year's Commission Opinion analyzing Otto Bock's acquisition of Freedom Innovations, two manufacturers of microprocessor prosthetic knees (MPKs). [In the matter of Otto Bock Healthcare North America, 2019-2 Trade Cases ¶ 80,990, 2019 WL 6003207 (F.T.C. Nov. 1, 2019)] Similar to Auto/Mate, Freedom was a smaller, but more innovative and aggressive competitor than the two larger prosthetic manufacturers, Otto Bock and Össur. Otto Bock argued that the transaction was unlikely to result in competitive harm because Össur, not Freedom, was its closest competitor. The Commission disagreed, emphasizing in its Opinion that, "a merger can cause unilateral effects even if the merging products are not each other's closest competitors" and noting that it is sufficient if "a significant fraction of the customers purchasing that product view products formerly sold by the other merging firm as their next-best choice"—and that a "significant fraction . . . need not approach a majority." Applying this principle, the Commission found sufficient evidence of closeness of competition because Otto Bock and Freedom competed vigorously before the merger and, at the time of the acquisition, Freedom was preparing to introduce a new MPK that it expected would take significant share away from Otto Bock.

As the *CDK* and *Otto Bock* matters demonstrate, parties that continue to focus on showing that the merging firms are not each other's closest competitor may be ignoring the full analysis necessary to convince the Bureau and the Commission that the merger does not raise competitive concerns. Because that fact is not dispositive, counsel should address all the ways in which the parties are important competitive constraints on each other (or other market participants) such that the merger, by removing this constraint, would allow the merged firm to raise prices, reduce quality, reduce innovation, or coordinate more effectively with remaining competitors. Merger review is not so myopic as to dismiss the impact of all but the closest competitor.

* * *

With this in mind, now read the court's analysis in *Oracle / PeopleSoft*. That case involved the proposed merger of two major suppliers of enterprise software, including software for financial management and human resources management. The court was unpersuaded by the Department of Justice's effort to show a distinctive zone of head-to-head competition between the parties that did not include a third player, SAP. The court's discussion walks through a variety of common types of evidence in a merger case. Is the court's approach in tension with the FTC blog post above, or just an application of the same approach to particular facts?

United States v. Oracle Corp.
331 F.Supp.2d 1098 (N.D. Cal. 2004)[632]

Judge Walker.

[1] In a unilateral effects case, a plaintiff is attempting to prove that the merging parties could unilaterally increase prices. Accordingly, a plaintiff must demonstrate that the merging parties would enjoy a post-merger monopoly or dominant position, at least in a "localized competition" space. [. . .]

---

[632] For a perspective from one of the lead lawyers, see Commissioner J. Thomas Rosch, *Lessons Learned from* United States v. Oracle Corp., *Remarks for Antitrust in the High Tech Sector: Mergers, Enforcement, and Standardization* (Jan. 31, 2012); for contemporary commentary, *see* Roundtable, *Unilateral Effects Analysis After* Oracle, ANTITRUST (Spring 2005) 8; R. Preston McAfee, David S. Sibley, and Michael

[2] Merely demonstrating that the merging parties' products are differentiated is not sufficient. Instead, a plaintiff must demonstrate product differentiation sufficient to sustain a small but significant and non-transitory price increase. [. . .]

[3] Price is one, but only one, of many ways in which to differentiate a product. A market of homogeneous goods can be seen as a market in which sellers have only one dimension in which to differentiate their product. One expects sellers in such a market to "differentiate" their products by lowering the price until price equals marginal cost. On the other hand, a differentiated product "market" is a market in which sellers compete along more dimensions than price. As a result, products competing against one another in a differentiated product market may have widely different prices. That products with widely different prices may, in fact, be in the same market complicates market definition considerably. [. . .]

[4] In sum, defining the relevant market in differentiated product markets is likely to be a difficult task due to the many non-price dimensions in which sellers in such markets compete. Further, it may be difficult to determine currently existing market power and separate this from enhanced market power due to the merger. [. . .]

[5] Plaintiffs [in this case] rest their theory of anticompetitive effects on an attempt to prove that Oracle and PeopleSoft are in a "localized" competition sphere (a "node") within the high function FMS [*i.e.*, financial management systems] and HRM [*i.e.*, human resources management] market. This sphere does not include SAP or any other vendors, and a merger of Oracle and PeopleSoft would, therefore, adversely affect competition in this localized market. Plaintiffs also offered evidence to show that SAP could not reposition itself to replace the localized competition that would allegedly be lost if Oracle and PeopleSoft merge.

[6] In attempting to prove localized competition between Oracle and PeopleSoft, plaintiffs relied on virtually the same kind of evidence used to prove the product market, including internal corporate documents, SAP executive testimony, customer and consultant firm testimony and expert testimony.

[7] **Internal documents.** Plaintiffs rely upon several quarterly "win/loss analysis" documents that were compiled by Oracle during 2003 to show that Oracle and PeopleSoft are each other's closest competitors. In Quarter 1 of 2003, plaintiffs offered evidence that Oracle lost to PeopleSoft 37 percent of the time when the two were in competition, while Oracle lost to SAP only 15 percent of the time the two competed. Plaintiffs then offered evidence from Quarter 3 in which Oracle explicitly states that PeopleSoft is our Number # 1 competitor and SAP is our Number # 2 competitor.

[8] But what plaintiffs failed to mention regarding the Quarter 3 findings is that Oracle lost to PeopleSoft 54 percent of the time, while they lost to SAP 53 percent of the time. Accordingly, what separates the "# 1 competitor" and "# 2 competitor" of Oracle is merely one percent. Moreover, these roughly equal loss ratios continued into Quarter 4 when Oracle lost to PeopleSoft 59 percent of the time, while losing to SAP 50 percent of the time. Accordingly, the court can draw no conclusions from the conflicting data within the win/loss reports upon which plaintiffs focus. In fact, these documents arguably negate a showing of localization between Oracle and PeopleSoft more than they support such a finding.

[9] **SAP executive testimony.** Plaintiffs attempt to localize PeopleSoft and Oracle by showing that many customers have a negative "perception" of SAP and that SAP is at a substantial disadvantage when it comes to competing for customers in the United States (the geographic market that the court has already rejected). In proving these negative perceptions, plaintiffs pointed to the testimony of SAP America's [executive] Knowles. At trial, Knowles agreed that SAP has had to deal with perceptions that SAP is too costly and difficult to implement. Further, plaintiffs cited evidence from consulting firms and Knowles stating that SAP has had trouble breaking into certain verticals in the United States.

[10] In deciding the merits of this argument, the court is again perplexed by the inconsistency within plaintiffs' own evidence. In trying to prove Oracle and PeopleSoft are in localized competition, plaintiffs tried to downplay SAP's presence in the United States and characterize SAP has being "disadvantaged" and unable to enter several

---

A. Williams, *Oracle's Acquisition of PeopleSoft:* U.S. v. Oracle (July 2007), https://vita.mcafee.cc/PDF/Oracle.pdf. For the DOJ's closing argument slides, see https://www.justice.gov/atr/case-document/closing-argument-presentation.

markets. But plaintiffs' own evidence on market shares negates such a finding. Even assuming the relevant geographic market in this case was the United States, [plaintiff's expert] Elzinga's calculations of market shares in so-called high function FMS has SAP ranked highest (above Oracle and PeopleSoft) with a 39 percent market share. Moreover, in the HRM high function market, plaintiffs' expert ranked SAP second with a 29 percent market share (beating Oracle). SAP is not a "disadvantaged" and "troubled" competitor in the United States. If it were, SAP should not be beating Oracle in both markets and beating PeopleSoft in the FMS market. Accordingly, the court cannot credit plaintiffs' argument that SAP is suffering from negative customer perceptions or is disadvantaged in competing against Oracle and PeopleSoft.

[11] **Customer and consulting firm testimony.** In furtherance of this localization theory, plaintiffs argued that customer testimony shows that Oracle and PeopleSoft present better alternatives in the United States than SAP. Plaintiffs support this assertion by citing the testimony of five customers who eliminated SAP from the final round of negotiations and instead chose to deal with Oracle and PeopleSoft.

[12] The court finds this evidence unpersuasive for two reasons. First, the court cannot take the self-interested testimony of five companies which chose to eliminate SAP from consideration, and from that sample draw the general conclusion that SAP does not present a competitive alternative to Oracle and PeopleSoft. Drawing generalized conclusions about an extremely heterogeneous customer market based upon testimony from a small sample is not only unreliable, it is nearly impossible. Second, the most persuasive testimony from customers is not what they say in court, but what they do in the market. And as Elzinga's statistics showed, customers are buying SAP FMS more than Oracle and PeopleSoft FMS. Customers are buying SAP HRM more than that of Oracle.

[13] Plaintiffs rely upon two of the Big Five consulting firms' testimony stating they believe SAP is often the third choice of many U.S. customers. According to BearingPoint's Keating, SAP has long been the least flexible of the three vendors in the way it has sold its HRM and FMS software. Also, Accenture's Bass testified that SAP was less likely to discount than Oracle and PeopleSoft. But the plaintiffs' own evidence discounts this argument. While it may be true that SAP has been the least flexible and least likely to discount, the evidence introduced by Elzinga shows that customers apparently are not deterred by SAP's inflexibility or higher pricing. Customers still buy SAP software over Oracle and PeopleSoft.

[14] Taken as a whole, the customer and consulting firm testimony falls short of proving that Oracle and PeopleSoft engage in competition to which SAP is simply not a party. Moreover, both PeopleSoft industry witnesses conceded there is no vertical in which SAP is not competitive with Oracle and PeopleSoft.

[15] **Expert testimony.** Finally, plaintiffs offered the testimony of Professor McAfee to show that PeopleSoft and Oracle are engaged in localized competition to which SAP is not a party. McAfee conducted three independent analyses to reach his conclusions.

[16] First, McAfee examined, in detail, twenty-five of Oracle's DAFs {*eds: Discount Approval Forms, an internal document used at Oracle to seek management approval for a discount to a customer*} in which Oracle salespersons had listed PeopleSoft as their justification for seeking a higher discount. Second, McAfee, using charts of discount trends provided by Oracle, ran a regression analysis to assess the effect of PeopleSoft's presence on Oracle's discount levels. . . . Based upon these . . . independent studies, McAfee concluded that in many instances PeopleSoft and Oracle are each other's closest competitor and a merger between the two would cause significant anticompetitive effects.

[17] *Twenty-five case studies.* At trial, McAfee showed the court several DAFs in which the presence of PeopleSoft had justified an Oracle salesperson seeking a steep discount. McAfee then picked out explicit language from the justification column to prove that when Oracle and PeopleSoft compete, they do so vigorously. For example, when seeking a discount on the Hallmark account, a salesperson's justification for a discount was an "EXTREMELY competitive situation against" PeopleSoft. Because of this competition, a higher discount was warranted. Likewise, in trying to win the Greyhound account Oracle wanted to cause a third straight loss for PeopleSoft and only aggressive proposals would win Greyhound over.

[18] These two examples are representative of the many that McAfee showed the court—clear examples of how vigorously PeopleSoft and Oracle compete when they go "head to head" against each other, he asserted. McAfee

concluded that such head to head competition between Oracle and PeopleSoft would be lost if this merger were consummated.

[19] *Regressions.* Next, in trying to show localized competition, McAfee used a regression technique to calculate what effect, if any, the presence of PeopleSoft or another competitor has on the discounts offered by Oracle. McAfee ran two regression analyses. In the first, McAfee was privy to sales representative surveys identifying the discount percentages given to Oracle customers that had purchased the E–Business Suite. The surveys also identified the competitor that Oracle had beaten to get the account. McAfee narrowed the sample to all sales that were over $500,000, in order to equate the sample with Elzinga's market definition. McAfee used these variables (competitor, net revenue, discount percentage) and ran the regressions. The data led McAfee to conclude that PeopleSoft has a .097 (9.7 percent) effect on the discount Oracle offers. In other words, when Oracle competes against PeopleSoft for the sale of Oracle's E–Business Suite, the consumer obtains a 9.7 percent greater discount than when Oracle competes against no one in selling the suite.

[20] Wanting to look at more than just the sale of the E–Business suite, McAfee then analyzed all of the DAFs that Elzinga had used in defining the product market and matched those with the data from the sales representative forms to create a larger sample with more variables. The DAFs listed the percentage requested along with the competitor justifying such a discount. Once McAfee ran this second regression, he concluded that PeopleSoft had a .136 effect on Oracle's discount rates (i.e., 13.6 percent greater discount). Accordingly, McAfee concluded that when PeopleSoft is competing against Oracle, Oracle's discounts are 9 to 14 percentage points greater.

[21] Based upon these DAF studies and regression analyses, it is safe for the court to conclude that Oracle and PeopleSoft do compete frequently for ERP customers and when they do compete, that competition can be vigorous. But these two contentions are not disputed by anyone in the case. Oracle concedes that PeopleSoft is a frequent rival. The court fails to understand what this undisputed fact is supposed to show about whether Oracle and PeopleSoft are competing head to head in a product space in which SAP is not a party. McAfee himself stated that from these twenty-five DAFs, he drew the broad conclusion that in many instances PeopleSoft and Oracle are each others' closest competitors. But these DAFs tell the court nothing about how often SAP competes against PeopleSoft or Oracle (a key factual issue if trying to exclude SAP) or whether that competition is equally fierce. What would have been more helpful to the court would have been the DAFs of PeopleSoft and SAP as well. Defendants introduced several SAP DAFs during trial, one showing a very aggressive competition against Oracle, so it is clear that such forms exist. A more complete DAF record would perhaps have evidenced localized competition between Oracle and PeopleSoft. But plaintiffs did not provide such DAFs to McAfee, nor is it clear whether they even sought to obtain such documents during discovery.

[22] Simply because Oracle and PeopleSoft often meet on the battlefield and fight aggressively does not lead to the conclusion that they do so in the absence of SAP. [. . .]

Oracle's Competitive Effects Rebuttal

[23] Oracle takes issue with all of the plaintiffs' evidence regarding the likelihood of anticompetitive unilateral effects.

[24] First, Oracle claims that the present case is not the type of case for which the doctrine of unilateral effects was created. Oracle offered Campbell's expert testimony that a fundamental assumption of the unilateral effects theory is not present in this case. Campbell testified that the unilateral effects doctrine is posited on the notion of a localized market powered by a seller and a group of purchasers located in product space or geographic space around that particular seller. This product space is defined by characteristics of the product or products within the space. Campbell offered a homey example of product space using breakfast cereal. A number of customers have characteristic preferences for their breakfast cereal that could create a product space within the entire breakfast cereal market. For example, some customers prefer cereal to be crunchy, sugar-free and high in fiber. These characteristics of the product will narrow the entire market down to a "space" in which only crunchy, sugarless, high fiber cereals occupy the space and only those companies that produce such cereal are competitors. Campbell called this space a "node," with the buyers being centered around this node. The unilateral effects theory is concerned about there being only one vendor operating inside the node, thereby being able to increase the price

unilaterally. Plaintiffs attempted to carve out a "node" for high function FMS and HRM software in the United States in which only Oracle and PeopleSoft compete. Accordingly, if a merger takes place, there will be only one vendor in this node with the ability unilaterally to reduce output and raise price within the node.

[25] Campbell asserted that the unilateral effects theory is predicated on the fundamental assumption that the consumers in the node have no "buyer power." He testified that the theory assumes that customers are unsophisticated buyers who will not be able to rebuff a price increase. This fundamental assumption does not hold in the case of the products in suit. Campbell asserted that the buyers of high function FMS and HRM are extremely sophisticated and knowledgeable and engage in extensive and intensive one-on-one negotiations with vendors. These customers clearly have a lot of power during these negotiations, Campbell claimed, and they are aware of this power. Campbell gave examples of high function consumers such as Emerson Electric and Daimler whose representatives testified that their companies have "leverage" and "power over people they deal with," and use their "size" and "the size of the deal" to gain better deals on software. Campbell concluded that the unilateral effects theory is dogma developed for a totally different context from the present case.

[26] Even assuming arguendo that a unilateral effects theory is appropriate for this case, Oracle attacks each piece of evidence that plaintiffs put forward attempting to prove localization between Oracle and PeopleSoft.

[27] Oracle objected to plaintiffs' characterization of SAP as a struggling firm with a substantial disadvantage which prevents it from being in a localized space with Oracle and PeopleSoft. Oracle claims that these SAP "struggling" assertions are "not remotely true" and are belied by the fact that SAP has over 22,000 professional service customers. While Oracle admits that SAP does not dominate the United States in the manner that it may "dominate elsewhere," non-domination does not equate with "struggling."

[28] Finally, Oracle takes aim at McAfee's expert testimony on anticompetitive effects. First, Oracle claims that McAfee's case studies based upon the Oracle DAFs do nothing more than show Oracle and PeopleSoft are frequent rivals. This evidence reveals nothing about localization between Oracle and PeopleSoft in a product space in which SAP is not encompassed. McAfee offered no insights regarding the characteristics of high function FMS and HRM that create the alleged product space between Oracle and PeopleSoft. Further, these case studies are devoid of any information about whether head to head competition between Oracle and SAP, or PeopleSoft and SAP, is equally vigorous.

[29] With regards to McAfee's regression analysis, Oracle argued the analysis was flawed from the outset. The data upon which McAfee based his regression were not based on any set of data identifying high function HRM and FMS software, but only on data involving broader suites of EAS. Accordingly, it is impossible to know if these alleged increased discount rates were the product of high function FMS and HRM, other ERP pillars or the bundling of all. Without this crucial information, the regression analysis shows nothing in regards to localization between Oracle and PeopleSoft in a high function FMS and HRM product space. [. . .]

[30] Finally, and perhaps most importantly, Oracle contends that plaintiffs have offered no econometric calculations in trying to prove localization. Oracle argues that proving localization requires extensive econometric analysis, such as diversion ratios, price-cost margins and the like, of which plaintiffs have offered none. When Oracle cross-examined plaintiffs' expert witnesses, both admitted that they did not even attempt to calculate diversion ratios, or cross-elasticities, or any other economically meaningful measurement of whether the products of Oracle and PeopleSoft are uniquely close substitutes for each other.

Findings of Fact: Unilateral Effects

[31] The court finds that the plaintiffs have wholly failed to prove the fundamental aspect of a unilateral effects case—they have failed to show a "node" or an area of localized competition between Oracle and PeopleSoft. In other words, plaintiffs have failed to prove that there are a significant number of customers (the "node") who regard Oracle and PeopleSoft as their first and second choices. If plaintiffs had made such a showing, then the court could analyze the potential for exercise of monopoly power over this "node" by a post-merger Oracle or the ability of SAP or Lawson to reposition itself within the node in order to constrain such an exercise of monopoly power.

[32] Plaintiffs' attempt to show localized competition based upon customer and expert testimony was flawed and unreliable. Moreover, plaintiffs' evidence was devoid of any thorough econometric analysis such as diversion ratios showing recapture effects. . . . [T]he only other courts explicitly to address unilateral effects based their rulings in part upon econometric evidence submitted by the parties. [. . .]

[33] In sum, the court finds that plaintiffs have failed to show an area of localized competition between Oracle and PeopleSoft. [. . .]

[34] Because plaintiffs have not shown by a preponderance of the evidence that the merger of Oracle and PeopleSoft is likely substantially to lessen competition in a relevant product and geographic market in violation of 15 U.S.C. § 7, the court directs the entry of judgment against plaintiffs and in favor of defendant Oracle Corporation.

NOTES

1) We have seen that courts consider many kinds of evidence—including economic expert analysis, market participant testimony, and ordinary-course documents—as well as information about market shares and market concentration. Which of these do you think are most reliable? Which are least reliable?

2) In practice, courts and agencies often pay particular attention to the views of customers, rather than those of the merging parties or competitors. Why do you think this is? What disadvantages apply to customer testimony as a guide to the likely effects of a merger?

3) Should the probative weight of parties' internal documents depend on whether they are consistent, or inconsistent, with the parties' arguments at the time of the merger review? How, if at all, should this matter?

4) Nascent competition cases involve a competitor that is already present in the relevant market, but which is still developing. What are the dangers of adopting too lax a standard in connection with acquisitions of nascent competitors? What are the dangers of a too-strict standard?[633]

5) Some have suggested that the acquisitions of potential and nascent competitors might be a particular problem in markets for digital products and services, and that we should have special rules for such markets. How would we test to see whether that is true? What kind of information would we need, and how would we collect it?

6) Two former federal enforcers have written that "the court's opinion [in Oracle/PeopleSoft] betrays a deep hostility to unilateral effects [theory] that interferes with careful antitrust analysis."[634] Do you agree? What features of the reasoning or opinion support your view?

7) One major concern for antitrust law and policy is the phenomenon of so-called "serial acquisitions": that is, multiple acquisitions by a firm in the same market, and particularly those such that each individual acquisition may have a small impact on competition but the overall effect may be significant. How do you think Section 7 should treat such practices?

8) Should we have complementary per se and "rule of reason" rules for unilateral effects analysis in mergers? How would you define a per se rule for unilateral effects?

9) Do you think a court reviewing the legality of a consummated merger should admit evidence of how the merged firm in fact priced following the deal?

b) Coordinated Effects

"Coordinated" anticompetitive effects arise when a merger or acquisition makes a market more susceptible to tacit or express coordination. As we saw in Chapter II, tacit collusion is a reduction in competition among firms that realize that it is in their interests to avoid aggressive competition and can sustain strategic interaction to that end. As you know, this kind of behavior is not itself illegal (assuming the participants do not enter into an actual

---

[633] *Compare, e.g.,* C. Scott Hemphill & Tim Wu, *Nascent Competitors,* 168 U. Penn. L. Rev. 1879 (2020), *with* John M. Yun, Bruce H. Kobayashi, Abbott B. Lipsky, Alexander Raskovich, & Joshua D. Wright, *Potential and Nascent Competition in Merger Review: Global Antitrust Institute Comment on the DOJ-FTC Request for Information on Merger Enforcement* (April 2022).

[634] Jonathan B. Baker & Carl Shapiro, *Reinvigorating Horizontal Merger Enforcement,* in Robert Pitofsky (ed.) HOW CHICAGO SCHOOL OVERSHOT THE MARK: THE EFFECT OF CONSERVATIVE ECONOMIC ANALYSIS ON U.S. ANTITRUST (2008) 238.

agreement) so merger control is often a critical opportunity to prevent the emergence of concentration levels, and other conditions, that make it more likely.[635]

As you might expect, in coordinated effects cases, courts and agencies pay close attention to the factors that make strategic interdependence particularly likely or particularly harmful. As you will remember from Chapter II, these factors include, among other things: high levels of concentration; transparency of price and other terms among the market participants; mechanisms to punish or retaliate against firms that violate the terms of coordination; symmetry of incentives among the participants; and so on.[636] When circumstances are otherwise—for example, when market participants are many or dissimilarly situated, or when their dealings are not transparent—then the implicit bargain of coordination may be shaky or unsustainable.

As a result, coordinated-effects analysis often focuses on factors that might increase the vulnerability of the market to coordination. Will the merger significantly increase concentration? Will it eliminate a disruptive maverick that has been thwarting efforts at tacit collusion? Will it leave the market more transparent, or the participants' incentives more closely aligned? Will it give coordinators better means of detecting or punishing cheating? And so on.

Horizontal Merger Guidelines § 7

7. Coordinated Effects

[1] A merger may diminish competition by enabling or encouraging post-merger coordinated interaction among firms in the relevant market that harms customers. Coordinated interaction involves conduct by multiple firms that is profitable for each of them only as a result of the accommodating reactions of the others. These reactions can blunt a firm's incentive to offer customers better deals by undercutting the extent to which such a move would win business away from rivals. They also can enhance a firm's incentive to raise prices, by assuaging the fear that such a move would lose customers to rivals.

[2] Coordinated interaction includes a range of conduct. Coordinated interaction can involve the explicit negotiation of a common understanding of how firms will compete or refrain from competing. Such conduct typically would itself violate the antitrust laws. Coordinated interaction also can involve a similar common understanding that is not explicitly negotiated but would be enforced by the detection and punishment of deviations that would undermine the coordinated interaction. Coordinated interaction alternatively can involve parallel accommodating conduct not pursuant to a prior understanding. Parallel accommodating conduct includes situations in which each rival's response to competitive moves made by others is individually rational, and not motivated by retaliation or deterrence nor intended to sustain an agreed-upon market outcome, but nevertheless emboldens price increases and weakens competitive incentives to reduce prices or offer customers better terms. Coordinated interaction includes conduct not otherwise condemned by the antitrust laws.

[3] The ability of rival firms to engage in coordinated conduct depends on the strength and predictability of rivals' responses to a price change or other competitive initiative. Under some circumstances, a merger can result in market concentration sufficient to strengthen such responses or enable multiple firms in the market to predict them more confidently, thereby affecting the competitive incentives of multiple firms in the market, not just the merged firm.

7.1 Impact of Merger on Coordinated Interaction

[4] The Agencies examine whether a merger is likely to change the manner in which market participants interact, inducing substantially more coordinated interaction. The Agencies seek to identify how a merger might significantly weaken competitive incentives through an increase in the strength, extent, or likelihood of coordinated conduct. There are, however, numerous forms of coordination, and the risk that a merger will induce adverse coordinated effects may not be susceptible to quantification or detailed proof. Therefore, the Agencies evaluate the risk of coordinated effects using measures of market concentration (see Section 5) in conjunction with an

---

[635] *See supra* § IV.B.
[636] *See supra* § II.H.

assessment of whether a market is vulnerable to coordinated conduct. See Section 7.2. The analysis in Section 7.2 applies to moderately and highly concentrated markets, as unconcentrated markets are unlikely to be vulnerable to coordinated conduct.

[5] Pursuant to the Clayton Act's incipiency standard, the Agencies may challenge mergers that in their judgment pose a real danger of harm through coordinated effects, even without specific evidence showing precisely how the coordination likely would take place. The Agencies are likely to challenge a merger if the following three conditions are all met: (1) the merger would significantly increase concentration and lead to a moderately or highly concentrated market; (2) that market shows signs of vulnerability to coordinated conduct (see Section 7.2); and (3) the Agencies have a credible basis on which to conclude that the merger may enhance that vulnerability. An acquisition eliminating a maverick firm (see Section 2.1.5) in a market vulnerable to coordinated conduct is likely to cause adverse coordinated effects.

7.2 Evidence a Market is Vulnerable to Coordinated Conduct

[6] The Agencies presume that market conditions are conducive to coordinated interaction if firms representing a substantial share in the relevant market appear to have previously engaged in express collusion affecting the relevant market, unless competitive conditions in the market have since changed significantly. Previous express collusion in another geographic market will have the same weight if the salient characteristics of that other market at the time of the collusion are comparable to those in the relevant market. Failed previous attempts at collusion in the relevant market suggest that successful collusion was difficult pre-merger but not so difficult as to deter attempts, and a merger may tend to make success more likely. Previous collusion or attempted collusion in another product market may also be given substantial weight if the salient characteristics of that other market at the time of the collusion are closely comparable to those in the relevant market.

[7] A market typically is more vulnerable to coordinated conduct if each competitively important firm's significant competitive initiatives can be promptly and confidently observed by that firm's rivals. This is more likely to be the case if the terms offered to customers are relatively transparent. Price transparency can be greater for relatively homogeneous products. Even if terms of dealing are not transparent, transparency regarding the identities of the firms serving particular customers can give rise to coordination, e.g., through customer or territorial allocation. Regular monitoring by suppliers of one another's prices or customers can indicate that the terms offered to customers are relatively transparent.

[8] A market typically is more vulnerable to coordinated conduct if a firm's prospective competitive reward from attracting customers away from its rivals will be significantly diminished by likely responses of those rivals. This is more likely to be the case, the stronger and faster are the responses the firm anticipates from its rivals. The firm is more likely to anticipate strong responses if there are few significant competitors, if products in the relevant market are relatively homogeneous, if customers find it relatively easy to switch between suppliers, or if suppliers use meeting-competition clauses.

[9] A firm is more likely to be deterred from making competitive initiatives by whatever responses occur if sales are small and frequent rather than via occasional large and long-term contracts or if relatively few customers will switch to it before rivals are able to respond. A firm is less likely to be deterred by whatever responses occur if the firm has little stake in the status quo. For example, a firm with a small market share that can quickly and dramatically expand, constrained neither by limits on production nor by customer reluctance to switch providers or to entrust business to a historically small provider, is unlikely to be deterred. Firms are also less likely to be deterred by whatever responses occur if competition in the relevant market is marked by leapfrogging technological innovation, so that responses by competitors leave the gains from successful innovation largely intact.

[10] A market is more apt to be vulnerable to coordinated conduct if the firm initiating a price increase will lose relatively few customers after rivals respond to the increase. Similarly, a market is more apt to be vulnerable to coordinated conduct if a firm that first offers a lower price or improved product to customers will retain relatively few customers thus attracted away from its rivals after those rivals respond.

[11] The Agencies regard coordinated interaction as more likely, the more the participants stand to gain from successful coordination. Coordination generally is more profitable, the lower is the market elasticity of demand.

[12] Coordinated conduct can harm customers even if not all firms in the relevant market engage in the coordination, but significant harm normally is likely only if a substantial part of the market is subject to such conduct. The prospect of harm depends on the collective market power, in the relevant market, of firms whose incentives to compete are substantially weakened by coordinated conduct. This collective market power is greater, the lower is the market elasticity of demand. This collective market power is diminished by the presence of other market participants with small market shares and little stake in the outcome resulting from the coordinated conduct, if these firms can rapidly expand their sales in the relevant market.

[13] Buyer characteristics and the nature of the procurement process can affect coordination. For example, sellers may have the incentive to bid aggressively for a large contract even if they expect strong responses by rivals. This is especially the case for sellers with small market shares, if they can realistically win such large contracts. In some cases, a large buyer may be able to strategically undermine coordinated conduct, at least as it pertains to that buyer's needs, by choosing to put up for bid a few large contracts rather than many smaller ones, and by making its procurement decisions opaque to suppliers.

* * *

An excellent example of a successful coordinated-effects challenge is our old friend *H&R Block*. In that case, the Department of Justice successfully persuaded the court that the reduction from three to two suppliers of free DIY tax services would give rise to coordinated effects. As in many other coordinated-effects cases, the court gave special attention to whether the merger would eliminate a player that had, before the transaction, been particularly disruptive to oligopolistic behavior. Such firms are sometimes called "mavericks," and their elimination through acquisition can be particularly harmful.[637]

United States v. H & R Block, Inc.
833 F.Supp.2d 36 (D.D.C. 2011)

Judge Howell.

[1] Having defined the relevant market as [digital do-it-yourself (or "DDIY")] tax preparation products, the Court must next consider the likely effects of the proposed acquisition on competition within that market. The government must now make out its prima facie case by showing that the merger would produce a firm controlling an undue percentage share of the relevant market, and would result in a significant increase in the concentration of firms in that market. Such a showing establishes a presumption that the merger will substantially lessen competition. [. . .]

[2] In this case, market concentration as measured by HHI is currently 4,291, indicating a highly concentrated market under the Merger Guidelines. The most recent measures of market share show Intuit with 62.2 percent of the market, HRB with 15.6 percent, and TaxACT with 12.8 percent. These market share calculations are based on data provided by the IRS for federal tax filings for 2010, the most recent data available.

[3] The defendants argue that market share calculations based exclusively on federal filing data are insufficient to meet the plaintiff's burden in establishing its alleged relevant product market, which includes both federal and state filings. The Court rejects this argument. State tax return products are typically sold as add-ons to or in combination with federal return products and the Court finds that there is little reason to conclude that the market share proportions within the state DDIY segment would be significantly different from federal DDIY. While, as defendants point out, many customers of federal tax return DDIY products do not also purchase state returns, that may be because they live in states without income tax or because their state returns are simple enough to prepare very easily without assistance. A reliable, reasonable, close approximation of relevant market share data is sufficient, however. Further, the defendants' own ordinary course of business documents analyze the market

---

[637] It is not always easy to identify a maverick in practice. *See, e.g.*, Taylor M. Owings, *Identifying a Maverick: When Antitrust Law Should Protect a Low-Cost Competitor*, 66 Vand. L. Rev. 323 (2013); Jonathan B. Baker, *Mavericks, Mergers, and Exclusion: Proving Coordinated Competitive Effects Under the Antitrust Laws*, 77 N.Y.U. L. Rev. 135 (2002).

based on IRS federal e-file data, without reference to state filings, even though the defendants' clearly sell state tax return products.

[4] The proposed acquisition in this case would give the combined firm a 28.4 percent market share and will increase the HHI by approximately 400, resulting in a post-acquisition HHI of 4,691. These HHI levels are high enough to create a presumption of anticompetitive effects. Accordingly, the government has established a prima facie case of anticompetitive effects.

[5] Upon the showing of a prima facie case, the burden shifts to defendants to show that traditional economic theories of the competitive effects of market concentration are not an accurate indicator of the merger's probable effect on competition in these markets or that the procompetitive effects of the merger are likely to outweigh any potential anticompetitive effects. [. . .]

[6] Merger law rests upon the theory that, where rivals are few, firms will be able to coordinate their behavior, either by overt collusion or implicit understanding in order to restrict output and achieve profits above competitive levels. The government argues that the elimination of TaxACT, one of the "Big 3" Digital DIY firms will facilitate tacit coordination between Intuit and HRB. Whether a merger will make coordinated interaction more likely depends on whether market conditions, on the whole, are conducive to reaching terms of coordination and detecting and punishing deviations from those terms. Since the government has established its prima facie case, the burden is on the defendants to produce evidence of structural market barriers to collusion specific to this industry that would defeat the ordinary presumption of collusion that attaches to a merger in a highly concentrated market.

[7] The defendants argue the primary reason that coordinated effects will be unlikely is that Intuit will have no incentive to compete any less vigorously post-merger. The defendants assert that the competition between Intuit and HRB's retail stores would be fundamentally nullified if Intuit decided to reduce the competitiveness of TurboTax. Further, defendants contend that Intuit has no incentive to reduce the competitiveness of its free product because it views its free product as a critical driver of new customers. Therefore, the defendants conclude that if HRB does not compete as aggressively as possible with its post-merger products, it will lose customers to Intuit.

[8] The most compelling evidence the defendants marshal in support of these arguments consists of documents and testimony indicating that Intuit engaged in a series of "war games" designed to anticipate and defuse new competitive threats that might emerge from HRB post-merger. The documents and testimony do indicate that Intuit and HRB will continue to compete for taxpayers' patronage after the merger—indeed, in the DDIY market, they would be the only major competitors. This conclusion, however, is not necessarily inconsistent with some coordination. As the Merger Guidelines explain, coordinated interaction involves a range of conduct, including unspoken understandings about how firms will compete or refrain from competing. *See* Merger Guidelines § 7.

[9] In this case, the government contends that coordination would likely take the form of mutual recognition that neither firm has an interest in an overall "race to free" in which high-quality tax preparation software is provided for free or very low prices. Indeed, the government points to an outline created as part of the Intuit "war games" regarding post-merger competition with HRB that also indicates an Intuit employee's perception that part of HRB's post-merger strategy would be to "not escalate free war: Make free the starting point not the end point for customers." Since, as defendants point out, DDIY companies have found "free" offers to be a useful marketing tool, it is unlikely that free offers would be eliminated. Rather, the government argues, it is more likely that HRB and Intuit may find it in their mutual interest to . . . offer a lower quality free product and maintain higher prices for paid products.

[10] The government points to a highly persuasive historical act of cooperation between HRB and Intuit that supports this theory. *Cf.* Merger Guidelines § 7.2 ("[M]arket conditions are conducive to coordinated interaction if firms representing a substantial share in the relevant market appear to have previously engaged in express collusion."). After TaxACT launched its free-for-all offer in the [Free File Alliance ("FFA")], Intuit proposed that the firms in the market limit their free FFA offers, a move which TaxACT opposed and which Mr. Dunn [TaxACT's founder] believed was an illegal restraint on trade. HRB, Intuit, and others then joined together and

successfully lobbied the IRS for limitations on the scope of the free offers through the FFA—limitations that remain in place today. This action illustrates how the pricing incentives of HRB and Intuit differ from those of TaxACT and it also shows that HRB and Intuit, although otherwise competitors, are capable of acting in concert to protect their common interests.

[11] The defendants also argue that coordinated effects are unlikely because the DDIY market consists of differentiated products and has low price transparency. To the contrary, the record clearly demonstrates that the players in the DDIY industry are well aware of the prices and features offered by competitors. Since DDIY products are marketed to a large swath of the American population and available via the Internet, DDIY firms can easily monitor their competitors' offerings and pricing. The fact that competitors may offer various discounts and coupons to some customers via email hardly renders industry pricing "not transparent," as defendants submit. Moreover, while collusion may, in some instances, be more likely in markets for homogenous products than differentiated products, product differentiation in this market would not necessarily make collusion more difficult.

[12] Other indicia of likely coordination are also present in the DDIY market. Transactions in the market are small, numerous, and spread among a mass of individual consumers, each of whom has low bargaining power; prices can be changed easily; and there are barriers to switching due to the "stickiness" of the DDIY products.

[13] Finally, the Court notes that the merger would result in the elimination of a particularly aggressive competitor in a highly concentrated market, a factor which is certainly an important consideration when analyzing possible anti-competitive effects. The evidence presented at the hearing from all parties demonstrated TaxACT's impressive history of innovation and competition in the DDIY market. Mr. Dunn's trial testimony revealed him to be a dedicated and talented entrepreneur and businessman, with deep knowledge and passion for providing high-quality, low-cost tax solutions. TaxACT's history of expanding the scope of its high-quality, free product offerings has pushed the industry toward lower pricing, even when the two major players were not yet ready to follow—most notably in TaxACT's introduction of free-for-all into the market.

[14] The government presses the argument that TaxACT's role as an aggressive competitor is particularly important by urging this Court to find that TaxACT is a maverick. In the context of antitrust law, a maverick has been defined as a particularly aggressive competitor that "plays a disruptive role in the market to the benefit of customers." Merger Guidelines § 2.1.5. The most recent revision of the Merger Guidelines endorses this concept and gives a few examples of firms that may be industry mavericks, such as where "one of the merging firms may have the incentive to take the lead in price cutting or a firm that has often resisted otherwise prevailing industry norms to cooperate on price setting or other terms of competition." *Id.*

[15] The parties have spilled substantial ink debating TaxACT's maverick status. The arguments over whether TaxACT is or is not a "maverick"—or whether perhaps it once was a maverick but has not been a maverick recently—have not been particularly helpful to the Court's analysis. The government even put forward as supposed evidence a TaxACT promotional press release in which the company described itself as a "maverick." This type of evidence amounts to little more than a game of semantic gotcha. Here, the record is clear that while TaxACT has been an aggressive and innovative competitor in the market, as defendants admit, TaxACT is not unique in this role. Other competitors, including HRB and Intuit, have also been aggressive and innovative in forcing companies in the DDIY market to respond to new product offerings to the benefit of consumers.

[16] The government has not set out a clear standard, based on functional or economic considerations, to distinguish a maverick from any other aggressive competitor. At times, the government has emphasized TaxACT's low pricing as evidence of its maverick status, while, at other times, the government seems to suggest that almost any competitive activity on TaxACT's part is a "disruptive" indicator of a maverick. For example, the government claims that most recently, TaxACT continued to disrupt the Digital DIY market by entering the boxed retail software segment of the market, which had belonged solely to HRB and Intuit. Credible evidence at the hearing, however, showed otherwise. . . . .

[17] What the Court finds particularly germane for the "maverick" or "particularly aggressive competitor" analysis in this case is this question: Does TaxACT consistently play a role within the competitive structure of this market that constrains prices? The Court finds that TaxACT's competition does play a special role in this market that

constrains prices. Not only did TaxACT buck prevailing pricing norms by introducing the free-for-all offer, which others later matched, it has remained the only competitor with significant market share to embrace a business strategy that relies primarily on offering high-quality, full-featured products for free with associated products at low prices.

[18] Moreover, as the plaintiff's expert, Dr. Warren-Boulton, explained, the pricing incentives of the merged firm will differ from those of TaxACT pre-merger because the merged firm's opportunity cost for offering free or very low-priced products will increase as compared to TaxACT now. In other words, the merged firm will have a greater incentive to migrate customers into its higher-priced offerings—for example, by limiting the breadth of features available in the free or low-priced offerings or only offering innovative new features in the higher-priced products.

[19] While the defendants oppose the government's maverick theory, they do not deny that TaxACT has been an aggressive competitor. Indeed, they submit that "that's why H & R Block wants to buy them." HRB contends that the acquisition of TaxACT will result in efficiencies and management improvements that will lead to better, more effective, and/or cheaper H & R Block digital products post-merger that are better able to compete with Intuit. . . . .

[20] Finally, the defendants suggest that coordinated effects are unlikely because of the ease of expansion for other competitors in the market. As detailed above in the Court's discussion of barriers to entry and expansion, the Court does not find that ease of expansion would counteract likely anticompetitive effects.

[21] Accordingly, the defendants have not rebutted the presumption that anticompetitive coordinated effects would result from the merger. To the contrary, the preponderance of the evidence suggests the acquisition is reasonably likely to cause such effects.

* * *

Compare the *H&R Block* analysis with that in the first *Arch Coal* case,[638] in which the court was having none of the FTC's argument that the acquisition by a coal mining company, Arch Coal, of its competitor, Triton, would give rise to coordinated effects. The FTC's case foundered on the court's conclusions that, *first*, the nature of the market was uncongenial to oligopoly effects, and, *second*, the target could not plausibly be described as a "maverick." As you read the following extract, remember that in 2004 the operative Horizontal Merger Guidelines were those issued in 1997, which provided that a merger "potentially raise[d] significant competitive concerns" if the post-merger HHI exceeded 1,800 and the transaction increased the HHI by more than 50 points.

FTC v. Arch Coal, Inc.
329 F. Supp. 2d 109 (D.D.C. 2004)

Judge Bates.

[1] Coal is the primary fuel that produces electric power for residential and business consumers across the United States. It is mined in various regions across the country, in either surface or underground mining operations, after which the coal is transported by rail, truck or barge to electrical generating plants. One-third of the coal produced annually in the United States—over 360 million tons—is produced from large-scale surface mining operations in the Southern Powder River Basin ("SPRB") region of Wyoming. Seven companies operate fourteen mines in the SPRB at this time.

[2] In May of 2003, Arch Coal, Inc. ("Arch"), the owner and operator of two SPRB mines (Black Thunder and Coal Creek) as well as other mining operations across the United States, and New Vulcan Coal Holdings, LLC ("New Vulcan"), the owner of two SPRB mines (North Rochelle and Buckskin), which it operates through its subsidiary Triton Coal Company, LLC ("Triton"), entered into a merger and purchase agreement under which

---

[638] For the final (or at least next) chapter of the story, *see* FTC v. Peabody Energy Corp., 492 F. Supp. 3d 865 (E.D. Mo. 2020) ("Arch Coal II") (granting preliminary injunction to block proposed JV between Arch Coal and Peabody that would have created a firm with 68% share and increased HHI from 2,707 to 4,965).

Arch would acquire Triton and its two SPRB mines. Hart–Scott–Rodino pre-merger notification was provided to the Federal Trade Commission ("FTC"), which in August 2003 requested additional information from Arch and New Vulcan. Arch subsequently informed the FTC that it intended to divest one of the acquired mines (Buckskin) to Peter Kiewit Sons, Inc. ("Kiewit"), a large company with some mining interests outside the SPRB, and in January 2004 a firm asset purchase agreement was entered by Arch and Kiewit. {*Eds.: in a footnote, the court explained that "A British Thermal Unit (Btu) is the amount of heat required to raise the temperature of one pound of water one degree Fahrenheit."*}

[3] Coal resources in the SPRB are controlled primarily by the federal government, and the vast majority of SPRB production is from lands subject to federal coal leases, with a small amount from state and private lands. The SPRB mines can be divided into three tiers based on coal quality, heat content, and mine location. Tier 1 mines typically produce a high Btu (8600–8900) coal and include the Antelope, Black Thunder, Jacobs Ranch, North Antelope/Rochelle, and North Rochelle mines. Tier 2 mines produce coals ranging from 8300 to 8550 Btu, and include Belle Ayr, Caballo/North Caballo, Coal Creek, and the Cordero Rojo complex. Tier 3 mines produce relatively low Btu coal (7900–8450) and include the Buckskin, Dry Fork, Eagle Butte, Fort Union, Rawhide, and Wyodak mines.

[4] Seven companies currently operate the fourteen mines in the SPRB. Four companies, each operating a Tier 1 mine, are considered the major producers of SPRB coal: Arch, Triton, Kennecott Energy Co. ("Kennecott"), and Peabody Holding Co. ("Peabody"). Arch operates the Black Thunder and Coal Creek mines; Triton operates the North Rochelle and Buckskin mines; Kennecott operates the Antelope, Jacobs Ranch and Cordero–Rojo mines; and Peabody operates the North Antelope/Rochelle, Caballo, and Rawhide mines. RAG American ("RAG") is another significant producer in the SPRB, but it only operates mines in Tiers 2 and 3 (Belle Ayr and Eagle Butte). Two small mining entities, Western Fuels and Wyodak, generally do not compete for business in the region and, therefore, are not recognized by most customers as feasible supply alternatives to the five larger producers. [. . .]

[5] There are currently five significant producers of SPRB coal: Peabody, Kennecott, Arch, RAG, and Triton. Post-merger, there will still be five significant producers of SPRB coal, with Kiewit replacing Triton as an SPRB producing entity. The percentages of the firms' market shares will change, to be sure, as Arch will acquire the North Rochelle mine and Kiewit will take over only Triton's Buckskin mine. However, Arch will remain third among the five producers.

[6] Based on the HHI calculation for the current SPRB coal market, it is highly concentrated. Whether market concentration is measured in terms of practical capacity, loadout capacity, production, or reserves, the post-merger market remains highly concentrated. The post-merger increase in HHI ranges from 49 points to 224 points, depending on which measure is used to calculate market concentration. . . .

[7] . . . The reserves data provided to the Court establish that the current market concentration (HHI) is 2054, and that post-merger it will be 2103, for an increase in HHI of 49. According to the Merger Guidelines, an increase in HHI of 50 points or more in a post-merger highly concentrated market raises significant competitive concerns. Although the HHI increase calculated on the basis of reserves is only 49, the Merger Guidelines state that: "the numerical divisions suggest greater precision than is possible with the available economic tools and information. Other things being equal, cases falling just above and just below a threshold present comparable competitive issues." Based on reserves, then, the proposed transaction may raise significant competitive concerns—although just barely. [. . .]

[8] [Various alternative measures] of market concentration in the SPRB presented by the parties . . . reflect an increase in HHI ranging from 49 to 224. Considering all these measures of market concentration, therefore, at a minimum the proposed transactions raise significant competitive concerns and if, as the Court believes may be appropriate, one departs from a strictly reserves-based approach . . . because of changes that have occurred in the coal market over the last thirty years, then there may even be a presumption of an anticompetitive increase in market power. Ignoring altogether the other measures of market concentration in favor of an exclusively reserves-based assessment seems unwarranted. The FTC has, therefore, satisfied its prima facie case burden.

[9] Nevertheless, it is important to note that this case is not one in which the post-merger increase in HHI produces an overwhelming statistical case for the likely creation or enhancement of anticompetitive market power. Indeed, the single best available measure of market concentration—reserves—produces an increase in HHI of only 49, which is actually below the level for significant concern in the highly concentrated SPRB market. The [alternative] measure plaintiffs urge . . . only produces an HHI increase of 224. Such HHI increases are far below those typical of antitrust challenges brought by the FTC and DOJ. For example, in *Heinz* the HHI increase was 510 based on a pre-merger HHI of 4775. In *Baker Hughes* the HHI increase was 1425, from 2878 pre-merger to 4303 post-merger. In *Staples* the average HHI increase in the several markets under consideration was 2715. And in FTC v. Libbey, Inc., 211 F.Supp.2d 34, 51 (D.D.C.2002), the impact of the original merger agreement (used by the court for its analysis) was an HHI increase of 1052. All of these levels of HHI increase dwarf even the highest increase arguably present here. Indeed, between 1999 and 2003, only twenty-six merger challenges out of 1,263 (two percent) occurred in markets with comparable concentration levels to those argued here.

[10] Thus, although the FTC has satisfied its prima facie case burden, the FTC's prima facie case is not strong. Certainly less of a showing is required from defendants to rebut a less-than-compelling prima facie case. Even assuming that the FTC's showing of an increase in HHI, and thus market concentration, warrants a presumption that the transactions will lessen competition, defendants have pointed out the shortcomings of statistics based on capacity or production, rather than on reserves, in providing the best assessment of the proposed merger's likely future effect on competition. Defendants have, therefore, successfully rebutted the presumption that the merger will substantially lessen competition and the Court will proceed to examine the issue of the likely competitive effects of the proposed merger in the relevant market, for which plaintiffs bear the ultimate burden of persuasion. As discussed below, an analysis of the SPRB market confirms that defendants have produced sufficient evidence to further rebut the FTC's prima facie case and that, ultimately, plaintiffs have not carried their burden of persuasion. [. . .]

[11] Plaintiffs [in a merger case] may seek to show that a merger will diminish competition by showing that it will facilitate coordinated interaction. That is, in fact, the thrust of plaintiffs' case here. The Merger Guidelines define coordinated interaction as actions by a group of firms that are profitable for each of them only as a result of the accommodating reactions of the others. This behavior includes tacit or express collusion, and may or may not be lawful in and of itself. Indeed, antitrust policy seeks particularly to inhibit the creation or reinforcement by merger of oligopolistic market structures in which tacit coordination can occur."

[12] A market is conducive to tacit coordination, then, where producers recognize their shared economic interests and their interdependence with respect to price and output decisions. Successful coordination requires two factors: (1) reaching terms of coordination that are profitable to the firms involved and (2) an ability to detect and punish deviations that would undermine the coordinated interaction. Merger Guidelines § 2.1. Coordination need not be complex or complete—instead, the terms of coordination may be imperfect and incomplete and still result in significant competitive harm. The Merger Guidelines provide, moreover, that the punishment of deviation will not always be direct and specific: "Credible punishment may not need to be any more complex than temporary abandonment of the terms of coordination by other firms in the market." Id. at § 2.12. But "where detection or punishment is likely to be slow, incentives to deviate are enhanced and coordinated interaction is unlikely to be successful." [. . .]

[13] The . . . question . . . is whether . . . coordinated interaction in the form of tacit output reduction is likely to occur in this market as a result of the proposed transactions. [. . .]

a. Interest in Production Discipline

[14] Producers in the SPRB have certainly evinced some past interest in price or production discipline. On April 25, 2000, Irl Engelhardt, Chairman and CEO of Peabody, gave a speech before the Western Coal Transportation Association, a meeting attended by SPRB coal producers and customers, in which he remarked on disciplining production in the coal industry. Engelhardt noted that "[o]ne example [of approaches in the coal industry] is making capital investments to improve productivity and lower costs. Nothing wrong here. Lower costs mean higher margins, right? They do unless the incremental production that results contributes to an oversupply situation." Engelhardt then commented that "[i]f coal producers would use growth in returns as their performance

metric, we believe more discipline would be applied to investments that would otherwise lead to oversupply situations." Engelhardt detailed the actions that Peabody was taking to address oversupply in the market:

> Peabody is focusing on profitability and high return investments in the Powder River Basin. Here are some recent steps that they have taken:
>
> > • In early 1999, Peabody suspended the 10–million–ton–per–year Rawhide Mine, one of the most productive mines in the United States;
> >
> > • Also in 1999, the company delayed a 30–million–ton–per–year capacity expansion at North Antelope/Rochelle until margins generate the proper returns; and
> >
> > • In April 2000, it idled a truck/shovel fleet at Caballo, producing 8 million tons per year, until market conditions improve.

[15] A month later, on May 23, 2000, Steven Leer, Chairman and CEO of Arch, addressed the Western Coal Council's 2000 Spring Coal Forum, attended by SPRB coal producers and customers. Leer posed the question "What can we do about oversupply?" His answer was "Produce less coal." In identifying a response to low coal prices, he provided the following information:

> Subliminal Messages
>
> • If you produce it, they will buy it
>
> • Outcome: Prices have suffered
>
> • Solution: Produce less coal.

[16] Leer also identified "produce less coal" as the solution to low prices resulting from the evaporating export market and huge stockpiles.

[17] Plaintiffs view these statements from SPRB producers as strong evidence of the type of production coordination that is likely if Arch's acquisition of Triton is allowed. Defendants have explained, however, that Leer's comments are simply an articulation of Arch's "market driven" business strategy, under which Arch will restrict its production when it believes that, due to oversupply, it cannot obtain returns it considers adequate. This approach is consistent with the accepted business objective of obtaining an adequate rate of return to fund expansion. Nonetheless, statements of the type made by Leer and Englehardt in 2000 are indicative of possible producer coordination to limit production, and warrant close scrutiny in an assessment of the likelihood of anticompetitive coordination in the SPRB market.

b. Feasibility of Coordinated Interaction

[18] There is evidence that coordination in the SPRB market is feasible. The differences that distinguish coal produced at one SPRB mine from that at another SPRB mine, such as Btu content, sulfur content, moisture and ash content, are similar to differences that distinguish crude oil produced from different wells. Standard adjustments are made in pricing to account for any specific differences that do exist in the coal from different SPRB mines. Furthermore, plaintiffs' expert concluded that the demand for SPRB coal is inelastic, i.e., the elasticity of demand is less than one. This means that a modest price increase in the highly concentrated SPRB market would be very profitable to producers because it would increase revenues, and therefore profits, even before taking into account the additional profits that would be realized from reductions in total costs as a result of any reduction in output.

[19] Barriers to entry into the SPRB coal market increase the likelihood of coordinated interaction. Certainly there are appreciable start-up costs associated with becoming an SPRB coal producer. The small and frequent transactions for SPRB coal also increase the likelihood of coordinated interaction, decrease the incentive to deviate from coordinated interaction, and increase the likelihood that deviations from coordinated interaction will be quickly detected. A typical transaction size in the SPRB coal market is less than one percent of the total market.

[20] Key market information relating to the other competitors in the SPRB coal market is available from numerous sources, which would theoretically permit the sharing of information among producers. These sources include: trade reports and conferences, industry analysts and consultants who publish reports containing annual production, production capacity, and cost-of-production by mine information for the SPRB coal market; governmental filings such as the Form 423 monthly reports required by the Federal Energy Regulatory Commission ("FERC") stating the quantity and quality of coal purchased and the delivered price for each source; coal company announcements that inform the public on market conditions, production costs, mine productivity, and whether a company is gaining an adequate return for its coal; the bidding process which, even though sealed under confidentiality provisions, nevertheless allows some information to be transmitted to producers from customers regarding how their bids compared to other bids from producers; and merger and joint venture negotiations which may allow for limited transfer of certain competitive information between producers.

[21] Given a stated interest by some SPRB producers in production discipline, these general features of the SPRB market would not appear to preclude coordinated interaction having anticompetitive effects. However, even though these factors and conditions make post-merger coordinated activity to limit production in the SPRB market feasible, whether anticompetitive coordination is likely requires closer examination of such factors as the past history of coordinated interaction, the SPRB market structure and dynamics, and the roles of "fringe" or "maverick" producers.

c. Existence of Actual Coordinated Interaction

[22] There is insufficient evidence to conclude that express or even tacit coordination has taken place in the SPRB market. Traditional factors that industrial organization economists consider when assessing the susceptibility of a market to coordinated interaction include whether producers recognize their mutual interest in competing less aggressively and whether producers with incentives to compete less aggressively communicate their intentions to one another. Plaintiffs' expert concluded that he would need to do additional analysis before he could offer conclusive testimony on whether coordinated interaction is occurring in the SPRB coal market. Plaintiffs have not produced sufficient evidence that such coordination to limit production has actually occurred.

[23] Based on a review of the evidence over time, it is unlikely that coordination has taken place in the SPRB, especially since the evidence through which the FTC attempts to show the existence of coordination is focused primarily on 2000 and 2001. The lynchpin of the FTC's position is the comments and actions of Arch with respect to "production discipline." Through 1999, Arch sold coal on an incremental basis, which meant it sold coal for anything more than the cost of producing it. Under what Arch calls its "market driven" approach, however, Arch will restrict its production when it believes that, due to oversupply, it cannot obtain returns that it considers adequate. On May 17, 2000, Arch announced that it planned to reduce production at its Coal Creek mine by as much as 10 million tons annually. Arch announced that it would no longer expand capacity to keep pace with growing demand for SPRB coal until SPRB price and margin increased to an acceptable level. Arch informed the industry that "moves such as the one we are taking today should have a positive impact on prices," in light of the "supply/demand fundamentals" for SPRB coal.

[24] On May 23, 2000, Arch's CEO Steven Leer drew attention to the fact that "Arch has been conscientious" and illustrated the statement by observing that Arch was idling the Coal Creek mine and had limited expansion at Black Thunder. Jon Kelly of Tuco (a utility) recalled that he found Leer's comments disturbing because there were representatives from Triton, Peabody, and Kennecott in the room. The speech was reported by the trade press to the coal industry as calling for reductions in coal production. A year later, on April 17, 2001, Leer gave an address at the Western Coal Transportation Association in Santa Fe, New Mexico, during which he presented a slide depicting the following information:

What's different today?

Supply/demand balance

Southern PRB

• Fewer producers, so greater potential for discipline

• Loadout and rail capacity create constraints

• Adding incremental production more expensive.

[25] The next year, Arch announced in a March 17, 2002 press release that it had recently cut production by seven percent. Arch announced the production cuts in 2002 despite the fact that the cuts would have a negative impact on earnings: "We are committed to being a market-driven producer. We believe it would be a mistake to sell coal into an oversupplied market, at prices that will not provide an adequate return."

[26] Although Arch made public announcements about cutting production and its commitment to being a market-driven producer, other SPRB producers chose not to follow Arch's strategy. [. . .]

[27] [T]here is no evidence that Arch sought to "punish" the producers who declined to restrict production, even if it had the means to do so. According to defendants' expert, public announcements about production made by Peabody, Kennecott, and Arch did not trigger a coordinated output reduction by coal producers, and were instead followed by enhanced output in the SPRB market. The totality of the evidence, then, establishes that although production restrictions were advocated and even practiced by Arch during 2000–2002, and broader coordination by SPRB producers to limit supply was feasible, no express or tacit coordination to limit production has actually occurred among the major SPRB coal producers.

d. Market Structure and Dynamics

[28] That observed conclusion is consistent with an assessment of the SPRB coal market. The structure and dynamics of the SPRB market may permit coordination, but do not make coordination likely. While barriers to entry into the SPRB market exist, and such barriers may facilitate the creation or enhancement of market power or its exercise, Merger Guidelines § 3.0, a substantial number of firms actively compete in the marketplace. Furthermore, heterogeneity of products and producers limit or impede the ability of firms to reach terms of coordination. See Merger Guidelines § 2.11. The evidence establishes that products in the SPRB market are heterogeneous; SPRB coal is different from one mine to another, and the SPRB mines and coal companies differ in many important respects, including their production costs, cost structures, contractual commitments, level of reserves, and financial viability.

[29] It is true that industry publications make some market information available among producers. However, the information published in those sources is limited, imperfect, and largely unreliable and untimely. Public data on coal pricing, capacity, and production levels are historical, not particularly comprehensive, and tend to lag behind the market by several months, if not more. [Mine Safety and Health Administration ("MSHA")] data is a good example. It provides on a quarterly or annual aggregated basis a snapshot of historic shipments, but provides no information about future shipments, long-term mine commitments, or the nature of any contracts a supplier may have with utilities, let alone the nature or date of the specific contract under which the reported shipments were made. FERC reports suffer similar deficiencies in that they, too, report only historic shipments, and the data only become available months after the reported shipments were made. Moreover, the shipments reflected in FERC reports are (like MSHA data) tied to contracts that were entered into years earlier. Thus, if a supplier signs a contract today for deliveries commencing in 2005, FERC data will not be reported until several months after the first shipment is sent in 2005. FERC data are reported on a delivered basis (i.e., the combined cost of the coal and transportation) and do not break out the cost of the coal alone. Because utilities treat their transportation costs as confidential, it is impossible accurately to determine the cost of the coal at the mine-mouth. [. . .]

[30] A market is conducive to tacit coordination where producers recognize their shared economic interests and their interdependence with respect to price and output decisions. Successful coordination requires both that firms reach terms of coordination that are profitable and that they be able detect and punish deviations from the coordinated interaction. In order for producers to be able to coordinate production, they would need a reliable reference point to attain agreement as to a lag in production. Supply and demand estimates in this marketplace, however, have been historically inaccurate and uncertain.

[31] Demand for SPRB coal is not predictable either in the short- or the long-term. The two largest demand drivers for coal consumption are the weather and the economy, and neither can accurately be predicted.

Unexpected weather and changes in economic conditions can result in utilities delaying receipt of coal under contract, advancing receipt of coal, choosing to increase or decrease inventories, or buying and selling coal on the spot market to meet immediate, unanticipated demand.

[32] The opaqueness of utility inventories also makes it difficult to predict the demand for SPRB coal from year to year. When utilities draw down inventories, they defer coal purchases, resulting in reduced demand; conversely, when utilities build up inventories, they drive up demand. Utilities do not disclose their inventory levels to suppliers. There are thus many different forecasts of future inventories, none of which is very accurate. As a result, predictions of future demand for coal vary dramatically, with no real consensus as to what future usage of electricity might be. Customers are no better at projecting demand. As Mr. Bales testified, he takes his own company's estimates of coal consumption "with a grain of salt." Demand estimates, particularly as they relate to coal prices, "would be pure speculation." Long-term, variable contracts further complicate efforts to forecast the demand for coal from year to year. [. . .]

[33] Tacit agreement would also be difficult to coordinate in this marketplace because the terms of agreement would be hard to communicate between producers, even though tacit agreement only requires producers to adopt a uniform strategy that is consistent with less aggressive competition. Moreover, there is no effective mechanism in the SPRB to discipline any producer that would deviate from the terms of coordination. Plaintiffs' economic expert posited no theory for punitive discipline among producers. Due to the nature of the confidential bidding and contracting process that gives producers incentives to submit aggressive bids to capture long term contracts, cheating would not be detected until well after the fact, if ever, and any punishment would come well after the fact as well. Such delays in detection or punishment generally mean that deviations are likely and that coordinated interaction is unlikely to succeed. [. . .]

e. Triton as a Market "Maverick"

[34] An important consideration when analyzing possible anticompetitive effects' is whether the acquisition would result in the elimination of a particularly aggressive competitor in a highly concentrated market. For purposes of a coordinated effects analysis, the Merger Guidelines define a "maverick" firm as one possessing a greater economic incentive to deviate from the terms of coordination than those of its rivals. Merger Guidelines § 2.12. FTC officials have noted that, in the context of an auction market, to be a maverick a firm must consistently compete aggressively when it bids, causing other firms to bid more aggressively when it is present. The loss of a firm that does not behave as a maverick is unlikely to lead to increased coordination.

[35] The evidence here does not support the proposition that Triton is, or will likely become, a maverick in the SPRB market. Triton is not presently a maverick in the market, particularly not over the last two to three years. Triton's North Rochelle mine is one of the highest cost mines in the SPRB. As a consequence, Triton has been forced to adopt a "last mine standing" sales strategy for its North Rochelle coal. Pursuant to this strategy, Triton bids its North Rochelle coal at a price that covers its cost plus a profit and waits for the market to come to that price as other mines in the SPRB sell out. This strategy is driven for the most part by Triton's debt financing obligations, which require Triton to obtain a sufficient return on its coal sales to meet bank commitments as they come due. Thus, Triton would rarely deviate from the "last mine standing" strategy.

[36] Because of these circumstances, Triton is wholly indifferent to competitors' production levels or their likely uncommitted tonnage in pricing its North Rochelle coal. Triton's goal is not to increase its market share by pricing under its competitors. Rather, Triton seeks to cover its cost and make a profit on each sale by waiting out the competition and obtaining the highest price possible. Given North Rochelle's high cost structure, therefore, Triton has been unable in recent years to be at all competitive on contract bids. The result, the Court concludes, is that Triton does not lead or even influence pricing in the market, does not compete aggressively, and does not have a history of bidding on contracts consistent with the behavior of a maverick in the SPRB market. [. . .]

[38] [P]laintiffs are not likely to succeed on the merits of their claim of a Clayton Act violation based on the novel theory of prospective tacit coordination on production limits.

* * *

Unusual Merger Theories: Ovation Pharmaceuticals

Concurring Statement of Commissioner J. Thomas Rosch, Federal Trade Commission v. Ovation Pharmaceuticals, Inc., FTC File No. 081-0156 (Dec. 16, 2008)

From time to time, courts and commentators have advanced unusual theories of harm in horizontal merger cases that do not fit easily into familiar buckets. One example is offered by FTC Commissioner Thomas Rosch in his concurrence in *Ovation?* In that matter, Ovation Pharmaceuticals had acquired the drug NeoProfen from Merck in a deal that the FTC challenged as a violation of Section 7. Commissioner Rosch voted for that complaint, but also expressed his desire to have challenged a separate Ovation acquisition: the purchase of the drug Indocin, designed for premature babies, from Merck.

Commissioner Rosch argued that the investigation showed that, before the deal, Merck had not raised the price of Indocin to monopoly levels because it was subject to "reputational constraints" that could harm sales of its many other, more profitable, drugs. Specifically: "if [Merck] sold at a monopoly price a product used to treat premature babies, that could damage its reputation and its sales of those more profitable products." But Ovation lacked Merck's larger product portfolio, and so had less (or no!) reputational concerns that would hold it back from monopoly pricing. He pointed to evidence that "after the transaction, Ovation began charging roughly 1300 percent more than the price at which Merck sold the same product." Thus, he concluded, "there is reason to believe that Merck's sale of Indocin to Ovation had the effect of enabling Ovation to exercise monopoly power in its pricing of Indocin, which Merck could not profitably do prior to the transaction." He would accordingly have alleged that the Indocin acquisition violated Section 7. Do you agree that this is or should be a theory of illegality under Section 7?[639] Can you imagine ways in which a defendant might use this argument to defend a deal—and does that change your view?

NOTES

1) If tacit collusion is not unlawful, why should we ban mergers on the ground that they will facilitate it?

2) Think about the proposition that the agencies will be more likely to infer coordinated effects if the market participants previously engaged in *express* collusion. What do you make of that? Is it an improper inference of future guilt based on past (possible?) misconduct? Double punishment for the earlier offense? A sensible response to actual evidence of competition in the market? Something else?

3) At least in principle, a "coordinated effects" theory could specify that the merged firm would engage in per se illegal price fixing as a result of the deal. What kind of circumstances would give rise to that effect?

4) If a merger can be challenged on the theory that the merged firm will have greater ability or incentive to engage in a price-fixing cartel, could it also be challenged on the theory that the merged firm will have the ability and incentive to violate the antitrust laws in other ways, such as by engaging in monopolization? What would a plausible fact pattern for such a claim look like?

5) Many scholars and commentators have suggested that the United States economy is becoming more concentrated.[640] Much of the data that is customarily cited is at the "sector" level rather than market-specific in the antitrust sense. How useful is this: what does it teach us, and what does it not teach? What other information would you want to review to determine whether we have a "concentration problem" in the United States?

6) When we are concerned about coordinated effects, are there remedies that could be imposed as an alternative to blocking the deal? If so, what might they look like? If not, why not?

7) Should we have complementary per se and "rule of reason" rules for coordinated effects analysis in mergers? How would you define a per se rule for coordinated effects?

8) Do you agree with Commissioner Rosch's assessment that a transaction that eliminates or reduces reputational constraints on pricing could violate Section 7? On the flip side of the same issue: should a party

---

[639] *See, e.g.*, Jonathan Gleklen, *The Emerging Antitrust Philosophy of FTC Commissioner Rosch*, ANTITRUST 46 (Spring 2009).

[640] Jonathan B. Baker, THE ANTITRUST PARADIGM: RESTORING A COMPETITIVE ECONOMY (2019), Ch. 1; Jan De Loecker & Jan Eeckhout, *The Rise of Market Power and the Macroeconomic Implications*, NBER Working Paper 23687 (Aug. 2017); John Kwoka, MERGERS, MERGER CONTROL, AND REMEDIES (2015); *see also* Carl Shapiro, *Antitrust in a Time of Populism*, 61 Int'l J. Indus. Org. 714 (2018) (noting limits of evidence).

be permitted to argue that reputational constraints would prevent or deter a price increase that would otherwise result from a challenged merger?

c) Future Competition: Mergers with Potential and Nascent Competitors

In appropriate circumstances, harm to competition that does not yet exist at the time of the proposed merger, but could or will arise in the future, can form the basis for a merger challenge. As we saw in Chapter II, an entity that does not compete with a particular firm today, but may compete with it in the future, is often called a "potential" competitor. An entity that is a new and minor competitor today, but promises to be a greater threat in future, is often called a "nascent" competitor. It can be hard to win nascent and potential competition merger cases—partly because success requires a plaintiff to prove that the future will be unlike the past in some important ways—but both the law and enforcement practice support bringing them, and they have enjoyed something of a renaissance in recent years.[641] The FTC's monopolization complaint against Facebook, for example, alleged harms to both nascent and potential competition from Facebook's acquisitions: specifically, the FTC alleged that Instagram was an existing and growing competitor with Facebook in the personal social networking market (*i.e.*, a nascent competitor), while WhatsApp was established in the mobile messaging market from which it threatened to enter the personal social networking market (*i.e.*, a potential competitor).[642]

When you read potential competition cases, it may be helpful to know that potential competition theories are sometimes broken down into two confusingly named subgroups: (1) "actual potential competition" cases, which frame the harm as the lost possibility that actual horizontal competition might exist in the future if the merger does not occur, following the entry of one firm into the other's market, and (2) "perceived potential competition" cases, which frame the harm as the loss of the disciplining power exerted by market participants' *perception*, before the merger, that such future entry might occur, regardless of whether or not it would actually do so. The perceived potential competition doctrine has been explicitly validated by the Supreme Court; the actual potential competition doctrine has not.[643] Lower courts have generally not doubted the validity of either doctrine.[644]

To see the difference, imagine that, today, the market participants in a relevant market *believe* that, if they increased their prices, Firm X, not currently in the market, would then find it rational to enter the market and compete vigorously, and imagine that this belief currently disciplines their competitive conduct. Imagine further that Firm X itself privately knows that it could not or would not in fact enter. Under those circumstances, Firm X would be

---

[641] For some recent nascent and potential competition cases brought by the agencies, *see, e.g.*, Complaint, FTC v. Meta Platforms, Inc., Case No. 3:22-cv-04325 (N.D. Cal., filed July 27, 2022); Complaint, United States v. Visa Inc., Case No. 3:20-cv-07810 (N.D. Cal. filed Nov. 5, 2020); First Amended Complaint, FTC v. Facebook, Inc., Case No. 1:20-cv-03590 (D.D.C. filed Aug. 19, 2021); Complaint, In the matter of Illumina, Inc., FTC Dkt. No. 9387 (F.T.C. filed Dec. 17, 2019).

[642] First Amended Complaint, FTC v. Facebook, Inc., Case No. 1:20-cv-03590 (D.D.C. filed Aug. 19, 2021).

[643] The potential competition doctrine is grounded in some landmark Supreme Court opinions from the 1960s and 1970s. *See, e.g.*, United States v. Marine Bancorporation, Inc., 418 U.S. 602, 624 (1974) (noting that a merger may violate Section 7 on a perceived potential competition theory "if the target market is substantially concentrated, if the acquiring firm has the characteristics, capabilities, and economic incentive to render it a perceived potential de noto entrant, and if the acquiring firm's premerger presence on the fringe of the target market in fact tempered oligopolistic behavior on the part of existing participants in that market," and acknowledging the actual-potential competition theory without adopting it); *id.* at 639 (expressly reserving judgment on the actual potential competition doctrine); United States v. Falstaff Brewing Corp., 410 U.S. 526 (1973) (noting, in what would now be called a perceived potential competition case, that Section 7 covers "the acquisition [of a market participant] by a company not competing in the market but so situated as to be a potential competitor and likely to exercise substantial influence on market behavior," and commenting that "The specific question with respect to this phase of the case is not what Falstaff's internal company decisions were but whether, given its financial capabilities and conditions in the New England market, it would be reasonable to consider it a potential entrant into that market."); *id.* at 559–70 (Marshall, J., concurring) (coining the distinction between an actual potential competitor and a perceived potential competitor, and discussing a variety of related evidentiary concerns); United States v. El Paso Nat. Gas Co., 376 U.S. 651, 659 (1964) (illustrating merging party's competitive "effect . . . merely as a potential competitor").

[644] *See, e.g.*, Ginsburg v. InBev NV/SA, 623 F.3d 1229, 1234 (8th Cir. 2010); Tenneco, Inc. v. FTC, 689 F.2d 346, 351 (2d Cir. 1982); Mercantile Texas Corp. v. Bd. of Governors of Fed. Rsrv. Sys., 638 F.2d 1255, 1264 (5th Cir. 1981); FTC v. Meta Platforms Inc.. No. 5:22-cv-04325, 2023 WL 2346238, at *21 (N.D. Cal. Feb. 3, 2023).

a perceived potential competitor, because the perceived threat of entry is exerting competitive discipline, but not an actual potential competitor, because in reality the threat is unfounded.[645]

CASENOTE: United States v. Marine Bancorporation
418 U.S. 602 (1974)

In what is, remarkably, one of the Supreme Court's most recent substantive merger decisions (!), the Court held in *Marine Bancorporation* in 1974 that Section 7 was not violated when the National Bank of Commerce—a national bank with its principal office in Seattle, Washington—acquired Washington Trust Bank ("WTB"), a state bank headquartered in Spokane almost 300 miles from Seattle. DOJ argued that, but for the transaction, NBC would find "an alternative and more competitive means for entering the Spokane market." DOJ also argued that the merger would end the existing "procompetitive influence that the acquiring bank presently exerts over Spokane banks due to the potential for its entry into that market." In other words, DOJ asserted what we would today call actual potential competition *and* perceived potential competition theories. The U.S. District Court for the Western District of Washington dismissed DOJ's complaint, and the government appealed.

The Supreme Court affirmed the district court's opinion. In a majority opinion authored by Justice Powell, the Court reiterated its recognition—at least in principle—of the perceived potential competition doctrine: that is, a theory of harm based on the claim that "the target market is substantially concentrated, . . . the acquiring firm has the characteristics, capabilities, and economic incentive to render it a perceived potential de novo entrant, and . . . the acquiring firm's premerger presence on the fringe of the target market in fact tempered oligopolistic behavior on the part of existing participants in that market."

The Court then considered DOJ's actual potential competition theory. The Court set out two key criteria against which such a claim, assuming its validity, would have to be considered: (1) whether "in fact NBC has available feasible means for entering the Spokane market other than by acquiring WTB"; and (2) whether such means "offer a substantial likelihood of ultimately producing deconcentration of that market or other significant procompetitive effects." In light of this standard, DOJ's claim did not fare well. State-law regulatory barriers made entry difficult, and the theoretical paths to entry suggested by DOJ were unavailing in light of evidence that they either had never been tried in practice, or that they seemed likely to produce entry at such a small scale that it was unlikely to produce "a reasonable prospect of long-term structural improvement or other benefits in the target market." In light of the claim's failure on the facts, the Court pointedly refused to express a view on the legal validity of the theory: "[S]ince the preconditions for [the] theory are not present, we do not reach it, and therefore we express no view on the appropriate resolution of the question[.]"

Finally, the Court circled back to perceived potential competition. Other market participants, the Court explained, could reasonably be assumed to be aware of the barriers that made NBC's entry into the Spokane market implausible. As such, it was not plausible that they lived in competitive fear of NBC's entry. "[I]t is improbable that NBC exerts any meaningful procompetitive influence over Spokane banks by standing in the wings."

With *Marine Bancorp*—and an outcome that seems to owe much to an awfully unpromising evidentiary record—the law of potential-competition mergers passed into the hands of the lower courts, where it has remained ever since.

Yamaha Motor demonstrates a potential competition theory at work in the hands of the Eighth Circuit. In that case, the parties—Yamaha and Brunswick—entered into a joint venture to make outboard motors for boats. They were not actually competing before the deal, as Yamaha was not yet supplying motors in the United States. But the question for the Eighth Circuit was whether Yamaha—which was making and selling outboard motors in most of

---

[645] Confusingly, this means that the actual potential competitor doctrine is concerned with a mere possible (or "potential") future effect, while the perceived potential competitor doctrine is concerned with a real and ongoing (or "actual") effect. Look: no one promised this stuff was going to make any sense.

the rest of the world before entering into the JV—was a sufficiently plausible entrant into the United States to make it an actual potential competitor, and thus make the deal harmful to actual potential competition.

Yamaha Motor Co., Ltd. v. FTC
657 F.2d 971 (8th Cir. 1981)

Judge Arnold.

[1] Brunswick is a diversified manufacturer whose products include recreational items. Brunswick began making outboard motors in 1961, when it acquired what is now called its Mercury Marine Division (Mercury). Brunswick is the second largest seller of outboard motors in the United States. Between 1971 and 1973 its share of the outboard motor market fluctuated between 19.8% and 22.6% by unit volume and between 24.2% and 26% by dollar volume. Brunswick also sells its Mercury outboards in Canada, Australia, Europe, and Japan.

[2] Before entering the joint venture, Brunswick, through Mercury, was considering development of a second line of outboards in an effort to increase its market share. Mariner was to become this second line, which Brunswick hoped would expand the dealer network carrying both the Mercury and Mariner brands.

[3] Yamaha is a Japanese corporation incorporated by Nippon Gakki Company, Ltd. In 1972, it made outboard motors, motorcycles, snowmobiles, and boats. Since 1961, Yamaha has sold snowmobiles, motorcycles, and spare parts to Yamaha International Corporation, a wholly owned subsidiary of Nippon Gakki, which distributes to the United States. In 1972, 40% of Yamaha's total sales were from exports to this country, and 70% of its total production was for export to some country other than Japan. Yamaha manufactures outboard motors through Sanshin Kogyo Company, Ltd., also a Japanese corporation. Since 1969, when Yamaha acquired 60% of Sanshin's stock, Sanshin has produced Yamaha brand outboard motors, and they are sold in most outboard motor markets throughout the world. [. . .]

[4] On November 21, 1972, Brunswick and Yamaha entered into a joint venture under which Brunswick, through Mariner, acquired 38% of the stock of Sanshin. Yamaha's share in Sanshin also became 38%, with the balance of the stock held by others not involved here. Sanshin was to produce outboard motors and sell its entire production to Yamaha. Some of the motors were to be sold by Yamaha under its own brand name, while the rest, physically identical, were to be resold by Yamaha to Mariner, to be marketed by it under the Mariner brand name. [. . .]

[5] The Commission's first ground involves application of a theory known as the "actual potential entrant doctrine." In essence the doctrine, under the circumstances of this case, would bar under s 7 acquisitions by a large firm in an oligopolistic market, if the acquisition eliminated the acquired firm as a potential competitor, and if the acquired firm would otherwise have been expected to enter the relevant market de novo. To put the question in terms applicable to the present case, would Yamaha, absent the joint venture, probably have entered the U.S. outboard-motor market independently, and would this new entry probably have increased competition more than the joint venture did? We stress the word "probably" in this formulation of the issue, because the question under Section 7 is not whether competition was actually lessened, but whether it "may be" lessened substantially. The question arises here, of course, not in the perhaps more common context of an outright acquisition of a competitor that might otherwise have entered, but in the form of acquisition of stock in a jointly owned company, an acquisition that necessarily foreclosed (for the duration of the joint venture) the independent entry of Yamaha, the other joint venturer.

[6] Although the Supreme Court has yet to rule specifically on the validity of the actual-potential-entrant doctrine, it has delineated two preconditions that must be present, prior to any resolution of the issue. First, it must be shown that the alleged potential entrant had available feasible means for entering the relevant market, and second, that those means offered a substantial likelihood of ultimately producing deconcentration of that market or other significant procompetitive effects. On this basis the Commission's decision is amply supported by the evidence.

[7] A finding that the first precondition exists, in essence, establishes whether the firm in question is an "actual potential entrant." It is clear that absent the joint venture, de novo entry into the United States market, in both the low and high horsepower submarkets, was Yamaha's only alternative, unless it was prepared to abandon the

United States market altogether, which is most unlikely. There is substantial evidence to support the finding that such entry into the United States market is an attractive alternative. The United States market for outboard engines is the largest and most sophisticated one in the world. In addition, at the time of the agreement, Yamaha was selling substantial numbers of outboard motors in every developed market in the world, except the United States. Yamaha's management had the requisite experience in the production and marketing of outboard motors in areas of the world other than Japan.

[8] There is also evidence that Yamaha had the technology needed to be a viable entrant into the United States market. Yamaha had long been a leader in other parts of the world in production of outboards in the low-horsepower range, and at the time of the agreement was engaged in an ambitious program of development of motors in the high-horsepower range. By 1969 Yamaha had plans to market a 25-horsepower engine in the United States. Engines with 25-horsepower and 55-horsepower ratings were exhibited by Yamaha at the 1972 and 1973 Tokyo boat shows, and the 55-horsepower model was marketed in Japan in 1973 and 1974. Thus Yamaha was close to possessing a "complete line" of models with a wide horsepower range suitable for entry into the United States market.

[9] Brunswick argues that possession of a network of marine dealers to sell and service the outboards was essential, that Yamaha lacked such a network, and that Yamaha was therefore in no position to enter the United States market.

[10] Engines in the high-horsepower range are sold predominantly through dealers, while the low-horsepower models are commonly sold by both dealers and mass merchandisers. The lack of a network of dealers is indeed an obstacle to viable participation in the United States market, but it is probably less so for Yamaha than for others. First, Yamaha, through its sales of motorcycles in the United States, had considerable name recognition. Next, there was evidence that most marine dealers enter into one-year contracts. Thus, recurring opportunities exist for a manufacturer to obtain new dealers. Last, many dealers carry more than one line of outboards, so Yamaha might have been able to persuade established dealers to carry a second line. Sales to mass merchandisers were also available, under the Yamaha brand name or some other brand name. We think the Commission was reasonable in finding that Yamaha had viable opportunities to market its wares effectively in the United States.

[11] As recounted above, the objective evidence of Yamaha's capacity to enter the United States market is substantial. There is also considerable evidence of Yamaha's subjective intent to enter the United States. Prior to the 1972 agreement Yamaha made two less-than-successful attempts to penetrate the United States market. The first attempt came in 1968 when it introduced low-horsepower models into the United States market on a limited scale. This effort failed primarily because the motors were too expensive, and Yamaha's one-cylinder, air-cooled engines were ill-suited to United States consumers, who preferred two-cylinder, water-cooled engines. In 1972 Sears Roebuck & Company offered a 1.5-horsepower Yamaha engine but discontinued the arrangement with Yamaha because the motors proved to be too expensive for Sears customers because of their high quality. These attempts at penetration, coupled with Yamaha's ambitious program to develop high-horsepower models, aimed specifically at the American consumer, indicate a high degree of interest in penetrating the United States market. The 55-h.p. motor that Yamaha exhibited at the 1972 Tokyo boat show was actually being marketed in Japan in 1973. A managing director of Yamaha testified that "with the addition of the 55 horsepower, that is about the time we can go into a developed market like the United States or Canada."

[12] The record amply supports the Commission's finding that Yamaha had the available feasible means for entering the American outboard-motor market. We next inquire whether those means offered a substantial likelihood of ultimately producing deconcentration of the United States market or other significant procompetitive effects. The Commission found that independent entry by Yamaha would certainly have had a significant procompetitive impact. Given the factual context of this case, support for this conclusion is easily found. We start by re-emphasizing the oligopolistic nature of the outboard-motor market in the United States. The top four firms had 98.6% of the dollar volume, and the top two, OMC and Brunswick, controlled 85.0% of the market by dollar volume. Any new entrant of Yamaha's stature would have had an obvious procompetitive effect leading to some deconcentration. Yamaha is a well-established international firm with considerable financial strength. In addition, the Yamaha brand name was familiar to American consumers, and Yamaha had considerable marketing experience in the United States. [. . .]

[13] Accordingly, the record supports the Commission's finding that . . . Yamaha was an actual potential entrant into the United States.

* * *

In *Yamaha Motor*, the plaintiff won, but things are not always so easy in potential-competition cases. In *Steris*, for example, the FTC challenged a merger under similar circumstances—between an in-market incumbent and a threatening entrant—and lost, despite fairly robust evidence of impending entry by the target into the acquirer's market.[646]

Nevertheless, such potential competition cases continue to be brought. The Department of Justice's challenge to the Visa / Plaid transaction is a good example. DOJ filed the following complaint; the parties abandoned the transaction.

Complaint, United States v. Visa Inc. and Plaid Inc.
Case No. 3:20-cv-07810 (N.D. Cal. filed Nov. 5, 2020)

1. Visa is "everywhere you want to be." Its debit cards are accepted by the vast majority of U.S. merchants, and it controls approximately 70% of the online debit transactions market. In 2019, there were roughly 500 million Visa debit cards in circulation in the United States. That same year, Visa processed approximately 43 billion debit transactions, including more than 10 billion online transactions. In 2019, Visa earned over $4 billion from its debit business, including approximately $2 billion from online debit. [. . .]

3. American consumers use debit cards to purchase hundreds of billions of dollars of goods and services on the internet each year. Many consumers buying goods and services online either prefer using debit or cannot access other means of payment, such as credit. Because of its ubiquity among consumers, merchants have no choice but to accept Visa debit despite perennial complaints about the high cost of Visa's debit service.

4. Visa's monopoly power in online debit is protected by significant barriers to entry and expansion. Visa connects millions of merchants to hundreds of millions of consumers in the United States. New challengers to Visa's monopoly would thus face a chicken-and-egg quandary, needing connections with millions of consumers to attract thousands of merchants and needing thousands of merchants to attract millions of consumers. Visa's Chief Financial Officer has acknowledged that building an extensive network like Visa's is "very, very hard to do" and "takes many years of investment," but "[i]f you can do that, then you can have a business [like Visa's] that has a relatively high margin." He explained that entry barriers are so significant that even well-funded companies with strong brand names struggle to enter online debit.

5. Mastercard, Visa's only longstanding rival in online debit services, has a much smaller market share of around 25%. For years, Mastercard has neither gained significant share from Visa nor restrained Visa's monopoly. Mastercard's participation in the online debit market has not translated into lower prices for consumers, and this appears unlikely to change. For example, Visa has long-term contracts with many of the nation's largest banks that restrict these banks' ability to issue Mastercard debit cards. Visa also has hamstrung smaller rivals by either erecting technical barriers, or entering into restrictive agreements that prevent rivals from growing their share in online debit, or both.

6. These entry barriers, coupled with Visa's long-term, restrictive contracts with banks, are nearly insurmountable, meaning Visa rarely faces any significant threats to its online debit monopoly. Plaid is such a threat.

7. Plaid is uniquely positioned to surmount these entry barriers and undermine Visa's monopoly in online debit services. Plaid powers some of today's most innovative financial technology ("fintech") apps, such as Venmo, Acorns, and Betterment. Plaid's technology allows fintechs to plug into consumers' various financial accounts, with consumer permission, to aggregate spending data, look up balances, and verify other personal financial information. Plaid has already built connections to 11,000 U.S. financial institutions and more than 200 million

---

[646] *See FTC v. Steris Corp.*, 133 F.Supp.3d 962 (N.D. Ohio 2015).

consumer bank accounts in the United States and growing. These established connections position Plaid to overcome the entry barriers that others face in attempting to provide online debit services.

8. While Plaid's existing technology does not compete directly with Visa today, Plaid is planning to leverage that technology, combined with its existing relationships with banks and consumers, to facilitate transactions between consumers and merchants in competition with Visa. Like Visa's online debit services, Plaid's new debit service would enable consumers to pay for goods and services online with money debited from their bank accounts. With this new online debit service, Plaid intended to "steal[] share" and become a "formidable competitor to Visa and Mastercard." Competition from Plaid likely would drive down prices for online debit transactions, chipping away at Visa's monopoly and resulting in substantial savings to merchants and consumers.

9. Visa feared that Plaid's innovative potential—on its own or in partnership with another company—would threaten Visa's debit business. In evaluating whether to consider Plaid as a potential acquisition target in March 2019, Visa's Vice President of Corporate Development and Head of Strategic Opportunities expressed concerns to his colleagues about the threat Plaid posed to Visa's established debit business, observing: "I don't want to be IBM to their Microsoft." This executive analogized Plaid to an island "volcano" whose current capabilities are just "the tip showing above the water" and warned that "[w]hat lies beneath, though, is a massive opportunity – one that threatens Visa." [. . .]

12. On January 13, 2020, Visa agreed to acquire Plaid in part to eliminate this existential risk and protect its monopoly in online debit. Visa offered approximately $5.3 billion for Plaid, "an unprecedented revenue multiple of over 50X" and the second-largest acquisition in Visa's history. Recognizing that the deal "does not hunt on financial grounds," Visa's CEO justified the extraordinary purchase price for Plaid as a "strategic, not financial" move because "[o]ur US debit business i[s] critical and we must always do what it takes to protect this business."

13. Monopolists cannot have "free reign to squash nascent, albeit unproven, competitors at will." *United States v. Microsoft Corp.*, 253 F.3d 34, 79 (D.C. Cir. 2001). Acquiring Plaid would eliminate the nascent but significant competitive threat Plaid poses, further entrenching Visa's monopoly in online debit. As a result, both merchants and consumers would be deprived of competition that would drastically lower costs for online debit transactions, leaving them with few alternatives to Visa's monopoly prices. Thus, the acquisition would unlawfully maintain Visa's monopoly in violation of Section 2 of the Sherman Act.

14. Visa's proposed acquisition also would violate Section 7 of the Clayton Act, which was "designed to arrest the creation of monopolies 'in their incipiency,'" *United States v. Gen. Dynamics Corp.*, 415 U.S. 486, 505 n.13 (1974), and similarly prohibits a monopolist from bolstering its monopoly through an acquisition that eliminates a nascent but significant competitive threat. The Supreme Court has explained that an acquisition can violate Section 7 when "the relative size of the acquiring corporation ha[s] increased to such a point that its advantage over its competitors threaten[s] to be 'decisive.'" *Brown Shoe Co. v. United States*, 370 U.S. 294, 321 n.36 (1962). Visa already has a decisive market position through its online debit monopoly, and would unlawfully extend that advantage by acquiring Plaid. For the reasons set forth in this Complaint, the proposed acquisition must be enjoined.

CASENOTE: FTC v. Meta Platforms, Inc. ("Meta/Within")
Case No. 5:22-cv-04325 (N.D. Cal. Feb. 3, 2023)

In 2022, the FTC sued Meta (formerly Facebook) to block its proposed acquisition of Within, a virtual-reality app developer. Meta supplied a set of virtual reality devices (including the "Quest" line of headsets), and also made certain apps that could run on those devices, including Beat Saber, a game in which users smash blocks with laser swords. Within supplied a subscription-based virtual reality service that allowed users to undertake fitness workouts in virtual reality. The FTC's theory was that the acquisition would lead to a loss of potential competition: Meta was an actual potential competitor *and* a perceived potential competitor of Within, because it both could in fact have entered the VR fitness app market and it visibly threatened to do so.

The court agreed with the FTC that there was a "VR dedicated fitness app" market. The court also agreed that that market was highly concentrated—citing *Marine Bancorp* for the proposition that this was a prerequisite for any successful potential-competition claim—whether calculated by revenue, hours spent, or monthly active users. But neither the actual potential competition claim nor the perceived potential competition claim succeeded.

Analyzing the actual potential competition claim, the court held that the FTC was required to show a "reasonable probability"—something *more* than 50%[647]—of entry by Meta, but-for the acquisition. And, while Meta undoubtedly had the necessary "financial and engineering capabilities," it could not currently create fitness content, lacked the studios to film VR workouts, and did not clearly have the necessary incentives to try to enter under its own steam. Moreover, the evidence did not indicate that Meta had considered *de novo* entry to be feasible, nor that any other approach (*e.g.*, a partnership with Peloton) was reasonably probable to work out. And turning to the perceived potential competition claim, the court concluded that the FTC had simply failed to muster sufficient evidence that "Meta's presence did in fact temper oligopolistic behavior or result in any other procompetitive benefits." The mere fact that Within had expressed some concern about unidentified "hypothetical potential entrants" was not enough.

The failure of the Meta/Within effort has meant another adverse holding on the FTC's potential-competition enforcement docket. Will the FTC's challenge to Facebook's acquisition of WhatsApp fare better?[648]

The protection of future competition is not limited to circumstances like *Yamaha Motor*, *Visa / Plaid*, and Meta/Within in which one company is already in the market. In rare cases, competition concerns can arise in markets that do not even exist yet. This was the case, for example, in the FTC's intervention in *Nielsen / Arbitron* in 2013, when the Commission acted to protect competition among cross-platform audience measurement tools, in a market for a service that did not yet exist.[649]

NOTES

1) In principle, a future-competition case could be built on either a coordinated effects theory or a unilateral effects theory. What would be the outline of the story of harm in each case?

2) Some commentators have expressed concerns that an unduly strict approach to nascent and potential competition could have the effect of cutting off an important incentive for investment in startups and, thus, deterring competition; others claim that this concern is overblown.[650] Do you think courts or agencies should consider such second-order impacts of antitrust enforcement: if so, how?

3) In its challenge to Facebook's acquisition of Instagram and WhatsApp, the FTC emphasized the contents of internal documents expressing expectations that the targets presented a serious competitive threat.[651] What are the advantages and disadvantages of such evidence as a guide to the competitive effects of an acquisition?

4) What is the relevance, for competitive analysis, of the documents quoted in paragraph 12 of the *Visa / Plaid* complaint (noting that the deal "does not hunt on financial grounds")?

d) Entry, Expansion, and Countervailing Power

We have already encountered the law and economics of entry barriers in Chapters II and III. But, as the Horizontal Merger Guidelines indicate, entry can be a particularly important consideration in merger cases. In particular, under certain circumstances, a clear enough prospect of competitive entry—or expansion by existing

---

[647] *See also, e.g.*, Mercantile Texas Corp. v. Bd. of Governors, 638 F.2d 1255, 1268–69 (5th Cir. 1981).

[648] Complaint, FTC v. Facebook, Case No. 1:20-cv-03590 (D.D.C. Aug. 19, 2021), ¶¶ 107–29.

[649] Statement of the Federal Trade Commission, In the Matter of Nielsen Holdings N.V. and Arbitron Inc., FTC File No. 131 0058 (Sept. 20, 2013) ("The Commission . . . has reason to believe that Nielsen and Arbitron are the best-positioned firms to develop (or partner with others to develop) [the relevant] service.").

[650] *Compare, e.g.*, Mark A. Lemley & Andrew McCreary, *Exit Strategy*, 101 B.U.L. Rev. 1 (2021) *with* D. Daniel Sokol, *Vertical Mergers and Entrepreneurial Exit*, 70 Fla. L. Rev. 1357 (2018).

[651] First Amended Complaint, FTC v. Facebook, Inc., Case No. 1:20-cv-03590 (D.D.C. filed Aug. 19, 2021) ¶ 84 (quoting internal document stating: "If Instagram continues to kick ass on mobile or if Google buys them, then over the next few years they could easily add pieces of their service that copy what we're doing now, and if they have a growing number of people's photos then that's a real issue for us."), ¶ 86 (quoting internal document stating "the potential for someone like Apple to use [Instagram] as a foothold."), ¶ 88 (quoting internatl document stating: "If [my analytical] framework holds true, then we should expect apps like Instagram to be able to grow quite large. If it has 15m users now, it might be able to reach 100-200m in the next 1-2 years.").

firms—can allay competitive concerns that a transaction would otherwise present. So too, in rare circumstances, can the power of buyers able to protect themselves from post-merger market power.

Countervailing Buyer Power

Section 8 of the Horizontal Merger Guidelines explain that, in certain circumstances, the presence of powerful buyers can allay competitive concerns that would otherwise be presented by a transaction: "The Agencies consider the possibility that powerful buyers may constrain the ability of the merging parties to raise prices. This can occur, for example, if powerful buyers have the ability and incentive to vertically integrate upstream or sponsor entry, or if the conduct or presence of large buyers undermines coordinated effects. However, the Agencies do not presume that the presence of powerful buyers alone forestalls adverse competitive effects flowing from the merger. Even buyers that can negotiate favorable terms may be harmed by an increase in market power. . . . Furthermore, even if some powerful buyers could protect themselves, the Agencies also consider whether market power can be exercised against other buyers."

The "power buyer" argument is seldom much help to merging parties, but it has been important in a small number of cases. A prominent example is DOJ's 1991 challenge to the lease by Archer-Daniels-Midland, an owner and operator of corn wet milling plants, of two additional such plants.[652] The transaction triggered the structural presumption (as it then stood), but the district court held that the parties had successfully rebutted the government's case. Noting that "the buying side of the . . . industry is populated by very large and sophisticated purchasers [with] a continuing trend toward increasing concentration on the buying side," the district court concluded that "this consolidation of buying power is an effective means of counteracting any potential market power that might be exercised by sellers." The court pointed out that "[b]uyers have successfully used a variety of tactics to obtain low prices from . . . suppliers, including playing off suppliers against one another, swinging volume back and forth among suppliers, disciplining sellers by cutting them off entirely, successfully insisting on year long or multi-year tolling agreements, and holding out the threat of inducing a new entrant into . . . production." As a result, "[t]here is no question that the size and sophistication of buyers in the . . . industry is a powerful [factor] that strongly mitigates against the possibility of any attempt by . . . suppliers to raise prices anticompetitively." Given additional evidence that coordination would be implausible following the merger, the court concluded that the defendant had successfully rebutted the affirmative case.

Predicting entry and expansion in response to post-merger supracompetitive pricing is a tricky business, as we shall see. It is easy for merging parties to cry "entry and expansion!" but it can be much harder to establish that entry will be fast enough or significant enough to protect against what would otherwise be harmful effects from a transaction.

Horizontal Merger Guidelines § 9

9. Entry

[1] The analysis of competitive effects in Sections 6 and 7 [of the HMGs] focuses on current participants in the relevant market. That analysis may also include some forms of entry. Firms that would rapidly and easily enter the market in response to a SSNIP are market participants and may be assigned market shares. *See* Sections 5.1 and 5.2. Firms that have, prior to the merger, committed to entering the market also will normally be treated as market participants. *See* Section 5.1. This section concerns entry or adjustments to pre-existing entry plans that are induced by the merger.

[2] As part of their full assessment of competitive effects, the Agencies consider entry into the relevant market. The prospect of entry into the relevant market will alleviate concerns about adverse competitive effects only if such entry will deter or counteract any competitive effects of concern so the merger will not substantially harm customers.

---

[652] United States v. Archer-Daniels-Midland Co., 781 F.Supp. 1400 (S.D Iowa 1991).

[3] The Agencies consider the actual history of entry into the relevant market and give substantial weight to this evidence. Lack of successful and effective entry in the face of non-transitory increases in the margins earned on products in the relevant market tends to suggest that successful entry is slow or difficult. Market values of incumbent firms greatly exceeding the replacement costs of their tangible assets may indicate that these firms have valuable intangible assets, which may be difficult or time consuming for an entrant to replicate.

[4] A merger is not likely to enhance market power if entry into the market is so easy that the merged firm and its remaining rivals in the market, either unilaterally or collectively, could not profitably raise price or otherwise reduce competition compared to the level that would prevail in the absence of the merger. Entry is that easy if entry would be timely, likely, and sufficient in its magnitude, character, and scope to deter or counteract the competitive effects of concern.

[5] The Agencies examine the timeliness, likelihood, and sufficiency of the entry efforts an entrant might practically employ. An entry effort is defined by the actions the firm must undertake to produce and sell in the market. Various elements of the entry effort will be considered. These elements can include: planning, design, and management; permitting, licensing, or other approvals; construction, debugging, and operation of production facilities; and promotion (including necessary introductory discounts), marketing, distribution, and satisfaction of customer testing and qualification requirements. Recent examples of entry, whether successful or unsuccessful, generally provide the starting point for identifying the elements of practical entry efforts. They also can be informative regarding the scale necessary for an entrant to be successful, the presence or absence of entry barriers, the factors that influence the timing of entry, the costs and risk associated with entry, and the sales opportunities realistically available to entrants.

[6] If the assets necessary for an effective and profitable entry effort are widely available, the Agencies will not necessarily attempt to identify which firms might enter. Where an identifiable set of firms appears to have necessary assets that others lack, or to have particularly strong incentives to enter, the Agencies focus their entry analysis on those firms. Firms operating in adjacent or complementary markets, or large customers themselves, may be best placed to enter. However, the Agencies will not presume that a powerful firm in an adjacent market or a large customer will enter the relevant market unless there is reliable evidence supporting that conclusion.

[7] In assessing whether entry will be timely, likely, and sufficient, the Agencies recognize that precise and detailed information may be difficult or impossible to obtain. The Agencies consider reasonably available and reliable evidence bearing on whether entry will satisfy the conditions of timeliness, likelihood, and sufficiency.

9.1 Timeliness

[8] In order to deter the competitive effects of concern, entry must be rapid enough to make unprofitable overall the actions causing those effects and thus leading to entry, even though those actions would be profitable until entry takes effect.

[9] Even if the prospect of entry does not deter the competitive effects of concern, post-merger entry may counteract them. This requires that the impact of entrants in the relevant market be rapid enough that customers are not significantly harmed by the merger, despite any anticompetitive harm that occurs prior to the entry.

[10] The Agencies will not presume that an entrant can have a significant impact on prices before that entrant is ready to provide the relevant product to customers unless there is reliable evidence that anticipated future entry would have such an effect on prices.

9.2 Likelihood

[11] Entry is likely if it would be profitable, accounting for the assets, capabilities, and capital needed and the risks involved, including the need for the entrant to incur costs that would not be recovered if the entrant later exits. Profitability depends upon (a) the output level the entrant is likely to obtain, accounting for the obstacles facing new entrants; (b) the price the entrant would likely obtain in the post-merger market, accounting for the impact of that entry itself on prices; and (c) the cost per unit the entrant would likely incur, which may depend upon the scale at which the entrant would operate.

9.3 Sufficiency

[13] Even where timely and likely, entry may not be sufficient to deter or counteract the competitive effects of concern. For example, in a differentiated product industry, entry may be insufficient because the products offered by entrants are not close enough substitutes to the products offered by the merged firm to render a price increase by the merged firm unprofitable. Entry may also be insufficient due to constraints that limit entrants' competitive effectiveness, such as limitations on the capabilities of the firms best placed to enter or reputational barriers to rapid expansion by new entrants. Entry by a single firm that will replicate at least the scale and strength of one of the merging firms is sufficient. Entry by one or more firms operating at a smaller scale may be sufficient if such firms are not at a significant competitive disadvantage.

* * *

As you might expect, merging parties routinely claim that there are one or more critical entrants poised to leap into the market and reshape competitive conditions. But agencies and courts generally examine these claims skeptically.[653] In two merger challenges we have met already—Staples / Office Depot II and H&R Block / TaxAct—the parties argued that entry and expansion would be sufficient to allay competitive concerns. In each case the court was unmoved. In particular, *Staples / Office Depot II* demonstrates a recurrent theme in recent merger challenges: merging parties who point to a "big tech" platform as a gamechanging entrant. As Judge Sullivan's opinion makes clear, the mere presence of a big tech platform—even one that has already begun to enter the relevant market—is not automatically enough to eliminate competitive concerns.

<h1 style="text-align:center">FTC v. Staples, Inc. ("Staples / Office Depot II")</h1>

190 F. Supp. 3d 100 (D.D.C. 2016)

Judge Sullivan.

{Eds.: The FTC's prima facie case is covered above.[654]}

[1] Defendants' sole argument in response to Plaintiffs' *prima facie* case is that the merger will not have anti-competitive effects because Amazon Business, as well as the existing patchwork of local and regional office supply companies, will expand and provide large B-to-B customers with competitive alternatives to the merged entity. Plaintiffs argue that there is no evidence that Amazon or existing regional players will expand in a timely and sufficient manner so as to eliminate the anticompetitive harm that will result from the merger.

[2] The prospect of entry into the relevant market will alleviate concerns about adverse competitive effects only if such entry will deter or counteract any competitive effects of concern so the merger will not substantially harm customers. Even in highly concentrated markets, Plaintiffs' prima facie case may be rebutted if there is ease of entry or expansion such that other firms would be able to counter any discriminatory pricing practices. Defendants carry the burden of showing that the entry or expansion of competitors will be timely, likely and sufficient in its magnitude, character, and scope to deter or counteract the competitive effects of concern. The relevant time frame for consideration in this forward looking exercise is two to three years.

[3] Defendants seize on Amazon's lofty vision for Amazon Business to be the preferred marketplace for all professional, business and institutional customers worldwide to support their contention that Amazon not only wants to take over the office supply industry, but desires to take over the world. Amazon Business may eventually transform the B-to-B office supply space. *See, e.g.*, DX05284 at 43 (Mr. Wilson's 2016 presentation in Baltimore:

---

[653] *See supra* § VIII.B.2.(a).

[654] *See, e.g.*, FTC v. Swedish Match, 131 F. Supp. 2d 151, 170–71 (D.D.C. 2000) ("The defendants' evidence on entry . . . is not sufficiently persuasive. As discussed above, the evidence shows falling sales volume, increased government regulation, shrinking shelf space, and brand loyalty, all of which will prevent new entry into this market. Demand in the [relevant] market has been declining at a rate of two to three percent per year, a trend which is expected to continue. Thus, there are fewer sales opportunities for new entrants. The steady decline in . . . demand has created excess capacity at . . . production facilities, and existing . . . producers could simply increase production as an effective competitive response to new entrants. [The] consumers are brand loyal, and regulatory restrictions have decreased the producers' ability to advertise their products. New entrants therefore would have a significant, uphill climb to take away market share from the incumbent producers.").

"It's still Day One." Amazon Business plans to "improve with: more selection; an increasing number of produce and business products [sic]; better personalization; a purchasing experience even better tailored for businesses."). The Court's unenviable task is to assess the likelihood that Amazon Business will, within the next three years, replace the competition lost from Office Depot in the B-to-B space as a result of the proposed merger.

[4] Amazon Business has a number of impressive strengths. For example, Amazon Business already enjoys great brand recognition and its consumer marketplace has a reputation as user-friendly, innovative and reliable. Amazon Business' strategy documents also reveal a number of priorities that, if successful, may revolutionize office supply procurement for large companies. . . .

[5] However, several significant institutional and structural challenges face Amazon Business. Plaintiffs point to a long list of what they view as Amazon Business' deficiencies, including, but not limited to: (1) lack of RFP experience; (2) no commitment to guaranteed pricing [redacted text]; (3) lack of ability to control third-party price and delivery; (4) inability to provide customer-specific pricing; (5) a lack of dedicated customer service agents dedicated to the B-to-B space; (6) no desktop delivery; (7) no proven ability to provide detailed utilization and invoice reports; and (8) lack of product variety and breadth. Although Amazon Business may successfully address some of these alleged weaknesses in the short term, the evidence produced during the evidentiary hearing does not support the conclusion that Amazon Business will be in a position to restore competition lost by the proposed merger within three years.

[6] First, despite entering the office supply business fourteen years ago, large B-to-B customers still do not view Amazon Business as a viable alternative to Staples and OfficeDepot. Moreover, Amazon Business' participation in RFPs has been "limited." Significantly, Amazon Business also has yet to successfully bid to be a large B-to-B customer's primary vendor. . . .

[7] The Court has considered whether Amazon Business' newly energized focus on the B-to-B space could transform the office supply industry for B-to-B customers in such a dramatic way that the RFP process may be "what dinosaurs do" in the future. However, during [the deposition of Vice President of Amazon Business, Prentis Wilson], he testified that Amazon Business does not seek to change the RFP process. During cross-examination, [counsel for Defendants, Diane Sullivan,] addressed this point with Mr. Wilson directly:

> Ms. Sullivan: And anybody that's been watching what's been going on in the world understands that the way the old companies are doing things, running around, trying to get RFPs and a contract is kind of the old world. The new world is going to be procurement officers sitting at their desks using platforms like the one you're developing?

> Mr. Wilson: I don't know—I mean, that's maybe one vision of what may happen. We'll see how the technology sort of evolves and where things land.

> Ms. Sullivan: But that's your plan, that that's going to be the new world?

> Mr. Wilson: Well, our plan is to bring Amazon Business shopping experience to customers. And we would like for them to be able to—to leverage it, and we would like to create a solution that they like.

[8] Mr. Wilson's testimony does not support the conclusion that Amazon Business seeks to make the RFP process obsolete. Defendants did not offer testimony from other industry experts or offer any other credible evidence that the RFP process will become obsolete within the next three years. The evidence before the Court simply does not support a finding that Amazon Business will, within the next three years, either compete for large RFPs in the same way that Office Depot does now, or so transform the industry as to make the RFP process obsolete.

[9] Second, Amazon Business' marketplace model is at odds with the large B-to-B industry. Similar to Amazon's consumer marketplace, half of all sales on Amazon Business are serviced by Amazon directly, while the other half are serviced by third-party sellers. Amazon does not control the price or delivery offered by third-party sellers. Mr. Wilson confirmed that this will not change. Amazon Business' lack of control over the price offered by third-party sellers contributes to Amazon Business' inability to offer guaranteed pricing. . . . [T]he record is devoid of evidence to support the proposition that large business would shift their entire office supply spend to Amazon Business in the next three years.

[10] Finally, although Amazon Business' 2020 revenue projection is an impressive $[redacted text], only [redacted text] percent of that is forecast to come from the sale of office supplies. This level of revenue for office supplies would give Amazon Business only a very small share in the relevant market. . . .

[11] . . . [D]uring Mr. Wilson's testimony about Amazon Business' ability to compete for RFPs, the Court engaged in this exchange:

> THE COURT: So, if one were to predict—if a vice president were to predict five years from now, you'd be in a much better position to respond, just predicting?
>
> THE WITNESS: That's our point, yes.
>
> THE COURT: Right. And that—the strength of that prediction is based upon what?
>
> THE WITNESS: Investment in resources.
>
> THE COURT: Right. And that's something that, I guess from a business point of view, you plan to do?
>
> THE WITNESS: I plan to request the resources.
>
> THE COURT: Right. Because you want to be as successful as you possibly can and compete, right?
>
> THE WITNESS: Absolutely.

[12] Critically, however, when the Court asked whether Mr. Wilson [text redacted in the court's opinion for confidentiality]. This answer, considered in light of Amazon Business' lack of demonstrated ability to compete for RFPs and the structural and institutional challenges of its marketplace model, leads the Court to conclude that Amazon Business will not be in a position to compete in the B-to-B space on par with the proposed merged entity within three years. . . . [I]t would be sheer speculation, based on the evidence, for the Court to conclude otherwise. If Amazon Business was more developed . . . the outcome of this case very well may have been different.

* * *

United States v. H & R Block, Inc.
833 F.Supp.2d 36 (D.D.C. 2011)

Judge Howell.

{Eds.: DOJ's prima facie case is covered above.[655]}

[1] Defendants argue that the likelihood of expansion by existing [digital do-it-yourself ("DDIY")] companies besides Intuit, HRB, and TaxACT will offset any potential anticompetitive effects from the merger. Courts have held that likely entry or expansion by other competitors can counteract anticompetitive effects that would otherwise be expected. According to the Merger Guidelines, entry or expansion must be "timely, likely, and sufficient in its magnitude, character, and scope to deter or counteract the competitive effects of concern." Merger Guidelines § 9. Determining whether there is ease of entry hinges upon an analysis of barriers to new firms entering the market or existing firms expanding into new regions of the market. In this case, the parties essentially agree that the proper focus of this inquiry is on the likelihood of expansion by existing competitors rather than new entry into the market.[28] Since the government has established its prima facie case, the defendants carry the burden to

---

[655] *See supra* § VIII.B.2.(b).

[28] New entrants to the market would not only face all of the barriers to expansion already faced by the existing small firms offering DDIY products, they would also have to develop their own products, including a software platform and a sufficient level of tax expertise. For entry to be considered timely, it typically must occur within approximately two years post-merger. *See* COMMENTARY ON THE HORIZONTAL MERGER GUIDELINES (2006) at 45–46 (discussing prior Merger Guidelines § 3.2, which specified that timely entry should occur within two years). It is unlikely that an entirely new entrant to the market could compete meaningfully with the established DDIY firms within that time frame.

show that ease of expansion is sufficient to fill the competitive void that will result if defendants are permitted to purchase their acquisition target.

[2] In describing the competitive landscape, the defendants note there are eighteen companies offering various DDIY products through the [Free File Alliance ("FFA")]. Most of these companies are very small-time operators, however. The defendants acknowledge this fact, but nevertheless contend that the companies TaxSlayer and TaxHawk are the two largest and most poised to replicate the scale and strength of TaxACT. Witnesses from TaxSlayer and TaxHawk were the only witnesses from other DDIY companies to testify at the hearing. As such, the Court's ease of expansion analysis will focus on whether these two competitors are poised to expand in a way that is "timely, likely, and sufficient in its magnitude, character, and scope to deter or counteract" any potential anticompetitive effects resulting from the merger.

[3] TaxHawk runs five different websites, including FreeTaxUSA.com, that all market the same underlying DDIY product. TaxHawk was founded in 2001, three years after TaxACT, although it has a significantly smaller market share of 3.2 percent. TaxHawk's vice-president and co-founder, Mr. Dane Kimber, testified that the company has the technical infrastructure to grow by five to seven times the number of customers in any given year. TaxHawk's marketing strategy relies substantially on search engine advertising and search term optimization, including by using the FreeTaxUSA.com domain name, which contains the keywords "free" and "tax." Despite having been in business for a decade, its products are functionally more limited than those of Intuit, HRB, and TaxACT in various ways. Although TaxHawk services the forms that cover most taxpayers, its program does not service all federal forms, it excludes two states' forms in their entirety, and it does not service city income tax forms for major cities that have income taxes—notably, New York City. In fact, Mr. Kimber testified that the company would likely need another decade before its DDIY products could fully support all the tax forms. The reason is that TaxHawk is what Mr. Kimber [testified that he] "likes to call a lifestyle company. We like the lifestyle we have as owners. We want our employees to have a life, if you will. I do feel we have the expertise to expand functionality more rapidly, but we choose not to." Mr. Kimber also testified that TaxHawk had suddenly experienced an unprecedented growth rate of over 60 percent since April 2011, But that the company had not done any analysis to attempt to explain this unanticipated (and presumably welcome) growth.

[4] TaxHawk's relaxed attitude toward its business stands in stark contrast to the entrepreneurial verve that was apparent throughout the testimony of Mr. Dunn [founder of TaxACT] and that has been rewarded by the impressive growth of TaxACT over the years. In short, TaxHawk is a very different company from TaxACT. TaxHawk is a small company that has developed a string of search-engine-optimized DDIY websites, which deliver a sufficient income stream to sustain its owners' comfortable lifestyle, without requiring maximal effort on their part. While TaxHawk's decision to prioritize a relaxed lifestyle over robust competition and innovation is certainly a valid one, expansion from TaxHawk that would allow it to compete on the same playing field as the merged company appears unlikely.

[5] After TaxHawk, TaxSlayer is the next largest DDIY competitor, with a 2.7 percent market share. TaxSlayer.com launched in 2003, although the same company started selling a software product to tax professionals several years earlier. TaxSlayer is part of the same corporate family as Rhodes Murphy, a tax firm that provides assisted tax preparation through sixteen retail offices in the Augusta, Georgia area. The company is a family business and James Brian Rhodes, the product manager of TaxSlayer and the son of the company's founder, testified at the hearing. Mr. Rhodes testified that, in the event of an increase in TaxACT's prices or a decrease in its quality, he believes that TaxSlayer is poised and ready to take those customers who would want to go elsewhere for lower prices. TaxSlayer's marketing strategy relies heavily on sponsorship of sporting events, including the Gator Bowl and NASCAR. TaxSlayer typically invests a significant amount of its budget in marketing. For example, TaxSlayer plans to spend $[amount redacted in the court's opinion for confidentiality] on marketing in 2012 based on 2011 revenues of $[amount redacted in the court's opinion for confidentiality]. Despite this high level of marketing spending, TaxSlayer's DDIY market share has not changed substantially since 2006, despite steady growth in TaxSlayer's revenue and number of units sold. Rather, TaxSlayer's growth in unit sales and revenue has come from maintaining the same slice of an expanding pie—the growing DDIY market.

[6] TaxSlayer's stable market share despite its significant marketing expenditure as a proportion of revenue points to what the government considers the key barrier to entry in this market—the importance of reputation and brand

in driving consumer behavior in purchasing DDIY products. Simply put, tax returns are highly personal documents that carry significant financial and legal consequences for consumers. Consumers, therefore, must trust and have confidence in their tax service provider. As one of TaxACT's bankers put it a confidential memorandum, tax filers must have confidence that sensitive data is being handled with care and that returns are processed in a secure, error-free and timely manner.

[7] Building a reputation that a significant number of consumers will trust requires time and money. As HRB's former CEO noted, it takes millions of dollars and lots of time to develop a brand. TaxACT's offering memoranda also point to the difficulty in building a brand in the industry as a barrier to competition. In the DDIY industry, the Big Three incumbent players spend millions on marketing and advertising each year to build and maintain their brands, dwarfing the combined spending of the smaller companies. For example, in tax year 2009, Intuit, HRB, and TaxACT collectively spent approximately over $100 million on marketing and advertising. By contrast, TaxSlayer and TaxHawk spent a significantly smaller amount.

[8] Even TaxACT's successful business strategy has been premised on the notion that it cannot outspend Intuit and HRB on marketing. The massive marketing expenditures of the two major DDIY firms create high per customer acquisition costs and limit the easy marketing channels that are open to smaller competitors. Rather than attempting to outspend HRB and Intuit, TaxACT's growth strategy has largely depended on providing great customer service, a great product, and a great customer experience and then relying on word-of-mouth referrals to spread the awareness of the brand. This process is inherently time-consuming and difficult to replicate.

[9] In support of their argument that TaxSlayer and TaxHawk are poised to expand in response to a price increase, the defendants emphasize that these companies are at about the same position in terms of customer base as TaxACT was in 2002, which was the year before it did the Free For All offer on the FFA. The government points out, however, that there are two flaws in this comparison, even assuming that TaxSlayer and TaxHawk were TaxACT's competitive equals. First, while these companies may have a similar number of customers to TaxACT in 2002 in absolute terms, TaxACT's market share at 8 percent was already significantly larger than the market shares of these firms today, despite the fact that TaxACT had been in the market for fewer years.

[10] Second, the DDIY market has matured considerably since 2002, in parallel with the general ripening of various online industries during the past decade. Notably, the pool of pen-and-paper customers has dwindled as DDIY preparation has grown. Thus, the "low hanging fruit" of DDIY customer acquisition may have been plucked. This trend suggests existing market shares may become further entrenched and that growing market share may be even harder, especially because there are barriers to switching from one DDIY product to another. For example, the hearing evidence showed that it is difficult to import prior-year tax return data across DDIY brands. If a taxpayer uses, say, TurboTax or TaxACT in one year, then when the taxpayer returns the next year, the program can automatically import the prior year's data, which is not only convenient but can also help the taxpayer identify useful tax information, such as carry forwards and available deductions. Currently, it is not possible to import much of this data if the taxpayer switches to a competitor's product. Thus, this feature lends a "stickiness" to each particular DDIY product once a customer has used it.

[11] Upon consideration of all of the evidence relating to barriers to entry or expansion, the Court cannot find that expansion is likely to avert anticompetitive effects from the transaction. The Court will next consider whether the evidence supports a likelihood of coordinated or unilateral anticompetitive effects from the merger.

* * *

So what does a successful entry showing look like? One such showing was managed by the parties in DOJ's challenge to the acquisition by Waste Management Services of its competitor EMV Ventures.

United States v. Waste Management, Inc.

743 F.2d 976 (2d Cir. 1984)

Judge Winter.

[1] WMI is in the solid waste disposal business. It provides services in twenty-seven states and had revenues of approximately $442 million in 1980. At the time of the acquisition, EMW was a diversified holding company that owned a subsidiary by the name of Waste Resources, which was in the waste disposal business in ten states and had revenues of $54 million in 1980.

[2] WMI and Waste Resources each had subsidiaries that operated in or near Dallas. WMI has one subsidiary, American Container Service ("ACS") in Dallas, and another, Texas Waste Management, in the Dallas suburb of Lewisville. Waste Resources had a Dallas subsidiary called Texas Industrial Disposal, Inc. ("TIDI"). WMI now operates TIDI as a WMI sub. [. . .]

[3] Based on revenue data, Judge Griesa [in the district court below] found that the combined market share of TIDI and ACS was 48.8%. He viewed that market share as prima facie illegal under *United States v. Philadelphia National Bank*, 374 U.S. 321, 364–66 (1963). Agreeing with appellants that entry into the product market is easy— indeed, individuals operating out of their homes can compete successfully "with any other company"—Judge Griesa nevertheless held that proof of ease of entry did not rebut the prima facie showing of illegality. The district court therefore ordered WMI to divest itself of TIDI. Because we conclude that potential entry into the relevant Dallas market by new firms or by firms now operating in Fort Worth is so easy as to constrain the prices charged by WMI's subs, we reverse on the grounds that the merged firm does not substantially lessen competition. [. . .]

[4] WMI does not claim that [the 48.8% combined market share of the parties] is too small a share to trigger the *Philadelphia National Bank* presumption. Rather, it argues that the presumption is rebutted by the fact that competitors can enter the Dallas waste hauling market with such ease that the finding of a 48.8% market share does not accurately reflect market power. WMI argues that it is unable to raise prices over the competitive level because new firms would quickly enter the market and undercut them. [. . .]

[5] . . . [W]e believe that entry into the relevant product and geographic market by new firms or by existing firms in the Fort Worth area is so easy that any anti-competitive impact of the merger before us would be eliminated more quickly by such competition than by litigation. Judge Griesa specifically found that individuals operating out of their homes can acquire trucks and some containers and compete successfully "with any other company." The government's response to this factual finding is largely to the effect that economies of scale are more important than Judge Griesa believed. As with his other findings of fact, however, this one is not clearly erroneous, as there are examples in the record of such entrepreneurs entering and prospering.

[6] In any event, entry by larger companies is also relatively easy. At existing prices most Fort Worth and Dallas haulers operate within their own cities, but it is clear from the record that Fort Worth haulers could easily establish themselves in Dallas if the price of trash collection rose above the competitive level. Although it may be true that daily travel from Fort Worth to Dallas and back is costly, there is no barrier to Fort Worth haulers' acquiring garage facilities in Dallas permitting them to station some of their trucks there permanently or for portions of each week. The risks of such a strategy are low since substantial business can be assured through bidding on contracts even before such garage facilities are acquired, as one Fort Worth firm demonstrated by winning such a contract and then opening a facility in a Dallas suburb. That example can hardly be ignored by WMI or other Dallas haulers (not to mention their customers) in arriving at contract bids. The existence of haulers in Fort Worth, therefore, constrains prices charged by Dallas haulers . [. . .]

[7] Judge Griesa's conclusion that "there is no showing of any circumstances, related to ease of entry or the trend of the business, which promises in and of itself to materially erode the competitive strength of TIDI and ACS" is consistent with our decision. TIDI and ACS may well retain their present market share. However, in view of the findings as to ease of entry, that share can be retained only by competitive pricing. Ease of entry constrains not only WMI, but every firm in the market. Should WMI attempt to exercise market power by raising prices, none of its smaller competitors would be able to follow the price increases because of the ease with which new

competitors would appear. WMI would then face lower prices charged by all existing competitors as well as entry by new ones, a condition fatal to its economic prospects if not rectified.

[8] The government argues that consumers may prefer WMI's services, even at a higher price, over those of a new entrant because of its "proven track record." We fail to see how the existence of good will achieved through effective service is an impediment to, rather than the natural result of, competition. The government also argues that existing contracts bind most customers to a particular hauler and thereby prevent new entrants from acquiring business. If so, they also prevent the price increases until new entrants can submit competitive bids.

[9] Given Judge Griesa's factual findings, we conclude that the 48.8% market share attributed to WMI does not accurately reflect future market power. Since that power is in fact insubstantial, the merger does not, therefore, substantially lessen competition in the relevant market and does not violate Section 7.

CASENOTE: Google/AdMob

FTC File No. 101 0031 (May 21, 2010)

Entry was a critical basis for the FTC's decision to permit Google to acquire the AdMob mobile ad network. In a May 2010 statement, the Commission explained that its unanimous vote to close the merger investigation was "difficult" because "the parties currently are the two leading mobile advertising networks, and the Commission was concerned about the loss of head-to-head competition between them." The Commission's investigation had generated "evidence that each of the merging parties viewed the other as its primary competitor, and that each firm made business decisions in direct response to this perceived competitive threat."

But during the merger review, Apple acquired the #3 mobile ad network, Quattro Wireless. The Commission concluded that: "Apple quickly will become a strong mobile advertising network competitor. Apple not only has extensive relationships with application developers and users, but also is able to offer targeted ads (heretofore a strength of AdMob) by leveraging proprietary user data gleaned from users of Apple mobile devices. Furthermore, Apple's ownership of the iPhone software development tools, and its control over the developers' license agreement, gives Apple the unique ability to define how competition among ad networks on the iPhone will occur and evolve."

The Commission expressed confidence that interplatform competition between Google Android and iPhone would protect against any effort by the merged firm to exercise market power on Android devices. In particular, because "applications are often made available to consumers in their current low- or no-cost form through advertising provided by mobile ad networks like AdMob," Google would be motivated to keep apps on the Android platform by providing competitive advertising terms. "To the extent Google were to exercise market power on Android after this acquisition, it would risk making Android less competitive against the iPhone and other platforms."

Unfortunately, the predicted competitive pressure from Apple on which the FTC relied so heavily did not take place.[656] What could the agency have done when this became clear?

NOTES

1) Should courts and agencies use the same legal test to assess whether a business should be considered (a) an entrant for the purposes of *reducing* competitive concerns presented by a merger, and (b) a potential competitor for the purposes of *generating* competitive concerns? Should burdens be different? For one perspective, *see* Keith Klovers, Alexandra Keck & Allison Simkins, *Treating Like Cases Alike: The Need for Consistency in the Forthcoming Merger Guidelines*, Comp. Pol'y Int'l (Nov. 2022).

2) Suppose that an agency concludes that the prospect of entry or expansion is sufficient to resolve competitive concerns, allows the merger to close, and the predicted entry or expansion does not occur. Does this mean that the agency was wrong—either factually or legally—in its assessment? When, if at all, should the agency sue?

---

[656] *See, e.g.*, Ragnar Kruse, *The downfall of the walled garden: Here's why iAd failed*, TECHCRUNCH (Mar. 28, 2016).

3) Should the HMGs state that a merger will be permitted if the merged firm will face a monopolist supplier or customer? *Compare, e.g.*, Tom Campbell, *Bilateral Monopoly in Mergers*, 74 Antitrust L.J. 521 (2007) *with* Jonathan B. Baker, Joseph Farrell, & Carl Shapiro, *Merger to Monopoly to Serve a Single Buyer: Comment*, 75 Antitrust L.J. 637 (2008).

C. Vertical Mergers

Vertical mergers combine firms at different levels of the supply chain (such as an upstream input supplier with a downstream manufacturer that uses the input, or an upstream content creator with a downstream distribution platform), or suppliers of complementary products and services, leading to a "vertically integrated" post-merger firm.[657] The term "vertical merger" is also often used to include mergers of suppliers of complements.

As we noted at the outset, as a class, these transactions are (generally) somewhat less likely than horizontal mergers to be competitively troubling: because the firms are not in competition, and because there are often efficiencies from integrating different stages of production. As a result, vertical integration may represent a move toward a more efficient way of doing business, with the result that the firm is better able to compete.[658] But individual vertical mergers can and do cause competitive problems, as we shall see, and the agencies have a considerable body of vertical merger enforcement practice, even if few cases have been litigated to judgment in recent decades.[659]

The most common concern in vertical merger cases is that, post-merger, the integrated firm will use its control over its upstream / downstream division to reduce competition in the downstream / upstream market, by either cutting off rivals entirely or by dealing with them on less favorable terms. For example, a vertical merger that combines a downstream firm with market power in the supply of equipment with an upstream firm with market power in the supply of a key component could enable the merged firm to "foreclose" downstream rivals' access to inputs, or upstream rivals' access to distribution or customers, in ways that might lead to an overall reduction in competition. It may be helpful to see this presented visually:

Figure 6: Input foreclosure

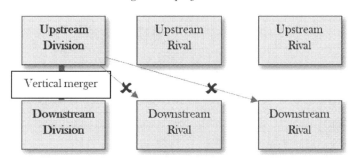

---

[657] Virtually all firms are vertically integrated to at least some extent, in that they combine more than one stage of production within the firm. (The very idea of a "production line," in which multiple different processes are applied in sequence, implies that the firm is active in successive stages of production.)

[658] *See, e.g.*, Oliver E. Williamson, *Economies as an Antitrust Defense: The Welfare Tradeoffs*, 58 Am. Econ. Rev. 18, 32 (1968) ("The logical boundaries of a firm are not necessarily those which have been inherited but rather are defined by the condition that the firm be unable to arrange a transaction internally more cheaply than the market. This is not something which is given once-for-all but depends both on technology and the extent of the market. Thus what may be regarded as 'vertical integration' under a historical definition of an industry might, in many instances, more accurately be characterized as a reorganization into a more efficient configuration. For example, as technology evolves processes that are more fully automated or as demand for a commodity increases sufficiently to warrant continuous processing techniques, combinatorial economies may result by serially linking activities within a single firm that had previously been done in separate specialty firm").

[659] *See* FTC, *Commentary on Vertical Merger Enforcement* (Dec. 2020); Steven C. Salop & Daniel P. Culley, *Vertical Merger Enforcement Actions: 1994-2016*, https://scholarship.law.georgetown.edu/facpub/1529/.

Figure 7: Customer / distribution foreclosure

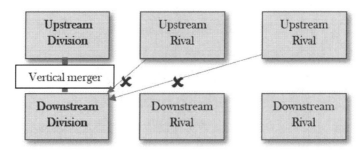

A vertical merger will not necessarily create (or strengthen) the incentive to foreclose rivals: after all, doing so means fewer sales for the foreclosing division. For foreclosure to be attractive, the expected additional profits to the division that competes with the targets of foreclosure must exceed the expected losses from the reduction in sales activity for the foreclosing division. Likewise, a vertical merger does not necessarily create (or strengthen) the ability to foreclose rivals. For a foreclosure strategy to have a significant effect on rivals, the division must have some degree of market power, or the targets of the foreclosure strategy will simply switch to an alternative source of inputs or distribution. Figuring out whether a merger will create or augment the ability or incentive to engage in harmful foreclosure, and weighing this effect against beneficial ones like cost savings and elimination of double marginalization ("EDM") incentive effects (*i.e.*, price reductions flowing from the integration of upstream and downstream divisions into a single decision-maker[660]) to determine the transaction's overall effect, can be a complex task.

Foreclosure is not the only way in which a vertical merger could harm competition. A merger that gives the merged firm access to competitively sensitive information about its rivals could harm competition by reducing rivals' incentive to compete aggressively.[661] A vertical merger could also improve market transparency or symmetry in a way that would facilitate coordination.[662]

Finally, remember that some transactions that appear vertical may also be horizontal: some vertical mergers involve parties who are, in addition to their vertical relationship, also potential horizontal competitors of one another. It is important not to forget this![663]

The most common theories of harm in vertical cases are set out in the Vertical Merger Guidelines.

Vertical Merger Guidelines § 4
(issued by FTC and DOJ 2020; FTC withdrew 2021)

4. Unilateral Effects

---

[660] *See infra* § VIII.D.2.

[661] *See, e.g.*, Complaint, United States v. UnitedHealth Group Inc., Case No. 1:22-cv-481 (D.D.C. filed Feb. 24, 2022) ¶ 12 ("Post-transaction, United . . . would have a strong incentive to use this data to weaken its health insurance rivals' competitiveness. The competitive insights that United would obtain by acquiring Change would allow United to slow its rivals' innovations, reverse-engineer its rivals' proprietary plan and payment rules, preempt their competitive strategies, and compete less vigorously for certain customers by understanding which employer groups pose more risk and have higher costs of treatment. This course would prove profitable to United while harming competition"), ¶ 88 ("With this data, UnitedHealthcare would have the ability to disadvantage its rivals, including by mimicking their innovative policies to make their rivals' healthcare plans less attractive to customers (relative to UnitedHealthcare). This would reduce the rivals' incentives to innovate in claims edits, which would also reduce innovation in commercial health insurance plan and provider network design."), ¶ 89 ("Innovation competition among health insurers would likely decline, because rival insurers would know that United could identify and appropriate the innovation through its access to the innovator's competitively sensitive edits. This harm to innovation would reduce competition in the sale of commercial health insurance to national accounts and large group employers, resulting in less affordable or lower quality plans.").

[662] *See, e.g.*, Steven C. Salop, *A Suggested Revision of the 2020 Vertical Merger Guidelines*, Working Paper, (December 31, 2021), https://papers.ssrn.com/sol3/papers.cfm?abstract_id=3839768, § 5.3 at 16 ("Coordinated effects may also arise when the merged firm gains access to rivals' sensitive competitive information, which may facilitate either (a) reaching a tacit agreement among market participants, (b) detecting cheating on such an agreement, or (c) punishing cheating firms.").

[663] See generally Alison Oldale, Bilal Sayyed & Andrew Sweeting, *A review of cases involving the loss of potential and nascent competition at the FTC, with particular reference to vertical mergers*, 6 Comp. L. & Pol'y Debate 60 (2020).

[1] A vertical merger may diminish competition between one merging firm and rivals that trade with, or could trade with, the other merging firm. This section discusses common types of unilateral effects arising from vertical mergers. Section (a) discusses foreclosure and raising rivals' costs. Section (b) discusses competitively sensitive information. These effects do not exhaust the types of possible unilateral effects.

a. Foreclosure and Raising Rivals' Costs

[2] A vertical merger may diminish competition by allowing the merged firm to profitably use its control of the related product to weaken or remove the competitive constraint from one or more of its actual or potential rivals in the relevant market. For example, a merger may increase the vertically integrated firm's incentive or ability to raise its rivals' costs by increasing the price or lowering the quality of the related product. The merged firm could also refuse to supply rivals with the related products altogether ("foreclosure").

[3] In identifying whether a vertical merger may diminish competition due to unilateral foreclosure or raising rivals' costs, the Agencies generally consider whether the following conditions are satisfied:

[4] **(1) Ability:** By altering the terms by which it provides a related product to one or more of its rivals, the merged firm would likely be able to cause those rivals (a) to lose significant sales in the relevant market (for example, if they are forced out of the market; if they are deterred from innovation, entry, or expansion, or cannot finance those activities; or if they have incentives to pass on higher costs through higher prices) or (b) to otherwise compete less aggressively for customers' business.

[5] This element would not be satisfied, and in turn a merger would rarely warrant close scrutiny for its potential to lead to foreclosure or raising rivals' costs, if rivals could readily switch purchases to alternatives to the related product, including self-supply, without any meaningful effect on the price, quality, or availability of products or services in the relevant market.

[6] The Agencies' review of the merged firm's rivals' ability to switch to alternatives to the related product may include, but is not limited to, the types of evidence the Agencies use to evaluate customer switching when implementing the hypothetical monopolist test, listed in Section 4.1.3 of the Horizontal Merger Guidelines.

[7] **(2) Incentive:** The merged firm, as a result of the merger, would likely find it profitable to foreclose rivals, or offer inferior terms for the related product, because it benefits significantly in the relevant market when rivals lose sales or alter their behavior in response to the foreclosure or to the inferior terms.

[8] This element would not be satisfied, and in turn a merger would rarely warrant close scrutiny for its potential to induce foreclosure or raise rivals' costs, if the merged firm would not benefit from a reduction in actual or potential competition with users of the related product in the relevant market.

[9] The Agencies' assessment of the effect of a vertical merger on the incentive to foreclose rivals or raise their costs by changing the terms of the related product will be fact-specific. For example, in the case of foreclosure, the Agencies generally consider whether the merged firm's gains in the relevant market would likely outweigh any losses from reduced sales of the related product.

[10] Mergers for which these conditions are met potentially raise significant competitive concerns and often warrant scrutiny.

[11] For mergers that warrant scrutiny, the Agencies will determine whether, based on an evaluation of the facts and circumstances of the relevant market, the merger may substantially lessen competition. This evaluation will generally include an assessment of the likely net effect on competition in the relevant market of all changes to the merged firm's unilateral incentives. The merged firm may foreclose its rivals or raise their costs by changing the terms offered for the related product, but a vertical merger can also change other incentives. The elimination of double marginalization, for example, can confer on the merged firm an incentive to set lower downstream prices. The price that a downstream firm pays for an input supplied by an independent upstream firm may include a markup over the upstream firm's marginal cost. If a downstream and an upstream firm merge, and the merged firm supplies itself with its own related product, it will have access to the input at cost. The likely merger-induced

increase or decrease in downstream prices would be determined by considering the impact of both these effects, as well as any other competitive effects. [. . .]

[12] Where sufficient relevant data are available, the Agencies may construct economic models designed to quantify the net effect on competition. The Agencies may employ merger simulation models to assist in this quantitative evaluation. These models often include independent price responses by non-merging firms and may incorporate feedback from the different effects on incentives. The Agencies do not treat merger simulation evidence as conclusive in itself, and they place more weight on whether merger simulations using reasonable models consistently predict substantial price increases than on the precise prediction of any single simulation. The Agencies may also determine that a merger may substantially lessen competition based on an evaluation of qualitative evidence of all potential effects. [. . .]

b. Access to Competitively Sensitive Information

[13] In a vertical merger, the transaction may give the combined firm access to and control of sensitive business information about its upstream or downstream rivals that was unavailable to it before the merger. For example, a downstream rival to the merged firm may have been a premerger customer of the upstream firm. Post-merger, the downstream component of the merged firm could now have access to its rival's sensitive business information. In some circumstances, the merged firm can use access to a rival's competitively sensitive information to moderate its competitive response to its rival's competitive actions. For example, it may preempt or react quickly to a rival's procompetitive business actions. Under such conditions, rivals may see less competitive value in taking procompetitive actions. Relatedly, rivals may refrain from doing business with the merged firm rather than risk that the merged firm would use their competitively sensitive business information as described above. They may become less effective competitors if they must rely on less preferred trading partners, or if they pay higher prices because they have fewer competing options.

5. Coordinated Effects

[14] In some cases, a vertical merger may diminish competition by enabling or encouraging postmerger coordinated interaction among firms in the relevant market that harms customers. Section 7 of the Horizontal Merger Guidelines describes how the Agencies evaluate coordinated effects.

[15] In particular, Section 7.1 notes that the Agencies are more likely to challenge a merger on the basis of coordinated effects when the relevant market shows signs of vulnerability to coordinated conduct, and the Agencies have a credible basis on which to conclude that the merger may enhance that vulnerability. Section 7.2 sets forth evidence relevant to evaluating whether a market is vulnerable to coordination. The theories of harm discussed in the Horizontal Merger Guidelines, as well as those discussed below, are not exhaustive, but rather are illustrations of the manner in which a merger may lessen competition due to coordinated effects.

[16] A vertical merger may enhance the market's vulnerability to coordination by eliminating or hindering a maverick firm that otherwise plays or would play an important role in preventing or limiting anticompetitive coordination in the relevant market. For example, the merged firm could use its control over a related product or service to harm the ability of a non-merging maverick to compete in the relevant market, thereby increasing the likelihood of coordinated interaction among the merged firm and rivals participating in that market.

[17] Coordinated effects may also arise in other ways, including when changes in market structure or the merged firm's access to confidential information facilitate (a) reaching a tacit agreement among market participants, (b) detecting cheating on such an agreement, or (c) punishing cheating firms.

* * *

Vertical merger policy is controversial. Some argue that the federal government and the courts have been too tolerant of vertical mergers.[664] Some scholars, including most notably Steven Salop, have proposed that alternative vertical merger guidelines could play a stronger role in articulating theories of harm in vertical cases.[665]

The leading modern case on vertical mergers is the Department of Justice's challenge to the merger of AT&T and Time Warner, which was litigated up to the D.C. Circuit. AT&T's DirecTV subsidiary was a downstream distributor of television to viewers; Time Warner was an upstream supplier of TV content, through its ownership of TV networks. The Department of Justice alleged that the merged firm would have the ability and incentive to foreclose competing distributors' access to Time Warner's programming. In the district court, Judge Leon was not convinced; and, on appeal, the D.C. Circuit agreed. Note the court's insistence that economic evidence must be consistent with so-called "real-world" evidence: that is, testimony from executives.

United States v. AT&T, Inc.
916 F.3d 1029 (D.C. Cir. 2019)

Judge Rogers.

[1] The video programming and distribution industry traditionally operates in a three-stage chain of production. Studios or networks create content. Then, programmers package content into networks and license those networks to video distributors. Finally, distributors sell bundles of networks to subscribers. For example, a studio may create a television show and sell it to Turner Broadcasting System ("Turner Broadcasting"), a programmer, which would package that television show into one of its networks, such as CNN or TNT. Turner Broadcasting would then license its networks to distributors, such as DirecTV or Comcast.

[2] Programmers license their content to distributors through affiliate agreements, and distributors pay "affiliate fees" to programmers. Programmers and distributors engage in what are oftentimes referred to as "affiliate negotiations," which, according to evidence before the district court, can be lengthy and complicated. If a programmer and a distributor fail to reach an agreement, then the distributor will lose the rights to display the programmer's content to its customers. This situation, known as a "blackout" or "going dark," is generally costly for both the programmer, which loses affiliate fee revenues, and the distributor, which risks losing subscribers. Therefore, blackouts rarely occur, and long-term blackouts are especially rare. The evidence indicated, however, that programmers and distributors often threaten blackouts as a negotiating tactic, and both may perform "go dark" analyses to estimate the potential impact of a blackout in preparation for negotiations.

[3] The evidence before the district court also showed that the industry has been changing in recent years. Multichannel video programming distributors ("MVPDs") offer live television content as well as libraries of licensed content "on demand" to subscribers. So-called "traditional" MVPDs distribute channels to subscribers on cable or by satellite. Recently, "virtual" MVPDs have also emerged. They distribute live videos and on-demand videos to subscribers over the internet and compete with traditional MVPDs for subscribers. Virtual MVPDs, such as DirecTV Now and YouTube TV, have been gaining market share, the evidence showed, because they are easy to use and low-cost, often because they offer subscribers smaller packages of channels, known as "skinny bundles."

[4] In addition, subscription video on demand services ("SVODs") have also emerged on the market. SVODs, such as Netflix, do not offer live video content but have large libraries of content that a viewer may access on demand. SVODs also offer low-cost subscription plans and have been gaining market share recently. Increasingly, cable customers are "cutting the cord" and terminating MVPD service altogether. Often these customers do not exit the entertainment field altogether, but instead switch to SVODs for entertainment service.

[5] Leading SVODs are vertically integrated, which means they create content and also distribute it. Traditional MVPDs typically are not vertically integrated with programmers. In 2009, however, Comcast Corporation

---

[664] *See, e.g.,* Jonathan B. Baker, THE ANTITRUST PARADIGM: RESTORING A COMPETITIVE ECONOMY (2019); Adil Abdela, Kristina Karlsson & Marshall Steinbaum, *Vertical Integration and the Market Power Crisis,* Roosevelt Institute Issue Brief (Apr. 2019); Steven C. Salop, *Invigorating Vertical Merger Enforcement,* 127 Yale L.J. 1962 (2018).

[665] *See* Steven C. Salop, *A Suggested Revision of the 2020 Vertical Merger Guidelines* (Dec. 31, 2021), https://papers.ssrn.com/sol3/papers.cfm?abstract_id=3839768.

("Comcast") (a distributor and the largest cable company in the United States) announced a $30 billion merger with NBC Universal, Inc. ("NBCU") (a content creator and programmer), whereby it would control popular video programming that included the NBC broadcast network and the cable networks of NBC Universal, Inc. The government sued to permanently enjoin the merger under Section 7, alleging that Comcast's "majority control of highly valued video programming would prevent rival video-distribution companies from competing against the post-merger entity." *United States v. Comcast*, 808 F.Supp.2d 145, 147 (D.D.C. 2011). The district court, with the defendants' agreement and at the government's urging, allowed the merger to proceed subject to certain remedies for the alleged anticompetitive conduct post-merger, including remedies ordered in a related proceeding before the Federal Communications Commission ("FCC"). One remedy in the Comcast-NBCU merger was an agreement by the defendants to submit, at a distributor's option, to "baseball style" arbitration — in which each side makes a final offer and the arbitrator chooses between them — if parties did not reach a renewal agreement. During the arbitration, the distributor would retain access to NBC content, thereby mitigating concerns that Comcast-NBCU may withhold NBC programming during negotiations in order to benefit Comcast's distribution subscriptions. Comcast-NBCU currently operates as a "vertically integrated" programmer and distributor.

[6] Now the government has again sued to halt a proposed vertical merger of a programmer and a distributor in the same industry. On October 22, 2016, AT&T Inc. announced its plan to acquire Time Warner Inc. ("Time Warner") as part of a $108 billion transaction. AT&T Inc. is a distribution company with two traditional MVPD products: DirecTV and U-verse. DirecTV transmits programming over satellite, while U-verse transmits programming over cable. Time Warner, by contrast, is a content creator and programmer and has three units: Warner Bros., Turner Broadcasting, and Home Box Office Programming ("HBO"). Warner Bros. creates movies, television shows, and other video programs. Turner Broadcasting packages content into various networks, such as TNT, TBS, and CNN, and licenses its networks to third-party MVPDs. HBO is a "premium" network that provides on-demand content to subscribers either directly through HBO Now or through licenses with third-party distributors. The merged firm would operate both AT&T MVPDs (DirecTV and U-verse) and Turner Broadcasting networks (which license to other MVPDs). The government alleged that "the newly combined firm likely would use its control of Time Warner's popular programming as a weapon to harm competition."

[7] A week after the government filed suit to stop the proposed merger, Turner Broadcasting sent letters to approximately 1,000 distributors "irrevocably offering" to engage in "baseball style" arbitration at any time within a seven-year period, subject to certain conditions not relevant here. According to President of Turner Content Distribution Richard Warren, the offer of arbitration agreements was designed to address the government's concern that as a result of being commonly owned by AT&T, Turner Broadcasting would have an incentive to drive prices higher and go dark with its affiliates. In the event of a failure to agree on renewal terms, Turner Broadcasting agreed that the distributor would have the right to continue carrying Turner networks pending arbitration, subject to the same terms and conditions in the distributor's existing contract.

[*]

[8] The government's increased leverage theory is that by combining Time Warner's programming and DirecTV's distribution, the merger would give Time Warner increased bargaining leverage in negotiations with rival distributors, leading to higher, supracompetitive prices for millions of consumers. Under this theory, Turner Broadcasting's bargaining position in affiliate negotiations will change after the merger due to its relationship with AT&T because the cost of a blackout will be lower. Prior to the merger, if Turner Broadcasting failed to reach a deal with a distributor and engaged in a long-term blackout, then it would lose affiliate fees and advertising revenues. After the merger, some costs of a blackout would be offset because some customers would leave the rival distributor due to Turner Broadcasting's blackout and a portion of those customers would switch to AT&T distributor services. The merged AT&T-Turner Broadcasting entity would earn a profit margin on these new customers. Because Turner Broadcasting would make a profit from switched customers, the cost of a long-term blackout would decrease after the merger and thereby give it increased bargaining leverage during affiliate negotiations with rival distributors sufficient to enable it to secure higher affiliate fees from distributors, which would result in higher prices for consumers.

[9] To support this theory of competitive harm, the government presented evidence purporting to show the real-world effect of the proposed merger. Specifically, it introduced statements in prior FCC filings by AT&T and

DirecTV that vertical integration provides an incentive to increase prices and poses a threat to competition. Various internal documents of the defendants were to the same effect. Third-party competitors, such as cable distributors, testified that the merger would increase Turner Broadcasting's bargaining leverage.

[10] The government also presented the expert opinion of Professor Carl Shapiro on the likely anticompetitive effect of the proposed merger. He opined, based on the economic theory of bargaining—here, the Nash bargaining theory—that Turner Broadcasting's bargaining leverage would increase after the merger because the cost of a long-term blackout would decrease. His quantitative model predicted net price increases to consumers. Specifically, his model predicted increases in fees paid by rival distributors for Turner Broadcasting content and cost savings for AT&T through elimination of double marginalization ("EDM"). The fee increases for rival distributors were based on the expected benefit to AT&T of a Turner Broadcasting blackout after the merger. Professor Shapiro determined the extent to which rival distributors and AT&T would pass on their respective cost increases and cost decreases to consumers. His model predicted: (1) an annual fee increase of $587 million for rival distributors to license Turner Broadcasting content, and cost savings of $352 million for AT&T; and (2) an annual net increase of $286 million in costs passed on to consumers in 2016, with increases in future years.

[11] AT&T responded by pointing to testimony of executives' past experience in affiliate negotiations, and presenting testimony by its experts critiquing Professor Shapiro's opinion and model. It purported to show through its own experts that the government's prima facie case inaccurately predicted the proposed merger's probable effect on competition. Professor Dennis Carlton's econometric analysis (also known as a regression analysis), showed that prior instances of vertical integration in the MVPD market had not had a statistically significant effect on content prices, pointing to data on the Comcast-NBCU merger in 2011 as well as prior vertical integration between News Corp.-DirecTV and Time Warner Cable-Time Warner Inc., which split in 2008 and 2009, respectively. Professor Carlton and Professor Peter Rossi critiqued the "inputs" used by Professor Shapiro in his quantitative model, opining for instance that values he used for subscriber loss rate and diversion rate were not calculated through reliable methods. Professor Carlton also opined that Professor Shapiro's quantitative model overestimated how quickly harm would occur because it failed to consider existing long-term contracts.

[12] Professor Shapiro, in turn, critiqued Professor Carlton's econometric analysis as comparing different types of vertical mergers. Regarding the "inputs" to his quantitative model, Professor Shapiro conceded that he was unaware the subscriber loss rate percentage he used (from a consultant report for Charter Communications, Inc.) had been changed after the report was presented to Charter executives. He also acknowledged that he had not considered the effects of the arbitration agreements offered by Turner Broadcasting and that to do so would require preparation of a new model.

[13] The district court acknowledged the uncertainty regarding the measure of proof for the government's burden because Section 7 does not require proof of certain harm. The government and AT&T had used various phrases to describe the government's burden, including that it must show an "appreciable danger" of competitive harm, or that it must show that harm is "likely" or "reasonably probable." The district court concluded that it need not articulate the differences between these phrases because even assuming the "reasonable probability" or "appreciable danger" formulations govern here its conclusions regarding the government's failure of proof would remain unchanged. Acknowledging also the lack of precedent and the complexity in establishing the correct approach in a Section 7 challenge to a proposed vertical merger, the district court viewed the outcome of the litigation to turn on whether, notwithstanding the proposed merger's conceded procompetitive effects, the government has met its burden of establishing, through "case-specific evidence," that the merger of AT&T and Time Warner, at this time and in this remarkably dynamic industry, is likely to substantially lessen competition in the manner it predicts. [. . .]

[14] The district court found that the government had failed to clear the first hurdle of showing that the proposed merger is likely to increase Turner [Broadcasting]'s bargaining leverage in affiliate negotiations. Although acknowledging, as Professor Shapiro had opined, that the Nash bargaining theory could apply in the context of affiliate fee negotiations, the district court found more probative the real-world evidence offered by AT&T than that offered by the government. The econometric analysis of AT&T's expert had examined real-world data from prior instances of vertical integration in the video programming and distribution industry and concluded that the bulk of the results show no significant results at all, but many do show a decrease in content prices. The district

court also credited the testimony of several industry executives—e.g., Madison Bond, lead negotiator for NBCU, and Coleman Breland and Richard Warren, lead negotiators for Turner Broadcasting—that vertical integration had not affected their affiliate negotiations in the past. By contrast, the testimony from third-party competitors that the merger would increase Turner Broadcasting's bargaining leverage was, the district court found, speculative, based on unproven assumptions, or unsupported. Although Professor Shapiro's opinion was that the Nash bargaining theory predicted an increase in Turner Broadcasting's post-merger bargaining leverage, leading to an increase in affiliate fees, the district court found, in view of the industry's dynamism in recent years, that Professor Shapiro's opinion (by contrast with Professor Carlton's) had not been supported by sufficient real-world evidence.

[15] Second, the district court found that Professor Shapiro's quantitative model, which estimated the proposed merger would result in future increases in consumer prices, lacked sufficient reliability and factual credibility to generate probative predictions of future competitive harm. Relying on critiques by Professor Carlton and Professor Rossi, the district court found errors in the model "inputs," for example, the value used for subscriber loss rate was not calculated through a reliable method. Neither the model nor Professor Shapiro's opinion accounted for the effect of the irrevocably-offered arbitration agreements, which the district court stated would have "real world effects" on negotiations and characterized "as extra icing on a cake already frosted," i.e., another reason the government had not met its first-level burden of proof.

[16] The district court therefore concluded that the government failed to present persuasive evidence that Turner Broadcasting's bargaining leverage would "materially increase" as a result of the merger, or that the merger would lead to "any raised costs" for rival distributors or consumers. It therefore did not address the balancing analysis offered by Professor Shapiro's quantitative model, nor the question whether any increased costs would result in a substantial lessening of competition.

[*]

[17] On appeal, the government contends that the district court (1) misapplied economic principles, (2) used internally inconsistent logic when evaluating industry evidence, and (3) clearly erred in rejecting Professor Shapiro's quantitative model. Undoubtedly the district court made some problematic statements, which the government identifies and this court cannot ignore. And in the probabilistic Section 7 world, uncertainty exists about the future real-world impact of the proposed merger on Turner Broadcasting's post-merger leverage. At this point, however, the issue is whether the district court clearly erred in finding that the government failed to clear the first hurdle in meeting its burden of showing that the proposed merger is likely to increase Turner Broadcasting's bargaining leverage.

[18] **(1) Application of economic principles.** The government contends that in evaluating the evidence in support of its increased leverage theory, the district court erroneously discarded or otherwise misapplied two economic principles—the Nash bargaining theory and corporate-wide profit maximization.

[19] *(a) Nash bargaining theory.* The Nash bargaining theory is used to analyze two-party bargaining situations, specifically where both parties are ultimately better off by reaching an agreement. The theory posits that an important factor affecting the ultimate agreement is each party's relative loss in the event the parties fail to agree: when a party would have a greater loss from failing to reach an agreement, the other party has increased bargaining leverage. In other words, the relative loss for each party affects bargaining leverage and when a party has more bargaining leverage, that party is more likely to achieve a favorable price in the negotiation.

[20] The district court had to determine whether the economic theory applied to the particular market by considering evidence about the structure, history, and probable future of the video programming and distribution industry. As one circuit has put it, the Nash theorem arrives at a result that follows from a certain set of premises, while the theory asserts nothing about what situations in the real world fit those premises. The district court concluded that the government presented insufficient real-world evidence to support the prediction under the Nash bargaining theory of a material increase of Turner Broadcasting's post-merger bargaining leverage in affiliate negotiations by reason of less-costly long-term blackouts. The government's real-world evidence consisted of statements by AT&T Inc. and DirecTV in FCC regulatory filings that vertical integration, such as in the proposed

Comcast-NBCU merger, can give distributors an incentive to charge higher affiliate fees and expert opinion and a quantitative model prepared by Professor Shapiro. The expert opinion and model were subject to deficiencies identified by AT&T's experts, some of which Professor Shapiro conceded. By contrast, AT&T's expert's econometric analysis of real-world data showed that content pricing in prior vertical mergers in the industry had not increased as the Nash bargaining theory and the model predicted. Given evidence the industry was now "remarkably dynamic," the district court credited CEO testimony about the null effect of vertical integration on affiliate negotiations.

[21] In other words, the record shows that the district court accepted the Nash bargaining theory as an economic principle generally but rejected its specific prediction in light of the evidence that the district court credited. The district court explained that its conclusion

> does not turn on defendants' protestations that the theory is "preposterous," "ridiculous," or "absurd." but instead on its evaluation of the shortcomings in the proffered third-party competitor testimony, the testimony about the complex nature of these negotiations and the low likelihood of a long-term Turner Broadcasting blackout, and the fact that real-world pricing data and experiences of individuals who have negotiated on behalf of vertically integrated entities all fail to support the government's increased-leverage theory.

[22] More concerning is the government's contention that the district court misapplied the Nash bargaining theory in a manner that negated its acceptance of the economics of bargaining by erroneously focusing on whether long-term blackouts would actually occur after the merger, rather than on the changes in stakes of such a blackout for Turner Broadcasting. The government points to the district court's statements that Professor Shapiro's testimony was undermined by evidence that a blackout would be infeasible. The district court also stated that there has never been, and is likely never going to be, an actual long-term blackout of Turner Broadcasting content. The district court noted that Turner Broadcasting would not be willing to accept the "catastrophic" affiliate fee and advertising losses associated with a long-term blackout.

[23] The question posed by the Nash bargaining theory is whether Turner Broadcasting would be more favorably positioned after the merger to assert its leverage in affiliate negotiations whereby the cost of its content would increase. Considered in isolation, the district court's statements could be viewed as addressing the wrong question. Considered as part of the district court's analysis of whether the stakes for Turner Broadcasting would change and if so by how much, the statements address whether the threat of long-term blackouts would be credible, as posited by the government's increased leverage theory. The district court found that after the merger the stakes for Turner Broadcasting would change only slightly, so its threat of a long-term blackout "will only be somewhat less incredible." Recognizing Professor Shapiro applied the Nash bargaining theory in opining that if a party's alternative to striking a deal improves, that party is more willing and able to push harder for a better deal because it faces less downside risk if the deal implodes, the district court rejected the assumption underlying the government's theory that Turner Broadcasting would gain increased leverage from this slight change in stakes. It relied on testimony that the small change in bargaining position from a less costly blackout would not cause Turner Broadcasting to take more risks, specifically noting the Time Warner CEO's analogy of the cost difference between having a 1,000-pound weight fall on Turner Broadcasting and a 950-pound weight fall on it—the difference being unlikely to change the risk Turner Broadcasting would be willing to take.

[24] The district court's statements identified by the government, then, do not indicate that the district court misunderstood or misapplied the Nash bargaining theory but rather, upon considering whether in the context of a dynamic market where a similar merger had not resulted in a "statistically significant increase in content costs," the district court concluded that the theory inaccurately predicted the post-merger increase in content costs during affiliate negotiations.

[25] Of course, it was not enough for the government merely to prove that after the merger the costs of a long-term blackout would change for Turner Broadcasting. Its theory is that Turner Broadcasting's bargaining leverage would increase sufficiently to enable it to charge higher prices for its content. The district court's focus on the slight change in the cost of a long-term blackout in finding Turner Broadcasting's bargaining leverage would not meaningfully change aligns with determining whether the government's evidence established that a change in the post-merger stakes for Turner Broadcasting would likely allow it to extract higher prices during affiliate

negotiations. The district court reasoned that because long-term blackouts are very costly and would therefore be infeasible for Turner Broadcasting even after the merger, there was insufficient evidence that a post-merger Turner Broadcasting would, or even could, drive up prices by threatening distributors with long-term blackouts. In finding the government failed to prove that Turner Broadcasting's post-merger negotiating position would materially increase based on its ownership by AT&T, the district court reached a fact-specific conclusion based on real-world evidence that, contrary to the Nash bargaining theory and government expert opinion on increased content costs, the post-merger cost of a long-term blackout would not sufficiently change to enable Turner Broadcasting to secure higher affiliate fees. Witnesses such as a Turner Broadcasting president Coleman Breland, AT&T executive John Stankey, and Time Warner CEO Jeff Bewkes, whom the district court credited, testified that after the merger blackouts would remain too costly to risk and that any change in that cost would not affect negotiations as the government's theory predicted.

[26] Not to be overlooked, the district court also credited the efficacy of Turner Broadcasting's "irrevocable" offer of arbitration agreements with a no-blackout guarantee. It characterized the no-blackout agreements as "extra icing on a cake already frosted." In crediting Professor Carlton's econometric analysis, the district court explained that it was appropriate to consider the analysis of the Comcast-NBCU merger because the Comcast-NBCU merger was similar to the proposed merger—a vertical merger in the video programming and distribution industry. There the government had recognized, especially in vertical mergers, that conduct remedies, such as the ones proposed in the Comcast case, can be a very useful tool to address the competitive problems while preserving competition and allowing efficiencies that may result from the transaction. Like there, the district court concluded the Turner arbitration agreements would have real-world effect.

[27] The post-merger arbitration agreements would prevent the blackout of Turner Broadcasting content while arbitration is pending. As mentioned, Turner Broadcasting "irrevocably offer[ed]" approximately 1,000 distributors agreements to engage in baseball style arbitration in the event the parties fail to reach a renewal agreement, and the offered agreement guarantees no blackout of Turner Broadcasting content once arbitration is invoked. AT&T's counsel represented the no-blackout commitment is "legally enforceable," and AT&T "will honor" the arbitration agreement offers. Consequently, the government's challenges to the district court's treatment of its economic theories becomes largely irrelevant, at least during the seven-year period. Counsel for Amici Curiae 27 Antitrust Scholars explained that arbitration agreements make the Nash bargaining model premised on two-party negotiations "substantially more complicated," and Professor Shapiro acknowledged that taking the arbitration agreements into account would require "a completely different model." [. . .]

[28] [T]he district court's finding of the efficacy of Turner Broadcasting's irrevocable offers of no-blackout arbitration agreements means the merger is unlikely to afford Turner Broadcasting increased bargaining leverage.

[29] *(b) Corporate-wide profit maximization.* Still, the government maintains that the reliance on past negotiation experience indicates that the district court misunderstood, and failed to apply, the principle of corporate-wide profit maximization by treating the principle as a question of fact, when "[t]he assumption of profit maximization is 'crucial' in predicting business behavior." This principle posits that a business with multiple divisions will seek to maximize its total profits. It was adopted as a principle of antitrust law in *Copperweld Corp. v. Independence Tube Corp.*, 467 U.S. 752, 771 . . . (1984), holding that a parent and a wholly-owned subsidiary are not capable of conspiracy against each other under Section 1 of the Sherman Antitrust Act. Companies with multiple divisions must be viewed as a single actor, and each division will act to pursue the common interests of the whole corporation.

[30] The district court never cited *Copperweld* in its opinion, which is troubling given the government's competitive harm theories and expert evidence based on economic principles. But the government's position that the district court never accepted this economic principle overlooks that it did accept Professor Shapiro's (and the Government's) argument that generally, a firm with multiple divisions will act to maximize profits across them. And it ignores that if the merged firm was unable to exert the leverage required by the government's increased leverage theory, then inquiring (as the district court did of Professor Shapiro) about an independent basis to conclude that the firm did have such leverage is not a rejection of the corporate-wide profit maximization principle.

[31] The government maintains that the district court's misapplication of the principle of corporate-wide profit maximization is evident from its statement the evidence suggests vertically integrated corporations have previously determined that the best way to increase company wide profits is for the programming and distribution components to separately maximize their respective revenues. Stating that the programming and distribution divisions would "separately maximize their respective revenues" is contrary to the maximization principle to the extent separate units would act against the merged entity's common interest. At this point in its opinion, however, the district court was explaining why "that profit-maximization principle is not inconsistent with testimony that the identity of a programmer's owner has not affected affiliate negotiations in real-world instances of vertical integration." The district court can be viewed as conveying its understanding that Turner Broadcasting's interest in spreading its content among distributors, not imposing long-term blackouts, would redound to the merged firm's financial benefit, not that Turner Broadcasting would act in a manner contrary to the merged firm's financial benefit. Industry executives testified that the identity of a programmer's owner has not affected affiliate negotiations in real-world instances of vertical integration. For instance, the Chair of Content Distribution at NBC Universal testified that at Comcast-NBCU, he "never once took into account the interest of Comcast cable in trying to negotiate a carriage agreement" for NBC Universal.

[32] To the extent the government maintains this testimony is irreconcilable with the legal principle of corporate-wide profit maximization, it gives no credence to the district court's focus on the best way to increase company wide profits, referring to the merged firm. In other words, the district court was explaining that real-world evidence reflected the profit-maximization principle. Even if the district court could have made clearer that it understood the principle was not a question of fact, the government does not explain how considering how that is done in a particular industry is contrary to the principle of corporate-wide profit maximization. [. . .]

[33] *(3) Rejection of Professor Shapiro's quantitative model.* Finally, the government contends that the district court clearly erred in rejecting Professor Shapiro's quantitative bargaining model. Specifically, that the district court erred in finding insufficient evidence to support Professor Shapiro's calculations of fee increases for rival distributors and in finding no proof of any price increase to consumers.

[34] Preliminarily, the court does not hold that quantitative evidence of price increase is required in order to prevail on a Section 7 challenge. Vertical mergers can create harms beyond higher prices for consumers, including decreased product quality and reduced innovation. Indeed, the Supreme Court upheld the Federal Trade Commission's Section 7 challenge to Ford Motor Company's proposed vertical merger with a major spark plug manufacturer without quantitative evidence about price increases. *Ford Motor Co. v. United States*, 405 U.S. 562, 567–69, 578 (1972). Here, however, the government did not present its challenge to the AT&T-Time Warner merger in terms of creating non-price related harms in the video programming and distribution industry, and we turn to the government's challenges to the district court's handling of the quantitative evidence regarding the proposed merger's predicted effect on consumer price.

[35] Professor Shapiro presented a quantitative model that predicted an annual net increase of $286 million being passed on to consumers in 2016, with increasing costs in future years. This figure was based on the model's predictions of an annual fee increase of $587 million for rival distributors to license Turner Broadcasting content and cost savings of $352 million for AT&T. The district court accepted Professor Shapiro's testimony about the $352 million cost savings from the merger. But it found that insufficient evidence supported the inputs and assumptions used to estimate the annual costs increases for rival distributors, crediting criticisms by Professor Carlton and Professor Rossi. Indeed, the district court found that the quantitative model as presented through Professor Shapiro's opinion testimony did not provide an adequate basis to conclude that the merger will lead to any raised costs for distributors or consumers, much less consumer harms that outweigh the conceded $350 million in annual cost savings to AT&T's customers.

[36] Whatever errors the district court may have made in evaluating the inputs for Professor Shapiro's quantitative model, the model did not take into account long-term contracts, which would constrain Turner Broadcasting's ability to raise content prices for distributors. The district court found that the real-world effects of Turner Broadcasting's existing contracts would be "significant" until 2021 and that it would be difficult to predict price increases farther into the future, particularly given that the industry is continually changing and experiencing increasing competition. This failure, the district court found, resulted in overestimation of how quickly the harms

would occur. Professor Shapiro acknowledged that predictions farther into the future, after the long-term contracts expire, are more difficult. Neither Professor Shapiro's opinion testimony nor his quantitative model considered the effect of the post-litigation offer of arbitration agreements, something he acknowledged would require a new model. And the video programming and distribution industry had experienced "ever-increasing competitiveness" in recent years. Taken together, the government's clear-error contention therefore fails. [. . .]

[37] Accordingly, because the district court did not abuse its discretion in denying injunctive relief, we affirm the district court's order denying a permanent injunction of the merger.

* * *

The merger proceeded, but the ending was not a happy one: the parties separated a few years after the deal closed.[666] In 2021, the FTC challenged another vertical merger: the federal government's first vertical merger challenge since *AT&T*. The case concerned the acquisition by medical technology business Illumina, a leading provider of DNA sequencing technology, of Grail, which was developing a multi-cancer early detection test. The case was tried before an FTC administrative law judge, Judge Chappell, who rejected the FTC's theory, three days after the European Commission had blocked the deal on EU competition grounds.[667] Judge Chappell was subsequently reversed by the Commission.[668] A wave of further vertical challenges followed.[669]

Although foreclosure is the most common concern in vertical cases, access to information was also at issue in DOJ's effort in 2022 to block the acquisition by Optum, a subsidiary of UnitedHealth Group ("UHG") (the country's largest health insurer, or "payer"), of Change Healthcare. Change was a health technology supplier and the country's largest electronic data interchange ("EDI") clearinghouse for transmitting data about insurance claims between healthcare providers and insurers. DOJ's challenge to the merger advanced two vertical theories: (1) that the merged firm would use its control over competitively sensitive information to weaken rivals' incentive to compete; and (2) that the merged firm would foreclose its insurer rivals' access to valuable EDI innovations (*i.e.*, traditional input foreclosure). In September 2022, the district court rejected both theories (as well as a horizontal theory not presented here). Among other things, the *United / Change* decision demonstrates the importance of supportive customer witnesses in any merger challenge—and the challenges of litigating without them.

United States v. UnitedHealth Group, Ltd.
__ F. Supp. 3d. __, 2022 WL 4365867 (D.D.C. Sept. 21, 2022)

Judge Nichols.

[1] [T]he Government advances two [vertical] theories of competitive harm. First, the Government argues that United's control over Change's EDI clearinghouse would give United the ability and incentive to use rivals' [competitively sensitive information] ("CSI") for its own benefit. Second, the Government argues that United's control over Change's EDI clearinghouse would give United the ability and incentive to foreclose rivals' access to key inputs on competitive terms by withholding innovations, thereby raising those rivals' costs. The effect of these actions, says the Government, would be to substantially lessen competition in the markets for national accounts and large group commercial health insurance.

1. The Government's Data-Misuse Theory Fails.

[2] Consider, first, the Government's data-misuse argument. The claim starts by contending that Optum, through its post-acquisition control of Change's EDI clearinghouse, will gain broad access and use rights to the claims data of UHC's rivals. The argument then posits that Optum will have an incentive to share the data—or at least the

666 *See* Victor Glass, *Culture Clash and the Failure of the AT&T/Time Warner Merger*, Rutgers Bus. Rev. 350 (Fall 2021).

667 *See* Initial Decision, In the Matter of Illumina, Inc., FTC Dkt. No. 9401 (Mar. 31. 2023).

668 *See* Opinion of the Commission, In the Matter of Illumina, Inc., FTC Dkt. No. 9401 (Sept. 9, 2022); Case M.10188, Illumina / Grail (prohibition decision of Sept. 6, 2022). For discussion of the FTC's Part 3 administrative litigation process, *see infra* Chapter XI.

669 *See* Complaint, In the matter of Lockheed Martin Corp., FTC Dkt. No. 9405 (F.T.C. filed Jan. 25, 2022); Complaint, In the matter of Nvidia Corp., FTC Dkt. No. 9404 (F.T.C. filed Dec. 2, 2021); Complaint, United States v. UnitedHealth Group, Ltd., Case No. 1:22-cv-00481 (D.D.C. filed Feb. 24, 2022); Complaint, In the Matter of Microsoft Corp, FTC Dkt. No. 9412 (F.T.C. filed Dec. 8, 2022).

competitively sensitive insights that can be gleaned from the data—with UHC. Knowing this, UHC's rivals will innovate less, out of fear that UHC will free ride off their innovations, thereby resulting in harm to competition in the relevant insurance markets. In essence, then, this vertical theory can be distilled to four steps, each of which the Government must establish is likely: (1) Optum will gain incremental access and use rights to the claims data of UHC's rivals; (2) Optum will have an incentive to share these data—or the competitively sensitive insights derived from the data—with UHC; (3) rival payers' fear of UHC using these data or insights will chill innovation; and (4) less innovation means less competition in the relevant markets.

[3] The evidence at trial highlighted weaknesses in each of these steps. But the central problem with this vertical claim is that it rests on speculation rather than real-world evidence that events are likely to unfold as the Government predicts. Governing law requires the Court to make a prediction about the future, and that prediction must be informed by record evidence and a fact-specific showing as to the proposed merger's likely effect on competition. Under this standard, antitrust theory and speculation cannot trump facts.

[4] The evidence adduced at trial established that, for it to be likely that the proposed acquisition would substantially lessen competition, United would have to uproot its entire business strategy and corporate culture; intentionally violate or repeal longstanding firewall policies; flout existing contractual commitments; and sacrifice significant financial and reputational interests. The Government has failed to show that United's post-merger incentives will lead it to take such extreme actions. Nor has the Government put forward real-world evidence that United's rivals are likely to innovate less out of fear that United will poach their data. No payer witness made that claim; in fact, all the payer witnesses testified to just the opposite. Although the Government's data-misuse argument has other shortcomings, these two defects stand out above the rest. [. . .]

[5] Also relevant are certain structural guarantees that exist to prevent CSI from being shared between Optum and UHC. The Court will discuss two of those structural protections: firewalls and customer contracts.

[6] Start with United's firewall policies. The evidence established, and the Court finds, that firewalls are an industry standard means of protecting CSI in the vertically integrated healthcare space. The evidence also established that, for over a decade—beginning well before the proposed acquisition here—United has maintained a corporate antitrust firewall that expressly prohibits the sharing of CSI between business units. That policy provides: "You must not participate in or facilitate communications that may reduce or eliminate competition between another Business Unit and its competitor(s)." The policy also requires employees to "exercise caution when communicating with a customer or supplier who is a competitor of another UHG Business Unit," and to "avoid serving as a conduit of information or an intermediary between the 'competitor' and the other Business Unit." The evidence does not reflect a single instance in which these firewalls have been breached. See, e.g., 8/5/22 PM Trial Tr. 42:24–43:2 (Dumont) ("Q. Have there been any violations of United's firewall policies where a UnitedHealthcare employee actually accessed Optum external customer data? A. Not that I'm aware of."); 8/4/22 AM Trial Tr. 101:6–10 (Wichmann) ("Q. Were you aware of any employees of United across the business segments using competitively-sensitive information learned from one business segment and applying it to another? A. No.").

[7] In May 2022, United took a related step by issuing guidance to address the Change transaction specifically and the data sharing principles that will apply post-merger. The evidence established, and the Court finds, that this transaction-specific policy was not designed to alter United's longstanding approach to information sharing, but rather was intended to memorialize existing practices and to address specific concerns raised in relation to the proposed acquisition. Among other things, the May 2022 policy provides:

- "The disclosure of External Customer CSI to UHG business units that are competitors of such External Customers is strictly prohibited."
- "The use of External Customer CSI to benefit UHG business units that are competitors of such External Customers is strictly prohibited."
- "UHG employees may not access External Customer CSI unless such access is necessary to perform their job responsibilities."
- "External Customer CSI shall be logically separated from other UHG business unit data within Electronic Data Sites. No employees of other UHG business units that are competitors of an External

Customer shall have access to the locations where External Customer CSI is stored within such Electronic Data Sites."

[8] . . . [T]he evidence at trial established, and the Court finds, that United will have strong legal, reputational, and financial incentives to protect rival payers' CSI after the proposed merger. Still, the Government's expert, Dr. Gowrisankaran, says that the costs of data misuse would be "negligible" for United, because even though United may lose "some business" as a result of the merger, other customers will just "assume the risk," and those customers are unlikely to later leave because they will never know if United misuses their data. This contention, in the Court's view, rests on speculation and is unsupported by any real-world evidence.

[9] The Government and Dr. Gowrisankaran are on firmer ground when they argue that United is a vertically integrated firm with an incentive to maximize its overall profits, not just the profits of an individual subsidiary like Optum. After all, it has long been a principle of antitrust law that a business with multiple divisions will seek to maximize its total profits. For this reason, the operations of a corporate enterprise organized into divisions must be judged as the conduct of a single actor, with each division pursuing the common interests of the whole. Here, the Government contends that United's corporate-wide interests and incentives will be to share CSI with UHC, even if doing so hurts Optum, because that is the best way to maximize corporate-wide profits.

[10] It is of course true that, in some cases, the optimal strategy for maximizing corporate-wide profits will be to leverage one division of the business to benefit another division. But it is also true that, in other cases, the best way to maximize corporate-wide profits will be for the first division to do business with as many customers as possible, including competitors of the sister division. It is consistent with the corporate-wide profit maximization principle to assess which strategy is the best way to increase company wide profits in a particular industry.

[11] Witty, the CEO of UHG, explained all this in his deposition testimony. The Government seizes upon his statement "that UnitedHealth Group needs to think about United at an enterprise level," while ignoring his observation that maximizing enterprise value "sometimes would involve separate business units' assets being worked together," and "sometimes individually," subject to "the important caveat of all of the rule sets" that limit UHG's conduct.

[12] And at trial, Witty testified that enterprise value would not be maximized—in fact, it would be harmed—if Optum shared competitively sensitive data with UHC. See 8/10/22 PM Trial Tr. 28:2–24 (Witty) ("Q. [The Government's] expert also testified that because of your enterprise approach, that that would cause people at OptumInsight to give data concerning UHC's rivals over to UHC so they could beat them in the marketplace. And what's your response to that? A. So again, first of all, that would be against the tone, the culture, the rules, everything that we stand for in the organization. . . . [And] it would be hugely destructive, not just to our reputation but to our economic interest."). The Government downplays the relative gains and losses between UHC and OptumInsight by focusing only on OptumInsight's revenue, rather than the revenue of Optum as a whole. But as the evidence demonstrated at trial, and as the Court finds, data misuse would place all of Optum's $63 billion in external revenue at risk, because customers think of Optum as a single unit. The trial evidence did not demonstrate that the potential gains to UHC would outweigh this potential loss.

[13] In sum, the evidence established that the Government's claim fails to account for all of United's post-merger incentives, including its incentives to preserve its multi-payer business model, to maintain its internal culture, and, ultimately, to protect its financial and reputational interests. The Government, at most, presented evidence that United would have some incentive (and ability) to exploit competitors' competitively sensitive data for its own economic benefit following the acquisition. But evidence that it could be possible to act in accordance with the Government's theories of harm is a far cry from evidence that the merged company is likely to do so. The Court must make a predictive judgment about the competitive effect of the proposed merger, and that prediction must be based on real-world evidence related to the structure, history, and probable future of the relevant markets. Here, that evidence—the widespread use of firewalls in the industry, United's history of compliance with its own firewalls, the customer contracts, and the convincing testimony from senior executives about United's practices and incentives—weighs strongly against the Government's position.

[14] Even if the Government had established that United's post-merger incentives would drive it to "misuse" Change's claims data, the Government also had to demonstrate a likely substantial lessening of competition. The Government based its theory of competitive harm here on reduced innovation by other payers. This theory of harm does not necessarily depend on United's actual misuse of rivals' data for competitive insights—according to the Government, United's rivals will reduce innovation because regardless of what United's going to do, United's rivals are going to think that United will act in its own interests.

[15] Yet the Government provided zero real-world evidence that rival payers are likely to reduce innovation. The Government did not call a single rival payer to offer corporate testimony that it would innovate less or compete less aggressively if the proposed merger goes through. Nor did any of the rival payer employees who did testify support the Government's theory. To the contrary, all the payer witnesses rejected the notion that the proposed merger would harm innovation.

2. The Government's Foreclosure Theory Fails.

[16] The Government's second vertical theory posits that United will have the ability and incentive to raise rival payers' costs by withholding or delaying the sale of EDI-related innovations—specifically, integrated platforms. The Government stresses that Optum and Change have long competed to develop their own integrated platforms—Optum, through an idea called the Transparent Network, and Change, through a concept called Real-Time Settlement—and that if United acquires Change, United would control the development of the only integrated platform that is also scaled. And if that happens, the Government contends, rival payers would likely be stuck with United, because no other firm is well-suited to build a competing platform. United could then foreclose access to the integrated platform, such as by withholding or delaying sales. And more than that, United would have an incentive to do so, because the downstream commercial health insurance markets are more lucrative than the upstream healthcare IT markets.

[17] The Government's foreclosure theory has significant flaws. To begin, the evidence overwhelmingly established, and the Court finds, that both Real-Time Settlement and Transparent Network are "concepts," not actual products. See 8/11/22 AM Trial Tr. 34:2–5 (Wukitch) ("Q. First of all, does Change Healthcare have an existing offering called Real-Time Settlement? A. No. It is a concept that's in development."); 8/3/22 PM Trial Tr. 57:1–10 (Joshi) ("So, Real-Time Settlement is a concept. It is not a product today. It is not close to being a product."); 8/5/22 PM Trial Tr. 120:25–122:11 (Schmuker) (noting that Optum cannot "say definitively" whether Transparent Network will ever be a marketable product). This fact puts the Government in an awkward position: It must prove that United will likely withhold from its rivals products that don't even exist. That may be why the Government did not define the relevant EDI-related innovation market. See 8/9/22 PM Trial Tr. 52:18–53:7 (Gowrisankaran) ("I didn't define the market for integrated platforms because these are products that are just being developed now.").

[18] Moreover, the evidence did not establish that Optum will likely withhold Transparent Network or Real-Time Settlement (if either becomes a product) from external payers. The evidence established, and the Court finds, that Optum has never withheld a product from external payers—in fact, it currently markets all of its payment integrity products to UHC's biggest rivals. When asked for his reaction to the Government's claim that Optum will withhold innovations from rival payers, former United CEO Wichmann testified that the allegation was "without foundation" because "the business is fiercely multi-payer." He also testified that in his 23 years at United, he could not "think of any instance where OptumInsight withheld products and services to rivals of UHC."

[19] The evidence also established, and the Court finds, that Optum has never sold one version of a product to UHC while selling a degraded version to other customers. [. . .]

[20] . . . [In unrebutted testimony,] various United executives . . . stated consistently their view that it is not in United's interests for Optum to abandon its multi-payer strategy. Witty, the CEO of UHG, was expressly asked at trial about this theory, and stated: "Of course, my responsibility is to maximize UnitedHealth Group's performance. That is maximized by developing great products, not just to the benefit of UHC but to all of our other clients. And the idea that we would develop something or acquire it, preclude its use from others, and then somehow expect it to stay a high-quality asset, I think, is nonsensical." He even stressed that leveraging Optum to

increase UHC's profits "would be a destruction of my whole fiduciary responsibility." The Court concludes that this testimony—and the similar testimony of a number of other United executives—is far more probative of post-merger behavior than Dr. Gowrisankaran's independent weighing of costs and benefits.

NOTES

1) Why would a merged firm with upstream monopoly power want to sell fewer inputs to downstream rivals?
2) Why do you think vertical mergers have not often been litigated in recent decades?
3) Do you think that different Vertical Merger Guidelines would or could have affected the outcome in the vertical cases discussed above?
4) In both *AT&T / Time Warner* and *UnitedHealth / Change*, the district court judge was persuaded that foreclosure was unlikely based in large point on testimony from party executives, despite economic analysis to the contrary. Under what circumstances do you think a court should credit party testimony over econometrics, and vice versa? Why?
5) "The agencies should prioritize bringing vertical merger cases—even at the expense of other meritorious merger cases that would otherwise be higher enforcement priorities—until they secure at least one victory in a vertical merger decision that can provide precedential support for future vertical merger enforcement." Do you agree or disagree with this statement of enforcement policy?
6) What do you make of the pre-emptive remedy offered by the parties in *AT&T / Time Warner*—how should a court react to that fact in litigation? What if the parties to a horizontal merger made a unilateral offer to charge only reasonable prices post-consummation, with a right to arbitrate in the event of a dispute?
7) Suppose that you are investigating a vertical merger that raises the prospect that the merged firm will have access to the confidential information of rivals. What questions would you want to prioritize in evaluating the merger and how would you examine them?
8) After *UnitedHealth* and *AT&T*, when do you think a court or agency should accept the argument that a merged firm would have the *ability* to inflict competitive harm but not the *incentive* to do so?

D. Procompetitive Benefits and Defenses

Merger analysis involves more than just an assessment of harms: it also involves a careful weighing of the merger's beneficial effects, as well as any legal defenses that could apply. Some defenses, like the "state action" defense, apply to all antitrust claims, including mergers: those will be discussed in Chapter IX.

In this Section, though, we will discuss three issues that are specific to mergers. The first is the proposition that a merger will lead to cost savings that will make the transaction beneficial, not harmful, to competition. This is sometimes, somewhat misleadingly, described as an efficiency "defense." While the legal status of efficiencies in merger review remains somewhat uncertain, the best view is probably that efficiencies do not constitute a defense to a merger that has been shown to be anticompetitive, but that efficiencies can be taken into account in figuring out whether a merger is anticompetitive in the first place. Whatever the precise legal framing, in practice agencies and courts give serious consideration to the effects of production cost savings arising from mergers, and the impact of those cost savings upon competition and consumers.

The second issue is not strictly an efficiency (in the sense of a production cost saving) so much as an incentive effect: the elimination of double marginalization ("EDM") specific to vertical mergers. EDM arises from the same impact of a vertical merger on incentives as does anticompetitive foreclosure: in each case, the change in incentives from the integration causes the integrated division to be treated more favorably than its unintegrated rivals, with ambiguous effects on competition and consumers.

The third issue is the "failing firm" defense. This is the argument—often made but seldom accepted—that one of the merging parties is failing and that even an anticompetitive transaction is better than the *even more anticompetitive* alternative of exit. We will also meet the somewhat related, but different, argument that a merging party is declining in competitive strength, such that existing market shares overstate its competitive importance.

1. Efficiencies

Mergers may have positive as well as negative effects on competition. In particular, they may reduce the costs of coordination in ways that would be more difficult or impossible through arms-length contracting. By combining the parties' existing assets, they may unlock economies of scale (*i.e.*, cost reductions from increased scale of operation) and scope (*i.e.*, cost reductions from supply of different products and services), or other synergies, that reduce the merged firm's costs and exert downward pressure on its prices. The result can be a more effective competitor, more intensive competition, and ultimately overall benefits for consumers.[670]

But merger efficiencies do not arise in every case, and in some cases negative efficiencies, or "diseconomies," may even result from a deal.[671] And even when they do arise, the merger may still be anticompetitive overall because the harmful tendencies outweigh the benefits. (Indeed, there is a considerable literature on the empirics of the net effects of mergers on price, quality, and innovation.[672]) The merger may also be unnecessary in order to achieve the benefits in question (*e.g.*, because the same benefits could be obtained through arm's-length contracting with less harm to competition). So a careful examination is necessary in every case before concluding that efficiencies justify a troubling merger.

Although, as we shall see, it is not clear whether the courts really accept an "efficiencies defense" to an otherwise-anticompetitive merger, the agencies generally do consider the impact of efficiencies.[673] The Horizontal Merger Guidelines state that efficiencies may constitute a reason to exercise prosecutorial discretion not to challenge a deal, so long as the claimed efficiencies satisfy certain criteria. In particular, efficiencies must be "cognizable"—that is, they must be specific to the proposed transaction and verifiable—and they must also be sufficiently substantial in magnitude to offset any anticompetitive harms from the transaction. They must also not arise from anticompetitive reductions in output. If these factors are all present, the merger guidelines indicate that the agencies will not challenge the deal.[674]

It was not always so. In the mid-century years, it was widely believed that mergers virtually never generated procompetitive efficiencies (or "economies"),[675] or that such efficiencies were actively harmful and a reason to prevent, rather than permit, mergers. In *Brown Shoe*, for example, the Court had given some lip service to the idea that efficiencies alone were not a cause for concern, noting:

> [A]t the same time that it sought to create an effective tool for preventing all mergers having demonstrable anti-competitive effects, Congress recognized the stimulation to competition that might flow from particular mergers. When concern as to the Act's breadth was expressed, supporters of the amendments indicated that it would not impede, for example, a merger between two small companies to enable the combination to compete more effectively with larger corporations dominating the relevant market, nor a merger between a corporation which is financially healthy and a failing one which no longer can be a vital competitive factor in the market. The deletion of the word "community" in the original Act's description of the relevant

---

[670] *See generally, e.g.*, Louis Kaplow, *Efficiencies in Merger Analysis*, 83 Antitrust L.J. 557 (2021); Herbert J. Hovenkamp, *Appraising Merger Efficiencies*, 24 Geo. Mason L. Rev. 703 (2017); Daniel A. Crane, *Rethinking Merger Efficiencies*, 110 Mich. L. Rev. 347 (2011).

[671] On diseconomies of scope, *see, e.g.*, Evan Rawley and Timothy S. Simcoe, *Diversification, Diseconomies of Scope, and Vertical Contracting: Evidence from the Taxicab Industry*, 57 Mgmt. Sci. 1534 (2010); Cynthia A. Montgomery, *Corporate Diversification*, 8 J. Econ. Persp. 163 (1994). On diseconomies of scale, *see, e.g.*, Oliver E. Williamson, *Hierarchical Control and Optimum Firm Size*, 75 J. Pol. Econ. 123 (1967).

[672] For a selection from the healthcare industry, *see, e.g.*, Nancy Beaulieu et al., *Changes in Quality of Care after Hospital Mergers and Acquisitions*, 382 New Eng. J. Med. 51 (Jan. 2, 2020); Gautam Gowrisankaran, Aviv Nevo, & Robert Town, *Mergers When Prices Are Negotiated: Evidence from the Hospital Industry*, 105(1) Am. Econ. Rev. 172 (2015); Patrick S. Romano & David J. Balan, *A Retrospective Analysis of the Clinical Quality Effects of the Acquisition of Highland Park Hospital By Evanston Northwestern Healthcare*, 18(1) Int'l J. Econ. Bus. 45 (2011); John E. Schneider et al., *The Effect of Physician and Health Plan Market Concentration on Prices in Commercial Health Insurance Markets*, 8(1) Int'l J. Health Care Fin. & Econ. 13 (2008); Vivian Ho & Barton H. Hamilton, *Hospital Mergers and Acquisitions: Does Market Consolidation Harm Patients?*, 19(5) J. Health Econ. 767 (2000).

[673] *See, e.g.*, Malcolm B. Coate & Andrew Heimert, *Merger Efficiencies at the Federal Trade Commission 1997-2007*, FTC BE Working Paper (Feb. 2009).

[674] HMGs § 10.

[675] George J. Stigler, *Mergers and Preventive Anti-Trust Policy*, 54 U. Pa. L. Rev. 176, 181 (1955) ("mergers which increase both concentration and competition are most uncommon"); Donald Dewey, *Mergers and Cartels: Some Reservations About Policy*, 51 Am. Econ. Rev. 255, 257 (1961) ("Most mergers . . . have virtually nothing to do with either the creation of market power or the realization of scale economies. They are merely a civilized alternative to bankruptcy or the voluntary liquidation that transfers assets from falling to rising firms.").

geographic market is another illustration of Congress' desire to indicate that its concern was with the adverse effects of a given merger on competition only in an economically significant "section" of the country. Taken as a whole, the legislative history illuminates congressional concern with the protection of competition, not competitors, and its desire to restrain mergers only to the extent that such combinations may tend to lessen competition.[676]

But the Court went on, later in *Brown Shoe*, to reject the idea that efficiencies might justify the transaction:

> A . . . significant aspect of this merger is that it creates a large national chain which is integrated with a manufacturing operation. The retail outlets of integrated companies, by eliminating wholesalers and by increasing the volume of purchases from the manufacturing division of the enterprise, can market their own brands at prices below those of competing independent retailers. Of course, some of the results of large integrated or chain operations are beneficial to consumers. Their expansion is not rendered unlawful by the mere fact that small independent stores may be adversely affected. It is competition, not competitors, which the Act protects. But we cannot fail to recognize Congress' desire to promote competition through the protection of viable, small, locally owned business. Congress appreciated that occasional higher costs and prices might result from the maintenance of fragmented industries and markets. It resolved these competing considerations in favor of decentralization. We must give effect to that decision.[677]

Likewise, in *Von's Grocery* the Court condemned a merger to a combined market share of 7.5% in a market with a postmerger HHI of less than 745 on the basis that, among other things, the transaction involved "two already powerful companies merging in a way which makes them even more powerful than they were before."[678] And the Court said outright in *FTC v. Procter & Gamble* that "Possible economies cannot be used as a defense to illegality. Congress was aware that some mergers which lessen competition may also result in economies but it struck the balance in favor of protecting competition."[679]

With the advent of scholarship suggesting that efficient mergers might improve competition,[680] and with the shift in antitrust law's emphasis from skepticism of size and success toward welfare impacts on consumers,[681] the picture began to change. Oliver Williamson's seminal article on *Economies as an Antitrust Defense* was published in 1968,[682] the same year that the Justice Department issued its first Merger Guidelines. These provided a kind of backhanded provision for an efficiencies defense, implicitly acknowledging the in-principle benefits of efficiencies though expressing doubt that the factual predicates would be established in many cases:

> Unless there are exceptional circumstances, the Department will not accept as a justification for an acquisition normally subject to challenge under its horizontal merger standards the claim that the merger will produce economies (i.e., improvements in efficiency) because, among other reasons, (i) the Department's adherence to the standards will usually result in no challenge being made to mergers of the kind most likely to involve companies operating significantly below the size necessary to achieve significant economies of scale; (ii) where substantial economies are potentially available to a firm, they can normally be realized through internal expansion; and

---

[676] Brown Shoe Co. v. United States, 370 U.S. 294, 319–20 (1962).

[677] Brown Shoe Co. v. United States, 370 U.S. 294 (1962)

[678] United States v. Von's Grocery Co., 384 U.S. 270 (1966).

[679] FTC v. Procter & Gamble Co., 386 U.S. 568, 580 (1967). *But see* id. at 603 (Harlan, J., concurring) ("The Commission [below]— in my opinion quite correctly—seemed to accept the idea that economies could be used to defend a merger, noting that a merger that results in increased efficiency of production, distribution or marketing may, in certain cases, increase the vigor of competition in the relevant market.").

[680] *See, e.g.*, Oliver E. Williamson, *Economies as an Antitrust Defense: The Welfare Tradeoffs*, 58 Am. Econ. Rev. 18 (1968) (arguing that significant competitive harms are necessary to offset modest efficiencies from a merger, and that antitrust agencies should consider efficiencies in the exercise of prosecutorial discretion); Henry G. Manne, *Mergers and the Market for Corporate Control*, 73 J. Pol. Econ. 110 (1965) (arguing that many mergers are driven by the existence of inefficiently managed firms that would be more productive under new ownership); Michael C. Jensen, *Takeovers: Their Causes and Consequences*, 2 J. Econ. Per. 21 (1988) (enumerating, among other things, various positive effects of mergers); 4 Robert Pitofsky, *Proposals for Revised United States Merger Enforcement in a Global Economy*, 81 Geo. L.J. 195 (1992) (proposing adoption of an efficiency defense).

[681] *See supra* § I.E.

[682] Oliver E. Williamson, *Economies as an Antitrust Defense: The Welfare Tradeoffs*, 58 Am. Econ. Rev. 18 (1968).

(iii) there usually are severe difficulties in accurately establishing the existence and magnitude of economies claimed for a merger.[683]

And through the 1970s, as we have seen, the Court began to embrace the value of efficiency in antitrust analysis, including by relaxing the *per se* rule against vertical nonprice distribution restraints in *GTE Sylvania*,[684] and by accepting the efficiency justification for a form of (what could be called) "price fixing" in *BMI*.[685] In 1980, Phillip Areeda and Donald Turner "became the first widely respected antitrust legal scholars to argue in favor of incorporating efficiencies into the merger review process on a broader scale than the 1968 Merger Guidelines [had] contemplated."[686] Since that time, the recognition of efficiencies as a consideration in merger review has gained ground unevenly in successive Merger Guidelines.[687] The courts too began to indicate, rather cautiously, that efficiency generation was a point in favor of, rather than against, the legality of a transaction in merger review. They remain cautious to this day, often indicating that efficiencies may at least play a role in evaluating whether a merger is anticompetitive, while acknowledging the uncertain legal status of efficiencies in a merger case.[688]

---

[683] U.S. Dept. of Justice, 1968 Merger Guidelines, § 10.

[684] Continental T.V., Inc. v. GTE Sylvania Inc., 433 U.S. 36 (1977).

[685] Broadcast Music, Inc. v. Columbia Broadcasting Sys., Inc., 441 U.S. 1 (1979).

[686] William Kolasky & Andrew Dick, *The Merger Guidelines and the Integration of Efficiencies into Antitrust Review of Horizontal Mergers*, 71 Antitrust L.J. 207, 216 (2003).

[687] *See, e.g.*, U.S. Dept. of Justice, 1982 Merger Guidelines, § V.A. at 29 ("In the overwhelming majority of cases, the Guidelines will allow firms to achieve available efficiencies through mergers without interference from the Department. Except in extraordinary cases, the Department will not consider a claim of specific efficiencies as a mitigating factor for a merger that would otherwise be challenged. Plausible efficiencies are far easier to allege than to prove. Moreover, even if the existence of efficiencies were clear, their magnitudes would be extremely difficult to determine."), *id.* at 29 n.53 ("At a minimum, the Department will require clear and convincing evidence that the merger will produce substantial cost savings resulting from the realization of scale economies, integration of production facilities, or multi-plant operations which are already enjoyed by one or more firms in the industry and that equivalent results could not be achieved within a comparable period of time through internal expansion or through a merger that threatened less competitive harm. In any event, the Department will consider such efficiencies only in resolving otherwise close cases."); U.S. Dept. of Justice, 1984 Merger Guidelines § 3.5 ("The primary benefit of mergers to the economy is their efficiency-enhancing potential, which can increase the competitiveness of firms and result in lower prices to consumers. Because the antitrust laws and, thus, the standards of the Guidelines, are designed to proscribe only mergers that present a significant danger to competition, they do not present an obstacle to most mergers. As a consequence, in the majority of cases, the Guidelines will allow firms to achieve available efficiencies through mergers without interference from the Department. Some mergers that the Department otherwise might challenge may be reasonably necessary to achieve significant net efficiencies. If the parties to the merger establish by clear and convincing evidence that a merger will achieve such efficiencies, the Department will consider those efficiencies in deciding whether to challenge the merger. Cognizable efficiencies include, but are not limited to, achieving economies of scale, better integration of production facilities, plant specialization, lower transportation costs, and similar efficiencies relating to specific manufacturing, servicing, or distribution operations of the merging firms. The Department may also consider claimed efficiencies resulting from reductions in general selling, administrative, and overhead expenses, or that otherwise do not relate to specific manufacturing, servicing, or distribution operations of the merging firms, although, as a practical matter, these types of efficiencies may be difficult to demonstrate. In addition, the Department will reject claims of efficiencies if equivalent or comparable savings can reasonably be achieved by the parties through other means. The parties must establish a greater level of expected net efficiencies the more significant are the competitive risks identified in Section 3."); U.S. Dept. of Justice & Fed. Trade Comm'n, 1992 Merger Guidelines § 4 (substantially following 1984 language but omitting the requirement to show efficiencies by "clear and convincing evidence"); U.S. Dept. of Justice & Fed. Trade Comm'n, 1997 Merger Guidelines § 4 (switching to extended treatment requiring and defining cognizability in a manner similar to the 2010 guidelines, reproduced above).

[688] *See, e.g.*, United States v. Anthem, Inc., 855 F.3d 345, 355 (D.C. Cir. 2017) ("[T]he circuit precedent that binds us allowed that evidence of efficiencies could rebut a prima facie showing, which is not invariably the same as an ultimate defense to Section 7 illegality. . . . [P]rudence counsels that the court should leave for another day whether efficiencies can be an ultimate defense to Section 7 illegality. We will proceed on the assumption that efficiencies as presented by Anthem could be such a defense under a totality of the circumstances approach[.]"); FTC v. Penn State Hershey Med. Ctr., 838 F.3d 327, 348 (3d Cir. 2016) (expressing some skepticism, reserving the issue, but analyzing efficiencies anyway); Saint Alphonsus Med. Ctr.–Nampa, Inc. v. St. Luke's Health Sys., Ltd., 778 F.3d 775, 790 (9th Cir. 2015) (assuming efficiencies may constitute a basis for concluding that a merger that would otherwise harm competition does not); FTC v. H.J. Heinz Co., 246 F.3d 708, 720–22 (D.C. Cir. 2001) (accepting and evaluating efficiency "defense"); FTC v. Tenet Health Care Corp., 186 F.3d 1045, 1054 (8th Cir. 1999) ("[T]he district court should . . . have considered evidence of enhanced efficiency in the context of the competitive effects of the merger."); FTC v. Univ. Health, Inc., 938 F.2d 1206, 1222 (11th Cir. 1991) ("[E]vidence that a proposed acquisition would create significant efficiencies benefiting consumers is useful in evaluating the ultimate issue—the acquisition's overall effect on competition. We think, therefore, that an efficiency defense to the government's prima facie case in section 7 challenges is appropriate in certain circumstances."); United States v. Aetna Inc., 240 F.Supp.3d 1 (D.D.C. 2017) ("Although the Supreme Court has never recognized the 'efficiencies' defense in a Section 7 case, the D.C. Circuit as well as the Horizontal Merger Guidelines recognize that, in some instances, efficiencies resulting from the merger may be considered in rebutting the government's prima facie case.") (internal quotation marks omitted); FTC v. Sysco Corp., 113 F. Supp. 3d 1, 81 (D.D.C. 2015) (same); FTC v. Swedish Match, 131 F. Supp. 2d 151, 171–72 (D.D.C. 2000) (stating that "[i]t is unclear whether a defense showing that the intended merger would create significant efficiencies in the

Today, the merger guidelines set out the agencies' modern approach in some detail, including the criteria that must be satisfied for the agencies to exercise their prosecutorial discretion not to challenge a merger.

Horizontal Merger Guidelines § 10

10. Efficiencies

[1] Competition usually spurs firms to achieve efficiencies internally. Nevertheless, a primary benefit of mergers to the economy is their potential to generate significant efficiencies and thus enhance the merged firm's ability and incentive to compete, which may result in lower prices, improved quality, enhanced service, or new products. For example, merger-generated efficiencies may enhance competition by permitting two ineffective competitors to form a more effective competitor, e.g., by combining complementary assets. In a unilateral effects context, incremental cost reductions may reduce or reverse any increases in the merged firm's incentive to elevate price. Efficiencies also may lead to new or improved products, even if they do not immediately and directly affect price. In a coordinated effects context, incremental cost reductions may make coordination less likely or effective by enhancing the incentive of a maverick to lower price or by creating a new maverick firm. Even when efficiencies generated through a merger enhance a firm's ability to compete, however, a merger may have other effects that may lessen competition and make the merger anticompetitive.

[2] The Agencies credit only those efficiencies likely to be accomplished with the proposed merger and unlikely to be accomplished in the absence of either the proposed merger or another means having comparable anticompetitive effects. These are termed merger-specific efficiencies.[13] Only alternatives that are practical in the business situation faced by the merging firms are considered in making this determination. The Agencies do not insist upon a less restrictive alternative that is merely theoretical.

[3] Efficiencies are difficult to verify and quantify, in part because much of the information relating to efficiencies is uniquely in the possession of the merging firms. Moreover, efficiencies projected reasonably and in good faith by the merging firms may not be realized. Therefore, it is incumbent upon the merging firms to substantiate efficiency claims so that the Agencies can verify by reasonable means the likelihood and magnitude of each asserted efficiency, how and when each would be achieved (and any costs of doing so), how each would enhance the merged firm's ability and incentive to compete, and why each would be merger-specific.

[4] Efficiency claims will not be considered if they are vague, speculative, or otherwise cannot be verified by reasonable means. Projections of efficiencies may be viewed with skepticism, particularly when generated outside of the usual business planning process. By contrast, efficiency claims substantiated by analogous past experience are those most likely to be credited.

[5] Cognizable efficiencies are merger-specific efficiencies that have been verified and do not arise from anticompetitive reductions in output or service. Cognizable efficiencies are assessed net of costs produced by the merger or incurred in achieving those efficiencies.

---

relevant, thereby offsetting any anticompetitive effects, may be used by a defendant to rebut the government's prima facie case," but analyzing efficiencies and finding them insufficient anyway because "speculative"); FTC v. Staples, Inc., 970 F.Supp. 1066, 1088–90 (D.D.C. 1997) (Staples I) (noting uncertainty of legal grounding but analyzing efficiencies anyway); U.S. v. Long Island Jewish Medical Center, 983 F.Supp. 121, 147 (E.D.N.Y. 1997) ("[T]he Court finds that, with regard to the so-called 'efficiencies defense,' the defendants must clearly demonstrate that the proposed merger itself will, in fact, create a net economic benefit for the health care consumer."); FTC v. Butterworth Health Corp., 946 F. Supp. 1285, 1300 (W.D. Mich. 1996) ("The courts have recognized that in certain circumstances, a defendant may rebut the government's prima facie case with evidence showing that the intended merger would create significant efficiencies in the relevant market.") (internal quotation marks and citation omitted), *aff'd sub nom.* FTC v. Butterworth Health Corp., 121 F.3d 708 (6th Cir. 1997); Cargill, Inc. v. Monfort of Colorado, Inc., 479 U.S. 104, 114–17 (1986) (rejecting theory of antitrust harm based on the merged firm becoming too competitive); United States v. LTV Corp., Case No. Civ-A-84-884, 1984 WL 21973, at *14 (D.D.C. Aug. 2, 1984) (approving proposed consent decree in a Tunney Act proceeding and noting: "The purpose of the present merger is to achieve savings in cost through increased efficiencies which will enable the surviving company to compete more effectively both here and in the export market. We cannot predict that these efforts will succeed, but we can say with some certainty, that without an opportunity to improve their acute financial predicament, their future will indeed be bleak.").

[13] The Agencies will not deem efficiencies to be merger-specific if they could be attained by practical alternatives that mitigate competitive concerns, such as divestiture or licensing. If a merger affects not whether but only when an efficiency would be achieved, only the timing advantage is a merger-specific efficiency.

[6] The Agencies will not challenge a merger if cognizable efficiencies are of a character and magnitude such that the merger is not likely to be anticompetitive in any relevant market.[14] To make the requisite determination, the Agencies consider whether cognizable efficiencies likely would be sufficient to reverse the merger's potential to harm customers in the relevant market, e.g., by preventing price increases in that market. In conducting this analysis, the Agencies will not simply compare the magnitude of the cognizable efficiencies with the magnitude of the likely harm to competition absent the efficiencies. The greater the potential adverse competitive effect of a merger, the greater must be the cognizable efficiencies, and the more they must be passed through to customers, for the Agencies to conclude that the merger will not have an anticompetitive effect in the relevant market. When the potential adverse competitive effect of a merger is likely to be particularly substantial, extraordinarily great cognizable efficiencies would be necessary to prevent the merger from being anticompetitive. In adhering to this approach, the Agencies are mindful that the antitrust laws give competition, not internal operational efficiency, primacy in protecting customers.

[7] In the Agencies' experience, efficiencies are most likely to make a difference in merger analysis when the likely adverse competitive effects, absent the efficiencies, are not great. Efficiencies almost never justify a merger to monopoly or near-monopoly. Just as adverse competitive effects can arise along multiple dimensions of conduct, such as pricing and new product development, so too can efficiencies operate along multiple dimensions. Similarly, purported efficiency claims based on lower prices can be undermined if they rest on reductions in product quality or variety that customers value.

[8] The Agencies have found that certain types of efficiencies are more likely to be cognizable and substantial than others. For example, efficiencies resulting from shifting production among facilities formerly owned separately, which enable the merging firms to reduce the incremental cost of production, are more likely to be susceptible to verification and are less likely to result from anticompetitive reductions in output. Other efficiencies, such as those relating to research and development, are potentially substantial but are generally less susceptible to verification and may be the result of anticompetitive output reductions. Yet others, such as those relating to procurement, management, or capital cost, are less likely to be merger-specific or substantial, or may not be cognizable for other reasons.

[9] When evaluating the effects of a merger on innovation, the Agencies consider the ability of the merged firm to conduct research or development more effectively. Such efficiencies may spur innovation but not affect short-term pricing. The Agencies also consider the ability of the merged firm to appropriate a greater fraction of the benefits resulting from its innovations. Licensing and intellectual property conditions may be important to this enquiry, as they affect the ability of a firm to appropriate the benefits of its innovation. Research and development cost savings may be substantial and yet not be cognizable efficiencies because they are difficult to verify or result from anticompetitive reductions in innovative activities.

* * *

Vertical Merger Guidelines § 6
(issued by FTC and DOJ 2020; FTC withdrew 2021)

6. Procompetitive Effects

[1] Vertical mergers combine complementary economic functions and eliminate contracting frictions, and therefore have the capacity to create a range of potentially cognizable efficiencies that benefit competition and consumers. Vertical mergers combine complementary assets, including those used at different levels in the supply chain, to make a final product. A single firm able to coordinate how these assets are used may be able to streamline

---

[14] The Agencies normally assess competition in each relevant market affected by a merger independently and normally will challenge the merger if it is likely to be anticompetitive in any relevant market. In some cases, however, the Agencies in their prosecutorial discretion will consider efficiencies not strictly in the relevant market, but so inextricably linked with it that a partial divestiture or other remedy could not feasibly eliminate the anticompetitive effect in the relevant market without sacrificing the efficiencies in the other market(s). Inextricably linked efficiencies are most likely to make a difference when they are great and the likely anticompetitive effect in the relevant market(s) is small so the merger is likely to benefit customers overall.

production, inventory management, or distribution. It may also be able to create innovative products in ways that would not likely be achieved through arm's-length contracts.

[2] The Agencies evaluate efficiency claims by the parties using the approach set forth in Section 10 of the Horizontal Merger Guidelines, as elaborated here. Cognizable efficiencies are merger-specific efficiencies that have been verified and do not arise from anticompetitive reductions in output or service. The Agencies do not challenge a merger if cognizable efficiencies are of a character and magnitude such that the merger is unlikely to be anticompetitive in any relevant market.

* * *

As we have seen, the HMGs are pretty clear: "The Agencies will not challenge a merger if cognizable efficiencies are of a character and magnitude such that the merger is not likely to be anticompetitive in any relevant market." And a number of courts have accepted that the assessment of efficiencies is required in merger analysis.[689]

Although the agencies have a settled practice of considering efficiencies when deciding whether to sue, the courts have not always been so willing to consider efficiencies as a mitigating factor when deciding whether to impose liability. Indeed, at the time of writing no circuit court of appeals has found that a *prima facie* case of harm to competition has been actually outweighed by efficiencies. (The closest thing to such a case is probably the states' challenge to the *Sprint / T-Mobile* merger, which we will meet below.)

Judicial caution in handling merger efficiencies was on display when the Department of Justice challenged a merger of two insurers in *Anthem / Cigna*. The D.C. Circuit expressed reservations about the legal status of the efficiencies defense; then-Judge Kavanaugh, in dissent, did not.

CASENOTE: United States v. Anthem, Inc.
855 F.3d 345 (D.C. Cir. 2017)

Anthem / Cigna concerned a proposed merger between the second- and third-largest sellers of health insurance to large companies in the United States. DOJ sued to block the deal, and the D.C. district court concluded that the transaction violated Section 7, as it would lessen competition in certain markets for the sale of health insurance. The parties appealed to the D.C. Circuit on the ground that the transaction would generate sufficient efficiencies— in the form of cost savings—to offset any threatened harm. The case presented an opportunity for the nation's most prominent antitrust court to clarify the role of efficiencies under Section 7. But, alas, that was not the outcome!

Judge Rogers, writing for the panel, cast plenty of doubt on the question of whether efficiencies could justify an otherwise-anticompetitive deal: "Despite . . . widespread acceptance of the potential benefit of efficiencies as an economic matter, *see, e.g.,* [Horizontal Merger] Guidelines § 10, it is not at all clear that they offer a viable legal defense to illegality under Section 7. In *FTC v. Procter & Gamble Co.,* 386 U.S. 568 . . . (1967), the Supreme Court enjoined a merger without any consideration of evidence that the combined company could purchase advertising at a lower rate. It held that '[p]ossible economies cannot be used as a defense to illegality. Congress was aware that some mergers which lessen competition may also result in economies but it struck the balance in favor of protecting competition.' In his concurrence, Justice Harlan . . . accepted the idea that economies could be used to defend a merger. No matter that Justice Harlan's view may be the more accepted today, the Supreme Court held otherwise[.]"

The court acknowledged that lower courts had generally assumed the relevance of efficiencies. Indeed, even the D.C. Circuit had previously suggested that, "in view of the trend among lower courts and secondary authority, that the Supreme Court [in *Procter & Gamble*] can be understood only to have rejected 'possible' efficiencies, while efficiencies that are verifiable can be credited."

---

[689] *See supra* note 688.

Ultimately, the court punted again on the legal status of efficiencies, confining its decision to the evidence. "In this expedited appeal, prudence counsels that the court should leave for another day whether efficiencies can be an ultimate defense to Section 7 illegality. We will proceed on the assumption that efficiencies as presented by Anthem could be such a defense under a totality of the circumstances approach, because Anthem has failed to show the district court clearly erred in rejecting Anthem's purported medical cost savings as an offsetting efficiency."

Justice Kavanaugh dissented, arguing that merger law had long left *Procter & Gamble* behind. "In landmark decisions in the 1970s—including *United States v. General Dynamics Corp.*, 415 U.S. 486 (1974) {*Eds.: this is excerpted later in this chapter*}, and *Continental T.V., Inc. v. GTE Sylvania Inc.*, 433 U.S. 36 (1977)—the Supreme Court indicated that modern antitrust analysis focuses on the effects on the consumers of the product or service, not the effects on competitors. In the horizontal merger context, the Supreme Court in the 1970s therefore shifted away from the strict anti-merger approach that the Court had employed in the 1960s[.]." Under the modern approach, "we must take account of the efficiencies and consumer benefits that would result from this merger." Concluding that the parties' claimed efficiencies were indeed verifiable, merger-specific, and resulted in benefits sufficient to outweigh the harms, Justice Kavanaugh would have held that the deal did not violate Section 7.

So what does an efficiencies analysis look like? Many courts have undertaken extensive analysis of actual and claimed efficiencies in merger cases.[690] One of the most extended and favorable judicial treatments of merger efficiency claims in recent history is found in the district court's decision in the states' challenge to the T-Mobile/Sprint merger. The transaction in that case—the merger of mobile network operators T-Mobile and Sprint—had triggered the structural presumption by a considerable margin.[691] But the court went on to hold that the presumption had been rebutted, emphasizing evidence that: (1) the transaction would turn the merged firm into a more efficient competitor, (2) Sprint was a weakened competitor that was unlikely to continue providing strong competitive pressure, and (3) remedies obtained as a result of FCC and DOJ review would "ameliorate any remaining concerns of anticompetitive effect."[692] In the following passage, the court applies the merger-specificity and verifiability tests to a complex trial record.

New York v. Deutsche Telekom AG
439 F.Supp.3d 179 (S.D.N.Y. 2020)[693]

Judge Marrero.

[1] It remains unclear whether and how a court may consider evidence of a merger's efficiencies. While the Supreme Court has previously stated that possible economies cannot be used as a defense to illegality, lower courts have since considered whether possible economies might serve not as justification for an illegal merger but as evidence that a merger would not actually be illegal. The trend among lower courts has thus been to recognize or

---

[690] *See, e.g.*, United States v. Anthem, Inc., 855 F.3d 345, 356–67 (D.C. Cir. 2017) (considering and rejecting claimed efficiencies defense in Anthem / Cigna health insurance merger); FTC v. Penn State Hershey Medical Center, 838 F.3d 327, 347–52 (3d Cir. 2016) (analyzing and reecting claimed efficiencies in hospital merger); FTC v. H.J. Heinz Co., 246 F.3d 708, 720–24 (D.C. Cir. 2001) (analyzing and rejecting claimed efficiencies in merger of baby food manufacturers); New York v. Deutsche Telekom AG, 439 F.Supp.3d 179 (S.D.N.Y. 2020) (considering efficiencies as part of a "totality of the circumstances" analysis); United States v. Aetna Inc., 240 F. Supp. 3d 1, 94–98 (D.D.C. 2017) (considering and rejecting claimed efficiencies defense in Aetna / Humana health insurance merger); FTC v. Staples, Inc., 970 F. Supp. 1066, 1088–90 (D.D.C. 1997 (analyzing and rejecting claimed efficiencies in first Staples / Office Depot merger).

[691] New York v. Deutsche Telekom AG, 439 F.Supp.3d 179, 206 (S.D.N.Y. 2020) ("By either measure, Plaintiff States have satisfied their prima facie burden. [Plaintiffs' expert Carl] Shapiro calculated that New T-Mobile would have a national market share of either 37.8 percent if measured by subscribers or 34.4 percent if measured by revenues, and the national HHI would increase by 679 points for a total HHI of 3186. The shares are higher in certain local markets. For example, the total HHIs for the local CMAs corresponding to Los Angeles and New York would be as high as 4158 and 4284 respectively, and market share in Los Angeles would be as high as 57 percent. These figures are more than enough to establish a presumption that the Proposed Merger would be anticompetitive. It bears repeating, however, that market shares and HHIs establish only a presumption, rather than conclusive proof of a transaction's likely competitive impact.").

[692] New York v. Deutsche Telekom AG, 439 F.Supp.3d 179, 207 (S.D.N.Y. 2020) (summarizing rebuttal evidence).

[693] For opposing perspectives on the deal and the remedy obtained by the Department of Justice, *see* Melody Wang & Fiona Scott Morton, *The Real Dish on the T-Mobile/Sprint Merger: A Disastrous Deal From the Start*, ProMarket (Apr. 23, 2021) (criticizing the transaction); Competitive Impact Statement, United States v. Deutsche Telekom AG, Case No. 1:19-cv-02232 (D.D.C. filed July 30, 2019) (explaining the DOJ view of the adequacy of the remedy).

at least assume that evidence of efficiencies may rebut the presumption that a merger's effects will be anticompetitive, even if such evidence could not be used as a defense to an actually anticompetitive merger.

[2] Additionally, the DOJ and FTC have indicated that they will not challenge a merger if its efficiencies indicate that the merger will not be anticompetitive in any relevant market. See Merger Guidelines § 10 (noting as an example that "merger-generated efficiencies may enhance competition by permitting two ineffective competitors to form a more effective competitor, e.g., by combining complementary assets"). Courts and the Merger Guidelines generally require that claimed efficiencies be both merger-specific and verifiable.

[3] Despite the skepticism that some courts have expressed . . . this Court will consider evidence of efficiencies, given courts' and federal regulators' increasingly consistent practice of doing so, and because Section 7 requires evaluation of a merger's competitive effects under the totality of the circumstances.

[4] Defendants project that the Proposed Merger would result in a variety of efficiencies that would be passed on to consumers through more aggressive service offers, leading to annual consumer welfare gains that will range from $540 million in 2020 to $18.17 billion by 2024. Defendants' claimed efficiencies include: (1) more than doubling the standalone firms' network capacity, which is projected to result in 15 times the speeds now offered by the four major [mobile network operators ("MNOs")] to consumers; (2) saving $26 billion in network costs and another $17 billion in other operating costs; (3) increasing network coverage to strengthen competition in underserved markets; and (4) accelerating the provision of 5G service. Defendants' bottom-line conclusion is that they will use these advantages to lower prices and thus compete more effectively against AT&T and Verizon. Even if the Court assumed that the efficiencies cited by Defendants would not, absent other circumstances, rebut Plaintiff States' prima facie case, the Court concludes that the efficiencies are sufficiently verifiable and merger-specific to merit consideration as evidence that decreases the persuasiveness of the prima facie case.

[5] The primary efficiency Defendants claim is the increased capacity that New T-Mobile would gain from adding Sprint's mid-band spectrum and 11,000 cell sites to T-Mobile's network. T-Mobile argues that these cell sites and spectrum would provide it with enough additional capacity to meet the market's projected growth in data consumption and thus avoid the erosion in quality of service that would result from saturating its existing capacity. The undisputed evidence at trial reflects that combining Sprint and T-Mobile's low-band and mid-band spectrum on one network will not merely result in the sum of Sprint and T-Mobile's standalone capacities, but will instead multiply the combined network's capacity because of a technological innovation referred to as "carrier aggregation" and certain physical properties governing the interaction of radios. Because mobile networks are the basis for mobile wireless telecommunications services, this increase in network capacity would translate to what T-Mobile's President of Technology, Neville Ray ("Ray"), described as an "inordinate amount" of new supply in the market. Not only would this excess capacity allow New T-Mobile to support additional subscribers at reduced marginal costs, it would improve the speeds at which current subscribers could use data services. Defendants argue that this is particularly important in a world where data-intensive streaming video now accounts for over 50 percent of the traffic on T-Mobile's network. Defendants project that the Proposed Merger would result in speeds averaging between 400 to 500 mbps, or at least 15 times current speeds.

[6] Defendants next note that the Proposed Merger would allow New T-Mobile to operate at reduced cost, projecting that roughly $26 billion in efficiencies will result from network cost synergies alone. They project that the retirement of Sprint's network would save $4.2 billion in operating costs per year. In addition to reduced operating costs and the benefits of combining spectrum on one network, that New T-Mobile will take over 11,000 of Sprint's existing towers would reduce the cost and delay that T-Mobile would otherwise incur from building new towers for future network development. By reducing these network costs while combining the standalone firms' customers onto one network, New T-Mobile would achieve economies of scale on par with those of market leaders AT&T and Verizon. Defendants also project savings from streamlined advertising, the closing of 3,000 redundant retail stores, and reducing the costs of billing and other professional "back office" services, which combine with the network cost savings for total net cost savings of $43 billion.

[7] Apart from capacity and cost benefits, Defendants claim that New T-Mobile will provide better coverage than Sprint customers currently receive because T-Mobile's low-band spectrum covers a broader range and penetrates through buildings more effectively than Sprint's mid-band holdings can. Having a broad range of spectrum would

allow New T-Mobile to dedicate each band of spectrum to its best use; it could prioritize the use of low-band in areas that mid-band and mmWave [(other categories of spectrum)] could not reach, while instead prioritizing the other two bands in areas correspondingly closer to the cell sites.

[8] Defendants further claim that the Proposed Merger would accelerate mobile wireless carriers' provision of 5G service in the United States. They argue that in fact, the mere announcement of the Proposed Merger has already procompetitively improved the rollout of 5G services. Defendants state that though AT&T and Verizon originally planned to deploy 5G service primarily on mmWave spectrum, they have since, in response to the prospect that New T-Mobile would deploy 5G services across its broader-reaching low-band and mid-band holdings, broadened the spectrum that they will use. Because spectrum must generally be dedicated to either 4G or 5G and carriers must continue to serve customers without 5G-capable handsets, acquiring Sprint's currently underused mid-band assets would allow New T-Mobile to dedicate spectrum to 5G more quickly than either standalone firm could. Apart from the greater spectral efficiency associated with 5G, Defendants state that faster adoption of 5G will also catalyze the earlier creation of new applications and services not currently possible in the [pre-5G] 4G/LTE environment.

[9] Defendants conclude that New T-Mobile would use these advantages to decrease consumer prices because doing so would actually be profitable. As New T-Mobile would have relatively low network marginal costs and more excess capacity to fill than AT&T and Verizon, it could rationally lower its prices and advertise the higher quality of its network to attract customers away from AT&T and Verizon, thus increasing competition in the [retail mobile wireless telecommunications services ("RMWTS")] Markets.

[10] Other courts have similarly noted that the incentive to use excess capacity given lower marginal costs, as well as the reduction of required capital and operational expenditures, increases the likelihood of competition rather than coordination.

[11] These cases and the record evidence confirm that there is substantial merit to Defendants' claims that the efficiencies arising from the Proposed Merger will lead T-Mobile to compete more aggressively to the ultimate benefit of all consumers, and in particular the subscribers of each of the four major competitors. Sprint customers would benefit from greater coverage, T-Mobile customers would benefit from greater speeds and 5G service sooner. And even AT&T and Verizon customers would benefit insofar as New T-Mobile continued T-Mobile's past practice of pushing AT&T and Verizon to adopt pro-consumer offerings.

[12] While Plaintiff States do not deny that generally the Proposed Merger could generate efficiencies, they respond that these efficiencies are not cognizable because they are neither merger-specific nor verifiable. The Court now considers both grounds pressed by Plaintiff States, concluding that these arguments lack sufficient merit to warrant disregard of Defendants' claimed efficiencies.

a. Merger Specificity

[13] Efficiencies are merger-specific if they cannot be achieved by either company alone, as otherwise those benefits could be achieved without the concomitant loss of a competitor. In this regard, the DOJ and FTC consider only alternatives that are practical in the business situation faced by the merging firms and do not insist upon a less restrictive alternative that is merely theoretical.

[14] Plaintiff States argue that Defendants' claimed efficiencies are not merger specific because Defendants have alternate means of increasing capacity and coverage, and because both Sprint and T-Mobile will inevitably provide 5G services on a nationwide basis. In particular, Plaintiff States emphasize that Defendants can alternatively increase capacity by acquiring spectrum through auctions and private transactions.

[15] Auctions present multiple issues for T-Mobile and Sprint. They are infrequent, their timing is uncertain, and it can take years for a contemplated auction to occur. There is no guarantee that Sprint or T-Mobile could win a substantial amount of spectrum at these auctions because AT&T and Verizon can leverage their higher market capitalization to dominate the auctions with high bids. Moreover, the spectrum that the FCC chooses to auction may not practically address the merging parties' needs. For example, while Sprint needs low-band spectrum, there have been no such auctions since 2015 and there are no future low-band auctions anticipated at this time.

[16] Similarly, while the mid-band "C-Band" spectrum that the FCC will eventually auction might address some of T-Mobile's needs, no date for the auction has been set, it could take years for the spectrum to actually become available for use after the auction, and T-Mobile would also need to deploy radios and handsets that can use this newly available spectrum. The mid-band CBRS spectrum that the FCC will auction is similarly impractical to address T-Mobile's requirements because the Department of Defense will always have priority over its use; as T-Mobile's rights are necessarily subordinate, its ability to use such spectrum for RMWTS purposes is inherently subject to uncertainty.

[17] Private transactions are certainly possible, as T-Mobile has consistently acquired spectrum through either this method or auctions in every year since 2013. But private transactions usually entail small amounts of spectrum and depend upon counterparties' willingness to part with their spectrum. Opportunities to acquire the desired bands of spectrum in any significant measure are thus infrequent. While T-Mobile or Sprint could theoretically spend another decade negotiating and acquiring the required spectrum bit-by-bit, doing so would clearly not allow for anywhere near the efficiencies of the Proposed Merger in anywhere near the same timeframe.

[18] Finally, even assuming that the standalone firms could acquire some additional capacity through auctions or private transactions, that capacity would not nearly approach the capacity that would result from combining the standalone firms' broad spectrum assets on one network. The combination of each firm's spectrum creates unused capacity without the need for, and without excluding the possibility of, New T-Mobile acquiring additional spectrum in the future. And because of the multiplicative effect associated with combining spectrum on one set of infrastructure, New T-Mobile's acquisition of additional spectrum would inherently create more capacity than if either standalone firm acquired the exact same amount of spectrum. While Plaintiff States' claims are not entirely without merit, the alternatives they cite all present significant practical difficulties and do not promise nearly the same capacity benefits that the combination of T-Mobile and Sprint's spectrum assets onto one network would achieve.

[19] With respect to coverage, Plaintiff States proposed at various points during trial that gaps in coverage could be filled by small cells through so-called "densification" projects. This is an interesting and potentially useful solution in more limited contexts, but its benefits are not comparable to those possible under the Proposed Merger. As Ray noted at trial, such small cells would need to be deployed by the millions to match the network coverage that would result from the Proposed Merger. As deployment costs for small cells could thus run well into the billions, densification is simply not a practical alternative at the nationwide scale suggested by Plaintiff States.

[20] Plaintiff States are correct that both Sprint and T-Mobile will provide 5G service without the Proposed Merger. But they fail to adequately acknowledge that the standalone firms' 5G networks will be materially more limited in their scope and require a longer timeframe to establish. Legere testified that while T-Mobile will deploy 5G across its low-band spectrum, that could not compare to the ability to provide 5G service to more consumers nationwide at faster speeds across the mid-band spectrum as well. Sprint's deployment of 5G has been limited to discrete and distant markets, and its prospects for deploying 5G more broadly are uncertain given mid-band spectrum's limited reach and Sprint's financial challenge . . . . And though Plaintiff States make much of the possibility that a technology called Dynamic Spectrum Sharing ("DSS") can allow spectrum to be used for either 4G or 5G, the evidence at trial reflected that the technology is still experimental, will not be deployed for at least a year, and currently results in a 20 to 30 percent loss of usable spectrum wherever it is deployed. Considering the significant uncertainty surrounding this technology, the Court is not persuaded that it promises nearly the same efficiencies as the Proposed Merger.

[21] Finally, Plaintiff States argue that rather than merging with each other, T-Mobile or Sprint could realize similar efficiencies through a merger with DISH. However, this argument seems speculative because both companies have previously attempted to negotiate with DISH and failed. The Court simply cannot presume that DISH would inevitably agree to a merger with T-Mobile or Sprint, particularly considering the record evidence that DISH plans to enter the RMWTS Market with a materially different 5G network and its own competitive strategy . . . . In sum, it may be that Defendants are not entirely incapable of improving their networks and services through means other the Proposed Merger. But none of those alternatives appear reasonably practical, especially in the short term, and neither company as a standalone can achieve the level of efficiencies promised by the

Proposed Merger. Accordingly, the Court concludes that Defendants' claimed efficiencies satisfy the merger-specific test.

Verifiability

[22] Courts consider efficiencies verifiable if they are not speculative and shown in what economists label "real" terms. The DOJ and FTC similarly state that efficiency claims will not be considered if they are vague, speculative, or otherwise cannot be verified by reasonable means. Projections of efficiencies may be viewed with skepticism, particularly when generated outside of the usual business planning process. By contrast, efficiency claims substantiated by analogous past experience are those most likely to be credited. Merger Guidelines § 10. The Merger Guidelines also note that efficiencies resulting from shifting production among facilities formerly owned separately, which enable the merging firms to reduce the incremental cost of production, are more likely to be susceptible to verification and are less likely to result from anticompetitive reductions in output.

[23] Most of Plaintiff States' criticisms regarding the verifiability of Defendants' claimed efficiencies center on the "Montana Model," which Defendants prepared to quantify the benefits of increased capacity for the purposes of this action. The Montana Model is an adaptation of a Network Engineering Model ("NEM") that T-Mobile uses in its ordinary course of business to predict which of its cell sites will become "congested," or reach a threshold capacity at which T-Mobile deems its customers would not receive the quality of service they expect. This "congestion threshold" is defined in terms of speed, as the NEM forecasts the speeds that consumers would require for their anticipated future uses. T-Mobile typically uses the NEM to plan solutions aimed at avoiding congestion, such as the deployment of small cells or the creation of new macro cell towers. The NEM is updated every year and forecasts network traffic over a five-year period, predicting consumer demand by incorporating information from T-Mobile's marketing teams and studies on likely future consumer applications and data demands. T-Mobile employees expressed satisfaction with the NEM at trial, noting that it predicts capacity needs at over 99 percent accuracy in the ordinary course of business.

[24] T-Mobile's Vice President of Network Technology, Ankur Kapoor ("Kapoor"), oversaw the creation of the Montana Model by adapting the NEM (which he regularly oversees) to account for both the advent of 5G and Sprint's future standalone performance. The adaptation for 5G required updating likely consumer uses to include 4K video streaming and AR and VR applications. The 5G adaptation also required a methodological change to calculate 5G speeds, as there was no actual data on 5G speeds at the time; Kapoor prepared this measure by using the most advanced LTE handset technology and cell site capabilities to project speeds and then factoring in the predicted spectral efficiency gains from 5G. The model also required that 4G sectors be upgraded to 5G if customers with 5G-capable handsets were present and experienced speeds lower than those normally provided in a 5G sector, because "leakage," or customers' transitioning from a higher quality sector to a lower quality sector, is actually the highest driver of T-Mobile customers' churn. Kapoor then adapted the NEM to model Sprint's future congestion by meeting with his counterparts at Sprint and incorporating the assumptions that then controlled under Sprint's April 2018 plan of record. Defendants' economic expert, Katz, then quantified the value of the resulting efficiencies by measuring the marginal costs required to solve network congestion and comparing New T-Mobile's marginal costs with those for standalone T-Mobile and Sprint. Katz also quantified the value of increased speeds by extrapolating from a 2012 study regarding the fixed in-home broadband services market, which he considered sufficiently analogous based on the increasing convergence between the mobile wireless (also called mobile broadband) and fixed in-home broadband markets. Based on these assumptions, Katz calculated that New T-Mobile's network marginal costs would be 1/10 of standalone T-Mobile's, and the value of its increased speeds would be over $15 per month per subscriber.

[25] Plaintiff States claim that Defendants' claimed efficiencies are unverifiable because the Montana Model was prepared for the purposes of litigation rather than in the ordinary course of business. They note as an example that the Montana Model predicts Sprint's future congestion even though Sprint does not do any similar modeling in the ordinary course of its business, and even though Sprint would not actually follow the April 2018 plan of record used to supply the Montana Model's inputs if the Proposed Merger did not occur. Plaintiff States add that the NEM is updated every year, whereas the Montana Model has not been updated since its completion in roughly September of 2018. They finally cite a letter from T-Mobile's counsel stating that "any model created in the ordinary course would not have attempted to model as far into the future" as the Montana Model does.

[26] The Court is not persuaded that these criticisms render the Montana Model so unreliable that it should not be credited to any degree. . . . Kapoor testified that the Montana Model follows the same core logic as the NEM, which suggests that though the Montana Model was initially created for litigation, it was nevertheless closely based on a model that has proven highly successful in the ordinary course of business. That T-Mobile now uses the Montana Model in the ordinary course of its business also confirms that it essentially tracks the logic of the undisputedly reliable NEM. The Montana Model used the inputs regarding Sprint that were available at the time of its creation, and it would be unreasonable to require constant updates every time Sprint considers a change of strategy. . . . Plaintiff States' criticisms are relevant and noted, but that does not mean that the Montana Model is without value. [. . .]

[27] As the Merger Guidelines explicitly note, efficiencies are generally more susceptible to verification where they result from combining separate facilities and thus reducing the incremental cost of production. No party in this action has disputed that combining Sprint and T-Mobile's network facilities will result in reduced network marginal costs and a large increase in capacity, which in the RMWTS Market effectively equates to supply or output. None of Plaintiff States' arguments challenge this basic reality. Their arguments instead go primarily to the weight that the Court accords to the model's output, rather than barring altogether any recognition of the model's results. As a practical matter, the model almost certainly cannot exactly quantify the extent to which each specific aspect of the Proposed Merger would benefit consumers, even if it is 99 percent accurate.

[28] As the Supreme Court noted almost sixty years ago, the predictive exercises demanded by Section 7 are not susceptible of a ready and precise answer in most cases. To expect otherwise in the dynamic and rapidly changing RMWTS Market is to invite almost certain disappointment. Section 7 calls for a predictive judgment, necessarily probabilistic and judgmental rather than demonstrable. Accordingly, the Court concludes that the Montana Model is sufficiently reliable to indicate that Defendants' claimed efficiencies will be substantial, even if not quite as large as the model's precise prediction.

[29] Of course, the Court need not, and does not, rest its conclusion of verifiability on the Montana Model alone. Indeed, despite the considerable trial time dedicated to the trustworthiness of the Montana Model, the Court is not persuaded that the model's results are particularly integral to a finding of verifiability or lack of it. As noted above, the Merger Guidelines state that efficiency claims may be verifiable if substantiated by analogous past experience. Defendants' claimed efficiencies are verifiable in significant part because of T-Mobile's successful acquisition of MetroPCS in 2013. T-Mobile actually underpredicted the efficiencies that would result from the MetroPCS merger: the merger resulted in network synergies of $9–10 billion rather than the $6–7 billion predicted. Those economies were realized in two years rather than the three predicted. Moreover, Metro's customers have more than doubled since the merger, and Metro's unlimited plans have decreased in price from $60 to $50.

[30] As multiple witnesses noted at trial, the integration of Sprint and T-Mobile would be very similar to the integration of T-Mobile and MetroPCS and could follow the same basic organizational structure and strategy. Although the Proposed Merger would take place on a larger geographic scale, T-Mobile witnesses noted that integration might actually be easier in the sense that over 80 percent of Sprint customers already use handsets compatible with T-Mobile's network, whereas T-Mobile had to provide MetroPCS customers with new handsets due to differences in voice technology protocols at the time of the MetroPCS merger. Considering T-Mobile has already overdelivered on its projected efficiencies in an analogous past merger, the Court is persuaded that the Proposed Merger's efficiencies are ultimately verifiable rather than speculative.

[31] In sum, the Court concludes that Defendants' proposed efficiencies are cognizable and increase the likelihood that the Proposed Merger would enhance competition in the relevant markets to the benefit of all consumers. However, mindful of the uncertainty in the state of the law regarding efficiencies and Plaintiff States' pertinent criticisms, the Court stresses that the Proposed Merger efficiencies it has recognized constitute just one of many factors that it considers and do not alone possess dispositive weight in this inquiry.

Out-of-Market Benefits and *PNB*

What if the efficiencies and harms are in different markets: such that the merger creates net benefits in one market but inflicts harm in another? Although the rule for similar situations in conduct cases remains unclear,[694] the general rule in merger cases is that such "out of market" efficiencies are normally <u>not</u> cognizable: that is, efficiencies in market A cannot be used to allay competitive concerns in market B.

The flagship authority for that proposition is none other than *Philadelphia National Bank*. The critical analysis in *PNB* itself occupied all of two paragraphs:

> [I]t is suggested that the increased lending limit of the resulting bank will enable it to compete with the large out-of-state bank, particularly the New York banks, for very large loans. We reject this application of the concept of countervailing power. If anticompetitive effects in one market could be justified by procompetitive consequences in another, the logical upshot would be that every firm in an industry could, without violating s 7, embark on a series of mergers that would make it in the end as large as the industry leader. For if all the commercial banks in the Philadelphia area merged into one, it would be smaller than the largest bank in New York City. This is not a case, plainly, where two small firms in a market propose to merge in order to be able to compete more successfully with the leading firms in that market. Nor is it a case in which lack of adequate banking facilities is causing hardships to individuals or businesses in the community. The present two largest banks in Philadelphia have lending limits of $8,000,000 each. The only business located in the Philadelphia area which find such limits inadequate are large enough readily to obtain bank credit in other cities.

> This brings us to appellees' final contention, that Philadelphia needs a bank larger than it now has in order to bring business to the area and stimulate its economic development. We are clear, however, that a merger the effect of which "may be substantially to lessen competition" is not saved because, on some ultimate reckoning of social or economic debits and credits, it may be deemed beneficial. A value choice of such magnitude is beyond the ordinary limits of judicial competence, and in any event has been made for us already, by Congress when it enacted the amended s 7. Congress determined to preserve our traditionally competitive economy. It therefore proscribed anticompetitive mergers, the benign and the malignant alike, fully aware, we must assume, that some price might have to be paid.

In a slight qualification to *PNB*'s rule, the Horizontal Merger Guidelines explain that the agencies, in the exercise of their prosecutorial discretion about whether to challenge a merger, will consider efficiencies in closely related markets under appropriate circumstances:

> The Agencies normally assess competition in each relevant market affected by a merger independently and normally will challenge the merger if it is likely to be anticompetitive in any relevant market. In some cases, however, the Agencies in their prosecutorial discretion will consider efficiencies not strictly in the relevant market, but so inextricably linked with it that a partial divestiture or other remedy could not feasibly eliminate the anticompetitive effect in the relevant market without sacrificing the efficiencies in the other market(s). Inextricably linked efficiencies are most likely to make a difference when they are great and the likely anticompetitive effect in the relevant market(s) is small so the merger is likely to benefit customers overall.[695]

2. EDM

EDM—the elimination of double marginalization[696]—is not a saving in the cost of production, and it is not a defense, in that it is not a separate ground for exculpation for a merger that would otherwise harm competition. Rather, it is an incentive effect that can arise as a consequence of the fact that a vertically merged firm will not attempt to maximize the profits of its upstream division and downstream division separately (*i.e.*, taking a maximum profit margin at each level in isolation), but will rather maximize its total profits. This will often involve

---

[694] *See* Chapter IV (noting that this is an open question in rule of reason analysis).
[695] Horizontal Merger Guidelines (2010) § X n.14.
[696] Also, electronic dance music.

setting a downstream price for its own downstream-division sales that will be lower than would arise in an unintegrated setting. The price will be lower because each firm will internalize the benefit to the other division from a reduction in its own price, as well as any benefit of its own in the form of increased sales. (As we have already seen, antitrust analysis invariably assumes that an integrated firm will attempt to maximize its overall profits.[697])

EDM arises from many, but not all, vertical mergers. Predicting the overall likely effects on consumers from the interaction of EDM (which tends to lower consumer prices) and foreclosure of rivals (which can exclude competition, resulting in consumer harm and higher prices) can require complex expert analysis.

Some basic prerequisites for a cognizable EDM effect include: (1) the downstream division and upstream division were actually dealing with one another before the transaction; (2) the downstream division and upstream division will actually deal with one another after the transaction; and (3) the parties would not achieve the same internalization without the transaction (or a similarly harmful measure).

EDM was front and center in some antitrust high drama, such as it is, when the FTC and DOJ issued Vertical Merger Guidelines in 2020, only for the FTC to withdraw from them in 2021 with sharp words for the treatment of EDM (among other issues), triggering equally heated reaction from commenters.

Vertical Merger Guidelines § 6
(issued by FTC and DOJ 2020; FTC withdrew 2021)

[1] Due to the elimination of double marginalization, mergers of vertically related firms will often result in the merged firm's incurring lower costs for the upstream input than the downstream firm would have paid absent the merger. This is because the merged firm will have access to the upstream input at cost, whereas often the downstream firm would have paid a price that included a markup. The elimination of double marginalization is not a production, research and development, or procurement efficiency; it arises directly from the alignment of economic incentives between the merging firms. Since the same source drives any incentive to foreclose or raise rivals' costs, the evidence needed to assess those competitive harms overlaps substantially with that needed to evaluate the procompetitive benefits likely to result from the elimination of double marginalization.

[2] Mergers of firms that make complementary products can lead to a pricing efficiency analogous to the elimination of double marginalization. Absent the merger, the merging parties would set the price for each complement without regard to the impact of lower prices for one on demand for the other. If the two merge, the merged firm has an incentive to set prices that maximize the profits of the firm as a whole, which may result in lower prices for each component. Any incentive to offer lower prices may be more pronounced if the merged firm can target lower prices at customers that buy both components from it.

[3] While it is incumbent upon the merging firms to provide substantiation for claims that they will benefit from the elimination of double marginalization, the Agencies may independently attempt to quantify its effect based on all available evidence, including the evidence they develop to assess the potential for foreclosure or raising rivals' costs. In verifying the elimination of double marginalization, the agencies typically examine the likely cost saving to the merged firm from self-supplying inputs that would have been purchased from independent suppliers absent the merger. Creditable quantifications of the elimination of double marginalization are generally of similar precision and reliability to the Agencies' quantifications of likely foreclosure, raising rivals' costs, or other competitive effects.

[4] In assessing the merger-specificity of the elimination of double marginalization, the Agencies typically examine whether it would likely be less costly for the merged firm to self-supply inputs following the merger than for the downstream firm to purchase them from one or more independent firms absent the merger. The merging parties' evidence about existing contracting practices is often the best evidence of the price the downstream firm would likely pay for inputs absent the merger. The Agencies also consider other evidence, such as contracts between

---

[697] United States v. AT&T, Inc., 916 F.3d 1029, 1043 (D.C. Cir. 2019) ("[A] business with multiple divisions will seek to maximize its total profits."); Copperweld Corp. v. Indep. Tube Corp., 467 U.S. 752, 770 (1984) ("[T]he operations of a corporate enterprise organized into divisions must be judged as the conduct of a single actor.").

similarly situated firms in the same industry and contracting efforts considered by the merging firms. The Agencies do not, however, reject the merger specificity of the elimination of double marginalization solely because it could theoretically be achieved but for the merger, if such practices are not reflected in documentary evidence. The Agencies will generally take the same approach to evaluate the likely contractual arrangements absent the transaction as the one they use when evaluating raising rivals' costs or foreclosure.

* * *

Statement of Chair Lina M. Khan, Commissioner Rohit Chopra, and Commissioner Rebecca Kelly Slaughter on the Withdrawal of the Vertical Merger Guidelines (Sept. 15, 2021)

[1] The VMGs' emphasis on a non-statutory efficiency defense leads to their most significant flaw—their treatment of the elimination of double marginalization (EDM). The VMGs identify EDM as the principal reason to treat vertical mergers distinctly from horizontal mergers, claim that EDM "often" causes vertical mergers to benefit consumers, and suggest the agencies will proactively evaluate its impact even when not substantiated by the parties. EDM is cited as a reason to discount both a merger's impact on pricing power and the likelihood of coordination among the remaining firms.

[2] The VMGs' reliance on EDM is theoretically and factually misplaced. It is theoretically flawed because the economic model predicting EDM is limited to very specific factual scenarios: mergers that involve one single-product monopoly buying another single-product monopoly in the same supply chain, where both charge monopoly prices pre-merger and the product from one firm is used as an input by the other in a fixed-proportion production process. Yet outside this limited context, economic theory does not predict that EDM will create downward pricing pressure.

[3] Empirical evidence suggests that we should be highly skeptical that EDM will even be realized—let alone passed on to end-users. In many cases, vertical integration does not even prompt firms to provide the upstream input to its own downstream division. Studies of mergers between hospitals and physician groups—which have led to significant concentration in many areas—suggest these vertical mergers have not achieved theorized efficiencies. Instead, they find that vertical consolidation has increased physician costs, hospital prices, and per capita medical spending, with larger effects in more concentrated markets. Nor have these cost increases been associated with improved medical care. Similarly, when AT&T acquired Direct TV, it successfully argued to the FCC that the merger would lead to downward pricing pressure due to EDM. Yet shortly after the merger, AT&T began raising prices instead.

[4] Withdrawing from the VMGs reflects the FTC's view that it is inappropriate for the Commission's analysis of whether a transaction may lead to a substantial lessening of competition to assume that EDM is likely to exist.

* * *

Carl Shapiro & Herbert Hovenkamp, How Will the FTC Evaluate Vertical Mergers?
ProMarket (Sept. 23, 2021)

[I]n its attempt to explain why it withdrew the 2020 VMGs, the FTC majority statement relied on specious economic arguments. The majority critiqued "the 2020 VMGs' flawed discussion of the purported procompetitive benefits (i.e., efficiencies) of vertical mergers, especially its treatment of the elimination of double marginalization ("EDM")." This "could become difficult to correct if relied on by courts."

The theory of EDM is that a vertical merger can promote competition by eliminating double markups that occur when two independent firms sell and then resell something. In some cases, EDM justifies a vertical merger, but in other cases it does not. In its withdrawal statement, however, the FTC majority wrote this:

> The VMGs' reliance on EDM is theoretically flawed because the economic model predicting EDM is limited to very specific factual scenarios: mergers that involve one single-product

monopoly buying another single-product monopoly in the same supply chain, where both charge monopoly prices pre-merger and the product from one firm is used as an input by the other in a fixed-proportion production process. Yet outside this limited context, economic theory does not predict that EDM will create downward pricing pressure.

This statement is flatly incorrect as a matter of microeconomic theory. EDM applies (a) to multi-product firms, (b) regardless of whether the firms at either level have monopoly power or charge monopoly prices, and (c) regardless of whether the downstream production process involves fixed proportions. All of this has been included in economics textbooks for decades, building on a seminal 1950 paper by Joseph Spengler. None of the conditions cited by the majority are required for EDM to apply, although they are clearly relevant when one is measuring EDM in a specific vertical merger. While EDM does not save every vertical merger, it should be part of any vertical merger inquiry and is not nearly as limited as the majority's statement suggests.

In drafting its statement, the majority appears not to have consulted with the FTC's own Bureau of Economics. As a result, we have the spectacle of a federal agency basing its policies on a demonstrably false claim that ignores relevant expertise. Perhaps we are naïve, but we had been hoping that would stop when Donald Trump left office.

When the FTC investigates vertical mergers, will it dismiss EDM in cases that do not fit the very narrow fact pattern which the majority (incorrectly) believes to be the only one in which EDM applies? That could lead to enforcement errors and the prospect of embarrassing losses in court.

In addition, the FTC Press Release argues that the 2020 Vertical Merger Guidelines' approach to efficiencies was inconsistent with the language of the Clayton Act because efficiencies "are not recognized by the statute as a defense to an unlawful merger." [. . .]

This is baffling. The statutory text prohibits mergers whose effect "may be substantially to lessen competition, or to tend to create a monopoly." Consider a merger between two of the smaller firms in a concentrated market. In the absence of any efficiencies, such a merger could well be illegal, by eliminating the direct competition between those two firms (unilateral effects) or by making it easier for the remaining firms to collude (coordinated effects). Suppose, however, that the merger would enable these two smaller firms to achieve economies of scale, with the result that output is higher and prices lower than without the merger. There is no logical sense in which that merger would "lessen competition," so the merger cannot violate the statute. The legality of the merger thus must hinge on those efficiencies, yet the new FTC would ignore them.

Inexplicably, the Chair also categorically dismisses "procompetitive effects" in merger analysis. How can that make any sense? If a merger will generate procompetitive effects and thus will promote competition, on what basis can the Chair claim that the merger will substantially lessen competition, a requirement that is explicit in the text of the statute? Indeed, if mergers never produced procompetitive effects they could be condemned under a per se rule, but neither the statutory language nor a century of enforcement history permits that. [. . .]

Our view is that Vertical Merger Guidelines should make clear that the merging parties bear the burden of establishing EDM, just as they bear the burden of establishing all efficiencies in horizontal as well as vertical mergers. In a recent paper, one of us has described how to determine whether the efficiencies associated with EDM are cognizable, and if so how to measure them,

Finally, merger review is not just about price effects. Often the effect of a merger on product quality and innovation is far more important. In vertical mergers, EDM receives a lot of attention because it is well understood and amenable to quantification. But we find it very helpful to think of EDM as just one example of a far more general concept: some supply chains are handled more efficiently within a single firm than through contract. An extensive economic literature about vertical integration and "make or buy" decisions teaches us that vertical integration can spur innovation and greatly benefit consumers, especially when new methods require risky investments and coordination throughout the supply chain. Oliver Williamson won a Nobel Prize in 2009 for his work on these issues. There are many powerful historical examples where vertical integration promoted innovation by firms producing technologically complex products, including sewing machines, farm equipment, and cameras, as documented by the great economic historian, Alfred Chandler in his 1977 masterpiece, "*The Visible Hand: The*

Managerial Revolution in American Business." If the FTC does not understand that basic point about how our economy operates, they are likely to cause real harm.

3. Failing and Flailing Firms

It is fairly common for a party to a proposed merger to argue to an agency or court that they are failing and that an—admittedly somewhat anticompetitive—transaction is the only alternative to an even worse outcome of complete market exit by one of the parties. Courts have long recognized that a merger may be lawful for this reason.[698]

Today, the Horizontal Merger Guidelines allow such a defense sparingly:

> . . . [A] merger is not likely to enhance market power if imminent failure, as defined below, of one of the merging firms would cause the assets of that firm to exit the relevant market. This is an extreme instance of the more general circumstance in which the competitive significance of one of the merging firms is declining: the projected market share and significance of the exiting firm is zero. If the relevant assets would otherwise exit the market, customers are not worse off after the merger than they would have been had the merger been enjoined.

> The Agencies do not normally credit claims that the assets of the failing firm would exit the relevant market unless all of the following circumstances are met: (1) the allegedly failing firm would be unable to meet its financial obligations in the near future; (2) it would not be able to reorganize successfully under Chapter 11 of the Bankruptcy Act; and (3) it has made unsuccessful good-faith efforts to elicit reasonable alternative offers that would keep its tangible and intangible assets in the relevant market and pose a less severe danger to competition than does the proposed merger. [A footnote here adds: "Any offer to purchase the assets of the failing firm for a price above the liquidation value of those assets will be regarded as a reasonable alternative offer. Liquidation value is the highest value the assets could command for use outside the relevant market."][699]

As this extract suggests, in practice, the agencies and courts alike tend to take a hard line when parties invoke this defense.[700] In *Otto Bock*, the FTC challenged the acquisition by Otto Bock of Freedom, an important competitor in the manufacture of microprocessor-equipped prosthetic knees. Among the parties' other arguments, they offered a "failing firm" defense on the basis that Freedom had been in some financial trouble. The Commission was unmoved.

Opinion of the Commission, In the Matter of Otto Bock HealthCare North America, Inc.

FTC Docket No. 9378, 2019-2 Trade Cases ¶ 80,990, 2019 WL 6003207 (F.T.C. Nov. 1, 2019)

Commissioner Chopra.

[1] Respondent argues that it has demonstrated the failing firm defense, which would be a complete defense to Complaint Counsel's showing of liability.

1. Legal Standard

[2] The Supreme Court first recognized the failing firm defense in *International Shoe Co. v. FTC*, 280 U.S. 291 (1930), where it refused to enjoin the acquisition of a failing corporation by the only available purchaser. The defense

---

[698] *See* Int'l Shoe Co. v. FTC, 280 U.S. 291, 302–03 (1930) ("In the light of the case . . . of a corporation with resources so depleted and the prospect of rehabilitation so remote that it faced the grave probability of a business failure with resulting loss to its stockholders and injury to the communities where its plants were operated, we hold that the purchase of its capital stock by a competitor (there being no other prospective purchaser), not with a purpose to lessen competition, but to facilitate the accumulated business of the purchaser and with the effect of mitigating seriously injurious consequences otherwise probable, is not in contemplation of law prejudicial to the public and does not substantially lessen competition or restrain commerce within the intent of the Clayton Act.").

[699] Horizontal Merger Guidelines § 11.

[700] *See, e.g.,* ProMedica Health System, Inc. v. F.T.C., 749 F.3d 559, 572 (6th Cir. 2014) (the "Hail-Mary pass of presumptively doomed mergers").

provides a safety valve for the parties when, in the absence of the proffered transaction, the competitive assets would otherwise exit the market. Horizontal Merger Guidelines § 11. The defense is, in a sense, a "lesser of two evils" approach, in which the possible threat to competition resulting from an acquisition is deemed preferable to the adverse impact on competition from the company's going out of business. The Horizontal Merger Guidelines explain that the antitrust agencies do not normally credit a failing firm defense unless all of the following circumstances are met: (1) the allegedly failing firm would be unable to meet its financial obligations in the near future; (2) it would not be able to reorganize successfully under Chapter 11 of the Bankruptcy Act; and (3) it has made unsuccessful good faith efforts to elicit reasonable alternative offers that would keep its tangible and intangible assets in the market and pose a less severe danger to competition than does the proposed merger. § 11. The Horizontal Merger Guidelines define a "reasonable alternative offer" as one that exceeds the liquidation value of the assets. A successful failing firm defense effectively permits a transaction that otherwise would violate the antitrust laws. Thus, the Supreme Court has narrowly confined the scope of the doctrine. The proponent of the defense bears the burden to prove each element, and failure to prove any element is fatal. [. . .]

[3] In order to demonstrate the first element of the defense, i.e., that Freedom was unable to meet financial obligations, Respondent cannot simply show that it had an imminent payment that exceeded its existing cash on hand. Rather, the analysis must account for the commercially reasonable options that firms in today's markets can pursue when facing a liquidity shortfall. To meet the first element, Respondent needs to prove that Freedom had resources so depleted and the prospect of rehabilitation so remote that it faced the grave probability of a business failure absent the challenged transaction. We find that Respondent failed to meet the first prong of the defense by demonstrating a grave probability of Freedom's failure. At the time of the Acquisition and during the approximately one year leading up to it, Freedom was engaged in a turnaround that had begun to show results. Freedom hired its new CEO, Mr. Smith, in April 2016. By December 2016, many of Freedom's financial metrics were starting to improve. [. . .]

[4] A second requirement of the failing firm defense is that a failing firm not be able to reorganize successfully under Chapter 11 of the Bankruptcy Act. As with the defense's other elements, Respondent bears the burden of proof. Respondent argues that Freedom considered and rejected the possibility of Chapter 11, determining that it would not have successfully emerged from the process. [. . .]

[5] Although this element is a closer call, we find that Respondent has not demonstrated that prospects for Chapter 11 reorganization were dim or nonexistent. . . . . Freedom had valuable products in its pipeline, including Quattro, that drove its projected revenue growth and underpinned its investment bankers' enterprise valuation. . . . Yet Freedom did not, it appears, explore the possibilities that could have helped it surmount its liquidity challenges and launch those products. [. . .]

[6] To sustain a failing firm defense, the proponent is called upon to demonstrate that the acquiring company was the only available purchaser. The antitrust enforcement agencies have implemented this element of the failing firm defense by focusing on the respondent's efforts to elicit reasonable alternative offers that would keep its tangible and intangible assets in the relevant market and pose a less severe danger to competition. Defendant's burden is quite heavy. Like the ALJ, we hold that Respondent failed to meet its burden. [. . .]

[7] Respondent states that Freedom preferred a refinancing to a sale, but that it could not obtain refinancing, such that a sale to a strategic acquirer became the only option. However, the evidence suggests that potential financing sources did express interest in Freedom, but on terms that the existing shareholders did not like. [. . .]

[8] As to the sales process, the evidence again shows that Freedom focused prematurely on Otto Bock. Freedom's representatives began to meet with Otto Bock regarding a potential sale in October 2016. Then, from October 2016 to April 2017, neither Freedom nor its investment banker contacted any potential alternative strategic buyers besides Otto Bock. They finally did so because they were not satisfied with Otto Bock's initial offer. Freedom's belated outreach to strategic acquirers besides Otto Bock suffered from shortcomings similar to those experienced with its refinancing efforts. [. . .]

[9] A respondent must make a sufficiently clear showing that it undertook a well-conceived and thorough canvass of the industry such as to ferret out viable alternative partners for merger. Here, Moelis contacted seven potential

strategic acquirers, but failed to contact several prosthetics makers who later expressed interest in Freedom. . . . Some of the firms that Moelis neglected were small, but two . . . are firms that Respondent now touts as capable of replacing competition lost by the Acquisition. And at least in some cases, approaching smaller companies in a given industry might be exactly what is required of a company seeking the protection of the failing company defense. [. . .]

[10] In sum, Freedom's executives and shareholders were focused on obtaining the highest possible offer, which is a different objective from searching for a reasonable alternative offer above Freedom's liquidation value. [. . .]

[11] Because Respondent failed to establish the three elements of the failing firm defense—*i.e.*, that Freedom would be unable to meet its financial obligations in the near future, that it would not be able to reorganize successfully under Chapter 11 of the Bankruptcy Act, and that it conducted a reasonable, good faith search for alternative offers that would keep its assets in the market and pose a less severe danger to competition—we find the defense inapplicable.

* * *

Ian Conner, On "Failing" Firms—and Miraculous Recoveries,
Competition Matters Blog (May 27, 2020)

Over the past few years, the [FTC's Bureau of Competition] has faced a surprising number of failing firm claims by merging parties. Even when the economy was booming, we heard many iterations of the same argument: The acquired firm is failing. The acquiring firm is failing. Both firms are failing (which presumably would justify the merger on the basis that if you tie two sinking rocks together, they're more likely to float). The entire industry is failing. But despite many claims and much time spent assessing the financial health of numerous firms, the Bureau rarely finds that the facts support a failing firm argument. Saying it doesn't make it so: if you want the Bureau to accept such an argument in your case, you had better actually be failing, and able to prove it.

It's important to remember the procompetitive rationale for entertaining claims that a firm is failing. The failing firm defense is just that, a defense. The merger that is being proposed is anticompetitive, but, assuming the elements of the failing firm defense are met, it is preferable to have the assets in the hands of the acquirer than see the assets exit the market completely. Note that failing is equated with reducing the acquired firm to nothing— not only does the business no longer exist, but the productive assets are also dismantled or redeployed for use outside the relevant market.

The failing firm defense has been described in every iteration of the Horizontal Merger Guidelines since 1982. Section 11 of the 2010 version of the Guidelines provide the most detailed iteration, and the Bureau has previously discussed the showing that is required to establish it in an individual case. As we noted there, the argument is often made, but rarely accepted.

Some commentators have suggested that the agencies may face a wave of mergers with failing firm arguments in the coming months, in light of current economic conditions in some sectors of the economy. And while no such wave has yet materialized—in fact, filings have fallen significantly from their recent annualized rate—parties contemplating such an argument should understand that the Bureau will not relax the stringent conditions that define a genuinely "failing" firm. We will continue to apply the test set out in the Guidelines and reflected in our long-standing practice, and in doing so we will require the same level of substantiation as we required before the COVID pandemic. As I noted previously, we have not relaxed, and will not relax, the intensity of our scrutiny or the vigor of our enforcement efforts. Consumers deserve the protection of the antitrust laws now as much as ever.

Finally, a cautionary note for those advising and representing merging parties: think twice before making apocalyptic predictions of imminent failure during a merger investigation. Candor before the agency remains paramount, and it has been striking to see firms that were condemned as failing rise like a phoenix from the ashes once the proposed transaction was abandoned in light of our competition concerns. No doubt some of these recoveries are due to the tireless efforts of the firm's leadership and employees to turn around a struggling business. But other examples have suggested to us that a serious effort to assess the standalone future of the company was not undertaken before representing that the failure of the merger would result in the imminent demise of that company. Counsel who make too many failing-firm arguments on behalf of businesses that go on to make miraculous recoveries may find that we apply particularly close scrutiny to similar claims in their future cases.

To be clear, we support vigorous competition and hope that firms that have been hard hit by the economic downturn recover quickly and remain viable competitors so that they can continue to serve their customers. We will accept solid evidence that a firm is failing, and step aside when justified by the full evidence. But we will not turn away from the challenges ahead by changing the rules that have served us well in the past, including during prior economic downturns. And we ask that counsel not make that job harder by seeking advantage from the suffering of some.

* * *

Although failing firm arguments seldom succeed, a lighter-lift version of the argument sometimes has better luck. Courts and agencies have on some occasions recognized that a firm might be declining in competitive importance, such that evidence of its past strength is a poor guide to its current, or expected future, importance to competition. This argument received its seminal statement in *General Dynamics*. It has become known as the "flailing firm" argument: it is not a defense in a strict sense (because it is really just an argument about the competitive effects of the merger, made by the defendant in an effort to rebut the plaintiff's affirmative case), but it is so similar in spirit to a failing-firm argument that the two are presented together here.[701]

In *General Dynamics* itself, the Court considered whether the acquisition of United Electric by General Dynamics would harm competition in a market for coal production, given (among other things) an argument advanced by the parties—and accepted by the district court—that historical data overstated United Electric's competitive vitality.

United States v. General Dynamics Corp.

415 U.S. 486 (1974)

Justice Stewart.

[1] [T]he District Court [below] found that the evidence did not support the Government's contention that the 1959 acquisition of United Electric [by General Dynamics] substantially lessened competition in any product or geographic market. . . . [T]he court found that United Electric's coal reserves were so low that its potential to compete with other coal producers in the future was far weaker than the aggregate production statistics relied on by the Government might otherwise have indicated. In particular, the court found that virtually all of United Electric's proved coal reserves were either depleted or already committed by long-term contracts with large customers, and that United Electric's power to affect the price of coal was thus severely limited and steadily diminishing. On the basis of these considerations, the court concluded: "Under these circumstances, continuation of the affiliation between United Electric and [General Dynamics] is not adverse to competition, nor would divestiture benefit competition even were this court to accept the Government's unrealistic produce and geographic market definitions." [. . .]

[2] In this case, the District Court relied on evidence relating to changes in the patterns and structure of the coal industry and in United Electric's coal reserve situation after the time of acquisition in 1959. Such evidence could not reflect a positive decision on the part of the merged companies to deliberately but temporarily refrain from anticompetitive actions, nor could it reasonably be thought to reflect less active competition than that which might have occurred had there not been an acquisition in 1959. As the District Court convincingly found, the trend toward increased dependence on utilities as consumers of coal and toward the near-exclusive use of long-term contracts was the product of inevitable pressures on the coal industry in all parts of the country. And, unlike evidence showing only that no lessening of competition has yet occurred, the demonstration of weak coal resources

---

[701] In *Arch Coal II* the parties tried an incautious version of this argument: that the proposed transaction would allow Arch to "focus on its most profitable operations in the hopes of earning positive margins." The court was bemused, and pointed out that "Arch's underlying logic . . . supports the Court's finding that the parties have the incentive and intention to maximize profits by cutting output." FTC v. Peabody Energy Corporation, 492 F. Supp. 3d 865, 901 (E.D. Mo. 2020).

necessarily and logically implied that United Electric was not merely disinclined but unable to compete effectively for future contracts. Such evidence went directly to the question of whether future lessening of competition was probable, and the District Court was fully justified in using it.

[3] [T]he Government contends that reliance on depleted and committed resources is essentially a "failing company" defense which must meet the strict limits placed on that defense by this Court's decisions[.] . . . A company invoking the defense has the burden of showing that its resources (were) so depleted and the prospect of rehabilitation so remote that it faced the grave probability of a business failure, and further that it tried and failed to merge with a company other than the acquiring one.

[4] The Government asserts that United Electric was a healthy and thriving company at the time of the acquisition and could not be considered on the brink of failure, and also that the appellees have not shown that Material Service was the only available acquiring company. These considerations would be significant if the District Court had found no violation of s 7 by reason of United Electric's being a failing company, but the District Court's conclusion was not, as the Government suggests, identical with or even analogous to such a finding. The failing-company defense presupposes that the effect on competition and the loss to the company's stockholders and injury to the communities where its plants were operated, will be less if a company continues to exist even as a party to a merger than if it disappears entirely from the market. It is, in a sense, a "lesser of two evils" approach, in which the possible threat to competition resulting from an acquisition is deemed preferable to the adverse impact on competition and other losses if the company goes out of business. The appellees' demonstration of United's weak reserves position, however, proved an entirely different point. Rather than showing that United would have gone out of business but for the merger with Material Service, the finding of inadequate reserves went to the heart of the Government's statistical prima facie case based on production figures and substantiated the District Court's conclusion that United Electric, even if it remained in the market, did not have sufficient reserves to compete effectively for long-term contracts. The failing-company defense is simply inapposite to this finding and the failure of the appellees to meet the prerequisites of that doctrine did not detract from the validity of the court's analysis. [. . .]

[5] Since we agree with the District Court that the Government's reliance on production statistics in the context of this case was insufficient, it follows that the judgment before us may be affirmed[.]

NOTES

1) Suppose that a court, reviewing a proposed transaction, is confident that the deal will harm some customers, but will benefit some others through the creation of efficiencies. What rule should the court apply to decide whether to permit the merger? Does it matter whether the "some" and "others" are within the same market—and if so, why?

2) Why do you think parties make the failing firm argument so frequently, but then—if the deal is blocked or abandoned—turn out to be just fine? (Bonus points for something more thoughtful than "everybody lies.")

3) Suppose that you represented a company that was genuinely on track for failure, but agency staff were skeptical. What evidence do you think would be most persuasive?

4) Is *General Dynamics* inconsistent with the logic of the structural presumption?

5) Should the agencies recognize a "national security" defense to a merger: that is, a defense for a merger that may harm competition but will advance national security? What questions would you want to ask to determine whether this would be a good idea? How would you formulate it in law?[702]

6) The HMGs say: "Efficiencies are difficult to verify and quantify, in part because much of the information relating to efficiencies is uniquely in the possession of the merging firms." Can you think of any other reasons?

---

[702] *See* Statement of Commissioner William E. Kovacic, with whom Chairman Deborah Platt Majoras and Commissioner J. Thomas Rosch Join, In the Matter of Lockheed Martin Corporation, The Boeing Company, and United Launch Alliance, L.L.C., FTC File No. 051 0165, Docket No. C-4188 (May 8, 2007); Analysis of Agreement Containing Consent Order to Aid Public Comment, In the Matter of The Boeing Company, Lockheed Martin Corporation, and United Launch Alliance, FTC File No. 051-0165 (Oct. 3, 2006).

E. Remedies

Merger remedies can be divided into two broad groups: structural remedies, which change the structure of the market (*e.g.*, by "breakup" or "divestiture"—that is, sale—of businesses or assets) and behavioral remedies, which instruct market participants to behave in particular ways or to refrain from behaving in particular ways.

We will talk more generally about antitrust remedies in Chapters XI (injunctions) and XII (damages). In this Chapter we will focus on the distinctive issues that arise in connection with remedies in merger, rather than conduct, cases. These remedies may be imposed by a court or agency (sua sponte or based on a proposal from an agency or litigating party) or—as we shall see at the end of this section—imposed by agreement between an agency and the merging parties. As a general matter, courts have emphasized that the agencies enjoy considerable discretion in remedying an unlawful transaction.[703]

1. Structural Merger Remedies

Structural remedies—orders to spin off, break up, or sell businesses—are (at least in theory) the default remedy in merger cases. In the simplest cases, if the acquisition by A of B, or the merger of A and B, is unlawful, then the natural fix is an injunction requiring that the transaction not go ahead (if the deal has not yet "closed" or been consummated), or, if the deal has already closed, an injunction requiring that the target be sold off again, or the merger be unwound. In slightly more complex cases, if an acquisition by A of B raises competitive concerns with respect to some of B's business units, but does not raise such concerns with respect to B's other business units, the parties might be required to divest the business units that give rise to the concerns, as long as a buyer can be found with the ability and incentive to run them as an effective competitive force. With that remedy in place, the parties may be able to proceed with the rest of the deal.

The agencies prefer structural remedies because it is usually safer to eliminate the merged firm's *ability* to engage in harmful conduct (*e.g.*, by eliminating the market power created by an unlawful transaction) than to try to manage its *incentives* by threatening penalties for detected misconduct. After all, monitoring is difficult, expensive, and uncertain. Market participants and agencies will not always be able to spot misconduct; and even when they do, they will not always be able to prove it to a judge—and seldom without considerable burden and expense. It is often cleaner and cheaper to solve a competitive problem at its root, by undoing the illegal transaction (or the illegal piece of the transaction), and let the parties and the agencies get on with their respective lives in relative peace.

Divestiture is easier in some cases than others. In practice, most federal government merger challenges deal with *proposed*, rather than consummated, transactions, because of the HSR premerger notification rules that require parties to give prior notice of large deals to the agencies. (We will discuss these rules in Chapter XI.) When the deal is merely proposed, a court can issue a simple order to prohibit or "block" the deal, solving the problem before it arises.

But some mergers have already been closed by the time they are challenged or ruled unlawful. This can happen, for example, if the transaction was not subject to HSR notification, such that the agencies did not become aware of the transaction until after the deal was done. It can also arise when the transaction was reviewed but not challenged at the time of the initial review, only for the agency to later conclude that enforcement action was appropriate.[704]

Requiring divestiture in a consummated merger case can be very difficult, and is often likened to "unscrambling eggs," as the two firms may no longer be meaningfully distinct. Courts and agencies generally do not want to impose a remedy that is not in the public interest: *i.e.*, not reasonably likely to restore competitive conditions to

---

[703] *See, e.g.*, Polypore Int'l, Inc. v. FTC, 686 F.3d 1208, 1218 (11th Cir. 2012) ("The Commission has broad discretion in the formulating of a remedy for unlawful practices."); Hospital Corp. of America v. FTC, 807 F.2d 1381 (7th Cir. 1986) (noting in a merger case that "the Commission has a broad discretion, akin to that of a court of equity, in deciding what relief is necessary to cure a violation of law and ensure against its repetition"); Olin Corp. v. FTC, 986 F.2d 1295, 1307 (9th Cir. 1993) ("[T]he Commission has broad discretion to cope with any unlawful practices disclosed by the record").

[704] *See infra* Chapter XI (describing the relationship between HSR and merger enforcement).

what they would have been but-for the unlawful transaction, or as close as possible. A divestiture that butchers the merged firm and results in one or two non-viable competitors is not likely to be in the public interest. The problems can be formidable:

> For many reasons, it may be hard to resurrect a competitor or form a new player that is able to exert the same competitive intensity that the target would have provided, but for the [consummated] merger in question. . . .
>
> . . . [T]he challenges here can come not only from "scrambled" assets, but also from lost business relationships: customers may have chosen new suppliers, employees may have left or taken different positions, suppliers may no longer be available for needed inputs. And degraded assets cause other challenges: machinery may have been actively destroyed or intellectual property may not have been properly upgraded. The companies may have shared confidential business information, knowhow, trade secrets, or proprietary data that were key to the competitive significance of the acquired firm. Additionally, the passage of time may have resulted in the loss of brand or reputational cachet. . . . Nevertheless, even when it is hard and may require assets and services beyond those acquired, breakup of the merged company to reestablish competition is still the most likely remedy for a consummated merger.[705]

In the past, federal courts have emphasized that divestiture is the preferred remedy in a merger case, at least in a government challenge.[706] In a classic remedial decision, the Supreme Court insisted on divestiture despite the parties' protestation that this would have unreasonably harsh consequences because of applicable tax laws. Note the Court's insistence on the clarity and effectiveness of structural relief—the "surer, cleaner" solution—rather than behavioral constraints designed to manage the parties' behavior while leaving the objectionable economic structure intact, as well as its explicit recognition of the practical difficulties of enforcement.

United States v. E.I. du Pont de Nemours & Co.
366 U.S. 316 (1961)

Justice Brennan.

[1] [In a previous proceeding the Court] held that du Pont's acquisition of the 23 percent of General Motors stock had led to the insulation from free competition of most of the General Motors market in automobile finishes and fabrics, with the resultant likelihood, at the time of suit, of the creation of a monopoly of a line of commerce, and, accordingly, that du Pont had violated s 7 of the Clayton Act. We did not, however, determine what equitable relief was necessary in the public interest. [. . .]

[2] [In the District Court on remand,] Du Pont objected that the Government's plan of complete divestiture entailed harsh income-tax consequences for du Pont stockholders and, if adopted, would also threaten seriously to depress the market value of du Pont and General Motors stock. Du Pont therefore proposed its own plan designed to avoid these results. The salient feature of its plan was substitution for the Government's proposed complete divestiture of a plan for partial divestiture in the form of a so-called 'pass through' of voting rights, whereby du Pont would retain all attributes of ownership of the General Motors stock, including the right to receive dividends and a share of assets on liquidation, except the right to vote. The vote was to be 'passed through' to du Pont's shareholders proportionally to their holdings of du Pont's own shares[.] [. . .]

[3] Before we examine the adequacy of the relief allowed by the District Court, it is appropriate to review some general considerations concerning that most drastic, but most effective, of antitrust remedies—divestiture. The key to the whole question of an antitrust remedy is of course the discovery of measures effective to restore competition. Courts are not authorized in civil proceedings to punish antitrust violators, and relief must not be

---

[705] Ian Conner, *Fixer Upper: Using the FTC's Remedial Toolbox to Restore Competition* (remarks of Feb. 8, 2020), 4. The reference in the text to destruction of acquired assets is not conjectural. *See, e.g.*, Analysis to Aid Public Comment, In the Matter of Charlotte Pipe and Foundry, FTC File No. 111-34, 2 ("After the Acquisition, Charlotte Pipe destroyed the CISP production equipment that it acquired from Star Pipe."). (How might this affect the objectives of a remedy?)

[706] California v. Am. Stores Co., 495 U.S. 271, 280–81 (1990) ("[I]n Government actions divestiture is the preferred remedy for an illegal merger or acquisition"). *See generally* Post-Trial Brief of the United States, United States v. AT&T Inc., Case No. 1:17-cv-2511 (D.D.C. filed May 8, 2018), 22–25 (expressing and explaining strong preference for structural relief and citing authorities).

punitive. But courts are authorized, indeed required, to decree relief effective to redress the violations, whatever the adverse effect of such a decree on private interests. Divestiture is itself an equitable remedy designed to protect the public interest. . . .

[4] If the Court concludes that other measures will not be effective to redress a violation, and that complete divestiture is a necessary element of effective relief, the Government cannot be denied the latter remedy because economic hardship, however severe, may result. Economic hardship can influence choice only as among two or more effective remedies. If the remedy chosen is not effective, it will not be saved because an effective remedy would entail harsh consequences. This proposition is not novel; it is deeply rooted in antitrust law and has never been successfully challenged. The criteria were announced in one of the earliest cases. In *United States v. American Tobacco Co.*, [221 U.S. 106, 185 (1911)], we said:

> In considering the subject three dominant influences must guide our action: 1, The duty of giving complete and efficacious effect to the prohibitions of the statute; 2, the accomplishing of this result with as little injury as possible to the interest of the general public; and, 3, a proper regard for the vast interests of private property which may have become vested in many persons as a result of the acquisition either by way of stock ownership or otherwise of interests in the stock or securities of the combination without any guilty knowledge or intent in any way to become actors or participants in the wrongs which we find to have inspired and dominated the combination from the beginning.

[5] The Court concluded in that case that, despite the alleged hardship which would be involved, only dissolution of the combination would be effective, and therefore ordered dissolution. Plainly, if the relief is not effective, there is no occasion to consider the third criterion.

[6] Thus, in this case, the adverse tax and market consequences which the District Court found would be concomitants of complete divestiture cannot save the remedy of partial divestiture through the 'pass through' of voting rights if, though less harsh, partial divestiture is not an effective remedy. We do not think that the 'pass through' is an effective remedy and believe that the Government is entitled to a decree directing complete divestiture.

[7] It cannot be gainsaid that complete divestiture is peculiarly appropriate in cases of stock acquisitions which violate s 7. That statute is specific and narrowly directed, and it outlaws a particular form of economic control—stock acquisitions which tend to create a monopoly of any line of commerce. The very words of s 7 suggest that an undoing of the acquisition is a natural remedy. Divestiture or dissolution has traditionally been the remedy for Sherman Act violations whose heart is intercorporate combination and control, and it is reasonable to think immediately of the same remedy when s 7 of the Clayton Act, which particularizes the Sherman Act standard of illegality, is involved. Of the very few litigated s 7 cases which have been reported, most decreed divestiture as a matter of course. Divestiture has been called the most important of antitrust remedies. It is simple, relatively easy to administer, and sure. It should always be in the forefront of a court's mind when a violation of s 7 has been found.

[8] The divestiture only of voting rights does not seem to us to be a remedy adequate to promise elimination of the tendency of du Pont's acquisition offensive to s 7. Under the decree, two-thirds of du Pont's holdings of General Motors stock will be voted by du Pont shareholders—upwards of 40 million shares. Common sense tells us that under this arrangement there can be little assurance of the dissolution of the intercorporate community of interest which we found to violate the law. The du Pont shareholders will ipso facto also be General Motors voters. It will be in their interest to vote in such a way as to induce General Motors to favor du Pont, the very result which we found illegal on the first appeal. It may be true, as appellees insist, that these shareholders will not exercise as much influence on General Motors as did du Pont when it held and voted the shares as a block. And it is true that there is no showing in this record that the du Pont shareholders will combine to vote together, or that their information about General Motors' activities will be detailed enough to enable them to vote their shares as strategically as du Pont itself has done. But these arguments misconceive the nature of this proceeding. The burden is not on the Government to show de novo that a 'pass through' of the General Motors vote, like du Pont's ownership of General Motors stock, would violate s 7. It need only appear that the decree entered leaves a substantial likelihood that the tendency towards monopoly of the acquisition condemned by s 7 has not been satisfactorily eliminated. We are

not required to assume, contrary to all human experience, that du Pont's shareholders will not vote in their own self-interest. Moreover, the General Motors management, which over the years has become accustomed to du Pont's special relationship, would know that the relationship continues to a substantial degree, and might well act accordingly. The same is true of du Pont's competitors. They might not try so vigorously to break du Pont's hold on General Motors' business, as if complete divestiture were ordered. And finally, the influence of the du Pont company itself would not be completely dissipated. For under the decree du Pont would have the power to sell its General Motors shares; the District Court expressly held that there would be nothing in the decree to prevent such dispositions. Such a sale would presumably restore the vote separated from the sold stock while du Pont owned it. This power to transfer the vote could conceivably be used to induce General Motors to favor du Pont products. In sum, the 'pass through' of the vote does not promise elimination of the violation offensive to s 7. . . .

[9] Du Pont replies, inter alia, that it would be willing for all of its General Motors stock to be disenfranchised, if that would satisfy the requirement for effective relief. This suggestion, not presented to the District Court, is distinctly an afterthought. If the suggestion is disenfranchisement only while du Pont retains the stock, it would not avoid the hazards inherent in du Pont's power to transfer the vote. If the suggestion is permanent loss of the vote, it would create a large and permanent separation of corporate ownership from control, which would not only run directly counter to accepted principles of corporate democracy, but also reduce substantially the number of voting General Motors shares, thereby making it easier for the owner of a block of shares far below an absolute majority to obtain working control, perhaps creating new antitrust problems for both General Motors and the Department of Justice in the future. And finally, we should be reluctant to effect such a drastic change in General Motors' capital structure, established under state corporation law.

[10] Appellees argue further that the injunctive provisions of the decree supplementary to the 'pass through' of voting rights adequately remove any objections to the effectiveness of the 'pass through.' Du Pont is enjoined, for example, from in any way influencing the choice of General Motors' officers and directors, and from entering into any preferential trade relations with General Motors. And, under . . . the decree, the Government may reapply in the future should this injunctive relief prove inadequate. Presumably this provision could be used to prevent the exercise of the power to transfer the vote. But the public interest should not in this case be required to depend upon the often cumbersome and time-consuming injunctive remedy. Should a violation of one of the prohibitions be thought to occur, the Government would have the burden of initiating contempt proceedings and of proving by a preponderance of the evidence that a violation had indeed been committed. Such a remedy would, judging from the history of this litigation, take years to obtain. Moreover, an injunction can hardly be detailed enough to cover in advance all the many fashions in which improper influence might manifest itself. And the policing of an injunction would probably involve the courts and the Government in regulation of private affairs more deeply than the administration of a simple order of divestiture. We think the public is entitled to the surer, cleaner remedy of divestiture. The same result would follow even if we were in doubt. For it is well settled that once the Government has successfully borne the considerable burden of establishing a violation of law, all doubts as to the remedy are to be resolved in its favor.

[11] We therefore direct complete divestiture.

CASENOTE: Chicago Bridge & Iron Co. N.V. v. FTC
534 F.3d 410 (5th Cir. 2008)

A viable divestiture may require that the company sell off more than just the acquired assets: the package may also include assets and resources from outside the relevant market where these are necessary to ensure competitive adequacy.[707] A great example is presented by the *Chicago Bridge* litigation. In that case, the Chicago Bridge & Iron Company had acquired assets from Pitt-Des Moines ("PDM") used for the business of making cryogenic storage tanks. The FTC found that the acquisition violated Section 7, and ordered that the merged firm should divide its cryogenic business into two equally competitive entities. The FTC insisted that the divestiture package should include not just the acquired cryogenic tank assets in the market of competitive concerns, but also acquired water

---

[707] See Ian Conner, Fixer Upper: Using the FTC's Remedial Toolbox to Restore Competition (remarks of Feb. 8, 2020), 5–6.

tank assets. On appeal, the merged firm argued that this relief was an abuse of the Commission's discretion, because it required divestiture outside the market of competitive concern. The Fifth Circuit disagreed.

The court began by emphasizing that the agencies enjoy considerable deference in the design of a merger remedy: "All doubts as to the remedy are to be resolved in [the FTC's] favor. The Commission is clothed with wide discretion in determining the type of order that is necessary to bring an end to the unfair practices found to exist. It has wide latitude for judgment and the courts will not interfere except where the remedy selected has no reasonable relation to the unlawful practices found to exist."

And here, the court held, the FTC had exercised this discretion appropriately, by mandating that the merged firm divest sufficient assets to create a new competitor "capable of competing for an equal share of the market similar to the situation pre-acquisition." The Commission had reasonably concluded that the creation of a viable competitor required the divestiture of not just the overlapping cryogenic-tank assets but also the target's water plant division. As a result, "the Commission did not abuse its discretion, but instead fashioned a remedy reasonably calculated to eliminate the anti-competitive effects of CB&I's acquisition in violation of the Clayton and FTC Acts."

So—what does this look like in practice? A divestiture order may sound like a simple matter: an instruction to sell off an acquired business. But in practice crafting an effective divestiture is always an intricate undertaking. Following the FTC's successful challenge to a consummated acquisition in the *Otto Bock* case, the buyer, Otto Bock, was ordered to sell off the target, Freedom. The full Final Order is more than 20 pages long, including almost six pages of definitions: the following extract includes some of the key provisions, giving a flavor of the kind of thing that divestiture orders must grapple with in practice. As you can imagine, the expertise of remedial specialists at the antitrust agencies is absolutely indispensable in designing merger remedies, even in fairly simple cases.

FTC, Final Order, In the Matter of Otto Bock HealthCare North America, Inc., FTC Dkt. No. 9378 (Nov. 1, 2019)

II.

IT IS FURTHER ORDERED that:

A. Otto Bock shall:

1. No later than ninety (90) days from the date this Order becomes final and effective, divest absolutely and in good faith, and at no minimum price, the Freedom Assets and Business to an Acquirer that receives the prior approval of the Commission and in a manner, including pursuant to a Divestiture Agreement, that receives the prior approval of the Commission;

Provided, however, that Otto Bock may retain any or all of the Divestiture Products Group A unless the Acquirer demonstrates to the Commission's satisfaction: (i) that any such asset is necessary to achieve the purpose of this Order; and (ii) that the Acquirer needs such asset to effectively operate the Freedom Business in a manner consistent with the purpose of this Order, and the Commission approves the divestiture with the divestiture of such asset.

Provided, however, that Otto Bock must divest any or all of the Divestiture Products Group B unless the Acquirer demonstrates to the Commission's satisfaction: (i) that any such asset is not necessary to achieve the purpose of this Order; and (ii) that the Acquirer does not need such asset to effectively operate the Freedom Business in a manner consistent with the purpose of this Order, and the Commission approves the divestiture without the divestiture of such asset.

2. Comply with all terms of the Divestiture Agreement approved by the Commission pursuant to this Order, which agreement shall be deemed incorporated by reference into this Order; and any failure by Otto Bock to comply with any term of the Divestiture Agreement shall constitute a failure to comply with this Order. The Divestiture Agreement shall not reduce, limit or contradict, or be construed to reduce, limit or contradict, the terms of this Order; *provided, however,* that nothing in this Order shall be construed

to reduce any rights or benefits of any Acquirer or to reduce any obligations of Otto Bock under such agreement; *provided further*, that if any term of the Divestiture Agreement varies from the terms of this Order ("Order Term"), then to the extent that Otto Bock cannot fully comply with both terms, the Order Term shall determine Otto Bock's obligations under this Order. Notwithstanding any paragraph, section, or other provision of the Divestiture Agreement, any failure to meet any condition precedent to closing (whether waived or not) or any modification of the Divestiture Agreement, without the prior approval of the Commission, shall constitute a failure to comply with this Order. [. . .]

5. Take all actions and shall effect all arrangements in connection with the divestiture of the Freedom Assets and Business necessary to ensure that the Acquirer can conduct the Freedom Assets and Business in substantially the same manner as operated prior to the Acquisition, including, but not limited to:

> a. Complying with the Hold-Separate Agreements, the Hold-Separate Manager Agreement, the Hold-Separate Monitor Agreement, or the Procedures, Terms, and Conditions Agreement or any term of the above Agreements,

> b. Providing Transitional Services,

> c. Providing the opportunity to recruit and employ all Freedom Employees.

6. Convey as of the Effective Date of Divestiture to the Acquirer the right to use any Licensed Intangible Property (to the extent permitted by the third-party licensor), if such right is needed for the operation of the Freedom Business by the Acquirer and if the Acquirer is unable, using commercially-reasonable efforts, to obtain equivalent rights from other third parties on commercially-reasonable terms and conditions.

7. Otto Bock shall:

> a. Place no restrictions on the use by the Acquirer of the Freedom Assets and Business, including any Intangible Property;

> b. On or before the Effective Date of Divestiture, provide to the Acquirer contact information about customers, Payors, and Suppliers for the Freedom Assets and Business;

> c. With respect to contracts with Freedom Business Suppliers, at the Acquirer's option and as of the Effective Date of Divestiture:

>> i. If such contract can be assigned without third-party approval, assign its rights under the contract to the Acquirer; and

>> ii. If such contract can be assigned to the Acquirer only with third-party approval, assist and cooperate with the Acquirer in obtaining:

>>> (a) Such third-party approval and in assigning the contract to the acquirer; or

>>> (b) A new contract.

8. At the request of the Acquirer, for two (2) years from the Effective Date of Divestiture, with the option of the Acquirer to renew for two six (6) month periods with written notification to Commission staff, except as otherwise approved by the Commission, and in a manner (including pursuant to an agreement) that receives the prior approval of the Commission:

> a. Otto Bock shall provide Transitional Services to the Acquirer sufficient to enable the Acquirer to conduct the Freedom Business in substantially the same manner that the Freedom Business was conducted prior to the Acquisition and during the Hold-Separate Period.

> b. Otto Bock shall provide the Transitional Services required by this Paragraph II.A.8 at substantially the same level and quality as such services are provided by Otto Bock in connection with the Hold-Separate Agreements. [. . .]

IV.

IT IS FURTHER ORDERED that:

A. From the date this Order becomes final and effective (without regard to the finality of the divestiture requirements herein) until the Effective Date of Divestiture, Otto Bock shall take such actions as are necessary to maintain the viability, marketability, and competitiveness of the Freedom Assets and Business, as provided in the Hold-Separate Agreements. Among other things that may be necessary, as provided for in the Hold-Separate Agreements, Otto Bock shall:

> 1. Maintain the operations of the Freedom Business relating to the Freedom Assets in the ordinary course of business and in accordance with the Hold-Separate Agreements;

> 2. Use best efforts to maintain and increase revenues of the Freedom Business, and to maintain at budgeted levels for the year 2018 or the current year, whichever are higher, all administrative, technical, and marketing support for the Freedom Business and in accordance with the Hold-Separate Agreements;

> 3. Use best efforts to maintain the current workforce and to retain the services of employees and agents in connection with the Freedom Business, including payments of bonuses as necessary, and maintain the relations and goodwill with customers. [. . .]

VII.

IT IS FURTHER ORDERED that:

A. If Otto Bock has not divested, absolutely and in good faith, the Freedom Assets and Business pursuant to the requirements of Paragraph II of this Order, within the time and manner required by Paragraph II of this Order, the Commission may at any time appoint one or more Persons as Divestiture Trustee to divest the Freedom Assets and Business, at no minimum price, and pursuant to the requirements of Paragraph II of this Order, in a manner that satisfies the requirements of this Order. [. . .]

VIII.

IT IS FURTHER ORDERED that:

A. Otto Bock shall submit the complete Divestiture Agreement to the Commission at ElectronicFilings@ftc.gov and bccompliance@ftc.gov no later than 30 days after the Divestiture Date.

B. Otto Bock shall submit verified written reports ("compliance reports") in accordance with the following:

> 1. Otto Bock shall submit: a. Interim compliance reports (i) no later than thirty (30) days after the Order becomes final and effective (without regard to the finality of the divestiture requirements herein), and every thirty (30) days thereafter until the divestiture of the Freedom Assets and Business is accomplished, and (ii) thereafter, every sixty (60) days (measured from the Effective Date of Divestiture) until the date Otto Bock completes its obligations under this Order; and b. Additional compliance reports as the Commission or its staff may request.

> 2. Otto Bock shall include in its compliance reports, among other things required by the Commission, a full description of the efforts being made to comply with the relevant Paragraphs of this Order, the identity of all parties contacted, copies of 20 all written communications to and from such parties, internal documents and communications, and all reports and recommendations concerning the divestiture, the date of divestiture, and a statement that the divestiture has been accomplished in the manner approved by the Commission. Each compliance report shall contain sufficient information and documentation to enable the Commission to determine independently whether Otto Bock is in compliance with each Paragraph of the Order. Conclusory statements that Otto Bock has complied with its obligations under the Order are insufficient.

2. Behavioral Merger Remedies

The term "behavioral remedy" is a capacious one: it encompasses any remedy or relief that amounts to an instruction to the merged firm to do something or to refrain from doing something. Behavioral remedies may play a role in cases that also involve a divestiture: for example, the merged firm might be required to divest certain business units (structural remedy) *and also* to provide certain inputs, licenses, or support to the divestiture buyer on an ongoing basis for a certain period (behavioral remedy). In other cases, relief may be entirely behavioral.

Behavioral remedies are always creatures of their unique circumstances, designed to solve particular problems in light of particular market circumstances. For example, if the competitive concern is that a merged firm's upstream division may "foreclose" rivals of the downstream division, a behavioral remedy might require that the merged firm deal with such rivals on a non-discriminatory basis. Likewise, if the competitive concern is that the merged firm might access rivals' competitively sensitive information, reducing their incentives or ability to compete vigorously with the merged firm, a behavioral remedy might require that such information be firewalled off from the rest of the merged firm.

The toolkit of behavioral remedies is very broad. They may include, for example:

- obligations to supply products, services, or data at particular prices, for free, or on non-discriminatory terms;
- obligations to license intellectual property rights at particular royalty rates, for free, or on non-discriminatory terms;
- obligations to refrain from tying, conditioning, or bundling products and services in particular ways;
- obligations to refrain from seeking or incentivizing partial or complete exclusivity, either with particular trading partners or with any trading partners;
- obligations to submit to, or to offer, arbitration with trading partners regarding particular terms of dealing;
- firewalls, which require information or data to be held confidentially within the merged firm;
- obligations to communicate, or to refrain from communicating, in particular ways with customers; and
- whistleblower protection rules prohibiting retaliation for complaining to a governmental agency.

In general, behavioral relief can present any or all of three main kinds of difficulty: (1) design difficulties (*i.e.*, a government agency working on a proposed settlement or proposed court order is not always able to understand the full implications of particular choices); (2) monitoring difficulties (*i.e.*, it can be hard for an agency or court to detect violations); and (3) enforcement difficulties (*i.e.*, demonstrating a violation to a court or agency may be a difficult, costly, and lengthy process).[708] These concerns inform the general view that structural remedies should be the starting point in merger control.[709] Purely behavioral relief is much more common in conduct cases, as we shall see in Chapter XI.

A good example of purely behavioral relief is the consent decree imposed in Northrop Grumman's acquisition of Orbital ATK. The concern in that case, which united Northrop (a "prime contractor" supplier of missiles to the U.S. Government, among other defense products) with Orbital ATK (a key supplier of solid rocket motors ("SRMs") used in missiles) was a vertical one: the threat that the merged firm might foreclosure rival missile prime contractors' access to Orbital ATK's SRM motors. The following extracts include the Commission's summary of its reasoning as well as the central terms of the order itself.[710] Again, the point is to give you a flavor of the detail

---

[708] *See, e.g.*, Saint Alphonsus Med. Ctr.-Nampa Inc. v. Saint Luke's Health Sys., Ltd., 778 F.3d 775, 793 (9th Cir. 2015) (behavioral remedies "risk excessive government entanglement in the market"); ProMedica Health Sys., Inc. v. FTC, 749 F.3d 559, 573 (6th Cir. 2014) (noting that "there are usually greater long term costs associated with monitoring the efficacy of a conduct remedy than with imposing a structural solution").

[709] *See, e.g.*, Post-Trial Brief of the United States, United States v. AT&T Inc., Case No. 1:17-cv-2511 (D.D.C. filed May 8, 2018), 25 ("The United States is not aware of any Section 7 case in which a court's order of exclusively behavioral relief over the objection of the United States survived appellate review. Behavioral relief has instead been ordered in conjunction with structural relief and at the request of the United States.").

[710] *See infra* § VIII.E.3 (consent remedies in merger cases).

and granularity with which behavioral merger remedies are specified, to demonstrate the intricacy of the task: do not agonize over the details here!

FTC, Analysis of Proposed Agreement Containing Consent Order to Aid Public Comment, In the Matter of Northrop Grumman Corporation and Orbital ATK, Inc.

FTC File No. 181-0005 (F.T.C. June 5, 2018)

[1] The Federal Trade Commission ("Commission") has accepted an Agreement Containing Consent Order ("Consent Agreement") designed to remedy the anticompetitive effects resulting from Northrop Grumman Corporation's ("Northrop") proposed acquisition of Orbital ATK, Inc. ("Orbital ATK"). Under the terms of the Consent Agreement, Northrop would be required to (1) continue to act as a non-discriminatory merchant supplier of Orbital ATK's solid rocket motors ("SRMs") rather than favor its now-vertically integrated missile system business, and (2) protect SRM and missile system competitors' competitively sensitive information from improper use or disclosure. [. . .]

[2] The Commission's Complaint alleges that the Acquisition is in violation of Section 5 of the FTC Act, as amended, 15 U.S.C. § 45, and that the acquisition, if consummated, would violate Section 7 of the Clayton Act, as amended, 15 U.S.C. § 18, and Section 5 of the FTC Act, as amended, 15 U.S.C. § 45, by lessening the competition in the United States market for missile systems. The Acquisition would provide Northrop with the ability and incentive to withhold its SRMs from competing missile system prime contractors, or only offer its SRMs at disadvantageous terms, thereby raising rivals' costs or otherwise undermining their ability to compete on future missile system bids. The Consent Agreement will remedy the alleged violations by prohibiting Northrop from discriminating against competing missile prime customers in supplying SRMs. [. . .]

[3] Northrop is one of only four companies capable of supplying missile systems to the United States Government. Missile systems provide essential national defense capabilities for the United States Government. The United States Armed Forces employ multiple types of missile systems, including short-range tactical missiles, longer-range strategic missiles, and missile defense interceptors designed to defeat ballistic missile threats. Each type of missile system purchased by DOD has unique capabilities and is designed specifically to perform its given mission(s).

[4] Orbital ATK is one of only two viable suppliers of SRMs for U.S. Government missile systems and the dominant supplier of large SRMs used for long-range strategic missiles. SRMs are used to propel tactical, missile defense, and strategic missiles to their intended targets. SRMs are used for virtually all missile systems purchased by the United States Government because they offer numerous advantages over all other existing propulsion technologies. [. . .]

[5] Following the Acquisition, Northrop will be one of only two viable suppliers of SRMs for U.S. Government missile systems. The choice of SRM can have a significant impact on the final determination of a missile system prime competition because the propulsion system is a critical element of the overall missile design. SRMs comprise a large portion of the cost of the integrated missile and their performance affects the range, accuracy, and payload capacity of the missile. Absent the protections of the Consent Agreement, Northrop would have the ability to disadvantage competitors for future missile prime contracts by denying or limiting their access to Northrop's SRM products and technologies, which would lessen the ability of Northrop's missile system competitors to compete successfully for a given missile system prime contract. The Acquisition would also give Northrop access, through the former Orbital ATK SRM business, to the proprietary information that rival missile prime contractors must share with its SRM vendor. Similarly, the Acquisition creates a risk that the proprietary, competitively sensitive information of a rival SRM supplier supporting Northrop's missile system business could be transferred to Northrop's vertically integrated SRM business. [. . .]

[6] The Consent Agreement remedies the acquisition's likely anticompetitive effects by requiring, whenever Northrop competes for a missile system prime contract, that Northrop must make its SRM products and related services available on a non-discriminatory basis to all other third-party competing prime contractors that wish to purchase them. The non-discrimination prohibitions of the Consent Agreement are comprehensive and apply to

any potential discriminatory conduct affecting price, schedule, quality, data, personnel, investment, technology, innovation, design, or risk.

[7] The Consent Agreement requires Northrop to establish firewalls to ensure that Northrop does not transfer or use any proprietary information that it receives from competing missile prime contractors or SRM suppliers in a manner that harms competition. These firewall provisions require that Northrop maintain separate firewalled teams to support offers of SRMs to different third-party missile prime contractors and to maintain these firewalled teams separate from the team supporting Northrop's missile prime contractor activities. The firewall provisions also prohibit Northrop's missile business from sharing proprietary information it may receive from third-party SRM suppliers with Northrop's SRM business.

[8] The Consent Agreement also provides that the [Department of Defense's] Under Secretary of Defense for Acquisition and Sustainment shall appoint a compliance officer to oversee Northrop's compliance with the Order. The compliance officer will have all the necessary investigative powers to perform his or her duties, including the right to interview respondent's personnel, inspect respondent's facilities, and require respondents to provide documents, data, and other information. The compliance officer has the authority to retain third-party advisors, at the expense of Northrop, as appropriate to perform his or her duties. Access to these extensive resources will ensure that the compliance officer is fully capable of overseeing the implementation of, and compliance with, the Order.

* * *

FTC, Decision & Order, In the Matter of Northrop Grumman Corporation and Orbital ATK, Inc.

FTC File No. 181-0005 (F.T.C. June 5, 2018)

II.

IT IS FURTHER ORDERED THAT:

A. Respondents shall not Discriminate in any Missile Competition where Northrop: (i) is currently competing to be the Prime Contractor; or (ii) has the capability to compete and has taken the steps identified in Paragraph IV. and continues to take steps to compete as a Prime Contractor. By way of example, Respondents shall:

> 1. Not Discriminate in developing or providing an Offer requested by or made to a Third Party Prime Contractor, or in supporting the proposal of the Third Party Prime Contractor in connection with the Offer;

> 2. Not Discriminate in providing SRM Information;

> 3. Not Discriminate regarding staffing, resource allocation, or design decisions in connection with SRMs and Related Services to be provided to any Third Party Prime Contractor;

> 4. Not Discriminate in making any Offers to, or entering into Collaborative Agreements or other similar arrangements with, any Third Party Prime Contractor, or in the negotiation of such Offers, agreements, or other arrangements with Third Party Prime Contractors; Provided, however, that no provision of this Order shall require Respondents to provide products, services or technologies, including SRMs and Related Services, to any Third Party without commercially reasonable terms or if it is commercially unreasonable because (i) the Northrop SRM Business does not have the technical capability to supply the Third Party Prime Contractor or (ii) the Northrop SRM Business does not have the capacity (and it is not commercially reasonable to expand its capacity) to provide SRMs or a Firewalled SRM Customer Team to one or more Prime Contractors that have requested such services or team because the number or burden of Prime Contractors seeking the benefit of Paragraph II.A. of this Order becomes unreasonably large, so long as Respondents are providing SRMs and Related Services to at least one Third Party Prime Contractor in the applicable Missile Competition;

5. Not Discriminate in making available for use in Missile Competitions any technologies for SRMs and Related Services developed by the Northrop SRM Business under independent research and development funding, government-funded research and development activities or other funds expended by the Northrop SRM Business; provided, however, that Respondents shall be under no obligation to disclose or offer the products or other results of any joint investment or development activity engaged in with one Prime Contractor (including Northrop) to any other Prime Contractor in the applicable Missile Competition;

6. Establish and maintain separate Firewalled SRM Customer Teams as required by Paragraph III. of this Order to support each Third Party Prime Contractor; and

7. As to each separate Firewalled SRM Customer Team, take all steps reasonably necessary to ensure that a Prime Contractor's Non-Public Missile Information is kept confidential and protected from unauthorized disclosure and use, including such steps as Respondents would take to protect their own Non-Public Information and as required pursuant to Paragraph III.

B. The provision of any protected information, technology, or product to the Respondents by any Third Party, or to any Third Party by the Respondents, pursuant to this Order shall be subject to appropriate customary confidentiality agreements on the treatment of competitively-sensitive, national security-sensitive, ITAR-controlled, and/or proprietary information. Notwithstanding any other provision of this Order, Respondents shall not be required to provide any information to any Persons, including at the DoD or a Third Party Prime Contractor, if they do not have the security clearance required to be eligible to receive such information. [. . .]

D. The purpose of the provisions of Paragraph II. of this Order is to assure that the Northrop SRM Business continues to provide its services to Third Party Prime Contractors in any Missile Competition after the Acquisition on a non-discriminatory basis and in the same manner and of the same performance level and quality as before the Acquisition, and to remedy the lessening of competition resulting from the Acquisition as alleged in the Commission's Complaint

III.

IT IS FURTHER ORDERED THAT Respondents shall protect a Third Party Prime Contractor's Non-Public Missile Information and Non-Public SRM Information in any Missile Competition where Northrop (i) is currently competing to be the Prime Contractor or (ii) has the capability to compete and has taken the steps identified in Paragraph IV. and continues to take steps to compete as a Prime Contractor. Specifically, Respondents shall take all actions as are reasonably necessary and appropriate to prevent access to, or the disclosure or use of, any Non-Public Missile Information or Non-Public SRM Information by or to any Person(s) not authorized to access, receive, or use such Non-Public Information pursuant to the terms of this Order, and shall develop and implement procedures and requirements to protect such Non-Public Information and to comply with the prohibitions and requirements of this Order, including, but not limited to, taking the following actions in any such Missile Competition covered by Paragraph II. of this Order to protect such Non-Public Information:

A. Northrop Firewalled SRM Customer Teams shall maintain firewalls and confidentiality protections, consistent with company practices and industry standards, and in compliance with the following requirements and prohibitions:

1. Northrop Personnel assigned to the Firewalled SRM Customer Teams shall receive training on the restrictions on the disclosure, use, and dissemination of Non-Public Information and, following completion of the relevant Missile Competition, will be reminded of their ongoing obligations with respect to such Non-Public Information;

2. Northrop Personnel assigned to the Firewalled SRM Customer Teams shall sign appropriate non-disclosure or equivalent agreements providing written acknowledgement of their responsibilities regarding the restrictions on the use and dissemination of Non-Public Information;

3. Northrop shall keep separate and limit access to Non-Public Missile Information and Non-Public SRM Information of the respective Firewalled SRM Customer Teams, e.g., by separating data in information

systems; physically separating, securing, and/or shielding prototypes, models, and hard copies of such NonPublic Information; utilizing identification badge hangers to identify members of Firewalled SRM Customer Teams; and employing other processes designed to confine the flow of such Non-Public Information to personnel who have permission to see it in connection with the Missile Competition;

4. No member of a Firewalled SRM Customer Team supporting a Third Party Prime Contractor in a Missile Competition where Northrop is currently competing to be the Prime Contractor or has the capability to compete and has taken the steps identified in Paragraph IV. and continues to take steps to compete as a Prime Contractor (i) may participate in any way, directly or indirectly, in support of Respondents' efforts to participate as a Prime Contractor in the Missile Competition, including the preparation or review of a proposal or other response to a Request for Information, Request for Proposal or similar inquiry from the Government Customer or (ii) disclose any Non-Public Missile Information to any Northrop Personnel outside the Firewalled SRM Customer Team, except as permitted in Paragraph III.A.5. or Paragraph III.D. of this Order; [. . .]

B. The Firewalled SRM Customer Teams shall protect all Non-Public Missile Information, such that, absent a Third Party Prime Contractor's prior written consent or otherwise as provided below, the Firewalled SRM Customer Teams shall not:

1. Disclose any of that Third Party Prime Contractor's Non-Public Missile Information to Northrop Personnel in a Firewalled SRM Customer Team supporting Northrop or another Third Party Prime Contractor, or

2. Use that Third Party Prime Contractor's Non-Public Missile Information for any purpose other than developing or providing an Offer requested by or made to that Third Party Prime Contractor, or in supporting the proposal of that Third Party Prime Contractor in connection with the Offer.

C. The Northrop Missile Business shall take all reasonable steps to protect any Non-Public SRM Information, and shall not provide, disclose, or otherwise make any Non-Public SRM Information available to the Northrop SRM Business. Northrop shall use Non-Public SRM Information only in Northrop's capacity as a Prime Contractor absent the prior written consent of the proprietor of the Non-Public SRM Information. [. . .]

V. IT IS FURTHER ORDERED THAT:

A. The Under Secretary of Defense for Acquisition and Sustainment shall appoint a Compliance Officer, who shall be an employee of the United States government not otherwise involved in Missile Competitions or in setting the requirements for or the procurement of SRMs, Missiles or Missile Systems. The Compliance Officer shall have the power and authority to oversee compliance by the Respondents with the terms of this Order.

B. To the extent reasonably necessary to perform his or her duties and responsibilities pursuant to this Order, and subject to any legally recognized privilege or other forms of protection of information, the Compliance Officer shall be authorized to and may, in the presence of counsel for Northrop:

1. during normal business hours, interview any of Respondents' personnel, upon three days' notice to that Respondent and without restraint or interference by Respondents, relating to any matters contained in this Order;

2. during normal business hours, inspect and copy any document in the possession, custody, or control of Respondents relating to any matters contained in this Order;

3. during normal business hours, obtain access to and inspect any systems or equipment, relating to any matters contained in this Order, to which Respondents' personnel have access;

4. during normal business hours, obtain access to and inspect any physical facility, building, or other premises, relating to any matters contained in this Order, to which Respondents' personnel have access; and

5. require Respondents to provide access to documents, data, and other information, relating to any matters contained in this Order, to the Compliance Officer in such form as the Compliance Officer may reasonably direct and within such time periods as the Compliance Officer may reasonably require.

C. Respondents shall timely comply with the Compliance Officer's reasonable requests relating to Respondents' compliance with their obligations pursuant to this Order, and the Compliance Officer shall not unreasonably withhold approval of any request for additional time.

VI.

IT IS FURTHER ORDERED THAT:

A. Respondents shall develop and implement written procedures and protocols and maintain a system of access and data controls, with the advice and assistance of the Compliance Officer, to comply with the requirements of this Order, which shall include, but not be limited to, procedures for:

1. Monitoring compliance;

2. Requiring and enforcing compliance with appropriate remedial action in the event of non-compliance;

3. Notifying the Compliance Officer and any Third Party Advisor of any noncompliance of the requirements of Paragraph III. of the Order.

B. Respondents shall design, maintain, and operate a Compliance Program to assure compliance with the requirements and prohibitions of this Order, which shall include, but not be limited to:

1. Designating an officer or other individual to supervise personally the design, maintenance, and operation of the Compliance Program, and to be available on an ongoing basis to respond to any questions by employees of Respondents;

2. Distributing a copy of the Order to all members of (i) a Firewalled SRM Customer Team; (ii) the TAS Group; (iii) the Management Oversight Group; or (iv) the Northrop Personnel who are developing a proposal or otherwise preparing for Northrop to compete as Prime Contractor in a Missile Competition

a. Within thirty (30) days of the date this Order becomes final; and

b. Annually within thirty (30) days of the anniversary of the date this Order becomes final until the Order terminates;

3. Training on the requirements of this Order for all members of (i) a Firewalled SRM Customer Team; (ii) the TAS Group; (iii) the Management Oversight Group; or (iv) the Northrop Personnel who are developing a proposal or otherwise preparing for Northrop to compete as a Prime Contractor in a Missile Competition;

4. The retention of documents and records sufficient to record Respondents' compliance with its obligations under this Paragraph VI. of this Order.

VII.

IT IS FURTHER ORDERED THAT:

A. Respondent Northrop shall notify the Commission and its staff, the DoD, and the Compliance Officer of the Acquisition Date no later than five days after the Acquisition Date. Respondent Northrop shall notify the Commission via email to the Secretary of the Commission with electronic copies to the Secretary at ElectronicFilings@ftc.gov, and shall provide notice to staff of the Compliance Division via email to bccompliance@ftc.gov.

B. Respondents shall submit verified written reports ("compliance reports") in accordance with the following:

1. [. . .]

2. Each compliance report shall set forth in detail the manner and form in which Respondents intend to comply, are complying, and have complied with this Order, including, as applicable:

> a. the name and status of all Missile Competitions where Northrop is a competitor (or, for potential future Missile Competitions, when Northrop has the capability to compete and has taken steps in anticipation of potentially competing pursuant to Paragraph IV.) to be the Prime Contractor;

> b. the identity of all Third Party Prime Contractors seeking SRMs from Northrop for any such Missile Competition and the status of such request for each Third Party Prime Contractor; and

> c. such other information as the Compliance Officer may request.

* * *

CASENOTE: The Evanston Hospital Remedy

In the matter of Evanston Northwestern Healthcare Corp., 2007 WL 2286195 (F.T.C. Aug. 6, 2007)

The legacy of the *Evanston Hospital* hospital merger litigation is a complicated one. In 2000, Evanston Northwestern Healthcare Corp. ("Evanston"), a two-hospital system, merged with Highland Park Hospital ("Highland"). Four years later (!), the FTC sued in Part 3 administrative court under Section 7. (The Part 3 process is described in more detail in Chapter XI.) The FTC's Administrative Law Judge ("ALJ") imposed liability and required divestiture of Highland, and the merging parties appealed to the Commission.

The Commission upheld the ALJ's decision on liability. The merged firm had "substantially" raised its prices after the deal, and the weight of econometric evidence tended to exclude most likely benign explanations for the price increase. The inference of competitive harm was also consistent with the documentary evidence: the Commission pointed out that "the merging parties' documents reflect that a primary motivation of the senior officials in agreeing to merge the hospitals was to increase their bargaining leverage with MCOs in order to raise prices." For example, the minutes of one meeting recorded an Evanston employee's comment that the deal "would be an opportunity to join forces and grow together rather than compete with each other." The Commission noted that these documents "reflect[ed] the merging parties' unvarnished contemporaneous analyses of the parties' market positions by their most senior officials. The statements are not simple bravado or unsubstantiated hyperbole from middle managers or sales representatives." The Commission concluded that the deal had enabled the merged firm to exercise market power, and that it had resulted in a price increase of at least 9–10%.

But things got sticky on remedy. The Commission began by acknowledging that structural remedies are "preferred" in merger cases, including by reason of divestiture's superior efficacy and lower monitoring costs, compared with behavioral relief. But the Commission concluded that a breakup would not be in the public interest in this case.

The Commission relied on a number of considerations to reach this conclusion. First, and perhaps most obviously, a long time had elapsed since the consummation of the deal in 2000 and the end of the litigation in 2007. This increased the difficulty of a divestiture remedy, as well as its costs and risks of failure. Second, the parties had implemented certain improvements to the acquired facilities: regardless of whether these were cognizable efficiencies under the merger guidelines, they constituted real benefits that a divestiture would jeopardize or reduce.

Third, the Commission emphasized its concern that a divestiture could harm the quality of patient care at Highland. There was particular reason to fear for Highland's cardiac surgery program: "Complaint counsel's [*i.e.*, the FTC staff's] expert . . . testified that it was not clear whether, without Evanston, Highland Park would have the volume that it needed to maintain the cardiac surgery program. If Highland Park lost its cardiac surgery program, or if the quality of its surgical program diminished, then the quality of patient care to the community would suffer. Highland Park would need to transport some or all of its patients needing emergency cardiac surgery to other hospitals, potentially creating life-threatening risks. The possibility of a delay in reestablishing cardiac surgery services at Highland Park is a significant factor that we must weigh in considering a remedy." In addition, Highland's ability to use the EPIC record keeping software would be imperiled, raising "concern[s] about the potential effects on patient care from the inevitable glitches involved in Highland Park's swapping out complex software systems."

As a result, the Commission opted for behavioral relief of a very unusual kind. "[W]e reject divestiture as a remedy and will impose an injunctive remedy that requires respondent to establish separate and independent negotiating teams—one for Evanston and Glenbrook Hospitals ("E&G"), and another for Highland Park. While not ideal, this remedy will allow [managed care organizations ("MCOs")] to negotiate separately again for these competing hospitals, thus re-injecting competition between them for the business of MCOs." The Commission warned that this would not signal a change in remedies policy for future cases: divestiture remained the preferred remedy.

Although this remedy is widely regarded as a unique effort to make the best of an unfortunate situation, the *Evanston Hospital* litigation itself claims a more positive legacy for merger enforcement. The case marked the first substantive victory for the antitrust agencies in many years in a merger case: the result of a multi-year program—the Merger Litigation Task Force, inaugurated by then-Director Joe Simons of the Bureau of Competition in August 2002 to figure out how to break the federal government's long losing streak in such cases.[711] In the years since *Evanston*, the Commission has lost just one hospital merger litigation.[712]

3. Negotiated Remedies in Merger Cases

Most merger "remedies" in practice are not imposed by courts after victory in litigation, but are negotiated between an agency and the merging parties.

Generally speaking, negotiated merger remedies arise in two types of situations. The first involves transactions that raise competitive concerns with respect to some business lines but not others. Thus, for example, suppose that Company A has a car business, a motorbike business, and a speedboat business, and that it plans to merge with Company B, which makes only speedboats. That deal might raise competitive concerns only with respect to speedboat markets. In this kind of situation, the merger would likely not raise competitive concerns as long as Company A's speedboat business was carved out of the deal by "divesting" (selling) it to another buyer that would operate it with equal competitive vigor. The second involves transactions that raise concerns that— notwithstanding the general preference for structural relief—really can be adequately addressed with a behavioral order, allowing the transaction to proceed with the remedy in place.

Most commonly, a negotiated divestiture remedy involves the company working with the antitrust agencies to identify the areas of competitive concern presented by the transaction, and then working to identify one or more potential "divestiture buyers" who would be suitable stewards of the divested businesses. The company and the agency then typically enter into a consent decree or settlement agreement—entered by a federal court for a DOJ case (and subject to Tunney Act review), or entered by the Commission or a federal court in an FTC case[713]—in which the merging parties agree to undertake the relevant divestiture, and perhaps to provide certain kinds of interim support for the divested business to help assure the continued viability of the divestiture package. The court and/or the FTC typically retains ongoing jurisdiction over the remedial order to ensure compliance with the terms. For example, the remedy in Northrop/Orbital ATK, excerpted above, was imposed by consent decree.

"DIY" Merger Remedies and Litigating the Fix

In some cases, merging parties might try to design their own divestiture in a "fix-it-first" move, by selling off the business units that are likely to raise concerns before turning to the ultimate transaction.[714] From the company's

---

[711] *See* Press Release, Federal Trade Commission Announces Formation of Merger Litigation Task Force (Aug. 28, 2002), ("The Task Force will be responsible for reinvigorating the Commission's hospital merger program[.]").

[712] FTC v. Thomas Jefferson Univ., 505 F. Supp. 3d 522, 527 (E.D. Pa. 2020).

[713] For discussion of agency procedures and the differences between FTC and DOJ litigations, *see infra* Chapter XI.

[714] We are setting aside here the applicability of HSR merger notification rules. *See infra* § XI.E.

perspective, this path has the advantage of avoiding the time and expense of agency engagement, but it runs the risk that the agency may conclude that the fix—in which agency staff did not participate—was competitively inadequate. And from the public's point of view, this path has the disadvantage of sacrificing agency oversight of the proposed deal (including the nature of the package and the adequacy of the buyer) and ongoing monitoring and jurisdiction to deal with any concerns.[715]

In other cases, merging parties might offer, or just unilaterally implement, a fix of some kind during an investigation or litigation. In a number of cases, courts have been willing to evaluate under Section 7 not the transaction as originally formulated and notified to the agencies under the HSR merger notification system, but as modified by the parties with divestitures or unilateral commitments.[716] "Litigating the fix" in this way can be a stiff challenge for an enforcement agency.[717]

In practice, the agencies' negotiated merger remedies appear generally, if imperfectly, successful. In January 2017, the FTC released a study of merger remedies between 2006 and 2012. The following extract summarizes some of its conclusions.

FTC, The FTC's Merger Remedies 2006-2012: A Report of the Bureaus of Competition and Economics (January 2017)

[1] The . . . study evaluated the success of each [consent] remedy and examined the remedy process more generally. Staff used three methods to conduct the study. First, staff examined 50 of the Commission's orders using a case study method. . . . [S]taff interviewed buyers of divested assets and the merged firms. Staff also interviewed other market participants and analyzed seven years of sales data gathered from significant competitors. Second, staff evaluated an additional 15 orders affecting supermarkets, drug stores, funeral homes, dialysis clinics, and other health care facilities by examining responses to questionnaires directed to Commission-approved buyers in the relevant transactions. Finally, staff evaluated 24 orders affecting the pharmaceutical industry using both internal and publicly available information and data. In all, staff reviewed 89 orders and conducted more than 200 interviews, analyzed sales data submitted by almost 200 firms, examined responses to almost 30 questionnaires, and reviewed significant additional information related to the pharmaceutical industry.

[2] In evaluating the 50 orders in the case study component, Commission staff considered a merger remedy to be successful only if it cleared a high bar—maintaining or restoring competition in the relevant market. Using that standard, all of the divestitures involving an ongoing business succeeded. Divestitures of limited packages of assets in horizontal, non-consummated mergers fared less well, but still achieved a success rate of approximately 70%.

[715] For some criticism of agency practices that might lead to more "off the books" remedies of this kind, see Noah J. Phillips, *Disparate Impact: Winners and Losers from the New M&A Policy* (remarks of Apr. 27, 2022) 8–9 ("Without a consent, there is nothing for enforcers to approve. Sure, this strategy probably will push a few otherwise settleable matters into expensive, uncertain litigation and force staff to review prior approval applications for transactions that would not otherwise merit investigation. Fine, companies will fix it first. And, yes, the agencies will be less effective and efficient as a result. But at least the leadership will be able to dodge some difficult and unpopular decisions. This is a political benefit, not a policy. I am very concerned we are going to start seeing deals with divestitures but without consents. There are today murmurings in the private bar that the agencies are refusing to engage on remedies, and instead are conveying their competitive concerns and leaving it up to the merging parties to attempt a resolution. This is fixing it first with a wink and a nod—and no enforceable agreement with the government. As a result, the public loses out on the protections that a consent agreement provides—including, ironically, prior approval policy. Only agency heads, who get to avoid the appearance of blessing mergers, gain. Reading strident dissents about failed remedies for years, it never occurred to me that one solution might be neither blocking nor remediating deals at all.").

[716] *See, e.g.*, United States v. AT&T, Inc., 916 F.3d 1029, 1042–43 (D.C. Cir. 2019) (relying in part on post-complaint "irrevocable offers" to arbitrate prices and terms with downstream trading partners); United States v. UnitedHealth Group, Ltd., __ F. Supp. 3d. __, 2022 WL 4365867, at *8–10 & n.5 (D.D.C. Sept. 21, 2022) (discussing the analytical framework for a DIY divestiture announced between HSR notification and complaint, pursuant to an agreement entered into following the complaint, indicating that the relevant transaction for legal analysis is the *modified* transaction, but applying a more pro-plaintiff test because the Court concluded that the same outcome would result); Initial Decision, In the matter of Illumina, Inc., and Grail Inc., FTC Dkt. No. 9401, 2022 WL 4199859 (F.T.C. 2022), § III.D.3. (declining to block deal, partly in light of an "open offer" that would protect against foreclosure).

[717] *See, e.g.*, Steven C. Salop & Jennifer Sturiale, *Fixing "Litigating the Fix,"* Georgetown Law Faculty Working Paper No. 2470 (October 2022); Katherine M. Ambrogi, *The Elephant in the Courtroom: Litigating the Premerger Fix in* Arch Coal *and Beyond*, 47 Wm. & Mary L. Rev. 1781 (2006); David Gelfand & Leah Brannon, *A Primer on Litigating the Fix*, 31 Antitrust 10 (2016).

Remedies addressing vertical mergers also succeeded. Overall, with respect to the 50 orders examined, more than 80% of the Commission's orders maintained or restored competition.

[3] For the remedies involving supermarkets, drug stores, funeral homes, dialysis clinics, and other health care facilities evaluated as part of the questionnaire portion of the study, the vast majority of the assets divested under those 15 orders are still operating in the relevant markets. And, with respect to the 24 orders affecting the pharmaceutical industry, the majority of buyers that acquired products on the market at the time of the divestiture continued to sell those products. Additionally, all of the divested assets relating to products that were in development and not available on the market at the time of the divestiture were successfully transferred to the approved buyers.

[4] The study also confirmed that the Commission's practices relating to designing, drafting, and implementing its merger remedies are generally effective, but it identified certain areas in which improvements can be made. Specifically, some buyers expressed concerns with the scope of the asset package, the adequacy of the due diligence, and the transfer of back-office functions. While the concerns raised may not have interfered with buyers' ability to compete in the relevant markets over the long term, they may have resulted in additional challenges that buyers had to work around or otherwise overcome. Staff has already taken various steps to address these concerns. They include asking additional targeted questions about remedy proposals to divest limited asset packages, asking more focused questions about financing, and monitoring the due diligence process even more carefully. Staff is also more closely scrutinizing buyers' back-office needs, and, in some cases, is considering additional order language. Finally, the study surprisingly revealed that there continued to be a reluctance among buyers to raise concerns with staff and independent monitors when they arose. Staff is increasing efforts to remind buyers of the benefits of reaching out to staff or monitors when issues arise.

* * *

In recent years, while the use of remedial consent decrees continues to be an indispensable part of the work of the federal agencies, the practice has attracted some criticism from commentators on the right and left.[718] In the following extracts, note the different treatment, less than ten years apart, of the options of litigation and settlement!

Deborah L. Feinstein, The Significance of Consent Orders in the Federal Trade Commission's Competition Enforcement Efforts, Remarks of Sept. 17, 2013

[1] I would like to start by discussing generally why the Commission settles rather than litigates in certain matters.

[2] Above all, although they are often lower profile, in appropriate cases, consent orders are as effective in maintaining or restoring competition as going to court. A well-crafted consent order can achieve divestitures necessary to preserve existing levels of competition, stop anticompetitive conduct, cause firms to take additional steps to restore competition, or clear away impediments to future competition. Where a consent order can address the harm the Commission alleges has occurred or is likely to occur without the need for litigation, there are enormous benefits to resolving matters through consent orders.

[3] First, resolving a matter through a consent order can lead to a quicker resolution of a matter. Litigation takes considerable time, and may prolong the anticompetitive effects of the illegal conduct and delay implementation of the remedy. The most obvious examples involve ongoing anticompetitive conduct or a consummated merger. Even where a merger is not consummated, obtaining relief quickly is important. Competition can be affected during the pendency of a merger. For example, customers and employees may go elsewhere because of the uncertainty related to the transaction. Plans of the parties may get put on hold while they consider what they might

---

[718] See Douglas H. Ginsburg & Joshua D. Wright, *Antitrust Settlements: The Culture of Consent* in Nicolas Charbit et al. (eds.) 1 WILLIAM E. KOVACIC: AN ANTITRUST TRIBUTE – LIBER AMICORUM (February 2013) (arguing that agencies can use consent decrees to extract more stringent relief than they would obtain in court); Open Markets Institute, Public Comments Submitted by the Open Markets Institute for the Antitrust Division's Roundtable on Antitrust Consent Decrees (Apr. 20, 2018) ("In many instances, consent decrees fail to strike at the root of anti-competitive conduct. They often serve as band-aid solutions that seek to regulate the harms generated by market power without addressing the underlying incentive and ability that firms have to wield it. Moreover, consent decrees can introduce unwieldy regulatory regimes that are both difficult to administer and susceptible to runarounds by the private parties they are intended to cover.").

do jointly if the transaction proceeds. And, although unlawful, there is always the potential for gun-jumping which can also harm competition.

[4] Second, in addition to being time-consuming, litigation is resource intensive. In this regard, the Commission seeks to be a good steward of public resources. Resolving a matter through a consent order frees up resources to be spent on investigating, and if necessary challenging other anticompetitive mergers or conduct. And it is not only Commission resources that are at stake. While decisions on fully litigated records may provide greater guidance on the state of the law, it is generally not good public policy to impose substantial costs on respondents and third parties to bring to trial matters that can be settled based on the sound application of law to the substantial record the Commission has developed during an investigation.

[5] Third, litigation is uncertain. And it is important, especially in unconsummated mergers, to achieve a remedy before the eggs are scrambled and a remedy becomes unavailable or less effective. Sometimes, even when we ultimately win, it can be a bittersweet victory. This was the outcome recently when the Commission settled its case challenging the acquisition of Palmyra Park Hospital by its only hospital competitor in Albany Georgia. [. . .]

[6] Fourth, litigation can be a blunt instrument—especially federal court injunction cases where a merger is either blocked or allowed to proceed in its entirety. In some cases, the decision to litigate is the result of rejecting a settlement proposal and accepting that the litigation outcome will be all or nothing. In contrast, a consent order allows us to be surgical in our approach—to eliminate the anticompetitive aspects of a transaction or conduct with the detailed information needed to do so while not adversely affecting procompetitive aspects of an arrangement.

[7] Finally, as I noted at the outset, in addition to maintaining or restoring competition, consents can provide significant guidance as to how the Commission views the competitive issues raised by a particular transaction or conduct.

* * *

Jonathan Kanter, Remarks to the New York State Bar Association Antitrust Section (Jan. 24, 2022)

[1] I would . . . like to touch briefly on how we remedy antitrust violations. . . . [Former AAG Robert] Jackson's wisdom guides us. "We should not spend great sums to obtain decrees which are economically unenforceable," he said, "and, when carried out in form, are often only lessons in futility."

[2] Like Jackson, I am focused on how a remedy will function. After the ink has dried and the press cycle has faded, does a settlement in fact restore competition? Does it preserve the competitive process? Most importantly, does our overall approach to remedies, carried out across cases and industries, protect competition as the law demands? We are law enforcers, not regulators.

[3] I am concerned that merger remedies short of blocking a transaction too often miss the mark. Complex settlements, whether behavioral or structural, suffer from significant deficiencies. Therefore, in my view, when the division concludes that a merger is likely to lessen competition, in most situations we should seek a simple injunction to block the transaction. It is the surest way to preserve competition.

[4] Let me explain why. First, determining the contours of a remedy that carves up a business to maintain competition assumes we can capture with precision the contours of competition in the market. Competition is not static, however. It is dynamic, complex and often multidimensional. How do we determine the appropriate divestiture for evolving business models and innovative markets?

[5] We must give full weight to the benefits of preserving competition that already exists in a market, rather than predicting whether a divestiture will actually serve to keep a market competitive. That will often mean that we cannot accept anything less than an injunction blocking the merger—full stop.

[6] Moreover, merger settlements that include partial divestitures too often result in what might be called "concentration creep." This happens when divested assets end up in the hands of someone that does not make

effective use of them. Divestiture buyers may lose interest in assets after acquiring them, or be less effective than they expected.

[7] Finally, settlements do not move the law forward. We need new published opinions from courts that apply the law in modern markets in order to provide clarity to businesses. This requires litigation that sets out the boundaries of the law as applied to current markets, and we need to be willing to take risks and ask the courts to reconsider the application of old precedents to those markets.

[8] That is not to say divestitures should never be an option. Sometimes business units are sufficiently discrete and complete that disentangling them from the parent company in a non-dynamic market is a straightforward exercise, where a divestiture has a high degree of success. But in my view those circumstances are the exception, not the rule.

F. Some Further Reading

Jonathan B. Baker, *Contemporary Empirical Merger Analysis*, 5 Geo. Mason L. Rev. 347 (1997)

Marissa Beck & Fiona Scott Morton, *Evaluating the Evidence on Vertical Mergers*, 59 Rev. Indus. Org. 273 (2021)

Eleanor Fox, *U.S. and European Merger Policy – Fault Lines and Bridges – Mergers That Create Incentives for Exclusionary Practices*, 10 Geo. Mason L. Rev. 471 (2002)

FTC, COMMENTARY ON VERTICAL MERGER ENFORCEMENT (Dec. 2020)

FTC & U.S. Department of Justice, COMMENTARY ON THE HORIZONTAL MERGER GUIDELINES (2006)

C. Scott Hemphill & Nancy Rose, *Mergers that Harm Sellers*, 127 Yale L.J. 2078 (2018)

Herbert Hovenkamp, *Prophylactic Merger Policy*, 70 Hastings L.J. 45 (2018)

Herbert Hovenkamp & Carl Shapiro, *Horizontal Mergers, Market Structure, and Burdens of Proof*, 127 Yale L.J. 1997 (2018)

Keith N. Hylton, Brown Shoe *Versus the Horizontal Merger Guidelines*, 39 Rev. Indus. Org. 95 (2011)

Francine Lafontaine & Margaret Slade, *Vertical Integration and Firm Boundaries*, 45 J. Econ. Lit. 629 (2007);

John Kwoka, MERGERS, MERGER CONTROL AND REMEDIES (2014)

Naomi R. Lamoureux, THE GREAT MERGER MOVEMENT IN AMERICAN BUSINESS, 1895–1904 (1985)

David J. Ravenscraft & F.M. Scherer, MERGERS, SELL-OFFS & ECONOMIC EFFICIENCY (1987)

Steven C. Salop, *A Suggested Revision of the 2020 Vertical Merger Guidelines* (December 2021)

Carl Shapiro, *The 2010 Horizontal Merger Guidelines: From Hedgehog to Fox in Forty Years*, 77 Antitrust L.J. 49 (2010)

IX. Immunities and Exemptions

A. Overview

Although the antitrust laws establish a set of ground rules that apply broadly across the U.S. economy, their coverage has been limited by a modest number of immunities and exemptions. Some of these, like the statutory immunity for labor unions, have been established by Congress; others have been "recognized" by the judiciary for a variety of reasons over the long history of the antitrust system. This chapter surveys some of the most important of these carveouts from the general reach of the antitrust laws.

In part, these immunities reflect the fact that economic competition (and, particularly, the version of "competition" that antitrust doctrine acknowledges and protects) is not always or automatically the highest, or only, relevant value in our society. Within its scope, as we have seen, antitrust doctrine tends to give little room for parties to advance arguments unrelated to competition, as the antitrust laws define it.[719] As a result, such values are accommodated, in part, through the introduction of immunities. For example, the recognition that atomistic competition among workers is not always desirable helps to underpin the immunity of certain labor practices.

In general, antitrust exemptions are fairly rare: Congress and the courts have created them infrequently and with great caution. The Supreme Court has emphasized that judicial exemptions are generally disfavored, and that all exceptions to the antitrust laws—judicial and legislative alike—should be construed narrowly.[720]

In the following pages, we will meet a series of exceptions and immunities, and consider the scope and rationale of each. Section B considers the immunity accorded to "petitioning" conduct under the "*Noerr-Pennington*" doctrine; Section C introduces the "state action" doctrine that protects the conduct of state governments (and some others acting under some measure of state governments' authority) from antitrust scrutiny; Section D describes the immunity for certain practices relating to labor; Section E briefly presents a variety of other, narrower, antitrust exemptions, covering activities from agriculture to baseball.

B. *"Noerr-Pennington"* Petitioning Immunity

The "*Noerr-Pennington*" doctrine protects so-called "petitioning"—that is, conduct that involves soliciting some form of government action—from antitrust liability. It covers conduct ranging from legislative and executive lobbying to litigation. The core concept is that the antitrust system should not deter or punish efforts to access the government, on the basis that freedom of recourse to courts and to the political branches is even more important than the protection of competition. As we shall see, the doctrine has been understood as a reflection of the values of the First Amendment, as well as an interpretation of the intent of the Sherman Act legislators.

But the exception is not limitless, and it does not give businesses free rein to use and abuse governmental processes in bad faith to harass and oppress rivals. One of the most important limits on the *Noerr-Pennington* doctrine is the "sham exception," which applies to very clear examples of bad behavior that lacks an objective basis. For example, if a monopolist uses baseless litigation in bad faith as a tool to drive up rivals' costs or punish competition, it may

---

[719] The seminal statement is National Soc. of Professional Engineers v. United States, 435 U.S. 679, 689 (1978) ("The early [antitrust] cases also foreclose the argument that because of the special characteristics of a particular industry, monopolistic arrangements will better promote trade and commerce than competition. That kind of argument is properly addressed to Congress and may justify an exemption from the statute for specific industries, but it is not permitted by the Rule of Reason."); *id.* at 692 ("the purpose of the analysis is to form a judgment about the competitive significance of the restraint; it is not to decide whether a policy favoring competition is in the public interest, or in the interest of the members of an industry. Subject to exceptions defined by statute, that policy decision has been made by the Congress."); *id.* at 695 ("The assumption that competition is the best method of allocating resources in a free market recognizes that all elements of a bargain—quality, service, safety, and durability—and not just the immediate cost, are favorably affected by the free opportunity to select among alternative offers. Even assuming occasional exceptions to the presumed consequences of competition, the statutory policy precludes inquiry into the question whether competition is good or bad.").

[720] *See, e.g.*, Union Lab. Life Ins. Co. v. Pireno, 458 U.S. 119, 126 (1982); Grp. Life & Health Inc. Co. v. Royal Drug Co., 440 U.S. 205, 231 (1979); Fed. Mar. Comm'n v. Seatrain Lines, Inc., 411 U.S. 726, 733 (1973).

not hide behind the *Noerr-Pennington* shield. As we shall see, the "sham" category is generally reserved for egregious misbehavior.[721]

The *Noerr-Pennington* doctrine was first recognized in a trio of Supreme Court cases: *Noerr*, *Pennington*, and *California Motor Trucking*.[722] In *Eastern R.R. Presidents Conference v. Noerr Motor Freight* in 1961, a group of truck operators and a group of railroads—competing for long-haul freight—accused one another of violating the antitrust laws through their respective lobbying campaigns. In their complaint, the truck operators alleged that the railroads had:

> engaged [a PR firm] to conduct a publicity campaign against the truckers designed to foster the adoption and retention of laws and law enforcement practices destructive of the trucking business, to create an atmosphere of distaste for the truckers among the general public, and to impair the relationships existing between the truckers and their customers. The campaign so conducted was described in the complaint as "vicious, corrupt, and fraudulent," first, in that the sole motivation behind it was the desire on the part of the railroads to injure the truckers and eventually to destroy them as competitors in the long-distance freight business, and, secondly, in that the defendants utilized the so-called third-party technique, that is, the publicity matter circulated in the campaign was made to appear as spontaneously expressed views of independent persons and civic groups when, in fact, it was largely prepared and produced by [the PR firm] and paid for by the railroads. The complaint then went on to supplement these more or less general allegations with specific charges as to particular instances in which the railroads had attempted to influence legislation by means of their publicity campaign. One of several such charges was that the defendants had succeeded in persuading the Governor of Pennsylvania to veto a measure known as the "Fair Truck Bill," which would have permitted truckers to carry heavier loads over Pennsylvania roads.[723]

The railroads came right back with a counterclaim, which in turn alleged "a malicious publicity campaign designed to destroy the railroads' business by law, to create an atmosphere hostile to the railroads among the general public, and to interfere with relationships existing between the railroads and their customers."[724]

Can, or should, conduct of this kind form the basis for an antitrust challenge? In the following extract, the Court considered that question. Holding that the antitrust laws could *not* be invoked to punish or prohibit lobbying efforts, the Court set out a rationale for what would become known as *Noerr-Pennington* immunity.

Eastern R. R. Presidents Conference v. Noerr Motor Freight, Inc.
365 U.S. 127 (1961)

Justice Black.

[1] We accept, as the starting point for our consideration of the case, the same basic construction of the Sherman Act adopted by the courts below—that no violation of the Act can be predicated upon mere attempts to influence the passage or enforcement of laws. It has been recognized, at least since the landmark decision of this Court in *Standard Oil Co., of New Jersey v. United States*, that the Sherman Act forbids only those trade restraints and monopolizations that are created, or attempted, by the acts of "individuals or combinations of individuals or corporations." Accordingly, it has been held that where a restraint upon trade or monopolization is the result of valid governmental action, as opposed to private action, no violation of the Act can be made out. These decisions rest upon the fact that under our form of government the question whether a law of that kind should pass, or if passed be enforced, is the responsibility of the appropriate legislative or executive branch of government so long as the law itself does not violate some provision of the Constitution.

---

[721] *See, e.g.*, Federal Trade Commission v. AbbVie Inc, 976 F.3d 327, 359–71 (3d Cir. 2020) (noting that "[g]enerally, a plaintiff seeking to show the sham litigation exception faces an uphill battle" and analyzing arguments) (internal quotation marks and citation omitted).

[722] Eastern R. R. Presidents Conference v. Noerr Motor Freight, Inc., 365 U.S. 127 (1961); United Mine Workers of America v. Pennington, 381 U.S. 657 (1965); Professional Real Estate Investors, Inc. v. Columbia Pictures Industries, Inc., 508 U.S. 46 (1993).

[723] Eastern R. R. Presidents Conference v. Noerr Motor Freight, Inc., 365 U.S. 127, 129–30 (1961).

[724] Eastern R. R. Presidents Conference v. Noerr Motor Freight, Inc., 365 U.S. 127, 132 (1961).

[2] We think it equally clear that the Sherman Act does not prohibit two or more persons from associating together in an attempt to persuade the legislature or the executive to take particular action with respect to a law that would produce a restraint or a monopoly. Although such associations could perhaps, through a process of expansive construction, be brought within the general proscription of "combination(s) in restraint of trade," they bear very little if any resemblance to the combinations normally held violative of the Sherman Act, combinations ordinarily characterized by an express or implied agreement or understanding that the participants will jointly give up their trade freedom, or help one another to take away the trade freedom of others through the use of such devices as price-fixing agreements, boycotts, market-division agreements, and other similar arrangements. This essential dissimilarity between an agreement jointly to seek legislation or law enforcement and the agreements traditionally condemned by s 1 of the Act, even if not itself conclusive on the question of the applicability of the Act, does constitute a warning against treating the defendants' conduct as though it amounted to a common-law trade restraint. And we do think that the question is conclusively settled, against the application of the Act, when this factor of essential dissimilarity is considered along with the other difficulties that would be presented by a holding that the Sherman Act forbids associations for the purpose of influencing the passage or enforcement of laws.

[3] In the first place, such a holding would substantially impair the power of government to take actions through its legislature and executive that operate to restrain trade. In a representative democracy such as this, these branches of government act on behalf of the people and, to a very large extent, the whole concept of representation depends upon the ability of the people to make their wishes known to their representatives. To hold that the government retains the power to act in this representative capacity and yet hold, at the same time, that the people cannot freely inform the government of their wishes would impute to the Sherman Act a purpose to regulate, not business activity, but political activity, a purpose which would have no basis whatever in the legislative history of that Act. Secondly, and of at least equal significance, such a construction of the Sherman Act would raise important constitutional questions. The right of petition is one of the freedoms protected by the Bill of Rights, and we cannot, of course, lightly impute to Congress an intent to invade these freedoms. Indeed, such an imputation would be particularly unjustified in this case in view of all the countervailing considerations enumerated above. For these reasons, we think it clear that the Sherman Act does not apply to the activities of the railroads at least insofar as those activities comprised mere solicitation of governmental action with respect to the passage and enforcement of laws. . . .

[4] [The District Court held below that] the railroads' sole purpose in seeking to influence the passage and enforcement of laws was to destroy the truckers as competitors for the long-distance freight business. But we do not see how this fact, even if adequately supported in the record, could transform conduct otherwise lawful into a violation of the Sherman Act. All of the considerations that have led us to the conclusion that the Act does not apply to mere group solicitation of governmental action are equally applicable in spite of the addition of this factor. The right of the people to inform their representatives in government of their desires with respect to the passage or enforcement of laws cannot properly be made to depend upon their intent in doing so. It is neither unusual nor illegal for people to seek action on laws in the hope that they may bring about an advantage to themselves and a disadvantage to their competitors. . . . Indeed, it is quite probably people with just such a hope of personal advantage who provide much of the information upon which governments must act. A construction of the Sherman Act that would disqualify people from taking a public position on matters in which they are financially interested would thus deprive the government of a valuable source of information and, at the same time, deprive the people of their right to petition in the very instances in which that right may be of the most importance to them. We reject such a construction of the Act and hold that, at least insofar as the railroads' campaign was directed toward obtaining governmental action, its legality was not at all affected by any anticompetitive purpose it may have had. [. . .]

[5] [T]he courts below rested their holding that the Sherman Act had been violated upon a finding that the purpose of the railroads was "more than merely an attempt to obtain legislation. It was the purpose and intent to hurt the truckers in every way possible even though they secured no legislation." Specifically, the District Court found that the purpose of the railroads was to destroy the goodwill of the truckers, among the public generally and among the truckers' customers particularly, in the hope that by doing so the over-all competitive position of the truckers would be weakened, and that the railroads were successful in these efforts to the extent that such injury was actually inflicted. The apparent effect of these findings is to take this case out of the category of those that

involve restraints through governmental action and thus render inapplicable the principles announced above. But this effect is only apparent and cannot stand under close scrutiny. There are no specific findings that the railroads attempted directly to persuade anyone not to deal with the truckers. Moreover, all of the evidence in the record, both oral and documentary, deals with the railroads' efforts to influence the passage and enforcement of laws. Circulars, speeches, newspaper articles, editorials, magazine articles, memoranda and all other documents discuss in one way or another the railroads' charges that heavy trucks injure the roads, violate the laws and create traffic hazards, and urge that truckers should be forced to pay a fair share of the costs of rebuilding the roads, that they should be compelled to obey the laws, and that limits should be placed upon the weight of the loads they are permitted to carry. In the light of this, the findings of the District Court that the railroads' campaign was intended to and did in fact injure the truckers in their relationships with the public and with their customers can mean no more than that the truckers sustained some direct injury as an incidental effect of the railroads' campaign to influence governmental action and that the railroads were hopeful that this might happen. Thus, the issue presented by the lower courts' conclusion of a violation of the Sherman Act on the basis of this injury is no different than the issue presented by the factors already discussed. It is inevitable, whenever an attempt is made to influence legislation by a campaign of publicity, that an incidental effect of that campaign may be the infliction of some direct injury upon the interests of the party against whom the campaign is directed. And it seems equally inevitable that those conducting the campaign would be aware of, and possibly even pleased by, the prospect of such injury. To hold that the knowing infliction of such injury renders the campaign itself illegal would thus be tantamount to outlawing all such campaigns. We have already discussed the reasons which have led us to the conclusion that this has not been done by anything in the Sherman Act.

[6] There may be situations in which a publicity campaign, ostensibly directed toward influencing governmental action, is a mere sham to cover what is actually nothing more than an attempt to interfere directly with the business relationships of a competitor and the application of the Sherman Act would be justified. But this certainly is not the case here. No one denies that the railroads were making a genuine effort to influence legislation and law enforcement practices. Indeed, if the version of the facts set forth in the truckers' complaint is fully credited, as it was by the courts below, that effort was not only genuine but also highly successful. Under these circumstances, we conclude that no attempt to interfere with business relationships in a manner proscribed by the Sherman Act is involved in this case.

* * *

A few years later, in *United Mine Workers of America v. Pennington* in 1965, the Court stated that "*Noerr* shields from the Sherman Act a concerted effort to influence public officials regardless of intent or purpose," and applied it to protect a union's actions in lobbying the Secretary of Labor and officials of the Tennessee Valley Authority.[725] The third seminal decision in the *Noerr-Pennington* line—*California Motor Transport*—came a few years later.

CASENOTE: California Motor Transport Co. v. Trucking Unlimited
404 U.S. 508 (1972)

In *California Motor Transport Co. v. Trucking Unlimited*, a group of trucking companies sued a group of their incumbent competitors for using litigation and agency action to hinder their access to the market, including by using state and federal proceedings to relentlessly oppose—in bad faith and regardless of the merits—the plaintiffs' ability to obtain, transfer, and register rights to operate their businesses. The Court grappled with two questions: first, whether petitioning protection should apply, in general, to conduct directed to the judiciary and administrative processes; and, second, under what circumstances a defendant might be deprived of petitioning immunity that would otherwise cover its conduct. In *Noerr*, the Court had pointed out that, at least in principle, there could be some limits for conduct that amounted to a "mere sham": and in doing so, it had raised but not answered the

---

[725] United Mine Workers of America v. Pennington, 381 U.S. 657, 670 (1965).

question of how "sham" behavior would be defined.[726] *California Motor Transport* now required the Court to take a clearer position on the law of sham petitioning.

The Court reiterated the importance of the *Noerr-Pennington* doctrine, and confirmed its general applicability to efforts to petition the judiciary and administrative agencies. However, the Court explained, this case was an unusual one. The complaint alleged "that the power, strategy, and resources of the [defendants] were used to harass and deter [plaintiffs] in their use of administrative and judicial proceedings so as to deny [the plaintiffs] free and unlimited access to those tribunals. The result, it is alleged, was that the machinery of the agencies and the courts was effectively closed to [plaintiffs], and [defendants] indeed became the regulators of the grants of rights, transfers and registrations to [plaintiffs]—thereby depleting and diminishing the value of the businesses of [plaintiffs] and aggrandizing [defendants'] economic and monopoly power." Crucially, the allegations here were "not that the conspirators sought to influence public officials, but that they sought to bar their competitors from meaningful access to adjudicatory tribunals and so to usurp that decisionmaking process." Indeed, the Court explained, the complaint here alleged that the defendants "instituted the proceedings and actions with or without probable cause, and regardless of the merits of the cases."

There were many cases, the Court pointed out, in which misconduct or abuse relating to governmental process can result in liability or illegality. "Perjury of witnesses is one example. Use of a patent obtained by fraud to exclude a competitor from the market may involve a violation of the antitrust laws." And "bribery of a public purchasing agent may constitute a violation of s 2(c) of the Clayton Act, as amended by the Robinson-Patman Act." In sum: "There are many other forms of illegal and reprehensible practice which may corrupt the administrative or judicial processes and which may result in antitrust violations. Misrepresentations, condoned in the political arena, are not immunized when used in the adjudicatory process." And such abuse does not "acquire immunity by seeking refuge under the umbrella of political expression."

So too here. "First Amendment rights may not be used as the means or the pretext for achieving substantive evils which the legislature has the power to control. . . . A combination of entrepreneurs to harass and deter their competitors from having free and unlimited access to the agencies and courts, to defeat that right by massive, concerted, and purposeful activities of the group are ways of building up one empire and destroying another. . . If these facts are proved, a violation of the antitrust laws has been established." The plaintiffs would be entitled to a trial on their claims.

California Motor Transport established beyond doubt that *Noerr-Pennington* immunity applied to efforts to petition the judicial and administrative organs of government, and that it was subject to a meaningful sham exception that was not merely theoretical. But the bounds of that sham exception would require further clarification.

Today the bounds of the "sham exception" are somewhat clearer. The leading treatment is found in *Professional Real Estate Investors, Inc. v. Columbia Pictures Industries, Inc.* In that case, Professional Real Estate Investors operated a resort in Palm Springs, California, and rented out videodiscs to guests for viewing in their hotel rooms.[727] Columbia, which owned the copyrights to the movies on certain videodiscs—and which offered a competing wired cable system for the viewing of movies in hotel rooms—sued PRE for copyright infringement; PRE counterclaimed for antitrust violations, alleging that "Columbia's copyright action was a mere sham that cloaked underlying acts of monopolization and conspiracy to restrain trade."[728] The Supreme Court's opinion provided some detailed guidance on the sham exception.

---

[726] Eastern R. R. Presidents Conference v. Noerr Motor Freight, Inc., 365 U.S. 127, 144 (1961) ("There may be situations in which a publicity campaign, ostensibly directed toward influencing governmental action, is a mere sham to cover what is actually nothing more than an attempt to interfere directly with the business relationships of a competitor and the application of the Sherman Act would be justified. But this certainly is not the case here. No one denies that the railroads were making a genuine effort to influence legislation and law enforcement practices. Indeed, if the version of the facts set forth in the truckers' complaint is fully credited, as it was by the courts below, that effort was not only genuine but also highly successful. Under these circumstances, we conclude that no attempt to interfere with business relationships in a manner proscribed by the Sherman Act is involved in this case.").

[727] Videodiscs were a hard-copy storage format for audiovisual content, and a predecessor to the DVD format (which was a dominant means of distributing audiovisual content, such as movies, before the advent of streaming services).

[728] Professional Real Estate Investors, Inc. v. Columbia Pictures Industries, Inc., 508 U.S. 46, 52 (1993).

Professional Real Estate Investors, Inc. v. Columbia Pictures Industries, Inc.

508 U.S. 46 (1993)

Justice Thomas.

[1] Those who petition government for redress are generally immune from antitrust liability. . . . *Noerr*, however, withheld immunity from "sham" activities because application of the Sherman Act would be justified when petitioning activity, ostensibly directed toward influencing governmental action, is a mere sham to cover an attempt to interfere directly with the business relationships of a competitor. In *Noerr* itself, we found that a publicity campaign by railroads seeking legislation harmful to truckers was no sham in that the "effort to influence legislation" was not only genuine but also highly successful.

[2] In *California Motor Transport Co. v. Trucking Unlimited*, we elaborated on *Noerr* in two relevant respects. First, we extended *Noerr* to the approach of citizens to administrative agencies and to courts. Second, we held that the complaint showed a sham not entitled to immunity when it contained allegations that one group of highway carriers sought to bar competitors from meaningful access to adjudicatory tribunals and so to usurp that decisionmaking process by instituting proceedings and actions with or without probable cause, and regardless of the merits of the cases. We left unresolved the question presented by this case—whether litigation may be sham merely because a subjective expectation of success does not motivate the litigant. We now answer this question in the negative and hold that an objectively reasonable effort to litigate cannot be sham regardless of subjective intent.

[3] Our original formulation of antitrust petitioning immunity required that unprotected activity lack objective reasonableness. *Noerr* rejected the contention that an attempt to influence the passage and enforcement of laws might lose immunity merely because the lobbyists' sole purpose was to destroy their competitors. Nor were we persuaded by a showing that a publicity campaign was intended to and did in fact injure competitors in their relationships with the public and with their customers, since such direct injury was merely an incidental effect of the campaign to influence governmental action. We reasoned that the right of the people to inform their representatives in government of their desires with respect to the passage or enforcement of laws cannot properly be made to depend upon their intent in doing so. In short, *Noerr* shields from the Sherman Act a concerted effort to influence public officials regardless of intent or purpose. [. . .]

[4] We now outline a two-part definition of "sham" litigation. First, the lawsuit must be objectively baseless in the sense that no reasonable litigant could realistically expect success on the merits. If an objective litigant could conclude that the suit is reasonably calculated to elicit a favorable outcome, the suit is immunized under *Noerr*, and an antitrust claim premised on the sham exception must fail. Only if challenged litigation is objectively meritless may a court examine the litigant's subjective motivation. Under this second part of our definition of sham, the court should focus on whether the baseless lawsuit conceals an attempt to interfere directly with the business relationships of a competitor, through the use of the governmental process—as opposed to the outcome of that process—as an anticompetitive weapon. This two-tiered process requires the plaintiff to disprove the challenged lawsuit's legal viability before the court will entertain evidence of the suit's economic viability. Of course, even a plaintiff who defeats the defendant's claim to *Noerr* immunity by demonstrating both the objective and the subjective components of a sham must still prove a substantive antitrust violation. Proof of a sham merely deprives the defendant of immunity; it does not relieve the plaintiff of the obligation to establish all other elements of his claim.

[5] Some of the apparent confusion over the meaning of "sham" may stem from our use of the word "genuine" to denote the opposite of "sham." The word "genuine" has both objective and subjective connotations. On one hand, "genuine" means "actually having the reputed or apparent qualities or character." Webster's Third New International Dictionary 948 (1986). "Genuine" in this sense governs Federal Rule of Civil Procedure 56, under which a "genuine issue" is one "that properly can be resolved only by a finder of fact because [it] may reasonably be resolved in favor of either party." *Anderson v. Liberty Lobby, Inc.*, 477 U.S. 242, 250 (1986) (emphasis added). On the other hand, "genuine" also means "sincerely and honestly felt or experienced." Webster's Dictionary, at 948. To be sham, therefore, litigation must fail to be "genuine" in both senses of the word. [. . .]

[6] We conclude that the Court of Appeals properly affirmed summary judgment for Columbia on PRE's antitrust counterclaim. Under the objective prong of the sham exception, the Court of Appeals correctly held that sham litigation must constitute the pursuit of claims so baseless that no reasonable litigant could realistically expect to secure favorable relief.

[7] The existence of probable cause to institute legal proceedings precludes a finding that an antitrust defendant has engaged in sham litigation. The notion of probable cause, as understood and applied in the common-law tort of wrongful civil proceedings, requires the plaintiff to prove that the defendant lacked probable cause to institute an unsuccessful civil lawsuit and that the defendant pressed the action for an improper, malicious purpose. Probable cause to institute civil proceedings requires no more than a reasonable belief that there is a chance that a claim may be held valid upon adjudication. Because the absence of probable cause is an essential element of the tort, the existence of probable cause is an absolute defense. Just as evidence of anticompetitive intent cannot affect the objective prong of *Noerr*'s sham exception, a showing of malice alone will neither entitle the wrongful civil proceedings plaintiff to prevail nor permit the factfinder to infer the absence of probable cause. When a court has found that an antitrust defendant claiming *Noerr* immunity had probable cause to sue, that finding compels the conclusion that a reasonable litigant in the defendant's position could realistically expect success on the merits of the challenged lawsuit. Under our decision today, therefore, a proper probable cause determination irrefutably demonstrates that an antitrust plaintiff has not proved the objective prong of the sham exception and that the defendant is accordingly entitled to *Noerr* immunity.

[8] The District Court and the Court of Appeals correctly found that Columbia had probable cause to sue PRE for copyright infringement. Where, as here, there is no dispute over the predicate facts of the underlying legal proceeding, a court may decide probable cause as a matter of law. . . .

[9] When the District Court entered summary judgment for PRE on Columbia's copyright claim in 1986, it was by no means clear whether PRE's videodisc rental activities intruded on Columbia's copyrights. At that time, the Third Circuit and a District Court within the Third Circuit had held that the rental of video cassettes for viewing in on-site, private screening rooms infringed on the copyright owner's right of public performance. Although the District Court and the Ninth Circuit distinguished these decisions by reasoning that hotel rooms offered a degree of privacy more akin to the home than to a video rental store, copyright scholars criticized both the reasoning and the outcome of the Ninth Circuit's decision. The Seventh Circuit expressly declined to follow the Ninth Circuit and adopted instead the Third Circuit's definition of a public place. In light of the unsettled condition of the law, Columbia plainly had probable cause to sue.

NOTES

1) Is petitioning conduct likely to be very anticompetitive in practice? What are the worst examples you can think of?

2) The rules on sham litigation require, among other things, that a suit not be objectively baseless. Is this standard too harsh, because some "objectively baseless" litigation surely turns out to be successful? (For example: can you think of any famous Supreme Court cases that seemed "objectively baseless" when filed? Or is it too lax, because it allows parties to file suits that they do not expect to succeed for purely malicious and anticompetitive reasons?

3) In *California Motor* the Court said: "Misrepresentations, condoned in the political arena, are not immunized when used in the adjudicatory process." After *PRE*, what is "sham" petitioning of a legislative or executive body? What kind of misrepresentation would be immune in a more traditionally "political" arena but not in a court? (And where do administrative agencies fit into this scheme?)

4) As we saw in Chapter VII, fraud on the Patent Office may be an antitrust violation (a "*Walker Process* claim"). Should there be a fraud exception to the *Noerr-Pennington* doctrine? How would you define it? Would you add any other exceptions?

5) If petitioning conduct is appropriate to accommodate the values of the Petition Clause, can you think of any other constitutional provisions that might provide a basis for an antitrust exemption?

C. State Action

The "state action" doctrine shields from antitrust liability certain conduct that can be attributed to the decisions of state and local governments. As the following extracts show, it is not quite clear whether the doctrine is best understood as an expression of the legislative history of the Sherman Act, as an independent accommodation for the constitutional value of federalism, or as something else.[729] The Court itself has referred to a wide variety of constitutional, legal, and practical concerns when describing the doctrine's foundations and functions.[730] Like other exemptions, the doctrine is construed narrowly.[731]

The defense was recognized in *Parker v. Brown*. In that case, a California state statute—the California Agricultural Prorate Act—had created a program to limit and control the production and sale of raisins, in order to "restrict competition among the growers and maintain prices." This program was supervised by California's Director of Agriculture, and backed up with civil and criminal sanctions (!). In other words, the California statute authorized the state government to supervise and enforce a raisin-growers' cartel.

Brown, a producer and packer of raisins based in California, chafed under the program's restrictions, and sued the Director of Agriculture, challenging the Act as (among other things) an antitrust violation. But the Court held that the Sherman Act was simply inapplicable to conduct of this kind.

Parker v. Brown
317 U.S. 341 (1943)

Chief Justice Stone.

[1] The California Agricultural Prorate Act authorizes the establishment, through action of state officials, of programs for the marketing of agricultural commodities produced in the state, so as to restrict competition among the growers and maintain prices in the distribution of their commodities to packers. The declared purpose of the Act is to "conserve the agricultural wealth of the State" and to "prevent economic waste in the marketing of agricultural crops" of the state. It authorizes the creation of an Agricultural Prorate Advisory Commission of nine members, of which a state official, the Director of Agriculture, is ex-officio a member. The other eight members are appointed for terms of four years by the Governor and confirmed by the Senate, and are required to take an oath of office.

[2] Upon the petition of ten producers for the establishment of a prorate marketing plan for any commodity within a defined production zone, and after a public hearing, and after making prescribed economic findings, showing that the institution of a program for the proposed zone will prevent agricultural waste and conserve agricultural wealth of the state without permitting unreasonable profits to producers, the Commission is authorized to grant the petition. . . .

---

[729] There is a lively and often critical literature on this doctrine. *See, e.g.*, Thomas B. Nachbar, *Antitrust and the Politics of State Action*, 60 Wm. & Mary L. Rev. 1395 (2019); Rebecca Haw Allensworth, *The New Antitrust Federalism*, 102 Va. L. Rev.. 1387 (2016); Alan J. Meese, *Antitrust Federalism and State Restraints of Interstate Commerce: An Essay for Professor Hovenkamp*, 100 Iowa L. Rev. 2161 (2015); Aaron Edlin & Rebecca Haw, *Cartels by Another Name: Should Licensed Occupations Face Antitrust Scrutiny?*, 162 U. Pa. L. Rev. 1093, 1098 (2014); John F. Hart, *"Sovereign" State Policy and State Action Antitrust Immunity*, 56 Fordham L. Rev. 535, 546–47 (1988); Merrick B. Garland, *Antitrust and State Action: Economic Efficiency and the Political Process*, 96 Yale L.J. 486 (1987); Thomas M. Jorde, *Antitrust and the New State Action Doctrine: A Return to Deferential Economic Federalism*, 75 Calif. L. Rev. 227, 230 (1987).

[730] *See, e.g.*, North Carolina State Bd. of Dental Examiners v. FTC, 574 U.S. 494, 503 (2015) ("If every duly enacted state law or policy were required to conform to the mandates of the Sherman Act, thus promoting competition at the expense of other values a State may deem fundamental, federal antitrust law would impose an impermissible burden on the States' power to regulate. . . . [*Parker v. Brown*] recognized Congress' purpose to respect the federal balance and to embody in the Sherman Act the federalism principle that the States possess a significant measure of sovereignty under our Constitution."); FTC v. Phoebe Putney Health System, Inc., 568 U.S. 216, 224–25 (2013) (text and legislative history); FTC. v. Ticor Title Ins. Co., 504 U.S. 621, 633 (1992) ("Our decision [in *Parker*] was grounded in principles of federalism. The principle of freedom of action for the States, adopted to foster and preserve the federal system, explains the later evolution and application of the *Parker* doctrine in our [subsequent] decisions[.]"); California Retail Liquor Dealers Ass'n v. Midcal Aluminum, Inc., 445 U.S. 97 (1980) (federalism and legislative intent).

[731] *See, e.g.*, FTC v. Phoebe Putney Health System, Inc., 568 U.S. 216, 225 (2013) ("disfavored").

[3] If the proposed program, as approved by the Commission, is consented to by 65 per cent in number of producers in the zone owning 51 per cent of the acreage devoted to production of the regulated crop, the Director is required to declare the program instituted.

[4] Authority to administer the program, subject to the approval of the Director of Agriculture, is conferred on the program committee. [The Act] declares that it shall be a misdemeanor, which is punishable by fine and imprisonment, for any producer to sell or any handler to receive or possess without proper authority any commodity for which a proration program has been instituted. Like penalty is imposed upon any person who aids or abets in the commission of any of the acts specified in the section, and it is declared that each infraction shall constitute a separate and distinct offense. [The Act] imposes a civil liability of $500 for each and every violation of any provision of a proration program. [. . .]

[5] The seasonal proration marketing program for raisins, with which we are now concerned, became effective on September 7, 1940. . . . The committee is required to establish receiving stations within the zone to which every producer must deliver all raisins which he desires to market. The raisins are graded at these stations [as standard, substandard, or inferior]. All inferior raisins are to be placed in the "inferior raisin pool," to be disposed of by the committee . . . All substandard raisins, and at least 20 per cent of the total standard and substandard raisins produced, must be placed in a "surplus pool." Raisins in this pool may . . . be disposed of only for "assured by-product and other diversion purposes," except that under certain circumstances the program committee may transfer standard raisins from the surplus pool to the stabilization pool. Fifty per cent of the crop must be placed in a "stabilization pool."

[6] Under the program the producer is permitted to sell . . . 30 per cent of his standard raisins, denominated "free tonnage," through ordinary commercial channels, subject to the requirement that he obtain a "secondary certificate" authorizing such marketing and pay a certificate fee of $2.50 for each ton covered by the certificate. . . . [B]ut no raisins, (other than those subject to special lending or pooling arrangements of the Federal Government) can be sold by the committee at less than the prevailing market price for raisins of the same variety and grade on the date of sale . . . .

[7] Appellee's bill of complaint challenges the validity of the proration program as in violation of the . . . Sherman Act. [. . .]

[8] . . . We may assume for present purposes that the California prorate program would violate the Sherman Act if it were organized and made effective solely by virtue of a contract, combination or conspiracy of private persons, individual or corporate. . . .

[9] But it is plain that the prorate program here was never intended to operate by force of individual agreement or combination. It derived its authority and its efficacy from the legislative command of the state and was not intended to operate or become effective without that command. We find nothing in the language of the Sherman Act or in its history which suggests that its purpose was to restrain a state or its officers or agents from activities directed by its legislature. In a dual system of government in which, under the Constitution, the states are sovereign, save only as Congress may constitutionally subtract from their authority, an unexpressed purpose to nullify a state's control over its officers and agents is not lightly to be attributed to Congress.

[10] The Sherman Act makes no mention of the state as such, and gives no hint that it was intended to restrain state action or official action directed by a state. The Act is applicable to "persons" including corporations, s 7, 15 U.S.C.A., and it authorizes suits under it by persons and corporations. A state may maintain a suit for damages under it, but the United States may not—conclusions derived not from the literal meaning of the words "person" and "corporation" but from the purpose, the subject matter, the context and the legislative history of the statute.

[11] There is no suggestion of a purpose to restrain state action in the Act's legislative history. The sponsor of the bill which was ultimately enacted as the Sherman Act declared that it prevented only "business combinations." That its purpose was to suppress combinations to restrain competition and attempts to monopolize by individuals and corporations, abundantly appears from its legislative history.

[12] True, a state does not give immunity to those who violate the Sherman Act by authorizing them to violate it, or by declaring that their action is lawful; and we have no question of the state or its municipality becoming a participant in a private agreement or combination by others for restraint of trade. Here the state command to the Commission and to the program committee of the California Prorate Act is not rendered unlawful by the Sherman Act since, in view of the latter's words and history, it must be taken to be a prohibition of individual and not state action. It is the state which has created the machinery for establishing the prorate program. Although the organization of a prorate zone is proposed by producers, and a prorate program, approved by the Commission, must also be approved by referendum of producers, it is the state, acting through the Commission, which adopts the program and which enforces it with penal sanctions, in the execution of a governmental policy. The prerequisite approval of the program upon referendum by a prescribed number of producers is not the imposition by them of their will upon the minority by force of agreement or combination which the Sherman Act prohibits. The state itself exercises its legislative authority in making the regulation and in prescribing the conditions of its application. The required vote on the referendum is one of these conditions.

[13] The state in adopting and enforcing the prorate program made no contract or agreement and entered into no conspiracy in restraint of trade or to establish monopoly but, as sovereign, imposed the restraint as an act of government which the Sherman Act did not undertake to prohibit.

* * *

Parker inaugurated a complex line of cases that attempt to define when and how "state action" enjoys privileged treatment under the antitrust laws. Very crudely, the modern framework can be reduced to four broad categories:

1. **"Sovereign" acts of the state,** including legislation, are effectively *per se* immune from antitrust liability.[732]
2. **The acts of municipal and local government** are beyond the reach of the Sherman Act if those acts are taken are pursuant to a "clearly articulated and affirmatively expressed" state policy.[733]
3. **The acts of private entities** are also immune from antitrust scrutiny if such conduct is undertaken pursuant to a "clearly articulated" state policy and "actively supervised" by the state government itself.[734] The "active supervision" prong reflects an effort "not to determine whether the State has met some normative standard, such as efficiency, in its regulatory practices," but rather "whether the State has exercised sufficient independent judgment and control so that the details of the rates or prices have been established as a product of deliberate state intervention, not simply by agreement among private parties. Much as in causation inquiries, the analysis asks whether the State has played a substantial role in determining the specifics of the economic policy. The question is not how well state regulation works but whether the anticompetitive scheme is the State's own."[735]
4. **The acts of state administrative agencies and boards** will be analyzed under *either* the framework for municipal and local government, *or* the framework for private conduct, depending not on whether the agency is formally designated as a government agency but rather on a substantive analysis of whether the agency is vulnerable to a "risk that active market participants will pursue private interests in restraining trade" through the agency's activities.[736] At least when "a controlling number of decisionmakers are active market participants in the occupation the board regulates," the acts of the

---

[732] *See, e.g.*, North Carolina State Bd. of Dental Examiners v. FTC, 574 U.S. 494, 504 (2015) ("State legislation and decisions of a state supreme court, acting legislatively rather than judicially, will satisfy this standard, and ipso facto are exempt from the operation of the antitrust laws because they are an undoubted exercise of state sovereign authority.") (citations and internal quotation marks omitted); Hoover v. Ronwin, 466 U.S. 558, 567–68 (1984).

[733] *See, e.g.*, FTC v. Phoebe Putney Health System, Inc., 568 U.S. 216, 225–26 (2013); City of Columbia v. Omni Outdoor Advert., Inc., 499 U.S. 365, 372 (1991); Town of Hallie v. Eau Claire, 471 U.S. 34, 46–47 (1985); Community Communications Co. v. City of Boulder, 455 U.S. 40, 52–56 (1982).

[734] North Carolina State Bd. of Dental Examiners v. FTC, 574 U.S. 494, 504–07 (2015); FTC v. Ticor Title Ins. Co., 504 U.S. 621, 631 (1992); Cal. Retail Liquor Dealers Ass'n v. Midcal Aluminum Inc., 445 U.S. 97, 105 (1980).

[735] FTC v. Ticor Title Ins. Co., 504 U.S. 621, 634–35 (1992).

[736] North Carolina State Bd. of Dental Examiners v. FTC, 574 U.S. 494, 510 (2015).

agency will be treated as private conduct: that is, subject to both the "clear articulation" and the "active supervision" tests.[737]

CASENOTE: FTC v. Phoebe Putney Health Sys., Inc., and "Clear Articulation"
568 U.S. 216 (2013)

Phoebe Putney involved an FTC challenge to a hospital merger. Specifically, it concerned the acquisition by the Phoebe Putney Health System ("PPHS"), which owned one of two hospitals in Dougherty County, GA, of the other, Palmyra Medical Center. PPHS was in turn owned by the Hospital Authority of Albany-Dougherty County: a county hospital authority created pursuant to a Georgia statute, the Hospital Authorities Law ("Law").

To defend the legality of the transaction, PPHS pointed to provisions of the Law empowering hospital authorities to "exercise public and essential governmental functions," and to the statutory delegation to such authorities of "all the powers necessary or convenient to carry out and effectuate" the purposes of the Law. The Law also specifically empowered hospital authorities to "acquire by purchase, lease, or otherwise and to operate projects," which included hospitals and other public health facilities. Hospital authorities were also prohibited from operating facilities for a profit: they were limited to covering expenses and maintaining reasonable reserves. PPHS argued that this statutory scheme created state-action immunity for the acquisition.

Writing for a unanimous Court, Justice Sotomayor rejected the state-action immunity defense on the ground that Georgia had not clearly articulated a policy of displacing competition. In so doing, the Court described the clear-articulation test in fairly demanding terms. It would be satisfied only "when it is clear that the challenged anticompetitive conduct is undertaken pursuant to a regulatory scheme that is the State's own." This means, among other things, "the State must have affirmatively contemplated the displacement of competition." Such a policy would be "sufficiently expressed where the displacement of competition was the inherent, logical, or ordinary result of the exercise of authority delegated by the state legislature. . . . [T]he State must have foreseen and implicitly endorsed the anticompetitive effects as consistent with its policy goals."

Here, the merging parties' "claim for state-action immunity fail[ed] because there [was] no evidence the State affirmatively contemplated that hospital authorities would displace competition by consolidating hospital ownership." Instead, the Law merely provided "general powers routinely conferred by state law upon private corporations." Such powers "should be, can be, and typically are used in ways that raise no federal antitrust concerns." And the mere fact that a reasonable legislature might have been able to anticipate that powers would be used in a way that would violate the antitrust laws "falls well short of clearly articulating an affirmative state policy to displace competition with a regulatory alternative." As Georgia had not clearly made such a choice, the claim of immunity failed and Section 7 applied to the transaction.

As you can imagine, state action immunity is particularly controversial when it protects private parties from antitrust scrutiny. Unsurprisingly, the courts have repeatedly had to adjudicate cases on this frontier.

The next two cases, *Midcal* and *North Carolina Dental*, illustrate some of the complexities in applying the state-action doctrine to the conduct of private parties. In *Midcal*, the Court dealt with the question: what constitutes a state policy to depart from the antitrust framework? The Court held that a state does not authorize private anticompetitive conduct merely by creating a scheme that permits, without requiring, action that violates the antitrust laws. And in *North Carolina Dental*, the Court grappled with the reality that many "state" licensing boards are in practice dominated by private incumbents, holding that a state board with a majority of private-competitor members should be treated just like a private actor for the purposes of assessing state-action immunity.[738]

---

[737] North Carolina State Bd. of Dental Examiners v. FTC, 574 U.S. 494, 511 (2015).

[738] Fun fact: the California Agricultural Prorate Commission—the state body at issue in *Parker*—appears to have been a majority-market-participant commission. Would *Parker* come out differently today? *See* H.E. Erdman, *The California Agricultural Prorate Act*, 16 J. Farm Econ. 624, 626 (1934) ("[The Commission] consists of nine members. Four of them are producers of agricultural commodities, one is an experienced commercial handler of fruits and vegetables, another a cooperative marketing handler, one an agricultural

---

CASENOTE: California Retail Liquor Dealers Ass'n v. Midcal Aluminum, Inc.

445 U.S. 97 (1980)

Despite its name, Midcal Aluminum was a wine distributor, which bought wine from producers and sold it to retailers. During the relevant time period, California law provided that wine producers must set price schedules that wholesalers and other wine distributors must then follow in reselling their wine. Pursuant to that law, E&J Gallo, a prominent wine producer, set a price schedule. But alas: Midcal violated the schedule by selling 27 cases of wine below the scheduled price. California's Department of Alcoholic Beverage Control charged Midcal with a violation of the statute, and Midcal went to state court to obtain an injunction against the state's wine pricing system on the ground that it violated the Sherman Act by mandating resale price maintenance. (As you will remember from Chapter VI, resale price maintenance was *per se* illegal in 1980.)

Several appeals later, the matter landed in the U.S. Supreme Court, where the Court acknowledged that "California's system for wine pricing plainly constitutes resale price maintenance in violation of the Sherman Act." Justice Powell's opinion grappled with a central question: did California's involvement immunize what would otherwise be illegal RPM? In particular, the Court focused on "whether the State's involvement in the price-setting program is sufficient to establish antitrust immunity under [*Parker.*]"

The Court held that California's legislative intervention was not enough to create state-action immunity. That immunity, the Court began by pointing out, "is grounded in our federal structure. In a dual system of government in which, under the Constitution, the states are sovereign, save only as Congress may constitutionally subtract from their authority, an unexpressed purpose to nullify a state's control over its officers and agents is not lightly to be attributed to Congress."

In the opinion's pivotal paragraph, the Court explained that California had satisfied the requirement of clear articulation. But the state would need to get its hands a little dirtier if it wanted to achieve active supervision:

> [The Court's prior] decisions establish two standards for antitrust immunity under *Parker v. Brown*. First, the challenged restraint must be one clearly articulated and affirmatively expressed as state policy; second, the policy must be actively supervised by the State itself. The California system for wine pricing satisfies the first standard. The legislative policy is forthrightly stated and clear in its purpose to permit resale price maintenance. The program, however, does not meet the second requirement for *Parker* immunity. The State simply authorizes price setting and enforces the prices established by private parties. The State neither establishes prices nor reviews the reasonableness of the price schedules; nor does it regulate the terms of fair trade contracts. The State does not monitor market conditions or engage in any "pointed reexamination" of the program. The national policy in favor of competition cannot be thwarted by casting such a gauzy cloak of state involvement over what is essentially a private price-fixing arrangement. As *Parker* teaches, a state does not give immunity to those who violate the Sherman Act by authorizing them to violate it, or by declaring that their action is lawful.

North Carolina State Bd. of Dental Examiners v. FTC

574 U.S. 494 (2015)

Justice Kennedy.

[1] In its Dental Practice Act ("Act"), North Carolina has declared the practice of dentistry to be a matter of public concern requiring regulation. Under the Act, the North Carolina State Board of Dental Examiners (Board) is the agency of the State for the regulation of the practice of dentistry. [. . .]

[2] The Act provides that six of the Board's eight members must be licensed dentists engaged in the active practice of dentistry. They are elected by other licensed dentists in North Carolina, who cast their ballots in elections

---

economist, and one a agriculturist employed by a metropolitan chamber of commerce. The last two supposedly represent consumers."); *see also id.* at 627 (committees appointed by the Commission consist of "five producers and two handlers").

conducted by the Board. The seventh member must be a licensed and practicing dental hygienist, and he or she is elected by other licensed hygienists. The final member is referred to by the Act as a "consumer" and is appointed by the Governor. . . . The Act does not create any mechanism for the removal of an elected member of the Board by a public official.

[3] Board members swear an oath of office, and the Board must comply with the State's Administrative Procedure Act, Public Records Act, and open-meetings law. The Board may promulgate rules and regulations governing the practice of dentistry within the State, provided those mandates are not inconsistent with the Act and are approved by the North Carolina Rules Review Commission, whose members are appointed by the state legislature. [. . .]

[4] In the 1990's, dentists in North Carolina started whitening teeth. Many of those who did so, including 8 of the Board's 10 members during the period at issue in this case, earned substantial fees for that service. By 2003, nondentists arrived on the scene. They charged lower prices for their services than the dentists did. Dentists soon began to complain to the Board about their new competitors. Few complaints warned of possible harm to consumers. Most expressed a principal concern with the low prices charged by nondentists.

[5] Responding to these filings, the Board opened an investigation into nondentist teeth whitening. A dentist member was placed in charge of the inquiry. Neither the Board's hygienist member nor its consumer member participated in this undertaking. The Board's chief operations officer remarked that the Board was "going forth to do battle" with nondentists. The Board's concern did not result in a formal rule or regulation reviewable by the independent Rules Review Commission, even though the Act does not, by its terms, specify that teeth whitening is "the practice of dentistry."

[6] Starting in 2006, the Board issued at least 47 cease-and-desist letters on its official letterhead to nondentist teeth whitening service providers and product manufacturers. Many of those letters directed the recipient to cease "all activity constituting the practice of dentistry"; warned that the unlicensed practice of dentistry is a crime; and strongly implied (or expressly stated) that teeth whitening constitutes the practice of dentistry. In early 2007, the Board persuaded the North Carolina Board of Cosmetic Art Examiners to warn cosmetologists against providing teeth whitening services. Later that year, the Board sent letters to mall operators, stating that kiosk teeth whiteners were violating the Act and advising that the malls consider expelling violators from their premises.

[7] These actions had the intended result. Nondentists ceased offering teeth whitening services in North Carolina. [. . .]

[8] In 2010, the Federal Trade Commission (FTC) filed an administrative complaint charging the Board with violating § 5 of the Federal Trade Commission Act. The FTC alleged that the Board's concerted action to exclude nondentists from the market for teeth whitening services in North Carolina constituted an anticompetitive and unfair method of competition. [. . .]

[9] In this case the Board argues its members were invested by North Carolina with the power of the State and that, as a result, the Board's actions are cloaked with Parker immunity. This argument fails, however. A nonsovereign actor controlled by active market participants—such as the Board—enjoys *Parker* immunity only if it satisfies two requirements: first that the challenged restraint be one clearly articulated and affirmatively expressed as state policy, and second that the policy be actively supervised by the State. The parties have assumed that the clear articulation requirement is satisfied, and we do the same. While North Carolina prohibits the unauthorized practice of dentistry, however, its Act is silent on whether that broad prohibition covers teeth whitening. Here, the Board did not receive active supervision by the State when it interpreted the Act as addressing teeth whitening and when it enforced that policy by issuing cease-and-desist letters to nondentist teeth whiteners. [. . .]

[10] Although state-action immunity exists to avoid conflicts between state sovereignty and the Nation's commitment to a policy of robust competition, *Parker* immunity is not unbounded. Given the fundamental national values of free enterprise and economic competition that are embodied in the federal antitrust laws, state-action immunity is disfavored, much as are repeals by implication.

[11] An entity may not invoke *Parker* immunity unless the actions in question are an exercise of the State's sovereign power. State legislation and decisions of a state supreme court, acting legislatively rather than judicially, will satisfy

this standard, and ipso facto are exempt from the operation of the antitrust laws because they are an undoubted exercise of state sovereign authority.

[12] But while the Sherman Act confers immunity on the States' own anticompetitive policies out of respect for federalism, it does not always confer immunity where, as here, a State delegates control over a market to a nonsovereign actor. For purposes of *Parker*, a nonsovereign actor is one whose conduct does not automatically qualify as that of the sovereign State itself. State agencies are not simply by their governmental character sovereign actors for purposes of state-action immunity. Immunity for state agencies, therefore, requires more than a mere facade of state involvement, for it is necessary in light of *Parker*'s rationale to ensure the States accept political accountability for anticompetitive conduct they permit and control.

[13] Limits on state-action immunity are most essential when the State seeks to delegate its regulatory power to active market participants, for established ethical standards may blend with private anticompetitive motives in a way difficult even for market participants to discern. Dual allegiances are not always apparent to an actor. In consequence, active market participants cannot be allowed to regulate their own markets free from antitrust accountability. Indeed, prohibitions against anticompetitive self-regulation by active market participants are an axiom of federal antitrust policy. So it follows that, under *Parker* and the Supremacy Clause, the States' greater power to attain an end does not include the lesser power to negate the congressional judgment embodied in the Sherman Act through unsupervised delegations to active market participants.

[14] *Parker* immunity requires that the anticompetitive conduct of nonsovereign actors, especially those authorized by the State to regulate their own profession, result from procedures that suffice to make it the State's own. The question is not whether the challenged conduct is efficient, well-functioning, or wise. Rather, it is whether anticompetitive conduct engaged in by nonsovereign actors should be deemed state action and thus shielded from the antitrust laws.

[15] To answer this question, the Court applies the two-part test set forth in *California Retail Liquor Dealers Assn. v. Midcal Aluminum, Inc.*, 445 U.S. 97, a case arising from California's delegation of price-fixing authority to wine merchants. Under *Midcal*, a state law or regulatory scheme cannot be the basis for antitrust immunity unless, first, the State has articulated a clear policy to allow the anticompetitive conduct, and second, the State provides active supervision of the anticompetitive conduct.

[16] *Midcal*'s clear articulation requirement is satisfied where the displacement of competition is the inherent, logical, or ordinary result of the exercise of authority delegated by the state legislature. In that scenario, the State must have foreseen and implicitly endorsed the anticompetitive effects as consistent with its policy goals. The active supervision requirement demands, inter alia, that state officials have and exercise power to review particular anticompetitive acts of private parties and disapprove those that fail to accord with state policy.

[17] The two requirements set forth in *Midcal* provide a proper analytical framework to resolve the ultimate question whether an anticompetitive policy is indeed the policy of a State. The first requirement—clear articulation—rarely will achieve that goal by itself, for a policy may satisfy this test yet still be defined at so high a level of generality as to leave open critical questions about how and to what extent the market should be regulated. Entities purporting to act under state authority might diverge from the State's considered definition of the public good. The resulting asymmetry between a state policy and its implementation can invite private self-dealing. The second *Midcal* requirement—active supervision—seeks to avoid this harm by requiring the State to review and approve interstitial policies made by the entity claiming immunity. [. . .]

[18] The Board argues entities designated by the States as agencies are exempt from *Midcal*'s second requirement. That premise, however, cannot be reconciled with the Court's repeated conclusion that the need for supervision turns not on the formal designation given by States to regulators but on the risk that active market participants will pursue private interests in restraining trade.

[19] State agencies controlled by active market participants, who possess singularly strong private interests, pose the very risk of self-dealing *Midcal*'s supervision requirement was created to address. This conclusion does not question the good faith of state officers but rather is an assessment of the structural risk of market participants' confusing their own interests with the State's policy goals.

[20] The Court applied this reasoning to a state agency in *Goldfarb*. There the Court denied immunity to a state agency (the Virginia State Bar) controlled by market participants (lawyers) because the agency had joined in what is essentially a private anticompetitive activity" for "the benefit of its members. This emphasis on the Bar's private interests explains why *Goldfarb*, though it predates *Midcal*, considered the lack of supervision by the Virginia Supreme Court to be a principal reason for denying immunity. [. . .]

[21] In important regards, agencies controlled by market participants are more similar to private trade associations vested by States with regulatory authority than to [state agencies with general regulatory powers and no private interests]. And as the Court [has observed], there is no doubt that the members of such associations often have economic incentives to restrain competition and that the product standards set by such associations have a serious potential for anticompetitive harm. For that reason, those associations must satisfy *Midcal*'s active supervision standard.

[22] The similarities between agencies controlled by active market participants and private trade associations are not eliminated simply because the former are given a formal designation by the State, vested with a measure of government power, and required to follow some procedural rules. *Parker* immunity does not derive from nomenclature alone. When a State empowers a group of active market participants to decide who can participate in its market, and on what terms, the need for supervision is manifest. The Court holds today that a state board on which a controlling number of decisionmakers are active market participants in the occupation the board regulates must satisfy *Midcal*'s active supervision requirement in order to invoke state-action antitrust immunity.

Foreign Governments and U.S. Antitrust Law

We have already seen that state governments enjoy a form of special treatment under the antitrust laws. So too—in different ways—do foreign governments! The relevant law here is somewhat convoluted: we will just sketch the outlines of three legal doctrines that may protect defendants in cases involving the conduct of foreign governments.

The "foreign sovereign compulsion" doctrine is the simplest of this family of rules.[739] It provides that a defendant will not generally be held liable for unlawful conduct that is genuinely compelled by a foreign sovereign.[740] The illegal conduct must be required, not merely encouraged, by the foreign government.[741]

The "act of state" doctrine centrally provides that the acts of foreign sovereigns within their respective jurisdictions must be conclusively presumed valid. This doctrine is not a principle of abstention, nor a rule to prevent courts from entertaining "cases and controversies that may embarrass foreign governments": it simply prohibits courts from entertaining arguments that the acts of foreign states are or may be invalid.[742] Courts have relied on this doctrine to dismiss antitrust claims that explicitly or implicitly target foreign-state acts. For example, the Fifth Circuit has invoked it to dismiss a challenge to the OPEC oil cartel, among other things because "[t]he granting of any relief to Appellants would effectively order foreign governments to dismantle their chosen means of exploiting the valuable natural resources within their sovereign territories."[743] Likewise, the Seventh Circuit has dismissed an antitrust challenge to a Canadian trade restriction that was "contained in agreements entered into by the Ontario government and approved of in legislation."[744] But not all courts agree that a challenge to an act's *legality* under the antitrust laws amounts to a challenge to its *validity* under the act-of-state doctrine! The Second

---

[739] It may also be unique to antitrust! *See* Unigestion Holding, S.A. v. UPM Tech., Inc., No. 3:15-CV-185-SI, 2022 WL 3017524, at *5 (D. Or. July 29, 2022) (foreign sovereign compulsion defense "appears only to apply in the context of antitrust cases").

[740] *See, e.g.*, Cont'l Ore Co. v. Union Carbide & Carbon Corp., 370 U.S. 690, 706–07 (1962); Mountain Crest SRL, LLC v. Anheuser-Busch InBev SA/NV, 937 F.3d 1067, 1080 (7th Cir. 2019); Mannington Mills, Inc. v. Congoleum Corp., 595 F.2d 1287, 1293 (3d Cir. 1979); Interamerican Ref. Corp. v. Texaco Maracaibo, Inc., 307 F. Supp. 1291, 1298 (D. Del. 1970).

[741] *See, e.g.*, Mannington Mills, Inc. v. Congoleum Corp., 595 F.2d 1287, 1293 (3d Cir. 1979); United States v. Brodie, 174 F. Supp. 2d 294, 299–300 (E.D. Pa. 2001); *see also* Societe Internationale Pour Participations Industrielles Et Commerciales, S.A. v. Rogers, 357 U.S. 197, 210 (1958) (requiring good faith effort to comply with U.S. law).

[742] W.S. Kirkpatrick & Co. v. Env't Tectonics Corp., Int'l, 493 U.S. 400, 409 (1990). *See also, e.g.*, Ricaud v. Am. Metal Co., 246 U.S. 304, 309 (1918) ("[W]hen it is made to appear that the foreign government has acted in a given way on the subject-matter of the litigation, the details of such action or the merit of the result cannot be questioned but must be accepted by our courts as a rule for their decision.").

[743] Spectrum Stores, Inc. v. Citgo Petroleum Corp., 632 F.3d 938, 955 (5th Cir. 2011).

[744] Mountain Crest SRL, LLC v. Anheuser-Busch InBev SA/NV, 937 F.3d 1067, 1085 (7th Cir. 2019).

Circuit has refused to exculpate a defendant on act-of-state grounds despite claims that the President of Haiti had issued directive to implement the challenged price-fixing scheme, on the basis that the plaintiff challenged the illegal conspiracy, not the validity of the legal acts.[745] Nor is this the only point of difference among the circuits: for example, the D.C. Circuit has suggested that a "commercial exception" should permit suit for acts that are commercial rather than governmental.[746]

The principle of international comity expresses respect for foreign sovereigns. It can be a basis for dismissal of an antitrust (or other) suit if there is a "true conflict" between the law of the United States and the law of another nation, such that compliance with both laws is impossible.[747] A true conflict is a necessary, but not sufficient, condition for a comity dismissal.[748] Other relevant factors, in an influential Third Circuit formulation, include: (1) the "[d]egree of conflict with foreign law or policy"; (2) the "[n]ationality of the parties"; (3) the "[r]elative importance of the alleged violation of conduct here compared to that abroad"; (4) the "[a]vailability of a remedy abroad and the pendency of litigation there"; (5) any "[e]xistence of intent to harm or affect American commerce and its foreseeability"; (6) the "[p]ossible effect upon foreign relations if the court exercises jurisdiction and grants relief"; (7) "[i]f relief is granted, whether a party will be placed in the position of being forced to perform an act illegal in either country or be under conflicting requirements by both countries"; (8) "[w]hether the [U.S.] court can make its order effective"; (9) "[w]hether an order for relief would be acceptable in this country if made by the foreign nation under similar circumstances"; and (10) "[w]hether a treaty with the affected nations has addressed the issue."[749] Other circuit courts have taken a similar approach.[750]

NOTES

1) Based on what you have read, do you think the state action doctrine is most plausibly understood as primarily grounded in (a) the legislative intent behind the Sherman Act; (b) the constitutional value of federalism; or (c) something else?

2) Should the state action doctrine apply even when the state action in question is in violation of some constitutional provision (*e.g.*, a protectionist measure that violates the dormant Commerce Clause doctrine)?

3) Why, if at all, should the state action doctrine apply to the actions of local governments? Do those governments have the same (or any) claim to independent constitutional dignity in our federal system?

4) When should we require affirmative evidence that the Sherman Act legislators did intend to cover some practice or phenomenon as a basis for applying the antitrust laws to that practice or phenomenon, rather than requiring affirmative evidence that they did not so intend as a basis for exempting it?

5) Should we be worried about local incumbents "capturing" state government and getting away with anticompetitive activity under cover of the state action doctrine? If so, what can we do about it? If not, why is this not a concern?

6) When and why should the reach of U.S. antitrust law be determined by the decisions of foreign governments?

D. Labor

It is not quite clear whether, and to what extent, any of the framers of the Sherman Act imagined that the federal antitrust laws—including the prohibition on combinations in "restraint of trade"—would or could be a weapon

---

[745] Celestin v. Caribbean Air Mail, Inc., 30 F.4th 133, 144–45 (2d Cir. 2022).

[746] *Compare* de Csepel v. Republic of Hung., 714 F.3d 591, 604 (D.C. Cir. 2013) with Spectrum Stores, Inc. v. Citgo Petroleum Corp., 632 F.3d 938, 955 n.16 (5th Cir. 2011) and Honduras Aircraft Registry, Ltd. V. Honduras, 129 F.3d 543, 550 (11th Cir. 1997).

[747] In Re: Vitamin C Antitrust Litig., 8 F.4th 136, 145 (2d Cir. 2021), cert. denied sub nom. Animal Sci. Prod., Inc. v. Hebei Welcome Pharm. Co., 143 S. Ct. 85 (2022).

[748] *See, e.g.*, Hartford Fire Ins. Co. v. California, 509 U.S. 764, 799 (1993) (finding no true conflict, thus no need to consider other factors).

[749] Mannington Mills, Inc. v. Congoleum Corp., 595 F.2d 1287, 1297–98 (3d Cir. 1979).

[750] *See, e.g.*, In Re: Vitamin C Antitrust Litig., 8 F.4th 136, 159 (2d Cir. 2021); Timberlane Lumber Co. v. Bank of Am., N.T. & S.A., 549 F.2d 597, 614 (9th Cir. 1976).

to be used against labor unions and their practices.[751] Nevertheless, in the Act's early years government prosecutors showed at least as much interest, and perhaps rather more, in using it for this purpose as for tackling practices by businesses. In a string of cases, the Sherman Act was pressed into service as an anti-labor device.[752] Congress eventually responded, enacting the Clayton Act of 1914 and the Norris-LaGuardia Act of 1932 to immunize certain labor activities from antitrust scrutiny.[753]

15 U.S.C. § 17

The labor of a human being is not a commodity or article of commerce. Nothing contained in the antitrust laws shall be construed to forbid the existence and operation of labor, agricultural, or horticultural organizations, instituted for the purposes of mutual help, and not having capital stock or conducted for profit, or to forbid or restrain individual members of such organizations from lawfully carrying out the legitimate objects thereof; nor shall such organizations, or the members thereof, be held or construed to be illegal combinations or conspiracies in restraint of trade, under the antitrust laws.

* * *

29 U.S.C. § 52

No restraining order or injunction shall be granted by any court of the United States, or a judge or the judges thereof, in any case between an employer and employees, or between employers and employees, or between employees, or between persons employed and persons seeking employment, involving, or growing out of, a dispute concerning terms or conditions of employment, unless necessary to prevent irreparable injury to property, or to a property right, of the party making the application, for which injury there is no adequate remedy at law, and such property or property right must be described with particularity in the application, which must be in writing and sworn to by the applicant or by his agent or attorney.

And no such restraining order or injunction shall prohibit any person or persons, whether singly or in concert, from terminating any relation of employment, or from ceasing to perform any work or labor, or from recommending, advising, or persuading others by peaceful means so to do; or from attending at any place where any such person or persons may lawfully be, for the purpose of peacefully obtaining or communicating information, or from peacefully persuading any person to work or to abstain from working; or from ceasing to patronize or to employ any party to such dispute, or from recommending, advising, or persuading others by peaceful and lawful means so to do; or from paying or giving to, or withholding from, any person engaged in such dispute, any strike benefits or other moneys or things of value; or from peaceably assembling in a lawful manner, and for lawful purposes; or from doing any act or thing which might lawfully be done in the absence of such dispute by any party thereto; nor shall any of the acts specified in this paragraph be considered or held to be violations of any law of the United States.

* * *

29 U.S.C. § 102

In the interpretation of this chapter and in determining the jurisdiction and authority of the courts of the United States, as such jurisdiction and authority are defined and limited in this chapter, the public policy of the United States is declared as follows:

---

[751] Compare, e.g., Sandeep Vaheesan, *Accommodating Capital and Policing Labor: Antitrust in the Two Gilded Ages*, 78 Md. L. Rev. 766, 779–83 (2019) *with* Herbert Hovenkamp, *Labor Conspiracies in American Law*, 1880-1930, 66 Tex. L. Rev. 919, 950–51 (1988).

[752] Loewe v. Lawlor, 208 U.S. 274 (1908); United States v. Debs, 64 F. 724 (C.C.N.D. Ill. 1894); United States v. Workingmen's Amalgamated Council, 54 F. 994 (C.C.E.D.La. 1893).

[753] For some perspectives on the history, *see, e.g.,* Hiba Hafiz, *Labor Antitrust's Paradox*, 86 U. Chi. L. Rev. 381, 383–91 (2019); Milton Handler, *Labor and Antitrust: A Bit of History*, 40 Antitrust L.J. 233 (1971); Ralph K. Winter, Jr., *Collective Bargaining and Competition: The Application of Antitrust Standards to Union Activities*, 73 Yale L.J. 14, 30–59 (1963); Hans B. Thorelli, THE FEDERAL ANTITRUST POLICY: ORIGINATION OF AN AMERICAN TRADITION (1955) 389–94; Archibald Cox, *Labor and the Antitrust Laws—A Preliminary Analysis*, 104 U. Pa. L. Rev. 252 (1955).

Whereas under prevailing economic conditions, developed with the aid of governmental authority for owners of property to organize in the corporate and other forms of ownership association, the individual unorganized worker is commonly helpless to exercise actual liberty of contract and to protect his freedom of labor, and thereby to obtain acceptable terms and conditions of employment, wherefore, though he should be free to decline to associate with his fellows, it is necessary that he have full freedom of association, self-organization, and designation of representatives of his own choosing, to negotiate the terms and conditions of his employment, and that he shall be free from the interference, restraint, or coercion of employers of labor, or their agents, in the designation of such representatives or in self-organization or in other concerted activities for the purpose of collective bargaining or other mutual aid or protection; therefore, the following definitions of, and limitations upon, the jurisdiction and authority of the courts of the United States are enacted.

* * *

29 U.S.C. § 104

No court of the United States shall have jurisdiction to issue any restraining order or temporary or permanent injunction in any case involving or growing out of any labor dispute to prohibit any person or persons participating or interested in such dispute (as these terms are herein defined) from doing, whether singly or in concert, any of the following acts:

(a)   Ceasing or refusing to perform any work or to remain in any relation of employment;

(b)   Becoming or remaining a member of any labor organization or of any employer organization, regardless of any such undertaking or promise as is described in section 103 of this title;

(c)   Paying or giving to, or withholding from, any person participating or interested in such labor dispute, any strike or unemployment benefits or insurance, or other moneys or things of value;

(d)   By all lawful means aiding any person participating or interested in any labor dispute who is being proceeded against in, or is prosecuting, any action or suit in any court of the United States or of any State;

(e)   Giving publicity to the existence of, or the facts involved in, any labor dispute, whether by advertising, speaking, patrolling, or by any other method not involving fraud or violence;

(f)   Assembling peaceably to act or to organize to act in promotion of their interests in a labor dispute;

(g)   Advising or notifying any person of an intention to do any of the acts heretofore specified;

(h)   Agreeing with other persons to do or not to do any of the acts heretofore specified; and

(i)   Advising, urging, or otherwise causing or inducing without fraud or violence the acts heretofore specified, regardless of any such undertaking or promise as is described in section 103 of this title. {*Eds.: Section 103, not reproduced here, provides that contracts in violation of the public policy stated in § 102—including so-called "yellow dog" contracts prohibiting union membership—are unenforceable.*}

* * *

29 U.S.C. § 105

No court of the United States shall have jurisdiction to issue a restraining order or temporary or permanent injunction upon the ground that any of the persons participating or interested in a labor dispute constitute or are engaged in an unlawful combination or conspiracy because of the doing in concert of the acts enumerated in section 104 of this title.

* * *

29 U.S.C. § 113

When used in this chapter, and for the purposes of this chapter—

(a)   A case shall be held to involve or to grow out of a labor dispute when the case involves persons who are engaged in the same industry, trade, craft, or occupation; or have direct or indirect interests therein; or who are employees of the same employer; or who are members of the same or an affiliated organization of employers or employees; whether such dispute is (1) between one or more employers or associations of employers and one or more employees or associations of employees; (2) between one or more employers or associations of employers and one or more employers or associations of employers; or (3) between one or more employees or associations of employees and one or more employees or associations of employees; or when the case involves any conflicting or competing interests in a "labor dispute" (as defined in this section) of "persons participating or interested" therein (as defined in this section).

(b)   A person or association shall be held to be a person participating or interested in a labor dispute if relief is sought against him or it, and if he or it is engaged in the same industry, trade, craft, or occupation in which such dispute occurs, or has a direct or indirect interest therein, or is a member, officer, or agent of any association composed in whole or in part of employers or employees engaged in such industry, trade, craft, or occupation.

(c)   The term "labor dispute" includes any controversy concerning terms or conditions of employment, or concerning the association or representation of persons in negotiating, fixing, maintaining, changing, or seeking to arrange terms or conditions of employment, regardless of whether or not the disputants stand in the proximate relation of employer and employee.

* * *

In *Hutcheson* in 1941, the Supreme Court indicated that these statutory provisions create an antitrust shield for actions that are in a union's self-interest and that do not involve combination with "non-labor groups."[754]

CASENOTE: United States v. Hutcheson
312 U.S. 219 (1941)

In *Hutcheson* the Supreme Court gave a seminal account of the function and scope of the statutory labor exemption. The case involved a criminal prosecution under Section 1 of a union: the United Brotherhood of Carpenters and Joiners of America (the "Carpenters"). In an unusual twist, the challenged practices—a strike, picketing, and an invitation to members to boycott the products of an employer, Anheuser-Busch—sprang from a dispute not between the Carpenters and the employer itself, but from a dispute between the Carpenters and another union, the International Association of Machinists. The Court was required to determine whether the apparently broad language of the statutory exemptions really immunized efforts by one union to pursue a dispute with another union, rather than with an employer.

In an opinion that emphasized the breadth of the statutory exemption, and the clarity of Congress's purpose in enacting it, the Court concluded that the Carpenters were entitled to immunity. "The Norris-LaGuardia Act removed the fetters upon trade union activities" that the federal courts had continued to apply after 1914 notwithstanding the language of the Clayton Act. Its underlying aim was to "restore the broad purpose which Congress thought it had formulated in the Clayton Act but which was frustrated." Correctly understood, the shield was a broad one: "So long as a union acts in its self-interest and does not combine with non-labor groups, the licit

---

[754] United States v. Hutcheson, 312 U.S. 219, 232 (1941) ("If the facts laid in the indictment come within the conduct enumerated in s 20 of the Clayton Act they do not constitute a crime within the general terms of the Sherman Law because of the explicit command of that section that such conduct shall not be 'considered or held to be violations of any law of the United States'. So long as a union acts in its self-interest and does not combine with non-labor groups, the licit and the illicit under s 20 are not to be distinguished by any judgment regarding the wisdom or unwisdom, the rightness or wrongness, the selfishness or unselfishness of the end of which the particular union activities are the means.").

and the illicit under [29 U.S.C. § 52] are not to be distinguished by any judgment regarding the wisdom or unwisdom, the rightness or wrongness, the selfishness or unselfishness of the end of which the particular union activities are the means. There is nothing remotely within the terms of [29 U.S.C. § 52] that differentiates between trade union conduct directed against an employer because of a controversy arising in the relation between employer and employee, as such, and conduct similarly directed but ultimately due to an internecine struggle between two unions seeking the favor of the same employer." The immunity therefore extended to the familiar activities of striking, picketing, and boycotting in which the Carpenters had engaged.

In the following extract, the Ninth Circuit wrestled with the meaning and application of this test in an antitrust suit brought by a construction company plaintiff, BE & K, against a number of unions.

USS-POSCO Indus. v. Contra Costa Cnty. Bldg. & Const. Trades Council, AFL-CIO

31 F.3d 800 (9th Cir. 1994)

Judge Kozinski.

[1] USS–POSCO Industries ("UPI") is a joint venture between USX Corporation (formerly U.S. Steel) and Pohang Iron and Steel Co. of South Korea, formed to modernize and operate an old steel facility in Pittsburg, California (PITCAL). Interested unions allegedly attempted to coerce UPI into awarding the general contract to a unionized contractor. After bidding, UPI nevertheless awarded the $350 million construction contract—involving over 800 jobs—to appellant BE & K, a merit-shop [*i.e.*, non-unionized] contractor.

[2] BE & K alleges the unions then began a campaign to eliminate non-union construction in Northern California by making an example of PITCAL. Although none of the unions had a collective bargaining agreement with BE & K, defendants allegedly filed automatic protests to BE & K's permits in order to cause it gratuitous expense and delay; lobbied for a local toxic waste disposal ordinance that would require BE & K to obtain more permits; sued to enforce the ordinance at the PITCAL site; encouraged BE & K's subcontractors to protest nonexistent safety violations; brought suit against BE & K for allegedly violating environmental laws (the Piledrivers suit); and brought numerous grievances, arbitrations and enforcement proceedings against BE & K's partner, Eichleay Constructors, Inc. (the Eichleay actions). According to BE & K, the unions' purpose was not to organize BE & K's employees, but to cause such delay and expense that future project owners would only hire unionized contractors and subcontractors.

[3] UPI and BE & K originally brought suit alleging unfair labor practices [but the district court found that the challenged conduct constituted valid attempts to petition the government and were therefore protected by *Noerr-Pennington* petitioning immunity.]

[4] [BE & K subsequently amended its complaint (twice), and some—but not all—of the amended allegations were again dismissed under *Noerr-Pennington.*]

[5] The unions then advised the district court they intended to seek partial summary judgment on the antitrust claim on the ground that the surviving allegations involved activities protected by the statutory labor exemption. The court ruled that, in order to overcome the statutory exemption, BE & K would have to prove *both* a combination with non-labor groups *and* an illegitimate purpose in such combination. The court then limited BE & K's discovery to the first of these elements. Because BE & K was unable to show a triable issue of fact as to whether there was a combination with non-labor groups, the court granted the unions' subsequent motion for partial summary judgment.

[6] BE & K stipulated to dismissal of its remaining claims with prejudice. It appeals only the antitrust claims and the imposition of sanctions.

[7] In United States v. Hutcheson, 312 U.S. 219, 232 (1941), the Supreme Court examined the "interlacing" Sherman, Clayton and Norris-LaGuardia Acts, and held that they gave unions a statutory exemption to the antitrust laws:[2]

> So long as a union acts in its self-interest and does not combine with non-labor groups, the licit and the illicit are not to be distinguished by any judgment regarding the wisdom or unwisdom, the rightness or wrongness, the selfishness or unselfishness of the end of which the particular union activities are the means.

[8] This passage has been read as establishing a two-prong test for the statutory labor exemption: (1) Did the union combine with a non-labor group? (2) Did the union act in its legitimate self-interest? A key question in this case is whether these two prongs of *Hutcheson* are to be read in the conjunctive (*i.e.*, that plaintiff must establish both elements in order to get around the exemption), or in the disjunctive (*i.e.*, that plaintiff can bypass the exemption by proving either element).

[9] The district court read the *Hutcheson* test in the conjunctive and granted summary judgment on the antitrust claim because BE & K was unable to establish a triable issue of fact as to the first element—whether the unions had combined with non-labor groups. BE & K appeals this ruling, arguing first, that the district court defined non-labor group too narrowly; and second, that BE & K should have been allowed to show the union acted for an improper purpose, as an alternative avenue for defeating the statutory labor exemption.

[10] . . . What constitutes a non-labor group for purposes of the antitrust laws has never been very clearly defined. It is possible, however, to derive a fair approximation of what the term means based on certain common-sense observations.

[11] On the one hand, when a labor union combines with an entity that is competing in the plaintiff's market, this normally is deemed to be a combination with a non-labor group, stripping the union of the statutory labor exemption. Thus, in most statutory labor exemption cases, the focus has been on whether the union combined with a competitor of the targeted employer.

[12] At the other end of the spectrum, labor unions carrying out their normal functions must be free to hire law firms, contract for lease space and negotiate with other business entities, without risking antitrust liability. Even though many of the entities that unions deal with on a daily basis cannot fairly be described as labor groups, they are not deemed "non-labor groups" for purposes of the statutory labor exemption. Were it otherwise, this requirement—which lies at the heart of the test announced by *Hutcheson*—would be rendered utterly meaningless in the sense that everything unions do would become a combination with a non-labor group and possibly subject to antitrust liability.

[13] To allow unions breathing space in carrying out their legitimate functions without giving them free rein to extend their substantial economic power into markets for goods and services other than labor, we conclude that the definition of non-labor group must not stray too far from the paradigm of the union combining with the employer's competitors. To constitute a non-labor group for purposes of the statutory labor exemption, therefore, the entity in question must operate in the same market as the plaintiff to a sufficient degree that it would be capable of committing an antitrust violation against the plaintiff, quite independent of the union's involvement.

[14] . . . [A] competitor of the plaintiff clearly falls within that definition, as would a supplier or purchaser of the plaintiff's goods or services. Other entities, though more remote, may nevertheless stand in such a relationship to the plaintiff that they are deemed to be operating in the same market. When the union combines with such an entity, it loses the protections of the antitrust exemption.

[15] BE & K took discovery on this issue and, although the initial order seemed to restrict discovery to BE & K's competitors, the court subsequently explained that it did not mean to cut off any discovery reasonably designed to identify contractors, manufacturers or other commercial entities with whom the defendants may have formed

---

[2] There is also a non-statutory exemption for agreements between unions and employers that are intimately related to the unions' vital concern with wages, hours and working conditions. As no such collective bargaining relationship existed here, the non-statutory exemption is not at issue.

illegal combinations. This was sufficiently broad to allow BE & K to identify anyone falling under the definition of non-labor group as explicated above, but BE & K has been able to point to no such entity. We therefore agree with the district court that BE & K has failed to raise a material issue of fact as to whether the unions combined with non-labor groups, and therefore did not carry its burden under this prong of the *Hutcheson* test.

[16] . . . The district court didn't allow BE & K discovery on the alternate prong of *Hutcheson* because it took the view that failure as to one prong was fatal to BE & K's case. In its most recent pronouncement on the subject, however, the Supreme Court clearly held that a union that combines only with other labor groups may nonetheless lose the statutory exemption under the second prong of *Hutcheson*. *H.A. Artists & Assocs. v. Actors' Equity Ass'n*, 451 U.S. 704 (1981), involved a challenge under the Sherman Act to certain rules of the Actors' Equity Union, including the exaction of a franchising fee from theatrical agents licensed by the union.

[17] The Supreme Court first inquired whether there was a combination between the union and any "non-labor groups," or persons who are not "parties to the labor dispute." The Court found that the theatrical agents were not a "non-labor group" for purposes of the statutory exemption. Had this been sufficient to establish the union's entitlement to the labor exemption, the Court could have stopped right there. Instead, it proceeded to evaluate whether the union's activities were undertaken in pursuit of its legitimate self-interest. While it found the union's activity generally exempt because the regulations were clearly designed to promote the union's legitimate self-interest, it found the fees that the union levied upon the agents might not be a permissible component of the exempt regulatory system. Because no evidence had been presented at trial to show that the costs justified the fees actually levied, the case was remanded for further factfinding.

[18] Had the Court in *H.A. Artists* eventually approved all aspects of the arrangement between the union and the agents, its examination of the fee structure might have been explainable on a belt-and-suspenders rationale. But the Court found fault with the fee structure—or at least found that there might be fault. Since *H.A. Artists* was an antitrust case, the only possible fault could be a violation of the antitrust laws. We read this as a clear holding that a union may violate the antitrust laws—in other words, that it may lose the benefit of the labor exemption—even when it does not combine with a non-labor group. Although, prior to *H.A. Artists*, there was some doubt on this point, there no longer is.

[19] What, then, does it mean for a union to pursue an illegitimate purpose? In the broadest sense, everything a union does serves its self-interest. But *Hutcheson* requires that it act in pursuit of its legitimate self-interest. Whether the interest in question is legitimate depends on whether the ends to be achieved are among the traditional objectives of labor organizations. Thus, if a union forces employers to funnel money into a commercial enterprise from which the union derives profits; or if it forces the employer to hire the union president's spouse; or if a union is involved in illegal activities unrelated to its mission, such as dealing drugs or gambling, those would not be objectives falling within the union's legitimate interest. In such cases, the unions cease to act as labor groups.

[20] Of course, the means employed by the union bear on the degree of scrutiny we will cast on the legitimacy of the union's interest. Thus, where a union engages in activities normally associated with labor disputes, these will be presumed to be in pursuit of the union's legitimate interest absent a very strong showing to the contrary. Where the union's activities are farther afield, the scrutiny is more searching.

[21] *H.A. Artists* casts a highly instructive light on this issue. The activity there—collection of franchise fees from the agents for the direct benefit of union members—was not a traditional union activity; it looked like the union may have been using its bargaining power with theatrical agents to generate a collateral source of revenue. The Court did not say the franchise fees violated the antitrust laws per se, but placed a substantial burden on the union to prove why this method of collecting revenues was not merely convenient but necessary. "Without the fees," the Court reasoned, "the dues of the union's members would perhaps have to be increased to offset the loss of a general revenue source," but there was "no reason to believe that any of its legitimate interests would be affected." The Court's concern thus seemed to be that the union may have funneled the market power granted to it by the labor laws into a money-making enterprise. That the money would then be used to finance labor-related activities was not, in the Court's view, exculpatory, unless the union could show it could not achieve those objectives some other way.

[22] Many of the activities of which BE & K complains are traditional organizational activities, closely related to traditional union ends. For example, the unions allegedly picketed and handbilled the plaintiffs' premises after BE & K refused to recognize them as the exclusive collective bargaining representative for the employees of BE & K and its subcontractors, and enter into a collective bargaining agreement with the defendants. And the unions encouraged work stoppages by unionized employees because of well-founded safety concerns at the project site.

[23] That these activities were not undertaken to unionize this particular employer but in order to eliminate non-union shops altogether by making an example of BE & K does not matter. Encouraging the use of unionized labor is an objective well within the legitimate interests of labor unions and, so long as this end is pursued by activities normally associated with labor disputes, there's a strong presumption that the unions are protected from antitrust liability by the statutory labor exemption.

[24] More troublesome are certain other activities allegedly undertaken by the unions, such as pressing frivolous lawsuits, automatically protesting against permits sought by BE & K, pressing for the passage of a regulatory measure and then agitating for its enforcement against BE & K—all allegedly to make an example of BE & K and discourage use of merit-shop contractors by parties such as UPI. Taking a cue from *H.A. Artists*, we cannot say that pursuing legitimate labor goals through this kind of activity is per se exempted from the antitrust laws. The question here, as in *H.A. Artists*, is whether the non-traditional means were appropriate—in other words, whether the non-traditional means were not only lawful, but necessary because the goals could not be achieved through traditional tactics. And the burden to show this lies with the unions.

[25] Because the district court erroneously construed *Hutcheson*'s two-part test in the conjunctive, it did not allow discovery on this issue. In this, we conclude, the district court erred. Plaintiff was entitled to try to raise a triable issue of fact on this point by gathering evidence in support of its allegations.

* * *

The statutory exemptions are supplemented by a penumbral "nonstatutory" zone of protection recognized by the Court.[755] In *Brown*, the Supreme Court considered a situation in which a group of employers—professional football club owners—had made a joint wage offer to a players' union. The offer was declined, and despite the impasse the club owners agreed to implement the wage offer. They were then sued for violating Section 1. The Court held that the agreement, growing directly from the collective-bargaining process, was immune from antitrust scrutiny, but left the outer bounds of this zone of immunity uncertain.

Brown v. Pro Football, Inc.
518 U.S. 231 (1996)

Justice Breyer.

[1] The question in this case arises at the intersection of the Nation's labor and antitrust laws. A group of professional football players brought this antitrust suit against football club owners. The club owners had bargained with the players' union over a wage issue until they reached impasse. The owners then had agreed among themselves (but not with the union) to implement the terms of their own last best bargaining offer. The question before us is whether federal labor laws shield such an agreement from antitrust attack. We believe that they do. This Court has previously found in the labor laws an implicit antitrust exemption that applies where

---

[755] *See, e.g.*, Brown v. Pro Football, Inc., 518 U.S. 231, 250 (1996) ("[T]he implicit ('nonstatutory') antitrust exemption applies to the employer conduct at issue here. That conduct took place during and immediately after a collective-bargaining negotiation. It grew out of, and was directly related to, the lawful operation of the bargaining process. It involved a matter that the parties were required to negotiate collectively. And it concerned only the parties to the collective-bargaining relationship."); Connell Const. Co. v. Plumbers & Steamfitters Loc. Union No. 100, 421 U.S. 616, 622 (1975) ("The nonstatutory exemption has its source in the strong labor policy favoring the association of employees to eliminate competition over wages and working conditions. Union success in organizing workers and standardizing wages ultimately will affect price competition among employers, but the goals of federal labor law never could be achieved if this effect on business competition were held a violation of the antitrust laws."); *see also* H. A. Artists & Assocs., Inc. v. Actors' Equity Ass'n, 451 U.S. 704, 714 (1981) ("While the Norris-LaGuardia Act's bar of federal-court labor injunctions is not explicitly phrased as an exemption from the antitrust laws, it has been interpreted broadly as a statement of congressional policy that the courts must not use the antitrust laws as a vehicle to interfere in labor disputes.").

needed to make the collective-bargaining process work. Like the Court of Appeals, we conclude that this need makes the exemption applicable in this case. [. . .]

[2] The immunity before us rests upon what this Court has called the "nonstatutory" labor exemption from the antitrust laws. The Court has implied this exemption from federal labor statutes, which set forth a national labor policy favoring free and private collective bargaining, which require good-faith bargaining over wages, hours, and working conditions; and which delegate related rulemaking and interpretive authority to the National Labor Relations Board (Board).

[3] This implicit exemption reflects both history and logic. . . . In the 1930's, when it subsequently enacted the labor statutes, Congress, as in 1914, hoped to prevent judicial use of antitrust law to resolve labor disputes—a kind of dispute normally inappropriate for antitrust law resolution. The implicit ("nonstatutory") exemption interprets the labor statutes in accordance with this intent, namely, as limiting an antitrust court's authority to determine, in the area of industrial conflict, what is or is not a "reasonable" practice. It thereby substitutes legislative and administrative labor-related determinations for judicial antitrust-related determinations as to the appropriate legal limits of industrial conflict.

[4] As a matter of logic, it would be difficult, if not impossible, to require groups of employers and employees to bargain together, but at the same time to forbid them to make among themselves or with each other any of the competition-restricting agreements potentially necessary to make the process work or its results mutually acceptable. Thus, the implicit exemption recognizes that, to give effect to federal labor laws and policies and to allow meaningful collective bargaining to take place, some restraints on competition imposed through the bargaining process must be shielded from antitrust sanctions.

[5] The petitioners and their supporters concede, as they must, the legal existence of the exemption we have described. They also concede that, where its application is necessary to make the statutorily authorized collective-bargaining process work as Congress intended, the exemption must apply both to employers and to employees. . . . Consequently, the question before us is one of determining the exemption's scope: Does it apply to an agreement among several employers bargaining together to implement after impasse the terms of their last best good-faith wage offer? We assume that such conduct, as practiced in this case, is unobjectionable as a matter of labor law and policy. On that assumption, we conclude that the exemption applies.

[6] Labor law itself regulates directly, and considerably, the kind of behavior here at issue—the post-impasse imposition of a proposed employment term concerning a mandatory subject of bargaining. Both the Board and the courts have held that, after impasse, labor law permits employers unilaterally to implement changes in pre-existing conditions, but only insofar as the new terms meet carefully circumscribed conditions. For example, the new terms must be "reasonably comprehended" within the employer's pre-impasse proposals (typically the last rejected proposals), lest by imposing more or less favorable terms, the employer unfairly undermined the union's status. The collective-bargaining proceeding itself must be free of any unfair labor practice, such as an employer's failure to have bargained in good faith. These regulations reflect the fact that impasse and an accompanying implementation of proposals constitute an integral part of the bargaining process. [. . .]

[7] Multiemployer bargaining itself is a well-established, important, pervasive method of collective bargaining, offering advantages to both management and labor. . . . [It] plays a significant role in a collective-bargaining process that itself constitutes an important part of the Nation's industrial relations system.

[8] In these circumstances, to subject the practice to antitrust law is to require antitrust courts to answer a host of important practical questions about how collective bargaining over wages, hours, and working conditions is to proceed—the very result that the implicit labor exemption seeks to avoid. And it is to place in jeopardy some of the potentially beneficial labor-related effects that multiemployer bargaining can achieve. That is because unlike labor law, which sometimes welcomes anticompetitive agreements conducive to industrial harmony, antitrust law forbids all agreements among competitors (such as competing employers) that unreasonably lessen competition among or between them in virtually any respect whatsoever. . . .

[9] If the antitrust laws apply, what are employers to do once impasse is reached? If all impose terms similar to their last joint offer, they invite an antitrust action premised upon identical behavior (along with prior or

accompanying conversations) as tending to show a common understanding or agreement. If any, or all, of them individually impose terms that differ significantly from that offer, they invite an unfair labor practice charge. Indeed, how can employers safely discuss their offers together even before a bargaining impasse occurs? A preimpasse discussion about, say, the practical advantages or disadvantages of a particular proposal invites a later antitrust claim that they agreed to limit the kinds of action each would later take should an impasse occur. . . . All this is to say that to permit antitrust liability here threatens to introduce instability and uncertainty into the collective-bargaining process, for antitrust law often forbids or discourages the kinds of joint discussions and behavior that the collective-bargaining process invites or requires. [. . .]

[10] [W]e hold that the implicit ("nonstatutory") antitrust exemption applies to the employer conduct at issue here. That conduct took place during and immediately after a collective-bargaining negotiation. It grew out of, and was directly related to, the lawful operation of the bargaining process. It involved a matter that the parties were required to negotiate collectively. And it concerned only the parties to the collective-bargaining relationship.

[11] Our holding is not intended to insulate from antitrust review every joint imposition of terms by employers, for an agreement among employers could be sufficiently distant in time and in circumstances from the collective-bargaining process that a rule permitting antitrust intervention would not significantly interfere with that process. We need not decide in this case whether, or where, within these extreme outer boundaries to draw that line. Nor would it be appropriate for us to do so without the detailed views of the [National Labor Relations] Board, to whose specialized judgment Congress intended to leave many of the inevitable questions concerning multiemployer bargaining bound to arise in the future.

CASENOTE: William Morris Endeavor Entertainment, LLC v. Writers Guild of America

432 F.Supp.3d 1127 (C.D. Cal. 2020)

The bounds of the statutory and nonstatutory labor exemptions were recently put at issue in the *Writers Guild* litigation. That case concerned an alleged effort by two writers' unions to end the practice of "packaging" by talent agencies. "Packaging" involves talent agencies charging fees ("packaging fees") for furnishing a group or set of creative individuals for a production (writers, actors, directors, etc.) to a movie studio, rather than taking a customary 10% commission from the relevant talented individuals.

The writers' unions had become concerned that the packaging-fee practice harmed writers by encouraging agencies to maximize their packaging fee rather than writers' compensation. As a result, they had adopted a "Code of Conduct" which forbade their members from accepting representation by any talent agency that: (1) received packaging fees; or (2) held any interest in a movie production company. Three Hollywood talent agencies sued the unions under Section 1, and the unions moved to dismiss the complaint, citing both the statutory and non-statutory antitrust exemptions. But the district court refused to dismiss the antitrust claims on either ground.

First, the court considered and rejected the unions' argument that the challenged conduct was covered by the statutory exemption. The plaintiffs had alleged that the defendants had compromised their immunity by combining with "non-labor groups," including: "(1) other talent agencies, (2) showrunners acting in a producer-only capacity who are thus exempt from the [writers' collective bargaining agreement, which covered only writers rather than producers], and (3) unlicensed lawyers and managers." The defendants argued that showrunners should be treated as a labor group because the employment of a showrunner on a production displaces the need to employ a writer. But the court rejected this argument, pointing out that the alleged conduct had embraced showrunners even when they were working in a role that did *not* displace a writer. The presence of plausible allegations of combination with non-labor groups precluded the application of the statutory exemption.

Second, the court considered and rejected the unions' effort to invoke the nonstatutory exemption. The court acknowledged two previous formulations of the nonstatutory exemption in the Ninth Circuit. In Phoenix Elec. Co. v. Nat'l Elec. Contractors Ass'n, 81 F.3d 858, 861 (9th Cir. 1996), the court of appeals had stated that: "[T]he parties to an agreement restraining trade are exempt from antitrust liability only if (1) the restraint primarily affects the parties to the agreement and no one else, (2) the agreement concerns wages, hours, or conditions of employment that are mandatory subjects of collective bargaining and (3) the agreement is produced from bona fide, arm's-length collective bargaining." And in California ex rel. Harris v. Safeway, Inc., 651 F.3d 1118, 1129 (9th Cir. 2011) (en banc), the court had more recently indicated that the nonstatutory exception should be guided by a totality-of-the-circumstances approach that included scrutiny of whether the challenged practice is an "extensively regulated and carefully circumscribed practice in labor negotiations," whether it relates to a "core subject matter" of collective bargaining, such as wages, hours, or working conditions, and whether it "operates primarily in the labor market with only tangential effects on the business market."

Under neither standard could the defendants qualify for the nonstatutory exemption. The *Phoenix Electric* formulation was inapposite because the plaintiffs had plausibly alleged that the conduct primarily affected a broader group than just the parties to the Code of Conduct. "In particular," the court explained, "Plaintiffs allege that the Code of Conduct's packaging restrictions prohibit actors and directors, who are not Defendants' members, from benefiting from packaging as well. Plaintiffs further allege that the Code of Conduct's packaging restrictions will reduce the amount of content created overall, resulting in harm to media consumers."

And the challenged conduct fell outside the more recent *Harris* formulation even more clearly. Plaintiffs had alleged that packaging had been accepted and endorsed by defendants themselves for "more than forty years," with no previous bans. They also alleged that the effort to prohibit packaging fees was not only overbroad, rather than circumscribed to reflect the "idiosyncratic" nature of individual packaging agreements, but that it also "has substantial effects on the larger media market, reducing employment for directors and actors, and reducing the overall amount of media content produced." In sum, the plaintiffs had alleged a claim sufficient to avoid the nonstatutory exemption.

As a result, neither the statutory nor the nonstatutory exemption would apply. The case would be permitted to proceed to discovery.

Today, the scope and application of the labor exemption remains controversial. In particular, the asymmetry of treatment between, on the one hand, employees who are members of a traditional labor union (who enjoy protected treatment under the antitrust exemption), and, on the other, gig workers who operate outside these traditional structures (who often do not) has attracted comment and criticism.[756]

CASENOTE: Columbia River Packers Ass'n v. Hinton
315 U.S. 143 (1942)

Columbia River exemplifies the relationship between antitrust's labor exemptions and the status of "employee"—rather than "independent contractor"—in labor law. In that case, Columbia River (a fish processing and canning business with facilities in Oregon, Washington, and Alaska) had been confronted with a demand by the Pacific Coast Fishermen's Union—which represented "independent entrepreneur[]" fishermen—to agree to buy only from Union fishermen. Columbia River refused, found that Union fishermen would not supply it with fish, and sued the Union for violating Section 1. The Union argued that its actions were immune from antitrust scrutiny, and the Ninth Circuit agreed.

But the Supreme Court, in a short and unanimous opinion, did not. The Court held that the challenged conduct did not arise from a "labor dispute" within the meaning of the Norris-LaGuardia Act [i.e., 29 U.S.C. § 113]. "That a dispute among businessmen over the terms of a contract for the sale of fish is something different from a controversy concerning terms or conditions of employment, or concerning the association of persons seeking to arrange terms or conditions of employment," held the Court, "calls for no extended discussion." The statutory exemption is intended to help workers "obtain acceptable terms and conditions of employment" and protection from "the interference, restraint, or coercion of employers of labor." Congress's attention "was focussed upon disputes affecting the employer-employee relationship . . . the Act was not intended to have application to disputes over the sale of commodities." And while it was true that the statute expressly covered circumstances in which the

---

[756] *See, e.g.*, Marina Lao, *Workers in the "Gig" Economy: The Case for Extending the Antitrust Labor Exemption*, 51 U.C. Davis L. Rev. 1543 (2018).

disputants were not in the relation of employer and employee, "the statutory classification, however broad, . . . does not expand the application of the Act to include controversies upon which the employer-employee relationship has no bearing."

The conclusion followed inexorably. "The sellers are not employees of the petitioners or of any other employer nor do they seek to be. On the contrary, their desire is to continue to operate as independent businessmen, free from such controls as an employer might exercise. That some of the fishermen have a small number of employees of their own, who are also members of the Union, does not alter the situation. For the dispute here, relating solely to the sale of fish, does not place in controversy the wages or hours or other terms and conditions of employment of these employees." As a result, there would be no antitrust immunity.

As Sanjukta Paul notes in the following extract, the decisions reflected in the law's definitions of "worker" and "collusion" raise sharp questions about antitrust's conceptual foundations.

Sanjukta M. Paul, The Enduring Ambiguities of Antitrust Liability for Worker Collective Action
47 Loyola U. Chi. L.J. (2016)

The labor exemption currently immunizes most worker collective action from antitrust liability. Employee status, much discussed in its impact on workers in terms of the receding reach of labor and employment law protections, is also the trigger for extending the grasp of antitrust regulation of workers' autonomous collective action to better their working conditions. In other words, a phenomenon that is commonly understood as exemplifying deregulation actually extends regulation over the conduct of workers even as it withdraws it from the conduct of employers. As a result, individual workers classified as independent contractors may be subject to antitrust prosecution for organizing for decent wages or working conditions under the price-fixing doctrine, regardless of the reasonableness of the wage or the broader social or economic outcome.

Assuming for the moment that the labor exemption does not apply to a given set of independent contractor workers, and that they are not able to prove that they are misclassified employees, the law of price-fixing is likely to govern their concerted action. The modern neoclassical interpretation of antitrust, which mostly still reigns, takes market actors as black boxes: they are just "firms," whether they are massive corporations or a single truck driver. [. . .]

Antitrust law itself, leaving aside how it plays out in the price-fixing or boycott doctrine or its application to labor, is . . . an embodiment of the fact that the market society is not some "natural" or default state of affairs but, on the contrary, the product of an affirmative and often costly set of policy decisions on the part of the state itself. Today, competition is something that courts undertake to promote, and various policies and practices by private actors are to be evaluated specifically according to whether they promote competition. This is truly a far cry from the original classicist position on markets, according to which almost anything a private actor did in furtherance of interest was, ipso facto, competition. The very idea that competition is a normative ideal separate from what firms actually do in furtherance of their economic self-interest makes space for affirmative state intervention (to bring affairs closer to that normative ideal). To be sure, the classicists had a notion of legitimate and illegitimate competition, but that distinction was drawn on the basis of moral or normative concepts distinct from competition itself. In the neoclassical framework, by contrast, competition itself is the normative benchmark used by antitrust. In other words, the classical framework put bounds on the acts of market actors, but on the basis of conflict between competition and other normative ideals. The neoclassical framework bounds the acts of market actors on the basis of ideal of competition itself. That fact betrays the irreducible normative content of the concept of competition as it is used by contemporary courts, over and above the content of the concept of competition employed by classicist courts.

The law of price-fixing is about preventing restraints on competition, or coordinated conduct that tends to have anti-competitive effects. The reason that I say there is an irreducible normative component in its application is that *some* restraints on competition are always present in a market; they function as the walls within which competition will take place. At the most basic level, these include all sorts of commercial regulation such as the rules defining and legally constituting the entities that will engage in competition, as well as industry-specific regulation.

The goal of "maximizing competition" is simply not tenable, as a practical and logical matter, without incorporating some kind of limits. Then it is an unavoidable question what those appropriate limits, embodied for example in the scope of the price-fixing law, are. The limits we actually have are arguably as much the result of historical accident as they are of rational economic science. Thus, the logic of price-fixing has an inherent openness or indeterminacy, such that effectively extrinsic normative considerations are necessary to determine the precise circumstances under which concerted action to constrict supply of a given commodity is prohibited by antitrust law. The role these considerations play is rarely overt; courts typically fold them under the concepts of "maximizing competition" or "legitimate competition."

This is particularly so with respect to antitrust's relationship to labor, which was formed under the pressure of normative considerations that would likely not be endorsed openly by today's courts. That relationship raises a set of normative questions no matter how it is constituted—not only if labor is exempted from antitrust prosecution. One can imagine a whole variety of arrangements relating antitrust law to labor—from total subjection of worker collective action to price-fixing, treating each worker as an individual firm, and with no labor exemption whatsoever, on one end; to a complete exemption for workers' organizations with no restrictions, on the other. Any of these arrangements would then simply become background legal facts; they would constitute the markets within which economic interactions take place.

* * *

In light of *Columbia River* and the concern with the employment relation that it (arguably) exemplifies, antitrust leans heavily on labor law for an account of what relationships can be labeled those of "employment." The following amicus brief, filed by DOJ with the National Labor Relations Board, gives an enforcer's perspective on the importance of labor law's employee / contractor distinction for antitrust analysis.

Brief of the United States Department of Justice as Amicus Curiae in Support of Neither Party, The Atlanta Opera, Inc.
National Labor Relations Board Case 10-RC-276292 (Feb. 10, 2022)

[1] . . . [T]he antitrust laws were intended by Congress to be interpreted in harmony with the aims of the labor laws, including the National Labor Relations Act of 1935 ("NLRA"), which encourages the practice and procedure of collective bargaining to restore equality of bargaining power between employers and employees. To harmonize these two bodies of law, including to preserve protections for worker organizing, courts have recognized both the "statutory" and "nonstatutory" labor exemptions from the antitrust laws.

[2] The statutory exemption excepts specific union activities, including secondary picketing and boycotts, from the operation of the antitrust laws. It has been interpreted broadly to cover substantially all, if not all, of the normal peaceful activities of labor union[s]. But it does not cover agreements between workers (or unions) and "non-labor groups," i.e., their employers.

[3] The nonstatutory labor exemption insulates certain agreements between workers and their employers imposed through the bargaining process from challenge under the antitrust laws, under the view that Congress intended rulemaking and interpretive authority on these topics to be delegated to the NLRB.

[4] In doing so, the exemption accommodates the congressional policy favoring collective bargaining under the NLRA. But that accommodation has limits. For example, the nonstatutory exemption offers no similar protection when a union and a nonlabor party agree to restrain competition in a business market, e.g., with an agreement on how much consumers will pay for a product. Nor does it protect agreements among competing employers— imposed outside the collective bargaining process—that restrain competition in labor markets, e.g., agreements to fix prices or allocate markets.

[*]

[5] A dramatic expansion during the past decade in the number and variety of workers who are categorized as independent contractors has created significant ambiguity about the appropriate treatment of such workers under antitrust law. While the statutory and nonstatutory labor exemptions provide important protections for worker organizing and bargaining, courts have historically held that these exemptions only protect employees and their unions, not independent contractors.[16] By contrast, concerted action by independent contractors traditionally has been subject to antitrust scrutiny.[17]

[6] Because of this distinction, if the NLRB adopts or maintains an ambiguous or overly narrow definition of "employee," certain workers . . . may be subjected to antitrust liability for organizing to improve their conditions— a risk that is heightened by the tendency of courts to construe the labor exemptions narrowly. Consistent with the reasoning in these and other cases, there may be potential benefits to extending certain labor protections to workers who seek to bargain with a single employer—including digital platforms and other firms whose business models have led to the proliferation of the "gig economy." Clarity as to employee status is important, in part, because the antitrust laws otherwise scrutinize collective action among independent contractors or independent professionals, where they are not employees.

[7] The potential for confusion with respect to the applicability of the labor exemption among both courts and workers is likely to be compounded by the growing number of states and other federal agencies which have recently adopted a broader definition of employment than that used in [the NLRB's *SuperShuttle DFW Inc.* decision, 367 NLRB No. 75 (2019)], thereby creating an interpretive split among labor regulators. Even if the Antitrust Division were to exercise its prosecutorial discretion not to pursue action against workers whose status as employees is unclear, the threat of private antitrust lawsuits and treble damages might nonetheless substantially chill worker organizing, since employers and other interested parties would remain free to pursue antitrust litigation. Such an outcome would leave affected workers with fewer tools to combat the exercise of monopsony power or superior bargaining leverage by employers in the manner that Congress intended when it passed the NLRA.

[8] In addition to harming workers, ambiguity about the definition of employment may also create uncertainty and risk of antitrust liability for employers. In general, firms can decide how much they pay their employees and, in turn, how much to charge consumers for their employees' services. But independent contractors generally cannot coordinate their pricing decisions absent some exemption from the antitrust laws. Nor can they do so through a third party. Thus, firms that set the prices at which their workers offer services to consumers may face uncertainty about their potential antitrust exposure if there is ambiguity about whether those workers are independent contractors rather than employees. [. . .]

[9] [T]he [Antitrust] Division supports clarifying the NLRB's definition of "employee." Evidence collected by the Division at our recent Labor Workshop as well as a growing body of legal and economic scholarship both support the view that labor markets are currently undergoing substantial change and disruption, including but not limited to changes resulting from the rise of the so-called "gig economy." Given these changes in the underlying economic realities, the Division believes that the NRLB is in a position to better protect both labor market competition and the welfare of workers by adopting a sound, up-to-date, consistent approach to worker classification that adequately protects workers' rights to organize. Such an effort would not only be consistent with the legislative history of the statutory sources of the antitrust labor exemptions, such as the Norris-LaGuardia Act, which were explicitly passed to clarify the Congress's interest in harmonizing antitrust law and labor law in a way that reflects the special status of labor organizing within our economic and political system, but would also would help to increase the effectiveness of antitrust enforcement and aid the Division's efforts to protect competition, particularly in markets where employee misclassification may harm competition.

---

[16] *See, e.g.*, [H.A. Artists & Assocs. v. Actors' Equity Ass'n, 451 U.S. 704, 717 n.20 (1981)] ("[A] party seeking refuge in the statutory exemption must be a bona fide labor organization, and not an independent contractor or entrepreneur."). Antitrust courts typically draw on common law principles to evaluate whether workers are employees or independent contractors. *See, e.g.*, United States v. Women's Sportswear Mfg. Ass'n, 336 U.S. 460, 463–64 (1949) ("The stitching contractor, although he furnishes chiefly labor, also utilizes the labor through machines and has his rentals, capital costs, overhead and profits. He is an entrepreneur, not a laborer."); Chamber of Com. of United States of Am. v. City of Seattle, 426 F. Supp. 3d 786, 788 (W.D. Wash. 2019).

[17] *See, e.g.*, Columbia River Packers Ass'n v. Hinton, 315 U.S. 143, 146-47 (1942) (agreements between fish sellers); [United States v. Women's Sportswear Mfg. Ass'n, 336 U.S. 460, 463–64 (1949)] (garment workers); FTC v. Superior Court Trial Lawyers' Ass'n, 493 U.S. 411 (1990) (trial lawyers).

* * *

In light of the preceding extracts, what do you make of the First Circuit's 2022 decision in *Confederación Hípica de Puerto Rico* to apply labor immunity to a group of independent-contractor jockeys who went on strike for higher pay? In that case—which surprised many observers—the First Circuit took a fresh look at the scope of the statutory exemption and concluded that it should not be limited to employer-employee bargaining at all. *Confederación Hípica* leaves observers wondering whether the scope of labor immunity might be somewhat broader than many had previously thought: and it challenges the idea that *Columbia River*—along with other cases like *Superior Court Trial Lawyers*, which you may remember from Chapter V—closes the door to labor immunity for independent contractors. The Supreme Court declined to grant cert, leaving lower courts to puzzle it over for now.[757]

Confederación Hípica de Puerto Rico, Inc. v. Confederación de Jinetes Puertorriqueños, Inc.

30 F.4th 306 (1st Cir. 2022)

Judge Lynch.

[1] The Sherman Antitrust Act usually forbids would-be competitors from staging a group boycott. Federal statutes and controlling Supreme Court case law create an exemption for certain conduct, commonly called the labor-dispute exemption.

[2] In this action, brought by an association of horse owners ("Hípica") and the owner of a racetrack ("Camerero") against a group of jockeys who demanded higher wages and refused to race, the district court erroneously determined that the labor-dispute exemption does not apply. The district court preliminarily and permanently enjoined the work stoppage, awarded summary judgment against the jockeys, their spouses and conjugal partnerships, and an association representing them ("Jinetes"), and imposed $1,190,685 in damages. [. . .]

[3] Puerto Rico is home to one horse-racing track, the Hipódromo Camarero in Canóvanas, which is operated by plaintiff Camarero. Horse owners hire jockeys on a race-by-race basis. Since 1989, the jockeys have been paid a $20 mount fee for each race they participate in. The fortunate jockeys who finish in the top five positions in each race share in the "purse"—the prize money for the top five horses. A Puerto Rico government agency, established in its current form in 1987, regulates the sport. It embodied the compensation structure we have described in regulations in 1989.

[4] The jockeys have long chafed at their employment conditions. They object to the mount fee, which is about one-fifth what jockeys receive in the mainland United States. They also complain about pre-race weigh-in procedures and about the conduct of racing officials.

[5] In early June 2016, those long-simmering grievances boiled over. On June 10, several jockeys delayed the start of a race to demand that racing officials discuss the weigh-in procedures. As a result of that delay, the officials fined those jockeys. The jockeys responded through a pair of associations: defendant Jinetes and a second smaller group ("AJP"). On behalf of dozens of jockeys, the associations disputed the fines and objected to jockey compensation. The associations then attempted to negotiate employment conditions with plaintiff Hípica, the representative of the horse owners. Those negotiations resolved none of the issues, and the racing regulators declined the jockeys' request to mediate.

[6] After negotiations failed, in pursuit of their demands for increased compensation, thirty-seven jockeys refused to race for three days. Jinetes claimed credit for organizing the work stoppage. As no jockeys had registered to ride on June 30, July 1, and July 2, 2016, Camerero canceled the races scheduled for those days.

---

[757] For a recent perspective, *see* Jack Samuel, *Confederación Hípica v. Confederación de Jinetes Puertorriqueños*, N.Y.U. L. Rev. Case Comments (Apr. 23, 2023).

[7] Hípica and Camerero sued the jockeys, their spouses and conjugal partnerships, and Jinetes, alleging that the defendants engaged in a group boycott in violation of federal antitrust law. The defendants counterclaimed, alleging that the plaintiffs violated federal civil rights and antitrust law. [. . .]

[8] T]here is an inherent tension between national antitrust policy, which seeks to maximize competition, and national labor policy, which encourages cooperation among workers to improve the conditions of employment. Most of the time, antitrust law forbids would-be competitors from colluding to increase prices. When the price is a laborer's wage, however, a different set of rules apply. That must be so, lest antitrust law waylay ordinary collective bargaining. Thus a pair of exemptions—one statutory and one nonstatutory—shield legitimate labor conduct from antitrust scrutiny. We deal here with the statutory exemption.

[9] The statutory labor-dispute exemption flows from both the Clayton Act and the Norris-LaGuardia Act. Through those two statutes, Congress exempted labor disputes from antitrust law.

[10] The Clayton Act declares that "[t]he labor of a human being is not a commodity or article of commerce," subject to antitrust law. 15 U.S.C. § 17. To implement that policy, the Norris-LaGuardia Act provides that persons participating or interested in a labor dispute may engage in an enumerated set of acts—including entering agreement to refuse to perform work—without falling afoul of the Sherman Act's prohibition on engaging in an unlawful combination or conspiracy. 29 U.S.C. §§ 104, 105. The Norris-LaGuardia Act defines a "labor dispute" by specifically providing that:

> (a) A case shall be held to involve or to grow out of a labor dispute when the case involves persons who are engaged in the same industry, trade, craft, or occupation; or have direct or indirect interests therein . . . when the case involves any conflicting or competing interests in a "labor dispute" . . . of "persons participating or interested" therein . . .

> (b) A person or association shall be held to be a person participating or interested in a labor dispute if relief is sought against him or it, and if he or it is engaged in the same industry . . . in which such dispute occurs, or has a direct or indirect interest therein, or is a member, officer, or agent of any association composed in whole or in part of employers or employees engaged in such industry . . . .

> (c) The term "labor dispute" includes any controversy concerning terms or conditions of employment, or concerning the association or representation of persons in negotiating, fixing, maintaining, changing, or seeking to arrange terms or conditions of employment, regardless of whether or not the disputants stand in the proximate relation of employer and employee.

29 U.S.C. § 113.

[11] The Supreme Court has explained that the statutory exemption applies when four conditions are met. First, the conduct must be undertaken by a bona fide labor organization. Second, the conduct must actually arise from a labor dispute, as defined under the Norris-LaGuardia Act. Once those two prerequisites are satisfied, we apply a further two-prong test: the organization must act in its self-interest and not combine with non-labor groups. To summarize, then, the statutory labor-dispute exemption applies to conduct arising (1) out of the actions of a labor organization and undertaken (2) during a labor dispute, (3) unilaterally, and (4) out of the self-interest of the labor organization.

[12] We discuss the elements of the exemption in turn. First, a labor organization is a "bona fide" group representing laborers. It need not be formally recognized as a union. Second, a labor dispute broadly encompasses any controversy concerning terms or conditions of employment. Third, a labor group acts unilaterally unless it coordinates with a nonlabor group. And fourth, a labor organization acts in its self-interest when its activities bear a reasonable relationship to a legitimate union interest.

[13] We apply the statutory framework, emphasizing the first two elements, as the second pair are not seriously disputed here. We conclude that the jockeys' action fell within the labor-dispute exemption. Jinetes, which advocates for the jockeys' terms of employment, is a labor organization. The defendants sought higher wages and safer working conditions, making this a core labor dispute. The plaintiffs make no assertion that the defendants

coordinated with any nonlabor group. And the defendants acted to serve their own economic interests. Because the dispute meets the statutory criteria, the labor-dispute exemption applies.

[14] The district court erred when it concluded that the jockeys' alleged independent-contractor status categorically meant they were ineligible for the exemption. We express no opinion on whether the jockeys are independent contractors, because, by the express text of the Norris-LaGuardia Act, a labor dispute may exist "regardless of whether or not the disputants stand in the proximate relation of employer and employee." 29 U.S.C. § 113(c). The Court interpreted that provision in New Negro Alliance v. Sanitary Grocery Co., 303 U.S. 552 (1938). There, a community association encouraged a boycott of a grocery store in protest of the store's refusal to hire black employees. The Supreme Court held that the association's conduct fell within the labor-dispute exemption because the association sought to influence the store's terms of employment. It explained that the text of the Norris-LaGuardia Act was intended to embrace controversies other than those between employers and employees; between labor unions seeking to represent employees and employers; and between persons seeking employment and employers. *New Negro Alliance* thus precludes an interpretation of the exemption limited to employees alone.

[15] The key question is not whether the jockeys are independent contractors or laborers but whether what is at issue is compensation for their labor. We draw that principle from Columbia River Packers Ass'n v. Hinton, 315 U.S. 143 (1942). In that case, a group of fishermen tried to force exclusive contracts on the canneries to which they sold fish. Relying on the fact that the fishermen were "independent entrepreneurs," the Supreme Court held that the labor-dispute exemption did not apply. Instead, it explained that the dispute "is altogether between fish sellers and fish buyers" and "relates solely to the sale of fish," without implicating "wages or hours or other terms and conditions of employment." From *Columbia River Packers*, thus, comes a critical distinction in applying the labor-dispute exemption: disputes about wages for labor fall within the exemption but those over prices for goods do not. Whether or not the jockeys are independent contractors does not by itself determine whether this dispute is within the labor-dispute exemption. [. . .]

[16] The plaintiffs also appear to advert to a line of cases holding unlawful private restraints of trade intended to influence government action. Yet they fare no better with that argument. Even if the jockeys ultimately sought to influence a political body through their work stoppage, their political activism would make no difference. As long as an employee-employer relationship—broadly understood—is at the core of the controversy, as here, then any political motivations for a work stoppage would not take a dispute out of the labor exemption.[4]

[17] As the labor-dispute exemption applies, the district court erred in granting the plaintiffs an injunction and summary judgment. The plaintiffs are legally precluded from prevailing on their antitrust claims. On remand, the district court must dismiss the complaint.

NOTES

1) How would you explain the best case for a labor exemption? Does that case suggest other areas in which an exemption might be appropriate?

2) Why do you think the courts generated a "non-statutory" antitrust exemption in addition to the immunity created by Congress?

3) Should the antitrust exemption for labor unions be limited to (a) formal employees and/or (b) members of a formal union? If so, why? If not, why not?

4) How, if at all, does or should the logic of the labor exemption (*i.e.*, permitting collusion among covered workers) relate to antitrust's treatment of firms (*i.e.*, permitting collusion among members of an incorporated firm)?

5) Section 6 of the Clayton Act says that "The labor of a human being is not a commodity or article of commerce." Doesn't that mean that *anything* related to a labor market is outside the scope of antitrust?[758]

---

[4] None of the Supreme Court's subsequent cases about politically motivated anticompetitive actions alter that rule. *See* Allied Tube & Conduit Corp. v. Indian Head, Inc., 486 U.S. 492, 499-501 (1988) (curtailing politically motivated boycott rule for sale of goods); FTC v. Superior Ct. Trial Laws. Ass'n, 493 U.S. 411, 425 (1990) (labor exemption not argued); *see also* Superior Ct. Trial Laws. Ass'n v. FTC, 856 F.2d 226, 230 n.6 (D.C. Cir. 1988).

[758] *See* Daniel A. Crane, *Antitrust Antitextualism*, 96 Notre Dame L. Rev. 1205, 1223–26 (2021).

6) How, and how persuasively, did the *Confederación Hípica* court: (a) conclude that statutory antitrust immunity was not chained to the employer/employee relation? (b) distinguish *FTC v. Superior Court Trial Lawyers* (in which, as you will remember from Chapter V, the Supreme Court held *per se* illegal an effort by D.C. criminal defense lawyers to strike for higher wages)? (It may take you a minute to find the reference.)

E. Other Exemptions

Beyond petitioning, state action, and labor, antitrust is subject to a variety of other exceptions and carveouts. This subsection presents a selection. But there are plenty of others not included here, including exemptions for shipping lines, medical residency matching programs, export cartels, and others.[759]

1. Implied Repeal

In very rare cases, courts will conclude that a later federal statute has repealed the antitrust laws, within its zone of application, by implication. The leading Supreme Court decision on this issue remains 2007's *Credit Suisse*: at the time, commentators feared that this decision would herald a wave of carveouts and subtractions from the antitrust laws, but in practice the category has remained largely unpopulated.[760]

Credit Suisse Securities (USA) LLC v. Billing
551 U.S. 264 (2007)

Justice Breyer.

[1] In January 2002, respondents, a group of 60 investors, filed two antitrust class-action lawsuits against petitioners, 10 leading investment banks. They sought relief under § 1 of the Sherman Act; § 2(c) of the Clayton Act; and state antitrust laws. The investors stated that between March 1997 and December 2000 the banks had acted as underwriters, forming syndicates that helped execute the IPOs of several hundred technology-related companies. Respondents' antitrust complaints allege that the underwriters abused the practice of combining into underwriting syndicates by agreeing among themselves to impose harmful conditions upon potential investors— conditions that the investors apparently were willing to accept in order to obtain an allocation of new shares that were in high demand.

[2] These conditions, according to respondents, consist of a requirement that the investors pay additional anticompetitive charges over and above the agreed-upon IPO share price plus underwriting commission. In particular, these additional charges took the form of (1) investor promises to place bids in the aftermarket at prices above the IPO price (*i.e.*, "laddering" agreements); (2) investor commitments to purchase other, less attractive securities (*i.e.*, "tying" arrangements); and (3) investor payment of "non-competitively determined" (*i.e.*, excessive) commissions, including the purchase of an issuer's shares in follow-up or "secondary" public offerings (for which the underwriters would earn underwriting discounts). The complaint added that the underwriters' agreement to engage in some or all of these practices artificially inflated the share prices of the securities in question.

[3] The underwriters moved to dismiss the investors' complaints on the ground that federal securities law impliedly precludes application of antitrust laws to the conduct in question. . . . The District Court agreed with petitioners and dismissed the complaints against them. The Court of Appeals for the Second Circuit reversed, however, and reinstated the complaints. We granted the underwriters' petition for certiorari. And we now reverse the judgment of the Court of Appeals. [. . .]

[4] Sometimes regulatory statutes explicitly state whether they preclude application of the antitrust laws. Where regulatory statutes are silent in respect to antitrust, however, courts must determine whether, and in what respects, they implicitly preclude application of the antitrust laws. Those determinations may vary from statute to statute,

---

[759] 15 U.S.C. § 37b (medical residency matching programs); 15 U.S.C. § 62 (export arrangements); 46 U.S.C. § 40307 (shipping lines).

[760] *See generally* Howard A. Shelanski, *The Case for Rebalancing Antitrust and Regulation*, 109 Mich. L. Rev. 683 (2011).

depending upon the relation between the antitrust laws and the regulatory program set forth in the particular statute, and the relation of the specific conduct at issue to both sets of laws. [. . .]

[5] This Court's prior decisions . . . make clear that, when a court decides whether securities law precludes antitrust law, it is deciding whether, given context and likely consequences, there is a clear repugnancy between the securities law and the antitrust complaint—or as we shall subsequently describe the matter, whether the two are clearly incompatible. Moreover, [previous cases], in finding sufficient incompatibility to warrant an implication of preclusion, have treated the following factors as critical: (1) the existence of regulatory authority under the securities law to supervise the activities in question; (2) evidence that the responsible regulatory entities exercise that authority; and (3) a resulting risk that the securities and antitrust laws, if both applicable, would produce conflicting guidance, requirements, duties, privileges, or standards of conduct. We also note (4) that in [previous cases] the possible conflict affected practices that lie squarely within an area of financial market activity that the securities law seeks to regulate. [. . .]

[6] These principles, applied to the complaints before us, considerably narrow our legal task. For the parties cannot reasonably dispute the existence here of several of the conditions that this Court previously regarded as crucial to finding that the securities law impliedly precludes the application of the antitrust laws.

[7] First, the activities in question here—the underwriters' efforts jointly to promote and to sell newly issued securities—is central to the proper functioning of well-regulated capital markets. The IPO process supports new firms that seek to raise capital; it helps to spread ownership of those firms broadly among investors; it directs capital flows in ways that better correspond to the public's demand for goods and services. Moreover, financial experts, including the securities regulators, consider the general kind of joint underwriting activity at issue in this case, including road shows and bookbuilding efforts essential to the successful marketing of an IPO. . . . Thus, the antitrust complaints before us concern practices that lie at the very heart of the securities marketing enterprise.

[8] Second, the law grants the SEC authority to supervise all of the activities here in question. Indeed, the SEC possesses considerable power to forbid, permit, encourage, discourage, tolerate, limit, and otherwise regulate virtually every aspect of the practices in which underwriters engage. Private individuals who suffer harm as a result of a violation of pertinent statutes and regulations may also recover damages.

[9] Third, the SEC has continuously exercised its legal authority to regulate conduct of the general kind now at issue. It has defined in detail, for example, what underwriters may and may not do and say during their road shows. It has brought actions against underwriters who have violated these SEC regulations. And private litigants, too, have brought securities actions complaining of conduct virtually identical to the conduct at issue here; and they have obtained damages.

[10] The preceding considerations show that the first condition (legal regulatory authority), the second condition (exercise of that authority), and the fourth condition (heartland securities activity) . . . are satisfied in this case as well. . . . [T]here is here no question of the existence of appropriate regulatory authority, nor is there doubt as to whether the regulators have exercised that authority. Rather, the question before us concerns the third condition: Is there a conflict that rises to the level of incompatibility? Is an antitrust suit such as this likely to prove practically incompatible with the SEC's administration of the Nation's securities laws? [. . .]

[11] [S]everal considerations taken together lead us to find that, even on . . . pro-respondent assumptions, securities law and antitrust law are clearly incompatible.

[12] First, to permit antitrust actions such as the present one still threatens serious securities-related harm. For one thing, an unusually serious legal line-drawing problem remains unabated. In the present context only a fine, complex, detailed line separates activity that the SEC permits or encourages (for which respondents must concede antitrust immunity) from activity that the SEC must (and inevitably will) forbid (and which, on respondents' theory, should be open to antitrust attack). [. . .]

[13] Under these standards, to distinguish what is forbidden from what is allowed requires an understanding of just when, in relation to services provided, a commission is "excessive," indeed, so "excessive" that it will remain permanently forbidden. And who but the SEC itself could do so with confidence?

[14] For another thing, evidence tending to show unlawful antitrust activity and evidence tending to show lawful securities marketing activity may overlap, or prove identical. Consider, for instance, a conversation between an underwriter and an investor about how long an investor intends to hold the new shares (and at what price), say, a conversation that elicits comments concerning both the investor's short and longer term plans. That exchange might, as a plaintiff sees it, provide evidence of an underwriter's insistence upon "laddering" or, as a defendant sees it, provide evidence of a lawful effort to allocate shares to those who will hold them for a longer time. [. . .]

[15] We believe it fair to conclude that, where conduct at the core of the marketing of new securities is at issue; where securities regulators proceed with great care to distinguish the encouraged and permissible from the forbidden; where the threat of antitrust lawsuits, through error and disincentive, could seriously alter underwriter conduct in undesirable ways, to allow an antitrust lawsuit would threaten serious harm to the efficient functioning of the securities markets.

[16] Second, any enforcement-related need for an antitrust lawsuit is unusually small. For one thing, the SEC actively enforces the rules and regulations that forbid the conduct in question. For another, as we have said, investors harmed by underwriters' unlawful practices may bring lawsuits and obtain damages under the securities law. Finally, the SEC is itself required to take account of competitive considerations when it creates securities-related policy and embodies it in rules and regulations. And that fact makes it somewhat less necessary to rely upon antitrust actions to address anticompetitive behavior.

[17] We also note that Congress, in an effort to weed out unmeritorious securities lawsuits, has recently tightened the procedural requirements that plaintiffs must satisfy when they file those suits. To permit an antitrust lawsuit risks circumventing these requirements by permitting plaintiffs to dress what is essentially a securities complaint in antitrust clothing.

[18] In sum, an antitrust action in this context is accompanied by a substantial risk of injury to the securities markets and by a diminished need for antitrust enforcement to address anticompetitive conduct. Together these considerations indicate a serious conflict between, on the one hand, application of the antitrust laws and, on the other, proper enforcement of the securities law. [. . .]

[19] The upshot is that all four elements . . . are present here: (1) an area of conduct squarely within the heartland of securities regulations; (2) clear and adequate SEC authority to regulate; (3) active and ongoing agency regulation; and (4) a serious conflict between the antitrust and regulatory regimes. We therefore conclude that the securities laws are "clearly incompatible" with the application of the antitrust laws in this context.

* * *

In *Trinko*—a monopolization case you will remember from Chapter VII—the Court relied on the existence of a parallel regulatory scheme in a somewhat softer way: as a reason to refrain from extending the reach of antitrust liability. The complaint in that case concerned Verizon's refusal to provide a competitor with necessary interconnection services: a complaint, the Court noted, that could have been addressed to a sectoral regulator—the Federal Communications Commission ("FCC")—under the Telecommunications Act 1996.[761]

Verizon Communications Inc. v. Law Offices of Curtis V. Trinko, LLP
540 U.S. 398 (2004)

Justice Scalia.

[1] [W]e do not believe that traditional antitrust principles justify adding the present case to the few existing exceptions from the proposition that there is no duty to aid competitors. Antitrust analysis must always be attuned to the particular structure and circumstances of the industry at issue. Part of that attention to economic context is an awareness of the significance of regulation. As we have noted, careful account must be taken of the pervasive federal and state regulation characteristic of the industry.

---

[761] For a thoughtful argument that this analysis depends on the effectiveness of the regulatory regime, *see* Michael A. Carrier, *Unsettling Drug Patent Settlements: A Framework for Presumptive Illegality*, 108 Mich. L. Rev. 37, 70–71 (2009).

[2] One factor of particular importance is the existence of a regulatory structure designed to deter and remedy anticompetitive harm. Where such a structure exists, the additional benefit to competition provided by antitrust enforcement will tend to be small, and it will be less plausible that the antitrust laws contemplate such additional scrutiny. Where, by contrast, there is nothing built into the regulatory scheme which performs the antitrust function, the benefits of antitrust are worth its sometimes considerable disadvantages. Just as regulatory context may in other cases serve as a basis for implied immunity, it may also be a consideration in deciding whether to recognize an expansion of the contours of § 2.

[3] The regulatory framework that exists in this case demonstrates how, in certain circumstances, regulation significantly diminishes the likelihood of major antitrust harm. Consider, for example, the statutory restrictions upon Verizon's entry into the potentially lucrative market for long-distance service. To be allowed to enter the long-distance market in the first place, an incumbent [local exchange carrier (LEC)] must be on good behavior in its local market. Authorization by the FCC requires state-by-state satisfaction of [Telecommunications Act 1996] § 271's competitive checklist, which . . . includes the nondiscriminatory provision of access to [unbundled network elements (UNEs)]. Section 271 applications to provide long-distance service have now been approved for incumbent LECs in 47 States and the District of Columbia.

[4] The FCC's § 271 authorization order for Verizon to provide long-distance service in New York discussed at great length Verizon's commitments to provide access to UNEs, including the provision of OSS. Those commitments are enforceable by the FCC through continuing oversight; a failure to meet an authorization condition can result in an order that the deficiency be corrected, in the imposition of penalties, or in the suspension or revocation of long-distance approval. Verizon also subjected itself to oversight by the PSC under a so-called "Performance Assurance Plan" (PAP). The PAP, which by its terms became binding upon FCC approval, provides specific financial penalties in the event of Verizon's failure to achieve detailed performance requirements. The FCC described Verizon's having entered into a PAP as a significant factor in its § 271 authorization, because that provided a strong financial incentive for post-entry compliance with the section 271 checklist, and prevented backsliding.

[5] The regulatory response to the OSS failure complained of in respondent's suit provides a vivid example of how the regulatory regime operates. When several competitive LECs complained about deficiencies in Verizon's servicing of orders, the FCC and PSC responded. The FCC soon concluded that Verizon was in breach of its sharing duties under § 251(c), imposed a substantial fine, and set up sophisticated measurements to gauge remediation, with weekly reporting requirements and specific penalties for failure. The PSC found Verizon in violation of the PAP even earlier, and imposed additional financial penalties and measurements with daily reporting requirements. In short, the regime was an effective steward of the antitrust function. {*Eds.: § 251(c) of the Telecommunications Act , 47 U.S.C. § 251(c), required Verizon to share "unbundled" elements of its network with competitors.*}

[6] Against the slight benefits of antitrust intervention here, we must weigh a realistic assessment of its costs. Under the best of circumstances, applying the requirements of § 2 can be difficult because the means of illicit exclusion, like the means of legitimate competition, are myriad. Mistaken inferences and the resulting false condemnations are especially costly, because they chill the very conduct the antitrust laws are designed to protect. The cost of false positives counsels against an undue expansion of § 2 liability. One false-positive risk is that an incumbent LEC's failure to provide a service with sufficient alacrity might have nothing to do with exclusion. Allegations of violations of § 251(c)(3) duties are difficult for antitrust courts to evaluate, not only because they are highly technical, but also because they are likely to be extremely numerous, given the incessant, complex, and constantly changing interaction of competitive and incumbent LECs implementing the sharing and interconnection obligations. Amici States have filed a brief asserting that competitive LECs are threatened with death by a thousand cuts, the identification of which would surely be a daunting task for a generalist antitrust court. Judicial oversight under the Sherman Act would seem destined to distort investment and lead to a new layer of interminable litigation, atop the variety of litigation routes already available to and actively pursued by competitive LECs.

2. Agricultural Cooperatives

The Capper-Volstead Act of 1922 creates a limited antitrust exception for certain cooperative activities in agricultural markets. Section 1 of the Act, codified at 7 U.S.C. § 291, creates the exemption; Section 2, codified at 7 U.S.C. § 292, aims to supervise and soften its effects.

17 U.S.C. § 291

Persons engaged in the production of agricultural products as farmers, planters, ranchmen, dairymen, nut or fruit growers may act together in associations, corporate or otherwise, with or without capital stock, in collectively processing, preparing for market, handling, and marketing in interstate and foreign commerce, such products of persons so engaged. Such associations may have marketing agencies in common; and such associations and their members may make the necessary contracts and agreements to effect such purposes: Provided, however, That such associations are operated for the mutual benefit of the members thereof, as such producers, and conform to one or both of the following requirements:

> First. That no member of the association is allowed more than one vote because of the amount of stock or membership capital he may own therein, or,

> Second. That the association does not pay dividends on stock or membership capital in excess of 8 per centum per annum.

And in any case to the following:

> Third. That the association shall not deal in the products of nonmembers to an amount greater in value than such as are handled by it for members.

* * *

17 U.S.C. § 292

If the Secretary of Agriculture shall have reason to believe that any such association monopolizes or restrains trade in interstate or foreign commerce to such an extent that the price of any agricultural product is unduly enhanced by reason thereof, he shall serve upon such association a complaint stating his charge in that respect, to which complaint shall be attached, or contained therein, a notice of hearing, specifying a day and place not less than thirty days after the service thereof, requiring the association to show cause why an order should not be made directing it to cease and desist from monopolization or restraint of trade. . . . .

* * *

The core rationale for the agricultural exemption is generally understood to be the persistent asymmetry of economic power between large, integrated incumbent buyers in the agricultural supply chain and individual growers.[762] In 1978, Justice Blackmun explained the point in *National Broiler*.

National Broiler Marketing Ass'n v. United States
436 U.S. 816 (1978)

Justice Blackmun.

[1] The Capper-Volstead Act removed from the proscription of the antitrust laws cooperatives formed by certain agricultural producers that otherwise would be directly competing with each other in efforts to bring their goods

---

[762] *See generally* Michael Kades, *Protecting livestock producers and chicken growers: Recommendations for reinvigorating enforcement of the Packers and Stockyards Act*, Center for Equitable Growth (May 2022); U.S. Dept. of Agriculture, *Antitrust Status of Farmer Cooperatives: The Story of the Capper Volstead Act* (Sept. 2002), https://www.rd.usda.gov/files/CIR59.pdf; David L. Baumer, Robert T. Masson, and Robin Abrahamson Masson, *Curdling the Competition: An Economic and Legal Analysis of the Antitrust Exemption for Agriculture*, 31 Vill. L. Rev. 183 (1986).

to market. But if the cooperative includes among its members those not so privileged under the statute to act collectively, it is not entitled to the protection of the Act. . . . .

[2] The Act protects "[p]ersons engaged in the production of agricultural products *as farmers, planters, ranchmen, dairymen, nut or fruit growers*" (emphasis added). A common-sense reading of this language clearly leads one to conclude that not all persons engaged in the production of agricultural products are entitled to join together and to obtain and enjoy the Act's benefits: The italicized phrase restricts and limits the broader preceding phrase "[p]ersons engaged in the production of agricultural products . . . ."

[3] The purposes of the Act, as revealed by the legislative history, confirm the conclusion that not all those involved in bringing agricultural products to market may join cooperatives exempt under the statute, and have the cooperatives retain that exemption. The Act was passed in 1922 to remove the threat of antitrust restrictions on certain kinds of collective activity, including processing and handling, undertaken by certain persons engaged in agricultural production. Similar organizations of those engaged in farming, as well as organizations of laborers, were already entitled, since 1914, to special treatment under § 6 of the Clayton Act. This treatment, however, had proved to be inadequate. Only nonstock organizations were exempt under the Clayton Act, but various agricultural groups had discovered that in order best to serve the needs of their members, accumulation of capital was required. With capital, cooperative associations could develop and provide the handling and processing services that were needed before their members' products could be sold. The Capper-Volstead Act was passed to make it clear that the formation of an agricultural organization with capital would not result in a violation of the antitrust laws, and that the organization, without antitrust consequences, could perform certain functions in preparing produce for market. . . . .

[4] Farmers were perceived to be in a particularly harsh economic position. They were subject to the vagaries of market conditions that plague agriculture generally, and they had no means individually of responding to those conditions. Often the farmer had little choice about who his buyer would be and when he would sell. A large portion of an entire year's labor devoted to the production of a crop could be lost if the farmer were forced to bring his harvest to market at an unfavorable time. Few farmers, however, so long as they could act only individually, had sufficient economic power to wait out an unfavorable situation. Farmers were seen as being caught in the hands of processors and distributors who, because of their position in the market and their relative economic strength, were able to take from the farmer a good share of whatever profits might be available from agricultural production. By allowing farmers to join together in cooperatives, Congress hoped to bolster their market strength and to improve their ability to weather adverse economic periods and to deal with processors and distributors.

[5] NBMA argues that this history demonstrates that the Act was meant to protect all those that must bear the costs and risks of a fluctuating market, and that all its members, because they are exposed to those costs and risks and must make decisions affected thereby, are eligible to organize in exempt cooperative associations. The legislative history indicates, however, and does it clearly, that it is not simply exposure to those costs and risks, but the inability of the individual farmer to respond effectively, that led to the passage of the Act. The congressional debates demonstrate that the Act was meant to aid not the full spectrum of the agricultural sector but, instead, to aid only those whose economic position rendered them comparatively helpless. It was very definitely, special-interest legislation. Indeed, several attempts were made to amend the Act to include certain processors who, according to preplanting contracts, paid growers amounts based on the market price of processed goods; these attempts were roundly rejected. Clearly, Congress did not intend to extend the benefits of the Act to the processors and packers to whom the farmers sold their goods, even when the relationship was such that the processor and packer bore a part of the risk.

[6] Petitioner suggests that agriculture has changed since 1922, when the Act was passed, and that an adverse decision here might simply accelerate an existing trend toward the absorption of the contract grower by the integrator, or might induce the integrators to rewrite their contracts with the contract growers to designate the latter as lessor-employees rather than independent contractors. We may accept the proposition that agriculture has changed in the intervening years, but, as the second Mr. Justice Harlan said, when speaking for the Court in another context, a statute is not an empty vessel into which this Court is free to pour a vintage that we think better suits present-day tastes. Considerations of this kind are for the Congress, not the courts.

* * *

The agricultural exemption reflects, in part, the idea that the creation of market power may in some cases help to "countervail" against existing market power on the other side of the bargaining table.[763] This idea underpins some calls for antitrust exemptions in other settings where some degree of market power is or may be present.[764] However, as other commentators have pointed out, there are reasons to approach the creation of "countervailing power" with real caution.

Laura M. Alexander, Countervailing Power: A Comprehensive Assessment of a Persistent but Troubling Idea (Oct. 15, 2020)

At a high level, the theory of countervailing power is that where a firm at one level of a supply chain enjoys market power, entities that transact with (and thus negotiate with) that firm should be allowed to either merge or collaborate, even if doing so would otherwise be anticompetitive or illegal, because doing so will enable them to more effectively bargain with the powerful counterparty.

While this argument may seem facially appealing, it is also deeply concerning. The arguments in favor of countervailing power as a response to increasing and seemingly intractable market concentration are not driven by methodological, fact-based analysis; indeed, the economic evidence strongly suggests that countervailing market power, particularly among intermediaries in the supply chain, leads to increased prices, inefficiency, and worse outcomes for consumers in most cases.

Moreover, the adverse legal and policy consequences of adapting antitrust laws and competition policy to recognize countervailing market power as a defense to market concentration are profound and may be underappreciated. What is often overlooked is that concentrated firms at the two levels do not have the incentive to charge competitive prices. To the contrary, after the buying firms are permitted to join together to countervail the power of the sellers, the now-concentrated firms at the two levels have the mutual incentive to exclude rivals and charge higher monopoly prices to consumers.

While countervailing market power may seem like a quick fix to the problem of increased concentration, in-depth analysis suggests it is a cure worse than the disease, at least insofar as competition remains the goal of antitrust. Simply put, countervailing power is not a competition-based response to market power. And, it is a response that risks significant additional harm to competition, consumers, and workers. [. . .]

What countervailing power does reliably do, is to improve the outcomes for the parties allowed to exercise it. . . . [I]t is this feature of the economics of countervailing power that has been behind the instances where lawmakers have instituted legislative solutions rooted in countervailing power. Antitrust exemptions, such as labor unions and agricultural cooperatives, for example, represent a policy decision to bolster the bargaining leverage of workers and family farms because we, as a society, determined that it is in our best interest to prioritize the living standards of these groups over competition in affected labor and agricultural markets. Allowing these groups to exercise countervailing power is viewed as a means toward that end.

3. Insurance

In 1945, Congress passed the McCarran-Ferguson Act, broadly exempting the "business of insurance" from antitrust scrutiny so long as it is subject to state law, and except for boycotts, coercion, and intimidation. This broad exemption remained undisturbed for more than 75 years until 2021, when it was cut back to subject much

---

[763] *See generally* GAO, *Dairy Cooperatives—Role and Effects of the Capper-Volstead Exemption*, GAO/RCED-90-186 (Sept. 1990).

[764] For thoughtful discussions, *see* Jonathan B. Baker, Joseph Farrell, & Carl Shapiro, *Merger to Monopoly to Serve a Single Buyer: Comment*, 75 Antitrust L.J. 637, 640-41 (2008); John B. Kirkwood, *Collusion to Control a Powerful Customer: Amazon, E-Books, and Antitrust Policy*, 69 U. Miami L. Rev. 1, 60 (2014). *Compare also* Written Testimony of Daniel Francis before U.S. Senate, Committee on the Judiciary, Subcommittee on Competition Policy, Antitrust, and Consumer Rights, Hearing on "Breaking the News: Journalism, Competition, and the Effects of Market Power on a Free Press" (February 2022) (opposing antitrust exemption) *with* Written Testimony of Hal J. Singer, before U.S. Senate, Committee on the Judiciary, Subcommittee on Competition Policy, Antitrust, and Consumer Rights, Hearing on "Breaking the News: Journalism, Competition, and the Effects of Market Power on a Free Press" (February 2022) (supporting antitrust exemption).

of the business of health insurance to antitrust scrutiny. In *Group Life*, the Supreme Court summarized the Act's history and purpose.

15 U.S.C. § 1012(b)

[A]fter June 30, 1948, the Act of July 2, 1890, as amended, known as the Sherman Act, and the Act of October 15, 1914, as amended, known as the Clayton Act, and the Act of September 26, 1914, known as the Federal Trade Commission Act, as amended, shall be applicable to the business of insurance to the extent that such business is not regulated by State Law.

* * *

15 U.S.C. § 1013(b)

Nothing contained in this chapter shall render the . . . Sherman Act inapplicable to any agreement to boycott, coerce, or intimidate, or act of boycott, coercion, or intimidation.

* * *

Grp. Life & Health Ins. Co. v. Royal Drug Co.
440 U.S. 205 (1979)

Justice Stewart.

[1] The [McCarran-Ferguson antitrust exemption] was enacted in 1945 in response to this Court's decision in *United States v. South-Eastern Underwriters Assn.*, 322 U.S. 533 (1944). The indictment in that case charged that the defendants had conspired to fix insurance rates and commissions, and had conspired to boycott and coerce noncooperating insurers, agents, and insureds. In the District Court the defendants had successfully demurred to the indictment on the ground that the insurance industry was not a part of interstate commerce subject to regulation under the Commerce Clause. On direct appeal, this Court reversed the judgment, holding that the business of insurance is interstate commerce, and that the Congress which enacted the Sherman Act had not intended to exempt the insurance industry from its coverage. [. . .]

[2] The primary concern of Congress in the wake of that decision was in enacting legislation that would ensure that the States would continue to have the ability to tax and regulate the business of insurance. This concern is reflected in §§ 1 and 2(a) of the [McCarran-Ferguson] Act . . . . A secondary concern was the applicability of the antitrust laws to the insurance industry. Months before this Court's decision in *South-Eastern Underwriters* was announced, proposed legislation to totally exempt the insurance industry from the Sherman and Clayton Acts had been introduced in Congress. Less than three weeks after the actual decision, the House of Representatives passed a bill which would also have provided the insurance industry with a blanket exemption from the antitrust laws, thus restoring the state of law that had existed before the decision in *South-Eastern Underwriters*.

[3] Congress, however, rejected this approach. Instead of a total exemption, Congress provided in § 2(b) that the antitrust laws "shall be applicable" unless the activities of insurance companies are the business of insurance and regulated by state law. Moreover, under § 3(b) the Sherman Act was made applicable in any event to acts of boycott, coercion, or intimidation. To allow the States time to adjust to the applicability of the antitrust laws to the insurance industry, Congress imposed a 3-year moratorium. After the expiration of the moratorium on July 1, 1948, however, Congress clearly provided that the antitrust laws would be applicable to the business of insurance "to the extent that such business is not regulated by State law."

[4] By making the antitrust laws applicable to the insurance industry except as to conduct that is the business of insurance, regulated by state law, and not a boycott, Congress did not intend to and did not overrule the South-Eastern Underwriters case. While the power of the States to tax and regulate insurance companies was reaffirmed, the McCarran-Ferguson Act also established that the insurance industry would no longer have a blanket exemption from the antitrust laws. It is true that § 2(b) of the Act does create a partial exemption from those laws. Perhaps more significantly, however, that section, and the Act as a whole, embody a legislative rejection of the

concept that the insurance industry is outside the scope of the antitrust laws—a concept that had prevailed before the *South-Eastern Underwriters* decision. [. . .]

[5] References to the meaning of the "business of insurance" in the legislative history of the McCarran-Ferguson Act strongly suggest that Congress understood the business of insurance to be the underwriting and spreading of risk. Thus, one of the early House Reports stated: "The theory of insurance is the distribution of risk according to hazard, experience, and the laws of averages. These factors are not within the control of insuring companies in the sense that the producer or manufacturer may control cost factors."

[6] Because of the widespread view that it is very difficult to underwrite risks in an informed and responsible way without intra-industry cooperation, the primary concern of both representatives of the insurance industry and the Congress was that cooperative ratemaking efforts be exempt from the antitrust laws. The passage of the McCarran-Ferguson Act was preceded by the introduction in the Senate Committee of a report and a bill submitted by the National Association of Insurance Commissioners on November 16, 1944. The views of the NAIC are particularly significant, because the Act ultimately passed was based in large part on the NAIC bill. The report emphasized that the concern of the insurance commissioners was that smaller enterprises and insurers other than life insurance companies were unable to underwrite risks accurately, and it therefore concluded:

> For these and other reasons this subcommittee believes it would be a mistake to permit or require the unrestricted competition contemplated by the antitrust laws to apply to the insurance business. To prohibit combined efforts for statistical and rate-making purposes would be a backward step in the development of a progressive business. We do not regard it as necessary to labor this point any further because Congress itself recently recognized the necessity for concert of action in the collection of statistical data and rate making when it enacted the District of Columbia Fire Insurance Rating Act. [. . .]

[7] The floor debates also focused simply on whether cooperative ratemaking should be exempt. Thus, Senator Ferguson, in explaining the purpose of the bill, stated:

> This bill would permit—and I think it is fair to say that it is intended to permit—rating bureaus, because in the last session we passed a bill for the District of Columbia allowing rating. What we saw as wrong was the fixing of rates without statutory authority in the States; but we believe that State rights should permit a State to say that it believes in a rating bureau. I think the insurance companies have convinced many members of the legislature that we cannot have open competition in fixing rates on insurance. If we do, we shall have chaos. There will be failures, and failures always follow losses.

[8] The consistent theme of the remarks of other Senators also indicated a primary concern that cooperative ratemaking would be protected from the antitrust laws. President Roosevelt, in signing the bill, also emphasized that the bill would allow cooperative rate regulation. He stated that "Congress did not intend to permit private rate fixing, which the Antitrust Act forbids, but was willing to permit actual regulation of rates by affirmative action of the States."

* * *

The insurance exemption was often criticized,[765] but it was not until January 2021 that the exemption was cut back through the introduction of language restoring ordinary-course antitrust scrutiny to most health insurance.

15 U.S.C. § 1013(c)

(1) Nothing contained in this chapter shall modify, impair, or supersede the operation of any of the antitrust laws with respect to the business of health insurance (including the business of dental insurance and limited-scope dental benefits).

---

[765] *See, e.g.*, Statement of Christine Varney, U.S. Dept. of Justice, before the Committee on the Judiciary, U.S. Senate, Hearing on Prohibiting Price Fixing and Other Anticompetitive Conduct in the Health Insurance Industry (Oct. 14, 2009) (summarizing criticism).

(2) Paragraph (1) shall not apply with respect to making a contract, or engaging in a combination or conspiracy—

> (A) to collect, compile, or disseminate historical loss data;

> (B) to determine a loss development factor applicable to historical loss data;

> (C) to perform actuarial services if such contract, combination, or conspiracy does not involve a restraint of trade; or

> (D) to develop or disseminate a standard insurance policy form (including a standard addendum to an insurance policy form and standard terminology in an insurance policy form) if such contract, combination, or conspiracy is not to adhere to such standard form or require adherence to such standard form.

4. Baseball

Perhaps the strangest antitrust exemption is the one enjoyed by the game of baseball. This judge-made exemption owes its existence to the following brief opinion of Justice Holmes in a 1922 case. Recent attention to sports antitrust—and particularly the Supreme Court decision in *NCAA v. Alston*—has encouraged some plaintiffs to take a fresh run at this strange exception from the reach of antitrust.

Fed. Baseball Club of Baltimore v. Nat'l League of Pro. Base Ball Clubs
259 U.S. 200 (1922)

Justice Holmes.

[1] This is a suit for threefold damages brought by the plaintiff in error under the Anti-Trust Acts of July 2, 1890. The defendants are the National League of Professional Base Ball Clubs and the American League of Professional Base Ball Clubs, unincorporated associations, composed respectively of groups of eight incorporated base ball clubs, joined as defendants; the presidents of the two Leagues and a third person, constituting what is known as the National Commission, having considerable powers in carrying out an agreement between the two Leagues; and three other persons having powers in the Federal League of Professional Base Ball Clubs, the relation of which to this case will be explained. It is alleged that these defendants conspired to monopolize the base ball business, the means adopted being set forth with a detail which, in the view that we take, it is unnecessary to repeat.

[2] The plaintiff is a base ball club incorporated in Maryland, and with seven other corporations was a member of the Federal League of Professional Base Ball Players, a corporation under the laws of Indiana, that attempted to compete with the combined defendants. It alleges that the defendants destroyed the Federal League by buying up some of the constituent clubs and in one way or another inducing all those clubs except the plaintiff to leave their League, and that the three persons connected with the Federal League and named as defendants, one of them being the President of the League, took part in the conspiracy. Great damage to the plaintiff is alleged. The plaintiff obtained a verdict for $80,000 in the Supreme Court and a judgment for treble the amount was entered, but the Court of Appeals, after an elaborate discussion, held that the defendants were not within the Sherman Act. . . . .

[3] The decision of the Court of Appeals went to the root of the case and if correct makes it unnecessary to consider other serious difficulties in the way of the plaintiff's recovery. A summary statement of the nature of the business involved will be enough to present the point. The clubs composing the Leagues are in different cities and for the most part in different States. The end of the elaborate organizations and sub-organizations that are described in the pleadings and evidence is that these clubs shall play against one another in public exhibitions for money, one or the other club crossing a state line in order to make the meeting possible. When as the result of these contests one club has won the pennant of its League and another club has won the pennant of the other League, there is a final competition for the world's championship between these two. Of course the scheme requires constantly repeated travelling on the part of the clubs, which is provided for, controlled and disciplined by the organizations, and this it is said means commerce among the States. But we are of opinion that the Court of Appeals was right.

[4] The business is giving exhibitions of base ball, which are purely state affairs. It is true that in order to attain for these exhibitions the great popularity that they have achieved, competitions must be arranged between clubs from different cities and States. But the fact that in order to give the exhibitions the Leagues must induce free persons to cross state lines and must arrange and pay for their doing so is not enough to change the character of the business. According to the distinction insisted upon in *Hooper v. California*, 155 U. S. 648, 655 [(1895)], the transport is a mere incident, not the essential thing. That to which it is incident, the exhibition, although made for money would not be called trade of commerce in the commonly accepted use of those words. As it is put by defendant, personal effort, not related to production, is not a subject of commerce. That which in its consummation is not commerce does not become commerce among the States because the transportation that we have mentioned takes place. To repeat the illustrations given by the Court below, a firm of lawyers sending out a member to argue a case, or the Chautauqua lecture bureau sending out lecturers, does not engage in such commerce because the lawyer or lecturer goes to another State.

[5] If we are right the plaintiff's business is to be described in the same way and the restrictions by contract that prevented the plaintiff from getting players to break their bargains and the other conduct charged against the defendants were not an interference with commerce among the States.

* * *

In *Flood v. Kuhn*, the Supreme Court effectively conceded that *Federal Baseball* was wrongly decided but declined to disturb it, on *stare decisis* grounds, and indicated that it would be up to Congress to fix the problem.[766] In 1998 Congress enacted a limited repeal of the baseball exemption.[767] And in *Alston* (a restraint of trade case you will remember from Chapter IV), the Supreme Court went out of its way to cast some doubt on this exemption:

> [T]his Court once dallied with something that looks a bit like an antitrust exemption for professional baseball. In *Federal Baseball Club of Baltimore, Inc. v. National League of Professional Baseball Clubs*, 259 U.S. 200 (1922), the Court reasoned that "exhibitions" of "base ball" did not implicate the Sherman Act because they did not involve interstate trade or commerce—even though teams regularly crossed state lines (as they do today) to make money and enhance their commercial success. But this Court has refused to extend *Federal Baseball*'s reasoning to other sports leagues—and has even acknowledged criticisms of the decision as "unrealistic" and "inconsistent" and "aberrational." Indeed, as we have seen, this Court has already recognized that the NCAA itself is subject to the Sherman Act.

> The orderly way to temper that Act's policy of competition is by legislation and not by court decision. The NCAA is free to argue that, because of the special characteristics of [its] particular industry, it should be exempt from the usual operation of the antitrust laws—but that appeal is properly addressed to Congress. Nor has Congress been insensitive to such requests. It has modified the antitrust laws for certain industries in the past, and it may do so again in the future. But until Congress says otherwise, the only law it has asked us to enforce is the Sherman Act, and that law is predicated on one assumption alone—competition is the best method of allocating resources in the Nation's economy. [768]

Private litigation followed,[769] and the Justice Department took the opportunity to speak up.

---

[766] 407 U.S. 258 (1972). Inexplicably, the opinion dedicates two pages to listing favorite baseball players. *Id.* at 262–64.

[767] See 15 U.S.C. § 26b. *See generally* John T. Wolohan, *The Curt Flood Act of 1998 and Major League Baseball's Federal Antitrust Exemption*, 9 Marq. Sports L. J. 347 (1999).

[768] NCAA v. Alston, 141 S.Ct. 2141, 2159–60 (2021).

[769] *See, e.g.*, Complaint, Nostalgic Partners, LLC v. Office of the Comm'r of Baseball, Case 1:21-cv-10876 (S.D.N.Y. filed Dec. 20, 2021) ¶ 4 ("Virtually no other business in the United States would have even *considered* such a brazen horizontal agreement among competing businesses. MLB and its Clubs, however, had no such qualms because for almost a century they have laid claim to an anomalous, judicially created "get-out-of-jail-free card" from antitrust scrutiny. The so-called "baseball exemption" from the Sherman Act was first articulated by the Supreme Court in *Federal Baseball Club v. National League*, 259 U.S. 200 (1922). If not for this anomalous precedent, MLB knows that the type of anticompetitive conduct challenged here would warrant per se condemnation. The time is at hand to cast the baseball exemption into the dust bin of antitrust history.").

Statement of Interest of the United States, Nostalgic Partners LLC v. Office of the Commissioner of Baseball,

Case No. 1:21-cv-10876 (S.D.N.Y. filed June 15, 2022)

[1] Baseball may be our national pastime, but our national economic policy long has been faith in the value of competition. The Sherman Act is a comprehensive charter of economic liberty aimed at preserving free and unfettered competition, and as important to the preservation of economic freedom and our free-enterprise system as the Bill of Rights is to the protection of our fundamental personal freedoms.

[2] The baseball exemption established in *Federal Baseball Club of Baltimore v. National League of Professional Baseball Clubs*, 259 U.S. 200 (1922), is a judicially created exception to this national economic policy established by Congress. The Supreme Court has itself recognized the exemption as an exception and an anomaly and an aberration confined to baseball. Just last year, the Court acknowledged that although it once dallied with something that looks a bit like an antitrust exemption for professional baseball, it has refused to extend *Federal Baseball*'s reasoning to other sports leagues. Accordingly, the Court has expressly declined to create similar exemptions for boxing, and football. Lower courts have likewise refused to recognize exemptions for other sports leagues. [. . .]

[3] In addition to being unique among sports leagues, the baseball exemption is also distinct among antitrust exemptions in that it was not created to reconcile competing legal authorities or substantive policy goals. For example, the "state-action doctrine" exempts certain actions taken by state governments from the scope of the federal antitrust laws. The Supreme Court has explained that nothing in the language of the Sherman Act or in its history suggested that Congress intended to restrict the sovereign capacity of the States to regulate their economies, and thus the state-action doctrine is intended to foster and preserve the federal system. Similarly, the nonstatutory labor exemption immunizes certain activity from the Sherman Act to accommodate . . . the congressional policy favoring collective bargaining.

[4] By contrast, the "baseball exemption" rests on a repudiated Commerce Clause rationale. In *Federal Baseball*, the Supreme Court concluded that "the business of giving exhibitions of base ball" involved "purely state affairs" and therefore did not satisfy the interstate-commerce element of the Sherman Act. [However, in later cases, including *Flood v. Kuhn*, 407 U.S. 258, 282 (1972), the Court has recognized that baseball is a business and that it involves interstate commerce.] [. . .]

[5] Thus, today, the baseball exemption that was born from *Federal Baseball*'s interstate commerce analysis persists as a freestanding exemption despite [the subsequent] repudiation of its original rationale. [. . .]

[6] While *Federal Baseball* and its progeny remain binding precedent, lower courts should narrowly construe the judicially created exemption for the business of baseball, and should not extend its scope beyond what the Supreme Court has articulated—conduct that is central to providing professional baseball games to the public. [. . .]

[7] [L]ower courts should not extend the baseball exemption beyond the scope recognized by the Supreme Court in its baseball [cases], which [have] limited the exemption to conduct that is central to the actual exhibition of professional baseball games. In *Federal Baseball*, the Court identified "[t]he business" at issue as "giving exhibitions of base ball." Indeed, the distinction the Court drew between exhibitions (games) and activity "incident" to the exhibitions, such as the teams' travel, was central to the Court's reasoning. "[O]ne or the other club cross[ed] a state line in order to make the meeting possible," the Court acknowledged, but the games themselves—the "business" in dispute—were "purely state affairs" and thus outside the scope of the Commerce Clause (as interpreted in *Federal Baseball*). [*Toolson v. N.Y. Yankees, Inc.*, 346 U.S. 356 (1953)] likewise characterized the scope of *Federal Baseball*'s holding as the business of providing public baseball games for profit between clubs of professional baseball players. [. . .]

[8] Thus, while the exemption may cover antitrust challenges to Major League Baseball's league structure and its reserve system, it would not cover conduct beyond the scope of the offering of exhibitions of professional baseball. Such conduct would include agreements between baseball teams and baseball card manufacturers to fix the prices at which cards are sold to consumers, or restraints on broadcasting baseball games.

NOTES

1) One consequence of *Trinko* is that a complainant with a possible Section 2 claim may be on *weaker* ground, not stronger ground, if the defendant is simultaneously violating a regulatory obligation. Is that a desirable result? Why, or why not?

2) The baseball example looks like an example of striking judicial innovation. But is it really different from other judge-created antitrust rules, like the state-action defense or the rule of reason? How?

3) If you could create one new antitrust exemption, which one would you create and why?

4) If you could abolish one existing exemption, what would you abolish and why?

5) Might we want an exemption from private enforcement without also creating an exemption from government enforcement (or the other way around)? Under what circumstances? What plausible examples can you suggest?

6) Should games and sports be subject to antitrust rules at all? Do you fear the use of antitrust to undermine or distort a fair and balanced competition? Would you fear or welcome the consequences of a general "games of recreation" antitrust exemption?

7) Should an antitrust exemption always, or usually, be accompanied by some kind of alternative measure to protect competition within the scope of the exemption?

8) How would you describe the standard that you think a legislature should apply when deciding whether or not to create an antitrust exemption?

F. Some Further Reading

Daniel A. Crane & Adam Hester, *State-Action Immunity and Section 5 of the FTC Act*, 115 Mich. L. Rev. 365 (2016).

FTC, REPORT OF THE STATE ACTION TASK FORCE (Sept. 2003)

GAO, *Dairy Cooperatives—Role and Effects of the Capper-Volstead Exemption*, GAO/RCED-90-186 (Sept. 1990)

Hiba Hafiz, *Labor Antitrust's Paradox*, 87 U. Chi. L. Rev. 381 (2020)

Michael Kades, *Protecting livestock producers and chicken growers: Recommendations for reinvigorating enforcement of the Packers and Stockyards Act*, Center for Equitable Growth (May 2022)

Marina Lao, *Workers in the "Gig" Economy: The Case for Extending the Antitrust Labor Exemption*, 51 U.C. Davis L. Rev. 1543 (2018)

Geoffrey Manne & Josh Wright, *A First Principles Approach to Antitrust Enforcement in the Agricultural Industry*, Comp. Pol'y Int'l (2010)

Doha Mekki, Statement before the Subcommittee on Antitrust, Competition Policy and Consumer Rights, Committee on the Judiciary, U.S. Senate, Antitrust and Economic Opportunity: *Competition in Labor Markets* (Oct. 29, 2019)

Sanjukta Paul, *Charting the Reform Path*, 120 Mich. L. Rev. 1265 (2022)

Eric A. Posner, HOW ANTITRUST FAILED WORKERS (2021)

Global Antitrust Institute, *Noncompete Clauses Used in Employment Contracts* (Feb. 2020)

Howard A. Shelanski, *The Case for Rebalancing Antitrust and Regulation*, 109 Mich. L. Rev. 683 (2011)

X. ANTITRUST AND INTELLECTUAL PROPERTY

A. Overview

Antitrust has many frontiers. The Sherman and Clayton Acts, and the policies they express, interact in a variety of ways with other areas of law, from contract (*e.g.*, when can a party to an agreement avoid its contractual obligation to perform on the ground that the agreement is anticompetitive?[770]) to constitutional law (*e.g.*, when is anticompetitive conduct constitutionally protected?[771]). But one of the most important, controversial, and heavily litigated frontiers is the one that antitrust shares with intellectual property law.

At the very highest level of generality, both the antitrust laws and the intellectual property laws represent efforts to promote the public interest by regulating the process of business rivalry. Thus, as we have seen throughout this book, the antitrust laws aim to promote social welfare by dividing market rivalry into competition "on the merits," which is protected and encouraged, and "anticompetitive" practices and transactions, which are often prohibited. The antitrust project rests on the expectation that sorting business rivalry into these two categories will benefit society through lower prices, better-quality products and services, and—importantly for this Chapter—increased innovation.

The intellectual property laws also aim to promote social welfare by regulating market rivalry. In particular, they reflect an effort to encourage certain kinds of investment by guaranteeing the ability to enjoy certain rewards from such investments. Each system of intellectual property law aims at this goal in a different way.

Patent law, copyright law, and trade secret law are focused on incentivizing innovation in particular. Patent law is arguably the most fully articulated branch of intellectual property law. It confers on the inventor of any "new and useful process, machine, manufacture, or composition of matter," any "distinct and new variety of plant," or any "new, original and ornamental design for an article of manufacture" an exclusive right to make, use, or sell the invention throughout the United States, or to authorize others to do so, for a term of years.[772] Copyright law confers on the creator of an original artistic or literary work exclusive rights (also of limited duration) to reproduce, adapt, distribute, or publicly perform or display that work.[773] Trade secret law protects certain kinds of confidential business information—such as formulas, designs, and compilations of information—from disclosure. In each case, the premise of the right is that the prospect of legal protection, and the ability to monetize that protection through profits or royalties, will encourage investment in the creation of desirable inventions, creative works, and valuable confidential business information. Or, to put it another way, the premise is that if others could "free ride" without restriction on the benefits of successful innovation, which is often costly and risky for those undertaking it, then there would be less innovation and society would be worse off as a result.

Of course, each of these mechanisms also suppresses some innovation. The enforcement of an IP right (or even the threat of enforcement) may suppress certain kinds of valuable innovation that copies or incorporates the patented invention, the copyrighted work, or the secret information. The existence of our intellectual property laws thus reflects a policy bet that the social benefits to innovation from recognizing and protecting IP rights will exceed the social costs (including forgone innovation as well as higher prices) of restricting or prohibiting certain forms of infringing activity.[774]

Trademark law is situated a little differently. Trademark law protects various indicia (words, symbols, sounds, etc.) used to identify the source of products and services, against unauthorized use by others in ways that would

---

[770] *See, e.g.*, Tampa Elec. Co. v. Nashville Coal Co., 365 U.S. 320 (1961).

[771] *See supra* Chapter IX (*Noerr-Pennington* and state action defenses).

[772] *See* 35 U.S.C. §§ 101, 154, 161, 171.

[773] *See* 17 U.S.C. § 106.

[774] The term "bet" is apt: we have, particularly for copyright law, less information about the social costs and benefits of protection than we would need to be sure about the balance of the trade. *See, e.g.*, Christopher Jon Sprigman, *Copyright and Creative Incentives: What We Know (And Don't)*, 55 HOUS. L. REV. 451 (2017).

undermine the relationship of identity and association that the mark expresses. The central purpose of trademark protection is to encourage a business to invest in its brand and reputation, safe in the knowledge that the benefits of that investment will not be appropriated by competitors, or diluted by third-party use of the mark. Thus, it too aims to protect against "free riding": but on investment in a brand and reputation rather than in innovation as such.

1. Are IP and Antitrust in Conflict?

Courts and commentators have disagreed for many years over whether the antitrust and IP systems are in a meaningful sense "in conflict" with one another.[775] The nature of the apparent conflict is easy to see. Some would-be copyists aim to compete in an economic sense against the rightsholder: for example, someone might create a pirate copy of a song or movie in an effort to win sales away from the rightsholder, or a competitor might infringe a rival's patent in an effort to create a better or cheaper mousetrap than the rival. We generally think of antitrust as encouraging competition among substitute protects or services: including lower-cost imitations of a successful rival. But in these and similar cases the intellectual-property laws may give an incumbent the power to stop—or at least to extract value from—certain kinds of competitive imitation. In such cases we might say that the competition-promoting project of antitrust is "yielding" to the investment-protecting project of intellectual property. Conversely, when a court concludes that a rightsholder has violated the antitrust laws by entering into a licensing agreement on particular terms, or by refusing to license at all, we might say that intellectual property is yielding to antitrust by protecting competition rather than the right of exclusion. In these and similar ways, we might think of antitrust and IP as taking opposing views of competition: antitrust exists to protect it, while IP law exists to protect against certain forms of it.

But the picture is more complicated. First, it is not clear that the tension we have described makes intellectual property uniquely, or even distinctively, situated in relation to antitrust. After all, the entire antitrust project is a limitation on the exercise of certain other rights and freedoms—property, contract, and so on—that are conferred by the state in order to promote social welfare in some sense. For example, the manufacturer of a product has a personal property right in its goods, which the legal system recognizes in part to promote innovation and investment. But antitrust directly limits that right when it prevents a monopolist manufacturer from, say, selling only to customers that commit to dealing exclusively with that manufacturer, or that agree to purchase a tying product as part of an anticompetitive tie. Likewise, a dominant incumbent that obtains exclusive contracts from key input suppliers and distributors has an affirmative right in contract to that exclusivity: but antitrust, of course, directly expropriates that right when it forbids the incumbent to exclude competition in that fashion. In these and other ways we can see that antitrust enforcement is centrally, and maybe wholly, a project in limiting the exercise of affirmative legal rights and freedoms that the legal system confers for other reasons.

Second, it is not even obvious that the IP laws' central preoccupation with the "right to exclude" is a particularly sharp challenge to the antitrust system. For one thing, the exclusion that intellectual property protects is not the exclusion that antitrust abhors. Modern patent and copyright centrally protect against *duplication*, not against

[775] *See, e.g.*, Christopher Jon Sprigman, *The Intersection of Patent and Antitrust Law* in Einer Elhauge (ed.), RESEARCH HANDBOOK ON THE ECONOMICS OF ANTITRUST LAW (2012) ("Given their fundamentally incompatible baseline assumptions regarding the consequences of competition for innovation, it makes little sense to insist . . . that there is no essential conflict between IP and the antitrust laws."); Herbert Hovenkamp, *The Antitrust-Intellectual Property Interface* in ABA Section of Antitrust Law, 3 ISSUES IN COMPETITION LAW AND POLICY (2008) ("The relation between intellectual property (IP) and antitrust policy has always been unstable and problematic. Courts have seen an inherent conflict between the two legal regimes. . . . [But] the conflict between IP and antitrust law is easily exaggerated, and the courts have been too ready to find conflicts where none existed."); R. Hewitt Pate, *Antitrust and Intellectual Property* (remarks of Jan. 24, 2003) ("Many observers, particularly in the antitrust community, contend there is a tension between antitrust and intellectual property, arguing that the antitrust laws seek to eliminate monopolies and encourage competition, while the intellectual property laws reward creators and inventors with a limited monopoly. . . . There may be legitimate room for debate. I would suggest, however, that this tension is overstated."); 1-800 Contacts, Inc. v. Fed. Trade Comm'n, 1 F.4th 102, 121–22 (2d Cir. 2021) ("When the restraint at issue in an antitrust action implicates IP rights, [the Supreme Court's *Actavis* decision] directs us to consider the policy goals of the relevant IP law."); SCM Corp. v. Xerox Corp., 645 F.2d 1195, 1203 (2d Cir. 1981) ("The conflict between the antitrust and patent laws arises in the methods they embrace that were designed to achieve reciprocal goals. While the antitrust laws proscribe unreasonable restraints of competition, the patent laws reward the inventor with a temporary monopoly that insulates him from competitive exploitation of his patented art."). *See generally, e.g.*, Michael A. Carrier, *Unraveling the Patent-Antitrust Paradox*, 150 U. Pa. L. Rev. 761 (2002); Louis Kaplow, *The Patent-Antitrust Intersection: A Reappraisal*, 97 Harv. L. Rev. 1813 (1984); Ward S. Bowman, Jr., PATENT AND ANTITRUST LAW: A LEGAL AND ECONOMIC APPRAISAL (1973); William F. Baxter, *Legal Restrictions on Exploitation of the Patent Monopoly: An Economic Analysis*, 76 Yale L.J. 267 (1966).

economic competition from functional substitutes as such. Moreover, the very process of competition that antitrust protects is itself constituted by exclusive economic rights. If every competitor could freely use its rivals' stores, employees, facilities, and production lines, or simply seize and sell their goods, there would be no competitive process at all. No-one—not even a monopolist—has a general antitrust obligation to let others use their competitive assets (let alone to do so without reasonable compensation), advertise on their facilities, take and sell their goods, use their machines, direct their employees, or prevent the bare and unconditional enforcement of their property rights. Indeed, antitrust is highly resistant to the idea that a rival has a presumptive right to compete against even a monopolist using the monopolist's own property, even when the property in question is commercially essential for access to a broader market.[776] So antitrust does not really recoil from the idea of exclusive property rights as such.

More subtly still: the exclusionary reach of the IP laws is more qualified, and more compatible with antitrust, than it may seem. As one of us has pointed out elsewhere, even "patent's remedies regime does not align with the theological argument that the patent law provides an 'unqualified' or 'categorical' property right."[777] Despite the popular conception that an injunction is the invariable remedy in an IP case, the remedy for infringement is often not exclusion but rather a right to participate in profits, in the form of a reasonable royalty.[778] That version of an "exclusive right"—the right to a reasonable fee—is very seldom threatened by antitrust enforcement: after all, even the elusive "essential facilities" doctrine allows a monopolist to charge a reasonable fee for access.[779] Nor, on the other side of the coin, is antitrust antagonistic to the unconditional enforcement of a exclusive property right. Throwing a trespassing rival off your property, for example, or filing a reasonably plausible suit for infringement of a property right, is virtually never an antitrust violation.[780] Thus, the tension between IP and antitrust turns out to be more a complicated matter than it might first appear: not a crude opposition, but something much more nuanced.

2. IP and Market Power

Regardless of whether intellectual property law and antitrust are truly in deep policy tension, the interaction between the two systems has presented no end of practical challenges and puzzles for courts and commentators over their long co-existence. One of the most important parts of this process has been the untangling of the relationship between intellectual property and market power.

For much of the 20th century, the Supreme Court was willing to infer the existence of market power, as a matter of law, from the existence of a patent.[781] That came to an end in 2006, with the Court's recognition in *Independent Ink*—a tying case—that market power in the antitrust sense must be proved in every such case.[782] This signaled a return to antitrust's regular rule of the road for the analysis of market power, and the rejection of special presumptions for cases involving IP rights.

Illinois Tool Works Inc. v. Independent Ink, Inc.

547 U.S. 28 (2006)

[1] Petitioners, Trident, Inc., and its parent, Illinois Tool Works Inc., manufacture and market printing systems that include three relevant components: (1) a patented piezoelectric impulse ink jet printhead; (2) a patented ink container, consisting of a bottle and valved cap, which attaches to the printhead; and (3) specially designed, but

---

[776] *See supra* Chapter VII.

[777] Christopher Jon Sprigman, *The Intersection of Patent and Antitrust Law* in Einer Elhauge (ed.), RESEARCH HANDBOOK ON THE ECONOMICS OF ANTITRUST LAW (2012) 358.

[778] *See* 35 U.S.C. § 284; eBay Inc. v. MercExchange, L.L.C., 547 U.S. 388 (2006).

[779] *See, e.g.*, Kerwin v. Casino, 802 F. App'x 723, 727 (3d Cir. 2020) (obligation under the doctrine is "reasonable access"); Gregory v. Fort Bridger Rendezvous Ass'n, 448 F.3d 1195, 1204 (10th Cir. 2006) (same); Aerotec Int'l, Inc. v. Honeywell Int'l, Inc., 836 F.3d 1171, 1185 (9th Cir. 2016) (same); Hecht v. Pro-Football, Inc., 570 F.2d 982, 992 (D.C. Cir. 1977) ("fair terms"). *See supra* § VII.E (describing essential facilities doctrine).

[780] *See, e.g.*, Professional Real Estate Investors, Inc. v. Columbia Pictures Industries, 508 U.S. 49, 65 (1993) (no antitrust liability for an "objectively plausible effort to enforce rights").

[781] *See, e.g.*, International Salt Co. v. United States, 332 U.S. 392 (1947).

[782] Illinois Tool Works Inc. v. Independent Ink, Inc., 547 U.S. 28, 42–43 (2006).

unpatented, ink. Petitioners sell their systems to original equipment manufacturers (OEMs) who are licensed to incorporate the printheads and containers into printers that are in turn sold to companies for use in printing barcodes on cartons and packaging materials. The OEMs agree that they will purchase their ink exclusively from petitioners, and that neither they nor their customers will refill the patented containers with ink of any kind.

[2] Respondent, Independent Ink, Inc., has developed an ink with the same chemical composition as the ink sold by petitioners. After an infringement action brought by Trident against Independent was dismissed for lack of personal jurisdiction, Independent filed suit against Trident seeking a judgment of noninfringement and invalidity of Trident's patents. In an amended complaint, it alleged that petitioners are engaged in illegal tying and monopolization in violation of §§ 1 and 2 of the Sherman Act. 15 U.S.C. §§ 1, 2. [. . .]

[3] Respondent [proposes] that we differentiate between tying arrangements involving the simultaneous purchase of two products that are arguably two components of a single product—such as the provision of surgical services and anesthesiology in the same operation, or the licensing of one copyrighted film on condition that the licensee take a package of several films in the same transaction—and a tying arrangement involving the purchase of unpatented goods over a period of time, a so-called "requirements tie." According to respondent, we should recognize a presumption of market power when faced with the latter type of arrangements because they provide a means for charging large volume purchasers a higher royalty for use of the patent than small purchasers must pay, a form of discrimination that "is strong evidence of market power."

[4] The opinion that imported the "patent equals market power" presumption into our antitrust jurisprudence, however, provides no support for respondent's proposed alternative. In [International Salt Co. v. U.S., 332 U.S. 392 (1947)] it was the existence of the patent on the tying product, rather than the use of a requirements tie, that led the Court to presume market power. Moreover, the requirements tie in that case did not involve any price discrimination between large volume and small volume purchasers or evidence of noncompetitive pricing. Instead, the leases at issue provided that if any competitor offered salt, the tied product, at a lower price, the lessee should be free to buy in the open market, unless appellant would furnish the salt at an equal price.

[5] . . . [T]he vast majority of academic literature recognizes that a patent does not necessarily confer market power. Similarly, while price discrimination may provide evidence of market power, particularly if buttressed by evidence that the patentee has charged an above-market price for the tied package, it is generally recognized that it also occurs in fully competitive markets. We are not persuaded that the combination of these two factors should give rise to a presumption of market power when neither is sufficient to do so standing alone. Rather, the lesson to be learned from *International Salt* and the academic commentary is the same: Many tying arrangements, even those involving patents and requirements ties, are fully consistent with a free, competitive market. For this reason, we reject both respondent's proposed rebuttable presumption and their narrower alternative.

[6] It is no doubt the virtual consensus among economists that has persuaded the enforcement agencies to reject the position that the Government took when it supported the per se rule that the Court adopted in the 1940's. In antitrust guidelines issued jointly by the Department of Justice and the Federal Trade Commission in 1995, the enforcement agencies stated that in the exercise of their prosecutorial discretion they "will not presume that a patent, copyright, or trade secret necessarily confers market power upon its owner." . . . While that choice is not binding on the Court, it would be unusual for the Judiciary to replace the normal rule of lenity that is applied in criminal cases with a rule of severity for a special category of antitrust cases.

[7] Congress, the antitrust enforcement agencies, and most economists have all reached the conclusion that a patent does not necessarily confer market power upon the patentee. Today, we reach the same conclusion, and therefore hold that, in all cases involving a tying arrangement, the plaintiff must prove that the defendant has market power in the tying product.

* * *

Even in the wake of *Independent Ink*, intellectual property rights may still contribute to market or monopoly power in an individual case. This may be easiest to see with patent rights. For example, suppose that a pharmaceutical company holds a strong patent protecting a technology that is necessary to satisfy a particular kind of demand: this might be the case for a particular molecule with important therapeutic effects, for which no adequate substitutes exist. Such a right may well create very substantial market power, or even monopoly power. The crucial question, with patents as with other assets, is whether there are reasonable substitutes for the right in question. Assessing this will often require an understanding of what rights exactly are controlled by the rightsholder, what demand exists for such rights, and what alternative technologies exist.[783] Pharmaceutical markets in particular may be very narrow, such that a patent right may confer something like monopoly power over a particular form of therapy for a particular medical indication.[784]

Copyright, too may confer some power over competition. Generally speaking, the copyright laws protect a narrower set of rights than the patent laws do: for example, they protect creative expression but not the ideas underlying it, leaving room for similar activity by rivals.[785] But, on the other hand, markets for creative works like novels and songs are often highly differentiated, with inelastic demand for particular kinds of output. As one commentator has argued: "because everyone has a favorite author, and is willing to pay a little more, drive a little further, or search a little harder for a particular work by a particular author, even a very narrow copyright would grant most authors, and certainly all popular authors, some degree of market power."[786] Judicial practice in defining antitrust markets for creative and cultural activities is sparse, and the common principles are not obvious.[787] But it is clear that in appropriate cases, the possession of copyright interests—including not only those pertaining to artistic work but also those protecting source and object code describing software interfaces such as APIs—can grant market power in the absence of reasonable substitutes for the protected works.

Trademark law and trade secret laws are, at least in general, somewhat less likely to be a source of market power.[788] The rights of a trademark owner only extend to avoiding confusion regarding the source of products, or damage to the identification value of the mark. However, trademark law can serve to protect market power that the trademark owner has acquired through investment in its brand and reputation. Indeed, the value proposition of a trademark rests on the idea that there is some inelastic demand for the output of the business in question, making the mark worth protecting. Likewise, trade secret laws have only a narrow preclusive effect: they do not restrict mimicry, independent discovery, or reverse engineering of the protected information. As a result, they may be less likely to grant the freedom from close substitute competition that patent and copyright law can create. However, in appropriate cases the underlying trade secret may relate to some inelastic demand, even to the point of market power: for example, a secret recipe that competitors are unable to duplicate or reverse-engineer may be the secret of the success of a dominant food or drink brand!

In sum, the relationship between IP rights and market power in the antitrust sense is complex, and generalities are probably not much help. In addition to the foregoing, it is also worth remembering that intellectual property rights (of all kinds) may be subject to various limitations and defenses, such as fair use doctrines, that may further limit

---

[783] *See, e.g.*, Intel Corp. v. Fortress Inv. Grp. LLC, 511 F. Supp. 3d 1006, 1024 (N.D. Cal. 2021) ("Without having an understanding of how many patents there are in a given product market, it is difficult to say that the relevant defendants' possession of their patents constitutes market power—even more so when taking into account that Plaintiffs have claimed . . . product markets that are relatively broad in scope.").

[784] *See generally, e.g.*, Michael A. Carrier, *Three Challenges for Pharmaceutical Antitrust*, 59 Santa Clara L. Rev. 615 (2020); Richard G. Frank & Raymond S. Hartman, *The Nature of Pharmaceutical Competition: Implications for Antitrust Analysis*, 22 Intl. J. Econ. Bus. 301 (2015); Herbert Hovenkamp, *Sensible Antitrust Rules for Pharmaceutical Competition*, 39 U.S.F. L. Rev. 11 (2004); David A. Balto & James F. Mongoven, *Antitrust Enforcement in Pharmaceutical Industry Mergers*, 54 Food & Drug L.J. 255 (1999).

[785] *See* 17 U.S.C. § 102(b) (setting out distinction between copyrightable expression and uncopyrightable ideas, principles, processes, methods of operation, etc.).

[786] Glynn S. Lunney Jr., *Reexamining Copyright's Incentives--Access Paradigm*, 49 Vand. L. Rev. 483, 519 (1996).

[787] *See, e.g.*, Le v. Zuffa, LLC, 216 F. Supp. 3d 1154, 1166–67 (D. Nev. 2016) (sustaining "elite mixed martial arts" as a relevant market for antitrust analysis at the motion to dismiss stage); In re Live Concert Antitrust Litig., 863 F. Supp. 2d 966, 984–99 (C.D. Cal. 2012) (rejecting under *Daubert* an expert report purporting to define a market for "live rock music concerts"); Christou v. Beatport, LLC, 849 F. Supp. 2d 1055, 1065 (D. Colo. 2012) (sustaining, for purposes of motion to dismiss, a market for "downloads of DRM-free, high fidelity Electronic Dance Music"); Navarra v. Marlborough Gallery, Inc., 820 F. Supp. 2d 477, 487 (S.D.N.Y. 2011) (rejecting as implausibly *broad* a market that combined original and replica ceramics by the same creator), *vacated on other grounds*, Case No. 10-CV-7547, 2012 WL 13210272 (S.D.N.Y. Apr. 4, 2012); Vitale v. Marlborough Gallery, Case No. 93 CIV. (PKL) 6276, 1994 WL 654494, at *4 (S.D.N.Y. July 5, 1994) (sustaining, for purposes of motion to dismiss, a market for Jackson Pollock paintings).

[788] *See, e.g.*, Clorox Co. v. Sterling Winthrop, Inc., 117 F.3d 50, 56 (2d Cir. 1997).

market power and permit economic competition with the rightsholder—including, for example, protection for certain kinds of comparative advertising through doctrines like trademark's "nominative fair use."[789]

3. IP and Specific Practices

Antitrust doctrine must not only navigate the relationship between IP and market power: it must also pronounce on the legality of the ways in which IP rights can be acquired, asserted, used, infringed, and licensed in ways that might affect competition. Over antitrust's long history, the views of courts and agencies regarding antitrust analysis of conduct involving IP rights has oscillated across a broad spectrum, ranging from intrusive intervention to broad deference and everything in between. There are many explanations for these shifts over time, including changing views of intellectual property rights, the evolving antitrust treatment of particular commercial practices (such as tying and resale price maintenance), and broader political and industrial trends.[790]

An iconic example of changing attitudes to IP practices is the fate of the DOJ Antitrust Division's (in)famous "Nine No Nos" for IP licensing, announced as DOJ antitrust enforcement policy in 1970. They provided:

> (1) "It is clear that it is unlawful to require a licensee to purchase unpatented materials from the licensor";
>
> (2) "[T]he Department views it as unlawful for a patentee to require a licensee to assign to the patentee any patent which may be issued to the licensee after the licensing arrangement is executed";
>
> (3) "The Department believes it is unlawful to attempt to restrict a purchaser of a patented product in the resale of that product";
>
> (4) "[A] patentee may not restrict his licensee's freedom to deal in the products or services not within the scope of the patent";
>
> (5) "[T]he Department believes it to be unlawful or a patentee to agree with his licensee that he will not, without the licensee's consent, grant further licenses to any other person";
>
> (6) "[T]he Department believes that mandatory package licensing is an unlawful extension of the patent grant";
>
> (7) "[T]he Department believes that it is unlawful for a patentee to insist, as a condition of the license, that his licensee pay royalties in an amount not reasonably related to the licensee's sales of products covered by the patent-for example, royalties on the total sales of products of the general type covered by the licensed patent";
>
> (8) "[I]t is pretty clearly unlawful for the owner of a process patent to attempt to place restrictions in his licensee's sales of products made by the use of the patented process"; and
>
> (9) ""[T]he Department of Justice considers it unlawful for a patentee to require a licensee to adhere to any specified or minimum price with respect to the licensee's sale of the licensed products."[791]

But the Nine No Nos did not survive the Chicago revolution, which brought a revision of antitrust's relationship with vertical practices in general and its treatment of IP rights in particular.[792] By 1986 the deputy head (and later head) of the Antitrust Division could remark that he looked upon IP policy speeches as "a way to atone for the

---

[789] *See* 15 U.S.C. § 107 (copyright fair use); 15 U.S.C. §1115(b)(4) (Lanham Act fair use); KP Permanent Make-Up, Inc. v. Lasting Impression I, Inc., 543 U.S. 111 (2004) (holding that fair use defense applies even where evidence shows consumer confusion).

[790] For a wide spectrum of approaches, *see, e.g.*, Federal Trade Commission v. Qualcomm Inc., 969 F.3d 974 (9th Cir. 2020) (deference to licensing practices); Illinois Tool Works Inc. v. Independent Ink, Inc., 547 U.S. 28, 42–43 (2006) (mandating rule of reason analysis for patent tying); United States v. Masonite Corp., 316 U.S. 265 (1942) (invalidating price restraints in a patent license); Morton Salt Co. v. G.S. Suppiger Co., 314 U.S. 488 (1942) (patent tying unlawful).

[791] *See* Abbott B. Lipsky Jr., *Current Antitrust Division Views on Patent Licensing Practices*, 50 Antitrust L.J. 515 (1981), *passim*, quoting Bruce Wilson, Department of Justice Luncheon Speech, *Law on Licensing Practices: Myth or Reality?* (Jan. 21, 1975).

[792] Abbott B. Lipsky Jr., *Current Antitrust Division Views on Patent Licensing Practices*, 50 Antitrust L.J. 515 (1981) (repudiating the No Nos); Richard Gilbert & Carl Shapiro, *Antitrust Issues in the Licensing of Intellectual Property: The Nine No-No's Meet the Nineties*, Brookings Papers: Microeconomics (1997); William D. Coston, *The Patent-Antitrust Interface: Are There Any No-No's Today?*, Venable LLP White Paper (Jan. 2013).

sins" of the earlier approach and of the Nine No Nos themselves.[793] The rapprochement of antitrust and IP continued with the 1995 Antitrust Guidelines for the Licensing of Intellectual Property, which stated that "[t]he intellectual property laws and the antitrust laws share the common purpose of promoting innovation and enhancing consumer welfare," a statement that the revised Guidelines repeated verbatim in 2017.[794] Today, none of the Nine No Nos is *per se* illegal: indeed, none is even presumptively unlawful.

Perspectives on the right relationship between antitrust and IP vary considerably. Some argue that the policy concerns underpinning the intellectual property laws require particular deference in cases involving IP rights; others argue that antitrust should apply with equal—or even particular—force in cases involving rights of this kind. In the following two extracts, a recent Antitrust Division head makes the case for some antitrust deference in the presence of IP rights, and an antitrust scholar makes the case for antitrust's equal (or perhaps greater?) dignity.

Makan Delrahim, The "New Madison" Approach to Antitrust and Intellectual Property Law (remarks of Mar. 16, 2018)

[1] The exchanges between Jefferson and Madison on the question of patent rights in 1788 are . . . illuminating of Madison's intellectual influence. Reflecting the general anti-monopoly sentiment at the time, Jefferson wrote from his post in Paris that "the benefit even of limited monopolies is too doubtful to be opposed to that of their general suppression."

[2] In response, Madison acknowledged that monopolies "are justly classed among the greatest nuisances in Government." But he recognized a limited exception for patents. "[I]s it clear," he asked Jefferson, "that as encouragement to literary works and ingenious discoveries, [monopolies] are not too valuable to be wholly renounced?" Madison answered his own question, demonstrating a nuanced understanding of how to balance concerns about monopolies with creating incentives to innovate: "Monopolies are sacrifices of the many to the few. . . . Where the power . . . is in the many not in the few, the danger can not be very great that the few will be thus favored. It is much more to be dreaded that the few will be unnecessarily sacrificed to the many." [. . .]

[3] There has been a shift in recent years toward what I would call a "retro-Jefferson" view of patents as conferring too much power that ought to be curbed, either through reinterpreting antitrust law or establishing patent policies of standard setting organization ("SSO") that favor implementers who practice on a patent when they build new technologies. Many advocates of reducing the power of intellectual property rights cite the so-called "hold-up" problem in the context of SSOs. As many of you know, I believe these concerns are largely misplaced. Instead, I favor what I call the "New Madison" approach to the application of antitrust law to intellectual property rights.

[4] The New Madison approach, if I may, has four basic premises that are aimed at ensuring that patent holders have adequate incentives to innovate and create exciting new technologies, and that licensees have appropriate incentives to implement those technologies.

[5] First, hold-up [of companies by patent holders for royalties reflecting the sunk value of their investments] is fundamentally not an antitrust problem, and therefore antitrust law should not be used as a tool to police . . . commitments that patent-holders make to standard setting organizations [to license their IP on fair, reasonable, and nondiscriminatory ("FRAND") terms].

[6] Second, standard setting organizations should not become vehicles for concerted actions by market participants to skew conditions for patented technologies' incorporation into a standard in favor of implementers because this can reduce incentives to innovate and encourage patent hold-out.

---

[793] Charles F. Rule, *The Administration's Views: Antitrust Analysis After the Nine No-No's*, 55 Antitrust L.J. 365 (1986)

[794] U.S. Dept. of Justice & Federal Trade Commission, ANTITRUST GUIDELINES FOR THE LICENSING OF INTELLECTUAL PROPERTY (Apr. 6, 1995); U.S. Dept. of Justice & Federal Trade Commission, ANTITRUST GUIDELINES FOR THE LICENSING OF INTELLECTUAL PROPERTY (Jan. 12, 2017).

[7] Third, because a key feature of patent rights is the right to exclude, standard setting organizations and courts should have a very high burden before they adopt rules that severely restrict that right or—even worse—amount to a de facto compulsory licensing scheme.

[8] Fourth, consistent with the fundamental right to exclude, from the perspective of the antitrust laws, a unilateral and unconditional refusal to license a patent should be considered per se legal. [. . .]

[9] The third premise of the New Madison approach to antitrust law and intellectual property is to respect the core of what it means to hold an IP right—namely, the right to exclude. In his letters to Thomas Jefferson, Madison acknowledged that state-conferred monopolies are "among the greatest nuisances in government," but maintained that these "nuisances" could be harnessed to serve the greater good of social progress and innovation through patent protection. His analogy of patents to the "common law . . . copyright of authors" in The Federalist Papers is telling because, at the time, the copyright of authors was understood as a property right. Equipping patent holders with the property right to exclude therefore goes hand-in-hand with the goals Madison envisioned for the U.S. patent regime.

[10] Understanding patent rights, once conferred, as a form of property right helps frame the current debate over injunctions, and demonstrates how far we've strayed off course. . . . In a worrisome trend, some commentators have suggested that the mere act of seeking an injunction order to prevent infringement [of a patent that has been incorporated into an industry standard] raises competition concerns, and, with a degree of hubris litigants have advanced such theories as a basis for antitrust liability. Taken together, these trends fundamentally transform the nature of patent rights away from their constitutional underpinnings. They convert a property rule into a liability rule, and amount to a troubling de facto compulsory licensing scheme. It is not difficult to understand why that is the case, particularly in the context of standard setting. If a patent holder effectively loses its right to an injunction whenever a licensing dispute arises, or is deterred from seeking an injunction due to the prospect of treble damages, an implementer can freely infringe, knowing that the most he or she will eventually have to pay is a reasonable royalty rate. Implementers have a strong incentive to pursue this course while holding out from taking a license due to the high injunction bar for innovators that make [commitments to a standard-setting organization to license their IP on FRAND terms]. It is a harmful arbitrage that should be discouraged.

[11] . . . Deterring the right to enjoin other parties from infringement—particularly competitors—seriously reduces incentives to innovate, much in the same way that the DOJ's enforcement policies in the 1970s prevented field of use restrictions in patent licensing. This can cause great harm to consumers, and is particularly problematic as more and more products and services come to depend on standardized technology.

[12] . . . [T]he fourth premise of the "New Madison" approach . . . is that a unilateral and unconditional refusal to license a valid patent should be per se legal. A refusal to license should not be a source for a competitor or customer to seek treble damages under the Sherman Act. That is because competition and consumers both benefit when inventors have full incentives to exploit their patent rights.

[13] This requires an assurance to inventors that they need not subsidize their competitors' business models if they prefer not to do so. The Supreme Court clarified as much in *Trinko*, explaining that a refusal to deal is not an antitrust violation if the parties have never done business with each other, because "there is no duty to aid competitors." A de facto compulsory licensing scheme turns this policy underlying the Sherman Act on its head.

[14] To that end, I urge scholars and policymakers to give careful consideration to the underlying policies of the *Trinko* decision. The Supreme Court emphasized that its earlier *Aspen Skiing* decision was merely a "limited exception" to the rule that there is no duty to deal under the antitrust laws. But some, particularly some of the newer enforcement agencies abroad, may think the "exception" leaves room for a licensee to bring an antitrust suit if a patent holder terminates or refuses to renew the licensing agreement. The licensor thus could be forced to litigate for years the consequences of a business decision stemming from changed competitive dynamics or a new licensing strategy. Antitrust laws should not be used to transform an inventor's one-time decision to offer a license to a competitor into a forever commitment that the inventor will continue licensing that competitor in perpetuity

* * *

Herbert Hovenkamp, *The Antitrust-Intellectual Property Interface*

ABA Section of Antitrust Law, 3 ISSUES IN COMPETITION LAW AND POLICY (2008)

Ever since the antitrust laws were passed, antitrust and IP have had to accommodate one another, but they have done so in different ways in different periods. The early twentieth century was an era of IP expansion and antitrust accommodation. During this period even when the Supreme Court saw fit to make IP yield, it frequently did so on "misuse" rather than antitrust grounds. {*Eds.: the "patent misuse" doctrine is a doctrine of IP law, not antitrust, that limits efforts to assert exclusive rights beyond the scope of a patent.*} By contrast, beginning during the New Deal and extending through the Warren era, the Supreme Court was more inclined to view patents as inherently anticompetitive and to interpret the antitrust laws expansively. The result was overly aggressive and sometimes even silly antitrust rules, such as those for patent ties, that found antitrust violations when the defendant had no real power and there was no realistic prospect of economic harm.

Today, we once again live in an era of IP expansionism. Indeed, the IP laws, particularly the Copyright Act, bear the marks of significant special interest capture. The result is provisions that are much more likely to protect IP holders' profits than to serve the constitutional purpose of the IP laws, which is to encourage innovation by searching for the right balance between the right to exclude and the need of every innovator to build on the work of others. By contrast, antitrust over the last three decades has become much more focused on protecting consumer welfare, neoclassically defined, and interest groups have had considerably less success in obtaining special interest legislation. As a result, application of the antitrust laws is more likely to serve the public interest than application of at least many IP provisions. This counsels against overly expansive interpretations of IP rights in the face of serious complaints of competitive harm.

At the policy level, antitrust is a more coherent enterprise than the IP regimes. While the point can certainly be exaggerated, the fact is that the neoclassical model of competition has become robustly established in both the antitrust academy and the federal judiciary. Courts have become far better at distinguishing anticompetitive practices from those that are procompetitive or harmless. While plenty of problems of administration remain, most of them have to do with the details of antitrust enforcement rather than its core policy.

IP policy cannot make the same set of claims. Most importantly, it lacks an empirically useable model for identifying the appropriate duration and scope of IP rights. An optimal IP policy would seek to maximize the social returns from innovation, less the costs of any monopoly output reductions and related dislocations that result, plus the costs of using the IP system, including the costs of identifying IP rights and negotiating licenses. Determining the optimal amount of protection is incredibly difficult. For example, as the scope and strength of IP rights increases, people have a greater incentive to innovate insofar as anticipated returns to completed innovations are greater, but a reduced incentive insofar as it becomes more costly to borrow the ideas of others. Further, while the IP statutes are largely general, optimal coverage almost certainly varies from industry to industry. For example, a shorter period of copyright protection for computer code would almost certainly further innovation in that market. The market life of computer code is a few years at the most. Under the current regime, there is no realistic chance that copyrighted code will ever enter the public domain while it has economic life remaining. Largely because of this uncertainty, the IP laws have become a playground for special interests, who have remarkable and generally unprecedented control over congressional agendas.

Of course, special interest capture of IP regimes is not a problem to be addressed under the antitrust laws, but rather by educating Congress and convincing courts to take legislative capture into account when interpreting statutes. At the same time, however, the current regime of unduly expansionist IP provisions and a decently grounded antitrust policy suggest that antitrust should not be as cautious as it has been in the past. When a challenged practice poses a true threat to competition and is not expressly permitted by the IP statutes, courts are well advised to err on the side of promoting the short-run competitive interests recognized in antitrust, rather than the cacophony of voices reflected in the IP laws.

* * *

Antitrust-IP cases arise in a range of settings. They may arise in government antitrust enforcement actions; in private antitrust claims brought by consumers (including as a class) or by competitors; as antitrust counterclaims to infringement suits brought by rightsholders against alleged infringers; or as challenges by licensees to terms and conditions demanded by licensors.

But we can group antitrust's most important engagements with intellectual property into three broad categories. First, in a very small number of circumstances, the acquisition and/or assertion of intellectual property rights may itself be challenged under the antitrust laws. This includes, for examples, mergers and acquisitions that involve the acquisition of IP portfolios; unilateral refusals to license intellectual property rights; and antitrust challenges to the mere assertion of IP rights. Second, a range of agreements and joint practices involving IP may be challenged as antitrust violations, from licensing agreements to settlements of infringement litigation. Third, antitrust has often been invoked in connection with the use and licensing of so-called "standard-essential patents" ("SEPs"): that is, patent rights over technologies that have been incorporated into standards adopted by standard-setting organizations ("SSOs").

In this chapter we will visit each of these theaters in turn. In Section B we will consider the antitrust analysis of the acquisition and assertion of IP rights. In Section C we will consider agreements and joint practices. Finally, in Section D we will encounter the standard-setting process and some aspects of its engagement with antitrust, including antitrust's complex relationship with so-called "FRAND commitments."

NOTES

1) In what ways are antitrust and IP in tension? Can you think of some concrete settings in which the goals of the IP laws and the goals of antitrust may be at odds for an antitrust agency, or for a court hearing an antitrust case? What guideposts can agencies and courts use to navigate that tension?

2) How, if at all, should antitrust's relationship with intellectual property differ from its relationship with other forms of property?

3) In what sense is it true, as the 1995 and 2017 IP Guidelines suggest, that both IP and antitrust law aim to maximize "consumer welfare"? Can you articulate a plausible and appealing alternative vision?

4) IP rights are premised in large part on the belief that IP rights incentivize innovation that leads to dynamic competition, resulting in far greater social benefit than the harms those rights create. Do you think that is a correct premise? How would we test whether it were true or false?

5) Do you agree with the holding in *Independent Ink*? Would a weak (*i.e.*, easily rebutted) presumption of market power have been a better or worse solution than the one articulated by the Court?

6) What is the basis for thinking that the innovation that the IP laws protect is more socially valuable than the innovation that those laws suppress?

7) As you read through this Chapter, consider whether antitrust law has developed a consistent account of its relationship to IP rights. Is such an account possible or desirable? Do we need a "theory" of antitrust's relationship to other bodies of law—and if so, which ones?

8) Are all IP rights equally worthy of antitrust deference, or are some more worthy than others?

9) How would you assess the antitrust risk of the Nine No Nos today?

10) What do you make of the claim in the previous extract that the intellectual-property laws have been more vulnerable to capture by special interests than the antitrust laws? Is antitrust enforcement vulnerable to capture?

B. Acquisition and Assertion of Intellectual Property

In certain circumstances, an agency or plaintiff might challenge the mere acquisition and assertion of intellectual property rights as a violation of the antitrust laws.[795] In this section we will consider three categories of such circumstances: mergers and acquisitions involving intellectual property; unilateral refusals to license intellectual property; and various forms of alleged "abuse" of the patent system, including "patent thicketing," "patent trolling," and "product hopping."

---

[795] *See, e.g.*, FTC, PATENT ASSERTION ENTITY ACTIVITY: AN FTC STUDY (Oct. 2016) 18 n.55 ("[T]he antitrust laws may forbid patent acquisitions or patent assertions that harm competition."). *See also* Fiona M. Scott Morton & Carl Shapiro, *Strategic Patent Acquisitions*, 79 Antitrust L.J. 463 (2014).

1. IP Issues in Merger Review

In some industries, intellectual property is critical to competitive effectiveness. Patented technology, for example, may be the key to a critical competitive advantage over rivals, and—where there are few or no substitutes for the protected technology—ownership of one or more patents may even confer market or even monopoly power. In such industries, merger analysis may involve a close focus on the parties' respective IP rights.

Nowhere is this clearer than in the pharmaceutical industry, where intellectual property often defines the competitive landscape. To simplify considerably, we can think of pharmaceutical competition as involving two main groups of businesses: "branded" businesses, which make massive investments in research and development and launch patent-protected drugs; and "generic" businesses, which market unpatented versions of existing branded drugs, generally at lower price points than branded drugs. Generic entry becomes possible once the patents have expired or have been shown to be invalid or not infringed by the relevant product, or pursuant to an agreement with the patent holder.

Competition among pharmaceutical drugs often takes place in narrow markets, with individual drugs tailored to highly specific clinical indications.[796] As a result, a branded drug may enjoy significant market power for the duration of its patent, with that power eroding considerably when the patent expires (or is invalidated) and generic entry begins.

As you might expect, generic drugs are typically priced much lower than their branded equivalents.[797] Interestingly, the entry of additional generic competitors after the first appears to have significant price effects, as a recent FDA study indicated. A recent FDA report found that successive entry by generics reduced prices until as many as nine generics were in the market.[798] (Generic entry sometimes causes an *increase* in the branded drug's own price: can you think of a reason why this might be?[799])

The Hatch-Waxman Act

The promotion of generic competition in pharma markets and the fostering of innovation were key objectives of the Hatch-Waxman Act, which was enacted in 1984 to stimulate competition in drug markets,[800] and amended in 2003.[801] There is a rich literature on Hatch-Waxman and its complex relationships with competition and antitrust.[802]

Among other things, Hatch-Waxman created a method for generic manufacturers to obtain accelerated approval from the Food and Drug Administration ("FDA") for their drugs, via an FDA filing known as an Abbreviated New Drug Application ("ANDA"). As part of that process, the filer of an ANDA must demonstrate that its drug is identical or equivalent in several important respects to an already-approved drug, as an alternative to conducting its own clinical studies of safety and effectiveness. It must also make a certification regarding the existence of patent rights, explaining how generic entry would not infringe any valid, unexpired patents. Among other alternatives, it

---

[796] *See, e.g.*, In re Nexium Antitrust Litig., 968 F. Supp. 2d 367, 388-89 (D. Mass. 2013) (properly constituted market may be comprised of single product; lower courts have ruled that both brand-name drug and its generic analogs can constitute a relevant antitrust market) (internal citation omitted); In re Brand Name Prescription Drugs Antitrust Litig., 186 F.3d 781, 787 (7th Cir. 1999) ("It would not be surprising . . . if every manufacturer of brand name prescription drugs had some market power.")

[797] Congressional Budget Office, *How Increased Competition from Generic Drugs Has Affected Prices and Returns in the Pharmaceutical Industry* (July 1998) 28 ("Generics . . . cost one-fourth less than the brand-name drugs, on average, at retail prices.").

[798] Ryan Conrad & Randall Lutter, FDA, *Generic Competition and Drug Prices: New Evidence Linking Greater Generic Competition and Lower Generic Drug Prices* (December 2019).

[799] Hint: who buys branded drugs after a low-cost generic is available? *See* Congressional Budget Office, *How Increased Competition from Generic Drugs Has Affected Prices and Returns in the Pharmaceutical Industry* (July 1998) 29; Richard G. Frank & David S. Salkever, Generic Entry and the Pricing of Pharmaceuticals, 6 J. of Econ. & Mgmt Strategy 75 (Spring 1997); Henry Grabowski & John M. Vernon, *Brand Loyalty, Entry and Price Competition In Pharmaceuticals After the 1984 Drug Act*, 35 J. L. & Econ. 331, 340 (1992).

[800] 21 U.S.C. § 355 *et seq.*

[801] Medicare Prescription Drug, Improvement, and Modernization Act of 2003.

[802] *See, e.g.*, C. Scott Hemphill & Mark A. Lemley, *Earning Exclusivity: Generic Drug Incentives and the Hatch-Waxman Act*, 77 Antitrust L.J. 947 (2011); Jaime F. Cardenas-Navia, *Thirty Years of Flawed Incentives: An Empirical and Economic Analysis of Hatch-Waxman Patent-Term Restoration*, 29 Berkeley Tech. L.J. 1301 (2014); Elizabeth Stotland Weiswasser & Scott D. Danzis, *The Hatch-Waxman Act: History, Structure, and Legacy*, 71 Antitrust L.J. 585 (2003).

may do so through a "Paragraph IV" certification stating that the patent for an already-approved branded drug is either not infringed or is invalid. Upon such a certification, the patent holder may file an infringement suit against the ANDA filer: if it does so within 45 days, the approval of the ANDA is stayed for a period of up to 30 months to allow the patent issues to be resolved. During this period, the FDA will not approve another ANDA. The stay ends early (*i.e.*, before the expiration of the 30-month period) if the relevant patents expire or a court determines that they are invalid or not infringed.

Many patent claims do not survive the test of Paragraph IV litigation: remarkably, a 2002 FTC study noticed that the generic applicant prevailed in 73% of the cases in which a court was required to adjudicate the validity and infringement of relevant patents.[803] (Of course, this is only a subset of the cases in which the Paragraph IV filing is made.)

In order to induce entry and to encourage challenges to weak patents, the first generic company to file an ANDA with a Paragraph IV certification is guaranteed 180 days of marketing exclusivity—that is, without competition from other generics—after launch. The profit available during this time may constitute a sizeable incentive.

Hatch-Waxman is widely understood to have stimulated generic entry in many pharmaceutical markets, and to have affected pharma competition in a variety of ways—not all of which were intended by the drafters.[804] As Scott Hemphill and Mark Lemley argued in 2011: "Pharmaceutical patent owners have responded to Hatch-Waxman with a sophisticated program of 'product lifecycle management,' which is code for finding ways to extend exclusivity as long as possible. They have filed multiple patents on variants of the same drug, listed patents with the FDA that don't cover the product, taken advantage of litigation rules to stay generic entry, and 'product-hopped' (made small changes to a product timed to prevent generic entry). Most of all, they have paid their potential generic competitors to abandon their challenges, keeping weak patents intact and preventing competition."[805]

We will consider the antitrust analysis of some of these practices below.

As you can imagine, the narrow-market nature of pharma competition and the centrality of patent rights have significant implications for the evaluation of mergers in the pharmaceutical industry. Such mergers are generally reviewed by the FTC's Mergers I division: generally, the Commission identifies "overlapping" product lines and requires divestiture of those products before allowing the rest of the transaction to proceed. Note that a relevant competing product may be already on the market or merely in a development pipeline: the agency prefers divestiture of the on-market product rather than the one in development.[806] (Why do you think that is?)

The standard modern approach is exemplified by the FTC's analysis of the Teva / Allergan merger, which consolidated the first and third-largest generic pharmaceutical manufacturers in the United States. As the following statement explained, the FTC applied not only the traditional approach: it also considered other theories of harm to competition.

---

[803] FTC, GENERIC DRUG ENTRY PRIOR TO PATENT EXPIRATION: AN FTC STUDY (July 2002) vi & n.8.

[804] *See, e.g.*, FTC, GENERIC DRUG ENTRY PRIOR TO PATENT EXPIRATION: AN FTC STUDY (July 2002) i ("Beyond any doubt, Hatch-Waxman has increased generic drug entry. Generic drugs now comprise more than 47 percent of the prescriptions filled for pharmaceutical products – up from 19 percent in 1984, when Hatch-Waxman was enacted. In spite of this record of success, two of the provisions governing generic drug approval prior to patent expiration (the 180-day exclusivity and the 30-month stay provisions) are susceptible to strategies that, in some cases, may have prevented the availability of more generic drugs. These provisions continue to have the potential for abuse."); Elizabeth Stotland Weiswasser & Scott D. Danzis, *The Hatch-Waxman Act: History, Structure, and Legacy*, 71 Antitrust L.J. 585, 607 (2003) ("Of the most frequently prescribed drugs on the market with expired patents, the share that have a generic competitor on the market has increased from 36 percent in 1984 to nearly 100 percent today.").

[805] C. Scott Hemphill & Mark A. Lemley, *Earning Exclusivity: Generic Drug Incentives and the Hatch-Waxman Act*, 77 Antitrust L.J. 947, 948 (2011).

[806] D. Bruce Hoffman, *It Only Takes Two to Tango: Reflections on Six Months at the FTC* (remarks of Feb. 2, 2018) 6–7.

Statement of the FTC, In the Matter of Teva Pharmaceuticals Industries Ltd. and Allergan plc

FTC Dkt No. C-4589 (July 27, 2016)

[1] Both Teva and Allergan are global pharmaceutical companies that are among the largest suppliers of generic pharmaceuticals in the United States. Teva is currently the largest generic drug company in the United States, with an overall generic market share of approximately 13%; Allergan is third, accounting for approximately 9% of generic sales. Although this merger combines two large sellers of generic drugs, the generic pharmaceutical industry as a whole remains relatively unconcentrated. Over two hundred firms sell generic drugs in the United States and the five largest suppliers account only for about half of overall generic sales. Following this transaction, the combined firm will likely have a 22% share of industry-wide sales across all generic product markets.

[2] Despite the industry's relatively low concentration, the Commission appreciates that the price, quality, and availability of generic pharmaceutical products have a significant impact on American consumers' daily lives and on healthcare costs nationwide. We therefore looked closely at every possible aspect of this transaction that could result in competitive harm. We examined not only particular product overlaps but also whether the combination between Teva and Allergan would result in other adverse consequences to competition. Our comprehensive investigation included the review of extensive documents from the merging parties and other industry players as well as interviews with dozens of customers and more than 50 competitors. We concluded that the substantial divestitures required by the consent order resolve the competitive concerns resulting from the transaction.

[3] As detailed in our complaint, we have reason to believe that, absent a remedy, the transaction would likely substantially reduce competition in 79 markets for pharmaceutical products, including oral contraceptives, steroidal medications, mental health drugs, and many other products. These markets include individual strengths of pharmaceutical products where Teva and Allergan currently offer competing products as well as products where there would likely be future competition absent the merger because one or both of the parties are developing competing products. To remedy the likely anticompetitive effects in each of the relevant markets, the consent order requires the divestiture of the products and related assets to specific acquirers that the Commission has closely vetted and approved. Where at least one dosage strength raised a competitive concern, we required Teva to divest all strengths. These divestitures, and the other relief contained in the proposed consent order, are designed to maintain competition in the relevant markets. [. . .]

[4] In assessing whether the combination of the parties' generic businesses would harm competition or create a firm with a greater ability to engage in anticompetitive conduct, we evaluated three additional potential theories of harm beyond individual product overlaps.

[5] First, we considered whether the merger would likely lead to anticompetitive effects from the bundling of generic products. Although both Teva and Allergan have broad generic drug portfolios today, the evidence did not show that the breadth of their portfolios significantly affects their ability to win business in individual drug product markets. Nor have they been able to use their portfolios to foreclose smaller competitors. Even with one of the broadest generic product portfolios in the industry, Teva's overall share of U.S. generic prescriptions has steadily declined from 2010 to 2015, and the share of total prescriptions filled by the five largest generic suppliers has similarly fallen during this period. Generic sales occur at the individual product level, and customers sometimes even break up purchases by specific strengths to obtain more favorable pricing. As a result, smaller firms with much smaller portfolios compete head-to-head against larger generic firms and are the leading suppliers in the markets for many individual generic treatments. Additionally, purchasers actively seek to diversify their supplier base by sourcing from smaller suppliers. On the facts here, we concluded that anticompetitive effects arising from the merged company's portfolio of products are unlikely to occur.

[6] Second, we examined whether the merger would likely decrease incentives to challenge the patents held by brand-name pharmaceutical companies and bring new generic drugs to market. The regulatory framework governing generic pharmaceuticals, the Hatch-Waxman Act, provides specific procedures for identifying and resolving patent disputes related to new generic drugs. Under the Hatch-Waxman Act, a company seeking to introduce a new generic drug may file what is commonly known as a "Paragraph IV challenge" to a brand-name

pharmaceutical product's patent. This filing triggers a process, including potential litigation, to resolve patent issues surrounding the proposed generic product's entry into the marketplace.

[7] We considered whether the merger would likely result in fewer or less effective Paragraph IV challenges, but the evidence did not support such a conclusion. A major incentive to file Paragraph IV challenges is the 180-day exclusivity period awarded to the first generic drug that the Food and Drug Administration approves in a market. The financial rewards associated with this "first-to-file" exclusivity period provide a strong incentive for generic drug companies of all sizes to challenge brand drug patents and litigate against brand drug companies. Indeed, first-to-file Paragraph IV challenges are not concentrated among a small group of firms. To the contrary, many firms, including small ones, have been active and successful first filers. In 2014, for example, twenty-five different companies were the first to file Paragraph IV challenges. For eight of those companies, that was their very first Paragraph IV challenge. Thus, while Teva and Allergan have actively filed Paragraph IV challenges, we found no evidence that either one has been better positioned to win the first-to-file race or that they have substantially greater incentives or ability to succeed in Paragraph IV challenges than many other generic companies. Nor did we see evidence that a merger between the two would diminish the combined firm's incentive to continue to pursue Paragraph IV challenges.

[8] Finally, we analyzed whether the proposed transaction might dampen incentives to develop new generic products. For example, certain types of generic drugs are especially difficult to develop. For the most part, however, the parties' in-house technical capabilities to develop complex generic drugs do not overlap. And to the extent that there are complex products for which both companies have engaged in development efforts, we found that there are a number of other firms with similar capabilities such that the transaction would not substantially lessen competition. Moreover, generic firms, including the merging parties, often partner with third parties (e.g., specialized contract development and manufacturing organizations) to obtain the technical capability to develop complex generic drugs. These types of partnership options will remain after the merger. The consent order addresses individual markets where the merger was likely to harm competition, including markets for difficult-to-develop products that are currently in the parties' pipelines.

[9] We therefore concluded that the proposed merger is unlikely to produce anticompetitive effects beyond the markets discussed above. That conclusion is necessarily limited to the facts of this case. Another set of facts presented by a different transaction might lead us to find that there are competitive concerns that extend beyond markets for individual pharmaceutical products.

***

The standard market-by-market approach to pharma merger enforcement has drawn criticism for being unduly narrow, and perhaps missing broader harms to competition.[807] But it is not clear what plausible alternatives exist, given the market-based nature of antitrust analysis. In 2021, the FTC announced the formation of a Pharmaceutical Task Force to reconsider enforcement policies in pharma markets.[808] The Task Force completed its main work in 2022, and the FTC has not yet announced any revisions to its approach.

The debate was exemplified in 2019 when Bristol-Myers Squibb, a major pharmaceutical manufacturer, sought to purchase Celgene, a manufacturer focused on drugs for cancer and inflammatory diseases, for $74 billion. The FTC applied the standard approach and required the parties to divest Celgene's market-leading psoriasis drug Otezla. At $13.4 billion, this was the largest merger divestiture that the federal government had ever required in a merger case.[809]

---

[807] *See, e.g.*, Diana L. Moss, American Antitrust Institute, *From Competition To Conspiracy: Assessing The Federal Trade Commission's Merger Policy in The Pharmaceutical Sector* (Sept. 2020).

[808] Pharmaceutical Task Force, Project No. P212900 (Docket No. FTC-2021-0025).

[809] *See* Press Release, FTC Requires Bristol-Myers Squibb Company and Celgene Corporation to Divest Psoriasis Drug Otezla as a Condition of Acquisition (Nov. 15, 2019).

Analysis Of Agreement Containing Consent Orders to Aid Public Comment, In the Matter of Bristol-Myers Squibb Company and Celgene Corporation
FTC File No. 191-0061 (Nov. 15, 2019)

[1] Headquartered in New York City, BMS researches, develops, manufactures, and sells prescription pharmaceutical products and biologic products in several therapeutic areas, including oncology, cardiology, virology, and inflammatory diseases. Among other products, BMS is developing an oral product to treat moderate-to-severe psoriasis. Like BMS, Celgene researches, develops, manufactures and sells prescription pharmaceutical products in the United States. Celgene markets eight products, including an oral treatment for moderate-to-severe psoriasis.

[2] Psoriasis is a chronic skin disease caused by an overactive immune system. The disease causes skin cells to multiply faster than normal and leads to a build-up of cells on the skin surface, forming bumpy red patches that are covered with white scales, known as plaques. The plaques can appear anywhere on the body, although they are most commonly found on the scalp, elbows, knees, and lower back. The severity of psoriasis (mild, moderate, or severe) is determined based upon the percentage of body surface area affected and the parts of the body that are affected. Typically, mild psoriasis covers less than 3 percent of the body, moderate psoriasis covers 3 to 10 percent of the body and severe psoriasis covers more than 10 percent of the body.

[3] When deciding how to treat psoriasis, dermatologists typically evaluate the severity of the disease, any risk factors or contraindications for the patient, and the patient's preferences. Dermatologists consider efficacy data, safety data, and side effect profile of each product, as well as mode of administration to select the appropriate treatment course for their patients. While many injectable and infused products are approved to treat moderate-to-severe psoriasis, a number of patients object to such injections or find them inconvenient. For those patients, dermatologists often select an oral product.

[4] Celgene's apremilast, marketed under the brand name Otezla, is a phosphodiesterase inhibitor. Otezla is the most popular oral product approved to treat moderate-to-severe psoriasis in the United States. Several older oral generic products, including methotrexate and acitretin, are approved by the U.S. Food and Drug Administration ("FDA") to treat psoriasis that does not respond to light, topical agents, and other forms of therapy. These drugs are still occasionally used in the treatment of psoriasis, but most doctors have moved to prescribing newer agents with better efficacy, better safety, or a more favorable side effect profile for patients with moderate-to-severe psoriasis who desire an oral treatment. BMS is developing BMS 986165, an oral, selective tyrosine kinase 2 inhibitor that is the most advanced oral treatment in development for moderate-to-severe psoriasis.

[5] The United States is the relevant geographic market in which to assess the competitive effects of the proposed Acquisition. Oral products to treat moderate-to-severe psoriasis are prescription pharmaceutical products and regulated by FDA. As such, products sold outside the United States, but not approved for sale in the United States, do not provide viable competitive alternatives for U.S. consumers.

[6] The proposed Acquisition would likely result in substantial competitive harm to consumers in the market for oral products to treat moderate-to-severe psoriasis. Celgene is currently the market leader and BMS would likely be the next entrant into the market. Upon entry, BMS 986165 likely will compete directly with, and take sales from, Otezla.

[7] Entry in the relevant market would not be timely, likely, or sufficient in magnitude, character, and scope to deter or counteract the anticompetitive effects of the proposed Acquisition. New entry would require significant investment of time and money for product research and development, regulatory approval by the FDA, developing clinical history supporting the long-term efficacy of the product, and establishing a U.S. sales and service infrastructure. Such development efforts are difficult, time-consuming, and expensive, and often fail to result in a competitive product reaching the market.

[8] The Consent Agreement eliminates the competitive concerns raised by the proposed Acquisition by requiring BMS and Celgene to divest Celgene's worldwide Otezla business, including its regulatory approvals, intellectual property, contracts, and inventory to Amgen. BMS and Celgene also must transfer all confidential business

information, research and development information, regulatory, formulation, and manufacturing reports related to the divested products, as well as provide access to employees who possess or are able to identify such information. Additionally, to ensure that the divestiture is successful and to maintain continuity of supply, the proposed Order requires BMS and Celgene to supply Amgen with Otezla for a limited time while Amgen establishes its own manufacturing capability. The provisions of the Consent Agreement ensure that Amgen becomes an independent, viable, and effective competitor in the U.S. market.

* * *

Dissenting Statement of Commissioner Rohit Chopra, In the Matter of Bristol-Myers Squibb Company and Celgene Corporation
FTC File No. 191-0061 (Nov. 15, 2019)

[1] When it comes to life-saving pharmaceuticals, the Federal Trade Commission should never ignore serious warning signs that most Americans see clearly. Many of us depend on prescription drugs to survive, but too many cannot afford the high costs. The argument that sky-high prices are necessary for innovation has been falling apart, as more evidence reveals that many new drugs seem to be designed to extend exclusivity, rather than providing meaningful therapeutic benefits.

[2] Predicting the anticompetitive effects of massive mergers in any industry is difficult. This is especially true in pharmaceuticals, where research and discovery are core to competition. Some evidence shows that these mergers have choked off innovation, creating harms that are immeasurable for those waiting for a cure.

[3] Over the years, the agency has worked to combat abuse of intellectual property and other anticompetitive conduct by pharmaceutical companies, achieving major victories in courts across the country. Our approach to pharmaceutical mergers, however, has focused primarily on reaching settlements, rather than litigation or in-depth merger studies. The agency has focused on seeking divestitures of individual products, usually to another major pharmaceutical player.

[4] There have been longstanding, bipartisan concerns about whether this strategy is truly working. For example, in 2005, as he reflected on his six years of service as Commissioner, Thomas Leary lamented that the agency's approach to these investigations mostly stayed the same, despite overarching concerns about other anticompetitive harms.

[5] During my time as a Commissioner, I have pushed for the agency to be more rigorous across all of our work by opening our eyes to new types of analysis and sources of evidence, while avoiding assumptions that may be outdated. Given some of the clear warning signs in the industry, we must approach our investigations of pharmaceutical mergers with careful scrutiny and great humility about our longstanding practices.

[6] This massive $74 billion merger between Bristol-Myers Squibb and Celgene may have significant implications for patients and inventors, so we must be especially vigilant. In my view, this transaction appears to be heavily motivated by financial engineering and tax considerations (as opposed to a genuine drive for greater discovery of lifesaving medications), without clear benefits to patients or the public. The buyer's incentives might also be distorted, given overlaps in ownership. In addition, there are also concerns about a history of anticompetitive conduct. Expansive investigation for mergers like these is time well spent.

[7] Again, with a few exceptions, many FTC Commissioners have primarily scrutinized pharmaceutical mergers based on an examination of whether there are any product overlaps between the merging corporations, or where there may be clear-cut incentives to foreclose rivals with the ability to compete. When there are no obvious overlaps or foreclosure possibilities, the Commission typically does not challenge any aspect of the transaction.

[8] I am deeply skeptical that this approach can unearth the complete set of harms to patients and innovation, based on the history of anticompetitive conduct of the firms seeking to merge and the characteristics of today's pharmaceutical industry when it comes to innovation. Will the merger facilitate a capital structure that magnifies incentives to engage in anticompetitive conduct or abuse of intellectual property? Will the merger deter formation of biotechnology firms that fuel much of the industry's innovation? How can we know the effects on competition

if we do not rigorously study or investigate these and other critical questions? Given our approach, I am not confident that the Commission has sufficient information to determine the full scope of potential harms to competition of this massive merger.

***

Dissenting Statement of Commissioner Rebecca Kelly Slaughter, In the Matter of Bristol-Myers Squibb Company and Celgene Corporation
FTC File No. 191-0061 (Nov. 15, 2019)

[1] The Federal Trade Commission has a long history of reviewing mergers between pharmaceutical manufacturers using an analytical framework that identifies specific product overlaps between the merging parties, including of drugs in development, and requiring divestitures of one of those products. This approach addresses significant competitive concerns in these mergers, but I am concerned that it does not fully capture all of the competitive consequences of these transactions.

[2] The consent decree in this case follows the Commission's standard approach. It remedies a serious concern about a drug-level overlap between BMS's development-stage BMS 986165 (or "TYK2") and Celgene's on-market Otezla for the treatment of moderate-to-severe psoriasis. This is important, and I support the Commission's effort to remedy this drug-level overlap. However, I remain concerned that this analytical approach is too narrow. In particular, I believe the Commission should more broadly consider whether any pharmaceutical merger is likely to exacerbate anticompetitive conduct by the merged firm or to hinder innovation.

[3] Several recent developments enhance my concerns. Branded drug prices have increased substantially in recent years, and pharmaceutical merger activity persists at a high pace. The high rate of drug company consolidation has coincided with a sea change in the structure of pharmaceutical research and development; recent studies suggest mergers may inhibit research, development, or approval in this changing environment. In addition, the pharmaceutical industry has long been the focus of anticompetitive conduct enforcement by both the Commission and private litigants, including for practices such as pay-for-delay settlements, sham litigation, and anticompetitive product hopping. We must carefully consider the facts in each specific merger to understand whether or how it may facilitate anticompetitive conduct, and therefore be more likely to result in a substantial lessening of competition.

[4] Going forward, I hope the Commission will take a more expansive approach to analyzing the full range of competitive consequences of pharmaceutical mergers. I urge not only the Commission, but also researchers and industry experts to think carefully and creatively about these cases, and in particular to study the effects of recent consummated mergers on drug research, development, and approval. Outside of merger enforcement, we should also continue to police aggressively business practices that suppress competition. Indeed, as Commissioner Chopra and I have explained elsewhere, we should unleash the full scope of our authority under Section 5 to combat high drug prices.

[5] The problem of high drug prices is too important to leave any potential solutions unexhausted. As a society, we should also consider all other policy interventions that would help combat high drug prices.

***

Statement of Commissioner Noah Joshua Phillips, In the Matter of Bristol-Myers Squibb Company and Celgene Corporation
FTC File No. 191-0061 (Nov. 15, 2019)

[1] I write to address the dissenting statements issued by my colleagues, Commissioners Chopra and Slaughter.

[2] From these statements, a reader unfamiliar with the U.S. antitrust laws could be forgiven for gleaning several inaccurate conclusions. First, companies in the U.S. may not merge unless the antitrust enforcement agencies permit them to do so. Second, to stop a merger, the government need not provide any theory as to why a merger

violates the law, nor any evidence to support that theory. Third, antitrust enforcement agencies can and should condemn mergers they cannot prove violate the law because the agencies deem the business justifications for the merger insufficient.

[3] The unfamiliar reader would be wrong on each count. That is not the law. (Nor, for that matter, is it sound policy.)

[4] The structural remedy agreed to by the merging parties in this case addresses every competition concern uncovered after an extensive investigation. Every one. But Commissioners Chopra and Slaughter still dissent. Why?

[5] Commissioner Chopra cites a study purporting to show that mergers "can choke off innovation." Okay. But how does this merger do that? Without an answer to that question, the logic is rather like saying an individual defendant is guilty of a crime because there is too much of that crime in society. Thank goodness that is not how our criminal justice system works.

[6] He next writes that we must approach our investigations of pharmaceutical mergers with careful scrutiny and with great humility. I agree completely. What I fail to see is how careful scrutiny and great humility lead to the conclusion, without any clearly articulated theory of liability or facts to support it, that this merger violates the law—or, again without any facts in support, that the remedy is inadequate.

[7] The next basis Commissioner Chopra offers for his dissent is his view that the merger is animated by financial and tax considerations, which he deems insufficient to justify the merger. Leaving aside the question of why he thinks the job of antitrust enforcers is to value-judge a merger beyond its impact upon competition, that gets the law precisely backwards. The parties get to merge unless we can show a harm to competition, not the other way round. [. . .]

[8] The dissenting commissioners both criticize the Commission's investigations of pharmaceutical mergers generally, expressing concern that they fail to capture all the harms to competition posed by such mergers. But, again, the most they offer is speculation about vaguely articulated harms, without reference to any evidence that this merger is likely to exacerbate them. Nor do the dissenters cite a previous case that resulted in anticompetitive effects that they insinuate the Commission missed. The dissenting statements mention various violations of the antitrust laws committed by firms in the pharmaceutical industry, but neither explains how this merger makes such conduct more likely. For decades, the Federal Trade Commission has pursued enforcement against many different kinds of anticompetitive conduct in the pharmaceutical industry. That work, critical to controlling healthcare costs for Americans, will continue.

[9] Neither dissenting commissioner argues that the consent order and associated divestiture are bad for competition or consumers, or identifies any additional remedy they believe is warranted. And neither proposes any basis to sue to stop the merger.[3] So, again, why dissent? At the end of the day, we are left only with the sense that Commissioners Chopra and Slaughter feel the merger will threaten competition and wish to dissociate themselves with it. To me, that is not enough. (Even if it were, a vote to join Commissioners Chopra and Slaughter would result, at the end of the day, in the merger without the remedy. Are they calling on their colleagues to vote with them?)

[10] Returning to our unfamiliar reader, here is how the law actually works. First, to block a merger outright, U.S. antitrust enforcement agencies must convince a judge that it violates the law. In this country, where people and companies are free to do what they wish with their property subject to the constraints imposed by the law, our judges are somewhat hostile to the notion that we should block a merger when the parties have agreed to address every problem that we can identify. Second, we need to articulate a viable theory of harm to competition posed by the merger and produce evidence to support that theory. Third, our job is to enforce the antitrust laws, which guard against particular (competitive) harms that mergers may present. Other parts of the government guard

---

[3] In fairness, Commissioner Chopra does state his view that the agency should litigate to block more pharmaceutical mergers outright. But he fails to answer whether the Commission should litigate this case, and—more importantly—on what legal and factual basis. That is the question we face today.

against other harms posed by mergers, for example the Committee on Foreign Investment in the United States, which looks at certain investments for their potential impact on national security, or the Securities and Exchange Commission, which reviews transactions to protect investors. Our job is not to opine on whether a merger is "good" or "bad" for society as a whole, or to use our authority to make sure firms merge for reasons that someone might like (innovation) as opposed to reasons that they may not (tax).

[11] In reviewing the dissenting statements, readers—unfamiliar and otherwise—would do well to keep all of that in mind.

* * *

Pharma mergers are not the only ones in which IP plays a key role. In other industries, too, intellectual property rights may also be central to the competitive analysis of mergers. In some cases, an entire acquisition may be of a package of intellectual property: IP rights constitute assets within the meaning of Section 7 and, in appropriate cases, a pure IP transaction may give rise to competitive concerns.[810] In other cases, IP issues merely play a significant role in the context of a broader deal. For example, in 2008, the FTC challenged the proposed acquisition by Flow—a manufacturer of waterjet cutting systems—of its competitor OMAX. The FTC was particularly concerned that OMAX's broad patents would preclude competitive entry in competition with the merged firm. As a result, it obtained a consent decree that required OMAX to grant royalty-free licenses to the relevant patents.[811]

CASENOTE: United States v. Bayer AG and Agricultural Patents
Competitive Impact Statement, Case No. 1:18-cv-01241 (D.D.C. May 29, 2018)

Markets for agricultural products, like those for pharmaceuticals, are often shaped by patent rights, and this means that patents may play a prominent role in both effects theories and in remedy packages. In the blockbuster Bayer / Monsanto transaction, for example, among other things, in framing a consent decree to resolve its competitive concerns, DOJ insisted on the divestiture by the merged firm of a package of intellectual property rights that played an important role in competition to supply "seed treatments": that is, coatings that protect seeds from various hazards.

DOJ's competitive impact statement, published to explain the competitive analysis that led to the proposed remedy, explained the basic concern that the parties would acquire market power in seed treatments without a meaningful threat of entry. "Developing a new, effective seed treatment is a slow, costly, and difficult process, and new seed treatments require extensive regulatory approvals before farmers can use them. Generic versions of the Bayer seed treatments . . . will not be available for at least the next several years due to various intellectual property protections. Neither expansion by existing seed treatments nor new seed treatments expected to launch in the next several years would prevent the anticompetitive effects of the proposed merger."

As a result, Bayer would have to give up its intellectual property. Specifically, the remedy required Bayer to "divest all intellectual property associated with its Poncho, VOTiVO, and TWO.0 seed treatment brands. . . . Because

---

[810] *See, e.g.*, Intel Corp. v. Seven Networks, LLC, 562 F. Supp. 3d 454, 464 (N.D. Cal. 2021) ("[T]he Court does not take issue with the general theory being put forward by Intel – *i.e.*, that aggregation of substitute patents could, in theory, harm competition in the same way as any merger or combination of competitors that lessens competition . . . The problem for Intel is that the SAC lacks sufficient facts to demonstrate the narrative has been carried out against the company, at least at this juncture."); U.S. Dept. of Justice, Press Release, CPTN Holdings LLC and Novell Inc. Change Deal in Order to Address Department of Justice's Open Source Concerns (Apr. 20, 2011) ("The Department of Justice announced today that in order to proceed with the first phase of their acquisition of certain patents and patent applications from Novell Inc., CPTN Holdings LLC and its owners have altered their original agreements to address the department's antitrust concerns. The department said that, as originally proposed, the deal would jeopardize the ability of open source software, such as Linux, to continue to innovate and compete in the development and distribution of server, desktop, and mobile operating systems, middleware, and virtualization products. Although the department will allow the transaction to proceed, it will continue investigating the distribution of the Novell patents to the CPTN owners. . . . In light of the department's competition concerns, CPTN and its owners made revisions to their formation agreements to acquire approximately 882 patents and patent applications from Novell. The department said that these changes were necessary to protect competition and innovation in the open source software community.").

[811] See Analysis of Agreement Containing Consent Order, *In the Matter of Flow International Corp.*, FTC File No. 081-0079 (July 10, 2008), 3.

VOTiVO and TWO.0 are each typically sold in combination with Poncho, divestiture of the intellectual property associated with all three products will allow BASF to offer American farmers the same packages of Poncho-branded seed treatments as Bayer does today." It also required that Bayer "divest all intellectual property associated with its ILeVO and COPe0 seed treatments, which are both based on the same active ingredient, fluopyram." In addition, reflecting the need to ensure that the remedy was genuinely effective, "Bayer also will transfer all intellectual property used by these divested seed treatment businesses, including all patents, licenses, know-how, trade names, and data or information collected on the products." In all, Bayer would provide the divestiture buyer (BASF) with "a perpetual, royalty-free license for all patents related to the use of fluopyram in seed treatments."

Although most of our discussion so far has focused on patents, in some cases other forms of IP may play a role in a merger case or a divestiture package. In Intuit / Credit Karma, for example, DOJ's divestiture required not just the divestiture of Credit Karma's digital do-it-yourself ("DDIY") tax preparation business, but also a "limited, non-exclusive license to use the Credit Karma trademarks for the Credit Karma Tax business during the [upcoming, *i.e.*, 2021] tax filing season."[812] This might seem odd: after all, the purpose of a trademark is normally to identify of the product or service provider. Why do you think DOJ required the merged firm to let the divestiture buyer—which of course was *not* Credit Karma—use Credit Karma's trademark?

NOTES

1) What kind of issues do you think the FTC's market-by-market approach to merger control might be missing? What could the FTC do differently? What about Congress?

2) Given the importance of effective drugs to American society, do you think strong patent protection is more desirable or less desirable in pharmaceutical markets than in other areas of the economy?

3) Are you surprised by the evidence that additional generic manufacturer entry after the first has significant price effects: for example, that prices are higher in a market with three generic suppliers than in a market with five or six? Do you think we would see similar results in other areas of the economy, or is generic pharmaceutical competition special in some respect? What do you think keeps prices higher when there are one, two, or three generics in the market?

4) Do any aspects of Hatch-Waxman's framework for generic drugs seem undesirable? What other ways could you imagine to incentivize generic entry and flush out weak patents, while still encouraging innovation and investment?

2. Refusal to License

Nowhere do antitrust and IP collide more directly than in an antitrust challenge to a unilateral refusal to license. In the paradigm case, a company with monopoly power is asked for a license by a business that is also a competitor in some market to which the license is an important input; the monopolist refuses to grant the license; and it is sued for monopolization under Section 2 as a result. Most courts considering this issue have held that a simple unilateral refusal to license a patent, without additional conduct, cannot be the basis for antitrust liability.[813]

Patent law itself does not generally impose an obligation to license. In fact, the Patent Act expressly states that "No patent owner otherwise entitled to relief for infringement or contributory infringement of a patent shall be denied relief or deemed guilty of misuse or illegal extension of the patent right by reason of his having . . . refused to license or use any rights to the patent."[814] In an early patent case not involving antitrust claims, *Continental Paper Bag Co. v. Eastern Paper Bag Co.*,[815] the Court noted that a firm holding patents on an improved machine was under no obligation to license the patents to rivals: "As to the suggestion that competitors were excluded from the use of

---

[812] Competitive Impact Statement, United States v. Intuit Inc., Case No. 1:20-cv-3441 (D.D.C. filed Dec. 10, 2020) ("[T]he Divestiture Assets include a limited, non-exclusive license to use the Credit Karma trademarks for the Credit Karma Tax business during the 2021 tax filing season.").

[813] A concerted agreement among competitors not to license IP is treated like any other boycott. *See, e.g.*, Primetime 24 Joint Venture v. Nat'l Broad. Co., Inc., 219 F.3d 92, 102–03 (2d Cir. 2000).

[814] 35 U.S.C. § 271(d)(4).

[815] 210 U.S. 405 (1908).

the new patent, we answer that such exclusion may be said to have been of the very essence of the right conferred by the patent, as it is the privilege of any owner of property to use or not use it, without question of motive."[816]

In the years since *Continental Paper Bag*, courts and commentators have pondered whether a refusal to license intellectual property should be subject to equal, lesser, or greater antitrust scrutiny than other refusals to deal. Some commentators have suggested that, because the refusal does nothing more than implement the right to exclude others from the subject matter of the patent grant, antitrust liability for a "pure" refusal to license is incompatible with the patent grant itself.[817] The IP Licensing Guidelines wink at the same point—without quite saying it—when they say that "[t]he antitrust laws generally do not impose liability upon a firm for a unilateral refusal to assist its competitors, in part because doing so may undermine incentives for investment and innovation."[818]

This view animated the Federal Circuit's holding in the *Xerox* case, in which the court considered whether refusal to grant licenses covering patented equipment parts and/or copyrighted manuals could give rise to antitrust liability.

CSU, L.L.C. v. Xerox Corporation

(In re Independent Service Organizations Antitrust Litigation)

203 F.3d 1322 (Fed. Cir. 2000)

Chief Judge Mayer.

[1] CSU, L.L.C. appeals the judgment of the United States District Court for the District of Kansas, dismissing on summary judgment CSU's claims that Xerox's refusal to sell patented parts and copyrighted manuals and to license copyrighted software violate the antitrust laws. Because we agree with the district court that CSU has not raised a genuine issue as to any material fact and that Xerox is entitled to judgment as a matter of law, we affirm.

[2] Xerox manufactures, sells, and services high-volume copiers. Beginning in 1984, it established a policy of not selling parts unique to its series 10 copiers to independent service organizations ("ISOs"), including CSU, unless they were also end-users of the copiers. In 1987, the policy was expanded to include all new products as well as existing series 9 copiers. Enforcement of this policy was tightened in 1989, and Xerox cut off CSU's direct purchase of restricted parts. Xerox also implemented an "on-site end-user verification" procedure to confirm that the parts ordered by certain ISOs or their customers were actually for their end-user use. Initially this procedure applied to only the six most successful ISOs, which included CSU.

[3] To maintain its existing business of servicing Xerox equipment, CSU used parts cannibalized from used Xerox equipment, parts obtained from other ISOs, and parts purchased through a limited number of its customers. For approximately one year, CSU also obtained parts from Rank Xerox, a majority-owned European affiliate of Xerox, until Xerox forced Rank Xerox to stop selling parts to CSU and other ISOs. In 1994, Xerox settled an antitrust lawsuit with a class of ISOs by which it agreed to suspend its restrictive parts policy for six and one-half years and to license its diagnostic software for four and one-half years. CSU opted out of that settlement and filed this suit alleging that Xerox violated the Sherman Act by setting the prices on its patented parts much higher for ISOs than for end-users to force ISOs to raise their prices. This would eliminate ISOs in general and CSU in particular as competitors in the relevant service markets for high speed copiers and printers.

[4] Xerox counterclaimed for patent and copyright infringement and contested CSU's antitrust claims as relying on injury solely caused by Xerox's lawful refusal to sell or license patented parts and copyrighted software. Xerox also claimed that CSU could not assert a patent or copyright misuse defense to Xerox's infringement counterclaims

[816] *Id.* at 429.

[817] *See, e.g.*, Herbert J. Hovenkamp, Mark D. Janis, & Mark A. Lemley, *Unilateral Refusals to License in the U.S.*, in Francois Lévêque & Howard Shelanski (eds.), ANTITRUST, PATENTS, AND COPYRIGHT: EU AND US PERSPECTIVES (2005) 15 ("[A]s a general rule there is no antitrust obligation either to use or license a patent."); Jonathan Glcklen, *Per Se Legality for Unilateral Refusals to License IP Is Correct as a Matter of Law and Policy*, Antitrust Source (July 2002); Jeffrey K. MacKie-Mason, *Antitrust Immunity for Refusals to Deal in (Intellectual) Property Is a Slippery Slope*, Antitrust Source (July 2002).

[818] U.S. Dept. of Justice & FTC, ANTITRUST GUIDELINES FOR THE LICENSING OF INTELLECTUAL PROPERTY (2017), 3.

based on Xerox's refusal to deal. The district court granted summary judgment to Xerox dismissing CSU's antitrust claims and holding that if a patent or copyright is lawfully acquired, the patent or copyright holder's unilateral refusal to sell or license its patented invention or copyrighted expression is not unlawful exclusionary conduct under the antitrust laws, even if the refusal to deal impacts competition in more than one market. The court also held, in both the patent and copyright contexts, that the right holder's intent in refusing to deal and any other alleged exclusionary acts committed by the right holder are irrelevant to antitrust law. This appeal followed. [. . .]

[5] Intellectual property rights do not confer a privilege to violate the antitrust laws. But it is also correct that the antitrust laws do not negate the patentee's right to exclude others from patent property. The commercial advantage gained by new technology and its statutory protection by patent do not convert the possessor thereof into a prohibited monopolist. The patent right must be coupled with violations of § 2, and the elements of [a] violation of 15 U.S.C. § 2 must be met. Determination of whether the patentee meets the Sherman Act elements of monopolization or attempt to monopolize is governed by the rules of application of the antitrust laws to market participants, with due consideration to the exclusivity that inheres in the patent grant.

[6] A patent alone does not demonstrate market power. The United States Department of Justice and Federal Trade Commission have issued guidance that, even where it exists, such market power does not impose on the intellectual property owner an obligation to license the use of that property to others. There is no reported case in which a court has imposed antitrust liability for a unilateral refusal to sell or license a patent. The patentee's right to exclude is further supported by section 271(d) of the Patent Act which states, in pertinent part, that "[n]o patent owner otherwise entitled to relief . . . shall be denied relief or deemed guilty of misuse or illegal extension of the patent right by reason of his having . . . (4) refused to license or use any rights to the patent[.]"

[7] The patentee's right to exclude, however, is not without limit. . . . [A] patent owner who brings suit to enforce the statutory right to exclude others from making, using, or selling the claimed invention is exempt from the antitrust laws, even though such a suit may have an anticompetitive effect, unless the infringement defendant proves one of two conditions. First, he may prove that the asserted patent was obtained through knowing and willful fraud within the meaning of *Walker Process Equipment, Inc. v. Food Machinery & Chemical Corp.*, 382 U.S. 172, 177 (1965). Or he may demonstrate that the infringement suit was a mere sham to cover what is actually no more than an attempt to interfere directly with the business relationships of a competitor. *See id.* (citing *Eastern R.R. Presidents Conference v. Noerr Motor Freight, Inc.*, 365 U.S. 127, 144 (1961)). Here, CSU makes no claim that Xerox obtained its patents through fraud in the Patent and Trademark Office; the *Walker Process* analysis is not implicated.

[8] Irrespective of the patent applicant's conduct before the Patent and Trademark Office, an antitrust claim can also be based on an allegation that a suit is baseless; in order to prove that a suit was within *Noerr*'s "sham" exception to immunity, an antitrust plaintiff must prove that the suit was both *objectively* baseless and *subjectively* motivated by a desire to impose collateral, anti-competitive injury rather than to obtain a justifiable legal remedy. Accordingly, if a suit is not objectively baseless, an antitrust defendant's subjective motivation is immaterial. CSU has alleged that Xerox misused its patents but has not claimed that Xerox's patent infringement counterclaims were shams.

[9] To support its argument that Xerox illegally sought to leverage its presumably legitimate dominance in the equipment and parts market into dominance in the service market, CSU relies on a footnote in *Eastman Kodak Co. v. Image Technical Services, Inc.*, 504 U.S. 451, 480 n. 29 (1992), that "the Court has held many times that power gained through some natural and legal advantage such as a patent, can give rise to liability if a seller exploits his dominant position in one market to expand his empire into the next." Notably, *Kodak* was a tying case when it came before the Supreme Court, and no patents had been asserted in defense of the antitrust claims against Kodak. Conversely, there are no claims in this case of illegally tying the sale of Xerox's patented parts to unpatented products. Therefore, the issue was not resolved by the *Kodak* language cited by CSU. Properly viewed within the framework of a tying case, the footnote can be interpreted as restating the undisputed premise that the patent holder cannot use his statutory right to refuse to sell patented parts to gain a monopoly in a market *beyond the scope of the patent.*

[10] The cited language from *Kodak* does nothing to limit the right of the patentee to refuse to sell or license in markets within the scope of the statutory patent grant. In fact, we have expressly held that, absent exceptional circumstances, a patent may confer the right to exclude competition altogether in more than one antitrust market.

[11] CSU further relies on the Ninth Circuit's holding on remand in *Image Technical Services* that "while exclusionary conduct can include a monopolist's unilateral refusal to license a [patent] or to sell its patented work, a monopolist's desire to exclude others from its protected work is a presumptively valid business justification for any immediate harm to consumers." [*Image Technical Servs. v. Eastman Kodak Co.*, 125 F.3d 1195, 1216 (9th Cir. 1997).] By that case, the Ninth Circuit adopted a rebuttable presumption that the exercise of the statutory right to exclude provides a valid business justification for consumer harm, but then excused as harmless the district court's error in failing to give any instruction on the effect of intellectual property rights on the application of the antitrust laws. It concluded that the jury must have rejected the presumptively valid business justification as pretextual. This logic requires an evaluation of the patentee's subjective motivation for refusing to sell or license its patented products for pretext. We decline to follow *Image Technical Services.*

[12] We have held that if a patent infringement suit is not objectively baseless, an antitrust defendant's subjective motivation is immaterial. We see no more reason to inquire into the subjective motivation of Xerox in refusing to sell or license its patented works than we found in evaluating the subjective motivation of a patentee in bringing suit to enforce that same right. In the absence of any indication of illegal tying, fraud in the Patent and Trademark Office, or sham litigation, the patent holder may enforce the statutory right to exclude others from making, using, or selling the claimed invention free from liability under the antitrust laws. We therefore will not inquire into his subjective motivation for exerting his statutory rights, even though his refusal to sell or license his patented invention may have an anticompetitive effect, so long as that anticompetitive effect is not illegally extended beyond the statutory patent grant. It is the infringement defendant and not the patentee that bears the burden to show that one of these exceptional situations exists and, in the absence of such proof, we will not inquire into the patentee's motivations for asserting his statutory right to exclude. Even in cases where the infringement defendant has met this burden, which CSU has not, he must then also prove the elements of the Sherman Act violation.

[13] We answer the threshold question of whether Xerox's refusal to sell its patented parts exceeds the scope of the patent grant in the negative. Therefore, our inquiry is at an end. Xerox was under no obligation to sell or license its patented parts and did not violate the antitrust laws by refusing to do so.

[*]

[14] The Copyright Act expressly grants a copyright owner the exclusive right to distribute the protected work by transfer of ownership, or by rental, lease, or lending. The owner of the copyright, if it pleases, may refrain from vending or licensing and content itself with simply exercising the right to exclude others from using its property.

[15] The Supreme Court has made clear that the property right granted by copyright law cannot be used with impunity to extend power in the marketplace beyond what Congress intended. The Court has not, however, directly addressed the antitrust implications of a unilateral refusal to sell or license copyrighted expression.

[16] The Tenth Circuit has not addressed in any published opinion the extent to which the unilateral refusal to sell or license copyrighted expression can form the basis of a violation of the Sherman Act. We are therefore left to determine how that circuit would likely resolve the issue; the precedent of other circuits is instructive in that consideration. The Fourth Circuit has rejected a claim of illegal tying, supported only by evidence of a unilateral decision to license copyrighted diagnostic software to some but not to others. In reaching this conclusion, the court recognized the copyright owner's exclusive right to sell, rent, lease, lend, or otherwise distribute copies of a copyrighted work, and concluded that Section 1 of the Sherman Act does not entitle a purchaser to buy a product that the seller does not wish to offer for sale.

[17] Perhaps the most extensive analysis of the effect of a unilateral refusal to license copyrighted expression was conducted by the First Circuit in [*Data General Corp. v. Grumman Sys. Support Corp.*, 36 F.3d 1147 (1st Cir. 1994)]. There, the court noted that the limited copyright monopoly is based on Congress' empirical assumption that the right to "exclude others from using their works creates a system of incentives that promotes consumer welfare in the long term by encouraging investment in the creation of desirable artistic and functional works of expression.

We cannot require antitrust defendants to prove and reprove the merits of this legislative assumption in every case where a refusal to license a copyrighted work comes under attack." The court went on to establish as a legal standard that while exclusionary conduct can include a monopolist's unilateral refusal to license a copyright, an author's desire to exclude others from use of its copyrighted work is a presumptively valid business justification for any immediate harm to consumers. The burden to overcome this presumption was firmly placed on the antitrust plaintiff. The court gave no weight to evidence showing knowledge that developing a proprietary position would help to maintain a monopoly in the service market in the face of contrary evidence of the defendant's desire to develop state-of-the-art diagnostic software to enhance its service and consumer benefit.

[18] As discussed above, the Ninth Circuit adopted a modified version of this *Data General* standard. Both courts agreed that the presumption could be rebutted by evidence that the monopolist acquired the protection of the intellectual property laws in an unlawful manner. The Ninth Circuit, however, extended the possible means of rebutting the presumption to include evidence that the defense and exploitation of the copyright grant was merely a pretextual business justification to mask anticompetitive conduct. The hazards of this approach are evident in both the path taken and the outcome reached. The jury in that case was instructed to examine each proffered business justification for pretext, and no weight was given to the intellectual property rights in the instructions. This permitted the jury to second guess the subjective motivation of the copyright holder in asserting its statutory rights to exclude under the copyright laws without properly weighing the presumption of legitimacy in asserting its rights under the copyright laws. While concluding that the failure to weigh the intellectual property rights was an abuse of discretion, the Ninth Circuit nevertheless held the error harmless because it thought the jury must have rejected the presumptive validity of asserting the copyrights as pretextual. This is in reality a significant departure from the First Circuit's central premise that rebutting the presumption would be an uphill battle and would only be appropriate in those rare cases in which imposing antitrust liability is unlikely to frustrate the objectives of the Copyright Act.

[19] We believe the First Circuit's approach is more consistent with both the antitrust and the copyright laws and is the standard that would most likely be followed by the Tenth Circuit in considering the effect of Xerox's unilateral right to refuse to license or sell copyrighted manuals and diagnostic software on liability under the antitrust laws. We therefore reject CSU's invitation to examine Xerox's subjective motivation in asserting its right to exclude under the copyright laws for pretext, in the absence of any evidence that the copyrights were obtained by unlawful means or were used to gain monopoly power beyond the statutory copyright granted by Congress. In the absence of such definitive rebuttal evidence, Xerox's refusal to sell or license its copyrighted works was squarely within the rights granted by Congress to the copyright holder and did not constitute a violation of the antitrust laws.

[20] Accordingly, the judgment of the United States District Court for the District of Kansas is affirmed.

CASENOTE: Image Tech. Servs., Inc. v. Eastman Kodak Co.
125 F.3d 1195 (9th Cir. 1997)

The *Xerox* court's rhetorical and substantive foil was the Ninth Circuit's decision in *Kodak*—which was itself a step beyond the First Circuit's *Data General*. *Kodak* dealt with the conduct of Eastman Kodak, which manufactured and sold photocopiers, while also selling replacement parts (and installation services for those parts) for its own copiers. In an effort to fend off competition from third-party suppliers of parts and services (independent service organizations or "ISOs"), Kodak stopped selling parts to those suppliers, and obtained commitments from its own contracted part manufacturers that they would also refuse to sell to the ISOs. The ISOs sued, alleging that Kodak was unlawfully tying parts to copiers in violation of Section 1 and was monopolizing the sale of parts under Section 2. A jury found Kodak liable.

The Ninth Circuit described the border between antitrust and IP as a "field of dissonance," and indicated that "[h]armonizing antitrust monopoly theory with the monopolies granted by intellectual property law requires that some weight be given to the intellectual property rights of the monopolist." The court appeared to assume that, under *Aspen Skiing* (note that *Trinko* had not yet been decided!), refusal to deal by a monopolist would result in liability under Section 2 if, but only if, the monopolist lacked a "legitimate business justification." And such a justification would be *presumed* in a case where the refusal corresponded to intellectual property rights: "exclusionary conduct can include a monopolist's unilateral refusal to license a patent or copyright, or to sell its patented or copyrighted work, a monopolist's desire to exclude others from its protected work is a *presumptively valid business justification* for any immediate harm to consumers." (Emphasis added.)

However, this presumption was rebuttable, including by evidence of "pretext." This could be established by "evidence suggest[ing] that the proffered business justification played no part in the decision to act." And, the court held, the record in this case suggested that the jury would have concluded that Kodak's justification was pretextual: "Kodak's parts manager testified that patents did not cross his mind at the time Kodak began the parts policy. Further, no distinction was made by Kodak between proprietary parts covered by tooling or engineering clauses and patented or copyrighted products. In denying Kodak's motion for a new trial, the district court commented that Kodak was not actually motivated by protecting its intellectual property rights. . . . [T]his case concerns a blanket refusal that included protected and unprotected products." As a result, IP was no defense.

NOTES

1) You have now seen the approach of the Federal Circuit in *Xerox* (which effectively immunizes pure refusals to license) and that of the Ninth in *Kodak* (which requires, but presumes, a business justification). Which is the better rule? If a "desire to exclude" is indeed a legitimate justification for the purposes of the Ninth Circuit's text, what should or could "pretextual" mean for this purpose?

2) Is it true, as a matter of patent law, that a patent creates a right to exclude which is "complete"? Can this idea be squared with the principle that patent law seeks to tie monetary damages to a reasonable royalty?[819] This award may be trebled for willful infringement,[820] but the Supreme Court has made clear that enhanced damages in patent "should generally be reserved for egregious cases typified by willful misconduct."[821] Similarly, awards of attorneys' fees in patent cases are limited to "exceptional cases."[822] U.S. patent law also provides for preliminary and permanent injunctions,[823] but since the Supreme Court's opinion in *eBay Inc. v. MercExchange, LLC*,[824] it has been clear that injunctions are not available as a matter of course, but rather the need for relief beyond monetary compensation must be established by the plaintiff according to traditional rules of equity. What, if anything, follows from all this for antitrust policy?

3) Both *Kodak* and *Xerox* involved copier firms cutting off independent copier repair firms from access to a range of copier parts. Why would firms like Xerox and Kodak want to cut off ISOs' access to replacement parts in the first place? Couldn't the patent holders garner whatever rents their patents might earn them by charging the ISOs higher prices for the patented parts? Why would the firms choose to limit competition in repair rather than just raising the price of parts? Chris Sprigman has raised two possible reasons for such a practice:

> [T]he cut-off may afford the copier firm additional rents via enhanced ability to price discriminate. Additionally, the cut-off may allow the copier firm to increase the length of time during which it will be able to extract rents.

> How might this be so? Prior to the cut-off, the ISOs are able to work with the copier firm's parts. Through their experience with the various parts, the ISOs may learn how to invent around the copier firm's patents and create functionally useful replacements that do not trespass upon the copier firm's IP. Similarly with parts covered by trade secret; via repeated use and interaction, the ISOs may unravel the secrets of a part's function or manufacture, thereby vitiating entirely the narrow trade secret protection. And once an ISO is able to provide a workable replacement (or, perhaps more often, a workable repair) for the copier firm's proprietary part, either through

---

[819] *See* 35 U.S.C. § 284 ("Upon finding for the claimant the court shall award the claimant damages adequate to compensate for the infringement, but in no event less than a reasonable royalty for the use made of the invention by the infringer, together with interest and costs as fixed by the court").

[820] *Id.*

[821] Halo Elecs., Inc. v. Pulse Elecs., Inc., 579 U.S. 93, 106 (2016).

[822] 35 U.S.C. § 285.

[823] 25 U.S.C. § 283.

[824] 547 U.S. 388 (2006).

a patent work-around or by piercing a trade secret, competition from the ISOs will dispel some of the rents that the copier firm currently enjoys.

After the cut-off, of course, the ISOs are deprived of much of their former opportunity to work with and learn from the copier firm's proprietary parts. So the motivation for the cut-off may be explained not only by the ability to extract rents in the short run, but additionally by the length of time during which rents may be extracted.

Should a firm's refusal to deal aimed at extending the period during which it is able to extract rents from its patent be shielded from antitrust liability? That is a much more difficult question than the one typically posited in cases like *Kodak* and *Xerox*.[825]

4) A small number of cases have considered the application of the "essential facilities" doctrine to IP licensing, and one or two have indicated a little receptivity to the idea in principle.[826] Are there any circumstances under which you think an IP right could be considered an essential facility that must be shared on reasonable terms with all who want a license? What if anything should be done if the owner of a patent that was needed to commercialize a COVID (or other pandemic) vaccine refused to license that patent to other vaccine-makers?

5) How would you analyze a refusal to license that was not absolute but which was, rather, aimed only at actual or potential competitors of the licensor? In other words, the licensing policy would be: "you can have a license at price X unless you are a competitor, in which case you may not have a license at all." Under what circumstances, if any, would that state an antitrust violation, and what would the remedy be? What if the licensor charged rivals a higher royalty, rather than just refusing to license them?

3. Unilateral "Abuse" of the Patent System: Thicketing, Trolling, and Hopping

In Chapter VII we saw that obtaining a patent by fraud can constitute unlawful monopolization: a so-called "*Walker Process*" claim.[827] In this section we will meet other unilateral conduct that may be challenged as an antitrust violation: namely, patent "thicketing"; patent "trolling"; and "product hopping."

(a) Patent Thicketing

Patent "thicketing" is an unflattering label for the practice of amassing a patent portfolio—usually alleged to be of dubious or low quality—in a manner that may harm competition. In the following extracts, the Department of Justice warns the Seventh Circuit against giving this theory any oxygen, and the Seventh Circuit agrees. Do you?

Brief for the United States of America as Amicus Curiae in Support of Appellees, UFCW Local 1500 Welfare Fund v. AbbVie Inc.
Case No. 20-2402 (7th Cir. filed Dec. 28, 2020)

[1] Plaintiffs-appellants allege that defendant-appellee AbbVie Inc. has maintained its monopoly in the market for the drug Humira by, among other conduct, filing hundreds of patent applications and thereby amassing a "patent thicket." Through this aspect of their theory, plaintiffs effectively would attach antitrust liability to the procurement of a large portfolio of patents, a result contrary to antitrust law and patent law.[1] Accordingly, in the interest of competition and innovation, the Court should exclude AbbVie's patent procurement from the alleged

---

[825] Christopher Jon Sprigman, *The Intersection of Patent and Antitrust Law*, in Einer Elhauge (ed.), RESEARCH HANDBOOK ON THE ECONOMICS OF ANTITRUST (2012) 351.

[826] *See, e.g.*, Bellsouth Advertising & Pub. Corp. v. Donnelley Information Pub., Inc., 719 F. Supp. 1551, 1566–67 (S.D. Fla. 1988) ("Although the doctrine of essential facilities has been applied predominantly to tangible assets, there is no reason why it could not apply, as in this case, to information wrongfully withheld. The effect in both situations is the same: a party is prevented from sharing in something essential to compete. . . . Donnelley is not precluded from attempting to prove intent by using the essential facilities doctrine in conjunction with other evidence that the Bell companies willfully maintained a monopoly."), *rev'd on other grounds*, 999 F.2d 1436 (11th Cir. 1993).

[827] Walker Process Equipment, Inc. v. Food Machinery & Chemical Corp., 382 U.S. 172, 177 (1965).

[1] This brief addresses the internal development of patents, not the acquisition of patents from third parties. In a number of circumstances, an acquisition of a patent(s) from a third party can give rise to antitrust concerns.

anticompetitive conduct when assessing the adequacy of plaintiffs' claim under Section 2 of the Sherman Act. [. . .]

[2] In their complaint, plaintiffs allege that AbbVie's development, acquisition, and enforcement of its patent thicket undertaken and executed without regard to the merits of the patents violates Section 2 of the Sherman Act. AbbVie obtained an "enormous portfolio of patents," by one estimate filing 247 patent applications and procuring 132 Humira-related patents. AbbVie "sought to obtain patents regardless of their merits," and, as a result, "many of its patents do not withstand scrutiny."

[3] AbbVie nonetheless threatened protracted litigation against any applicants for a Humira biosimilar. "Regardless of the ultimate merits" of AbbVie's patents, "the sheer volume of patents and claims" deterred or delayed entry of biosimilar competitors. "Few if any companies could litigate all of AbbVie's patents; indeed, few could even parse through the morass of patents to determine whether any were valid and infringed." [. . .]

[4] Plaintiffs seek an unwarranted extension of Section 2 liability, endeavoring to base liability, in part, on mere patent procurement. Filing patent applications, even hundreds, can promote innovation and competition, the shared goals of patent and antitrust law. Accordingly to avoid chilling such procompetitive conduct, courts recognize Section 2 liability for conduct involving patent procurement only in limited circumstances.

[5] Plaintiffs have not alleged such circumstances and have not presented a cognizable theory of liability related to AbbVie's patent procurement. They have not alleged any use of the application process—as opposed to the outcome of process—to exclude competitors, and therefore have failed to allege sham petitioning with respect to AbbVie's patent procurement. Indeed, the process costs of applying for patents fall entirely on AbbVie. Once the Patent and Trademark Office (USPTO) grants a patent, the patentee, of course, can impose costs on a competitor by asserting the patent, as AbbVie did here in patent dances and in litigation. However, imposing assertion costs is improper only in limited circumstances, e.g., sham litigation or the assertion of a patent obtained by fraud (a *Walker Process* claim). The mere fact of asserting numerous validly obtained patents is not enough to give rise to antitrust liability.

[6] Plaintiffs have waived any *Walker Process* claim. In any event, they have not attempted to allege fraud on the USPTO with regard to the vast majority of the patent procurement. Accordingly, and in order not to upset the Supreme Court's suitable accommodation of antitrust law and patent law, and thereby discourage innovation, the Court should not consider AbbVie's patent procurement, or the mere fact of its numerous patents, as part of plaintiffs' Section 2 claim. More broadly, the Court should decline plaintiffs' invitation to use antitrust law to redress alleged deficiencies in the patent system and the regulatory framework. As the district court correctly concluded, that is a job for Congress, not the courts. [. . .]

[7] Ordinarily, there is no limitation on a company's freedom to generate its own patents. Courts therefore have concluded that the mere accumulation of patents, no matter how many, is not in and of itself illegal. The reasons for this rule are straightforward, but critical. Put simply, we do not wish to discourage innovation, even by monopolists. The prospect of a patent drives innovation, a shared goal of antitrust law and patent law. Thus, a vigorous research program directed toward improving one's competitive position via the development of patented inventions will not by itself be grounds for antitrust challenge, even if the program ultimately results in the entity achieving a dominant or monopoly position in the field.

[8] Additionally, imposing liability for the mere accumulation of patents could have unwanted collateral consequences. The patent system is designed to facilitate the disclosure of inventions in exchange for a limited period of exclusivity. This disclosure can facilitate follow-on innovation. Imposing antitrust liability merely for filing large numbers of patent applications may cause innovators to abandon the patent system and instead rely on trade secrets to protect investment in research and development, which could hamper follow-on innovation rather than advance it.

[9] Relatedly, a patentee's conduct in obtaining or enforcing a patent generally is protected by the *Noerr-Pennington* doctrine. Under this doctrine, those who petition government for redress are generally immune from antitrust liability. [. . .]

[10] *Walker Process* sometimes is viewed as the patent-litigation version of a broader "misrepresentation" exception to *Noerr*. The logic of this exception is that, where government action is procured through intentional fraud, the outcome properly is attributed to the private party whose fraud procured the outcome, not the government actor who unwittingly relied on the fraudulent representation.

[11] In and of itself, however, procuring large numbers of patents does not implicate either the sham or Walker-Process exception to *Noerr-Pennington* protection. It therefore follows that, without more, procuring a large portfolio of patents cannot constitute anticompetitive conduct sufficient to ground a Section 2 claim.

* * *

<h2 style="text-align:center">Mayor and City Council of Baltimore v. AbbVie Inc.</h2>
Case No. 20-2402 (7th Cir. Aug. 1, 2022)

Judge Easterbrook.

[1] [. . .] [W]hat's wrong with having lots of patents? If AbbVie made 132 inventions, why can't it hold 132 patents? The patent laws do not set a cap on the number of patents any one person can hold—in general, or pertaining to a single subject. Tech companies such as Cisco, Qualcomm, Intel, Microsoft, and Apple have much larger portfolios of patents. Thomas Edison alone held 1,093 U.S. patents. When the FTC challenged Qualcomm's patent practices, it objected to licensing terms rather than the sheer size of the portfolio—and the FTC lost in the end. [. . .]

[2] The payors insist that AbbVie's patents are weak—too weak to monopolize the sales of such an important drug. This argument leaves us cold. Weak patents are valid; to say they are weak is to say that their scope is limited, not that they are illegitimate. [. . .]

[3] Trying to conjure liability out of successful petitions for governmental aid in blocking competition runs into the *Noerr-Pennington* doctrine. This doctrine, rooted in the First Amendment, deems petitioning a protected activity.

[4] Unsuccessful petitioning can be a source of liability when the petitioner runs up rivals' costs and so stifles competition independent of a petition's success. An example would be filing a frivolous suit, as many a suit is more costly to defend than to prosecute. The Justices held in BE&K Construction Co. v. NLRB, 536 U.S. 516 (2002), that no one has a constitutional right to pursue baseless litigation. *Professional Real Estate* says that petitioning exceeds the scope of the *Noerr-Pennington* doctrine when the petitioner tries to interfere directly with the business relationships of a competitor, through the use of the governmental process—as opposed to the outcome of that process—as an anticompetitive weapon. But the payors express concern about the successful outcome of AbbVie's petitioning, not about costs imposed by the process of petitioning. Patent applications, successful or not, do not impose costs on rivals; only issued patents do so.

[5] Doubtless it is possible to use properly issued patents in a way that *Noerr-Pennington* does not protect. For example, if AbbVie were to assert irrelevant patents against producers of biosimilar drugs, that might come within the scope of *BE&K Construction*. The payors contend that AbbVie listed some irrelevant patents in the litigation it commenced against would-be entrants, but they do not contend that AbbVie listed only irrelevant patents in those suits. What's more, the sifting of wheat from chaff is a job for the judges hearing those patent cases. The would-be entrants . . . were free to make arguments along these lines; a separate antitrust suit by strangers to the patent litigation does not justify an effort to adjudicate by proxy what might have happened in the patent litigation, but didn't.

(b) Patent Trolling

"Patent trolling" is an unflattering label sometimes applied to the business model of a "patent assertion entity" ("PAE"). This business model involves obtaining patents in order to assert them against entities practicing the patents, in order to obtain "holdup" rents, through the threat of an injunction, from those who have already sunk investments into the patented technology. As Fiona Scott Morton and Carl Shapiro describe it:

> The pure PAE business model involves purchasing patents, often in large numbers, and obtaining revenues by asserting those patents, with no conventional lines of business. By definition, pure PAEs have no financial interest in targeted products or substitutes or complements to them. The core competency of PAEs is to acquire and monetize patents. [. . .]
>
> PAEs seek to keep abreast of industry knowledge and trends so that they can locate valuable patents and purchase them inexpensively. Indeed, having good information about potential licensees and past licensing deals or settlement terms is critical to the PAE business model. Some PAEs require their business partners to sign very stringent non-disclosure agreements to keep this information private.
>
> PAEs adopt diverse business strategies to exploit these opportunities. Some PAEs are mass aggregators, purchasing thousands of patents. Aggregating related patents can enhance monetization if litigation by the PAE based on the combined portfolio is profitable while litigation of the smaller constituent portfolios is not. A large portfolio may especially be needed if many of the patents involved are weak. Mass aggregation of related but weak patents may thus allow the PAE to achieve a rather novel type of scale economy. Other PAEs assert a small number of patents against many targets. One version of this involves assertions that have elements of nuisance suits, where targets can settle for less than the cost of litigation.[828]

There is room for reasonable disagreement about the right legal and social response to the activity of PAEs. On the one hand, obtaining and monetizing patents is exactly what the Patent Act is supposed to facilitate. It hardly seems fair to punish businesses for rationally exercising the valuable rights that the federal government has itself conferred on them. On the other hand, the extraction of surprise holdup rents by entities that engage in no innovation—from those that do!—does not seem the most sympathetic or socially beneficial use of the intellectual property laws.

Antitrust's toolkit does not contain many devices for deterring the activities of PAEs. In general, antitrust doctrine recognizes that "sham litigation"—that is, the prosecution of objectively baseless lawsuits against rivals—may constitute a means of unlawful monopolization when it operates to exclude a monopolist's rivals and thus to create or maintain market power.[829] But the paradigm PAE does not itself practice the patents: it is not active in the same market as its targets, and thus cannot be liable for monopolizing a market in which it is not present.[830] More complex cases can involve a practice known as "privateering" in which a practicing entity (*i.e.*, a competitor) transfers a patent portfolio to a PAE under circumstances in which the PAE is likely to assert them against its rivals, raising their costs.[831] Mark Popofsky and Michael Laufert have argued that antitrust can reach such transfers when they are structured in ways that raise rivals' costs by: (1) increasing the "ability or incentives to enforce the transferred patents"; (2) disaggregate a patent portfolio in order to expose rivals to "royalty stacking" (*i.e.*, extraction of value in excess of a reasonable royalty through multiple independent holdup threats); or (3) involve violation of a previous commitment to limit royalties to a reasonable rate.[832]

The principal difficulty in an antitrust challenge to "patent trolling" is the broad protection from antitrust liability afforded under the *Noerr-Pennington* doctrine to any use of the court system that is not objectively baseless.[833] In a lengthy analysis of a monopolization challenge to infringement litigation from a significant PAE, the U.S. District Court for the District of Maryland applied the doctrine and concluded that the room for antitrust to operate is limited. The decision was subsequently affirmed by the Federal Circuit on other grounds.[834]

---

[828] Fiona M. Scott Morton & Carl Shapiro, *Strategic Patent Acquisitions*, 79 Antitrust L.J. 463, 464, 470 (2014).

[829] *See* Chapters VII, IX.

[830] *See, e.g.*, Spanish Broad. Sys. of Fla., Inc. v. Clear Channel Commc'ns, Inc., 376 F.3d 1065, 1075 (11th Cir. 2004).

[831] *See, e.g.*, Jay P. Kesan, Anne Layne-Farrar & David L. Schwartz, *Understanding Patent "Privateering": A Quantitative Assessment*, 16 J. Empirical Leg. Stud. 343 (2019); Jorge Lemus & Emil Temnyalov, *Patent privateering, litigation, and R&D incentives*, 48 RAND J. Econ. 1004 (2017); Matthew Sipe, *Patent Privateers and Antitrust Fears*, 22 Mich. Telecomm. & Tech. L. Rev. 191 (2016); Mark S. Popofsky & Michael D. Laufert, *Antitrust Attacks On Patent Assertion Entities*, 79 Antitrust L.J. 445, 455 (2014).

[832] Mark S. Popofsky & Michael D. Laufert, *Antitrust Attacks On Patent Assertion Entities*, 79 Antitrust L.J. 445, 456–57 (2014); *see also* Michael A. Carrier, *Patent Assertion Entities: Six Actions the Antitrust Agencies Can Take*, Comp. Pol'y Int'l (Jan. 2013).

[833] *See supra* Chapter IX.

[834] Intell. Ventures I LLC v. Cap. One Fin. Corp., 937 F.3d 1359 (Fed. Cir. 2019).

Intellectual Ventures I LLC v. Capital One Financial Corp.

280 F. Supp. 3d 691 (D. Md. 2017)

Judge Grimm.

[1] The essence of Capital One's antitrust claim is that IV is a "patent troll,"[3] and not just any patent troll, but a veritable Dovregubben.[4] Capital One asserts that IV's business practice is to acquire a vast portfolio of thousands of patents that purportedly deal with technology essential to the types of services offered by commercial banks (such as ATM transactions, mobile banking, on-line banking, and credit card transactions). It then employs an aggressive marketing scheme whereby it makes an "offer" for banks to license (Capital One really would prefer to say "extorts" banks to license) its entire portfolio for a period of years at a jaw-droppingly high price. But, Capital One insists, when the banks ask for details about the patents covered in the portfolio in order to determine whether their services infringe them, IV refuses to disclose sufficient information to enable them to make an intelligent decision about whether they should agree to the license. And, if the bank balks at licensing the entire portfolio at IV's take-it-or-leave-it price, IV then threatens to file a patent infringement claim against the bank regarding only a few of the patents in the portfolio. Adding insult to injury, IV then makes it clear that should it lose the patent infringement case, it will simply file another (and if needed, another, and so on) regarding a different set of its patents, until the prospect of endless high-cost litigation forces the bank to capitulate and license the entire portfolio.

[2] Capital One characterizes IV's business model as comprised of three components:

> *accumulate* a vast portfolio of patents purportedly relating to essential commercial banking services, *conceal* the details of those patents so that the banks cannot determine whether their products infringe any of IV's patents, and serially *litigate* to force the banks to capitulate and license the portfolio at exorbitant cost. This conduct, Capital One insists, constitutes monopolization under § 2 of the Sherman Act, attempted monopolization under § 2 of the Sherman Act, and unlawful asset acquisition under § 7 of the Clayton Act.

[3] Nonsense, IV indignantly responds. It counters Capital One's charges by arguing that it legitimately purchased or otherwise acquired its large portfolio of patents that relate to multiple technology markets. It then offers to license its portfolio to banks (and other types of businesses), beginning its negotiation with an opening offer, and expecting the bank to counteroffer, thereby initiating a back-and-forth exchange that it hopes will result in a mutually-agreeable licensing fee. IV vehemently denies that it conceals the details of its individual patents or that Capital One could not determine what they relate to by reviewing publicly available information. As IV sees things, when Capital One declined to make a counter offer to its opening bid, it then selected a number of its patents and brought suit against Capital One, first in the Eastern District of Virginia, and then, when that suit was unsuccessful, in this Court, with respect to a different set of patents. Moreover, IV claims that Capital One is, in essence, an "efficient infringer"—an entity that engages in its business without care for whether it infringes on patents held by others, with the knowledge that a patent infringement case is expensive to bring, and many patent holders lack the funds to do so to protect their rights. As such, Capital One can play the odds, infringing patents with near impunity until the rare patent holder with the resources to sue does so, and then negotiate a favorable license fee.

[4] IV points out that each of its patents is presumptively valid, and that it has an absolute right to file litigation to enforce them. And, in IV's view, if enforcing its patents through litigation has any monopoly effect (which IV denies it does), it has immunity under the *Noerr–Pennington* doctrine. . . .

[5] IV also asserts that Capital One's antitrust theory is fundamentally flawed, because no liability can attach unless Capital One can prove that IV exercises monopoly power within a relevant market. Monopoly power is the power to control prices or exclude competition. IV insists that it does neither, because the correct market definition

---

[3] A "patent troll" is an individual or company who acquires by purchase or application to the Patent and Trademark Office a patent that he uses not to protect an invention but to obtain a license fee from, or legal judgment against, an alleged infringer. Patent trolls are also known as patent assertion entities (PAEs), and non-practicing entities (NPEs).

[4] Dovregubben was the Troll King in Henrik Ibsen's 1867 play *Peer Gynt*.

would recognize that what IV owns is a series of patents that relate to multiple, distinct technology markets. And IV could exercise monopoly power only if Capital One can show that its patents include those affecting alternative substitute technologies that Capital One otherwise could turn to in order to avoid having to license IV's patents. Capital One has not made this showing, IV contends, entitling it to summary judgment.

[6] Underlying the legal issues in this case are two important but competing policies. On one hand, we value innovation that leads to new inventions that advance science and technology, protecting that creative effort by issuing patents. A patent, by its very nature, vests its owner with a type of legal monopoly, which it can enforce against anyone who infringes the patent. Enforcing a patent through litigation protects this monopoly, even though in other circumstances we view monopolies as harmful.

[7] The other important policy implicated by this case, of course, is the strong desire to ensure vigorous competition in the marketplace, so that consumers (whether businesses or individuals) can purchase at the lowest possible price. To promote the benefits of robust competition, antitrust law aims to prevent a company from having the ability to control the price of its product or exclude competitors to the extent that it can charge sustained supracompetitive prices (prices substantially above what a competitive price would be if consumers could simply buy a close substitute product from a competitor at lower cost).

[8] The exercise of monopoly power with regard to a single patent (or even a few patents) usually does not offend antitrust law. But it is another matter to acquire a vast portfolio of patents that are essential to technology employed by an entire industry and then to compel its licensing at take-it-or-leave-it prices because it is not economically feasible to determine if alternative technologies, not covered by the accumulation of patents, are available. This acquisition and compelled licensing could amount to the ability to exercise monopoly power on an entirely different scale. [. . .]

[9] . . . Antitrust law is designed to prevent the acquisition and exercise of monopoly power.

[10] Each of the above important competing policies is at play in this case. Capital One argues, through its highly credentialed and impressive economic expert, Professor Fiona Scott Morton of Yale University, that IV possesses monopoly power in connection with its large financial services patent portfolio, which touches on essential technologies that commercial banks have heavily invested in and cannot realistically design around to avoid the reach of IV's patents. Because of the size of this portfolio (between 7,725 and 35,000 patents, depending on whether Capital One or IV's expert is correct), IV is able to charge supracompetitive prices to license the portfolio. And IV's concealment of the details regarding the patents leaves Capital One unable (without incurring ruinous cost) to ferret out the particulars of each patent and assess whether it infringes any patents. Also at play is IV's aggressive policy of threatening (and bringing) expensive serial patent infringement suits. IV's aggregation of such a large portfolio, combined with its concealment and aggressive litigation strategies will, according to Capital One, eventually force it to capitulate and pay IV's supracompetitive price to license the entire portfolio.

[11] As Professor Scott Morton sees it, antitrust analysis commonly used to determine whether a proposed merger will result in anticompetitive effects, simply does not work for the facts of this case. That is because merger analysis is ex ante, focusing on whether, if the merger is approved, the new entity will be able to charge a small but significant non-transitory increase in price (referred to as "SSNIP") that it could maintain over time without competition from others making that price increase unsustainable. Put differently, SSNIP analysis is best done before the entity of interest has acquired monopoly power. Scott Morton reasons that this case requires ex post analysis because Capital One already had incurred significant costs to acquire the technology to compete with other commercial banks in essential services such as on-line banking, remote banking, and ATM and credit card transactions when IV began licensing its massive financial services patent portfolio. In other words, IV already had acquired monopoly power when it approached Capital One to license its patents. Because Capital One already had incurred substantial sunk costs in the technology in which it had invested, it was unable to design around IV's enormous portfolio to adopt non-infringing technologies the way it could have done if it knew of the breadth and scope of IV's patents before it incurred the cost of the technologies it adopted.

[12] Under her proposed ex post analysis, it is IV's conduct after having acquired monopoly power that is critical to antitrust scrutiny. Through its trio of patent aggregation, concealment and litigation, IV has acquired

insurmountable bargaining power enabling it to exercise "hold-up" power by demanding take-it-or-leave-it supracompetitive prices to license its financial services portfolio. And even though it has resisted doing so to date, eventually Capital One will be forced to capitulate to the threat of exorbitantly expensive patent litigation to purchase a license that it does not want, despite the fact that IV's singular lack of success in prosecuting any of its patent suits against IV (or other banks) suggests that its massive portfolio is in truth composed of nothing more than an amalgamation of weak patents. And, but for IV's practice of accumulation, concealment and litigation, it could never command a price to license its portfolio of weak patents at anything near the supracompetitive price it sought from Capital One. [. . .]

[13] Pure humbug, counters IV, through its equally well-credentialed and impressive economic expert, Professor Richard Gilbert from the University of California, Berkley. He challenges Professor Scott Morton's market definition, arguing that the proper definition is not a "cluster" of financial services patents constituting a single product, but rather a collection of patents that relate to multiple distinct technology markets. Professor Gilbert relies on the Antitrust Guidelines for the Licensing of Intellectual Property issued jointly by the U.S. Department of Justice and the Federal Trade Commission ("Guidelines"). The Guidelines state, relevantly, that "[a]lthough the intellectual property right confers the power to exclude with respect to the specific product, process, or work in question, there will often be sufficient actual or potential close substitutes for such product, process, or work to prevent the exercise of market power." Id. § 2.2, at 4. The flaw in Capital One's antitrust analysis, according to Professor Gilbert, is its failure to analyze the distinct technology markets for which IV does have patents to determine whether there are alternative close substitutes that Capital One could turn to in order to avoid having to license from IV. [. . .]

[14] If the only issue raised in IV's summary judgment motion was whether there are genuine disputes of material fact that would entitle it to judgment as a matter of law on the issues of possession of monopoly power in a relevant market and the willful acquisition or maintenance of that power as distinguished from growth or development as a consequence of a superior product, business acumen, or historic accident, I would deny the motion and allow the case to proceed to trial. This is because I have concluded from the record before me that Capital One has identified admissible evidence to establish a genuine dispute as to these issues, precluding summary judgment. But as next will be seen, there are further legal issues which, when resolved, require the granting of IV's motion. [. . .]

[15] Antitrust law proscribes the willful acquisition or maintenance of monopoly power within a market, as well as attempts to monopolize. In contrast, a patent creates a legal monopoly. Additionally, those who petition government for redress are generally immune from antitrust liability under what is known as *Noerr-Pennington* immunity. This holds true for parties who file suit in court. And, patent holders that believe that their patents have been infringed may seek to enforce their rights under the patent through patent litigation. Thus, when a party challenges a patent holder's efforts to enforce its patents through litigation, the court must determine whether the patent holder is exercising the lawful restraint on trade of the patent monopoly or the illegal restraint prohibited broadly by the Sherman Act. To do so, courts must balance the privileges of a patent holder under its patent grants with the prohibitions of the Sherman Act against combinations and attempts to monopolize.

[16] IV contends that under the First Amendment and the *Noerr-Pennington* doctrine, Intellectual Ventures I and Intellectual Ventures II, like other patent owners, are entitled to petition a court for a redress of their grievances, that is, IV may sue corporations like Capital One for patent infringement without being sued under the antitrust laws for bringing suit. On that basis, it argues that, for Capital One to proceed on its antitrust claims against IV based on IV's patent litigation activities, Capital One must establish that an exception to *Noerr-Pennington* exists such that IV was not entitled to exercise its right to sue. According to IV, Capital One has failed to prove that IV's claims were "objectively baseless," as it had to do to prove that IV was not exempt from antitrust liability. IV asserts that Capital One instead tried to prove that IV's claims were "unsuccessful," which IV insists is not enough.

[17] Capital One counters that *Noerr-Pennington* immunity simply does not apply because the litigation conduct is part of a broader monopolistic scheme, and *Noerr* does not insulate the entire scheme. Insofar as Capital One argues that IV's aggregation of patents to create market power would support substantial Section 2 and Section 7 claims on its own, and that the concealment and misdirection at the heart of IV's extortive licensing strategy would be anticompetitive even if IV had never filed a lawsuit, this contention is contrary to Capital One's pleadings. Capital One alleges that IV has eliminated banks' access to substitutes for IV's license, both in the form of other

patent licenses and banking-product designs, through a carefully orchestrated campaign of patent aggregation, concealment, and sham litigation, and that IV's use of patent accumulations to cut off banks' design and license choices, as weapons in negotiation, and to provide fuel for repeated sham litigation, violates Section 2 of the Sherman Act.

[18] And, while patent acquisition and aggregation is the focus of the Clayton Act claim, acquisition is actionable under the Clayton Act only where the effect of such acquisition may be substantially to lessen competition, or to tend to create a monopoly. To establish this effect, Capital One relies on IV's purported "campaign," which could not succeed absent the allegedly sham litigation. [. . .]

[19] Under [Prof. Real Est. Invs., Inc. v. Columbia Pictures Indus., Inc., 508 U.S. 49 (1993)], what I need to determine is whether a reasonable litigant in IV's position could realistically expect to succeed on the merits of its claims in this Court because, if it could, the litigation was not objectively baseless and therefore not sham litigation. . . .

[20] Fatally, Capital One cannot establish that IV's litigation against it was objectively baseless because there were too many indicia of probable cause. Most significantly, in this case, it is undisputed that the parties selected and the Court appointed an independent Special Master (with significant experience handling patent litigation), who wrote two comprehensive reports and recommendations regarding the merits of four of IV's patent claims after the parties submitted cross-motions for summary judgment on patent validity under 35 U.S.C. § 101. Prior to issuing those reports and recommendations, the Special Master resolved multiple discovery disputes; reviewed the parties' extensive formal briefing, as well as supplemental letter briefing that the Special Master requested and twenty-seven exhibits; and heard argument. Under the Special Master's detailed and insightful analysis, IV did succeed on two of its patent claims: the Special Master recommended a judgment of patent eligibility for the '084 and '002 Patents. ECF No. 298. This fact alone is sufficient to show that a reasonable litigant could realistically expect to succeed on the merits, and it vitiates the notion that the loss before Judge Trenga meant that IV no longer could reasonably believe that it could prevail in this court. And, next to this fact, any other disputes are scintillae.

[21] Moreover, various other undisputed facts also support the finding that IV's litigation in this Court was not objectively baseless. First, there is the presumptive validity of each of the nine patents that were the subjects of IV's claims against Capital One. Second, IV filed both suits before the Supreme Court decided Alice Corp. Pty. v. CLS Bank Int'l, [573 U.S. 208 (2014)] (holding that claims disclosing a computer-implemented scheme for mitigating settlement risk by using a third-party intermediary were not patent eligible under 35 U.S.C. § 101.) . . . I considered *Alice* and the parameters it set for eligibility in concluding that two of the patents before me were not actually patent-eligible. The Special Master did not consider post-*Alice* cases and found that the same patents were patent eligible. This shows that when IV filed suit, before *Alice* was decided, it was realistic to expect success on the merits, at least with regard to these two patents.

[22] Third, IV has not filed any additional suits against Capital One post-*Alice*. Fourth, IV withdrew specific claims when it was persuaded that it would not prevail, suggesting that it reasonably believed it could prevail on the others. Fifth, IV appealed my summary judgment rulings, an extra step that one who did not expect to succeed likely would not bother taking. Sixth, while Capital One incurred significant costs defending IV's patent claims, IV also incurred substantial litigation expenses. The litigation before me has involved nineteen attorneys for IV, as well as a Special Master and an economic consultant, the costs of whom the parties have shared. The docket includes almost 700 entries, and the documents in support of the parties' pending summary judgment briefing exceed 13,000 pages. Seventh, IV did not file for these patents with the Patent and Trademark Office; it acquired them and was entitled to rely on their presumptive validity. Eighth, Judge Trenga ruled that IV's patent infringement action was not an "exceptional case" marked by "unreasonable conduct" that would justify an award of attorneys' fees to Capital One pursuant to 35 U.S.C. § 285. Ninth, IV incurred the significant expense of designating nine experts on objective reasonableness—in comparison to Capital One's failure to designate any—something IV hardly would have done had it thought its underlying patent claims were objectively baseless. Under these circumstances, no reasonable factfinder could conclude that IV lacked probable cause. [. . .]

[23] In sum, not only is Capital One not a competitor of IV, but more significantly, a reasonable litigant in IV's position realistically could have expected to succeed on the merits of its claims in this Court. Therefore, the litigation was not objectively baseless. Consequently, it was not sham litigation, and IV is entitled to *Noerr-Pennington* immunity, as its patent litigation is integral to Capital One's antitrust claims.

(c) Product Hopping

"Product hopping" is the practice of making non-improving changes to a product before the expiry of a patent in order to obtain a fresh term of patent exclusivity. This category includes so-called "hard switch" cases, in which the original is withdrawn from the market, and "soft switch" cases, in which the original product is maintained but demand is directed to the new product. The term is primarily used in the pharmaceutical context, where it centrally refers to the reformulation of an original drug into a new form, such that generic versions of the original are no longer substitutable for the new one (*e.g.*, from chewable to injectable, or with a different dosage), combined with an effort to encourage clinicians to prescribe the new drug rather than the original.[835] If such a switch is accomplished before a generic drug enters,[836] the generic will arrive on the market only to find that it is not in fact a substitute for the branded drug at which it was aimed—such that it will not be prescribed as a substitute.[837] And a generic seeking approval as a substitute for the *new* version of the branded drug will have to start the long regulatory process again.

The core antitrust concern in such cases is that the product hopper is abusing the patent system—and perhaps other regulatory systems too[838]—in order to extend monopoly and keep out rivals. But this concern is qualified by reluctance to impose antitrust liability for any—or even the combination—of three activities that sound, at least at first blush, like they should virtually always be lawful: the introduction of a new product; the withdrawal of an old product; and the otherwise-lawful acquisition and exercise of rights under the Patent Act. As a result, there is plenty of controversy about the wisdom of antitrust control of product hopping.[839]

Courts and agencies have now had some opportunities to weigh in on the question, and they have expressed a variety of views.[840] The following pages present three perspectives: the FTC's take, as expressed in a 2015 amicus brief on appeal from a district court decision that had expressed skepticism of the product-hopping theory of liability, and the views of the Second and Third Circuits.

---

[835] Michael A. Carrier & Steve D. Shadowen, *Product Hopping: A New Framework*, 92 Notre Dame L. Rev. 167, 171 (2016) (defining a product hop as a reformulation of this kind plus the encouragement to clinicians).

[836] *See supra* notes 800–805 and accompanying text.

[837] Michael A. Carrier & Steve D. Shadowen, *Product Hopping: A New Framework*, 92 Notre Dame L. Rev. 167, 176 (2016).

[838] Other regulatory systems that may be abused include state drug product selection laws (which govern substitution of generics for branded drugs) and FDA citizen petition rules (which are intended to allow citizens to raise concerns, but which may be used by incumbents to hinder and deter entry).

[839] *See, e.g.*, Dennis W. Carlton, Fredrick A. Flyer & Yoad Shefi, *Does The FTC's Theory Of Product Hopping Promote Competition?*, 12 J. Comp. L. 7 Econ. 495 (2016); Michael A. Carrier & Steve D. Shadowen, *Product Hopping: A New Framework*, 92 Notre Dame L. Rev. 167 (2016); M. Sean Royall, Ashley E. Johnson & Jason C. McKenney, *Antitrust Scrutiny of "Product Hopping,"* 28 Antitrust 71 (2013); Michael Carrier, *Provigil: A Case Study of Anticompetitive Behavior*, 3 Hast.. Sci. & Tech. L.J. 441 (2011); Stacey L. Dogan & Mark A. Lemley, *Antitrust Law and Regulatory Gaming*, 87 Tex. L. Rev. 685, 687–88, 708–17 (2009); *see also, e.g.*, Steve D. Shadowen et al., *Anticompetitive Product Changes in the Pharmaceutical Industry*, 41 Rutgers L.J. 1, 44–45 (2009).

[840] *See, e.g.*, Abbott Labs. v. Teva Pharms. USA, Inc., 432 F. Supp. 2d 408 (D. Del. 2006) (denying motion to dismiss and indicating that the rule of reason should be applied to hard-switch product hopping); Walgreen Co. v. AstraZeneca Pharmaceuticals L.P., 534 F. Supp. 2d 146 (D.D.C. 2008) (dismissing complaint alleging a soft switch); In re Suboxone Antitrust Litigation, 64 F. Supp. 3d 665 (E.D. Pa. 2014) (denying motion to dismiss in a case falling somewhere between "hard" and "soft" switching); Mylan Pharms. Inc. v. Warner Chilcott Pub. Ltd. Co., 838 F.3d 421 (3d Cir. 2016) (granting summary judgment for defendant given evidence of nonpretextual purposes, additional competitors, and lack of coercion); New York ex rel. Schneiderman v. Actavis PLC, 787 F.3d 638 (2d Cir. 2015) (granting preliminary injunction to prevent a hard switch); *see also* Brief for FTC as Amicus Curiae, Mylan Pharm., Inc. v. Warner Chilcott Pub. Co., Case No. 12-3824 (E.D. Pa. filed Nov. 21, 2012).

Brief For Amicus Curiae Federal Trade Commission Supporting Plaintiff-Appellant, Mylan Pharmaceuticals, Inc. v. Warner-Chilcott PLC

Case No. 15-2236 (3d Cir. filed Sept. 30, 2015)

[1] A typical product-hopping scheme works as follows. A brand-name pharmaceutical company expects generic rivals to win FDA approval to compete with the company's profitable brand-name drug using automatically substitutable AB-rated equivalents. To thwart such substitution, the brand-name company introduces minor changes to the drug's formulation, such as therapeutically insignificant tweaks to dosage levels or to the form of administration (e.g., capsules vs. tablets).

[2] Before generic equivalents have a chance to enter, the brand-name manufacturer then takes various steps to extinguish demand for the original version. For example, the manufacturer might restrict or eliminate the supply of the original formulation, increase its effective price to patients, or flood physician offices with free samples of the revised formulation but not the original to divert prescriptions to the revised formulation. That shift in prescriptions is generally a one-way street: once doctors prescribe a medicine and find that it works, they are generally reluctant to switch users back to the original formulation even if a cheaper generic version of it later becomes available. Theoretically, third-party payors (e.g., insurers) should have incentives to persuade physicians to switch patients back to generic versions of the original drugs—for example, by announcing that they will deny coverage when a patient shows up at the pharmacy with a prescription for the more expensive new formulation. Empirical research suggests, however, that such efforts have been generally ineffective in influencing physicians' responses to product-hopping behavior. 11

[3] Shifting the market to the reformulated product in this manner can thwart generic entry. As noted, effective generic competition generally depends on automatic substitution at the pharmacy. But automatic substitution ordinarily requires an FDA determination of therapeutic equivalence—an "AB rating." In general, because an AB rating is specific to dosage and form, a pharmacist cannot automatically substitute a generic drug that differs even slightly from the dosage or form of the prescribed brand-name drug. Thus, if a brand-name manufacturer tweaks its brand-name product shortly before anticipated generic entry and begins eliminating the market for the original formulation, it can impede competition from would-be generic entrants, which have sought FDA approval to sell a generic version only of the original formulation and not the replacement. The foiled generic entrant can try to make conforming changes to its own product, but it cannot sell its reformulated version without restarting the FDA approval process (and under certain circumstances provoking patent litigation and automatic regulatory stays). The brand-name manufacturer's well-timed tweaks to its drugs can thus create an ever-retreating horizon of generic competition at the expense of consumers. [. . .]

[4] . . . [T]he Second Circuit recently held in [New York ex rel. Schneiderman v. Actavis PLC, 787 F.3d 638 (2d Cir. 2015)] that a pharmaceutical manufacturer can violate Section 2 if it uses a product-hopping scheme to foreclose rival generic manufacturers from their most efficient distribution channel: automatic substitution at the pharmacy for AB-rated drugs. In that case, a brand-name manufacturer altered the formula for an anti-Alzheimer's drug to avoid automatic generic substitution, and it took various steps, including sharply limiting supply of the legacy version, to ensure that most physicians would prescribe only the reformulated version before the expected date of generic entry. The Second Circuit concluded that because Defendants' forced switch through something other than competition on the merits has the effect of significantly reducing usage of rivals' products and hence protecting its own monopoly, it is anticompetitive. [. . .]

[5] The Second Circuit is hardly alone in so ruling. A number of courts and leading commentators have concluded that, in various circumstances, product-hopping can violate Section 2 of the Sherman Act. The district court [below] departed from that growing consensus by adopting broad rationales that would bar product-hopping liability in almost all circumstances. [. . .]

[6] Genuine pharmaceutical innovation is also unlikely to be chilled simply because antitrust law may hold brand-name manufacturers liable for minor product tweaks that have little or no therapeutic value and serve only to avoid generic competition. First, a manufacturer that incorporates a genuine innovation in its reformulated product can offer that fact as a procompetitive justification. Second, as the *Namenda* court observed, actionable

product-hopping conduct typically consists not only of a product reformulation, but also calculated efforts to damage or destroy the market for the original formulation. A company is unlikely to face potential antitrust liability if it does not take targeted steps to damage the market for the original formulation and instead allows the marketplace itself to choose between that formulation and the modified version. But when a brand-name company conducts an anticompetitive product hop with no countervailing justification, the benefits of antitrust enforcement—the promotion of competition and efficient pricing—outweigh any residual risk of chilling actual pharmaceutical innovation. Indeed, if anything, foreclosing antitrust liability in those circumstances might itself sometimes chill genuine innovation.

Product Hopping in the Courts

New York ex rel. Schneiderman v. Actavis PLC, 787 F.3d 638 (2d Cir. 2015); Mylan Pharms. Inc. v. Warner Chilcott Pub. Ltd. Co., 838 F.3d 421 (3d Cir. 2016)

Two prominent discussions of the antitrust assessment of product hopping can be found in the Second Circuit's 2015 decision in *Schneiderman* and the Third Circuit's 2016 decision in *Mylan Pharmaceuticals*.

In *Schneiderman* the Second Circuit granted a preliminary injunction on the theory that a challenge to a "hard switch" had demonstrated a substantial likelihood of success under Section 2. In that case, defendants (Actavis and its subsidiary) had introduced a new version of its Alzheimer's medication, Namenda XR, into the market and "effectively withdr[ew]" the previous version, Namenda IR. This, the court explained, "forced Alzheimer's patients . . . to switch to XR (to which generic IR is not therapeutically equivalent) and would likely impede generic competition by precluding generic substitution through state drug substitution laws."

The Second Circuit approached this practice with a fairly aggressive standard of liability under Section 2. "Well-established case law," the court explained, "makes clear that product redesign is anticompetitive when it coerces consumers and impedes competition." The court relied on its own 1979 decision in Berkey Photo, Inc. v. Eastman Kodak Co., 603 F.2d 263 (2d Cir. 1979), in which it had indicated in *dicta* that Kodak might have faced antitrust liability in that case if it had introduced a desirable new film that only interoperated with Kodak's own newly-developed camera *and had also* ceased to produce its existing film, which was compatible with other manufacturers' cameras. The competitive concern in such a case would be "coercion" of customers to buy Kodak's camera. The *Schneiderman* court cited *Berkey Photo* for the proposition that "[N]either product withdrawal nor product improvement alone is anticompetitive. But . . . when a monopolist combines product withdrawal with some other conduct, the overall effect of which is to coerce consumers rather than persuade them on the merits, and to impede competition, its actions are anticompetitive under the Sherman Act."

Applying that principle to Actavis's conduct, the court held that, while a soft switch would have been lawful, the "hard switch crosses the line from persuasion to coercion and is anticompetitive. As long as Defendants sought to persuade patients and their doctors to switch from Namenda IR to Namenda XR while both were on the market (the soft switch) and with generic IR drugs on the horizon, patients and doctors could evaluate the products and their generics on the merits in furtherance of competitive objectives." The hard switch had eliminated this option, forcing patients to switch when they did not want to do so. The court noted evidence that "Defendants devised the hard switch because they projected that only 30% of memantine-therapy patients would voluntarily switch to Namenda XR prior to generic entry. Defendants' hard switch was expected to transition 80 to 100% of Namenda IR patients to XR prior to generic entry, and thereby impede generic competition."

Defendants raised a series of purported justifications, but the court dismissed them: "All of Defendants' procompetitive justifications for withdrawing IR are pretextual. The record is replete with evidence showing that Defendants were, in the words of Defendants' own CEO, trying to put up barriers or obstacles to generic competition." Of particular note, defendants argued that they were attempting to avoid "free riding," by preventing generics from siphoning off profits from investment in Namenda. But the court rejected that argument out of hand. What defendants were labeling "free riding" was in fact "authorized by law," the "explicit goal of state substitution laws," and consistent with "the goals of the Hatch-Waxman Act by promoting drug competition[.]" Defendants' broader argument, that "antitrust scrutiny of the pharmaceutical industry will . . . deter innovation," met the same fate: "immunizing product hopping from antitrust scrutiny may deter significant innovation by encouraging manufacturers to focus on switching the market to trivial or minor product reformulations rather than investing in the research and development necessary to develop riskier, but medically significant innovations."

In *Mylan Pharmaceuticals* the Third Circuit also confronted a hard switch, but with a different outcome. In that case, the pharmaceutical manufacturer Mayne had for many years been manufacturing and selling (through its U.S. distributor, Warner Chilcott) both branded and generic versions of its drug Doryx—an *unpatented* delayed-release version of doxycycline hyclate, an oral antibiotic—in capsule form. In 1997, Mayne and Warner decided to try to revive flagging profits by switching the market from the old capsules to new, branded-only tablets. Among other things, they stopped selling the capsules to drug wholesalers, removed the capsules from Warner's website, informed market participants that capsules had been "replaced" with tablets, bought back some existing inventory of capsules, and even destroyed some capsule stock.

Then, beginning in 2007, Mayne and Warner began a process of making multiple alterations to the Doryx tablets, each of which required FDA approval: and, crucially, each of which "required generic manufacturers to file, and await approval of, a new ANDA demonstrating the similarities between their product and the reformulated Doryx product in order to continue selling generics that were AB-rated to the newest Doryx product," and each of which was followed by withdrawal of the older version. Mylan, a generic pharmaceutical manufacturer attempting to keep up with the ever-changing Doryx tablet, sued under Sections 1 and 2.

The court of appeals held that the conduct of Mayne and Warner was not anticompetitive or unlawful. Among other things, Mylan had in fact been able to get to market with a generic version of Doryx, and had reaped "generous profits" from doing so.

But even setting this aside, the court credited "strong evidence of non-pretextual purposes for their various product changes." The switch from capsules to tablets was consistent with evidence linking doxycycline capsules to esophageal problems. Instead, the capsule version "was ultimately banned in France and Sweden, and Defendants faced a products liability lawsuit in Michigan regarding the same problem." The various modifications to the tablets were also supported by evidence of nonpretextual purposes: for example, the switch to a higher-dose tablet could be understood as a response to the availability of competing drugs at various dosage levels, while the introduction of scoring lines on the tablets enabled consumers to "more effectively self-dose" at various levels.

The court expressly acknowledged and distinguished the Second Circuit's *Namenda* decision. Unlike the *Namenda* case, Mayne and Warner here saw "no patent cliffs on the horizon," and they faced significant competition in the relevant market. The *Mylan* court also emphasized the different procedural posture: "*Namenda* merely upheld a preliminary injunction, unlike this case, which proceeded through full discovery and resulted in a robust record void of any evidence of anticompetitive conduct." The *Mylan* court also emphasized that its holding did not "rule out the possibility that certain insignificant design or formula changes, combined with other coercive conduct, could present a closer call with respect to establishing liability in future cases."

After *Schneiderman* and *Mylan*, the door to antitrust liability for product hopping remains somewhat open in the federal courts, albeit wider in some circuits than others.

NOTES

1) "Antitrust is so deferential to minimally plausible uses of the courts that it is virtually powerless to control a wide array of harmful patent abuses." Do you agree? How might Congress fix these problems?

2) Is the power that a PAE wields fairly described as market or monopoly power? How, if it all, does it differ from the power of: (a) any other input supplier; or (b) any entity in a position to threaten to inflict economic harm on a business?

3) Should antitrust have a normative "theory" of the legitimacy of business models, such that PAE activity is treated by antitrust in a more hostile manner than other business models? If so, what other business models should be treated in this way?

4) Is "coercion" an appealing basis for a test of the legality of product hopping? What is the best definition of that concept?

5) Many businesses—supplying everything from stereo systems to software—introduce improved versions of their products and withdraw the original. Does product-hopping law imply that this practice may create antitrust risk outside the pharmaceutical industry? Or is this theory of harm tied to the special nature of pharma regulation?

6) On one view, the "hard switch" product-hopping cases can be understood as a refusal to assist a competitor by continuing to supply a product that the generic pharmaceutical company needs to remain on the market. Can these decisions be reconciled with the courts' hostility to antitrust liability for unilateral refusals to deal?

C. Agreements Involving Intellectual Property

In the previous section we considered purely unilateral conduct: in this section we will turn to agreements and joint conduct involving intellectual property. We will focus on two categories of agreement: intellectual property licenses and agreements settling infringement suits.

1. Licensing Agreements

In general, patent licensing agreements are treated much like other vertical agreements: thus, the rule of reason governs vertical restraints like territorial restrictions.[841] Exclusive licenses, too, which may effectively substitute the licensee for the licensor, are analyzed under the rule of reason.[842] The IP Guidelines state three broad principles to guide courts and businesses:

> (a) [F]or the purpose of antitrust analysis, the Agencies apply the same analysis to conduct involving intellectual property as to conduct involving other forms of property, taking into account the specific characteristics of a particular property right;

> (b) the Agencies do not presume that intellectual property creates market power in the antitrust context; and

> (c) the Agencies recognize that intellectual property licensing allows firms to combine complementary factors of production and is generally procompetitive.[843]

Courts have sometimes struggled with the question of when and how licensing agreements may violate the antitrust laws, particularly in cases where the licensor is a competitor of its own licensees. In the following two extracts, two courts entertain arguments that a license agreement is being used to "tax" rivals' sales and thus maintain monopoly power—with very different results.

Caldera, Inc. v. Microsoft Corp.

87 F. Supp. 2d 1244 (D. Utah 1999)

Chief Judge Benson.

---

[841] Generac Corp. v. Caterpillar Inc., 172 F.3d 971, 977 (7th Cir. 1999) ("[T]his particular agreement was a vertical one in which Generac played the role of supplier and Caterpillar both upstream supplier of the trademark, and downstream purchaser of the finished goods. Unlike horizontal agreements, vertical agreements are per se illegal under Sherman Act § 1 only if they impose minimum price restraints. . . . Vertical non-price restraints, such as the territorial and marketing restrictions at issue in this case, are evaluated under the rule of reason."); Miller Insituform, Inc. v. Insituform of N. Am., Inc., 605 F. Supp. 1125, 1130 (M.D. Tenn. 1985) ("Even if the antitrust laws do apply to the territorial restrictions in INA's patent licensing scheme, such vertical allocations of markets are not per se illegal, but are subject to scrutiny under the rule of reason."); Am. Key Corp. v. Cumberland Assocs., 579 F. Supp. 1245, 1256 (N.D. Ga. 1983) ("As between Sears and Cole plaintiff arguably has established that a contract or combination does in fact exist. The licensing agreement between Sears and Cole is a de facto exclusive dealing agreement similar to a vertical exclusive territory agreement or a franchising agreement. Such agreements are not per se illegal but are governed by the rule of reason.").

[842] See, e.g., Am. Needle, Inc. v. New Orleans La. Saints, Case No. 04-cv-7806, 2014 WL 1364022, at *1 (N.D. Ill. Apr. 7, 2014) ("[D]efendants contend that the exclusive license arrangement encouraged additional licensee commitment and had numerous procompetitive effects, including improvements in product design, quality, distribution, and coordination of styles with other apparel items. These contentions are sufficiently supported by evidence and expert opinion to be facially plausible.").

[843] U.S. Dept. of Justice and FTC, ANTITRUST GUIDELINES FOR THE LICENSING OF INTELLECTUAL PROPERTY (2017) § 2.0 at 2.

[1] Caldera . . . alleges that Microsoft's two and three-year per processor licensing agreements with minimum commitments provisions were anticompetitive and unlawful under [the] antitrust laws. Under these agreements an original equipment manufacturer (OEM) was required to pay Microsoft a royalty on every machine the OEM shipped regardless of whether the machine contained [Microsoft's] MS DOS or another operating system. The effect of such an arrangement was that an OEM who chose to install [a competing product, DR DOS,] would pay two royalties on the same machine. Moreover, Caldera asserts that Microsoft required OEMs to make large minimum commitments with up-front payments and that Microsoft's pricing structure rewarded OEMs that made overly-optimistic minimum commitments. Accordingly, OEMs regularly had large prepaid balances when the licenses expired. OEMs would forfeit these balances unless they renewed their licenses with Microsoft. Although Microsoft offered other licensing agreements, Caldera claims that Microsoft coerced OEMs into entering per-processor licenses by offering significant discounts on MS DOS licensed under a per processor agreement. Caldera contends that this conduct was anticompetitive and therefore in violation of both Sections 1 and 2 of the Sherman Antitrust Act.

[2] Ordinarily, the Rule of Reason is employed to determine whether particular concerted action violates Section 1 of the Sherman Act. That is, the fact finder weighs all of the circumstances of a case in deciding whether a restrictive practice should be prohibited as imposing an unreasonable restraint on competition. Here, the alleged facts that OEMs entered into per processor licensing agreements with Microsoft at Microsoft's suggestion and that Microsoft used economic pressure to give OEMs an incentive to enter into per processing agreements is enough evidence of restraint of trade to allow Caldera to proceed on its Section 1 claim. Therefore, the Court denies Microsoft's motion for summary judgment on Caldera's Section 1 claims relating to licensing practices.

[3] Turning to the strength of Caldera's Section 2 claim, the parties agree that the standard for determining whether Microsoft's licensing agreements constitute illegal exclusive dealings was established in Tampa Electric Co. v. Nashville Coal Co., 365 U.S. 320 (1961). In *Tampa Electric* the United States Supreme Court addressed the validity of a requirements contract under the Clayton Act. In evaluating whether an exclusive dealing arrangement violates antitrust law, the Court developed a two-part test: first, the agreement at issue must be exclusive; and second, the agreement must have an adverse effect on competition.

[4] Microsoft argues because per processor agreements did not require an OEM covered by such an agreement to purchase all operating systems from Microsoft it is not an exclusive agreement and Caldera cannot meet the first prong of the *Tampa Electric* test. However, a contract need not be denominated exclusive nor must exclusivity be an express condition of a contract, in order for it to be exclusive under Section 2. An agreement with the "practical effect" of exclusivity is covered. The effect of per processor licenses was that an OEM had to pay two royalties on a computer shipped with an operating system other than MS DOS. A fact-finder could reasonably conclude that this effect coupled with the significant discount offered OEMs who participated in per processor agreements resulted in an agreement with the practical effect of exclusivity.

[5] Microsoft also contends that because new OEMs were always entering the market and a certain number of MS DOS licenses were expiring at any given time, competition was not foreclosed. However, determining whether competition has been foreclosed in a given market requires first, defining the product market, and second, identifying the geographic market by careful selection of the market area in which the seller operates, and to which the purchaser can practicably turn for supplies. Moreover, the competition foreclosed by the contract must be found to constitute a substantial share of the relevant market. That is to say, the opportunities for other traders to enter into or remain in that market must be significantly limited.

[6] The Supreme Court further stated in *Tampa Electric* that to determine whether competition has been significantly limited it is necessary to weigh the probable effect of the contract on the relevant area of effective competition, taking into account the relative strength of the parties, the proportionate volume of commerce involved in relation to the total volume of commerce in the relevant market area, and the probable immediate and future effects which preemption of that share of the market might have on effective competition therein. Applying this to the instant case, Microsoft has not defined the relevant market or properly weighed the factors outlined in *Tampa Electric* to determine whether per processor licenses had a substantial effect on competition. Therefore, Microsoft has not met its burden on this issue for purposes of summary judgment.

[7] Finally, unlike the plaintiff in *Tampa Electric*, Caldera offers Microsoft's licensing scheme as part of a bigger picture of anticompetitive behavior by Microsoft. It is not a discrete claim of exclusive dealing. Microsoft's per processor agreements may not amount to a finding of Section 2 liability standing alone, however, use of per processor licenses viewed in context with other alleged anticompetitive behavior may give rise to a Section 2 violation as complained of by Caldera.

* * *

FTC v. Qualcomm Inc.
969 F.3d 974 (9th Cir. 2020)

Judge Callahan.

[1] This case asks us to draw the line between *anti*competitive behavior, which is illegal under federal antitrust law, and *hyper*competitive behavior, which is not. The Federal Trade Commission ("FTC") contends that Qualcomm Incorporated ("Qualcomm") violated [Sections 1 and 2 of] the Sherman Act by unreasonably restraining trade in, and unlawfully monopolizing, the code division multiple access ("CDMA") and premium long-term evolution ("LTE") cellular modem chip markets. After a ten-day bench trial, the district court agreed and ordered a permanent, worldwide injunction prohibiting several of Qualcomm's core business practices. We granted Qualcomm's request for a stay of the district court's injunction pending appeal. At that time, we characterized the district court's order and injunction as either "a trailblazing application of the antitrust laws" or "an improper excursion beyond the outer limits of the Sherman Act." We now hold that the district court went beyond the scope of the Sherman Act, and we reverse.

[2] Founded in 1985, Qualcomm dubs itself "the world's leading cellular technology company." Over the past several decades, the company has made significant contributions to the technological innovations underlying modern cellular systems, including third-generation ("3G") CDMA and fourth-generation ("4G") LTE cellular standards—the standards practiced in most modern cellphones and "smartphones." Qualcomm protects and profits from its technological innovations through its patents, which it licenses to original equipment manufacturers ("OEMs") whose products (usually cellphones, but also smart cars and other products with cellular applications) practice one or more of Qualcomm's patented technologies.

[3] Qualcomm's patents include cellular standard essential patents ("SEPs"), non-cellular SEPs, and non-SEPs. Cellular SEPs are patents on technologies that international standard-setting organizations ("SSOs") choose to include in technical standards practiced by each new generation of cellular technology. SSOs—also referred to as standards development organizations ("SDOs")—are global collaborations of industry participants that "establish technical specifications to ensure that products from different manufacturers are compatible with each other." Cellular SEPs are necessary to practice a particular cellular standard. Because SEP holders could prevent industry participants from implementing a standard by selectively refusing to license, SSOs require patent holders to commit to license their SEPs on fair, reasonable, and nondiscriminatory ("FRAND") terms before their patents are incorporated into standards.

[4] Some of Qualcomm's SEPs and other patents relate to CDMA and premium LTE technologies—that is, the way cellular devices communicate with the 3G and 4G cellular networks—while others relate to other cellular and non-cellular applications and technologies, such as multimedia, cameras, location detecting, user interfaces, and more. Rather than license its patents individually, Qualcomm generally offers its customers various "patent portfolio" options, whereby the customer/licensee pays for and receives the right to practice all three types of Qualcomm patents (SEPs, non-cellular SEPs, and non-SEPs).

[5] Qualcomm's patent licensing business is very profitable, representing around two-thirds of the company's value. But Qualcomm is no one-trick pony. The company also manufactures and sells cellular modem chips, the hardware that enables cellular devices to practice CDMA and premium LTE technologies and thereby communicate with each other across cellular networks. This makes Qualcomm somewhat unique in the broader cellular services industry. Companies such as Nokia, Ericsson, and Interdigital have comparable SEP portfolios but do not compete with Qualcomm in the modem chip markets. On the other hand, Qualcomm's main

competitors in the modem chip markets—companies such as MediaTek, HiSilicon, Samsung LSI, ST-Ericsson, and VIA Telecom (purchased by Intel in 2015)—do not hold or have not held comparable SEP portfolios.

[6] Like its licensing business, Qualcomm's modem chip business has been very successful. From 2006 to 2016, Qualcomm possessed monopoly power in the CDMA modem chip market, including over 90% of market share. From 2011 to 2016, Qualcomm possessed monopoly power in the premium LTE modem chip market, including at least 70% of market share. During these timeframes, Qualcomm leveraged its monopoly power to "charge monopoly prices on [its] modem chips." Around 2015, however, Qualcomm's dominant position in the modem chip markets began to recede, as competitors like Intel and MediaTek found ways to successfully compete. Based on projections from 2017 to 2018, Qualcomm maintains approximately a 79% share of the CDMA modem chip market and a 64% share of the premium LTE modem chip market.[4]

[7] Qualcomm licenses its patent portfolios exclusively at the OEM level, setting the royalty rates on its CDMA and LTE patent portfolios as a percentage of the end-product sales price. This practice is not unique to Qualcomm. As the district court found, "[f]ollowing Qualcomm's lead, other SEP licensors like Nokia and Ericsson have concluded that licensing only OEMs is more lucrative, and structured their practices accordingly." OEM-level licensing allows these companies to obtain the maximum value for their patented technologies while avoiding the problem of patent exhaustion, whereby "the initial authorized [or licensed] sale of a patented item terminates all patent rights to that item." Due to patent exhaustion, if Qualcomm licensed its SEPs further "upstream" in the manufacturing process to competing chip suppliers, then its patent rights would be exhausted when these rivals sold their products to OEMs. OEMs would then have little incentive to pay Qualcomm for patent licenses, as they could instead become "downstream" recipients of the already exhausted patents embodied in these rivals' products.

[8] Because rival chip manufacturers practice many of Qualcomm's SEPs by necessity, Qualcomm offers these companies what it terms "CDMA ASIC Agreements," wherein Qualcomm promises not to assert its patents in exchange for the company promising not to sell its chips to unlicensed OEMs. These agreements, which essentially function as patent-infringement indemnifications, include reporting requirements that allow Qualcomm to know the details of its rivals' chip supply agreements with various OEMs. But they also allow Qualcomm's competitors to practice Qualcomm's SEPs royalty-free.

[9] Qualcomm reinforces these practices with its so-called "no license, no chips" policy, under which Qualcomm refuses to sell modem chips to OEMs that do not take licenses to practice Qualcomm's SEPs. Otherwise, because of patent exhaustion, OEMs could decline to take licenses, arguing instead that their purchase of chips from Qualcomm extinguished Qualcomm's patent rights with respect to any CDMA or premium LTE technologies embodied in the chips. This would not only prevent Qualcomm from obtaining the maximum value for its patents, it would result in OEMs having to pay more money (in licensing royalties) to purchase and use a competitor's chips, which are unlicensed. Instead, Qualcomm's practices, taken together, are "chip supplier neutral"—that is, OEMs are required to pay a per-unit licensing royalty to Qualcomm for its patent portfolios regardless of which company they choose to source their chips from.

[10] Although Qualcomm's licensing and modem chip businesses have made it a major player in the broader cellular technology market, the company is not an OEM. That is, Qualcomm does not manufacture and sell cellphones and other end-use products (like smart cars) that consumers purchase and use. Thus, it does not "compete"—in the antitrust sense—against OEMs like Apple and Samsung in these product markets. Instead, these OEMs are Qualcomm's *customers*. [. . .]

[11] Qualcomm's competitors in the modem chip markets contend that Qualcomm's business practices, in particular its refusal to license them, have hampered or slowed their ability to develop and retain OEM customer bases, limited their growth, delayed or prevented their entry into the market, and in some cases forced them out of the market entirely. These competitors contend that this result is not just anticompetitive, but a violation of Qualcomm's contractual commitments to two cellular SSOs—the Telecommunications Industry Association ("TIA") and Alliance for Telecommunications Industry Solutions ("ATIS")—to license its SEPs "to all applicants"

on FRAND terms.[9] Qualcomm argues that it has no antitrust duty to deal with its rivals, and in any case OEM-level licensing is consistent with Qualcomm's SSO commitments because only OEM products (*i.e.*, cellphones, tablets, etc.) "practice" or "implement" the standards embodied in Qualcomm's SEPs. Furthermore, Qualcomm argues that it substantially complies with the TIA and ATIS requirements by not asserting its patents against rival chipmakers. [. . .]

[12] "To safeguard the incentive to innovate, the possession of monopoly power will not be found unlawful [under § 2] unless it is accompanied by an element of anticompetitive *conduct*." Accordingly, plaintiffs are required to prove "anticompetitive abuse or leverage of monopoly power, or a predatory or exclusionary means of attempting to monopolize the relevant market." "[T]o be condemned as exclusionary, a monopolist's act must have an 'anticompetitive effect' "—that is, it "must harm the competitive *process* and thereby harm consumers." [. . .]

[13] . . . [N]ovel business practices—*especially* in technology markets—should not be conclusively presumed to be unreasonable and therefore illegal without elaborate inquiry as to the precise harm they have caused or the business excuse for their use. Because innovation involves new products and business practices, courts' and economists' initial understanding of these practices will skew initial likelihoods that innovation is anticompetitive and the proper subject of antitrust scrutiny. [. . .]

[14] . . . [We] focus on the impact, if any, of Qualcomm's practices in the area of effective competition: the markets for CDMA and premium LTE modem chips. [. . .]

[15] . . . [T]he district court's primary theory of anticompetitive harm [was] Qualcomm's imposition of an "anticompetitive surcharge" on rival chip suppliers via its licensing royalty rates. According to the district court,

> Qualcomm's unreasonably high royalty rates enable Qualcomm to control rivals' prices because Qualcomm receives the royalty even when an OEM uses one of Qualcomm's rival's chips. Thus, the "all-in" price of any modem chip sold by one of Qualcomm's rivals effectively includes two components: (1) the nominal chip price; and (2) Qualcomm's royalty surcharge.

[16] This central component of the district court's ruling is premised on the district court's findings that Qualcomm's royalty rates are (1) "unreasonably high" because they are improperly based on Qualcomm's monopoly chip market share and handset price instead of the "fair value of Qualcomm's patents," and (2) anticompetitive because they raise costs to OEMs, who pass the extra costs along to consumers and are forced to invest less in other handset features. The FTC agrees with this aspect of the district court's ruling, pointing out that its "reasonableness" determination regarding Qualcomm's royalty rates is a factual finding subject to clear error review and arguing that this finding "was supported by overwhelming evidence."

[17] We hold that the district court's "anticompetitive surcharge" theory fails to state a cogent theory of anticompetitive harm. . . . [E]ven if we were to accept the district court's conclusion that Qualcomm's royalty rates are unreasonable, we conclude that the district court's surcharging theory still fails as a matter of law and logic. [. . .]

[18] . . . [E]ven assuming that a deviation between licensing royalty rates and a patent portfolio's "fair value" could amount to "anticompetitive harm" in the antitrust sense, the primary harms the district court identified here were to the OEMs who agreed to pay Qualcomm's royalty rates—that is, Qualcomm's *customers*, not its *competitors*. These harms were thus located outside the "areas of effective competition"—the markets for CDMA and premium LTE modem chips—and had no direct impact on competition in those markets.

[19] Regardless of the "reasonableness" of Qualcomm's royalty rates, the district court erred in finding that these royalties constitute an "artificial surcharge" on rivals' chip sales. In *Caldera, Inc. v. Microsoft Corp.*, 87 F. Supp. 2d 1244 (D. Utah 1999), the primary case relied upon by the district court for its surcharging theory, Microsoft required OEMs "to pay [it] a royalty on every machine the OEM shipped regardless of whether the machine

---

[9] Under the TIA contract, Qualcomm agreed to make its SEPs "available to all applicants under terms and conditions that are reasonable and non-discriminatory and only to the extent necessary for the practice of any or all of the Normative portions for the field of use of practice of the Standard." Under the ATIS contract, Qualcomm committed to making its SEPs "available to applicants desiring to utilize the license for the purpose of implementing the standard under reasonable terms and conditions that are demonstrably free of any unfair discrimination."

contained MS DOS or another operating system." This resulted in OEMs having to pay two royalties instead of one for a portion of their product base unless they chose to exclusively install Microsoft's operating system in their products. Microsoft's policy thus had "the practical effect of exclusivity," as it imposed a naked tax on rivals' software even when the end-product—an individual computer installed with a non-Microsoft operating system—contained no added value from Microsoft. The *Caldera* court held that this hidden surcharge, combined with Microsoft's related practices that were designed to secure exclusivity, were sufficient to defeat Microsoft's motion for summary judgment on the question of whether its policy amounted to anticompetitive conduct in violation of § 2.

[20] Qualcomm's licensing royalties are qualitatively different from the per-unit operating-system royalties at issue in *Caldera*. When Qualcomm licenses its SEPs to an OEM, those patent licenses have value—indeed, they are necessary to the OEM's ability to market and sell its cellular products to consumers—regardless of whether the OEM uses Qualcomm's modem chips or chips manufactured and sold by one of Qualcomm's rivals. And unlike *Caldera*, where OEMs who installed non-Microsoft operating systems in some of their products were required to pay royalties for both the actual operating system *and* MS DOS (which was not installed), here OEMs do not pay twice for SEP licenses when they use non-Qualcomm modem chips. Thus, unlike Microsoft's practice, Qualcomm's practice does not have the "practical effect of exclusivity." Even the FTC concedes that "this case differs from *Caldera* in [that] Qualcomm holds patents practiced by its rivals' chips, and no one disputes that Qualcomm is entitled to collect a royalty equal to the reasonable value of those patents."

[21] In its complaint and in its briefing, the FTC suggests that Qualcomm's royalty rates impose an anticompetitive surcharge on its rivals' sales not for the reasons at play in *Caldera*, but rather because Qualcomm uses its licensing royalties to charge anticompetitive, ultralow prices on its own modem chips—pushing out rivals by squeezing their profit margins and preventing them from making necessary investments in research and development. But this type of "margin squeeze" was rejected as a basis for antitrust liability in [*Pac. Bell Tel. Co. v. Linkline Commc'ns, Inc.*, 555 U.S. 438, 451-52 (2009)]. There, multiple digital subscriber line ("DSL") high-speed internet service providers complained that AT & T was selling them access to AT & T's must-have telephone lines and facilities at inflated wholesale rates and then shifting those increased profits to charge ultra-low rates for DSL services at retail, effectively squeezing these DSL competitors out of the market. The Court rejected the plaintiffs' assertion of anticompetitive harm, holding that AT & T was under no antitrust duty to deal with its competitors on the wholesale level, and that the plaintiffs failed to introduce evidence of predatory pricing (that is, charging below cost) at the retail level.

[22] Here, not only did the FTC offer no evidence that Qualcomm engaged in predatory pricing, the district court's entire antitrust analysis is premised on the opposite proposition: that Qualcomm "charge[s] monopoly prices on modem chips." Indeed, the district court faulted Qualcomm for lowering its prices only when other companies introduced CDMA modem chips to the market to effectively compete. We agree with Qualcomm that this is exactly the type of "garden-variety price competition that the law encourages," and are aware of no authority holding that a monopolist may not lower its rates in response to a competitor's entry into the market with a lower-priced product.

[23] As with its critique of Qualcomm's royalty rates, the district court's analysis of Qualcomm's "no license, no chips" policy focuses almost exclusively on alleged "anticompetitive harms" to OEMs—that is, impacts outside the relevant antitrust market. The district court labeled Qualcomm's policy "anticompetitive conduct against OEMs" and an "anticompetitive practice in patent license negotiations." But the district court failed to identify how the policy directly impacted Qualcomm's competitors or distorted "the area of effective competition." Although OEMs consistently described Qualcomm's "no license, no chips" policy as "unique in the industry," none articulated a cogent theory of anticompetitive harm. Instead, they objected to Qualcomm's licensing royalty rates, which they have to pay *regardless* of whether they chose to purchase their chips from Qualcomm or a competitor (or else risk a patent infringement suit from Qualcomm).

[24] According to the FTC, the problem with "no license, no chips" is that, under the policy, "Qualcomm will not sell chips to a cellphone [OEM] like Apple or Samsung unless the OEM agrees to a license that requires it to pay a substantial per-phone surcharge *even on phones that use rivals' chips*." But this argument is self-defeating: if the condition imposed on gaining access to Qualcomm's chip supply applies regardless of whether the OEM chooses

Qualcomm or a competitor (in fact, this appears to be the essence of Qualcomm's policy), then the condition by definition does not distort the "area of effective competition" or impact competitors. At worst, the policy raises the "all-in" price that an OEM must pay for modem chips (chipset + licensing royalties) regardless of which chip supplier the OEM chooses to source its chips from. As we have already discussed, whether that all-in price is reasonable or unreasonable is an issue that sounds in patent law, not antitrust law. Additionally, it involves potential harms to Qualcomm's *customers*, not its competitors, and thus falls outside the relevant antitrust markets.

[25] The district court stopped short of holding that the "no license, no chips" policy itself violates antitrust law. For good reason: neither the Sherman Act nor any other law prohibits companies like Qualcomm from (1) licensing their SEPs independently from their chip sales and collecting royalties, and/or (2) limiting their chip customer base to licensed OEMs. As we have noted, as a general rule, businesses are free to choose the parties with whom they will deal, as well as the prices, terms, and conditions of that dealing. Indeed, the FTC accepts that this is the state of the law when it concedes that "Qualcomm holds patents practiced by its rivals' chips, and is entitled to collect a royalty on them.

[26] . . . If Qualcomm were to refuse to license its SEPs to OEMs unless they first agreed to purchase Qualcomm's chips ("no chips, no license"), then rival chip suppliers indeed might have an antitrust claim under both §§ 1 and 2 of the Sherman Act based on exclusionary conduct. This is because OEMs cannot sell their products *without* obtaining Qualcomm's SEP licenses, so a "no chips, no license" policy would essentially force OEMs to either purchase Qualcomm's chips or pay for *both* Qualcomm's and a competitor's chips (similar to the no-win situation faced by OEMs in the *Caldera* case). But unlike a hypothetical "no chips, no license" policy, "no license, no chips" is chip-neutral: it makes no difference whether an OEM buys Qualcomm's chip or a rival's chips. The policy only insists that, whatever chip source an OEM chooses, the OEM pay Qualcomm for the right to practice the patented technologies embodied in the chip, as well as in other parts of the phone or other cellular device. [. . .]

[27] Anticompetitive behavior is illegal under federal antitrust law. Hypercompetitive behavior is not. Qualcomm has exercised market dominance in the 3G and 4G cellular modem chip markets for many years, and its business practices have played a powerful and disruptive role in those markets, as well as in the broader cellular services and technology markets. The company has asserted its economic muscle "with vigor, imagination, devotion, and ingenuity." It has also "acted with sharp elbows—as businesses often do." Our job is not to condone or punish Qualcomm for its success, but rather to assess whether the FTC has met its burden under the rule of reason to show that Qualcomm's practices have crossed the line to "conduct which unfairly tends to destroy competition itself." We conclude that the FTC has not met its burden.

NOTES

1) Should antitrust law treat intellectual property licensing agreements differently from other agreements?

2) Are restraints in an IP license always "intrabrand" and thus of secondary concern to antitrust under *GTE Sylvania* (look back at Chapter VI for a fuller discussion)? If not, when is an IP licensing restraint an intrabrand one?

3) The *Caldera* court indicated that an analysis of the per-processor license under Section 1 should turn on different questions than the analysis under Section 2. Do you agree?

4) In light of the extracts from *Caldera* and *Qualcomm* that you have just read: which of the following, if any, should violate Section 2?

    a. A dominant chip manufacturer requires its chip customers to agree that they will pay a $10 fee every time they purchase a chip from a rival.

    b. A dominant chip manufacturer requires its chip customers to agree that they will pay a $10 fee every time they purchase a chip from *any chip supplier*, including itself—and it reduces its own chip price by $10 to avoid losing any chip sales.

    c. A dominant chip manufacturer requires its chip customers to agree that they will pay a $11 fee every time they purchase a chip from any chip supplier—reducing its own chip price by $10 to avoid losing any chip sales—and it throws in an IP license of value $1/chip to those customers.

    d. A dominant chip manufacturer requires its chip customers to agree that they will pay a $11 fee every time they purchase a chip from *any chip supplier*—reducing its own chip price by $10 to avoid losing any chip sales—and it throws in an IP license of uncertain value/chip to those customers?

5) The court in *Qualcomm* notes (at paragraph 6 of the extract) that eventually other chip competitors entered the market and began to erode Qualcomm's very high market share. What is the significance of that fact? If Qualcomm was able to leverage its IP licensing strategy to exclude competitors for 2 years, should that be remedied as an antitrust violation? Five years? Ten years? Six months? Does it matter that antitrust litigation typically takes multiple years from complaint to resolution, even setting aside time required for pre-complaint investigation?

2. Infringement Settlements

Some of the most challenging policy questions on the antitrust / IP interface arise in connection with settlements of intellectual property infringement litigation. In the core case, the basic fact pattern is commonly something like this: (1) two businesses are actually or potentially active in the same market (*i.e.*, they are at least potential competitors), setting aside all questions of intellectual property; (2) one of them asserts an intellectual property right which, if valid and infringed by the other, would confer the power to exclude the other from the market (or at least to take a price reflecting the value of the right); (3) the parties resolve the actual or threatened litigation between them by entering into a settlement agreement that permits *less* competition that would exist if no intellectual property were in play, but *more* competition than would exist if the rightsholder's intellectual property were valid, infringed, and fully asserted. And, crucially: (4) there is some reason to doubt the validity or infringement of the intellectual property right.

What is antitrust to do? On the one hand, agreements between rivals not to compete are a central evil—perhaps *the* central evil—of antitrust. And it is not obvious that the invocation of a questionable IP claim by one of the rivals changes anything about that situation. On the other hand, there is certainly no general right to compete using a rival's property. And if the intellectual property is indeed valid (which, in the case of a patent right, must be presumed by statute[844]) and if a patent-holder can prove that it has been infringed, then there may very well be *no* lawful competition to be had. On a third hand, we might not want to make the result of an antitrust challenge itself depend on a full trial of the validity and infringement of the IP right—creating a kind of turducken litigation combining some of the most notoriously lengthy and expensive forms of dispute resolution—so a court must likely adjudicate the issue without knowing for sure whether the IP rights in question are indeed valid and infringed. [845] And finally: what role for the policy principle that settlement agreements are to be encouraged?[846]

The leading case on the antitrust treatment of IP settlements—indeed, on the antitrust-IP frontier in general—is the Supreme Court's 2013 *Actavis* decision. *Actavis* dealt with so-called "pay for delay" or "reverse payment" agreements, in which incumbent branded drug companies would enter into agreements with generic would-be entrants who were first to file an ANDA with a Paragraph IV certification challenging the incumbent's patent.[847] In the most common version of a pay-for-delay settlement: the generic would agree to drop its challenge to the validity of the brand's patent; the brand would agree to make a sizeable payment to the generic; and the parties would agree that the generic would have the right to enter the market after a period of delay, but before the expiration of the patent term.

There are significant interests on both sides here. The core competition concern is that "the holder of a dodgy patent may be paying off a would-be competitor and splitting the profits of undeserved monopoly."[848] But then: why shouldn't a patent holder be entitled to avoid the enormous costs and burdens of litigation—as well as the commercial risk of having a key patent invalidated by an adverse decision—with a deal that allows new entry within the term of a (presumed-valid) patent? And a large payment from incumbent to generic need not indicate

---

[844] 35 U.S.C. § 282.

[845] *But see* Rebecca S. Eisenberg & Daniel A. Crane, *Patent Punting: How FDA and Antitrust Courts Undermine the Hatch-Waxman Act to Avoid Dealing with Patents*, 21 Mich. Telecomm. & Tech. L. Rev. 197 (2015) (criticizing "patent punting" by courts).

[846] *See, e.g.*, McDermott, Inc. v. AmClyde, 511 U.S. 202, 215 (1994) ("[P]ublic policy wisely encourages settlements.").

[847] *See supra* notes 800–805 and accompanying text.

[848] Daniel Francis, *Making Sense of Monopolization*, 84 Antitrust L.J. 779, 810–11 (2022). *See generally* C. Scott Hemphill, *Paying for Delay: Pharmaceutical Patent Settlement as a Regulatory Design Problem*, 81 N.Y.U. L. Rev. 1553 (2006); Jon Liebowitz, Chairman, FTC, *"Pay for Delay" Settlements in the Pharmaceutical Industry: How Congress Can Stop Anticompetitive Conduct, Protect Consumers' Wallets, and Help Pay for Health Care Reform (the $35 Billion Solution)* 3 (remarks of June 23, 2009).

that the patent is a particularly weak one: it could just represent the high value of the patent to the holder, rather than a high chance of invalidity.

When this issue came up for decision by the Supreme Court, lower courts had taken a range of positions, from a blanket rule that pay-for-delay agreements limiting competition within the scope of a patent claim were *per se* legal, as the Eleventh Circuit had held below,[849] to presumed *illegality* of such agreements, as the Third Circuit had held.[850] The Court took a middle road.

FTC v. Actavis, Inc.
570 U.S. 136 (2013)

Justice Breyer.

[1] Company A sues Company B for patent infringement. The two companies settle under terms that require (1) Company B, the claimed infringer, not to produce the patented product until the patent's term expires, and (2) Company A, the patentee, to pay B many millions of dollars. Because the settlement requires the patentee to pay the alleged infringer, rather than the other way around, this kind of settlement agreement is often called a "reverse payment" settlement agreement. And the basic question here is whether such an agreement can sometimes unreasonably diminish competition in violation of the antitrust laws.

[2] In this case, the Eleventh Circuit dismissed a Federal Trade Commission (FTC) complaint claiming that a particular reverse payment settlement agreement violated the antitrust laws. In doing so, the Circuit stated that a reverse payment settlement agreement generally is "immune from antitrust attack so long as its anticompetitive effects fall within the scope of the exclusionary potential of the patent." And since the alleged infringer's promise not to enter the patentee's market expired before the patent's term ended, the Circuit found the agreement legal and dismissed the FTC complaint. In our view, however, reverse payment settlements such as the agreement alleged in the complaint before us can sometimes violate the antitrust laws. We consequently hold that the Eleventh Circuit should have allowed the FTC's lawsuit to proceed.

[3] Apparently most if not all reverse payment settlement agreements arise in the context of pharmaceutical drug regulation, and specifically in the context of suits brought under statutory provisions allowing a generic drug manufacturer (seeking speedy marketing approval) to challenge the validity of a patent owned by an already-approved brand-name drug owner. We consequently describe four key features of the relevant drug-regulatory framework established by the Drug Price Competition and Patent Term Restoration Act of 1984. That Act is commonly known as the Hatch-Waxman Act.

[4] First, a drug manufacturer, wishing to market a new prescription drug, must submit a New Drug Application to the federal Food and Drug Administration (FDA) and undergo a long, comprehensive, and costly testing process, after which, if successful, the manufacturer will receive marketing approval from the FDA.

[5] Second, once the FDA has approved a brand-name drug for marketing, a manufacturer of a generic drug can obtain similar marketing approval through use of abbreviated procedures. The Hatch-Waxman Act permits a generic manufacturer to file an Abbreviated New Drug Application specifying that the generic has the "same active ingredients as," and is "biologically equivalent" to, the already-approved brand-name drug. The Hatch-Waxman process, by allowing the generic to piggy-back on the pioneer's approval efforts, "speed[s] the introduction of low-cost generic drugs to market," thereby furthering drug competition.

[6] Third, the Hatch-Waxman Act sets forth special procedures for identifying, and resolving, related patent disputes. It requires the pioneer brand-name manufacturer to list in its New Drug Application the "number and the expiration date" of any relevant patent. And it requires the generic manufacturer in its Abbreviated New Drug Application to "assure the FDA" that the generic "will not infringe" the brand-name's patents.

---

[849] FTC v. Watson Pharmaceuticals, Inc., 677 F.3d 1298, 1312 (11th Cir. 2012).
[850] In re K–Dur Antitrust Litigation, 686 F.3d 197, 214–218 (3d Cir. 2012).

[7] The generic can provide this assurance in one of several ways. It can certify that the brand-name manufacturer has not listed any relevant patents. It can certify that any relevant patents have expired. It can request approval to market beginning when any still-in-force patents expire. Or, it can certify that any listed, relevant patent "is invalid or will not be infringed by the manufacture, use, or sale" of the drug described in the Abbreviated New Drug Application. Taking this last-mentioned route (called the "paragraph IV" route), automatically counts as patent infringement. If the brand-name patentee brings an infringement suit within 45 days, the FDA then must withhold approving the generic, usually for a 30-month period, while the parties litigate patent validity (or infringement) in court. If the courts decide the matter within that period, the FDA follows that determination; if they do not, the FDA may go forward and give approval to market the generic product.

[8] Fourth, Hatch-Waxman provides a special incentive for a generic to be the first to file an Abbreviated New Drug Application taking the paragraph IV route. That applicant will enjoy a period of 180 days of exclusivity (from the first commercial marketing of its drug). During that period of exclusivity no other generic can compete with the brand-name drug. If the first-to-file generic manufacturer can overcome any patent obstacle and bring the generic to market, this 180-day period of exclusivity can prove valuable, possibly worth several hundred million dollars. Indeed, the Generic Pharmaceutical Association said in 2006 that the vast majority of potential profits for a generic drug manufacturer materialize during the 180-day exclusivity period. The 180-day exclusivity period, however, can belong only to the first generic to file. Should that first-to-file generic forfeit the exclusivity right in one of the ways specified by statute, no other generic can obtain it.

[9] In 1999, Solvay Pharmaceuticals, a respondent here, filed a New Drug Application for a brand-name drug called AndroGel. The FDA approved the application in 2000. In 2003, Solvay obtained a relevant patent and disclosed that fact to the FDA, as Hatch-Waxman requires.

[10] Later the same year another respondent, Actavis, Inc. (then known as Watson Pharmaceuticals), filed an Abbreviated New Drug Application for a generic drug modeled after AndroGel. Subsequently, Paddock Laboratories, also a respondent, separately filed an Abbreviated New Drug Application for its own generic product. Both Actavis and Paddock certified under paragraph IV that Solvay's listed patent was invalid and their drugs did not infringe it. A fourth manufacturer, Par Pharmaceutical, likewise a respondent, did not file an application of its own but joined forces with Paddock, agreeing to share the patent litigation costs in return for a share of profits if Paddock obtained approval for its generic drug.

[11] Solvay initiated paragraph IV patent litigation against Actavis and Paddock. Thirty months later the FDA approved Actavis' first-to-file generic product, but, in 2006, the patent-litigation parties all settled. Under the terms of the settlement Actavis agreed that it would not bring its generic to market until August 31, 2015, 65 months before Solvay's patent expired (unless someone else marketed a generic sooner). Actavis also agreed to promote AndroGel to urologists. The other generic manufacturers made roughly similar promises. And Solvay agreed to pay millions of dollars to each generic—$12 million in total to Paddock; $60 million in total to Par; and an estimated $19–$30 million annually, for nine years, to Actavis. The companies described these payments as compensation for other services the generics promised to perform, but the FTC contends the other services had little value. According to the FTC the true point of the payments was to compensate the generics for agreeing not to compete against AndroGel until 2015.

[12] On January 29, 2009, the FTC filed this lawsuit against all the settling parties . . . . The FTC's complaint (as since amended) alleged that respondents violated § 5 of the Federal Trade Commission Act by unlawfully agreeing to share in Solvay's monopoly profits, abandon their patent challenges, and refrain from launching their low-cost generic products to compete with AndroGel for nine years. The District Court held that these allegations did not set forth an antitrust law violation. It accordingly dismissed the FTC's complaint. The FTC appealed.

[13] The Court of Appeals for the Eleventh Circuit affirmed the District Court. It wrote that "absent sham litigation or fraud in obtaining the patent, a reverse payment settlement is immune from antitrust attack so long as its anticompetitive effects fall within the scope of the exclusionary potential of the patent." The court recognized that "antitrust laws typically prohibit agreements where one company pays a potential competitor not to enter the market." But, the court found that "reverse payment settlements of patent litigation present atypical cases because one of the parties owns a patent." Patent holders have a "lawful right to exclude others from the market"; thus a

patent "conveys the right to cripple competition." The court recognized that, if the parties to this sort of case do not settle, a court might declare the patent invalid. But, in light of the public policy favoring settlement of disputes (among other considerations) it held that the courts could not require the parties to continue to litigate in order to avoid antitrust liability. . . .

[14] Solvay's patent, if valid and infringed, might have permitted it to charge drug prices sufficient to recoup the reverse settlement payments it agreed to make to its potential generic competitors. And we are willing to take this fact as evidence that the agreement's "anticompetitive effects fall within the scope of the exclusionary potential of the patent." But we do not agree that that fact, or characterization, can immunize the agreement from antitrust attack.

[15] For one thing, to refer, as the Circuit referred, simply to what the holder of a valid patent could do does not by itself answer the antitrust question. The patent here may or may not be valid, and may or may not be infringed. "[A] *valid* patent excludes all except its owner from the use of the protected process or product." And that exclusion may permit the patent owner to charge a higher-than-competitive price for the patented product. But an *invalidated* patent carries with it no such right. And even a valid patent confers no right to exclude products or processes that do not actually infringe. The paragraph IV litigation in this case put the patent's validity at issue, as well as its actual preclusive scope. The parties' settlement ended that litigation. The FTC alleges that in substance, the plaintiff agreed to pay the defendants many millions of dollars to stay out of its market, even though the defendants did not have any claim that the plaintiff was liable to them for damages. That form of settlement is unusual. And, for reasons discussed [below], there is reason for concern that settlements taking this form tend to have significant adverse effects on competition.

[16] Given these factors, it would be incongruous to determine antitrust legality by measuring the settlement's anticompetitive effects solely against patent law policy, rather than by measuring them against procompetitive antitrust policies as well. And indeed, contrary to the Circuit's view that the only pertinent question is whether the settlement agreement falls within the legitimate scope of the patent's exclusionary potential, this Court has indicated that patent and antitrust policies are both relevant in determining the "scope of the patent monopoly"— and consequently antitrust law immunity—that is conferred by a patent. [. . .]

[17] . . .[T]he Hatch-Waxman Act itself does not embody a statutory policy that supports the Eleventh Circuit's view. Rather, the general procompetitive thrust of the statute, its specific provisions facilitating challenges to a patent's validity, and its later-added provisions requiring parties to a patent dispute triggered by a paragraph IV filing to report settlement terms to the FTC and the Antitrust Division of the Department of Justice, all suggest the contrary. . . .

[18] The Eleventh Circuit's conclusion finds some degree of support in a general legal policy favoring the settlement of disputes. The Circuit's related underlying practical concern consists of its fear that antitrust scrutiny of a reverse payment agreement would require the parties to litigate the validity of the patent in order to demonstrate what would have happened to competition in the absence of the settlement. Any such litigation will prove time consuming, complex, and expensive. The antitrust game, the Circuit may believe, would not be worth that litigation candle.

[19] We recognize the value of settlements and the patent litigation problem. But we nonetheless conclude that this patent-related factor should not determine the result here. Rather, five sets of considerations lead us to conclude that the FTC should have been given the opportunity to prove its antitrust claim.

[20] *First,* the specific restraint at issue has the "potential for genuine adverse effects on competition." The payment in effect amounts to a purchase by the patentee of the exclusive right to sell its product, a right it already claims but would lose if the patent litigation were to continue and the patent were held invalid or not infringed by the generic product. Suppose, for example, that the exclusive right to sell produces $50 million in supracompetitive profits per year for the patentee. And suppose further that the patent has 10 more years to run. Continued litigation, if it results in patent invalidation or a finding of noninfringement, could cost the patentee $500 million in lost revenues, a sum that then would flow in large part to consumers in the form of lower prices.

[21] We concede that settlement on terms permitting the patent challenger to enter the market before the patent expires would also bring about competition, again to the consumer's benefit. But settlement on the terms said by the FTC to be at issue here—payment in return for staying out of the market—simply keeps prices at patentee-set levels, potentially producing the full patent-related $500 million monopoly return while dividing that return between the challenged patentee and the patent challenger. The patentee and the challenger gain; the consumer loses. Indeed, there are indications that patentees sometimes pay a generic challenger a sum even larger than what the generic would gain in profits if it won the paragraph IV litigation and entered the market. The rationale behind a payment of this size cannot in every case be supported by traditional settlement considerations. The payment may instead provide strong evidence that the patentee seeks to induce the generic challenger to abandon its claim with a share of its monopoly profits that would otherwise be lost in the competitive market.

[22] But, one might ask, as a practical matter would the parties be able to enter into such an anticompetitive agreement? Would not a high reverse payment signal to other potential challengers that the patentee lacks confidence in its patent, thereby provoking additional challenges, perhaps too many for the patentee to "buy off?" Two special features of Hatch-Waxman mean that the answer to this question is "not necessarily so." First, under Hatch-Waxman only the first challenger gains the special advantage of 180 days of an exclusive right to sell a generic version of the brand-name product. And as noted, that right has proved valuable—indeed, it can be worth several hundred million dollars. Subsequent challengers cannot secure that exclusivity period, and thus stand to win significantly less than the first if they bring a successful paragraph IV challenge. That is, if subsequent litigation results in invalidation of the patent, or a ruling that the patent is not infringed, that litigation victory will free not just the challenger to compete, but all other potential competitors too (once they obtain FDA approval). The potential reward available to a subsequent challenger being significantly less, the patentee's payment to the initial challenger (in return for not pressing the patent challenge) will not necessarily provoke subsequent challenges. Second, a generic that files a paragraph IV after learning that the first filer has settled will (if sued by the brand-name) have to wait out a stay period of (roughly) 30 months before the FDA may approve its application, just as the first filer did. These features together mean that a reverse payment settlement with the first filer (or, as in this case, *all* of the initial filers) "removes from consideration the most motivated challenger, and the one closest to introducing competition." The dissent may doubt these provisions matter, but scholars in the field tell us that "where only one party owns a patent, it is virtually unheard of outside of pharmaceuticals for that party to pay an accused infringer to settle the lawsuit." It may well be that Hatch-Waxman's unique regulatory framework, including the special advantage that the 180-day exclusivity period gives to first filers, does much to explain why in this context, but not others, the patentee's ordinary incentives to resist paying off challengers (*i.e.*, the fear of provoking myriad other challengers) appear to be more frequently overcome.

[23] *Second,* these anticompetitive consequences will at least sometimes prove unjustified. As the FTC admits, offsetting or redeeming virtues are sometimes present. The reverse payment, for example, may amount to no more than a rough approximation of the litigation expenses saved through the settlement. That payment may reflect compensation for other services that the generic has promised to perform—such as distributing the patented item or helping to develop a market for that item. There may be other justifications. Where a reverse payment reflects traditional settlement considerations, such as avoided litigation costs or fair value for services, there is not the same concern that a patentee is using its monopoly profits to avoid the risk of patent invalidation or a finding of noninfringement. In such cases, the parties may have provided for a reverse payment without having sought or brought about the anticompetitive consequences we mentioned above. But that possibility does not justify dismissing the FTC's complaint. An antitrust defendant may show in the antitrust proceeding that legitimate justifications are present, thereby explaining the presence of the challenged term and showing the lawfulness of that term under the rule of reason.

[24] *Third,* where a reverse payment threatens to work unjustified anticompetitive harm, the patentee likely possesses the power to bring that harm about in practice. At least, the size of the payment from a branded drug manufacturer to a prospective generic is itself a strong indicator of power—namely, the power to charge prices higher than the competitive level. An important patent itself helps to assure such power. Neither is a firm without that power likely to pay large sums to induce others to stay out of its market. In any event, the Commission has referred to studies showing that reverse payment agreements are associated with the presence of higher-than-competitive profits—a strong indication of market power.

[25] *Fourth*, an antitrust action is likely to prove more feasible administratively than the Eleventh Circuit believed. The Circuit's holding does avoid the need to litigate the patent's validity (and also, any question of infringement). But to do so, it throws the baby out with the bath water, and there is no need to take that drastic step. That is because it is normally not necessary to litigate patent validity to answer the antitrust question (unless, perhaps, to determine whether the patent litigation is a sham). An unexplained large reverse payment itself would normally suggest that the patentee has serious doubts about the patent's survival. And that fact, in turn, suggests that the payment's objective is to maintain supracompetitive prices to be shared among the patentee and the challenger rather than face what might have been a competitive market—the very anticompetitive consequence that underlies the claim of antitrust unlawfulness. The owner of a particularly valuable patent might contend, of course, that even a small risk of invalidity justifies a large payment. But, be that as it may, the payment (if otherwise unexplained) likely seeks to prevent the risk of competition. And, as we have said, that consequence constitutes the relevant anticompetitive harm. In a word, the size of the unexplained reverse payment can provide a workable surrogate for a patent's weakness, all without forcing a court to conduct a detailed exploration of the validity of the patent itself.

[26] *Fifth*, the fact that a large, unjustified reverse payment risks antitrust liability does not prevent litigating parties from settling their lawsuit. They may, as in other industries, settle in other ways, for example, by allowing the generic manufacturer to enter the patentee's market prior to the patent's expiration, without the patentee paying the challenger to stay out prior to that point. Although the parties may have reasons to prefer settlements that include reverse payments, the relevant antitrust question is: What are those reasons? If the basic reason is a desire to maintain and to share patent-generated monopoly profits, then, in the absence of some other justification, the antitrust laws are likely to forbid the arrangement. [. . .]

[27] The FTC urges us to hold that reverse payment settlement agreements are presumptively unlawful and that courts reviewing such agreements should proceed via a "quick look" approach, rather than applying a "rule of reason." We decline to do so. In [California Dental Ass'n v. FTC, 526 U.S. 756 (1999)] {*Eds.: You may remember this case from Chapter V*}, we held (unanimously) that abandonment of the "rule of reason" in favor of presumptive rules (or a "quick-look" approach) is appropriate only where an observer with even a rudimentary understanding of economics could conclude that the arrangements in question would have an anticompetitive effect on customers and markets. We do not believe that reverse payment settlements, in the context we here discuss, meet this criterion.

[28] That is because the likelihood of a reverse payment bringing about anticompetitive effects depends upon its size, its scale in relation to the payor's anticipated future litigation costs, its independence from other services for which it might represent payment, and the lack of any other convincing justification. The existence and degree of any anticompetitive consequence may also vary as among industries. These complexities lead us to conclude that the FTC must prove its case as in other rule-of-reason cases.

[29] To say this is not to require the courts to insist, contrary to what we have said, that the Commission need litigate the patent's validity, empirically demonstrate the virtues or vices of the patent system, present every possible supporting fact or refute every possible pro-defense theory. As a leading antitrust scholar has pointed out, there is always something of a sliding scale in appraising reasonableness, and as such the quality of proof required should vary with the circumstances.

[30] As in other areas of law, trial courts can structure antitrust litigation so as to avoid, on the one hand, the use of antitrust theories too abbreviated to permit proper analysis, and, on the other, consideration of every possible fact or theory irrespective of the minimal light it may shed on the basic question—that of the presence of significant unjustified anticompetitive consequences. We therefore leave to the lower courts the structuring of the present rule-of-reason antitrust litigation. We reverse the judgment of the Eleventh Circuit. And we remand the case for further proceedings consistent with this opinion. . . .

Chief Justice Roberts, with whom Justice Scalia and Justice Thomas join, dissenting.

[31] [. . .] A patent carves out an exception to the applicability of antitrust laws. The correct approach should therefore be to ask whether the settlement gives Solvay monopoly power beyond what the patent already gave it.

The Court, however, departs from this approach, and would instead use antitrust law's amorphous rule of reason to inquire into the anticompetitive effects of such settlements. This novel approach is without support in any statute, and will discourage the settlement of patent litigation. [. . .]

[32] We have never held that it violates antitrust law for a competitor to refrain from challenging a patent. And by extension, we have long recognized that the settlement of patent litigation does not by itself violate the antitrust laws. Like most litigation, patent litigation is settled all the time, and such settlements—which can include agreements that clearly violate antitrust law, such as licenses that fix prices, or agreements among competitors to divide territory—do not ordinarily subject the litigants to antitrust liability.

[33] The key, of course, is that the patent holder—when doing anything, including settling—must act within the scope of the patent. If its actions go beyond the monopoly powers conferred by the patent, we have held that such actions are subject to antitrust scrutiny. If its actions are within the scope of the patent, they are not subject to antitrust scrutiny, with two exceptions concededly not applicable here: (1) when the parties settle sham litigation, and (2) when the litigation involves a patent obtained through fraud on the Patent and Trademark Office.

[34] Thus, under our precedent, this is a fairly straight-forward case. Solvay paid a competitor to respect its patent—conduct which did not exceed the scope of its patent. . . . As in any settlement, Solvay gave its competitors something of value (money) and, in exchange, its competitors gave it something of value (dropping their legal claims). In doing so, they put an end to litigation that had been dragging on for three years. Ordinarily, we would think this a good thing.

[35] Today, however, the Court announces a new rule. It is willing to accept that Solvay's actions did not exceed the scope of its patent. But it does not agree that this is enough to immunize the agreement from antitrust attack. According to the majority, if a patent holder settles litigation by paying an alleged infringer a "large and unjustified" payment, in exchange for having the alleged infringer honor the patent, a court should employ the antitrust rule of reason to determine whether the settlement violates antitrust law.

[36] The Court's justifications for this holding are unpersuasive. First, the majority explains that "the patent here may or may not be valid, and may or may not be infringed." Because there is "uncertainty" about whether the patent is actually valid, the Court says that any questions regarding the legality of the settlement should be "measur[ed]" by "procompetitive antitrust policies," rather than "patent law policy." This simply states the conclusion. The difficulty with such an approach is that a patent holder acting within the scope of its patent has an obvious defense to any antitrust suit: that its patent allows it to engage in conduct that would otherwise violate the antitrust laws. But again, that's the whole point of a patent: to confer a limited monopoly. The problem, as the Court correctly recognizes, is that we're not quite certain if the patent is actually valid, or if the competitor is infringing it. But that is always the case, and is plainly a question of patent law. [. . .]

[37] . . . A patent exempts its holder from the antitrust laws only insofar as the holder operates within the scope of the patent. When the holder steps outside the scope of the patent, he can no longer use the patent as his defense. The majority points to *no* case where a patent settlement was subject to antitrust scrutiny merely because the validity of the patent was uncertain. Not one. It is remarkable, and surely worth something, that in the 123 years since the Sherman Act was passed, we have never let antitrust law cross that Rubicon.

[38] Next, the majority points to the "general procompetitive thrust" of the Hatch-Waxman Act, the fact that Hatch-Waxman "facilitat[es] challenges to a patent's validity," and its "provisions requiring parties to [such] patent dispute[s] to report settlement terms to the FTC and the Antitrust Division of the Department of Justice." The Hatch-Waxman Act surely seeks to encourage competition in the drug market. And, like every law, it accomplishes its ends through specific provisions. . . . But it should by now be trite—and unnecessary—to say that "no legislation pursues its purposes at all costs" and that "it frustrates rather than effectuates legislative intent simplistically to assume that *whatever* furthers the statute's primary objective must be the law." . . . Indeed, for whatever it may be worth, Congress has repeatedly declined to enact legislation addressing the issue the Court takes on today. [. . .]

[39] The majority suggests that "[a]pparently most if not all reverse payment settlement agreements arise in the context of pharmaceutical drug regulation." This claim is not supported empirically by anything the majority cites,

and seems unlikely. The term "reverse payment agreement"—coined to create the impression that such settlements are unique—simply highlights the fact that the party suing ends up paying. But this is no anomaly, nor is it evidence of a nefarious plot; it simply results from the fact that the patent holder plaintiff is a defendant against an invalidity counterclaim—not a rare situation in intellectual property litigation. Whatever one might call them, such settlements—paying an alleged infringer to drop its invalidity claim—are a well-known feature of intellectual property litigation, and reflect an intuitive way to settle such disputes. To the extent there are not scores and scores of these settlements to point to, this is because such settlements—outside the context of Hatch–Waxman—are private agreements that for obvious reasons are generally not appealed, nor publicly available. [. . .]

[40] The majority seems to think that *even if* the patent is valid, a patent holder violates the antitrust laws merely because the settlement took away some chance that his patent would be declared invalid by a court. This is flawed for several reasons.

[41] First, a patent is either valid or invalid. The parties of course don't know the answer with certainty at the outset of litigation; hence the litigation. But the same is true of any hard legal question that is yet to be adjudicated. Just because people don't know the answer doesn't mean there is no answer until a court declares one. Yet the majority would impose antitrust liability based on the parties' subjective uncertainty about that legal conclusion.

[42] The Court does so on the assumption that offering a "large" sum is reliable evidence that the patent holder has serious doubts about the patent. Not true. A patent holder may be 95% sure about the validity of its patent, but particularly risk averse or litigation averse, and willing to pay a good deal of money to rid itself of the 5% chance of a finding of invalidity. What is actually motivating a patent holder is apparently a question district courts will have to resolve on a case-by-case basis. The task of trying to discern whether a patent holder is motivated by uncertainty about its patent, or other legitimate factors like risk aversion, will be made all the more difficult by the fact that much of the evidence about the party's motivation may be embedded in legal advice from its attorney, which would presumably be shielded from discovery. . . .

[43] The irony of all this is that the majority's decision may very well discourage generics from challenging pharmaceutical patents in the first place. Patent litigation is costly, time consuming, and uncertain. Generics enter this risky terrain only after careful analysis of the potential gains if they prevail and the potential exposure if they lose. Taking the prospect of settlements off the table—or limiting settlements to an earlier entry date for the generic, which may still be many years in the future—puts a damper on the generic's expected value going into litigation, and decreases its incentive to sue in the first place. The majority assures us, with no support, that everything will be okay because the parties can settle by simply negotiating an earlier entry date for the generic drug manufacturer, rather than settling with money. But it's a matter of common sense, confirmed by experience, that parties are more likely to settle when they have a broader set of valuable things to trade.

[44] . . . I would keep things as they were and not subject basic questions of patent law to an unbounded inquiry under antitrust law, with its treble damages and famously burdensome discovery. . . .

* * *

As we have already seen, in *1-800-Contacts* the Second Circuit held that a trademark settlement that involved commitments to not to bid on advertising that responded to competitors' trademarked keywords should be analyzed under the rule of reason.[851] In that case, the Second Circuit applied its earlier *Clorox* decision. Did *Clorox* fully anticipate *Actavis*?

CASENOTE: Clorox Co. v. Sterling Winthrop, Inc.
117 F.3d 50 (2d Cir. 1997)

Clorox was a tale of two trademarks: PINE-SOL and LYSOL. Their respective owners, Clorox and Reckitt, were competitors in the all-purpose household cleaning market: Clorox through its PINE-SOL line, and Reckitt through its LYSOL line. Both trademarks were of long standing. The PINE-SOL trademark had been used since

---

[851] *See supra* Chapter V.

at least 1945, and was federally registered in 1957. The LYSOL mark—particularly associated with aerosol spray disinfectants—was the senior mark: it had been federally registered for disinfectants in 1906, and for cleaning products in general in the 1920s. Both trademarks had passed through various hands over their long history before ending up with Clorox and Reckitt respectively.

Throughout the long shared history of the two trademarks, their respective owners had continually sparred, and litigated, regarding their respective rights of use and the risks of confusion between the two marks. On three occasions—in 1956, 1967, and 1987—the marks' respective owners settled litigation between them by reaching agreements on the ways in which the parties could use their marks (and particularly the ways in which the PINE-SOL owner could use its mark, given the LYSOL owner's objective to keep PINE-SOL out of the disinfectant space). For example, in 1956, the owner of the PINE-SOL mark agreed to use the trademark only in connection with preparations that used pine oil as an active ingredient. In 1967, that agreement was amended to provide that the owner of the PINE-SOL mark would not use it on any "disinfectant product," to permit the PINE-SOL owner to introduce products in certain categories (such as soaps), and to require that it discontinue a PINE-SOL spray disinfectant that had triggered suit from the LYSOL owner.

But the crucial agreement was the 1987 one, in which the PINE-SOL owner obtained permission to market a "multi-purpose pump spray household cleaner with disinfecting properties," subject to certain conditions. Those conditions provided that, among other things: (1) only one "form, scent, or formula" of the PINE-SOL basic liquid cleaner and pump spray could be sold in any geographic area at one time; (2) the original PINE-SOL product would be advertised primarily as a cleaner, not a disinfectant; and (3) PINE-SOL products could not be sold as anything other than generic cleaners (rather than, say, bathroom cleaners, or for other special purposes). In the same agreement, the LYSOL owner obtained permission to market a "pine action" cleaner under the LYSOL mark.

The resulting peace was not destined to last. In 1992, Clorox—by now the owner of the PINE-SOL mark—aired a commercial that, in the view of the owner of the LYSOL mark, emphasized PINE-SOL's disinfectant properties. The owner of the LYSOL mark sued (of course) to enjoin the commercial. In return, Clorox filed its own lawsuit, alleging that the 1987 agreement violated Section 1 and Section 2 by limiting Clorox's freedom to compete and by perpetuating a monopoly in certain cleaner-disinfectant markets. The district court granted summary judgment for the defendant on the ground that the 1987 agreement was not anticompetitive, and Clorox appealed.

Reviewing this long and sorry history, the Second Circuit began its legal analysis by noting that "Clorox challenges a trademark agreement," and that such agreements "are common, and favored, under the law." As the agreement did not create any restraint that was recognized as *per se* illegal, the rule of reason would govern.

Applying that standard, Clorox faced a "difficult task" of showing competitive harm. Trademarks, unlike other forms of IP, are "by their nature non-exclusionary." In particular, "[b]ecause a trademark merely enables the owner to bar others from use of the mark, as distinguished from competitive manufacture and sale of identical goods bearing another mark, the opportunity for effective antitrust misuse of a trademark" was very limited. The court concluded that the 1987 agreement imposed a particularly modest restriction: "it does not in any way restrict Clorox from producing and selling products that compete directly with the LYSOL brand, so long as they are marketed under a brand name other than PINE–SOL. Accordingly, at first blush it would not appear to restrict Clorox's, much less any other competitor's, ability to compete[.]"

Clorox argued that this restriction was, in reality, not so modest. In the realm of mass-marketed consumer products, it claimed, established brand names are critical. Accordingly, if deprived of the ability to use the PINE–SOL name, Clorox could not "effectively penetrate the alleged disinfectant cleaning markets dominated by the popular LYSOL brand."

But the court was not persuaded. For one thing, the CLOROX trademark itself was "a megabrand with substantial brand equity." Indeed, Clorox "has enjoyed great success in extending its own name into new cleaning-market niches, and developing new products under new names in the past." Moreover, there were many other competitors in the market able to exert competitive pressure against the LYSOL line of products. "The overall household cleaning industry is the battleground of some of the largest corporations in the country, wielding numerous megabrands. The industry is made up of firms with the resources to develop new products and market them, as these companies have repeatedly done. . . . Each of these major corporations, like Clorox, has significant goodwill attached to its own name, and to the trademarks it owns." In light of the abundant opportunities for competition, the court concluded that "[t]he agreement simply does not significantly restrict Clorox's, or other competitors', ability to enter [the alleged relevant] markets."

For completeness's sake, the court also pointed out that the 1987 agreement was supported by procompetitive justifications. In particular, "trademark agreements are favored in the law as a means by which parties agree to market products in a way that reduces the likelihood of consumer confusion and avoids time-consuming litigation." As a result:

> in the absence of any evidence that the provisions relating to trademark protection are auxiliary to an underlying illegal agreement between competitors . . . and absent exceptional circumstances, we believe the parties' determination of the scope of needed trademark protections is entitled to substantial weight. At the time of the execution of such an agreement, the parties are in the best position to determine what protections are needed and how to resolve disputes concerning earlier trademark agreements between themselves. While the intent of the parties may not always be determinative, it is usually unwise for courts to second-guess such decisions. In the absence of evidence to the contrary it is reasonable to presume that such arms-length agreements are pro-competitive.

In so holding, the Second Circuit marked out the line to which it would return almost 25 years later in the *1-800 Contacts* litigation.[852]

NOTES

1) Has the *Actavis* Court provided a workable standard for assessing reverse payment settlement agreements? Specifically, is the size of the payment a good proxy for the likelihood that the defendant would have prevailed in the litigation, and would have entered but for the settlement? What is a "large" payment?

2) In 2019 the FTC issued a report assessing how pharmaceutical companies were adjusting their behavior in the post-*Actavis* environment. The FTC found that the pharma industry was now "largely avoiding reverse payments," although they were finding other ways to settle that were less likely to draw antitrust scrutiny, including, for example, by pegging payments to anticipated savings in litigation costs. *See Then, Now, and Down the Road: Trends in Pharmaceutical Patent Settlements after FTC v. Actavis,* https://www.ftc.gov/enforcement/competition-matters/2019/05/then-now-down-road-trends-pharmaceutical-patent-settlements-after-ftc-v-actavis.

3) At paragraph 25 of the *Actavis* extract, the Court says something very interesting: "the payment (if otherwise unexplained) likely seeks to prevent the risk of competition. And, as we have said, that consequence constitutes the relevant anticompetitive harm." And the Court indicates in the same paragraph that this reasoning applies even when the risk is "small." Is this consistent with antitrust's approach to the loss of a "small" risk of competition in Section 1, Section 2, or Section 7 cases?[853]

4) When, if ever, should a restrictive trademark agreement like the one in *Clorox* be condemned? Would your answer change if the agreement dealt with patent rights rather than a trademark?

5) Do you agree with the *Clorox* court's observations at paragraph 19 that: "[T]he parties are in the best position to determine what protections are needed and how to resolve disputes concerning earlier trademark agreements between themselves. While the intent of the parties may not always be determinative, it is usually unwise for courts to second-guess such decisions. In the absence of evidence to the contrary it is reasonable to presume that such arms-length agreements are [procompetitive]"? Who is injured, and who is benefited, by an anticompetitive agreement of this kind?

6) Federal trademark law contains a doctrine of "nominative fair use" that is intended to insulate at least some uses of trademarks for the purpose of comparative advertising. Are the potential competitive harms created by trademark agreements like the one in *Clorox* and *1-800-Contacts* (see Chapter V) better handled through

---

[852] *See supra* § V.D.

[853] *Compare, e.g.,* FTC v. Steris Corp., 133 F.Supp.3d 962 (N.D. Ohio 2015) (potential competition merger case).

antitrust, or through legislative and judicial development of trademark's internal doctrines, such as nominative fair use, in a way that is sensitive to competition concerns? And are those options substitutes or complements?

D. Standard Setting and Standard-Essential Patents

A fertile source of controversy and antitrust litigation is the field of "standard-setting," or "standards development," activity. This is the—mostly private and voluntary—process of collaboration among market participants, through an array of various standard setting organizations ("SSOs"; also standards development organizations ("SDOs")) to establish industry standards. Prominent SSOs include the Institute of Electrical and Electronics Engineers ("IEEE"), the American National Standards Institute ("ANSI"), the Internet Engineering Task Force ("IETF"), the International Organization for Standardization ("ISO"), the International Telecommunications Union ("ITU"), the World Wide Web Consortium (W3C), and many others.

These SSOs create and amend technical standards that enable products made by different manufacturers to interoperate with one another. Many commonplace technologies have been made possible by one or more SSOs at their heart: for example, the IEEE 802.11 standard sets out the technological basis for the "wi-fi" wireless access to the Internet. Likewise, Bluetooth, USB, 5G cellular networks, and "tap" payment technologies all rely on extensive SSO activity. In these and countless other areas of the economy, the presence of a standard permits a large number of companies to manufacture equipment that complies with the standard and thus can interoperate with all other standard-compliant technology.

Standardized technology often implicates patent rights, which are known as "Standard-Essential Patents" ("SEPs") when they cover some aspect of an adopted standard. This is an important consideration in the design of a standard: the existence and nature of IP rights can affect an SSO's choice between alternative technologies. For example, an SSO might prefer to incorporate a technology that can be licensed for free, or for a low royalty, than one that can be used only at great cost. Most market participants would not welcome the prospect of making a significant investment in a standardized technology only to be "held up" after the fact by a patent-holder aiming to extract the benefits of the investment through the threat of an injunction.

SSOs have developed several practices in an attempt to address the threat of patent holdup. First, many SSOs impose disclosure obligations on all participants, requiring that they declare, in advance, any intellectual property that may read on a proposed standard. This addresses the risk that a participant might encourage the SSO to adopt a particular technology and then assert IP rights over it after the standard is finalized and investments have been made. Second, many SSOs require that all participants commit to license any intellectual property implicated by a standard on "fair, reasonable, and nondiscriminatory" ("FRAND") terms. Importantly, each SSO works differently: their respective intellectual property rights ("IPR") policies impose different obligations of disclosure and licensing. And—as you might expect—the meaning of "FRAND" is far from clear in many cases. But courts have held that the FRAND commitment is an enforceable contractual obligation and can be vindicated by an ordinary contract action, on the theory that potential licensees are third-party beneficiaries of the promise made to the SSO.[854]

Activity of this kind—even though it involves competitors collaborating to choose market "standards"—is obviously necessary for the development and maintenance of an open system. As such, courts, Congress, and the agencies have recognized that standard-setting activity is generally procompetitive and should be analyzed under the rule of reason.[855]

---

[854] *See, e.g.*, Microsoft Corp. v. Motorola, Inc., 696 F.3d 872, 884 (9th Cir. 2012); Broadcom Corp. v. Qualcomm Inc., 501 F.3d 297, 304, 313–14 (3d Cir. 2007); *see also* Cont'l Auto. Sys., Inc. v. Avanci, LLC, 485 F. Supp. 3d 712, 728 (N.D. Tex. 2020), *aff'd sub nom.* Cont'l Auto. Sys., Inc. v. Avanci, L.L.C., No. 20-11032, 2022 WL 2205469 (5th Cir. June 21, 2022).

[855] *See, e.g.*, Allied Tube & Conduit Corp. v. Indian Head, Inc., 486 U.S. 492, 501 (1988) ("When . . . private associations promulgate safety standards based on the merits of objective expert judgments and through procedures that prevent the standard-setting process from being biased by members with economic interests in stifling product competition, those private standards can have significant procompetitive advantages. It is this potential for procompetitive benefits that has led most lower courts to apply rule-of-reason analysis to product standard-setting by private associations."); Standards Development Organization Act of 2004, codified at 15

However, SSOs have always given rise to a healthy docket of antitrust cases. In the remainder of this chapter we will encounter three kinds of antitrust concern: (1) deception of the SSO in order to obtain market or monopoly power (*e.g.*, failing to disclose intellectual property that may read on the standard); (2) violations of FRAND commitments under circumstances where the extraction of supra-FRAND royalties may harm competition; and (3) manipulation of the SSO process as a vehicle for collusion among, or exclusion of, competitors.

1. IP Concealment

A classic form of antitrust misconduct in an SSO involves obtaining monopoly power through deception regarding the existence of IP rights. In the paradigm case, an SSO participant intentionally deceives a standard-setting organization by failing to disclose (or affirmatively denying) its possession of relevant patent rights, only to assert those rights with a flourish after the relevant technology has been incorporated into the standard.[856] This can be a violation of the antitrust laws, in particular where an alternative technology would have been incorporated into the standard but-for the deceptive concealment of IP rights.[857]

The following two extracts demonstrate two variations on this story. In *Rambus*, the FTC challenged Rambus's deception of an SSO. But the Commission's case foundered on the FTC's failure to prove that, if Rambus *had* disclosed its patents, the SSO would have incorporated another technology, rather than just extracting a FRAND commitment from Rambus. In *Unocal*, an oil company had engaged in some misleading conduct regarding a standards-setting process for gasoline to reduce air pollution in California. The two matters proceeded on very different paths: in *Rambus*, the Commission imposed liability but lost on appeal to the D.C. Circuit; in *Unocal*, it obtained full relief as part of a consent decree entered at the time Unocal's merger with Chevron was approved.

Rambus v. FTC

522 F.3d 456 (D.C. Cir. 2008)

Judge Williams.

[1] Rambus Inc. develops computer memory technologies, secures intellectual property rights over them, and then licenses them to manufacturers in exchange for royalty payments. In 1990, Rambus's founders filed a patent application claiming the invention of a faster architecture for dynamic random access memory ("DRAM"). In recent years, Rambus has asserted that patents issued to protect its invention cover four technologies that a private standard-setting organization ("SSO") included in DRAM industry standards.

[2] Before an SSO adopts a standard, there is often vigorous competition among different technologies for incorporation into that standard. After standardization, however, the dynamic typically shifts, as industry members begin adhering to the standard and the standardized features start to dominate. In this case, 90% of DRAM production is compliant with the standards at issue, and therefore the technologies adopted in those standards—

U.S.C. § 4301-06 ("In any action under the antitrust laws, or under any State law similar to the antitrust laws, the conduct of- (1) any person in making or performing a contract to carry out a joint venture, or (2) a standards development organization while engaged in a standards development activity, shall not be deemed illegal per se; such conduct shall be judged on the basis of its reasonableness, taking into account all relevant factors affecting competition, including, but not limited to, effects on competition in properly defined, relevant research, development, product, process, and service markets. For the purpose of determining a properly defined, relevant market, worldwide capacity shall be considered to the extent that it may be appropriate in the circumstances."); David A. Balto, *Standard Setting in a Network Economy* (remarks of Feb. 17, 2000).

[856] For a classic example of this in action, *see, e.g.*, Complaint, *In the Matter of Dell Computer Corp*, FTC Dkt. No. C-3658 (filed May 20 1996) ¶¶ 7-8 ("After committee approval of the VL-bus design standard, VESA sought the approval of the VL-bus design standard by all of its voting members. On July 20, 1992, Dell voted to approve the preliminary proposal for the VL-bus standard. As part of this approval, a Dell representative certified in writing that, to the best of his knowledge, 'this proposal does not infringe on any trademarks, copyrights, or patents' that Dell possessed. On August 6, 1992, Dell gave final approval to the VL-bus design standard. As part of this final approval, the Dell representative again certified in writing that, to the best of his knowledge, 'this proposal does not infringe on any trademarks, copyrights, or patents' that Dell possessed. After VESA's VL-bus design standard became very successful, having been included in over 1.4 million computers sold in the eight months immediately following its adoption, Dell informed certain VESA members who were manufacturing computers using the new design standard that their 'implementation of the VL-bus is a violation of Dell's exclusive rights.' Dell demanded that these companies meet with its representatives to 'determine the manner in which Dell's exclusive rights will be recognized.' Dell followed up its initial demands by meeting with several companies, and it has never renounced the claimed infringement.").

[857] Broadcom Corp. v. Qualcomm Inc., 501 F.3d 297, 314 (3d Cir. 2007).

including those over which Rambus claims patent rights—enjoy a similar level of dominance over their alternatives.

[3] After lengthy proceedings, the Federal Trade Commission determined that Rambus, while participating in the standard-setting process, deceptively failed to disclose to the SSO the patent interests it held in four technologies that were standardized. Those interests ranged from issued patents, to pending patent applications, to plans to amend those patent applications to add new claims; Rambus's patent rights in all these interests are said to be sufficiently connected to the invention described in Rambus's original 1990 application that its rights would relate back to its date. Finding this conduct monopolistic and in violation of § 2 of the Sherman Act, 15 U.S.C. § 2, the Commission went on to hold that Rambus had engaged in an unfair method of competition and unfair or deceptive acts or practices prohibited by § 5(a) of the Federal Trade Commission Act ("FTC Act"), id. § 45(a).

[4] Rambus petitions for review. We grant the petition, holding that the Commission failed to sustain its allegation of monopolization. Its factual conclusion was that Rambus's alleged deception enabled it either to acquire a monopoly through the standardization of its patented technologies rather than possible alternatives, or to avoid limits on its patent licensing fees that the SSO would have imposed as part of its normal process of standardizing patented technologies. But the latter—deceit merely enabling a monopolist to charge higher prices than it otherwise could have charged—would not in itself constitute monopolization. . . .

[5] During the early 1990s, the computer hardware industry faced a "memory bottleneck": the development of faster memory lagged behind the development of faster central processing units, and this risked limiting future gains in overall computer performance. To address this problem, Michael Farmwald and Mark Horowitz began collaborating during the late 1980s and invented a higher-performance DRAM architecture. Together, they founded Rambus in March 1990 and filed Patent Application No. 07/510,898 ("the '898 application") on April 18, 1990.

[6] As originally filed, the '898 application included a 62-page written description of Farmwald and Horowitz's invention, 150 claims, and 15 technical drawings. Under the direction of the Patent Office, acting pursuant to 35 U.S.C. § 121, Rambus effectively split the application into several (the original one and 10 "divisionals"). Thereafter, Rambus amended some of these applications and filed additional continuation and divisional applications.

[7] While Rambus was developing a patent portfolio based on its founders' inventions, the computer memory industry was at work standardizing DRAM technologies. The locus of those efforts was the Joint Electron Device Engineering Council ("JEDEC")—then an "activity" of what is now called the Electronics Industries Alliance ("EIA") and, since 2000, a trade association affiliated with EIA and known as the JEDEC Solid State Technology Association. Any company involved in the solid state products industry could join JEDEC by submitting an application and paying annual dues, and members could receive JEDEC mailings, participate in JEDEC committees, and vote on pending matters.

[8] One JEDEC committee, JC 42.3, developed standards for computer memory products. Rambus attended its first JC 42.3 meeting as a guest in December 1991 and began formally participating when it joined JEDEC in February 1992. At the time, JC 42.3 was at work on what became JEDEC's synchronous DRAM ("SDRAM") standard. The committee voted to approve the completed standard in March 1993, and JEDEC's governing body gave its final approval on May 24, 1993. The SDRAM standard includes two of the four technologies over which Rambus asserts patent rights — programmable CAS latency and programmable burst length.

[9] Despite SDRAM's standardization, its manufacture increased very slowly and asynchronous DRAM continued to dominate the computer memory market, so JC 42.3 began to consider a number of possible responses — among them specifications it could include in a next-generation SDRAM standard. As part of that process, JC 42.3 members received a survey ballot in October 1995 soliciting their opinions on features of an advanced SDRAM — which ultimately emerged as the double data rate ("DDR") SDRAM standard. Among the features voted on were the other two technologies at issue here: on-chip phase lock and delay lock loops ("on-chip PLL/DLL") and dual-edge clocking. The Committee tallied and discussed the survey results at its December 1995 meeting, which was Rambus's last as a JEDEC member. Rambus formally withdrew from JEDEC by letter dated

June 17, 1996, saying (among other things) that the terms on which it proposed to license its proprietary technology "may not be consistent with the terms set by standards bodies, including JEDEC."

[10] JC 42.3's work continued after Rambus's departure. In March 1998 the committee adopted the DDR SDRAM standard, and the JEDEC Board of Directors approved it in 1999. This standard retained SDRAM features including programmable CAS latency and programmable burst length, and it added on-chip PLL/DLL and dual-edge clocking; DDR SDRAM, therefore, included all four of the technologies at issue here.

[11] Starting in 1999, Rambus informed major DRAM and chipset manufacturers that it held patent rights over technologies included in JEDEC's SDRAM and DDR SDRAM standards, and that the continued manufacture, sale, or use of products compliant with those standards infringed its rights. It invited the manufacturers to resolve the alleged infringement through licensing negotiations. A number of manufacturers agreed to licenses; others did not, and litigation ensued.

[12] On June 18, 2002, the Federal Trade Commission filed a complaint under § 5(b) of the FTC Act, 15 U.S.C. § 45(b), charging that Rambus engaged in unfair methods of competition and unfair or deceptive acts or practices in violation of the Act. Specifically, the Commission alleged that Rambus breached JEDEC policies requiring it to disclose patent interests related to standardization efforts and that the disclosures it did make were misleading. By this deceptive conduct, it said, Rambus unlawfully monopolized four technology markets in which its patented technologies compete with alternative innovations to address technical issues relating to DRAM design — markets for latency, burst length, data acceleration, and clock synchronization technologies.

[13] Proceedings began before an administrative law judge, who in due course dismissed the Complaint in its entirety. He concluded that Rambus did not impermissibly withhold material information about its intellectual property, and that, in any event, there was insufficient evidence that, if Rambus had disclosed all the information allegedly required of it, JEDEC would have standardized an alternative technology.

[14] Complaint Counsel [i.e., FTC staff] appealed the ALJ's Initial Decision to the Commission, which reopened the record to receive additional evidence and did its own plenary review. On July 31, 2006 the Commission vacated the ALJ's decision and set aside his findings of fact and conclusions of law. The Commission found that while JEDEC's patent disclosure policies were "not a model of clarity," members expected one another to disclose patents and patent applications that were relevant to technologies being considered for standardization, plus (though the Commission was far less clear on these latter items) planned amendments to pending applications or "anything they're working on that they potentially wanted to protect with patents down the road." Based on this interpretation of JEDEC's disclosure requirements, the Commission held that Rambus willfully and intentionally engaged in misrepresentations, omissions, and other practices that misled JEDEC members about intellectual property information "highly material" to the standard-setting process.

[15] The Commission focused entirely on the allegation of monopolization. In particular, the Commission held that the evidence and inferences from Rambus's purpose demonstrated that but for Rambus's deceptive course of conduct, JEDEC either would have excluded Rambus's patented technologies from the JEDEC DRAM standards, or would have demanded RAND assurances [i.e., assurances of reasonable and nondiscriminatory license fees], with an opportunity for ex ante licensing negotiations. Rejecting Rambus's argument that factors other than JEDEC's standards allowed Rambus's technologies to dominate their respective markets, the Commission concluded that Rambus's deception of JEDEC significantly contributed to its acquisition of monopoly power.

[16] After additional briefing by the parties, the Commission rendered a separate remedial opinion and final order. It held that it had the authority in principle to order compulsory licensing, but that remedies beyond injunctions against future anticompetitive conduct would require stronger proof that they were necessary to restore competitive conditions. Applying that more demanding burden to Complaint Counsel's claims for relief, the Commission refused to compel Rambus to license its relevant patents royalty-free because there was insufficient evidence that absent Rambus's deception JEDEC would have standardized non-proprietary technologies instead of Rambus's; thus, Complaint Counsel had failed to show that such a remedy was necessary to restore competition that would have existed in the but for world. Instead, the Commission decided to compel licensing at reasonable royalty rates, which it calculated based on what it believed would have resulted from negotiations between Rambus

and manufacturers before JEDEC committed to the standards. The Commission's order limits Rambus's royalties for three years to 0.25% for JEDEC-compliant SDRAM and 0.5% for JEDEC-compliant DDR SDRAM (with double those royalties for certain JEDEC-compliant, non-DRAM products); after those three years, it forbids any royalty collection.

[17] Rambus moved for reconsideration, and the Commission denied the motion in relevant part on April 27, 2007. Rambus timely petitioned for our review of both the Commission's Final Order and its Denial of Reconsideration, and we consolidated those petitions.

[18] Rambus challenges the Commission's determination that it engaged in unlawful monopolization—and thereby violated § 5 of the FTC Act—on a variety of grounds, of which two are most prominent. First, it argues that the Commission erred in finding that it violated any JEDEC patent disclosure rules and thus that it breached any antitrust duty to provide information to its rivals. Second, it asserts that even if its nondisclosure contravened JEDEC's policies, the Commission found the consequences of such nondisclosure only in the alternative: that it prevented JEDEC either from adopting a non-proprietary standard, or from extracting a RAND commitment from Rambus when standardizing its technology. As the latter would not involve an antitrust violation, says Rambus, there is an insufficient basis for liability.

[19] We find the second of these arguments to be persuasive, and conclude that the Commission failed to demonstrate that Rambus's conduct was exclusionary under settled principles of antitrust law. Given that conclusion, we need not dwell very long on the substantiality of the evidence, which we address only to express our serious concerns about the breadth the Commission ascribed to JEDEC's disclosure policies and their relation to what Rambus did or did not disclose.

[20] In this case under § 5 of the FTC Act, the Commission expressly limited its theory of liability to Rambus's unlawful monopolization of four markets in violation of § 2 of the Sherman Act. Therefore, we apply principles of antitrust law developed under the Sherman Act, and we review the Commission's construction and application of the antitrust laws de novo.

[21] It is settled law that the mere existence of a monopoly does not violate the Sherman Act. In addition to the possession of monopoly power in the relevant market, the offense of monopolization requires the willful acquisition or maintenance of that power as distinguished from growth or development as a consequence of a superior product, business acumen, or historical accident. In this case, Rambus does not dispute the nature of the relevant markets or that its patent rights in the four relevant technologies give it monopoly power in each of those markets. The critical question is whether Rambus engaged in exclusionary conduct, and thereby acquired its monopoly power in the relevant markets unlawfully.

[22] To answer that question, we adhere to two antitrust principles. First, to be condemned as exclusionary, a monopolist's act must have anticompetitive effect. That is, it must harm the competitive process and thereby harm consumers. In contrast, harm to one or more competitors will not suffice. Second, it is the antitrust plaintiff—including the Government as plaintiff—that bears the burden of proving the anticompetitive effect of the monopolist's conduct.

[23] The Commission held that Rambus engaged in exclusionary conduct consisting of misrepresentations, omissions, and other practices that deceived JEDEC about the nature and scope of its patent interests while the organization standardized technologies covered by those interests. Had Rambus fully disclosed its intellectual property, "JEDEC either would have excluded Rambus's patented technologies from the JEDEC DRAM standards, or would have demanded RAND assurances, with an opportunity for ex ante licensing negotiations." But the Commission did not determine that one or the other of these two possible outcomes was the more likely. The Commission's conclusion that Rambus's conduct was exclusionary depends, therefore, on a syllogism: Rambus avoided one of two outcomes by not disclosing its patent interests; the avoidance of either of those outcomes was anticompetitive; therefore Rambus's non-disclosure was anticompetitive.

[24] We assume without deciding that avoidance of the first of these possible outcomes was indeed anticompetitive; that is, that if Rambus's more complete disclosure would have caused JEDEC to adopt a different (open, non-proprietary) standard, then its failure to disclose harmed competition and would support a monopolization claim.

But while we can assume that Rambus's non-disclosure made the adoption of its technologies somewhat more likely than broad disclosure would have, the Commission made clear in its remedial opinion that there was insufficient evidence that JEDEC would have standardized other technologies had it known the full scope of Rambus's intellectual property. Therefore, for the Commission's syllogism to survive—and for the Commission to have carried its burden of proving that Rambus's conduct had an anticompetitive effect—we must also be convinced that if Rambus's conduct merely enabled it to avoid the other possible outcome, namely JEDEC's obtaining assurances from Rambus of RAND licensing terms, such conduct, alone, could be said to harm competition. We are not convinced.

[25] Deceptive conduct—like any other kind—must have an anticompetitive effect in order to form the basis of a monopolization claim. Even an act of pure malice by one business competitor against another does not, without more, state a claim under the federal antitrust laws, without proof of a dangerous probability that the defendant would monopolize a particular market. Even if deception raises the price secured by a seller, but does so without harming competition, it is beyond the antitrust laws' reach. Cases that recognize deception as exclusionary hinge, therefore, on whether the conduct impaired rivals in a manner tending to bring about or protect a defendant's monopoly power. . . . The focus of our antitrust scrutiny, therefore, was properly placed on the resulting harms to competition rather than the deception itself. [. . .]

[26] But an otherwise lawful monopolist's use of deception simply to obtain higher prices normally has no particular tendency to exclude rivals and thus to diminish competition. [. . .]

[27] Here, the Commission expressly left open the likelihood that JEDEC would have standardized Rambus's technologies even if Rambus had disclosed its intellectual property. Under this hypothesis, JEDEC lost only an opportunity to secure a RAND commitment from Rambus. But loss of such a commitment is not a harm to competition from alternative technologies in the relevant markets. Indeed, had JEDEC limited Rambus to reasonable royalties and required it to provide licenses on a nondiscriminatory basis, we would expect less competition from alternative technologies, not more; high prices and constrained output tend to attract competitors, not to repel them.

[28] Scholars in the field have urged that if nondisclosure to an SSO enables a participant to obtain higher royalties than would otherwise have been attainable, the "over-charge can properly constitute competitive harm attributable to the nondisclosure," as the overcharge will distort competition in the downstream market. The contention that price-raising deception has downstream effects is surely correct, but that consequence was equally surely true in [NYNEX Corp. v. Discon, Inc., 525 U.S. 128 (1998)] (though perhaps on a smaller scale) and equally obvious to the Court. The Commission makes the related contention that because the ability to profitably restrict output and set supracompetitive prices is the sine qua non of monopoly power, any conduct that permits a monopolist to avoid constraints on the exercise of that power must be anticompetitive. But again, as in *NYNEX*, an otherwise lawful monopolist's end-run around price constraints, even when deceptive or fraudulent, does not alone present a harm to competition in the monopolized market.

[29] Thus, if JEDEC, in the world that would have existed but for Rambus's deception, would have standardized the very same technologies, Rambus's alleged deception cannot be said to have had an effect on competition in violation of the antitrust laws; JEDEC's loss of an opportunity to seek favorable licensing terms is not as such an antitrust harm. Yet the Commission did not reject this as being a possible—perhaps even the more probable—effect of Rambus's conduct. We hold, therefore, that the Commission failed to demonstrate that Rambus's conduct was exclusionary, and thus to establish its claim that Rambus unlawfully monopolized the relevant markets.

[30] Our conclusion that the Commission failed to demonstrate that Rambus inflicted any harm on competition requires vacatur of the Commission's orders.

* * *

Analysis of Proposed Consent Order to Aid Public Comment, In the Matter of Union Oil Company of California,

FTC Dkt. No. 9305 (June 10, 2005)

[1] The Complaint alleges that Respondent Union Oil engaged in a series of acts to subvert state regulatory standard-setting procedures relating to low emissions gasoline. To address California's serious air pollution problems, the California Air Resources Board ("CARB") initiated proceedings in the late 1980s to set regulations and standards governing the composition of low emissions, reformulated gasoline ("RFG"). The Complaint alleges that Union Oil actively participated in CARB RFG rulemaking proceedings and engaged in a pattern of bad-faith, deceptive conduct, exclusionary in nature, that enabled it to undermine competition and harm consumers. The Complaint states that Union Oil also engaged in deceptive and exclusionary conduct through its participation in two private industry groups – the Auto/Oil Air Quality Improvement Program ("Auto/Oil") and the Western States Petroleum Association ("WSPA"). According to the Complaint, Union Oil thereby illegally monopolized, attempted to monopolize, and otherwise engaged in unfair methods of competition in violation of Section 5 of the FTC Act in both the technology market for the production and supply of CARB-compliant "summer-time" gasoline, and the downstream "summer-time" gasoline product market.

[2] Union Oil is a public corporation, organized in, and doing business under, the laws of California. Union Oil is a wholly-owned operating subsidiary of Unocal Corporation, a holding company incorporated in Delaware. Prior to 1997, Union Oil owned and operated refineries in California as a vertically-integrated producer, refiner, and marketer of petroleum products. In 1997, Union Oil sold its west coast refining, marketing, and transportation assets. Currently, Union Oil's primary business activities involve oil and gas exploration and production.

[3] The Complaint alleges that during the CARB "Phase 2" RFG rulemaking proceedings in 1990–1994, Union Oil made a series of materially false and misleading statements. According to the allegations in the Complaint, Union Oil willfully and intentionally:

> a. Represented to CARB and other participants that Union Oil's emissions research results showing, inter alia, the relationships between certain gasoline properties and automobile emissions, were "nonproprietary," in "the public domain," or otherwise were available to CARB, industry members, and the general public – without disclosing that Union Oil intended to assert its proprietary interests (as manifested in pending patent claims) in the results of this research;

> b. Represented to CARB that a "predictive model" – i.e., a mathematical model that predicts whether the emissions that would result from varying certain gasoline properties in a fuel are equivalent to the emissions resulting from a specified and fixed fuel formulation – would be "cost-effective" and "flexible," without disclosing that Union Oil's assertion of its proprietary interests would undermine the cost-effectiveness and flexibility of such a model; and

> c. Made statements and comments to CARB and other industry participants relating to the cost-effectiveness and flexibility of the regulations that further reinforced the materially false and misleading impression that Union Oil had relinquished or would not enforce any proprietary interests in its emissions research results.

[4] According to the Complaint, Union Oil continued to conceal its intention to obtain a competitive advantage through the enforcement of its proprietary interests relating to RFG even after Union Oil received notice that the pending patent claims were allowed and issued. The Complaint alleges that Union Oil thereby led CARB and two private industry groups—Auto/Oil and WSPA (and their respective industry members)—to believe that Union Oil did not have, or would not enforce, any proprietary interests or intellectual property rights associated with its emissions research results.

[5] The Complaint alleges that Union Oil's conduct caused CARB to adopt Phase 2 "summer-time" RFG regulations that substantially overlapped with Union Oil's concealed pending patent claims. But for Union Oil's deception, according to the Complaint, CARB would not have adopted RFG regulations substantially incorporating Union Oil's proprietary interests; the terms on which Union Oil was later able to enforce its proprietary interests would have been substantially different; or both.

[6] The Complaint alleges that but for Union Oil's deceptive conduct, industry participants in Auto/Oil and WSPA would have taken actions including, but not limited to, (a) advocating that CARB adopt regulations that minimized or avoided infringement of Union Oil's patent claims; (b) advocating that CARB negotiate license terms substantially different from those that Union Oil was later able to obtain; and/or (c) incorporating knowledge of Union Oil's pending patent rights in their capital investment and refinery reconfiguration decisions to avoid and/or minimize potential infringement.

[7] According to the Complaint, Union Oil did not announce the existence of its proprietary interests and patent rights relating to RFG until January 1995—shortly before the relevant CARB Phase 2 RFG regulations were to go into effect. The Complaint alleges that, by that time, the refining industry had spent billions of dollars in capital expenditures to modify their refineries to comply with the CARB Phase 2 RFG regulations, in reliance on Union Oil's representations that its research results were in "the public domain." The Complaint states that once CARB and the refiners had become locked into the Phase 2 regulations, Union Oil commenced vigorous enforcement of its patent rights through litigation and licensing, and obtained four additional patents based on the same RFG research results.

[8] Union Oil's misrepresentations, according to the Complaint, have harmed competition and led directly to the acquisition of monopoly power for the technology to produce and supply California "summer-time" reformulated gasoline (mandated for up to eight months of the year, from approximately March through October). The Complaint alleges that Union Oil's conduct also permitted it to undermine competition and harm consumers in the downstream product market for "summer-time" reformulated gasoline in California. The Complaint alleges that without recourse, Union Oil's conduct would continue materially to cause or threaten to cause further substantial injury to competition and to consumers.

[9] According to the Complaint, Union Oil's enforcement of its RFG patents has resulted, inter alia, in a jury determination of a 5.75 cents per gallon royalty on gasoline produced by major California refiners comprising approximately 90 percent of the current refining capacity of CARB-compliant RFG in the California market. The Complaint alleges that Union Oil also has publicly announced that it will license its RFG patent portfolio, with fees ranging from 1.2 to 3.4 cents per gallon, to "non-litigating" refiners.

[10] The Complaint alleges that Unocal's conduct could result in an estimated annual cost of more than $500 million to the refining industry. According to the Complaint, Union Oil's own economic expert has testified under oath that 90 percent of any royalty would be passed through to consumers in the form of higher gasoline prices. [. . .]

[11] In order to remedy the alleged anticompetitive effects, Union Oil has agreed to take several actions. First, it will cease and desist from any and all efforts, and will not undertake any new efforts to: (a) assert or enforce any of Union Oil's Relevant U.S. Patents against any person; (b) recover any damages or costs for alleged infringements of any of the Relevant U.S. Patents; or (c) collect any fees, royalties or other payments, in cash or in kind, for the practice of any of the Relevant U.S. Patents, including but not limited to fees, royalties, or other payments, in cash or in kind, to be collected pursuant to any License Agreement. . . .

[12] Second, the Proposed Consent Order requires that, within thirty (30) days following the Merger Effective Date, Union Oil shall file, or cause to be filed, with the United States Patent and Trademark Office, the necessary documents pursuant to 35 U.S.C. § 253, 37 C.F.R. § 1.321, and the Manual of Patent Examining Procedure to disclaim or dedicate to the public the remaining term of the Relevant U.S. Patents. The Proposed Consent Order further requires that Union Oil shall correct as necessary, and shall not withdraw or seek to nullify, any disclaimers or dedications filed pursuant to the Proposed Consent Order.

[13] Third, the Proposed Consent Order requires that, within thirty (30) days following the Merger Effective Date, Union Oil shall move to dismiss, with prejudice, all pending legal actions relating to the alleged infringement of any Relevant U.S. Patents, including but not limited to the following actions pending in the United States District Court for the Central District of California: Union Oil Company of California v. Atlantic Richfield Company, et al., Case No. CV-95-2379-CAS and Union Oil Company of California v. Valero Energy Corporation, Case No. CV-02- 00593 SVW.

[14] Paragraph V of the Proposed Consent Order requires Union Oil to distribute a copy of the Proposed Consent Order and the Complaint in this matter to certain interested parties, including (1) any person that Union Oil has contacted regarding possible infringement of any of the Relevant U.S. Patents, (2) any person against which Union Oil is, or was, involved in any legal action regarding possible infringement of any of the Relevant U.S. Patents, (3) any licensee or other Person from which Union Oil has collected any fees, royalties or other payments, in cash or in kind, for the practice of the Relevant U.S. Patents, and (4) any person that Union Oil has contacted with regard to the possible collection of any fees, royalties or other payments, in cash or in kind, for the practice of the Relevant U.S. Patents.

NOTES

1) A recurrent feature in SSO disclosure / deception cases is the lack of clarity in the patent disclosure policies of SSOs. Do you think SSOs tend to hire bad lawyers? Or can you think of other reasons why patent disclosure rules may often be incompletely described?

2) The remedy in *Unocal* (paragraphs 11–14) seems pretty severe, especially compared to the FTC's intended remedy in *Rambus* (paragraph 16). Under what circumstances do you think that a court ought to impose the *Unocal* remedy rather than the (attempted) *Rambus* one as a response to SSO deception?

3) Is it fair to say that the analysis in *Rambus* presumes that the existence (or not) of a FRAND commitment is immaterial to determining whether monopoly power exists? Do you agree with that premise?

4) Was the FTC's case against Unocal stronger or weaker than its case against Rambus? Why do you think Unocal did not litigate?[858]

5) What counts as deception? Is it enough if the patent holder does not affirmatively disclose an IP right but does not affirmatively deny having any such rights: in that case, is the risk appropriately borne by other participants? What if the patent holder innocently fails to spot that its IP reads on a proposed standard? What if the patent disclosure rules of the SSO are at odds with the participants' actual practices and expectations?[859]

6) At the same time the *Rambus* appeal was pending before the D.C. Circuit, the Commission announced it had reached a settlement with Negotiated Data Solutions (N-Data) to resolve charges that N-Data violated Section 5 of the FTC Act by failing to honor a licensing commitment made by its predecessor company.[860] N-Data acquired patents from National Semiconductor that had been incorporated into the IEEE's standard for "autonegotiation"—a process, used on basically every computer sold in the U.S., that allows Ethernet devices made by different manufacturers to work together. National Semiconductor had committed to IEEE that its relevant patents would be licensed at fair, reasonable and non-discriminatory—so-called "FRAND"—royalty rates. According to the FTC's complaint, even though N-Data was aware of National Semiconductor's agreement with the IEEE when N-Data acquired the patents, N-Data refused to honor it. Under the settlement, N-Data agreed not to enforce its patents without first offering to license its technology according to National Semiconductor's initial IEEE commitment. Unlike in *Rambus*, the FTC pursued the N-Data matter exclusively using the broader standards under Section 5 of the FTC Act rather than invoking the traditional monopolization standards in Section 2 of the Sherman Act. How do you think the allegations against N-Data would have been analyzed under Section 2?

2. Other FRAND Violations

Setting aside cases in which a monopolist gets its IP incorporated into a standard by concealing the existence of intellectual property, some argue that a breach of a FRAND commitment may itself constitute an antitrust problem. To see the core concern, suppose that a monopolist contributes its intellectual property to a standard that it will practice along with its rivals, subject to a FRAND commitment. Then, after the technology is

---

[858] *See generally* Statement of the Federal Trade Commission, *In the Matter of Union Oil Company of California*, Dkt. No. 9305 and *Chevron/Unocal*, File No. 051-0125 (June 10 ,2005) (announcing a vote to accept "two linked consent agreements that resolve both the Commission's monopolization case against Unocal Corporation's subsidiary Union Oil Company of California and any antitrust concerns arising from Chevron Corporation's pending acquisition of Unocal").

[859] *See* D. Bruce Hoffman & Joseph J. Simons, *Known unknowns: Uncertainty and its implication for antitrust policy and enforcement in the standard-setting context*, 57 Antitrust Bull. 89, 101 (2012) ("Where it can be shown that the SSO's participants, in general, expected one another to behave in a way that, although reasonable, is at odds with the formal, written rules of the organization, the expected rule should govern in place of the written one.").

[860] *See* In re Negotiated Data Solutions LLC, File No. 051 0094 (FTC 2008), www. ftc.gov/os/caselist/0510094/index.shtm.

standardized, the monopolist charges an exorbitant royalty, or simply refuses to license, to the surprise and dismay of all.

On the one hand, this sure sounds like the monopolist is engaging in conduct that raises its rivals' costs, violates the FRAND commitment on which the other market participants have relied, and reduces its rivals' ability to compete with its own product monopoly. On the other hand, though, *Rambus v. FTC* (excerpted above) and *NYNEX Corp. v. Discon, Inc.* (which you may remember from Chapter VII), both hold that the evasion of a price cap is not creation of monopoly power for the purposes of antitrust law. And if the monopolist's rivals—who knew perfectly well from the start that a FRAND commitment is an awfully vague thing to trust in—have access to the same remedies in contract to vindicate that FRAND promise, then what's the harm to competition?

Views differ deeply about the merits of theories of competitive harm centering on FRAND violations. The following extracts—two academic and two judicial—give a flavor of some of the debate. In the first two extracts, Makan Delrahim and Herbert Hovenkamp give dueling accounts of the role of antitrust in responding to FRAND violations in the SSO context. In the latter two, the Ninth and Third Circuits adjudicate different claims regarding Qualcomm's participation in various standard-setting organizations: in the FTC case, the Ninth Circuit held that Qualcomm's refusal to grant licenses to rival chip makers—an alleged violation of its FRAND commitments— was not a violation of Section 2. In the case brought by Broadcom regarding separate conduct, the Third Circuit refused to dismiss the claim under Rule 12, explicitly holding that the breach of a "false promise" to license on FRAND terms could constitute unlawful monopolization.

Makan Delrahim, Take It to the Limit: Respecting Innovation Incentives in the Application of Antitrust Law (Nov. 10, 2017)

Antitrust Law Should Not Police FRAND Commitments to SSOs

. . . I respectfully submit that enforcers and courts should be mindful of the proper application of antitrust law to standard setting. There is a growing trend supporting what I would view as a misuse of antitrust or competition law, purportedly motivated by the fear of so-called patent hold-up, to police private commitments that IP holders make in order to be considered for inclusion in a standard. This trend is troublesome. If a patent holder violates its commitments to an SSO, the first and best line of defense, I submit, is the SSO itself and its participants.

These commitments are typically contractual in nature. More specifically, SSOs often impose obligations on IP holders seeking to have their technology evaluated and, if selected, incorporated into a standard to engage in fair, reasonable, and nondiscriminatory licensing of their technology—what we call "FRAND" or "RAND" commitments. Disputes inevitably arise regarding what licensing fees or practices are "reasonable," and "nondiscriminatory," as you would expect with free-market negotiations. We should be most concerned, however, when this dispute involves concerted action, on either side—the implementers or the innovators.

If a patent holder is alleged to have violated a commitment to a standard setting organization, that action may have some impact on competition. But, I respectfully submit, that does not mean the heavy hand of antitrust necessarily is the appropriate remedy for the would-be licensee—or the enforcement agency. There are perfectly adequate and more appropriate common law and statutory remedies available to the SSO or its members. [. . .]

Under the existing statutory scheme, it is not the duty or the proper role of antitrust law to referee what unilateral behavior is reasonable for patent holders in this context. Patent holders make decisions every day about how to exploit their property rights, knowing that the consequence of those actions may be to subject themselves to contractual or other common law liability. The blunt application of antitrust law to such unilateral conduct throws those decisions into disarray, threatening to punish IP holders with onerous penalties that can deter other innovators from taking the necessary R&D investment risk to develop the next great technological leap forward.

More importantly, refraining from imposing antitrust penalties gives teeth to more appropriate common law remedies and allows SSOs to live up to their promise. In a breach of contract action, a party can litigate the facts regarding what constitutes a "reasonable" or "nondiscriminatory" rate or commitment. If there is a violation of a reasonableness standard, the factfinder can decide it, like they do in other instances of contract violations. Antitrust enforcers should exercise greater humility and enforce the antitrust laws in a manner that best promotes dynamic competition for the benefit of consumers.

* * *

Herbert Hovenkamp, FRAND and Antitrust
105 Cornell L. Rev. 1683 (2020)

Although the fact that a patent is FRAND-encumbered does not determine antitrust liability in either direction, it is hardly irrelevant. On the market power question, the fact that a patent has been declared standard essential and subjected to FRAND requirements is certainly important. Depending on the degree of path dependence, a patent may have become essential to practicing a particular standard, or implementers may have invested substantial sunk costs into the technology it covers. In that case, extraction may be more costly than simply paying more, or else the firm may exit from the market. These are all fact questions, but they can weigh heavily in a determination of market power.

We suggest that FRAND status creates a presumption of sufficient market power, which can be defeated by a showing that firms operating under the SSO can find a suitable substitute for the FRAND-encumbered patent in question, readily and at low cost. For example, the presumption would likely be defeated by a finding that firms operating under the standard are not infringers, which is simply another way of saying that the patent has been mis-declared as standard essential. [. . .]

[W]hile violation of a FRAND commitment on a SEP is not necessarily an antitrust violation, two important antitrust requirements, power and anticompetitive effects, can be heavily affected by SEP status. Conditionally refusing to license a FRAND-encumbered patent when the relevant agreement requires licensing is clearly a breach of contract, but it can also be an antitrust violation when these conditions are met.

Conditional dealing is unlawful under the antitrust laws only when both power and anticompetitive effects are shown. Conventionally, the relevant anticompetitive effects are market foreclosure or raising rivals' costs. Here, the primary question is whether the condition made it more costly or impossible for a participating firm to operate on the network. Under the restraint of trade standard of section 1 of the Sherman Act, antitrust harm also includes reduced output and higher prices in output markets. Depending on the facts, the victims could be either excluded rivals; those whose costs have been increased; or else downstream firms, including consumers, forced to pay higher prices.

* * *

One aspect of the *Qualcomm* litigation concerned an allegation that Qualcomm had engaged in a non-deceptive FRAND violation. The FTC argued that Qualcomm's FRAND commitments to various SSOs—governing SEPs practiced by other chip makers and device makers alike—required that Qualcomm grant licenses to other chip-makers, rather than only to device manufacturers (original equipment manufacturers, or "OEMs"), and that its failure to license other chip-makers was anticompetitive. Qualcomm denied any such duty, pointed out that it had committed not to sue any other chip-makers, and it preferred to license only at the device level of the supply chain. The Ninth Circuit agreed with Qualcomm, distinguishing the Third Circuit's earlier decision in *Broadcom v. Qualcomm*. Take look at both opinions.

FTC v. Qualcomm Inc.
969 F.3d 974 (9th Cir. 2020)

Judge Callahan.

[1] Qualcomm's competitors in the modem chip markets contend that Qualcomm's business practices, in particular its refusal to license them, have hampered or slowed their ability to develop and retain OEM customer bases, limited their growth, delayed or prevented their entry into the market, and in some cases forced them out of the market entirely. These competitors contend that this result is not just anticompetitive, but a violation of Qualcomm's contractual commitments to two cellular SSOs—the Telecommunications Industry Association

("TIA") and Alliance for Telecommunications Industry Solutions ("ATIS")—to license its SEPs "to all applicants" on FRAND terms. Qualcomm argues that it has no antitrust duty to deal with its rivals, and in any case OEM-level licensing is consistent with Qualcomm's SSO commitments because only OEM products (i.e., cellphones, tablets, etc.) "practice" or "implement" the standards embodied in Qualcomm's SEPs. Furthermore, Qualcomm argues that it substantially complies with the TIA and ATIS requirements by not asserting its patents against rival chipmakers. [. . .]

[2] [T]he FTC contends that this court may . . . hold that Qualcomm engaged in anticompetitive conduct in violation of § 2. This is so, the FTC urges, because (1) Qualcomm entered into a voluntary contractual commitment to deal with its rivals as part of the SSO process, which is itself a derogation from normal market competition, and (2) Qualcomm's breach of this contractual commitment satisfies traditional Section 2 standards in that it tends to impair the opportunities of rivals and does not further competition on the merits. We disagree.

[3] Even if the district court is correct that Qualcomm is contractually obligated via its SSO commitments to license rival chip suppliers—a conclusion we need not and do not reach—the FTC still does not satisfactorily explain how Qualcomm's alleged breach of this contractual commitment itself impairs the opportunities of rivals. It argues the breach facilitates Qualcomm's collection of a surcharge from rivals' customers. But this refers to a distinct business practice, licensing royalties, and alleged harm to OEMs, not rival chipmakers. In any case, Qualcomm's royalties are "chip-supplier neutral" because Qualcomm collects them from all OEMs that license its patents, not just "rivals' customers." The FTC argues that Qualcomm's breach directly impacts rivals by otherwise deterring their entry and investment. But this ignores that [Qualcomm allows competing chip makers] to practice Qualcomm's SEPs (royalty-free) before selling their chips to downstream OEMs. Furthermore, in order to make out a § 2 violation, the anticompetitive harm identified must be to competition itself, not merely to competitors. The FTC identifies no such harm to competition.

[4] The FTC's conclusion that OEM-level licensing does not further competition on the merits is not only belied by MediaTek and Intel's entries into the modem chip markets in the 2015–2016 timeframe, it also gives inadequate weight to Qualcomm's reasonable, procompetitive justification that licensing at the OEM and chip-supplier levels simultaneously would require the company to engage in "multi-level licensing," leading to inefficiencies and less profit. Qualcomm's procompetitive justification is supported by at least two other companies—Nokia and Dolby—with similar SEP portfolios to Qualcomm's. More critically, this part of the FTC's argument skips ahead to an examination of Qualcomm's procompetitive justifications, failing to recognize that the burden does not shift to Qualcomm to provide such justifications unless and until the FTC meets its initial burden of proving anticompetitive harm. Because the FTC has not met its initial burden under the rule of reason framework, we are less critical of Qualcomm's procompetitive justifications for its OEM-level licensing policy—which, in any case, appear to be reasonable and consistent with current industry practice.

[5] The FTC points to one case, *Broadcom Corp. v. Qualcomm Inc.*, 501 F.3d 297 (3rd Cir. 2007), as support for its argument that a company's breach of its SSO commitments may rise to the level of an antitrust violation. But in that earlier antitrust action against Qualcomm, the alleged anticompetitive conduct was not Qualcomm's practice of licensing at the OEM level while not enforcing its patents against rival chip suppliers; instead, Broadcom asserted that Qualcomm intentionally deceived SSOs by inducing them to standardize one of its patented technologies, which it then licensed at "discriminatorily higher" royalty rates to competitors and customers using non-Qualcomm chipsets. The Broadcom court held that Qualcomm's intentionally false promise to license [its SEP] on FRAND terms coupled with an SDO's reliance on that promise and Qualcomm's subsequent discriminatory pricing sufficiently alleged actionable anticompetitive conduct under § 2 to overcome Qualcomm's motion to dismiss.

[6] Here, the district court found neither intentional deception of SSOs on the part of Qualcomm nor that Qualcomm charged discriminatorily higher royalty rates to competitors and OEM customers using non-Qualcomm chips. Instead, it is undisputed that Qualcomm's current royalty rates—which the district court found "unreasonably high" . . . —are based on the patent portfolio chosen by the OEM customer regardless of where the OEM sources its chips. Furthermore, competing chip suppliers are permitted to practice Qualcomm's SEPs freely without paying any royalties at all. Thus, the Third Circuit's "intentional deception" exception to the general rule that breaches of SSO commitments do not give rise to antitrust liability does not apply to this case.

[7] Finally, we note the persuasive policy arguments of several academics and practitioners with significant experience in SSOs, FRAND, and antitrust enforcement, who have expressed caution about using the antitrust laws to remedy what are essentially contractual disputes between private parties engaged in the pursuit of technological innovation. The Honorable Paul R. Michel, retired Chief Judge of the Court of Appeals for the Federal Circuit, argues that it would be a mistake to use the hammer of antitrust law to resolve FRAND disputes when more precise scalpels of contract and patent law are effective. Judge Michel notes that while antitrust policy has its place as a policy lever to enhance market competition, the rules of contract and patent law are better equipped to handle commercial disputes between the world's most sophisticated companies about FRAND agreements. Echoing this sentiment, a former FTC Commissioner, Joshua Wright, argues that the antitrust laws are not well suited to govern contract disputes between private parties in light of remedies available under contract or patent law, and that imposing antitrust remedies in pure contract disputes can have harmful effects in terms of dampening incentives to participate in standard-setting bodies and to commercialize innovation.

[8] In short, we are not persuaded by the FTC's argument that we should adopt an additional exception, beyond the *Aspen Skiing* exception that the FTC concedes does not apply here, to the general rule that businesses are free to choose the parties with whom they will deal, as well as the prices, terms, and conditions of that dealing. We therefore decline to hold that Qualcomm's alleged breach of its SSO commitments to license its SEPs on FRAND terms, even assuming there was a breach, amounted to anticompetitive conduct in violation of § 2. [. . .]

[9] [A further] problem with the district court's "unreasonable royalty rate" conclusion is that it erroneously assumes that royalties are "anticompetitive"—in the antitrust sense—unless they precisely reflect a patent's current, intrinsic value and are in line with the rates other companies charge for their own patent portfolios. Neither the district court nor the FTC provides any case law to support this proposition, which sounds in patent law, not antitrust law. See 35 U.S.C. § 284 (entitling a patent owner to "damages adequate to compensate for the infringement, but in no event less than a *reasonable royalty* for the use made of the invention by the infringer" (emphasis added)). We decline to adopt a theory of antitrust liability that would presume anticompetitive conduct any time a company could not prove that the "fair value" of its SEP portfolios corresponds to the prices the market appears willing to pay for those SEPs in the form of licensing royalty rates.

* * *

Broadcom Corp. v. Qualcomm Inc.

501 F.3d 297 (3d Cir. 2007)

Judge Barry.

[1] [Broadcom's] Complaint alleged that Qualcomm induced the [European Telecommunications Standards Institute ("ETSI")] and other SDOs to include its proprietary technology in the UMTS standard by falsely agreeing to abide by the SDOs' policies on [intellectual property rights ("IPRs")], but then breached those agreements by licensing its technology on non-FRAND terms. The intentional acquisition of monopoly power through deception of an SDO, Broadcom posits, violates antitrust law.

[2] The Complaint also alleged that Qualcomm ignored its FRAND commitment to the ETSI and other SDOs by demanding discriminatorily higher (i.e., non-FRAND) royalties from competitors and customers using chipsets not manufactured by Qualcomm. Qualcomm, the Complaint continued, has a 90% share in the market for CDMA-path chipsets, and by withholding favorable pricing in that market, coerced cellular telephone manufacturers to purchase only Qualcomm-manufactured UMTS-path chipsets. These actions are alleged to be part of Qualcomm's effort to obtain a monopoly in the UMTS chipset market because it views competition in that market as a long-term threat to its existing monopolies in CDMA technology. [. . .]

[3] . . . [W]e must determine whether Broadcom has stated actionable anticompetitive conduct with allegations that Qualcomm deceived relevant SDOs into adopting the UMTS standard by committing to license [certain relevant] technology on FRAND terms and, later, after lock-in occurred, demanding non-FRAND royalties. As Qualcomm is at pains to point out, no court nor agency has decided this precise question and, in that sense, our decision will break new ground. The authorities we have cited in our lengthy discussion that has preceded this

point, however, decidedly favor a finding that Broadcom's allegations, if accepted as true, describe actionable anticompetitive conduct.

[4] To guard against anticompetitive patent hold-up, most SDOs require firms supplying essential technologies for inclusion in a prospective standard to commit to licensing their technologies on FRAND terms. (E.g., IEEE Br. 9 & n. 13 (stating that under IEEE bylaws, the absence of irrevocable FRAND assurances will preclude approval of standards known to incorporate essential, proprietary technologies).) A firm's FRAND commitment, therefore, is a factor—and an important factor—that the SDO will consider in evaluating the suitability of a given proprietary technology vis-a-vis competing technologies.

[5] The FRAND commitment, or lack thereof, is, moreover, a key indicator of the cost of implementing a potential technology. During the critical competitive period that precedes adoption of a standard, technologies compete in discrete areas, such as cost and performance characteristics. Misrepresentations concerning the cost of implementing a given technology may confer an unfair advantage and bias the competitive process in favor of that technology's inclusion in the standard.

[6] A standard, by definition, eliminates alternative technologies. When a patented technology is incorporated in a standard, adoption of the standard eliminates alternatives to the patented technology. Although a patent confers a lawful monopoly over the claimed invention, its value is limited when alternative technologies exist. That value becomes significantly enhanced, however, after the patent is incorporated in a standard. Firms may become locked in to a standard requiring the use of a competitor's patented technology. The patent holder's IPRs, if unconstrained, may permit it to demand supracompetitive royalties. It is in such circumstances that measures such as FRAND commitments become important safeguards against monopoly power.

[7] We hold that (1) in a consensus-oriented private standard-setting environment, (2) a patent holder's intentionally false promise to license essential proprietary technology on FRAND terms, (3) coupled with an SDO's reliance on that promise when including the technology in a standard, and (4) the patent holder's subsequent breach of that promise, is actionable anticompetitive conduct. This holding follows directly from established principles of antitrust law and represents the emerging view of enforcement authorities and commentators, alike. Deception in a consensus-driven private standard-setting environment harms the competitive process by obscuring the costs of including proprietary technology in a standard and increasing the likelihood that patent rights will confer monopoly power on the patent holder. Deceptive FRAND commitments, no less than deceptive nondisclosure of IPRs, may result in such harm.

[8] . . . Having now held that a firm's deceptive FRAND commitment to an SDO may constitute actionable anticompetitive conduct, we conclude quickly and easily that Claim 1 states a claim for monopolization under § 2 of the Sherman Act. [. . .]

[9] [T]he Complaint . . adequately alleged that Qualcomm obtained and maintained its market power willfully, and not as a consequence of a superior product, business acumen, or historic accident. Qualcomm excluded competition and refused to compete on the merits. As discussed above, the alleged anticompetitive conduct was the intentional false promise that Qualcomm would license its [relevant] technology on FRAND terms, on which promise the relevant SDOs relied in choosing the [relevant] technology for inclusion in the UMTS standard, followed by Qualcomm's insistence on non-FRAND licensing terms. Qualcomm's deceptive conduct induced relevant SDOs to incorporate a technology into the UMTS standard that they would not have considered absent a FRAND commitment. Although the Complaint did not specifically allege that Qualcomm made its false statements in a consensus-oriented environment . . . this omission is not fatal in light of allegations that FRAND assurances were required, as well as allegations concerning the SDOs' reliance on Qualcomm's assurances. Together, these allegations satisfy the second element of a § 2 claim. [. . .]

[10] A firm is generally under no obligation to cooperate with its rivals. . . . Here . . . Qualcomm is alleged to have actively marketed its . . . technology for inclusion in an industry-wide standard, and to have voluntarily agreed to license that technology on FRAND terms. We note, albeit in passing, that the Court in [*Trinko*] pointed as well to the extensive regulatory framework that created oversight functions and remedies that the antitrust laws were unsuited to augment. No such regulatory framework exists here.

NOTES

1) When, if ever, should antitrust liability result from the violation of a FRAND commitment?

2) Should the antitrust analysis of FRAND violations ever distinguish based on whether the promise, or the subsequent conduct, was in "good faith"? What would "good faith" mean for this purpose?

3) When should conduct that would otherwise be an antitrust violation be treated differently because of the availability of another cause of action (*e.g.*, contract or tort)? When might the entities with those remedies and the entities who are injured be different?

4) Many innovators have vast patent portfolios with many thousands of patents. How could, or should, a court determine the FRAND value of such a portfolio?

3. SSO Manipulation

Finally, some SSO activities may raise antitrust concerns based on alleged capture or manipulation of the process. Courts, including the Supreme Court, have been willing to impose antitrust liability when such conduct has turned the SSO into a vehicle for collusion or exclusion. However, because *all* SSO activity involves competitor collaboration, and involves the selection of some technologies at the expense of others, it can be challenging to be sure that concerns about collusion and exclusion are well founded.

A trio of famous Supreme Court cases—*Radiant Burners, Hydrolevel, and Allied Tube*—frame the landscape for antitrust claims alleging SSO manipulation. We will meet them in turn. In *Radiant Burners*, the plaintiff alleged that the SSO was going beyond establishing voluntary standards and was engaging in an unwarranted group boycott—a coordinated refusal to deal—that foreclosed the plaintiff's access to customers. In *Hydrolevel*, the plaintiff alleged that the defendant SSO had been effectively commandeered by a competitor in order to declare the plaintiff's product baselessly unsafe. And in *Allied Tube* the plaintiff alleged that the SSO process had been "stacked" in order to elicit an anticompetitive outcome.

Radiant Burners, Inc. v. Peoples Gas Light & Coke Co.

364 U.S. 656 (1961)

Per curiam.

[1] The question here is whether petitioner's complaint stated a claim upon which relief could be granted. Petitioner is engaged at Lombard, Illinois, in the manufacture and sale in interstate commerce of a ceramic gas burner, known as the "Radiant Burner," for the heating of houses and other buildings. Claiming that American Gas Association, Inc. (AGA), a membership corporation doing business in the Northern District of Illinois and in other States, and 10 of its numerous members[1] who also are doing business in the Northern District of Illinois, combined and conspired to restrain interstate commerce in the manufacture, sale and use of gas burners in violation of s 1 of the Sherman Act, petitioner brought this action against those parties for treble damages and an injunction in the United States District Court for the Northern District of Illinois.

[2] The complaint included the following allegations: American Gas Association operates testing laboratories wherein it purports to determine the safety, utility and durability of gas burners. It has adopted a seal of approval which it affixes on such gas burners as it determines have passed its tests. Its tests are not based on objective standards, but are influenced by respondents, some of whom are in competition with petitioner, and thus its determinations can be made arbitrarily and capriciously. Petitioner has twice submitted its Radiant Burner to AGA for approval but it has not been approved, although it is safer and more efficient than, and just as durable as, gas burners which AGA has approved. Because AGA and its . . . members, . . . effectuate the plan and purpose of the unlawful combination and conspiracy alleged herein by refusing to provide gas for use in the plaintiff's

---

[1] Of the 10 members of AGA who were joined with it as defendants, two are public utilities engaged in the distribution of gas in the Northern District of Illinois, namely, The Peoples Gas Light & Coke Company and Northern Illinois Gas Company; two are pipeline companies engaged in transporting natural gas in interstate commerce into the Northern District of Illinois, namely, Natural Gas Pipeline of America and Texas-Illinois Natural Gas Co.; the other six are manufacturers of gas burners, namely, Autogas Company, Crown Stove Works, Florence Stove Company, Gas Appliance Service, Inc., Norge Sales Corporation, and Sellers Engineering Company.

Radiant Burner(s) which are not approved by AGA, petitioner's gas burners have been effectively excluded from the market, as its potential customers will not buy gas burners for which they cannot obtain gas, and in consequence petitioner has suffered and is suffering the loss of substantial profits.

[3] Respondents moved to dismiss for failure of the complaint to state a claim upon which relief could be granted. . . .

[4] We think the decision of the Court of Appeals does not accord with our recent decision in Klor's, Inc. v. Broadway-Hale Stores, 359 U.S. 207 [(1959) (condemning as *per se* illegal a purported group boycott) {*Eds.: see supra § V.B.3.*}]. The allegation in the complaint that AGA and its Utility members, including Peoples and Northern, effectuate the plan and purpose of the unlawful combination and conspiracy by refusing to provide gas for use in the plaintiff's Radiant Burners because they are not approved by AGA clearly shows one type of trade restraint and public harm the Sherman Act forbids. It is obvious that petitioner cannot sell its gas burners, whatever may be their virtues, if, because of the alleged conspiracy, the purchasers cannot buy gas for use in those burners. The conspiratorial refusal to provide gas for use in the plaintiff's Radiant Burners because they are not approved by AGA therefore falls within one of the classes of restraints which from their nature or character are unduly restrictive, and hence forbidden by both the common law and the statute.

CASENOTE: American Society of Mechanical Engineers, Inc. v. Hydrolevel Corp.
456 U.S. 556 (1982)

Hydrolevel presents a striking example of SSO misuse. In that case, McDonnell & Miller, Inc. ("M&M"), had long dominated the market for a certain type of boiler component: "low-water fuel cutoffs," which switched off a boiler when the water level dropped too low. But after decades of incumbency, a new entrant, Hydrolevel, appeared with an improved fuel cutoff: one which, unlike M&M's product, included a novel time-delay function which prevented the cutoff from firing prematurely. In 1971, Hydrolevel won a key customer away from M&M.

M&M decided to respond to this competitive threat: not in the marketplace, but through its own deep involvement in the American Society of Mechanical Engineers ("ASME"). ASME was a nonprofit trade society of the mechanical engineering profession, with more than 90,000 members, responsible for promulgating more than 400 codes and standards that were frequently incorporated by reference into the laws of many states and the ordinances of major cities. One of ASME's codes was the Boiler and Pressure Vessel Code, which had been adopted as law by no fewer than 46 states. An M&M employee, John James, was vice-chair of the subcommittee responsible for drafting those portions of the code relating to low-water fuel cutoffs. In another cozy detail, the chair of the subcommittee, T.R. Hardin, worked for a firm controlled by IT&T, which was soon to acquire M&M.

James and other M&M employees met with Hardin and cooked up a plan. M&M would send a letter to ASME asking whether a fuel cutoff that used a time delay was compliant with ASME's code. In the ordinary course, this letter would be referred to Hardin to draft a response, which could be sent as unofficial correspondence to avoid any need to refer it to the broader subcommittee. The reply drafted by Hardin, of course, would interpret the Code to prohibit the use of time delays—and that letter, in turn, could be used to deter M&M's customers from dealing with Hydrolevel.

The plan worked as intended. Hydrolevel was forced to sell its assets for liquidation value—but not before filing suit under Sections 1 and 2 against the successor to M&M and ASME itself.

Justice Blackmun's opinion for the Court emphasized that "a standard-setting organization like ASME can be rife with opportunities for anticompetitive activity. . . Although, undoubtedly, most [members] serve ASME without concern for the interests of their corporate employers, some may well view their positions with ASME, at least in part, as an opportunity to benefit their employers." And the "great influence of ASME's reputation" created an opportunity for anticompetitive manipulation. Here, M&M had inappropriately "use[d] ASME's reputation to hinder Hydrolevel's competitive threat."

Liability was appropriate not just for the successor to M&M, but also for ASME itself, as long as ASME's agents had acted with the apparent authority (*i.e.*, the reasonable appearance of agency authority) of ASME itself. The

Court underscored the importance of the resulting incentives: if ASME was made to answer for the conduct of agents with apparent authority, "it is much more likely that similar antitrust violations will not occur in the future. Pressure will be brought on the organization to see to it that its agents abide by the law. Only ASME can take systematic steps to make improper conduct on the part of all its agents unlikely, and the possibility of civil liability will inevitably be a powerful incentive for ASME to take those steps. Thus, a rule that imposes liability on the standard-setting organization—which is best situated to prevent antitrust violations through the abuse of its reputation—is most faithful to the congressional intent that the private right of action deter antitrust violations."

With the great power of a standard-setting organization came great responsibility. "When ASME's agents act in its name, they are able to affect the lives of large numbers of people and the competitive fortunes of businesses throughout the country. By holding ASME liable under the antitrust laws for the antitrust violations of its agents committed with apparent authority, we recognize the important role of ASME and its agents in the economy, and we help to ensure that standard-setting organizations will act with care when they permit their agents to speak for them. We thus make it less likely that competitive challengers like Hydrolevel will be hindered by agents of organizations like ASME in the future."

Allied Tube & Conduit Corp. v. Indian Head, Inc.
486 U.S. 492 (1988)

Justice Brennan.

[1] The National Fire Protection Association (Association) is a private, voluntary organization with more than 31,500 individual and group members representing industry, labor, academia, insurers, organized medicine, firefighters, and government. The Association, among other things, publishes product standards and codes related to fire protection through a process known as "consensus standard making." One of the codes it publishes is the National Electrical Code (Code), which establishes product and performance requirements for the design and installation of electrical wiring systems. Revised every three years, the Code is the most influential electrical code in the nation. A substantial number of state and local governments routinely adopt the Code into law with little or no change; private certification laboratories, such as Underwriters Laboratories, normally will not list and label an electrical product that does not meet Code standards; many underwriters will refuse to insure structures that are not built in conformity with the Code; and many electrical inspectors, contractors, and distributors will not use a product that falls outside the Code.

[2] Among the electrical products covered by the Code is electrical conduit, the hollow tubing used as a raceway to carry electrical wires through the walls and floors of buildings. Throughout the relevant period, the Code permitted using electrical conduit made of steel, and almost all conduit sold was in fact steel conduit. Starting in 1980, respondent began to offer plastic conduit made of polyvinyl chloride. Respondent claims its plastic conduit offers significant competitive advantages over steel conduit, including pliability, lower installed cost, and lower susceptibility to short circuiting. In 1980, however, there was also a scientific basis for concern that, during fires in high-rise buildings, polyvinyl chloride conduit might burn and emit toxic fumes.

[3] Respondent initiated a proposal to include polyvinyl chloride conduit as an approved type of electrical conduit in the 1981 edition of the Code. Following approval by one of the Association's professional panels, this proposal was scheduled for consideration at the 1980 annual meeting, where it could be adopted or rejected by a simple majority of the members present. Alarmed that, if approved, respondent's product might pose a competitive threat to steel conduit, petitioner, the Nation's largest producer of steel conduit, met to plan strategy with, among others, members of the steel industry, other steel conduit manufacturers, and its independent sales agents. They collectively agreed to exclude respondent's product from the 1981 Code by packing the upcoming annual meeting with new Association members whose only function would be to vote against the polyvinyl chloride proposal.

[4] Combined, the steel interests recruited 230 persons to join the Association and to attend the annual meeting to vote against the proposal. Petitioner alone recruited 155 persons—including employees, executives, sales agents, the agents' employees, employees from two divisions that did not sell electrical products, and the wife of a national sales director. Petitioner and the other steel interests also paid over $100,000 for the membership, registration,

and attendance expenses of these voters. At the annual meeting, the steel group voters were instructed where to sit and how and when to vote by group leaders who used walkie-talkies and hand signals to facilitate communication. Few of the steel group voters had any of the technical documentation necessary to follow the meeting. None of them spoke at the meeting to give their reasons for opposing the proposal to approve polyvinyl chloride conduit. Nonetheless, with their solid vote in opposition, the proposal was rejected and returned to committee by a vote of 394 to 390. Respondent appealed the membership's vote to the Association's Board of Directors, but the Board denied the appeal on the ground that, although the Association's rules had been circumvented, they had not been violated.

[5] In October 1981, respondent brought this suit in Federal District Court, alleging that petitioner and others had unreasonably restrained trade in the electrical conduit market in violation of § 1 of the Sherman Act. [. . .]

[6] In this case, the restraint of trade on which liability was predicated was the Association's exclusion of respondent's product from the Code, and no damages were imposed for the incorporation of that Code by any government. The relevant context is thus the standard-setting process of a private association. Typically, private standard-setting associations, like the Association in this case, include members having horizontal and vertical business relations. There is no doubt that the members of such associations often have economic incentives to restrain competition and that the product standards set by such associations have a serious potential for anticompetitive harm. Agreement on a product standard is, after all, implicitly an agreement not to manufacture, distribute, or purchase certain types of products. Accordingly, private standard-setting associations have traditionally been objects of antitrust scrutiny. When, however, private associations promulgate safety standards based on the merits of objective expert judgments and through procedures that prevent the standard-setting process from being biased by members with economic interests in stifling product competition, those private standards can have significant procompetitive advantages. It is this potential for procompetitive benefits that has led most lower courts to apply rule-of-reason analysis to product standard-setting by private associations. [. . .]

[7] Although we do not here set forth the rules of antitrust liability governing the private standard-setting process, we hold that at least where, as here, an economically interested party exercises decision-making authority in formulating a product standard for a private association that comprises market participants, that party enjoys no *Noerr* immunity [*i.e.*, immunity for conduct that amounts to petitioning the government] from any antitrust liability flowing from the effect the standard has of its own force in the marketplace.

[8] This conclusion does not deprive state and local governments of input and information from interested individuals or organizations or leave petitioner without ample means to petition those governments. Petitioner, and others concerned about the safety or competitive threat of polyvinyl chloride conduit, can, with full antitrust immunity, engage in concerted efforts to influence those governments through direct lobbying, publicity campaigns, and other traditional avenues of political expression. To the extent state and local governments are more difficult to persuade through these other avenues, that no doubt reflects their preference for and confidence in the nonpartisan consensus process that petitioner has undermined. Petitioner remains free to take advantage of the forum provided by the standard-setting process by presenting and vigorously arguing accurate scientific evidence before a nonpartisan private standard-setting body. And petitioner can avoid the strictures of the private standard-setting process by attempting to influence legislatures through other forums. What petitioner may not do (without exposing itself to possible antitrust liability for direct injuries) is bias the process by, as in this case, stacking the private standard-setting body with decisionmakers sharing their economic interest in restraining competition.

Justice White, with whom Justice O'Connor joins, dissenting.

[9] [. . .] The Court's decision is unfortunate . . . . There are now over 400 private organizations preparing and publishing an enormous variety of codes and standards. State and local governments necessarily, and as a matter of course, turn to these proposed codes in the process of legislating to further the health and safety of their citizens. The code that is at issue in this case, for example, was adopted verbatim by 25 States and the District of Columbia; 19 others adopted it with only minor changes. It is the most widely disseminated and adopted model code in the world today. There is no doubt that the work of these private organizations contributes enormously to the public interest and that participation in their work by those who have the technical competence and experience to do so should not be discouraged.

[10] The Court's decision today will surely do just that. It must inevitably be the case that codes such as the NEC will set standards that some products cannot satisfy and hence in the name of health and safety will reduce or prevent competition, as was the case here. Yet, putative competitors of the producer of such products will now think twice before urging in the course of the code-making process that those products not be approved; for if they are successful (or even if they are not), they may well become antitrust defendants facing treble-damages liability unless they can prove to a court and a jury that they had no evil motives but were merely presenting and vigorously arguing accurate scientific evidence before a nonpartisan private standard-setting body. In this case, for example, even if Allied had not resorted to the tactics it employed, but had done no more than successfully argue in good faith the hazards of using respondent's products, it would have inflicted the same damage on respondent and would have risked facing the same antitrust suit, with a jury ultimately deciding the health and safety implications of the products at issue.

[11] The Court's suggestion that its decision will not affect the ability of these organizations to assist state and local governments is surely wrong. The Court's holding is that at least where, as here, an economically interested party exercises decisionmaking authority in formulating a product standard for a private association that comprises market participants, that party enjoys no *Noerr* immunity from any antitrust liability flowing from the effects the standard has of its own force in the marketplace. This description encompasses the structure and work of all such organizations as we now know them. The Court is saying, in effect, that where a private organization sets standards, the participants can be sued under the antitrust laws for any effects those standards have in the marketplace other than those flowing from their adoption into law. But the standards will have some effect in the marketplace even where they are also adopted into law, through publicity and other means, thus exposing the participants to liability. Henceforth, therefore, any private organization offers such standards at its peril, and without any of the breathing room enjoyed by other participants in the political process.

[12] The alternative apparently envisioned by the Court is that an organization can gain the protection of the *Noerr* doctrine as long as nobody with any economic interest in the product is permitted to exercise decisionmaking authority (i.e., vote) on its recommendations as to particular product standards. Insisting that organizations like the NFPA conduct themselves like courts of law will have perverse effects. Legislatures are willing to rely on such organizations precisely because their standards are being set by those who possess an expert understanding of the products and their uses, which are primarily if not entirely those who design, manufacture, sell, and distribute them. Sanitizing such bodies by discouraging the active participation of those with economic interests in the subject matter undermines their utility.

[13] I fear that exposing organizations like the NFPA to antitrust liability will impair their usefulness by inhibiting frank and open discussion of the health and safety characteristics of new or old products that will be affected by their codes. The Court focuses on the tactics of petitioner that are thought to have subverted the entire process. But it is not suggested that if there are abuses, they are anything more than occasional happenings. The Court does speculate about the terrible practices that applying *Noerr* in this context could lead us to condone in future cases, but these are no more than fantasies, since nothing of the sort occurred in the wake of *Noerr* itself. It seems to me that today's decision is therefore an unfortunate case of overkill.

NOTES

1) In *Allied Tube* the Court held that private SSOs should not be treated as governmental entities for the purposes of *Noerr-Pennington* petitioning immunity, even when they are in practice closely related to government action. In what circumstances or settings do you think that holding could do most harm?

2) Suppose that an SSO includes both implementers (*i.e.*, patent-practicing entities) and innovators (*i.e.*, patent-holding entities). What rules might you create to protect against collusion? What about to protect against exclusion? Do you think implementers or innovators are better situated to abuse the standard-setting process?

3) Do the trio of Supreme Court cases above suggest that antitrust courts should evaluate whether an SSO has a "biased" process? How could it measure this in practice?

4) Is every SSO a group boycott waiting to be sued?

5) We have addressed a number of cases in which IP owners have acted to harmed implementers of standardized technology. Are there also risks when SSO members may act collectively to disadvantage IP owners? What if

an SSO's rules only allow the standardization of technologies that are licensed royalty-free? Is that a procompetitive collaboration, a *per se* illegal buyer cartel, or something else?

E. Some Further Reading

Rebecca S. Eisenberg & Daniel A. Crane, *Patent Punting: How FDA and Antitrust Courts Undermine the Hatch-Waxman Act to Avoid Dealing with Patents*, 21 Mich. Telecomm. & Tech. L. Rev. 197 (2015)

Robin Feldman, *Patent and Antitrust: Differing Shades of Meaning*, 13 Va. J.L. & Tech. 5 (2008)

Robin Feldman & W. Nicholson Price II, *Patent Trolling: Why Bio & Pharmaceuticals Are at Risk*, 17 Stan. Tech. L. Rev. 773 (2014)

FTC, PATENT ASSERTION ENTITY ACTIVITY: AN FTC STUDY (Oct. 2016)

FTC, GENERIC DRUG ENTRY PRIOR TO PATENT EXPIRATION: AN FTC STUDY (July 2002)

C. Scott Hemphill, *Intellectual Property and Competition Law*, in Rochelle C. Dreyfuss & Justine Pila (eds.), OXFORD HANDBOOK OF INTELLECTUAL PROPERTY LAW (2017)

Herbert Hovenkamp, Mark D. Janis, Mark A. Lemley, Christopher R. Leslie & Michael A. Carrier, IP AND ANTITRUST: AN ANALYSIS OF ANTITRUST PRINCIPLES APPLIED TO INTELLECTUAL PROPERTY LAW (2021)

Keith N. Hylton & Wendy Xu, *Error Costs, Ratio Tests, and Patent Antitrust Law*, 56 Rev. Indus. Org. 563 (2020)

Noah Joshua Phillips, *IP and Antitrust Laws: Promoting Innovation in a High-Tech Economy* (remarks of Mar. 20, 2019)

Rebecca Kelly Slaughter, *SEPs, Antitrust, and the FTC* (remarks of Oct. 29, 2021)

Christopher Jon Sprigman, *The Intersection of Patent and Antitrust Law* in Einer Elhauge (ed.), RESEARCH HANDBOOK ON THE ECONOMICS OF ANTITRUST LAW (2012)

U.S. Department of Justice & FTC, ANTITRUST ENFORCEMENT AND INTELLECTUAL PROPERTY RIGHTS: PROMOTING INNOVATION AND COMPETITION (April 2007)

U.S. Dept. of Justice and FTC, ANTITRUST GUIDELINES FOR THE LICENSING OF INTELLECTUAL PROPERTY (2017)

XI. GOVERNMENT ENFORCEMENT

A. Overview

At the forefront of antitrust enforcement in the United States are the two federal antitrust agencies: the Federal Trade Commission and the U.S. Department of Justice. At the FTC, the Bureau of Competition (often "BC" or "the Bureau" in antitrust-speak) handles most antitrust enforcement work, with support from the Bureau of Economics, while DOJ's antitrust enforcement is housed in the Antitrust Division (often "ATR" or "the Division"). These two agencies bring many of the United States's most complex and important antitrust cases, handle the vast majority of the nation's merger and conduct government-enforcement workload, and play a critical role in developing antitrust policy and doctrine. In addition to the federal enforcers, the 50 states—along with the District of Columbia, Guam, and Puerto Rico—play an important role in detecting and combating antitrust violations.

This Chapter takes a look at these government enforcers and some aspects of their operation and relationships. Sections B and C introduce the nation's two federal antitrust enforcers in turn. Section D explores the unusual fact that we have two antitrust enforcers rather than one, and considers some of the implications (and the resulting litigation). Section E completes our examination of the federal institutions with a look at the Hart-Scott-Rodino ("HSR") Act, which structures the merger review process that represents the majority of each agency's civil workload. In Section F, we will briefly meet the state Attorneys-General, an important additional source of antitrust enforcement authority in the United States. Finally, in Section G, we will turn to antitrust remedies in the context of government enforcement, as we examine the injunctive relief that constitutes the usual remedy in government antitrust cases. In the next Chapter we will complete our survey of remedies when we consider damages: although the Justice Department and the states can sue for damages under the Sherman Act, on behalf of the federal government and state citizens respectively, damages are primarily important in connection with private litigation. (We will touch briefly on government damages and private injunctions in Chapter XII.)

B. The Federal Trade Commission

The Federal Trade Commission is an independent and bipartisan administrative agency, created in 1914 by the Federal Trade Commission Act. The FTC was created to augment the federal government's powers of economic regulation and to supplement the Department of Justice's existing antitrust jurisdiction.[861]

1. Structure and Organization

The FTC is overseen by a Commission of five Commissioners serving staggered seven-year terms, of whom no more than three may come from one political party, and each of whom is nominated by the President and confirmed by the Senate.[862] One Commissioner is designated by the President to serve as Chair of the agency. The President may remove a Commissioner only for cause—specifically for "inefficiency, neglect of duty, or malfeasance in office"—an arrangement that the Supreme Court authorized as consistent with the constitutional balance of institutional powers in its *Humphrey's Executor* decision in 1935. The case is notable for the unusual facts

---

[861] *See, e.g.*, Marc Winerman & William E. Kovacic, *The William Humphrey and Abram Myers Years: The FRC from 1925 to 1929*, 77 Antitrust L.J. 701 (2011); Marc Winerman & William E. Kovacic, *Outpost Years for a Start-Up Agency: The FTC from 1921–1925*, 77 Antitrust L.J. 145 (2010); Gerald Berk, LOUIS D. BRANDEIS AND THE MAKING OF REGULATED COMPETITION, 1900–1932 (2009); Marc Winerman, *The Origins of the Federal Trade Commission: Concentration, Cooperation, Control, and Competition*, 71 Antitrust L.J. 1 (2003); ABA, REPORT OF THE AMERICAN BAR ASSOCIATION SECTION OF ANTITRUST LAW SPECIAL COMMITTEE TO STUDY THE ROLE OF THE FEDERAL TRADE COMMISSION, *reprinted at* 59 Antitrust L. J. 43 (1989); James C. Lang, *The Legislative History of the Federal Trade Commission Act*, 13 Washburn L.J. 6 (1974); Richard A. Posner, *The Federal Trade Commission*, 37 U. Chi. L. Rev. 47 (1969); ABA, REPORT OF THE ABA COMMISSION TO STUDY THE FEDERAL TRADE COMMISSION (1969); George Rublee, *The Original Plan and Early History of the Federal Trade Commission*, 11 Proc. Academy of Pol. Sci. in the City of N.Y. 114 (1926).

[862] 15 U.S.C. § 41.

that gave rise to litigation, for its distinctive picture of the FTC's function and powers, and for its status as a magnet for criticism.[863]

Humphrey's Executor v. United States
295 U.S. 602 (1935)

Justice Sutherland.

[1] William E. Humphrey, the decedent, on December 10, 1931, was nominated by President Hoover to succeed himself as a member of the Federal Trade Commission, and was confirmed by the United States Senate. He was duly commissioned for a term of seven years, expiring September 25, 1938; and, after taking the required oath of office, entered upon his duties. On July 25, 1933, President Roosevelt addressed a letter to the commissioner asking for his resignation, on the ground "that the aims and purposes of the Administration with respect to the work of the Commission can be carried out most effectively with personnel of my own selection," but disclaiming any reflection upon the commissioner personally or upon his services. The commissioner replied, asking time to consult his friends. After some further correspondence upon the subject, the President on August 31, 1933, wrote the commissioner expressing the hope that the resignation would be forthcoming, and saying: "You will, I know, realize that I do not feel that your mind and my mind go along together on either the policies or the administering of the Federal Trade Commission, and, frankly, I think it is best for the people of this country that I should have a full confidence."

[2] The commissioner declined to resign; and on October 7, 1933, the President wrote him: "Effective as of this date you are hereby removed from the office of Commissioner of the Federal Trade Commission."

[3] Humphrey never acquiesced in this action, but continued thereafter to insist that he was still a member of the commission, entitled to perform its duties and receive the compensation provided by law at the rate of $10,000 per annum. [. . .]

[4] [Under the FTC Act, the]first commissioners appointed [were] to continue in office for terms of three, four, five, six, and seven years, respectively; and their successors are to be appointed for terms of seven years—any commissioner being subject to removal by the President for inefficiency, neglect of duty, or malfeasance in office. The words of the act are definite and unambiguous. {*Eds.: In other words, under the Act, the President could not remove a Commissioner without cause.*} . . .

[5] The commission is to be nonpartisan; and it must, from the very nature of its duties, act with entire impartiality. It is charged with the enforcement of no policy except the policy of the law. Its duties are neither political nor executive, but predominantly quasi judicial and quasi legislative. Like the Interstate Commerce Commission, its members are called upon to exercise the trained judgment of a body of experts appointed by law and informed by experience.

[6] The legislative reports in both houses of Congress clearly reflect the view that a fixed term was necessary to the effective and fair administration of the law. In the report to the Senate . . . the Senate Committee on Interstate Commerce, in support of the bill which afterwards became the act in question, after referring to the provision fixing the term of office at seven years, so arranged that the membership would not be subject to complete change at any one time, said: "The work of this commission will be of a most exacting and difficult character, demanding persons who have experience in the problems to be met—that is, a proper knowledge of both the public requirements and the practical affairs of industry. It is manifestly desirable that the terms of the commissioners shall be long enough to give them an opportunity to acquire the expertness in dealing with these special questions concerning industry that comes from experience." [. . .]

[7] The debates in both houses demonstrate that the prevailing view was that the Commission was not to be subject to anybody in the government but only to the people of the United States; free from political domination

---

[863] *See, e.g.,* Daniel A. Crane, *Debunking* Humphrey's Executor, 83 Geo. Wash. L. Rev. 1835 (2015); Sen. Mike Lee, *Take Care Act* (June 7, 2019), https://www.lee.senate.gov/2019/6/take-care-act-floor-remarks.

or control or the probability or possibility of such a thing; to be separate and apart from any existing department of the government—not subject to the orders of the President. [. . .]

[8] Thus, the language of the act, the legislative reports, and the general purposes of the legislation as reflected by the debates, all combine to demonstrate the congressional intent to create a body of experts who shall gain experience by length of service; a body which shall be independent of executive authority, except in its selection, and free to exercise its judgment without the leave or hindrance of any other official or any department of the government. To the accomplishment of these purposes, it is clear that Congress was of opinion that length and certainty of tenure would vitally contribute. And to hold that, nevertheless, the members of the commission continue in office at the mere will of the President, might be to thwart, in large measure, the very ends which Congress sought to realize by definitely fixing the term of office.

[9] We conclude that the intent of the act is to limit the executive power of removal to the causes enumerated, the existence of none of which is claimed here. . . .

[10] . . . To support its contention that the removal provision of section 1 [of the FTC Act], as we have just construed it, is an unconstitutional interference with the executive power of the President, the government's chief reliance is Myers v. United States, 272 U.S. 52 [(1926).] . . . [T]he narrow point actually decided [in *Myers*] was only that the President had power to remove a postmaster of the first class, without the advice and consent of the Senate as required by act of Congress. [. . .]

[11] The office of a postmaster is so essentially unlike the office now involved that the decision in the *Myers* Case cannot be accepted as controlling our decision here. A postmaster is an executive officer restricted to the performance of executive functions. He is charged with no duty at all related to either the legislative or judicial power. The actual decision in the *Myers* Case finds support in the theory that such an officer is merely one of the units in the executive department and, hence, inherently subject to the exclusive and illimitable power of removal by the Chief Executive, whose subordinate and aid he is. Putting aside dicta, which may be followed if sufficiently persuasive but which are not controlling, the necessary reach of the decision goes far enough to include all purely executive officers. It goes no farther; much less does it include an officer who occupies no place in the executive department and who exercises no part of the executive power vested by the Constitution in the President.

[12] The Federal Trade Commission is an administrative body created by Congress to carry into effect legislative policies embodied in the statute in accordance with the legislative standard therein prescribed, and to perform other specified duties as a legislative or as a judicial aid. Such a body cannot in any proper sense be characterized as an arm or an eye of the executive. Its duties are performed without executive leave and, in the contemplation of the statute, must be free from executive control. In administering the provisions of the statute in respect of "unfair methods of competition," that is to say, in filling in and administering the details embodied by that general standard, the commission acts in part quasi legislatively and in part quasi judicially. In making investigations and reports thereon for the information of Congress under section 6, in aid of the legislative power, it acts as a legislative agency. Under section 7, which authorizes the commission to act as a master in chancery under rules prescribed by the court, it acts as an agency of the judiciary. To the extent that it exercises any executive function, as distinguished from executive power in the constitutional sense, it does so in the discharge and effectuation of its quasi legislative or quasi judicial powers, or as an agency of the legislative or judicial departments of the government.

[13] If Congress is without authority to prescribe causes for removal of members of the trade commission and limit executive power of removal accordingly, that power at once becomes practically all-inclusive in respect of civil officers with the exception of the judiciary provided for by the Constitution. The Solicitor General, at the bar, apparently recognizing this to be true, with commendable candor, agreed that his view in respect of the removability of members of the Federal Trade Commission necessitated a like view in respect of the Interstate Commerce Commission and the Court of Claims. We are thus confronted with the serious question whether not only the members of these quasi legislative and quasi judicial bodies, but the judges of the legislative Court of Claims, exercising judicial power, continue in office only at the pleasure of the President.

[14] We think it plain under the Constitution that illimitable power of removal is not possessed by the President in respect of officers of the character of those just named. The authority of Congress, in creating quasi legislative or quasi judicial agencies, to require them to act in discharge of their duties independently of executive control cannot well be doubted; and that authority includes, as an appropriate incident, power to fix the period during which they shall continue, and to forbid their removal except for cause in the meantime. For it is quite evident that one who holds his office only during the pleasure of another cannot be depended upon to maintain an attitude of independence against the latter's will.

[15] The fundamental necessity of maintaining each of the three general departments of government entirely free from the control or coercive influence, direct or indirect, of either of the others, has often been stressed and is hardly open to serious question. So much is implied in the very fact of the separation of the powers of these departments by the Constitution; and in the rule which recognizes their essential coequality. The sound application of a principle that makes one master in his own house precludes him from imposing his control in the house of another who is master there. James Wilson, one of the framers of the Constitution and a former justice of this court, said that the independence of each department required that its proceedings "should be free from the remotest influence, direct or indirect, of either of the other two powers." And Mr. Justice Story in the first volume of his work on the Constitution (4th Ed.) s 530, citing No. 48 of the Federalist, said that neither of the departments in reference to each other "ought to possess, directly or indirectly, an overruling influence in the administration of their respective powers."

[16] The power of removal here claimed for the President falls within this principle, since its coercive influence threatens the independence of a commission, which is not only wholly disconnected from the executive department, but which, as already fully appears, was created by Congress as a means of carrying into operation legislative and judicial powers, and as an agency of the legislative and judicial departments.

***

Daniel A. Crane, Debunking *Humphrey's Executor*
83 Geo. Wash. L. Rev. 1835 (2015)

With a hundred years of natural experiment, it is worth pausing to consider the actual experience of the FTC and ask whether the Court's quartet of assumptions in *Humphrey's Executor* were correct.

In fact, they were largely incorrect—or, at least, fail to capture the dominant character of the FTC over time. First, the FTC's independence and nonpartisanship are overstated. Work in political science and economics has shown that the FTC tends to be compliant to the will of Congress and particular congresspersons. This may create some separation of powers between the FTC and other executive branch agencies that pursue similar goals under the will of the President, but separation of powers is a different justification than the sort of technocratic independence suggested in *Humphrey's Executor*.

Second, the FTC is not uniquely expert. For much of its history, presidents appointed Commissioners as a matter of political patronage rather than expertise in competition and consumer protection. Even as the FTC grew into a more professional and expert agency in the last several decades, it enjoyed no comparative advantage in expertise over purely executive agencies, like the Justice Department's Antitrust Division, which fulfills almost identical functions. Third, the description of the FTC as "quasi-legislative" has been more wrong than right. In its original antitrust capacity—the sole capacity it had at the time of *Humphrey's Executor*—the FTC has not been legislative at all, issuing virtually no substantive rules. It has issued some consumer protection rules in the last few decades, although rulemaking remains a very limited portion of its docket. Finally, adjudication is a very small part of what the agency does. A new empirical study, reported in this Essay, shows that the FTC's predominant mode of law enforcement is through consent decrees, which involve no adjudication, and that the FTC is more prone to sue in federal district court as a plaintiff than to adjudicate matters administratively in the event there is adjudication.

The upshot is that the FTC has essentially become the executive agency that the *Humphrey's Executor* Court denied it was. The FTC functions primarily by enforcing the antitrust and consumer protection laws as a plaintiff, no more expert than the executive branch agencies doing the same thing. The principal structural difference from the executive branch agencies is that the FTC is beholden to Congress rather than to the President.

***

The core of the agency is its three Bureaus: the Bureau of Competition, the Bureau of Consumer Protection, and the Bureau of Economics. They are complemented by Offices which report to the Chair, dealing with competition and consumer-protection policy, international affairs, and congressional relations, among others.

The FTC's antitrust enforcement arm is the Bureau of Competition. Led by a Director and managed by a "front office" that includes Deputy Directors and a rotating group of Counsel—experienced attorneys on detail from the Bureau's divisions—the Bureau includes:

- Four merger enforcement divisions:
    - Mergers I, which primarily investigates mergers involving pharmaceuticals, medical devices, defense, and tech businesses;
    - Mergers II, which primarily investigates mergers involving semiconductors, chemicals, heavy industries, and computer hardware / software;
    - Mergers III, which primarily investigates mergers involving oil and gas and a range of consumer and consumer-facing products and services; and
    - Mergers IV, which primarily investigates mergers involving hospital and physicians as well as retail businesses;
- Three divisions focused on conduct enforcement:
    - the Technology Enforcement Division, which primarily investigates practices (and some transactions) in digital markets;
    - the Health Care division, which primarily investigates practices in pharmaceutical and healthcare markets; and
    - the Anticompetitive Practices Division, which primarily investigates practices in other markets;
- And three other divisions:
    - the Compliance division (which advises on matters of remedy and investigates compliance matters);
    - the Premerger Notification Office (which handles merger notifications under the HSR merger review process and conducts the initial review of all merger filings);
    - the Office of Policy & Coordination (which provides policy and research support to the rest of the Bureau).

The work of the Bureau of Competition is also supported by the staff of the FTC's Regional Offices in New York, San Francisco, and Seattle. Overall, the FTC budgeted for 675 full-time equivalent (FTE) staff dedicated to competition work in Fiscal Year 2023.[864]

Crucial support for the antitrust enforcement function is provided by the Ph.D. economists in the Bureau of Economics, who work alongside attorneys on investigations and litigations. BE economists occasionally serve as testifying experts in the FTC's antitrust actions. The FTC supplements BE with extensive use of economists from private consulting firms to advise on, and testify in, antitrust matters. The expenses of so doing represent a significant portion of the Commission's enforcement budget.[865]

---

[864] FTC, CONGRESSIONAL BUDGET JUSTIFICATION FISCAL YEAR 2024 (Mar. 13, 2023), 8.

[865] FTC, CONGRESSIONAL BUDGET JUSTIFICATION FISCAL YEAR 2024 (Mar. 13, 2023), 11 ("Expert witnesses are a critical element of all antitrust litigations, where explaining complex market dynamics to generalist judges is essential. . . . . It is commonplace for defendants in FTC litigations to outspend the Commission by a significant amount on expert support[.]").

A majority vote of the Commission is required to undertake key actions, including to issue a complaint, to authorize compulsory process (*i.e.*, civil investigative demands or subpoenas), or to voluntarily withdraw or settle a case.[866]

2. Powers and Functions

a) FTC Act Section 5

The FTC's two principal functions—competition and consumer protection—are reflected in Section 5(a) of the FTC Act, 15 U.S.C. § 45(a), which prohibits "unfair methods of competition" ("UMC") and "unfair or deceptive acts and practices" ("UDAP"). The latter language, which forms the basis for the FTC's consumer protection enforcement authority, was added by Congress in 1938 after the FTC's efforts at consumer protection were blocked by the Supreme Court for want of statutory authority.[867] The FTC also issues guidance (alone and with DOJ) and is active as an amicus in antitrust cases.

The statutory prohibition on UMC, plus the Clayton Act, forms the accepted basis for the FTC's antitrust enforcement authority. As the Supreme Court put it in 1948, the FTC's mandate to prohibit UMC reflected "a strong congressional purpose not only to continue enforcement of the Sherman Act by the Department of Justice and the Federal District Courts but also to supplement that enforcement through the administrative process of the new Trade Commission."[868] But the limits of its substantive scope is unclear. Courts and commentators generally agree that the phrase "unfair methods of competition" includes *at least* all the conduct prohibited by the antitrust laws and at least some margin more, but they disagree about how much more broadly it reaches: that is, what the set of "standalone" Section 5 violations might be.[869]

It is broadly agreed that "invitations to collude"—that is, unilateral and unaccepted proposals to enter into a nakedly anticompetitive agreement, which do not generally violate the antitrust laws—violate Section 5.[870] But the consensus more or less stops there. After a trio of adverse decisions in the 1980s,[871] and with a couple of exceptions,[872] the FTC generally gave up the effort to assert "standalone" Section 5 theories other than those dealing with invitations to collude. (At least: until the effort, beginning in 2022, to reboot Section 5! We will come to that shortly.)

One case in the 1980s trio was *du Pont*, in which the FTC challenged the parallel but non-collusive use of practices that facilitated oligopolistic pricing by producers of "antiknock" gasoline additives. Specifically, the FTC's complaint charged that the producers had violated Section 5 by engaging, without agreement, in parallel practices including: (1) selling at a "delivered" price that included the cost of transportation; (2) using MFN clauses (see Chapter VI!) in their contracts with buyers; (3) using contractual provisions that required 30 days' notice of any

---

[866] Compulsory process is increasingly authorized on a categorical "omnibus" basis, rather than for individual matters. *See, e.g.*, FTC, Press Release, Federal Trade Commission Authorizes Three New Compulsory Process Resolutions for Investigations (Aug. 26, 2022).

[867] *See* FTC v. Raladam Co., 283 U.S. 643, 649 (1931). For some history, *see* J. Howard Beales, *The FTC's Use of Unfairness Authority: Its Rise, Fall, and Resurrection* (May 30, 2003).

[868] FTC v. Cement Inst., 333 U.S. 683, 692 (1948).

[869] See FTC v. Sperry & Hutchinson Co., 405 U.S. 233, 242 (1972); for a wide range of perspectives, *see generally* Sandeep Vaheesan, *Resurrecting "A Comprehensive Chapter of Economic Liberty": The Latent Power of the Federal Trade Commission*, 19 U. Pa. L. Bus. L. 645 (2017); Tim Wu, *Section 5 and "Unfair Methods of Competition": Protecting Competition or Increasing Uncertainty?"*, Colum. Pub. L. Research Paper 14-508 (2016); Debbie Feinstein, *A Few Words About Section 5*, COMPETITION MATTERS (Mar. 13, 2015); James C. Cooper, *The Perils of Excessive Discretion: The Elusive Meaning of Unfairness in Section 5 of the FTC Act*, 3 J. Antitrust Enf't 87, 88 (2015); William Kovacic & Marc Winerman, *Competition Policy and the Application of Section 5 of the Federal Trade Commission Act*, 20 Minn. J. Int'l L. 274 (2010); Susan A. Creighton & Thomas G. Krattenmaker, *Appropriate Role(s) for Section 5*, Antitrust Source (Feb. 2009); ABA, REPORT OF THE AMERICAN BAR ASSOCIATION SECTION OF ANTITRUST LAW SPECIAL COMMITTEE TO STUDY THE ROLE OF THE FEDERAL TRADE COMMISSION, *reprinted at* 59 Antitrust L. J. 43 (1989); Neil W. Averitt, *The Meaning of "Unfair Methods of Competition" in Section 5 of the Federal Trade Commission Act*, 21 B.C. L. Rev. 227 (1980); Eugene R. Baker & Daniel J. Baum, *Section 5 of the Federal Trade Commission Act: A Continuing Process of Redefinition*, 7 Villanova L. Rev. 517 (1962).

[870] *See, e.g.*, Analysis to Aid Public Comment, In the Matter of Fortiline, LLC, File No. 151-0000 (F.T.C. Aug. 9, 2016); Analysis to Aid Public Comment, In the Matter of U-Haul Int'l, Inc., File No. 081-0157 (F.T.C. June 9, 2010).

[871] E.I. du Pont de Nemours & Co. v. FTC, 729 F.2d 128 (2d Cir. 1984); Official Airline Guides, Inc. v. FTC, 630 F.2d 920 (2d Cir. 1980); Boise Cascade Corp. v. FTC, 637 F.2d 573 (9th Cir. 1980).

[872] *See, e.g.*, Complaint, In the Matter of Negotiated Data Solutions LLC., FTC File No. 51-94 (F.T.C. filed Sept. 23, 2008).

change in prices; and (4) giving advance notice of price increases to the press. Each of these practices had been used by Ethyl Corporation when it had been the sole supplier in the market; other firms, upon entering the market, had embarked on the practices as well. Such behavior would generally not violate the Sherman Act, given the absence of either agreement or individual monopoly power: the Second Circuit held that it did not violate Section 5 of the FTC Act either. In the process, the court indicated that there are some limits on the reach of the unfairness prohibition. The FTC would take this message to heart, cutting back its efforts to apply Section 5 beyond the antitrust laws.

E.I. du Pont de Nemours & Co. v. FTC
729 F.2d 128 (2d Cir. 1984)

Judge Mansfield.

[1] Congress' use of the vague general term "unfair methods of competition" in § 5 without defining what is "unfair" was deliberate. The statute's legislative history reveals that, in reaction to the relatively narrow terms of the Sherman Act as limited by the Supreme Court's adoption of the Rule of Reason in Standard Oil Co. v. United States, 221 U.S. 1 (1911), Congress sought to provide broad and flexible authority to the Commission as an administrative body of presumably practical men with broad business and economic expertise in order that they might preserve business' freedom to compete from restraints. Congress' aim was to protect society against oppressive anti-competitive conduct and thus assure that the conduct prohibited by the Sherman and Clayton Acts would be supplemented as necessary and any interstices filled. Indeed, Congress, in the process of drafting § 5, gave up efforts to define specifically which methods of competition and practices are competitively harmful and abandoned a proposed laundry list of prohibited practices for the reason that there were too many practices to define and many more unforeseeable ones were yet to be created by ingenious business minds. The specific practices that might be barred were left to be defined by the Commission, applying its expertise, subject to judicial review. Congress did not, however, authorize the Commission under § 5 to bar any business practice found to have an adverse effect on competition. Instead, the Commission could proscribe only "unfair" practices or methods of competition. Review by the courts was essential to assure that the Commission would not act arbitrarily or without explication but according to definable standards that would be properly applied.

[2] During the period since the enactment of the Federal Trade Commission Act the courts have established certain principles bearing on the scope of the Commission's powers. Although the Commission may under § 5 enforce the antitrust laws, including the Sherman and Clayton Acts, it is not confined to their letter. It may bar incipient violations of those statutes, and conduct which, although not a violation of the letter of the antitrust laws, is close to a violation or is contrary to their spirit. In prosecuting violations of the spirit of the antitrust laws, the Commission has, with one or two exceptions, confined itself to attacking collusive, predatory, restrictive or deceitful conduct that substantially lessens competition.

[3] The Commission here asks us to go further and to hold that the "unfair methods of competition" provision of § 5 can be violated by non-collusive, non-predatory and independent conduct of a non-artificial nature, at least when it results in a substantial lessening of competition. We recognize that § 5 invests the Commission with broad powers designed to enable it to cope with new threats to competition as they arise. As the Supreme Court stated in *FTC v. Sperry & Hutchinson Co.*, 405 U.S. 233, 244 (1972):

> Thus, legislative and judicial authorities alike convince us that the Federal Trade Commission does not arrogate excessive power to itself if, in measuring a practice against the elusive, but congressionally mandated standard of fairness, it, like a court of equity, considers public values beyond simply those enshrined in the letter or encompassed in the spirit of the antitrust laws.

[4] However, as the Court noted in the same case, appropriate standards must be adopted and applied to protect a respondent against abuse of power. As the Commission moves away from attacking conduct that is either a violation of the antitrust laws or collusive, coercive, predatory, restrictive or deceitful, and seeks to break new ground by enjoining otherwise legitimate practices, the closer must be our scrutiny upon judicial review. A test based solely upon restraint of competition, even if qualified by the requirement that the conduct be "analogous"

to an antitrust violation, is so vague as to permit arbitrary or undue government interference with the reasonable freedom of action that has marked our country's competitive system.

[5] The term "unfair" is an elusive concept, often dependent upon the eye of the beholder. A line must therefore be drawn between conduct that is anticompetitive and legitimate conduct that has an impact on competition. Lessening of competition is not the substantial equivalent of "unfair methods" of competition. Section 5 is aimed at conduct, not at the result of such conduct, even though the latter is usually a relevant factor in determining whether the challenged conduct is "unfair." Nor does the statute obligate a business to engage in competition; if that were the case, many acceptable pricing and market decisions would be barred. A manufacturer, for instance, would be prevented from making a concededly lawful change in its distribution system, designed to increase sales efficiency, by unilaterally reducing the number of its wholesalers, since the effect would be to diminish substantial competition at the wholesaler level. Similarly, if anticompetitive impact were the sole test, the admittedly lawful unilateral closing of a plant or refusal to expand capacity could be found to be "unfair." The holder of a valid product patent could be prevented from exercising its lawful monopoly to charge whatever the traffic would bear, even though "a monopolist, as long as he has no purpose to restrain competition or to enhance or expand his monopoly, and does not act coercively, retains [the right to trade with whom he wishes]."

[6] When a business practice is challenged by the Commission, even though, as here, it does not violate the antitrust or other laws and is not collusive, coercive, predatory or exclusionary in character, standards for determining whether it is "unfair" within the meaning of § 5 must be formulated to discriminate between normally acceptable business behavior and conduct that is unreasonable or unacceptable. Otherwise the door would be open to arbitrary or capricious administration of § 5; the FTC could, whenever it believed that an industry was not achieving its maximum competitive potential, ban certain practices in the hope that its action would increase competition. The mere existence of an oligopolistic market structure in which a small group of manufacturers engage in consciously parallel pricing of an identical product does not violate the antitrust laws. It represents a condition, not a "method;" indeed it could be consistent with intense competition. Labelling one producer's price change in such a market as a "signal," parallel price changes as "lock-step," or prices as "supracompetitive," hardly converts its pricing into an "unfair" method of competition. To so hold would be to condemn any such price increase or moves, however independent; yet the FTC has not suggested that § 5 authorizes it to ban all price increases in an oligopolistic market. On the contrary, it states that "Section 5 should not prohibit oligopolistic pricing alone, even supracompetitive parallel prices, in the absence of specific conduct which promotes such a result." This fine distinction creates doubt as to the types of otherwise legitimate conduct that are lawful and those that are not. The doubt is increased by the Commission's concession that price uniformity is normal in a market with few sellers and homogeneous products, such as that in the antiknock compound industry.

[7] In view of this patent uncertainty the Commission owes a duty to define the conditions under which conduct claimed to facilitate price uniformity would be unfair so that businesses will have an inkling as to what they can lawfully do rather than be left in a state of complete unpredictability. The Commission's decision in the present case does not provide any guidelines; it would require each producer not only to assess the general conduct of the antiknock business but also that of each of its competitors and the reaction of each to the other, which would be virtually impossible. Some idea of the fickleness and uncertainty of the FTC's position in the present case can be gathered from its ambivalent view towards some of the practices which it attacks. Certain otherwise-legitimate practices were declared unlawful only when used cumulatively with other practices. Others were found unfair when used by certain producers (Du Pont and Ethyl) but not when used by others (PPG and Nalco). Press announcements of price increases and contractual 30-day price increase notice requirements were held permissible but giving buyers a few days additional notice was found to be unfair even though there was no proof that the extra days made any competitive difference. Indeed, with or without the additional days' notice the initiator of a price increase was not precluded from withdrawing or modifying it within the 30-day period or from extending the 30-day notice period itself. Thus the FTC's rulings and order appear to represent uncertain guesswork rather than workable rules of law.

[8] In our view, before business conduct in an oligopolistic industry may be labelled "unfair" within the meaning of § 5 a minimum standard demands that, absent a tacit agreement, at least some indicia of oppressiveness must exist such as (1) evidence of anticompetitive intent or purpose on the part of the producer charged, or (2) the

absence of an independent legitimate business reason for its conduct. If, for instance, a seller's conduct, even absent identical behavior on the part of its competitors, is contrary to its independent self-interest, that circumstance would indicate that the business practice is "unfair" within the meaning of § 5. In short, in the absence of proof of a violation of the antitrust laws or evidence of collusive, coercive, predatory, or exclusionary conduct, business practices are not "unfair" in violation of § 5 unless those practices either have an anticompetitive purpose or cannot be supported by an independent legitimate reason. To suggest, as does the Commission in its opinion, that the defendant can escape violating § 5 only by showing that there are "countervailing procompetitive justifications" for the challenged business practices goes too far.

[9] In the present case the FTC concedes that the petitioners did not engage in the challenged practices by agreement or collusively. Each acted independently and unilaterally. There is no evidence of coercive or predatory conduct. If the petitioners nevertheless were unable to come forward with some independent legitimate reason for their adoption of these practices, the Commission's argument that they must be barred as "unfair" when they have the effect of facilitating conscious price parallelism and interdependence might have some merit. But the evidence is overwhelming and undisputed, as the ALJ found, that each petitioner independently adopted its practices for legitimate business reasons which we have described.

[10] The tenuousness of the Commission's finding that the challenged practices are "unfair" is illustrated by the fact that it does not tell us when the practices became unlawful: at the time of their original adoption by Ethyl when it was the sole manufacturer of antiknock compounds, when Du Pont entered the market in 1948, when PPG entered in 1961, when Nalco appeared on the scene in 1964, or at some other time. The matter is of some importance for the reason that during the period from 1948 (when Du Pont entered) to 1974 Ethyl's share of the market fell from 100% to 33%. Du Pont's share likewise fell from 50% in 1961, the time of PPG's entry, to 38% in 1974. In the meantime PPG and Nalco, using aggressive competitive measures, captured substantial shares of the market. If the challenged business practices engaged in by the four producers were "unfair" during the 1974-1979 period one would expect that they would be viewed as unfair during the 1960s. Yet the evidence is clear beyond doubt that they did not "facilitate" conscious price parallelism during that earlier period; indeed, from 1960 to 1974 the price of one ingredient of antiknock compounds, TEL (tetraethyl lead) increased only 17% while the price of the other, TML (tetramethyl lead) fell 10%, even though the overall price index rose 57% during the same period. This casts doubt upon the FTC's selection of the 1974-1979 period as indicative of the effect of the business practices at issue. It is difficult to believe that a practice deemed lawful when competitive forces were producing changes in the market became "unfair" when market conditions stabilized.

[11] The Commission contends that although the business practices at issue here might not be unfair under other market conditions, they assume that unlawful character when adopted in a concentrated or oligopolistic market in which a few producers sell a homogenous product, demand is inelastic, prices are "supracompetitive," and barriers to entry are high. It is argued that in such a milieu the practices assist the producers in independently maintaining prices at higher levels than would otherwise be the case. Perhaps this argument would be acceptable if the market were clearly as so described and a causal connection could be shown between the practices and the level of prices. Indeed the Commission majority concedes that "facilitating practices will be found to violate § 5 as unfair methods of competition only if the weight of the evidence shows that competition has been substantially lessened" and that it was required to "establish a clear nexus between the challenged conduct and adverse competitive effects before invoking our authority in this regard." But the record does not contain substantial evidence supporting many of the Commission's conclusions or showing a causal connection between the challenged practices and market prices. Indeed, it appears to be riddled with deficiencies and inconsistencies, many of which are noted by Chairman Miller in his dissent.

[12] In the first place, price uniformity and parallelism was much more limited than the FTC would have it. During the relevant period (1974-1979) Nalco extended price discounts on more than 80% of its sales and PPG on more than one-third of its sales, the latter increasing to 58% of its sales in 1979 as the sellers competed for fewer buyers in a diminishing market. Although there was for the most part price parallelism on the part of Du Pont and Ethyl, they effectively met the price discounts of the other two producers by providing competition in the form of extensive services which had the effect of retaining old customers or luring away new ones. Thus the total package, including free valuable services and discounts, presents a picture of a competitive market in which large,

sophisticated and aggressive buyers were making demands and were satisfied with the results. To the extent that there was price uniformity, that condition is as consistent with competitive as with anticompetitive behavior.

[13] The problems faced by anyone thinking of entering the market were not "barriers" in the usual sense used by economists, such as requirements for high capital investment or advanced technological know-how. The main problem has been that market demand, due to factors uncontrolled by petitioners, is sharply declining. A dying market, which will soon dry up altogether, does not attract new entries. Absent some reasonable prospect that a price reduction would increase demand-and there is none-it is not surprising that existing producers have not engaged in as much price competition as might exist under other conditions. To suggest that industry-wide use of delivered instead of f.o.b. pricing {*Eds.: f.o.b. = "free on board," or not including transportation costs*} restrained price competition in such a market ignores the de minimis part freight charges played in the price paid by customers. It also overlooks the fact that f.o.b. pricing is not necessarily more competitive than delivered pricing.

[14] In short, we do not find substantial evidence in this record as a whole that the challenged practices significantly lessened competition in the antiknock industry or that the elimination of those practices would improve competition.

* * *

In 2015, the FTC issued a brief "Statement of Enforcement Principles" relating to the meaning of the UMC prohibition, tying it to the principles of antitrust enforcement.

FTC, Statement of Enforcement Principles Regarding "Unfair Methods of Competition" Under Section 5 of the FTC Act (2015)

In deciding whether to challenge an act or practice as an unfair method of competition in violation of Section 5 on a standalone basis, the Commission adheres to the following principles:

- the Commission will be guided by the public policy underlying the antitrust laws, namely, the promotion of consumer welfare;
- the act or practice will be evaluated under a framework similar to the rule of reason, that is, an act or practice challenged by the Commission must cause, or be likely to cause, harm to competition or the competitive process, taking into account any associated cognizable efficiencies and business justifications; and
- the Commission is less likely to challenge an act or practice as an unfair method of competition on a standalone basis if enforcement of the Sherman or Clayton Act is sufficient to address the competitive harm arising from the act or practice.

* * *

But in 2021, the Commission withdrew the Statement, and signaled a determination to take a fresh, and broader, look at the scope of Section 5.[873] In November 2022, a new policy statement emerged (as did a vigorous dissent![874]).

---

[873] FTC, Statement of the Commission on the Withdrawal of the Statement of Enforcement Principles Regarding "Unfair Methods of Competition" Under Section 5 of the FTC Act (July 9, 2021).

[874] *See* Dissenting Statement of Commissioner Christine S. Wilson Regarding the "Policy Statement Regarding the Scope of Unfair Methods of Competition Under Section 5 of the Federal Trade Commission Act" (July 9, 2021), https://www.ftc.gov/system/files/ftc_gov/pdf/P221202Section5PolicyWilsonDissentStmt.pdf ("Instead of a law enforcement document, [the Statement] resembles the work of an academic or a think tank fellow who dreams of banning unpopular conduct and remaking the economy. It does not reflect the thinking of litigators who know that legal precedent cannot be ignored, case-specific facts and evidence must be analyzed, and the potential for anticompetitive effects must be assessed. It does not reflect the approach of experienced policy makers who recognize the necessity of considering the business rationales for, and benefits of, conduct so that agency action does not harm consumers and the economy. And it does not exhibit the input of those with counseling and in-house experience who understand the need to provide workable rules so that 'honest businesses' can map the boundaries of lawful conduct.").

FTC, Policy Statement Regarding the Scope of Unfair Methods of Competition Under Section 5 of the Federal Trade Commission Act (Nov. 10, 2022)

[1] Pursuant to the FTC's analysis of the decided cases and prior enforcement actions, this policy statement describes the key principles of general applicability concerning whether conduct is an unfair method of competition. Consistent with the Supreme Court's interpretation of the FTC Act in at least twelve decisions, this statement makes clear that Section 5 reaches beyond the Sherman and Clayton Acts to encompass various types of unfair conduct that tend to negatively affect competitive conditions. [. . .]

[2] In enacting Section 5, Congress's aim was to create a new prohibition broader than, and different from, the Sherman and Clayton Acts. Congress purposely introduced the phrase, "unfair methods of competition," in the FTC Act to distinguish the FTC's authority from the definition of "unfair competition" at common law. It also made clear that Section 5 was designed to extend beyond the reach of the antitrust laws. Concluding that a static definition would soon become outdated, Congress wanted to give the Commission flexibility to adapt to changing circumstances. [. . .]

[3] Relying on the text, structure, legislative history of Section 5, precedent, and the FTC's experience applying the law, this statement describes the most significant general principles concerning whether conduct is an unfair method of competition under Section 5 of the FTC Act.

[4] Conduct must be a "method of competition" to violate Section 5. A method of competition is conduct undertaken by an actor in the marketplace—as opposed to merely a condition of the marketplace, not of the respondent's making, such as high concentration or barriers to entry. The conduct must implicate competition, but the relationship can be indirect. For example, misuse of regulatory processes that can create or exploit impediments to competition (such as those related to licensing, patents, or standard setting) constitutes a method of competition. Conversely, violations of generally applicable laws by themselves, such as environmental or tax laws, that merely give an actor a cost advantage would be unlikely to constitute a method of competition.

[5] The method of competition must be unfair, meaning that the conduct goes beyond competition on the merits. Competition on the merits may include, for example, superior products or services, superior business acumen, truthful marketing and advertising practices, investment in research and development that leads to innovative outputs, or attracting employees and workers through the offering of better employment terms.

[6] There are two key criteria to consider when evaluating whether conduct goes beyond competition on the merits. First, the conduct may be coercive, exploitative, collusive, abusive, deceptive, predatory, or involve the use of economic power of a similar nature. It may also be otherwise restrictive or exclusionary, depending on the circumstances, as discussed below. Second, the conduct must tend to negatively affect competitive conditions. This may include, for example, conduct that tends to foreclose or impair the opportunities of market participants, reduce competition between rivals, limit choice, or otherwise harm consumers.

[7] These two principles are weighed according to a sliding scale. Where the indicia of unfairness are clear, less may be necessary to show a tendency to negatively affect competitive conditions. Even when conduct is not facially unfair, it may violate Section 5. In these circumstances, more information about the nature of the commercial setting may be necessary to determine whether there is a tendency to negatively affect competitive conditions. The size, power, and purpose of the respondent may be relevant, as are the current and potential future effects of the conduct.

[8] The second principle addresses the tendency of the conduct to negatively affect competitive conditions—whether by affecting consumers, workers, or other market participants. In crafting Section 5, Congress recognized that unfair methods of competition may take myriad forms and hence that different types of evidence can demonstrate a tendency to interfere with competitive conditions. Because the Section 5 analysis is purposely focused on incipient threats to competitive conditions, this inquiry does not turn to whether the conduct directly caused *actual* harm in the specific instance at issue. Instead, the second part of the principle examines whether the respondent's conduct has a tendency to generate negative consequences; for instance, raising prices, reducing output, limiting choice, lowering quality, reducing innovation, impairing other market participants, or reducing the likelihood of potential or nascent competition. These consequences may arise when the conduct is examined

in the aggregate along with the conduct of others engaging in the same or similar conduct, or when the conduct is examined as part of the cumulative effect of a variety of different practices by the respondent. Moreover, Section 5 does not require a separate showing of market power or market definition when the evidence indicates that such conduct tends to negatively affect competitive conditions. Given the distinctive goals of Section 5, the inquiry will not focus on the "rule of reason" inquiries more common in cases under the Sherman Act, but will instead focus on stopping unfair methods of competition in their incipiency based on their tendency to harm competitive conditions.

[9] In the event that conduct prima facie constitutes an unfair method of competition, liability normally ensues under Section 5 absent additional evidence. There is limited caselaw on what, if any, justifications may be cognizable in a standalone Section 5 unfair methods of competition case, and some courts have declined to consider justifications altogether. [. . .]

[10] If parties in these cases choose to assert a justification, the subsequent inquiry would not be a net efficiencies test or a numerical cost-benefit analysis. The unfair methods of competition framework explicitly contemplates a variety of non-quantifiable harms, and justifications and purported benefits may be unquantifiable as well. The nature of the harm is highly relevant to the inquiry; the more facially unfair and injurious the harm, the less likely it is to be overcome by a countervailing justification of any kind. In addition, whether harmed parties share in the purported benefits of the practice may be relevant to the inquiry.

[11] Some well-established limitations on what defenses are permissible in an antitrust case apply in the Section 5 context as well. It is the party's burden to show that the asserted justification for the conduct is legally cognizable, non-pretextual, and that any restriction used to bring about the benefit is narrowly tailored to limit any adverse impact on competitive conditions. In addition, the asserted benefits must not be outside the market where the harm occurs. Finally, it is the party's burden to show that, given all the circumstances, the asserted benefits outweigh the harm and are of the kind that courts have recognized as cognizable in standalone Section 5 cases. [. . .]

[12] A non-exclusive set of examples of conduct that have been found to violate Section 5 include:

- Practices deemed to violate Sections 1 and 2 of the Sherman Act or the provisions of the Clayton Act, as amended (the antitrust laws).
- Conduct deemed to be an incipient violation of the antitrust laws. Incipient violations include conduct by respondents who have not gained full-fledged monopoly or market power, or by conduct that has the tendency to ripen into violations of the antitrust laws. Past examples of such use of Section 5 of the FTC Act include:
  - o invitations to collude,
  - o mergers, acquisitions, or joint ventures that have the tendency to ripen into violations of the antitrust laws,
  - o a series of mergers, acquisitions, or joint ventures that tend to bring about the harms that the antitrust laws were designed to prevent, but individually may not have violated the antitrust laws, and
  - o loyalty rebates, tying, bundling, and exclusive dealing arrangements that have the tendency to ripen into violations of the antitrust laws by virtue of industry conditions and the respondent's position within the industry.
- Conduct that violates the spirit of the antitrust laws. This includes conduct that tends to cause potential harm similar to an antitrust violation, but that may or may not be covered by the literal language of the antitrust laws or that may or may not fall into a "gap" in those laws. As such, the analysis may depart from prior precedent based on the provisions of the Sherman and Clayton Acts. Examples of such violations, to the extent not covered by the antitrust laws, include:
  - o practices that facilitate tacit coordination,
  - o parallel exclusionary conduct that may cause aggregate harm,
  - o conduct by a respondent that is undertaken with other acts and practices that cumulatively may tend to undermine competitive conditions in the market,

- ○ fraudulent and inequitable practices that undermine the standard-setting process or that interfere with the Patent Office's full examination of patent applications,
- ○ price discrimination claims such as knowingly inducing and receiving disproportionate promotional allowances against buyers not covered by Clayton Act,
- ○ de facto tying, bundling, exclusive dealing, or loyalty rebates that use market power in one market to entrench that power or impede competition in the same or a related market,
- ○ a series of mergers or acquisitions that tend to bring about the harms that the antitrust laws were designed to prevent, but individually may not have violated the antitrust laws,
- ○ mergers or acquisitions of a potential or nascent competitor that may tend to lessen current or future competition,
- ○ using market power in one market to gain a competitive advantage in an adjacent market by, for example, utilizing technological incompatibilities to negatively impact competition in adjacent markets,
- ○ conduct resulting in direct evidence of harm, or likely harm to competition, that does not rely upon market definition,
- ○ interlocking directors and officers of competing firms not covered by the literal language of the Clayton Act,
- ○ commercial bribery and corporate espionage that tends to create or maintain market power,
- ○ false or deceptive advertising or marketing which tends to create or maintain market power, or
- ○ discriminatory refusals to deal which tend to create or maintain market power.

***

The FTC's authority to enforce Section 5 is subject to some jurisdictional carveouts. Most importantly, banks (including federal credit unions), common carriers, air carriers, and entities subject to the Packers and Stockyards Act are all beyond the FTC's reach under Section 5.[875] In addition, due to a peculiarity of the definition of "corporation" in 15 U.S.C. § 44, nonprofits fall outside Section 5's reach, preventing the FTC from tackling practices by, for example, nonprofit hospitals.[876] (*California Dental* established that the FTC can challenge nonprofit actors organized to promote the profit of their members.[877]) These create gaps in the FTC's powers, within which the Department of Justice alone must fulfil the enforcement function. In addition to its powers under Section 5, the FTC also has authority to enforce Section 7 of the Clayton Act directly.[878]

b) FTC Act Section 6(b)

The FTC has a unique power under Section 6(b) of the FTC Act, 15 U.S.C. § 46, to conduct market studies by means of compulsory process and to compel businesses subject to Section 5 to respond under oath. The FTC has used this power to conduct reports on a wide variety of topics, some of which have led to further enforcement or policy action.[879]

3. Enforcement Procedure

FTC antitrust enforcement begins with an investigation, which is almost invariably handled by a conduct or merger division in the Bureau of Competition. Such investigations typically begin with an informal or voluntary phase (in which potential targets as well as customers, trading partners, and competitors are invited to submit documents and information and/or to participate in interviews) following which the Commission may vote to

---

[875] 15 U.S.C. § 45.

[876] 15 U.S.C. § 44 (defining corporation, in relevant part, as "organized to carry on business for its own profit or that of its members").

[877] California Dental Ass'n v. FTC, 526 U.S. 756, 766–67 (1999) (holding that "proximate relation to lucre must appear" but that "[n]onprofit entities organized on behalf of for-profit members have the same capacity and derivatively, at least, the same incentives as for-profit organizations to engage in unfair methods of competition or unfair and deceptive acts").

[878] *See* 15 U.S.C. § 21(a)

[879] *See, e.g.*, FTC, PATENT ASSERTION ENTITY ACTIVITY: AN FTC STUDY (Oct. 2016); FTC, Press Release, FTC Issues Orders to Nine Social Media and Video Streaming Services Seeking Data About How They Collect, Use, and Present Information (Dec. 14, 2020); FTC, Press Release, FTC to Examine Past Acquisitions by Large Technology Companies (Feb. 11, 2020).

authorize the use of compulsory process—that is, civil investigative demands ("CIDs") and subpoenas[880]—with which compliance is mandatory.[881] Some investigations are governed by so-called "omnibus resolutions," providing pre-authorization for the use of compulsory process in certain categories of cases.[882]

The FTC has an unusual choice of venues in which to pursue enforcement litigation. It may file administrative litigation, pursuant to Part 3 of the FTC Rules of Practice, to obtain entry of a cease and desist order.[883] This typically involves an initial trial before an FTC Administrative Law Judge, with plenary review by the Commission itself.[884] A respondent may appeal from a decision of the Commission to any federal circuit court of appeals.[885] On appeal, factual findings are reviewed to determine whether they are supported by substantial evidence, while conclusions of law are reviewed *de novo* with some limited deference to the FTC's view of whether a particular practice is "unfair" under Section 5.[886] Violations of an FTC order are punishable by civil penalties of up to $50,120 per violation.[887]

Administrative litigation presents the slightly odd prospect of the Commission first voting to bring a case, and then sitting in an adjudicative capacity to decide the case that it has, itself, authorized. In order to separate the functions of prosecutor and adjudicator, once the Commission votes to file a complaint in Part 3, a firewall (the "Part 3 wall") is raised between the litigating staff and members of the Commission, including the Chair.[888] But criticism of this arrangement persists. (Indeed, as we shall see later in this Chapter, this feature of the FTC has been a target of litigation.)

Maureen K. Ohlhausen, Administrative Litigation at the FTC: Effective Tool for Developing the Law or Rubber Stamp?
J. Comp. L. & Econ. (2016)

[T]he FTC's administrative litigation process . . . stands accused of being a rigged system. In a Part 3 proceeding, the FTC serves prosecutorial and adjudicative roles. After a staff investigation and recommendation, and following party meetings, the Commissioners may vote out a Part 3 complaint if they find "reason to believe" that a section 5 violation occurred and that the action would serve the public interest. An independent administrative law judge (ALJ) subsequently reaches an initial decision, based on a full trial. The Commissioners, however, then decide the merits of the case without deferring to the ALJ's factual or legal findings pursuant to their regulatory authority. Due-process objections result. The worry is that, once the FTC authorizes a Part 3 complaint, liability is inevitable no matter how the ALJ rules or what new facts or legal issues emerge. To evidence those claims, some commentators have argued that the Commission almost always rules in complaint counsel's favor. Is such criticism accurate? [. . .]

[C]onsider five findings. First, a recurring claim is that the FTC always imposes liability. That claim is true, but only for recent cases, which are relatively few. Although the Commission found liability in 92 percent of its 12 Part

---

[880] The Commission must have "reason to believe" the recipient is in possession, custody, or control of relevant information before issuing a CID. *See* 15 U.S.C § 57b-1(c). *See also* 15 U.S.C. § 49 (subpoena power).

[881] *See generally* 16 C.F.R. Part 2 (nonadjudicative procedures).

[882] *See, e.g.*, FTC, Resolution Directing Use of Compulsory Process Regarding Acts or Practices Affecting Healthcare Markets, FTC File No. P210100 (July 1, 2021)

[883] *See* 15 U.S.C. § 45(b) (cease and desist order); 16 C.F.R. Part 3.

[884] *See* 16 C.F.R. § 3.52 (appeal from initial decision to Commission).

[885] 15 U.S.C. § 45(c) (allowing appellate review in "any circuit where the method of competition or the act or practice in question was used or where such person, partnership, or corporation resides or carries on business").

[886] 15 U.SC. § 21(c) (appeal court review of factual findings limited to determining whether such findings are supported by "substantial evidence"); FTC v. Indiana Fed'n of Dentists, 476 U.S. 447, 454 (1986) (under the substantial evidence test, "the court must accept the Commission's findings of fact if they are supported by such relevant evidence as a reasonable mind might accept as adequate to support a conclusion"); *id.* at 454 ("The legal issues presented—that is, the identification of governing legal standards and their application to the facts found—are, by contrast, for the courts to resolve, although even in considering such issues the courts are to give some deference to the Commission's informed judgment that a particular commercial practice is to be condemned as 'unfair.'").

[887] 15 U.S.C. 45(*l*). Penalties are annually adjusted for inflation. *See* FTC, Press Release, *FTC Publishes Inflation-Adjusted Civil Penalty Amounts for 2023* (Jan. 6, 2023).

[888] *See* 5 U.S.C. § 554(d) (APA requirement of separation between investigational and adjudicative functions).

3 decisions in the last decade, it dismissed 29 percent of the 143 Part 3 matters in which it made a liability-dismissal decision since January 1977. The Commission dismissed 16 percent of Part 3 matters on the merits. Those dismissals do not include the 21 matters in which the Commission found liability, but also trimmed counts or respondents, suggesting careful review. Notably, the Commission dismissed 40 percent of Part 3 antitrust complaints overall. And, of the antitrust matters adjudicated on the merits, 29 percent were dismissed.

Second, although the Commission dismissed more administrative cases historically—36 percent from 1987 to 1996, for example—its recent trend of finding liability coincides with a higher rate of success before the appellate courts. . . . .

Third, what of the criticism that the Commission is biased in deciding the merits simply because it previously instituted the proceedings? In fact, in 72 percent of Part 3 cases, the commissioners who authorized the administrative litigation had either left or no longer formed a majority at the liability-dismissal stage. . . . .

Fourth, a fascinating question is whether the Commission finds liability more often when the same majority authorized the Part 3 complaint. If claims of bias have merit, the FTC should be more likely to dismiss when different commissioners authorized the case. The results are the opposite. When the same Commission majority endured—that is, when "bias" would presumably exist—it dismissed 33 percent of cases. When a different majority decided the case than voted out the complaint, however, it was less likely to dismiss—doing so in 27 percent of matters.

* * *

Under certain circumstances the FTC may bring suit in federal district court under Section 13(b) of the FTC Act, 15 U.S.C. § 53(b). Sometimes district-court litigation is an alternative to the administrative process, but in other cases it may be a complement. In particular, because the remedy in a Part 3 case is limited to a cease and desist order, the FTC cannot use the administrative process to obtain interim relief, such as a preliminary injunction to block a merger. In those cases, the FTC may seek a preliminary injunction in district court *and* simultaneously move forward with administrative litigation to obtain a permanent injunction.[889]

But Section 13(b) is not a blank check to bring any antitrust suit in federal court: by contrast, the language of the provision sets up some important limitations on when the FTC can go to court, and what it can get when it does.[890] Here is the text of the statute.

15 U.S.C. § 53(b)

(b)Temporary restraining orders; preliminary injunctions

Whenever the Commission has reason to believe—

(1) that any person, partnership, or corporation is violating, or is about to violate, any provision of law enforced by the Federal Trade Commission, and

(2) that the enjoining thereof pending the issuance of a complaint by the Commission and until such complaint is dismissed by the Commission or set aside by the court on review, or until the order of the Commission made thereon has become final, would be in the interest of the public—

the Commission by any of its attorneys designated by it for such purpose may bring suit in a district court of the United States to enjoin any such act or practice. Upon a proper showing that, weighing the equities and considering the Commission's likelihood of ultimate success, such action would be in the public interest, and after notice to the defendant, a temporary restraining

---

[889] *See, e.g.*, FTC v. Thomas Jefferson Univ., 505 F. Supp. 3d 522, 527 (E.D. Pa. 2020) ("The Federal Trade Commission and Pennsylvania Office of Attorney General, collectively the Government, seek to preliminarily enjoin a proposed merger between Thomas Jefferson University and the Albert Einstein Healthcare Network pending an administrative determination of whether the combination violates Section 7 of the Clayton Act.").

[890] For one perspective on the role of 13(b) over time, *see* Stephen Calkins, *Civil Monetary Remedies Available to Federal Antitrust Enforcers*, 40 U.S.F. L. Rev. 567 (2006).

order or a preliminary injunction may be granted without bond: Provided, however, That if a complaint is not filed within such period (not exceeding 20 days) as may be specified by the court after issuance of the temporary restraining order or preliminary injunction, the order or injunction shall be dissolved by the court and be of no further force and effect: Provided further, That in proper cases the Commission may seek, and after proper proof, the court may issue, a permanent injunction. Any suit may be brought where such person, partnership, or corporation resides or transacts business, or wherever venue is proper under section 1391 of title 28. In addition, the court may, if the court determines that the interests of justice require that any other person, partnership, or corporation should be a party in such suit, cause such other person, partnership, or corporation to be added as a party without regard to whether venue is otherwise proper in the district in which the suit is brought. In any suit under this section, process may be served on any person, partnership, or corporation wherever it may be found.

* * *

The peculiar language of Section 13(b) sets up at least three possible limitations on the FTC's powers as a district-court litigant: first, the "is violating, or is about to violate" language might mean that the FTC is unable to go to district court to seek a remedy for past antitrust violations; second, the brief reference to "a permanent injunction" might mean that certain forms of equitable relief—such as disgorgement of profits or restitution of ill-gotten gains—are unavailable; and, third, that the "in a proper case" language might mean that injunctive relief is available in only a subset of litigated matters. All three of these issues were litigated in recent years: the FTC won one but lost two others, with dramatic implications for the scope of the agency's remedial powers.

FTC v. Shire ViroPharma, Inc.

917 F.3d 147 (3d Cir. 2019)

Chief Judge Smith.

[1] Section 13(b) requires that the FTC have reason to believe a wrongdoer "is violating" or "is about to violate" the law. We conclude that this language is unambiguous; it prohibits existing or impending conduct. Simply put, Section 13(b) does not permit the FTC to bring a claim based on long-past conduct without some evidence that the defendant "is" committing or "is about to" commit another violation.

[2] The plain language of Section 13(b) is reinforced by its history. Generally, where the text of a statute is unambiguous, the statute should be enforced as written and only the most extraordinary showing of contrary intentions in the legislative history will justify a departure from that language. When Congress added Section 13(b), the provision was expected to be used for obtaining injunctions against illegal conduct pending completion of FTC administrative hearings. See S. Rep. No. 93-151, at 30 (1973) ("The purpose of [Section 13(b)] is to permit the [FTC] to bring an immediate halt to unfair or deceptive acts or practices when [a]t the present time such practices might continue for several years until agency action is completed."). The provision was not designed to address hypothetical conduct or the mere suspicion that such conduct may yet occur. Nor was it meant to duplicate Section 5, which already prohibits past conduct. [. . .]

[3] The FTC's arguments to the contrary are unconvincing. The FTC contends that relief under Section 13(b) is appropriate when it shows a reasonable likelihood that past violations will recur. In other words, when a defendant has already violated the law but the illegal conduct has ceased, injunctive relief should be granted if 'there exists some cognizable danger of recurrent violation.

[4] The FTC borrows its "likelihood of recurrence" standard from the common law standard for an award of injunctive relief. A party can generally obtain injunctive relief for past conduct that is likely to recur; the wrongdoer cannot avoid an injunction by voluntarily ceasing its illegal conduct. Although injunctive relief can survive discontinuance of the illegal conduct, the moving party must satisfy the court that relief is needed. The necessary determination is that there exists some cognizable danger of recurrent violation, something more than the mere possibility which serves to keep the case alive.

[5] The FTC insists that other courts have consistently applied the likelihood of recurrence standard in Section 13(b) cases. This is true, and unsurprising, given that Section 13(b) explicitly authorizes the FTC to obtain injunctions. But none of the cases cited by the FTC considers the issue presented here—the meaning of Section 13(b)'s threshold requirement that a party "is" violating or "is about to" violate the law. [. . .]

[6] [T]he FTC trots out the old adage that a remedial statute like the FTC Act should be construed broadly. Because Section 13(b)'s "is" or "is about to" requirement allegedly conflicts with the remedial purpose of the FTC Act, the FTC says we should disregard the plain meaning of that language. Of course, none of the authority the FTC cites stands for the broad proposition that we can ignore clear statutory language if it does not promote a remedial interpretation.

[7] The FTC points to a parade of horribles that it predicts will result if we uphold the District Court's decision. *See*, *e.g.*, Br. Of Appellant [FTC] 35 ("Limiting the FTC's Section 13(b) authority to cases of ongoing or imminent violation would make it easy for wrongdoers to evade Congress' purposes in creating the regime. As soon as a potential defendant got wind that the FTC was investigating its activities, it could simply stop those activities and render itself immune from suit in federal court unless the FTC could allege and prove an imminent re-violation."). But there is no reason to believe that our decision today unnecessarily restricts the FTC's ability to address wrongdoing. Section 5 authorizes administrative proceedings based on past violations. And, of course, if the FTC believes that a wrongdoer is "about to violate" the law during the pendency of an administrative proceeding, it could then come to court and obtain an injunction under Section 13(b).

[8] The FTC's understandable preference for litigating under Section 13(b), rather than in an administrative proceeding, does not justify its expansion of the statutory language. If the FTC wants to recover for a past violation—where an entity "has been" violating the law—it must use Section 5(b). If the FTC instead chooses to use Section 13(b), it must plead that a violation of the law "is" occurring or "is about to" occur. Here, the FTC wants to use the most advantageous aspects of each statutory provision—to punish Shire for a past violation using the less onerous enforcement mechanism. But the FTC's attempt to squeeze Shire's conduct into the "about to violate" category distorts Section 13(b) beyond its intended purpose. Section 13(b) cannot accommodate the FTC's interpretation—that "about to violate" means only that a violation could recur at some future point.

[9] In short, we reject the FTC's contention that Section 13(b)'s "is violating" or "is about to violate" language can be satisfied by showing a violation in the distant past and a vague and generalized likelihood of recurrent conduct. Instead, "is" or "is about to violate" means what it says—the FTC must make a showing that a defendant is violating or is about to violate the law.

CASENOTE: FTC v. Surescripts, LLC, and The Idea of a "Proper Case"

424 F.Supp.3d 92 (D.D.C. 2020)

When the FTC sued the e-prescribing platform Surescripts for using loyalty discounts to induce exclusivity, it did so in federal court, pursuant to Section 13(b) of the FTC Act. As noted above, that provision states that "in proper cases the Commission may seek, and after proper proof, the court may issue, a permanent injunction."

In moving to dismiss the FTC's complaint, Surescripts argued that the language "in proper cases" should act as a meaningful limit on the scope of Section 13(b). In particular, Surescripts argued that injunctive relief should be available only in "routine, straightforward" cases. And the FTC's challenge to its loyalty discounts, Surescripts argued, was not a routine case: "it involves complex and novel issues of antitrust law, such as how to understand the two-sided e-prescription markets" in light of *AmEx*. Surescripts pointed to some legislative history suggesting that Congress may have intended the FTC to seek permanent injunctions in district court in routine cases in which it was not attempting to develop or extend the law. In opposing Surescripts's motion, the FTC's argued that Surescripts was overreading the language. A "proper" case, the FTC argued, is "any case in which a permanent injunction would be 'appropriate,' i.e., any case in which a law enforced by the FTC has been violated and equitable remedies are needed to make harmed consumers whole."

The district court agreed with the FTC. It was true, the court allowed, that a "proper case" could not mean "any case." The phrase "proper case" could be understood as an effort to distinguish between cases that were proper for a permanent, rather than preliminary, injunction—or as a reference to cases that did not rely on the FTC's "scientific expertise." But, leaving the boundaries of the zone for another day, it was enough that this case was an effort to enforce existing law, not to define new legal standards: "The FTC grounds its legal argument here in Circuit precedent, and does not seek to rely on its agency expertise to develop the law. Under such circumstances, the Court concludes that the complaint adequately alleges a 'proper case.'"

Surescripts thus gave the FTC a robust win on the "proper case" question, but it did not entirely foreclose future efforts by defendants to make some hay out of this enigmatic turn of phrase in Section 13(b).

AMG Cap. Mgmt., LLC v. FTC
141 S. Ct. 1341 (2021)

Justice Breyer.

[1] [S]everal considerations, taken together, convince us that § 13(b)'s "permanent injunction" language does not authorize the Commission directly to obtain court-ordered monetary relief. For one thing, the language refers only to injunctions. It says, "in proper cases the Commission may seek, and after proper proof, the court may issue, a permanent injunction." 15 U.S.C. § 53(b). An "injunction" is not the same as an award of equitable monetary relief. We have, however, sometimes interpreted similar language as authorizing judges to order equitable monetary relief.

[2] But if this language alone is not enough, there is more. The language and structure of § 13(b), taken as a whole, indicate that the words "permanent injunction" have a limited purpose—a purpose that does not extend to the grant of monetary relief. Those words are buried in a lengthy provision that focuses upon purely injunctive, not monetary, relief.

{Eds.: the Court here quoted Section 13(b), reproduced above.}

[3] Taken as a whole, the provision focuses upon relief that is prospective, not retrospective. Consider the words "is violating" and "is about to violate" (not "has violated") setting forth when the Commission may request injunctive relief. Consider too the words "pending the issuance of a complaint," "until such complaint is dismissed," "temporary restraining order," "preliminary injunction," and so forth in the first half of the section. These words reflect that the provision addresses a specific problem, namely, that of stopping seemingly unfair practices from taking place while the Commission determines their lawfulness. And the appearance of the words "permanent injunction" (as a proviso) suggests that those words are directly related to a previously issued preliminary injunction. They might also be read, for example, as granting authority for the Commission to go one step beyond the provisional and ("in proper cases") dispense with administrative proceedings to seek what the words literally say (namely, an injunction). But to read those words as allowing what they do not say, namely, as allowing the Commission to dispense with administrative proceedings to obtain monetary relief as well, is to read the words as going well beyond the provision's subject matter. In light of the historical importance of administrative proceedings, that reading would allow a small statutory tail to wag a very large dog.

[4] Further, the structure of the Act beyond § 13(b) confirms this conclusion. Congress in § 5(l) and § 19 gave district courts the authority to impose limited monetary penalties and to award monetary relief in cases where the Commission has issued cease and desist orders, *i.e.*, where the Commission has engaged in administrative proceedings. Since in these provisions Congress explicitly provided for "other and further equitable relief," 15 U. S. C. § 45(l), and for the "refund of money or return of property," § 57b(b), it likely did not intend for § 13(b)'s more cabined "permanent injunction" language to have similarly broad scope. [. . .]

[5] It is highly unlikely that Congress would have enacted provisions expressly authorizing conditioned and limited monetary relief if the Act, via § 13(b), had already implicitly allowed the Commission to obtain that same monetary relief and more without satisfying those conditions and limitations. Nor is it likely that Congress, without mentioning the matter, would have granted the Commission authority so readily to circumvent its traditional § 5 administrative proceedings.

[6] At the same time, to read § 13(b) to mean what it says, as authorizing injunctive but not monetary relief, produces a coherent enforcement scheme: The Commission may obtain monetary relief by first invoking its administrative procedures and then § 19's redress provisions (which include limitations). And the Commission may use § 13(b) to obtain injunctive relief while administrative proceedings are foreseen or in progress, or when it seeks only injunctive relief. By contrast, the Commission's broad reading would allow it to use § 13(b) as a substitute for § 5 and § 19. For the reasons we have just stated, that could not have been Congress' intent. Cf. *Whitman v. American Trucking Assns., Inc.*, 531 U.S. 457, 468, (2001) ("Congress does not hide elephants in mouseholes").

4. Competition Rulemaking Authority

In addition to its power to sue violators of Section 5 and conduct market studies under Section 6(b), the FTC has some power to undertake some rulemaking.

The FTC's principal rulemaking powers are aimed at consumer protection. The most important source of such authority is the Magnuson-Moss Act, codified at 15 U.S.C. § 57a. This is reserved for consumer-protection matters,[891] and requires the FTC to follow a lengthy process (including the publication of an advance notice of proposed rulemaking, followed by a notice of proposed rulemaking, followed by informal hearings, and finally judicial review before the D.C. Circuit at the behest of any interested person) before enforcing the rule.[892] The FTC also has some narrow authorities to make particular kinds of rules, subject to the Administrative Procedures Act, created by individual federal statutes over the years.[893]

But the FTC also has some statutory authority that can arguably be understood to authorize competition rulemaking. In particular, the FTC has power under Section 6(g) of the FTC Act, 15 U.S.C. § 46(g), to "[f]rom time to time classify corporations and (except as provided [in the Magnuson-Moss Act]) to make rules and regulations for the purpose of carrying out the provisions of this subchapter." The "subchapter" in question—15 U.S.C. §§ 41–58—includes among other things Section 5 of the FTC Act, 15 U.S.C. § 5.

The meaning of this Section 6(g) language is deeply controversial. Some commentators suggest that this statutory language creates a broad rulemaking power to "carry[] out" the FTC's function to prohibit unfair methods of competition—that is, a power to engage in general competition rulemaking—and they cite a 1973 D.C. Circuit opinion, *National Petroleum Refiners Association*, in support of this reading.[894] Other commentators argue that this language is a slender reed on which to hang a broad competition rulemaking power, and point to more recent cases that appear inconsistent with the earlier one.[895] To muddy the waters a little further: there appears to be exactly one example of pure UMC rulemaking in the FTC's history between 1914 and 2022. The "Tailored Clothing Rule" was promulgated in 1967 to clarify the application of the Robinson-Patman Act (which, as you may recall, prohibits certain forms of price discrimination) to promotional allowances in the tailored clothing industry: that rule was never enforced and was repealed in 1994.[896]

In 2023, the FTC called the question: launching a rulemaking effort aimed at the prohibition of labor non-compete agreements.[897] The Chair's Statement accompanying the Notice of Proposed Rule-Making pointed to *National*

---

[891] 15 U.S.C. § 57a(a).

[892] *See generally, e.g.,* Jeffrey S. Lubbers, *It's Time to Remove the "Mossified" Procedures for FTC Rulemaking*, 83 G.W.L. Rev. 1979 (2015); Kurt Walters, *Reassessing the Mythology of Magnuson-Moss: A Call to Revive Section 18 Rulemaking at the FTC*, 16 Harv. L. & Pol'y Rev. 519 (2022).

[893] *See, e.g.,* 15 U.S.C. § 68d (wool labeling).

[894] *See, e.g.,* Rohit Chopra & Lina M. Khan, *The Case for "Unfair Methods of Competition" Rulemaking*, 87 U. Chi. L. Rev. 357 (2020).

[895] *See, e.g.,* Maureen K. Ohlhausen & Ben Rossen, *Dead End Road: National Petroleum Refiners Association and FTC "Unfair Methods of Competition" Rulemaking*, in Daniel A. Crane (ed.) RULEMAKING AUTHORITY OF THE FEDERAL TRADE COMMISSION (2022).

[896] *See* 59 Fed. Reg. 8527 (Feb. 23, 1994) (recounting nature of rule, history, and reason for rescission).

[897] FTC, Press Release, FTC Proposes Rule to Ban Noncompete Clauses, Which Hurt Workers and Harm Competition (Jan. 5, 2023).

Petroleum Refiners Association as "the only case that directly addresses the FTC's Section 6(g) rulemaking authority" and representing the "current state of the law."[898]

We turn now to that case. In *National Petroleum Refiners Association*, the FTC had promulgated a rule stating that the failure to post "octane rating numbers" for gasoline at service stations was *both* an unfair method of competition *and* an unfair or deceptive act or practice. (The case thus involved a mingling of antitrust and consumer protection functions through the enaction of a rule.) The D.C. Circuit was asked to decide whether Section 6(g) supported the enaction of the rule, and it held that it did.

Nat'l Petroleum Refiners Ass'n v. FTC
482 F.2d 672 (D.C. Cir. 1973)

Judge Skelly Wright.

[1] Our duty here is not simply to make a policy judgment as to what mode of procedure—adjudication alone or a mixed system of rule-making and adjudication, as the Commission proposes—best accommodates the need for effective enforcement of the Commission's mandate with maximum solicitude for the interests of parties whose activities might be within the scope of the statutory standard of illegality. The Federal Trade Commission is a creation of Congress, not a creation of judges' contemporary notions of what is wise policy. The extent of its powers can be decided only by considering the powers Congress specifically granted it in the light of the statutory language and background. The question to be answered is not what the Commission thinks it should do but what Congress has said it can do. [. . .]

[2] [T]he [Federal] Trade Commission Act includes a provision which specifically provides for rule-making by the Commission to implement its adjudicatory functions under Section 5 of the Act. Section 6(g) of the Act, 15 U.S.C. § 46(g), states that the Commission may "[f]rom time to time . . . classify corporations and . . . make rules and regulations for the purpose of carrying out the provisions of [relevant sections] of this title."

[3] According to appellees, however, this rule-making power is limited to specifying the details of the Commission's nonadjudicatory, investigative and informative functions spelled out in the other provisions of Section 6 and should not be read to encompass substantive rulemaking in implementation of Section 5 adjudications. We disagree for the simple reason that Section 6(g) clearly states that the Commission "may" make rules and regulations for the purpose of carrying out the provisions of Section 5 and it has been so applied. [. . .]

[4] [I]t is at least arguable that [previous] cases go no farther than to justify utilizing Section 6(g) to promulgate procedural, as opposed to substantive, rules for administration of the Section 5 adjudication and enforcement powers. But we see no reason to import such a restriction on the "rules and regulations" permitted by Section 6(g). On the contrary, as we shall see, judicial precedents concerning rule-making by other agencies and the background and purpose of the Federal Trade Commission Act lead us liberally to construe the term "rules and regulations." The substantive rule here unquestionably implements the statutory plan. Section 5 adjudications–trial type proceedings–will still be necessary to obtain cease and desist orders against offenders, but Section 5 enforcement through adjudication will be expedited, simplified, and thus "carried out" by use of this substantive rule. And the overt language of both Section 5 and Section 6, read together, supports its use in Section 5 proceedings. [. . .]

[5] Our belief that "rules and regulations" in Section 6(g) should be construed to permit the Commission to promulgate binding substantive rules as well as rules of procedure is reinforced by the construction courts have given similar provisions in the authorizing statutes of other administrative agencies. There is, of course, no doubt that the approved practices of agencies with similar statutory provisions is a relevant factor in arriving at a sound interpretation of the Federal Trade Commission's power here. [. . .]

---

[898] Statement of Chair Lina M. Khan Joined by Commissioner Rebecca Kelly Slaughter and Commissioner Alvaro M. Bedoya Regarding the Notice of Proposed Rulemaking to Restrict Employers' Use of Noncompete Clauses, FTC File No. P201200 (Jan. 5, 2023) 4 n.12.

[6] The need to interpret liberally broad grants of rule-making authority like the one we construe here has been emphasized time and again by the Supreme Court. [. . .]

[7] [W]hile we believe the historical evidence is indecisive of the question before us, we are convinced that the broad, undisputed policies which clearly motivated the framers of the Federal Trade Commission Act of 1914 would indeed be furthered by our view as to the proper scope of the Commission's rule-making authority. The multiplicity of differing plans proposed for a trade commission prior to 1914 and during the intensive debates in 1914 immediately preceding enactment of the Trade Commission Act demonstrates, of course, that proponents of the agency were hardly agreed on exactly what powers the agency should assume. But the variety of plans and the proponents of the agency all unquestionably shared deep objections to the existing structure of judicial monopolization of cases involving unfair, anticompetitive business practices. Those who believed from the start in a commission with independent enforcement powers, as the Commission was finally given in the 1914 legislation, and those who believed the Commission should have lesser powers, agreed that entrusting enforcement of congressional policy to prevent undue incursions on competition exclusively to the courts was a serious mistake. The courts were said to lack sufficient expertise in matters of economic complexity, their decisions were said to be wanting in the clarity planners of complicated business transactions and innovations required, and finally and most importantly, the courts lacked both the resources and the skill to proceed with speed and expedition in the trial and disposition of complicated cases involving economic questions. This concern over judicial delay, inefficiency and uncertainty was echoed time and again throughout the 1914 debates over the form a commission would take.

[8] In determining the legislative intent, our duty is to favor an interpretation which would render the statutory design effective in terms of the policies behind its enactment and to avoid an interpretation which would make such policies more difficult of fulfillment, particularly where, as here, that interpretation is consistent with the plain language of the statute. In the absence of an unmistakable directive, we cannot construe the Act in a manner which runs counter to the broad goals which Congress intended it to effectuate. Indeed, as Mr. Justice Harlan put it in a case involving a question of the Federal Power Commission's power under a general rule-making provision to alter radically its customary modes of proceeding, [t]his Court has repeatedly held that the width of administrative authority must be measured in part by the purposes for which it was conferred. This view was reiterated just a few weeks ago by Mr. Chief Justice Burger, writing for the Court:

> Where the empowering provision of a statute states simply that the agency may make such rules and regulations as may be necessary to carry out the provisions of this Act, we have held that the validity of a regulation promulgated thereunder will be sustained so long as it is reasonably related to the purposes of the enabling legislation.

Mourning v. Family Publications Service, Inc., 411 U.S. 356, 369 (1973). In short, where a statute is said to be susceptible of more than one meaning, we must not only consult its language; we must also relate the interpretation we provide to the felt and openly articulated concerns motivating the law's framers. In this way we may be sure we are construing the statute rather than constructing a new one. [. . .]

[9] Despite the import of Section 6(g)'s plain language, the overwhelming judicial support given to expansive agency readings of statutory rule-making authorizations that are not flatly inconsistent with other statutory provisions, and the incontestable relationship between the broad policies behind the 1914 Act and the utility of substantive rule-making power, appellees argue that substantive rule-making represents a sufficiently important innovation in Commission practice for us to balk at authorizing its use on the basis of an arguably ambiguous statute in the absence of very firm indications of affirmative and specific legislative intent. Indeed, courts have assumed such a stance toward novel assertions of agency powers. . . .

[10] [But unlike some earlier cases], this case does not involve nearly so drastic a departure from accustomed modes of agency proceeding. The rule here does not bypass the Commission's statute-based cease-and-desist proceedings. It merely supplements them. Moreover, in light of the concern evident in the legislative history that the Commission give attention to the special circumstances of individual businesses in proceeding against them, the Commission should administer any rules it might promulgate in much the same way that courts have ordinarily required other agencies to administer rules that operate to modify a regulated party's rights to a full hearing. That is, some opportunity must be given for a defendant in a Section 5 proceeding to demonstrate that the special

circumstances of his case warrant waiving the rule's applicability, as where the rationale of the rule does not appear to apply to his own situation or a compelling case of hardship can be made out. [. . .]

[11] Any fears that the agency could successfully use rule-making power as a means of oppressive or unreasonable regulation seem exaggerated in view of courts' general practice in reviewing rules to scrutinize their statement of basis and purpose to see whether the major issues of policy pro and con raised in the submissions to the agency were given sufficient consideration. The Commission is hardly free to write its own law of consumer protection and antitrust since the statutory standard which the rules may define with greater particularity is a legal standard. Although the Commission's conclusions as to the standard's reach are ordinarily shown deference, the standard must get its final meaning from judicial construction.

[12] As we suggested earlier, our task in determining the meaning of this legislation is the usual one of starting from the areas where the legislative intent is readily discernible, and projecting to fair and reasonable corollaries of that intent for the specific issue before us. It is as clear as it is unlimited: "The Commission shall also have power . . . to make rules and regulations for the purpose of carrying out the provisions of Section 5." Ambiguous legislative history cannot change the express legislative intent. The Commission is using rule-making to carry out what the Congress agreed was among its central purposes: expedited administrative enforcement of the national policy against monopolies and unfair business practices. Under the circumstances, since Section 6(g) plainly authorizes rule-making and nothing in the statute or in its legislative history precludes its use for this purpose, the action of the Commission must be upheld.

[13] Our conclusion as to the scope of Section 6(g) is not disturbed by the fact that the agency itself did not assert the power to promulgate substantive rules until 1962 and indeed indicated intermittently before that time that it lacked such power. As the Supreme Court put it in *United States v. Morton Salt Co.*, [338 U.S. 632 (1950),] a case which involved what was thought to be a novel assertion of the FTC's statutory authority:

> The fact that powers long have been unexercised well may call for close scrutiny as to whether they exist; but if granted, they are not lost by being allowed to lie dormant, any more than nonexistent powers can be prescripted by an unchallenged exercise. We know that unquestioned powers are sometimes unexercised from lack of funds, motives of expediency, or the competition of more immediately important concerns. We find no basis for holding that any power ever granted to the Trade Commission has been forfeited by [nonuse].

[. .]

[14] [Courts have not hesitated] in construing broad grants of rule-making power to permit promulgation of rules with the force of law as a means of agency regulation of otherwise private conduct. . . .

[15] The need to interpret liberally broad grants of rule-making authority like the one we construe here has been emphasized time and again by the Supreme Court. [. . .]

[16] There is little disagreement that the Commission will be able to proceed more expeditiously, give greater certainty to businesses subject to the Act, and deploy its internal resources more efficiently with a mixed system of rule-making and adjudication than with adjudication alone. With the issues in Section 5 proceedings reduced by the existence of a rule delineating what is a violation of the statute or what presumptions the Commission proposes to rely upon, proceedings will be speeded up. For example, in an adjudication proceeding based on a violation of the octane rating rule at issue here, the central question to be decided will be whether or not pumps owned by a given refiner are properly marked. Without the rule, the Commission might well be obliged to prove and argue that the absence of the rating markers in each particular case was likely to have injurious and unfair effects on consumers or competition. Since this laborious process might well have to be repeated every time the Commission chose to proceed subsequently against another defendant on the same ground, the difference in administrative efficiency between the two kinds of proceedings is obvious. Furthermore, rules, as contrasted with the holdings reached by case-by-case adjudication, are more specific as to their scope, and industry compliance is more likely simply because each company is on clearer notice whether or not specific rules apply to it. [. . .]

[17] [The] relationship between rule-making's probable benefits and the broad concerns evident when the FTC was created, together with the express language of Section 6(g), help persuade us that any purported ambiguity of the statute be resolved in favor of the Commission's claim. [. . .]

[18] A more troubling obstacle to the Commission's position here is the argument that Congress was made fully aware of [a] formerly restrictive view of the Commission's power and passed a series of laws granting limited substantive rule-making authority to the Commission in discrete areas allegedly on the premise that the 1914 [legislative] debate withheld such authority. Where there has been evidence of congressional knowledge of and acquiescence in a long-standing agency construction of its own powers, courts have occasionally concluded that the agency construction had received a de facto ratification by Congress.

[19] But de facto ratification through acquiescence in an administrative construction is not lightly attributed. The argument before us is not that Congress, by a combination of its knowledge of the agency construction and its inaction . . . could be said to have accepted the construction. Even in these cases it can be argued quite plausibly that imputing ratification in this fashion fails to take into account significant practical aspects of the legislative process: those legislators actually aware of the construction in question may not have been so concerned as to raise it to the attention of most members, and even in the event some legislators were deeply troubled by the construction, the press of other business was such as to keep the question on the "back burner." Here the situation is different. The view that the Commission lacked substantive rule-making power has been clearly brought to the attention of Congress and, rather than simply failing to act on the question, Congress, in expanding the agency's powers in several discrete areas of marketing regulation, affirmatively enacted limited grants of substantive rule-making authority in the Wool Products Act of 1939, the Fur Products Labeling Act of 1951, the Flammable Fabrics Act of 1953 as amended in 1967, the Textile Fiber Products Identification Act of 1958, and the Fair Packaging and Labeling Act of 1967. Thus it is argued that Congress would not have granted the agency such powers unless it had felt that otherwise the agency lacked rule-making authority.

[20] Conceding the greater force of this argument than one premised on congressional inaction, we believe it must not be accepted blindly. In such circumstances, it is equally possible that Congress granted the power out of uncertainty, understandable caution, and a desire to avoid litigation. While this argument, like any theory requiring us to draw inferences from congressional action or inaction, may be speculative, we believe it cannot be ignored here. For there is ample evidence that, while some of the limited rule-making legislation may well have been influenced by the belief that the 1914 Act did not grant the Commission substantive rule-making power, at least during the passage of the Packaging and Labeling Act of 1967, this assumption was not accepted and was thought by many congressmen to be an open question, despite the protestations of the Commission's chairman that the agency was powerless under the 1914 Act. . . . [I]mputing congressional ratification to a disputed administrative construction of its powers is, in the words of the Supreme Court, shaky business. Where there is solid reason, as there plainly is here, to believe that Congress, in fact, has not wholeheartedly accepted the agency's viewpoint and instead enacted legislation out of caution and to eliminate the kind of disputes that invariably attend statutory ambiguity, we believe that relying on the de facto ratification argument is unwise. In such circumstances, we must perform our customary task of coming to an independent judgment as to the statute's meaning, confident that if Congress believes that its creature, the Commission, thus exercises too much power, it will repeal the grant.

[21] In sum, we must respectfully register our disagreement with the District Court's painstaking opinion. Its result would render the Commission ineffective to do the job assigned it by Congress.

The Supreme Court and Administrative Agency Power

Alabama Ass'n of Realtors v. Dept. of Health and Human Servs., 141 S.Ct. 2485 (2021); West Virginia v. EPA, 142 S.Ct. 2587 (2022)

Despite what you have just read, there is considerable doubt whether the approach outlined in *National Petroleum Refiners Association* would be followed today. The Supreme Court's 2021 decision in *Alabama Association of Realtors* and its 2022 decision in West Virginia exemplify current skepticism in the federal judiciary about broad (and particularly novel) assertions of agency power—even when statutory text can be read to confer considerable power.

In *Alabama Association of Realtors*, the Center for Disease Control had enacted an eviction moratorium in reliance on a broad delegated rulemaking power. The statutory power—§ 361(a) of the Public Health Service Act—empowered the Surgeon General, with the approval of the Secretary of Health and Human Services, to: "make and enforce such regulations as in his judgment are necessary to prevent the introduction, transmission, or spread of communicable diseases from foreign countries into the States or possessions, or from one State or possession into any other State or possession." The next sentence continued: "For purposes of carrying out and enforcing such regulations, the Surgeon General may provide for such inspection, fumigation, disinfection, sanitation, pest extermination, destruction of animals or articles found to be so infected or contaminated as to be sources of dangerous infection to human beings, and other measures, as in his judgment may be necessary."

The Supreme Court struck down the eviction moratorium for want of authority.[899] First, the Court pointed out, the second sentence of § 361(a) "informs" the first, by illustrating the kinds of measures that might be necessary to respond to disease within the meaning of the provision. An eviction moratorium "relates to interstate infection far more indirectly" than do the various activities in the second, making it a "stretch" to imagine that the first sentence contained such a power.

But even if the text were more ambiguous, the Court held, "the sheer scope of the CDC's claimed authority under § 361(a) would counsel against the Government's interpretation. We expect Congress to speak clearly when authorizing an agency to exercise powers of vast economic and political significance. That is exactly the kind of power that the CDC claims here. At least 80% of the country, including between 6 and 17 million tenants at risk of eviction, falls within the moratorium." In addition, the eviction moratorium intruded into "an area that is the particular domain of state law: the landlord-tenant relationship. Our precedents require Congress to enact exceedingly clear language if it wishes to significantly alter the balance between federal and state power and the power of the Government over private property."

More generally, reading § 361(a) to give the CDC the power to block evictions "would give the CDC a breathtaking amount of authority. It is hard to see what measures this interpretation would place outside the CDC's reach, and the Government has identified no limit in § 361(a) beyond the requirement that the CDC deem a measure necessary. Could the CDC, for example, mandate free grocery delivery to the homes of the sick or vulnerable? Require manufacturers to provide free computers to enable people to work from home? Order telecommunications companies to provide free high-speed Internet service to facilitate remote work?" Such an "unprecedented" reading of § 361(a) would dramatically break with the historical use and understanding of the provision. Indeed, "[s]ince [its] enactment in 1944, no regulation premised on it has even begun to approach the size or scope of the eviction moratorium."

The following year, in 2022, the Court decided West Virginia v. Environmental Protection Agency, holding among other things that "something more than a merely plausible textual basis for . . . agency action is necessary" to justify assertions of power in ways that would amount to an "extraordinary grant of regulatory authority" or work a "radical or fundamental change" in a statutory scheme. The Court would henceforth presume that "Congress intends to make major policy decisions itself, not leave those decisions to agencies": in such "major question" cases, "clear congressional authorization for the power [the agency] claims" would be required. In that case, the Court applied the major-questions doctrine to conclude that the EPA lacked power, under the Clean Air Act, to cap CO_2 emissions pursuant to a "generation shifting" plan designed to spur a transition to cleaner energy sources.

Plainly these cases indicate a much less charitable approach to agency efforts to implement broad policy initiatives pursuant to capacious but ambiguous statutory language. Do they imply the end of *National Petroleum Refiners*?

NOTES

1) What kinds of practices should constitute "unfair methods of competition" that do not constitute violations of the antitrust laws? Why?

---

[899] *See also* West Virginia v. EPA, 142 S. Ct. 2587, 2609 (2022) (holding that for "major" policy decisions, "something more than a merely plausible textual basis for the agency action is necessary," and "[t]he agency instead must point to 'clear congressional authorization' for the power it claims").

2) In what respects is the 2022 Section 5 policy statement different from the 2015 one? In what respects is it different from the rules imposed by the antitrust statutes?

3) When Congress created the FTC, why do you think it left DOJ with power to enforce the antitrust laws after doing so?

4) The market-study power allows the FTC to require compulsory production of documents and information from companies.

    a. What three market studies would you undertake and why? Specify the recipients, the nature of the specifications in the studies, and the payoff of the study for antitrust enforcement and policy.

    b. The market study power is limited in practice by the OMB requirement for burdensome additional process (under the Paperwork Reduction Act) for studies with more than nine respondents. What effect do you think this has in practice? Is it a good rule?[900]

5) Does it add value to have antitrust and consumer protection (from "unfair" and "deceptive" acts and practices) under the same roof at the FTC?

6) Imagine that the FTC was given plenary rulemaking power by Congress to enact rules to prevent unfair methods of competition, defined as violations of the antitrust laws. (In other words, assume a broad rulemaking power but a narrow definition of UMC under Section 5.). What rules would you write and why?

7) When should the FTC use its internal administrative litigation process rather than litigating in district court? Should this option exist at all?

8) Do you think the FTC has competition rulemaking power today? Do you think it should have?

9) Do you think the reasoning in *Humphrey's Executor* is undermined by the later introduction of the FTC's power to litigate in district courts?

C. The Department of Justice

The Department of Justice was the nation's first antitrust enforcer, and is the only federal criminal antitrust authority.

1. Structure and Organization

The Antitrust Division of the Department of Justice is led by an Assistant Attorney General ("AAG") for the Antitrust Division, and managed by a front office that also includes Deputy Assistant Attorneys General and a number of Counsel. The AAG reports to the Attorney General and serves at the pleasure of the President.

The Division consists of the following sub-components:

- Seven civil sections, which handle merger and nonmerger matters in their respective industries:
    - the Defense, Industrials, and Aerospace Section;
    - the Financial Services, Fintech, and Banking Section;
    - the Healthcare and Consumer Products Section;
    - the Media, Entertainment, and Communications Section;
    - the Technology and Digital Platforms Section;
    - the Transportation, Energy, and Agriculture Section; and
    - a Civil Conduct Task Force to coordinate and facilitate nonmerger enforcement;
- Criminal enforcement units:
    - two Criminal Sections based in Washington, D.C.;
    - criminal enforcement teams in Chicago, New York, and San Francisco;
    - a Procurement Collusion Strike Force to tackle bid-rigging and other crimes affecting government procurement;
- an Economic Analysis Group; and

---

[900] *See, e.g.,* FTC, PATENT ASSERTION ENTITY ACTIVITY: AN FTC STUDY (Oct. 2016) 37 (noting that the FTC began the process of obtaining authorization in September 2013, eventually receiving approval in August 2014). *See generally, e.g., Methodologies for Conducting Market Studies—Note by the United States,* OECD Working Paper DAF/COMP/WP3/WD(2017)19 (May 26, 2017) (detailing FTC's approach to market studies under 6(b), including the OMB requirements).

- a variety of other offices handling policy, appellate, international, administrative, and other matters.

Overall, the Antitrust Division reported 1,022 "direct authorized positions" for Fiscal Year 2023.[901] The Division works closely with other components of the Department of Justice, including the Office of the Solicitor General, which leads and coordinates work on Supreme Court matters and advises on some appeals.[902]

2. Powers and Functions

Just like the FTC, the DOJ's civil investigations commonly begin with an informal or voluntary phase, featuring voluntary interviews and productions of documents and information, which may progress to the issue of compulsory process—CIDs—with the approval of the Assistant Attorney General.[903] The Antitrust Division Manual sets out helpful guidance on DOJ's conduct of civil antitrust investigations.[904]

DOJ enforces the Sherman Act and the Clayton Act directly. Pursuant to 15 U.S.C. § 25, DOJ may file suit in district court "to prevent and restrain" antitrust violations. DOJ may also sue under the antitrust laws to recover treble damages for injuries suffered by the United States (*e.g.*, when the federal government is itself an injured customer or supplier).[905] As a result, DOJ faces none of the complexities or controversies raised by the FTC's unique structure, nor must it struggle with the peculiarities of Section 13(b) of the FTC Act. Like the FTC, DOJ issues guidance to consumers and businesses, and files amicus briefs and statements of interest in antitrust cases.

The Expediting Act

From 1903 to 1974, a statute called the Expediting Act provided for direct appeal from a district court to the Supreme Court—bypassing the courts of appeal—in civil antitrust cases brought by DOJ. The statute aimed to empower the Court to build a coherent national antitrust jurisprudence.[906] But it came with real costs. In *Brown Shoe*, for example, Justice Clark complained that the Act "deprives the parties of an intermediate appeal and this Court of the benefit of consideration by a Court of Appeals,"[907] while Justice Harlan grumbled that there was "much to be said in favor of relieving this Court of the often arduous task of searching through voluminous trial testimony any exhibits to determine whether a single district judge's findings of fact are supportable."[908] In 1974, Congress amended the Act, allowing direct appeal only if the district court certifies that "immediate consideration of the appeal by the Supreme Court is of general public importance in the administration of justice."[909] President Ford's signing statement noted that the change would "halt the practice of clogging the Supreme Court docket by taking all antitrust appeals directly to that tribunal, thus denying it the wisdom and advice of the U.S. Circuit Courts of Appeals."[910] Perhaps coincidentally, the Court's last substantive merger decision was in 1975.[911]

The Justice Department also has unique statutory authority to undertake certain kinds of antitrust investigations, including those relating to certain kinds of telecommunications, banks, railroads, and airlines, including by virtue of carveouts from FTC jurisdiction.[912]

---

[901] https://www.justice.gov/d9/2023-03/atr_bs_section_ii_omb_cleared_3.8.23.pdf.

[902] The FTC generally has independent litigating authority (*i.e.*, independent of DOJ), including some limited independence to litigate in the Supreme Court. *See* 15 U.S.C. § 56.

[903] 15 U.S.C. § 1312.

[904] *See* https://www.justice.gov/atr/division-manual.

[905] 15 U.S.C. § 15a.

[906] Robert C. Bonges, *The Antitrust Expediting Act—A Critical Reappraisal*, 63 Mich. L. Rev. 1240, 1242 (1965); W. Wallace Kirkpatrick, *Antitrust to the Supreme Court: The Expediting Act*, 37 Geo. Wash. L. Rev. 746, 748 (1969).

[907] Brown Shoe Co. v. United States, 370 U.S. 294, 355 (1962) (Clark, J., concurring).

[908] Brown Shoe Co. v. United States, 370 U.S. 294, 364 (1962) (Harlan, J., concurring in part and dissenting in part).

[909] 15 U.S.C. § 29(b).

[910] Statement by the President re: S.782 Antitrust Procedures and Penalties Act (Dec. 21, 1974), https://www.fordlibrarymuseum.gov/library/document/0055/1668810.pdf.

[911] United States v. Citizens and Southern Nat'l Bank, 422 U.S. 86 (1975).

[912] *See supra* notes 875–876 and accompanying text.

However, the Department of Justice does face some unique constraints as a civil enforcer. Unlike the Federal Trade Commission (which simply makes proposed consent decrees available for public comment before they are finally entered by the Commission), DOJ is subject to the Tunney Act, which provides for federal court review of DOJ consent decrees to determine that the settlement is in the public interest.[913] (The Tunney Act was enacted as a response to Congressional concern regarding the Nixon Administration's interference with a DOJ investigation of ITT.[914]) As part of that process, DOJ files with the court a "Competitive Impact Statement" explaining why the proposed remedy resolves the relevant antitrust concerns, and the court reviews the settlement and evidence bearing on its suitability.

Tunney Act review has sometimes led to changes in relief. Most famously, following the district court's Tunney Act review of the blockbuster consent decree breaking up AT&T in 1982, Judge Greene required additional provisions to be added to address his concerns.[915] But there is room for some disagreement about the scope of review and the extent to which DOJ should enjoy deference.[916] The next extract, taken from one such statement, states DOJ's view of the purpose and scope of Tunney Act review; the following note sets out Judge Leon's perspective.

Competitive Impact Statement, United States v. Intuit Inc.
Case No. 1:20-cv-3441 (D.D.C. filed Dec. 10, 2020)

[1] The Clayton Act, as amended by the [Antitrust Procedures and Penalties Act], requires that proposed consent judgments in antitrust cases brought by the United States be subject to a 60-day comment period, after which the Court shall determine whether entry of the proposed Final Judgment "is in the public interest." In making that determination, the Court, in accordance with the statute as amended in 2004, is required to consider:

> (A) the competitive impact of such judgment, including termination of alleged violations, provisions for enforcement and modification, duration of relief sought, anticipated effects of alternative remedies actually considered, whether its terms are ambiguous, and any other competitive considerations bearing upon the adequacy of such judgment that the court deems necessary to a determination of whether the consent judgment is in the public interest; and

> (B) the impact of entry of such judgment upon competition in the relevant market or markets, upon the public generally and individuals alleging specific injury from the violations set forth in the complaint including consideration of the public benefit, if any, to be derived from a determination of the issues at trial.

15 U.S.C. § 16(e)(1)(A) & (B). In considering these statutory factors, the Court's inquiry is necessarily a limited one as the government is entitled to broad discretion to settle with the defendant within the reaches of the public interest.

[2] As the U.S. Court of Appeals for the District of Columbia Circuit has held, under the APPA a court considers, among other things, the relationship between the remedy secured and the specific allegations in the government's complaint, whether the proposed Final Judgment is sufficiently clear, whether its enforcement mechanisms are sufficient, and whether it may positively harm third parties. With respect to the adequacy of the relief secured by the proposed Final Judgment, a court may not make de novo determination of facts and issues. Instead, the balancing of competing social and political interests affected by a proposed antitrust consent decree must be left, in the first instance, to the discretion of the Attorney General. The court should bear in mind the flexibility of the public interest inquiry: the court's function is not to determine whether the resulting array of rights and liabilities is one that will best serve society, but only to confirm that the resulting settlement is within the reaches of the

---

[913] 15 U.S.C. § 16.

[914] *See* George Lardner Jr., *On Tape, Nixon Outlines 1971 "Deal" to Settle Antitrust Case Against ITT*, WASHINGTON POST (Jan. 4, 1997).

[915] United States v. AT&T Co., 552 F. Supp. 131 (D.D.C. 1982). *See also* Memorandum Order, United States v. Comcast Corp., Case No, 1:11-cv-106 (D.D.C. filed Sept. 1, 2011) (ordering additional relief pursuant to consent decree in light of hearing).

[916] For a thoughtful overview of the issues, *see, e.g.*, Alexandra P. Clark, *Leaving Judicial Review with the Judiciary: The Misplaced Role of Agency Deference in Tunney Act Public Interest Review*, 78 Wash. & Lee L. Rev. 925 (2022). *See also, e.g.*, Darren Bush, *The Death of the Tunney Act at the Hands of an Activist D.C. Circuit*, 63 Antitrust Bull. 113 (2018).

public interest. More demanding requirements would have enormous practical consequences for the government's ability to negotiate future settlements, contrary to congressional intent. The Tunney Act was not intended to create a disincentive to the use of the consent decree.

[3] The United States' predictions about the efficacy of the remedy are to be afforded deference by the Court. The ultimate question is whether the remedies obtained by the Final Judgment are so inconsonant with the allegations charged as to fall outside of the reaches of the public interest.

[4] Moreover, the Court's role under the APPA is limited to reviewing the remedy in relationship to the violations that the United States has alleged in its complaint, and does not authorize the Court to construct its own hypothetical case and then evaluate the decree against that case. Because the "court's authority to review the decree depends entirely on the government's exercising its prosecutorial discretion by bringing a case in the first place, it follows that "the court is only authorized to review the decree itself, and not to effectively redraft the complaint to inquire into other matters that the United States did not pursue.

CASENOTE: Tunney Act in Action: United States v. CVS Health Corp.
407 F. Supp. 3d 45 (D.D.C. 2019)

Despite some of the language in the preceding extract, the full reach of the Tunney Act was demonstrated in 2019 when Judge Leon of the U.S. District Court for the District of Columbia undertook an extensive review— effectively, a mini-trial—of the proposed resolution of the CVS / Aetna merger. His opinion contains an extended discussion of the role and nature of Tunney Act review, and offers an interesting complement to DOJ's perspective above.

The court began by underscoring the importance of the Tunney Act: "Industry players, consumer groups, and state regulatory bodies have all raised concerns about CVS's acquisition of Aetna. The merger combines two healthcare giants. Its effects, for better or worse, will be felt by millions of consumers. As I explained to the parties near the outset of this case, with so much at stake, the congressionally mandated public interest inquiry must be thorough. Indeed, if the Tunney Act is to mean anything, it surely must mean that no court should rubberstamp a consent decree approving the merger of one of the largest companies in the United States and the nation's third-largest health-insurance company, simply because the Government requests it!"

The court then outlined the government's obligations during the Tunney Act process: (1) the government must "publish its proposed final judgment and a competitive impact statement in the Federal Register at least sixty days before the effective date of the proposed judgment"; (2) during this 60-day period, the government "must receive and consider written comments about its proposed judgment"; (3) once the period ends, it must "publish a response to those comments in the Federal Register and file the same response with the Court," and "publish the proposed final judgment and competitive impact statement in a newspaper of general circulation in the district where the case is pending and to furnish the competitive impact statement to members of the public upon request."

In addition to these steps, the court explained, the Tunney Act requires the court to "determine that the entry of such judgment is in the public interest." In this case, the court was far from satisfied with the government's written responses to the comments received. The response was "rife with conclusory assertions that merely reiterate the Government's confidence in its proposed remedy, but shed little light on the reasons for that confidence. Indeed, the Government's perfunctory response to the public comments was particularly disappointing in light of the volume and quality of the comments to which it was responding!"

As a result, the court decided to take an unusual step. "Rather than risk an uninformed public interest determination that relied too heavily on responses like these from the Government, I decided to hold hearings on the Motion to Enter the Proposed Final Judgment. The hearings were designed to assist the Court in evaluating the public record. The parties and the amici were given the opportunity to propose up to three witnesses who could be called to testify. The Court alone would decide which of those witnesses it believed would be most helpful to its analysis and how much time would be allotted to each witness. In the end, the amici were allowed to call a combined total of three witnesses who were permitted to testify for a total of four hours. CVS and the Government were allowed the same combined total of witnesses and the same combined total number of hours of testimony.

To reinforce my repeated emphasis that the hearings were not a trial, cross-examination was not permitted. Only the Court was allowed to ask follow-up questions during the direct examination of each witness."

The court's public-interest determination would be guided by the language of the Tunney Act, 15 U.S.C. § 16(e)(1), which required the court to consider: "(A) the competitive impact of such judgment, including termination of alleged violations, provisions for enforcement and modification, duration of relief sought, anticipated effects of alternative remedies actually considered, whether its terms are ambiguous, and any other competitive considerations bearing upon the adequacy of such judgment that the court deems necessary to a determination of whether the consent judgment is in the public interest; and (B) the impact of entry of such judgment upon competition in the relevant market or markets, upon the public generally and individuals alleging specific injury from the violations set forth in the complaint." In exercising this function, Judge Leon allowed, a court cannot "force the government to make a claim. The Government, alone, chooses which causes of action to allege in its complaint." But this does not mean the court should be blinkered: "[W]hile the Government is certainly entitled to great deference—if not a presumption of accuracy—when it contends that a proposed final judgment is in the public interest, evidence by third parties that persuasively demonstrates actual or likely harm to the public interest will overcome that presumption and the proposed final judgment will be denied."

In this case, as it turned out, the hearing had vindicated the government's position. The variety of concerns raised by amici had "shed a healthy light on this merger," but had not "persuasively demonstrate[ed] that the concerns currently exist or are likely to develop." Indeed, "the markets at issue are not only very competitive today, but are likely to remain so post-merger." Accordingly, there was no basis for rebuttal of the presumption in favor of the government's position, and the government's motion to enter the final judgment would be granted.

Unlike the FTC, DOJ has a criminal antitrust jurisdiction. This enforcement function is part of the Justice Department's overall (*i.e.*, non-antitrust) criminal enforcement program. The criminal program represents a significant share of DOJ's resource allocation and enforcement activity: in calendar year 2019, for example, DOJ initiated 38 criminal grand jury investigations and filed 26 criminal cases, compared to 72 merger and 18 non-merger civil investigations and 19 civil cases.[917]

In recent decades, criminal antitrust enforcement had been aimed only at conduct that is *per se* illegal under Section 1 of the Sherman Act: as we saw in Chapters IV and V, this includes price-fixing, market division, and bid-rigging. But the Division has recently signaled an expansion of its criminal enforcement program on at least two fronts.

First, the Division has undertaken for the first time criminal enforcement efforts relating to the fixing of wages by employers. The pathbreaking effort here was the prosecution of Neeraj Jindal and John Rogers in the U.S. District Court for the Eastern District of Texas for fixing wages to be paid to physical therapists. As we saw in Chapter V, the defendants argued that, while their conduct was nakedly anticompetitive, the fact that they were fixing purchase prices for labor rather than sale prices for other products or services meant that criminal scrutiny was inappropriate, including because they were denied fair notice that their conduct could be criminally prosecuted. The court disagreed and agreed with the Division that price-fixing and wage-fixing should be treated alike under Section 1, including in criminal cases. (However, the defendants were subsequently acquitted of wage-fixing by a jury.[918])

In a second—and rather more far-reaching—development, the Justice Department has recently launched an effort to criminally prosecute monopolization cases:

> One enforcement tool that the division has not recently utilized is Section 2. But unlike labor market collusion, Section 2 has not always been underenforced. Historically, the division didn't shy away from bringing criminal monopolization charges, frequently alongside Section 1 charges, when companies and executives committed flagrant offenses intended to monopolize markets.

---

[917] U.S. Dept. of Justice, *Antitrust Division Workload Statistics FY2010–19*, https://www.justice.gov/atr/file/788426/download.

[918] *See* U.S. Dept. of Justice, Press Release, Former Health Care Staffing Executive Convicted of Obstructing FTC Investigation into Wage-Fixing Allegations (Apr. 14, 2022).

Our job is straightforward: We enforce the laws that Congress passes. When it comes to criminal antitrust, that means prosecuting violations of not just Section 1, but also Section 2. Moving forward we intend to do our job as law enforcers and fully prosecute violations of our competition laws.

Section 2 is a criminal statute that's been on the books for over 130 years. It has been a felony for more than 40 years, which Congress reaffirmed in 2004 when it increased the felony penalties. Yet, since the late 1970s, the Antitrust Division effectively ignored Section 2 when it came to criminal enforcement. Going forward, the division will no longer ignore Section 2. A long history of Section 2 prosecutions and accompanying case law show us the way forward. If the facts and the law, and a careful analysis of department policies guiding our use of prosecutorial discretion, warrant a criminal Section 2 charge, the division will not hesitate to enforce the law.[919]

As we saw in Chapter VII, the law of monopolization is complex and enigmatic: as a result, many commentators expressed surprise that the Justice Department would take its criminal enforcement program in this direction. Among other things, courts have rejected constitutional fair-notice challenges to criminal enforcement under Section 1 because prosecution is limited to a reasonably clear set of *per se* offenses.[920]

In October 2022, DOJ pushed this program ahead by obtaining a guilty plea to criminal attempted monopolization in a case involving "highway crack-sealing services." As the press release explained:

> The president of a paving and asphalt contractor based in Billings, Montana, has pleaded guilty to attempting to monopolize the market for highway crack-sealing services in Montana and Wyoming.

> According to the one-count felony charge filed on Sept. 19 in the U.S. District Court for the District of Montana, Nathan Nephi Zito attempted to monopolize the markets for highway crack-sealing services in Montana and Wyoming by proposing that his company and its competitor allocate regional markets. The charge states that as early as January 2020, Zito approached a competitor about a "strategic partnership" and proposed that the competitor stop competing with Zito's company for highway crack-sealing projects administered by Montana and Wyoming. In return, Zito's company would stop competing with the competitor for projects administered by South Dakota and Nebraska. Zito offered to pay his competitor $100,000 as additional compensation for lost business in Montana and Wyoming. Zito further proposed that he and his competitor enter into a sham transaction to disguise their collusion. The charge states that Zito intended to monopolize the highway crack-sealing services markets in Montana and Wyoming. Today, the District Court accepted the guilty plea that was allocuted on Oct. 14, when Zito admitted to the facts contained in the charge.

> "Congress criminalized monopolization and attempted monopolization to combat criminal conduct that subverts competition," said Assistant Attorney General Jonathan Kanter of the Justice Department's Antitrust Division. "The Justice Department will continue to prosecute blatant and illegitimate monopoly behavior that subjects the American public to harm."[921]

The charged conduct here appears to have amounted to an invitation to collude: a practice that had been hitherto regarded as a matter warranting only civil antitrust enforcement under Section 5 of the FTC Act.[922] Why do you

---

[919] Richard A. Powers, *Effective Antitrust Enforcement: The Future Is Now* (remarks of June 3, 2022); *see also* Jonathan Kanter, *Remarks at 2022 Spring Enforcers Summit* (Apr. 4, 2022) ("We will aggressively pursue enforcement of the criminal antitrust laws to protect consumers, workers and businesses harmed by unlawful collusion and monopolization.").

[920] *See, e.g.*, Bouie v. City of Columbia, 378 U.S. 347, 350 (1964); United States v. Miller, 771 F.2d 1219, 1225 (9th Cir. 1985) ("The sufficiency of fair notice of the acts proscribed by a statute must be examined in the context of the conduct with which a defendant is charged. . . . A defendant cannot challenge a statute on the ground that it may not give fair notice that conduct other than that with which he is charged is forbidden. . . . The indictment charges Miller with price-fixing. Because price-fixing has repeatedly been held to be per se illegal under the Sherman Act . . . Miller could not have had any reasonable doubt that his conduct violated section one."); United States v. Cinemette Corp. of Am., 687 F. Supp. 976, 979 (W.D. Pa. 1988) ("In light of the decision in *Professional Engineers* . . .and the substantial case law holding that restrictions upon competitive bidding constitute price-fixing, a per se violation of the Sherman Act, the Court finds little merit in defendants' claims that they were not given fair notice that split agreements could constitute violations of § 1.").

[921] U.S. Dept. of Justice, Press Release, Executive Pleads Guilty to Criminal Attempted Monopolization (Oct. 31, 2022).

[922] *See supra* note 870 and accompanying text.

think DOJ chose to pursue a criminal enforcement path under Section 2 here? Further prosecutions have followed.[923]

The DOJ Cartel Leniency Program

One of the most significant challenges in fighting cartels is finding them. Cartel agreements are seldom publicized by their participants, and it can be difficult to spot collusive behavior in the marketplace. In order to aid the detection and prosecution of price-fixing cartels and other criminal practices (like bid-rigging schemes), DOJ has developed a highly successful leniency program to obtain information and cooperation from a surprising place: the cartel participants themselves.[924]

The core of the program is simple. DOJ grants immunity from criminal prosecution, and significant protection from civil prosecution,[925] to the first participant in an individual cartel to come forward, disclose the cartel to DOJ, and cooperate fully with the Department's investigation and prosecution efforts, while also making best efforts to provide restitution to victims.[926] Subsequent applicants for a particular cartel do not qualify for the protection of the leniency scheme, although they may obtain some benefits—in the form of Division support for a sentencing reduction—if they are first to self-report a *second* cartel while cooperating in the investigation into the first. Priority order is determined by a "marker" system that ensures that the first entity to contact DOJ and request leniency will be the protected applicant if it satisfies the substantive criteria for leniency.

The prospect of leniency for the first applicant, leaving the applicant's competitors to face investigation, prosecution, and penalties, is intended to have a destabilizing effect on cartels. It creates strong incentives for cartel participants to inform the authorities and cooperate against their competitors: thus undermining what may already be a fragile relationship among the cartelists.

NOTES

1) Should DOJ expand its criminal antitrust program beyond *per se* violations of the antitrust laws? To what?

2) The cartel leniency program has been successful. Could, and should, we introduce something similar for non-criminal antitrust violations? If so, what might it look like, and how would it work?

3) Should the DOJ Antitrust Division be apolitical, responsive to the views of the White House, both, or neither? Explain your view.

---

[923] U.S. Dept. of Justice, Press Release, Criminal Charges Unsealed Against 12 Individuals in Wide-Ranging Scheme to Monopolize Transmigrante Industry and Extort Competitors Near U.S.-Mexico Border (Dec. 6, 2022).

[924] *See generally* U.S. Dept. of Justice Antitrust Division Manual § 7-3.300 ("Antitrust Division Leniency Policy and Procedures"), https://www.justice.gov/atr/page/file/1490246/download; *see also* Antitrust Division Leniency FAQs, https://www.justice.gov/atr/page/file/1490311/download.

[925] Specifically, limitation of liability to single damages for conduct individually attributable to the applicant, rather than treble damages for the conduct of the conspiracy as a whole. 15 U.S.C. § 7a-1(a).

[926] "Type A" leniency may be granted to an applicant if: "1. At the time the applicant reports the illegal activity, the Antitrust Division has not received information about the illegal activity from any other source; 2. The applicant, upon its discovery of the illegal activity, promptly reports it to the Antitrust Division; 3. The applicant reports its participation in the illegal activity with candor and completeness and makes a confession of wrongdoing that is truly a corporate act, as opposed to isolated confessions of directors, officers, and employees; 4. The applicant provides timely, truthful, continuing, and complete cooperation to the Antitrust Division throughout its investigation; 5. The applicant uses best efforts to make restitution to injured parties, to remediate the harm caused by the illegal activity, and to improve its compliance program to mitigate the risk of engaging in future illegal activity; and 6. The applicant did not coerce another party to participate in the illegal activity and clearly was not the leader or originator of that activity." Type B leniency may be granted to an organization that does not qualify for Type A leniency if: "1. At the time the applicant reports the illegal activity, the Antitrust Division does not yet have evidence against the applicant that, in the Antitrust Division's sole discretion, is likely to result in a sustainable conviction against the applicant; 2. The applicant, upon its discovery of the illegal activity, promptly reports it to the Antitrust Division; 3. The applicant reports its participation in the illegal activity with candor and completeness and makes a confession of wrongdoing that is truly a corporate act, as opposed to isolated confessions of directors, officers, and employees; 4. The applicant provides timely, truthful, continuing, and complete cooperation that advances the Antitrust Division's investigation; 5. The applicant uses best efforts to make restitution to injured parties, to remediate the harm caused by the illegal activity, and to improve its compliance program to mitigate the risk of engaging in future illegal activity; 6. The applicant did not coerce another party to participate in the illegal activity and clearly was not the leader or originator of that activity; and 7. The applicant is the first to qualify for leniency for the illegal activity reported and the Antitrust Division determines that granting leniency to the applicant would not be unfair to others." U.S. Dept. of Justice Antitrust Division Manual § 7-3.300 ("Antitrust Division Leniency Policy and Procedures"), https://www.justice.gov/atr/page/file/1490246/download

4) As *CVS / Aetna* demonstrates, the Tunney Act can be used to run something like a mini-trial in which the nominal "parties" are aligned and the judge is testing their joint position. Is this desirable? What concerns or challenges might arise in this context?

5) As noted above, the Expediting Act was repealed in 1974; the last substantive Supreme Court merger decision was in 1975.[927] Do you think these are related? Should we bring back the Expediting Act?

D. The Two-Agency Model

In general, the two federal antitrust agencies typically enjoy a close and cooperative relationship. The agencies work together to avoid duplicative investigations through the "clearance" process, a somewhat informal system of allocating proposed investigations to one agency or another based, first, on statutory power (antitrust investigations in some industries, like airlines, are allocated to DOJ by statute); second, on comparative expertise and experience (a critical consideration in practice: for example, the FTC has unparalleled experience in handling hospital and physician mergers, while the DOJ has unrivalled expertise in certain agricultural markets); and, finally, on relative workload at the time the matter arises. Most of the time, this process works well enough to avoid generating significant headaches for either the agencies or for parties who appear before them.

But the overlapping jurisdiction of the antitrust agencies is, at least, not an obvious way to structure an antitrust enforcement system. The existence of two agencies, with different structures, internal processes, and leadership may strike an observer as odd, and it certainly raises some questions.

There is plenty to be said in defense of the arrangement. There are some striking complementarities between the Department of Justice, on the one hand (which can be highly responsive to democratic changes in the White House), and the Federal Trade Commission (which—given the staggered seven-year terms of the members of its bipartisan Commission—has a history of continuing policy and enforcement programs across multiple Administrations[928]). In addition, each agency has unique advantages that the other does not: for example, the Department of Justice has the power to conduct criminal prosecutions, and faces no threat of "deadlock" due to recusals or vacancies; while the Federal Trade Commission has some unique tools—including the market study power in Section 6(b), the ability to serve as a specialized antitrust court for administrative litigation, and very significant policy resources—that are well adapted to bringing specialized expertise to bear on complex civil matters. In addition, the FTC's simultaneous role as a consumer protection regulator (including its role as the nation's leading privacy enforcer) creates scope for competition concerns to be addressed in a manner that is sensitive to consumer protection ones, and vice versa. The two-agency model is also, of course, exactly what Congress intended in enacting the FTC Act.

However, there are also fair grounds for worry and for criticism on prudential grounds (setting aside here the concern expressed by some, noted above, that the FTC's structure may be constitutionally unsound[929]). These include:

- **Risk of actual conflict.** Critics point to the risk—and occasionally the reality—that the agencies will take different positions on antitrust enforcement and policy issues. This came to an unfortunate head in the *Qualcomm* litigation, in which the Department of Justice intervened in an FTC antitrust enforcement action, before the Ninth Circuit, on the side of the defendant and against the FTC(!).[930] In 2023, the U.S.

---

[927] United States v. Citizens and Southern Nat'l Bank, 422 U.S. 86 (1975).

[928] For example, in recent decades the FTC has pursued long, cross-Administration, bipartisan campaigns to roll back the scope of state-action immunity, invigorate hospital merger enforcement, and enforce the antitrust laws on the IP/antitrust frontier.

[929] *See supra* note 863 and accompanying text.

[930] *See, e.g.*, Brief of the United States of America as Amicus Curiae in Support of Appellant and Vacatur, FTC v. Qualcomm Inc., Case No. 19-16122 (9th Cir. Aug. 30, 2019) (supporting Qualcomm in its litigation with the FTC); Brief for the United States as Amicus Curiae, FTC v. Schering-Plough Corp., No 05-723 (May 2006) (opposing the FTC's petition for certiorari in its first pharmaceutical patent "reverse payment" case and criticizing the FTC's approach).

Government Accountability Office published a study of the jurisdictional overlap between the agencies, concluding that interagency conflicts are rare.[931]

- **Divergent positions on enforcement and policy.** More generally, the agencies have divided in recent years on enforcement policy relating to the interaction between antitrust and intellectual property, with the FTC generally favoring more aggressive antitrust enforcement in this area, while the Justice Department—at least during the Trump Administration—favored greater deference to the perceived demands of IP policy.[932]

- **Nonpublic procedures.** Critics also charge that there is some procedural unfairness in the fact that businesses are subject to the jurisdiction of two agencies, with different leadership and policy preferences, and that antitrust matters are allocated between those agencies through a largely informal, nonpublic, and non-transparent "clearance" process. Divergences in substantive law or policy—for example, the FTC's unilateral withdrawal from the Vertical Merger Guidelines in 2021, with DOJ declining to follow suit—have fueled this criticism.[933]

- **Possibility of parallel proceedings.** One could imagine circumstances under which the FTC and DOJ were both investigating the same practice or transaction. The Supreme Court has expressly held that such parallel proceedings are legally unobjectionable, in light of the broader reach of Section 5 of the FTC Act,[934] but such an outcome might—at a minimum—raise sharp questions about whether federal enforcement resources were being efficiently and prudently deployed.

A prominent challenge to this arrangement was filed in 2020 by Axon Enterprise, a manufacturer of police body cameras that acquired Vievu, a key rival, triggering an FTC administrative challenge to unwind the merger. Axon responded by filing a complaint for declaratory judgment in federal district court in Arizona, mounting a facial challenge to the dual-enforcement system, as well as the constitutional soundness of the FTC itself. (The ensuing litigation prompted the Supreme Court to rule unanimously that federal courts may hear constitutional challenges to the FTC's structure even while administrative proceedings are pending.[935])

Complaint, Axon Enterprise, Inc. v. FTC
Case No. 2:20-cv-14 (D. Ariz. filed Jan. 3, 2020)

1. Plaintiff Axon Enterprise, Inc. ("Axon") brings this case to challenge the unconstitutional structure and processes employed by Defendant, the Federal Trade Commission ("FTC" or "Commission"), to prohibit lawful mergers and extract unwarranted settlements. The FTC exists as a Constitutional anomaly. In one hand, it wields a mighty sword—the power to not only prosecute cases, but to judge them too; in the other, a massive shield—near-total protection from political accountability, with the Commissioners who direct its actions subject to neither democratic election nor at-will removal by the President. For decades, the agency has leveraged that power against American companies indiscriminately—including, most recently, Axon. No longer. [. . .]

30. Because the DOJ and FTC have dual jurisdiction to review mergers, the agencies have created a "clearance" process to decide which agency will investigate a merger. Over the years, the agencies have reached a series of informal, non-public understandings as to how they will divvy up merger investigations. Clearance is an opaque, black-box process. The agencies maintain complete control over the structure and implementation of the clearance process and have total discretion to decide which agency will undertake a particular merger investigation. Merging parties have no insight or input into which agency will investigate their merger. Moreover, clearance rules and procedures are not mandated by statute, subject to Congressional scrutiny, or promulgated through notice-and-comment rulemaking.

---

[931] GAO, ANTITRUST: DOJ AND FTC JURISDICTIONS OVERLAP, BUT CONFLICTS ARE INFREQUENT, GAO-23-105790 (Jan. 2023).

[932] *See, e.g.*, Anita Alanko, *New Madison Approach to Antitrust Law and IP Law*, 28 Cath. U. J. L. & Tech 219, 238–41 (2020) (noting divergence)

[933] *See* U.S. Dept. of Justice, Press Release, Justice Department Issues Statement on the Vertical Merger Guidelines (Sept. 15, 2021).

[934] FTC v. Cement Inst., 333 U.S. 683, 694 (1948).

[935] Axon Enterprise, Inc. v. FTC, 598 U.S. __, No. 21-86 (Apr. 14, 2023).

31. Which agency reviews a consummated transaction is critical. The DOJ's only means of unwinding a consummated merger is to sue in federal court. The FTC, on the other hand, has the option to sue in federal court under Section 13(b) of the Act, or to commence an internal administrative hearing before either a single Commissioner or an ALJ on the FTC's payroll.

32. The FTC's internal administrative hearing provides none of the substantive or procedural protections enjoyed by litigants in federal district court. These proceedings are, instead, fraught with Due Process and Equal Protection deficiencies.

- Federal district court judges are Article III impartial fact-finders who owe no allegiances to the DOJ. In contrast, any FTC Commissioner (including one who voted to sue the defendant) is permitted to preside over the administrative hearing; and, at best, an ALJ appointed by the FTC and on the FTC's payroll will preside.

- Federal court proceedings are governed by the Federal Rules of Evidence and Federal Rules of Civil Procedure. Neither apply in FTC administrative proceedings.

- The DOJ must satisfy a more rigorous standard of finding that a merger or acquisition "substantially lessens competition," whereas the FTC can satisfy a less onerous "unfair competition" standard in the administrative context.

- Litigants in federal court can appeal adverse decisions to impartial circuit court judges. Decisions rendered in FTC administrative proceedings must first be appealed to the same FTC Commissioners who voted to sue the defendant at the outset.

- The DOJ cannot change the findings made by the district court when appealing a decision to the circuit court. However, the FTC Commissioners, on appeal, can ignore and completely change the merits decision rendered in the administrative proceedings *before* the defendant appeals to the circuit court.

- Different appellate standards of review also apply depending on where the case originated. The district court's factual findings in a DOJ case are reviewed for "clear error," whereas "[t]he findings of the Commission as to the facts, if supported by evidence, shall be *conclusive*." 15 U.S.C. § 45(c) (emphasis added).

33. Given the inherently biased and unfair nature of administrative hearings at the FTC and the limited review of its factual findings on appeal, it is no surprise that the agency believes itself to be virtually untouchable in its internal arena. [. . .]

36. Worse still, the FTC lacks any political check on how it exercises its unfair procedures against the companies that happen to fall within its bailiwick. Although Article II "vested" all "executive Power" in the President, Art. II, § 1, cl. 1, and charged the President alone with "tak[ing] Care that the Laws be faithfully executed," Art. II, § 3, the FTC enforces the antitrust laws outside of Presidential control. [. . .]

40. FTC Commissioners, however, are shielded from at-will Presidential removal—and hence from the key mechanism of democratic accountability—in violation of Article II. The FTC is headed by five Commissioners, nominated by the President and confirmed by the Senate, each serving a 7-year term. 15 U.S.C. § 41. But once appointed, the Commissioners are not subject to removal by the President absent a finding of "inefficiency, neglect of duty, or malfeasance in office." Id. This means FTC Commissioners are not politically accountable for their actions. So long as the Commissioners stop short of "malfeasance," the President can do nothing but stand by and watch, no matter how much he disagrees with them. Moreover, because the FTC-appointed ALJ can also only be removed for "good cause" in accordance with statutory procedures, 5 U.S.C. § 7521(a), (b)(1), an impermissible "dual-layer of protection" even further restricts Executive control.

41. This means that crucial law enforcement actions, sometimes with massive consequences for the American economy (and here, for public safety), are currently taken by individuals not elected by the People, and not controlled by the President. That runs directly contrary to Article II and the democratic principles underlying the Constitution. [. . .]

COUNT I (Violation of Axon's Fifth Amendment Rights) [. . .]

58. The imminent administrative proceeding, in which the FTC will act as prosecutor, judge, and jury, violates Axon's Due Process rights, including but not limited to depriving Axon of the ability to make its case before a neutral arbiter.

59. By arbitrarily subjecting Axon to unfair procedures before an administrative body, rather than to a fair trial before a neutral judge appointed in accordance with Article III of the Constitution with the procedural protections of a federal court, the FTC has violated Axon's Equal Protection rights. [. . .]

COUNT II (The FTC's Structure Violates Article II) [. . .]

62. The FTC's actions separately violate Axon's Constitutional rights because the agency's structure, on its face, is unconstitutional under Article II. In particular, Article II requires that Executive officials exercising law-enforcement power be removable at will by the President. Although the FTC clearly exercises law-enforcement power—including but not limited to Axon's case—its Commissioners are shielded from at-will removal. Moreover, ALJs appointed by the FTC, who also can only be removed for cause, create an impermissible dual-layer of insulation. Because the agency's structure violates Article II, any actions taken against Axon under its present structure are invalid.

COUNT III (Declaratory Judgment that Axon's Acquisition Did Not Violate Antitrust Laws) [. . .]

64. Axon's acquisition of Vievu did not violate Clayton Act § 7 or any other antitrust law. The acquisition was not likely to substantially lessen competition and in fact has not done so.

NOTES

1) How would you allocate enforcement authority between the agencies?
2) How important is it that antitrust enforcement is: (a) responsive to political change; or (b) bipartisan? Why?
3) The clearance process for allocating investigations between the agencies is nonpublic and effectively unreviewable. Is this a problem?
4) Suppose that you are the head of the Antitrust Division (or FTC Chair) and the FTC (or the Division) files a complaint with which you disagree. Specifically, you think the enforcement action represents bad and harmful policy. What should you do?
5) Does the FTC's 2022 Section 5 statement affect the strength of Axon's constitutional objections?

E. Merger Review and the Hart-Scott-Rodino ("HSR") Act

Both agencies allocate a majority of their civil enforcement resources (including personnel and dollars) to merger enforcement: indeed, merger review is sometimes described as the agencies' primary function. To get a sense of the relative importance of merger review compared to conduct investigations, take a look at this DOJ workload chart covering 2010–19:

U.S. Department of Justice Antitrust Division Workload Statistics FY 2010–2019: Investigations

Total Investigations Initiated, by Primary Type of Conduct	2010	2011	2012	2013	2014	2015	2016	2017	2018	2019
Sherman §1 - Restraint of Trade [inc. civil and criminal]	46	47	31	25	30	39	42	38	44	52
Sherman §2 - Monopoly	2	2	2	2	0	3	1	0	0	6
Clayton §7 - Mergers	64	90	74	65	81	67	65	55	65	72
Others	3	3	0	0	2	2	4	7	5	4

Source: _https://www.justice.gov/atr/file/788426/download_ (footnotes omitted)

The merger review function at both agencies is governed by the Hart-Scott-Rodino Act, 15 U.S.C. § 18a, which sets out the statutory framework for premerger notification in the United States and establishes a timeline under which most merger review is conducted. The Premerger Notification Office ("PNO") of the FTC administers the HSR system on behalf of both agencies. The HSR statute is supplemented by implementing regulations,[936] and by informal interpretations issued by PNO.[937]

HSR was enacted in 1976 to create a system in which a purchaser that plans to undertake a merger or acquisition of a certain size must notify that transaction to the antitrust agencies *before* consummating the deal (*i.e.*, before the buyer actually becomes the owner of the target). The central purpose of the Act is to impose a "waiting period" to give the agencies a chance to review the deal, during which time the parties may not consummate the transaction.[938]

Under the Act, only certain mergers are "reportable" or subject to the notification obligation. The requirements are somewhat intricate, adjusted every year for inflation, and subject to some exceptions and special rules,[939] but in very broad terms (and with effect from February 27, 2023):

- transactions valued up to $111.4 million are not reportable;
- transactions valued at more than $445.5 million are reportable;
- transactions valued at between $111.4 million and $445.5 million are reportable *if*:
  - one party has assets or annual sales of at least $22.3 million *and*
  - the other party has assets or annual sales of at least $222.7 million.[940]

Under the Act, if a transaction is reportable, merger review begins with a "merger notification": a form, a fee, and a set of materials containing basic information about the proposed transaction.[941] An "initial waiting period" then follows—in most cases, 30 days after the notification[942]—in which the agencies have an opportunity to decide whether further investigation is appropriate, to determine which agency will be cleared to conduct that investigation, and (at least to some extent) conduct an initial review of the transaction. This may involve requesting and receiving some documents and information from the parties and/or from other market participants.

During the initial waiting period, the HSR Act forbids the parties from closing the deal. For the purposes of the antitrust laws, the merging parties are still considered separate entities during this time: coordination on commercial or competitive matters may, accordingly, constitute an antitrust violation. (Improper coordination with the other side of a deal that has been proposed but not consummated is often known as "jumping the gun" or a "gun-jumping violation."[943])

The agencies may grant early termination of the waiting period if they conclude there are no competitive concerns and further delay is unwarranted.[944] At the time of writing, however, this practice is suspended—the agencies cited

---

[936] 16 C.F.R. Parts 801–03.

[937] *See* https://www.ftc.gov/legal-library/browse/hsr-informal-interpretations.

[938] For thoughtful discussion of the HSR system, its history, and its purposes, *see* Statement of Commissioners Noah Joshua Phillips and Christine S. Wilson Regarding the Fiscal Year 2020 Hart-Scott Rodino Annual Report to Congress (Nov. 8, 2021); Noah Phillips, *The Repeal of Hart-Scott-Rodino*, Global Comp. Rev. (Oct. 6, 2021); William J. Baer, *Reflections on 20 Years of Merger Enforcement under the Hart-Scott-Rodino Act*, 65 Antitrust L.J. 825 (1997); Joe Sims & Deborah P. Herman, *The Effect of Twenty Years of Hart-Scott-Rodino on Merger Practice: A Case Study in the Law of Unintended Consequences Applied to Antitrust Legislation*, 65 Antitrust L.J. 865 (1997); William J. Kolasky, Jr. & James W. Lowe, *The Merger Review Process at the Federal Trade Commission: Administrative Efficiency and the Rule of Law*, 49 Admin. L. Rev. 889 (1997); James W. Mullenix, *The Premerger Notification Program at The Federal Trade Commission*, 57 Antitrust L.J. 125, 130-31 (1988); Irving Scher, *Emerging Issues Under the Antitrust Improvements Act of 1976*, 77 Colum. L. Rev. 679, 681-82 (1977).

[939] *See, e.g.*, 15 U.S.C. § 18a(c) (listing various categories of exempt transactions); 16 C.F.R. Part 802 (exemption rules).

[940] *See generally* 16 C.F.R. Part 801 (coverage rules).

[941] See 16 C.F.R. Part 803, Appendix A (HSR Form); Appendix B (instructions for completing the form).

[942] *See* 15 U.S.C. § 18a(b)(1)(B) (30 day default and 15-day period for cash tender offers); 11 U.S.C. §363(b) (abbreviated waiting period for certain filings in connection with a bankruptcy proceeding); FTC Premerger Notification Office Informal Interpretation 1307002 (July 19, 2013) (interpreting same).

[943] A number of merging parties have fallen into this trap. *See, e.g.*, U.S. Dept. of Justice, Press Release, Justice Department Reaches Settlement with Duke Energy Corporation for Violating Premerger Notification and Waiting Period Requirements (Jan. 18, 2017); U.S. Dept. of Justice, Press Release, Justice Department Settles Lawsuit Against Computer Associates For Illegal Pre-Merger Coordination (Apr. 23, 2002). *See generally, e.g.*, M. Howard Morse, *Mergers and Acquisitions: Antitrust Limitations on Conduct Before Closing*, 57 Bus. Lawyer 1463 (2002).

[944] 15 U.S.C. § 18a(b)(2); 16 C.F.R. § 803.11.

the transition to a new Administration and the volume of HSR requests as a reason to suspend the practice for a short time.[945]

At the expiration of the initial waiting period, the agency must decide whether to do nothing and simply let the waiting period expire (thus leaving the parties free to close their deal), or whether to issue a "Second Request." This is a demand pursuant to the HSR Act for additional documents and information relating to the transaction. Typically, a Second Request requires the production of a very significant amount of material, representing months of work by the company's employees and attorneys. When a Second Request is issued, a new waiting period begins, and runs until 30 days after the parties have substantially complied with the Second Request.[946] The HSR rules allow a party to withdraw and immediately refile a notification once (a "pull and refile") without needing to pay an additional filing fee.[947]

HSR violations (which might include failure to produce relevant materials, or violations of the suspensory obligation) are punishable by statutory penalties of up to $50,120 per day.[948] Failure to substantially comply with a notification requirement of a Second Request may also result in an order to comply, an extension of the statutory waiting period, or other equitable relief.[949]

The following brief extract from the FTC's public Model Second Request should give you a flavor of what a Second Request looks like in practice, and the kinds of information that are included.

FTC, Model Second Request (revised October 2021)

REQUEST FOR ADDITIONAL INFORMATION AND DOCUMENTARY MATERIAL ISSUED TO [COMPANY]

Unless modified by agreement with the staff of the Federal Trade Commission, each Specification of this Request for Additional Information and Documentary Material (the "Request") requires a complete search of "the Company" as defined in Definition D1 of the Definitions, which appear after the following Specifications. If the Company believes that the required search or any other part of the Request can be narrowed in any way that is consistent with the Commission's need for documents and information, you are encouraged to discuss any questions and possible modifications with the Commission representatives identified in Instruction I(11) of this Request. All modifications to this Request must be agreed to in writing by a Commission representative. Submit the information requested in Specifications 1 and 10(a) of this Request promptly to facilitate discussions about any potential modifications to this Request including the scope of the Company's search or interrogatory response obligations.

SPECIFICATIONS

1. Submit:

> (a) one copy of each organization chart and personnel directory in effect since January 1, [Yr-2] for the Company as a whole and for each of the Company's facilities or divisions involved in any activity relating to any Relevant Product [Service];
>
> (b) a list of all agents and representatives of the Company, including, but not limited to, all attorneys, consultants, investment bankers, product distributors, sales agents, and other Persons retained by the Company in any capacity relating to the Proposed Transaction or any Relevant Product [Service] (excluding those retained solely in connection with environmental, tax, human resources, pensions, benefits, ERISA, or OSHA issues);

---

[945] FTC, Press Release, FTC, DOJ Temporarily Suspend Discretionary Practice of Early Termination (Feb. 4, 2021).

[946] *See* 15 U.S.C. § 18a(e)(1).

[947] 16 C.F.R. § 803.12.

[948] 15 U.S.C. § 18a(g); FTC, Press Release, FTC Publishes Inflation-Adjusted Civil Penalty Amounts for 2023 (Jan. 6, 2023).

[949] 15 U.S.C. § 18a(g).

(c) for each Person identified in response to Specification 1(b), the agent's or representative's title, business address, and telephone number, as well as a description of that Person's responsibilities in any capacity relating to the Proposed Transaction or any Relevant Product [Service] provided in any Relevant Area; and

(d) a Data Map for the Company.

2. List each Relevant Product manufactured or sold [Service provided] by the Company in the Relevant Area, and for each:

    (a)   provide a detailed description of the product [service] [including its end uses]; and

    (b)   state [the brand name and] the division, subsidiary, or affiliate of the Company that manufactures or sells [provides] or has manufactured or sold [provided] the product [service].

3. For each Relevant Product [Service] listed in response to Specification 2 above, state or provide:

(a) the Company's Sales to all customers in each Relevant Area, stated separately in units and dollars;

(b) [that portion of the Company's Sales to customers in each Relevant Area, stated separately in units and dollars, that were of products manufactured in the U.S.;]

(c) [that portion of the Company's Sales to customers in each Relevant Area, stated separately in units and dollars, that were of products manufactured outside the U.S.;]

(d) that portion of the Company's Sales to customers in each Relevant Area, stated separately in units and dollars, that were of products purchased from sources outside the Company and resold by the Company rather than of products manufactured by the Company;

(e) the names and addresses of the [XX] Persons who purchased the greatest unit and dollar amounts of the Relevant Product [Service] from the Company in each Relevant Area;

(f) [a sample contract for each customer type]; and

(g) the name, address, estimated Sales, and estimated market share of the Company and each of the Company's competitors in each Relevant Area in the manufacture or sale of the Relevant Product [provision of the Relevant Service].

4. State the location of each facility that manufactures or sells [including distribution centers, etc.], or has manufactured or sold, any Relevant Product [provides or has provided any Relevant Service] in the Relevant Area for the Company, and for each such facility state: the current nameplate and practical capacity and the [annual, monthly] capacity utilization rate for production of each Relevant Product manufactured at the facility, specifying all other factors used to calculate capacity; the number of shifts normally used at the facility; and the feasibility of increasing capacity [by X% or more], including the costs and time required.

5. For each Relevant Product manufactured or sold [Service provided] in the Relevant Area, submit (a) one copy of all current selling aids and promotional materials and (b) all documents relating to advertising [and marketing] Plans and strategies.

6. Submit all documents relating to the Company's or any other Person's Plans relating to any Relevant Product [Service] [in the Relevant Area], including, but not limited to, business plans; short-term and long-range strategies and objectives; expansion or retrenchment plans; research and development efforts; presentations to management committees, executive committees, and boards of directors; and budgets and financial projections. For regularly prepared budgets and financial projections, the Company need only submit one copy of final year-end documents for prior years, and cumulative year-to-date documents for the current year.

7. Submit all documents relating to competition in the manufacture or sale of any Relevant Product [provision of any Relevant Service] in the Relevant Area, including, but not limited to, market studies, forecasts and surveys, and all other documents relating to:

(a) the Sales, market share, or competitive position of the Company or any of its competitors;

(b) the relative strength or weakness of Persons producing or selling each Relevant Product [providing each Relevant Service];

(c) supply and demand conditions;

(d) attempts to win customers from other Persons and losses of customers to other Persons, [including, but not limited to, all sales personnel call reports and win/loss reports];

(e) allegations by any Person that any Person that manufactures or sells any Relevant Product [provides any Relevant Service] is not behaving in a competitive manner, including, but not limited to, customer and competitor complaints; and threatened, pending, or completed lawsuits; and

(f) any actual or potential effect on the supply, demand, cost, or price of any Relevant Product [Service] as a result of competition from any other possible substitute product [service].

8. Submit:

(a) all documents relating to the Company's or any other Person's price lists, pricing Plans, pricing policies, pricing forecasts, pricing strategies, price structures, pricing analyses, price zones, and pricing decisions relating to any Relevant Product [Service] in the Relevant Area; and

(b) all studies, analyses, or assessments of the pricing or profitability of any Relevant Product [Service] sold or provided by the Company, [by third-party distributors/lessee dealers/etc.], or through other channels of trade in any Relevant Area.

9. Identify the Person(s) at the Company responsible for creating or monitoring price strategy, [price zones,] pricing practices, and pricing policies for the Relevant Product [Service] in the Relevant Area. Describe in detail the Company's pricing strategy, pricing practices, and pricing policies, including, but not limited to:

(a) a description regarding how, and how often, the prices for each Relevant Product [Service] in each Relevant Area are determined;

(b) whether, and how, pricing based on customer characteristics, presence of other competitors, or other factors are used by the Company in determining the prices for each Relevant Product [Service] in each Relevant Area; and

(c) [whether, and how, price zones and/or pricing based on geographic areas, the presence of local competitors, or other factors are used by the Company for each Relevant Product [Service] in each Relevant Area.]

10. Identify each electronic database used or maintained by the Company in connection with any Relevant Product [Service] at any time after January 1, [Yr-3], that contains information concerning the Company's (i) products [services] and product codes; (ii) facilities; (iii) production; (iv) shipments; (v) bids or sales proposals; (vi) sales; (vii) prices; (viii) margins; (ix) costs, including but not limited to production costs, distribution costs, standard costs, expected costs, and opportunity costs; (x) patents or other intellectual property; (xi) research or development projects; or (xii) customers.

{Eds: the full Model Second Request has 30 specifications, 16 definitions, and 11 instructions!}

* * *

In practice, the baseline timing (*i.e.*, substantial compliance plus 30 days) is often modified by entry into a negotiated "timing agreement" with the reviewing agency.[950] In this agreement, the parties and the agency

---

[950] See FTC Model Timing Agreement (Feb. 27, 2019), https://www.ftc.gov/system/files/attachments/merger-review/ftc_model_timing_agreement_2-27-19_0.pdf

typically agree that the parties will provide something less than full substantial compliance with the Second Request, in exchange for giving the agency a longer period of time in which to review the transaction after receiving the materials.

The HSR system transformed merger review. It gave the agencies the opportunity to detect and investigate troubling deals before they happen, and it gives businesses a measure of confidence that a merger is unlikely to be challenged by the agencies after it has been reviewed.[951] But the HSR system does *not* provide affirmative "clearance"—in the sense of positive approval—of a deal. The antitrust agencies can challenge deals after HSR review, and even after a Second Request. Indeed, the HSR Act expressly says so: "Any action taken by the Federal Trade Commission or the Assistant Attorney General or any failure of the Federal Trade Commission or the Assistant Attorney General to take any action under this section shall not bar any proceeding or any action with respect to such acquisition at any time under any other section of this Act or any other provision of law."[952] And, on rare occasions, the agencies have been willing to do so in practice.[953] But whether and when it is sound policy to challenge an HSR-reviewed merger, and whether the fact of a previous HSR review should weigh against a later challenge, is a matter of considerable controversy.[954]

A recent judicial discussion of this issue arose in the second motion-to-dismiss decision in the *Facebook* litigation. Facebook argued that the FTC's challenge to its consummated acquisitions of Instagram and WhatsApp was inappropriate, including because both transactions were notified under the HSR system, and the Instagram deal proceeded to a Second Request. The court held that this was no barrier to the suit.

FTC v. Facebook, Inc.
Case No. 20-3590, 2022 WL 103308 (D.D.C. Jan. 11, 2022)

Judge Boasberg.

[1] As required by the Hart-Scott-Rodino Act, 15 U.S.C. § 18a, the FTC reviewed the acquisition of Instagram prior to closing to assess whether it posed anticompetitive concerns. Whereas most mergers are cleared quickly, in this instance the review took over four months. During that scrutiny, the agency took the rare step of requiring the submission by the parties of additional information or documentary material relevant to the proposed acquisition. Eventually, however, Facebook and Instagram satisfied the agency's concerns, and in August (over four months after the merger was announced), the Commission voted 5-0 to allow it to proceed without any challenge or conditions.

[2] Facebook's acquisition of WhatsApp was also subject to Hart-Scott-Rodino Act pre-merger review, but the FTC, once again, did not block it. Although the FTC again conveniently omits any mention of this review in its Complaint, the Court may take judicial notice of that public agency action.

[3] Facebook thus argues that because the FTC unconditionally cleared both acquisitions under Section 7 of the Clayton Act, which Congress enacted to address incipient threats to competition that Section 2 would not condemn, it is hypocritical for the agency to now claim that the acquisitions run afoul of Section 2. The FTC, for its part, counters that HSR filings do not result in acquisitions being approved or blessed by the FTC or DOJ, that the HSR Act merely established reporting requirements for acquisitions over a certain size, and that the prior HSR reviews are simply beside the point here.

[4] The FTC has the better argument, at least insofar as its HSR reviews at the time of the acquisitions do not bear significantly on the issue now before the Court. The HSR Act does not require the FTC to reach a formal determination as to whether the acquisition under review violates the antitrust laws. On the contrary, it merely obliges the parties to the merger to report certain information to the agency and to wait to consummate the deal

---

[951] For a variety of perspectives on HSR, *see* supra note 938.

[952] 15 U.S.C. § 18a(i)(1).

[953] *See, e.g.*, Complaint, United States v. Parker-Hannifin Corp., Case No. 1:17-cv-01354 (D. Del. filed Sept., 26, 2017); Menesh S. Patel, *Merger Breakups*, 2020 Wis. L. Rev. 975, 990–91 (2020) (noting same).

[954] *See, e.g.*, Timothy J. Muris & Jonathan E. Nuechterlein, *First Principles for Review of Long-Consummated Mergers*, 5 Criterion J. on Innovation 29 (2020).

until the expiration of the statutory waiting period, which the FTC may extend while it gathers additional information. Indeed, while the FTC conducted an investigation of the challenged acquisitions here and eventually voted to close the investigation, its closing letter to Facebook expressly stated, "This action is not to be construed as a determination that a violation may not have occurred, just as the pendency of an investigation should not be construed as a determination that a violation has occurred. The Commission reserves the right to take such further action as the public interest may require." That letter is in keeping with the Act's explicit language making clear that the FTC can bring post-review challenges, notwithstanding the previous closing of HSR review without an antitrust-violation determination: "Any action taken by the Federal Trade Commission or the Assistant Attorney General or any failure of the Federal Trade Commission or the Assistant Attorney General to take any action under this section shall not bar any proceeding or any action with respect to such acquisition at any time under any other section of this Act or any other provision of law." 15 U.S.C. § 18a(i)(1).

[5] In light of that reality, the FTC's decisions to close the investigations into Facebook's acquisitions do not provide a basis to grant the company's Motion. The Commission could have decided to close the investigations for many reasons, and it would be improper to draw a merits conclusion about the legality of the mergers on the basis of those decisions, especially at the motion-to-dismiss stage. *Cf. Steves & Sons, Inc. v. JELD-WEN, Inc.*, 988 F.3d 690, 713–14 (4th Cir. 2021) (affirming district court's exclusion of evidence relating to Department of Justice's investigation of merger without challenging it and holding that Department's "decision not to pursue the matter isn't probative as to the merger's legality because many factors may motivate such a decision, including the Department's limited resources").

NOTES

1) How many different values does a merger review process serve? In what order do you think it is important that merger review be: (a) fast; (b) thorough; and (c) final?

2) Under what circumstances, if any, should the fact of a previous HSR review (without a challenge) weigh against an agency challenge to a consummated transaction, either (a) as a matter of law, or (b) as a matter of enforcement policy? Why? What impact, if any, should it have on a *private* challenge by an injured customer?

3) Some merging parties have received "close at your own risk" letters from the FTC at the end of the HSR waiting period, stating that the agency will not sue to block the deal but that the parties are on notice that the agency may investigate further and/or take enforcement action in the future. When, if ever, should the agencies send such letters?

4) As earlier noted, the Early Termination program has been suspended. Is there an argument that it should be removed permanently from the HSR procedures? What are the best arguments in favor of, and against, the Early Termination program?

5) A transaction may have a high valuation without raising competition concerns; conversely, it may have a low valuation and present a serious threat to competition. So why does the size of the parties matter for HSR reportability? Can you think of better criteria for reportability?

6) If you were designing or amending the HSR statute, what penalties or other consequences would you apply to an acquiror that has misrepresented facts, or withheld documents, in an HSR filing? *See* 15 U.S.C. § 18a(g).

F. The States

The fifty states, plus the District of Columbia, Guam, and Puerto Rico, are active to varying degrees in antitrust enforcement. The level and depth of state involvement varies widely. Some states include teams with experience and expertise to litigate significant antitrust matters: in particular, among others, New York, California, Colorado, Washington state, and Texas have established reputations as prominent actors in antitrust enforcement. In addition, states cooperate to investigate and pursue matters that affect more than one jurisdiction.[955]

---

[955] This has been the case in some recent tech enforcement actions. *See, e.g.*, New York v. Facebook, Inc., Case No. 1:20-cv-3589 (D.D.C. filed Dec. 9, 2020); United States v. Google, Case No 1:20-cv-3010 (D.D.C. filed Oct. 20, 2020); Colorado v. Google LLC, Case No. 1:20-cv-3715 (D.D.C. filed Dec. 17, 2020); Texas v. Google, Case No. 4:20-cv-957 (E.D. Tex. filed Dec. 16, 2020).

Under the federal antitrust laws, states may bring suit to obtain injunctive relief to protect themselves as direct victims of antitrust wrongdoing, under the provision that entitles private parties to injunctive relief, or on behalf of their citizens in what is sometimes called a "parens patriae" action.[956] States may also sue for treble damages suffered by them or by their citizens.[957] 15 U.S.C. § 15f directs the Attorney General of the United States to notify a State AG when the federal AG has filed an antitrust suit and has "reason to believe that any State attorney general would be entitled to bring an action under this Act based substantially on the same alleged violation of the antitrust laws."[958]

In addition to its powers under the federal antitrust system, every state has its own antitrust and competition laws. Although these usually resemble federal antitrust law—including equivalents of Sherman Act Sections 1 and 2, Clayton Act Section 7, and FTC Act Section 5—closely, some states' laws exhibit important differences. For example, California's unfair-competition law was of critical importance in the antitrust battle between Epic Games and Apple.[959] Many states allow indirect purchasers—such as those who buy at an overcharge from an intermediary that buys from an antitrust wrongdoer—to sue for damages: as we shall see in Chapter XII, federal law does not.[960] Some states are considering significant change to their antitrust statutes in ways that would create serious divergence from federal antitrust law.[961] The Supreme Court has held that federal antitrust law does not preempt state antitrust statutes that reach more broadly,[962] although other federal statutes have been held to do so on occasion.[963] While the vast majority of state antitrust enforcement is civil, there is a limited amount of state criminal enforcement.[964]

In practice, while relatively few states have the resources to undertake major antitrust litigations alone, they often serve as critical partners to the federal agencies.[965] State Attorneys-General may be the first to learn about anticompetitive practices or transactions, bringing them to the attention of the federal enforcers and working with

---

[956] Georgia v. Pennsylvania Railroad Co., 324 U.S. 439 (1945) ("Georgia, suing for her own injuries, is a 'person' within the meaning of s 16 of the Clayton Act, 15 U.S.C.A. s 26; she is authorized to maintain suits to restrain violations of the anti-trust laws or to recover damages by reason thereof. But Georgia is not confined to suits designed to protect only her proprietary interests. The rights which Georgia asserts, parens patriae, are those arising from an alleged conspiracy of private persons whose price-fixing scheme, it is said, has injured the economy of Georgia. . . . There is no apparent reason why those suits should be excluded from the purview of the anti-trust acts."); Hawaii v. Standard Oil Co. of Cal., 405 U.S. 251, 261 (1972) ("Hawaii plainly qualifies as a person . . . whether it sues in its proprietary capacity or as parens patriae."). *See also* Memorandum Amicus Curiae of the United States Regarding Microsoft Corporation's Motion for Dismissal of the Non-Settling States' Demand for Equitable Relief, United States v. Microsoft Corp., Civil Action No. 98-1233 (D.D.C. filed Apr. 15, 2002) 4–9 (discussing same and collecting authorities).

[957] 15 U.S.C. § 15c (parens patriae damages); 15 U.S.C. § 15 (injured-person damages).

[958] 15 U.S.C. § 15f.

[959] Epic Games, Inc. v. Apple Inc., 559 F. Supp. 3d 898, 1052–53 (N.D. Cal. 2021) ("As a competitor who claims to have suffered injury from Apple's unfair practices, [to sue under California's Unfair Competition Law,] Epic Games must show that Apple's conduct (1) threatens an incipient violation of an antitrust law, (2) violates the policy or spirit of one of those laws because its effects are comparable to or the same as a violation of the law, or (3) otherwise significantly threatens or harms competition. These findings must be tethered to some legislatively declared policy or proof of some actual or threatened impact on competition. As a quasi-consumer, on the other hand, Epic Games has several tests available for showing unfairness. Although some courts have continued to apply the "tethering" test stated above, others have applied a "balancing" test that requires the challenged business practice to be immoral, unethical, oppressive, unscrupulous, or substantially injurious to consumers based on the court's weighing of the utility of the defendant's conduct against the gravity of the harm to the alleged victim. Stated otherwise, the balancing test involves an examination of that practice's impact on its alleged victim, balanced against the reasons, justifications and motives of the alleged wrongdoer.").

[960] *See infra* § XII.C.

[961] *See, e.g.*, N.Y. Senate Bill S933C, https://legislation.nysenate.gov/pdf/bills/2021/S933C (proposed "abuse of dominance" bill).

[962] California v. ARC Am. Corp., 490 U.S. 93, 102 (1989) ("Given the long history of state common-law and statutory remedies against monopolies and unfair business practices, it is plain that this is an area traditionally regulated by the States. . . . Congress intended the federal antitrust laws to supplement, not displace, state antitrust remedies. . . . And on several prior occasions, the Court has recognized that the federal antitrust laws do not pre-empt state law.").

[963] *See, e.g.*, Connell Const. Co. v. Plumbers & Steamfitters Loc. Union No. 100, 421 U.S. 616, 635 (1975).

[964] *See, e.g.*, Office of the New York Attorney General, Press Release, *A.G. Schneiderman Announces Bust Of Broome County Waste Management Cartel For Colluding To Rig Bids And Fix Prices* (Apr. 9, 2018), https://ag.ny.gov/press-release/2018/ag-schneiderman-announces-bust-broome-county-waste-management-cartel-colluding.

[965] For a very different perspective, *see* Richard Posner, *Antitrust in the New Economy*, 68 Antitrust L.J. 925, 940–42 (2001) (refusing to "make a fetish of federalism" and arguing that the states should be stripped of their authority to enforce the federal antitrust laws for reasons including "the poor quality of the briefs and arguments").

them on investigations; and if matters proceed to litigation, states may serve as important partners in court.[966] The support of a state Attorney General not only means that more talented litigators with local knowledge are available for an enforcement effort: it may also may help to reassure a judge that the competitive concerns are shared by those with local expertise, rather than being a theoretical concern held only by distant D.C. regulators.

Stephen Calkins, Perspectives on State and Federal Antitrust Enforcement
53 Duke L.J. 673 (2003)

The most accepted roles for the states are ones derived from the states' comparative advantages. Three advantages stand out: familiarity with local markets, familiarity with and representation of state and local institutions, and ability to send money to injured individuals.

1. Familiarity with Local Markets. For all the talk about globalization of competition, antitrust enforcement is routinely concerned about competition in local markets. Almost half of the FTC's merger complaints make allegations involving local markets, which should not be surprising given the number of challenges to mergers in groceries, gasoline retailing, construction, natural gas transportation, and health care. Intimate knowledge about local competitive conditions is essential to effective antitrust enforcement. State attorneys general have a clear comparative advantage in understanding local markets. . . .

2. Familiarity with Local Institutions. State attorneys general are more likely than federal enforcers to know and be known and be trusted by state and local government officials. They are thus uniquely situated to help prevent anticompetitive harm from being inflicted on or by government agencies. Government and nonprofit entities play major roles, even in the United States' capitalist economy. . . . Although federal enforcers regularly engage in "competition advocacy," as it is called, no Washington-based voice is likely to be listened to as carefully as the voice of the state attorney general.

3. Compensating Individuals. State attorneys general recover money for injured individuals in two ways. First, states implicitly represent taxpayers by recovering overcharges exacted from state purchasing operations. Beyond that, state attorneys general are the only governmental officials specifically authorized by federal statute to recover monetary relief in treble damages for natural persons injured by Sherman Act violations. The Justice Department has no such power, and the FTC finds authority for a court to award consumer redress only by implication (and very rarely invokes the authority in antitrust cases). {*Eds.: this extract was written before the Supreme Court's decision in* AMG Capital.}

* * *

The final point mentioned in this extract—the states' power to obtain consumer redress—has acquired additional importance with the FTC's loss in *AMG Capital* of its power to obtain equitable monetary relief in district court. The continuing ability of state enforcers to do so ensures that at least one path to this form of redress remains open.[967]

Of course, the federal and state enforcers do not always see eye to eye on every issue, and some friction is a hallmark of any polycentric system. Thus, sometimes one or more states may take a different position on antitrust enforcement from the federal agencies: for example, state AGs may litigate when the federal government declines to do so.[968] In Sprint / T-Mobile, famously, the Antitrust Division negotiated a consent decree that, in the view of the Department of Justice, resolved the competitive concerns, but a group of state Attorneys-General disagreed and filed suit in an (unsuccessful) effort to block the deal.[969] In rejecting the challenge, the court treated DOJ's

---

[966] *See, e.g.*, FTC, Press Release, FTC and Commonwealth of Pennsylvania Challenge Proposed Merger of Two Major Philadelphia-area Hospital Systems (Feb. 27, 2020); U.S. Dept. of Justice, Press Release, Justice Department Sues Monopolist Google For Violating Antitrust Laws (Oct. 20, 2020) (noting suit along with 11 State AGs).

[967] *See generally* Schonette Walker, Steve Scannell & Abigail Wood, *Bridging the Gorge: States Prevent Retention of Ill-Gotten Profits Through Disgorgement*, Comp. Pol'y Int'l (Aug. 2021).

[968] *See, e.g.*, California v American Stores, 495 U.S. 271 (1990) (states permitted to sue for injunctive relief, notwithstanding FTC negotiation of a consent order).

[969] New York v. Deutsche Telekom AG, 439 F.Supp.3d 179 (S.D.N.Y. 2020).

decision as "informative but not decisive."[970] This episode generated some high-profile controversy about the relationship between federal and state antitrust enforcement.[971]

Statement of Interest of the United States of America, New York v. Deutsche Telekom
Case No. 1:19-cv-5434 (S.D.N.Y. filed Dec. 20, 2019)

[1] The United States, through the Department of Justice's Antitrust Division and the FCC, investigated the proposed merger of T-Mobile US, Inc. ("T-Mobile") and Sprint Corporation ("Sprint"). The Antitrust Division (along with a number of state Attorneys General) and the FCC concluded that consumers would benefit from the combination of T-Mobile and Sprint accompanied by the divestitures and other relief the Antitrust Division (in its proposed Final Judgment) and the FCC (in its order) secured to protect competition and promote the public interest. This outcome benefits consumers through the combination's enhanced output—the increased availability of a higher quality mobile wireless network for consumers. Specifically, TMobile has committed to providing 5G coverage to 85% of the rural population within three years, and 90% of the rural population within six years. In addition, the relief the Antitrust Division and the FCC secured will maintain the competitive structure of the industry through a substantial divestiture of assets from T-Mobile to DISH Network Corporation ("DISH"), which has committed to building a nationwide network that will put its idle spectrum holdings into use by mobile wireless consumers for the first time. As a result, the relief the Antitrust Division (and a number of state Attorneys General) and the FCC secured means consumers in rural areas will gain new access to high quality 5G networks and consumers nationwide will continue to have four fully competitive options for their mobile wireless services.

[2] A group of thirteen states and the District of Columbia (the "Litigating States") seek to block the merger in its entirety. In doing so, they ask this court to undo the benefits of the relief secured by the Antitrust Division (and our fellow state Attorneys General) and the FCC. The Litigating States face a high bar in their challenge. To win a permanent injunction that would block the merger, they must convince the court their request to block the merger in its entirety is in the public interest, among other obstacles. In other words, they must convince this honorable court that it is not merely acceptable, but beneficial to the public, to deprive consumers nationwide of a higher quality T-Mobile network and DISH's commitment to build a nationwide retail mobile wireless network, and to deprive consumers in rural states, which have disproportionately chosen to support the Antitrust Division's settlement rather than join in this litigation, of new access to 5G networks. Indeed, that the Litigating States' proposed remedy will affirmatively harm consumers in rural states by denying them these benefits weighs strongly against a nationwide injunction. [. . .]

[3] . . . The proposed Final Judgment outlines a structural settlement that preserves the existence of a fourth competitor in the nationwide market for retail mobile wireless service. The settlement requires T-Mobile to divest to DISH certain retail wireless business and network assets, and supporting assets and provide to DISH all services, access, and assets necessary, to facilitate DISH building and operating its own mobile wireless services network and to enable it to compete in the marketplace. This is intended to ensure the development of a new national facilities-based mobile wireless carrier competitor to ultimately remedy the anticompetitive harms that flow from the change in the market structure that otherwise would have occurred as a result of the merger. Further, DISH

---

[970] New York v. Deutsche Telekom AG, 439 F.Supp.3d 179, 224 (S.D.N.Y. 2020) ("Not only have the FCC and DOJ conditioned the transaction before the Court, the Court will accord their views some deference. Where federal regulators have carefully scrutinized the challenged merger, imposed various restrictions on it, and stand ready to provide further consideration, supervision, and perhaps invalidation of asserted anticompetitive practices[,] we have a unique indicator that the challenged practice may have redeeming competitive virtues and that the search for those values is not almost sure to be in vain. Indeed, the Supreme Court has looked to the views of federal regulators on multiple occasions for assistance in conducting its Section 7 analysis. As Plaintiff States note, however, the views of the FCC and DOJ cannot simply be adopted entirely at face value, as their assessment of a merger's legality may be guided by considerations that are outside the scope of Section 7. Ultimately, the Court will treat the views of the FCC and DOJ as informative but not conclusive. . . . [M[indful that the agencies are intimately familiar with this technical subject matter, as well as the competitive realities involved, the Court treats their views and actions as persuasive and helpful evidence in analyzing the competitive effect of this merger[.]") (cleaned up).

[971] See, e.g., Michael Murray, U.S. Department of Justice, Antitrust Federalism (remarks of Aug. 31, 2020) (explaining DOJ perspective on deference owed to federal enforcers' decisions).

will bring spectrum (that it currently has no obligation to build out in this way) into service as a mobile broadband 5G service that will serve consumers across the country.

[4] The Antitrust Division reached these conclusions in its role as the enforcer of the federal antitrust law on behalf of consumers nationwide. This required, among other things, considering the interests of differently situated consumers. Ultimately, the proposed Final Judgment fulfills the twin goals of a merger remedy. It permits the merger to proceed, enabling rural, and other, consumers to benefit from its promised efficiencies, while adopting remedies that will protect consumers in and bring new competition to urban areas that may have been at greater risk without this settlement. Currently, ten states—Arkansas, Colorado, Florida, Kansas, Louisiana, Nebraska, Ohio, Oklahoma, South Dakota, and Texas—have joined the Antitrust Division's suit seeking approval of its settlement, and three more states—Arizona, New Mexico, and Utah—have publicly supported the deal. [. . .]

[5] Just as the existence of the remedies secured by the Antitrust Division and the FCC are important factors in this court's equitable relief analysis, so too are the conclusions of both agencies that the remedies they secured are in the public's interest. Giving weight to these determinations is all the more justified here, where granting the Litigating States' request for a nationwide injunction would directly conflict with the Antitrust Division's proposed Final Judgment and the FCC's order, effectively displacing these remedies and preventing the merger's significant procompetitive efficiencies from flowing to consumers. [. . .]

[6] Both the Antitrust Division and the FCC had the ability to pursue a nationwide injunction to block the merger, but after an extensive review and analysis, instead chose to secure other relief. After studying the merger for fifteen months on the basis of its antitrust expertise and from the perspective of the nation as a whole, the Antitrust Division reached a settlement that provided substantial long-term benefits for American consumers by allowing consumers to benefit from the transaction's efficiencies while protecting them from its harms. Similarly, the FCC conducted a thorough and lengthy investigation, informed by its expertise regarding competition among providers of various telecommunications services and its nationwide perspective, and concluded that the proposed transaction, as modified by the FCC's own set of conditions, would be in the public interest. [. . .]

[7] As Congress recognized, state government bodies do not hold the same policy concerns as federal government bodies. In representing the rights and interests of their residents, they do not consider the rights and interests of the nation as a whole. In particular, they do not possess the expansive view of federal enforcers who regularly oversee antitrust investigations and make remedy recommendations on a national scale. They have neither the authority nor the responsibility to act on behalf of the nation, and while their concerns are not invalid, they are bound by state borders. [. . .]

[8] The Litigating States' strong interest in this merger does not justify their attempt to substitute their judgment for the nationwide perspective of the United States. The United States does not intend to discourage private party plaintiffs—whether states, businesses, or individuals—from spending their time and effort assisting the federal government in antitrust enforcement. The Clayton Act was enacted not merely to provide private relief, but to serve as well the high purpose of enforcing the antitrust laws. At the same time, states cannot and should not displace the federal government's role as the nation's federal antitrust enforcer. When a group of states attempts to do so by seeking relief that quite arguably may benefit certain citizens while harming others, such a remedy is not in the public interest, and, respectfully, should not satisfy this court's test for injunctive relief.

* * *

In other circumstances, however, the Antitrust Division has argued that *no* inference ought to be drawn from a federal agency's decision not to challenge a transaction, in the adjudication of a subsequent challenge by another plaintiff. In an amicus brief filed in the *Steves and Sons v. JELD-WEN* private merger challenge, the Division denied that the defendant could rely on the Justice Department's decision not to intervene, urging the court that:

> [N]o inference should be drawn from the Division's closure of its investigations into JELD-WEN's proposed and consummated acquisition of CMI. As the United States has stated twice previously in this case in response to JELD-WEN's assertions, there are many reasons why the Antitrust Division might close an investigation or choose not to take an enforcement action. The

Division's decision not to challenge a particular transaction is not confirmation that the transaction is competitively neutral or procompetitive.[972]

Are these positions consistent? Are there reasons of principle why a decision to affirmatively accept a remedy might warrant different treatment from a decision not to take enforcement action?

NOTES

1) What are the benefits and risks of increased state-level antitrust enforcement activity? When and why should we allocate national tax dollars to support state rather than federal antitrust enforcement?

2) State antitrust laws usually follow the contours of the federal antitrust statutes, but they do not always do so. Is this a reason for concern, a cause for celebration, or both? Explain.

3) Are there circumstances under which a court should defer to a state enforcer's view rather than the contrary view of the federal agencies?

4) Are there any reasons why it might not be optimal for the states have power to sue for parens patriae damages on behalf of their citizens?

5) What kinds of interstate cooperation could help improve the effectiveness of state enforcement? How?[973]

G. Remedies I: Injunctive Relief

The primary remedy in government cases—whether brought by the FTC, DOJ, or state governments—is usually injunctive relief: that is, a court order designed to terminate and remedy the antitrust violation, after liability has been established. (Damages—the signature remedy in private cases, although sometimes available to government plaintiffs—are considered in the next chapter.) In the following extract, Doug Melamed gives a very brief tour of the most important purposes of an antitrust remedy.

A. Douglas Melamed, Afterword: The Purposes of Antitrust Remedies
76 Antitrust L.J. 359 (2009)

Broadly speaking, antitrust remedies serve four different purposes:

(1) *Compensation of victims of unlawful conduct.* The most straightforward purpose is compensation of those who have been harmed by the unlawful conduct. . . .

(2) *Punishment and deterrence of unlawful conduct.* Furthering the punishment and deterrence objectives requires remedies the ex ante anticipation of which would cause economic actors to expect conduct that violates the antitrust laws to be ultimately unprofitable. . . . .

(3) Terminating and preventing the recurrence of unlawful conduct. There is probably no dispute that a determination that the defendant has violated the antitrust laws should at the very least be cessation of the unlawful conduct and some kind of assurance that the unlawful conduct will not be resumed in the near future. . . . .

(4) Restoring competitive conditions to the market harmed by the unlawful conduct. Questions regarding this remedial objective are in some ways the most difficult and controversial. Restorative remedies can include divestiture and mandatory injunctions. They can be problematic for three basic reasons. They could impose a disproportionate and inequitable burden on the defendant. They could wittingly or unwittingly substitute government regulation for market competition. And they could fail to achieve their purpose because of the inability of those fashioning the remedy fully to understand the markets and to foresee the future. In these ways, the cure of restorative remedies could be worse than the disease.

* * *

---

[972] Brief for the United States of America as Amicus Curiae in Support of Appellee Steves And Sons, Inc., Steves and Sons, Inc. v. JELD-WEN, Inc., Case No. 19-1397, at *15 (4th Cir. filed Aug. 23, 2019).

[973] The National Association of Attorneys General is very active in facilitating antitrust cooperation. *See* https://www.naag.org/issues/antitrust/.

Antitrust injunctions may be preliminary (*i.e.*, granted on an interim basis, usually to preserve the status quo, pending some more extensive proceeding) or permanent (*i.e.*, reflecting a full and final merits adjudication). The agencies are situated a little differently with respect to their access to injunctive relief. When the FTC contemplates permanent proceedings in administrative court, preliminary relief—such as an injunction preventing the parties closing a notified transaction after the expiration of the HSR waiting period—is only available in district court, because the Commission (and its ALJs) can only award a permanent cease-and-desist order.[974] As a result, the FTC has a practice, in merger cases, of filing complaints simultaneously in administrative court (seeking permanent relief) *and* in federal district court (seeking a preliminary injunction, and perhaps a temporary restraining order preventing the parties from closing the deal during the preliminary injunction proceedings). DOJ, by contrast, has no power to litigate administratively and no limits on its ability to litigate in district court: as a result, DOJ's practice usually involves a combined proceeding in federal district court to obtain both preliminary and permanent injunctive relief.

The agencies also face slightly different standards when seeking preliminary relief. DOJ's power to obtain an injunction is grounded in Section 15 of the Clayton Act, 15 U.S.C. § 25, which rests on the same standards for preliminary relief that apply to all litigants, including the provisions of Federal Rule of Civil Procedure 65. The generally applicable standard typically requires the government to show "a reasonable likelihood of success on the merits" as well as a favorable "balance of equities": most courts do not separately require the government to make a separate showing of irreparable injury.[975] By contrast, the FTC's power to seek a preliminary injunction is grounded in Section 13(b) of the FTC Act, as the district court explained in the FTC's (successful) effort to enjoin a New Jersey hospital merger:

> Pursuant to Section 13 of the FTC Act, the FTC can file suit in district court seeking a preliminary injunction to prevent a merger [or to restrain other conduct] pending a FTC administrative adjudication whenever the Commission has reason to believe that a corporation is violating, or is about to violate [the antitrust laws.] The standard for granting a preliminary injunction under the FTC Act is not the same as the standard used to grant injunctive relief under Federal Rule of Civil Procedure 65. Rather, a court should issue a preliminary injunction pursuant to Section [13(b)] "[u]pon a proper showing that, weighing the equities and considering the Commission's likelihood of ultimate success, such action would be in the public interest."

> Under Section 13(b), a court first considers the FTC's likelihood of success on the merits. Next, the court weighs the equities to determine whether a preliminary injunction is in the public interest. The question is whether the harm that the Defendants will suffer if the merger is delayed will, in turn, harm the public more than if the injunction is not issued. Ultimately, in deciding whether to preliminarily enjoin a merger[,] doubts are to be resolved against the transaction.

> The FTC must show that it has a likelihood of success of demonstrating, during the administrative proceeding, that the proposed merger [or conduct] violates [a relevant provision of law.] . . . [A]t the preliminary injunction stage, the FTC does not need to establish that the proposed [practice or transaction is unlawful]. Rather, the FTC need only show that there is a reasonable probability that the challenged [practice or] transaction will [be unlawful].[976]

---

[974] The remedial powers of the ALJ and Commission in administrative proceedings are limited to issuing a permanent cease-and-desist order. Interim or preliminary relief is not available. 15 U.S.C. § 45(b).

[975] *See, e.g.*, United States v. Siemens Corp., 621 F.2d 499, 505 (2d Cir. 1980) ("The proper test for determining whether preliminary relief should be granted in a Government-initiated antitrust suit is whether the Government has shown a reasonable likelihood of success on the merits and whether the balance of equities tips in its favor. . . . [O]nce the Government demonstrates a reasonable probability that s 7 has been violated, irreparable harm to the public should be presumed.").

[976] FTC v. Hackensack Meridian Health, Inc., No. CV 20-18140, 2021 WL 4145062, at *14 (D.N.J. Aug. 4, 2021), aff'd, 30 F.4th 160 (3d Cir. 2022). *See also, e.g.*, FTC v. Whole Foods Market, Inc., 548 F.3d 1028 (D.C. Cir. 2008) ("[A] district court must not require the FTC to prove the merits, because, in a § 53(b) preliminary injunction proceeding, a court is not authorized to determine whether the antitrust laws are about to be violated. That responsibility lies with the FTC. Not that the court may simply rubber-stamp an injunction whenever the FTC provides some threshold evidence; it must exercise independent judgment about the questions § 53(b) commits to it. Thus, the district court must evaluate the FTC's chance of success on the basis of all the evidence before it, from the defendants as well as from the FTC. The district court should bear in mind the FTC will be entitled to a presumption against the merger on the merits, and therefore does not need detailed evidence of anticompetitive effect at this preliminary phase. Nevertheless, the merging parties are entitled to oppose a § 53(b) preliminary injunction with their own evidence,

Courts have wide discretion in designing antitrust injunctive relief. The Supreme Court has stated that the touchstone is "whether the relief represents a reasonable method of eliminating the consequences of the illegal conduct."[977] This often includes what is known as "fencing-in" relief: that is, prohibitions on conduct that may not violate the antitrust laws in its own right, but which presents an unacceptable risk of illegality or harm given the circumstances following the violation. And when an antitrust agency is involved, courts exhibit considerable deference to the agency's judgment in designing an effective remedy.

National Lead exemplifies these principles. In that case, the FTC had determined that sellers of lead pigments had entered into an anticompetitive conspiracy that involved the use of "zone delivered pricing": that is, flat delivered pricing within particular geographic zones. The Commission issued an order requiring the participants to refrain from any conspiracy or agreement to use zone pricing, or any other system that resulted in identical prices to customers. The Commission also prohibited the participants from *unilaterally* using any pricing mechanism that resulted in identical prices with competitors as a result of zone delivered pricing. The participants objected to this latter limitation which, they argued, was an impermissible overreach. The Supreme Court thus faced the question: could the FTC ban a noncollusive and usually lawful pricing practice as part of a remedial order, when that same conduct could not be prohibited in its own right? The Court had no difficulty in saying yes.

FTC v. National Lead Co.
352 U.S. 419 (1957)

Justice Clark.

[1] The Court has held that the Commission is clothed with wide discretion in determining the type of order that is necessary to bring an end to the unfair practices found to exist. In *Jacob Siegel Co. v. Federal Trade Commission*, 327 U.S. 608 (1946), the Court named the Commission "the expert body to determine what remedy is necessary to eliminate the unfair or deceptive trade practices which have been disclosed. It has wide latitude for judgment and the courts will not interfere except where the remedy selected has no reasonable relation to the unlawful practices found to exist." Thereafter, in *FTC v. Cement Institute*, 333 U.S. 683 (1948), the Court pointed out that the Congress, in passing the Act, "felt that courts needed the assistance of men trained to combat monopolistic practices in the framing of judicial decrees in antitrust litigation." In the light of this, the Court reasoned, it should not "lightly modify" the orders of the Commission. Again, in *FTC v. Ruberoid Co.*, [343 U.S. 470, 473 (1952)] we said that "if the Commission is to attain the objectives Congress envisioned, it cannot be required to confine its road block to the narrow lane the transgressor has traveled; it must be allowed effectively to close all roads to the prohibited goal, so that its order may not be bypassed with impunity." We pointed out there that Congress had placed the primary responsibility for fashioning orders upon the Commission. These cases narrow the issue to the question: Does the remedy selected have a reasonable relation to the unlawful practices found to exist? We believe that it does. . . .

[2] . . . [T]he Commission correctly considered the circumstances under which the illegal acts occurred. Those in utter disregard of law . . . call for repression by sterner measures than where the steps could reasonably have been thought permissible. Respondents made no appeal here from some of the findings as to their guilt. Having lost the battle on the facts, they hope to win the war on the type of decree. They fight for the right to continue to use individually the very same weapon with which they carried on their unlawful enterprise. The Commission concluded that this must not be permitted. It was not obliged to assume, contrary to common experience, that a violator of the antitrust laws will relinquish the fruits of his violation more completely than it requires. Although

---

and that evidence may force the FTC to respond with a more substantial showing."); FTC v. Swedish Match, 131 F. Supp. 2d 151, 156 (D.D.C. 2000) ("The question before this Court is whether the FTC has made a showing that raises questions going to the merits so serious, substantial, difficult, and doubtful as to make them fair ground for thorough investigation, study, deliberation and determination by the Commission in the first instance and ultimately by the Court of Appeals. . . . [T]he Commission must show that there is a reasonable probability that the challenged acquisition will substantially lessen competition.") (internal quotation marks and citations omitted).

[977] Nat'l Soc. of Prof. Engineers v. United States, 435 U.S. 679, 698 (1978). *See also* Jacob Siegel Co. v. FTC, 327 U.S. 608, 613 (1946) ("The Commission is the expert body to determine what remedy is necessary to eliminate the unfair or deceptive trade practices which have been disclosed. It has wide latitude for judgment and the courts will not interfere except where the remedy selected has no reasonable relation to the unlawful practices found to exist.").

the zone plan might be used for some lawful purposes, decrees often suppress a lawful device when it is used to carry out an unlawful purpose. In such instances the Court is obliged not only to suppress the unlawful practice but to take such reasonable action as is calculated to preclude the revival of the illegal practices.

* * *

Over the long life of the antitrust project, courts and agencies have developed a robust toolkit of remedial provisions for antitrust cases. As we saw in discussing merger remedies in Chapter VIII,[978] these can crudely be divided into "structural" and "behavioral" remedies. Structural remedies work by severing the economic connections between businesses or business units; behavioral remedies work by establishing rules for what businesses must do (*i.e.*, affirmative duties) or must not do (*i.e.*, prohibitions). Structural remedies have the advantage that, if correctly designed, they eliminate the incentive for the relevant firm to engage in harmful conduct; behavioral remedies tend to leave that incentive intact, requiring ongoing interpretation, monitoring, and enforcement to guard against violations (and leaving open the possibility that the business will engage in behaviors that undermine the remedy without literally violating its terms).

1. Structural remedies

"Divestiture" of all or part of a merger or acquisition target. As we have already seen, the most common and important remedy in a merger case is a requirement to divest (*i.e.*, sell off) the assets that would, if acquired or retained, constitute an antitrust violation. Sometimes the divestiture amounts to a complete block on the entire proposed transaction: on other occasions, it is enough to spin off the competitively-troubling business units, such that the rest of the transaction can proceed. As you may remember, a successful divestiture must satisfy a number of tests: it must include a "package" of assets—including facilities, employees, IP, brands, information, and so on—that is commercially viable (this may mean that the package includes more than simply the assets that literally give rise to the competitive problems), and it must be to a buyer that can credibly commit to operating the package as a competitive force. A buyer that will simply strip business and sell off the component parts, or just under-invest in the business and let it decline, may not represent much of a solution to the competitive problem.

Look back at Chapter VIII for more information about divestiture remedies in a merger case.

"Breakup." Sometimes a synonym for "divestiture," the concept of "breakup" as an antitrust remedy tends to connote something beyond just blocking all or part of a proposed or consummated acquisition. In particular, the term tends to be used in an informal sense to mean a divestiture as a remedy for something other than an acquisition of the relevant business units: for example, the "breakup" of a company in response to a conduct violation such as monopolization. The breakup of AT&T in 1982 remains the most prominent example of such a remedy in modern antitrust history.[979]

Breakup of this kind remains very rare in conduct (*i.e.*, nonmerger) cases.[980] It was originally ordered by the district court in *Microsoft*, only for this instruction to be vacated by the D.C. Circuit, and the parties to subsequently reach a settlement that left Microsoft intact.[981] Nonetheless, while commenting on the possibility of divestiture in light of the district court's decision, the D.C. Circuit provided some helpful—and somewhat pointed—guidance on the role of the breakup remedy and the conditions under which it would be appropriate. What follows is, first, the district court's judgment on remedy—requiring that Microsoft's operating system business be separated from its applications business—followed by the D.C. Circuit's perspective on appeal.

---

[978] *See supra* § VIII.E (merger remedies).

[979] *See* United States v. American Tel. and Tel. Co., 552 F. Supp. 131 (D.D.C. 1982) (accepting consent decree pursuant to the Tunney Act); Joseph D. Kearney, *From the Fall of the Bell System to the Telecommunications Act: Regulation of Telecommunications under Judge Greene*, 50 Hastings L.J. 1395 (1999); Christopher S. Yoo, *The Enduring Lessons of the Breakup of AT&T: A Twenty-Five Year Retrospective*, 61 Fed. Commc'ns. L.J. (2008). *See also* Robert W. Crandall *The AT&T Divestiture: Was It Necessary? Was It A Success?* Presentation to DOJ (Mar. 28, 2007), https://www.justice.gov/sites/default/files/atr/legacy/2007/04/10/222440.pdf.

[980] *See generally, e.g.,* Spencer Weber Waller, *The Past, Present, and Future of Monopolization Remedies*, 76 Antitrust L.J. 11, 14–16 (2009); Robert Crandall, *The Failure of Structural Remedies in Sherman Act Monopolization Cases*, 80 Or. L. Rev. 109 (2001); Neil W. Averitt, *Structural Remedies in Competition Cases under the Federal Trade Commission Act*, 40 Ohio St. L.J. 779 (1979).

[981] Stipulation & Revised Proposed Final Judgment, United States v. Microsoft Corp., Case No. 98-1232 (Nov. 6, 2001).

Note: as you may remember from Chapter VII, the district court judge, Judge Thomas Penfield Jackson, had engaged in misconduct during the trial that gave rise to an appearance of impropriety and bias against Microsoft (although the circuit court concluded that there was no actual bias).

United States v. Microsoft Corp.

97 F. Supp. 2d 59 (D.D.C. June 7, 2000)

Judge Jackson.

[1] These cases are before the Court for disposition of the sole matter presently remaining for decision by the trial court, namely, entry of appropriate relief for the violations of the Sherman Act, §§ 1 and 2, and various state laws committed by the defendant Microsoft Corporation as found by Court in accordance with its Findings of Fact and Conclusions of Law. Final judgment will be entered contemporaneously herewith. No further proceedings will be required.

[2] The Court has been presented by plaintiffs with a proposed form of final judgment that would mandate both conduct modification and structural reorganization by the defendant when fully implemented. Microsoft has responded with a motion for summary rejection of structural reorganization and a request for months of additional time to oppose the relief sought in all other respects. Microsoft claims, in effect, to have been surprised by the "draconian" and "unprecedented" remedy the plaintiffs recommend. What it proposes is yet another round of discovery, to be followed by a second trial—in essence an ex post and de facto bifurcation of the case already considered and rejected by the Court.

[3] Microsoft's profession of surprise is not credible. From the inception of this case Microsoft knew, from well-established Supreme Court precedents dating from the beginning of the last century, that a mandated divestiture was a possibility, if not a probability, in the event of an adverse result at trial. . . . Its failure to anticipate and to prepare to meet such an eventuality gives no reason to afford it an opportunity to do so now.

[4] These cases have been before the Court, and have occupied much of its attention, for the past two years, not counting the antecedent proceedings. Following a full trial Microsoft has been found guilty of antitrust violations, notwithstanding its protests to this day that it has committed none. The Court is convinced for several reasons that a final—and appealable—judgment should be entered quickly. It has also reluctantly come to the conclusion, for the same reasons, that a structural remedy has become imperative: Microsoft as it is presently organized and led is unwilling to accept the notion that it broke the law or accede to an order amending its conduct.

[5] First, despite the Court's Findings of Fact and Conclusions of Law, Microsoft does not yet concede that any of its business practices violated the Sherman Act. Microsoft officials have recently been quoted publicly to the effect that the company has "done nothing wrong" and that it will be vindicated on appeal. The Court is well aware that there is a substantial body of public opinion, some of it rational, that holds to a similar view. It is time to put that assertion to the test. If true, then an appellate tribunal should be given early opportunity to confirm it as promptly as possible, and to abort any remedial measures before they have become irreversible as a practical matter.

[6] Second, there is credible evidence in the record to suggest that Microsoft, convinced of its innocence, continues to do business as it has in the past, and may yet do to other markets what it has already done in the PC operating system and browser markets. Microsoft has shown no disposition to voluntarily alter its business protocol in any significant respect. Indeed, it has announced its intention to appeal even the imposition of the modest conduct remedies it has itself proposed as an alternative to the non-structural remedies sought by the plaintiffs.

[7] Third, Microsoft has proved untrustworthy in the past. In earlier proceedings in which a preliminary injunction was entered, Microsoft's purported compliance with that injunction while it was on appeal was illusory and its explanation disingenuous. If it responds in similar fashion to an injunctive remedy in this case, the earlier the need for enforcement measures becomes apparent the more effective they are likely to be.

[8] Finally, the Court believes that extended proceedings on the form a remedy should take are unlikely to give any significantly greater assurance that it will be able to identify what might be generally regarded as an optimum

remedy. As has been the case with regard to Microsoft's culpability, opinion as to an appropriate remedy is sharply divided. There is little chance that those divergent opinions will be reconciled by anything short of actual experience. The declarations (and the "offers of proof") from numerous potential witnesses now before the Court provide some insight as to how its various provisions might operate, but for the most part they are merely the predictions of purportedly knowledgeable people as to effects which may or may not ensue if the proposed final judgment is entered. In its experience the Court has found testimonial predictions of future events generally less reliable even than testimony as to historical fact, and cross-examination to be of little use in enhancing or detracting from their accuracy.

[9] In addition to its substantive objections, the proposed final judgment is also criticized by Microsoft as being vague and ambiguous. Plaintiffs respond that, to the extent it may be lacking in detail, it is purposely so to allow Microsoft itself to propose such detail as will be least disruptive of its business, failing which plaintiffs will ask the Court to supply it as the need appears.

[10] Plaintiffs won the case, and for that reason alone have some entitlement to a remedy of their choice. Moreover, plaintiffs' proposed final judgment is the collective work product of senior antitrust law enforcement officials of the United States Department of Justice and the Attorneys General of 19 states, in conjunction with multiple consultants. These officials are by reason of office obliged and expected to consider—and to act in—the public interest; Microsoft is not. The proposed final judgment is represented to the Court as incorporating provisions employed successfully in the past, and it appears to the Court to address all the principal objectives of relief in such cases, namely, to terminate the unlawful conduct, to prevent its repetition in the future, and to revive competition in the relevant markets. Microsoft's alternative decree is plainly inadequate in all three respects.

[11] The final judgment proposed by plaintiffs is perhaps more radical than might have resulted had mediation been successful and terminated in a consent decree. It is less so than that advocated by four disinterested amici curiae. It is designed, moreover, to take force in stages, so that the effects can be gauged while the appeal progresses and before it has been fully implemented. And, of course, the Court will retain jurisdiction following appeal, and can modify the judgment as necessary in accordance with instructions from an appellate court or to accommodate conditions changed with the passage of time. [. . .]

[12] Upon the record at trial and all prior and subsequent proceedings herein, it is this 7th day of June, 2000, hereby:

ORDERED, ADJUDGED, AND DECREED as follows:

1. Divestiture

> a. Not later than four months after entry of this Final Judgment, Microsoft shall submit to the Court and the Plaintiffs a proposed plan of divestiture. . . .

> b. Following approval of a final plan of divestiture by the Court (the "Plan") . . . Microsoft shall implement such Plan.

> c. The Plan shall provide for the completion . . . of the following steps:

>> i. The separation of the Operating Systems Business from the Applications Business, and the transfer of the assets of one of them (the "Separated Business") to a separate entity along with (a) all personnel, systems, and other tangible and intangible assets (including Intellectual Property) used to develop, produce, distribute, market, promote, sell, license and support the products and services of the Separated Business, and (b) such other assets as are necessary to operate the Separated Business as an independent and economically viable entity.

>> ii. Intellectual Property that is used both in a product developed, distributed, or sold by the Applications Business and in a product developed, distributed, or sold by the Operating Systems Business as of April 27, 2000, shall be assigned to the Applications Business, and the Operating Systems Business shall be granted a perpetual, royalty-free license to license and distribute such Intellectual Property in its products[.] [. . .]

d. Until Implementation of the Plan, Microsoft shall:

i. preserve, maintain, and operate the Operating Systems Business and the Applications Business as ongoing, economically viable businesses, with management, sales, products, and operations of each business held as separate, distinct and apart from one another as they were on April 27, 2000, except to provide the accounting, management, and information services or other necessary support functions provided by Microsoft prior to the entry of this Final Judgment; [. . .]

iii. take no action that undermines, frustrates, interferes with, or makes more difficult the divestiture required by this Final Judgment without the prior approval of the Court[.] [. . .]

2. Provisions Implementing Divestiture

a. After Implementation of the Plan, and throughout the term of this Final Judgment, neither the Operating Systems Business nor the Applications Business, nor any member of their respective Boards of Directors, shall acquire any securities or assets of the other Business; no Covered Shareholder holding securities of either the Operating Systems Business or the Applications Business shall acquire any securities or assets of or shall be an officer, director, or employee of the other Business; and no person who is an officer, director, or employee of the Operating Systems Business or the Applications Business shall be an officer, director, or employee of the other Business.

b. After Implementation of the Plan and throughout the term of this Final Judgment, the Operating Systems Business and the Applications Business shall be prohibited from:

i. merging or otherwise recombining, or entering into any joint venture with one another;

ii. entering into any Agreement with one another under which one of the Businesses develops, sells, licenses for sale or distribution, or distributes products or services (other than the technologies referred to in the following sentence) developed, sold, licensed, or distributed by the other Business;

iii. providing to the other any APIs, Technical Information, Communications Interfaces, or technical information that is not simultaneously published, disclosed, or made readily available to ISVs, IHVs, and OEMs; and

iv. licensing, selling or otherwise providing to the other Business any product or service on terms more favorable than those available to any similarly situated third party.

* * *

<h2 style="text-align:center">United States v. Microsoft Corp.</h2>
<h3 style="text-align:center">253 F.3d 34 (D.C. Cir. 2001) (en banc)</h3>

Per curiam.

[1] As a general matter, a district court is afforded broad discretion to enter that relief it calculates will best remedy the conduct it has found to be unlawful. This is no less true in antitrust cases. And divestiture is a common form of relief in successful antitrust prosecutions: it is indeed the most important of antitrust remedies.

[2] On remand, the District Court must reconsider whether the use of the structural remedy of divestiture is appropriate with respect to Microsoft, which argues that it is a unitary company. By and large, cases upon which plaintiffs rely in arguing for the split of Microsoft have involved the dissolution of entities formed by mergers and acquisitions. On the contrary, the Supreme Court has clarified that divestiture has traditionally been the remedy for Sherman Act violations whose heart is intercorporate combination and control, and that complete divestiture is particularly appropriate where asset or stock acquisitions violate the antitrust laws.

[3] One apparent reason why courts have not ordered the dissolution of unitary companies is logistical difficulty. As the court explained in *United States v. Alcoa*, 91 F. Supp. 333, 416 (S.D.N.Y. 1950), a "corporation, designed to

operate effectively as a single entity, cannot readily be dismembered of parts of its various operations without a marked loss of efficiency." A corporation that has expanded by acquiring its competitors often has preexisting internal lines of division along which it may more easily be split than a corporation that has expanded from natural growth. Although time and corporate modifications and developments may eventually fade those lines, at least the identifiable entities preexisted to create a template for such division as the court might later decree. With reference to those corporations that are not acquired by merger and acquisition, Judge Wyzanski accurately opined in *United Shoe*:

> United conducts all machine manufacture at one plant in Beverly, with one set of jigs and tools, one foundry, one laboratory for machinery problems, one managerial staff, and one labor force. It takes no Solomon to see that this organism cannot be cut into three equal and viable parts.

United States v. United Shoe Machine Corp., 110 F.Supp. 295, 348 (D.Mass. 1953).

[4] Depending upon the evidence, the District Court may find in a remedies proceeding that it would be no easier to split Microsoft in two than United Shoe in three. Microsoft's Offer of Proof in response to the court's denial of an evidentiary hearing included proffered testimony from its President and CEO Steve Ballmer that the company "is, and always has been, a unified company without free-standing business units. Microsoft is not the result of mergers or acquisitions." Microsoft further offered evidence that it is "not organized along product lines," but rather is housed in a single corporate headquarters and that it has only one sales and marketing organization which is responsible for selling all of the company's products, one basic research organization, one product support organization, one operations department, one information technology department, one facilities department, one purchasing department, one human resources department, one finance department, one legal department and one public relations department.

[5] If indeed Microsoft is a unitary company, division might very well require Microsoft to reproduce each of these departments in each new entity rather than simply allocate the differing departments among them.

[6] In devising an appropriate remedy, the District Court also should consider whether plaintiffs have established a sufficient causal connection between Microsoft's anticompetitive conduct and its dominant position in the OS market. Mere existence of an exclusionary act does not itself justify full feasible relief against the monopolist to create maximum competition. Rather, structural relief, which is designed to eliminate the monopoly altogether requires a clearer indication of a significant causal connection between the conduct and creation or maintenance of the market power. Absent such causation, the antitrust defendant's unlawful behavior should be remedied by an injunction against continuation of that conduct.

[7] [In this case,] we have found a causal connection between Microsoft's exclusionary conduct and its continuing position in the operating systems market only through inference. Indeed, the District Court expressly did not adopt the position that Microsoft would have lost its position in the OS market but for its anticompetitive behavior. If the court on remand is unconvinced of the causal connection between Microsoft's exclusionary conduct and the company's position in the OS market, it may well conclude that divestiture is not an appropriate remedy.

[8] While we do not undertake to dictate to the District Court the precise form that relief should take on remand, we note again that it should be tailored to fit the wrong creating the occasion for the remedy.

* * *

Today, breakups are back on the menu of policy discussion. Tim Wu, for example, has argued that "[t]here is an unfortunate tendency within enforcement agencies to portray breakup and dissolutions as off the table or only for extremely rare cases. There is no legal reason for that presumption[.]"[982] The next couple of extracts give two different perspectives on the breakup option.

---

[982] Tim Wu, THE CURSE OF BIGNESS: ANTITRUST IN THE NEW GILDED AGE (2018) 132–33.

Noah J. Phillips, We Need to Talk: Toward a Serious Conversation About Breakups (remarks of Apr. 30, 2019)

[1] Using antitrust to break up companies was never common practice in U.S. history, even in the law's early days. Of the single-firm monopolization cases brought by the government, fewer than 20% resulted in substantial divestiture, whether the sample runs from 1890 through 1939 or is extended through 1999. Focusing only on non-merger cases, the percentage drops below 10%. The most famous antitrust breakups are Standard Oil in 1911 and AT&T in 1984. The contrasts between the two are instructive, but neither experience should whet our appetite for breaking up companies without a good basis and the right conditions.

The Standard Oil Breakup (1911)

[2] You might be surprised to learn that the breakup of Standard Oil, the infamous Rockefeller oil trust, formally ended earlier this month [*i.e.*, April 2019], when the Department of Justice (DOJ) moved a court to end the 1911 decree, from 108 years ago. The government sued Standard Oil under Sections 1 and 2 of the Sherman Act. The complaint alleged that the Standard Oil Company of New Jersey, some 70 subsidiary corporations and partnerships, and seven individuals conspired to restrain trade in petroleum, refined oil, and other petroleum products, and attempted to and did monopolize those lines of commerce. The lower court held the defendants liable under Sections 1 and 2, and ordered the dissolution of Standard Oil. The Supreme Court affirmed the breakup ruling.

[3] [But *Standard Oil*] was not so much a case about anticompetitive conduct[:] the breakup remedy was really aimed at the combination it sought to undo. . . . [W]hile the Supreme Court affirmed Standard Oil's antitrust liability based on the combinations creating the trust and the trust's exclusionary conduct, the illegality of the trust's 1882 formation and subsequent reorganization was essential to the breakup order. [. .]

The AT&T Breakup (1984)

[4] The next breakup on which I want to focus is AT&T, in 1984, perhaps the other most significant use of Section 2 to split up a large American company. The DOJ filed its complaint against AT&T in 1974, alleging that the company, Western Electric, and Bell Telephone Laboratories had violated Section 2. The government claimed an unlawful combination and conspiracy between the defendants, the Bell Operating Companies (the "Baby Bells"), and others, which allegedly allowed AT&T to maintain control over the two other defendants and the Baby Bells, to limit competition from other telecomm providers, and to maintain a monopolistic manufacturing and purchasing relationship between Western Electric and the Bell System. The discovery process lasted seven years, with trial beginning in January 1981. Many months later, but still one month before the very long trial was scheduled to end, the parties agreed on settlement terms that were approved by the court, with modifications, in August of that year.

[5] The final decree was complex and multifaceted; so I will focus on the provisions relating to the divestiture of the Baby Bells and their impact on long-distance services. The purpose of the breakup was to boost competition in this market, not competition between the Baby Bells, which were to become regional monopolies. The government's theory was that owning the Baby Bells allowed AT&T to foreclose competition in long-distance services and telecomm equipment, by denying long-distance competitors the necessary local interconnections to the Baby Bells. So, in addition to splitting them up, the decree also required the Baby Bells to make their switching facilities equally accessible to long-distance providers.

[6] Judge Posner called the breakup of AT&T arguably the most successful structural remedy in U.S. antitrust history. He was speaking in relative terms, and I think he's probably right. There is strong evidence and broad consensus that that the telecommunication industry's competitiveness increased following the 1984 breakup. . . . Unlike *Standard Oil* . . . AT&T's high pre-divestiture share of the long-distance market had been stable, and fell significantly after the breakup, as competitors entered or expanded. That suggests the divestiture achieved gains that market forces and regulatory measures had failed to deliver, though the organization of the Baby Bells and the regulatory structure of the telecommunications industry played significant roles. [. . .]

[7] [A]gencies and courts are not, like politicians and pundits, champing at the bit to break up companies. While the law contemplates doing so—and doing so sometimes is warranted—enforcement experience and economic research show us that the treatment may be worse than the disease and, in some cases, simply not doable.

High Uncertainty

[8] Seeking a breakup remedy in an antitrust case requires a judgment that the resulting market structure will leave competition and consumers better off. Consider that for a moment: breaking up a company is, quite directly, the government using the force of law to substitute its vision of how an industry can and should be structured, for how the market has actually worked. That alone should make one pause and appreciate the gravity of the proposal. Antitrust enforcers are not industrial planners. As Judge Easterbrook wrote, we should "fall prey to the nirvana fallacy, the belief that if a cost or flaw in existing affairs can be identified, it must follow that some other state of affairs (the 'remedy') is better."

[9] When we seek a divestiture in a merger case, we know how competition looks. The remedy seeks to preserve competition as it is (or recently was), not an untested state of affairs that we regulators might believe superior. Although some uncertainty remains in merger cases, it is far less than the uncertainty of breakups in non-merger cases. In a non-merger case, if we wish to restructure a market, why do we presume our vision for how that market ought to work will, in fact, work, much less actually work better? These are tough questions. And antitrust requires that they be answered only by one agency and one (or a few) judges.

[10] My argument here rests on the small-c conservative principle that, the greater the proposed interference with the status quo of a complex system like a market, the less confident we should be of the desired outcome, both that it will be the outcome and, if so, that it will be desirable. This principle acknowledges the nirvana fallacy and counters with a sober assessment of our limited ability to control complexity and guard against unintended consequences.

* * *

Rory Van Loo, In Defense of Breakups: Administering A "Radical" Remedy
105 Cornell L. Rev. 1955 (2020)

Antitrust debates [about the breakup remedy] fail to consider the insights generated by routine private sector breakups. One-third of mergers and acquisitions (M&A)—more appropriately termed reorganizations—are divestitures. These divestitures include some of the largest deals of the last decade, including Fox's sale of its 20th Century Fox production arm for $71 billion to Disney, eBay's spinoff of PayPal, and Hewlett-Packard's decision to split itself down the middle to create two of the one hundred largest U.S. companies. Despite meaningful differences, the prevalence of these deals alone is informative because what antitrust observers have come to view as drastic is commonplace in the business world.

Moreover, scholars in other fields—notably strategic management, finance, and organizational behavior—have studied voluntary private sector breakups extensively. They have shown how these voluntary divestitures add value and how better process design can improve their implementation. Of course, it is important to recognize that even if antitrust breakups are costly and lower the firm's value, they may be economically beneficial by deterring executives from pursuing anticompetitive deals. But by remaining disconnected from the extensive business scholarship on divestitures, the antitrust literature has exaggerated breakups' costs and governmental incompetence in administering them.

Regulatory scholarship can also improve the antitrust conceptualization of breakups. Antitrust scholars focus far more on ex post enforcement actions and legal cases, whereas scholars in environmental law and other regulatory fields extensively analyze the monitoring of firms and design of regulatory processes. In particular, the literature in those other fields is in dialogue with a prominent strand of research, associated with administrative law, arguing for collaborative governance.

Approaching breakup administration less as an adversarial law enforcement procedure and more as collaborative governance could streamline the process, which would speak to one of the biggest critiques of breakups: delay.

Also, collaborative governance aims to leverage business sector expertise to compensate for administrative agency sophistication shortfalls and information asymmetries. Most concretely, this would mean not only leveraging the monopoly's resources, but also involving independent third-party M&A consultants. Thus, by drawing on the collaborative governance literature it becomes possible to see beyond the limitations that breakups faced decades ago and adopt a more realistic assessment of how they would work today.

The implications of a more informed view of breakup administrability are far-reaching. A misguided view of breakups may help explain what many observers see as decades of weak antitrust enforcement, leading to charges that the deck is stacked in favor of large powerful firms. Executives know that if they execute an anticompetitive merger by quickly integrating the companies, antitrust enforcers or courts will fear breaking up the resulting company. Ironically, unfounded fears of doing harm through breakups may lead to either harmful inaction or weaker remedies that are more likely to prove wasteful. If widespread and unfounded resistance to administering breakups has contributed substantially to the presence of monopolies, it has imposed considerable costs on society.

Once breakups are understood as a normal part of business affairs, and as capable of being co-administered with the private sector, courts and enforcers can deploy them more readily as an antitrust remedy. That shift helps to solve the antitrust problem of what to do after an anticompetitive merger has occurred. But it also informs debates about how to handle monopolies that achieved their dominance in other ways. At the very least, the intuitive resistance to breakups needs to end. Unless and until greater evidence is produced that breakups harm society, judges should be less hesitant to approve breakups, enforcers less tentative to pursue them, and policymakers less resistant to write laws that deploy them.

2. Behavioral remedies

As we saw in the context of merger remedies, the toolkit of behavioral remedies is broad: we will meet just a handful of examples here.

Prohibitions on specific practices or contract terms. The most fundamental form of behavioral relief is an obligation to terminate the challenged practices, and to refrain from similar behavior in future. For example, in resolving allegations that the Alabama Board of Dental Examiners had unlawfully imposed an anticompetitive obligation on teeth-aligning providers to purchase the services of a licensed dentist, the remedial order required the Board to cut it out—to refrain from imposing that obligation, or a similar one, during the term of the order:

Decision and Order, In the matter of Board of Dental Examiners of Alabama
FTC Docket No. C-4757 (Dec. 20, 2021)

IT IS . . . ORDERED that Respondent, in connection with its activities in or affecting commerce . . . shall cease and desist from, directly or indirectly:

> A. Requiring any Non-Dentist Provider affiliated with any Clear Aligner Platform to have on-site supervision by a Dentist when performing Intraoral Scanning; and

> B. Prohibiting, restricting, impeding, or discouraging any (i) Clear Aligner Platform or (ii) Dentist or Non-Dentist Provider affiliated with any Clear Aligner Platform from providing or facilitating the provision of Clear Aligner Therapy through remote treatment;

> *Provided, however,* nothing in this Order shall prohibit Respondent from filing, or causing to be filed, a court action against a Non-Dentist Provider, Dentist, or Clear Aligner Platform for an alleged violation of the Alabama Dental Practice Act;

> *For the avoidance of doubt,* and other than as set out above in Paragraphs II.A. and II.B., this Order shall not be construed as preventing Respondent from pursuing any administrative remedies against a Dentist or Non-Dentist Provider pursuant to and in accordance with the Alabama Dental Practice Act and Chapter 270 of the Alabama Administrative Code.

* * *

Nondiscrimination. Where there is concern that a business subject to an antitrust remedy may suppress or exclude competition by foreclosing competitors' access to relevant inputs or distribution channels, a remedial order may require the business to make such inputs available on nondiscriminatory terms.

In the following extract, the FTC required Victrex, a supplier of polyetheretherketone (mercifully abbreviated to "PEEK") that had engaged in the unlawful use of exclusivity commitments, to refrain from discriminating against customers that dealt with a competing PEEK supplier.

Decision and Order, In the matter of Victrex PLC
FTC Docket No. C-4586 (July 13, 2016)

IT IS . . . ORDERED that [. . .]

B.   Respondents shall cease and desist from discriminating against, penalizing, or otherwise retaliating against any Customer for the reason, in whole or in part, that the Customer engages in, or intends to engage in, the research, development, testing, manufacture, production, distribution, purchase, marketing, promotion, or sale of any Customer Product using a Competing PEEK, or otherwise refuses to enter into or continue any condition, agreement, contract, understanding, or other requirement that imposes Exclusivity. Examples of practices prohibited under this Paragraph include but are not limited to the following, when the result, in whole or in part, of prohibited discrimination or retaliation for use of Competing PEEK or refusal to accede to Exclusivity:

1. Terminating, suspending, delaying, or threatening or proposing thereto, sales of Respondents' PEEK to the Customer, either generally or with respect to particular forms or grades of PEEK;

2. Denying, or threatening or proposing to deny, the Customer access to Respondents' FDA Master File;

3. Auditing the Customer's purchases or sales of Competing PEEK;

4. Withdrawing or modifying, or threatening or proposing thereto, favorable Sales Terms or Product Support to the Customer;

5. Providing, or threatening or proposing thereto, less favorable Sales Terms or Product Support to the Customer;

6. Withholding from the Customer any form or grade of Respondents' PEEK;

7. Refusing to deal with the Customer on terms and conditions generally available to other Customers; and

8. Notwithstanding the existence or non-existence of any severability or other provisions in Respondents' agreement(s) or contract(s) with any Customer(s), terminating, suspending, or requiring renegotiation of any term of any agreement or contract for the purchase and sale of Respondents' PEEK, as a result of the Exclusivity terms or other terms inconsistent with this Order being waived, invalid, illegal, or unenforceable.

For the avoidance of doubt, it shall not constitute, in and of itself, a violation of this Order for Respondents to engage in the conduct described in Paragraph II.B(1-7) above, when such conduct results from independent and verifiable business reasons unrelated to a Customer's use of Competing PEEK or refusal to accede to Exclusivity

* * *

Compelled dealing (supply / interoperation / licensing). Under certain circumstances, a remedial order may require that a business make some kind of supply, infrastructure, interoperability, intellectual property, or other assets or facilities available to others. Such an order may go further and require that such access be on particular terms: for example, nondiscriminatory terms, for no more than a "fair and reasonable" rate or price, or on other terms and conditions that a court or agency may consider appropriate.

A well-known, if unusual, example of this kind of thing was the FTC's negotiated remedy in the Google / MMI case, entered to resolve concerns that Google might use a package of acquired patent rights in a manner harmful to competition and in violation of previous commitments that those patents would be licensed on FRAND (*i.e.*, fair, reasonable, and non-discriminatory) terms. The consent decree in that case obliged Google to negotiate in good faith toward a license with potential licensees.

In the matter of Motorola Mobility LLC
FTC Dkt. No. C-4410 (F.T.C. July 23, 2013)

IT IS . . . ORDERED that:

A. Respondents shall, within sixty (60) days of receiving a written request by a Potential Licensee for a license to Respondents' [relevant patents] ("Requested License"), provide a written response and begin negotiation with such Potential Licensee for the Requested License. Respondents' written response pursuant to this paragraph shall be in good faith compliance with their FRAND Commitments and all other provisions of this Order.

B. Respondents shall not sell or assign any FRAND Patent to any Third Party unless such Third Party agrees: (i) to become a successor to Respondents' FRAND Commitments to the extent the FRAND Patent is subject to such FRAND Commitments, (ii) not to seek Covered Injunctive Relief on the basis of Infringement of the FRAND Patent except to the extent Respondents would be permitted to seek such Covered Injunctive Relief by the terms of this Order, and (iii) to condition further assignment of the FRAND Patent on the assignee agreeing to the terms of this subparagraph V.B.

* * *

Prior approval / notification. In some cases, it may be appropriate to impose an obligation to provide advance notice, or even seek affirmative permission, before engaging in certain conduct. For example, in the Victrex case mentioned above, the FTC required Victrex to agree to give 60 days' notice before terminating a customer. The remedial language aimed to protect Victrex's right to terminate a customer in appropriate circumstances, while preserving the FTC's ability to monitor the company's conduct in exercising this right.

Decision and Order, In the matter of Victrex PLC
FTC Docket No. C-4586 (July 13, 2016)

Notwithstanding any other provision of this Order, if:

1. Respondents timely deliver the Order and [relevant exhibits] to a Customer with an applicable Legacy Contract as required by [the Order]; and

2. the Customer has not indicated that it will comply with the terms of [the Order] by counter-signing and delivering [the relevant exhibit] to Respondents,

it shall not constitute a violation of this Order for Respondents to (i) enforce existing Exclusivity terms in a Legacy Contract, but only as applied to [certain products], or (ii) enforce terms under a Legacy Contract . . . .

Provided, however, that as to any Customer that has counter-signed and delivered [the relevant exhibit to this Order] to Respondents, Respondents shall submit to the Commission written notice of any communication from any Respondent to the Customer that the Customer has breached the terms set forth in Exhibit C. Respondents shall submit any such notice to the Commission at least sixty (60) days prior to exercising any right of termination resulting from the alleged breach, during which time the Customer shall be given the opportunity to cure the alleged breach.

* * *

Equitable monetary relief. In principle, an antitrust remedy might require that a business found guilty of antitrust violations hand over the profits of the illegal conduct, or otherwise make redress or restitution to injured parties.[983] The leading example of this remedy remains the FTC's consent decree in Cephalon, which contemplated total relief in excess of $1 billion.[984] At the time of writing, however, following the decision in *AMG Capital*, neither federal agency has the power to seek such a remedy in court (although there is no reason why monetary relief could not be included in a negotiated consent decree).[985] Legislative reform may re-open this avenue for consumer redress.

Other "fencing-in" relief. Remedial orders may also include a wide variety of provisions designed to "fence in" the risk of further violations, including be prohibiting conduct that would not itself be illegal or harmful.

Ian Conner, Fixer Upper: Using the FTC's Remedial Toolbox to Restore Competition (remarks of Feb. 8, 2020)

[1] Our remedial orders can (and do) do more than just repeat the antitrust laws by prohibiting conduct that is already unlawful and otherwise leaving the respondent free to go about its business. Commission remedial orders commonly include prohibitions that go beyond the complained of behavior and seek to, in the words of the Supreme Court, effectively to close all roads to the prohibited goal. This is obviously both necessary and appropriate because those caught violating the antitrust laws must expect some fencing in.

[2] Fencing-in relief is exemplified by our 2016 order in *Victrex*. In that case, the Commission alleged that Victrex, Inc., monopolized sales of a high-performance polymer by committing medical device companies to deal exclusively with Victrex. The Commission's order not only banned explicitly exclusive contracts, but also banned contract terms that would have an equivalent effect, such as market-share discounts or retroactive volume discounts that could result in de facto exclusivity. Even though Victrex had not used such pricing policies in the past, and even though such agreements are not automatically unlawful under the Sherman Act, the Commission's order simply took them off the table, to ensure that Victrex would stay away from conduct that would have an equivalent effect to its original violation of the law. [. . .]

[3] Other provisions in an order may require the respondent to mitigate the impact of its previous unlawful conduct in some way. For instance, the Commission may require respondents to notify customers who might have been affected by the illegal conduct, for example by giving them the option to terminate an existing contract without facing an action for breach by the respondent. In the *Victrex* order, for example, the Commission required respondents to notify all customers with existing contracts that required exclusivity and give them the opportunity to change the terms of their contracts. The Commission may also require notice to individuals who need to know that the Respondent's conduct will or may change in the future because of the order. The Commission can also prohibit the inclusion of certain similar terms in future agreements.

* * *

The potential scope of fencing-in relief is very broad. In 2022, for example, Judge Cote of the U.S. District Court for the Southern District of New York relied on both federal and state antitrust law to impose an unusual antitrust remedy for a particularly flagrant and harmful example of monopolization. In that case, infamous "Pharma Bro" Martin Shkreli had entered into a comprehensive (and highly successful) scheme to monopolize markets for the drug Daraprim, harming toxoplasmosis patients across the country. His ultimate reward: a lifetime ban from the pharmaceutical industry.

---

[983] Unlike damages, equitable monetary relief is generally measured by reference to the amount of an unjust gain, not an unjust injury. *See generally* Einer R. Elhauge, *Disgorgement as an Antitrust Remedy*, 76 Antitrust L.J. (2009).

[984] Stipulated Order for Permanent Injunction and Equitable Monetary Relief, FTC v. Cephalon, Inc., Case No. 2:08-CV-2141 (E.D. Pa. June 17, 2015) ("The Cephalon Parties shall pay One Billion and Two Hundred Million Dollars . . . as equitable monetary relief, which shall be used for a settlement fund . . . in accordance with the terms of this Order, including the Settlement Fund Disbursement Agreement, attached hereto as Exhibit A.").

[985] *But see* Schonette Walker, Steve Scannell & Abigail Wood, *Bridging the Gorge: States Prevent Retention of Ill-Gotten Profits Through Disgorgement*, Comp. Pol'y Int'l (Aug. 2021) (states' powers to obtain EMR).

FTC v. Shkreli

Case No. 20-CV-706, 2022 WL 135026 (S.D.N.Y. Jan. 14, 2022)

Judge Cote.

[1] The Plaintiffs [the FTC and a number of state AGs] seek a lifetime ban against Shkreli participating in the pharmaceutical industry. Banning an individual from an entire industry and limiting his future capacity to make a living in that field is a serious remedy and must be done with care and only if equity demands. Shkreli's egregious, deliberate, repetitive, long-running, and ultimately dangerous illegal conduct warrants imposition of an injunction of this scope.

[2] The Plaintiffs presented a wealth of evidence that Shkreli conducted a comprehensive scheme that violated the antitrust laws of the United States and the competition laws of the seven States. The FTC and the States are empowered by federal and State law to seek comprehensive equitable relief. The Plaintiffs have demonstrated that a lifetime ban against Shkreli's future participation in the pharmaceutical industry will protect the public from suffering a repetition of the unlawful schemes proven in this case.

[3] Without a lifetime ban, there is a real danger that Shkreli will engage in anticompetitive conduct within the pharmaceutical industry again. Shkreli established two companies, Retrophin and Vyera, with the same anticompetitive business model: Acquiring sole-source drugs for rare diseases so that he could profit from a monopolist scheme on the backs of a dependent population of pharmaceutical distributors, healthcare providers, and the patients who needed the drugs. The Daraprim scheme was particularly heartless and coercive. Daraprim must be administered within hours to those suffering from active toxoplasma encephalitis.

[4] Moreover, in the face of public opprobrium, Shkreli doubled down. He refused to change course and proclaimed that he should have raised Daraprim's price higher.

[5] The context in which Shkreli conducted his schemes cannot be ignored. He cynically took advantage of the requirements of a federal regulatory scheme designed to protect the health of a nation by ensuring that its population has access to drugs that are not only effective but also safe. He recklessly disregarded the health of a particularly vulnerable population, those with compromised immune systems. His scheme burdened those patients, their loved ones, and their healthcare providers.

[6] A lifetime ban would not deprive Shkreli of the opportunity to practice a profession or to exercise a lawful skill for which he trained. In his trial testimony Shkreli does not even express a clear desire to return to the pharmaceutical industry. He reports that he is considering pursuing opportunities "within and outside" the pharmaceutical industry upon his release from prison.

[7] The risk of a recurrence here is real. Shkreli has not expressed remorse or any awareness that his actions violated the law. While he takes full responsibility in his direct testimony for the increase of Daraprim's price from $17.50 to $750 per pill, he denies responsibility for virtually anything else. He argues in his testimony that he is not responsible for Vyera's anticompetitive contracts because he did not negotiate or sign the exclusive supply agreements or the restrictive distribution agreements. He has also denied that what happened here was egregious, arguing that the Plaintiffs have not proven that any patient died due to the price he set for Daraprim. He chose to not even attend the trial.

[8] Shkreli presents several legal arguments against a lifetime industry ban. He contends that it amounts to a penalty beyond the proper scope of a court's power in equity. He argues that an industry ban is uncommon and reserved only for the most egregious cases and for cases of fraud. He argues that a ban of this scope is not narrowly tailored to match the challenged conduct. For the reasons laid out above, these arguments are unavailing. This is an egregious case; death is not the only relevant metric. If a court sitting in equity is powerless to impose a lifetime industry ban to protect the public against a repetition of the conduct proven at this trial, then the public could rightfully ask whether its wellbeing has been adequately weighed.

[9] Shkreli appears to suggest that any injunction could be limited to banning him from acquiring commercial assets or engaging in the "day-to-day affairs of commercializing medicine." There is no reason to believe that a

narrowly crafted injunction will succeed in providing adequate protection against a repetition of illegal conduct. Shkreli has demonstrated that he can and will adapt to restrictions. With help at times from a contraband phone, Shkreli managed to control his company even from federal prison.

[10] Shkreli's anticompetitive conduct at the expense of the public health was flagrant and reckless. He is unrepentant. Barring him from the opportunity to repeat that conduct is nothing if not in the interest of justice. "If not now, when?" Mishnah, Pirkei Avot 1:14.

***

NOTES

1) Why do enforcers often prefer structural remedies? Under what circumstances should behavioral remedies be preferred?

2) In what ways do merger and conduct remedies differ? In what respects are they similar?

3) When and how, if at all, can agencies feasibly enforce nondiscrimination obligations?

4) Should agencies be able to require parties to give remedies that go beyond the termination or prohibition of likely violations of law? Why, or why not? In particular, should the agencies be able to negotiate a remedial obligation:

    a. to terminate and refrain from lawful conduct that may be harmful to competition but would not violate the antitrust laws?

    b. to terminate and refrain from lawful conduct that would not harm competition but may be undesirable for other reasons?

    c. to terminate individual executives?

    d. to pay money to the government or private parties that the agencies could not obtain in a court-ordered remedy?

5) What do you think makes a good divestiture buyer? How can the agencies feasibly (and swiftly) screen for those qualities? What kind of process would you design for this purpose?

6) In cases in which a narrow divestiture of a single business unit or product line would, in principle, eliminate competitive concerns, when if ever do you think that an agency should sue to block the whole transaction? On what legal basis could they do so? What if the parties sold off the troubling business unit first, fixing the problem before turning to the main transaction (this is called a "fix it first" remedy)?

7) Are there any advantages to a negotiated consent decree rather than a fix-it-first remedy?

8) What should be the result of a "failed" divestiture: that is, the sale or exit of a divested business unit some time after the remedy is imposed or accepted?

H. Some Further Reading

Gerald Berk, LOUIS D. BRANDEIS AND THE MAKING OF REGULATED COMPETITION, 1900–32 (2009) Chs. 3–4

Rohit Chopra & Lina M. Khan, *The Case for "Unfair Methods of Competition" Rulemaking*, 87 U. Chi. L. Rev. 357 (2020)

Ian Conner, *Fixer Upper: Using the FTC's Remedial Toolbox to Restore Competition* (Feb. 8, 2020)

Daniel A. Crane (ed.) RULEMAKING AUTHORITY OF THE FEDERAL TRADE COMMISSION (2022)

FTC & U.S. Dept. of Justice, Hart-Scott-Rodino Annual Report: Fiscal Year 2020, https://www.ftc.gov/system/files/documents/reports/hart-scott-rodino-annual-report-fiscal-year-2020/fy2020_-_hsr_annual_report_-_final.pdf

Sen. Mike Lee, S.633—One Agency Act, 117th Cong. (2021–2022), https://www.congress.gov/bill/117th-congress/senate-bill/633/text

Maureen K. Ohlhausen, *Administrative Litigation at the FTC: Effective Tool for Developing the Law or Rubber Stamp?* J. Comp. L. & Econ. (2016)

Joe Sims & Deborah P. Herman, *The Effect of Twenty Years of Hart-Scott-Rodino on Merger Practice: A Case Study in the Law of Unintended Consequences Applied to Antitrust Legislation*, 65 Antitrust L.J. 865 (1997)

Marc Winerman, *The Origins of the Federal Trade Commission: Concentration, Cooperation, Control, and Competition*, 71 Antitrust L.J. 1 (2003)

XII. PRIVATE ENFORCEMENT

A. Overview

Despite the prominence and importance of the federal agencies, most federal antitrust cases in the United States are not brought by the Department of Justice, the FTC, or the State Attorneys-General. Rather, most antitrust litigation and adjudication is the result of private enforcement: that is, lawsuits brought by consumers, competitors, and trading partners.[986]

- **Consumer lawsuits** are commonly brought as class actions pursuant to Federal Rule of Civil Procedure 23,[987] represented by class counsel who are typically compensated with a share of the recovery.[988] Among other things, this is because the harm suffered by individual consumers may be too small to justify the considerable costs of antitrust litigation for any individual plaintiff.

- **Competitor lawsuits** are often brought by rivals complaining of exclusion, or of conduct that will increase the defendant's market power. (Competitors generally cannot sue for collusive conduct by rivals, regardless of whether they have been invited to participate in the collusion or not: can you see why?) Courts entertaining such claims—and agencies entertaining competitor complaints—usually take a skeptical look at the allegations to make sure rivals are not just using the antitrust laws as a means of harming a competitor.

- **Trading partner lawsuits** are generally brought by sellers to, or buyers from, the defendant(s). Such claims may involve allegations that the defendant(s) have increased their market power through collusion or exclusion, resulting in (or threatening) the imposition of adverse terms of dealing—such as supracompetitive prices—on the trading partner. Here too, courts and agencies must screen complaints to be sure that a trading partner is not just seeking additional leverage over a bargaining partner in order to secure better terms.

Private antitrust cases tend to be of two kinds: private litigation brought in the wake of, or alongside, government enforcement action, and independent suits brought by market participants on their own initiative.[989] (Studies have shown that private litigation often involves much more than just riding the coat-tails of government enforcers.[990])

---

[986] *Compare, e.g., Judicial Business of the U.S. Courts*, Table C-2 (555 civil antitrust cases filed in the 12 months ending Sept. 30, 2021; 672 antitrust cases filed in the 12 months ending Sept. 30, 2020) *with* U.S. Dept. of Justice, *Antitrust Division Workload Statistics FY 2010–2019*, 5 (10 civil cases filed in 2018; 19 civil cases filed in 2019) *and* FTC, *Annual Performance Report for Fiscal Year 2020 and Annual Performance Plan for Fiscal Years 2021 and 2022* (FY 2020), 46 ("In FY 2020, the [FTC] concluded 27 matters in which it took action to maintain competition, including 11 consent orders and 11 abandoned transactions, focusing its efforts on markets with the greatest impact on American consumers. This fiscal year saw a continuation of the Commission's ambitious antitrust litigation docket, with 11 active litigations from the current or prior years."). *See also* Steven C. Salop & Lawrence J. White, *Economic Analysis of Private Antitrust Litigation*, 74 Geo. L. J. 1001, 1002 (1986) (private and public enforcement numbers for 1941–1984). *But see* Jonathan M. Jacobson & Tracy Greer, *Twenty-One Years of Antitrust Injury: Down the Alley with* Brunswick v. Pueblo Bowl-o-Mat, 66 Antitrust L.J. 273, 275 (1998) ("Despite the breadth of the statutory language, private antitrust actions in the initial decades of antitrust were very rare. From 1899 to 1939, only 157 treble damage actions were recorded, with only 14 recoveries by plaintiffs, totaling less than $275,000."); *id.* at 276 (dating the "explosion" of private litigation to a string of decisions between 1946 and 1961).

[987] *See generally, e.g.*, Christine P. Bartholomew, *Antitrust Class Actions in the Wake of Procedural Reform*, 97 Indiana L.J. 1315 (2022); *see also, e.g.*, Joshua P. Davis & Robert H. Lande, *Defying Conventional Wisdom: The Case for Private Antitrust Enforcement*, 48 Ga. L. Rev. 1, 5 (2013) (describing class actions as "the most important type of private [antitrust] cases").

[988] *See* American Antitrust Institute, *The Critical Role of Private Antitrust Enforcement In The United States, Commentary On: 2020 Antitrust Annual Report: Class Action Filings In Federal Court* (Aug. 4, 2021) 10 (empirical data on class action attorney fees).

[989] For some (now somewhat dated) comparative empirical work across the two classes of case, *see* Thomas E. Kauper & Edward A. Snyder, *An Inquiry into the Efficiency of Private Antitrust Enforcement: Follow-on and Independently Initiated Cases Compared*, 74 Geo. L. J. 1163 (1986).

[990] Joshua P. Davis & Robert H. Lande, *Toward an Empirical and Theoretical Assessment of Private Antitrust Enforcement*, 36 Sea. U. L. Rev. 1269, 1292-93 (2013) (Study of 20 successful private cases finding that 50% were not preceded by government action, and that $8.36 billion of the $10.7 billion in total victim recovery involved cases that either preceded government enforcement or significantly expanded the scope of recovery the government sought); John C. Coffee, Jr., *Understanding the Plaintiffs Attorney: The Implications of Economic Theory for Private Enforcement of Law Through Class and Derivative Actions*, 86 Colum. L. Rev. 669, 681 n.36 (1986) ("Although the conventional wisdom has long been that class actions tend to 'tag along' on the heels of governmentally initiated suits, a recent study

Private Injunctive Relief and Government Damages Actions

We have generally organized this book so that injunctive relief is covered in Chapter XI on government enforcement, while damages are covered in this Chapter XII on private enforcement. That's because injunctive relief is the focus of most government actions, while damages tend to be a central issue in private litigation. (This allocation also helps to keep the lengths of the chapters fairly balanced!) But it obscures two important points: first, private plaintiffs can and do sue for injunctions; and, second, government plaintiffs can and do sue for damages. And although those facts do not raise a host of important complexities, it is worth pointing out a couple of things.

Private injunctions first. Private plaintiffs and states (which are also persons under the antitrust laws[991]) are entitled to sue for injunctions to terminate and remedy antitrust violations.[992] Private plaintiffs are not treated identically to the federal government for all purposes, however, even in an injunction case. First, in order to obtain preliminary injunctive relief, a private plaintiff must not only show a substantial probability of success and a favorable balance of equities: a private litigant must also generally demonstrate a threat of irreparable harm.[993] Second, in order to obtain permanent injunctive relief, a private plaintiff must satisfy the *eBay* standards that apply to permanent injunctive relief generally: "(1) that it has suffered an irreparable injury; (2) that remedies available at law, such as monetary damages, are inadequate to compensate for that injury; (3) that, considering the balance of hardships between the plaintiff and defendant, a remedy in equity is warranted; and (4) that the public interest would not be disserved by a permanent injunction."[994]

As just as private plaintiffs can obtain injunctive relief, the United States (through the Department of Justice) and the states are also empowered by statute to assert certain damages claims for antitrust violations, pursuant to Sections 4a and 4c of the Clayton Act respectively.[995] The United States is limited under Section 4a to recoveries for injuries suffered in its own right to its "business or property": that is, as a buyer, seller, or (conceivably) competitor.[996] The states, by contrast, may sue either for their own damages (as "persons" like any others under Section 4) or for damages suffered by their citizens (in a "parens patriae" litigation under Section 4c).[997] Neither state nor federal governments may sue for broader "damage to the economy" caused by an antitrust violation:

---

of antitrust litigation by Professors Kauper and Snyder has placed this figure at less than 20% of private antitrust actions filed between 1976 and 1983.").

[991] *See supra* § XI.F; Georgia v. Pennsylvania Railroad Co., 324 U.S. 439 (1945); Hawaii v. Standard Oil Co. of Cal., 405 U.S. 251, 261 (1972).

[992] 15 U.S.C. § 26.

[993] *See, e.g.*, St. Luke's Hosp. v. ProMedica Health Sys., Inc., 8 F.4th 479, 485 (6th Cir. 2021) ("Four factors guide our review of a district court's preliminary injunction: (1) the likelihood of success on the merits, (2) the threat of irreparable harm absent an injunction, (3) the risk of harm to others, and (4) the broader public interest."); AlliedSignal, Inc. v. B.F. Goodrich Co., 183 F.3d 568, 573 (7th Cir. 1999) ("To prevail on a motion for preliminary injunction, the moving party must meet the threshold burden of establishing (1) some likelihood of prevailing on the merits; and (2) that in the absence of the injunction, he will suffer irreparable harm for which there is no adequate remedy at law. If the moving party clears both of these prerequisites, a district court engages in a 'sliding scale' analysis by balancing the harms to the parties and the public interest.").

[994] eBay Inc. v. MercExchange, L.L.C., 547 U.S. 388, 391 (2006).

[995] 15 U.S.C. § 15a ("Whenever the United States is hereafter injured in its business or property by reason of anything forbidden in the antitrust laws it may sue therefor in the United States district court for the district in which the defendant resides or is found or has an agent, without respect to the amount in controversy, and shall recover threefold the damages by it sustained and the cost of suit."); 15 U.S.C. § 15c ("Any attorney general of a State may bring a civil action in the name of such State, as parens patriae on behalf of natural persons residing in such State, in any district court of the United States having jurisdiction of the defendant, to secure monetary relief as provided in this section for injury sustained by such natural persons to their property by reason of any violation of sections 1 to 7 of this title."); 15 U.S.C. § 15c(a)(2) (providing for trebling and simple interest in parens patriae suits).

[996] Hawaii v. Standard Oil Co. of California, 405 U.S. 251, 265 (1972) ("The legislative history of [Section 4a of the Clayton Act] makes it quite plain that the United States was authorized to recover, not for general injury to the national economy or to the Government's ability to carry out its functions, but only for those injuries suffered in its capacity as a consumer of goods and services.").

[997] 15 U.S.C. § 15 (injured person may sue for damages); Hawaii v. Standard Oil Co. of Cal., 405 U.S. 251, 261 (1972) ("Hawaii plainly qualifies as a person under both sections of the statute [i.e., Section 4 and Section 4c], whether it sues in its proprietary capacity or as parens patriae.").

> harm to "business or property" is the only relevant kind of harm in an antitrust case for government, just as for private, plaintiffs.[998]

Private litigants—as well as State AGs—may benefit from antitrust's signature private remedy: treble damages.[999] Although somewhat unusual, treble damages are not unique to antitrust: among other things, they are available under federal law for certain kinds of patent infringement, trademark counterfeiting, and RICO violations.[1000] And they have been available in antitrust (or at least antitrust-like) cases since at least the 1623 Statute of Monopolies, which allowed a plaintiff to recover "three times so much as the damages which he or they sustained by means or occasion of being . . . hindered, grieved, disturbed, or disquieted" by violations of the statute.

Why have treble damages? Trebling serves multiple functions, of which the most obvious are deterrence of wrongdoing and compensation of victims.[1001] It is widely believed that many antitrust violations go undetected,[1002] and that in many cases the costs, complexities, uncertainties, and delays of antitrust litigation may dissuade plaintiffs from attempting to recover for what may be fairly modest individual injuries. Thus, trebling can be understood as an effort to correct the resulting under-deterrence, by increasing both plaintiffs' incentive to litigate and the consequences for defendants of a loss in court.[1003] (The low success rate of rule-of-reason cases may also tend to reduce the deterrence effect of threatened litigation.[1004]) The Supreme Court has expressly recognized the important role that private litigation plays in deterring antitrust wrongdoing.[1005]

Nor is deterrence the only function of the treble-damages rule. By encouraging victims to sue for their loss, trebling may help to promote compensation. Robert Lande has even argued that the apparent "windfall" for victims above compensation from trebling may be illusory because, all things considered, the "treble" damages provision simply balances out other limitations on the right to recover for harms arising from antitrust violations, such that it would be more accurate to think of antitrust damages as amounting to "single" damages only.[1006] Likewise, as DOJ and the FTC monitor private-litigation dockets, such litigation may serve a function of notifying the agencies of matters for investigation and potential enforcement action, including the filing of amicus briefs and/or statements of

---

[998] Hawaii v. Standard Oil Co. of Cal., 405 U.S. 251, 262, 92 S. Ct. 885, 891, 31 L. Ed. 2d 184 (1972) ("[Congress] could have . . . required violators to compensate federal, state, and local governments for the estimated damage to their respective economies caused by the violations. But, this remedy was not selected."); *id.* at 265 ("[Section] 4, which uses identical language [to Section 4a], does not authorize recovery for economic injuries to the sovereign interests of a State").

[999] 15 U.S.C. § 15, § 15c.

[1000] *See, e.g.*, 35 U.S.C. § 284 (in patent infringement cases "the court may increase the damages up to three times the amount found or assessed"); 15 U.S.C. § 1117 (in certain cases involving the intentional counterfeiting of a mark or designation "the court shall, unless the court finds extenuating circumstances, enter judgment for three times such profits or damages"); 18 U.S.C. § 1964(c) (plaintiff "shall recover threefold the damages he sustains and the cost of the suit, including a reasonable attorney's fee"). *See also, e.g.*, Cal. Bus. & Prof. Code § 17082.

[1001] *See, e.g.*, Am. Soc. of Mech. Engineers, Inc. v. Hydrolevel Corp., 456 U.S. 556, 575–76 (1982) ("[T]reble damages serve as a means of deterring antitrust violations and of compensating victims[.]").

[1002] *See, e.g.*, Peter G. Bryant & E. Woodrow Eckard, *Price Fixing: The Probability of Getting Caught*, 73(3) Rev. Econ. & Stats. 531, 535 (1991) ("The probability of getting caught in a given year is at most between 0.13 and 0.17.").

[1003] For a variety of perspectives on this elusive balance, *see, e.g.*, Joshua P. Davis & Robert H. Lande, *Defying Conventional Wisdom: The Case for Private Antitrust Enforcement*, 48 Ga. L. Rev. 1, 35–37 (2013) (noting: that defendants benefit from an "interest free loan" through the lack of prejudgment interest; costs and burdens of litigation; difficulties of detection; and superior resources of some defendants); Daniel A. Crane, *Optimizing Private Antitrust Enforcement*, 63 Vand. L. Rev. 673, 677 (2010); Robert H. Lande & Joshua P. Davis, *Benefits from Private Antitrust Enforcement: An Analysis of Forty Cases*, 42 U.S.F. L. Rev. 879 (2008); Robert H. Lande, *Wealth Transfers as the Original and Primary Concern of Antitrust: The Efficiency Interpretation Challenged*, 50 Hastings L.J. 871, 911-35 (1999); Steven C. Salop & Lawrence J. White, *Economic Analysis of Private Antitrust Litigation*, 74 Geo. L.J. 1001, 1017–24 (1986); Michael K. Block & Joseph Gregory Sidak, *The Cost of Antitrust Deterrence: Why Not Hang a Price Fixer Now and Then?*, 68 Geo L.J. 1131 (1980); Lawrence Vold, *Are Threefold Damages under the Anti-Trust Act Penal or Compensatory?*, 28 Ky. L. J. 177, 122–25 (1940).

[1004] *See* Michael A. Carrier, *The Rule of Reason: An Empirical Update for the 21st Century*, 16 Geo. Mason L. Rev. 827 (2009).

[1005] *See, e.g.*, Pfizer, Inc. v. Government of India, 434 U.S. 308, 314–15 (1978) (acknowledging the effects of damages actions on both compensation and deterrence); Perma Life Mufflers, Inc. v. Int'l Parts Corp., 392 U.S. 134, 139 (1968) ("[T]he purposes of the antitrust laws are best served by insuring that the private action will be an ever-present threat to deter anyone contemplating business behavior in violation of the antitrust laws."), *overruled on other grounds*, Copperweld Corp. v. Independence Tube Corp., 467 U.S. 752 (1984).

[1006] Robert H. Lande, *Are Antitrust "Treble" Damages Really Single Damages?*, 54 Ohio St. L.J. 115 (1993). *See also* Robert H. Lande, *Multiple Enforcers and Multiple Remedies: Why Antitrust Damage Levels Should be Raised*, 16 Loy. Consumer L.Rev. 329 (2004).

interest: thus, trebling can be seen as part of an information-gathering system that helps to alert federal enforcers to antitrust violations.[1007]

But trebling has plenty of critics. For one thing, the aptness of trebling to promote optimal deterrence is unclear. Many commentators express concerns that treble damages, combined with the high costs of litigation—particularly the burdens of discovery for large defendants—may allow plaintiffs to "hold up" defendants even on the basis of speculative or weak claims.[1008] Additionally, there may be reasons to doubt the assumption that damages promote deterrence, given the vast separation of time between conduct and penalty, as well as the prospect that individual misfeasant employees may have long since moved on by the time of a remedy.[1009] The Supreme Court has expressed its own concern about the use of antitrust litigation by rivals or trading partners to inflict meritless holdup.[1010] And some have worried that broad private remedies may encourage courts to trim substantive liability rules too narrowly.[1011]

The relationship of trebling to compensation is also hard to define with any precision. On the one hand, purchaser plaintiffs may well have passed on the amount of an overcharge to their own customers, such that they end up overcompensated when they recover damages for harm borne largely by others.[1012] On the other, antitrust litigation leaves some harm uncompensated. Among other things, much of the social harm from an antitrust violation may be found in the "deadweight loss" representing harm to those who would be willing to buy a product or service at the competitive price but do not do so at the supracompetitive price, but this harm is not reflected in antitrust damages claims because such individuals generally do not bring antitrust suits.[1013] At the end of the day, it would be a remarkable thing if a factor of three—the number chosen by the framers of the 1623 Statute of Monopolies—just happened to be the optimal multiplier for an ideal antitrust damages rule.

All this fuels a long-running and lively debate about the desirability of treble damages.[1014] Unfortunately, we do not really know many of the critical facts on which a full assessment of the costs and benefits of existing (and

---

[1007] United States, *Relationship Between Public and Private Antitrust Enforcement*, OECD Working Paper DAF/COMP/WP3/WD(2015)11 (June 15, 2015), 8 ("The Antitrust Division and FTC monitor the cases closely and participate as amicus curiae where important principles are implicated.").

[1008] Joshua P. Davis & Robert H. Lande, *Defying Conventional Wisdom: The Case for Private Antitrust Enforcement*, 48 Ga. L. Rev. 1, 33–35 (2013) (collecting concerns of other commentators that private suits may lead to excessive recoveries, prompt "extortionate settlements," and create opportunities for class counsel to "sell out" their clients); Daniel A. Crane, *Optimizing Private Antitrust Enforcement*, 63 Vand. L. Rev. 673, 680–81 (2010); Stephen Calkins, *Reflections on* Matsushita *and "Equilibrating Tendencies": Lessons for Competition Authorities*, 82 Antitrust L.J.201 (2018).

[1009] Daniel A. Crane, *Optimizing Private Antitrust Enforcement*, 63 Vand. L. Rev. 673, 697 (2010) ("[I]t is implausible that the threat of future private litigation does much to deter anticompetitive behavior").

[1010] *See, e.g.*, Bell Atlantic Corp. v. Twombly, 550 U.S. 544, 546 (2007) ("The requirement of allegations suggesting an agreement serves the practical purpose of preventing a plaintiff with a largely groundless claim from taking up the time of a number of other people, with the right to do so representing an in terrorem increment of the settlement value. It is one thing to be cautious before dismissing an antitrust complaint in advance of discovery, but quite another to forget that proceeding to antitrust discovery can be expensive. That potential expense is obvious here, where plaintiffs represent a putative class of at least 90 percent of subscribers to local telephone or high-speed Internet service in an action against America's largest telecommunications firms for unspecified instances of antitrust violations that allegedly occurred over a 7-year period. It is no answer to say that a claim just shy of plausible entitlement can be weeded out early in the discovery process, given the common lament that the success of judicial supervision in checking discovery abuse has been modest.").

[1011] *See, e.g.*, Daniel A. Crane, *Antitrust Antifederalism*, 96 Calif. L. Rev. 1, 41 (2008) ("[C]ourts often establish sharply underinclusive liability norms in private antitrust cases . . . [And] because it is often the same statute that courts must construe in both public and private cases, the courts have tended to apply private litigation liability rules to public litigation as well.").

[1012] *See infra* § XII.C (describing indirect purchaser rule).

[1013] *See, e.g.*, David C. Hjelmfelt & Channing D. Strother Jr., *Antitrust Damages for Consumer Welfare Loss*, 39 Clev. St. L. Rev. 505 (1991).

[1014] See, e.g., Joshua P. Davis & Robert H. Lande, *Defying Conventional Wisdom: The Case for Private Antitrust Enforcement*, 48 Ga. L. Rev. 1 (2013); Edward D. Cavanagh, *Detrebling Antitrust Damages in Monopolization Cases*, 76 Antitrust L.J. 97 (2009); Herbert Hovenkamp, THE ANTITRUST ENTERPRISE: PRINCIPLE AND EXECUTION (2005) 66–68; Steven C. Salop & Lawrence J. White, *Economic Analysis of Private Antitrust Litigation*, 74 Geo. L.J. 1001, 1034 (1986); William Breit & Kenneth G. Elzinga, *Private Antitrust Enforcement: The New Learning*, 28 J. L. & Econ. 405, 438 (1985) (summarizing proposals); Frank H. Easterbrook, *Detrebling Antitrust Damages*, 28 J. L. & Econ. 445 (1985).

plausible alternative) antitrust damages rules would depend.[1015] In 2007, the Antitrust Modernization Commission considered, and rejected, arguments for limiting or repealing the treble-damages rule.

Antitrust Modernization Commission, Report and Recommendations (April 2007)

[1] Treble damages serve five related and important goals:

(1) Deterring anticompetitive conduct;

(2) Punishing violators of the antitrust laws;

(3) Forcing disgorgement of the benefits of anticompetitive conduct from those violators;

(4) Providing full compensation to victims of anticompetitive conduct; and

(5) Providing an incentive to victims to act as "private attorneys general."

[2] Although it has been argued that, in certain circumstances, something more or less than treble damages would better advance one or more of these goals, the Commission concludes that an insufficient case has been made for changing the treble damages rule, either universally or in specified instances. The Commission concludes that, on balance, the treble damages rule well serves the defined goals.

[3] *Deterrence.* The first broadly recognized purpose of treble damages is deterrence. To eliminate the incentive to engage in anticompetitive conduct, a violator must be exposed to forfeiture of potential gains from such conduct. Treble damages compensate for the reality that some anticompetitive conduct is likely to evade detection and challenge. If a company realizes that its anticompetitive conduct has only a 50 percent chance of being detected, and if its liability were limited to single damages, it would be more likely to engage in that conduct because the reward exceeds the risk.

[4] *Punishment of violators.* The second recognized purpose of treble damages is to punish offenders, similar to punitive damages under the common law and other statutes. This reason is closely related to the deterrence justification: providing a multiple of damages helps deter such conduct and highlights societal disapproval of such conduct. Furthermore, in addition to raising prices, anticompetitive conduct causes allocative inefficiency (for example, forgone purchases and substitution of less optimal alternatives) that, while reducing consumer welfare, is not reflected in damage calculations. Treble damages help to ensure that the violator pays damages that more fully reflect the harm to society caused by the anticompetitive conduct.

[5] *Disgorgement of gains.* Treble damages also serve the purpose of requiring the disgorgement of unlawfully obtained gains (or profits) that result from anticompetitive conduct. Preventing violators from profiting removes incentives to engage in such conduct and thereby enhances deterrence.

[6] *Compensation to victims.* A fourth purpose of treble damages is to ensure full compensation to the victims of anticompetitive conduct. Indeed, in light of the fact that some damages may not be recoverable (e.g., compensation for interest prior to judgment, or because of the statute of limitations and the inability to recover "speculative" damages) treble damages help ensure that victims will receive at least their actual damages.

[7] *Creating incentives for "private attorneys general."* Finally, providing treble damages creates incentives for private enforcement of the antitrust laws. This is of particular importance in light of limited government resources to identify and prosecute all anticompetitive conduct. Incentives for private enforcement reinforce the other objectives of treble damages by increasing the likelihood that claims will be brought against violators, thereby enhancing deterrence, appropriate disgorgement and punishment, and compensation to victims.

[1015] Joshua P. Davis & Robert H. Lande, *Defying Conventional Wisdom: The Case for Private Antitrust Enforcement*, 48 Ga. L. Rev. 1, 15 (2013) ("Having set forth what we would like to know to evaluate private antitrust enforcement, it is striking how little we actually do know. Most of the key questions remain unanswered. The great bulk of the argument about private enforcement of the antitrust laws has been premised on unsubstantiated or insufficiently substantiated claims."). For a recent study, *see* Huntington National Bank & USF School of Law, *2020 Antitrust Annual Report: Class Action Filings in Federal Court* (Aug. 2021).

[8] The Commission was not presented with substantial evidence or empirical support that treble damages do not advance these goals. However, some have argued that treble damages, along with other remedies, can over-deter some conduct that may not be anticompetitive and result in duplicative recovery. No actual cases or evidence of systematic overdeterrence were presented to the Commission, however.

[9] The Commission carefully considered a variety of circumstances in which it was proposed that the damages multiplier might be decreased (or increased). . . . [T]he Commission considered the following (among others): (1) providing treble damages only in cases where the conduct is clearly unlawful and devoid of competitive benefit; (2) limiting damages to single damages when the conduct is overt; and, (3) placing the damages multiplier in the discretion of the trial judge. Ultimately, the Commission declined to recommend these approaches . . . .

[10] There is broad consensus that treble damages are appropriate for hard-core cartel conduct. Even those who advocate eliminating treble damages in some circumstances agree that price-fixing and similar conduct should be subject to treble damages. Moreover, some argue that the multiplier should be higher in these cases to compensate for the low likelihood of detection. Nonetheless, because the Commission recommends retention of a single, uniform multiplier in all antitrust cases, and because hard-core cartel conduct is often subject to criminal prosecution, the Commission does not recommend any increase to the multiplier for hard-core conduct.

[11] The Commission also declines to recommend a change to provide for only single damages in rule of reason cases. Several fundamentally similar proposals were advanced to the Commission to limit treble damages to per se antitrust violations, where the conduct is clearly unlawful and bereft of procompetitive benefits. These advocates argue that in cases other than those—where conduct may be procompetitive or is subject to unclear legal standards—treble damages may deter or "chill" potentially procompetitive behavior. Although such concerns are reasonable, the Commission concluded that statutorily defining whether conduct was a per se violation or subject to the rule of reason would prove difficult.

[12] Furthermore, there is anticompetitive conduct that is not per se unlawful can cause as much damage as per se violations such as price-fixing. Indeed, eliminating treble damages for such cases could greatly hamper incentives to bring actions, and thus reduce deterrence too much.

[14] The Commission also evaluated, but declined to recommend, limiting treble damages to conduct that is covert. For conduct that is publicly open (or "overt")—such as mergers, and most joint ventures, distribution contracts, and single-firm conduct—the probability of detection is close to 100 percent. By comparison, much covert cartel activity likely goes undetected. Given that a principal justification for treble damages is to account for the likelihood of detection, there may be no need for multiple damages where the public is aware of the conduct or it is otherwise overt. The Commission declined to recommend the creation of such a distinction, however, because some overt conduct, such as aspects of a legitimate joint venture, may be a disguised cartel, or otherwise cause severe harm. As with the proposed division between per se and rule of reason conduct, such a distinction might result in increased litigation over whether treble damages are available on the facts of the conduct.

[15] In light of the concerns with these two proposals, as well as several other similar proposals, the Commission also considered, but rejected, a rule that would leave the decision whether to award treble damages to the discretion of a judge. A court may be best positioned to evaluate the severity of the violation, in light of a range of possible factors, and tailor the penalty accordingly. This approach would allow a court to decline to award treble damages if, for example, the questions of fact are close or the legal standards unclear, the conduct was overt, or the conduct had sizable procompetitive benefits. Allowing judges to award only single damages in such cases would therefore potentially reduce overdeterrence and the chilling of procompetitive conduct that may result from mandatory trebling. It would also avoid the need for drafting a statute that defines types of conduct that are and are not subject to treble damages. The Commission concluded, however, that such an approach would increase the length and cost of trials as the parties contest factual issues relevant to the factors to be considered. Moreover, judges would be required potentially to balance multiple, conflicting factors, leading to inconsistency across courts and forum shopping.

* * *

The prospect of competitor antitrust lawsuits, in particular, can raise real challenges for antitrust policy. Courts and commentators often have significant unease about empowering firms to impose high costs—in the form of litigation expenses as well as exposure to treble damages and the risk of business-breaking injunctions—on their rivals, and the fear that antitrust litigation might be, or become, an anticompetitive weapon is widespread.[1016] (As we have already seen, meritless litigation against rivals can be a tool of monopolization: and, perhaps ironically, this tactic may work as well with an antitrust case as any other kind of litigation.[1017]) And yet competitors may be uniquely well placed to spot antitrust violations before they have resulted in enduring market harm.[1018]

Despite the controversies, private litigation remains of tremendous practical importance to the enforcement and development of modern antitrust. Federal agencies and state enforcers suffer from acute resource limitations, and can investigate only a relatively small proportion of the matters brought to their attention.[1019] Private enforcement allows many more alleged antitrust violations to be challenged, investigated, and remedied, and it provides an opportunity for development of the law.[1020] And privately litigated disputes are often just as important and complex as those pursued by the federal agencies. Indeed, some of the most famous and important antitrust precedents— including *Trinko, Aspen Skiing, Twombly, Tampa Electric, Jefferson Parish, LePage's, PeaceHealth, Brooke Group, Matsushita, Monsanto*, and many more—are the result of private litigation rather than government action.

The rest of this Chapter explores ways in which the courts have, for many decades, set important boundaries on who can sue under the antitrust laws, and what they can recover for, in ways that might surprise a reader of the statutory text. Indeed, on the face of it, the statutory rights to damages and injunctive relief are framed broadly. The statutory damages provision is found at 15 U.S.C. § 15a:

> [A]ny person who shall be injured in his business or property by reason of anything forbidden in the antitrust laws may sue therefor in any district court of the United States in the district in which the defendant resides or is found or has an agent, without respect to the amount in controversy, and shall recover threefold the damages by him sustained, and the cost of suit, including a reasonable attorney's fee. The court may award under this section, pursuant to a motion by such person promptly made, simple interest on actual damages for the period beginning on the date of service of such person's pleading setting forth a claim under the antitrust laws and ending on the date of judgment, or for any shorter period therein, if the court finds that the award of such interest for such period is just in the circumstances.

And the private plaintiff's right to an injunction is found at 15 U.S.C. § 26, framed in similarly broad terms:

> Any person, firm, corporation, or association shall be entitled to sue for and have injunctive relief, in any court of the United States having jurisdiction over the parties, against threatened loss or damage by a violation of the antitrust laws . . . when and under the same conditions and principles as injunctive relief against threatened conduct that will cause loss or damage is granted by courts of equity, under the rules governing such proceedings, and upon the execution of proper bond against damages for an injunction improvidently granted and a showing that the danger of irreparable loss or damage is immediate, a preliminary injunction may issue[.] . . . In any action under this section in which the plaintiff substantially prevails, the court shall award the cost of suit, including a reasonable attorney's fee, to such plaintiff.

But in practice these rights to relief have turned out to be narrower than the statutory language would suggest. Specifically, the Supreme Court has imposed some important limitations on the rights of a private person to obtain redress in antitrust litigation, giving rise to some important (and sometimes complicated) lines of authority with

---

[1016] *See, e.g.*, R.P. McAfee, & N. Vakkur, *The Strategic Abuse of Antitrust Laws*, 1 J. Strate. Mgmt. Educ. 3 (2004); Edward A. Snyder & Thomas E. Kauper, *Misuse of the Antitrust Laws: The Competitor Plaintiff*, 90 Mich. L. Rev.. 551 (1991); William J. Baumol & Janusz A. Ordover, *Use of Antitrust to Subvert Competition*, 28 J. L. & Econ. 247 (1985).

[1017] *See supra* § VII.G.6, § IX.B (sham litigation as an antitrust violation).

[1018] Herbert Hovenkamp, THE ANTITRUST ENTERPRISE: PRINCIPLE AND EXECUTION (2005) 68–72.

[1019] *See, e.g.*, Holly Vedova, *Adjusting merger review to deal with the surge in merger filings*, Competition Matters (Aug. 3, 2021) (emphasizing FTC's limited resources).

[1020] American Antitrust Institute, *The Critical Role of Private Antitrust Enforcement In The United States Commentary On: 2020 Antitrust Annual Report: Class Action Filings In Federal Court* (Aug. 4, 2021); Steven C. Salop & Lawrence J. White, *Economic Analysis of Private Antitrust Litigation*, 74 Geo. L.J. 1001 (1986) (noting detection function). Note, however, the concern mentioned above: that private-plaintiff cases might lead to the adoption of narrower substantive liability rules than might be the case in a government-only system. *See supra* note 1011.

which a private plaintiff must contend. One of these lines established what is known today as the "antitrust injury" requirement: in essence it limits the kinds of injuries for which a plaintiff can seek antitrust redress. Another important line is the "indirect purchaser" rule: in essence it provides that only individuals dealing directly with the defendant may sue. As Dan Crane has pointed out, these rules—regardless of whether one might think them wise, fair, or socially desirable—represent something like policy innovation by the Court, rather than a reflection of anything fairly discernible in the text or even legislative history of the antitrust laws.[1021]

This chapter will give a short tour of some of the distinctive issues attending private enforcement of the antitrust laws. In Section B we will encounter the concept of antitrust standing and one of its most important facets: the "antitrust injury" doctrine. In Section C we will examine another critical facet: the controversial "indirect purchaser rule" that limits which participants in the supply chain are entitled to bring an antitrust claim. In Section D we will consider some of the methods (and challenges) of proving antitrust damages in complex real-world markets. In Section E we will consider the question of timing, through the doctrines of limitations and laches. Finally, in Section F we will briefly explore the relationship between private and government enforcement.

B. Antitrust Standing

In order to sue for private relief, a plaintiff must have "antitrust standing." (Not to be confused with Article III standing![1022]) This is a complex and multifaceted concept, but it has two cores: the first core is a test of whether the injury suffered by the plaintiff is the kind of harm that is appropriate for redress through antitrust litigation; the second core is a test of whether the plaintiff is the right kind of entity to be suing for the harm.[1023] In this Section we will meet some leading versions of the standing test, and the critical requirement that an antitrust plaintiff has suffered "antitrust injury."

1. The Elements of Standing

In *Associated General Contractors of California*, the Court gave a lengthy explanation of its decision to deny relief to a union that was suing for antitrust violations—including a group boycott—that had harmed the union's interests by diverting business to nonunionized firms. *AGC* is a slightly odd case: the theory of antitrust violation was unusual, complex, and not well defined. But it prompted the Court to set out its views about antitrust standing in particular detail.

In reading this passage, notice how the Court appeals to a broad array of policy concerns rooted in the nature of the claimed harm *and* the identity of the plaintiff. What rules emerge? And which concerns, if any, do you find persuasive?

Associated Gen. Contractors of California, Inc. v. California State Council of Carpenters
459 U.S. 519 (1983)

Justice Stevens.

[1] This case arises out of a dispute between parties to a multiemployer collective bargaining agreement. The plaintiff unions allege that, in violation of the antitrust laws, the multiemployer association and its members coerced certain third parties, as well as some of the association's members, to enter into business relationships with nonunion firms. This coercion, according to the complaint, adversely affected the trade of certain unionized firms

---

[1021] Daniel A. Crane, *Antitrust Antitextualism*, 96 Notre Dame L. Rev. 1205, 1226–29 (2021).

[1022] *See, e.g.*, Potter v. Cozen & O'Connor, 46 F.4th 148, 156 (3d Cir. 2022) ("Antitrust standing, like shareholder standing, is not an Article III standing doctrine, but rather one that is variously characterized as prudential or a matter of 'statutory standing.'").

[1023] For discussions of various aspects of antitrust standing doctrine, *see, e.g.*, Herbert Hovenkamp, Apple v. Pepper, *Rationalizing Antitrust's Indirect Purchaser Rule*, 120 Colum. L. Rev. Forum 14 (2020); Roger D. Blair & Jeffrey L. Harrison, *Reexamining the Role of Illinois Brick in Modern Antitrust Standing Analysis*, 68 Geo. Wash. L. Rev. 1 (1999); Joseph F. Brodley, *Antitrust Standing in Private Merger Cases: Reconciling Private Incentives and Public Enforcement Goals*, 94 Mich. L. Rev. 1 (1995); Robert P. Taylor, *Antitrust Standing: Its Growing-or More Accurately Its Shrinking-Dimensions*, 55 Antitrust L.J. 515 (1986).

and thereby restrained the business activities of the unions. The question presented is whether the complaint sufficiently alleges that the unions have been "injured in [their] business or property by reason of anything forbidden in the antitrust laws" and may therefore recover treble damages under § 4 of the Clayton Act. 15 U.S.C. § 15. Unlike the majority of the Court of Appeals for the Ninth Circuit, we agree with the District Court's conclusion that the complaint is insufficient. [. . .]

[2] . . . [T]he Union's most specific claims of injury involve matters that are not subject to review under the antitrust laws. The amended complaint alleges that the defendants have breached their collective bargaining agreements in various ways, and that they have manipulated their corporate names and corporate status in order to divert business to nonunion divisions or firms that they actually control. Such deceptive diversion of business to the nonunion portion of a so-called "double-breasted" operation might constitute a breach of contract, an unfair labor practice, or perhaps even a common-law fraud or deceit, but in the context of the bargaining relationship between the parties to this litigation, such activities are plainly not subject to review under the federal antitrust laws. Similarly, the charge that the defendants advocated, encouraged, induced, and aided nonmembers to refuse to enter into collective bargaining relationships with the Union does not describe an antitrust violation.

[3] The Union's antitrust claims arise from alleged restraints caused by defendants in the market for construction contracting and subcontracting. The complaint alleges that defendants "coerced" two classes of persons: (1) landowners and others who let construction contracts, i.e., the defendants' customers and potential customers; and (2) general contractors, i.e., defendants' competitors and defendants themselves. Coercion against the members of both classes was designed to induce them to give some of their business—but not necessarily all of it—to nonunion firms. Although the pleading does not allege that the coercive conduct increased the aggregate share of nonunion firms in the market, it does allege that defendants' activities weakened and restrained the trade of certain contractors. Thus, particular victims of coercion may have diverted particular contracts to nonunion firms and thereby caused certain unionized subcontractors to lose some business.

[4] We think the Court of Appeals properly assumed that such coercion might violate the antitrust laws. An agreement to restrain trade may be unlawful even though it does not entirely exclude its victims from the market. Coercive activity that prevents its victims from making free choices between market alternatives is inherently destructive of competitive conditions and may be condemned even without proof of its actual market effect. [. . .]

[5] The class of persons who may maintain a private damage action under the antitrust laws is broadly defined in § 4 of the Clayton Act. 15 U.S.C. § 15. That section provides:

> Any person who shall be injured in his business or property by reason of anything forbidden in the antitrust laws may sue therefor in any district court of the United States in the district in which the defendant resides or is found or has an agent, without respect to the amount in controversy, and shall recover threefold the damages by him sustained, and the cost of suit, including a reasonable attorney's fee.

[6] A literal reading of the statute is broad enough to encompass every harm that can be attributed directly or indirectly to the consequences of an antitrust violation. Some of our prior cases have paraphrased the statute in an equally expansive way. But before we hold that the statute is as broad as its words suggest, we must consider whether Congress intended such an open-ended meaning.

[7] The critical statutory language was originally enacted in 1890 as § 7 of the Sherman Act. The legislative history of the section shows that Congress was primarily interested in creating an effective remedy for consumers who were forced to pay excessive prices by the giant trusts and combinations that dominated certain interstate markets. That history supports a broad construction of this remedial provision. A proper interpretation of the section cannot, however, ignore the larger context in which the entire statute was debated. [. . .]

[8] In 1890, notwithstanding general language in many state constitutions providing in substance that every wrong shall have a remedy, a number of judge-made rules circumscribed the availability of damages recoveries in both tort and contract litigation—doctrines such as foreseeability and proximate cause, directness of injury, certainty of damages, and privity of contract. Although particular common-law limitations were not debated in Congress, the frequent references to common-law principles imply that Congress simply assumed that antitrust damages

litigation would be subject to constraints comparable to well-accepted common-law rules applied in comparable litigation. [. . .]

[5] An antitrust violation may be expected to cause ripples of harm to flow through the Nation's economy; but despite the broad wording of § 4 there is a point beyond which the wrongdoer should not be held liable. It is reasonable to assume that Congress did not intend to allow every person tangentially affected by an antitrust violation to maintain an action to recover threefold damages for the injury to his business or property.

[9] It is plain, therefore, that the question whether the Union may recover for the injury it allegedly suffered by reason of the defendants' coercion against certain third parties cannot be answered simply by reference to the broad language of § 4. Instead, as was required in common-law damages litigation in 1890, the question requires us to evaluate the plaintiff's harm, the alleged wrongdoing by the defendants, and the relationship between them. [. . .]

[10] There is a similarity between the struggle of common-law judges to articulate a precise definition of the concept of "proximate cause," and the struggle of federal judges to articulate a precise test to determine whether a party injured by an antitrust violation may recover treble damages. It is common ground that the judicial remedy cannot encompass every conceivable harm that can be traced to alleged wrongdoing. In both situations the infinite variety of claims that may arise make it virtually impossible to announce a black-letter rule that will dictate the result in every case. Instead, previously decided cases identify factors that circumscribe and guide the exercise of judgment in deciding whether the law affords a remedy in specific circumstances.

[11] The factors that favor judicial recognition of the Union's antitrust claim are easily stated. The complaint does allege a causal connection between an antitrust violation and harm to the Union and further alleges that the defendants intended to cause that harm. As we have indicated, however, the mere fact that the claim is literally encompassed by the Clayton Act does not end the inquiry. [. . .]

[12] A number of other factors may be controlling. In this case it is appropriate to focus on the nature of the plaintiff's alleged injury. As the legislative history shows, the Sherman Act was enacted to assure customers the benefits of price competition, and our prior cases have emphasized the central interest in protecting the economic freedom of participants in the relevant market. [. . .]

[13] In this case, however, the Union was neither a consumer nor a competitor in the market in which trade was restrained. It is not clear whether the Union's interests would be served or disserved by enhanced competition in the market. As a general matter, a union's primary goal is to enhance the earnings and improve the working conditions of its membership; that goal is not necessarily served, and indeed may actually be harmed, by uninhibited competition among employers striving to reduce costs in order to obtain a competitive advantage over their rivals. At common law—as well as in the early days of administration of the federal antitrust laws—the collective activities of labor unions were regarded as a form of conspiracy in restraint of trade. Federal policy has since developed not only a broad labor exemption from the antitrust laws, but also a separate body of labor law specifically designed to protect and encourage the organizational and representational activities of labor unions. Set against this background, a union, in its capacity as bargaining representative, will frequently not be part of the class the Sherman Act was designed to protect, especially in disputes with employers with whom it bargains. In each case its alleged injury must be analyzed to determine whether it is of the type that the antitrust statute was intended to forestall. [. . .]

[14] An additional factor is the directness or indirectness of the asserted injury. In this case, the chain of causation between the Union's injury and the alleged restraint in the market for construction subcontracts contains several somewhat vaguely defined links. According to the complaint, defendants applied coercion against certain landowners and other contracting parties in order to cause them to divert business from certain union contractors to nonunion contractors. As a result, the Union's complaint alleges, the Union suffered unspecified injuries in its business activities. It is obvious that any such injuries were only an indirect result of whatever harm may have been suffered by "certain" construction contractors and subcontractors.

[15] If either these firms, or the immediate victims of coercion by defendants, have been injured by an antitrust violation, their injuries would be direct and . . . they would have a right to maintain their own treble damages

actions against the defendants. An action on their behalf would encounter none of the conceptual difficulties that encumber the Union's claim. The existence of an identifiable class of persons whose self-interest would normally motivate them to vindicate the public interest in antitrust enforcement diminishes the justification for allowing a more remote party such as the Union to perform the office of a private attorney general. Denying the Union a remedy on the basis of its allegations in this case is not likely to leave a significant antitrust violation undetected or unremedied.

[16] Partly because it is indirect, and partly because the alleged effects on the Union may have been produced by independent factors, the Union's damages claim is also highly speculative. There is, for example, no allegation that any collective bargaining agreement was terminated as a result of the coercion, no allegation that the aggregate share of the contracting market controlled by union firms has diminished, no allegation that the number of employed union members has declined, and no allegation that the Union's revenues in the form of dues or initiation fees have decreased. Moreover, although coercion against certain firms is alleged, there is no assertion that any such firm was prevented from doing business with any union firms or that any firm or group of firms was subjected to a complete boycott. Other than the alleged injuries flowing from breaches of the collective bargaining agreements—injuries that would be remediable under other laws—nothing but speculation informs the Union's claim of injury by reason of the alleged unlawful coercion. Yet, as we have recently reiterated, it is appropriate for § 4 purposes to consider whether a claim rests at bottom on some abstract conception or speculative measure of harm.

[17] The indirectness of the alleged injury also implicates the strong interest, identified in our prior cases, in keeping the scope of complex antitrust trials within judicially manageable limits. These cases have stressed the importance of avoiding either the risk of duplicate recoveries on the one hand, or the danger of complex apportionment of damages on the other. [. . .]

[18] The same concerns should guide us in determining whether the Union is a proper plaintiff under § 4 of the Clayton Act. . . . In this case, if the Union's complaint asserts a claim for damages under § 4, the District Court would face problems of identifying damages and apportioning them among directly victimized contractors and subcontractors and indirectly affected employees and union entities. It would be necessary to determine to what extent the coerced firms diverted business away from union subcontractors, and then to what extent those subcontractors absorbed the damage to their businesses or passed it on to employees by reducing the workforce or cutting hours or wages. In turn it would be necessary to ascertain the extent to which the affected employees absorbed their losses and continued to pay union dues.

[19] We conclude, therefore, that the Union's allegations of consequential harm resulting from a violation of the antitrust laws, although buttressed by an allegation of intent to harm the Union, are insufficient as a matter of law. Other relevant factors—the nature of the Union's injury, the tenuous and speculative character of the relationship between the alleged antitrust violation and the Union's alleged injury, the potential for duplicative recovery or complex apportionment of damages, and the existence of more direct victims of the alleged conspiracy—weigh heavily against judicial enforcement of the Union's antitrust claim. Accordingly, we hold that, based on the allegations of this complaint, the District Court was correct in concluding that the Union is not a person injured by reason of a violation of the antitrust laws within the meaning of § 4 of the Clayton Act. The judgment of the Court of Appeals is reversed.

* * *

It is now very clear that the elements of standing include *at least* antitrust injury: that is, injury of the kind that the antitrust laws are intended to address. We will focus on antitrust injury in the next Section. But, beyond the antitrust-injury test, the other components of standing can be harder to pin down. The Eleventh Circuit, for example, describes antitrust standing as a matter of two questions: first, whether the plaintiff has shown antitrust injury; second, whether the plaintiff is an "efficient enforcer" of the antitrust laws.[1024] (We will consider the

---

[1024] *See, e.g.*, Sunbeam Television Corp. v. Nielsen Media Rsch., Inc., 711 F.3d 1264, 1271 (11th Cir. 2013); Ekbatani v. Cmty. Care Health Network, LLC, Case No. 21-12322, 2022 WL 31793, at *1 (11th Cir. Jan. 4, 2022).

efficient-enforcer test in the next section.) The Second Circuit takes the same view.[1025] The Fifth Circuit makes it three questions: (1) whether the plaintiff has suffered injury-in-fact proximately caused by the defendant's conduct; (2) antitrust injury; and (3) "proper plaintiff status, which assures that other parties are not better situated to bring suit."[1026] But a number of other circuits, including the Fourth, apply a five-factor assessment, exemplified by its 2007 *Novell* decision.[1027] Do these factors set out an appealing framework for figuring out who can bring an antitrust claim?

Novell, Inc. v. Microsoft Corp.

505 F.3d 302 (4th Cir. 2007)

Judge Duncan.

[1] Novell seeks treble damages under § 4 of the Clayton Act for injuries allegedly suffered as a result of Microsoft's anticompetitive conduct in violation of §§ 1 and 2 of the Sherman Act. . . . Two of [Novell's] claims allege that Microsoft's conduct injured competition in the market for PC operating systems, a market in which Novell's products did not directly compete. [Microsoft moved to dismiss these claims on the basis that] Novell, as neither a consumer nor a competitor in the relevant market, lacks antitrust standing to bring them. Microsoft appeals the [district court's] denial of this motion to dismiss. [. . .]

[2] Novell is a software company that owned WordPerfect, a word-processing application, and Quattro Pro, a spreadsheet application, from 1994 until 1996. WordPerfect and Quattro Pro are office-productivity applications, which Novell marketed together as an office-productivity package called PerfectOffice. Microsoft is a software company that owns Windows, a personal-computer ("PC") operating system, as well as office-productivity applications of its own. [. . .]

[3] Novell concedes that its products did not directly compete in the market for PC operating systems. Nevertheless, Novell contends that the technological connection between operating systems and applications gives rise to a significant barrier to entry into the operating-systems market and thus protects Microsoft's Windows monopoly. Novell maintains that its office-productivity applications could perform well on a variety of operating systems and that, during the relevant time period, they were the dominant office-productivity applications in the market. The thrust of Novell's argument is that its popular applications, though themselves not competitors or potential competitors to Microsoft's Windows, offered competing operating systems the prospect of surmounting the applications barrier to entry and breaking the Windows monopoly. That is, Novell argues its products could provide a path onto the operating-system playing field for an actual competitor of Windows, because a competing operating system, running the popular Novell software applications, would offer consumers an attractive alternative to Windows. [. . .]

[4] Novell's present claims echo the government's theory in [United States v. Microsoft Corp., 253 F.3d 34 (D.C. Cir. 2001) (en banc)]. Just as the middleware threat posed by Java and Navigator came from outside the Microsoft dominated PC operating-system market, Novell now argues that its products, though also outside the relevant market, similarly threatened Microsoft Windows.

[5] Novell alleges three specific unlawful actions on the part of Microsoft that harmed its products and also harmed competition in the PC operating-systems market. First, Novell claims Microsoft withheld from Novell key technical information necessary to make well-functioning office-productivity applications for Windows 95, an updated version of Windows launched by Microsoft during the period that Novell owned WordPerfect and Quattro Pro. [. . .]

[1025] Laydon v. Cooperatieve Rabobank U.A., 51 F.4th 476, 488 (2d Cir. 2022). *See also* Marion Diagnostic Ctr., LLC v. Becton Dickinson & Co., 29 F.4th 337, 347 (7th Cir. 2022) ("In addition to satisfying Article III standing, the Providers must show that they have suffered an antitrust injury and that they are the proper parties to bring suit.").

[1026] Pulse Network, L.L.C. v. Visa, Inc., 30 F.4th 480, 488 (5th Cir. 2022).

[1027] *See also, e.g.*, Lifewatch Servs. Inc. v. Highmark Inc., 902 F.3d 323, 341–42 (3d Cir. 2018); Knevelbaard Dairies v. Kraft Foods, Inc., 232 F.3d 979, 987 (9th Cir. 2000).

[6] Second, Novell argues that Microsoft impeded Novell's access to distribution channels, including original equipment manufacturers ("OEMs"). OEMs manufacture PCs and typically preinstall an operating system and certain commonly used applications. Because Windows's monopoly in the operating-system market means most consumers want to buy Windows-equipped PCs, OEMs desire Windows licenses that enable them to install Windows on PCs. Novell asserts that OEMs' dependence on Windows licenses furnished Microsoft with leverage that it used to impose restrictive and exclusionary agreements on OEMs. . . .

[7] Finally . . . Novell claims that Microsoft required it, as a condition of being certified as Windows-compatible, to use Windows-specific technologies that degraded the performance of Novell's office-productivity applications on other operating systems. This requirement neutralized Novell's applications' purported advantage of working well on a variety of operating systems. Novell claims that such an advantage, along with Novell's applications' popularity, could have enabled other operating systems to bridge the "moat" that protected Microsoft's Windows monopoly.

[8] In a private antitrust action, a plaintiff must go beyond a showing that it meets the Article III standing requirements of injury, causation, and redressability; it must also demonstrate "antitrust standing." Section 4 of the Clayton Act, 15 U.S.C. § 15, provides:

> [A]ny person who shall be injured in his business or property by reason of anything forbidden in the antitrust laws may sue . . . and shall recover threefold the damages by him sustained, and the cost of suit, including a reasonable attorney's fee.

[9] Although a literal reading of § 4 is "broad enough to encompass every harm that can be attributed directly or indirectly to the consequences of an antitrust violation," the Supreme Court has interpreted the provision more restrictively. *See Assoc. Gen. Contractors of Cal., Inc. v. Cal. State Council of Carpenters ("AGC")*, 459 U.S. 519, 529–30 (1983). Congress did not intend the antitrust laws to provide a remedy in damages for all injuries that might conceivably be traced to an antitrust violation. An antitrust violation may be expected to cause ripples of harm to flow through the Nation's economy; but despite the broad wording of § 4 there is a point beyond which the wrongdoer should not be held liable.

[10] A plaintiff sufficiently connected to the violation propagating these ripples of harm is said to have "antitrust standing." The Supreme Court has held that a multi-factor analysis is required to determine whether a private plaintiff has antitrust standing. These factors circumscribe and guide courts' judgments on whether plaintiffs have antitrust standing. The Courts of Appeals have since relied on the *AGC* factors to determine antitrust standing. This court recently had the occasion to apply the *AGC* factors, distilling them to five:

> (1) the causal connection between an antitrust violation and harm to the plaintiffs, and whether that harm was intended; (2) whether the harm was of a type that Congress sought to redress in providing a private remedy for violations of the antitrust laws; (3) the directness of the alleged injury; (4) the existence of more direct victims of the alleged antitrust injury; and (5) problems of identifying damages and apportioning them among those directly and indirectly harmed.

[11] The first two of these antitrust-standing factors together encompass the concept of "antitrust injury." Antitrust injury has been defined as injury of the type the antitrust laws were intended to pre-vent and that flows from that which makes the defendants' acts unlawful. The other three *AGC* factors focus on the directness or remoteness of the plaintiff's alleged anti-trust injury.

[12] Before applying the *AGC* factors to the facts of this case, however, we must first consider Microsoft's argument that Novell's claims fail as a threshold matter. Microsoft asks us to adopt a bright-line rule that only consumers or competitors in the relevant market have antitrust standing to bring private treble-damages claims under § 4. Were we to adopt this proffered rule, Microsoft argues, we would be compelled to find, before reaching the five-factor analysis, that Novell does not have standing in this case because its products did not directly compete in the operating-system market.

[13] We must decline to adopt Microsoft's "consumer-or-competitor" rule. We note that the Supreme Court has rejected the utility of the very type of bright-line approach on which Microsoft seeks to rely: "The infinite variety of claims that may arise make it virtually impossible to announce a black-letter rule that will dictate the result in

every case." *AGC*, 459 U.S. at 536. In fact, a careful examination of the cases on which Microsoft relies for support of its proposed rule reveals that in most instances the claims were defeated by the absence of an antitrust injury, rather than the plaintiff's failure to demonstrate consumer or competitor status. [. . .]

[14] Having rejected Microsoft's argument that a bright-line consumer-or-competitor rule strips Novell of antitrust standing, we now consider whether the five *AGC* factors, as formulated in our decision in [Kloth v. Microsoft, 444 F.3d 312 (4th Cir. 2006)], compel dismissal of Novell's claims on antitrust-standing grounds. The first two factors— "(1) the causal connection between an antitrust violation and harm to the plaintiffs, and whether that harm was intended; and (2) whether the harm was of a type that Congress sought to redress in providing a private remedy for violations of the antitrust laws"—are closely related. They ensure that the plaintiff claims the proper type of injury to be accorded antitrust standing. The other factors, which involve examination of the directness or remoteness of the plaintiff's injury and the ease or difficulty of apportioning damages, may further constrict the number of private plaintiffs eligible to bring a treble-damages action under the federal antitrust laws.

[15] We begin by reviewing the first two *AGC* factors. For ease of analysis, we reverse their order and examine first whether Novell has alleged an injury that the antitrust laws were intended to prevent, and then the causal connection between Microsoft's conduct and Novell's injuries. It is helpful in this regard to briefly revisit the purposes of antitrust laws. [. . .]

[16] Taking Novell's allegations as true, as we must, the injury that Novell alleges here is plainly an injury to competition that the anti-trust laws were intended to forestall. Microsoft's activities, Novell claims, were intended to and did restrain competition in the PC operating-system market by keeping the barriers to entry into that market high. Thus, we conclude that Novell has alleged harm of the type the antitrust laws were intended to prevent.

[17] We now turn to the second facet of antitrust injury: the causal connection between Novell's injuries and Microsoft's alleged antitrust violations. Novell claims that its market share in the office-productivity-applications market was eroded as a result of Microsoft's activity, which was designed to and effectively did elevate the barriers to entry into the PC operating-systems market. As chronicled earlier in this opinion, Novell complains that Microsoft withheld key technical information from its software designers, disadvantaging Novell in preparing for the launch of the Windows 95 operating system; that Microsoft exploited its monopoly power to require or encourage OEMs to refrain from installing Novell's products on their computers, cutting off Novell's distribution channels; and that Microsoft required Novell to use Windows-specific technologies in order to be certified as Windows-compatible, degrading Novell's products' performance on other operating systems and harming their advantageous compatibility. All of these activities allegedly had the effect of thwarting the ability of Novell's products to lower the applications barrier to entry into the operating-system market, therefore harming competition in that market. [. . .]

[18] In sum, the first two *AGC* factors weigh in favor of granting Novell antitrust standing. The facts alleged by Novell, taken as true for the purposes of this appeal, are sufficient to demonstrate that Novell suffered an antitrust injury and that its injury can be traced to Microsoft's alleged antitrust violations. While the showing of an antitrust injury demonstrates that a case is of the type for which antitrust standing is recognized, such a showing is not necessarily sufficient to demonstrate that the particular plaintiff has antitrust standing. Thus, we now turn to an analysis of the remaining *AGC* factors. [. . .]

[19] The latter three *AGC* factors require us to consider the directness of the alleged injury; the existence of more direct victims of the alleged antitrust injury; and problems of identifying damages and apportioning them among those directly and indirectly harmed. These additional factors are intended to further restrict entry into the federal courts for private enforcement of the antitrust laws. [. . .]

[20] Considerations of the directness of the plaintiff's injury and of the existence of more-directly harmed parties are closely related. Anti-trust law favors granting standing to the most direct victims of defendants' anticompetitive conduct and denying standing to more remote victims on the theory that the direct victims have the greatest motivation to act as private attorney[s] general and to vindicate the public interest in antitrust enforcement. Further, compensating only direct victims avoids duplicative recoveries. Therefore, the existence of an identifiable, more-directly harmed class of victims with the incentive to sue under the antitrust laws weighs against granting

standing to a more remote plaintiff. If, however, there is no more-directly harmed party with motivation to act as a private attorney general than the plaintiff, the risk of duplicative recoveries on the one hand, or the danger of complex apportionment of damages on the other is mitigated. [. . .]

[21] Here, Novell alleges that its software applications' popularity, quality, and ability to function well on multiple operating systems posed a potential threat to Microsoft's Windows monopoly by offering competing PC operating systems a bridge across the applications barrier to entry (i.e., the "moat" that protects Windows's monopoly) into that market. Novell claims that because of this threat, Microsoft directly targeted its products. As noted above, Microsoft's specific intent with respect to Novell is not the decisive factor, but it is evidence that Microsoft viewed Novell as a threat that could enable competitors to gain a foothold in the operating-systems market. Furthermore, Microsoft's withholding of information from Novell's software developers relating to Windows 95 clearly has no more direct victim than Novell. Finally, Microsoft's exclusive deals with OEMs that ensured that Novell's products would not be preinstalled on new PCs built by those OEMs directly curtailed Novell's distribution channels.

[22] Although Microsoft argues that a long list of better-situated plaintiffs than Novell exists, it mentions none by name or by category. Nevertheless, we surmise that such plaintiffs might include potentially competing operating systems, the OEMs who were restrained from installing Novell's products on computers they manufactured, or even consumers who purchased computers installed with Microsoft products at an inflated price because of a lack of competition. Without addressing whether plaintiffs representing each of these groups would have antitrust standing, we note that none of these parties has sued Microsoft on the theory that Microsoft's alleged destruction of Novell's dominant office-productivity applications harmed competition in the PC operating-system market. It may be that OEMs, for example, are too dependent on relationships with Microsoft for their business livelihood to have the incentive to pursue claims under § 4. This suggests that Novell may be the best-situated plaintiff to assert these claims. Indeed, today Novell may be one of the few private plaintiffs whose claims in this regard are neither time-barred nor too tenuous to support antitrust standing. [. . .]

[23] Finally, we turn to the fifth *AGC* factor which considers whether a finding of antitrust standing would lead to problems of identifying damages and apportioning them among those directly and indirectly harmed. Cases where this factor has been found to bar standing often involve potential plaintiffs indirectly injured by the allegedly anticompetitive behavior, raising the specter of complex apportionment of damages among, or duplicative recoveries by, direct and indirect victims of such conduct. Because we have already determined, on the record before us, that Microsoft's allegedly anticompetitive conduct was directly aimed at Novell, there is little risk that any damages Novell might prove would need to be allocated or apportioned among any more-directly injured parties.

[24] We therefore find that the *AGC* factors favor granting standing to Novell . . . . We thus affirm the district court's denial of Microsoft's motion to dismiss as to these claims on the antitrust-standing issue.

2. Antitrust Injury

A long line of cases have focused on the first core of antitrust standing: the requirement that the plaintiff must demonstrate the "right" kind of injury, including by establishing what the Court calls "antitrust injury."[1028]

The seminal case on antitrust injury is *Brunswick*—a case which pre-dated *AGC* by a few years—in which a plaintiff complained that a competitor had been allowed to consummate an unlawful anticompetitive merger. The plaintiff's claimed injury in that case arose not from an anticompetitive overcharge, but from the fact that it faced competition from the merged firm, and suffered competitive losses as a result. The Third Circuit saw no problem with such a suit: after all, the plaintiff's injuries were fairly traceable to the defendant's unlawful actions.[1029] But

---

[1028] There is a huge literature on antitrust injury. *See, e.g.*, Ronald W. Davis, *Standing on Shaky Ground: The Strangely Elusive Doctrine of Antitrust Injury*, 70 Antitrust L.J. 697 (2003); Jonathan M. Jacobson & Tracy Greer, *Twenty-One Years of Antitrust Injury: Down the Alley with* Brunswick v. Pueblo Bowl-o-Mat, 66 Antitrust L.J. 273 (1998); Roger D. Blair & Jeffrey L. Harrison, *Rethinking Antitrust Injury*, 42 Vand. L. Rev. 1539 (1989); William H. Page, *Antitrust Damages and Economic Efficiency: An Approach to Antitrust Injury*, 47 U. Chi. L. Rev. (1979).

[1029] *See* NBO Indus. Treadway Companies, Inc. v. Brunswick Corp., 523 F.2d 262, 265 (3d Cir. 1975), *vacated sub nom.* Brunswick Corp. v. Pueblo Bowl-O-Mat, Inc., 429 U.S. 477 (1977).

the Supreme Court invoked the underlying purposes of the antitrust laws to conclude that this kind of "injury" could not be the basis for antitrust litigation.

Brunswick Corp. v. Pueblo Bowl-O-Mat, Inc.
429 U.S. 477 (1977)

Justice Marshall.

[1] Petitioner [Brunswick Corp.] is one of the two largest manufacturers of bowling equipment in the United States. Respondents [including Pueblo Bowl-O-Mat, Inc.] are three of the 10 bowling centers owned by Treadway Companies, Inc. Since 1965, petitioner has acquired and operated a large number of bowling centers, including six in the markets in which respondents operate. [. . .]

[2] Respondents initiated this action in June 1966, alleging . . . that these acquisitions might substantially lessen competition or tend to create a monopoly in violation of s 7 of the Clayton Act. Respondents sought damages . . . for three times "the reasonably expectable profits to be made (by respondents) from the operation of their bowling centers." Respondents also sought a divestiture order, an injunction against future acquisitions, and such "other further and different relief" as might be appropriate . . .

[3] Trial was held in the spring of 1973, following an initial mistrial due to a hung jury. To establish a s 7 violation, respondents sought to prove that because of its size, petitioner had the capacity to lessen competition in the markets it had entered by driving smaller competitors out of business. To establish damages, respondents attempted to show that had petitioner allowed the defaulting centers to close, respondents' profits would have increased. At respondents' request, the jury was instructed in accord with respondents' theory as to the nature of the violation and the basis for damages. The jury returned a verdict in favor of respondents in the amount of $2,358,030, which represented the minimum estimate by respondents of the additional income they would have realized had the acquired centers been closed. As required by law, the District Court trebled the damages. It also awarded respondents costs and attorneys' fees totaling $446,977.32, and, sitting as a court of equity, it ordered petitioner to divest itself of the centers involved here. Petitioner appealed.

[4] . . . [On appeal, the Third Circuit] found that a properly instructed jury could have concluded that petitioner was a "giant" whose entry into a "market of pygmies" might lessen horizontal retail competition, because such a "giant" "has greater ease of entry into the market, can accomplish cost-savings by investing in new equipment, can resort to low or below cost sales to sustain itself against competition for a longer period, and can obtain more favorable credit terms." [. . .]

[5] The issue for decision is a narrow one. Petitioner does not presently contest the Court of Appeals' conclusion that a properly instructed jury could have found the acquisitions unlawful. Nor does petitioner challenge the Court of Appeals' determination that the evidence would support a finding that had petitioner not acquired these centers, they would have gone out of business and respondents' income would have increased. Petitioner questions only whether antitrust damages are available where the sole injury alleged is that competitors were continued in business, thereby denying respondents an anticipated increase in market shares. [. . .]

[6] Section 4 [of the Clayton Act, 15 U.S.C. § 15]. . . is in essence a remedial provision. It provides treble damages to "(a)ny person who shall be injured in his business or property by reason of anything forbidden in the antitrust laws . . . ." Of course, treble damages also play an important role in penalizing wrongdoers and deterring wrongdoing, as we also have frequently observed. It nevertheless is true that the treble-damages provision, which makes awards available only to injured parties, and measures the awards by a multiple of the injury actually proved, is designed primarily as a remedy.

[7] Intermeshing a statutory prohibition against acts that have a potential to cause certain harms with a damages action intended to remedy those harms is not without difficulty. Plainly, to recover damages respondents must prove more than that petitioner violated s 7, since such proof establishes only that injury may result. Respondents contend that the only additional element they need demonstrate is that they are in a worse position than they would have been had petitioner not committed those acts. The Court of Appeals agreed, holding compensable

any loss causally linked to the mere presence of the violator in the market. Because this holding divorces antitrust recovery from the purposes of the antitrust laws without a clear statutory command to do so, we cannot agree with it.

[8] Every merger of two existing entities into one, whether lawful or unlawful, has the potential for producing economic readjustments that adversely affect some persons. But Congress has not condemned mergers on that account; it has condemned them only when they may produce anticompetitive effects. Yet under the Court of Appeals' holding, once a merger is found to violate s 7, all dislocations caused by the merger are actionable, regardless of whether those dislocations have anything to do with the reason the merger was condemned. This holding would make s 4 recovery entirely fortuitous, and would authorize damages for losses which are of no concern to the antitrust laws.

[9] Both of these consequences are well illustrated by the facts of this case. If the acquisitions here were unlawful, it is because they brought a "deep pocket" parent into a market of "pygmies." Yet respondents' injury[—]the loss of income that would have accrued had the acquired centers gone bankrupt[—]bears no relationship to the size of either the acquiring company or its competitors. Respondents would have suffered the identical "loss" but no compensable injury had the acquired centers instead obtained refinancing or been purchased by "shallow pocket" parents as the Court of Appeals itself acknowledged. Thus, respondents' injury was not of the type that the statute was intended to forestall.

[10] But the antitrust laws are not merely indifferent to the injury claimed here. At base, respondents complain that by acquiring the failing centers petitioner preserved competition, thereby depriving respondents of the benefits of increased concentration. The damages respondents obtained are designed to provide them with the profits they would have realized had competition been reduced. The antitrust laws, however, were enacted for the protection of competition not competitors. It is inimical to the purposes of these laws to award damages for the type of injury claimed here.

[11] Of course, Congress is free, if it desires, to mandate damages awards for all dislocations caused by unlawful mergers despite the peculiar consequences of so doing. But because of these consequences, we should insist upon a clear expression of a congressional purpose, before attributing such an intent to Congress. We can find no such expression in either the language or the legislative history of s 4. To the contrary, it is far from clear that the loss of windfall profits that would have accrued had the acquired centers failed even constitutes "injury" within the meaning of s 4. And it is quite clear that if respondents were injured, it was not "by reason of anything forbidden in the antitrust laws": while respondents' loss occurred "by reason of" the unlawful acquisitions, it did not occur "by reason of" that which made the acquisitions unlawful.

[12] We therefore hold that the plaintiffs to recover treble damages on account of s 7 violations, they must prove more than injury causally linked to an illegal presence in the market. Plaintiffs must prove antitrust injury, which is to say injury of the type the antitrust laws were intended to prevent and that flows from that which makes defendants' acts unlawful. The injury should reflect the anticompetitive effect either of the violation or of anticompetitive acts made possible by the violation. It should, in short, be the type of loss that the claimed violations . . . would be likely to cause.

* * *

Brunswick thus stands for the principle that, in order to bring a private action for an illegal merger or other antitrust violation, a plaintiff must be injured by the *loss of competition* resulting from the challenged transaction or practice, not from the mere fact of the illegal practice, and certainly not from additional competition!

Although *Brunswick* itself involved an action for damages following a merger, it soon became a landmark in the law of private antitrust enforcement more generally. In *McCready* in 1982, for example, the same principle was applied to a Section 1 damages claim[1030]; in *Cargill* in 1986 the Court confirmed that it applies to actions for an injunction[1031]; and later, in *Atlantic Richfield* in 1990, it was applied even to a *per se* antitrust violation.[1032]

These cases cemented the view of antitrust's purpose that underpinned *Brunswick*. In *Cargill*, just as in *Brunswick* itself, the plaintiff's core complaint was the merged firm would be a successful competitor to whom the plaintiff would lose share and profits. But again—as you may remember from Chapter I—the Court held the door closed:

> Monfort's first claim is that after the merger, Excel would lower its prices to some level at or slightly above its costs in order to compete with other packers for market share. Excel would be in a position to do this because of the multi-plant efficiencies its acquisition of Spencer would provide. To remain competitive, Monfort would have to lower its prices; as a result, Monfort would suffer a loss in profitability, but would not be driven out of business. The question is whether Monfort's loss of profits in such circumstances constitutes antitrust injury. [. . .]

> *Brunswick* holds that the antitrust laws do not require the courts to protect small businesses from the loss of profits due to continued competition, but only against the loss of profits from practices forbidden by the antitrust laws. The kind of competition that Monfort alleges here, competition for increased market share, is not activity forbidden by the antitrust laws. It is simply, as petitioners claim, vigorous competition. To hold that the antitrust laws protect competitors from the loss of profits due to such price competition would, in effect, render illegal any decision by a firm to cut prices in order to increase market share. The antitrust laws require no such perverse result, for it is in the interest of competition to permit dominant firms to engage in vigorous competition, including price competition."[1033]

Of course, these limitations are not complete, and, in the years since *Brunswick*, plenty of private plaintiffs have succeeded in showing antitrust injury.

CASENOTE: Steves and Sons, Inc. v. JELD-WEN, Inc.
988 F.3d 690 (4th Cir. 2021)

A high-profile success in showing antitrust injury was managed by Steves and Sons, in a prominent recent private merger challenge. The case took place in markets for doors and for the "doorskin" inputs used to make them. Before the relevant transaction took place, there were three major suppliers of doorskins, each of which was also vertically integrated downstream into doors: Jeld-Wen, CMI, and Masonite. There were also a number of unintegrated downstream door suppliers (or "independents"), of which Steves was one.

In 2012, Jeld-Wen acquired CMI, having given Steves and two other large independents long-term supply contracts to help win their support for the deal. Accordingly, Steves did not oppose the transaction when DOJ initially reviewed it. DO allowed the deal to close without challenge. But problems soon started. The quality of doors that Steves received from Jeld-Wen began to fall, and prices began to rise (even though Jeld-Wen's own costs were falling). In 2014, Masonite announced that it would stop selling doorskins to independents altogether. Later that year, Jeld-Wen gave notice to Steves of termination of supply under the existing contract (triggering a 7-year contractual notice period). In June 2016, Steves filed a private challenge to the merger. Among other things, Jeld-Wen argued that the existence of the supply contract between Steves and Jeld-Wen meant that Steves had not suffered *antitrust* injury, but merely contract damages. Steves prevailed at trial, and Jeld-Wen appealed.

On appeal, the Fourth Circuit directly evaluated whether Steves's complaint was "simply a contract claim masquerading as a candidate for treble damages." It approached this question by asking "whether Steves would have suffered an identical loss if Jeld-Wen had breached the Supply Agreement absent the merger."

The court concluded that Steves had indeed established antitrust injury arising from the merger. That injury took a number of forms. First, the merger eliminated Steves's opportunity to buy doorskins from CMI, the acquisition

---

[1030] Blue Shield of Virginia v. McCready, 457 U.S. 465, 482–83 (1982).

[1031] Cargill, Inc. v. Monfort of Colo., Inc., 479 U.S. 104, 122 (1986).

[1032] Atl. Richfield Co. v. USA Petroleum Co., 495 U.S. 328, 341–45 (1990).

[1033] Cargill, Inc. v. Monfort of Colo., Inc., 479 U.S. 104, 114–16 (1986).

target, as an alternative to Jeld-Wen's doorskins: access to CMI would have mitigated the harm from the contract breach. Second, the merger eliminated Steves's opportunity to buy from Masonite: a reasonable jury could have concluded that Masonite's refusal to offer reasonable terms to Steves was a consequence of the duopoly created by the transaction. Had the merger not taken place, the court reasoned, Masonite would likely have agreed to sell doorskins to Steves on more favorable terms. Third, the merger caused Jeld-Wen to degrade its performance of the contract to Steves in ways that did not constitute contract breaches. For example, "the contract didn't require Jeld-Wen to supply high-quality products, maintain a liberal reimbursement policy, or come within 3% of other suppliers' prices. Competition incentivized Jeld-Wen to do those things, and the merger reduced that incentive." Finally, the court noted, it appeared that Jeld-Wen subjectively intended to inflict injury on Steves of exactly the kind the antitrust laws were intended to prevent: "Jeld-Wen sought to leverage its enhanced market power to hurt its customers, including Steves. And that intent is relevant to our antitrust-injury analysis."

In a final effort, Jeld-Wen argued that Steves had failed to quantify the "antitrust impact" of the merger on its business. Specifically, Steves had failed to "construct a hypothetical market in which the merger never happened and show how it would have been better off therein. And Steves failed to do that, Jeld-Wen insists, because it didn't try to quantify the price of doorskins in this hypothetical market". But the court rejected this argument too. There was no requirement under existing law to show "antitrust impact" in a sense different from "antitrust injury." Nor had Jeld-Wen asked for such an jury instruction at trial. Here, ultimately, it was enough that "Steves could prove causation by demonstrating that the merger (1) kept it from buying from other suppliers, thereby exacerbating its contract damages, and (2) disincentivized JELD-WEN from offering quality products and customer service. A reasonable jury could find that Steves succeeded in its proof."

NOTES

1) Why shouldn't a plaintiff who is injured by an antitrust violation be able to sue for that harm? What is the best justification for allowing an injury from illegal conduct to go uncompensated and unpunished? What is the best argument for allowing *anyone* injured by unlawful conduct to sue for it, regardless of the precise means of causation?

2) How would you define "antitrust injury" to someone with no background in antitrust?

3) Do you prefer the Fourth Circuit's five-factor standing test or the Eleventh Circuit's two-part test? In what circumstances would they give different results?

4) When and why is it appropriate for a court to deny recovery to a plaintiff who has in fact brought a claim, and who is in other respects a proper plaintiff, on the ground that other entities, who have not in fact sued, might be "better placed" to do so? Are you aware of other areas of law in which we take this approach?

5) Does the availability of federal and state enforcement counsel in favor of a narrow approach to antitrust standing for private plaintiffs? If so, should a court consider whether a case is likely to attract government enforcers as part of the standing analysis?

3. The Indirect Purchaser Rule

One of the most important and controversial threads of antitrust standing doctrine is the so-called "indirect purchaser rule."[1034] The rule has two main elements. The first, established in *Hanover Shoe* in 1968, is the proposition that a defendant cannot raise the *defensive* argument that an antitrust private plaintiff in fact avoided injury by "passing on" its harm to purchasers further down the supply chain (*e.g.*, in the form of increased downstream prices). The second, established in *Illinois Brick* in 1977, is the proposition that a plaintiff cannot *offensively* bring suit on the ground that it was the recipient of such a passed-on overcharge from an intermediate

---

[1034] *See, e.g.*, William Breit & Kenneth G. Elzinga, *Private Antitrust Enforcement: The New Learning*, 28 J. L. & Econ. 405, 420 (1985) ("The limitation *Illinois Brick* placed on private actions, its candid departure from the compensation goal, its obvious concern with ruinous awards, and its concern about litigating complex economic issues of cause and effect are well known and oft debated."); William M. Landes & Richard A. Posner, *Should Indirect Purchasers Have Standing to Sue under the Antitrust Laws? An Economic Analysis of the Rule of* Illinois Brick, 46 U. Chi. L. Rev. 602 (1979). The Court appears to regard the indirect-purchaser rule as a component of standing doctrine. *See, e.g.*, *Nat'l Football League v. Ninth Inning, Inc.*, 141 S. Ct. 56, 57 (2020) (Kavanaugh, J., statement respecting denial of certiorari) (doubting antitrust standing by reason of the indirect-purchaser rule). *See also* Roger D. Blair & Jeffrey L. Harrison, *Reexamining the Role of* Illinois Brick *in Modern Standing Analysis*, 68 Geo. Wash. L. Rev. 1 (1999).

agent in the supply chain between the plaintiff and the defendant. Together, these propositions mean that direct purchasers must do the suing and recovering, even when the harms were distributed further down the chain.

Start by reading the Court's reasoning in *Hanover Shoe*. How many reasons does the Court give for denying the passing-on (or, sometimes, just "pass-on") defense? Are they all persuasive?

Hanover Shoe, Inc. v. United Shoe Machinery Corp.

392 U.S. 481 (1968)

Justice White.

[1] Section 4 of the Clayton Act provides that any person "who shall be injured in his business or property by reason of anything forbidden in the antitrust laws may sue therefor and shall recover threefold the damages by him sustained." We think it sound to hold that when a buyer shows that the price paid by him for materials purchased for use in his business is illegally high and also shows the amount of the overcharge, he has made out a prima facie case of injury and damage within the meaning of s 4.

[2] If in the face of the overcharge the buyer does nothing and absorbs the loss, he is entitled to treble damages. This much seems conceded. The reason is that he has paid more than he should and his property has been illegally diminished, for had the price paid been lower his profits would have been higher. It is also clear that if the buyer, responding to the illegal price, maintains his own price but takes steps to increase his volume or to decrease other costs, his right to damages is not destroyed. Though he may manage to maintain his profit level, he would have made more if his purchases from the defendant had cost him less. We hold that the buyer is equally entitled to damages if he raises the price for his own product. As long as the seller continues to charge the illegal price, he takes from the buyer more than the law allows. At whatever price the buyer sells, the price he pays the seller remains illegally high, and his profits would be greater were his costs lower. [. . .]

[3] United seeks to limit the general principle that the victim of an overcharge is damaged within the meaning of s 4 to the extent of that overcharge. The rule, United argues, should be subject to the defense that economic circumstances were such that the overcharged buyer could only charge his customers a higher price because the price to him was higher. It is argued that in such circumstances the buyer suffers no loss from the overcharge. This situation might be present, it is said, where the overcharge is imposed equally on all of a buyer's competitors and where the demand for the buyer's product is so inelastic that the buyer and his competitors could all increase their prices by the amount of the cost increase without suffering a consequent decline in sales.

[4] We are not impressed with the argument that sound laws of economics require recognizing this defense. A wide range of factors influence a company's pricing policies. Normally the impact of a single change in the relevant conditions cannot be measured after the fact; indeed a businessman may be unable to state whether, had one fact been different (a single supply less expensive, general economic conditions more buoyant, or the labor market tighter, for example), he would have chosen a different price. Equally difficult to determine, in the real economic world rather than an economist's hypothetical model, is what effect a change in a company's price will have on its total sales. Finally, costs per unit for a different volume of total sales are hard to estimate. Even if it could be shown that the buyer raised his price in response to, and in the amount of, the overcharge and that his margin of profit and total sales had not thereafter declined, there would remain the nearly insuperable difficulty of demonstrating that the particular plaintiff could not or would not have raised his prices absent the overcharge or maintained the higher price had the overcharge been discontinued. Since establishing the applicability of the passing-on defense would require a convincing showing of each of these virtually unascertainable figures, the task would normally prove insurmountable. On the other hand, it is not unlikely that if the existence of the defense is generally confirmed, antitrust defendants will frequently seek to establish its applicability. Treble-damage actions would often require additional long and complicated proceedings involving massive evidence and complicated theories.

[5] In addition, if buyers are subjected to the passing-on defense, those who buy from them would also have to meet the challenge that they passed on the higher price to their customers. These ultimate consumers, in today's case the buyers of single pairs of shoes, would have only a tiny stake in a lawsuit and little interest in attempting a class action. In consequence, those who violate the antitrust laws by price fixing or monopolizing would retain the

fruits of their illegality because no one was available who would bring suit against them. Treble-damage actions, the importance of which the Court has many times emphasized, would be substantially reduced in effectiveness.

[6] Our conclusion is that Hanover proved injury and the amount of its damages for the purposes of its treble-damage suit when it proved that United had overcharged it during the damage period and showed the amount of the overcharge; United was not entitled to assert a passing-on defense. We recognize that there might be situations—for instance, when an overcharged buyer has a pre-existing 'cost-plus' contract, thus making it easy to prove that he has not been damaged—where the considerations requiring that the passing-on defense not be permitted in this case would not be present. We also recognize that where no differential can be proved between the price unlawfully charged and some price that the seller was required by law to charge, establishing damages might require a showing of loss of profits to the buyer.

* * *

Nine years later, the *Hanover Shoe* was on the other foot: this time it was a plaintiff who was pointing to the fact of some passing-on by a direct trading partner. In that case—*Illinois Brick*—the Court held that the plaintiffs were equally forbidden from pointing to the fact of passing-on in order to recover from a defendant higher up the supply chain.

Illinois Brick Co. v. Illinois
431 U.S. 720 (1977)

Justice White.

[1] Respondent State of Illinois, on behalf of itself and respondent local governmental entities, brought this antitrust treble-damages action under s 4 of the Clayton Act, alleging that petitioners had engaged in a combination and conspiracy to fix the prices of concrete block in violation of s 1 of the Sherman Act. The complaint alleged that the amounts paid by respondents for concrete block were more than $3 million higher by reason of this price-fixing conspiracy. The only way in which the antitrust violation alleged could have injured respondents is if all or part of the overcharge was passed on by the masonry and general contractors to respondents, rather than being absorbed at the first two levels of distribution.

[2] Petitioner manufacturers moved for partial summary judgment against all plaintiffs that were indirect purchasers of concrete block from petitioners, contending that as a matter of law only direct purchasers could sue for the alleged overcharge. The District Court granted petitioners' motion, but the Court of Appeals reversed, holding that indirect purchasers such as respondents in this case can recover treble damages for an illegal overcharge if they can prove that the overcharge was passed on to them through intervening links in the distribution chain.

[3] We granted certiorari to resolve a conflict among the Courts of Appeals on the question whether the offensive use of pass-on authorized by the decision below is consistent with *Hanover Shoe*'s restrictions on the defensive use of pass-on. We hold that it is not, and we reverse. We reach this result in two steps. First, we conclude that whatever rule is to be adopted regarding pass-on in antitrust damages actions, it must apply equally to plaintiffs and defendants. Because *Hanover Shoe* would bar petitioners from using respondents' pass-on theory as a defense to a treble-damages suit by the direct purchasers (the masonry contractors), we are faced with the choice of overruling (or narrowly limiting) *Hanover Shoe* or of applying it to bar respondents' attempt to use this pass-on theory offensively. Second, we decline to abandon the construction given s 4 in *Hanover Shoe* that the overcharged direct purchaser, and not others in the chain of manufacture or distribution, is the party "injured in his business or property" within the meaning of the section in the absence of a convincing demonstration that the Court was wrong in *Hanover Shoe* to think that the effectiveness of the antitrust treble-damages action would be substantially reduced by adopting a rule that any party in the chain may sue to recover the fraction of the overcharge allegedly absorbed by it.

[4] [We first] consider the . . . position, adopted by our dissenting Brethren, by the United States as amicus curiae, and by lower courts that have allowed offensive use of pass-on, that the unavailability of a pass-on theory to a

defendant should not necessarily preclude its use by plaintiffs seeking treble damages against that defendant. Under this view, *Hanover Shoe*'s rejection of pass-on would continue to apply to defendants unless direct and indirect purchasers were both suing the defendant in the same action; but it would not bar indirect purchasers from attempting to show that the overcharge had been passed on to them. We reject this position for two reasons.

[5] First, allowing offensive but not defensive use of pass-on would create a serious risk of multiple liability for defendants. Even though an indirect purchaser had already recovered for all or part of an overcharge passed on to it, the direct purchaser would still recover automatically the full amount of the overcharge that the indirect purchaser had shown to be passed on; similarly, following an automatic recovery of the full overcharge by the direct purchaser, the indirect purchaser could sue to recover the same amount. The risk of duplicative recoveries created by unequal application of the Hanover Shoe rule is much more substantial than in the more usual situation where the defendant is sued in two different lawsuits by plaintiffs asserting conflicting claims to the same fund. [. . .]

[6] Second, the reasoning of *Hanover Shoe* cannot justify unequal treatment of plaintiffs and defendants with respect to the permissibility of pass-on arguments. The principal basis for the decision in *Hanover Shoe* was the Court's perception of the uncertainties and difficulties in analyzing price and output decisions "in the real economic world rather than an economist's hypothetical model," and of the costs to the judicial system and the efficient enforcement of the antitrust laws of attempting to reconstruct those decisions in the courtroom. This perception that the attempt to trace the complex economic adjustments to a change in the cost of a particular factor of production would greatly complicate and reduce the effectiveness of already protracted treble-damages proceedings applies with no less force to the assertion of pass-on theories by plaintiffs than it does to the assertion by defendants. [. . .]

[7] We are left, then, with two alternatives: either we must overrule *Hanover Shoe* (or at least narrowly confine it to its facts), or we must preclude respondents from seeking to recover on their pass-on theory. We choose the latter course. [. . .]

[8] Permitting the use of pass-on theories under s 4 essentially would transform treble-damages actions into massive efforts to apportion the recovery among all potential plaintiffs that could have absorbed part of the overcharge from direct purchasers to middlemen to ultimate consumers. However appealing this attempt to allocate the overcharge might seem in theory, it would add whole new dimensions of complexity to treble-damages suits and seriously undermine their effectiveness.

[9] As we have indicated, potential plaintiffs at each level in the distribution chain are in a position to assert conflicting claims to a common fund the amount of the alleged overcharge by contending that the entire overcharge was absorbed at that particular level in the chain. A treble-damages action brought by one of these potential plaintiffs (or one class of potential plaintiffs) to recover the overcharge implicates all three of the interests that have traditionally been thought to support compulsory joinder of absent and potentially adverse claimants: the interest of the defendant in avoiding multiple liability for the fund; the interest of the absent potential plaintiffs in protecting their right to recover for the portion of the fund allocable to them; and the social interest in the efficient administration of justice and the avoidance of multiple litigation. [. . .]

[10] [A]llowing indirect purchasers to recover using pass-on theories, even under the optimistic assumption that joinder of potential plaintiffs will deal satisfactorily with problems of multiple litigation and liability, would transform treble-damages actions into massive multiparty litigations involving many levels of distribution and including large classes of ultimate consumers remote from the defendant. In treble-damages actions by ultimate consumers, the overcharge would have to be apportioned among the relevant wholesalers, retailers, and other middlemen, whose representatives presumably should be joined. And in suits by direct purchasers or middlemen, the interests of ultimate consumers are similarly implicated.

[11] There is thus a strong possibility that indirect purchasers remote from the defendant would be parties to virtually every treble-damages action (apart from those brought against defendants at the retail level). The Court's concern in *Hanover Shoe* to avoid weighing down treble-damages actions with the massive evidence and complicated theories, involved in attempting to establish a pass-on defense against a direct purchaser applies a fortiori to the

attempt to trace the effect of the overcharge through each step in the distribution chain from the direct purchaser to the ultimate consumer. We are no more inclined than we were in *Hanover Shoe* to ignore the burdens that such an attempt would impose on the effective enforcement of the antitrust laws. [. . .]

[12] The concern in *Hanover Shoe* for the complexity that would be introduced into treble-damages suits if pass-on theories were permitted was closely related to the Court's concern for the reduction in the effectiveness of those suits if brought by indirect purchasers with a smaller stake in the outcome than that of direct purchasers suing for the full amount of the overcharge. The apportionment of the recovery throughout the distribution chain would increase the overall costs of recovery by injecting extremely complex issues into the case; at the same time such an apportionment would reduce the benefits to each plaintiff by dividing the potential recovery among a much larger group. Added to the uncertainty of how much of an overcharge could be established at trial would be the uncertainty of how that overcharge would be apportioned among the various plaintiffs. This additional uncertainty would further reduce the incentive to sue. The combination of increasing the costs and diffusing the benefits of bringing a treble-damages action could seriously impair this important weapon of antitrust enforcement.

[13] We think the longstanding policy of encouraging vigorous private enforcement of the antitrust laws supports our adherence to the *Hanover Shoe* rule, under which direct purchasers are not only spared the burden of litigating the intricacies of pass-on but also are permitted to recover the full amount of the overcharge. We recognize that direct purchasers sometimes may refrain from bringing a treble-damages suit for fear of disrupting relations with their suppliers. But on balance, and until there are clear directions from Congress to the contrary, we conclude that the legislative purpose in creating a group of private attorneys general to enforce the antitrust laws under s 4, is better served by holding direct purchasers to be injured to the full extent of the overcharge paid by them than by attempting to apportion the overcharge among all that may have absorbed a part of it.

[14] It is true that, in elevating direct purchasers to a preferred position as private attorneys general, the *Hanover Shoe* rule denies recovery to those indirect purchasers who may have been actually injured by antitrust violations. Of course, as Mr. Justice BRENNAN points out in dissent, from the deterrence standpoint, it is irrelevant to whom damages are paid, so long as some one redresses the violation. But s 4 has another purpose in addition to deterring violators and depriving them of the fruits of their illegality; it is also designed to compensate victims of antitrust violations for their injuries. *Hanover Shoe* does further the goal of compensation to the extent that the direct purchaser absorbs at least some and often most of the overcharge. In view of the considerations supporting the *Hanover Shoe* rule, we are unwilling to carry the compensation principle to its logical extreme by attempting to allocate damages among all those within the defendant's chain of distribution, especially because we question the extent to which such an attempt would make individual victims whole for actual injuries suffered rather than simply depleting the overall recovery in litigation over pass-on issues. Many of the indirect purchasers barred from asserting pass-on claims under the *Hanover Shoe* rule have such a small stake in the lawsuit that even if they were to recover as part of a class, only a small fraction would be likely to come forward to collect their damages. And given the difficulty of ascertaining the amount absorbed by any particular indirect purchaser, there is little basis for believing that the amount of the recovery would reflect the actual injury suffered.

Justice Brennan, dissenting, joined by Justices Marshall and Blackmun.

[15] Today's decision flouts Congress' purpose and severely undermines the effectiveness of the private treble-damages action as an instrument of antitrust enforcement. For in many instances, the brunt of antitrust injuries is borne by indirect purchasers, often ultimate consumers of a product, as increased costs are passed along the chain of distribution. In these instances, the Court's decision frustrates both the compensation and deterrence objectives of the treble-damages action. Injured consumers are precluded from recovering damages from manufacturers, and direct purchasers who act as middlemen have little incentive to sue suppliers so long as they may pass on the bulk of the illegal overcharges to the ultimate consumers. [. . .]

[16] *Hanover Shoe* confronted the Court with the choice . . . of interpreting s 4 in a way that might overcompensate the plaintiff, who had certainly suffered some injury, or of defining it in a way that under-deters the violator by allowing him to retain a portion of his ill-gotten overcharges. The Court chose to interpret s 4 so as to allow the plaintiff to recover for the entire overcharge. This choice was consistent with recognition of the importance of the

treble-damages action in deterring antitrust violations. But *Hanover Shoe* certainly did not imply that an indirect purchaser would not also have a cause of action under s 4 when the illegal overcharges were passed on to him.

[17] Despite the superficial appeal of the argument that *Hanover Shoe* should be applied "consistently," thus precluding plaintiffs and defendants alike from proving that increased costs were passed along the chain of distribution, there are sound reasons for treating offensive and defensive passing-on cases differently. The interests at stake in "offensive" passing-on cases, where the indirect purchasers sue for damages for their injuries, are simply not the same as the interests at stake in the *Hanover Shoe*, or "defensive" passing-on situation. There is no danger in this case, for example, as there was in *Hanover Shoe*, that the defendant will escape liability and frustrate the objectives of the treble-damages action. Rather, the same policies of insuring the continued effectiveness of the treble-damages action and preventing wrongdoers from retaining the spoils of their misdeeds favor allowing indirect purchasers to prove that overcharges were passed on to them. *Hanover Shoe* thus can and should be limited to cases of defensive assertion of the passing-on defense to antitrust liability, where direct and indirect purchasers are not parties in the same action. . . . The attempt to transform a rejection of a defense because it unduly hampers antitrust enforcement into a reason for a complete refusal to entertain the claims of a certain class of plaintiffs seems an ingenious attempt to turn the decision (in *Hanover Shoe*) and its underlying rationale on its head.

CASENOTE: Apple Inc. v. Pepper
139 S.Ct. 1514 (2019)

Unfortunately, despite the effort in *Illinois Brick* to maintain a bright-line rule, that bright line is harder to see in some cases than others. In *Pepper*, the Supreme Court considered the case of the operator of an app-store platform that deals with both developers and consumers. The complaint in that case was that Apple had engaged in anticompetitive conduct that resulted in overcharging for apps in the iPhone App Store. Can consumers sue Apple on the theory that they purchase the apps from Apple? Or do consumers "really" purchase from app developers, who set the price of the apps in the store?

The Court held that that question had an easy answer. "In this case, unlike in *Illinois Brick*, the iPhone owners are not consumers at the bottom of a vertical distribution chain who are attempting to sue manufacturers at the top of the chain. There is no intermediary in the distribution chain between Apple and the consumer. The iPhone owners purchase apps directly from the retailer Apple, who is the alleged antitrust violator. The iPhone owners pay the alleged overcharge directly to Apple. The absence of an intermediary is dispositive. Under *Illinois Brick*, the iPhone owners are direct purchasers from Apple and are proper plaintiffs to maintain this antitrust suit."

Apple, of course, had offered another view: "Apple's theory is that *Illinois Brick* allows consumers to sue only the party who sets the retail price, whether or not that party sells the good or service directly to the complaining party. . . . Here, Apple argues that the app developers, not Apple, set the retail price charged to consumers, which according to Apple means that the consumers may not sue Apple."

But there were three things wrong, in the Court's telling, with Apple's position. First, the statutory text and the weight of *Illinois Brick* cut against it, by setting a bright-line rule in the interests of administrability: "When there is no intermediary between the purchaser and the antitrust violator, the purchaser may sue." Second, it was economically arbitrary, turning on the intricacies of retailers' contracts with the upstream party. "[U]nder Apple's rule a consumer could sue a monopolistic retailer when the retailer set the retail price by marking up the price it had paid the manufacturer or supplier for the good or service," but not "a monopolistic retailer when the manufacturer or supplier set the retail price and the retailer took a commission on each sale." Third, if accepted, it would offer an easy way for retailers to structure deals with their upstream suppliers to evade antitrust liability.

Finally, the Court turned to what it took to be the three foundations of the *Illinois Brick* rule: (1) the imperative to facilitate more efficient enforcement of the antitrust laws; (2) the need to avoid complex damages calculations; and (3) the elimination of duplicative damages. Here, the first principle would be violated by "[l]eaving consumers at the mercy of monopolistic retailers simply because upstream suppliers could also sue the retailers." The second principle could not be understood to mean antitrust immunity "any time that a damages calculation might be complicated." And the third was consistent with allowing recovery here: "If the iPhone owners prevail, they will be entitled to the full amount of the unlawful overcharge that they paid to Apple. The overcharge has not been passed on by anyone to anyone." *Illinois Brick* did not enact a rule against liability from multiple classes of injured victims, whose harms my not be duplicative of one another. Apple would have to face the claims of the consumer plaintiffs.

However easy or difficult it may be to apply in practice, the rule in *Illinois Brick* is controversial, as it often involves allowing some (*i.e.*, direct purchasers) to recover for harm they have not in fact suffered while prohibiting others (*i.e.*, indirect purchasers) from recovering for harm that they have in fact sustained.

Perhaps unsurprisingly, many states have enacted statutes allowing indirect purchasers to recover for violations of state antitrust law.[1035] The resulting complexity informed the recommendation of the Antitrust Modernization Commission in 2007 to overrule the indirect-purchaser rule, at least in significant part.[1036]

Antitrust Modernization Commission, Report and Recommendations (April 2007)

[1] Direct and indirect purchaser litigation would be more efficient and more fair if it took place in one federal court for all purposes, including trial, and did not result in duplicative recoveries, denial of recoveries to persons who suffered injury, and windfall recoveries to persons who did not suffer injury. To facilitate this, Congress should enact a comprehensive statute with the following elements:

- Overrule *Illinois Brick* and *Hanover Shoe* to the extent necessary to allow both direct and indirect purchasers to sue to recover for actual damages from violations of federal antitrust law. Damages in such actions could not exceed the overcharges (trebled) incurred by direct purchasers. Damages should be apportioned among all purchaser plaintiffs—both direct and indirect—in full satisfaction of their claims in accordance with the evidence as to the extent of the actual damages they suffered.
- Allow removal of indirect purchaser actions brought under state antitrust law to federal court to the full extent permitted under Article III.
- Allow consolidation of all direct and indirect purchaser actions in a single federal forum for both pre-trial and trial proceedings.
- Allow for certification of classes of direct purchasers, consistent with current practice, without regard to whether the injury alleged was passed on to customers of the direct purchasers.

[. . .]

[2] The conflict between federal and state policies on indirect purchaser damage actions has created a variety of problems. Absent the consolidation of federal and state cases involving direct and indirect purchasers, defendants must respond to complaints about the same conduct in multiple courts. Burdensome and uncoordinated discovery increases costs to defendants and disadvantages plaintiffs as well, because they do not have access to materials produced in other actions. . . . With trials proceeding in at least two, and maybe more, different courts, a defendant may be liable for duplicative damages—the amount of the overcharge to the direct purchaser in the first instance, plus whatever overcharges the direct purchaser was able to pass on to indirect purchasers. Correspondingly, direct purchasers may receive "windfall" awards exceeding their actual damages. Furthermore, when all parties are not before a single court, it can be difficult to negotiate and implement a global settlement. Defendants also may confront costs due to the asymmetric application of collateral estoppel: a finding by one court that the defendant did violate the antitrust law may be used by plaintiffs to establish liability in other suits, but a finding in one suit that the defendant did not violate the antitrust laws may not be used by the defendant to seek dismissal of other suits. [. . .]

[1035] *See, e.g.*, Cal. Bus. & Prof. Code § 16750(a). The Supreme Court has sustained these "repealer" statutes against preemption challenge. California v. ARC Am. Corp., 490 U.S. 93, 101 (1989) ("There is no claim that the federal antitrust laws expressly pre-empt state laws permitting indirect purchaser recovery.").

[1036] Some members of the Commission dissented from this recommendation.

[3] To the maximum extent possible, a single federal court should hear all proceedings relevant to actions by direct and indirect purchasers alleging the same antitrust violation. To accomplish this, federal law should permit direct and indirect purchasers to recover the actual damages they suffer as the result of antitrust violations. The first step toward these goals is to overrule *Illinois Brick* and *Hanover Shoe* legislatively to the extent necessary to allow both direct and indirect purchasers to sue under federal law to recover for actual damages they suffer from antitrust violations resulting in an overcharge. Overruling *Illinois Brick* would increase fairness by ensuring that all indirect purchasers, not just those in states permitting such actions, could recover treble their actual damages under federal law for injuries attributable to antitrust violations. Overruling *Hanover Shoe* would limit direct purchasers to recovering treble their actual damages, rather than the full overcharge regardless of pass on, and will thus promote fairness by preventing windfall damage recoveries.

[4] Legislative overruling of *Illinois Brick* may encourage the resolution of direct and indirect purchaser litigation in a single forum, because indirect purchasers may choose to sue under federal antitrust laws rather than to bring state claims. In conjunction with the procedural components of the Commission's recommendation, this also should make resolution of all claims in a single forum easier. Federal recognition of indirect purchaser standing also will promote the development of a body of federal law governing the allocation of damages among direct and indirect purchasers. [. . .]

[5] To be sure, determinations of how to allocate damages among direct and indirect purchasers will often involve complex economic assessments of the extent to which each purchaser in the chain of distribution has suffered harm that can be traced to the overcharge. The federal courts have shown great ability to handle such complex economic issues, however, and they will develop rules and procedures to handle these issues. Consolidating all claims in a single proceeding will facilitate an appropriate allocation of relief among the claimants by the court. In addition, once all parties are before a single court, a global settlement becomes possible. Many of these disputes are likely to be settled; once liability and total damages are established, allocations of damages may often be determined by settlements among the claimants. Furthermore, limiting damages to the amount of the initial overcharge should streamline resolution of the litigation. Indeed, once the amount of overcharge has been determined, it may be possible to resolve the issues of how to allocate those damages among direct and indirect purchasers without the further involvement of the defendants.

NOTES

1) What is the best justification for the rule against indirect purchaser suits?
2) Does *Hanover Shoe* necessarily imply *Illinois Brick*?
3) Is there any point at all in keeping the *Illinois Brick* rule given the widespread availability of state-law causes of action for indirect purchasers?
4) Could *Apple v. Pepper* have plausibly come out any other way: that is, is there a sensible reading of the law on indirect-purchaser claims other than the one given by the Court? [1037]
5) Who is the direct purchaser of auctioneering services: the seller of the goods, the buyer, both, or neither? Do any of the following matter:
   a. which party literally hands over the cash to the auctioneer?
   b. whether the auctioneer styles the fee as a percentage commission on the value of the sale or a flat fee?
   c. whether either party negotiates with the auctioneer to reduce the fee?
   d. the nature of the challenged antitrust wrongdoing by the auctioneer?

4. "Efficient Enforcers"

In many circuits, even a direct purchaser may fail to establish antitrust standing if a court concludes that it would not be an "efficient enforcer" of the antitrust laws. Different circuits approach this analysis in different ways, but courts often consider: the directness and remoteness of the plaintiff's claimed injury; the existence of alternative

---

[1037] *See* Brief of Petitioner [Apple Inc.], Apple Inc. v. Pepper, Case No. 17-204 (Aug. 10. 2018).

(and better-situated) plaintiffs; and the extent to which damages are or may be speculative, uncertain, complex, or duplicative.[1038]

In *Gelboim*, the Second Circuit provided a detailed explanation of its own approach to this inquiry, in the context of an alleged conspiracy to depress the LIBOR interbank rate (broadly speaking, a price for interbank loans), but left it to the district court on remand to apply the resulting framework to the facts of the conspiracy.

CASENOTE: Gelboim v. Bank of Am. Corp.

823 F.3d 759 (2d Cir. 2016)

That case concerned an alleged conspiracy among 16 banks to depress the London Interbank Offered Rate ("LIBOR"), an indexed rate approximating the average rate of interest at which certain banks may borrow. The banks were sued by purchasers of financial instruments for which the rate of return was indexed to LIBOR: thus, depressing the LIBOR index also reduced their return.

The Second Circuit set out in some detail an analytical framework for determining whether the plaintiffs were "efficient enforcers of the antitrust laws." The court formulated the basic test as follows: "The four efficient enforcer factors are: (1) the directness or indirectness of the asserted injury, which requires evaluation of the chain of causation linking appellants' asserted injury and the Banks' alleged price-fixing; (2) the existence of more direct victims of the alleged conspiracy; (3) the extent to which appellants' damages claim is highly speculative; and (4) the importance of avoiding either the risk of duplicate recoveries on the one hand, or the danger of complex apportionment of damages on the other."

With respect to the first factor, the court highlighted that some of the plaintiffs had bought their financial instruments from entities that were not alleged to be part of the conspiracy. The court noted that this raised a complex issue in private-damages law: "umbrella" claims. These are suits involving allegations that the defendants' misconduct enabled or incentivized *other* market participants to raise their prices, and they are the subject of a circuit split in modern damages law.[1039] The court raised a concern that allowing umbrella recoveries could produce damages "disproportionate to wrongdoing .... Requiring the Banks to pay treble damages to every plaintiff who ended up on the wrong side of an independent LIBOR-denominated derivative swap would, if appellants' allegations were proved at trial, not only bankrupt 16 of the world's most important financial institutions, but also vastly extend the potential scope of antitrust liability in myriad markets where derivative instruments have proliferated."

With respect to the second factor, the court again raised concerns about the fact that plaintiff's theory of damages reached very broadly, including victims who had never dealt with the defendants. The court indicated that "not every victim of an antitrust violation needs to be compensated under the antitrust laws in order for the antitrust laws to be efficiently enforced," and emphasized that "one peculiar feature of this case is that remote victims (who acquired LIBOR-based instruments from any of thousands of non-defendant banks) would be injured to the same extent and in the same way as direct customers of the Banks. The bondholders, for example, purchased their

---

[1038] *See, e.g.*, Inform Inc. v. Google LLC, Case No. 21-13289, 2022 WL 3703958, at *5 (11th Cir. Aug. 26, 2022) ("We consider several non-exhaustive factors in determining whether a plaintiff would be an efficient enforcer of the antitrust laws, including the directness of the injury; the remoteness of the injury; whether other plaintiffs are better suited to bring suit; whether the damages are highly speculative; whether the calculation of damages would be highly complex and run the risk of duplicative recoveries; and whether the plaintiff would be able to efficiently and effectively enforce the judgment."); Kochert v. Greater Lafayette Health Servs., Inc., 463 F.3d 710, 718 (7th Cir. 2006) (listing factors: "(1) the causal connection between the alleged anti-trust violation and the harm to the plaintiff; (2) improper motive; (3) whether the injury was of a type that Congress sought to redress with the antitrust laws; (4) the directness between the injury and the market restraint; (5) the speculative nature of the damages; (6) the risk of duplicate recoveries or complex damages apportionment"); B-S Steel Of Kansas, Inc. v. Texas Indus., Inc., 439 F.3d 653, 667 (10th Cir. 2006) (listing factors: "(1) the causal connection between the antitrust violation and the plaintiff's potential injury; (2) the defendant's intent or motivation; (3) the nature of the plaintiff's potential injury—*i.e.*, whether it is one intended to be redressed by the antitrust laws; (4) the directness or the indirectness of the connection between the plaintiff's potential injury and the market restraint resulting from the alleged antitrust violation") (cleaned up).

[1039] *See, e.g.*, Roger D. Blair & Christine Durrance, *Umbrella Damages: Toward a Coherent Antitrust Policy*, 36 Contemp. Econ. Pol'y 241 (2018); *see also* U.S. Gypsum Co. v. Indiana Gas Co., Inc., 306 F.3d 469 (7th Cir.2002); In Re Coordinated Pretrial Proceedings in Petroleum Prods. Antitrust Litigation, 691 F. 2d 1335 (9th Cir. 1982); Mid-West Paper Products Co. v. Continental Group, 596 F. 2d 573 (3d. Cir. 1979); In re Beef Industry Antitrust Litig., 600 F.2d 1148 (5th Cir. 1979).

bonds from other sources. Crediting the allegations of the complaints, an artificial depression in LIBOR would injure anyone who bought bank debt pegged to LIBOR from any bank anywhere. So in this case directness may have diminished weight."

With respect to the third factor, the court indicated that the key question would be "whether the damages would necessarily be highly speculative. And as to that, this case presents some unusual challenges. The disputed transactions were done at rates that were negotiated, notwithstanding that the negotiated component was the increment above LIBOR. And the market for money is worldwide, with competitors offering various increments above LIBOR, or rates pegged to other benchmarks, or rates set without reference to any benchmark at all."

Finally, with respect to the fourth factor, the court pointed to the vast array of investigations and litigations around the world regarding the alleged conspiracy. "The transactions that are the subject of investigation and suit are countless and the ramified consequences are beyond conception. Related proceedings are ongoing in at least several countries. Some of those government initiatives may seek damages on behalf of victims, and for apportionment among them. Others may seek fines, injunctions, disgorgement, and other remedies known to United States courts and foreign jurisdictions. It is wholly unclear on this record how issues of duplicate recovery and damage apportionment can be assessed."

The court left it to the district court to work out how these factors should be applied to the complex, messy, and unfolding facts of the LIBOR conspiracy.

NOTES

1) Should we have an "efficient enforcer" rule, in addition to our other rules about antitrust injury and standing? If so, what should that rule be and why? If not, what undesirable outcomes are we accepting as the cost of giving up that rule?

2) Do you agree that a damages plaintiff is a "private attorney general" acting to "vindicate the public interest"? Why, or why not?

3) What policy considerations weigh in favor of and against accepting "umbrella" claims? How do you think the Supreme Court will (or should) resolve the circuit split?

C. Remedies II: Proving Antitrust Damages

Although private plaintiffs may obtain injunctive relief, treble damages are often of central importance in private litigation. Earlier in this chapter, we discussed the theory and practice of "trebling": now we consider what goes into the pre-trebled damages measure itself. Section 4 of the Clayton Act, 15 U.S.C. § 15, sets out the basic antitrust damages rule: "Except as provided in subsection (b), any person who shall be injured in his business or property by reason of anything forbidden in the antitrust laws may sue therefor in any district court of the United States in the district in which the defendant resides or is found or has an agent, without respect to the amount in controversy, and shall recover threefold the damages by him sustained, and the cost of suit, including a reasonable attorney's fee."

The "damage" measure is intended to capture the harmful incidence of an unlawful practice or transaction: that is, the damage "by [the plaintiff] sustained."[1040] The starting point in calculating it is the determination of what have happened in a "but-for world" (or a "counterfactual") in which the challenged conduct did not take place. The problem in practice, of course, is that this can be very difficult to prove.[1041]

Modern damages law lives in the shadow of the Court's 1946 decision in *Bigelow*, a suit for damages from an alleged anticompetitive conspiracy that excluded the plaintiffs from access to movie distribution. The plaintiffs alleged loss of profits of more than $120,000 over five years, based on the assumption that, had the defendants not engaged in their unlawful conduct, the plaintiffs would have continued to earn whatever profits they were earning

---

[1040] 15 U.S.C. § 15a.

[1041] *See generally*, e.g., Roger D. Blair & William H. Page, *"Speculative" Antitrust Damages*, 70 Wash. L. Rev. 423 (1995).

before the conduct began. The matter reached the Supreme Court with respect to damages only: the defendants (respondents in the Supreme Court) argued that it was simply too difficult to quantify the impact of the conduct on plaintiffs' (petitioners') profits, as there was no particular reason to think that the plaintiffs would have continued to make their pre-conduct profits rather than some other amount. The Court was unsympathetic.

Bigelow v. RKO Radio Pictures
327 U.S. 251 (1946)

Chief Justice Stone.

[1] . . . The Circuit Court of Appeals concluded that the jury [had] accepted the comparison of plaintiffs' earnings before and after the adoption of [the relevant conduct] as establishing the measure of petitioners' damage. But it held that this proof did not furnish a proper measure of damage for the reason that, while petitioners' earnings were known and proved for both the four and five year periods in question, it could not be proved what their earnings would have been during the five year period in the absence of the illegal distribution of films. It thought that the mere fact that earnings of the Jackson Park Theatre was greater before the adoption of [the conduct] did not serve to show what petitioners' earnings would have been afterwards, in the absence of [that conduct]. [. . .]

[2] Respondents' argument is, that notwithstanding the force of this evidence, it is impossible to establish any measure of damage, because the unlawful system which respondents have created has precluded petitioners from showing that other conditions affecting profits would have continued without change unfavorable to them during the critical period if that system had not been established, and petitioners had conducted their business in a free competitive market. [. . .]

[3] Respondents [argue] that, without the conspiracy, the conditions of purchase of films might not have been the same after as they were before [the conduct began]; that in any case it is not possible to say what those conditions would have been if the restraints had not been imposed, and that those conditions cannot be ascertained, because respondents have not removed the restraint. Hence, it is said, petitioners' evidence does not establish the fact of damage, and that further, the standard of comparison which the evidence sets up is too speculative and uncertain to afford an accurate measure of the amount of the damage. [. . .]

[4] . . . [E]ven where the defendant by his own wrong has prevented a more precise computation, the jury may not render a verdict based on speculation or guesswork. But the jury may make a just and reasonable estimate of the damage based on relevant data, and render its verdict accordingly. In such circumstances juries are allowed to act on probable and inferential as well as upon direct and positive proof. Any other rule would enable the wrongdoer to profit by his wrongdoing at the expense of his victim. It would be an inducement to make wrongdoing so effective and complete in every case as to preclude any recovery, by rendering the measure of damages uncertain.

[5] Failure to apply it would mean that the more grievous the wrong done, the less likelihood there would be of a recovery.

[6] [T]he most elementary conceptions of justice and public policy require that the wrongdoer shall bear the risk of the uncertainty which his own wrong has created. That principle is an ancient one, and is not restricted to proof of damage in antitrust suits, although their character is such as frequently to call for its application. In cases of collision where the offending vessel has violated regulations prescribed by statute, and in cases of confusion of goods, the wrongdoer may not object to the plaintiff's reasonable estimate of the cause of injury and of its amount, supported by the evidence, because not based on more accurate data which the wrongdoer's misconduct has rendered unavailable. And in cases where a wrongdoer has incorporated the subject of a plaintiff's patent or trademark in a single product to which the defendant has contributed other elements of value or utility, and has derived profits from the sale of the product, this Court has sustained recovery of the full amount of defendant's profits where his own wrongful action has made it impossible for the plaintiff to show in what proportions he and the defendant have contributed to the profits.

[7] The constant tendency of the courts is to find some way in which damages can be awarded where a wrong has been done. Difficulty of ascertainment is no longer confused with right of recovery for a proven invasion of the plaintiff's rights.

[8] The evidence here was ample to support a just and reasonable inference that petitioners were damaged by respondents' action, whose unlawfulness the jury has found, and respondents do not challenge. The comparison of petitioners' receipts before and after respondents' unlawful action impinged on petitioners' business afforded a sufficient basis for the jury's computation of the damage, where the respondents' wrongful action had prevented petitioners from making any more precise proof of the amount of the damage.

* * *

Bigelow thus stands for two propositions: (1) the plaintiff should have a reasonable margin of benefit-of-doubt in proving up antitrust damages, and (2) comparison of before-and-after profits may be one way in which such proof can be furnished.

In scrutinizing damages claims in modern cases, courts often stress the importance this reasonable margin of doubt, and have often endorsed mechanisms like "yardstick" or "benchmarking" evidence (*i.e.*, the use of a comparable market as a kind of natural experiment for what would have happened absent the conduct), or simple before-and-after comparisons (*i.e.*, use of the *status quo ante* as a rough proxy for a counterfactual).[1042] But, at least in theory, these are not the only paths to proof: "a plaintiff may prove damages by a different measure tailored to the facts of the case, so long as the estimates and assumptions used rest on adequate data."[1043]

In practice, what this means is that damages arguments can depend heavily on expert analysis, and that a district court plays a critical role in limiting through *Daubert* motions practice the set of theories and arguments that make it to a factfinder in an antitrust trial.[1044]

CASENOTE: Conwood Co., L.P. v. U.S. Tobacco Co.
290 F.3d 768 (6th Cir. 2002)

A variety of methods can be seen in action in *Conwood*, a well-known monopolization case that we encountered in Chapter VII. In that case, the defendant, U.S. Tobacco Co. ("USTC"), was found to have maintained its monopoly by abusing a category-captain position, including the removal and destruction of trade display racks displaying rivals' products. *Conwood* also happens to be a terrifically controversial case dealing with the calculation of antitrust damages.

Conwood's expert, Dr. Leftwich, offered what he described as a "regression" analysis to prove the amount of harm inflicted by USTC on Conwood. He analyzed whether, during the relevant period (1990–97), there was a relationship between Conwood's market share at the start of the period and its share at the end. He concluded that in cases where Conwood started out with a "foothold," its share increased by a higher amount: in states where Conwood had at least 15% share in 1990, it grew on average by 6.5%; in states where it had at least 20% in 1990, it grew on average by 8.1%. Conwood argued that it could be inferred from these relationships that Conwood's market share would have increased by the same amounts in states where it did *not* have a foothold, but for USTC's

---

[1042] *See, e.g.*, Lehrman v. Gulf Oil Corp., 500 F.2d 659, 667 (5th Cir. 1974) ("There are two generally recognized methods of proving lost profits: (1) the before and after theory; and (2) the yardstick test. The before and after theory compares the plaintiff's profit record prior to the violation with that subsequent to it. The before and after theory is not easily adaptable to a plaintiff who is driven out of business before he is able to compile an earnings record sufficient to allow estimation of lost profits. Therefore, the yardstick test is sometimes employed. It consists of a study of the profits of business operations that are closely comparable to the plaintiff's. Although allowances can be made for differences between the firms, the business used as a standard must be as nearly identical to the plaintiff's as possible.").

[1043] Eleven Line, Inc. v. N. Texas State Soccer Ass'n, Inc., 213 F.3d 198, 207 (5th Cir. 2000).

[1044] *See* Daubert v. Merrell Dow Pharmaceuticals, Inc., 509 U.S. 579, 592–95 (1993) (trial judge must make preliminary assessment of whether reasoning or methodology of expert is "scientifically valid" and "properly can be applied" to relevant facts, including: (1) testability; (2) subjection to peer review and publication; (3) known error rate; and (4) general acceptance by scientific community—amounting to a "flexible" inquiry to assess relevance and reliability).

conduct. The district court denied USTC's *Daubert* motion to exclude this expert evidence, and the jury appears to have accepted it.

On appeal, the Sixth Circuit held that it was not an abuse of the court's discretion to allow Dr. Leftwich to testify. Among other things, Dr. Leftwich indicated that he had evaluated some alternative explanations (*i.e.*, other than USTC's wrongdoing) for Conwood's slower growth in non-foothold states, and could not find such a relationship. He conducted a "before and after" test to see whether there was a relationship between foothold and market share growth in the seven years before 1990, and found no such relationship. Dr. Leftwich also conducted what he described as a "yardstick" analysis of another market in which Conwood was active but USTC was not—the loose-leaf tobacco market—and found no statistically significant relationship between foothold and market share growth. The court noted that regression, before-and-after, and yardstick analysis are all "generally accepted methods for proving antitrust damages."

As many commentators have since pointed out, the difficulty with Dr. Leftwich's testimony was that Conwood's better share growth between 1990 and 1997 in markets where it had a meaningful presence in 1990 tells us nothing useful about the effects of the challenged conduct. In a paper written after the litigation, the defendants' expert pointed out that: (1) the "before and after" analysis presented by Conwood's expert did not show a drop in profits during the relevant period, but rather an *increase* in Conwood's market share during that period; (2) in the "yardstick" market used by Conwood's expert—the loose leaf tobacco market, which was unaffected by the defendants' conduct—Conwood actually *lost* market share during the violation period; (3) the "regression" analysis was entirely disconnected from the alleged acts of monopolization.[1045] Herbert Hovenkamp, too, has offered an extended critique of the analysis, including the following observation:

> Before [regression analysis] can be meaningful there must be some good reason for believing that consistency of growth rates is closely related to the presence of exclusionary practices. For example, the Hubble Telescope was launched on April 25, 1990, the same year the plaintiff's claimed injuries began. The expert could just as plausibly have testified that "the launching of the Hubble Telescope caused Conwood to have slow growth in states where its share was low to begin with."[1046]

The damages award at trial, after trebling, was $1.05 billion.

Conwood aside, the latitude afforded to plaintiffs in proving damages has a limit, and different courts may define that limit in different ways. In *Marshfield Clinic*, for example, the Seventh Circuit—in an opinion written by Judge Posner—clearly felt that the plaintiff's experts had failed to take reasonable steps to isolate the harm attributable to an illegal market-division scheme. At trial, the plaintiff had won a sizeable jury verdict, but on appeal the Seventh Circuit had thrown out all the claims except those relating to the illegal division of markets. And, as the following extract demonstrates, the court of appeals was unsatisfied with the plaintiff's purported quantification of the harm resulting from that market division. As a result, it reversed the district court's damages award in its entirety, leaving the plaintiff with injunctive relief only.

Blue Cross and Blue Shield United of Wisconsin v. Marshfield Clinic
152 F.3d 588 (7th Cir. 1998)

Judge Posner.

[1] Blue Cross bought services from a seller [the Marshfield Clinic] that had agreed with other sellers to refrain from competing for customers, and it is likely, whether or not provable with the degree of precision required to ground an award of damages, that unless the defendant is enjoined Blue Cross will have to pay Marshfield Clinic more than if the Clinic were not a member of an anticompetitive conspiracy directed in part against the plaintiff, the conspiracy that the suit seeks to destroy.

[1045] D.H. Kaye, *Adversarial Econometrics in* United States Tobacco Co. v. Conwood Co., 43 Jurimetrics 343 (2003).

[1046] Herbert Hovenkamp, THE ANTITRUST ENTERPRISE: PRINCIPLE AND EXECUTION (2005) 88. *See also, e.g.,* Joshua D. Wright, *Antitrust Analysis of Category Management:* Conwood v United States Tobacco Co., 17 Sup. Ct. Econ. Rev. 311, 333–35 (2009).

[2] A more difficult question is whether the [district court] judge was right to conclude that Blue Cross could not prove what damages it had sustained as a result of the division of markets. The usual way to measure damages in such a case would be to compare the prices that the Marshfield Clinic charged Blue Cross before and during the conspiracy, or inside and outside the region covered by the conspiracy, or during the conspiracy and after it ended (if it has ended—the injunction issued by the district court before the first appeal was in effect for less than six weeks before we stayed it pending the appeal), correcting by various statistical techniques for any non-conspiratorial factors that might have caused the prices that are being compared to be different from each other. This method or congeries of methods was unavailable to Blue Cross, however, because the division of markets embraced the entire period and region in which the necessary data are obtainable; at least Blue Cross made no effort to show otherwise. Instead it compared the Marshfield Clinic's prices for medical services between 1988 and 1995 with the prices charged by other providers of medical care for the same services during the same period elsewhere in Wisconsin, on the theory that those other prices, properly adjusted, are what Blue Cross would have had to pay the Clinic and the Clinic's competitors had it not been for the conspiracy.

[3] This—the so-called "yardstick" method of computing antitrust damages—was not improper. But the qualification "properly adjusted" is at least as vital as when the plaintiff is trying to prove damages by comparing the defendant's prices at one period or in one area with its prices in another period or another area rather than (as under the yardstick approach) comparing the defendant's prices with the prices of other sellers. Any non-conspiratorial factors likely to have made the prices charged by the Marshfield Clinic higher than the prices charged by other health-care providers had to be taken into account in order to make a responsible estimate of the prices that Blue Cross would have paid had it not been for the conspiracy.

[4] The most important factors were the amount and quality of the Marshfield Clinic's service and its market share. The significance of market share is that even though the Marshfield Clinic was not proved to have monopoly power, it does have a large market share throughout north-central Wisconsin, which might confer enough market power on it to enable it all by itself, without dividing markets with its competitors, to charge a price somewhat above the average for the state. The larger a firm's market share is, the larger is the percentage increase that the other firms in the market must make in their output to offset the effect of the firm's curtailing its output in order to drive the market price above the competitive level. For example, if a firm has 50 percent of the market and as a corollary to jacking its price above the existing, competitive level reduces its output by 20 percent (say from 1,000 to 800 units), the other firms will have to increase their output by an average of 20 percent (from 1,000 to 1,200 units) in order to offset completely the reduction in the output of the dominant firm. This may be difficult for them to do, at least in the near term, and so the dominant firm, though not a monopolist, will be able to get away, at least for a time, with its price hike. That may have been the situation of the Marshfield Clinic.

[5] To make the necessary corrections and thus establish that there was enough evidence to enable a jury to make a responsible estimate of damages, Blue Cross submitted to the district court multiple reports by two economic experts, John Beyer and Thomas McGuire. Beyer's two reports, which compute a range of damages exceeding $7 million from the division of markets, are worthless. They attribute the entire difference between the prices of the Marshfield Clinic and the prices of other Wisconsin providers of medical services to the division of markets, with no correction for any other factor except differences in the treatment mix. Statistical studies that fail to correct for salient factors, not attributable to the defendant's misconduct, that may have caused the harm of which the plaintiff is complaining do not provide a rational basis for a judgment.

[6] McGuire's reports are more promising, though as his bottom line is a damages figure only $11,000 below the lower of Beyer's highest two estimates, it is a little hard to take seriously. For how is it that after making the subtractions that Beyer failed to make, McGuire came up with essentially the same figure? And is it purely a coincidence that this number, after trebling, would give Blue Cross the same $20 million judgment (actually a little more) that it won in the first trial, even though the division of markets was among the least important of the many antitrust violations charged in this suit? Of course it is possible that the alleged violations were redundant; like the assassins of Rasputin, who drowned him after poisoning and shooting him in order to make sure he was really dead, the Marshfield Clinic may have stacked the division of markets on top of other practices any one of which would have had the same effect on its customers' prices. But this observation cannot help Blue Cross. For only one

of the practices was illegal, the division of markets. If it added nothing to the price effects of the legal practices, it did not cause Blue Cross any harm. [. . .]

[7] McGuire did try to correct for differences in the quality of the services rendered by the Marshfield Clinic compared to the statewide average; but quality and quantity are not the same. If the Clinic because of its reputation . . . for high quality gets referred to it patients who are sicker than average and so require longer treatment, the average price per patient will be higher simply as a function of the more expensive or protracted care required on average by a sicker patient. As far as the record discloses, this is all there is to the higher average price charged by the Marshfield Clinic. McGuire also failed to correct for the effect of market share on the Clinic's prices. In sum, no reasonable jury could estimate the plaintiff's damages from the reports of the plaintiff's experts.

[8] In addition to those reports, there is some nonexpert evidence of damages, consisting of discounts of 15 or 20 percent that the Clinic gave to some of its coconspirators. But this evidence would not enable a reasonable jury to estimate the plaintiff's damages either. The discounts were given in exchange for bulk referrals, and there is no evidence that customers of the Marshfield Clinic, even so large a customer as Blue Cross, would have gotten equivalent discounts had the clinic been competing rather than conspiring. They might have, but no evidence was presented that they probably would have.

[9] We are not saying that Blue Cross did not in fact lose any money as a result of the division of markets. It may well have, as we suggested in discussing the issue of the injunction. (But remember that there is a difference between an actual and a threatened harm. And there is also, and here critically, a difference between an actual and a quantifiable harm and also between a quantifiable and a quantified harm—and only the last supports an award of damages.) The Clinic's own economic experts estimated that the division of markets may have caused the Clinic's prices to be between .4 and .9 percent higher than they would otherwise have been. Blue Cross, however, did not cite that estimate in its briefs to us, and this raises an interesting question of waiver or forfeiture. [. . .]

[10] So the district judge was right to throw out the damages claim on summary judgment but wrong to throw out the injunction as well and therefore premature in pronouncing the defendant the winner of this lawsuit.

NOTES

1) What, if anything, was wrong with the *Conwood* expert evidence? Do you agree that it was effectively worthless and that the judge should have excluded it under *Daubert*?
2) Do you agree with the following statement: "In an antitrust case, damages are generally less important than injunctions to both plaintiffs and defendants." Explain your answer.
3) What kinds of cases are private litigants more likely to bring than government enforcers? What about vice versa?
4) Class action plaintiffs' counsel commonly receive around 30% of any recovery as contingent fees, amounting to many millions of dollars. Recoveries of individual plaintiffs are often small. Does this suggest that something is amiss? Explain.
5) Which is the more important goal for antitrust damages law: compensation or deterrence? Why? In what respects does existing law fail to optimally serve that goal? Do we ever have to choose between the two?
6) Suppose you are asked to advise a jurisdiction that is setting up an antitrust enforcement system for the first time. Would you advise it to adopt private treble damages?

D. Limitations and Laches

Private plaintiffs and states, unlike the federal government, face a four-year statute of limitations for civil antitrust claims.[1047] But the application of a statute of limitations to an antitrust claim can be more complicated than it appears: in particular, it is not always clear when a violation is completed and when it is ongoing.

[1047] 15 U.S.C. § 15b. *See also* 15 U.S.C. § 16(i) (tolling civil limitations during a government antitrust suit); 18 U.S.C. § 3282 (five year limitations period in a federal criminal case).

The following two cases deal respectively with an unlawful price-fixing conspiracy and an unlawful acquisition. Do they indicate the only sensible results? Are they consistent with one another? Should they be?

In the adorably named *Pre-Filled Propane Tank Antitrust Litigation*, the plaintiffs were direct purchasers of—you guessed it—pre-filled propane tanks, alleging a conspiracy among suppliers to charge supracompetitive prices for the tanks. The plaintiffs argued that the four-year statute of limitations should be calculated from the most recent occasion on which a defendant had, pursuant to the conspiracy, either sold a tank at an anticompetitive overcharge or communicated about the conspiracy. The Eighth Circuit, sitting *en banc*, declined to consider the communication theory but agreed that each sale at an anticompetitive overcharge restarted the four-year statute of limitations.[1048]

In re Pre-Filled Propane Tank Antitrust Litigation
860 F.3d 1059 (8th Cir. 2017) (en banc)

Judge Benton.

[1] Actions under Section 1 of the Sherman Act must be filed "within four years after the cause of action accrued." 15 U.S.C. § 15b. Generally, the period commences on the date the cause of action accrues, that being, the date on which the wrongdoer commits an act that injures the business of another.

[2] Plaintiffs allege a continuing violation—an exception to the general rule—which restarts the statute of limitations period each time the defendant commits an overt act. An overt act has two elements: (1) it must be a new and independent act that is not merely a reaffirmation of a previous act, and (2) it must inflict new and accumulating injury on the plaintiff. [. . .]

[3] Plaintiffs allege two types of overt acts within the limitations period: (1) Defendants' sales to Plaintiffs at artificially inflated prices; and (2) conspiratorial communications between Defendants about pricing and fill levels. The first type of act is at issue here—whether sales at artificially inflated prices are overt acts that restart the statute of limitations. Also at issue is whether Plaintiffs allege a continuing violation exception sufficient to restart the statute of limitations. [. . .]

[4] The Supreme Court of the United States addressed the first issue in *Klehr v. A.O. Smith Corporation*, 521 U.S. 179 (1997). The Supreme Court defined a continuing violation under antitrust law:

> Antitrust law provides that, in the case of a continuing violation, say, a price-fixing conspiracy that brings about a series of unlawfully high priced sales over a period of years, each overt act that is part of the violation and that injures the plaintiff, e.g., each sale to the plaintiff, starts the statutory period running again, regardless of the plaintiff's knowledge of the alleged illegality at much earlier times.

Klehr, 521 U.S. at 189. [. . .]

[5] Every other circuit to consider this issue applies *Klehr*, holding that each sale in a price-fixing conspiracy is an overt act that restarts the statute of limitations.

[6] The other issue is whether the amended complaint adequately pleads a continuing violation sufficient to restart the statute of limitations. Under *Klehr*, Plaintiffs must allege: (1) a price-fixing conspiracy; (2) that brings about a series of unlawfully high priced sales during the class period; and (3) sales to the plaintiffs during the class period. In paragraph 111 of the amended complaint, Plaintiffs allege all three necessary elements:

> Plaintiffs purchased Filled Propane Exchange Tanks from Blue Rhino or AmeriGas on multiple occasions during the Class Period. On each occasion, Plaintiffs purchased Filled Propane Exchange Tanks containing only 15 pounds of propane, pursuant to the conspiracy, but sold at the price they would have been charged for 17-pound tanks but for the conspiracy. As

---

[1048] Note that this does not mean that the plaintiff can recover damages for earlier injuries! *See, e.g.*, CSX Transportation, Inc. v. Norfolk S. Ry. Co., Case No. 2:18CV530, 2023 WL 25344, at *6 (E.D. Va. Jan. 3, 2023) (discussing this issue in detail).

Defendants kept prices constant despite the fill level reduction, this amounted to an effective price increase of 13%. [. . .]

[7] [T]he allegations of a price-fixing conspiracy are sufficient. Plaintiffs plead that Defendants "conspired and acted in concert to eliminate competition by reducing the amount of propane they would put in their tanks, thereby raising the per-pound price of propane across the country as well as by dividing the market for Filled Propane Exchange Tanks in violation of federal antitrust law." Even more specifically, they plead that "Blue Rhino's President, Tod Brown, and AmeriGas's Director of National Accounts, Ken Janish, exchanged seven phone calls on June 18 and 19, 2008, during which AmeriGas agreed that if Blue Rhino reduced its fill levels to 15 pounds per tank, AmeriGas would follow suit." Defendants later "engaged in dozens of calls, emails, and in-person meetings to coordinate a unified front that would leave the largest retailers and then the entire industry with no choice but to accept their demands." "[N]o later than spring 2008," Defendants "reduced their fill levels from 17 pounds per tank to 15 pounds per tank while maintaining the same price per 'full' tank, for the purpose of increasing their margins on the sale of propane exchange tanks." "This collusion effectively raised the prices charged to Plaintiffs by more than 13% per pound." [. . .]

[8] According to Defendants, Plaintiffs' allegation that the propane conspiracy succeeded made the maintenance of fill levels and prices mere "unabated inertial consequences" and not overt acts continuing the conspiracy. But the question here is not whether the amended complaint alleges other overt acts in addition to sales to the Plaintiffs; the issue is whether the amended complaint alleges that the conspiracy continued when the sales took place. If so, under *Klehr*, each sale to the plaintiff, is an overt act that restarts the statute of limitations.

[9] In any event, this court has never applied the "unabated inertial consequences" test to a horizontal price-fixing conspiracy, let alone one where Plaintiffs allege that "sales pursuant to the conspiracy continued throughout the Class Period," and "Defendants continued to have regular communications regarding pricing, fill levels, and market allocation until at least late 2010." In context, Defendants' conspiracy "succeeded" in "forc[ing] Walmart and other large retailers to accept the fill reduction" and raising the "wholesale prices at which [they] sold propane in Filled Propane Exchange Tanks to retailers throughout the United States." This success did not end the conspiracy, but rather was a precondition to the price-fixing scheme Plaintiffs allege continued into the class period. [. . .]

[10] The amended complaint alleges sufficient factual matter, accepted as true, to show a continuing violation to restart the statute of limitations, and, therefore, to state a claim to relief that is plausible on its face. Because it is not clear from the face of the complaint that the action is barred by the applicable limitations period, the district court erred in granting the motion to dismiss.

CASENOTE: Reveal Chat Holdco, LLC v. Facebook, Inc.
471 F. Supp. 3d 981 (N.D. Cal. 2020)

In *Reveal Chat*, a private plaintiff challenged, among other things, the acquisition by Facebook of Instagram and WhatsApp. The district court held that the continuing violation doctrine was not triggered by Facebook's subsequent holding and integration of the assets, with the result that the statute of limitations was not suspended.

The court began its analysis by noting that, in the Ninth Circuit, a continuing violation requires "an overt act [by the defendant] during the limitations period that meets two criteria: 1) It must be a new and independent act that is not merely a reaffirmation of a previous act; and 2) it must inflict new and accumulating injury on the plaintiff." Here, the plaintiffs had argued that Facebook had engaged in a continuing violation, after the acquisitions of Instagram and WhatsApp, by announcing in March 2019 the continued technical integration of those apps. This announcement of further integration, according to the plaintiff, inflicted "a new and accumulating injury."

But the court took a different view. "The continuing violation doctrine does not make sense in the context of anticompetitive mergers, and therefore it should not apply to Section 7 claims under the Clayton Act. Section 7 of the Clayton Act is the mechanism for challenging a potentially anticompetitive merger, and it has a statute of limitations within which mergers must be challenged. If the continuing violation doctrine applied, every business decision could qualify as a continuing violation to restart the statute of limitations as long as the firm continued to desire to be merged. This would write the statute of limitations out of the law by allowing a merger to be challenged indefinitely. This cannot be the case because unlike a conspiracy or the maintaining of a monopoly, a merger is a discrete act, not an ongoing scheme, and once the merger is completed, the plan to merge is completed, and no overt acts can be undertaken to further that plan. Thus, the Court agrees with the Eighth Circuit and the Central District of California that the continuing violation doctrine does not apply in the context of Section 7 claims under the Clayton Act." To the extent that the plaintiff alleged that the acquisition constituted a violation of the Sherman Act as well, the same conclusion would apply under that statute also.

Limitations is not the only time-bar on private suits. The doctrine of laches also limits the period within which a complaint may be filed: this equitable doctrine generally precludes suit by reason of an inequitable delay in filing a complaint.[1049] Laches was front-and-center in the States' challenge to Facebook's 2012 and 2014 acquisitions of Instagram and WhatsApp, filed in 2020.

New York v. Facebook, Inc.
549 F. Supp. 3d 6 (D.D.C. 2021)

Judge Boasberg.

[1] Although what constitutes an "unreasonable delay" in filing suit is generally a fact-intensive question, in the context of injunctive actions under Section 16 [of the Clayton Act], many courts have held that the Clayton Act's four-year statute of limitation on damages actions should be used as a guideline for computing the laches period. As . . . courts explain, [t]he doctrine of laches is premised upon the same principles that underlie statutes of limitation: the desire to avoid unfairness that can result from the prosecution of stale claims.

[2] The starting presumption, then, is that regardless of whether a Section 16 plaintiff seeks damages or an injunction, it must file its lawsuit within four years from the accrual of the claim. Generally, a Section 7 action challenging the initial acquisition of another company's stocks or assets accrues at the time of the merger or acquisition, giving the plaintiff four years from that time to sue. . . . Following the lead of the parties and the cases, [the court] uses the terms "acquisition" and "merger" interchangeably for purposes of this analysis.

[3] This presumptive four-year laches period is particularly appropriate for challenges to acquisitions. The traditional remedy in such cases, which Plaintiffs seek here, is divestiture of the acquired assets and/or stock. Such a remedy, if ordered well after the merger has closed, will usually prejudice the defendant by inflicting substantial hardship and competitive disadvantage, especially where its business operations have been combined with those of the acquired company. For that reason, where the equity relief sought in a merger challenge is retroactive in character, such as divestiture of illegally acquired assets, Areeda and Hovenkamp argue that the four-year time limit should be absolute. Indeed, as they note, courts frequently find a divestiture remedy clearly unfair and unwarranted after delays in filing much shorter than four years—sometimes only months or even days after the merger's announcement. [. . .]

[4] Given these precedents, the Court concludes that Plaintiffs' challenges to Facebook's 2012 and 2014 acquisitions are barred by laches. Going by the four-year "guideline" alone, which is generous compared to the decisions set out above, and which prominent authorities argue "should be absolute," the States missed their window to sue by years. In the case of the Instagram acquisition, the comparable statute of limitations time period had run twice over by the time they filed. The Court is aware of no case, and the States provide none, in which a plaintiff other than the United States (against which laches does not apply), whether a state or a private party, was awarded equitable relief after such long post-acquisition delays in filing suit. Having thus slumbered on their rights, Plaintiffs' equitable claims are now barred.

[1049] *See, e.g.*, Russell v. Todd, 309 U.S. 280, 287 (1940) (defining laches as "the principle that equity will not aid a plaintiff whose unexcused delay, if the suit were allowed, would be prejudicial to the defendant").

[5] That result is confirmed by applying the standard laches elements. In brief, Plaintiffs' years-long delay in bringing this action was inexcusable as each challenged act was highly publicized, and Facebook would be prejudiced by the unreasonable delay.

[6] First, the States' long delays were unreasonable and unjustified as a matter of law. Both acquisitions were, per Plaintiffs' allegations, publicly announced, and the States were thus aware or certainly should have been aware of them from those points onward. The Complaint itself makes clear that concerns as to the effects of both on competition were apparent at the time. Plaintiffs allege that Facebook was the dominant player in Personal Social Networking Services at least as early as 2011, before either acquisition. Their position in this case, furthermore, is that when the acquiring firm is a dominant firm or monopolist, competitive harm from the acquisition of even a potential competitor can be predicted with considerably more confidence, indicating a harsh rule against such mergers.

[7] As to each acquisition, moreover, either judicially noticeable facts or the Complaint's allegations provide objective confirmation of contemporaneous antitrust concerns. After Facebook announced its plans to purchase Instagram in April 2012, the FTC conducted a highly publicized, four-month-long investigation to determine whether the proposed acquisition would violate Section 7 of the Clayton Act. Although the agency ultimately allowed the merger to proceed with no action, the States' choice not to assert their own concerns at that time, let alone at any time in the next eight years, "bear[s] upon the issue of laches. . . . .

[8] Second, prejudice to Facebook, were equitable relief to be awarded now, is also apparent. As an initial matter, the bare fact of delay beyond the analogous four-year statute of limitations creates a rebuttable presumption of prejudice. The facts alleged in the Complaint, moreover, confirm the existence of economic prejudice here. According to the States, for the last five-plus years Facebook has made business decisions and allocated firm resources based on holding Instagram and WhatsApp, and it has also integrated their offerings to some extent into its core business. Although short of full business integration, Defendant's expanded use of and investment in the acquired assets establishes economic prejudice resulting from Plaintiffs' delay.

[9] Equitable relief would similarly prejudice Facebook's shareholders, especially those who invested within the last several years, by which point the WhatsApp and Instagram acquisitions had become old news. [. . .]

[10] The States, unsurprisingly, object to the foregoing analysis on a number of grounds. The Court marches through each, but ultimately sticks to its guns.

a. Applicability of Laches

[11] Plaintiffs first maintain that the usual laches framework does not properly govern in cases brought by states suing *parens patriae* and in the public interest. They cite no authority for that contention . . . . The dearth of cases . . . applying laches to bar merger challenges by states, however, does not somehow establish that states are immune from the doctrine. It instead seems to reflect the fact that there are very few cases like the present one, in which state plaintiffs delayed years and years in seeking equitable relief from an allegedly unlawful acquisition.

[12] At any rate, to the extent that the question of laches' applicability to Section 16 suits by state plaintiffs is open, [*Gov't of Puerto Rico v. Carpenter Co.*, 442 F. Supp. 3d 464, 474 (D.P.R. 2020) (granting motion to dismiss on laches grounds)] had the correct answer. The only other case that is close to being on point, *California v. American Stores Co.*, [495 U.S. 271, (1990)], also supports the applicability of laches to state merger challenges. There, California sued in its capacity as parens patriae under Section 16 to unwind the merger of two supermarket chains, claiming that it violated Section 7. . . . Throughout its opinion, the Court repeatedly referred to the suit as a "private action under § 16 of the Clayton Act," and emphasized that despite its holding, equitable defenses such as laches may protect consummated transactions from belated attacks by private parties under Section 16. [. . .]

[13] In expanding the universe of antitrust enforcers beyond the United States itself, Congress thus drew no distinction between states and private litigants: both simply came within the statute's authorization of any person to sue for and have injunctive relief against threatened loss or damage by a violation of the antitrust laws. As such, the Congressional judgment was that states, like private parties, are entitled to relief under Section 16 under the same conditions and principles as injunctive relief against threatened conduct that will cause loss or damage is

granted by courts of equity—"conditions and principles" that have always included the bar of laches against plaintiffs whose unreasonable delay prejudices the defendant. [. . .]

[14] Although the doctrine of laches therefore applies to parens patriae suits such as this one, the Court does not mean to suggest that the presence of state plaintiffs has zero effect on the analysis. Laches is an equitable doctrine, and in the balancing of the equities, it is of course relevant that this suit is brought not by a competitor hoping to seriously interfere with a rival's business operations, but rather by many of the states of the Union. Even giving the States' interests significantly more weight than a private actor's would receive, however, does not lead to a different result. Plaintiffs waited six and eight years, compared to the four-year guideline statute of limitations, to challenge two highly publicized acquisitions—one of an existing nascent competitor, one of a potential future competitor—by a firm that they allege was already a "dominant" monopolist. To hold that laches did not apply in those circumstances would essentially declare the States immune from the doctrine for all practical purposes. While many might welcome such a regime as a matter of policy, it is not the system we have.

b. Ongoing Violation

[15] The States next posit that even if laches applies, their "Complaint is timely," despite the long delays between the mergers at issue and their filing, "because the[y] allege ongoing conduct" by Facebook. They appear to contend, albeit not with perfect clarity . . . that . . . the Instagram and WhatsApp acquisitions themselves are "ongoing" because Facebook still holds the purchased assets. {*Eds: for brevity and clarity we are omitting reference to a second theory here.*}

[16] As noted above, the general rule is that courts measure the reasonableness of a private plaintiff's delay in suing for divestiture relative to the announcement of the transaction and its subsequent consummation. . . .

[17] . . . The States contend that they may . . . seek equitable relief now, no matter what has come before, because time has made clear the more recent continuing anticompetitive effects of the Instagram and WhatsApp acquisitions. [. . .]

[18] [None of the Supreme Court cases cited by the States], however, [either] hold nor imply that the limitations or laches period for challenging a merger is forever tolled. The cases merely clarify that a violation of Section 7 . . . can arise (and persist) not only at the time of the merger, but also at any time afterward so long as the acquired assets are still held. That is a principle of substantive liability; it says nothing about when a plaintiff's cause of action accrues, or, by the same token, when it becomes time barred (or when delay becomes unreasonable). Areeda & Hovenkamp helpfully analogize to the doctrine of adverse possession: The fact that each day of a trespasser's occupancy constitutes a trespass, and thus a violation, does not operate so as to toll the statute of limitations, which accrues when the injury is first actionable. At some point, a trespasser's violation of the law, despite being ongoing, is immunized from suit. By the same token, even if Facebook's continued holding of Instagram and WhatsApp violates Section 7 in some sense at this very moment, that does not make a present challenge timely. Such a result would write the statute of limitations for Section 7 damages actions out of the Clayton Act and similarly eliminate the laches defense that Congress expected to govern Section 16's cause of action for injunctive relief. [. . .]

c. Prospective Relief

[19] The States next argue that because they have alleged ongoing harm flowing from the damage to competition caused by the WhatsApp and Instagram acquisitions, that renders the relief they seek prospective, and laches generally does not apply to bar claims for prospective injunctive relief. As to the remedy of divestiture, that argument makes little sense; indeed, it would mean that all of the cases applying laches in merger challenges were wrongly decided. Although divestiture is a form of equitable relief, it is not generally thought of as prospective but rather retroactive in character, as it is aimed at unwinding a transaction. The fact that the challenged acquisitions allegedly continue to cause ongoing harm does not affect that characterization; on the contrary, where a plaintiff's complaint is that it is experiencing continuing, present adverse effects of past action, a reparative or backward-looking decree such as a divestiture order is the appropriate remedy. [. . .]

[20] Down to their last card, Plaintiffs maintain that dismissing a claim based on laches at the Rule 12(b)(6) stage is generally improper because laches is an affirmative defense, as to which the defendant, here Facebook, bears the burden of proof. . . .

[21] The Court is aware that the D.C. Circuit has echoed the warning that a complaint seldom will disclose undisputed facts clearly establishing the laches defense. "Seldom," though, does not mean "never." Just as a district court must retain the power to insist upon some specificity in pleading before allowing a potentially massive factual controversy to proceed, so too must it retain the power to avoid sending the parties into discovery when there is no reasonable likelihood, based on the events related in the complaint, that Plaintiffs will ultimately be entitled to the injunctive relief they seek. . . .

[22] Ultimately, this antitrust action is premised on public, high-profile conduct nearly all of which occurred over six years ago—before the launch of the Apple Watch or Alexa or Periscope, when Kevin Durant still played for the Oklahoma City Thunder, and when Ebola was the virus dominating headlines. The Complaint's allegations themselves make clear that the States could easily have brought suit then, just as they make clear that any equitable relief this Court could or would order now would greatly prejudice both Facebook and third parties. The system of antitrust enforcement that Congress has established does not exempt Plaintiffs here from the consequences of their choice to do nothing over the last half decade. The Court accordingly finds that, as a matter of law, their challenges to Facebook's acquisitions . . . are barred by the doctrine of laches or otherwise furnish no basis for the injunctive relief sought.

* * *

Laches is not always such a good friend to merging parties. In the *Steves* private merger challenge discussed earlier in this chapter, the defendant raised a laches defense on the ground that the deal was announced in 2012 but Steves had not sued until 2016. The Fourth Circuit was unmoved.

Steves and Sons, Inc. v. JELD-WEN, Inc.

988 F.3d 690 (4th Cir. 2021)

Judge Diaz.

[1] Laches is a defense to a divestiture request. For the defense to succeed, JELD-WEN must prove both (1) that Steves unreasonably delayed in bringing suit and (2) that Steves's unreasonable delay prejudiced JELD-WEN. The district court found that JELD-WEN satisfied neither element, and we review that finding for abuse of discretion.

[2] As to unreasonable delay, JELD-WEN makes three points. None is persuasive. [. . .]

[3] First, JELD-WEN contends that a nearly four-year delay after a merger's consummation is presumptively unreasonable. We disagree. Laches turns on the particular circumstances of the case, militating against a singular focus on a merger's closing date. And we measure delay not from the date of the challenged action, but from when the plaintiff discovers or with reasonable diligence could have discovered the facts giving rise to his cause of action, and was able to pursue a claim.

[4] Some courts have relied on laches to dismiss post-consummation challenges to mergers. None of the plaintiffs in those cases, however, offered a good excuse for their delay. So, those cases don't support a singular focus on the date that a merger is consummated.

[5] Nor is such a focus warranted by the hardships of unwinding a completed merger. While those hardships factor into the prejudice stage of the laches analysis, they don't obviate our need to consider whether the plaintiff's delay was unreasonable. And even if a defendant's laches defense fails, it can still prevent divestiture by showing that the balance of hardships (one of the four equitable factors) tips in its favor. Thus, there's no need for the hardships of unwinding a merger to bleed into our review of whether Steves's delay was reasonable. [. . .]

[6] JELD-WEN's second argument is that Steves had notice of its injury right after the merger was announced and thus shouldn't have waited until fall 2014 to pursue relief. Specifically, Steves knew that the merger, by

removing a competitor from the market, would hinder it from buying doorskins from other suppliers and weaken JELD-WEN's incentive to provide good service. Further, Masonite stopped selling Steves any doorskins in 2012, so for those next two years, Steves knew that its only option was to buy from JELD-WEN—yet Steves didn't seek relief.

[7] Again, we disagree with JELD-WEN. It's true that Steves knew about the two injuries that support its past-damages claim in 2012. But Steves lacked notice of the threatened injury on which its divestiture claim is based—its potential loss of access to doorskins in 2021—until 2014, when JELD-WEN indicated that it was terminating the Supply Agreement and Masonite announced that it would stop selling to the Independents entirely. Before then, Steves's access to doorskins was contractually protected for the foreseeable future. The Supply Agreement was set to renew perpetually, and JELD-WEN's CEO had referred to it as a "life time [sic]" deal.

[8] Moreover, Masonite had previously sought a long-term agreement with Steves, so Steves had reason to believe that it had a fallback if its relationship with JELD-WEN soured. That fallback vanished in 2014, when Masonite announced its strategy to kill off the Independents. JELD-WEN's notice of termination and Masonite's announcement are key facts giving rise to Steves's cause of action, which Steves couldn't have discovered before 2014.

[9] The injuries that Steves suffered prior to 2014 wouldn't have supported a divestiture claim. Absent the threat to its survival that emerged only then, Steves couldn't have shown any of the first three *eBay* factors—a threatened irreparable injury, inadequacy of legal remedies, and that the balance of hardships tipped in its favor—because its earlier injuries were compensable by money damages (as evidenced by the award that Steves received in this case).

[10] Logic dictates that unreasonable delay does not include any period of time before Steves was able to pursue a claim. And, as the Supreme Court has explained, laches doesn't require a plaintiff to sue soon, or forever hold [their] peace. In other words, a plaintiff need not challenge an illegal act immediately after it happens; it may wait until it can estimate whether the act threatens it with irreparable harm. Thus, it was reasonable for Steves to wait to pursue relief until 2014, when it learned that the merger threatened its access to doorskins (and thus its survival) after September 2021. [. . .]

[11] JELD-WEN's last argument about delay is that Steves lacks a good excuse for not seeking divestiture between 2014 and 2016. But evidence supports the district court's finding that Steves spent that time diligently exhausting its alternative remedies. Specifically, Steves reached out to Masonite and foreign suppliers, explored building its own doorskin plant, engaged in settlement talks and mediation with JELD-WEN, and asked for (and cooperated with) a Justice Department investigation. Moreover, between September 2015 and June 2016, JELD-WEN signed a series of agreements with Steves reciting their mutual desire to settle their dispute. It would disserve the strong policy in favor of nonjudicial dispute resolution if a defendant successfully could assert that a period of settlement attempts—i.e., efforts to find nonjudicial remedies—contributes to the establishment of laches, particularly when the defendant has expressed a desire to settle.

[12] In short, the district court didn't abuse its discretion in finding that Steves's delay was reasonable, and thus properly denied JELD-WEN's laches defense. As JELD-WEN didn't prove unreasonable delay, we need not address whether the delay prejudiced JELD-WEN.

Fraudulent Concealment

In antitrust cases, as in other settings, courts are often willing to recognize that the statute of limitations should not begin to run if the defendant is fraudulently concealing its wrongdoing. Courts customarily require for this purpose: (1) that the concealment be intentional; (2) that it successfully prevented the plaintiff from learning of the existence of the illegality; and (3) that the plaintiff's ignorance was not traceable to a lack of due diligence.[1050] Courts formulate the concealment test differently: for example, the Second Circuit recognizes that conduct may be "self-concealing" by its nature, while the Ninth Circuit requires that the defendant "affirmatively misled" the

---

[1050] *See, e.g.*, Chandler v. Phoenix Servs., L.L.C., 45 F.4th 807, 815 (5th Cir. 2022); Edmonson v. Eagle Nat'l Bank, 922 F.3d 535, 557 (4th Cir. 2019); Hexcel Corp. v. Ineos Polymers, Inc., 681 F.3d 1055, 1060 (9th Cir. 2012); State of N.Y. v. Hendrickson Bros., 840 F.2d 1065, 1083 (2d Cir. 1988).

plaintiff. Do you think the test for concealment of (alleged) price-fixing and bid-rigging conspiracies should be the same as the test for concealment of, say, (alleged) exclusionary vertical contracts and mergers?

NOTES

1) When is an antitrust case untimely?

2) Which of the considerations identified by the Eighth Circuit in *Ginsburg* do you find most compelling?

3) When is the "best" time for a State AG to challenge a merger that may turn out to be harmful to competition: and does the *Facebook* decision on this point seem likely to result in better or worse enforcement practices? What positive and negative effects can you foresee?

4) Is there a good reason to apply the doctrine of laches against state government enforcers but not against federal government enforcers?

5) Suppose that an acquisition of a target company violates Section 7. Should the continued holding of the target constitute an ongoing violation for the purposes of applicable time bars? Should it constitute an ongoing violation for the purposes of Section 13(b) of the FTC Act (which limits the FTC's district-court litigation authority to ongoing and imminent violations of law)?

6) Consumers generally do not know the terms of the nonpublic dealings between upstream companies in the supply chain, so would often not be well placed to learn about anticompetitive agreements and other practices. What ideal rule would optimally balance fairness and efficiency here?

E. Interaction of Private and Government Enforcement

An important character is often found lurking, one way or another, in and around private antitrust litigation: the federal government. Sometimes the federal government will involve itself directly, by filing amicus briefs or statements of interest in order to make its position known on matters of significance.[1051]

But the federal government can be an important figure even when it is not present. Plaintiffs and defendants alike sometimes try to make some hay out of the fact that the antitrust agencies either have, or have not, taken particular action. For example, a plaintiff might argue that its allegations are more plausible because a government investigation or litigation is pending. Conversely, a defendant might argue that the court should be reluctant to draw inferences in favor of a private plaintiff when the federal agencies have chosen not to investigate—or have investigated but chose not to take further action.

The following three extracts give a flavor of some different perspectives on the interaction between decisions of various actual or potential antitrust enforcers. In *Steves*, the district court had excluded any evidence relating to a DOJ investigation; on appeal, the Fourth Circuit found no abuse of discretion in so doing. In *Deutsche Telekom*—the challenge to the Sprint/T-Mobile merger—the district court accorded "some deference" to the fact that DOJ had accepted a consent decree rather than suing to block the transaction (note that the plaintiffs in that case were states, not private plaintiffs), ultimately rejecting the states' challenge to the deal. Finally, in *In re Graphics Processors*, the district court explicitly declined to treat the fact of an ongoing federal antitrust investigation as a basis to infer plausibility of a private suit. Some other courts have taken a different view.[1052]

You may remember from Chapter XI that the Justice Department said in its own brief in the *Steves* case that the court should place no weight of any kind on the Justice Department's inaction in that case, stating:

> [N]o inference should be drawn from the Division's closure of its investigations into JELD-WEN's proposed and consummated acquisition of CMI. As the United States has stated twice

---

[1051] *See, e.g.*, Statement of Interest of the United States, Nostalgic Partners LLC v. Office of the Commissioner of Baseball, Case No. 1:21-cv-10876 (S.D.N.Y. filed June 15, 2022); *Amicus Curiae* Brief of the Federal Trade Commission, Staley v. Gilead Sciences, Inc., Case 3:19-cv-2573 (N.D. Cal. Oct. 25, 2019).

[1052] *See, e.g.*, Hinds Cty., Miss. v. Wachovia Bank N.A., 700 F. Supp. 2d 378, 394 (S.D.N.Y. 2010) ("Although pending government investigations may not, standing alone, satisfy an antitrust plaintiff's pleading burden, government investigations may be used to bolster the plausibility of § 1 claims."); Starr v. Sony BMG Music Ent., 592 F.3d 314, 324 (2d Cir. 2010) (noting in support of a plausibility finding that "defendants' price-fixing is the subject of a pending investigation by the New York State Attorney General and two separate investigations by the Department of Justice.").

previously in this case in response to JELD-WEN's assertions, there are many reasons why the Antitrust Division might close an investigation or choose not to take an enforcement action. The Division's decision not to challenge a particular transaction is not confirmation that the transaction is competitively neutral or procompetitive.[1053]

However, you may also remember statements by the Justice Department indicating that when it decides to *accept* a remedy, that decision should receive some deference in the event of a state-AG challenge to the same transaction.[1054]

As you read these passages, consider whether you think there are, or should be, clear or consistent rules about the inferences that a court should take from agency action or inaction. In light of what you know about agency powers, priorities, incentives, and resources, how should courts react to the knowledge that an agency is, or is not, investigating or litigating? Should juries be told? Are there any dangers with sharing this information? Conversely, how should agencies respond to the pendency or possibility of ongoing private litigation? How might the incentives of private litigants differ from those of the agencies, or the public interest?

Steves and Sons, Inc. v. JELD-WEN, Inc.
988 F.3d 690 (4th Cir. 2021)

Judge Diaz.

[1] JELD-WEN criticizes the exclusion of evidence related to the Justice Department's investigations of the merger. Specifically, the district court forbade evidence that the Department had twice investigated the merger without challenging it. The court also permitted evidence that Steves had stated (in 2012) that it didn't object to the merger and (in 2015) that the prices that it was paying JELD-WEN had been flat, while barring evidence that these statements were made to the Justice Department. The court limited JELD-WEN to asking Steves's witnesses whether Steves had made official statements to that effect.

[2] We conclude that the district court acted within its discretion. The Department's decision not to pursue the matter isn't probative as to the merger's legality because many factors may motivate such a decision, including the Department's limited resources.

[3] And in general, a defendant may not use an enforcement authority's decision not to take action as a sword because inaction on the part of the government cannot be used to prove innocence. In short, evidence of the Department's decision could have misled the jury into thinking that the Department deemed the merger to be legal when no such determination had been made.

[4] Similarly, the jury didn't need to know to whom Steves made its statements. Indeed, admitting that evidence might have misled the jury by calling attention to the Department's decision not to challenge the merger.

***

New York v. Deutsche Telekom AG
439 F. Supp. 3d 179 (S.D.N.Y. 2020)

Judge Marrero.

[1] Prior to and during the pendency of this action, the FCC and DOJ each heavily scrutinized the Proposed Merger and considered its likely effect on competition. Those agencies' conditional approval of the Proposed Merger does not immunize it from Plaintiff States' antitrust challenge or this Court's judicial scrutiny. Nevertheless, the reality remains that the Court must now assess the Proposed Merger as conditioned by both regulators after lengthy review.

[1053] Brief for the United States of America as Amicus Curiae in Support of Appellee Steves and Sons, Inc., Steves and Sons, Inc. v. JELD-WEN, Inc., Case No. 19-1397, at *15 (4th Cir. filed Aug. 23, 2019).

[1054] Michael Murray, Deputy Assistant Attorney General, U.S. Department of Justice, *Antitrust Federalism* (remarks of Aug. 31, 2020).

[2] Not only have the FCC and DOJ conditioned [*i.e.*, imposed negotiated remedies on] the transaction before the Court, the Court will accord their views some deference. Where federal regulators have carefully scrutinized the challenged merger, imposed various restrictions on it, and stand ready to provide further consideration, supervision, and perhaps invalidation of asserted anticompetitive practices we have a unique indicator that the challenged practice may have redeeming competitive virtues and that the search for those values is not almost sure to be in vain. Indeed, the Supreme Court has looked to the views of federal regulators on multiple occasions for assistance in conducting its Section 7 analysis. As Plaintiff States note, however, the views of the FCC and DOJ cannot simply be adopted entirely at face value, as their assessment of a merger's legality may be guided by considerations that are outside the scope of Section 7. Ultimately, the Court will treat the views of the FCC and DOJ as informative but not conclusive.

[3] As set forth above in the Court's Findings of Fact, although the FCC recognized the potential for the Proposed Merger to increase mobile wireless speeds, accelerate the provision of 5G service, and expand mobile wireless telecommunications services to underserved rural areas, the FCC nevertheless acknowledged that an unconditioned Proposed Merger could have potentially harmful effects in densely populated areas with price-conscious consumers. To mitigate these concerns, the FCC required that T-Mobile commit to providing its promised speed, 5G, and coverage benefits by setting clear targets with associated penalties. And the FCC sought to address the potential harm to price-conscious consumers by requiring the divestiture of the most successful part of Sprint's business, its prepaid subsidiary Boost, to an independent buyer on terms that would enable that buyer to compete aggressively for the benefit of such price-conscious customers. After extensive review, the DOJ concluded that the Proposed Merger, if unconditioned, could substantially lessen competition in the RMWTS Market. In order to achieve the benefits that the Proposed Merger could provide, the DOJ supplemented the FCC commitments by proposing that Sprint divest Boost to the well-resourced potential entrant DISH, that an independent monitor appointed by DOJ ensure DISH would take advantage of the low wholesale rates provided by an MVNO agreement, and that DISH build out its own 5G network within three years to become a nationwide MNO capable of replacing Sprint.

[4] Plaintiff States point out that some of the conditions contemplated by the FCC and DOJ, such as the MVNO agreement and transfer of spectrum licenses, have yet to receive formal approval. The Court declines to assume at present that the FCC and DOJ will, either through their regulatory review processes or lax enforcement, frustrate the conditions that they negotiated themselves over a period of 15 months.

[5] Having been tasked with independently reviewing the legality of the Proposed Merger, the Court is not bound by the conclusions of these regulatory agencies. Similarly, the Court does not simply adopt their conclusions wholesale. Nonetheless, mindful that the agencies are intimately familiar with this technical subject matter, as well as the competitive realities involved, the Court treats their views and actions as persuasive and helpful evidence in analyzing the competitive effect of this merger as conditioned by the factors described below.

* * *

In re Graphics Processing Units Antitrust Litig.
527 F. Supp. 2d 1011 (N.D. Cal. 2007)

Judge Alsup.

[1] The *Twombly* decision reiterated that allegations of antitrust conspiracy are governed by Rule 8, and not the heightened standard of Rule 9(b). The Supreme Court's concern in that instance was that the allegations were insufficiently particularized to render plaintiffs' entitlement to relief plausible.

[2] Plaintiffs allege in conclusory fashion that defendants fixed prices pursuant to an agreement, but that allegation is simply too conclusory to show a plausible entitlement to relief. As the Supreme Court noted in *Twombly*, parallel conduct does not suggest conspiracy, and a conclusory allegation of agreement at some unidentified point does not supply facts adequate to show illegality. Plaintiffs have not pleaded that defendants ever met and agreed to fix prices; they plead at most that defendants had the opportunity to do so because they attended many of the same

meetings. They then attempt to correlate the release of products with those meetings. Given the sheer number of meetings attended by both defendants, every product release will follow on the heels of a meeting. [. . .]

[3] In support of their allegations, plaintiffs point out that the Antitrust Division of the Department of Justice has served defendants with subpoenas and is conducting a grand jury investigation. The investigation, however, carries no weight in pleading an antitrust conspiracy claim. It is unknown whether the investigation will result in indictments or nothing at all. Because of the grand jury's secrecy requirement, the scope of the investigation is pure speculation. It may be broader or narrower than the allegations at issue. Moreover, if the Department of Justice made a decision not to prosecute, that decision would not be binding on plaintiffs. The grand jury investigation is a non-factor.

***

NOTES

1) When and why should an agency refrain from action because private litigation is ongoing or likely?
2) In what ways, if any, should the law offer protection from private litigation as part of a cartel leniency program? Explain.
3) If an agency negotiates a settlement agreement to resolve antitrust concerns, when and to what extent should the court defer to that settlement in a subsequent challenge by private plaintiffs? How about state-government plaintiffs?
4) "The agencies can do more good, more efficiently, by filing thoughtful amicus briefs in ten private cases than by bringing one of their own." Do you agree? Why?
5) If you were a judge, would you be more likely to find a complaint plausible if you knew the same allegations were the subject of a federal government investigation? What if you knew that the investigation had resulted in the filing of a complaint? What if it was a state investigation rather than a federal one?

F. Some Further Reading

Daniel A. Crane, *Optimizing Private Antitrust Enforcement*, 63 Vand. L. Rev. 673 (2010)

Joshua P. Davis & Robert H. Lande, *Defying Conventional Wisdom: The Case for Private Antitrust Enforcement*, 48 Ga. L. Rev. 1 (2013)

Herbert Hovenkamp, THE ANTITRUST ENTERPRISE: PRINCIPLE AND EXECUTION (2005) Ch. 3

Jonathan M. Jacobson & Tracy Greer, *Twenty-One Years of Antitrust Injury: Down the Alley with* Brunswick v. Pueblo Bowl-o-Mat, 66 Antitrust L.J. 273 (1998)

William Kolasky, *Antitrust Litigation: What's Changed in Twenty Five Years?* 27 ANTITRUST (2012)

Robert H. Lande, *Wealth Transfers as the Original and Primary Concern of Antitrust: The Efficiency Interpretation Challenged*, 50 Hastings L.J. 871 (1999)

UC Hastings Law Center for Litigation and Courts & Huntington National Bank, *2021 Antitrust Annual Report: Class Action Filings in Federal Court* (April 2022)

United States, *Relationship Between Public and Private Antitrust Enforcement*, OECD Working Paper DAF/COMP/WP3/WD(2015)11 (June 15, 2015)

Made in United States
Troutdale, OR
12/30/2023